Diagram Symbols

The entries in this table are given roughly in order of appearance in the textbook, but consistency has been maintained in later chapters as well.

Mechanics

Symbol	Meaning
	displacement vector, component displacement
	velocity vector, component velocity
	acceleration vector
	force vector, component force
	momentum vector
	angle marking
	rotational motion

Thermodynamics

Symbol	Meaning
	energy transfer by heat
	energy transfer by work
	cycle or process

Waves and Electromagnetism

Symbol	Meaning
	ray (light or sound)
	positive charge
	negative charge
	electric field lines
	electric field vector
	electric current
	magnetic field lines
	magnetic field vector (into page, out of page)

HOLT
Physics

HOLT, RINEHART AND WINSTON

Harcourt Brace & Company

Austin • New York • Orlando • Atlanta • San Francisco • Boston • Dallas • Toronto • London

Authors

Raymond A. Serway
North Carolina State University

Jerry S. Faughn
Eastern Kentucky University

Cover Photo: The Image Bank

Cover Design: Marc Cooper

Printed in the United States of America

      6 048 01 00

ISBN 0-03-050597-6

Staff Credits

Editorial

Ellen Standafer, Executive Editor

William Wahlgren, Managing Editor

Mark Grayson, Senior Editor

Project Editors
Angela Berenstein
Angela P. Cole
Anthony King
April Smith
John Stokes

Copyeditors
Steve Oelenberger, Copyediting
  Supervisor
Amy Dariewicz
Denise Haney
Tania Hannan

Editorial Staff
Tanu'e White

New Media

Randy Merriman, Vice President

Kate Bennett, Associate Director

Linda Miller, Technology Project Editor

Peter Leighton, Courseware Manager

Tom Upshaw, Courseware Developer

Jamie Lane, Associate Courseware
  Developer

Virgil McCullough, Production Manager

Art, Design, and Photo

BOOK DESIGN
Diane Motz, Art Director, Book
Marc Cooper, Senior Designer
Sally Bess
Julie Ray
Karen Luciani

PHOTO RESEARCH
Peggy Cooper, Photo Research
  Manager
Mavournea Hay
Mike Gobbi

IMAGE SERVICES
Elaine Tate, Art Buyer Supervisor
Linda Richey
Linda Wilbourn

NEW MEDIA DESIGN
Susan Michael, Art Director
Carey Smith, Design Manager

BOOK AND MEDIA DESIGN
Joe Melomo, Design Manager
Neel Heisel
Lisa Walston

Production

Mimi Stockdell, Senior Production
  Manager

Beth Sample, Production Coordinator

Sara Carroll-Downs, Senior Secretary

Manufacturing

Jenine Street, Manufacturing
  Coordinator

Media Production

Kim Anderson, Production Manager

Susan Mussey, Production Coordinator

Nancy Hargis, Production Supervisor

Research and Curriculum

Kathy McKee, Director

Joyce Herbert

Patty Kolar

Mike Tracy

Acknowledgments

Contributing Writers

Robert W. Avakian
Instructor
Trinity School
Midland, TX

Phillip G. Bunce
James Bowie High School
Austin, TX

Robert Davisson
Science Writer
Delaware, OH

Judith R. Edgington, Ph.D.
Physics/Science Education
Consultant and Curriculum Designer
Austin, TX

John W. Jewett Jr., Ph.D.
Professor of Physics
Physics Department
California State Polytechnic University
Pomona, CA

Seth Madej
Associate Producer
Pulse of the Planet radio series
Jim Metzner Productions, Inc.
Yorktown Heights, NY

Jim Metzner
Executive Producer
Pulse of the Planet radio series
Yorktown Heights, NY

Lab Reviewers

Christopher Barnett
Richard DeCoster
Elizabeth Ramsayer
Joseph Serpico
Niles West High School
Niles, IL

Gregory Puskar
Laboratory Manager
Physics Department
West Virginia University
Morgantown, WV

Richard Sorensen
Vernier Software
Portland, OR

Lee Sennholtz
Martin Taylor
Central Scientific Company
Franklin Park, IL

Text Reviewers

John A. Adamowski
Chairperson
Science Department
Fenton High School
Bensenville, IL

John Ahlquist, M.S.
Chemistry/Physics Teacher
Science Department
Anoka High School
Anoka, MN

Stephen D. Baker
Physics Department
Rice University
Houston, TX

Maurice Belanger
Science Department Head
Nashua High School
Nashua, NH

Larry G. Brown, Ph.D.
Science and Computer Science
 Instructor
Science Department
Morgan Park Academy
Chicago, IL

David S. Coco, Ph.D.
Senior Research Physicist
Applied Research Laboratories
University of Texas at Austin
Austin, TX

William K. Conway, Ph.D.
Advanced Placement Physics
 Teacher
Science Department
Lake Forest High School
Lake Forest, IL

Brad de Young
Department of Physics & Physical
 Oceanography
Memorial University
St. John's, Newfoundland, Canada

Bill Deutschman, Ph.D.
President
Oregon Laser Consultants
Klamath Falls, OR

Fred E. Ellis, Ph.D.
Physics & Geology
University of Texas-Pan American
Edinburg, TX

William D. Ellis
Advanced Placement Physics
 Instructor
Chairman: Science Department
Butler Senior High School
Butler, PA

Bruce Esser
Physics Teacher
Marian High School
Omaha, NE

Scott Fricke, Ph.D.
Schlumberger Oilfield Services
Sugarland, TX

David J. Hamilton, Ed.D.
Physics Teacher
Benjamin Franklin High School
Portland, OR

Sally P. Hicks, Ph.D.
Department of Physics
University of Dallas
Irving, TX

John L. Hubisz, Ph. D.
Physics Department
North Carolina State University
Raleigh, NC

Robert C. Hudson
Associate Professor Emeritus
Physics Department
Roanoke College
Salem, VA

William H. Ingham, Ph.D.
Professor
Department of Physics
James Madison University
Harrisonburg, VA

Douglas C. Jenkins
Chairman
Science Department
Warren Central High School
Bowling Green, KY

David S. Jones
Physics Teacher
Miami Sunset Senior High School
Miami, FL

Roger Kassebaum
Physics Department
Millard North High School
Omaha, NE

Mervin W. Koehlinger, M.S.
Physics Instructor
Concordia Lutheran High School
Fort Wayne, IN

Karen B. Kwitter, Ph.D.
Professor of Astronomy
Williams College
Williamstown, MA

William Lash
Westwood High School
Austin, TX

Norman A. Mankins
Science Curriculum Specialist
Canton City Schools
Canton, OH

John McGehee
Physics Teacher
Palos Verdes Peninsula High School
Rolling Hills Estates, CA

Ralph McGrew
Engineering Science Department
Broome Community College
Binghamton, NY

Clement J. Moses, Ph.D.
Associate Professor of Physics
Physics Department
Utica College
Utica, NY

Richard L. Pitter, Ph.D.

Alvin M. Saperstein, Ph.D.
Professor of Physics and Fellow of
    Center for Peace and
    Conflict Studies
Department of Physics and
    Astronomy
Wayne State University
Detroit, MI

Debra A. Schell
Physics Teacher
Austintown Fitch High School
Austintown, OH

Edwin R. Schweber
Physics Teacher
Solomon Schechter Day School
West Orange, NJ

Joseph A. Taylor
Physics Instructor
Middletown Area High School
Middletown, PA

Leonard L. Thompson
Physics and Meteorology Teacher
Science Department
North Allegheny Sr. High School
Wexford, PA

Thomas H. Troland, Ph.D.
Physics Department
University of Kentucky
Lexington, KY

John T. Vieira
Science Department Head
B.M.C. Durfee High School
Fall River, MA

Mary L. White
Coastal Ecology Institute
Louisiana State University
Baton Rouge, LA

Jerome Williams
Professor Emeritus
Oceanography Department
U.S. Naval Academy
Annapolis, MD

Tim Wright
Physics Instructor
Stevens Point Area Senior High
    School
Stevens Point, WI

Carol J. Zimmerman, Ph.D.
Exxon Exploration Company
Houston, TX

G. Patrick Zober, M.S.
Science Curriculum Coordinator
Yough Senior High School
Herminie, PA

Patricia I. Zober
APC Physics Teacher
Ringgold High School
Monongahela, PA

CONTENTS

5120 N

1520 N   950 N

4050 N

8 Rotational Equilibrium and Dynamics   276

9 Fluid Mechanics   316

Before charging

During charging

After charging

25 Subatomic Physics — 894

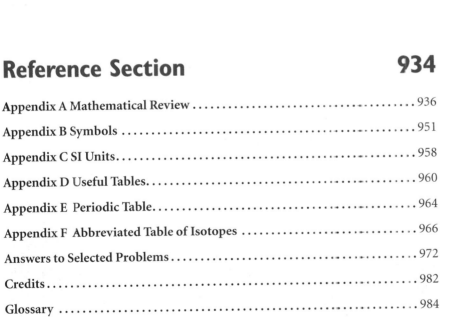

Baryons — Mesons

Reference Section — 934

Laboratory Experiments

Quick Labs

PHYSICS ON THE EDGE

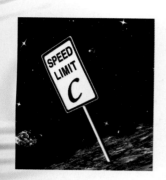

Science • Technology • Society

Timelines

SAFETY IN THE PHYSICS LABORATORY

Systematic, careful lab work is an essential part of any science program because lab work is the key to progress in science. In this class, you will practice some of the same fundamental laboratory procedures and techniques that experimental physicists use to pursue new knowledge.

The equipment and apparatus you will use involve various safety hazards, just as they do for working physicists. You must be aware of these hazards. Your teacher will guide you in properly using the equipment and carrying out the experiments, but you must also take responsibility for your part in this process. With the active involvement of you and your teacher, these risks can be minimized so that working in the physics laboratory can be a safe, enjoyable process of discovery.

These safety rules always apply in the lab:

1. **Always wear a lab apron and safety goggles.**
   Wear these safety devices whenever you are in the lab, not just when you are working on an experiment.

2. **No contact lenses in the lab.**
   Contact lenses should not be worn during any investigations using chemicals (even if you are wearing goggles). In the event of an accident, chemicals can get behind contact lenses and cause serious damage before the lenses can be removed. If your doctor requires that you wear contact lenses instead of glasses, you should wear eye-cup safety goggles in the lab. Ask your doctor or your teacher how to use this very important and special eye protection.

3. **Personal apparel should be appropriate for laboratory work.**
   On lab days avoid wearing long necklaces, dangling bracelets, bulky jewelry, and bulky or loose-fitting clothing. Loose, flopping, or dangling items may get caught in moving parts, accidentally contact electrical connections, or interfere with the investigation in some potentially hazardous manner. In addition, chemical fumes may react with some jewelry, such as pearl jewelry, and ruin them. Cotton clothing is preferable to clothes made of wool, nylon, or polyester. Tie back long hair. Wear shoes that will protect your feet from chemical spills and falling objects. Do not wear open-toed shoes or sandals or shoes with woven leather straps.

4. **NEVER work alone in the laboratory.**
   Work in the lab only while under the supervision of your teacher. Do not leave equipment unattended while it is in operation.

5. **Only books and notebooks needed for the experiment should be in the lab.**
   Only the lab notebook and perhaps the textbook should be in the lab. Keep other books, backpacks, purses, and similar items in your desk, locker, or designated storage area.

6. **Read the entire experiment before entering the lab.**
   Your teacher will review any applicable safety precautions before the lab. If you are not sure of something, ask your teacher.

7. **Heed all safety symbols and cautions written in the experimental investigations and handouts, posted in the room, and given verbally by your teacher.**
   They are provided for a reason: YOUR SAFETY.

8. **Know the proper fire-drill procedures and the locations of fire exits and emergency equipment.**
Make sure you know the procedures to follow in case of a fire or emergency.

9. **If your clothing catches on fire, do not run; WALK to the safety shower, stand under it, and turn it on.**
Call to your teacher while you do this.

10. **Report all accidents to the teacher immediately, no matter how minor.**
In addition, if you get a headache, feel sick to your stomach, or feel dizzy, tell your teacher immediately.

11. **Report all spills to your teacher immediately.**
Call your teacher rather than trying to clean a spill yourself. Your teacher will tell you if it is safe for you to clean up the spill; if not, your teacher will know how the spill should be cleaned up safely.

12. **Student-designed inquiry investigations, such as the Invention Labs in the *Laboratory Experiments* manual, must be approved by the teacher before being attempted by the student.**

13. **DO NOT perform unauthorized experiments or use equipment and apparatus in a manner for which they are not intended.**
Use only materials and equipment listed in the activity equipment list or authorized by your teacher. Steps in a procedure should only be performed as described in the book or lab manual or as approved by your teacher.

14. **Stay alert in the lab, and proceed with caution.**
Be aware of others near you or your equipment when you are about to do something in the lab. If you are not sure of how to proceed, ask your teacher.

15. **Horseplay and fooling around in the lab are very dangerous.**
Laboratory equipment and apparatus are not toys; never play in the lab or use lab time or equipment for anything other than their intended purpose.

16. **Food, beverages, chewing gum, and tobacco products are NEVER permitted in the laboratory.**

17. **NEVER taste chemicals. Do not touch chemicals or allow them to contact areas of bare skin.**

18. **Use extreme CAUTION when working with hot plates or other heating devices.**
Keep your head, hands, hair, and clothing away from the flame or heating area, and turn the devices off when they are not in use. Remember that metal surfaces connected to the heated area will become hot by conduction. Gas burners should only be lit with a spark lighter. Make sure all heating devices and gas valves are turned off before leaving the laboratory. Never leave a hot plate or other heating device unattended when it is in use. Remember that many metal, ceramic, and glass items do not always look hot when they are hot. Allow all items to cool before storing.

19. **Exercise caution when working with electrical equipment.**
Do not use electrical equipment with frayed or twisted wires. Be sure your hands are dry before using electrical equipment. Do not let electrical cords dangle from work stations; dangling cords can cause tripping or electrical shocks.

20. **Keep work areas and apparatus clean and neat.**
Always clean up any clutter made during the course of lab work, rearrange apparatus in an orderly manner, and report any damaged or missing items.

21. **Always thoroughly wash your hands with soap and water at the conclusion of each investigation.**

SAFETY SYMBOLS

Remember that the safety symbols shown here represent hazards that apply to a specific activity, but the numbered rules given on the previous pages always apply to all work in the laboratory.

Waste Disposal

- Never put broken glass or ceramics in a regular waste container. Use a dustpan, brush, and heavy gloves to carefully pick up broken pieces and dispose of them in a container specifically provided for this purpose.

- Dispose of chemicals as instructed by your teacher. Never pour hazardous or radioactive chemicals into a regular waste container or down the drain.

Heating Safety

- When using a burner or hot plate, always wear goggles and an apron to protect your eyes and clothing. Tie back long hair, secure loose clothing, and remove loose jewelry.

- Never leave a hot plate unattended while it is turned on.

- Wire coils may heat up rapidly. If heating occurs, open the switch immediately, and handle the equipment with a hot mitt.

- Allow all equipment to cool before storing it.

- If your clothing catches on fire, walk to the emergency lab shower and use the shower to put out the fire.

Hand Safety

- Perform this experiment in a clear area. Attach masses securely. Falling, dropped, or swinging objects can cause serious injury.

- Use a hot mitt to handle resistors, light sources, and other equipment that may be hot. Allow all equipment to cool before storing it.

Glassware Safety

- If a thermometer breaks, notify the teacher.

- Do not heat glassware that is broken, chipped, or cracked. Use tongs or a hot mitt to handle heated glassware and other equipment because it does not always look hot when it is hot. Allow all equipment to cool before storing it.

- If a bulb breaks, notify your teacher immediately. Do not remove broken bulbs from sockets.

Electrical Safety

- Never close a circuit until it has been approved by your teacher. Never rewire or adjust any element of a closed circuit.

- Never work with electricity near water; be sure the floor and all work surfaces are dry.

- If the pointer on any kind of meter moves off scale, open the circuit immediately by opening the switch.

- Do not work with any batteries, electrical devices, or magnets other than those provided by your teacher for this purpose.

Chemical Safety

- Do not eat or drink anything in the laboratory. Never taste chemicals or touch them with your hands.

- Do not allow radioactive materials to come into contact with your skin, hair, clothing, or personal belongings. Although the materials used in this lab are not hazardous when used properly, radioactive materials can cause serious illness and may have permanent effects.

Clothing Protection

- Tie back long hair, secure loose clothing, and remove loose jewelry to prevent their getting caught in moving or rotating parts or coming into contact with hazardous chemicals.

Eye Protection

- Wear eye protection, and perform this experiment in a clear area. Swinging objects can cause serious injury.

- Avoid looking directly at a light source, as this may cause permanent eye damage.

CHAPTER 1

The Science of Physics

PHYSICS IN ACTION

The sails of this boat billow out round and full. As the boat begins moving forward faster and faster, a ball on the deck rolls toward the stern. The boat pitches back and forth gently as it slices through the waves. Water slaps against the hull, occasionally spraying the crew and keeping them cool in the hot sun.

At first, this scene seems to have little to do with physics. Many people associate physics with complicated concepts studied by white-coated scientists working in laboratories with intricate machinery.

But physics can be used to explain anything in the physical world—from why the ball moves to the back as the boat speeds up to why different parts of the sail have different colors.

- *How are the principles of physics applied to sailboat design?*
- *How can the principles of physics be used to predict how a sailboat will move under various conditions?*

1-1
What is physics?

THE TOPICS OF PHYSICS

Many people consider physics to be a difficult science that is far removed from their lives. This may be because many of the world's most famous physicists study topics such as the structure of the universe or the incredibly small particles within an atom, often using complicated tools to observe and measure what they are studying.

But physics is simply the study of the physical world. Everything around you can be described and understood using the tools of physics. The goal of physics is to use a small number of basic concepts, equations, and assumptions to describe the physical world. Once the physical world has been described this way, the physics principles involved can be used to make predictions about a broad range of phenomena. For example, the same physics principles that are used to predict the interactions between two planets can also be used to predict the paths of two colliding galaxies or the trajectory of a basketball during a free throw.

Many of the inventions, appliances, tools, and buildings we live with today are made possible by the application of physics principles. Every time you take a step, catch a ball, open a door, whisper, or check your image in a mirror, you are unconsciously using your knowledge of physics. **Figure 1-1** indicates how the areas of physics apply to building and operating a car.

Figure 1-1
Without knowledge of many of the areas of physics, making cars would be impossible.

Thermodynamics Efficient engines, use of coolants

Electromagnetism
Battery, starter, headlights

Optics Headlights, rear-view mirrors

Vibrations and mechanical waves
Shock absorbers, radio speakers, sound insulation

Mechanics Spinning motion of the wheels, tires that provide enough friction for traction

Physics is everywhere

We are surrounded by principles of physics in our everyday lives. In fact, most people know much more about physics than they realize. When you buy a carton of ice cream at the store and put it in the freezer at home, you do it because intuitively you know enough about the laws of physics to know that the ice cream will melt if you leave it on the counter.

Any problem that deals with temperature, size, motion, position, shape, or color involves physics. Physicists categorize the topics they study in a number of different ways. **Table 1-1** shows some of the major areas of physics that will be described in this book.

People who design, build, and operate sailboats need a working knowledge of the principles of physics. Designers figure out the best shape for the boat's hull so that it remains stable and floating yet quick-moving and maneuverable. This design requires knowledge of the physics of fluids. Determining the most-efficient shapes for the sails and how to arrange them requires an understanding of the science of motion and its causes. Balancing loads in the construction of a sailboat requires knowledge of mechanics. Some of the same physics principles can also explain how the keel keeps the boat moving in one direction even when the wind is from a slightly different direction.

Table 1-1	Areas within physics	
Name	**Subjects**	**Examples**
Mechanics	motion and its causes	falling objects, friction, weight, spinning objects
Thermodynamics	heat and temperature	melting and freezing processes, engines, refrigerators
Vibrations and wave phenomena	specific types of repetitive motions	springs, pendulums, sound
Optics	light	mirrors, lenses, color, astronomy
Electromagnetism	electricity, magnetism, and light	electrical charge, circuitry, permanent magnets, electromagnets
Relativity	particles moving at any speed, including very high speeds	particle collisions, particle accelerators, nuclear energy
Quantum mechanics	behavior of submicroscopic particles	the atom and its parts

Make observations and collect data that lead to a question.

↓

Formulate and objectively test hypotheses by experiments.

↓

Interpret results, and revise the hypothesis if necessary.

↓

State conclusions in a form that can be evaluated by others.

Figure 1-2
Physics, like all other sciences, is based on the scientific method.

model

a replica or description designed to show the structure or workings of an object, system, or concept

THE SCIENTIFIC METHOD

When scientists look at the world, they see a network of rules and relationships that determine what will happen in a given situation. Everything you will study in this course was learned because someone looked out at the world and asked questions about how things work.

When physicists try to explain how things work, they use the *scientific method*. The steps of the scientific method are summarized in **Figure 1-2.** This simple, step-by-step chart is easy to understand, but, in reality, most scientific work is not so easily separated. Sometimes, exploratory experiments are performed as a part of the first step in order to generate observations that can lead to a focused question and further work. A revised hypothesis may require more experiments.

Physics uses models that describe only part of reality

How is physics distinct from chemistry, biology, or the other sciences? One difference is the scope of the subject matter, as briefly referred to earlier in this section. Another difference is that although the physical world is very complex, physicists often use simple **models** to explain the most fundamental features of various phenomena. They use this approach because it is usually impossible to describe all aspects of a phenomenon at the same time. A common technique that physicists use to analyze an event or observation is to break it down into different parts. Then physicists decide which parts are important to what they want to study and which parts can be disregarded.

For example, let's say you wish to study the motion of the ball shown in **Figure 1-3.** There are many observations that can be made about the situa-

Figure 1-3
This basketball game involves great complexity.

tion, including the ball's surroundings, size, spin, weight, color, time in the air, speed, and sound when hitting the ground. The first step toward simplifying this complicated situation is to decide what to study, the **system.** Typically, a single object and the items that immediately affect it are the focus of attention. Once you decide that the ball and its motion are what you want to study, you can eliminate all information about the surroundings of the ball except information that affects its motion, as indicated in **Figure 1-4(a).**

(a)

(b)

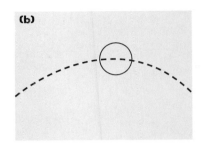

Figure 1-4
To analyze the motion of the basketball, isolate **(a)** what will affect its motion. Then draw a diagram **(b)** that includes only that information.

You can disregard characteristics of the ball that have little or no effect on its motion, such as the ball's color and its sound when bouncing against the floor. In some studies of motion, even the ball's spin and size are disregarded, and the change in the ball's position will be the only quantity investigated, as shown in **Figure 1-4(b).**

In effect, the physicist studies the motion of a ball by first creating a simple model of the ball and its motion. Unlike the real ball, the model object the physicist analyzes is isolated; it has no color, spin, or size, and it makes no noise on impact. Frequently, a model can be summarized with a diagram, like the one in **Figure 1-4(b).** Another way to summarize these models is to build a computer simulation or small-scale replica of the situation.

Without models to simplify matters, situations such as building a car or sailing a boat would be too complex to study. For instance, analyzing the motion of the sailboat is made easier by imagining that the push on the boat from the wind is steady and consistent. The boat is also treated as if it were a single point with a certain mass being pushed through the water. In other words, the color of the boat, the model of the boat, and the details of its shape are left out of the analysis. Furthermore, the water the boat moves through is treated as if it were a perfectly smooth-flowing liquid with no internal friction. In spite of these simplifications, the analysis can still make useful predictions of how the sailboat will move.

Models can help build hypotheses

A scientific hypothesis is a reasonable explanation for observations—one that can be tested with additional experiments. The process of simplifying and modeling a situation can help you identify the relevant variables and identify a hypothesis for testing.

Consider the example of Galileo's "thought experiment," in which he modeled the behavior of falling objects in order to develop a hypothesis about how objects fell. At the time Galileo published his work on falling objects, in 1638, scientists believed that a heavy object would fall faster than a lighter object.

In Galileo's thought experiment, he imagined two identical objects being released at the same time from the same height, so that they should fall with the same speed. Galileo then imagined tying the two objects together while they were falling. Both scenarios are represented in **Figure 1-5.**

If common belief were correct, the two objects tied together would suddenly fall faster than they had fallen before because they would be one heavy object instead of two lighter ones. But Galileo believed that tying the two objects together should not cause such a sudden change in how they fell. As a result of this reasoning, Galileo hypothesized that all objects fall at the same rate in the absence of air resistance, no matter what size they are.

Figure 1-5

Galileo used the thought experiment represented by this diagram as a way to organize his thoughts about falling bodies. Heavy objects must fall as fast as lighter ones **(a)**, or else two bricks tied together would fall faster than they would if kept separate **(b)**.

(a)

What does happen: Heavy objects fall as fast as lighter ones.

(b)

What does not happen: Heavy objects do *not* fall faster than lighter ones.

Models help guide experimental design

Galileo performed many experiments to test his hypothesis. To be certain he was observing differences due to weight, he kept all other variables the same: the objects he tested had the same size (but different weights) and were measured falling from the same point.

The measuring devices at that time were not precise enough to measure the motion of objects falling in air, and there was no way to eliminate air resistance. So Galileo used the motion of a ball rolling down a series of smooth ramps as a model of the motion of a falling ball. The steeper the ramp, the closer the model came to representing a falling object. These ramp experiments provided data that matched the predictions Galileo made in his hypothesis.

Like Galileo's hypothesis, any hypothesis must be tested in a **controlled experiment.** In an experiment to test a hypothesis, you must change one variable at a time to determine what influences the phenomenon you are observing. Galileo performed a series of experiments using balls of different weights on one ramp before determining the time they took to roll down a steeper ramp.

controlled experiment

experiment involving manipulation of a single variable or factor

The best physics hypotheses can make predictions in new situations

Until the invention of the air pump, it was not possible to perform direct tests of Galileo's hypothesis by observing objects falling in the absence of air resistance. But even though it was not completely testable, Galileo's hypothesis was used to make reasonably accurate predictions about the motion of many objects, from raindrops to boulders (even though they all experience air resistance).

Even if some experiments produce results that support a certain hypothesis, at any time another experiment may produce results that do not support the hypothesis. When this occurs, scientists repeat the experiment until they are sure that the results are not in error. If the unexpected results are confirmed, the hypothesis must be abandoned or revised. That is why the last step of the scientific method is so important. A conclusion is valid only if it can be verified by other people.

Section Review

1. Name the areas of physics.

2. Identify the area of physics that is most relevant to each of the following situations. Explain your reasoning.
   a. a high school football game
   b. food preparation for the prom
   c. playing in the school band
   d. lightning in a thunderstorm
   e. wearing a pair of sunglasses outside in the sun

3. What are the activities involved in the scientific method?

4. Give two examples of ways that physicists model the physical world.

5. **Physics in Action** Identify the area of physics involved in each of the following tests of a lightweight metal alloy proposed for use in sailboat hulls:
   a. testing the effects of a collision on the alloy
   b. testing the effects of extreme heat and cold on the alloy
   c. testing whether the alloy can affect a magnetic compass needle

1-2
Measurements in experiments

NUMBERS AS MEASUREMENTS

Physicists perform experiments to test hypotheses about how changing one variable in a situation affects another variable. An accurate analysis of such experiments requires numerical measurements.

Numerical measurements are different from the numbers used in a mathematics class. In mathematics, a number like 7 can stand alone and be used in equations. In science, measurements are more than just a number. For example, a measurement reported as 7 leads to several questions. What physical quantity is being measured—length, mass, time, or something else? If it is length that is being measured, what units were used for the measurement—meters, feet, inches, miles, or light-years?

The description of *what kind* of physical quantity is represented by a certain measurement is called *dimension*. In the next several chapters, you will encounter three basic dimensions: length, mass, and time. Many other measurements can be expressed in terms of these three dimensions. For example, physical quantities, such as force, velocity, energy, volume, and acceleration, can all be described as combinations of length, mass, and time. In later chapters, we will need to add two other dimensions to our list, for temperature and for electric current.

The description of *how much* of a physical quantity is represented by a certain numerical measurement depends on the *units* with which the quantity is measured. For example, small distances are more easily measured in millimeters than in kilometers or light-years.

SI is the standard measurement system for science

When scientists do research, they must communicate the results of their experiments with each other and agree on a system of units for their measurements. In 1960, an international committee agreed on a system of standards, such as the standard shown in **Figure 1-6,** and designations for the fundamental quantities needed for measurements. This system of units is called the Système International (SI). In SI, there are only seven base units, each describing a single dimension, such as length, mass, or time. The units of length, mass, and

Figure 1-6
The official standard kilogram mass is a platinum-iridium cylinder kept in a sealed container at the International Bureau of Weights and Measures at Sèvres, France.

Table 1-2   SI Standards

Unit	Original standard	Current standard
Meter (length)	1/10 000 000 distance from equator to North Pole	the distance traveled by light in a vacuum in 3.3×10^{-9} s
Kilogram (mass)	mass of 0.001 cubic meters of water	the mass of a specific platinum-iridium alloy cylinder
Second (time)	(1/60) (1/60) (1/24) = 0.000 01574 average solar days	9 192 631 700 times the period of a radio wave emitted from a cesium-133 atom

time are the meter, kilogram, and second, respectively. In most measurements, the units for these quantities will be abbreviated as m, kg, and s, respectively.

Not every observation can be described using one of these units, but the units can be combined to form derived units. Derived units are formed by combining the seven base units with multiplication or division. For example, speeds are typically expressed in units of meters per second (m/s), one unit divided by another unit.

In other cases, it may appear that a new unit that is not one of the base units is being introduced, but often these new units merely serve as shorthand ways to refer to combinations of units. For example, forces and weights are typically measured in units of newtons (N), but a newton is defined as being exactly equivalent to one kilogram multiplied by meters per second squared ($kg \bullet m/s^2$). Derived units, such as newtons, will be explained throughout this book as they are introduced.

These units are defined by the standards described in **Table 1-2** and are reproduced so that every meterstick, kilogram mass, and clock in the world is calibrated to give consistent results. We will use SI units throughout this book because they are almost universally accepted in science and industry.

SI uses prefixes to accommodate extremes

Physics is a science that describes a broad range of topics, and requires a wide range of measurements, from very large to very small. For example, distance measurements can range from the distances between stars (about 100 000 000 000 000 000 m) to the distances between atoms in a solid (0.000 000 0001 m). Because these numbers can be extremely difficult to read and write, they are often expressed in powers of 10 (1×10^{17} m or 1×10^{-10} m).

Another approach commonly used in SI is to combine the units with prefixes that symbolize certain powers of 10, as shown in **Figure 1-7.** The most

Figure 1-7
The mass of this mosquito can be expressed several different ways: 1×10^{-5} kg, 0.01 g, or 10 mg.

Table 1-3
Some prefixes for powers of 10 used with metric units

Power	Prefix	Abbreviation	Power	Prefix	Abbreviation
10^{-18}	atto-	a	10^{-1}	deci-	d
10^{-15}	femto-	f	10^{1}	deka-	da
10^{-12}	pico-	p	10^{3}	kilo-	k
10^{-9}	nano-	n	10^{6}	mega-	M
10^{-6}	micro-	μ (Greek letter *mu*)	10^{9}	giga-	G
			10^{12}	tera-	T
10^{-3}	milli-	m	10^{15}	peta-	P
10^{-2}	centi-	c	10^{18}	exa-	E

Quick Lab

Metric Prefixes

MATERIALS LIST

✔ balance (0.01 g precision or better)
✔ 50 sheets of loose-leaf paper

Record the following measurements (with appropriate units and metric prefixes):
- the mass of a single sheet of paper
- the mass of exactly 10 sheets of paper
- the mass of exactly 50 sheets of paper

Use each of these measurements to determine the mass of a single sheet of paper. How many different ways can you express each of these measurements? Use your results to estimate the mass of one ream (500 sheets) of paper. How many ways can you express this mass? Which is the most practical approach? Give reasons for your answer.

common prefixes and their symbols are shown in **Table 1-3.** For example, the length of a housefly, 5×10^{-3} m, is equivalent to 5 millimeters (mm), and the distance of a satellite 8.25×10^{5} m from Earth's surface can be expressed as 825 kilometers (km). A year, which is 3.2×10^{7} s, can also be expressed as 32 megaseconds (Ms).

Converting a measurement from its prefix form is easy to do. You can build conversion factors from any equivalent relationship, including those in **Table 1-3,** such as 1.609 km = 1 mi and 3600 s = 1 h. Just put the quantity on one side of the equation in the numerator and the quantity on the other side in the denominator, as shown below for the case of the conversion 1 mm = 1×10^{-3} m. Because these two quantities are equal, the following equations are also true:

$$\frac{1 \text{ mm}}{10^{-3} \text{ m}} = 1 \quad \text{and} \quad \frac{10^{-3} \text{ m}}{1 \text{ mm}} = 1$$

Thus, any measurement multiplied by either one of these fractions will be multiplied by 1. The number and the unit will change, but the quantity described by the measurement will stay the same.

To convert measurements, use the conversion factor that will cancel with the units you are given to provide the units you need, as shown in the example below. Typically, the units to which you are converting should be placed in the numerator. It is useful to cross out units that cancel to help keep track of them.

$$\text{Units } \textit{don't} \text{ cancel: } 37.2 \text{ mm} \times \frac{1 \text{ mm}}{10^{-3} \text{ m}} = 3.72 \times 10^{4} \frac{\text{mm}^2}{\text{m}}$$

$$\text{Units } \textit{do} \text{ cancel: } 37.2 \text{ mm} \times \frac{10^{-3} \text{ m}}{1 \text{ mm}} = 3.72 \times 10^{-2} \text{ m}$$

(a)

Figure 1-8
When determining area by multiplying measurements of length and width, be sure the measurements are expressed in the same units.

Both dimension and units must agree

Measurements of physical quantities must be expressed in units that match the dimensions of that quantity. For example, measurements of length cannot be expressed in units of kilograms because units of kilograms describe the dimension of mass. It is very important to be certain that a measurement is expressed in units that refer to the correct dimension. One good technique for avoiding errors in physics is to check the units in an answer to be certain they are appropriate for the dimension of the physical quantity that is being sought in a problem or calculation.

If several people make independent measurements of the same physical quantity, they may each use different units. As an example, consider **Figure 1-8(a),** which shows two people measuring a room to determine the area of carpet necessary to cover the floor. It is possible for one person to measure the length of the room in meters and for the other person to measure the width of the room in centimeters. When the numbers are multiplied to find the area, they will give a difficult-to-interpret answer in units of cm•m, as shown in **Figure 1-8(b).** On the other hand, if both measurements are made using the same units, the calculated area is much easier to intepret because it is expressed in units of m², as shown in **Figure 1-8(c).** Suppose that the measurements were made in different units, as in the example above. Because centimeters and meters are both units of length, one unit can be easily converted to the other. In order to avoid confusion, it is better to make the conversion to the same units before doing any more arithmetic.

(b)

$$2035 \text{ cm}$$
$$\times \ 12.5 \text{ m}$$
$$\overline{1017.5}$$
$$4070$$
$$\underline{2035}$$
$$25437.5$$

about ? ?

$2.54 \times 10^4 \text{ cm•m}$

(c)

$$20.35 \text{ m}$$
$$\times \ 12.5 \text{ m}$$
$$\overline{10.175}$$
$$40.70$$
$$\underline{203.5}$$
$$254.375$$

about ✓

$2.54 \times 10^2 \text{ m}^2$

Metric prefixes

PROBLEM

A typical bacterium has a mass of about 2.0 fg. Express this measurement in terms of grams and kilograms.

SOLUTION

Given: mass = 2.0 fg

Unknown: mass = ? g   mass = ? kg

Build conversion factors from the relationships given in **Table 1-3.** Two possibilities are shown below.

$$\frac{1 \times 10^{-15} \text{ g}}{1 \text{ fg}} \text{ and } \frac{1 \text{ fg}}{1 \times 10^{-15} \text{ g}}$$

Only the first one will cancel the units of fg to give units of g.

$$2.0 \text{ fg} \times \frac{1 \times 10^{-15} \text{ g}}{1 \text{ fg}} = \boxed{2.0 \times 10^{-15} \text{ g}}$$

Then, take this answer and use a similar process to cancel the units of g to give units of kg.

$$2.0 \times 10^{-15} \text{ g} \times \frac{1 \text{ kg}}{1 \times 10^{3} \text{ g}} = \boxed{2.0 \times 10^{-18} \text{ kg}}$$

Metric prefixes

1. A human hair is approximately 50 μm in diameter. Express this diameter in meters.

2. The distance between the sun and the Earth is about 1.5×10^{11} m. Express this distance with an SI prefix and in kilometers.

3. The average mass of an automobile in the United States is about 1.440×10^{6} g. Express this mass in kilograms.

4. A hydrogen atom has a diameter of about 10 nm.
   a. Express this diameter in meters.
   b. Express this diameter in millimeters.
   c. Express this diameter in micrometers.

5. A typical radio wave has a period of 1 μs. Express this period in seconds.

ACCURACY AND PRECISION

Because theories are based on observation and experiment, careful measurements are very important in physics. But in reality, no measurement is perfect. In describing the imperfection, there are two factors to consider: a measurement's **accuracy** and a measurement's **precision.** Although these terms are often used interchangeably in everyday speech, they have specific meanings in a scientific discussion.

Problems with accuracy are due to error

Experimental work is never free of error, but it is important to minimize error in order to obtain accurate results. Human error can occur, for example, if a mistake is made in reading an instrument or recording the results. The best way to avoid human error is to take repeated measurements to be certain they are consistent.

If some measurements are taken using one method and some are taken using a different method, another type of error, called method error, will result. Method error can be greatly reduced by standardizing the method of taking measurements. For example, when measuring a length with a meterstick, choose a line of sight directly over what is being measured, as shown in **Figure 1-9(a).** If you are too far to one side, you are likely to overestimate or underestimate the measurement, as shown in **Figure 1-9(b)** and **(c).** This problem is due to the phenomenon known as *parallax*. Another example of parallax is the fact that the speedometer reading reported by a car's driver is more accurate than the speedometer reading as seen from the passenger seat in an automobile.

Another type of error is instrument error. If a meterstick or balance is not calibrated properly, this will introduce error into any measurements made with the device. For this reason, it is important to be careful with lab equipment. For example, rough handling can damage balances. If a wooden meterstick gets wet, it can warp, making accurate measurements difficult.

accuracy

the extent to which a reported measurement approaches the true value of the quantity measured

precision

the degree of exactness or refinement of a measurement

(a) (b) (c)

Figure 1-9
If you measure this window by keeping your line of sight directly over the measurement **(a),** you will find that it is 165.2 cm long. If you do not keep your eye close to the mark, **(b)** and **(c),** you may report a measurement with some error.

Figure 1-10
Even though this ruler is only marked in centimeters and half-centimeters, if you estimate, you can use it to report measurements to a precision of a millimeter.

significant figures

those digits in a measurement that are known with certainty plus the first digit that is uncertain

Because the ends of a meterstick can be easily damaged or worn, it is best to minimize instrument error by making measurements with a portion of the scale that is in the middle of the meterstick. Instead of measuring from the end (0 cm), try measuring from the 10 cm line.

Precision describes the limitations of the measuring instrument

Poor accuracy involves errors that can often be corrected. On the other hand, precision describes how exact a measurement can possibly be. For example, a measurement of 1.325 m is more precise than a measurement of 1.3 m. A lack of precision is typically due to limitations of the measuring instrument and is not the result of human error or lack of calibration. For example, if a meterstick is divided only into centimeters, it will be difficult to measure something only a few millimeters thick with it.

In many situations, you can improve the precision of a measurement. This can be done by making a reasonable estimation of where the mark on the instrument would have been. Suppose that in a laboratory experiment you are asked to measure the length of a pencil with a meterstick marked in millimeters, as shown in **Figure 1-10.** The end of the pencil lies somewhere between 18 cm and 18.5 cm. The length you have actually measured is slightly more than 18 cm. You can make a reasonable estimation of how far between the two marks the end of the pencil is and add a digit to the end of the actual measurement. In this case, the end of the pencil seems to be less than half way between the two marks, so you would report the measurement as 18.2 cm.

Significant figures help keep track of imprecision

It is important to record the precision of your measurements so that other people can understand and interpret your results. A common convention used in science to indicate precision is known as **significant figures.**

In the case of the measurement of the pencil as about 18.2 cm, the measurement has three significant figures. The significant figures of a measurement include all the digits that are actually measured (18 cm), plus one *estimated* digit. Note that the number of significant figures is determined by the precision of the markings on the measuring scale.

The last digit is reported as a 0.2 (for the estimated 0.2 cm past the 18 cm mark). Because this digit is an estimate, the true value for the measurement is actually somewhere between 18.15 cm and 18.25 cm.

When the last digit in a recorded measurement is a zero, it is difficult to tell whether the zero is there as a place holder or as a significant digit. For example, if a length is recorded as 230 mm, it is impossible to tell whether this number has two or three significant digits. In other words, it can be difficult to know whether the measurement of 230 mm means the measurement is known to be between 225 mm and 235 mm or is known more precisely to be between 229.5 mm and 230.5 mm.

One way to solve such problems is to report all values using scientific notation. In scientific notation, the measurement is recorded to a power of 10, and all of the figures given are significant. For example, if the length of 230 cm has two significant figures, it would be recorded in scientific notation as 2.3×10^2 cm. If it has three significant figures, it would be recorded as 2.30×10^2 cm.

Scientific notation is also helpful when the zero in a recorded measurement appears in front of the measured digits. For example, a measurement such as 0.000 15 cm should be expressed in scientific notation as 1.5×10^{-4} cm if it has two significant figures. The three zeros between the decimal point and the digit 1 are not counted as significant figures because they are present only to locate the decimal point and to indicate the order of magnitude. The rules for determining how many significant figures are in a measurement that includes zeros are shown in **Table 1-4.**

Significant figures in calculations require special rules

In calculations, the number of significant figures in your result depends on the number of significant figures in each measurement. For example, if someone reports that the height of a mountaintop, like the one shown in **Figure 1-11,** is 1710 m, that implies that its actual height is between 1705 and 1715 m. If another person builds a pile of rocks 0.20 m high on top of the mountain, that would not suddenly make the mountain's new height known accurately enough to be measured as 1710.20 m. The final answer cannot be more precise than the least precise measurement used to find the answer. Therefore, the answer should be rounded off to 1710 m even if the pile of rocks is included.

Figure 1-11
If a mountain's height is known with an uncertainty of 5 m, the addition of 0.20 m of rocks will not appreciably change the height.

Table 1-4	Rules for determining whether zeros are significant figures
Rule	**Examples**
1. Zeros between other nonzero digits are significant.	**a.** 50.3 m has three significant figures. **b.** 3.0025 s has five significant figures.
2. Zeros in front of nonzero digits are not significant.	**a.** 0.892 kg has three significant figures. **b.** 0.0008 ms has one significant figure.
3. Zeros that are at the end of a number and also to the right of the decimal are significant.	**a.** 57.00 g has four significant figures. **b.** 2.000 000 kg has seven significant figures.
4. Zeros at the end of a number but to the left of a decimal are significant if they have been measured or are the first estimated digit; otherwise, they are *not* significant. In this book, they will be treated as *not* significant.	**a.** 1000 m may contain from one to four significant figures, depending on the precision of the measurement, but in this book it will be assumed that measurements like this have one significant figure. **b.** 20 m may contain one or two significant figures, but in this book it will be assumed to have one significant figure.

Similar rules apply to multiplication. Suppose that you calculate the area of a room by multiplying the width and length. If the room's dimensions are 4.6 m by 6.7 m, the product of these values would be 30.82 m^2. However, this answer contains four significant figures, which implies that it is more precise than the measurements of the length and width. Because the room could be as small as 4.55 m by 6.65 m or as large as 4.65 m by 6.75 m, the area of the room is known only to be between 30.26 m^2 and 31.39 m^2. The area of the room can have only two significant figures because each measurement has only two. So it must be rounded off to 31 m^2. **Table 1-5** summarizes the two basic rules for determining significant figures when you are performing calculations.

Table 1-5   Rules for calculating with significant figures

Type of calculation	Rule	Example
addition or subtraction	The final answer should have the same number of digits to the right of the decimal as the measurement with the *smallest* number of digits *to the right of the decimal.*	97.3 + 5.85 103.15 $\xrightarrow{\text{round off}}$ 103.2
multiplication or division	The final answer has the same number of significant figures as the measurement having the *smallest* number of *significant figures.*	123 × 5.35 658.05 $\xrightarrow{\text{round off}}$ 658

Calculators do not pay attention to significant figures

When you use a calculator to analyze problems or measurements, you may be able to save time because the calculator can do the math more quickly than you. However, the calculator does not keep track of the significant figures in your measurements.

Calculators often exaggerate the precision of your final results by returning answers with as many digits as the display can show. To reinforce the correct approach, the answers to the sample problems in this book will always show only the number of significant figures that the measurements justify.

In order to provide answers with the correct number of significant figures, it will sometimes be necessary to round the results of a calculation. The rules described in **Table 1-6** will be used. In this book, the results of a calculation will be rounded after each type of mathematical operation. For example, the result of a series of multiplications should be rounded using the multiplication/division rule before it is added to another number. Similarly, the sum of several numbers should be rounded according to the addition/subtraction rule before the sum is multiplied by another number. You should consult your teacher to find out whether to round this way or to delay rounding until the end of all calculations.

Table 1-6   Rules for rounding

What to do	When to do it	Examples
round down	• whenever the digit following the last significant figure is a 0, 1, 2, 3, or 4	30.24 becomes 30.2
	• if the last significant figure is an even number and the next digit is a 5, with no other nonzero digits	32.25 becomes 32.2 32.65000 becomes 32.6
round up	• whenever the digit following the last significant figure is a 6, 7, 8, or 9	22.49 becomes 22.5
	• if the digit following the last significant figure is a 5 followed by a nonzero digit	54.7501 becomes 54.8
	• if the last significant figure is an odd number and the next digit is a 5, with no other nonzero digits	54.75 becomes 54.8 79.3500 becomes 79.4

Section Review

1. Which SI units would you use for the following measurements?
   a. the length of a swimming pool
   b. the mass of the water in the pool
   c. the time it takes a swimmer to swim a lap

2. Convert the following measurements as indicated.
   a. 6.20 mg in kg
   b. 3×10^{-9} s in ms
   c. 88.0 km in m

3. The following students measure the density of a piece of lead three times. The density of lead is actually 11.34 g/cm^3. Considering all of the results, which person's results were accurate? Which were precise? Were any both accurate and precise?
   a. Rachel: 11.32 g/cm^3, 11.35 g/cm^3, 11.33 g/cm^3
   b. Daniel: 11.43 g/cm^3, 11.44 g/cm^3, 11.42 g/cm^3
   c. Leah: 11.55 g/cm^3, 11.34 g/cm^3, 11.04 g/cm^3

4. Perform these calculations, following the rules for significant figures.
   a. $26 \times 0.02584 = ?$
   b. $15.3 \div 1.1 = ?$
   c. $782.45 - 3.5328 = ?$
   d. $63.258 + 734.2 = ?$

1-3
The language of physics

- **Interpret data in tables and graphs, and recognize equations that summarize data.**

- **Distinguish between conventions for abbreviating units and quantities.**

- **Use dimensional analysis to check the validity of expressions.**

- **Perform order-of-magnitude calculations.**

MATHEMATICS AND PHYSICS

Just as physicists create simplified models to better understand the real world, they use the tools of mathematics to analyze and summarize their observations. Then they can use the mathematical relationships among physical quantities to help predict what will happen in new situations.

Tables, graphs, and equations can make data easier to understand

There are many ways to organize data. Consider the experiment shown in **Figure 1-12,** which tests Galileo's hypothesis by dropping a table-tennis ball and a golf ball in a vacuum and measuring how far each ball falls during a certain time interval. You record your results as a set of numbers corresponding to the times of the fall and the distance each ball falls. A convenient way to analyze the data is to form a table like **Table 1-7.** A clear trend can be seen in the data. The more time that passes after each ball is dropped, the farther the ball falls.

Table 1-7	Data from dropped-ball experiment	
Time (s)	Distance golf ball falls (cm)	Distance table-tennis ball falls (cm)
0.067	2.20	2.20
0.133	8.67	8.67
0.200	19.60	19.59
0.267	34.93	34.92
0.333	54.34	54.33
0.400	78.40	78.39

Figure 1-12
This experiment tests Galileo's hypothesis by having two balls with different masses dropped simultaneously.

A better method for analyzing the data is to construct a graph of the distance the balls fall in each time interval, as shown in **Figure 1-13.** Using the graph, you can reconstruct the table by noting the values along the distance and time axes for each of the points shown.

In addition, because the graph shows an obvious pattern, we can draw a smooth curve through the data points to make estimations for times when we have no data, such as 0.225 s. The shape of the graph also provides information about the relationship between time and distance.

Figure 1-13

The graph of these data provides a convenient way to summarize the data and indicate the relationship between the time an object has been falling and the distance it has fallen.

We can also use the following equation to describe the relationship between the variables in the experiment:

(change in position in meters) = $4.9 \times$ (time of fall in seconds)^2

This equation allows you to reproduce the graph and make predictions about the change in position for any arbitrary time during the fall.

Physics equations indicate relationships

While mathematicians use equations to describe relationships between variables, physicists use the tools of mathematics to describe measured or predicted relationships between physical quantities in a situation. For example, one or more variables may affect the outcome of an experiment. In the case of a prediction, the physical equation is a compact statement based on a model of the situation. It shows how two or more variables are thought to be related. Many of the most important equations in physics do not contain numbers. Instead, they represent a simple description of the relationship between physical quantities.

To make expressions as simple as possible, physicists often use letters to describe specific quantities in an equation. For example, the letter v is used to denote speed. Sometimes, Greek letters are used to describe mathematical operations. For example, the Greek letter Δ (delta) is often used to mean "difference or change in," and the Greek letter Σ (sigma) is used to mean "sum" or "total."

With these conventions, the word equation above can be written as follows:

$$\Delta y = 4.9\Delta t^2$$

The abbreviation Δy indicates the change in a ball's position, and Δt indicates the time elapsed.

As you saw in Section 1-2, the units these quantities are measured in are also often abbreviated with symbols consisting of a letter or two. Most physics books provide some clues to help you keep track of which letters refer to quantities and variables and which letters are used to indicate units. Typically,

CONCEPT PREVIEW

The differences between quantities denoted with boldfaced symbols and those denoted with italicized symbols will be further described in Chapter 3.

variables and other specific quantities are abbreviated with letters that are **boldfaced** or *italicized*. Units are abbreviated with regular letters (sometimes called roman letters). Some examples of variable symbols and the abbreviations for the units that measure them are shown in **Table 1-8.**

As you continue to study physics, carefully note the introduction of new variable quantities, and recognize which units go with them. The tables provided in Appendix A can help you keep track of these abbreviations.

Table 1-8	**Abbreviations for variables and units**		
Quantity	**Symbol**	**Units**	**Unit abbreviations**
change in position	$\Delta x, \Delta y$	meters	m
time interval	Δt	seconds	s
mass	m	kilograms	kg

EVALUATING PHYSICS EXPRESSIONS

Like most models physicists build to describe the world around them, physics equations are valid only if they can be used to make predictions about situations. Although an experiment is the best way to test the validity of a physics expression, several techniques can be used to evaluate whether expressions are likely to be valid.

Dimensional analysis can weed out invalid equations

Suppose a car, such as the one in **Figure 1-14,** is moving at a speed of 88 km/h and you want to know how long it will take it to travel 725 km. How can you decide a good way to solve the problem?

You can use a powerful procedure called *dimensional analysis.* Dimensional analysis makes use of the fact that *dimensions can be treated as algebraic quantities.* For example, quantities can be added or subtracted only if they have the same dimensions, and the two sides of any given equation must have the same dimensions.

Let us apply this technique to the problem of the car moving at a speed of 88 km/h. This measurement is given in dimensions of length over time. The total distance traveled has the dimension of length. Multiplying these numbers together gives the dimensions indicated below. Clearly, the result of this calculation does not have the dimensions of time, which is what you are trying to calculate. That is,

$$\frac{\text{length}}{\text{time}} \times \text{length} = \frac{\text{length}^2}{\text{time}}, \text{ or } \frac{88 \text{ km}}{1.0 \text{ h}} \times 725 \text{ km} = \frac{6.4 \times 10^4 \text{ km}^2}{1.0 \text{ h}}$$

Figure 1-14
Dimensional analysis can be a useful check for many types of problems, including those involving the length of time it would take for this car to travel 725 km if it moves with a speed of 88 km/h.

To calculate an answer that will have the dimension of time, you should take the distance and *divide* it by the speed of the car, as follows:

$$\text{length} \div \frac{\text{length}}{\text{time}} = \frac{\text{length} \times \text{time}}{\text{length}} = \text{time} \qquad \frac{725 \text{ km} \times 1.0 \text{ h}}{88 \text{ km}} = 8.2 \text{ h}$$

In a very simple example like this one, you might be able to solve the problem without dimensional analysis. But in more-complicated situations, dimensional analysis is a wise first step that can often save you a great deal of time.

Order-of-magnitude estimations check answers

Because the scope of physics is so wide and the numbers may be astronomically large or subatomically small, it is often useful to estimate an answer to a problem before trying to solve it exactly. This kind of estimate is called an *order-of-magnitude* calculation, which means determining the power of 10 that is closest to the actual numerical value of the quantity. Once you have done this, you will be in a position to judge whether the answer you get from a more exacting procedure is correct.

For example, consider the car trip described in the discussion of dimensional analysis. We must divide the distance by the speed to find the time. The distance, 725 km, is closer to 10^3 km (1000 km) than to 10^2 km (100 km), so we use 10^3 km. The speed, 88 km/h, is about 10^2 km/h (100 km/h).

$$\frac{10^3 \text{ km}}{10^2 \text{ km/h}} = 10 \text{ h}$$

This estimate indicates that the answer should be closer to 10 than to 1 or to 100 (10^2). If you perform the calculation, you will find that the correct answer is 8.2 h, which certainly fits this range.

Order-of-magnitude estimates can also be used to estimate numbers in situations in which little information is given. For example, how could you estimate how many gallons of gasoline are used annually by all of the cars in the United States?

First, consider that the United States has about 250 million people. Assuming that each family of about five people has a car, an estimate of the number of cars in the country is 50 million.

Next, decide the order of magnitude of the average distance each car travels every year. Some cars travel as few as 1000 mi per year, while others travel more than 100 000 mi per year. The appropriate order of magnitude to include in the estimate is 10 000 mi, or 10^4 mi, per year.

If we assume that cars average 20 mi for every gallon of gas, each car needs about 500 gal per year.

$$\left(\frac{10\ 000 \text{ mi}}{1 \text{ year}} \right) \left(\frac{1 \text{ gal}}{20 \text{ mi}} \right) = 500 \text{ gal/year for each car}$$

You have seen the signs before. "Billions of Hamburgers Sold." "Over a Million Satisfied Customers." These are pretty large numbers. Who counted all of those burgers and customers? Can these claims be trusted?

For most large numbers, such as the number of stars in the universe, the exact quantity is not known. Nobody really needs the exact number of burgers, customers, or stars, so no one is paid to make an exact count. Typically, these numbers are estimates from other data, such as the amount of raw materials consumed, the sales income of a company, or the number of stars in a very small patch of sky.

To see how this works, consider M&M's™ chocolate candies. How many of these candies have been eaten over all of time? According to the head office of Mars, Inc., the manufacturer of M&M's candies, "well over 100 million candies a day have been consumed" for the last 10 years. To keep up with this rate of consumption, 10 years (3650 days) would require the production of the following number of candies:

$$\frac{10^8 \text{ candies}}{\text{day}} \times (3.6 \times 10^3 \text{ days}) = 3.6 \times 10^{11} \text{ candies}$$

M&M's candies have been produced in large quantities since 1942. Assuming that the average production rate for each decade is at least half the amount for the last 10 years, we can say that more than 1.3×10^{12}, or 1 trillion, M&M's candies have been eaten over time.

But if no one is counting, can you be sure these claims are reasonable? You can test the validity of these claims by making an order-of-magnitude estimate of what this would mean for a single person and deciding whether it seems reasonable.

Is it reasonable to assume that over 100 million M&M's candies are eaten every day? First consider how many people are likely to be consuming these candies. The population of the United States is about 250 million people. Not all people in the United States eat M&M's candies, but these candies are also sold in many other countries, so a number like 200 million potential consumers seems about right.

Next, examine these numbers on a per-person (or *per capita*) basis by dividing the number eaten per day by the number of people who do the eating.

$$\frac{10^8 \text{ candies/day}}{2 \times 10^8 \text{ people}} = 0.5 \text{ candies per day per person}$$

Is it likely that 200 million people would carefully cut their M&M's candies in half? No, this number is an average over the period of one day. Instead of considering the average per day, it may be more appropriate to consider a longer period of time, like a month. Certainly it is possible to imagine a typical consumer eating 15 candies during a month. This would mean that the average consumer would consume a regular-sized packet every three months or so.

Thus, the claim that 100 million M&M's candies are eaten daily seems reasonable based on the estimates. Breaking large numbers like this down in terms of *per capita* consumption can help identify whether they are reasonable.

Multiplying this by the estimate of the total number of cars in the United States gives an annual consumption of more than 2×10^{10} gallons.

$$(5 \times 10^7 \text{ cars})\left(\frac{500 \text{ gal}}{1 \text{ car}}\right) = 2.5 \times 10^{10} \text{ gal}$$

This corresponds to a yearly consumer expenditure of more than $20 billion! Even so, this estimate may be low because we haven't accounted for commercial consumption and two-car families.

Section Review

1. Which of the following graphs best matches the data shown below?

Volume of air (m^3)	Mass of air (kg)
0.50	0.644
1.50	1.936
2.25	2.899
4.00	5.159
5.50	7.096

(a)

(b)

(c)

Figure 1-15

2. Which of the following equations best matches the data from item 1?
   a. $(\text{mass})^2 = 1.29 \,(\text{volume})$ b. $(\text{mass})(\text{volume}) = 1.29$
   c. $\text{mass} = 1.29 \,(\text{volume})$ d. $\text{mass} = 1.29 \,(\text{volume})^2$

3. Indicate which of the following physics symbols denote units and which denote variables or quantities.
   a. C   b. c c. C d. t e. T   f. T

4. Determine the units of the quantity described by the following combinations of units:
   a. kg (m/s) (1/s)   b. (kg/s) (m/s^2)
   c. (kg/s) $(\text{m/s})^2$ d. (kg/s) (m/s)

5. Which of the following is the best order of magnitude estimate in meters of the height of a mountain?
   a. 1 m   b. 10 m   c. 100 m   d. 1000 m

CHAPTER 1
Summary

KEY TERMS

accuracy (p. 15)

controlled experiment (p. 9)

model (p. 6)

precision (p. 15)

significant figures (p. 16)

system (p. 7)

KEY IDEAS

Section 1-1 What is physics?

- Physics is the study of the physical world, from motion and energy to light and electricity.
- Physics uses the scientific method to discover general laws that can be used to make predictions about a variety of situations.
- A common technique in physics for analyzing a complex situation is to disregard irrelevant factors and create a model that describes the essence of a system or situation.

Section 1-2 Measurements in experiments

- Physics measurements are typically made and expressed in SI, a system that uses a set of base units and prefixes to describe measurements of physical quantities.
- *Accuracy* describes how close a measurement is to reality. *Precision* describes the limitations of the measuring device used.
- Significant figures are used to indicate which digits in a measurement are actual measurements and which are estimates.
- Significant-figure rules provide a means to ensure that calculations do not report results that are more precise than the data used to make them.

Section 1-3 The language of physics

- Physicists make their work easier by summarizing data in tables and graphs and by abbreviating quantities in equations.
- Dimensional analysis can help identify whether a physics expression is a valid one.
- Order-of-magnitude calculations provide a quick way to evaluate the appropriateness of an answer.

Variable symbols		
Quantities		**Units**
$\Delta x, \Delta y$ change in position	m	meters
Δt time interval	s	seconds
m mass	kg	kilograms

THE SCIENCE OF PHYSICS

Review questions

1. Refer to **Table 1-1** on page 5 to identify at least two areas of physics involved in the following:
   a. building a louder stereo system in your car
   b. bungee jumping
   c. judging how hot a stove burner is by looking at it
   d. cooling off on a hot day by diving into a swimming pool

2. Which of the following scenarios fits the approach of the scientific method?
   a. An auto mechanic listens to how a car runs and comes up with an idea of what might be wrong. The mechanic tests the idea by adjusting the idle speed. Then the mechanic decides his idea was wrong based on this evidence. Finally, the mechanic decides the only other problem could be the fuel pump, and he consults with the shop's other mechanics about his conclusion.
   b. Because of a difference of opinions about where to take the class trip, the class president holds an election. The majority of the students decide to go to the amusement park instead of to the shore.
   c. Your school's basketball team has advanced to the regional playoffs. A friend from another school says their team will win because their players want to win more than your school's team does.
   d. A water fountain does not squirt high enough. The handle on the fountain seems loose, so you try to push the handle in as you turn it. When you do this, the water squirts high enough that you can get a drink. You make sure to tell all your friends how you did it.

3. You have decided to select a new car by using the scientific method. How might you proceed?

4. Consider the phrase, "The quick brown fox jumped over the lazy dog." Which details of this situation would a physicist who is modeling the path of a fox ignore?

SI UNITS

Review questions

5. List an appropriate SI base unit (with a prefix as needed) for measuring the following:
   a. the time it takes to play a CD in your stereo
   b. the mass of a sports car
   c. the length of a soccer field
   d. the diameter of a large pizza
   e. the mass of a single slice of pepperoni
   f. a semester at your school
   g. the distance from your home to your school
   h. your mass
   i. the length of your physics-lab room
   j. your height

6. If you square the speed expressed in m/s, in what units will the answer be expressed?

7. If you divide a force measured in newtons (1 newton = 1 kg·m/s^2) by a speed expressed in m/s, in what units will the answer be expressed?

Conceptual questions

8. The height of a horse is sometimes given in units of "hands." Why was this a poor standard of length before it was redefined to refer to exactly 4 in.?

9. Explain the advantages in having the meter officially defined in terms of the distance light travels in a given time rather than as the length of a specific metal bar.

10. Einstein's famous equation indicates that $E = mc^2$, where c is the speed of light and m is the object's mass. Given this, what are the SI units for E?

Practice problems

11. Convert each of the following to the units shown:

    a. 2 dm expressed in mm

    b. 2 h 10 min expressed in s

    c. 16 g expressed in μg

    d. 0.75 km expressed in cm

    e. 0.675 mg expressed in g

    f. 462 μm expressed in cm

    g. 35 km/h expressed in m/s

(See Sample Problem 1A.)

12. If a metric ton is 1.000×10^3 kg, how many 85 kg people can safely occupy an elevator that can hold a maximum mass of exactly 1 metric ton?
(See Sample Problem 1A.)

13. Use the fact that the speed of light in a vacuum is about 3.00×10^8 m/s to determine how many kilometers a pulse from a laser beam travels in exactly 1 h.
(See Sample Problem 1A.)

14. Use the SI prefixes in **Table 1-3** on page 12 to convert these *hypothetical* units of measure into appropriate quantities:

    a. 10 rations

    b. 2000 mockingbirds

    c. 10^{-6} phones

    d. 10^{-9} goats

    e. 10^{18} miners

(See Sample Problem 1A.)

ACCURACY, PRECISION, AND SIGNIFICANT FIGURES

Review questions

15. Can a set of measurements be precise but not accurate? Explain.

16. How many significant figures are in the following measurements?

    a. 300 000 000 m/s

    b. 25.030°C

    c. 0.006 070°C

    d. 1.004 J

    e. 1.305 20 MHz

17. **Figure 1-16** shows photographs of unit conversions on the labels of some grocery-store items. Check the accuracy of these conversions. Are the manufacturers using significant figures correctly?

(a)

(b)

(c)

(d)

Figure 1-16

18. The value of the speed of light is now known to be $2.997\ 924\ 58 \times 10^8$ m/s. Express the speed of light in the following ways:

    a. with three significant figures

    b. with five significant figures

    c. with seven significant figures

19. How many significant figures are there in the following measurements?

    a. 78.9 ± 0.2 m

    b. 3.788×10^9 s

    c. 2.46×10^6 kg

    d. 0.0032 mm

20. Carry out the following arithmetic operations:

    a. find the sum of the measurements 756 g, 37.2 g, 0.83 g, and 2.5 g

    b. find the quotient of 3.2 m/3.563 s

    c. find the product of 5.67 mm $\times \pi$

    d. find the difference of 27.54 s and 3.8 s

21. A fisherman catches two sturgeons. The smaller of the two has a measured length of 93.46 cm (two decimal places and four significant figures), and the larger fish has a measured length of 135.3 cm (one decimal place and four significant figures). What is the total length of the two fish?

22. A farmer measures the distance around a rectangular field. The length of each long side of the rectangle is found to be 38.44 m, and the length of each short side is found to be 19.5 m. What is the total distance around the field?

DIMENSIONAL ANALYSIS AND ORDER-OF-MAGNITUDE ESTIMATES

Review questions

Note: In developing answers to order-of-magnitude calculations, you should state your important assumptions, including the numerical values assigned to parameters used in the solution. Since only order-of-magnitude results are expected, do not be surprised if your results differ from those of other students.

23. Suppose that two quantities, *A* and *B*, have different dimensions. Which of the following arithmetic operations *could* be physically meaningful?
    a. $A + B$
    b. A/B
    c. $A \times B$
    d. $A - B$

24. Estimate the order of magnitude of the length in meters of each of the following:
    a. a ladybug
    b. your leg
    c. your school building
    d. a giraffe
    e. a city block

25. If an equation is dimensionally correct, does this mean that the equation is true?

26. The radius of a circle inscribed in any triangle whose sides are *a*, *b*, and *c* is given by the following equation, in which *s* is an abbreviation for $(a + b + c) \div 2$. Check this formula for dimensional consistency.

$$r = \sqrt{\frac{(s-a)(s-b)(s-c)}{s}}$$

27. The period of a simple pendulum, defined as the time necessary for one complete oscillation, is measured in time units and is given by the equation

$$T = 2\pi \sqrt{\frac{L}{g}}$$

where *L* is the length of the pendulum and *g* is the acceleration due to gravity, which has units of length divided by time squared. Check this equation for dimensional consistency.

Conceptual questions

28. In a desperate attempt to come up with an equation to solve a problem during an examination, a student tries the following: (velocity in m/s)^2 = (acceleration in m/s^2) × (time in s). Use dimensional analysis to determine whether this equation might be valid.

29. Estimate the number of breaths taken during 70 years, the average life span of a person.

30. Estimate the number of times your heart beats in a day.

31. Estimate the magnitude of your age, as measured in units of seconds.

32. An automobile tire is rated to last for 50,000 mi. Estimate the number of revolutions the tire will make in its lifetime.

33. Imagine that you are the equipment manager of a professional baseball team. One of your jobs is to keep a supply of baseballs for games in your home ballpark. Balls are sometimes lost when players hit them into the stands as either home runs or foul balls. Estimate how many baseballs you have to buy per season in order to make up for such losses. Assume your team plays an 81-game home schedule in a season.

34. A chain of hamburger restaurants advertises that it has sold more than 50 billion hamburgers over the years. Estimate how many pounds of hamburger meat must have been used by the restaurant chain to make 50 billion hamburgers and how many head of cattle were required to furnish the meat for these hamburgers.

35. Estimate the number of piano tuners living in New York City (population ≈ 7.5 million). This problem was first proposed by the physicist Enrico Fermi, who was well known for his ability to quickly make order-of-magnitude calculations.

36. Estimate the number of table-tennis balls that would fit (without being crushed) into a room that is 4 m long, 4 m wide, and 3 m high. Assume that the diameter of a ball is 3.8 cm.

MIXED REVIEW PROBLEMS

37. Calculate the circumference and area for the following circles. (Use the following formulas: circumference $= 2\pi r$ and area $= \pi r^2$.)

   a. a circle of radius 3.5 cm

   b. a circle of radius 4.65 cm

38. A billionaire offers to give you $5 billion if you will count out the amount in $1 bills or a lump sum of $5000. Which offer should you accept? Explain your answer. Assume that you can count at an average rate of one bill per second, and be sure to allow for the fact that you need about 10 h a day for sleeping and eating.

39. A quart container of ice cream is to be made in the form of a cube. What should be the length of one side in meters for the container to have the appropriate volume? (Use the following conversion: 4 quarts $= 3.786 \times 10^{-3}$ m^3.)

40. You can obtain a rough estimate of the size of a molecule with the following simple experiment: Let a droplet of oil spread out on a fairly large but smooth water surface. The resulting "oil slick" that forms on the surface of the water will be approximately one molecule thick. Given an oil droplet with a mass of 9.00×10^{-7} kg and a density of 918 kg/m^3 that spreads out to form a circle with a radius of 41.8 cm on the water surface, what is the approximate diameter of an oil molecule?

Technology & Learning

Graphing calculators

Program your graphing calculator to display graphs showing the relationship between the mass and length of wire made of three different substances. All three kinds of wire have a diameter of 0.50 cm. Then find the masses of each kind of wire at the following lengths:

a. 0.3 cm

b. 3.8 cm

c. 5.2 cm

d. 7.3 cm

Press [Y=] and [CLEAR] to clear any functions. Then enter the functions shown in the table below.

Press [WINDOW] and set Xmin to 0, Xmax to 10, Xscl to 1, Ymin to 0, Ymax to 3, and Yscl to 0.1. Then press [GRAPH].

The calculator will display three graphs. Each graph represents one type of wire. The mass of the wire in grams is plotted on the *y*-axis, and the length of the wire in centimeters is plotted on the *x*-axis.

Press [TRACE], and use the right/left arrow keys to trace along the curves. To switch from one graph to the next one, use the up/down arrow keys.

Keystrokes	Display
1. [8] [.] [9] [6] [×] [X,T,θ] [×] [2nd] [π] [×] [.] [2] [5] [x²] [ENTER]	Y1 = 8.96*X*π*.25²
2. [2] [.] [7] [0] [×] [X,T,θ] [×] [2nd] [π] [×] [.] [2] [5] [x²] [ENTER]	Y2 = 2.70*X*π*.25²
3. [1] [0] [.] [4] [9] [×] [X,T,θ] [×] [2nd] [π] [×] [.] [2] [5] [x²] [ENTER]	Y3 = 10.49*X*π*.25²

41. An ancient unit of length called the cubit was equal to six palms, where a palm was the combined width of the four fingers of a hand. It has been said that Noah's ark was 300 cubits long, 50 cubits wide, and 30 cubits high. Estimate the volume of the ark in cubic meters. Also estimate the volume of a typical home, and compare it with the ark's volume.

42. If one micrometeorite (a sphere with a diameter of 1.0×10^{-6} m) struck each square meter of the moon each second, how many years would it take to cover the moon with micrometeorites to a depth of 1.0 m? (Hint: Consider a cubic box, 1.0 m on a side, on the moon, and find how long it would take to fill the box with micrometeorites.)

43. One cubic centimeter (1.0 cm^3) of water has a mass of 1.0×10^{-3} kg at 25°C. Determine the mass of 1.0 m^3 of water at 25°C.

44. Assuming biological substances are 90 percent water and the density of water is 1.0×10^3 kg/m^3, estimate the masses (density multiplied by volume) of the following:
   a. a spherical cell with a diameter of 1.0 μm (volume $= \frac{4}{3}\pi r^3$)
   b. a fly, which can be approximated by a cylinder 4.0 mm long and 2.0 mm in diameter (volume $= \ell\pi r^2$)

45. The radius of the planet Saturn is 5.85×10^7 m, and its mass is 5.68×10^{26} kg.
   a. Find the density of Saturn (its mass divided by its volume) in grams per cubic centimeter. (The volume of a sphere is given by $\frac{4}{3}\pi r^3$.)
   b. Find the surface area of Saturn in square meters. (The surface area of a sphere is given by $4\pi r^2$.)

Alternative Assessment

Performance assessment

1. Imagine that you are a member of your state's highway board. In order to comply with a bill passed in the State Legislature, all of your state's highway signs must show distances in miles and kilometers. Two plans are before you. One plan suggests adding metric equivalents to all highway signs as follows: Dallas 300 mi (483 km). Proponents of the other plan say that the first plan makes the metric system seem more cumbersome, so they propose replacing the old signs with new signs every 50 km as follows: Dallas 300 km (186 mi). Participate in a class debate about which plan should be followed.

2. Can you measure the mass of a five-cent coin with a bathroom scales? Record the mass in grams displayed by your scales as you place coins on the scales, one at a time. Then divide each measurement by the number of coins to determine the approximate mass of a single five-cent coin, but remember to follow the rules for significant figures in calculations. Which estimate do you think is the most accurate? Which is the most precise?

Portfolio projects

3. Find out who were the Nobel laureates for physics last year, and research their work. Alternatively, explore the history of the Nobel Prizes. Who founded the awards? Why? Who delivers the award? Where? For either topic, summarize your findings in a brochure, poster, or computer presentation.

4. You have a clock with a second hand, a ruler marked in millimeters, a graduated cylinder marked in milliliters, and scales sensitive to 1 mg. How would you measure the mass of a drop of water? How would you measure the period of a swing? How would you measure the volume of a paper clip? How can you improve the accuracy of your measurements? Write the procedures clearly so that a partner can follow them and obtain reasonable results.

5. Create a poster or other presentation depicting the possible ranges of measurement for a dimension, such as distance, time, temperature, speed, or mass. Depict examples ranging from the very large to the very small. Include several examples that are typical of your own experiences.

CHAPTER 1
Laboratory Exercise A

PHYSICS AND MEASUREMENT

In this laboratory exercise, you will gain experience making measurements as a physicist. All measurements will be made using SI units to the precision allowed by your instruments.

SAFETY

- Review lab safety guidelines. Always follow correct procedures in the lab.

PREPARATION

1. Read the entire lab procedure, and plan the steps you will take.

2. Prepare a data table in your lab notebook with seven columns and five rows, as shown below. In the first row, label the second through seventh columns *Trial 1, Trial 2, Trial 3, Trial 4, Trial 5*, and *Trial 6*. In the first column, label the second through fifth rows *Length (cm), Width (cm), Thickness (cm)*, and *Mass (kg)*.

	Trial 1	Trial 2	Trial 3	Trial 4	Trial 5	Trial 6
Length (cm)						
Width (cm)						
Thickness (cm)						
Mass (kg)						

PROCEDURE

Measuring length, width, thickness, and mass

3. Use a meterstick to measure the length of the wood block. Record all measured digits plus one estimated digit.

4. Follow the same procedure to measure the width and thickness of the block. Repeat all measurements two more times. Record your data.

5. Carefully adjust the balance to make sure it is at zero when there is no mass on it. Your teacher will show you how to adjust the balances in your classroom to zero. Use the balance to find the mass of the block, as shown in **Figure 1-17.** Record the measurement in your data table.

6. Repeat the mass measurement three more times, and record the values in your data table. Each time, place the block on a different side.

7. For Trials 4–6, repeat steps 3 through 6 with the second wood block.

ANALYSIS AND INTERPRETATION

Calculations and data analysis

1. Organizing data   Using your data, calculate the volume of the wood block for each trial. The equation for the volume of a rectangular block is
volume = length × width × thickness.

2. Analyzing data   Use your measurements from different trials to answer the following questions.

    a. For each block, what is the difference between the smallest length measurement and the largest length measurement?

    b. For each block, what is the difference between the smallest calculated volume and the largest calculated volume?

    c. Based on your answers to (a) and (b), how does multiplying several length measurements together to find the volume affect the precision of the result?

Conclusions

3. Interpreting results   For each trial, find the ratio between the mass and the volume. Based on your data, what is the relationship between the mass and volume?

4. Evaluating methods   For each type of measurement you made, explain how error could have affected your results. Consider method error and instrument error. How could you find out whether error had a significant effect on your results for each part of the lab?

Figure 1-17

Step 3: Always record measurements to the precision allowed by your instruments.

Step 5: Make sure you know how to use the balances in your classroom. The balance should read zero when there is no mass on it. The number of significant figures in your measurement will be determined by your instruments.

CHAPTER 1
Laboratory Exercise B

OBJECTIVES

- Use typical laboratory equipment to measure the distance and time of an observed motion.
- Measure distance and time in SI units.
- Determine the appropriate number of significant figures for various measurements.
- Use graphs and data analysis to examine the relationships between measured physical quantities.

MATERIALS LIST

✔ meterstick
✔ rectangular wooden block

PROCEDURE

CBL AND SENSORS

✔ C-clamp
✔ CBL
✔ CBL motion detector
✔ graphing calculator with link cable
✔ support stand and clamp
✔ thin foam pad

STOPWATCH

✔ stopwatch

TIME AND MEASUREMENT

Many fields of physics require experimenters to study events that take place over time. In this laboratory exercise, you will become familiar with the kinds of equipment used to make these measurements, such as metersticks and stopwatches; or motion detectors, CBL, and graphing calculators. All measurements will be made using SI units to the precision allowed by your instruments.

SAFETY

- **Perform this lab in a clear area. Falling or dropped masses can cause serious injury.**

PREPARATION

1. Determine whether you will be using the CBL and sensors or the stopwatch. Read the entire lab for the appropriate procedure, and plan the steps you will take.

2. Prepare a data table in your lab notebook with three columns and seven rows. In the first row, label the columns *Trial*, *Distance (m)*, and *Time (s)*. Label the second through seventh rows *1, 2, 3, 4, 5,* and *6*.

Trial	Distance (m)	Time (s)
1		
2		
3		
4		
5		
6		

Stopwatch procedure begins on page 36.

PROCEDURE

CBL AND SENSORS

Measuring distance and time

3. This exercise should be performed with a partner. Perform this in a clear area away from other groups. Connect the CBL to the calculator with the unit-to-unit link cable using the ports located on each unit. Connect the motion detector to the SONIC port.

4. Set up the apparatus as shown in **Figure 1-18.** Securely clamp the motion detector to the support stand so that it faces downward, over the edge of the table. Make sure the motion detector is far enough away from the edge of the table that the signal will not hit the tabletop, clamp, or table leg.

5. Use a meterstick to measure a distance 0.5 m below the motion detector, and mark the point with tape on the table or stand. This is the starting position from which the blocks will be dropped from rest. Measure the height of the tape mark above the floor. Record this distance in your data table.

6. Start the program PHYSICS on your graphing calculator. Select option *SET UP PROBES* from the MAIN MENU. Enter 1 for the number of probes. Select the motion detector from the list.

7. Select the *MONITOR INPUT* option from the DATA COLLECTION menu. Test to be sure the motion detector is positioned properly.

   a. Read the CBL measurement for the distance between the motion detector and the floor. Measure the distance with a meterstick to confirm the CBL value. If the CBL reading is too low, adjust the motion detector to make sure the signal is not hitting the table instead of the floor.

   b. Cover the floor under the motion detector with a foam pad to reduce feedback.

   c. Hold the wooden block directly beneath the motion detector, and move the block up and down, reading the CBL measurements. Make sure the motion detector is not detecting other objects, such as the stand base, the tabletop, or the table leg. When the probe is functioning correctly, press + on the calculator to return to the MAIN MENU.

8. Select the *COLLECT DATA* option. Enter 0.02 for the time between samples. Enter 99 for the number of samples.

   a. Check the values you entered, and press ENTER. If the values are correct, select *USE TIME SETUP* to continue. If you made a mistake entering the time values, select *MODIFY SETUP*, reenter the values, and continue.

Figure 1-18

Step 4: The motion detector should be clamped securely to the stand, and the base of the stand should be clamped to the table if possible. Tape the cord to the stand to keep it out of the way.

Step 7: With the CBL in MONITOR INPUT mode, move the wooden block up and down below the motion detector to check the readings.

b. If you are given a choice on the TIME GRAPH menu, select *NON-LIVE DISPLAY.* Otherwise, continue to the next step.

9. One student should hold the block horizontally between flat hands, as shown in **Figure 1-19.** Position the block directly below the motion detector and level with the 0.5 m mark.

10. Turn on the CBL and the graphing calculator. When the area is clear of people and objects, one student should press ENTER on the graphing calculator. As soon as the motion detector begins to click, the student holding the block should release the block by pulling both hands out to the side. Releasing the block this way will prevent the block from twisting as it falls, which could affect the results of this experiment.

11. When the motion detector has stopped clicking and the CBL displays DONE, press ENTER on the graphing calculator to get to the SELECT CHANNELS menu. Select the *SONIC* option, and then select *DISTANCE* to plot a graph of distance in meters against time in seconds. The graph should have a smooth shape. If it has spikes or black lines, repeat the trial to obtain a smooth graph, and continue on to the next step.

12. Examine the graph to find the section of the curve that represents the block's motion. On the far left and far right, the curve represents the position of the block before and after its motion. The middle section of the curve represents the motion of the falling block. Sketch the graph in your lab notebook.

13. Use the arrow keys to trace the graph. The x and y coordinates will be displayed as the cursor moves along the graph. Select a point from the beginning of the block's motion and another point from the end. Find the time interval between the two points by finding the difference between their x values. Record this in your data table as the time in seconds. Find the distance moved by the block during that time by finding the difference between the y values of the two points. Record this in your data table as the distance. Press ENTER on the graphing calculator.

14. Repeat for two more trials, recording all data in your data table. Try to drop the block from exactly the same height each time.

15. Switch roles so that the student who dropped the block is now operating the CBL, and repeat the experiment. Perform three trials. Record all data in your data table.

Analysis and Interpretation begins on page 37.

PROCEDURE

STOPWATCH

Measuring distance and time

3. Perform this exercise with a partner. One partner will drop the wooden block from a measured height, and the other partner will measure the time it takes the block to fall to the floor. Perform this in a clear area away from other groups.

4. One student should hold the wooden block with arms held straight out in front at shoulder height. Hold the block between your hands, as shown in **Figure 1-19.** Use the meterstick to measure the

height of the wood block in this position. Record this distance in your data table.

5. Use the stopwatch to time the fall of the block. Make sure the area is clear, and inform nearby groups that you are about to begin. The student holding the block should release it by pulling both hands straight out to the sides. The student with the stopwatch should begin timing the instant the block is released and stop timing as soon as the block hits the floor. In your data table, record the time required for the block to fall.

6. Repeat for two more trials, recording all data in your data table. Try to drop the block from exactly the same height each time.

7. Switch roles, and repeat steps 4 through 6. Perform three trials. Record all data in your data table.

Figure 1-19
Step 4: Hold the block between your hands.
Step 5: Release the block by pulling both hands straight out to the sides. It may take some practice to release the block so that it falls straight down without turning.

ANALYSIS AND INTERPRETATION

Calculations and data analysis

1. **Organizing data**   Did the block always fall from the same height in the same amount of time? Explain how you found the answer to this question.

2. **Graphing data**   Using the data from all trials, make a scatter plot of the distance versus the time of the block's fall. Use a graphing calculator, computer, or graph paper.

Conclusions

3. **Evaluating methods**   For each type of measurement you made, explain how error could have affected your results. Consider method error and instrument error. How could you find out whether error had a significant effect on your results for each part of the lab?

Extensions

4. **Evaluating data**   If there is time and your teacher approves, conduct the following experiment. Have one student drop the wooden block from shoulder height while all other class members time the fall. Perform three trials. Compare results each time. What does this exercise suggest about accuracy and precision in the laboratory?

Motion in One Dimension

PHYSICS IN ACTION

The electric bullet trains in Japan have been running at speeds of 200 km/h since October 1964. Newer trains can achieve speeds of over 270 km/h. Unlike traditional locomotives, each car on the Japanese trains is powered by a motor that also acts as a brake. The individually powered cars can achieve much higher speeds than a long chain of cars pulled by a locomotive engine, and the bullet trains can accelerate and decelerate much more quickly. This allows the quiet bullet trains to be used for travel across Japan and within the cities.

- When the speed of the trains increased by 70 km/h, how much less time did it take to travel 97 km from Tokyo to Mount Fuji?

- How far before a station must the train begin to slow in order to stop directly in front of the platform?

CONCEPT REVIEW

Significant figures (Section 1-2)

SI measurements (Section 1-2)

Graphs and tables (Section 1-3)

2-1
Displacement and velocity

2-1 SECTION OBJECTIVES

- **Describe motion in terms of displacement, time, and velocity.**

- **Calculate the displacement of an object traveling at a known velocity for a specific time interval.**

- **Construct and interpret graphs of position versus time.**

displacement

the change in position of an object

DISPLACEMENT

Imagine that you want to travel from Eugene, Oregon, to Salem, the state capital. There are many ways to get to Salem. Depending on the mode of transportation you choose and the route you take, the trip could take from a few hours to several days. Whether you travel by plane, by car, or on foot, the straight-line distance between your beginning point and your end point will always be the same. To describe the results of your motion from one city to the other, you must be able to specify both the distance from your starting point to your destination and the direction of your travel.

As you move from one position to another, the length of the straight line drawn from your initial position to your final position is your **displacement.** Displacement is the change in position of an object. **Figure 2-1** shows the line between Eugene and Salem along which displacement is measured.

In SI, displacement is measured in meters. One meter is a little longer than one yard. The straight-line distance between Eugene and Salem is approximately 75 000 m.

The concept of displacement is usually used when describing objects that have moved. When an object is at rest, its displacement is zero because its position does not change no matter how much time has elapsed.

Displacement is not equal to distance traveled

The displacement from Eugene to Salem is defined as the change in position between the two cities; this means that the displacement is the same no matter what path you follow to get there. Any path connecting the two cities will result in the same displacement, even if you travel all the way around the world.

Figure 2-2 shows the unusual path of a confused football player. He receives a kickoff at his own goal, runs down the field to within inches of a touchdown, and then runs back

Figure 2-1

Although the distance you travel from Eugene to Salem may vary, your displacement will always be the straight-line distance between the two cities.

toward his own goal until he is tackled at the exact location where he first caught the ball. During this run, his displacement is zero. In other words, there is no change in position during this time interval because his initial position and his final position are exactly the same. Displacement should not be confused with the distance traveled. The football player traveled almost 200 yards, yet his displacement is zero because he ended up where he began.

Coordinate systems are used to describe motion

Yard lines and numbers make it easy to determine displacements during a football game. Applying a set of markers to other situations makes it easier to measure displacements. For example, in **Figure 2-3**, it is useful to place a stick marked in meters under the gecko's feet. You can then mark the gecko's initial position and its final position to find a value for its displacement in meters.

In effect, the measuring stick is used to define a coordinate system. In this case, the gecko is moving from left to right, and the measuring stick serves as the x-axis. The gecko moves along the x-axis from an initial position, x_i, to a final position, x_f. The change in the gecko's position is the difference between its final and initial coordinates, or $x_f - x_i$.

Figure 2-2
The football player ran a great distance, but his displacement during the given time interval is zero because his final position is the same as his original position.

Figure 2-3
A gecko moving along the x-axis from x_i to x_f undergoes a displacement of $\Delta x = x_f - x_i$.

DISPLACEMENT

$$\Delta x = x_f - x_i$$

displacement = change in position = final position − initial position

---

The Greek letter delta (Δ) before the x denotes a *change* in the position of the gecko.

The values of x_i and x_f are determined by their positions on the axis. If the gecko moves from an initial position of $x_i = -3$ m to a final position of $x_f = 5$ m, its displacement is equal to 8 m. That is, the displacement is as follows:

$$\Delta x = x_f - x_i = 5 \text{ m} - (-3 \text{ m}) = 5 \text{ m} + 3 \text{ m} = 8 \text{ m}$$

Conceptual Challenge

1. Space shuttle

A space shuttle takes off from Florida and circles Earth several times, finally landing in California. While the shuttle is in flight, a photographer flies from Florida to California to take pictures of the astronauts when they step off the shuttle. Who undergoes the greater displacement, the photographer or the astronauts?

2. Roundtrip

What is the difference between the displacement of the photographer flying from Florida to California and the displacement of the astronauts flying from California back to Florida?

Figure 2-4

When the gecko is climbing a tree, the displacement is measured on the y-axis. Again, the gecko's position is determined by the position of the same point on its body.

Figure 2-4 shows a gecko that has run up a tree. In this case, place the measuring stick parallel with the tree. The measuring stick in this position will serve as the y-axis. The gecko's initial and final positions will be indicated by y_i and y_f, and the displacement is denoted as Δy.

Displacement can be positive or negative

From the equation for displacement, we see that Δx is positive if x_f is greater than x_i and negative if x_f is less than x_i. Displacement is an example of a quantity that has both magnitude and direction. In the one-dimensional motion that we have been describing, there are only two directions in which an object can move, and these can be specified by plus and minus signs. In this book, unless otherwise noted, displacements to the right will be considered positive and displacements to the left will be considered negative. Similarly, upward displacements will be considered positive and downward displacements will be considered negative. **Table 2-1** gives examples of determining displacements for a variety of situations.

The choice of right as positive and left as negative is what is known in physics as a *convention*. A convention is a system that is chosen for convenience and consistency, not necessarily because it has to be that way. In other words, the positive direction could be to the left and the negative direction could be to the right. As long as you are consistent and use the same convention all the time, you will get the same results no matter which convention you use. However, when scientists compare their results, it is very important that they know which convention they are using so that they can be sure they are talking about the same thing.

Table 2-1   Positive and negative displacements

Positive

$\Delta x = x_f - x_i = 80 \text{ cm} - 10 \text{ cm} = +70 \text{ cm}$

$\Delta x = x_f - x_i = 12 \text{ cm} - 3 \text{ cm} = +9 \text{ cm}$

$\Delta x = x_f - x_i = 6 \text{ cm} - (-10 \text{ cm}) = +16 \text{ cm}$

Negative

$\Delta x = x_f - x_i = 20 \text{ cm} - 80 \text{ cm} = -60 \text{ cm}$

$\Delta x = x_f - x_i = 0 \text{ cm} - 15 \text{ cm} = -15 \text{ cm}$

$\Delta x = x_f - x_i = -20 \text{ cm} - (-10 \text{ cm}) = -10 \text{ cm}$

VELOCITY

A bullet train does not always travel the straight-line distance between two points, but travelers can get from one city to another in less time on the train than it would take them to drive a car along a straight road between the two cities. This is because the train moves much faster than a car does, so that it can cover a greater distance in a shorter time than the car can. The displacement—the straight-line distance from one city to the other—is the same whether the travelers drive or take the train, but the bullet train allows them to make that displacement in less time. The quantity that measures how fast something moves from one point to another is *velocity*.

Average velocity is displacement in a given time

To calculate the average velocity of an object, you must know the object's displacement. You must also know the time the object left its initial position and the time it arrived at its final position. **Average velocity** is equal to the displacement divided by the time during which the displacement occurred. In SI, the unit of velocity is meters per second (m/s).

CONCEPT PREVIEW

In Chapter 3, you will learn how to specify displacement in two dimensions.

average velocity

total displacement divided by the time interval during which the displacement occurred

AVERAGE VELOCITY

$$v_{avg} = \frac{\Delta x}{\Delta t} = \frac{x_f - x_i}{t_f - t_i}$$

$$\text{average velocity} = \frac{\text{change in position}}{\text{change in time}} = \frac{\text{displacement}}{\text{time interval}}$$

SAMPLE PROBLEM 2A

Finding the average velocity

PROBLEM

During a race on level ground, Andra covers 825 m in 137 s while running due west. Find Andra's average velocity.

SOLUTION

Given: $\Delta x = 825$ m to the west
              $\Delta t = 137$ s

Unknown: $v_{avg} = ?$

Use the average velocity equation.

$$v_{avg} = \frac{\Delta x}{\Delta t}$$

$$v_{avg} = \frac{\Delta x}{\Delta t} = \frac{825 \text{ m}}{137 \text{ s}} = 6.02 \text{ m/s to the west}$$

CALCULATOR SOLUTION

The calculator answer is 6.02189781, but both the values for the displacement and the time have three significant figures, so the velocity must be reported as 6.02 m/s.

Finding the average velocity

1. Heather and Matthew take 34 min to walk eastward along a straight road to a store 2.0 km away. What is their average velocity in m/s?

2. Eugene is 75.0 km due south of Salem. If Joe rides from Salem to Eugene on his bike in 6.00 h, what is his average velocity?

3. If the bus stop is 0.68 km down the street from the museum and it takes you 9.5 min to walk north from the bus stop to the museum entrance, what is your average velocity?

4. Simpson drives his car with an average velocity of 24 m/s toward the east. How long will it take him to drive 560 km on a perfectly straight highway?

5. How much time would Simpson save by increasing his average velocity to 26 m/s east?

6. A bus traveled south along a straight path for 3.2 h with an average velocity of 88 km/h, stopped for 20.0 min, then traveled south for 2.8 h with an average velocity of 75 km/h.

    a. What is the average velocity for the total trip?
    b. What is the displacement for the total trip?

Imagine taking a trip in a car along a perfectly straight highway. At the end of your journey, it is simple to calculate your average velocity. The car's odometer gives you the distance traveled, a compass can give you the direction, and a watch can supply the time interval. For example, if you left your house at 10 A.M. and arrived at your friend's house—located 370 km (230 mi) to the west—at 3 P.M., your average velocity for the trip would be as follows.

$$v_{avg} = \frac{\Delta x}{\Delta t} = \frac{370 \text{ km}}{5.0 \text{ h}} = 74 \text{ km/h to the west}$$

However, you probably did not travel at 74 km/h (46 mi/h) at every moment of your trip. You may have stopped for lunch or to buy gas. You probably also spent some time stopped at red lights or driving more slowly because of traffic or road construction. On the other hand, while you were on the freeway, you were driving at 88 km/h (55 mi/h).

The average velocity is equal to the constant velocity you would need to have to cover the given displacement in a given time interval. That is, if you left your house and maintained a velocity of 74 km/h to the west at every moment, it would take 5.0 h for you to travel 370 km.

Velocity is not the same as speed

In everyday usage, the terms *speed* and *velocity* are used interchangeably. In physics, however, there is a distinction between these two quantities. As we have seen, velocity has both magnitude and direction. That is, velocity indicates not only how fast something moves but also the direction of its motion. Speed has no direction, only magnitude. The average velocity depends on the total displacement, but the average speed is equal to the distance traveled divided by the time interval.

Velocity can be interpreted graphically

The runner in **Figure 2-5** completes a 400 m race in 55.00 s. The starting line, x_i, is at zero and the finish line, x_f, is at 400 m. The position of the runner is measured at 11.00 s intervals. These values are shown in **Table 2-2.** As you can see, the runner travels a greater distance in the second time interval than in the first, and then continues speeding up to cover larger distances in the next two time intervals.

When these points are plotted on a graph, the slope of the line connecting one point and the next point indicates the average velocity between those points. On a graph, this means that the slope of the line connecting the initial point (t_i, x_i) and the final point (t_f, x_f) is equal to the average velocity of the runner. To better understand this, compare the equation for the slope of the line with the equation for the average velocity.

Figure 2-5
The velocity of this runner can be analyzed throughout the race by plotting the runner's position against time.

Table 2-2 Positions of a runner at specific instants of time	
t (s)	x (m)
0.00	0
11.00	60
22.00	135
33.00	220
44.00	315
55.00	400

$$\text{slope of a line} \qquad\qquad \text{average velocity}$$

$$\text{slope} = \frac{\text{rise}}{\text{run}} = \frac{\text{change in vertical coordinates}}{\text{change in horizontal coordinates}} \qquad v_{avg} = \frac{\Delta x}{\Delta t} = \frac{x_f - x_i}{t_f - t_i}$$

This relationship between the slope of the position-time graph and the average velocity is very useful to physicists. Because the slope is equal to the velocity, you can tell a lot about the velocity of an object by the shape of its position-time graph. A steeper slope represents a greater change in position in a given time than a more gradual slope, so a steeper slope represents a larger velocity. A position-time graph that is parallel to the time axis indicates that the position remains constant over time; in other words, the object

Conceptual Challenge

1. Book on a table A book is moved once around the edge of a tabletop with dimensions 1.75 m × 2.25 m. If the book ends up at its initial position, what is its displacement? If it completes its motion in 23 s, what is its average velocity? What is its average speed?

2. Travel Car A travels from New York to Miami at a speed of 25 m/s. Car B travels from New York to Chicago, also at a speed of 25 m/s. Are the velocities of the cars equal? Explain.

(a)

(b)

Figure 2-6

The solid line represents the runner's actual position as a function of time. The dotted line **(a)** represents the average velocity of the runner. The straight line drawn between two points over a shorter time interval **(b)** shows the average velocity for that time.

Did you know?

When you use a car's speedometer to check your speed, the speedometer tells you the *instantaneous speed* of the car. The speedometer's reading is speed, the magnitude of velocity. In order to give a reading of velocity, the speedometer would have to indicate not only how fast you are driving but also in what direction.

is at rest. Finding the slope of the line allows you to find the average velocity of an object over a long time interval or a short one.

Figure 2-6 is a graph of the position of the runner at every moment, from the beginning of the race (x_i at time t_i) to the end of the race (x_f at time t_f). Notice that time is graphed on the *x*-axis and position is graphed on the *y*-axis. Each point on the graph (t, x) represents the position of the runner at a specific time. If the runner left the starting line and maintained a constant velocity at every moment of the race until crossing the finish line, all these points would be on a straight line. This line is shown as a dotted line in part **(a)** on the graph.

The slope of the dotted line is Δx divided by the time interval for the motion, Δt. Therefore, the average velocity of the runner from t_i to t_f is equal to the slope of the straight line joining the initial and final points when the runner's position is plotted versus time.

How would you find the exact velocity of the runner at $t = 16.50$ s? The line representing the average velocity does not tell us very much about the velocity at that point on the curve. However, we can come closer to finding the velocity at $t = 16.50$ s by finding the average velocity over a very small time interval. For example, if we draw the line whose slope is the average velocity during the time interval from $t = 11.00$ s to $t = 33.00$ s, we see that this line is closer to the curve at $t = 22.00$ s than the line representing the average velocity for the entire race. This is shown in part **(b)** on the graph.

As the time interval becomes smaller and smaller, the slope of the line representing the average velocity is closer to the curve for that time interval. When the time interval is infinitesimally small, the line will be tangent to the curve at that point. The slope of this tangent line is equal to the value of the *instantaneous velocity* at that point.

1. Does knowing the displacement between the positions of two objects give you enough information to locate the objects? Explain.

2. What is the shortest possible time in which a bacterium could move at a speed of 3.5 mm/s across a petri dish with a diameter of 8.4 cm?

3. **Figure 2-7** shows position-time graphs of the straight-line movement of two brown bears in a wildlife preserve. Which bear has the greater average velocity over the entire period? Which bear has the greater velocity at $t = 10.0$ min? Is the velocity of bear A always positive? Is the velocity of bear B ever negative?

Figure 2-7

4. A child can push a shopping cart at a speed of 1.5 m/s. How long would it take this child to push the cart down an aisle with a length of 9.3 m?

5. An athlete swims from the north end to the south end of a 50.0 m pool in 20.0 s and makes the return trip to the starting position in 22.0 s.
   a. What is the average velocity for the first half of the swim?
   b. What is the average velocity for the second half of the swim?
   c. What is the average velocity for the roundtrip?

6. Two students walk in the same direction along a straight path, at a constant speed—one at 0.90 m/s and the other at 1.90 m/s.
   a. Assuming that they start at the same point and the same time, how much sooner does the faster student arrive at a destination 780 m away?
   b. How far would the students have to walk so that the faster student arrives 5.50 min before the slower student?

2-2
Acceleration

2-2 SECTION OBJECTIVES

- **Describe motion in terms of changing velocity.**

- **Compare graphical representations of accelerated and nonaccelerated motions.**

- **Apply kinematic equations to calculate distance, time, or velocity under conditions of constant acceleration.**

CHANGES IN VELOCITY

The new bullet trains have a top speed of about 300 km/h. Because a train stops to load and unload passengers, it spends very little time traveling at that top speed. Most of the time the train is in motion, its velocity is either increasing or decreasing. It loses speed as it slows down to stop and gains speed as it pulls away and heads for the next station.

Acceleration measures changes in velocity

Similarly, when a shuttle bus approaches a stop, the driver begins to apply the brakes to slow down 5.00 s before actually reaching the stop. The speed changes from 9.00 m/s to 0.00 m/s over a time of 5.00 s. Sometimes, however, the shuttle stops much more quickly. For example, if the driver slams on the brakes to avoid hitting a dog, the bus slows from 9.00 m/s to 0.00 m/s in just 1.50 s.

Clearly these two stops are very different, even though the shuttle's velocity changes by the same amount in both. What is different in these two examples is the time interval during which the change in velocity occurs. As you can imagine, this difference has a great effect on the motion of the bus, as well as on the comfort and safety of the passengers. A sudden change in velocity feels very different from a slow, gradual change.

The quantity that describes the rate of change of velocity in a given time interval is called **acceleration.** The magnitude of the acceleration is calculated by dividing the total change in an object's velocity by the time interval in which the change occurs.

acceleration

the rate of change of velocity

AVERAGE ACCELERATION

$$a_{avg} = \frac{\Delta v}{\Delta t} = \frac{v_f - v_i}{t_f - t_i}$$

$$\text{average acceleration} = \frac{\text{change in velocity}}{\text{change in time}}$$

Acceleration has dimensions of length divided by time squared. The units of acceleration in SI are meters per second per second, which is equal to meters per second squared, as shown below. When measured in these units, acceleration describes how much the velocity changes in each second.

$$\frac{(m/s)}{s} = \frac{m}{s} \times \frac{1}{s} = \frac{m}{s^2}$$

Average acceleration

PROBLEM

As a shuttle bus comes to a normal stop, it slows from 9.00 m/s to 0.00 m/s in 5.00 s. Find the average acceleration of the bus.

SOLUTION

Given:

$v_i = 9.00$ m/s

$v_f = 0.00$ m/s

$\Delta t = 5.00$ s

Unknown: $a_{avg} = ?$

Use the equation for average acceleration.

$$a_{avg} = \frac{\Delta v}{\Delta t}$$

$$\Delta v = v_f - v_i = 0.00 \text{ m/s} - 9.00 \text{m/s} = -9.00 \text{ m/s}$$

$$a_{avg} = \frac{-9.00 \text{ m/s}}{5.00 \text{ s}} = \frac{-1.80 \text{ m/s}}{\text{s}}$$

$$\boxed{a_{avg} = -1.80 \text{ m/s}^2}$$

Average acceleration

1. When the shuttle bus comes to a sudden stop to avoid hitting a dog, it slows from 9.00 m/s to 0.00 m/s in 1.50 s. Find the average acceleration of the bus.

2. A car traveling initially at 7.0 m/s accelerates to a velocity of 12.0 m/s in 2.0 s. What is the average acceleration of the car?

3. Turner's treadmill starts with a velocity of −1.2 m/s and speeds up at regular intervals during a half-hour workout. After 25 min, the treadmill has a velocity of −6.5 m/s. What is the average acceleration of the treadmill during this period?

4. If a treadmill starts at a velocity of −2.7 m/s and has a velocity of −1.3 m/s after 5.0 min, what is the average acceleration of the treadmill?

5. With an average acceleration of −0.50 m/s^2, how long will it take a cyclist to bring a bicycle with an initial velocity of +13.5 m/s to a complete stop?

Figure 2-8
High-speed trains like this can travel at speeds of about 300 km/h (186 mi/h).

Figure 2-9
When the velocity in the positive direction is increasing, the acceleration is positive. When the velocity is constant, there is no acceleration. When the velocity in the positive direction is decreasing, the acceleration is negative.

Acceleration has direction and magnitude

Figure 2-8 shows a high-speed train pulling out of a station. Imagine that the train is moving to the right, so that the displacement and the velocity are positive. The velocity increases in magnitude as the train picks up speed. Therefore, the final velocity will be greater than the initial velocity, and Δv will be positive. When Δv is positive, the acceleration is positive.

On long trips with no stops, the train may travel for an extended time at a constant velocity. In this situation, since the velocity is not changing, $\Delta v = 0$ m/s. When the velocity is constant, the acceleration is equal to zero.

Imagine that the train, still traveling in the positive direction, slows down as it approaches the next station. In this case, the velocity is still positive, but the acceleration is negative. This is because the initial velocity is larger than the final velocity, so Δv will be negative.

The slope and shape of the graph describe the object's motion

As with all motion graphs, the slope and shape of the velocity-time graph in **Figure 2-9** allow a detailed analysis of the train's motion over time. When the train leaves the station, its speed is increasing over time. The line on the graph plotting this motion slopes up and to the right, as at point **A** on the graph.

When the train moves with a constant velocity, the line on the graph continues to the right but it is straight, with a slope equal to zero. This indicates that the train's velocity is constant, as at point **B** on the graph.

Finally, as the train approaches the station, its velocity decreases over time. The line on the graph plotting this motion slopes down to the right, as at point **C** on the graph. This downward slope indicates that the velocity is decreasing over time.

A negative value for the acceleration does not always indicate a deceleration. For example, if the train were moving in the negative direction, the acceleration would be negative when the train gained speed to leave a station and positive when the train lost speed to enter a station.

Conceptual Challenge

1. Fly ball If a baseball has zero velocity at some instant during a game, is the acceleration of the baseball necessarily zero at that instant? Explain, and give examples.

2. Runaway train If a passenger train is traveling on a straight track with a negative velocity and a positive acceleration, is its velocity increasing or decreasing?

3. Hike-and-bike trail When Jennifer is out for a ride, she slows down on her bike as she approaches a group of hikers on a trail. Explain how her acceleration can be positive even though her speed is decreasing.

Table 2-3 shows how the signs of the velocity and acceleration combine to describe an object's motion. From this table, you can see that a negative acceleration can describe an object that is speeding up (when the velocity is negative) and an object that is slowing down (when the velocity is positive). Use this table to check your answers to problems involving acceleration.

Table 2-3	Velocity and acceleration	
v_i	a	Motion
+	+	speeding up
−	−	speeding up
+	−	slowing down
−	+	slowing down
− or +	0	constant velocity
0	− or +	speeding up from rest
0	0	remaining at rest

MOTION WITH CONSTANT ACCELERATION

Figure 2-10 is a strobe photograph of a ball moving from left to right with constant acceleration. The time interval between successive images is 0.10 s. As the ball's velocity increases, the ball travels a greater distance during each time interval. Because the acceleration is constant, the velocity increases by exactly the same amount during each time interval. Because the velocity increases by the same amount in each time interval, the displacement for each time interval increases by the same amount. The relationships between displacement, velocity, constant acceleration, and time can be written as equations that can apply to any object moving with constant acceleration.

Figure 2-10
The motion in this picture took place in a little over 1.00 s. In this short time interval, your eyes could only detect a blur. This photo shows what really happens within that time.

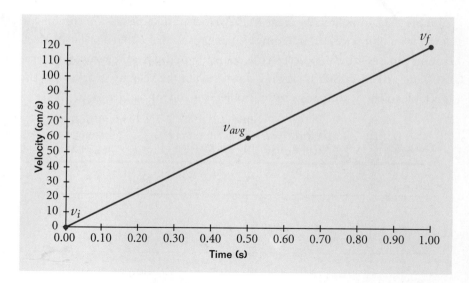

Figure 2-11

If a ball moved for the same time with a constant velocity equal to v_{avg}, it would have the same displacement as the ball in **Figure 2-10** moving with constant acceleration.

Did you know?

Decreases in speed are sometimes called decelerations. Despite the sound of the name, decelerations are really a special case of acceleration in which the magnitude of the velocity—or the speed—decreases with time.

Displacement depends on acceleration, initial velocity, and time

Figure 2-11 is a graph of the ball's velocity plotted against time. The initial, final, and average velocities are marked on the graph. We know that the average velocity is equal to displacement divided by the time interval.

$$v_{avg} = \frac{\Delta x}{\Delta t}$$

For an object moving with constant acceleration, the average velocity is equal to the average of the initial velocity and the final velocity.

$$v_{avg} = \frac{v_i + v_f}{2} \qquad \text{average velocity} = \frac{\text{initial velocity} + \text{final velocity}}{2}$$

To find an expression for the displacement in terms of the initial and final velocity, we can set the expressions for average velocity equal to each other.

$$\frac{\Delta x}{\Delta t} = v_{avg} = \frac{v_i + v_f}{2}$$

$$\frac{\text{displacement}}{\text{time interval}} = \frac{\text{initial velocity} + \text{final velocity}}{2}$$

Multiplying both sides of the equation by Δt leaves us with an expression for the displacement of the ball as a function of time. This equation can be used to find the displacement of any object moving with constant acceleration.

DISPLACEMENT WITH CONSTANT ACCELERATION

$$\Delta x = \tfrac{1}{2}(v_i + v_f)\Delta t$$

displacement $= \tfrac{1}{2}$(initial velocity + final velocity)(time interval)

Displacement with constant acceleration

PROBLEM

A racing car reaches a speed of 42 m/s. It then begins a uniform negative acceleration, using its parachute and braking system, and comes to rest 5.5 s later. Find how far the car moves while stopping.

SOLUTION

Given: $v_i = 42$ m/s $v_f = 0$ m/s
$\Delta t = 5.5$ s

Unknown: $\Delta x = ?$

Use the equation for displacement from page 52.

$$\Delta x = \tfrac{1}{2}(v_i + v_f)\Delta t$$

$$\Delta x = \tfrac{1}{2}(42 \text{ m/s} + 0 \text{ m/s})\,(5.5 \text{ s})$$

$$= \tfrac{1}{2}(42 \text{ m/s})\,(5.5 \text{ s})$$

$$\Delta x = (21 \text{ m/s})\,(5.5 \text{ s})$$

$$\boxed{\Delta x = 120 \text{ m}}$$

CALCULATOR SOLUTION

The calculator answer is 115.5. However, the velocity and time values have only two significant figures each, so the answer must be reported as 120 m.

Displacement with constant acceleration

1. A car accelerates uniformly from rest to a speed of 23.7 km/h in 6.5 s. Find the distance the car travels during this time.

2. When Maggie applies the brakes of her car, the car slows uniformly from 15.00 m/s to 0.00 m/s in 2.50 s. How many meters before a stop sign must she apply her brakes in order to stop at the sign?

3. A jet plane lands with a velocity of +100 m/s and can accelerate at a maximum rate of −5.0 m/s^2 as it comes to rest. Can this plane land at an airport where the runway is 0.80 km long?

4. A driver in a car traveling at a speed of 78 km/h sees a cat 100 m away on the road. How long will it take for the car to accelerate constantly to a stop in exactly 99 m?

5. A car enters the freeway with a speed of 23 km/h and accelerates to a speed of 86 km/h in 3.5 min. How far does the car move while accelerating?

Final velocity depends on initial velocity, acceleration, and time

What if the final velocity of the ball is not known but we still want to calculate the displacement? If we know the initial velocity, the acceleration, and the elapsed time, we can find the final velocity. We can then use this value for the final velocity to find the total displacement of the ball.

By rearranging the equation for acceleration, we can find a value for the final velocity.

$$a = \frac{v_f - v_i}{t_f - t_i} = \frac{v_f - v_i}{\Delta t}$$

$$a\Delta t = v_f - v_i$$

By adding the initial velocity to both sides of the equation, we get an equation for the final velocity of the ball.

$$a\Delta t + v_i = v_f$$

VELOCITY WITH CONSTANT ACCELERATION

$$v_f = v_i + a\Delta t$$

final velocity = initial velocity + (acceleration × time interval)

You can use this equation to find the final velocity of an object moving with constant acceleration after it has accelerated at a constant rate for any time interval, whether the time interval is a single minute or half an hour.

If you want to know the displacement of an object with constant acceleration for a certain time interval, you can obtain another useful expression for displacement by substituting the expression for v_f into the expression for Δx.

$$\Delta x = \tfrac{1}{2}(v_i + v_f)\Delta t$$

$$\Delta x = \tfrac{1}{2}(v_i + a\Delta t + v_i)\Delta t$$

$$\Delta x = \tfrac{1}{2}[2v_i\Delta t + a(\Delta t)^2]$$

CONCEPT PREVIEW

Galileo's achievements in the science of mechanics paved the way for Newton's development of the laws of motion, which we will study in Chapter 4.

DISPLACEMENT WITH CONSTANT ACCELERATION

$$\Delta x = v_i\Delta t + \tfrac{1}{2}a(\Delta t)^2$$

displacement = (initial velocity × time interval) +
$$\tfrac{1}{2}\text{ acceleration} \times (\text{time interval})^2$$

This equation is useful not only for finding how far an object travels under constant acceleration but also for finding the distance required for an object to reach a certain speed or to come to a stop.

Velocity and displacement with constant acceleration

PROBLEM

A plane starting at rest at one end of a runway undergoes a constant acceleration of 4.8 m/s^2 for 15 s before takeoff. What is its speed at takeoff? How long must the runway be for the plane to be able to take off?

SOLUTION

Given: $v_i = 0$ m/s $a = 4.8$ m/s^2 $\Delta t = 15$ s

Unknown: $v_f = ?$ $\Delta x = ?$

Use the equation for the velocity of a constantly accelerated object from page 54.

$$v_f = v_i + a\Delta t$$
$$v_f = 0 \text{ m/s} + (4.8 \text{ m/s}^2)(15 \text{ s})$$

$$\boxed{v_f = 72 \text{ m/s}}$$

Use the equation for the displacement from page 54.

$$\Delta x = v_i \Delta t + \tfrac{1}{2}a(\Delta t)^2$$
$$\Delta x = (0 \text{ m/s})(15 \text{ s}) + \tfrac{1}{2}(4.8 \text{ m/s}^2)(15 \text{ s})^2$$

$$\boxed{\Delta x = 540 \text{ m}}$$

Velocity and displacement with constant acceleration

1. A car with an initial speed of 23.7 km/h accelerates at a uniform rate of 0.92 m/s^2 for 3.6 s. Find the final speed and the displacement of the car during this time.

2. An automobile with an initial speed of 4.30 m/s accelerates at the rate of 3.00 m/s^2. Find the final speed and the displacement after 5.0 s.

3. A car starts from rest and travels for 5.0 s with a uniform acceleration of −1.5 m/s^2. What is the final velocity of the car? How far does the car travel in this time interval?

4. A driver of a car traveling at −15 m/s applies the brakes, causing a uniform acceleration of +2.0 m/s^2. If the brakes are applied for 2.5 s, what is the velocity of the car at the end of the braking period? How far has the car moved during the braking period?

Time can be found from displacement and velocities

So far, all of the equations for constantly accelerated motion have required knowing the time interval. But we can also obtain an expression that relates displacement, velocity, and acceleration without using the time interval. This method involves rearranging one equation to solve for Δt and substituting that expression in another equation. This equation makes it possible to find the final velocity of an accelerated object without knowing how long it has been accelerating. Start with the equation for displacement from page 52.

$$\Delta x = \tfrac{1}{2}(v_i + v_f)\Delta t \quad \text{Now, multiply both sides by 2.}$$

$$2\Delta x = (v_i + v_f)\Delta t \quad \text{Next, divide both sides by } (v_i + v_f)$$
$$\text{to solve for } \Delta t.$$

$$\left(\frac{2\Delta x}{v_i + v_f}\right) = \Delta t$$

Now that we have an expression for Δt, we can substitute this expression into the equation for the final velocity.

$$v_f = v_i + a(\Delta t)$$

$$v_f = v_i + a\left(\frac{2\Delta x}{v_i + v_f}\right)$$

In its present form, this equation is not very helpful because v_f appears on both sides. To solve for v_f, first subtract v_i from both sides of the equation.

$$v_f - v_i = a\left(\frac{2\Delta x}{v_i + v_f}\right)$$

Next, multiply both sides by $(v_i + v_f)$ to get all the velocities on the same side of the equation.

$$(v_f - v_i)(v_f + v_i) = 2a\Delta x = v_f^2 - v_i^2$$

Add v_i^2 to both sides to solve for v_f^2.

FINAL VELOCITY AFTER ANY DISPLACEMENT

$$v_f^2 = v_i^2 + 2a\Delta x$$

$$\textbf{(final velocity)}^2 = \textbf{(initial velocity)}^2 + 2\textbf{(acceleration)}\textbf{(displacement)}$$

When using this equation, you must take the square root of the right side of the equation to find the final velocity. Remember that the square root may be either positive or negative. If you have been consistent in your use of the sign convention, you will be able to determine which value is the right answer by reasoning based on the direction of the motion.

Final velocity after any displacement

PROBLEM

A baby sitter pushing a stroller starts from rest and accelerates at a rate of 0.500 m/s². What is the velocity of the stroller after it has traveled 4.75 m?

SOLUTION

1. DEFINE

Given: $v_i = 0$ m/s $a = 0.500$ m/s²

$\Delta x = 4.75$ m

Unknown: $v_f = ?$

Diagram:

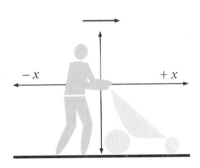

Choose a coordinate system. The most convenient one has an origin at the initial location of the stroller. The positive direction is to the right.

2. PLAN

Choose an equation or situation: Because the initial velocity, acceleration, and displacement are known, the final velocity can be found using the equation from page 56.

$$v_f^2 = v_i^2 + 2a\Delta x$$

3. CALCULATE

Substitute the values into the equation: Remember to take the square root in the final step.

$$v_f^2 = (0 \text{ m/s})^2 + 2(0.500 \text{ m/s}^2)(4.75 \text{ m})$$
$$v_f^2 = 4.75 \text{ m}^2/\text{s}^2$$
$$v_f = \pm\sqrt{4.75 \text{ m}^2/\text{s}^2} = \pm 2.18 \text{ m/s}$$

$$\boxed{v_f = +2.18 \text{ m/s}}$$

4. EVALUATE

Because the stroller is moving to the right from rest with a positive acceleration, we expect the final velocity to be positive. **Table 2-3** shows that an object with a positive acceleration and a positive velocity is speeding up. However, a negative velocity and a positive acceleration indicates that the object is slowing down. Because the stroller starts from rest, only a positive velocity makes sense as the answer.

Final velocity after any displacement

1. Find the velocity after the stroller has traveled 6.32 m.

2. A car traveling initially at +7.0 m/s accelerates at the rate of +0.80 m/s^2 for a distance of 245 m.

   a. What is its velocity at the end of the acceleration?
   b. What is its velocity after it accelerates for 125 m?
   c. What is its velocity after it accelerates for 67 m?

3. A gull soaring in a straight line with an initial velocity of −32 m/s accelerates at a rate of +3.0 m/s^2 for 9.0 s. What is the gull's velocity at the end of the acceleration?

4. An aircraft has a liftoff speed of 120 km/h.

   a. What minimum constant acceleration does this require if the aircraft is to be airborne after a take-off run of 240 m?
   b. How long does it take the aircraft to become airborne?

5. A car accelerates in a straight line from rest at the rate of 2.3 m/s^2.

   a. What is the speed of the car after it has traveled 55 m?
   b. How long does it take the car to travel 55 m?

With the four equations presented in this section, you will find that it is possible to solve any problem involving one-dimensional motion with constant acceleration. For your convenience, the equations that are used most often are listed in **Table 2-4.**

The first column of the table gives the equations in their standard form. The second column gives the form to use for an object that starts at rest and then undergoes constantly accelerated motion. For an object initially at rest, $v_i = 0$. Using this value for v_i in the equations in the first column will result in the equations in the second column. Referring back to the sample problems in this chapter will guide you through using these equations to solve many problems.

Table 2-4
Equations for constantly accelerated straight-line motion

Form to use when accelerating object has an initial velocity	Form to use when accelerating object starts from rest
$\Delta x = \frac{1}{2}(v_i + v_f)\Delta t$	$\Delta x = \frac{1}{2}(v_f)\Delta t$
$v_f = v_i + a(\Delta t)$	$v_f = a(\Delta t)$
$\Delta x = v_i(\Delta t) + \frac{1}{2}a(\Delta t)^2$	$\Delta x = \frac{1}{2}a(\Delta t)^2$
$v_f^2 = v_i^2 + 2a\Delta x$	$v_f^2 = 2a\Delta x$

1. Marissa's car accelerates at a rate of +2.60 m/s^2. How long does it take for Marissa's car to accelerate from a speed of 88.5 km/h to a speed of 96.5 km/h?

2. A bowling ball with a negative initial velocity slows down as it rolls down the lane toward the pins. Is the bowling ball's acceleration positive or negative as it rolls toward the pins?

3. Nathan accelerates his skateboard along a straight path from rest to 12.5 m/s in 2.5 s.
   a. What is Nathan's acceleration?
   b. What is Nathan's displacement during this time interval?
   c. What is Nathan's average velocity during this time interval?

4. Two cars are moving in the same direction in parallel lanes along a highway. At some instant, the instantaneous velocity of car A exceeds the instantaneous velocity of car B. Does this mean that car A's acceleration is greater than car B's? Explain, and use examples.

5. The velocity-versus-time graph for a shuttle bus moving along a straight path is shown in **Figure 2-12.**

   a. Identify the time intervals during which the velocity of the shuttle bus is constant.
   b. Identify the time intervals during which the acceleration of the shuttle bus is constant.
   c. Find the value for the average velocity of the shuttle bus during each time interval identified in **b.**
   d. Find the acceleration of the shuttle bus during each time interval identified in **b.**

Figure 2-12

16

   e. Identify the times at which the velocity of the shuttle bus is zero.
   f. Identify the times at which the acceleration of the shuttle bus is zero.
   g. Explain what the shape of the graph reveals about the acceleration in each time interval.

6. Is the shuttle bus in item 5 always moving in the same direction? Explain, and refer to the time intervals shown on the graph.

2-3
Falling objects

free fall

motion of an object falling with a constant acceleration

Figure 2-13
When there is no air resistance, all objects fall with the same acceleration regardless of their masses.

FREE FALL

On August 2, 1971, a demonstration was conducted on the moon by astronaut David Scott. He simultaneously released a hammer and a feather from the same height above the moon's surface. The hammer and the feather both fell straight down and landed on the lunar surface at exactly the same moment. Although the hammer is more massive than the feather, both objects fell at the same rate. That is, they traveled the same displacement in the same amount of time.

Freely falling bodies undergo constant acceleration

In **Figure 2-13,** a feather and an apple are released from rest in a vacuum chamber. The trapdoor that released the two objects was opened with an electronic switch at the same instant the camera shutter was opened. The two objects fell at exactly the same rate, as indicated by the horizontal alignment of the multiple images.

It is now well known that in the absence of air resistance all objects dropped near the surface of a planet fall with the same constant acceleration. Such motion is referred to as **free fall.**

The amount of time that passed between the first and second images is equal to the amount of time that passed between the fifth and sixth images. The picture, however, shows that the displacement in each time interval did not remain constant. Therefore, the velocity was not constant. The apple and the feather were accelerating.

Compare the displacement between the first and second images to the displacement between the second and third images. As you can see, within each time interval the displacement of the feather increased by the same amount as the displacement of the apple. Because the time intervals are the same, we know that the velocity of each object is increasing by the same amount in each time interval. In other words, the apple and the feather are falling with the same constant acceleration.

The free-fall acceleration is denoted with the symbol g. At the surface of Earth the magnitude of g is approximately 9.81 m/s^2, or 981 cm/s^2, or 32 ft/s^2. Unless stated otherwise, this book will use the value 9.81 m/s^2 for calculations. This acceleration is directed downward, toward the center of the Earth. In our usual choice of coordinates, the downward direction is negative. Thus, the acceleration of objects in free fall is $a = -g = -9.81$ m/s^2.

What goes up, must come down

Figure 2-14 is a strobe photograph of a ball thrown up into the air with an initial upward velocity of +10.5 m/s. The photo on the left shows the ball moving up from its release to the top of its path, and the photo on the right shows the ball moving down from the top of its path. Everyday experience shows that when we throw an object up in the air, it will continue to move upward for a short time, stop momentarily at the peak, and then change direction and begin to fall. Because the object changes direction, it may seem like the velocity and acceleration are both changing. Actually, objects thrown into the air have a downward acceleration as soon as they are released.

In the photograph on the left, the upward displacement of the ball between each successive image is smaller and smaller until the ball stops and finally begins to move with an increasing downward velocity, as shown on the right. As soon as the ball is released with an initial upward velocity of +10.5 m/s, it has an acceleration of -9.81 m/s^2. After 1.0 s ($\Delta t = 1.0$ s) the ball's velocity will change by -9.81 m/s to 0.69 m/s upward. After 2.0 s ($\Delta t = 2.0$ s) the ball's velocity will again change by -9.81 m/s, to -9.12 m/s.

The graph in **Figure 2-15** shows the velocity of the ball plotted against time. As you can see, there is an instant when the velocity of the ball is equal to 0 m/s. This happens at the instant when the ball reaches the peak of its upward motion and is about to begin moving downward. From the graph and the calculations in the preceding paragraph, you can see that this occurs after the ball has been moving for approximately 1.0 s. Although the velocity is zero at the instant the ball reaches the peak, the acceleration is equal to -9.81 m/s^2 at every instant regardless of the magnitude or direction of the velocity. The straight-line slope of the graph indicates that the acceleration is constant at every moment.

(a)   **(b)**

Figure 2-14
At the very top of its path, the ball's velocity is zero, but the ball's acceleration is -9.81 m/s^2 at every point—both when it is moving up **(a)** and when it is moving down **(b)**.

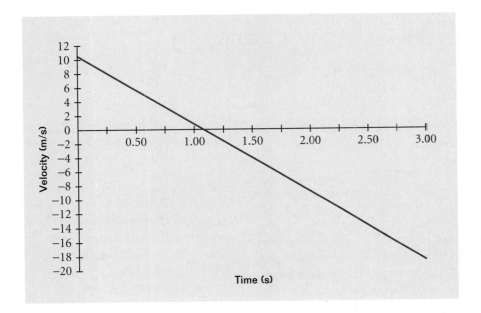

Figure 2-15
On this velocity-time graph, the slope of the line, which is equal to the ball's acceleration, is constant from the moment the ball is released ($t = 0.00$) and throughout its motion.

Freely falling bodies always have the same downward acceleration

It may seem a little confusing to think of something that is moving upward, like the ball in the example, as having a downward acceleration. Thinking of this motion as motion with a positive velocity and a negative acceleration may help. The downward acceleration is the same when an object is moving up, when it is at rest at the top of its path, and when it is moving down. The only things changing are the magnitude of the velocity and the direction of the velocity.

When an object is thrown up in the air, it has a positive velocity and a negative acceleration. From **Table 2-3,** we see that this means the object is slowing down. From the example of the ball and from everyday experience, we know that this makes sense. The object continues to move upward, but with a smaller and smaller velocity. In the photograph of the ball, this decrease in speed is shown by the smaller and smaller displacements as the ball moves up to the top of its path.

At the top of its path, the object's velocity has decreased until it is zero. Although it is impossible to see this because it happens so quickly, the object is actually at rest for an instant. Even though the velocity is zero, however, the acceleration is still -9.81 m/s^2.

Then the object begins moving down. When it is moving down, it has a negative velocity. From **Table 2-3,** we see that a negative acceleration and a negative velocity indicate an object that is speeding up. In fact, this is what happens when objects undergo free-fall acceleration. Objects that are falling toward Earth move faster and faster as they fall. In the photograph of the ball in **Figure 2-14,** this increase in speed is shown by the greater and greater displacements between the images as the ball falls.

Knowing the free-fall acceleration makes it easy to calculate the velocity, time, and displacement of many different motions using the equations for constantly accelerated motion. Because the acceleration is the same throughout the entire motion, you can study the motion of a freely-falling object during any time interval.

CONCEPT PREVIEW

In Chapter 7 we will study how to deal with variations in g with altitude.

Quick Lab

Time Interval of Free Fall

MATERIALS LIST

✔ 1 meterstick or ruler

 SAFETY CAUTION

Avoid eye injury; do not swing metersticks.

Your reaction time affects your performance in all kinds of activities—from sports to driving to catching something that you drop. Your reaction time is the time interval between an event and your response to it.

Determine your reaction time by having a friend hold a meterstick vertically between the thumb and index finger of your open hand. The meterstick should be held so that the zero mark is between your fingers with the 1 cm mark above it.

You should not be touching the meterstick. Without warning you, your friend should release the meterstick so that it falls between your thumb and your finger. Catch the meterstick as quickly as you can. You can calculate your reaction time from the free-fall acceleration and the distance the meterstick has fallen through your grasp.

Falling object

PROBLEM

Jason hits a volleyball so that it moves with an initial velocity of 6.0 m/s straight upward. If the volleyball starts from 2.0 m above the floor, how long will it be in the air before it strikes the floor? Assume that Jason is the last player to touch the ball before it hits the floor.

SOLUTION

1. DEFINE **Given:** $v_i = +6.0$ m/s $a = -9.81$ m/s^2

$\Delta y = -2.0$ m

Unknown: $\Delta t = ?$

Diagram: Choose a coordinate system. Place the starting point of the ball at the origin ($y_i = 0$ at $t_i = 0$).

2. PLAN **Choose the equation(s) or situation:** Both the time interval and the final velocity are unknown. Therefore, first solve for v_f using the equation that does not require time.

$$v_f^2 = v_i^2 + 2a\Delta y$$

Then the equation for v_f that does involve time can be used to solve for Δt.

$$v_f = v_i + a\Delta t$$

Rearrange the equation(s) to isolate the unknown(s): No rearrangement is necessary to calculate v_f, but the second equation must be rearranged to solve for Δt.

$$\Delta t = \frac{v_f - v_i}{a}$$

3. CALCULATE **Substitute the values into the equation:** First find the velocity of the ball at the moment that it hits the floor.

$$v_f^2 = v_i^2 + 2a\Delta y = (6.0 \text{ m/s})^2 + 2(-9.81 \text{ m/s}^2)(-2.0 \text{ m})$$

$$v_f^2 = 36 \text{ m}^2/\text{s}^2 + 39 \text{ m}^2/\text{s}^2 = 75 \text{ m}^2/\text{s}^2$$

When you take the square root to find v_f, the answer will be either positive or negative. In this case, select the negative answer because the ball will be moving toward the floor, in the negative direction.

$$v_f = \sqrt{75 \text{ m}^2/\text{s}^2} = \pm 8.7 \text{ m/s}$$

$$v_f = -8.7 \text{ m/s}$$

continued on
next page

Next, use this value of v_f in the second equation to solve for Δt.

$$\Delta t = \frac{v_f - v_i}{a} = \frac{-8.7 \text{ m/s} - 6.0 \text{ m/s}}{-9.81 \text{ m/s}^2} = \frac{-14.7 \text{ m/s}}{-9.81 \text{ m/s}^2}$$

$$\boxed{\Delta t = 1.50 \text{ s}}$$

4. EVALUATE Because the velocity will decrease by 9.81 m/s in 1 s and because v_i is only 6.0 m/s, it will take a little less than 1 s for the ball to reach its maximum height. Once the ball is at its maximum height, it will take less than 1 s to fall to its original position and a little additional time to fall the final 2.0 m to the floor. Therefore, a total time of between 1.0 s and 2.0 s is reasonable.

PRACTICE 2F

Falling object

1. Calculate the displacement and velocity of the volleyball 0.50 s after Jason hits it.

2. Stephanie serves the volleyball from a height of 0.80 m and gives it an initial velocity of +7.6 m/s straight up.
   a. How high will it go?
   b. How long will it take the ball to reach its maximum height? (Hint: At maximum height, $v = 0$ m/s.)

3. A tennis ball is thrown vertically upward with an initial velocity of +8.0 m/s.
   a. What will its speed be when it returns to its starting point?
   b. How long will it take for it to reach its starting point?

4. A flowerpot falls from a windowsill 25.0 m above the sidewalk.
   a. How fast is the flowerpot moving when it strikes the ground?
   b. How much time does a passerby on the sidewalk below have to move out of the way before the flowerpot hits the ground?

5. A robot probe drops a camera off the rim of a 24-km-deep crater on Mars, where the free-fall acceleration is -3.7 m/s^2. Find the time required for the camera to reach the crater floor and the velocity with which it hits.

6. Maria throws an apple vertically upward from a height of 1.3 m with an initial velocity of +2.4 m/s.
   a. Will the apple reach Maria's friend in a treehouse 5.3 m above the ground?
   b. If the apple is not caught, how long will the apple be in the air before it hits the ground?

1. A coin is tossed upward.
   a. What happens to its velocity while it is in the air?
   b. Does its acceleration increase, decrease, or remain constant while it is in the air?

2. A pebble is dropped down a well and hits the water 1.5 s later. Using the equations for motion with constant acceleration, determine the distance from the edge of the well to the water's surface.

3. A ball is thrown vertically upward. What are its velocity and acceleration when it reaches its maximum altitude? What is its acceleration just before it hits the ground?

4. Two children are bouncing small rubber balls. One child simply drops a ball. At the same time, the second child throws a ball downward so that it has an initial speed of 10 m/s. What is the acceleration of each ball while in motion?

5. A gymnast practices two dismounts from the high bar on the uneven parallel bars. During one dismount, she swings up off the bar with an initial upward velocity of + 4.0 m/s. In the second, she releases from the same height but with an initial downward velocity of −3.0 m/s. How do the final velocities of the gymnast as she reaches the ground differ? What is her acceleration in each case?

6. **Figure 2-16** is a position-time graph of the straight-line motion of a basketball. Use the graph to sketch the path of the basketball and to sketch a velocity-time graph of the basketball's motion.
   a. Is the velocity of the basketball constant?
   b. Is the acceleration of the basketball constant?
   c. What is the initial velocity of the basketball?

Figure 2-16

Time Dilation

Earlier in this chapter, you worked with equations that describe motion in terms of a time interval (Δt). Before Einstein developed the special theory of relativity, everyone assumed that Δt must be the same for any observer, whether that observer is at rest or in motion with respect to the event being measured. This idea is often expressed by the statement that time is *absolute*.

The relativity of time

In 1905, Einstein challenged the assumption that time is absolute in a paper titled "The Electrodynamics of Moving Bodies," which contained his special theory of relativity. One of the consequences of this theory is that Δt *does* depend on the observer's motion. Consider a passenger in a train that is moving uniformly with respect to an observer standing beside the track, as shown in **Figure 2-17.** The passenger on the train shines a pulse of light toward a mirror directly above him and measures the amount of time it takes for the pulse to return. Because the passenger is moving along with the train, he sees the pulse of light travel directly up and then directly back down, as in **Figure 2-17(a).** The observer beside the track, however, sees the pulse hit the mirror at an angle, as in **Figure 2-17(b),** because the train is moving with respect to the track. Thus, the distance the light travels according to the observer is *greater* than the distance the light travels according to the passenger.

One of the postulates of Einstein's theory of relativity, which follows from James Clerk Maxwell's equations about light waves, is that the speed of light is the same for *any* observer, even when there is motion between the source of light and the observer. Light is different from all other phenomena in this respect. Although this postulate seems counterintuitive, it was strongly supported by an experiment performed in 1849 by Armand Fizeau. But if the speed of light is the same for both the passenger on the

Mirror

Passenger's perspective
(a)

(b)   Observer's perspective

Figure 2-17

(a) A passenger on a train sends a pulse of light toward a mirror directly above. **(b)** Relative to a stationary observer beside the track, the distance the light travels is greater than that measured by the passenger.

train and the observer beside the track while the distances traveled are different, the time intervals observed by each person must also be different. Thus, the observer beside the track sees the light travel a greater distance and measures a longer time interval than the passenger does. This effect is known as *time dilation*.

Calculating time dilation

This time dilation is given by the following equation, where Δt represents the time interval according to the person beside the track (the stationary system) and $\Delta t'$ represents the time interval according to the passenger on the train (the moving system):

$$\Delta t = \frac{\Delta t'}{\sqrt{1 - \dfrac{v^2}{c^2}}}$$

In this equation, v represents the speed between the two systems, and c is the speed of light in a vacuum, 3.00×10^8 m/s. At speeds with which we are familiar, where v is much smaller than c, $\dfrac{v^2}{c^2}$ is such a small fraction that Δt is almost equal to $\Delta t'$ as shown in **Table 2-5.** That is why we do not observe the effects of time dilation in our typical experiences. But when speeds are closer to the speed of light, time dilation becomes more noticeable. As seen by this equation, time dilation becomes infinite as v approaches the speed of light.

So far, we have considered this event in terms of the observer beside the track being stationary and the passenger on the train being in motion. According to Einstein, however, the motion between the train and the track is *relative*; that is, either system can be considered to be in motion with respect to the other. For the passenger, the train is stationary and the observer beside the track is in motion. If the light experiment is repeated by the observer beside the track, then the passenger would see the light travel a greater distance than the observer would. Hence, according to the passenger, it is the observer beside the track whose clock runs more slowly. Thus, each observer sees the other observer's clock as running slower than his own. Because either perspective is valid, both observations are correct.

Experimental verification

The effects we have been considering hold true for all physical processes, including chemical and biological reactions. Scientists have empirically demonstrated time dilation by comparing the lifetime of muons (a type of unstable elementary particle) traveling at $0.9994c$ with the lifetime of stationary muons. In another experiment, atomic clocks on jet planes flying around the world were compared with identical clocks at the U.S. Naval Observatory. In both cases, time dilations were observed and the amounts of the dilations matched the predictions of Einstein's theory within the limits of experimental error.

Table 2-5
Time dilations

Moving system ($\Delta t'$)	Stationary system (Δt)
$v = 0$	$v = 0.1c$
$v = 0$	$v = 0.5c$
$v = 0$	$v = 0.9c$
$v = 0$	$v = 0.99c$
$v = 0$	$v = 0.999c$
$v = 0$	$v = 0.9999c$
	+

CHAPTER 2
Summary

KEY TERMS

acceleration (p. 48)

average acceleration (p. 48)

average velocity (p. 43)

constant acceleration (p. 51)

displacement (p. 40)

free fall (p. 60)

free-fall acceleration (p. 60)

velocity (p. 43)

Key Symbols

Quantities		Units	
x	position	m	meters
y	position	m	meters
Δx	displacement	m	meters
Δy	displacement	m	meters
v	velocity	m/s	meters per second
a	acceleration	m/s^2	meters per second^2
g	free-fall acceleration	m/s^2	meters per second^2

KEY IDEAS

Section 2-1 Displacement and velocity

- Displacement is a change of position in a certain direction, not the total distance traveled.
- The average velocity of an object during some time interval is equal to the displacement of the object divided by the time interval. Like displacement, velocity indicates both size and direction.
- The average velocity of an object is given by the following equation:

$$v_{avg} = \frac{\Delta x}{\Delta t} = \frac{x_f - x_i}{t_f - t_i}$$

- The average velocity is equal to the slope of the straight line connecting the initial and final points on a graph of the position of the object versus time.

Section 2-2 Acceleration

- The average acceleration of an object during a certain time interval is equal to the change in the object's velocity divided by the time interval. Acceleration has both magnitude and direction.
- The direction of the acceleration is not always the same as the direction of the velocity. The direction of the acceleration depends on the direction of the motion and on whether the velocity is increasing or decreasing.
- The average acceleration of an object is given by the following equation:

$$a_{avg} = \frac{\Delta v}{\Delta t} = \frac{v_f - v_i}{t_f - t_i}$$

- The average acceleration is equal to the slope of the straight line connecting the initial and final points on the graph of the velocity of the object versus time.
- The equations on page 58 are valid whenever acceleration is constant.

Section 2-3 Falling objects

- An object thrown or dropped in the presence of Earth's gravity experiences a constant acceleration directed toward the center of Earth. This acceleration is called the free-fall acceleration, or the acceleration due to gravity.
- Free-fall acceleration is the same for all objects, regardless of mass.
- The value for free-fall acceleration used in this book is $a = -g = -9.81 \text{ m/s}^2$.
- In this book, the direction of the free-fall acceleration is considered to be negative because the object accelerates toward Earth.

DISPLACEMENT AND VELOCITY

Review questions

1. On the graph in **Figure 2-18,** what is the total distance traveled during the recorded time interval? What is the displacement?

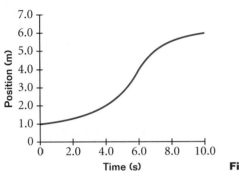

Figure 2-18

2. On a position-time graph such as **Figure 2-18,** what represents the velocity?

3. Sketch a position-time graph for each of the following situations:
   a. an object at rest
   b. an object with constant positive velocity
   c. an object with constant negative velocity

4. The position-time graph for a bug crawling along a line is shown in **Figure 2-19.** Determine whether the velocity is positive, negative, or zero at each of the times marked on the graph.

5. Use the position-time graph in **Figure 2-19** to answer the following questions:
   a. During which time interval(s) is the velocity decreasing?
   b. During which time interval(s) is the velocity increasing?

Figure 2-19

Conceptual questions

6. If the average velocity of a duck is zero in a given time interval, what can you say about the displacement of the duck for that interval?

7. Velocity can be either positive or negative, depending on the direction of the displacement. The time interval, Δt, is always positive. Why?

Practice problems

8. El Paso is 1142 km south of Denver. If a bus makes the trip in 15.08 h, what is its average velocity? (See Sample Problem 2A.)

9. If you live 10.0 km from your school and the bus takes 0.53 h to reach the school driving due east, what is the average velocity of the bus? (See Sample Problem 2A.)

10. **Figure 2-20** is the position-time graph for a squirrel running along a clothesline.

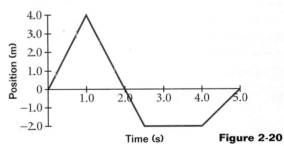

Figure 2-20

   a. What is the squirrel's displacement during the time interval from $t = 0.0$ s to $t = 3.0$ s?
   b. What is the squirrel's average velocity during this interval?
   (See Sample Problem 2A.)

11. The Olympic record for the marathon is 2 h, 9 min, 21 s. The marathon distance is 42.19 km. Determine the average speed in m/s of a runner achieving this record. (See Sample Problem 2A.)

12. Two cars are traveling on a desert road, as shown in **Figure 2-21.** After 5.0 s, they are side by side at the next telephone pole. The distance between the poles is 70.0 m. Identify the following quantities:

    a. the displacement of car A after 5.0 s
    b. the displacement of car B after 5.0 s
    c. the average velocity of car A during 5.0 s
    d. the average velocity of car B during 5.0 s

(See Sample Problem 2A.)

Figure 2-21

13. Sally travels by car from one city to another. She drives for 30.0 min at 80.0 km/h, 12.0 min at 105 km/h, and 45.0 min at 40.0 km/h, and she spends 15.0 min eating lunch and buying gas.

    a. Determine the average speed for the trip.
    b. Determine the total distance traveled.

(See Sample Problem 2A.)

14. Emily takes a trip, driving with a constant velocity of 89.5 km/h to the north except for a 22.0 min rest stop. If Emily's average velocity is 77.8 km/h to the north, how long does the trip take?
(See Sample Problem 2A.)

15. To qualify for the finals in a racing event, a race car must achieve an average speed of 250 km/h on a track with a total length of 1600 m. If a particular car covers the first half of the track at an average speed of 230 km/h, what minimum average speed must it have in the second half of the event to qualify?
(See Sample Problem 2A.)

16. A tortoise can run with a speed of 10.0 cm/s, and a hare can run exactly 20 times as fast. In a race, they both start at the same time, but the hare stops to rest for 2.00 min. The tortoise wins by 20.0 cm.

    a. How long does the race take?
    b. What is the length of the race?

(See Sample Problem 2A.)

17. Runner A is initially 6.0 km west of a flagpole and is running with a constant velocity of 9.0 km/h due east. Runner B is initially 5.0 km east of the flagpole and is running with a constant velocity of 8.0 km/h due west. How far are the runners from the flagpole when their paths cross?
(See Sample Problem 2A.)

VELOCITY AND ACCELERATION

Review questions

18. What is the acceleration for a turtle moving with a constant velocity of 0.25 m/s to the right?

19. Sketch the velocity-time graphs for the following motions.

    a. a city bus moving with a constant velocity
    b. a wheelbarrow speeding up at a uniform rate moving in the positive direction
    c. a tiger speeding up at a uniform rate moving in the negative direction
    d. an iguana slowing down at a uniform rate moving in the positive direction
    e. a camel slowing down at a uniform rate moving in the negative direction

Conceptual questions

20. The strobe photographs in **Figure 2-22** show a disk moving from left to right under different conditions. The time interval between images is constant. Assuming that the direction to the right is positive, identify the following types of motion in each photograph.

    a. the acceleration is positive
    b. the acceleration is negative
    c. the velocity is constant

Figure 2-22

21. If a car is traveling eastward, can its acceleration be westward? Explain, and use examples.

Practice problems

22. A car traveling in a straight line has a velocity of +5.0 m/s. After 4.0 s, its velocity is +8.0 m/s. What is the car's average acceleration in this time interval? (See Sample Problem 2B.)

23. A car traveling at +7.0 m/s accelerates at the rate of +0.80 m/s^2 for an interval of 2.0 s. Find v_f. (See Sample Problem 2D.)

24. A snowmobile has an initial velocity of +3.0 m/s.
    a. If it accelerates at the rate of +0.50 m/s^2 for 7.0 s, what is the final velocity?
    b. If it accelerates at the rate of −0.60 m/s^2, how long will it take to reach a complete stop?
    (See Sample Problem 2D.)

25. A car moving westward along a straight, level road increases its velocity uniformly from +16 m/s to +32 m/s in 10.0 s.
    a. What is the car's acceleration?
    b. What is its average velocity?
    c. How far did it move while accelerating?
    (See Sample Problem 2C.)

26. A ball initially at rest rolls down a hill with an acceleration of 3.3 m/s^2. If it accelerates for 7.5 s, how far will it move? (See Sample Problem 2D.)

27. A plane starting at rest at the south end of a runway undergoes a constant acceleration of +1.6 m/s^2 for a distance of 1600 m before takeoff.
    a. What is the plane's velocity at takeoff?
    b. What is the time required for takeoff?
    (See Sample Problem 2F.)

28. A bus slows down uniformly from 75.0 km/h (21 m/s) to 0.0 km/h in 220 m. How long does it take to stop? (See Sample Problem 2F.)

29. A car accelerates from rest at −3.00 m/s^2.
    a. What is the velocity at the end of 5.0 s?
    b. What is the displacement after 5.0 s?
    (See Sample Problem 2D.)

30. A car starts from rest and travels for 5.0 s with a uniform acceleration of +1.5 m/s^2. The driver then applies the brakes, causing a uniform acceleration of −2.0 m/s^2. If the brakes are applied for 3.0 s, how fast is the car going at the end of the braking period, and how far has it gone from its start? (See Sample Problem 2D.)

31. A car accelerates uniformly from rest to a speed of 65 km/h (18 m/s) in 12 s. Find the distance the car travels during this time. (See Sample Problem 2C.)

32. A boy sledding down a hill accelerates at 1.40 m/s^2. If he started from rest, in what distance would he reach a speed of 7.00 m/s? (See Sample Problem 2C.)

33. The velocity-time graph for an object moving along a straight path is shown in **Figure 2-23.** Find the average accelerations during the time intervals 0.0 s to 5.0 s, 5.0 s to 15.0 s, and 0.0 s to 20.0 s. (See Sample Problem 2B.)

Figure 2-23

34. A speedboat increases its velocity from 25 m/s to the west to 35 m/s to the west in a distance of 250 m.
    a. Find the magnitude of the boat's acceleration.
    b. Find the time it takes the boat to travel this distance.
    (See Sample Problem 2C.)

35. A plane lands with a velocity of +120 m/s and accelerates at a maximum rate of −6.0 m/s^2.
    a. From the instant the plane touches the runway, what is the minimum time needed before it can come to rest?
    b. Can this plane land on a naval aircraft carrier where the runway is 0.80 km long?
    (See Sample Problem 2D.)

FALLING OBJECTS

Conceptual questions

36. A ball is thrown vertically upward.

  a. What happens to the ball's velocity while the ball is in the air?

  b. What is its velocity when it reaches its maximum altitude?

  c. What is its acceleration when it reaches its maximum altitude?

  d. What is its acceleration just before it hits the ground?

  e. Does its acceleration increase, decrease, or remain constant?

37. Figure 2-24 is a strobe image of two falling balls released simultaneously. The ball on the left side is solid, and the ball on the right side is a hollow table-tennis ball. Analyze the motion of both balls in terms of velocity and acceleration.

Figure 2-24

38. A juggler throws a bowling pin into the air with an initial velocity v_i. Another juggler drops a pin at the same instant. Compare the accelerations of the two pins while they are in the air.

39. A bouquet is thrown upward.

  a. Will the value for the bouquet's displacement be the same no matter where you place the origin of the coordinate system?

  b. Will the value for the bouquet's velocity be the same?

  c. Will the value for the bouquet's acceleration be the same?

Practice problems

40. A worker drops a wrench from the top of a tower 80.0 m tall. With what velocity does the wrench strike the ground?
(See Sample Problem 2C.)

41. A physics student throws a softball straight up into the air. The ball was in the air for a total of 3.56 s before it was caught at its original position.

  a. What was the initial velocity of the ball?

  b. How high did it rise?

(See Sample Problem 2F.)

42. A gumdrop is released from rest at the top of the Empire State Building, which is 381 m tall. Disregarding air resistance, calculate the displacement and velocity of the gumdrop after 1.00, 2.00, and 3.00 s.
(See Sample Problem 2F.)

43. A small sandbag is dropped from rest from a hovering hot-air balloon.

  a. After 2.0 s, what is the velocity of the sandbag?

  b. After 2.0 s, how far below the hot-air balloon is the sand bag?

(See Sample Problem 2D.)

44. A ball thrown vertically upward is caught by the thrower after 5.0 s.

  a. Find the initial velocity of the ball.

  b. Find the maximum height it reaches.

(See Sample Problem 2D.)

45. A peregrine falcon dives at a pigeon. The falcon starts downward from rest with free-fall acceleration. If the pigeon is 76.0 m below the initial position of the falcon, how long does it take the falcon to reach the pigeon? Assume that the pigeon remains at rest.
(See Sample Problem 2F.)

46. A ball is thrown upward from the ground with an initial speed of 25 m/s; at the same instant, a ball is dropped from rest from a building 15 m high. After how long will the balls be at the same height?
(See Sample Problem 2F.)

47. A ball is thrown vertically upward with a speed of 25.0 m/s from a height of 2.0 m.

  a. How high does the ball rise?

  b. How long does it take to reach its highest point?

  c. How long does the ball take to hit the ground after it reaches its highest point?

  d. What is the ball's velocity when it returns to the level from which it started?

(See Sample Problem 2D.)

48. A rocket moves upward, starting from rest with an acceleration of $+29.4 \text{ m/s}^2$ for 4.00 s. It runs out of fuel at the end of the 4.00 s but does not stop. How high does it rise above the ground?
(See Sample Problem 2F.)

49. Two students are on a balcony 19.6 m above the street. One student throws a ball vertically downward at 14.7 m/s. At the same instant, the other student throws a ball vertically upward at the same speed. The second ball just misses the balcony on the way down.

    a. What is the difference in the time the balls spend in the air?

    b. What is the velocity of each ball as it strikes the ground?

    c. How far apart are the balls 0.800 s after they are thrown?

(See Sample Problem 2F.)

MIXED REVIEW PROBLEMS

50. If the average speed of an orbiting space shuttle is 31 800 km/h, determine the time required for it to circle Earth. Make sure you consider the fact that the shuttle is orbiting about 320.0 km above Earth's surface. Assume that Earth's radius is 6380 km.

51. A train travels between stations 1 and 2, as shown in **Figure 2-25.** The engineer of the train is instructed to start from rest at station 1 and accelerate uniformly between points A and B, then coast with a uniform velocity between points B and C, and finally accelerate uniformly between points C and D until the train stops at station 2. The distances AB, BC, and CD are all equal, and it takes 5.00 min to travel between the two stations. Assume that the uniform accelerations have the same magnitude, even when they are opposite in direction.

Figure 2-25

a. How much of this 5.00 min period does the train spend between points A and B?

b. How much of this 5.00 min period does the train spend between points B and C?

c. How much of this 5.00 min period does the train spend between points C and D?

52. Two cars travel westward along a straight highway, one at a constant velocity of 85 km/h, and the other at a constant velocity of 115 km/h.

    a. Assuming that both cars start at the same point, how much sooner does the faster car arrive at a destination 16 km away?

    b. How far must the cars travel for the faster car to arrive 15 min before the slower car?

53. A small first-aid kit is dropped by a rock climber who is descending steadily at 1.9 m/s. After 2.5 s, what is the velocity of the first-aid kit, and how far is the kit below the climber?

54. A small fish is dropped by a pelican that is rising steadily at 0.50 m/s.

    a. After 2.5 s, what is the velocity of the fish?

    b. How far below the pelican is the fish after 2.5 s?

55. A ranger in a national park is driving at 56 km/h when a deer jumps onto the road 65 m ahead of the vehicle. After a reaction time of t s, the ranger applies the brakes to produce an acceleration of -3.0 m/s^2. What is the maximum reaction time allowed if the ranger is to avoid hitting the deer?

56. A speeder passes a parked police car at 30.0 m/s. The police car starts from rest with a uniform acceleration of 2.44 m/s^2.

    a. How much time passes before the speeder is overtaken by the police car?

    b. How far does the speeder get before being overtaken by the police car?

57. An ice sled powered by a rocket engine starts from rest on a large frozen lake and accelerates at $+13.0 \text{ m/s}^2$. At t_1 the rocket engine is shut down and the sled moves with constant velocity v until t_2. The total distance traveled by the sled is 5.30×10^3 m and the total time is 90.0 s. Find t_1, t_2, and v.
(See Appendix A for hints on solving quadratic equations.)

58. At the 5800 m mark, the sled in the previous question begins to accelerate at -7.0 m/s^2. Use your answers from item 57 to answer the following questions.

    a. What is the final position of the sled when it comes to rest?

    b. How long does it take for the sled to come to rest?

59. A tennis ball with a velocity of $+10.0$ m/s to the right is thrown perpendicularly at a wall. After striking the wall, the ball rebounds in the opposite direction with a velocity of -8.0 m/s to the left. If the ball is in contact with the wall for 0.012 s, what is the average acceleration of the ball while it is in contact with the wall?

60. A parachutist descending at a speed of 10.0 m/s loses a shoe at an altitude of 50.0 m.

    a. When does the shoe reach the ground?

    b. What is the velocity of the shoe just before it hits the ground?

61. A mountain climber stands at the top of a 50.0 m cliff hanging over a calm pool of water. The climber throws two stones vertically 1.0 s apart and observes that they cause a single splash when they hit the water. The first stone has an initial velocity of $+2.0$ m/s.

    a. How long after release of the first stone will the two stones hit the water?

    b. What is the initial velocity of the second stone when it is thrown?

    c. What will the velocity of each stone be at the instant both stones hit the water?

62. A model rocket is launched straight upward with an initial speed of 50.0 m/s. It accelerates with a constant upward acceleration of 2.00 m/s^2 until its engines stop at an altitude of 150 m.

    a. What is the maximum height reached by the rocket?

    b. When does the rocket reach maximum height?

    c. How long is the rocket in the air?

Technology & Learning

Graphing calculators

In this exercise, you will program your graphing calculator to display graphs of displacement and speed for a falling body. Then identify the displacement and speed for a hailstone after the following time intervals (assuming that the hailstone starts from rest and that there is no air resistance):

    a. 2.9 s   **b.** 4.3 s   **c.** 5.4 s   **d.** 7.2 s

Press [Y=] and [CLEAR] to clear any functions. Then enter the functions in the table shown below.

Press [WINDOW] and set Xmin to 0, Xmax to 15, Xscl to 1, Ymin to 0, Ymax to 300, and Yscl to 25. Then press [GRAPH].

The calculator will display two graphs. For the upper graph, the x value corresponds to the time in seconds and the y value corresponds to the displacement in meters. For the other graph, the x value corresponds to the time in seconds and the y value corresponds to the speed in meters per second.

Press [TRACE] and use the arrow keys to trace along the curve. To switch from one graph to the next, use the up/down arrow keys.

Keystrokes	Display
1. [4] [.] [9] [×] [X,T,θ] [x^2] [ENTER]	Y1 = 4.9*X^2
2. [9] [.] [8] [×] [X,T,θ] [ENTER]	Y2 = 9.8*X

63. A professional race-car driver buys a car that can accelerate at $+5.9 \text{ m/s}^2$. The racer decides to race against another driver in a souped-up stock car. Both start from rest, but the stock-car driver leaves 1.0 s before the driver of the sports car. The stock car moves with a constant acceleration of $+3.6 \text{ m/s}^2$.

  a. Find the time it takes the sports-car driver to overtake the stock-car driver.

  b. Find the distance the two drivers travel before they are side by side.

  c. Find the velocities of both cars at the instant they are side by side.

(See Appendix A for hints on solving quadratic equations.)

64. Two cars are traveling along a straight line in the same direction, the lead car at 25 m/s and the other car at 35 m/s. At the moment the cars are 45 m apart, the lead driver applies the brakes, causing the car to have an acceleration of -2.0 m/s^2.

  a. How long does it take for the lead car to stop?

  b. Assume that the driver of the chasing car applies the brakes at the same time as the driver of the lead car. What must the chasing car's minimum negative acceleration be to avoid hitting the lead car?

  c. How long does it take the chasing car to stop?

65. One swimmer in a relay race has a 0.50 s lead and is swimming at a constant speed of 4.00 m/s. The swimmer has 50.0 m to swim before reaching the end of the pool. A second swimmer moves in the same direction as the leader. What constant speed must the second swimmer have in order to catch up to the leader at the end of the pool?

Alternative Assessment

Performance assessment

1. Can a boat moving eastward accelerate to the west? What happens to the boat's velocity? Name other examples of objects accelerating in the direction opposite their motion, including one with numerical values. Create diagrams and graphs.

2. The next time you are a passenger in a car, record the numbers displayed on the clock, the odometer, and the speedometer as frequently as you can for about 10 min. Create different representations of the car's motion, including maps, charts, and graphs. Exchange your representations with someone who made a different trip, and attempt to reconstruct their trip based on their report.

3. Two stones are thrown from a cliff at the same time with the same speed, one upward and one downward. Which stone, if either, hits the ground first? Which, if either, hits with the higher speed? In a group discussion, make your best argument for each possible prediction. Set up numerical examples and solve them to test your prediction.

Portfolio projects

4. Research typical values for velocities and acceleration of various objects. Include many examples, such as different animals, means of transportation, sports, continental drift, light, subatomic particles, and planets. Organize your findings for display on a poster or some other form.

5. Research Galileo's work on falling bodies. What did he want to demonstrate? What opinions or theories was he trying to refute? What arguments did he use to persuade others that he was right? Did he depend on experiments and observations, logic, or other approaches?

6. The study of various motions in nature requires devices for measuring periods of time. Prepare a presentation on a specific type of clock, such as water clocks, sand clocks, pendulum clocks, wind-up clocks, atomic clocks, or biological clocks. Who invented or discovered the clock? What scale of time does it measure? What are the principles or phenomena behind each clock? Can they be calibrated?

CHAPTER 2
Laboratory Exercise

MEASURING TIME AND MOTION

In this experiment, you will measure time intervals and displacements and determine the velocity and acceleration of free-falling bodies, using either a CBL™ unit with a motion detector or a recording timer.

- **CBL with motion detector**   The motion detector emits short bursts of ultrasonic waves and then "listens" for the echo of these waves as they return to it. Then the CBL uses the speed of the ultrasonic waves and the time it took for the waves to return to the motion detector to determine the distance to the object.

- **Recording timer**   A recording timer measures the time it takes an object to move a short distance by making marks at regular time intervals on a strip of paper attached to the moving object. As the paper tape is pulled through the timer, the distance between two dots on the tape is the distance the tape moved during one back-and-forth vibration of the clapper, the *period* of the timer.

OBJECTIVES

- Measure motion in terms of the change in distance during a period of the timer or motion detector.
- Compare the speed and acceleration of different falling masses at different stages of free fall.
- Compare the experimental value for the average acceleration to the accepted value for free-fall acceleration.

MATERIALS LIST

✔ C-clamp
✔ meterstick
✔ masking tape

PROCEDURE

CBL AND SENSORS

✔ balance
✔ CBL motion detector
✔ CBL
✔ thin foam pad
✔ graphing calculator with link cable
✔ support stand with V-clamp
✔ wood blocks, 3 different masses

RECORDING TIMER

✔ cellophane tape
✔ recording timer and paper tape
✔ set of hooked masses
✔ stopwatch

SAFETY

- **Tie back long hair, secure loose clothing, and remove loose jewelry to prevent their getting caught in moving or rotating parts.**
- **Attach masses securely. Falling or dropped masses can cause serious injury.**

PREPARATION

1. Determine whether you will be using the CBL and sensors procedure or the recording timer procedure. Read the entire lab for the appropriate procedure, and plan what measurements you will take.

2. Prepare a data table with six columns and five rows in your lab notebook. In the first row, label the first two columns *Trial* and *Mass (kg)*. The space for the third through sixth columns should be labeled *Distance (m)*. Under this common label, columns 3–6 should be labeled *A–B*, *C–D*, *E–F*, and *G–H*. In the first column, label the second through fifth rows *1, 2, 3,* and *4*.

Recording timer procedure begins on page 79.

PROCEDURE

CBL AND SENSORS

Setting up the motion detector

3. Connect the CBL to the calculator with the unit-to-unit link cable using the link ports located on each unit. Connect the motion detector to the SONIC port.

4. Set up the apparatus as shown in **Figure 2-26.** Place the ring stand near the edge of the lab table. Use the C-clamp to clamp the base of the ring stand securely to the table. Position the clamp so that it protrudes as little as possible.

5. Using the V-clamp, securely clamp the motion detector to the ring stand so that it faces down, over the edge of the table. Make sure the motion detector is far enough away from the edge of the table that the signal will not hit the table top, clamp, or table leg.

6. Use a meterstick to measure a distance 0.5 m below the motion detector and mark the point with tape on the ring stand. This is the starting position from which the blocks will be dropped from rest.

7. Start the program PHYSICS on your graphing calculator.

8. Select option *SET UP PROBES* from the MAIN MENU. Enter 1 for the number of probes. Select the motion detector from the list.

9. Select the *MONITOR INPUT* option from the DATA COLLECTION menu. Test to be sure the motion detector is positioned properly.

a. Read the CBL measurement for the distance between the motion detector and the floor. Make sure the reading is a reasonable distance, or measure the distance with a meterstick to make sure the CBL gives the same value. If the CBL reading is too low, adjust the motion detector to make sure the signal is not hitting the table.

b. Cover the floor under the motion detector with a foam pad to reduce unwanted feedback.

c. Hold the wooden block directly beneath the motion detector, and move it up and down, reading the CBL measurements. Make sure the motion detector is not "seeing" other objects, such as the stand base, the table top, or the table leg. When the probe is functioning correctly, press "+" on the calculator to return to the MAIN MENU.

Figure 2-26

Step 9: With the CBL in MONITOR INPUT mode, move the wooden block up and down below the motion detector to check the readings.

Step 11: Hold the block flat and parallel to the tape mark.

Step 12: Release the block by pulling hands straight out to the sides. It may take some practice to release the block so that it falls straight down without turning. If the block turns while falling, the motion detector will measure the distance to the closest part of the block and introduce error into your results.

10. Select the *COLLECT DATA* option. Enter 0.02 for the time between samples. Enter 99 for the number of samples.

   a. Check the values you entered and press ENTER. If the values are correct, select *USE TIME SETUP* to continue. If you made a mistake entering the time values, select *MODIFY SETUP*, reenter the values, and continue.

   b. If you are given a choice on the TIME GRAPH menu, select *NON-LIVE DISPLAY*. Otherwise, continue to step 11.

Speed and acceleration of a falling object

11. Find the mass of the first wooden block, and label the block with tape. Record the mass in your data table. Hold the block horizontally between your hands, with your hands flat. Position the block directly below the motion detector and level with the 0.5 m mark.

12. Turn on the CBL and the graphing calculator. When the area is clear of people and objects, one student should press ENTER on the graphing calculator. As soon as the motion detector begins to click, the student holding the block should release the block by pulling both hands out to the side. Releasing the block this way will prevent the block from twisting as it falls, which may affect the results of this experiment.

13. When the motion detector has stopped clicking and the CBL displays DONE, press ENTER on the graphing calculator to get to the SELECT CHANNELS menu. Select the *SONIC* option, and then select *DISTANCE* to plot a graph of the distance in meters against time in seconds. (Note: The graph should have a smooth shape. If it has spikes or black lines, repeat the trial to obtain a smooth graph, then continue on to the next step.)

14. Use the arrow keys to trace along the curve. On the far left and the far right, the curve represents the position of the block before and after its motion. The middle section of the curve represents the motion of the falling block. Sketch this graph in your lab notebook.

   a. Choose a point on the curve at the beginning of this middle section. Press the right arrow key once to select the next point. The difference between the *x* values for these two readings will be 0.02 s, the time interval between successive readings. Find the difference between the *y* values of these two points, and record it as *A–B* for *Trial 1* in your data table.

   b. Press the right arrow key three times to move to another point on the curve. Press the right arrow key once to select the next point. Find the difference between the *y* values of these two points and record that as *C–D* for *Trial 1* in your data table.

   c. Choose two more pairs of points along the curve. Select points at even intervals along the curve so that the first pair is at the beginning of the block's motion, and the last pair is at the end. Find the difference between the *y* values of each pair of points. Record them as *E–F* and *G–H* for *Trial 1*. Press ENTER to return to the SELECT CHANNELS menu.

15. Select the *SONIC* option again, and select *VELOCITY* to plot a graph of the velocity in m/s against time in seconds. Examine how the velocity of the block changed during the experiment. Sketch this graph in your lab notebook. Press ENTER.

16. Select the *SONIC* option again, and select *ACCELERATION* to plot a graph of the acceleration in m/s^2 against time in seconds. Examine how the acceleration of the block changed during the experiment. Sketch this graph in your lab notebook. Press ENTER.

17. Repeat this procedure using different wood blocks. Drop each block from the same level in each trial. Record all data for each trial.

Analysis and Interpretation begins on page 80.

PROCEDURE

RECORDING TIMER

Calibrating the timer

3. Prepare a second data table with three columns and five rows in your lab notebook. Label this table *Calibration*. In the first row, label the columns *Trial*, *Time (s)*, and *No. of dots*. Fill in the first column by labeling the second through fifth rows *1, 2, 3,* and *4* for the number of trials.

4. Clamp the recording timer to the table to hold the timer in place. Choose a location that will allow you to pull a long section of paper tape through the timer in a straight line without hitting any obstacles. **Do not plug in the timer until your teacher approves your setup.**

5. Insert a strip of paper tape about 2.0 m long into the timer so that the paper can move freely and will be marked as it moves. Lay the tape flat behind the timer. One student should hold the end of the tape in front of the timer.

6. When your teacher approves your setup, plug the timer into the wall socket.

7. One student should start the timer and the stopwatch at the same time that the student holding the free end of the tape begins pulling the tape through the timer at a steady pace by walking away from the timer.

    a. After exactly 3.0 s, the first student should turn off the timer and stop the watch, just as the student with the tape stops walking. Mark the first and last dots on the tape. Tear or cut the dotted strip of tape from the roll and label it with the trial number and the time interval as measured by the stopwatch.

    b. Repeat this procedure three more times. Label all tapes.

8. Count the number of dots for each trial, starting with the second dot. Record this in your data table.

    a. Compute the period of the timer for each trial by dividing the 3.0 s time interval by the number of dots recorded in the table.

    b. Find the average value for the period of the recording timer. Use this value for all your calculations.

Figure 2-27

Step 4: Clamp the timer to the edge of the table so the tape can be pulled through parallel to the floor for the calibration step. If your timer will not mount on a ring stand as shown, leave it clamped to the table throughout the experiment.

Step 5: Thread the tape through the timer and make sure the paper tape is *under* the carbon disk.

Step 9: When the timer is mounted on the ring stand, tape the cord to the stand to keep it out of the way.

Step 11: Use a piece of tape to mark the stand at the starting point, and start the mass from the same point for all trials.

Speed and acceleration of a falling object

9. Set up the apparatus as shown in **Figure 2-27**. If possible, clamp the recording timer to a stand as shown. If the timer cannot be mounted on the stand, clamp the timer to the edge of the table as before. Cut a length of paper tape that is at least 20 cm longer than the distance between the timer and the floor. Thread the end of the tape through the timer.

10. Fold the end of the paper tape and fasten it with cellophane tape to make a loop. Hook a 200 g mass through the looped end of the paper tape, as shown.

11. Position the mass at a convenient level near the timer, as shown. Hold the mass in place by holding the tape behind the timer. Make sure the area is clear of people and objects. Simultaneously start the timer and release the tape so the mass falls to the floor. Stop the timer when the mass hits the floor.

12. Label the tape with the mass used. Label the second and third dots A and B, respectively. Count four dots from B and label the seventh and eighth dots C and D, respectively. Label the twelfth and thirteenth dots E and F, and label the seventeenth and eighteenth dots G and H.

13. Repeat this procedure using different, larger masses, such as 300 g and 400 g masses. Drop each mass from the same level in each trial. Label all tapes, and record all data.

14. On each tape, measure the distance between A and B, between C and D, and so on. Record the distance in meters in your data table.

ANALYSIS AND INTERPRETATION

Calculations and data analysis

1. **Organizing data** For each trial with the falling mass, find the magnitude of the average velocity, v_{avg}.

   a. **CBL and probeware** Divide the distance A–B by 0.02 s, the time interval between distance readings. Repeat this calculation for the other distances you recorded for each trial.

   b. **Recording timer** Divide the distance A–B by the average period of the timer. Repeat this calculation for the other marked distances for each trial.

2. **Analyzing results** Using the results from item 1, calculate the average acceleration.

   a. **CBL and probeware** Find the change of speed between the distance A–B and the distance C–D, between the distance C–D and the distance E–F, and so on. (Hint: Remember to use the total time interval—A–D, C–F, E–H—for each calculation.)

   b. **Recording timer** Find the change of speed between the distance A–B and the distance C–D, between the distance C–D and the distance E–F, and so on. (Hint: Remember to use the total time interval for each calculation. For example, for the first calculation, use the time interval from A to D.)

3. Graphing data Use your data to plot the following graphs for each trial. On each graph, label the axes and indicate the trial number. Use a graphing calculator, computer, or graph paper.

    a. position versus time

    b. velocity versus time

    c. acceleration versus time

4. Evaluating data Use the values for the average acceleration for all four trials to find the average value.

5. Evaluating data Use the accepted value for the free-fall acceleration given in the text and the average of your results from item 4.

    a. Determine the absolute error of your results using the following equation:

$$\text{absolute error} = |\,\text{experimental} - \text{accepted}\,|$$

    b. Determine the relative error of your results using the following equation:

$$\text{relative error} = \frac{(\text{experimental} - \text{accepted})}{\text{accepted}}$$

Conclusions

6. Relating ideas Based on your results, how long would it take a 1000 kg mass to reach the floor if it were dropped from the same height as the masses in this experiment?

7. Interpreting graphs Calculate the slope of each velocity-time graph from item 3b above.

8. Evaluating data Find the average value for the slope of the velocity-time graphs. What is the relationship between this value and the values you found for the average accelerations of the masses?

Extensions

9. Devise a plan to perform this experiment to study the motion of an object thrown straight up into the air. Make sure you take into account any special safety requirements or equipment you might need to use. If there is time and your teacher approves your plan, perform the experiment. Use your data to plot graphs of the position, velocity, and acceleration versus time.

CHAPTER 3

Two-Dimensional Motion and Vectors

PHYSICS IN ACTION

Although the streams of water of the Place de la Concorde fountain in Paris, France, seem to flow through transparent pipes, they are actually fired in highly concentrated solitary streams. Each of the streams follows a parabolic path, just like the path a baseball follows when it is thrown through the air. In this chapter you will analyze two-dimensional motion and solve problems involving objects projected into the air.

- *Why does all of the water in a stream follow the same path?*
- *How does the angle at which the water is fired affect its path?*

CONCEPT REVIEW

Displacement   (Section 2-1)

Velocity   (Section 2-1)

Acceleration   (Section 2-2)

Free fall   (Section 2-3)

3-1
Introduction to vectors

scalar

a physical quantity that has only a magnitude but no direction

vector

a physical quantity that has both a magnitude and a direction

SCALARS AND VECTORS

In Chapter 2 our discussion of motion was limited to two directions, forward and backward. Mathematically, we described these directions of motion with a positive or negative sign. This chapter explains a method of describing the motion of objects that do not travel along a straight line.

Vectors indicate direction; scalars do not

Each of the physical quantities we will encounter in this book can be categorized as either a scalar or a vector quantity. A **scalar** is a quantity that can be completely specified by its magnitude with appropriate units; that is, a scalar has magnitude but no direction. Examples of scalar quantities are speed, volume, and the number of pages in this textbook. A **vector** is a physical quantity that has both direction and magnitude.

As we look back to Chapter 2, we can see that displacement is an example of a vector quantity. An airline pilot planning a trip must know exactly how far and which way to fly. Velocity is also a vector quantity. If we wish to describe the velocity of a bird, we must specify both its speed (say, 3.5 m/s) and the direction in which the bird is flying (say, northeast). Another example of a vector quantity is acceleration, which was also discussed in Chapter 2.

Vectors are represented by symbols

In physics, quantities are often represented by symbols, such as *t* for time. To help you keep track of which symbols represent vector quantities and which are used to indicate scalar quantities, this book will use **boldface** type to indicate vector quantities. Scalar quantities are designated by the use of *italics*. Thus, to describe the speed of a bird without giving its direction, you would write $v = 3.5$ m/s. But a velocity, which includes a direction, is written as **v** = 3.5 m/s to the northeast. Handwritten, a vector can be symbolized by showing an arrow drawn above the abbreviation for a quantity, such as $\vec{v} = 3.5$ m/s to the northeast.

One way to keep track of vectors and their directions is to use diagrams. In diagrams, vectors are shown as arrows that point in the direction of the vector. The length of a vector arrow in a diagram is related to the vector's magnitude. For example, in **Figure 3-1** the arrows represent the velocities of the two soccer players running toward the soccer ball.

Figure 3-1

The lengths of the vector arrows represent the magnitudes of these two soccer players' velocities.

Because the player on the right of the soccer ball is moving faster, the arrow representing that velocity is longer than the arrow representing the velocity of the player on the left.

Vectors can be added graphically

When adding vectors, you must make certain that they have the same units and describe similar quantities. For example, it would be meaningless to add a velocity vector to a displacement vector because they describe different physical quantities. Similarly, it would be meaningless, as well as incorrect, to add two displacement vectors that are not expressed in the same units (in meters, in feet, and so on).

Section 2-1 covered vector addition and subtraction in one dimension. For instance, consider the confused football player from Chapter 2 who ran 100 yards, then turned around and ran back to his starting position. Because the two parts of his displacement are equal and opposite, his displacement during his run equals 0 yards. The answer found by adding two vectors, such as the player's displacement running down field and his displacement running back, is called the **resultant.**

Consider a student walking to school. The student walks 350 m to a friend's house, then 740 m to the school, as shown in **Figure 3-2.** The student's total displacement during his walk to school is in a direction from his house to the school, as shown by the dotted line. This direct path is the *vector sum* of the student's displacement from his house to his friend's house and his displacement from the friend's house to school. How can this resultant displacement be found?

One way to find the magnitude and direction of the student's total displacement is to draw the situation to scale on paper. Use a reasonable scale, such as 50 m on land equals 1 cm on paper. First draw the vector representing the student's displacement from his house to his friend's house, giving the proper direction and scaled magnitude. Then draw the vector representing his walk to the school, starting with the tail at the head of the first vector. Again give its scaled magnitude and the right direction. The magnitude of the resultant vector can then be determined by using a ruler to measure the length of the vector pointing from the tail of the first vector to the head of the second vector. The length of that vector can then be multiplied by 50 (or whatever scale you have chosen) to get the actual magnitude of the student's total displacement in meters.

The direction of the resultant vector may be determined by using a protractor to measure the angle between the first vector and the resultant.

resultant

a vector representing the sum of two or more vectors

Figure 3-2

A student walks from his house to his friend's house **(a),** then from his friend's house to the school **(b).** The student's resultant displacement **(c)** can be found using a ruler and a protractor.

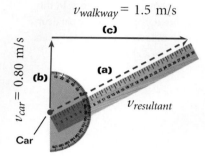

$v_{walkway} = 1.5$ m/s

(c)

(b)

(a)

$v_{car} = 0.80$ m/s

$v_{resultant}$

Car

Figure 3-3

The resultant velocity **(a)** of a toy car moving at a velocity of 0.80 m/s **(b)** across a moving walkway with a velocity of 1.5 m/s **(c)** can be found using a ruler and a protractor.

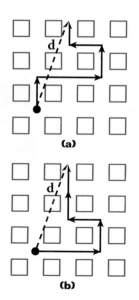

(a)

(b)

Figure 3-4

A marathon runner's displacement, **d,** will be the same regardless of whether the runner takes path **(a)** or **(b)**.

PROPERTIES OF VECTORS

Now consider a case in which two or more vectors act at the same point. When this occurs, it is possible to find a resultant vector that has the same net effect as the combination of the individual vectors. Imagine looking down from the second level of an airport at a toy car moving at 0.80 m/s across a moving walkway that moves at 1.5 m/s, as graphically represented in **Figure 3-3.** How can you determine what the car's resultant velocity will look like from your vantage point?

Vectors can be moved parallel to themselves in a diagram

Note that the car's resultant velocity while moving from one side of the walkway to the other will be the combination of two independent velocities. Thus, the car traveling for t seconds can be thought of as traveling first at 0.80 m/s across the walkway for t seconds, then down the walkway at 1.5 m/s for t seconds. In this way, we can draw a given vector anywhere in the diagram as long as the vector is parallel to its previous alignment and still points in the same direction. Thus, you can draw one vector with its tail starting at the tip of the other as long as the size and direction of each vector do not change.

Determining a resultant vector by drawing a vector from the tail of the first vector to the tip of the last vector is known as the *triangle method of addition.*

Again, the magnitude of the resultant vector can be measured using a ruler, and the angle can be measured with a protractor. In the next section, we will develop a technique for adding vectors that is less time-consuming because it involves a calculator instead of a ruler and protractor.

Vectors can be added in any order

When two or more vectors are added, the sum is independent of the order of the addition. This idea is demonstrated by a runner practicing for a marathon along city streets, as represented in **Figure 3-4.** In **(a)** the runner takes one path during a run, and in **(b)** the runner takes another. Regardless of which path the runner takes, the runner will have the same total displacement, expressed as **d.** Similarly, the vector sum of two or more vectors is the same regardless of the order in which the vectors are added, provided that the magnitude and direction of each vector remain the same.

To subtract a vector, add its opposite

Vector subtraction makes use of the definition of the negative of a vector. The negative of a vector is defined as a vector with the same magnitude as the original vector but opposite in direction. For instance, the negative of the velocity of a car traveling 30 m/s to the west is −30 m/s to the west, or 30 m/s to the east. Thus, as shown below, adding a vector to its negative vector gives zero.

$$v_1 + (-v_1) = 30 \text{ m/s} + (-30 \text{ m/s}) = 30 \text{ m/s} - 30 \text{ m/s} = 0 \text{ m/s}$$

When adding vectors in two dimensions, you can add a negative vector to a positive vector that does not point along the same line by using the triangle method of addition.

Multiplying or dividing vectors by scalars results in vectors

There are mathematical operations in which vectors can multiply other vectors, but they are not necessary for the scope of this book. This book does, however, make use of vectors multiplied by scalars, with a vector as the result. For example, if a cab driver obeys a customer who tells him to go twice as fast, that cab's original velocity vector, $\mathbf{v_{cab}}$, is multiplied by the scalar number 2. The result, written $2\mathbf{v_{cab}}$, is a vector with a magnitude twice that of the original vector and pointing in the same direction.

On the other hand, if another cab driver is told to go twice as fast in the opposite direction, this is the same as multiplying by the scalar number -2. The result is a vector with a magnitude two times the initial velocity but pointing in the opposite direction, $-2\mathbf{v_{cab}}$.

Section Review

1. Which of the following quantities are scalars, and which are vectors?
   a. the acceleration of a plane as it takes off
   b. the number of passengers on the plane
   c. the duration of the flight
   d. the displacement of the flight
   e. the amount of fuel required for the flight

2. A roller coaster moves 85 m horizontally, then travels 45 m at an angle of 30.0° above the horizontal. What is its displacement from its starting point? Use graphical techniques.

3. A novice pilot sets a plane's controls, thinking the plane will fly at 250 km/h to the north. If the wind blows at 75 km/h toward the southeast, what is the plane's resultant velocity? Use graphical techniques.

4. While flying over the Grand Canyon, the pilot slows the plane's engines down to one-half the velocity in item 3. If the wind's velocity is still 75 km/h toward the southeast, what will the plane's new resultant velocity be? Use graphical techniques.

5. **Physics in Action** The water used in many fountains is recycled. For instance, a single water particle in a fountain travels through an 85 m system and then returns to the same point. What is the displacement of a water particle during one cycle?

3-2
Vector operations

3-2 SECTION OBJECTIVES

- **Identify appropriate coordinate systems for solving problems with vectors.**

- **Apply the Pythagorean theorem and tangent function to calculate the magnitude and direction of a resultant vector.**

- **Resolve vectors into components using the sine and cosine functions.**

- **Add vectors that are not perpendicular.**

Figure 3-5
A gecko's displacement while climbing a tree can be represented by an arrow pointing along the *y*-axis.

COORDINATE SYSTEMS IN TWO DIMENSIONS

In Chapter 2, the motion of a gecko climbing a tree was described as motion along the *y*-axis. The direction of the displacement of the gecko along the axis was denoted by a positive or negative sign. The displacement of the gecko can now be described by an arrow pointing along the *y*-axis, as shown in **Figure 3-5.** A more versatile system for diagraming the motion of an object, however, employs vectors and the use of both the *x*- and *y*-axes simultaneously.

The addition of another axis not only helps describe motion in two dimensions but also simplifies analysis of motion in one dimension. For example, two methods can be used to describe the motion of a jet moving at 300 m/s to the northeast. In one approach, the coordinate system can be turned so that the plane is depicted as moving along the *y*-axis, as in **Figure 3-6(a).** The jet's motion also can be depicted on a two-dimensional coordinate system whose axes point north to south and west to east, as shown in **Figure 3-6(b).**

The problem with the orientation in the first case is that the axis must be turned again if the direction of the plane changes. Also, it will become difficult to describe the direction of another plane that is not traveling exactly northeast. Thus, axes are often designated with the positive *y*-axis pointing north and the positive *x*-axis pointing east, as shown in **Figure 3-6(b).**

Similarly, when analyzing the motion of objects thrown into the air, orienting the *y*-axis perpendicular to the ground, and therefore parallel to the direction of free-fall acceleration, greatly simplifies things.

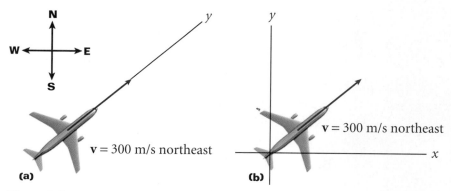

(a)   **(b)**

Figure 3-6
A plane traveling northeast at a velocity of 300 m/s can be represented as either **(a)** moving along a *y*-axis chosen to point to the northeast or **(b)** moving at an angle of 45° to both the *x*- and *y*-axes, which line up with west-east and north-south, respectively.

There are no firm rules for applying coordinate systems to situations involving vectors. As long as you are consistent, the final answer will be correct regardless of the system you choose. Perhaps the best choice for orienting axes is the approach that makes solving the problem easiest.

DETERMINING RESULTANT MAGNITUDE AND DIRECTION

In Section 3-1, the magnitude and direction of a resultant were found graphically by making a drawing with an appropriate scale. There are, however, drawbacks to this approach; it is time-consuming, and the accuracy of the answer depends on how carefully the diagram is drawn and measured. There is a better, simpler method. The magnitude and direction of the resultant of two perpendicular vectors can be calculated using the Pythagorean theorem and the tangent function.

Use the Pythagorean theorem to find the magnitude of the resultant

Imagine a tourist climbing a pyramid in Egypt. The tourist knows the height and width of the pyramid and would like to know the distance covered in a climb from the bottom to the top of the pyramid.

As can be seen in **Figure 3-7,** the magnitude of the tourist's vertical displacement, Δy, is the height of the pyramid, and the magnitude of the horizontal displacement, Δx, equals the distance from one edge of the pyramid to the middle, or half the pyramid's width. Notice that these two vectors are perpendicular and form a right triangle with the displacement, **d.**

As shown in **Figure 3-8(a),** the Pythagorean theorem states that for any right triangle, the square of the hypotenuse—the side opposite the right angle—equals the sum of the squares of the other two sides, or legs.

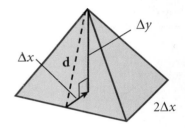

Figure 3-7
Because the base and height of a pyramid are perpendicular, we can find a tourist's total displacement, **d,** if we know the height, Δy, and width, $2\Delta x$, of the pyramid.

PYTHAGOREAN THEOREM FOR RIGHT TRIANGLES

$$a^2 = b^2 + c^2$$

$$(\text{length of hypotenuse})^2 = (\text{length of one leg})^2 + (\text{length of other leg})^2$$

In **Figure 3-8(b),** the Pythagorean theorem is applied to find the tourist's displacement. The square of the displacement is equal to the sum of the

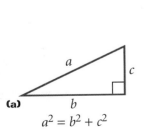

(a)
$$a^2 = b^2 + c^2$$

(b)
$$d^2 = \Delta x^2 + \Delta y^2$$

Figure 3-8
(a) The Pythagorean theorem can be applied to any right triangle. **(b)** It can also be applied to find the magnitude of a resultant displacement.

$$\tan\theta = \frac{\text{opp}}{\text{adj}}$$

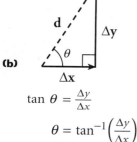

$$\tan\theta = \frac{\Delta y}{\Delta x}$$

$$\theta = \tan^{-1}\left(\frac{\Delta y}{\Delta x}\right)$$

Figure 3-9

(a) The tangent function can be applied to any right triangle, and **(b)** it can also be used to find the direction of a resultant displacement.

square of the horizontal displacement and the square of the vertical displacement. Using this method, you can find out the magnitude of the tourist's displacement, *d*.

Use the tangent function to find the direction of the resultant

In order to completely describe the tourist's displacement, you must also know the direction of the tourist's motion. Because **Δx, Δy,** and **d** form a right triangle, as shown in **Figure 3-9(b),** the tangent function can be used to find the angle *θ*, which denotes the direction of the tourist's displacement.

For any right triangle, the tangent of an angle is defined as the ratio of the opposite and adjacent legs with respect to a specified acute angle of a right triangle, as shown in **Figure 3-9(a).**

DEFINITION OF THE TANGENT FUNCTION FOR RIGHT TRIANGLES

$$\tan\theta = \frac{\text{opp}}{\text{adj}}$$

$$\text{tangent of angle} = \frac{\text{opposite leg}}{\text{adjacent leg}}$$

The inverse of the tangent function, shown below, indicates the angle.

$$\theta = \tan^{-1}\left(\frac{\text{opp}}{\text{adj}}\right)$$

SAMPLE PROBLEM 3A

Finding resultant magnitude and direction

PROBLEM

An archaeologist climbs the Great Pyramid in Giza, Egypt. If the pyramid's height is 136 m and its width is 2.30×10^2 m, what is the magnitude and the direction of the archaeologist's displacement while climbing from the bottom of the pyramid to the top?

SOLUTION

1. DEFINE **Given:** $\Delta y = 136$ m $\Delta x = \frac{1}{2}(\text{width}) = 115$ m

Unknown: $d = ?$ $\theta = ?$

Diagram: Choose the archaeologist's starting position as the origin of the coordinate system. The positive *y*-axis points up and the positive *x*-axis points toward the center of the pyramid.

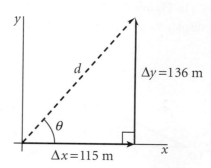

2. PLAN　**Choose an equation(s) or situation:** The Pythagorean theorem can be used to find the magnitude of the archaeologist's displacement. The direction of the displacement can be found by using the tangent function.

$$d^2 = \Delta x^2 + \Delta y^2$$
$$\tan \theta = \frac{\Delta y}{\Delta x}$$

Rearrange the equation(s) to isolate the unknown(s):

$$d = \sqrt{\Delta x^2 + \Delta y^2}$$
$$\theta = \tan^{-1}\left(\frac{\Delta y}{\Delta x}\right)$$

3. CALCULATE　**Substitute the values into the equation(s) and solve:**

$$d = \sqrt{(136 \text{ m})^2 + (115 \text{ m})^2}$$

$$\boxed{d = 178 \text{ m}}$$

$$\theta = \tan^{-1}\left(\frac{136 \text{ m}}{115 \text{ m}}\right)$$

$$\boxed{\theta = 49.8°}$$

CALCULATOR SOLUTION

Be sure your calculator is set to calculate angles measured in degrees. Most calculators have a button labeled "DRG" that, when pressed, toggles between degrees, radians, and grads.

4. EVALUATE　Because d is the hypotenuse, the archaeologist's displacement should be longer than the height and width. The angle is expected to be more than 45° because the height is greater than half of the width.

PRACTICE 3A

Finding resultant magnitude and direction

1. While following the directions on a treasure map, a pirate walks 45.0 m north, then turns and walks 7.5 m east. What single straight-line displacement could the pirate have taken to reach the treasure?

2. Emily passes a soccer ball 6.0 m directly across the field to Kara, who then kicks the ball 14.5 m directly down the field to Luisa. What is the ball's total displacement as it travels between Emily and Luisa?

3. A hummingbird flies 1.2 m along a straight path at a height of 3.4 m above the ground. Upon spotting a flower below, the hummingbird drops directly downward 1.4 m to hover in front of the flower. What is the hummingbird's total displacement?

RESOLVING VECTORS INTO COMPONENTS

components of a vector

the projections of a vector along the axes of a coordinate system

In the pyramid example, the horizontal and vertical parts that add up to give the tourist's actual displacement are called **components.** The *x* component is parallel to the *x*-axis. The *y* component is parallel to the *y*-axis. These components can be either positive or negative numbers with units.

Any vector can be completely described by a set of perpendicular components. When a vector points along a single axis, as do the quantities in Chapter 2, the second component of motion is equal to zero.

By breaking a single vector into two components, or *resolving* it into its components, an object's motion can sometimes be described more conveniently in terms of directions, such as north to south or up and down.

To illustrate this point, let's examine a scene on the set of a new action movie. For this scene a biplane travels at 95 km/h at an angle of 20° relative to the ground. Attempting to film the plane from below, a camera team travels in a truck, keeping the truck beneath the plane at all times, as shown in **Figure 3-10.** How fast must the truck travel to remain directly below the plane?

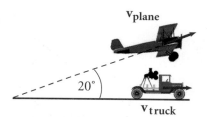

Figure 3-10

A truck carrying a film crew must be driven at the correct velocity to enable the crew to film the underside of a biplane flying at an angle of 20° to the ground at a speed of 95 km/h.

To find out the velocity that the truck must maintain to stay beneath the plane, we must know the horizontal component of the plane's velocity. Once more, the key to solving the problem is to recognize that a right triangle can be drawn using the plane's velocity and its *x* and *y* components. The situation can then be analyzed using trigonometry.

The sine and cosine functions are defined in terms of the lengths of the sides of such right triangles. The sine of an angle is the ratio of the leg opposite that angle to the hypotenuse.

DEFINITION OF THE SINE FUNCTION FOR RIGHT TRIANGLES

$$\sin \theta = \frac{\text{opp}}{\text{hyp}} \qquad \text{sine of an angle} = \frac{\text{opposite leg}}{\text{hypotenuse}}$$

In **Figure 3-11,** the leg opposite the 20° angle represents the *y* component, v_y, which describes the vertical speed of the airplane. The hypotenuse, **v**$_{plane}$, is the resultant vector that describes the airplane's total motion.

The cosine of an angle is the ratio between the leg adjacent to that angle and the hypotenuse.

Figure 3-11

To stay beneath the biplane, the truck must be driven with a velocity equal to the *x* component (v_x) of the biplane's velocity.

DEFINITION OF THE COSINE FUNCTION FOR RIGHT TRIANGLES

$$\cos \theta = \frac{\text{adj}}{\text{hyp}} \qquad \text{cosine of an angle} = \frac{\text{adjacent leg}}{\text{hypotenuse}}$$

In **Figure 3-11,** the leg adjacent to the 20° angle represents the *x* component, v_x, which describes the horizontal speed of the airplane. This *x* component equals the speed that the truck must maintain to stay beneath the plane.

Resolving vectors

PROBLEM

Find the component velocities of a helicopter traveling 95 km/h at an angle of 35° to the ground.

SOLUTION

1. DEFINE   **Given:** $v = 95$ km/h $\theta = 35°$

Unknown: $v_x = ?$ $v_y = ?$

Diagram: The most convenient coordinate system is one with the x-axis directed along the ground and the y-axis directed vertically.

2. PLAN   **Choose an equation(s) or situation:** Because the axes are perpendicular, the sine and cosine functions can be used to find the components.

$$\sin \theta = \frac{v_y}{v}$$

$$\cos \theta = \frac{v_x}{v}$$

Rearrange the equation(s) to isolate the unknown(s):

$$v_y = v(\sin \theta)$$
$$v_x = v(\cos \theta)$$

3. CALCULATE   **Substitute the values into the equation(s) and solve:**

$$v_y = (95 \text{ km/h})(\sin 35°)$$

$$\boxed{v_y = 54 \text{ km/h}}$$

$$v_x = (95 \text{ km/h})(\cos 35°)$$

$$\boxed{v_x = 78 \text{ km/h}}$$

4. EVALUATE   Because the component velocities form a right triangle with the helicopter's actual velocity, the Pythagorean theorem can be used to check whether the magnitudes of the components are correct.

$$v^2 = v_x^2 + v_y^2$$
$$(95)^2 \approx (78)^2 + (54)^2$$
$$9025 \approx 9000$$

The slight difference is due to rounding.

CALCULATOR SOLUTION

When using your calculator to solve a problem, perform trigonometric functions such as *sin, cos,* and *tan* first, before multiplication.

Resolving vectors

1. How fast must a truck travel to stay beneath an airplane that is moving 105 km/h at an angle of 25° to the ground?

2. What is the magnitude of the vertical component of the velocity of the plane in item 1?

3. Find the horizontal and vertical components of the 125 m displacement of a superhero who flies down from the top of a tall building at an angle of 25° below the horizontal.

4. A child rides a toboggan down a hill that descends at an angle of 30.5° to the horizontal. If the hill is 23.0 m long, what are the horizontal and vertical components of the child's displacement?

5. A truck drives up a hill with a 15° incline. If the truck has a constant speed of 22 m/s, what are the horizontal and vertical components of the truck's velocity?

6. A skier squats low and races down an 18° ski slope. During a 5 s interval, the skier accelerates at 2.5 m/s^2. What are the horizontal (perpendicular to the direction of free-fall acceleration) and vertical components of the skier's acceleration during this time interval?

7. What are the horizontal and vertical components of a cat's displacement when it is climbing 5 m directly up a tree?

ADDING VECTORS THAT ARE NOT PERPENDICULAR

Until this point, all of the vector-addition problems in Section 3-2 have concerned vectors that are perpendicular to one another. However, many objects move in a less rigid manner—moving in one direction, then turning at an acute angle before continuing their motion.

Suppose that a plane initially travels 50 km at an angle of 35° to the ground, then climbs at only 10° for 220 km. How can you determine the magnitude and direction for the vector denoting the total displacement of the plane?

Because the original displacement vectors do not form a right triangle, it is not possible to directly apply the tangent function or the Pythagorean theorem when adding the original two vectors.

Determining the magnitude and the direction of the resultant can be achieved by resolving each of the plane's displacement vectors into their x and *y* components. Then the components along each axis can be added together. As shown in **Figure 3-12,** these vector sums will be the two perpendicular components of the resultant, **d.** The magnitude of the resultant can then be found using the Pythagorean theorem, and its direction can be found using the tangent function.

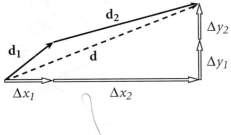

Figure 3-12
Add the components of the actual displacement vector to find two components that form a right triangle with the resultant vector.

Adding vectors algebraically

PROBLEM

A hiker walks 25.5 km from her base camp at 35° south of east. On the second day, she walks 41.0 km in a direction 65° north of east, at which point she discovers a forest ranger's tower. Determine the magnitude and direction of her resultant displacement between the base camp and the ranger's tower.

SOLUTION

1. Select a coordinate system, draw a sketch of the vectors to be added, and label each vector.

Figure 3-13 depicts the situation drawn on a coordinate system. The positive *y*-axis points north and the positive *x*-axis points east. The origin of the axes is the base camp. In the chosen coordinate system, the hiker's direction during the first day is signified by a negative angle because clockwise movement from the positive *x*-axis is conventionally considered to be a negative angle.

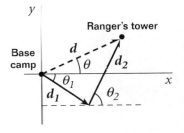

Figure 3-13

Given: $\theta_1 = -35°$ $\theta_2 = 65°$ $d_1 = 25.5$ km $d_2 = 41.0$ km
Unknown: $d = ?$ $\theta = ?$

2. Find the *x* and *y* components of all vectors.

Make a separate sketch for each day. The values for each of the components can be determined by using the sine and cosine functions. Because the hiker's angle on the first day is negative, the *y* component of her displacement during that day is negative.

$$\sin \theta = \frac{\Delta y}{d}$$

$$\cos \theta = \frac{\Delta x}{d}$$

continued on next page

For day 1: $\Delta x_1 = d_1 (\cos \theta_1) = (25.5 \text{ km}) [\cos (-35°)]$
(Figure 3-14)

$\Delta x_1 = 21 \text{ km}$

$\Delta y_1 = d_1 (\sin \theta_1) = (25.5 \text{ km}) [\sin (-35°)]$

$\Delta y_1 = -15 \text{ km}$

For day 2: $\Delta x_2 = d_2 (\cos \theta_2) = (41.0 \text{ km}) (\cos 65°)$
(Figure 3-15)

$\Delta x_2 = 17 \text{ km}$

$\Delta y_2 = d_2 (\sin \theta_2) = (41.0 \text{ km}) (\sin 65°)$

$\Delta y_2 = 37 \text{ km}$

Figure 3-14

Figure 3-15

3. **Find the total displacement for both the x and y directions.**

First add together the x components to find the total displacement in the x direction. Then perform the same operation for the y direction.

$\Delta x_{tot} = \Delta x_1 + \Delta x_2 = 21 \text{ km} + 17 \text{ km} = 38 \text{ km}$

$\Delta y_{tot} = \Delta y_1 + \Delta y_2 = -15 \text{ km} + 37 \text{ km} = 22 \text{ km}$

4. **Use the Pythagorean theorem to find the magnitude of the resultant vector.**

Because the components are now perpendicular, the Pythagorean theorem can be used to find the magnitude of the resultant.

$$d^2 = (\Delta x_{tot})^2 + (\Delta y_{tot})^2$$

$$d = \sqrt{(\Delta x_{tot})^2 + (\Delta y_{tot})^2} = \sqrt{(38 \text{ km})^2 + (22 \text{ km})^2}$$

$$\boxed{d = 44 \text{ km}}$$

5. **Use a suitable trigonometric function to find the angle the resultant vector makes with the x-axis.**

The direction of the resultant can be found using the tangent function.

$$\theta = \tan^{-1}\left(\frac{\Delta y}{\Delta x}\right)$$

$$\theta = \tan^{-1}\left(\frac{\Delta y_{tot}}{\Delta x_{tot}}\right) = \tan^{-1}\left(\frac{22 \text{ km}}{38 \text{ km}}\right)$$

$$\boxed{\theta = (3.0 \times 10^1)° \text{ north of east}}$$

6. **Evaluate your answer.**

If the diagram is drawn to scale, compare the algebraic results with the drawing. The calculated magnitude seems reasonable because the distance from the base camp to the ranger's tower is longer than the distance hiked during the first day and slightly longer than the distance hiked during the second day. The calculated direction of the resultant seems reasonable because the angle in **Figure 3-13** looks to be about 30°.

Adding vectors algebraically

1. A football player runs directly down the field for 35 m before turning to the right at an angle of 25° from his original direction and running an additional 15 m before getting tackled. What is the magnitude and direction of the runner's total displacement?

2. A plane travels 25 km at an angle of 35° to the ground, then changes direction and travels 515 km at an angle of 22° to the ground. What is the magnitude and direction of the plane's total displacement?

3. During a rodeo, a clown runs 8.0 m north, turns 35° east of north, and runs 3.5 m. Then, after waiting for the bull to come near, the clown turns due east and runs 5.0 m to exit the arena. What is the clown's total displacement?

Section Review

1. Identify a convenient coordinate system for analyzing each of the following situations:
   a. a dog walking along a sidewalk
   b. an acrobat walking along a high wire
   c. a submarine submerging at an angle of 30° to the horizontal
   d. a person climbing a ladder at an angle of 70° to the ground

2. Apply the Pythagorean theorem to find the magnitude of the resultant velocity vector for the following perpendicular velocities:
   a. a fish swimming at 3.0 m/s across a river that moves at 5.0 m/s
   b. a surfer traveling at 1.0 m/s across a wave that is traveling at 6.0 m/s

3. Find the direction of the resultant velocities for each situation in item 2.

4. Find the component vectors along the directions noted in parentheses.
   a. a car displaced northeast by 10.0 km (north and east)
   b. a duck accelerating away from a hunter at 2.0 m/s^2 at an angle of 35° to the ground (horizontal and vertical)
   c. a submarine moving at 10.0 m/s toward the surface at an angle of 35° to the ocean floor (horizontal and vertical)

5. Find the resultant displacement of a fox searching for mice in a prairie. First the fox heads 55° north of west for 10.0 m; then it turns and heads west for 5.0 m.

3-3
Projectile motion

3-3 SECTION OBJECTIVES

- **Recognize examples of projectile motion.**

- **Describe the path of a projectile as a parabola.**

- **Resolve vectors into their components and apply the kinematic equations to solve problems involving projectile motion.**

Figure 3-16
When the long jumper is in the air, his velocity has both a horizontal and a vertical component.

TWO-DIMENSIONAL MOTION

In the last section, quantities such as displacement and velocity were shown to be vectors that can be resolved into components. In this section, these components will be used to understand and predict the motion of objects thrown into the air.

Use of components avoids vector multiplication

How can you know the displacement, velocity, and acceleration of a ball at any point in time during its flight? All of the kinematic equations from Chapter 2 could be rewritten in terms of vector quantities. However, when an object is propelled into the air in a direction other than straight up or down, the velocity, acceleration, and displacement of the object do not all point in the same direction. This makes the vector forms of the equations difficult to solve.

One way to deal with these situations is to avoid using the complicated vector forms of the equations altogether. Instead, apply the technique of resolving vectors into components. Then you can apply the simpler one-dimensional forms of the equations for each component. Finally, you can recombine the components to determine the resultant.

Components simplify projectile motion

When a long jumper approaches his jump, he runs along a straight line, which can be called the *x*-axis. When he jumps, as shown in **Figure 3-16,** he begins to move perpendicular to the ground as well. Movement in this plane can be depicted using both the *x*- and *y*-axes.

Note that in **Figure 3-17** the jumper's velocity vector is resolved into its two component vectors. This way, the jumper's motion can be analyzed using the kinematic equations applied to one direction at a time.

Figure 3-17

(a) A long jumper's velocity while sprinting along the runway can be represented by a single vector.
(b) Once the jump is made, the jumper's velocity at any instant can be described by the components of the velocity.

(a)

v_y
v_x

(b)

In this section, we will focus on the form of two-dimensional motion called **projectile motion.** Objects that are thrown or launched into the air and are subject to gravity are called *projectiles*. Some examples of projectiles are softballs, footballs, and arrows when they are projected through the air. Even a long jumper can be considered a projectile.

projectile motion

motion of objects moving in two dimensions under the influence of gravity

Path without air resistance

Path with air resistance

(a)

(b)

Figure 3-18

(a) If air resistance were neglected, a frog jumping into the air would be represented as traveling along a parabola. **(b)** With air resistance, the frog would travel along a shorter path, which would not be a parabola.

Projectiles follow parabolic trajectories

The path of a projectile is a curve called a parabola, as shown in **Figure 3-18(a).** Many people mistakenly believe that projectiles eventually fall straight down, much like a cartoon character does after running off a cliff. However, if an object has an initial horizontal velocity in any given time interval, there will be horizontal motion throughout the flight of the projectile. Note that for the purposes of samples and exercises in this book, the horizontal velocity of the projectile will be considered constant. This velocity would not be constant if we accounted for air resistance. With air resistance, a projectile slows down as it collides with air particles. Hence, as shown in **Figure 3-18(b),** the true path of a projectile traveling through Earth's atmosphere is not a parabola.

Projectile motion is free fall with an initial horizontal velocity

To understand the motion a projectile undergoes, first examine **Figure 3-19.** The red ball was dropped, while the yellow ball was launched horizontally. Disregarding air resistance, both balls hit the ground at the same time.

By examining each ball's position in relation to the horizontal lines and to one another, it is evident that the two balls fall at the same rate. This may seem impossible because one is given an initial velocity and the other begins from rest. But if the motion is analyzed one component at a time, it makes sense.

First, consider the red ball that falls straight down. It has no motion in the horizontal direction. In the vertical direction, it starts from rest ($v_{y,i} = 0$ m/s) and proceeds in free fall. Thus, the kinematic equations from Chapter 2 can be applied to analyze the vertical motion of the falling ball. Note that the acceleration, a, can be rewritten as $-g$ because the only vertical component of acceleration is free-fall acceleration.

Figure 3-19

This is a strobe photograph of two table-tennis balls released at the same time. Even though the yellow ball is given an initial horizontal velocity and the red ball is simply dropped, both balls fall at the same rate.

VERTICAL MOTION OF A PROJECTILE

$$\Delta y = -\tfrac{1}{2} g (\Delta t)^2$$

$$v_{y,f} = -g \Delta t$$

$$v_{y,f}^2 = -2g \Delta y$$

Now consider the components of motion of the yellow ball that is launched in **Figure 3-19.** This ball undergoes the same horizontal displacement during each time interval. This means that the ball's horizontal velocity remains constant (if air resistance is assumed to be negligible). Thus, when using the kinematic equations from Chapter 2 to analyze the horizontal motion of a projectile, the initial horizontal velocity is equal to the horizontal velocity throughout the projectile's flight. A projectile's horizontal motion is described by the following equation.

HORIZONTAL MOTION OF A PROJECTILE

$$\Delta x = v_x \Delta t$$

$$v_x = v_{x,i} = \text{constant}$$

Next consider the initial motion of the launched yellow ball in **Figure 3-19.** Despite having an initial horizontal velocity, the launched ball has no initial velocity in the vertical direction. Just like the red ball that falls straight down, the launched yellow ball is in free fall. Its vertical motion is described by the same free-fall equations. In any time interval, the launched ball undergoes the same vertical displacement as the ball that falls straight down. This is why both balls reach the ground at the same time.

To find the velocity of a projectile at any point during its flight, find the vector sum of the components of the velocity at that point. Use the Pythagorean theorem to find the magnitude of the velocity, and use the tangent function to find the direction of the velocity.

Quick Lab

Projectile Motion

MATERIALS LIST

- ✔ 2 identical balls
- ✔ slope or ramp

Roll a ball off a table. At the instant the rolling ball leaves the table, drop a second ball from the same height above the floor. Do the two balls hit the floor at the same time? Try varying the speed at which you roll the first ball off the table. Does varying the speed affect whether the two balls strike the ground at the same time? Now try dropping one ball while tossing the other into the air at an angle. Which of these balls strikes the floor first? What does this tell you about the vertical components of the initial velocity of each ball? Next roll one of the balls down a slope. Drop the other ball from the base of the slope at the instant the first ball leaves the slope. Which of the balls hits the ground first in this situation?

Projectiles launched horizontally

PROBLEM

A movie director is shooting a scene that involves dropping a stunt dummy out of an airplane and into a swimming pool. The plane is 10.0 m above the ground, traveling at a velocity of 22.5 m/s in the positive x direction. The director wants to know where in the plane's path the dummy should be dropped so that it will land in the pool.

SOLUTION

1. DEFINE

Given: $\Delta y = -10.0$ m $\quad g = 9.81$ m/s^2 $\quad v_x = 22.5$ m/s
$v_{y,i} = 0$ m/s

Unknown: $\Delta t = ?$ $\quad \Delta x = ?$

Diagram: The initial velocity vector of the stunt dummy only has a horizontal component. Choose the coordinate system oriented so that the positive y direction points upward and the positive x direction points to the right.

$v_{x,i} = v_x = 22.5$ m/s

$a_y = -g$

2. PLAN

Choose an equation(s) or situation:

The dummy drops with no initial vertical velocity. Because air resistance is neglected, the dummy's horizontal velocity remains constant.

$$\Delta y = -\tfrac{1}{2}g\Delta t^2$$
$$\Delta x = v_x \Delta t$$

Rearrange the equation(s) to isolate the unknown(s):

$$\frac{2\Delta y}{-g} = \Delta t^2$$

$$\Delta t = \sqrt{\frac{2\Delta y}{-g}} \text{ where } \Delta y \text{ is negative}$$

3. CALCULATE First find the time it takes for the dummy to reach the ground.

$$\Delta t = \sqrt{\frac{2\Delta y}{-g}} = \sqrt{\frac{2(-10.0 \text{ m})}{-9.81 \text{ m/s}^2}} = 1.43 \text{ s}$$

Find out how far horizontally the dummy can travel during this period of time.

$$\Delta x = v_x \Delta t = (22.5 \text{ m/s})(1.43 \text{ s})$$

$$\boxed{\Delta x = 32.2 \text{ m}}$$

4. EVALUATE The stunt dummy will have to drop from the plane when the plane is at a horizontal distance of 32.2 m from the pool. The distance is within the correct order of magnitude, given the other values in this problem.

Projectiles launched horizontally

1. A pelican flying along a horizontal path drops a fish from a height of 5.4 m while traveling 5.0 m/s. How far does the fish travel horizontally before it hits the water below?

2. Give both the horizontal and vertical components of the velocity of the fish from item 1 before the fish enters the water.

3. Find the instantaneous velocity of the stunt dummy in Sample Problem 3D as it hits the water.

4. A cat chases a mouse across a 1.0 m high table. The mouse steps out of the way, and the cat slides off the table at a speed of 5.0 m/s. Where does the cat strike the floor?

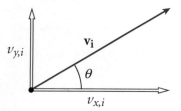

Figure 3-20

An object is projected with an initial velocity, v_i, at an angle of θ. By resolving the initial velocity into its x and y components, the kinematic equations can be applied to describe the motion of the projectile throughout its flight.

Use components to analyze objects launched at an angle

Let us examine a case in which a projectile is launched at an angle to the horizontal, as shown in **Figure 3-20.** The projectile has an initial vertical component of velocity as well as a horizontal component of velocity.

Suppose the initial velocity vector makes an angle θ with the horizontal. Again, to analyze the motion of such a projectile, the object's motion must be resolved into its components. The sine and cosine functions can be used to find the horizontal and vertical components of the initial velocity.

$$v_{x,i} = v_i (\cos \theta) \quad \text{and} \quad v_{y,i} = v_i (\sin \theta)$$

We can substitute these values for $v_{x,i}$ and $v_{y,i}$ into the kinematic equations from Chapter 2 to obtain a set of equations that can be used to analyze the motion of a projectile launched at an angle.

PROJECTILES LAUNCHED AT AN ANGLE

$$\Delta x = v_i(\cos \theta)\Delta t$$
$$v_x = v_i (\cos \theta) = \text{constant}$$
$$\Delta y = v_i(\sin \theta)\Delta t - \tfrac{1}{2}g(\Delta t)^2$$
$$v_{y,f} = v_i(\sin \theta) - g\Delta t$$
$$v_{y,f}^2 = v_i^2(\sin \theta)^2 - 2g\Delta y$$

Instead of having vertical motion that starts from rest, a projectile launched at an angle has an initial vertical value. This vertical motion is similar to that of an object that is thrown straight up with an initial velocity.

Projectiles launched at an angle

PROBLEM

A zookeeper finds an escaped monkey hanging from a light pole. Aiming her tranquilizer gun at the monkey, the zookeeper kneels 10.0 m from the light pole, which is 5.00 m high. The tip of her gun is 1.00 m above the ground. The monkey tries to trick the zookeeper by dropping a banana, then continues to hold onto the light pole. At the moment the monkey releases the banana, the zookeeper shoots. If the tranquilizer dart travels at 50.0 m/s, will the dart hit the monkey or the banana?

SOLUTION

1. **Select a coordinate system.**

As shown in **Figure 3-21**, the positive y-axis points up along the tip of the gun, and the positive x-axis points along the ground toward the light pole. Because the dart leaves the gun at a height of 1.00 m, the vertical distance to the monkey (and to the banana) is 4.00 m rather than 5.00 m.

Figure 3-21

2. **Use the tangent function to find the initial angle that the initial velocity makes with the x-axis.**

$$\theta = \tan^{-1}\left(\frac{\Delta y}{\Delta x}\right) = \tan^{-1}\left(\frac{4.00 \text{ m}}{10.0 \text{ m}}\right)$$

$$\theta = 21.8°$$

3. **Choose a kinematic equation to solve for time.**

First rearrange the equation for motion along the x-axis to isolate the unknown, Δt, which is the time it takes the bullet to travel the horizontal distance from the tip of the gun to the pole.

$$\Delta x = v_i(\cos \theta)\Delta t$$

$$\Delta t = \frac{\Delta x}{v_i \cos \theta} = \frac{10.0 \text{ m}}{(50.0 \text{ m/s})(\cos 21.8°)}$$

$$\Delta t = 0.215 \text{ s}$$

4. **Using your knowledge of free fall, find out how far each object will fall during this time.**

For the banana:

This is a free-fall problem where $v_i = 0$.

$$\Delta y = -\frac{1}{2}g(\Delta t)^2 = -\frac{1}{2}(9.81 \text{ m/s}^2)(0.215 \text{ s})^2$$

$$\Delta y = -0.227 \text{ m}$$

continued on next page

Thus, the banana will be 0.227 m below its starting point.

For the dart:

$$\Delta y = v_i(\sin \theta)\Delta t - \tfrac{1}{2}g(\Delta t)^2$$
$$\Delta y = (50.0 \text{ m/s})(\sin 21.8°)(0.215 \text{ s}) - \tfrac{1}{2}(9.81 \text{ m/s}^2)(0.215 \text{ s})^2$$
$$\Delta y = 3.99 \text{ m} - 0.227 \text{ m}$$
$$\Delta y = 3.76 \text{ m}$$

The dart will be 3.76 m above its starting point.

5. Analyze the results.

By rearranging our equation for displacement, we can find the final height of both the banana and the dart. Note that the banana began 5.00 m above the ground and the dart began 1.00 m above the ground.

$$y_f = y_i + \Delta y$$
$$y_{banana, f} = 5.00 \text{ m} + (-0.227 \text{ m}) = \boxed{4.77 \text{ m above the ground}}$$

$$y_{dart, f} = 1.00 \text{ m} + 3.76 \text{ m} = \boxed{4.76 \text{ m above the ground}}$$

This shows that the dart hits the banana, rather than the monkey. The slight difference is due to rounding.

PRACTICE 3E

Projectiles launched at an angle

1. In a scene in an action movie, a stuntman jumps from the top of one building to the top of another building 4.0 m away. After a running start, he leaps at an angle of 15° with respect to the flat roof while traveling at a speed of 5.0 m/s. Will he make it to the other roof, which is 2.5 m shorter than the building he jumps from?

2. A golfer can hit a golf ball a horizontal distance of over 300 m on a good drive. What maximum height would a 301.5 m drive reach if it were launched at an angle of 25.0° to the ground? (Hint: At the top of its flight, the ball's vertical velocity will be zero.)

3. Salmon often jump waterfalls to reach their breeding grounds. Starting 2.00 m from a waterfall 0.55 m in height, at what minimum speed must a salmon jumping at an angle of 32.0° leave the water to continue upstream?

4. A quarterback throws the football to a receiver who is 31.5 m down the field. If the football is thrown at an initial angle of 40.0° to the ground, at what initial speed must the quarterback throw the ball? What is the ball's highest point during its flight?

1. Which of the following are examples of projectile motion?
   a. an airplane taking off
   b. a tennis ball lobbed over a net
   c. a plastic disk sailing across a lawn
   d. a hawk diving to catch a mouse
   e. a parachutist drifting to Earth
   f. a frog jumping from land into the water

2. Which of the following exhibit parabolic motion?
   a. a flat rock skipping across the surface of a lake
   b. a three-point shot in basketball
   c. the space shuttle while orbiting Earth
   d. a ball bouncing across a room
   e. a cliff diver
   f. a life preserver dropped from a stationary helicopter
   g. a person skipping

3. An Alaskan rescue plane drops a package of emergency rations to a stranded party of explorers, as illustrated in **Figure 3-22**. The plane is traveling horizontally at 100.0 m/s at a height of 50.0 m above the ground. What horizontal distance does the package travel before striking the ground?

$v_{plane} = 100.0$ m/s

50.0 m

Figure 3-22

4. Find the velocity (magnitude and direction) of the package in item 3 just before it hits the ground.

5. During a thunderstorm, a tornado lifts a car to a height of 125 m above the ground. Increasing in strength, the tornado flings the car horizontally with an initial speed of 90.0 m/s. How long does the car take to reach the ground? How far horizontally does the car travel before hitting the ground?

6. **Physics in Action**   Streams of water in a fountain shoot from one level to the next. A particle of water in a stream takes 0.50 s to travel between the first and second level. The receptacle on the second level is a horizontal distance of 1.5 m away from the spout on the first level. If the water is projected at an angle of 33°, what is the initial speed of the particle?

7. **Physics in Action**   If a water particle in a stream of water in a fountain takes 0.35 s to travel from spout to receptacle when shot at an angle of 67° and an initial speed of 5.0 m/s, what is the vertical distance between the levels of the fountain?

3-4
Relative motion

FRAMES OF REFERENCE

If you are moving at 80 km/h north and a car passes you going 90 km/h, to you the faster car seems to be moving north at 10 km/h. Someone standing on the side of the road would measure the velocity of the faster car as 90 km/h toward the north. This simple example demonstrates that velocity measurements depend on the **frame of reference** of the observer.

Velocity measurements differ in different frames of reference

Observers using different frames of reference may measure different displacements or velocities for an object in motion. That is, two observers moving with respect to each other would generally not agree on some features of the motion.

Let us return to the example of the stunt dummy that is dropped from an airplane flying horizontally over Earth with a constant velocity. As shown in **Figure 3-23(a),** a passenger on the airplane would describe the motion of the dummy as a straight line toward Earth, whereas an observer on the ground would view the trajectory of the dummy as that of a projectile, as shown in **Figure 3-23(b).** Relative to the ground, the dummy would have a vertical component of velocity (resulting from free-fall acceleration and equal to the velocity measured by the observer in the airplane) *and* a horizontal component of velocity given to it by the airplane's motion. If the airplane continued to move horizontally with the same velocity, the dummy would enter the swimming pool directly beneath the airplane (assuming negligible air resistance).

(a)

(b)

Figure 3-23
When viewed from the plane **(a),** the stunt dummy (represented by the maroon dot) falls straight down. When viewed from a stationary position on the ground **(b),** the stunt dummy follows a parabolic projectile path.

RELATIVE VELOCITY

The case of the faster car overtaking your car was easy to solve with a minimum of thought and effort, but you will encounter many situations in which a more systematic method of solving such problems is beneficial. To develop this method, write down all the information that is given and that you want to know in the form of velocities with subscripts appended.

$\mathbf{v_{se}}$ = +80 km/h north (Here the subscript *se* means the velocity of the *slower* car with respect to *Earth*.)

$\mathbf{v_{fe}}$ = +90 km/h north (The subscript *fe* means the velocity of the *fast* car with respect to *Earth*.)

We want to know $\mathbf{v_{fs}}$, which is the velocity of the fast car with respect to the slower car. To find this, we write an equation for $\mathbf{v_{fs}}$ in terms of the other velocities, so on the right side of the equation the subscripts start with *f* and eventually end with *s*. Also, each velocity subscript starts with the letter that ended the preceding velocity subscript.

$$\mathbf{v_{fs}} = \mathbf{v_{fe}} + \mathbf{v_{es}}$$

The boldface notation indicates that velocity is a vector quantity. This approach to adding and monitoring subscripts is similar to vector addition, in which vector arrows are placed head to tail to find a resultant.

If we take north to be the positive direction, we know that $\mathbf{v_{es}} = -\mathbf{v_{se}}$ because an observer in the slow car perceives Earth as moving south at a velocity of 80 km/h while a stationary observer on the ground (Earth) views the car as moving north at a velocity of 80 km/h. Thus, this problem can be solved as follows:

$$\mathbf{v_{fs}} = +90 \text{ km/h} - 80 \text{ km/h} = +10 \text{ km/h}$$

The positive sign means that the fast car appears (to the occupants of the slower car) to be moving north at 10 km/h.

There is no general equation to work relative velocity problems; instead, you should develop the necessary equations on your own by following the above technique for writing subscripts.

Conceptual Challenge

1. Elevator acceleration A boy bounces a small rubber ball in an elevator that is going down. If the boy drops the ball as the elevator is slowing down, is the ball's acceleration relative to the elevator less than or greater than it's acceleration relative to the ground?

2. Aircraft carrier Why does a plane landing on an aircraft carrier approach the carrier from the rear instead of from the front?

Relative velocity

PROBLEM

A boat heading north crosses a wide river with a velocity of 10.00 km/h relative to the water. The river has a uniform velocity of 5.00 km/h due east. Determine the boat's velocity with respect to an observer on shore.

SOLUTION

1. DEFINE   **Given:** $\mathbf{v_{br}}$ = 10.00 km/h due north (velocity of the *boat, b,* with respect to the *river, r*)

$\mathbf{v_{re}}$ = 5.00 km/h due east (velocity of the *river, r,* with respect to *Earth, e*)

Unknown: $\mathbf{v_{be}}$ = ?

Diagram:

2. PLAN   **Choose an equation(s) or situation:** To find $\mathbf{v_{be}}$, write the equation so that the subscripts on the right start with *b* and end with *e*.

$$\mathbf{v_{be}} = \mathbf{v_{br}} + \mathbf{v_{re}}$$

As in Section 3-2, we use the Pythagorean theorem to calculate the magnitude of the resultant velocity and the tangent function to find the direction.

$$(v_{be})^2 = (v_{br})^2 + (v_{re})^2$$

$$\tan \theta = \frac{v_{re}}{v_{br}}$$

Rearrange the equation(s) to isolate the unknown(s):

$$v_{be} = \sqrt{(v_{br})^2 + (v_{re})^2}$$

$$\theta = \tan^{-1}\left(\frac{v_{re}}{v_{br}}\right)$$

3. CALCULATE   **Substitute the known values into the equation(s) and solve:**

$$v_{be} = \sqrt{(10.00 \text{ km/h})^2 + (5.00 \text{ km/h})^2}$$

$$\boxed{v_{be} = 11.18 \text{ km/h}}$$

$$\theta = \tan^{-1}\left(\frac{5.00}{10.00}\right)$$

$$\boxed{\theta = 26.6°}$$

4. EVALUATE   The boat travels at a speed of 11.18 km/h in the direction 26.6° east of north with respect to Earth.

Relative velocity

1. A passenger at the rear of a train traveling at 15 m/s relative to Earth throws a baseball with a speed of 15 m/s in the direction opposite the motion of the train. What is the velocity of the baseball relative to Earth as it leaves the thrower's hand? Show your work.

2. A spy runs from the front to the back of an aircraft carrier at a speed of 3.5 m/s. If the aircraft carrier is moving forward at 18.0 m/s, how fast does the spy appear to be running when viewed by an observer on a nearby stationary submarine? Show your work.

3. A ferry is crossing a river. If the ferry is headed due north with a speed of 2.5 m/s relative to the water and the river's velocity is 3.0 m/s to the east, what will the boat's velocity be relative to Earth? (Hint: Remember to include the direction in describing the velocity.)

4. A pet-store supply truck moves at 25.0 m/s north along a highway. Inside, a dog moves at 1.75 m/s at an angle of 35.0° east of north. What is the velocity of the dog relative to the road?

Section Review

1. Describe the motion of the following objects if they are observed from the stated frames of reference:
   a. a person standing on a platform viewed from a train traveling north
   b. a train traveling north viewed by a person standing on a platform
   c. a bouncing ball dropped by a boy walking at a speed of 1 m/s viewed by the boy
   d. a bouncing ball dropped by a boy walking 1 m/s as seen by a nearby viewer who is stationary

2. A woman on a 10-speed bicycle travels at 9 m/s relative to the ground as she passes a little boy on a tricycle going in the opposite direction. If the boy is traveling at 1 m/s relative to the ground, how fast does the boy appear to be moving relative to the woman? Show your work.

3. A girl at an airport rolls a ball north on a moving walkway that moves east. If the ball's speed with respect to the walkway is 0.15 m/s and the walkway moves at a speed of 1.50 m/s, what is the velocity of the ball with respect to the ground?

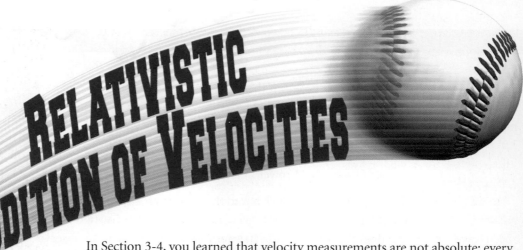

RELATIVISTIC ADDITION OF VELOCITIES

PHYSICS ON THE EDGE

In Section 3-4, you learned that velocity measurements are not absolute; every velocity measurement depends on the frame of reference of the observer with respect to the moving object. For example, imagine that someone riding a bike toward you at 25 m/s (v) throws a softball toward you. If the bicyclist measures the softball's speed (u') to be 15 m/s, you would perceive the ball to be moving toward you at 40 m/s (u) because you have a different frame of reference than the bicyclist does. This is expressed mathematically by the equation $u = v + u'$, which is also known as the classical addition of velocities.

The speed of light

As stated in the "Time dilation" feature in Chapter 2, according to Einstein's special theory of relativity, the speed of light is absolute, or independent of all frames of reference. If, instead of a softball, the bicyclist were to shine a beam of light toward you, both you and the bicyclist would measure the light's speed as 3.0×10^8 m/s. This would remain true even if the bicyclist were moving toward you at 99 percent of the speed of light. Thus, Einstein's theory requires a different approach to the addition of velocities. Einstein's modification of the classical formula, which he derived in his 1905 paper on special relativity, covers both the case of the softball and the case of the light beam.

$$u = \frac{v + u'}{1 + (vu'/c^2)}$$

In this equation, u is the velocity of an object in one reference frame, u' is the velocity of that same object in another reference frame, v is the velocity of one reference frame relative to the other, and c is the speed of light.

The universality of Einstein's equation

How does Einstein's equation cover both cases? First we shall consider the bicyclist throwing a softball. Because c^2 is such a large number, the vu'/c^2 term in the denominator is very small for velocities typical of our everyday experience. As a result, the denominator of the equation is nearly equal to 1. Hence, for speeds that are small compared with c, the two theories give nearly the same result, $u = v + u'$, and the classical addition of velocities can be used.

However, when speeds approach the speed of light, vu'/c^2 increases, and the denominator becomes greater than 1 and less than 2. When this occurs, the difference between the two theories becomes significant. For example, if a bicyclist moving toward you at 80 percent of the speed of light were to throw a ball to you at 70 percent of the speed of light, you would observe the ball moving toward you at about 96 percent of the speed of light rather than the 150 percent of the speed of light predicted by classical theory. In this case, the difference between the velocities predicted by each theory cannot be ignored, and the relativistic addition of velocities must be used.

In this last example, it is significant that classical addition predicts a speed greater than the speed of light (1.5c), while the relativistic addition predicts a speed less than the speed of light (0.96c). In fact, no matter how close the speeds involved are to the speed of light, the relativistic equation yields a result less than the speed of light, as seen in **Table 3-1.**

How does Einstein's equation cover the second case, in which the bicyclist shines a beam of light toward you? Einstein's equation predicts that any object traveling at the speed of light ($u' = c$) will appear to travel at the speed of light ($u = c$) for an observer in any reference frame:

$$u = \frac{v + u'}{1 + (vu'/c^2)} = \frac{v + c}{1 + (vc/c^2)} = \frac{v + c}{1 + (v/c)} = \frac{v + c}{(c + v)/c} = c$$

This corresponds with our earlier statement that the bicyclist measures the beam of light traveling at the same speed that you do, 3.0×10^8 m/s, even though you have a different reference frame than the bicyclist does. This occurs regardless of how fast the bicycle is moving because v (the bicycle's speed) cancels from the equation. Thus, Einstein's relativistic equation successfully covers both cases. This shows that Einstein's equation is a more general case of the classical equation, which is simply the limiting case.

Figure 3-24
According to Einstein's relativistic equation for the addition of velocities, material particles can never reach the speed of light.

Table 3-1	Classical and relativistic addition of velocities		
		Classical addition	**Relativistic addition**
Speed between frames (v)	Speed in A (u')	Speed in B (u)	Speed in B (u)
25 m/s	15 m/s	40 m/s	40 m/s
100 000.00 m/s	100 000.00 m/s	200 000.00 m/s	199 999.9 m/s
50% of c	50% of c	300 000 000 m/s	240 000 000 m/s
90% of c	90% of c	540 000 000 m/s	298 342 541 m/s
99.99% of c	99.99% of c	599 940 000 m/s	299 999 999 m/s

CHAPTER 3
Summary

KEY TERMS

components of a vector (p. 92)

frame of reference (p. 106)

projectile motion (p. 99)

resultant (p. 85)

scalar (p. 84)

vector (p. 84)

KEY IDEAS

Section 3-1 Introduction to vectors

- A scalar is a quantity completely specified by only a number with appropriate units, whereas a vector is a quantity that has magnitude and direction.
- Vectors can be added graphically using the triangle method of addition, in which the tail of one vector is placed at the head of the other. The resultant is the vector drawn from the tail of the first vector to the head of the last vector.

Section 3-2 Vector operations

- The Pythagorean theorem and the tangent function can be used to find the magnitude and direction of a resultant vector.
- Any vector can be resolved into its component vectors using the sine and cosine functions.

Section 3-3 Projectile motion

- Neglecting air resistance, a projectile has a constant horizontal velocity and a constant downward free-fall acceleration.
- In the absence of air resistance, projectiles follow a parabolic path.

Section 3-4 Relative motion

- If the frame of reference is denoted with subscripts ($\mathbf{v_{ab}}$ is the velocity of a with respect to b), then the velocity of an object with respect to a different frame of reference can be found by adding the known velocities so that the subscript starts with the letter that ends the preceding velocity subscript, $\mathbf{v_{ab}} = \mathbf{v_{ac}} + \mathbf{v_{cb}}$.
- If the order of the subscripts is reversed, there is a change in sign, for example, $\mathbf{v_{cd}} = -\mathbf{v_{dc}}$.

Diagram symbols

⟶	displacement vector
⟶	velocity vector
⟹	acceleration vector
------▶	resultant vector
⟹	component

Variable symbols

Quantities		Units	
$\mathbf{d}$ (vector)	displacement	m	meters
$\mathbf{v}$ (vector)	velocity	m/s	meters/second
$\mathbf{a}$ (vector)	acceleration	m/s^2	meters/second^2
Δx (scalar)	horizontal component	m	meters
Δy (scalar)	vertical component	m	meters

VECTORS AND THE GRAPHICAL METHOD

Review questions

1. The magnitude of a vector is a scalar. Explain this statement.

2. If two vectors have unequal magnitudes, can their sum be zero? Explain.

3. What is the relationship between instantaneous speed and instantaneous velocity?

4. What is another way of saying −30 m/s west?

5. Is it possible to add a vector quantity to a scalar quantity? Explain.

6. Vector **A** is 3.00 units in length and points along the positive *x*-axis. Vector **B** is 4.00 units in length and points along the negative *y*-axis. Use graphical methods to find the magnitude and direction of the following vectors:
   a. **A** + **B**
   b. **A** − **B**
   c. **A** + 2**B**
   d. **B** − **A**

7. Each of the displacement vectors **A** and **B** shown in **Figure 3-25** has a magnitude of 3.00 m. Graphically find the following:
   a. **A** + **B**
   b. **A** − **B**
   c. **B** − **A**
   d. **A** − 2**B**

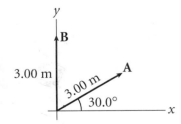

Figure 3-25

8. A dog searching for a bone walks 3.50 m south, then 8.20 m at an angle of 30.0° north of east, and finally 15.0 m west. Use graphical techniques to find the dog's resultant displacement vector.

9. A man lost in a maze makes three consecutive displacements so that at the end of the walk he is back where he started, as shown in **Figure 3-26**. The first displacement is 8.00 m westward, and the second is 13.0 m northward. Use the graphical method to find the third displacement.

Figure 3-26

Conceptual questions

10. If **B** is added to **A,** under what conditions does the resultant have the magnitude equal to *A* + *B*?

11. Give an example of a moving object that has a velocity vector and an acceleration vector in the same direction and an example of one that has velocity and acceleration vectors in opposite directions.

12. A student accurately uses the method for combining vectors. The two vectors she combines have magnitudes of 55 and 25 units. The answer that she gets is either 85, 20, or 55. Pick the correct answer, and explain why it is the only one of the three that can be correct.

13. If a set of vectors laid head to tail forms a closed polygon, the resultant is zero. Is this statement true? Explain your reasoning.

VECTOR OPERATIONS

Review questions

14. Can a vector have a component equal to zero and still have a nonzero magnitude?

15. Can a vector have a component greater than its magnitude?

16. Explain the difference between vector addition and vector resolution.

17. If the component of one vector along the direction of another is zero, what can you conclude about these two vectors?

18. How would you add two vectors that are not perpendicular or parallel?

Conceptual questions

19. If $\mathbf{A} + \mathbf{B} = 0$, what can you say about the components of the two vectors?

20. Under what circumstances would a vector have components that are equal in magnitude?

21. The vector sum of three vectors gives a resultant equal to zero. What can you say about the vectors?

Practice problems

22. A girl delivering newspapers covers her route by traveling three blocks west, four blocks north, then six blocks east.
  a. What is her resultant displacement?
  b. What is the total distance she travels?
  (See Sample Problem 3A.)

23. A submarine dives 110.0 m at an angle of 10.0° below the horizontal. What are the horizontal and vertical components of the submarine's displacement?
  (See Sample Problem 3B.)

24. A quarterback takes the ball from the line of scrimmage, runs backward for 10.0 yards, then runs sideways parallel to the line of scrimmage for 15.0 yards. At this point, he throws a 50.0-yard forward pass straight down the field. What is the magnitude of the football's resultant displacement?
  (See Sample Problem 3A.)

25. A golfer takes two putts to sink his ball in the hole once he is on the green. The first putt displaces the ball 6.00 m east, and the second putt displaces it 5.40 m south. What displacement would put the ball in the hole in one putt?
  (See Sample Problem 3A.)

26. A person walks 25.0° north of east for 3.10 km. How far would another person walk due north and due east to arrive at the same location?
  (See Sample Problem 3B.)

27. A roller coaster travels 41.1 m at an angle of 40.0° above the horizontal. How far does it move horizontally and vertically?
  (See Sample Problem 3B.)

28. A shopper pushing a cart through a store moves 40.0 m south down one aisle, then makes a 90.0° turn and moves 15.0 m. He then makes another 90.0° turn and moves 20.0 m. Find the shopper's total displacement. Note that you are not given the direction moved after any of the 90.0° turns, so there could be more than one answer.
  (See Sample Problem 3A.)

29. A person walks the path shown in **Figure 3-27**. The total trip consists of four straight-line paths. At the end of the walk, what is the person's resultant displacement measured from the starting point?
  (See Sample Problem 3C.)

Figure 3-27

PROJECTILE MOTION

Review questions

30. A bullet is fired horizontally from a pistol, and another bullet is dropped simultaneously from the same height. Neglecting air resistance, which bullet hits the ground first?

31. If a rock is dropped from the top of a sailboat's mast, will it hit the deck at the same point whether the boat is at rest or in motion at constant velocity?

32. Does a ball dropped out of the window of a moving car take longer to reach the ground than one dropped at the same height from a car at rest?

33. A rock is dropped at the same instant that a ball at the same elevation is thrown horizontally. Which will have the greater velocity when it reaches ground level?

Practice problems

34. The fastest recorded pitch in Major League Baseball, thrown by Nolan Ryan in 1974, was clocked at 162.3 km/h (100.8 mi/h). If a pitch were thrown horizontally with this velocity, how far would the ball fall vertically by the time it reached home plate, 18.3 m (60.0 ft) away?
(See Sample Problem 3D.)

35. A ball is fired from the ground with an initial speed of 1.70×10^3 m/s (approximately five times the speed of sound) at an initial angle of 55.0° to the horizontal. Neglecting air resistance, find
  a. the ball's horizontal range.
  b. the amount of time the ball is in motion.
(See Sample Problem 3E.)

36. A person standing at the edge of a seaside cliff kicks a stone over the edge with a speed of 18 m/s. The cliff is 52 m above the water's surface, as shown in **Figure 3-28.** How long does it take for the stone to fall to the water? With what speed does it strike the water?
(See Sample Problem 3D.)

Figure 3-28

$v_i = +18$ m/s

$h = 52$ m

g

37. A daredevil is shot out of a cannon at 45.0° to the horizontal with an initial speed of 25.0 m/s. A net is positioned a horizontal distance of 50.0 m from the cannon. At what height above the cannon should the net be placed in order to catch the daredevil?
(See Sample Problem 3E.)

38. A place kicker must kick a football from a point 36.0 m (about 40.0 yd) from the goal, and the ball must clear the crossbar, which is 3.05 m high. When kicked, the ball leaves the ground with a speed of 20.0 m/s at an angle of 53° to the horizontal.
  a. By how much does the ball clear or fall short of clearing the crossbar?
  b. Does the ball approach the crossbar while still rising or while falling?
(See Sample Problem 3E.)

39. A ball player hits a home run, and the baseball just clears a wall 21.0 m high located 130.0 m from home plate. The ball is hit at an angle of 35.0° to the horizontal, and air resistance is negligible. Assume the ball is hit at a height of 1.0 m above the ground.
  a. What is the initial speed of the ball?
  b. How much time does it take for the ball to reach the wall?
  c. Find the velocity components and the speed of the ball when it reaches the wall.
(See Sample Problem 3E.)

40. A daredevil jumps a canyon 12 m wide. To do so, he drives a car up a 15° incline.
  a. What minimum speed must he achieve to clear the canyon?
  b. If the daredevil jumps at this minimum speed, what will his speed be when he reaches the other side?
(See Sample Problem 3E.)

41. A 2.00 m tall basketball player attempts a goal 10.0 m from the basket (3.05 m high). If he shoots the ball at a 45.0° angle, at what initial speed must he throw the basketball so that it goes through the hoop without striking the backboard?
(See Sample Problem 3D.)

42. When a water gun is fired while being held horizontally at a height of 1.00 m above ground level, the water travels a horizontal distance of 5.00 m. A child holds the same gun in a horizontal position while sliding down a 45.0° incline at a constant speed of 2.00 m/s. If the child fires the gun when it is 1.00 m above the ground and the water takes 0.329 s to reach the ground, how far will the water travel horizontally?
(See Sample Problem 3E.)

43. A spy in a speed boat is being chased down a river by government officials in a larger craft. If the spy travels at 26 m/s and the officials travel at a speed of 15 m/s, how far from each other will the two vessels land after they fly off a 5.0 m waterfall?

44. A ship maneuvers to within 2500 m of an island's 1800 m high mountain peak and fires a projectile at an enemy ship 610 m on the other side of the peak, as illustrated in **Figure 3-29.** If the ship shoots the projectile with an initial velocity of 250 m/s at an angle of 75°, how close to the enemy ship does the projectile land? How close (vertically) does the projectile come to the peak?
(See Sample Problem 3E.)

Figure 3-29

RELATIVE MOTION

Review questions

45. Explain the statement, "All motion is relative."

46. What is a frame of reference?

47. When we describe motion, what is a common frame of reference?

48. A small airplane is flying at 50 m/s toward the east. A wind of 20 m/s toward the east suddenly begins to blow, giving the plane a velocity of 70 m/s east.

    a. Which of these are component vectors?
    b. Which is the resultant?
    c. What is the magnitude of the wind velocity?

49. A ball is thrown upward in the air by a passenger on a train that is moving with constant velocity.

    a. Describe the path of the ball as seen by the passenger. Describe the path as seen by a stationary observer outside the train.
    b. How would these observations change if the train were accelerating along the track?

Practice problems

50. The pilot of a plane measures an air velocity of 165 km/h south. An observer on the ground sees the plane pass overhead at a velocity of 145 km/h toward the north. What is the velocity of the wind that is affecting the plane?
(See Sample Problem 3F.)

51. A river flows due east at 1.50 m/s. A boat crosses the river from the south shore to the north shore by maintaining a constant velocity of 10.0 m/s due north relative to the water.

    a. What is the velocity of the boat as viewed by an observer on shore?
    b. If the river is 325 m wide, how far downstream has the boat moved by the time it reaches the north shore?

(See Sample Problem 3F.)

52. The pilot of an aircraft wishes to fly due west in a 50.0 km/h wind blowing toward the south. The speed of the aircraft in the absence of a wind is 205 km/h.

    a. In what direction should the aircraft head?
    b. What should its speed be relative to the ground?

(See Sample Problem 3F.)

53. A hunter wishes to cross a river that is 1.5 km wide and that flows with a speed of 5.0 km/h. The hunter uses a small powerboat that moves at a maximum speed of 12 km/h with respect to the water. What is the minimum time necessary for crossing?
(See Sample Problem 3F.)

54. A swimmer can swim in still water at a speed of 9.50 m/s. He intends to swim directly across a river that has a downstream current of 3.75 m/s.

    a. What must the swimmer's heading be?
    b. What is his velocity relative to the bank?

(See Sample Problem 3F.)

MIXED REVIEW PROBLEMS

55. A motorboat heads due east at 12 m/s across a river that flows toward the south at a speed of 3.5 m/s.

    a. What is the resultant velocity relative to an observer on the shore?
    b. If the river is 1360 m wide, how long does it take the boat to cross?

56. A ball is thrown straight upward and returns to the thrower's hand after 3.00 s in the air. A second ball is thrown at an angle of 30.0° with the horizontal. At what speed must the second ball be thrown so that it reaches the same height as the one thrown vertically?

57. An escalator is 20.0 m long. If a person stands on the escalator, it takes 50.0 s to ride from the bottom to the top.

    a. If a person walks up the moving escalator with a speed of 0.500 m/s relative to the escalator, how long does it take the person to get to the top?

    b. If a person walks down the "up" escalator with the same relative speed as in item (a), how long does it take to reach the bottom?

58. A ball is projected horizontally from the edge of a table that is 1.00 m high, and it strikes the floor at a point 1.20 m from the base of the table.

    a. What is the initial speed of the ball?

    b. How high is the ball above the floor when its velocity vector makes a 45.0° angle with the horizontal?

59. How long does it take an automobile traveling 60.0 km/h to become even with a car that is traveling in another lane at 40.0 km/h if the cars' front bumpers are initially 125 m apart?

60. The eye of a hurricane passes over Grand Bahama Island. It is moving in a direction 60.0° north of west with a speed of 41.0 km/h. Exactly three hours later, the course of the hurricane shifts due north, and its speed slows to 25.0 km/h, as shown in **Figure 3-30**. How far from Grand Bahama is the hurricane 4.50 h after it passes over the island?

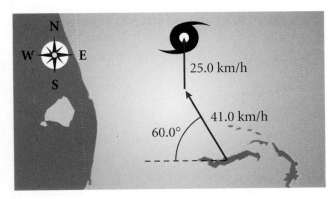

Figure 3-30

61. A car is parked on a cliff overlooking the ocean on an incline that makes an angle of 24.0° below the horizontal. The negligent driver leaves the car in neutral, and the emergency brakes are defective. The car rolls from rest down the incline with a constant acceleration of 4.00 m/s² and travels 50.0 m to the edge of the cliff. The cliff is 30.0 m above the ocean.

    a. What is the car's position relative to the base of the cliff when the car lands in the ocean?

    b. How long is the car in the air?

62. A boat moves through a river at 7.5 m/s relative to the water, regardless of the boat's direction. If the water in the river is flowing at 1.5 m/s, how long does it take the boat to make a round trip consisting of a 250 m displacement downstream followed by a 250 m displacement upstream?

63. A golf ball with an initial angle of 34° lands exactly 240 m down the range on a level course.

    a. Neglecting air friction, what initial speed would achieve this result?

    b. Using the speed determined in item (a), find the maximum height reached by the ball.

64. A water spider maintains an average position on the surface of a stream by darting upstream (against the current), then drifting downstream (with the current) to its original position. The current in the stream is 0.500 m/s relative to the shore, and the water spider darts upstream 0.560 m (relative to a spot on shore) in 0.800 s during the first part of its motion. Use upstream as the positive direction.

    a. Determine both the velocity of the water spider relative to the water during its dash upstream and its velocity during its drift downstream.

    b. How far upstream relative to the water does the water spider move during one cycle of this upstream and downstream motion?

    c. What is the average velocity of the water spider relative to the water?

65. A car travels due east with a speed of 50.0 km/h. Rain is falling vertically with respect to Earth. The traces of the rain on the side windows of the car make an angle of 60.0° with the vertical. Find the velocity of the rain with respect to the following:

    a. the car

    b. Earth

66. A shopper in a department store can walk up a stationary (stalled) escalator in 30.0 s. If the normally functioning escalator can carry the standing shopper to the next floor in 20.0 s, how long would it take the shopper to walk up the moving escalator? Assume the same walking effort for the shopper whether the escalator is stalled or moving.

67. If a person can jump a horizontal distance of 3.0 m on Earth, how far could the person jump on the moon, where the free-fall acceleration is $g/6$ and $g = 9.81$ m/s^2? How far could the person jump on Mars, where the acceleration due to gravity is $0.38g$?

68. A science student riding on a flatcar of a train moving at a constant speed of 10.0 m/s throws a ball toward the caboose along a path that the student judges as making an initial angle of 60.0° with the horizontal. The teacher, who is standing on the ground nearby, observes the ball rising vertically. How high does the ball rise?

69. A football is thrown toward a receiver with an initial speed of 18.0 m/s at an angle of 35.0° above the horizontal. At that instant, the receiver is 18.0 m from the quarterback. In what direction and with what constant speed should the receiver run to catch the football at the level at which it was thrown?

Technology & Learning

Graphing calculators

Program your graphing calculator to create a graph of height versus time so that you can predict how high a vertically thrown baseball will go and how long it will remain in flight, given the following initial speeds for a ball traveling straight upward:

a. 25 m/s

b. 35 m/s

c. 75 m/s

Open a new program by pressing [PRGM] [▶] [▶] [ENTER]. Name the program "BASEBALL" and press [ENTER]. Then enter the program shown in the table below.

To exit the program editor, press [2nd] [QUIT]. To run the program, press [PRGM], select "BASEBALL," and press [ENTER] [ENTER]. Enter the value for initial velocity, pressing [ENTER] afterward.

The calculator will provide the graph of the displacement function versus time. The x value corresponds to the time in seconds, and the y value corresponds to the height in meters. (If the graph is not visible, press [WINDOW] and change the settings for the graph window.)

Press [TRACE], and use the arrow keys to trace along the curve to the highest point of the graph. The y value there will be the greatest height the ball reaches. Trace the curve to the right, where the y value (height) is zero. The x value will be the duration of the ball's flight.

Keystrokes	Display
	PROGRAM: BASEBALL
1. [PRGM] [▶] [2] [ALPHA] [V] [ENTER]	:PROMPT V
2. [ALPHA] ["] [ALPHA] [V] [X,T,θ] [−] [4] [.] [9] [X,T,θ] [x^2] [ALPHA] ["] [STO▶] [2nd] [Y-VARS] [1] [1] [ENTER]	:"VX–4.9 X^2" → Y1
3. [PRGM] [▶] [4] [ENTER]	:DISPGRAPH

70. A rocket is launched at an angle of 53° above the horizontal with an initial speed of 75 m/s, as shown in **Figure 3-31.** It moves for 25 s along its initial line of motion with an acceleration of 25 m/s². At this time its engines fail and the rocket proceeds to move as a free body.

Figure 3-31

   a. What is the rocket's maximum altitude?
   b. What is the rocket's total time of flight?
   c. What is the rocket's horizontal range?

Alternative Assessment

Performance assessment

1. Work in cooperative groups to analyze a game of chess in terms of displacement vectors. Make a model chessboard, and draw arrows showing all the possible moves for each piece as vectors made of horizontal and vertical components. Then have two members of your group play the game while the others keep track of each piece's moves. Be prepared to demonstrate how vector addition can be used to explain where a piece would be after several moves.

2. Use a garden hose to investigate the laws of projectile motion. Design experiments to investigate how the angle of the hose affects the range of the water stream. (Assume that the initial speed of water is constant and is determined by the pressure indicated by the faucet's setting.) What quantities will you measure, and how will you measure them? What variables do you need to control? What is the shape of the water stream? How can you reach the maximum range? How can you reach the highest point? Present your results to the rest of the class and discuss the conclusions.

3. How would a physics expert respond to the following suggestions made by three airline executives? Write a script of the expert's response for performance in front of the class.
   Airline Executive A: Since the Earth rotates from west to east, we could operate "static flights"—helicopters that begin by hovering above New York City could begin their landing four hours later, when San Francisco arrives below.

   Airline Executive B: This could work for one-way flights, but the return trip would take 20 hours.
   Airline Executive C: That will never work. It's like when you throw a ball up in the air; it comes back to the same point.
   Airline Executive A: That's only because the Earth's motion is not significant during that short a time.

Portfolio projects

4. You are helping NASA engineers design a basketball court for a colony on the moon. How do you anticipate the ball's motion compared with its motion on Earth? What changes will there be for the players—how they move and how they throw the ball? What changes would you recommend for the size of the court, the basket height, and other regulations in order to adapt the sport to the moon's low gravity? Create a presentation or a report presenting your suggestions, and include the physics concepts behind your recommendations.

5. There is conflicting testimony in a court case. A police officer claims that his radar monitor indicated that a car was traveling at 176 km/h (110 mi/h). The driver argues that the radar must have recorded the relative velocity because he was only going 88 km/h (55 mi/h). Is it possible that both are telling the truth? Could one be lying? Prepare scripts for expert witnesses, for both the prosecution and the defense, that use physics to justify their positions before the jury. Create visual aids to be used as evidence to support the different arguments.

CHAPTER 3
Laboratory Exercise

VELOCITY OF A PROJECTILE

In this experiment, you will determine the horizontal velocity of a projectile and compare the effects of different inclined planes on the projectile motion of a ball.

SAFETY

• Tie back long hair, secure loose clothing, and remove loose jewelry to prevent their getting caught in moving or rotating parts.

• Perform this experiment in a clear area. Falling or dropped masses can cause serious injury.

PREPARATION

1. Read the entire lab, and plan what measurements you will take.

2. Prepare a data table in your lab notebook with five columns and nine rows. In the first row, label the columns *Trial, Height of ramp (m), Length of ramp (m), Displacement* Δx *(m), Displacement* Δy *(m)*. In the first column, label the second through ninth rows *1, 2, 3, 4, 5, 6, 7,* and *8*.

3. Set up the inclined plane at any angle, as shown in **Figure 3-32(a)**. Tape the aluminum to the end of the plane and to the table. Leave at least 5 cm between the bottom end of the inclined plane and the edge of the table.

4. In front of the table, place the box to catch the ball after it bounces. Perform a practice trial to find the correct placement of the box. Use masking tape to secure the box to the floor. Cover the floor with white paper. Cover the white paper with the carbon paper, carbon side down. Tape the paper down.

5. Use a piece of cord and tape to hang a washer from the edge of the table so that the washer hangs a few centimeters above the floor. Mark the floor directly beneath the washer with tape. Move the washer to another point on the table edge, and repeat. Connect the two marks on the floor with masking tape.

PROCEDURE

6. Use tape to mark a starting line near the top of the inclined plane. Measure the height of the ramp from the tabletop to the tape mark. Measure

the length along the ramp from the tape mark to the tabletop. Measure the distance from the top of the tabletop to the floor. Enter these values in the data table for *Trial 1* as *Height of ramp (m)*, *Length of ramp (m)*, and *Displacement Δy*.

7. Place the metal ball on the inclined plane at the tape mark. Keep the area around the table clear of people and obstructions. Release the ball from rest so that it rolls down the inclined plane, off the table onto the carbon paper, and bounces into the box.

8. Lift the carbon paper. There should be a heavy carbon mark on the white paper where the ball landed. Label the mark with the trial number.

9. Replace the carbon paper and repeat this procedure as *Trial 2*.

10. With the inclined plane in the same position, place another tape mark about halfway down the inclined plane. Measure and record the height and length of the inclined plane from this mark. Use this mark as the starting point for *Trial 3* and *Trial 4*. Record all data.

11. Raise or lower the inclined plane and repeat the procedure. Perform two trials for each tape mark as *Trials 5, 6, 7,* and *8*. For each trial, measure the distance from the carbon mark to the tape line. Record this distance as *Displacement Δx*.

ANALYSIS AND INTERPRETATION

Calculations and data analysis

1. **Organizing data**   Find the time interval for the ball's motion from the edge of the table to the floor using the equation for the vertical motion of a projectile from page 100, where Δy is the *Displacement Δy* recorded in your data table. For this equation, Δy is negative. The result is the time interval for each trial.

2. **Organizing data**   Using the time interval from item 1 and the value for *Displacement Δx*, calculate the average horizontal velocity for each trial during the ball's motion from the edge of the table to the floor.

Conclusions

3. **Inferring conclusions**   What is the relationship between the height of the inclined plane and the horizontal velocity of the ball? Explain.

4. **Inferring conclusions**   What is the relationship between the length of the inclined plane and the horizontal velocity of the ball? Explain.

Figure 3-32

Step 3: Use tape to cover the sharp edges of the aluminum sheet before taping it to the end of the plane. The aluminum keeps the ball from bouncing as it rolls onto the table.

Step 4: Place a soft cloth in the box as shown. Throughout the lab, be careful not to have too much contact with the carbon paper.

Step 5: This tape line will serve as the baseline for measuring the horizontal distance traveled by the projectile.

Forces and the Laws of Motion

PHYSICS IN ACTION

At General Motors' Milford Proving Grounds, in Michigan, technicians place a crash-test dummy behind the wheel of a new car. While the car accelerates and slams into a concrete barrier, the scientists watch computer screens that display data from sensors implanted in the dummy. These sensors report the acceleration and forces acting on the dummy during the collision. The technicians study the data from the crash to design safer cars and more-effective restraint systems.

In this chapter you will study forces and learn to analyze motion in terms of force.

- *What are the forces acting on a dummy during a car crash?*
- *Why are seat belts necessary to keep dummies in their seats during a crash?*

CONCEPT REVIEW

Acceleration (Section 2-2)

Kinematic equations (Section 2-2)

Vector diagrams (Section 3-1)

Forces and the Laws of Motion **123**

4-1
Changes in motion

4-1 SECTION OBJECTIVES

- **Explain how force affects the motion of an object.**
- **Distinguish between contact forces and field forces.**
- **Interpret and construct free-body diagrams.**

force

the cause of an acceleration, or the change in an object's motion

FORCE

When we think of **force**, we usually imagine a *push* or a *pull* exerted on some object. For instance, you exert a force on a ball when you throw or kick it, and you exert a force on a chair when you sit in it. Force represents the interaction of an object with its environment.

Forces cause changes in motion

Notice that force is defined as causing a *change* in the motion of an object. Some examples of this are shown in **Figure 4-1.** In many cases, force does cause a stationary object to move, as when you throw a ball. Force also causes moving objects to stop, as when brakes stop your car or when a ball is caught. A force can also cause a moving object to change its direction, such as when you use the steering wheel to turn your car or when a tennis ball collides with a racket and bounces off in another direction.

  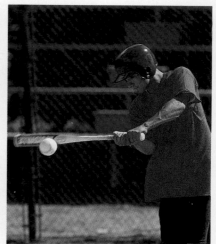

Figure 4-1
Force can cause objects to
(a) start moving, **(b)** stop moving, or **(c)** change direction.

The SI unit of force is the newton

The SI unit of force is the newton, named after Sir Isaac Newton (1642–1727), whose work contributed much to the modern understanding of force and motion. The newton (N) is defined as the amount of force that, when acting on a 1 kg mass, produces an acceleration of 1 m/s^2. Therefore, $1 \text{ N} = 1 \text{ kg} \times 1 \text{ m/s}^2$.

The weight of an object is a measure of the magnitude of the gravitational force exerted on the object. It is the result of the interaction of an object's mass with the gravitational field of another object, such as Earth. Many of the terms

Table 4-1   Units of mass, acceleration, and force

System	Mass	Acceleration	Force
SI	kg	m/s^2	$N = kg \cdot m/s^2$
cgs	g	cm/s^2	$dyne = g \cdot cm/s^2$
Avoirdupois	slug	ft/s^2	$lb = slug \cdot ft/s^2$

Did you know?

The abbreviation for the pound, lb, comes from *libra*, the Latin word for pound, a unit of measure that has been used since medieval times to measure weight.

and units you use every day to talk about weight are really units of force that can be converted to the SI unit of newtons. For example, a $\frac{1}{4}$ lb stick of margarine has a weight equivalent to a force of about 1 N, as shown in the following conversions:

$$1 \text{ lb} = 4.448 \text{ N}$$
$$1 \text{ N} = 0.225 \text{ lb}$$

Forces can act through contact or at a distance

If you pull on a spring, the spring stretches. If you pull on a wagon, the wagon moves. When a football is caught, its motion is stopped. These pushes and pulls are examples of **contact forces,** so named because they result from physical contact between two objects. This kind of force is usually easy to identify when you analyze a situation.

Another class of forces—called **field forces**—does not involve physical contact between two objects. One example of this kind of force is the force of gravity. Whenever an object falls to Earth, it is accelerated by Earth's gravity. In other words, Earth exerts a force on the object, even when it is not in immediate physical contact with the object.

Another common example of a field force is the attraction or repulsion between electrical charges. You can observe this force by rubbing a balloon against your hair and then observing how little pieces of paper appear to jump up and cling to the balloon's surface, as shown in **Figure 4-2.** The paper is pulled by the balloon's electric field.

The theory of fields was developed as a tool to explain how objects could exert force on each other without touching. According to this theory, the presence of an object affects the space around it so that a force is exerted on any other object placed within that space. This region of influence is called a field. Objects exert forces on one another when their fields come into contact. For example, an object falls to Earth because of the interaction between the object and the gravitational field of Earth.

Field forces are especially important in the study of particle physics. The known fundamental forces in nature, which act on elementary particles, are all field forces. This means that elementary particles have no actual contact—all their interactions are the results of field forces.

contact force

force that arises from the physical contact of two objects

field force

force that can exist between objects, even in the absence of physical contact between the objects

Figure 4-2
The electric field around the balloon exerts an attractive force on the pieces of paper.

FORCE DIAGRAMS

If you give a toy car a small push, it will not move as far as it will when you give a harder push. The effect of a force depends on its magnitude, and the magnitude of the force of the second push is greater. The effect of a force on an object's motion also depends on the direction of the force. For example, if you push the toy car first from behind and then from the front, using the same amount of force each time, the car will move in a different direction each time.

Force is a vector

Because the effect of a force depends on its magnitude and direction, force is a vector quantity. Diagrams that show force vectors as arrows, like **Figure 4-3(a)**, are called **force diagrams.** In this book, the arrows used to represent forces are blue. The tail of the arrow is attached to the object on which the force is acting. These diagrams can be used as tools in analyzing collisions and other situations.

At this point, we will disregard the size and shape of objects and assume that all forces act on a point at the center of an object. In force diagrams, all forces are drawn as if they act on that point, no matter where the force is applied.

A free-body diagram shows the forces on one object

Once engineers analyzing a test-car crash have identified all the forces involved, they isolate the car from the other objects in its environment. One of their goals is to determine which forces affect the car and its passengers. **Figure 4-3(b)** is a free-body diagram. It represents the same collision as the force diagram **(a),** but it shows only the car and the forces acting on it. The forces exerted *by* the car on other objects are not included in the free-body diagram because they do not affect the motion of the car.

A free-body diagram is used to analyze only the forces affecting the motion of a single object. Free-body diagrams are constructed and analyzed just like other vector diagrams. In Section 4-2, you will learn to use them to find component and resultant forces. In this section, you will learn to draw a free-body diagram for situations in this book.

force diagram

a diagram of the objects involved in a situation and the forces exerted on the objects

Quick Lab

Force and Changes in Motion

MATERIALS LIST

✔ 1 toy car
✔ 1 book

Use a toy car and a book to model a car colliding with a brick wall while traveling at a constant velocity. Observe the motion of the car before and after the crash. Identify as many changes in its motion, such as a change in speed or in direction, as you can. Make a list of all the changes, and try to identify the forces that caused them. Make a force diagram of the collision.

(a) **(b)**

Figure 4-3
In a force diagram **(a)**, vector arrows represent all the forces acting in a situation. A free-body diagram **(b)** shows only the forces acting on the object of interest—in this case, the car.

A free-body diagram helps to analyze a situation

The photograph in **Figure 4-4(a)** shows a car being pulled by a tow truck. In a situation like this, there are many forces acting on the car. The tow truck exerts a force on the car in the direction of the cable, the road exerts forces on the car, and the car is also acted on by a gravitational force. The relationships between these forces help describe the motion of the car as it is being towed. A free-body diagram of the car will show all the forces acting on the car and how they affect the motion of the car as it is towed.

To draw a free-body diagram of the car, you must first isolate and identify all the forces acting on the car. The figures shown in **(b)** through **(f)** show all the steps required to draw a free-body diagram of the car. Following these general steps will allow you to draw a free-body diagram to isolate the forces acting on a single object for any situation. Before you begin identifying any of the forces acting in the situation, draw a diagram to represent the isolated object under consideration.

A simple diagram of the car is shown in step **(b).** It is often helpful to draw a very simple shape with some distinguishing characteristics that will help you visualize the object. In this case, the car is shown with a very simple shape that is positioned in the same way as the car in the photograph. Positioning the car in the same way will help you draw the arrows representing the forces in the correct positions. Free-body diagrams are often drawn using simple squares, circles, or even points to represent the object. In most cases in this book, free-body diagrams will use shapes that help you visualize the specific situations.

The next step is to draw and label vector arrows representing all external forces acting on the object. The diagram in **(c)** shows the force exerted by the towing cable attached to the car. The arrow is shown originating at the center of the car because all forces are assumed to act on a single point at the center of the object.

When you draw the arrow representing the force, it is important to label the arrow either with the size of the force or a name that will distinguish it from the other forces acting on the car. In this case, the force the tow truck exerts on the car is 5 800 N. The arrow is shown pointing in the same direction as the force of the cable on the car.

The gravitational force acting on the car is 14 700 N, directed toward the center of Earth. This force is shown in part **(d).** The road exerts an upward

Figure 4-4(a)

The steps for drawing a free-body diagram to analyze the forces acting on this car are shown in **(b)** through **(f).**

(b)

(c) 5 800 N

(d) 5 800 N

14 700 N

Figure 4-4(b–d)

(e)

13 690 N

5 800 N

14 700 N

(f)

13 690 N

5 800 N

775 N

14 700 N

Figure 4-4(e–f)

force on the car equal to 13 690 N, as shown in part **(e)**. Because of the interaction between the road and the car's tires, the road also exerts a backward force on the car equal to 775 N, as shown in part **(f)**.

Make sure that only the forces acting on the car are included in your free-body diagram. Even though the car exerts forces on other objects, the only forces that should be included in the free-body diagram are the forces exerted on the car.

The figure in part **(f)** is the completed free-body diagram of the car being towed. Compare the free-body diagram to the car in the photograph. Although the two images of the car are very different, there is a strong resemblance between them. As you learn more about physics, the free-body diagram may begin to look more and more like the real image of the car because it reveals more information about the car in physics terms than the photograph does.

A free-body diagram can be used to find the net external force acting on an object, using the rules for vector analysis from Chapter 3.

Section Review

1. List three examples of each of the following:
   a. a force causing an object to start moving
   b. a force causing an object to stop moving
   c. a force causing an object to change direction

2. Give three examples of field forces described in this section and three examples of contact forces you observe in everyday life. Explain how you know that these are forces.

3. Draw a free-body diagram of a football being kicked. Assume that the only forces acting on the ball are the force of gravity and the force exerted by the kicker.

4. **Physics in Action**   Draw a force diagram of a crash-test dummy in a car at the moment of collision. For this problem, assume that the forces acting on the car are 19 600 N downward, 17 800 N forward, and 25 000 N backward. The forces acting on the dummy are 585 N downward, 175 N backward, and 585 N upward.

5. **Physics in Action**   Use the information given above to draw a free-body diagram showing only the forces acting on the car in item 4. Label all forces.

6. **Physics in Action**   Use the information given above to draw a free-body diagram showing only the forces acting on the dummy in item 4. Label all forces.

Indestructible Alloy

Impervium? Eternium? What do you call a nearly unbreakable metal? Dr. Richard Waterstrat has been pondering that question ever since he invented an alloy that is nearly impervious to wear.

Several years ago at the National Institute for Standards and Technology, Dr. Waterstrat was developing a metal for use in artificial hips and knees. Because the alloy would be implanted into the human body, it needed to be both nontoxic and crack-resistant.

He made one alloy by mixing three metals— zirconium, palladium, and ruthenium. The alloy seemed promising, so Dr. Waterstrat sent it down to the machine shop to prepare a sample for testing. Soon after, Dr. Waterstrat received a call from a worker in the shop who reported that he was unable to cut the alloy in a lathe, using conventional methods. At first, Dr. Waterstrat thought that the metal might simply be too hard to cut. But closer examination revealed that a very thin fibrous layer had formed wherever force had been applied to the metal. The crystalline structure of the alloy's surface had changed in response to the force to prevent new damage. The metal had actually "healed itself."

"The new crystals are harder and stronger than the original crystals," Dr. Waterstrat explained, "and that reinforces or 'heals' the defects that form as a result of the applied stress, making the material, in fact, stronger than it was to begin with. So the unusual wear-resistance is due to the fact that the metal is continually forming crystals under stress to resist further wear."

Dr. Waterstrat's alloy not only was resistant to cracking but also was found to be nearly impervious to wear. He submitted the alloy to a test to measure its wear-resistance, its ability to withstand intense wear over a long period of time. After a pin was rubbed against the metal for 5 million cycles, the alloy showed practically no wear. Artificial joints are constantly subjected to wear, so it seemed that Dr. Waterstrat had finally found his ideal metal. While the alloy is still being perfected for use in joint replacements, there are other applications for which it might be used. Any piece of metal that is subject to extreme wear, such as drill bits, bearings in machinery, or needles in sewing machines, could be coated with the wonder metal. The alloy also seems to be corrosion-resistant, suggesting that it could be used as the metal contact in an electric circuit, a part that is constantly subjected to high wear and corrosion. The indestructible alloy is here; now all it needs is a name.

4-2
Newton's first law

- **Explain the relationship between the motion of an object and the net external force acting on it.**

- **Determine the net external force on an object.**

- **Calculate the force required to bring an object into equilibrium.**

INERTIA

A hovercraft like the one in **Figure 4-5** glides along the surface of the water on a cushion of air. Physicists and engineers study examples like this to determine exactly what effect forces have on the motion of objects.

The first step is to examine the motion of the object before forces are applied. A common misconception is that an object with no force acting on it will always be at rest. To test whether this is true, consider the example of sliding a block on different surfaces. First imagine a block on a deep, thick carpet. If you apply a force by pushing the block, it will begin sliding, but soon after you remove the force, the block will come to rest. Next imagine pushing the same block across a smooth waxed floor. When you push with the same force, the block will slide much farther before coming to rest.

With examples like this, Galileo realized in the 1630s that a block sliding on a perfectly smooth surface would slide forever in the absence of an applied force. He concluded correctly that it is not the nature of an object to *stop* once it is set in motion; rather, it is an object's nature to *maintain its state of motion.*

This concept was further developed by Newton in 1687 and has come to be known as **Newton's first law of motion.**

Figure 4-5
A hovercraft maintains its state of motion by floating on a cushion of air above the water. Air provides less resistance to motion than water does.

inertia

the tendency of an object to maintain its state of motion

NEWTON'S FIRST LAW
An object at rest remains at rest, and an object in motion continues in motion with constant velocity (that is, constant speed in a straight line) unless it experiences a net external force.

The tendency of an object not to accelerate is called **inertia.** Newton's first law is often referred to as the *law of inertia* because it states that in the absence of forces a body will preserve its state of motion. In simpler terms, Newton's first law says that *when the net external force on an object is zero, its acceleration (or the change in its motion) is zero.*

Net external force can be determined by a change in motion

Consider a car traveling at a constant velocity. Newton's first law tells us that the net external force on the car must be equal to zero. However, **Figure 4-6** shows that there are many forces acting on a car in motion. The vector $F_{forward}$ represents the forward force of the road on the tires. The vector $F_{resistance}$, which acts in the opposite direction, represents the backward force the air exerts on the car to resist its motion. The vector $F_{gravity}$ represents the downward force of gravity on the car, and the vector $F_{ground-on-car}$ represents the upward force the ground exerts on the car.

To understand how a car can maintain a constant velocity under the influence of so many forces, it is necessary to understand the distinction between external force and net external force.

An *external force* is a single force that acts on an object as a result of the interaction between the object and its environment. All four forces in **Figure 4-6** are external forces acting on the car.

The **net external force** is the vector sum of all the forces acting on a body. When all external forces acting on an object are known, the net external force can be found using the methods for finding resultant vectors. That means an object's acceleration is determined by the combination of all the forces acting on it. The net external force is equivalent to the one force that would produce the same effect on the object as all the external forces combined. In other words, the object's motion is the same as if the net external force were the only force acting on the object.

Consider **Figure 4-7,** in which two teams are playing tug-of-war. If both teams pull on the rope with equal but opposite force **(a),** the net external force on the rope is equal to zero. The knot in the center of the rope will be at rest, even though forces are pulling the rope in opposite directions. When one team increases the force of its pull **(b),** the knot will experience a net external force equal to the difference in the forces, and it will move in the direction of the greater pull.

Examples like this show how an object can be in equilibrium even when many forces act on it. For example, although there are four forces acting on the car in **Figure 4-6,** the car will maintain its constant velocity as long as the vector sum of these forces is equal to zero.

Figure 4-6
Although there are several forces acting on this car, the vector sum of the forces is zero, so the car moves at a constant velocity.

net external force

the total force resulting from a combination of external forces on an object; sometimes called the resultant force

Figure 4-7
When both teams pull with equal but opposite force **(a),** the knot is at rest, but when the team on the right applies a greater force **(b),** the knot accelerates to the right.

Net external force

PROBLEM

Derek left his physics book on top of a drafting table, as shown in Figure 4-8. The table is inclined at a 35° angle. Find the net external force acting on the book, and determine whether the book will remain at rest in this position.

Figure 4-8

SOLUTION

1. **Define the problem and identify the variables.**

   Given: $F_{gravity\text{-}on\text{-}book} = 22$ N

   $F_{friction} = 11$ N

   $F_{table\text{-}on\text{-}book} = 18$ N

   Unknown: $F_{net} = ?$

   Diagram:

   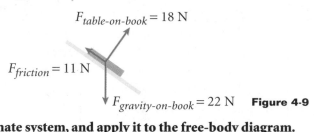

   $F_{table\text{-}on\text{-}book} = 18$ N

   $F_{friction} = 11$ N

   $F_{gravity\text{-}on\text{-}book} = 22$ N   **Figure 4-9**

2. **Select a coordinate system, and apply it to the free-body diagram.**

   Choose the x-axis parallel to and the y-axis perpendicular to the incline of the table, as shown in **Figure 4-10.** This is the most convenient coordinate system because only the force of gravity on the book needs to be resolved into x and y components. All other forces are either along the x-axis or the y-axis.

   Figure 4-10

3. **Find the x and y components of all vectors.**

   Draw a sketch as shown in **Figure 4-11** to find the x component and y component of the vector $\mathbf{F_{gravity\text{-}on\text{-}book}}$. The force of gravity acts at a 90° angle to the surface of Earth, and the x-axis is at a 35° angle to Earth's surface. Therefore, θ, the angle between the weight vector and the x-axis, is the third angle in this right triangle and is equal to 55°.

   Figure 4-11

$$\cos \theta = \frac{F_{g,x}}{F_g}$$

$$F_{g,x} = F_g \cos \theta = (22 \text{ N}) (\cos 55°) = 13 \text{ N}$$

$$\sin \theta = \frac{F_{g,y}}{F_g}$$

$$F_{g,y} = F_g \sin \theta = (22 \text{ N}) (\sin 55°) = 18 \text{ N}$$

4. **Find the net external force in both the x and y directions.**

   For the x direction: $\Sigma F_x = F_{g,x} - F_{friction}$

$$\Sigma F_x = 13 \text{ N} - 11 \text{ N} = 2 \text{ N}$$

Figure 4-12

For the y direction: $\Sigma F_y = F_{table\text{-}on\text{-}book} - F_{g,y}$

$$\Sigma F_y = 18\ \text{N} - 18\ \text{N} = 0\ \text{N}$$

5. **Find the net external force.**

The net force in the y direction is equal to zero, so the net external force is equal to the net force in the x direction, 2 N, acting in the positive x direction.

6. **Evaluate your answer.**

Apply the net external force to the drawing of the book on the table. The force acts on the book in the downhill direction. Therefore, the book will experience an acceleration in the downhill direction, and it will slide off the table, as shown **Figure 4-13.**

$F_{net} = 2\ \text{N}$

Figure 4-13

Net external force

1. A man is pulling on his dog with a force of 70.0 N directed at an angle of +30.0° to the horizontal.

   a. Find the x component of this force.

   b. Find the y component of this force.

2. The man pulls with a force of 25.0 N at an angle of 18.0° to the horizontal.

   a. Find the x component of this force.

   b. Find the y component of this force.

3. A crate is pulled to the right with a force of 85 N, to the left with a force of 115 N, upward with a force of 565 N, and downward with a force of 236 N.

   a. Find the net external force in the x direction.

   b. Find the net external force in the y direction.

   c. Find the magnitude and direction of the net external force on the crate.

Mass is a measurement of inertia

Imagine a basketball and a golf ball at rest side by side on the ground. Newton's first law tells us that both remain at rest as long as no net external force acts on them. Now imagine supplying a net force by striking each ball with a golf club. If the two are struck with equal force, the golf ball will accelerate much more than the basketball. Both balls tend to maintain their states of motion, but the basketball will experience a smaller acceleration because it maintains its state of motion more successfully. That is, it has more inertia than the golf ball.

As you can see, the inertia of an object is directly proportional to its mass. The greater the mass of a body, the less the body accelerates under an applied force. Similarly, an object with little mass will undergo a large acceleration under the same force. Therefore, mass, which is a measure of the amount of matter in an object, is also a measure of the inertia of an object.

Inertia is the tendency of an object to maintain its state of motion unless acted on by a net force

Inertia is the principle underlying the operation of seat belts. The purpose of a seat belt is to prevent serious injury by holding a passenger firmly in place in the event of a sudden stop. Your seat belt may also lock when you slow down or turn a corner.

Imagine a crash-test dummy not wearing a seat belt at the moment of a collision. Even after the car stops, the dummy will continue to move forward with the same velocity until acted on by some force. In this case, the force stopping the dummy would be the force exerted on the dummy by the dashboard of the car.

Figure 4-14 illustrates how one type of shoulder harness operates. Under normal conditions, the ratchet turns freely to allow the harness to wind or unwind along the pulley. In a collision, the car undergoes a large acceleration and rapidly comes to rest. The large mass under the seat, because of its inertia, continues to slide forward along the tracks. The pin connection between the mass and the rod causes the rod to pivot and lock the ratchet wheel in place. At this point the harness no longer unwinds, and the seat belt holds the passenger firmly in place.

Figure 4-14

When the car suddenly slows down, inertia causes the large mass under the seat to continue moving, which activates the lock on the safety belt.

EQUILIBRIUM

equilibrium

the state of a body in which there is no change in its motion

The bob on the fishing line in **Figure 4-15(a)** is at rest. Objects that are either at rest or moving with constant velocity are said to be in **equilibrium.** Newton's first law describes objects in equilibrium, whether they are at rest or moving with a constant velocity. Newton's first law states one condition that must be true for equilibrium: the net external force acting on a body in

Inertia

MATERIALS LIST

✔ Skateboard or cart
✔ Several toy balls with different masses

SAFETY CAUTION

Perform this experiment away from walls and furniture that can be damaged.

Place a small ball near the back of a skateboard or cart. Push the skateboard across the floor into a wall or other solid barrier. Observe what happens to the ball when the skateboard hits the wall. Perform several trials, placing the ball in different positions, such as in the middle of the skateboard and near the front of the skateboard. Repeat all trials using balls with different masses, and compare the results. Perform this experiment at different speeds, and compare the results.

equilibrium must be equal to zero. Therefore, we know that the net external force on the fishing bob is equal to zero.

Imagine that a fish bites the bait, as shown in **(b).** The fish exerts a force on the line. Because a net external force is acting on the line, the bob accelerates. To return the bob to equilibrium, the person fishing must apply a force to the fishing line.

The force that brings an accelerating object into equilibrium must be equal and opposite to the force causing the object to accelerate. Therefore, if the person pulls on the line and applies a force to the bob equal and opposite to the force exerted by the fish, the net external force on the bob is equal to zero. This is shown in **Figure 4-15(c).**

An object is in equilibrium when the vector sum of the forces acting on it is equal to zero. Usually, the easiest way to determine whether a body is in equilibrium is to assign a coordinate system and resolve all forces into their x and y components. The x and y components are represented by outlined arrows. When the sum of all forces in the x direction is equal to zero (that is, $\Sigma F_x = 0$) and the sum of all forces in the y direction is equal to zero (that is, $\Sigma F_y = 0$), then the vector sum of *all* forces acting on the body is equal to zero, and the body is in equilibrium.

(a)

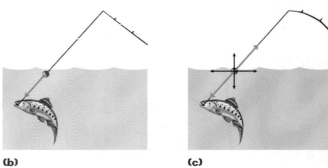

(b)   (c)

Figure 4-15
The bob on this fishing line is at rest **(a).** When it is acted on by a net external force, it accelerates **(b),** until an equal and opposite external force is applied and the net external force is zero **(c).**

Section Review

1. Can an object be in equilibrium if only one force acts on it?

2. If a car is traveling westward with a constant velocity of 20 m/s, what is the net external force acting on it?

3. If a car is accelerating downhill under a net force of 3674 N, what force must the brakes exert to cause the car to have a constant velocity?

4. **Physics in Action**   The sensor in the torso of a crash-test dummy records the magnitude of the net external force acting on it. If the dummy is thrown forward with a force of 130.0 N while simultaneously being hit from the side with a force of 4500.0 N, what force will the sensor report?

5. **Physics in Action**   What force will the seat belt have to exert on the dummy in item 4 to hold the dummy in the seat?

4-3

Newton's second and third laws

4-3 SECTION OBJECTIVES

- **Describe the acceleration of an object in terms of its mass and the net external force acting on it.**

- **Predict the direction and magnitude of the acceleration caused by a known net external force.**

- **Identify action-reaction pairs.**

- **Explain why action-reaction pairs do not result in equilibrium.**

NEWTON'S SECOND LAW

From Newton's first law, we know that an object with no net external force acting on it is in a state of equilibrium. We also know that an object experiencing a net external force undergoes a change in its motion. But exactly how much does a known force affect the motion of an object?

Force is proportional to mass and acceleration

Imagine pushing a stalled car through a level intersection, as shown in **Figure 4-16.** Because a net force causes an object to accelerate, the speed of the car will increase. When you push the car by yourself, however, the acceleration will be so small that it will take a long time for you to notice an increase in the car's speed. If you get several friends to help you, the net force on the car is much greater and the car will soon be moving so fast that you will have to run to keep up with it. This happens because the acceleration of an object is directly proportional to the net external force acting on it.

Experience pushing objects reveals that the mass of an object also affects its acceleration. It requires much less force to accelerate a low-mass object than it does to accelerate a high-mass object the same amount. That is why safety engineers have designed special safety restraints for children and babies. The lightest crash-test dummy will experience an acceleration 13 times greater than the acceleration experienced by the heaviest dummy when both are acted on by the same force. This is because an object with smaller mass has less inertia, or tendency to maintain its state of motion, than an object with greater mass.

Figure 4-16

A small force on an object causes a small acceleration **(a),** but a larger force causes a larger acceleration **(b).**

(a) (b)

Newton's second law relates force, mass, and acceleration

Observations such as these are quantifiable using **Newton's second law,** which states the relationships between mass, force, and acceleration.

NEWTON'S SECOND LAW

The acceleration of an object is directly proportional to the net external force acting on the object and inversely proportional to the mass of the object.

According to Newton's second law, if the same force is applied to two objects of different masses, the object with greater mass will experience a smaller acceleration, and the object with less mass will experience a greater acceleration.

In equation form, we can state Newton's law as

$$\Sigma \mathbf{F} = m\mathbf{a}$$

net external force = mass × acceleration

where **a** is the acceleration of the object, m is its mass, and $\Sigma \mathbf{F}$ represents the *vector sum of all external forces acting on the object.* This relationship makes it possible to determine exactly what effect a given force will have on an object's motion, when the mass of the object is known.

SAMPLE PROBLEM 4B

Newton's second law

PROBLEM

A 5.5 kg watermelon is pushed across a table. If the acceleration of the watermelon is 4.2 m/s² to the right, find the net external force exerted on the watermelon.

SOLUTION

Given: $m = 5.5$ kg
          $\mathbf{a} = 4.2$ m/s², to the right

Unknown: $\Sigma \mathbf{F} = ?$

Use Newton's second law.

$$\Sigma \mathbf{F} = m\mathbf{a}$$

$$\Sigma \mathbf{F} = (5.5 \text{ kg})(4.2 \text{ m/s}^2)$$

$$\Sigma \mathbf{F} = 23 \text{ kg} \cdot \text{m/s}^2$$

$$\boxed{\Sigma \mathbf{F} = 23 \text{ N, to the right}}$$

CALCULATOR SOLUTION

Your calculator will give you the answer of 23.1 for the net external force. Because all values have only two significant digits, this value must be rounded down to 23.

Newton's second law

1. The net external force on the propeller of a 0.75 kg model airplane is 17 N forward. What is the acceleration of the airplane?

2. The net external force on a golf cart is 390 N north. If the cart has a total mass of 270 kg, what are the magnitude and direction of its acceleration?

3. A car has a mass of 1.50×10^3 kg. What force is required to accelerate the car at 4.5 m/s^2 to the east?

4. A 2.0 kg mass starts from rest at the top of an inclined plane 85 cm long and slides down to the bottom in 0.50 s. What net external force acts on the mass along the incline?

5. A ball pushed with a force of 13.5 N accelerates at 6.5 m/s^2 to the right. What is the mass of the ball?

In solving problems, it is often easier to break the Newton's-law equation into components. That is, the sum of forces acting in the x direction equals the mass times the acceleration in the x direction ($\Sigma F_x = ma_x$), and the sum of forces in the y direction equals the mass times the acceleration in the y direction ($\Sigma F_y = ma_y$). Note that if the net external force is zero, then $\mathbf{a} = 0$, which corresponds to the equilibrium situation where $\mathbf{v}$ is either constant or zero.

Conceptual Challenge

1. Gravity and rocks

The force of gravity is twice as great on a 20 N rock as it is on a 10 N rock. Why doesn't the 20 N rock have a greater free-fall acceleration?

2. Leaking truck

A truck loaded with sand accelerates at 0.5 m/s^2 on the highway. If the driving force on the truck remains constant, what happens to the truck's acceleration if sand leaks at a constant rate from a hole in the truck bed?

NEWTON'S THIRD LAW

We have seen that a force is exerted on an object when that object interacts with some other object in its environment. Consider a moving car colliding with a concrete barrier. The car exerts a force on the barrier at the moment of collision, just as you apply force to a door when you push it or to a ball when you kick it. Furthermore, the barrier exerts a force on the car so that the car rapidly slows down after coming into contact with the barrier.

Forces always exist in pairs

From examples like this, Newton recognized that a single isolated force cannot exist. Instead, *forces always exist in pairs.* The car exerts a force on the barrier, and the barrier exerts a force on the car. Newton described this type of situation with his **third law of motion.**

NEWTON'S THIRD LAW

If two bodies interact, the magnitude of the force exerted on object 1 by object 2 is equal to the magnitude of the force simultaneously exerted on object 2 by object 1, and these two forces are opposite in direction.

An alternative statement of this law is that *for every action there is an equal and opposite reaction.* This statement is also commonly referred to as Newton's third law of motion.

When two objects interact with one another, the forces they exert on each other are called an **action-reaction pair.** One force is referred to as the *action,* and the other force is called the *reaction.* These names sometimes cause confusion because they are used a little differently in physics than they are in everyday speech. In everyday speech, we use the word *reaction* to refer to something that happens *after* and *in response to* an event. In physics, however, the reaction force occurs at exactly the same time as the action force.

Because the forces coexist, either force can be called the action or reaction. For example, we could call the force the car exerts on the barrier the action and the force the barrier exerts on the car the reaction. If you choose to call the force the barrier exerts on the car the action and the force the car exerts on the barrier the reaction, it is perfectly all right to do so.

Action-reaction forces act on different objects

The most important thing to remember about action-reaction pairs is that each force acts on a different object. Consider the task of driving a nail into a block of wood, as illustrated in **Figure 4-17.** To accelerate the nail and drive it into the block, the hammer exerts a force on the nail. According to Newton's third law, the nail exerts a force on the hammer equal to the force the hammer exerts on the nail.

The concept of action-reaction pairs is a common source of confusion because many people assume incorrectly that the equal and opposite forces balance one another and make any change in the state of motion impossible. If the nail exerts a force on the hammer equal to the force the hammer exerts on the nail, why doesn't the nail remain at rest?

Action-reaction pairs do not result in equilibrium because they act on different objects. The motion of the nail is affected only by the forces acting on the nail. The force the nail exerts on the hammer affects only the hammer, not the nail. To determine whether the nail will accelerate, draw a free-body diagram to isolate the forces acting on the nail alone.

Figure 4-18 is a free-body diagram showing the horizontal forces acting on the nail. The force that the nail exerts on the hammer is not included because it does not affect the motion of the nail. As you can see, the nail is driven into the wood because there is a net external force acting on the nail.

action-reaction pair

a pair of simultaneous equal but opposite forces resulting from the interaction of two objects

Figure 4-17
The nail exerts a force on the hammer equal and opposite to the force the hammer exerts on the nail.

Figure 4-18
The net external force acting on the nail drives it into the wood.

Field forces also exist in pairs

The concept of action-reaction pairs also applies to field forces. For example, consider the gravitational force exerted by Earth on an object. During calibration at the crash-test site, engineers calibrate the sensors in the heads of crash-test dummies by removing the heads and dropping them from a known height.

The force Earth exerts on a dummy's head is $\mathbf{F_g}$. Let's call this force the action. What is the reaction? Because $\mathbf{F_g}$ is the force exerted on the falling head by Earth, the reaction to $\mathbf{F_g}$ is the force exerted on Earth by the falling head.

According to Newton's third law, the force of the dummy on Earth is equal to the force of Earth on the dummy. Thus, as a falling object accelerates toward Earth, Earth also accelerates toward the object.

The thought that Earth accelerates toward the dummy's head may seem to contradict our experience. One way to make sense of this is to refer to Newton's second law. The mass of Earth is much greater than that of the dummy's head. Therefore, while the dummy's head undergoes a large acceleration due to the force of Earth, the acceleration of Earth due to this reaction force is negligibly small because of its enormous mass.

CONCEPT PREVIEW

Gravitational force is covered in Chapter 7, Section 7-3.

Section Review

1. A 6.0 kg object undergoes an acceleration of 2.0 m/s^2.
   a. What is the magnitude of the net external force acting on it?
   b. If this same force is applied to a 4.0 kg object, what acceleration is produced?

2. A child pulls a wagon with a horizontal force, causing it to accelerate. Newton's third law says that the wagon exerts an equal and opposite force on the child. How can the wagon accelerate? (*Hint:* Draw a free-body diagram for each object to help you answer this question.)

3. Identify the action-reaction pairs in the following situations:
   a. a person takes a step
   b. a snowball hits someone in the back
   c. a baseball player catches a ball
   d. a gust of wind strikes a window

4. The forces acting on a sailboat are 390 N north and 180 N east. If the boat (including crew) has a mass of 270 kg, what are the magnitude and direction of its acceleration?

5. **Physics in Action** If a small sports car collides head-on with a massive truck, which vehicle experiences the greater impact force? Which vehicle experiences the greater acceleration? Explain.

WEIGHT

Why does a heavy object, such as a bowling ball, feel heavier than a lighter object, such as a tennis ball? Because the **weight** of an object is defined as the magnitude of the force of gravity on that object, a larger weight represents a larger force. The force exerted on the ball by Earth, $\mathbf{F_g}$, is a vector quantity, directed toward the center of Earth. The magnitude of this force, F_g, is a scalar quantity called weight.

When the mass and the acceleration due to gravity are known, the weight of an object can be calculated using the equation $F_g = mg$, where g is the magnitude of the acceleration due to gravity, or the free-fall acceleration. In this book, $g = 9.81 \text{ m/s}^2$ unless otherwise specified.

Because the weight of the object is dependent on gravity, weight depends on location. For example, an astronaut who weighs 800 N (180 lb) on Earth weighs only about 130 N (30 lb) on the moon because the acceleration due to the moon's gravity is much smaller than g. The astronaut in **Figure 4-19** weighs much less on the moon than on Earth. In contrast, the mass of an object is a scalar quantity that does not change with the object's location.

Furthermore, objects on Earth weigh less at higher altitudes than at sea level because g decreases with increasing distance from the center of Earth. As a result, weight, unlike mass, is not an inherent property of an object. Therefore, if you want to lose weight without losing mass, move to the top of a mountain or weigh yourself at an altitude of 9000 m during an airplane flight.

THE NORMAL FORCE

Imagine a television set at rest on a table. We know that the force of gravity is acting on the television. How do we use Newton's laws to explain why the television does not continue to fall toward the center of Earth?

An analysis of the forces acting on the television will reveal the forces that cause equilibrium. First, we know that the force acting on a freely falling object is the downward force of gravity, $\mathbf{F_g}$. Because the television is in equilibrium, we know that another force, equal in magnitude to $\mathbf{F_g}$ but in the opposite direction, must be acting on it. This force is the force exerted on the television by the table. This force is called the **normal force, $\mathbf{F_n}$.**

weight

the magnitude of the force of gravity acting on an object

Figure 4-19
On the moon, astronauts weigh much less than they do on Earth because the acceleration due to the moon's gravity is so much less than Earth's.

normal force

a contact force exerted by one object on another in a direction perpendicular to the surface of contact

(b)

Figure 4-20
The normal force, **F$_n$**, is always perpendicular to the surface, not necessarily opposite the force of gravity.

The word *normal* is used because the direction of the contact force is perpendicular to the table surface, and one meaning of the word *normal* is "perpendicular." **Figure 4-20(a)** shows the forces acting on the television.

The normal force is always perpendicular to the contact surface, but it is not always opposite in direction to the force of gravity acting on an object. For example, if an object is on a surface that is not horizontal, the normal force will be perpendicular to the surface. **Figure 4-20(b)** shows a refrigerator on a ramp. The normal force, **F$_n$,** is perpendicular to the surface of the ramp. The normal force is equal and opposite to the component of **F$_g$** that is perpendicular to the ramp.

THE FORCE OF FRICTION

Consider a jug of juice at rest on a table, as in **Figure 4-21(a).** Because the jug is at rest, it is in equilibrium, and we know from Newton's first law that the net external force acting on it is zero. Newton's second law tells us that any force applied to the jug will cause it to accelerate and to remain in motion unless acted on by another force. However, experience tells us that the jug won't move at all if we apply a very small horizontal force. Even when we apply a force large enough to move the jug, it will stop moving almost as soon as we remove this applied force.

Friction opposes the applied force

When the jug is at rest, the only forces acting on it are the force of gravity and the normal force exerted by the table. These forces are equal and opposite, so the jug is in equilibrium. When you push the jug with a small horizontal force, as shown in **(b),** the table exerts an equal force in the opposite direction. This force, friction, causes the net external force on the jug to be zero. Because of this force, the jug remains in equilibrium. The jug remains at rest. If you push harder on the jug, it will suddenly begin to move, as shown in **(c).**

Figure 4-21

(a)

(b)

(c)

(a) Because this jug of juice is in equilibrium, any horizontal force applied to it should cause the jug to accelerate.

(b) When a small force is applied, the jug remains in equilibrium because the friction force is equal but opposite to the applied force.

(c) When a larger force is applied, the jug begins to move as soon as the applied force exceeds the opposing friction force.

The frictional force that keeps the jug from moving is called the force of **static friction** ($\mathbf{F_s}$). Until the applied force is large enough to move the jug, the force of static friction is equal to the applied force and opposite in direction ($\mathbf{F_s} = -\mathbf{F}$). As the applied force increases, the force of static friction also increases; if the applied force decreases, the force of static friction also decreases.

When the applied force is as great as it can be without causing the jug to move, the force of static friction reaches its maximum value, $\mathbf{F_{s,max}}$. The magnitude of $\mathbf{F_{s,max}}$ is determined by the interaction between the jug and the table. When the applied force exceeds the maximum force of static friction between the juice jug and the table, the jug begins to move with an acceleration to the left. The net external force acting on the jug is equal to the difference between the applied force and the maximum force of static friction ($\mathbf{F} - \mathbf{F_{s,max}}$).

Kinetic friction is less than static friction

As soon as the jug of juice begins to move, the retarding frictional force becomes less than $\mathbf{F_{s,max}}$. We call the retarding force on an object in motion the force of **kinetic friction** ($\mathbf{F_k}$). Once the object is in motion, the net external force acting on the object is equal to the difference between the applied force and the force of kinetic friction ($\mathbf{F} - \mathbf{F_k}$). This net external force produces an acceleration in the $-x$ direction.

Experiments show that frictional force arises from the interaction of the two surfaces in contact with each other. Because the surfaces are rough and uneven, contact is made at only a few points. **Figure 4-22** is a magnified view of the contact between two surfaces.

When an object is stationary, the contact points between it and the surface on which it rests are said to be "cold-welded." Cold-welding, or surface adhesion, is caused by intermolecular forces exerted on the molecules of the object and the surface at the points of contact. Essentially, these forces create bonds between the molecules of the two surfaces. While the object is in motion, these small welds cannot form and the frictional force decreases. This is why kinetic friction is less than static friction.

Friction depends on the surfaces in contact

A sled moves much faster down an icy hill than down the same hill covered with soft, wet snow. The direction of the force of kinetic friction is the same in both examples, but the magnitude of the friction force between the ice and the sled is lower than that between the snow and the sled.

Experimental observations show that the magnitude of the friction force is proportional to the magnitude of the normal force a surface exerts on an object. We can write this proportion as $F_{friction} \propto F_n$. For the sled on different surfaces, the normal force is the same. The forces of kinetic friction are different because the force of kinetic friction also depends on the composition and qualities of the surfaces in contact.

static friction

the force exerted on a motion-less body by its environment to resist an external force

kinetic friction

the force exerted on a moving object

Figure 4-22
On the microscopic level, even very smooth surfaces make contact at only a few points.

coefficient of friction

the ratio of the force of friction to the normal force acting between two objects

To express the relationship between frictional forces and the properties of different surfaces, we use a symbol that relates the normal force to the frictional force for different surfaces. This symbol, μ, the lowercase Greek letter *mu*, is called the **coefficient of friction,** and it is used to find the value for the friction force between two surfaces. The coefficient of static friction is the ratio of the maximum value of the force of static friction to the normal force.

$$\mu_s = \frac{F_{s,max}}{F_n}$$

The ratio of the force of kinetic friction to the normal force is called the coefficient of kinetic friction. It is given by the following ratio.

$$\mu_k = \frac{F_k}{F_n}$$

Table 4-2   Coefficients of friction (approximate values)

	μ_s	μ_k		μ_s	μ_k
Steel on steel	0.74	0.57	Waxed wood on wet snow	0.14	0.1
Aluminum on steel	0.61	0.47	Waxed wood on dry snow	—	0.04
Rubber on dry concrete	1.0	0.8	Metal on metal (lubricated)	0.15	0.06
Rubber on wet concrete	—	0.5	Ice on ice	0.1	0.03
Wood on wood	0.4	0.2	Teflon on Teflon	0.04	0.04
Glass on glass	0.9	0.4	Synovial joints in humans	0.01	0.003

Coefficient of friction is a ratio of forces

Experimental values for the coefficients of static and kinetic friction have revealed that typical values of μ range from around 0.01 to 1.5. **Table 4-2** shows some experimental values for μ for different materials. For example, the coefficients of friction between the skis and the wet snow in **Figure 4-23** range from $\mu_s = 0.14$ to $\mu_k = 0.1$. The value for the coefficient of kinetic friction is always lower than the value for static friction.

A value of 1.0 for the coefficient of static friction indicates a force of static friction equal to the normal force. In the earlier example of pushing a jug of juice across a table, assume that $\mu_s = 1.0$. To move the jug across the table, you would need a horizontal force equal in magnitude to the normal force.

In this case, we know that the normal force is equal in magnitude to the weight of the jug. Therefore, you would have to exert a force equal in magnitude to the weight of the jug to cause the jug to move. If the coefficient of static friction were equal to 1.5, you would have to exert a force 1.5 times the weight of the jug in order to cause it to move.

Figure 4-23
The coefficients of friction between waxed wood and snow affect the acceleration of this skier on the slopes.

Coefficients of friction

PROBLEM

A 24 kg crate initially at rest on a horizontal surface requires a 75 N horizontal force to set it in motion. Find the coefficient of static friction between the crate and the floor.

SOLUTION

Given: $F_{s,max} = 75$ N $\quad m = 24$ kg

Unknown: $\mu_s = ?$

Use the equation for the coefficient of static friction.

$$\mu_s = \frac{F_{s,max}}{F_n}$$

$$\mu_s = \frac{F_{s,max}}{mg} = \frac{75 \text{ N}}{24 \text{ kg} \times 9.81 \text{ m/s}^2}$$

$$\boxed{\mu_s = 0.32}$$

CALCULATOR SOLUTION

The answer your calculator will return for the coefficient of friction is 0.3185524975. The value for the mass has only two significant digits, so the answer must be rounded up to 0.32.

Coefficients of friction

1. Once the crate is in motion, a horizontal force of 53 N keeps the crate moving with a constant velocity. Find μ_k, the coefficient of kinetic friction, between the crate and the floor.

2. A museum curator moves artifacts into place on many different display surfaces. Use the values in **Table 4-2** to find $F_{s,max}$ and F_k for the following situations:

   a. moving a 145 kg aluminum sculpture across a horizontal steel platform
   b. pulling a 15 kg steel sword across a horizontal steel shield
   c. pushing a 227 kg wood bed on a wood floor
   d. sliding a 0.55 kg glass amulet on a glass display case

3. A 25 kg chair initially at rest on a horizontal floor requires a 365 N horizontal force to set it in motion. Once the chair is in motion, a 327 N horizontal force keeps it moving at a constant velocity.

   a. Find the coefficient of static friction between the chair and the floor.
   b. Find the coefficient of kinetic friction between the chair and the floor.

Overcoming friction

PROBLEM

A student moves a box of books by attaching a rope to the box and pulling with a force of 90.0 N at an angle of 30.0°, as shown in Figure 4-24. The box of books has a mass of 20.0 kg, and the coefficient of kinetic friction between the bottom of the box and the sidewalk is 0.50. Find the acceleration of the box.

Figure 4-24

SOLUTION

1. DEFINE

Given:

$$m = 20.0 \text{ kg} \quad \mu_k = 0.50$$
$$\mathbf{F_{applied}} = 90.0 \text{ N at } \theta = 30.0°$$

Unknown: $\mathbf{a} = ?$

Diagram:

Figure 4-25

2. PLAN

Choose the equation(s) or situation:

First find the normal force $\mathbf{F_n}$ by applying the first condition of equilibrium in the vertical direction.

$$\Sigma F_y = 0$$

Calculate the force of kinetic friction on the box.

$$F_k = \mu_k F_n$$

Apply Newton's second law along the horizontal direction to find the acceleration of the box.

$$\Sigma F_x = ma_x$$

3. CALCULATE

Choose a convenient coordinate system, and find the x and y components of all forces.

The diagram in **Figure 4-26** shows the most convenient coordinate system. Find the y component of $\mathbf{F_{applied}}$.

$$F_{applied,y} = (90.0 \text{ N})(\sin 30.0°) = 45.0 \text{ N}$$

Find the x component of $\mathbf{F_{applied}}$.

$$F_{applied,x} = (90.0 \text{ N})(\cos 30.0°) = 77.9 \text{ N}$$

Use the mass to find the force of gravity acting on the box.

$$\mathbf{F_g} = (20.0 \text{ kg})(9.81 \text{ m/s}^2) = 196 \text{ N, downward}$$

Figure 4-26

To find the normal force, find the sum of all forces in the y direction, set them equal to zero, and solve for F_n.

$$\Sigma F_y = F_n + F_{applied, y} - F_g = 0$$

$$F_n + 45.0 \text{ N} - 196 \text{ N} = 0$$

$$F_n = -45.0 \text{ N} + 196 \text{ N} = 151 \text{ N}$$

Use the normal force to find the force of kinetic friction.

$$F_k = \mu_k F_n = (0.50)(151 \text{ N}) = 75.5 \text{ N (to the left)}$$

Determine the horizontal acceleration using Newton's second law.

$$\Sigma F_x = F_{applied, x} - F_k = ma_x$$

$$\Sigma F_x = 77.9 \text{ N} - 75.5 \text{ N} = (20.0 \text{ kg})(a_x)$$

$$a_x = \frac{77.9 \text{ N} - 75.5 \text{ N}}{20.0 \text{ kg}} = \frac{2.4 \text{ N}}{20.0 \text{ kg}} = \frac{2.4 \text{ kg} \cdot \text{m/s}^2}{20.0 \text{ kg}}$$

$$\boxed{a_x = 0.12 \text{ m/s}^2 \text{ (to the right)}}$$

4. EVALUATE The normal force is not equal in magnitude to the weight because the y component of the student's pull on the rope helps support the box.

Overcoming friction

1. A box of books weighing 325 N moves with a constant velocity across the floor when it is pushed with a force of 425 N exerted downward at an angle of 35.2° below the horizontal. Find μ_k between the box and the floor.

2. A student moves a box of books down the hall by pulling on a rope attached to the box. The student pulls with a force of 185 N at an angle of 25° above the horizontal. The box has a mass of 35 kg. and μ_k between box and floor is 0.27. Find the acceleration of the box.

3. The student in item 2 moves the box up a ramp inclined at 12° with the horizontal. If the box starts from rest at the bottom of the ramp and is pulled at an angle of 25° with respect to the incline and with the same 185 N force, what is the acceleration up the ramp? Assume that $\mu_k = 0.27$.

4. A 75 kg box slides down a 25° ramp with an acceleration of 3.6 m/s².
    a. Find μ_k between the box and the ramp.
    b. What acceleration would a 175 kg box have on this ramp?

Air resistance is a form of friction

Another type of friction, the retarding force produced by air resistance, is important in the analysis of the motion of cars and other vehicles that move through air. Whenever an object moves through a fluid medium such as air or water, the fluid provides a resistance to the object's motion. The force of air resistance, $\mathbf{F_R}$, acts in the direction opposite the direction of the car's motion.

The magnitude of $\mathbf{F_R}$ is usually proportional to the car's speed. That is, $F_R \propto v$. Thus, the force of air resistance increases with increasing speed. When $\mathbf{F_R}$ is equal to the force acting in the opposite direction, the acceleration is zero and the car moves at a constant speed.

A similar situation occurs when an object falls through air. As a free-falling body accelerates, its velocity increases. As the velocity increases, the resistance of the air to the object's motion also constantly increases. When the upward force of air resistance balances the downward force of gravity, the net force on the object is zero, and the object's acceleration is zero. Once this condition is reached, the object continues to move downward with a constant maximum speed called the terminal speed.

Consumer Focus *Driving and Friction*

*A*ccelerating a car seems simple to the driver. It is just a matter of pressing on a pedal or turning a wheel. But what are the forces involved?

The reason a car moves is that as its wheels turn, they push back against the road. It is actually the reaction force of the road pushing on the car that causes the car to accelerate. Without the friction between the tires and the road, the wheels would not be able to exert this force, and the car would not experience a reaction force. Thus, acceleration (whether speeding up, slowing down, or changing direction) requires this friction. Water and snow provide less friction and therefore reduce the amount of control the driver has over the direction and speed of the car.

As a car moves slowly over an area of water on the road, the water is squeezed out from under the tires. If the car moves too quickly, there is not enough time for the weight of the car to squeeze the water out from under the tires. The water trapped between the tires and the road will actually lift the tires and car off the road, a phenomenon called *hydroplaning*. When this occurs, there is very little friction between the tires and the water, and the car becomes difficult to control. To prevent hydroplaning, rain tires like the ones shown in **Figure 4-27** keep water from accumulating between the tire and the road. Deep channels down the center of the tire provide a place for the water to accumulate, and slightly curved grooves in the tread channel the water outward.

Because snow moves even less easily than water, snow tires are designed differently than rain tires. Snow tires have several deep grooves in their tread, enabling the tire to cut through the snow and make contact with the pavement. In the most extreme conditions, these deep grooves push against the snow and, like the paddle blades of a river-boat, use the snow's inertia to provide resistance.

Figure 4-27

1. Draw a free-body diagram for each of the following objects:
   a. a projectile in motion in the presence of air resistance
   b. a rocket leaving the launch pad with its engines operating
   c. a heavy crate being pushed across a rough surface

2. A bag of sugar has a mass of 2.26 kg.
   a. What is its weight in newtons on the moon, where the acceleration due to gravity is one-sixth that on Earth?
   b. What about on Jupiter, where the acceleration due to gravity is 2.64 times that on Earth?

3. A block of mass $m = 2.0$ kg is held in equilibrium on an incline of angle $\theta = 60.0°$ by a horizontal force.
   a. Determine the magnitude of this horizontal force (disregard friction).
   b. Determine the normal force exerted by the incline on the block.

4. A 55 kg ice skater, initially at rest on a flat skating rink, requires a 198 N horizontal force to be set in motion. However, after the skater is in motion, a horizontal force of 175 N keeps her moving at a constant speed. Find the coefficients of static and kinetic friction between the skates and the ice.

5. The force of air resistance acting on a falling object is approximated by the statement that it is proportional to the object's velocity and directed upward. If the object falls fast enough, will the force of air resistance eventually exceed the weight of the object and cause it to accelerate upward? Explain your answer.

6. The graph in **Figure 4-28** shows the relationship between the applied force and the force of friction.
   a. What is the relationship between the forces at point A?
   b. What is the relationship between the forces at point B?

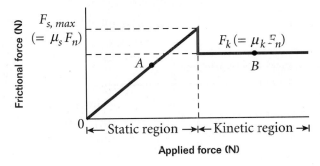

Figure 4-28

CHAPTER 4
Summary

KEY TERMS

action-reaction pair (p. 139)

coefficient of friction (p. 144)

contact force (p. 125)

equilibrium (p. 134)

field force (p. 125)

force (p. 124)

force diagram (p. 126)

inertia (p. 130)

kinetic friction (p. 143)

net external force (p. 131)

normal force (p. 141)

static friction (p. 143)

weight (p. 141)

KEY IDEAS

Section 4-1 Changes in motion
- Force is a vector quantity that causes changes in motion.
- Force can act either through the physical contact of two objects (contact force) or at a distance (field force).
- A free-body diagram shows only the forces that act on one object. These are the only forces that affect the motion of that object.

Section 4-2 Newton's first law
- The tendency of an object to maintain its state of motion is called inertia. Mass is the physical quantity used to measure inertia.
- The net external force acting on an object is the vector sum of all the forces acting on it. An object is in a state of equilibrium when the net external force on it is zero.

Section 4-3 Newton's second and third laws
- The net external force acting on an object is equal to the product of the mass of the object and its acceleration.
- When two bodies exert force on each other, the forces are equal in magnitude and opposite in direction. These forces are called action-reaction pairs. Forces always exist in pairs.

Section 4-4 Everyday forces
- The weight of an object is equal to the mass of the object times the acceleration due to gravity.
- A normal force is a contact force exerted by one surface on another in a direction perpendicular to the surface of contact.
- Friction is a force between two surfaces that acts in a direction opposite to the direction of the motion of one of the surfaces. The force of friction between two surfaces is proportional to the normal force.

Variable symbols

Quantities	Units	Conversions
F (vector) force	N newtons	$= kg \cdot m/s^2$
F (scalar)		
μ coefficient of friction	(no units)	

CHAPTER 4
Review and Assess

FORCES AND NEWTON'S FIRST LAW

Review questions

1. Is it possible to have motion in the absence of a force? Explain.

2. If an object is at rest, can we conclude that no external forces are acting on it?

3. An object thrown into the air stops at the highest point in its path. Is it in equilibrium at this point? Explain.

4. State Newton's first law.

5. What physical quantity is a measure of the amount of inertia an object has?

Conceptual questions

6. A large crate is placed on the bed of a truck but not tied down.
   a. As the truck accelerates forward, the crate slides across the bed until it hits the tailgate. Explain what causes this.
   b. If the driver slammed on the brakes, what could happen to the crate?

7. A beach ball is left in the bed of a pickup truck. Describe what happens to the ball when the truck accelerates forward.

Practice problems

8. Draw a free-body diagram representing each of the following objects:
   a. a ball in free fall in the presence of air resistance
   b. a helicopter lifting off a landing pad
   c. an athlete running along a horizontal track
   (See Sample Problem 4A.)

9. Draw a force diagram for each of the following situations:
   a. A chair is pushed forward with a force of 185 N, the force of Earth on the chair is 155 N downward, and the floor exerts a force of 155 N upward on the chair. Draw a free-body diagram of the chair.
   b. The force of Earth on a cake on a plate is 8.9 N downward, the plate exerts a force of 11.0 N upward on the cake, and a knife exerts a downward force of 2.1 N on the cake. Draw a free-body diagram of the cake.
   (See Sample Problem 4A.)

10. Four forces act on a hot-air balloon, shown from the side in **Figure 4-29**. Find the magnitude and direction of the resultant force on the balloon. (See Sample Problem 4A.)

5120 N

1520 N   950 N

4050 N

Figure 4-29

11. Two lifeguards pull on ropes attached to a raft. If they pull in the same direction, the raft experiences a net external force of 334 N to the right. If they pull in opposite directions, the raft experiences a net external force of 105 N to the left.
   a. Draw a free-body diagram representing the raft for each situation.
   b. Find the force exerted by each lifeguard on the raft. (Disregard any other forces acting on the raft.)
   (See Sample Problem 4A.)

12. A dog pulls on a pillow with a force of 5 N at an angle of 37° above the horizontal. Find the x and y components of this force.
(See Sample Problem 4A.)

NEWTON'S SECOND AND THIRD LAWS

Review questions

13. Earth is attracted to an object with a force equal to and opposite the force Earth exerts on the object. Explain why Earth's acceleration is not equal to and opposite that of the object.

14. Explain Newton's second law in terms of inertia.

15. An astronaut on the moon has a 110 kg crate and a 230 kg crate. How do the forces required to lift the crates straight up on the moon compare with the forces required to lift them on Earth?

16. Draw a force diagram to identify all the action-reaction pairs that exist for a horse pulling a cart.

17. Draw a free-body diagram of the cart from item 16.

Conceptual questions

18. A space explorer is moving through space far from any planet or star and notices a large rock, taken as a specimen from an alien planet, floating around the cabin of the ship. Should the explorer push it gently or kick it toward the storage compartment? Why?

19. Explain why a rope climber must pull downward on the rope in order to move upward. Discuss the force exerted by the climber's arms in relation to the weight of the climber during the various stages of each "step" up the rope.

Practice problems

20. What net external force is required to give a 25 kg suitcase an acceleration of 2.2 m/s² to the right? Draw a free-body diagram of the suitcase.
(See Sample Problem 4B.)

21. What acceleration will you give to a 24.3 kg box if you push it with a force of 85.5 N?
(See Sample Problem 4B.)

22. An 1850 kg car is moving to the right at a constant velocity of 1.44 m/s.
    a. What is the net force on the car?
    b. What would be the net force on the car if it were moving to the left?
(See Sample Problem 4B.)

23. A freight train has a mass of 1.5×10^7 kg. If the locomotive can exert a constant pull of 7.5×10^5 N, how long would it take to increase the speed of the train from rest to 85 km/h?
(See Sample Problem 4B.)

24. A 5.0 kg bucket of water is raised from a well by a rope. If the upward acceleration of the bucket is 3.0 m/s², find the force exerted by the rope on the bucket of water.
(See Sample Problem 4B.)

25. A boat moves through the water with two forces acting on it. One is a 2.10×10^3 N forward push by the motor, and the other is a 1.80×10^3 N resistive force due to the water.
    a. What is the acceleration of the 1200 kg boat?
    b. If it starts from rest, how far will it move in 10.0 s?
    c. What will its velocity be at the end of this time interval?
(See Sample Problem 4B.)

26. Two forces are applied to a car in an effort to accelerate it, as shown in **Figure 4-30.**
    a. What is the resultant of these two forces?
    b. If the car has a mass of 3200 kg, what acceleration does it have? Disregard friction.
(See Sample Problem 4B.)

450 N   30.0°   10.0°   380 N

Figure 4-30

27. A 3.00 kg ball is dropped from the roof of a building 176.4 m high. While the ball is falling to Earth, a horizontal wind exerts a constant force of 12.0 N on it.

  a. How far from the building does the ball hit the ground?

  b. How long does it take to hit the ground?

  c. What is its speed when it hits the ground?

(See Sample Problem 4B.)

28. A block with a mass of 5.0 kg is held in equilibrium on an incline of angle $\theta = 30.0°$ by the horizontal force, **F**, as shown in **Figure 4-31**. Find the magnitude of **F**. Find the normal force exerted by the incline on the block. (Disregard friction.) (See Sample Problem 4B.)

Figure 4-31

29. A 2.0 kg mass starts from rest and slides down an inclined plane 8.0×10^{-1} m long in 0.50 s. What net force is acting on the mass along the incline? (See Sample Problem 4B.)

30. A shopper in a supermarket pushes a loaded 32 kg cart with a horizontal force of 12 N.

  a. How far will the cart move in 3.5 s, starting from rest? (Disregard friction.)

  b. How far will the cart move in 3.5 s if the shopper places an 85 N child in the cart before pushing?

(See Sample Problem 4B.)

31. A 75 kg person escapes from a burning building by jumping from a window 25 m above a catching net. Assuming that air resistance exerts a 95 N force on the person during the fall, determine the person's velocity just before hitting the net. (See Sample Problem 4B.)

32. The parachute on a race car that weighs 8820 N opens at the end of a quarter-mile run when the car is traveling 35 m/s. What total retarding force must be supplied by the parachute to stop the car in a distance of 1100 m? (See Sample Problem 4B.)

33. A 1250 kg car is pulling a 325 kg trailer. Together, the car and trailer have an acceleration of 2.15 m/s^2 directly forward.

  a. Determine the net force on the car.

  b. Determine the net force on the trailer.

(See Sample Problem 4B.)

WEIGHT, FRICTION, AND NORMAL FORCE

Review questions

34. Explain the relationship between mass and weight.

35. A 0.150 kg baseball is thrown upward with an initial speed of 20.0 m/s.

  a. What is the force on the ball when it reaches half its maximum height?

  b. What is the force on the ball when it reaches its peak? (Disregard air resistance.)

36. Draw a force diagram showing the weight and normal forces on a laundry basket in each of the following situations:

  a. at rest on a horizontal surface

  b. at rest on a ramp inclined 12° above the horizontal

  c. at rest on a ramp inclined 25° above the horizontal

  d. at rest on a ramp inclined 45° above the horizontal

37. If the basket in item 36 has a mass of 5.5 kg, find the magnitude of the normal force for the situations described in (a) through (d).

38. Explain how placing an object on an inclined plane instead of on a horizontal surface affects the forces acting on the object.

39. A massive metal object on a rough metal surface may undergo contact welding to that surface. Discuss how this affects the frictional forces that arise between object and surface.

Conceptual questions

40. Imagine an astronaut in space at the midpoint between two stars of equal mass. If all other objects are infinitely far away, how much does the astronaut weigh? Explain your answer.

41. Although the frictional force between two surfaces may decrease as the surfaces are smoothed, it will increase if the surfaces are made extremely smooth and flat. Explain.

42. Analyze the motion of a rock dropped in water in terms of its speed and acceleration. Assume that a resistive force acting on the rock increases as the velocity increases.

43. A sky diver falls through the air. As the speed of the sky diver increases, what happens to the sky diver's acceleration? What is the acceleration when the sky diver reaches terminal speed?

44. A ball is held in a person's hand.

  a. Identify all the external forces acting on the ball and the reaction force to each.

  b. If the ball is dropped, what force is exerted on it while it is falling? Identify the reaction force in this case. (Disregard air resistance.)

Practice problems

45. A loaf of bread weighs 5.30 N on Earth.

  a. What should it weigh, in newtons, on the moon, where the acceleration due to gravity is one-sixth that on Earth?

  b. What should it weigh on Jupiter, where g is 2.64 times Earth's gravity?

  (See Sample Problem 4C.)

46. A 2.26 kg book is dropped from a height of 1.5 m.

  a. What is its acceleration?

  b. What is its weight in newtons?

  (See Sample Problem 4C.)

47. A 3.46 kg briefcase is sitting at rest on a level floor.

  a. What is its acceleration?

  b. What is its weight in newtons?

  (See Sample Problem 4C.)

48. A 2.00 kg block is in equilibrium on an incline of angle $\theta = 60.0°$. Find F_n of the incline on the block. (See Sample Problem 4C.)

49. A 5.4 kg bag of groceries is in equilibrium on an incline of angle $\theta = 15°$. Find the normal force of the incline on the bag. (See Sample Problem 4C.)

50. Find the force exerted by each cable to support the 625 N bag in **Figure 4-32.** (See Sample Problem 4B.)

Figure 4-32

51. A box of books weighing 319 N is shoved across the floor by a force of 485 N exerted downward at an angle of 35° below the horizontal.

  a. If μ_k between the box and the floor is 0.57, how long does it take to move the box 4.00 m, starting from rest?

  b. If μ_k between the box and the floor is 0.75, how long does it take to move the box 4.00 m, starting from rest?

  (See Sample Problem 4D.)

52. A 95 kg clock initially at rest on a horizontal floor requires a 650 N horizontal force to set it in motion. After the clock is in motion, a horizontal force of 560 N keeps it moving with a constant speed. Find μ_s and μ_k between the clock and the floor. (See Sample Problem 4D.)

53. A box slides down a 30.0° ramp with an acceleration of 1.20 m/s². Determine the coefficient of kinetic friction between the box and the ramp. (See Sample Problem 4D.)

54. A 40.0 kg wagon is towed up a hill inclined at 18.5° with respect to the horizontal. The tow rope is parallel to the incline and exerts a force of 140 N on the wagon. Assume that the wagon starts from rest at the bottom of the hill, and disregard friction.

  a. How fast is the wagon going after moving 30.0 m up the hill?

  b. How fast is the wagon going after moving 80.0 m up the hill?

  (See Sample Problem 4D.)

55. A clerk moves a box of cans down an aisle by pulling on a rope attached to the box. The clerk pulls with a force of 185.0 N at an angle of 25.0° with the horizontal. The box has a mass of 35.0 kg, and the coefficient of kinetic friction between box and floor is 0.450. Find the acceleration of the box. (See Sample Problem 4D.)

56. A car is traveling at 50.0 km/h on a flat highway.

    a. If the coefficient of friction between the road and the tires on a rainy day is 0.100, what is the minimum distance needed for the car to stop?

    b. What is the stopping distance when the surface is dry and the coefficient of friction is 0.600?

(See Sample Problem 4D.)

57. A 4.00 kg block is pushed along the ceiling with a constant applied force of 85.0 N that acts at an angle of 55.0° with the horizontal, as in **Figure 4-33**. The block accelerates to the right at 6.00 m/s². Determine the coefficient of kinetic friction between the block and the ceiling.
(See Sample Problem 4D.)

85 N

55°

Figure 4-33

58. A 35 kg box rests on the back of a truck. The coefficient of static friction between the box and the truck bed is 0.300.

    a. When the truck accelerates forward, what happens to the box?

    b. Find the maximum acceleration the truck can have before the box slides.

(See Sample Problem 4D.)

59. A girl coasts down a hill on a sled, reaching the bottom with a speed of 7.0 m/s. The coefficient of friction between the sled's runners and the snow is 0.050, and the girl and sled together weigh 645 N. How far does the sled travel on the surface before coming to rest?
(See Sample Problem 4D.)

60. A 3.00 kg block starts from rest at the top of a 30.0° incline and slides 2.00 m down the incline in 1.50 s.

    a. Find the acceleration of the block.

    b. Find the coefficient of kinetic friction between the block and the incline.

    c. Find the frictional force acting on the block.

    d. Find the speed of the block after it has slid a distance of 2.00 m.

(See Sample Problem 4D.)

61. The coefficient of static friction between the 3.00 kg crate and the 35.0° incline of **Figure 4-34** is 0.300.

What is the minimum force, F, that must be applied to the crate perpendicular to the incline to prevent the crate from sliding down the incline?
(See Sample Problem 4D.)

Figure 4-34

62. Two blocks with masses of 45.0 kg and 25.5 kg are stacked on a table with the heavier block on top. The coefficient of static friction is 0.60 between the two blocks and 0.30 between the bottom block and the table. A horizontal force is slowly applied to the top block until one of the blocks moves.

    a. Where does slippage occur first, between the two blocks or between the bottom block and the table? Explain.

    b. What value of the coefficient of static friction between the bottom block and the table would change the answer to part (a)?

(See Sample Problem 4D.)

63. **Figure 4-35** shows a plot of the speed of a person's body during a chin-up. All motion is vertical and the mass of the person (excluding the arms) is 64.0 kg. Find the magnitude of the force exerted on the body by the arms at 0.50 s intervals.
(See Sample Problem 4C.)

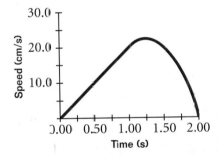

Figure 4-35

64. A hockey puck is hit on a frozen lake and starts moving with a speed of 12.0 m/s. Exactly 5.00 s later, its speed is 6.00 m/s.

    a. What is its average acceleration?

    b. What is the average value of the coefficient of kinetic friction between puck and ice?

    c. How far does the puck travel during this 5.00 s interval?

(See Sample Problem 4D.)

65. A truck driver slams on the brakes and skids to a stop through a displacement Δx.

    a. If the truck had double the mass, find the truck's "skidding distance" in terms of Δx. (Hint: Increasing the mass increases the normal force.)

    b. If the initial velocity of the truck were halved, what would be the truck's "skidding distance" in terms of Δx?

66. The board sandwiched between two other boards in **Figure 4-36** weighs 95.5 N. If the coefficient of friction between the boards is 0.663, what must be the magnitude of the horizontal forces acting on both sides of the center board to keep it from slipping downward?

Figure 4-36

Technology Learning

Graphing calculators

Program your graphing calculator to create a graph of normal force versus force of static friction to determine what applied force would be necessary to keep the objects in each of the following situations sliding:

a. a 25 N wooden box resting on a wooden table-top, with $\mu_k = 0.20$

b. a 325 N wooden box on the same tabletop

c. a 25 N steel box resting on a steel countertop, with $\mu_k = 0.57$

d. a 325 N steel box on the same countertop

Press [Y=] and [CLEAR] to clear any functions.

Open a new program by pressing [PRGM] [▶] [▶] [ENTER]. Name the program "FRICTION" and press

[ENTER]. Then enter the program in the table below.

To exit the program editor, press [2nd] [QUIT]. To run the program, press [PRGM], select "FRICTION," and press [ENTER] [ENTER]. Enter the value for the coefficient of friction and press [ENTER].

The calculator will provide a graph of the force of friction versus the normal force. (If the graph is not visible, press [WINDOW], change the settings for the graph window, then press [GRAPH].)

Press [TRACE], and use the arrow keys to trace along the curve. The x value corresponds to the normal force in newtons, and the y value corresponds to the force of friction in newtons.

After you have finished using the graph for one coefficient of friction, press [2nd] [QUIT] and run the program for the next one.

Keystrokes	Display
	PROGRAM: FRICTION
1. [PRGM] [▶] [3] [ALPHA] ["] [ALPHA] [M] [ALPHA] [U] [2nd] [TEST] [1] [ALPHA] ["] [ENTER]	:DISP"MU="
2. [PRGM] [▶] [1] [ALPHA] [K] [ENTER]	:INPUT K
3. [ALPHA] ["] [ALPHA] [K] [×] [X,T,θ] [ALPHA] ["] [STO▶] [2nd] [Y-VARS] [1] [1] [ENTER]	:"K∗X" → Y₁
4. [PRGM] [▶] [4] [ENTER]	:DISPGRAPH

67. Refer to the diagram in **Figure 4-37** to answer the following questions.

Figure 4-37

  a. What is the minimum force of friction between the table and the 150 N block required to hold both blocks in equilibrium?

  b. What would the coefficient of static friction between the 150 N block and the table have to be to ensure that both blocks would be held in equilibrium?

68. Three blocks are in contact with each other on a frictionless horizontal surface, as in **Figure 4-38**. A horizontal force, **F**, is applied to m_1. For this problem, $m_1 = 2.00$ kg, $m_2 = 3.00$ kg, $m_3 = 4.00$ kg, and $F = 180$ N to the right.

  a. Find the acceleration of the blocks.
  b. Find the resultant force on each block.
  c. Find the magnitude of the contact forces between the blocks.

Figure 4-38

Alternative Assessment

Performance assessment

1. Predict what will happen in the following test of the laws of motion. You and a partner face each other, each holding a bathroom scale. Place the scales back to back and slowly begin pushing on them. Record the measurements of both scales at the same time. Perform the experiment. Which of Newton's laws have you verified?

2. You can keep a 3 kg book from dropping by pushing it horizontally against a wall. Draw force diagrams and identify all the forces involved. How do they combine to result in a zero net force? Will the force you must supply to hold the book up be different for different types of walls? Design a series of experiments to test your answer. Identify exactly which measurements will be necessary and what equipment you will need. If your teacher approves your plan, perform the experiments and present your analysis and conclusions to the class.

Portfolio projects

3. Research how the work of scientists Antoine Lavoisier, Isaac Newton, and Albert Einstein related to the study of mass. Which might have said the following?

  a. The mass of a body is a measure of the quantity of matter in it.

  b. The mass of a body is its resistance to a change in motion.

  c. The mass of a body depends on its velocity.

  To what extent are these statements compatible or contradictory? Create a presentation, such as a poster, video, or computer presentation, of these scientists' conceptions of the meaning of mass.

4. Imagine an airplane with a series of special instruments anchored to its walls: a pendulum, a 100 kg mass on a spring balance, and a sealed half-full aquarium. What will happen to each instrument when the plane takes off, makes turns, slows down, lands, etc.? If possible, test your responses by simulating the experience in elevators, car rides, and other situations with similar instruments and with your body sensations. Write a report comparing your predictions with your experiences.

5. Research the effects of snow, ice, and water on friction and gliding in the context of skiing, ice skating, hockey, mountain climbing, and other activities. Explain how athletes in these sports need and use friction. Explain how friction—or its absence—can diminish these athletes' performance. How do your findings relate to your personal experience? Prepare a report or presentation and use specific examples.

CHAPTER 4
Laboratory Exercise

OBJECTIVES

- Compare the accelerations of a mass acted on by different forces.
- Compare the accelerations of different masses acted on by the same force.
- Examine the relationships between mass, force, acceleration, and Newton's laws of motion.

MATERIALS LIST

- ✔ balance
- ✔ calibrated masses and holder
- ✔ cord
- ✔ dynamics cart
- ✔ mass hanger
- ✔ meterstick
- ✔ pulley with table clamp

PROCEDURE

CBL AND SENSORS

- ✔ CBL
- ✔ CBL force sensor with CBL-DIN adapter
- ✔ CBL motion detector
- ✔ graphing calculator with link cable
- ✔ support stand with V-jaw clamp
- ✔ rod and parallel clamp
- ✔ tape
- ✔ 25 cm × 25 cm square of poster board

RECORDING TIMER

- ✔ C-clamp
- ✔ recording timer and tape
- ✔ stopwatch

FORCE AND ACCELERATION

Newton's second law states that any net external force applied to a mass causes the mass to accelerate according to the equation $\mathbf{F} = m\mathbf{a}$. Because of frictional forces, experience does not always seem to support this. For example, when you are driving a car you must apply a constant force to keep the car moving with a constant velocity. In the absence of friction, the car would continue to move with a constant velocity after the force was removed. The continued application of force would cause the car to accelerate.

In this lab, you will study the motion of a dynamics cart pulled by the weight of masses falling from a table to the floor. The cart is set up so that any applied force will cause it to move with a constant velocity. In the first part of the experiment, the total mass will remain constant while the force acting on the cart will be different for each trial. In the second part, the force acting on the cart will remain constant, but the total mass will change for each trial.

SAFETY

- Tie back long hair, secure loose clothing, and remove loose jewelry to prevent its getting caught in moving or rotating parts.
- Attach masses securely. Falling or dropped masses can cause serious injury.

PREPARATION

1. Determine whether you will be using the CBL and sensors or the recording timer to take your measurements. Read the entire lab procedure for the appropriate method. Plan the steps you will take.

2. Prepare a data table in your lab notebook with six columns and six rows. In the first row, label the first through sixth columns *Trial, Total mass (kg), Accelerating mass (kg), Accelerating force (N), Time interval (s),* and *Distance (m)*. In the first column, label the second through sixth rows *1, 2, 3, 4,* and *5*.

3. Choose a location where the cart will be able to move a considerable distance without any obstacles and where you will be able to clamp the pulley to a table edge.

Recording-timer procedure begins on page 161.

PROCEDURE

CBL AND SENSORS

Apparatus setup

4. Connect the CBL to the calculator with the unit-to-unit link cable using the link ports located on each unit. Connect the force sensor to the CH1 port on the CBL and connect the motion detector to the SONIC port. Turn on the CBL and the graphing calculator.

5. Start the program PHYSICS on your graphing calculator.

    a. Select option *SET UP PROBES* from the MAIN MENU. Enter 2 for the number of probes. Select the motion detector. Next, select the appropriate force sensor from the list; your teacher will tell you what kind of force sensor you are using. Enter 1 for the channel number. Select *USED STORED* from the CALIBRATION menu.

    b. Select the *COLLECT DATA* option from the MAIN MENU. Select the *TIME GRAPH* option from the DATA COLLECTION menu. Enter 0.02 for the time between samples. Enter 99 for the number of samples. Check the values you entered and press ENTER. Press ENTER to continue. If you made a mistake entering the time values, select MODIFY SETUP, reenter the values, and continue.

6. Securely tape the force sensor to the dynamics cart, as shown in **Figure 4-39.** Tape the poster board to the opposite end of the dynamics cart to make a flat vertical surface.

7. Set up the apparatus as shown in **Figure 4-39.** Clamp the pulley to the table edge using a table clamp, rod, and parallel clamp so that it is level with the force sensor hook. Position the motion detector so that the cart will move away from it in a straight line. To keep the motion detector from moving during the experiment, securely clamp it to the ring stand. Place a piece of tape 0.5 m in front of the motion detector to serve as a starting line for the cart.

Constant mass with varying force

8. Carefully measure the mass of the cart assembly on the platform balance, making sure that the cart does not roll or fall off the balance. Then load it with masses equal to 0.60 kg. Lightly tape the masses to the cart to hold them in place. Add these masses to the mass of the cart.

9. Attach one end of the cord to a small mass hanger and the other end of the cord to the force sensor. Pass the cord over the pulley and fasten a small mass to the end to offset the frictional force on the cart.

Figure 4-39

Step 7: Make sure the motion detector has a clear view of the cart. For all trials, start the cart from the same position.

Step 14: Using the CBL with the graphing calculator will allow you to view graphs of the motion after each trial.

The mass is correct when the car moves forward with a constant velocity when you give it a push. *This counterweight should stay on the string throughout the entire experiment.* Add the mass of the counterweight to the mass of the cart and masses, and record the sum as *Total mass* in your data table.

10. For the first trial, remove a 0.10 kg mass from the cart, and securely fasten it to the end of the cord along with the counterweight. Record 0.10 kg as the *Accelerating mass* in the data table.

11. Place the cart at the piece of tape 0.5 m in front of the motion detector. Place the cart so the poster board end is closest to the motion detector and lined up with the tape line. Keep the force sensor cord clear so that the cart will be able to move freely.

12. Make sure the CBL and the graphing calculator are turned on. Make sure the area under the falling mass is clear of obstacles. Press ENTER on the calculator to begin collecting data, and release the cart simultaneously. The motion detector will begin to click as it collects data.

13. Carefully stop the cart when the 0.10 kg mass hits the floor. *Do not let the cart fall off the table.*

14. When the motion detector stops clicking and the CBL displays *DONE*, press ENTER on the graphing calculator. Select the *ANALOG* option from the SELECT CHANNELS menu. This will plot a graph of the force sensor reading against time. Use the arrow keys to trace along the curve. The *y* value is the force in newtons; it should be fairly constant. Record this value as the *Accelerating force* in the data table. Press ENTER.

15. Select the *SONIC* option, and then select the *DISTANCE* option to plot a graph of the distance in meters against time. Use the arrow keys to trace along the curve. On the far left and the far right, the flat portion of the curve represents the positions of the cart before and after its motion. The middle section of the curve represents the motion of the cart. Choose a point on the curve near the begin-

ning of this middle section, and choose another point near the end.

16. Find the difference between the *y* values of these two points, and record it as the *Distance* for *Trial 1* in your data table. Find the difference between the *x* values for these two readings to find the time elapsed between measurements. Record this as the *Time interval* for *Trial 1* in your data table. Press ENTER on the calculator.

- Select the *SONIC* option again, and select the *VELOCITY* option to plot a graph of the velocity in m/s against time. Examine how the velocity of the cart changed during the experiment. Press ENTER.

- Select the *SONIC* option again, and select the *ACCELERATION* option to plot a graph of the acceleration in m/s^2 against time. Examine how the acceleration of the cart changed during the experiment. Press ENTER.

17. Replace the 0.10 kg mass in the cart. Remove 0.20 kg from the cart, and attach it securely to the end of the cord. Repeat the procedure.

18. Leave the 0.20 kg on the end of the cord, and attach the 0.10 kg mass from the cart securely to the end of the cord. Repeat the procedure.

Constant force with varying mass

19. For the two trials in this part of the experiment, keep 0.30 kg and the counterweight on the string. Be sure to include this mass when recording the total mass for these three trials.

20. Add 0.50 kg to the cart. Tape the mass to the cart to keep it in place. Run the experiment and record the total mass, accelerating mass, accelerating force, distance, and time under *Trial 4* in your data table.

21. Tape 1.00 kg to the cart, and repeat the procedure. Record the data under *Trial 5* in your data table.

Analysis and Interpretation begins on page 162.

PROCEDURE

RECORDING TIMER

Apparatus setup

4. Set up the apparatus as shown in **Figure 4-40.** Clamp the pulley to the edge of the table so that it is level with the top of the cart. Clamp the recording timer to a ring stand or to the edge of the table to hold it in place. If the timer is clamped to the table, leave 0.5 m between the timer and the initial position of the cart. Insert the carbon disk, and thread tape through the guides under the disk. When your teacher approves your setup, plug the timer into a wall outlet.

5. If you have not used the recording timer before, refer to the lab for Chapter 2 for instructions. Calibrate the recording timer with the stopwatch or use the previously determined value for the timer's period.

6. Record the value for the timer's period at the top of the data table.

7. Fasten the timing tape to one end of the cart.

Constant mass with varying force

8. Carefully measure the mass of the cart assembly on the platform balance, making sure that the cart does not roll or fall off the balance. Then load it with masses equal to 0.60 kg. Lightly tape the masses to the cart to hold them in place. Add these masses to the mass of the cart.

9. Attach one end of the cord to a small mass hanger and the other end of the cord to the cart. Pass the cord over the pulley and fasten a small mass to the end to offset the frictional force on the cart. The mass is correct when the car moves forward with a constant velocity when you give it a push. *This counterweight should stay on the string throughout the entire experiment.* Add the mass of the counterweight to the mass of the cart and masses, and record the sum as *Total mass* in your data table.

10. For the first trial, remove a 0.10 kg mass from the cart, and securely fasten it to the end of the string along with the counterweight. Record 0.10 kg as the *Accelerating mass* in the data table.

11. Hold the cart by holding the tape behind the timer. Make sure the area under the falling mass is clear of obstacles. Start the timer and release the tape simultaneously.

12. Carefully stop the cart when the 0.10 kg mass hits the floor, and then stop the timer. ***Do not let the cart fall off the table.***

13. Remove the tape and label it.

Figure 4-40

Step 4: Make sure the clamp protrudes as little as possible from the edge of the table.

Step 7: Fold the end of the recording tape over the edge of the rail on the cart and tape it down.

Step 10: Always hold the cart when you are removing and adding masses. When you are ready, release the cart from the same position each time.

14. Use a meterstick to measure the distance the weights fell. Record the *Distance* in your data table.

15. On the tape, measure this distance starting from the first clear dot. Mark the end of this distance. Count the number of dots between the first dot and this mark.

16. Calculate and record the *Time interval* represented by the number of dots. Fasten a new timing tape to the end of the cart.

17. Replace the 0.10 kg mass in the cart. Remove 0.20 kg from the cart and attach it securely to the end of the cord. Repeat the procedure, and record the results in your data table as *Trial 2*.

18. Leave the 0.20 kg on the end of the cord and attach the 0.10 kg mass from the cart securely to the end of the cord. Repeat the procedure, and record the results in your data table as *Trial 3*.

Constant force with varying mass

19. For the two trials in this part of the experiment, keep 0.30 kg and the counterweight on the string. Be sure to include this mass when recording the total mass for these three trials.

20. Add 0.50 kg to the cart. Tape the mass to the cart to keep it in place. Run the experiment and record the total mass, accelerating mass, accelerating force, distance, and time under *Trial 4* in your data table.

21. Tape 1.00 kg to the cart and repeat the procedure. Record the data under *Trial 5* in your data table.

ANALYSIS AND INTERPRETATION

Calculations and data analysis

1. Analyzing data   Using the Newton's second law equation, $\mathbf{F} = m\mathbf{a}$, where $a = g$, calculate the force acting on the accelerating mass in each trial.

   a. CBL and sensors   Compare these values to the force values in your data table. Are they the same? If not, why not?

   b. Recording timer   Enter these values in your data table as the *Accelerating force* for each trial.

2. Applying ideas   Use your values for the distance and time to find the acceleration of the cart for each trial using the equation $\Delta x = \frac{1}{2}a\Delta t^2$ for constantly accelerated motion.

3. Graphing data   Using the data from *Trials 1–3*, plot a graph of the accelerations of the cart versus the accelerating forces. Use a graphing calculator, computer, or graph paper.

4. Interpreting graphs   Based on your graph from item 3, what is the relationship between the acceleration of the cart and the accelerating force? Explain how your graph supports your answer.

5. Graphing data   Using the data from *Trials 3–5*, plot a graph of the total masses versus the accelerations. Use a graphing calculator, computer, or graph paper.

6. Interpreting graphs Based on your graph from item 5, what is the relationship between the total mass and the acceleration? Explain how your graph supports your answer.

Conclusions

7. Evaluating methods Why does the mass in *Trials 1–3* remain constant even though masses are removed from the cart during the trials?

8. Evaluating methods Do the carts move with the same velocity and acceleration as the accelerating masses that are dropped? If not, why not?

9. Applying conclusions Do your data support Newton's second law? Use your data and your analysis of your graphs to support your conclusions.

10. Applying ideas A team of automobile safety engineers developed a new type of car and performed some test crashes to find out whether the car is safe. The engineers tested the new car by involving it in a series of different types of accidents. For each test, the engineers applied a known force to the car and measured the acceleration of the car after the crash. The graph in **Figure 4-41** shows the acceleration of the car plotted against the applied force. Compare this with the data you collected and the graphs you made for this experiment to answer the following questions.

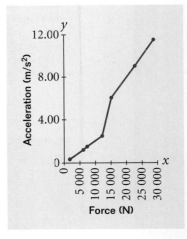

Figure 4-41

a. Based on the graph, what is the relationship between the acceleration of the new car and the force of the collision?

b. Does this graph support Newton's second law? Use your analysis of this graph to support your conclusions.

c. Does the data from the crash tests meet your expectations based on this lab? Explain what you think may have happened to affect the results. If you were on the engineering team, how would you find out whether your results were in error?

Extensions

11. Critical thinking How would your results be affected if you used the mass of the cart and its contents instead of the total mass? Predict what would happen if you performed *Trials 1–3* again keeping the mass of the cart and its contents constant while varying the accelerating mass. If there is time and your teacher approves your plan, go into the lab and try it. Plot your data using a graphing calculator, computer, or graph paper.

Physics and Its World *Timeline 1540–1690*

1540
1550
1560
1570
1580
1590
1600
1610

1556 – Akbar becomes ruler of the Moghul Empire in North India, Pakistan, and Afghanistan. By ensuring religious tolerance, he establishes greater unity in India, making it one of the world's great powers.

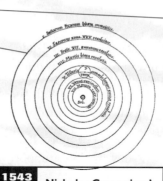

1543 — **Nicholas Copernicus'** *On the Revolutions of the Heavenly Bodies* is published. It is the first work on astronomy to provide an analytical basis for the motion of the planets, including Earth, around the sun.

1543 – Andries van Wesel, better known as Andreas Vesalius, completes his *Seven Books on the Structure of the Human Body.* It is the first work on anatomy to be based on the dissection of human bodies.

1564 – English writers **Christopher Marlowe** and **William Shakespeare** are born.

1586 – Kabuki theater is developed in Japan.

1588 – Queen Elizabeth I of England sends the English fleet to repel the invasion by the Spanish Armada. The success of the English navy marks the beginning of Great Britain's status as a major naval power.

1592

$$\Delta x = v_i \Delta t + \frac{1}{2} a (\Delta t)^2$$

Galileo Galilei is appointed professor of mathematics at the University of Padua. While there, he performs experiments on the motions of bodies.

1605 – The first part of **Miguel de Cervantes's** *Don Quixote* is published.

1609

$$T^2 \propto a^3$$

New Astronomy, by **Johannes Kepler**, is published. In it, Kepler demonstrates that the orbit of Mars is elliptical rather than circular.

1608 – The first telescopes are constructed in the Netherlands. Using these instruments as models, **Galileo** constructs his first telescope the following year.

1637 – **René Descartes's** *Discourse on Method* is published. According to Descartes's philosophy of rationalism, the laws of nature can be deduced by reason.

1644 – The Ch'ing, or Manchu, Dynasty is established in China. China becomes the most prosperous nation in the world, then declines until the Ch'ing Dynasty is replaced by the Chinese Republic in 1911.

1656 – The first paintings of Dutch artist **Jan Vermeer** are produced around this time. Vermeer's paintings portray middle- and working-class people in everyday situations.

1669 – Danish geologist **Niclaus Steno** correctly determines the structure of crystals and identifies fossils as organic remains.

1678

$$c = f\lambda$$

Christian Huygens completes the bulk of his *Treatise on Light*, in which he presents his model of secondary wavelets, known today as Huygens' principle. The completed book is published 12 years later.

1687

$$F = ma$$

Issac Newton's masterpiece, the *Mathematical Principles of Nature*, is published. In this extensive work, Newton systematically presents a unified model of mechanics.

Physics and Its World 1540–1690   **165**

CHAPTER 5

Work and Energy

PHYSICS IN ACTION

This whimsical piece of art is a type of audio-kinetic sculpture. Balls are raised to a high point on the curved blue track. As the balls roll down the track, they turn levers, spin rotors, and bounce off elastic membranes.

As each ball travels along the track, the total energy remains unchanged. The types of energy that are involved—whether associated with the ball's motion, the ball's position above the ground, or friction—vary in ways that keep the total energy constant.

In this chapter, you will learn about work and the different types of energy that are relevant to mechanics.

- *How many different kinds of energy are used in this sculpture?*
- *How are work, energy, and power related in the functioning of this sculpture?*

CONCEPT REVIEW

Kinematics (Section 2-2)

Newton's second law (Section 4-3)

Force of friction (Section 4-4)

5-1
Work

5-1 SECTION OBJECTIVES

- **Recognize the difference between the scientific and the ordinary definitions of *work*.**

- **Define *work*, relating it to force and displacement.**

- **Identify where work is being performed in a variety of situations.**

- **Calculate the net work done when many forces are applied to an object.**

work

the product of the magnitudes of the component of a force along the direction of displacement and the displacement

DEFINITION OF WORK

Many of the terms you have encountered so far in this book have meanings in physics that are similar to their meanings in everyday life. In its everyday sense, the term *work* means doing something that takes physical or mental effort. But in physics, work has a distinctly different meaning. Consider the following situations:

- A student holds a heavy chair at arm's length for several minutes.
- A student carries a bucket of water along a horizontal path while walking at constant velocity.

It might surprise you to know that under the scientific definition of work there is no work done on the chair or the bucket, even though effort is required in both cases. We will return to these examples later.

A force that causes a displacement of an object does work on the object

Imagine that your car has run out of gas, like the car shown in **Figure 5-1,** and you have to push it down the road to the gas station. If you push the car with a constant force, the **work** you do on the car is equal to the magnitude of the force, F, times the magnitude of the displacement of the car. Using the symbol d instead of Δx for displacement, work can be defined as follows:

$$W = Fd$$

Work is not done on an object unless the object is moved due to the action of a force. The application of a force alone does not constitute work. That is why no work is done on the chair when a student holds the chair at arm's length. Even though the student exerts a force to support the chair, the chair does not move. The student's tired arms suggest that a considerable amount of work is being done, which is indeed true. However, work is done *within the student's body.* Work is not done on the chair.

Work is done only when components of a force are parallel to a displacement

When the force on an object and the object's displacement are in different directions, the component of the force that is in the direction of the object's displacement does work. Components of the force perpendicular to a displacement do no work.

Figure 5-1
This person exerts a constant force on the car, displacing it to the left. The work done on the car by the person is equal to the force times the displacement.

For example, imagine you push a crate along the ground. If the force you exert is horizontal, all of your effort moves the crate. If your force is other than horizontal, only the horizontal component of your applied force causes a displacement and does work. If the angle between the force and the direction of the displacement is θ, as in **Figure 5-2,** work can be written as follows:

$$W = Fd(\cos \theta)$$

If $\theta = 0°$, then cos $0° = 1$ and $W = Fd$, which is the definition of work given earlier. If $\theta = 90°$, however, then cos $90° = 0$ and $W = 0$. This is why no work is done on a bucket of water being carried by a student walking horizontally. The upward force exerted to support the bucket is perpendicular to the displacement of the bucket, resulting in no work done on the bucket.

Finally, if many constant forces are acting on an object, you can find the *net* work done by first finding the net force.

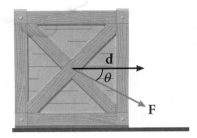

$$W = Fd(\cos \theta)$$

Figure 5-2
The work done on this crate is equal to the force times the displacement times the cosine of the angle between them.

NET WORK DONE BY A CONSTANT NET FORCE

$$W_{net} = F_{net}d(\cos \theta)$$

net work = net force × displacement × cosine of the angle between them

---

Work has dimensions of force times length. In the SI system, work has a unit of N•m, or joules (J). The work done in lifting an apple from your waist to the top of your head requires about 1 J. Three pushups require about 1000 J.

SAMPLE PROBLEM 5A

Work

PROBLEM

How much work is done on a vacuum cleaner pulled 3.0 m by a force of 50.0 N at an angle of 30.0° above the horizontal?

SOLUTION

Given: $F = 50.0$ N $\theta = 30.0°$ $d = 3.0$ m

Unknown: $W = ?$

Use the equation for net work done by a constant force:

$$W = Fd(\cos \theta)$$

Only the horizontal component of the applied force is doing work on the vacuum cleaner.

$$W = (50.0 \text{ N})(3.0 \text{ m})(\cos 30.0°)$$

$$\boxed{W = 130 \text{ J}}$$

Work

1. A tugboat pulls a ship with a constant net horizontal force of 5.00×10^3 N, causing the ship to move through a harbor. How much work does the tugboat do on the ship if each moves a distance of 3.00 km?

2. A weight lifter lifts a set of weights a vertical distance of 2.00 m. If a constant net force of 350 N is exerted on the weights, how much work does the weight lifter do on the weights?

3. A shopper in a supermarket pushes a cart with a force of 35 N directed at an angle of 25° downward from the horizontal. Find the work done by the shopper on the cart as the shopper moves along a 50.0 m length of aisle.

The sign of work is important

Work is a scalar quantity and can be positive or negative, as shown in **Figure 5-3**. Work is positive when the component of force is in the same direction as the displacement. For example, when you lift a box, the work done by the force you exert on the box is positive because that force is upward, in the same direction as the displacement. Work is negative when the force is in the direction opposite the displacement. For example, the force of kinetic friction

Figure 5-3
Depending on the angle, an applied force can either cause a moving car to slow down (left), resulting in negative work done on the car, or speed up (right), resulting in positive work done on the car.

between a sliding box and the floor is opposite to the displacement of the box, so the work done by the force on the box is negative. If you are very careful in applying the equation for work, your answer will have the correct sign: $\cos \theta$ is negative for angles greater than 90° but less than 270°.

If the work done on an object results only in a change in the object's speed, the sign of the net work on the object tells you whether the object's speed is increasing or decreasing. If the net work is positive, the object speeds up and the net force does work *on* the object. If the net work is negative, the object slows down and work is done *by* the object on another object.

Section Review

1. For each of the following statements, identify whether the everyday or the scientific meaning of work is intended.

   a. Jack had to work against time as the deadline neared.
   b. Jill had to work on her homework before she went to bed.
   c. Jack did work carrying the pail of water up the hill.
   d. Jill works 20 hours a week.

2. If a neighbor pushes a lawnmower four times as far as you do but exerts only half the force, which one of you does more work? By how much?

3. For each of the following cases, indicate whether the work done on the second object in each example will have a positive or a negative value.

   a. The road exerts a friction force on a speeding car skidding to a stop.
   b. A rope exerts a force on a bucket as the bucket is raised up a well.
   c. Air exerts a force on a parachute as the parachutist slowly falls to Earth.
   d. The Earth exerts a force on a bobsled as it moves down a track.

4. Determine whether work is being done in each of the following examples:

   a. a train engine pulling a loaded boxcar initially at rest
   b. a tug of war that is evenly matched
   c. a crane lifting a car

5. A worker pushes a 1.50×10^3 N crate with a horizontal force of 345 N a distance of 24.0 m. Assume the coefficient of kinetic friction between the crate and the floor is 0.220.

   a. How much work is done by the worker on the crate?
   b. How much work is done by the floor on the crate?
   c. What is the net work done on the crate?

6. **Physics in Action** A 0.075 kg ball in a kinetic sculpture is raised 1.33 m above the ground by a motorized vertical conveyor belt. A constant frictional force of 0.350 N acts in the direction opposite the conveyor belt's motion. How much total work is done in raising the ball?

5-2 SECTION OBJECTIVES

- Identify several forms of energy.

- Calculate kinetic energy for an object.

- Distinguish between kinetic and potential energy.

- Classify different types of potential energy.

- Calculate the potential energy associated with an object's position.

kinetic energy

energy of an object due to its motion

KINETIC ENERGY

Think about the images that the following words bring to your mind: *zoom, race, zip, hover.* Which of these words do you associate with the word *energetic?* Answering this question should give you some idea of the meaning of **kinetic energy.**

Kinetic energy depends on speed and mass

Kinetic energy is energy associated with an object in motion. Thus, the kinetic energy of an object depends on the speed of the object. Its kinetic energy increases as its speed increases. Because the word *hover,* unlike the other words, does not convey a sense of motion, a hovering object, such as a hot-air balloon, has little kinetic energy. Objects that zoom, race, or zip probably have a lot of kinetic energy.

But kinetic energy depends on more than an object's speed. For example, if a bowling ball and a volleyball are traveling at the same speed, as shown in **Figure 5-4(a)** and **(b),** which do you think has more kinetic energy? You may think that because they are moving with identical speeds they have exactly the same kinetic energy. However, the bowling ball has more kinetic energy than the volleyball traveling at the same speed because the bowling ball has more mass than the volleyball. Kinetic energy depends on both an object's mass and its speed. The kinetic energy of an object with mass m and speed v, when treated as a particle, can be determined using the following equation:

KINETIC ENERGY

$$KE = \frac{1}{2} m v^2$$

$$\textbf{kinetic energy} = \tfrac{1}{2} \times \textbf{mass} \times (\textbf{speed})^2$$

Kinetic energy is a scalar quantity, and the SI unit for kinetic energy (and all other forms of energy) is the joule. Recall that a joule is also used as the basic unit for work.

Figure 5-4
Kinetic energy, the energy of motion, depends on more than just an object's speed. These balls are moving at the same speed, but the bowling ball **(a)** has more kinetic energy than the volleyball **(b).**

Kinetic energy

PROBLEM

A 7.00 kg bowling ball moves at 3.00 m/s. How much kinetic energy does the bowling ball have? How fast must a 2.45 g table-tennis ball move in order to have the same kinetic energy as the bowling ball?

SOLUTION

Given: The subscripts b and t indicate the bowling ball and the table-tennis ball, respectively.

$$m_b = 7.00 \text{ kg} \qquad m_t = 2.45 \text{ g} \qquad v_b = 3.00 \text{ m/s}$$

Unknown: $KE_b = ? \quad v_t = ?$

Use the kinetic energy equation:

$$KE_b = \frac{1}{2} m_b v_b^2 = (0.5)(7.00 \text{ kg})(3.00 \text{ m/s})^2 = 31.5 \text{ J}$$

$$KE_t = \frac{1}{2} m_t v_t^2 = KE_b = 31.5 \text{ J}$$

$$v_t = \sqrt{\frac{2KE_b}{m_t}} = \sqrt{\frac{(2)(31.5 \text{ J})}{2.45 \times 10^{-3} \text{ kg}}}$$

$3g \times \dfrac{1kg}{1000g}$

$$\boxed{v_t = 1.60 \times 10^2 \text{ m/s}}$$

Kinetic energy

1. Calculate the kinetic energy of an 8.0×10^4 kg airliner flying at 600.0 km/h.

2. Two bullets have masses of 3.0 g and 6.0 g, respectively. Both are fired with a speed of 40.0 m/s. Which bullet has more kinetic energy? What is the ratio of their kinetic energies?

3. Two 3.0 g bullets are fired with velocities of 40.0 m/s and 80.0 m/s, respectively. What are their kinetic energies? Which bullet has more kinetic energy? What is the ratio of their kinetic energies?

4. A running student has half the kinetic energy that his younger brother has. The student speeds up by 1.3 m/s, at which point he has the same kinetic energy as his brother. If the student's mass is twice as large as his brother's mass, what were the original speeds of both the student and his brother? (See Appendix A for hints on solving quadratic equations.)

Figure 5-5
Energy is present in this example, but it is not kinetic energy because there is no motion. What kind of energy is it?

potential energy

energy associated with an object due to its position

gravitational potential energy

potential energy associated with an object due to its position relative to the Earth or some other gravitational source

Did you know?

Another commonly used unit for energy besides the joule is the kilowatt-hour (kW•h). It is equal to 3.6×10^6 J. Electrical energy is often measured in kilowatt-hours.

POTENTIAL ENERGY

Consider the balanced boulder shown in **Figure 5-5.** While the boulder remains balanced, it has no kinetic energy. If it becomes unbalanced it will fall vertically to the desert floor, gaining kinetic energy as it falls. A similar example is when an arrow is set, ready to be released on a bent bow. Once the arrow is in flight, it will have kinetic energy.

Potential energy is stored energy

These examples suggest that there is another form of energy besides kinetic energy, an energy that is associated not only with the speed of an object, but with the position of an object in relation to other objects or to a reference point. Kinetic energy describes an object in motion, but **potential energy** describes an object that has the potential to move because of its position with respect to some other location. Unlike kinetic energy, potential energy depends not only on the properties of an object but also on the object's interaction with its environment.

Gravitational potential energy depends on height from a zero level

In Chapter 3 we saw how gravitational force influences the motion of a projectile. If an object is thrown up in the air, the force of gravity will cause the object to eventually fall back down, provided the object was not thrown too hard. Similarly, the force of gravity will cause the unbalanced boulder in the previous example to fall. The energy associated with an object due to the object's position relative to a gravitational source is called **gravitational potential energy.**

Imagine an egg falling off a table. As it falls, it gains kinetic energy. But where does the egg's kinetic energy come from? It comes from the gravitational potential energy that is associated with the egg's initial position on the table relative to the floor. Gravitational potential energy can be determined using the following equation:

GRAVITATIONAL POTENTIAL ENERGY

$$PE_g = mgh$$

gravitational potential energy = mass × free-fall acceleration × height

The SI unit for gravitational potential energy, as with kinetic energy, is the joule. Note that the definition for gravitational potential energy in this chapter is valid only when the free-fall acceleration is constant over the entire height, such as at any point near the Earth's surface. Furthermore, gravitational potential energy depends on both the height and the free-fall acceleration, neither of which is a property of an object.

Suppose you drop a volleyball from a second-floor roof and it lands on the first-floor roof of an adjacent building (see **Figure 5-6**). If the height is measured from the ground, the gravitational potential energy is not zero because the ball is still above the ground. But if the height is measured from the first-floor roof, the potential energy is zero.

Gravitational potential energy is a result of an object's position, so it must be measured relative to some *zero level*. The zero level is the vertical coordinate at which gravitational potential energy is defined to be zero. This zero level is arbitrary, but it is chosen to make a specific problem easier to solve. In many cases, the statement of the problem suggests what to use as a zero level.

Figure 5-6
If B is the zero level, then the gravitational potential energy is converted to kinetic energy as the ball falls from A to B. If C is the zero level, then only part of the total gravitational potential energy is converted to kinetic energy during the fall from A to B.

Elastic potential energy depends on distance compressed or stretched

Imagine you are playing with a spring on a tabletop. You push a block into the spring, compressing the spring, and then release the block. The block slides across the tabletop. The kinetic energy of the block came from the stored energy in the stretched or compressed spring. This potential energy is called **elastic potential energy.** Elastic potential energy is stored in any compressed or stretched object, such as a spring or the stretched strings of a tennis racket or guitar.

The length of a spring when no external forces are acting on it is called the *relaxed length* of the spring. When an external force compresses or stretches the spring, elastic potential energy is stored in the spring. The amount of energy depends on the distance the spring is compressed or stretched from its relaxed length, as shown in **Figure 5-7.** Elastic potential energy can be determined using the following equation:

elastic potential energy

the potential energy in a stretched or compressed elastic object

---

ELASTIC POTENTIAL ENERGY

$$PE_{elastic} = \frac{1}{2}kx^2$$

$$\text{elastic potential energy} = \frac{1}{2} \times \text{spring constant} \times \left(\begin{array}{c}\text{distance compressed}\\\text{or stretched}\end{array}\right)^2$$

The symbol k is called the **spring constant,** or force constant. For a flexible spring, the spring constant is small, whereas for a stiff spring, the spring constant is large. A spring constant is measured in the SI system with units of N/m.

spring constant

a parameter that expresses how resistant a spring is to being compressed or stretched

Distance compressed

Compressed length of spring

Relaxed length of spring

Figure 5-7
The distance to use in the equation for elastic potential energy is the distance the spring is compressed or stretched from its relaxed length.

Potential energy

PROBLEM

A 70.0 kg stuntman is attached to a bungee cord with an unstretched length of 15.0 m. He jumps off a bridge spanning a river from a height of 50.0 m. When he finally stops, the cord has a stretched length of 44.0 m. Treat the stuntman as a point mass, and disregard the weight of the bungee cord. Assuming the spring constant of the bungee cord is 71.8 N/m, what is the total potential energy relative to the water when the man stops falling?

SOLUTION

1. DEFINE   **Given:**

$m = 70.0$ kg $k = 71.8$ N/m

$h = 50.0$ m $- 44.0$ m $= 6.0$ m

$x = 44.0$ m $- 15.0$ m $= 29.0$ m

$PE = 0$ at river level

Unknown: $PE_{tot} = ?$

Diagram:

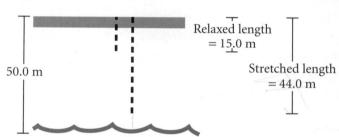

2. PLAN   **Choose an equation(s) or situation:** The zero level for gravitational potential energy is chosen to be at the surface of the water. The total potential energy is the sum of the gravitational and elastic potential energy.

$$PE_{tot} = PE_g + PE_{elastic}$$

$$PE_g = mgh$$

$$PE_{elastic} = \tfrac{1}{2}kx^2$$

3. CALCULATE   **Substitute values into equations:**

$$PE_g = (70.0 \text{ kg})(9.81 \text{ m/s}^2)(6.0 \text{ m}) = 4.1 \times 10^3 \text{ J}$$

$$PE_{elastic} = \tfrac{1}{2}(71.8 \text{ N/m})(29.0 \text{ m})^2 = 3.02 \times 10^4 \text{ J}$$

$$PE_{tot} = 4.1 \times 10^3 \text{ J} + 3.02 \times 10^4 \text{ J}$$

$$\boxed{PE_{tot} = 3.43 \times 10^4 \text{ J}}$$

4. EVALUATE   One way to evaluate the answer is to make an order-of-magnitude estimate. The gravitational potential energy is on the order of 10^2 kg $\times$ 10 m/s^2 $\times$ 10 m $= 10^4$ J. The elastic potential energy is on the order of 1×10^2 N/m $\times$ 10^2 m^2 $= 10^4$ J. Thus, the total potential energy should be on the order of 2×10^4 J. This is close to the actual answer.

Potential energy

1. If the stuntman in Sample Problem 5C changes bungee cords, what will the spring constant of the new cord be if the total potential energy is the same as in Sample Problem 5C and the man stops 12.0 m above the water level? Assume the unstretched cord has a length of 15.0 m.

2. The staples inside a stapler are kept in place by a spring with a relaxed length of 0.115 m. If the spring constant is 51.0 N/m, how much elastic potential energy is stored in the spring when its length is 0.150 m?

3. A spring with a force constant of 5.2 N/m has a relaxed length of 2.45 m. When a mass is attached to the end of the spring and allowed to come to rest, the vertical length of the spring is 3.57 m. Calculate the elastic potential energy stored in the spring.

4. A 40.0 kg child is in a swing that is attached to ropes 2.00 m long. Find the gravitational potential energy associated with the child relative to the child's lowest position under the following conditions:

   a. when the ropes are horizontal
   b. when the ropes make a 30.0° angle with the vertical
   c. at the bottom of the circular arc

MECHANICAL ENERGY

We have seen examples of objects that have either kinetic or potential energy. The description of the motion of many objects, however, often involves a combination of kinetic and potential energy as well as different forms of potential energy. For example, consider the motion of the different parts of a clock, as shown in **Figure 5-8.** The pendulum swings back and forth. At the highest point of its swing, there is only gravitational potential energy associated with its position. At other points in its swing, the pendulum is in motion, so it has kinetic energy as well. Elastic potential energy is also present in the many springs that are part of the inner workings of the clock.

The expressions for kinetic, gravitational potential, and elastic potential energy are relatively simple. Unfortunately, expressions for other forms of energy—such as chemical potential energy—are not as easy.

We can often ignore these other forms of energy because their influence is negligible or because they are not relevant to the situation being analyzed. In most situations that we are concerned with, these forms of energy are not involved in the motion of objects. In ignoring these other forms of energy, it is useful to define a quantity called **mechanical energy.** The mechanical energy is

Figure 5-8
Total potential energy and kinetic energy must be taken into account in order to describe the total energy of the clock.

mechanical energy

the sum of kinetic energy and all forms of potential energy

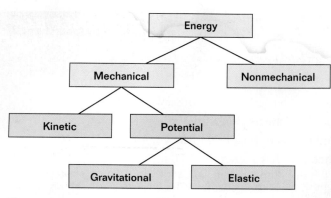

Figure 5-9

Energy can be classified in a number of ways.

the sum of kinetic energy and all forms of potential energy associated with an object or group of objects.

$$ME = KE + \Sigma PE$$

All energy that is not mechanical energy is classified as *nonmechanical energy.* Do not be confused by the term *mechanical energy.* It is not necessarily related to machines, and it is not a unique form of energy. It is merely a way of classifying energy, as shown in **Figure 5-9.** As you learn about new forms of energy in this book, you will be able to add them to this chart.

Section Review

1. What forms of energy are involved in the following situations?
   a. a bicycle coasting along a level road
   b. heating water
   c. throwing a football
   d. winding the hairspring of a clock

2. How do the forms of energy in item 1 differ from one another? Be sure to discuss mechanical versus nonmechanical, kinetic versus potential, and gravitational versus elastic.

3. A pinball bangs against a bumper, giving the ball a speed of 42 cm/s. If the ball has a mass of 50.0 g, what is the ball's kinetic energy in joules?

4. A spoon is raised 21.0 cm above a table. If the spoon and its contents have a mass of 30.0 g, what is the gravitational potential energy associated with the spoon at that height relative to the surface of the table?

5. A 65 kg diver is poised at the edge of a 10.0 m high platform. Calculate the gravitational potential energy associated with the position of the diver. Assume the zero level is at the surface of the pool.

6. What is the kinetic energy of a 1250 kg car moving at 45.0 km/h?

7. The force constant of a spring in a child's toy car is 550 N/m. How much elastic potential energy is stored in the spring if the spring is compressed a distance of 1.2 cm?

8. A 25.0 kg falling object strikes the ground with a speed of 12.5 m/s. If the kinetic energy of the object when it hits the ground is equal to the gravitational potential energy at some height above the ground, what is the height?

5-3
Conservation of energy

CONSERVED QUANTITIES

When we say that something is *conserved,* we mean that it remains constant. If we have a certain amount of a conserved quantity at some instant of time, we will have that same amount at a later time. This does not mean that the quantity cannot change form during that time, but if we consider all the forms that the quantity can take, we will find that we always have the same amount.

For example, the amount of money you now have is not a conserved quantity because it is likely to change over time. For the moment, however, let us assume that you do not spend the money you have, so your money is conserved. This means that if you have a dollar in your pocket, you will always have that same amount, although it may change form. One day it may be in the form of a bill. The next day you may have a hundred pennies, and the next day you may have an assortment of dimes and nickels. But when you total the change, you always have the equivalent of a dollar. It would be nice if money was like this, but of course it isn't. Because money is often acquired and spent, it is not a conserved quantity.

An example of a conserved quantity that you are already familiar with is mass. For instance, imagine that a light bulb is dropped on the floor and shatters into many pieces, as shown in **Figure 5-10.** No matter how the bulb shatters, the total mass of all of the pieces together is the same as the mass of the intact light bulb because mass is conserved.

Mechanical energy is often conserved

Imagine a 75 g egg located on a countertop 1.0 m above the ground. The egg is knocked off the edge and falls to the ground. Because the acceleration of the egg is constant as it falls, you can use the kinematic formulas from Chapter 2 to determine the speed of the egg and the distance the egg has fallen at any subsequent time. The distance fallen can then be subtracted from the initial height to find the height of the egg above the ground at any subsequent time. For example, after 0.10 s, the egg will have a speed of 0.98 m/s and will have fallen a distance 0.05 m, corresponding to a height above the ground of 0.95 m. Once the speed of the egg and its height above the ground are known as a function of time, you can use what you have learned in this chapter to calculate both the kinetic energy of the egg and the

Figure 5-10
The mass of the light bulb, whether whole or in pieces, is constant and thus conserved.

Quick Lab

Potential Energy

MATERIALS LIST

✔ medium-sized spring (spring balance)

✔ assortment of small balls, each having a different mass

✔ ruler

✔ tape

✔ scale or balance

SAFETY CAUTION

Students should wear goggles to perform this lab.

First determine the mass of each of the balls. Then tape the ruler to the side of a tabletop so that the ruler is vertical. Place the spring vertically on the tabletop near the ruler, and compress the spring with one of the balls. Release the ball, and measure the maximum height it achieves in the air. Repeat this process five times, and average the result. From the data, can you predict how high each of the other balls will rise? Test your predictions. (Hint: Assume mechanical energy is conserved.)

Table 5-1   **Forms of energy for a falling egg**

Time (s)	Height (m)	Speed (m/s)	PE_g (J)	KE (J)	ME (J)
0.00	1.0	0.00	0.74	0.00	0.74
0.10	0.95	0.98	0.70	0.036	0.74
0.20	0.80	2.0	0.59	0.15	0.74
0.30	0.56	2.9	0.41	0.33	0.74
0.40	0.22	3.9	0.16	0.58	0.74

gravitational potential energy associated with the position of the egg at any subsequent time. Adding the kinetic and potential energy gives the total mechanical energy at each position.

In the absence of friction, the total mechanical energy remains the same. This is called *conservation of mechanical energy*. Although the amount of mechanical energy is constant, mechanical energy itself can change form. For instance, consider the forms of energy for the falling egg, as shown in **Table 5-1.** As the egg falls, the potential energy is continuously converted into kinetic energy. If the egg were thrown up in the air, kinetic energy would be converted into gravitational potential energy. In either case, mechanical energy is conserved. The conservation of mechanical energy can be written symbolically as follows:

CONSERVATION OF MECHANICAL ENERGY

$$ME_i = ME_f$$

**initial mechanical energy = final mechanical energy
(in the absence of friction)**

The mathematical expression for the conservation of mechanical energy depends on the forms of potential energy in a given problem. For instance, if the only force acting on an object is the force of gravity, as in the egg example, the conservation law can be written as follows:

$$\tfrac{1}{2}mv_i^2 + mgh_i = \tfrac{1}{2}mv_f^2 + mgh_f$$

If other forces (except friction) are present, simply add the appropriate potential energy terms associated with each force. For instance, if the egg happened to compress or stretch a spring as it fell, the conservation law would also include an elastic potential energy term on each side of the equation.

In situations in which frictional forces are present, the principle of mechanical energy conservation no longer holds because kinetic energy is not simply converted to a form of potential energy. This special situation will be discussed more thoroughly on page 183.

Conservation of mechanical energy

PROBLEM

Starting from rest, a child zooms down a frictionless slide with an initial height of 3.00 m. What is her speed at the bottom of the slide? Assume she has a mass of 25.0 kg.

SOLUTION

1. DEFINE **Given:** $h = h_i = 3.00$ m $m = 25.0$ kg $v_i = 0.0$ m/s

$h_f = 0$ m

Unknown: $v_f = ?$

2. PLAN **Choose an equation(s) or situation:** The slide is frictionless, so mechanical energy is conserved. Kinetic energy and gravitational potential energy are the only forms of energy present.

$$KE = \tfrac{1}{2}mv^2 \qquad PE = mgh$$

The zero level chosen for gravitational potential energy is the bottom of the slide. Because the child ends at the zero level, the final gravitational potential energy is zero.

$$PE_{g,f} = 0$$

The initial gravitational potential energy is measured at the top of the slide.

$$PE_{g,i} = mgh_i = mgh$$

Because the child starts at rest, the initial kinetic energy at the top is zero.

$$KE_i = 0$$

Therefore, the final kinetic energy is as follows:

$$KE_f = \tfrac{1}{2}mv_f^2$$

3. CALCULATE **Substitute values into the equations:**

$$PE_{g,i} = (25.0 \text{ kg})(9.81 \text{ m/s}^2)(3.00 \text{ m}) = 736 \text{ J}$$
$$KE_f = (0.500)(25.0 \text{ kg})v_f^2$$

Now use the calculated quantities to evaluate the final velocity.

$$ME_i = ME_f$$
$$PE_i + KE_i = PE_f + KE_f$$
$$736 \text{ J} + 0 \text{ J} = 0 \text{ J} + (0.500)(25.0 \text{ kg})v_f^2$$

$$\boxed{v_f = 7.67 \text{ m/s}}$$

CALCULATOR SOLUTION

Your calculator should give an answer of 7.67333, but because the answer is limited to three significant figures, it should be rounded to 7.67.

continued on next page

4. EVALUATE The expression for the square of the final speed can be written as follows:

$$v_f^2 = \frac{2mgh}{m}$$

Notice that the masses cancel, so the final speed does not depend on the mass of the child. This makes sense because the acceleration of an object due to gravity does not depend on the mass of the object.

PRACTICE 5D

Conservation of mechanical energy

1. A bird is flying with a speed of 18.0 m/s over water when it accidentally drops a 2.00 kg fish. Assuming the altitude of the bird is 5.40 m, and disregarding friction, what is the speed of the fish when it hits the water?

2. A 755 N diver drops from a board 10.0 m above the water's surface.
   a. Find the diver's speed 5.00 m above the water's surface.
   b. Find the diver's speed just before striking the water.

3. If the diver in item 2 leaves the board with an initial downward speed of 2.00 m/s, find the diver's speed when striking the water.

4. An Olympic high jumper leaps over a horizontal bar. The jumper's center of mass is raised 0.25 m during the jump. Calculate the minimum speed with which the athlete must leave the ground to perform this feat.

5. A pendulum 2.0 m long is released from rest when the support string is at an angle of 25.0° with the vertical. What is the speed of the bob at the bottom of the swing?

Energy conservation occurs even when acceleration varies

If the slope of the slide in Sample Problem 5D were constant, the acceleration along the slide would also be constant, and the kinematic formulas from Chapter 2 could have been used to solve the problem. However, you do not know the shape of the slide. Thus, the acceleration may not be constant, and the kinematic formulas could not be used.

But now we can apply a new method to solve such a problem. Because the slide is frictionless, mechanical energy is conserved. We simply equate the initial mechanical energy to the final mechanical energy and ignore all the details in the middle. The shape of the slide is not a contributing factor to the system's mechanical energy as long as friction can be ignored.

Mechanical energy is not conserved in the presence of friction

If you have ever used a sanding block to sand a rough surface, such as in **Figure 5-11,** you may have noticed that you had to keep applying a force to keep the block moving. This is because kinetic friction between the moving block and the surface causes the kinetic energy of the block to be converted into a nonmechanical form of energy. As you continue to exert a force on the block, you are replacing the kinetic energy that is lost due to kinetic friction. The observable result of this energy dissipation is that the sanding block and the tabletop become warmer.

In the presence of kinetic friction, nonmechanical energy is no longer negligible and mechanical energy is no longer conserved. This does not mean that energy in general is not conserved—total energy is *always* conserved. However, the mechanical energy is converted into forms of energy that are much more difficult to account for, and the mechanical energy is therefore considered to be "lost."

(a)

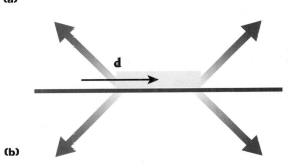

(b)

Figure 5-11
As the block slides **(a),** its kinetic energy tends to decrease because of friction. The force from the hand keeps it moving. Kinetic energy is dissipated into the block and surface **(b).**

Section Review

1. If the spring of a jack-in-the-box is compressed a distance of 8.00 cm from its relaxed length and then released, what is the speed of the toy head when the spring returns to its natural length? Assume the mass of the toy head is 50.0 g, the spring constant is 80.0 N/m, and the toy head moves only in the vertical direction. Also disregard the mass of the spring. (Hint: Remember that there are two forms of potential energy in the problem.)

2. You are designing a roller coaster in which a car will be pulled to the top of a hill of height h and then, starting from a momentary rest, be released to roll freely down the hill and toward the peak of the next hill, which is 1.1 times as high. Will your design be successful? Explain.

3. Is conservation of mechanical energy likely to hold in these situations?
   a. a hockey puck sliding on a frictionless surface of ice
   b. a toy car rolling on a carpeted floor
   c. a baseball being thrown into the air

4. **Physics in Action** What parts of the kinetic sculpture on pages 166 and 167 involve the conversion of one form of energy to another? Is mechanical energy conserved in these processes?

5-4
Work, energy, and power

5-4 SECTION OBJECTIVES

- Apply the work–kinetic energy theorem to solve problems.

- Relate the concepts of energy, time, and power.

- Calculate power in two different ways.

- Explain the effect of machines on work and power.

work–kinetic energy theorem

the net work done on an object is equal to the change in the kinetic energy of the object

THE WORK–KINETIC ENERGY THEOREM

Imagine that a person kicks a sled initially at rest on a frozen pond, as shown in **Figure 5-12.** There is kinetic friction between the sled and the ice, so the sled slows down and eventually stops. How far does the sled move?

Clearly, mechanical energy is not conserved, but there is a relationship between the work done on the sled and the change in the kinetic energy of the sled. This relationship is known as the **work–kinetic energy theorem** and is written as follows:

> **WORK–KINETIC ENERGY THEOREM**
>
> $$W_{net} = \Delta KE$$
>
> **net work = change in kinetic energy**

Notice that the type of force acting on the object is not specified in the work–kinetic energy theorem. Because it could be any force, the theorem applies to all objects universally. There is an alternative form for the work–kinetic energy theorem that is useful when the work is done by friction:

$$W_{friction} = \Delta ME$$

If a problem does not involve friction, then $W_{friction} = 0$ and the above equation can be simplified.

$$\Delta ME = 0$$
$$ME_i = ME_f$$

This is a statement of conservation of mechanical energy. Notice that the work–kinetic energy theorem in either form demonstrates that work is a method of transferring energy. A force that is perpendicular to the displacement of an object does no work on the object because no energy is transferred.

In solving problems, it is important to make a distinction between the two expressions $W = Fd(\cos \theta)$ and $W_{net} = \Delta KE$. The first expression applies to the work done by one object on another and is the definition of work. The second expression applies only to the net force on an object and relates the net work done on an object to the change in kinetic energy.

Figure 5-12
The net energy transferred to the sled by work equals the change in the sled's kinetic energy.

Work–kinetic energy theorem

PROBLEM

On a frozen pond, a person kicks a 10.0 kg sled, giving it an initial speed of 2.2 m/s. How far does the sled move if the coefficient of kinetic friction between the sled and the ice is 0.10?

SOLUTION

1. DEFINE

Given: $m = 10.0 \text{ kg}$ $v_i = 2.2 \text{ m/s}$ $v_f = 0 \text{ m/s}$ $\mu_k = 0.10$

Unknown: $d = ?$

Diagram:

2. PLAN

Choose an equation(s) or situation: This problem can be solved using the definition of work and the work–kinetic energy theorem.

$$W_{net} = F_{net}d(\cos \theta)$$
$$W_{net} = \Delta KE$$

The initial kinetic energy is given to the sled by the person.

$$KE_i = \frac{1}{2}mv_i^2$$

Because the sled comes to rest, the final kinetic energy is zero.

$$KE_f = 0$$
$$\Delta KE = KE_f - KE_i = -\frac{1}{2}mv_i^2$$

The net work done on the sled is provided by the force of kinetic friction.

$$W_{net} = F_{net}d(\cos \theta) = \mu_k mgd(\cos \theta)$$

The force of kinetic friction is in the direction opposite d.

$$\theta = 180°$$

3. CALCULATE

Substitute values into the equations:

$$W_{net} = (0.10)(10.0 \text{ kg})(9.81 \text{ m/s}^2) \, d \, (\cos 180°)$$
$$= (-9.8 \text{ N})d$$
$$\Delta KE = -KE_i = -(0.50)(10.0 \text{ kg})(2.2 \text{ m/s})^2 = -24 \text{ J}$$

Use the work–kinetic energy theorem to solve for d.

$$W_{net} = \Delta KE$$
$$(-9.8 \text{ N})d = -24 \text{ J}$$

continued on next page

$$\boxed{d = 2.4 \text{ m}}$$

CALCULATOR SOLUTION

Your calculator should give an answer of 2.44898, but because the answer is limited to two significant figures, this should be rounded to 2.4.

4. EVALUATE Note that because the direction of the force of kinetic friction is opposite the displacement, the net work done is negative. Also, according to Newton's second law, the acceleration of the sled is about -1 m/s^2 and the time it takes the sled to stop is about 2 s. Thus, the distance the sled traveled in the given amount of time should be less than the distance it would have traveled in the absence of friction.

$$2.4 \text{ m} < (2.2 \text{ m/s})(2 \text{ s}) = 4.4 \text{ m}$$

PRACTICE 5E

Work–kinetic energy theorem

1. A 2.0×10^3 kg car moves down a level highway under the actions of two forces. One is a 1140 N forward force exerted on the wheels by the road. The other is a 950 N resistive force exerted on the car by the air. Use the work–kinetic energy theorem to find the speed of the car after it has moved a distance of 20.0 m, assuming the car starts from rest.

2. A 2.10×10^3 kg car starts from rest at the top of a driveway 5.0 m long that is sloped at 20.0° with the horizontal. If an average friction force of 4.0×10^3 N impedes the motion, what is the speed of the car at the bottom of the driveway?

3. A 10.0 kg crate is pulled up a rough incline with an initial speed of 1.5 m/s. The pulling force is 100.0 N parallel to the incline, which makes an angle of 15.0° with the horizontal. Assuming the coefficient of kinetic friction is 0.40 and the crate is pulled a distance of 7.5 m, find the following:
   a. the work done by the Earth's gravity on the crate
   b. the work done by the force of friction on the crate
   c. the work done by the puller on the crate
   d. the change in kinetic energy of the crate
   e. the speed of the crate after it is pulled 7.5 m

POWER

power

the rate at which energy is transferred

The rate at which work is done is called **power.** More generally, power is the rate of energy transfer by any method. Like the concepts of energy and work, power has a specific meaning in science that differs from its everyday meaning.

Imagine you are producing a play and you need to raise and lower the curtain between scenes in a specific amount of time. You decide to use a motor that will pull on a rope connected to the top of the curtain rod. Your assistant finds three motors but doesn't know which one to use. One way to decide is to consider the power output of each motor.

If the work done on an object is W in a time interval Δt, then the power delivered to the object over this time interval is written as follows:

POWER

$$P = \frac{W}{\Delta t}$$

power = work ÷ time

It is sometimes useful to rewrite this equation in an alternative form by substituting the definition of work into the definition of power.

$$W = Fd$$
$$P = \frac{W}{\Delta t} = F\frac{d}{\Delta t}$$

The distance moved per unit time is just the speed of the object.

POWER (ALTERNATIVE FORM)

$$P = Fv$$

power = force × speed

The SI unit of power is the *watt*, W, which is defined to be 1 J/s. The *horsepower*, hp, is another unit of power that is sometimes used. One horsepower is equal to 746 W.

The watt is perhaps most familiar to you from your everyday experience with light bulbs (see **Figure 5-13**). A dim light bulb requires about 40 W to operate, while a bright bulb can require up to 500 W. Decorative lights need about 0.7 W each for indoor lights and 7.0 W each for outdoor lights.

Figure 5-13
The wattage of each of these bulbs tells you the rate at which energy is converted by the bulb. The bulbs in this photo require wattages ranging from 0.7 W to 200 W.

Conceptual Challenge

1. Mountain roads Many mountain roads are built so that they zigzag up the mountain rather than go straight up toward the peak. Discuss the advantages of such a design from the viewpoint of energy conservation and power.

2. Light bulbs A light bulb is described as *having* 60 watts. What's wrong with this phrase?

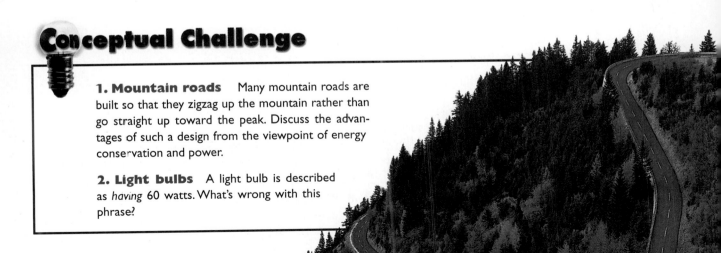

Power

PROBLEM

A 193 kg curtain needs to be raised 7.5 m in as close to 5.0 s as possible. Three motors are available. The power ratings for the three motors are listed as 1.0 kW, 3.5 kW, and 5.5 kW. Which motor is best for the job?

SOLUTION

Given: $m = 193$ kg $\quad \Delta t = 5.0$ s $\quad d = 7.5$ m

Unknown: $P = ?$

Use the power equation from page 187.

$$P = \frac{W}{\Delta t} = \frac{Fd}{\Delta t} = \frac{mgd}{\Delta t}$$

$$= \frac{(193 \text{ kg})(9.81 \text{ m/s}^2)(7.5 \text{ m})}{5.0 \text{ s}}$$

$$P = 2.8 \times 10^3 \text{ W} = 2.8 \text{ kW}$$

The best motor to use is the 3.5 kW motor. The 1.0 kW motor will not lift the curtain fast enough, and the 5.5 kW motor will lift the curtain too fast.

Power

1. A 1.0×10^3 kg elevator carries a maximum load of 800.0 kg. A constant frictional force of 4.0×10^3 N retards the elevator's motion upward. What minimum power, in kilowatts, must the motor deliver to lift the fully loaded elevator at a constant speed of 3.00 m/s?

2. A 1.50×10^3 kg car accelerates uniformly from rest to 10.0 m/s in 3.00 s.
   a. What is the work done on the car in this time interval?
   b. What is the power delivered by the engine in this time interval?

3. A car with a mass of 1.50×10^3 kg starts from rest and accelerates to 18.0 m/s in 12.0 s. Assume that air resistance remains constant at 400.0 N during this time. What is the average power developed by the engine?

4. A rain cloud contains 2.66×10^7 kg of water vapor. How long would it take for a 2.00 kW pump to raise the same amount of water to the cloud's altitude, 2.00 km?

Machines with different power ratings do the same work in different time intervals

In Sample Problem 5F, the three motors would lift the curtain at different rates because the power output for each motor is different. This means that each motor would do work on the curtain at different rates, thus transferring energy to the curtain at different rates.

In a given amount of time, each motor would do different amounts of work on the curtain. The 5.5 kW motor would do the most amount of work in a given time, and the 1.0 kW motor would do the least amount of work in the same time. Yet they would all perform the same total amount of work in lifting the curtain. The important difference is that the more powerful motor could do the work in a shorter time interval.

CONCEPT PREVIEW

Machines will be discussed further in Chapter 8.

Section Review

1. A 50.0 kg parachutist jumps out of an airplane at a height of 1.00 km. The parachute opens, and the jumper lands on the ground with a speed of 5.00 m/s. By what amount was the jumper's mechanical energy reduced due to air resistance during this jump? What was the average force of air friction during the jumper's descent if the parachute opened immediately after jumping?

2. A 50.0 kg student climbs 5.00 m up a rope at a constant speed. If the student's power output is 200.0 W, how long does it take the student to climb the rope? How much work does the student do?

3. How are energy, time, and power related?

4. Two movers have to lift a refrigerator onto a truck, as shown in **Figure 5-14**. One of the movers wants to lift the refrigerator vertically, but the other mover wants to roll it up a ramp by applying a force parallel to the ramp. Assume the height of the truck is 1.5 m, the length of the ramp is 5.0 m, and the weight of the refrigerator is 1200.0 N. Calculate the force and the total work required in each case. Which method is easier?

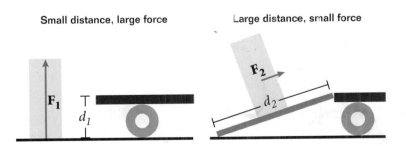

Small distance, large force   Large distance, small force

Figure 5-14

The Equivalence of MASS and ENERGY

Einstein's $E_0 = mc^2$ is one of the most famous equations of the twentieth century. This equation was a surprise to Einstein, who discovered it through his work with relative velocity and kinetic energy.

Relativistic kinetic energy

In the "Relativistic addition of velocities" feature, in Chapter 3, you learned how Einstein's special theory of relativity modifies the classical addition of velocities. Because of this, the classical equation for kinetic energy ($KE = \frac{1}{2}mv^2$) must also be modified for relativity. In 1905, Einstein derived a new equation for kinetic energy based on the principles of special relativity:

$$KE = \frac{mc^2}{\sqrt{1 - \left(\frac{v^2}{c^2}\right)}} - mc^2$$

In this equation, m is the mass of the object, v is the velocity of the object, and c is the speed of light. (Some texts distinguish between a rest mass, m_0, and a relativistic mass, m; in this book, relativistic mass is not used, and m always refers to rest mass.) Although it isn't immediately obvious, this equation reduces to the classical equation $KE = \frac{1}{2}mv^2$ for speeds that are small compared with the speed of light, as shown in **Figure 5-15.**

Einstein's relativistic expression for kinetic energy has been confirmed by experiments in which electrons are accelerated to extremely high speeds in particle accelerators. In all cases, the experimental data correspond to Einstein's equation rather than to the classical equation. Nonetheless, the difference between the two theories at low speeds (relative to c) is so minimal that the classical equation can be used in all such cases when the speed is much less than c.

Figure 5-15

This graph of kinetic energy versus velocity for both the classical and relativistic equations shows that the two theories are in agreement when v is much less than c. Note that v is always less than c in the relativistic case.

Rest energy

The second term of Einstein's equation for kinetic energy, $-mc^2$, is required so that $KE = 0$ when $v = 0$. Note that this term is independent of velocity. This suggests that the *total* energy of an object equals its kinetic energy plus some additional form of energy equal to mc^2. The mathematical expression of this additional energy is the familiar Einstein equation:

$$E_0 = mc^2$$

This equation shows that an object has a certain amount of energy (E_0), known as *rest energy*, simply by virtue of its mass. The rest energy of a body is equal to its mass, m, multiplied by the speed of light squared, c^2. Thus, the mass of a body is a measure of its rest energy. This equation is significant because rest energy is an aspect of special relativity that was not predicted by classical physics.

Experimental verification

The magnitude of the conversion factor between mass and rest energy ($c^2 = 9 \times 10^{16}$ m^2/s^2) is so great that even a very small mass has a huge amount of rest energy. Nuclear reactions utilize this relationship by converting mass (rest energy) into other forms of energy. For example, in nuclear fission, which is the energy source of nuclear power plants, the nucleus of an atom is split into two or more nuclei. Taken together, the mass of these nuclei is slightly less than the mass of the original nucleus, and a very large amount of energy is released. In typical nuclear reactions, about one-thousandth of the initial mass is converted from rest energy into other forms of energy. This change in mass, although very small, can be detected experimentally.

Another type of nuclear reaction that converts mass into energy is fusion, which is the source of energy for our sun and other stars. About 4.5 million tons of the sun's mass is converted into other forms of energy every second. Fortunately, the sun has enough mass to last approximately 5 billion more years.

Most of the energy changes encountered in your typical experiences are much smaller than the energy changes that occur in nuclear reactions. As a result, the change in mass is even less than that observed in nuclear reactions. Such changes are far too small to be detected experimentally. Thus, for typical cases, the classical equation still holds, and mass and energy can be thought of as separate.

Before Einstein's theory of relativity, conservation of energy and conservation of mass were regarded as two separate laws. The equivalence between mass and energy reveals that in fact these two laws are one. In the words of Einstein, "Prerelativity physics contains two conservation laws of fundamental importance. . . . Through relativity theory, they melt together into *one* principle."

Figure 5-16
Electrons in the Stanford Linear Accelerator, in California, (SLAC) reach 99.999999967 percent of the speed of light. At such great speeds, the difference between classical and relativistic theories becomes significant.

Figure 5-17
Our sun uses a nuclear reaction called fusion to convert mass to energy. About 90 percent of the stars, including our sun, fuse hydrogen, while some older stars fuse helium.

CHAPTER 5
Summary

KEY TERMS

elastic potential energy
(p. 175)

gravitational potential
energy (p. 174)

kinetic energy (p. 172)

mechanical energy (p. 177)

potential energy (p. 174)

power (p. 186)

spring constant (p. 175)

work (p. 168)

work–kinetic energy
theorem (p. 184)

KEY IDEAS

Section 5-1 Work
- Work is done on an object only when a net force acts on the object to displace it in the direction of a component of the net force.
- The amount of work done on an object is given by the following equation, where θ is the angle between the applied force, F, and the displacement of the object, d:

$$W = Fd(\cos \theta)$$

Section 5-2 Energy
- Objects in motion possess kinetic energy due to their mass and velocity.
- Potential energy is energy associated with an object's position. Two forms of potential energy discussed in this chapter are gravitational potential energy and elastic potential energy.
- Mechanical energy is the total kinetic and potential energy present in a given situation.

Section 5-3 Conservation of energy
- Energy can change form but can never be created or destroyed.
- In the absence of friction, mechanical energy is conserved, so the amount of mechanical energy remains constant.

Section 5-4 Work, energy, and power
- The net work done on or by an object is equal to the change in the kinetic energy of the object.
- Power is the rate at which work is done or the rate of energy transfer.
- Machines with different power ratings do the same amount of work in different time intervals.

Variable symbols

Quantities		Units		Conversions
W	work	J	joule	$= N \bullet m$ $= kg \bullet m^2/s^2$
KE	kinetic energy	J	joule	
PE_g	gravitational potential energy	J	joule	
$PE_{elastic}$	elastic potential energy	J	joule	
P	power	W	watt	$= J/s$

WORK

Review questions

1. Can the speed of an object change if the net work done on it is zero?

2. Discuss whether any work is being done by each of the following agents and, if so, whether the work is positive or negative.
   a. a chicken scratching the ground
   b. a person studying
   c. a crane lifting a bucket of concrete
   d. the force of gravity on the bucket in (c).

3. Furniture movers wish to load a truck using a ramp from the ground to the rear of the truck. One of the movers claims that less work would be required if the ramp's length were increased, reducing its angle with the horizontal. Is this claim valid? Explain.

Conceptual questions

4. A pendulum swings back and forth, as shown in **Figure 5-18.** Does the tension force in the string do work on the pendulum bob? Does the force of gravity do work on the bob? Explain your answers.

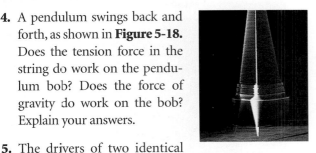

Figure 5-18

5. The drivers of two identical cars heading toward each other apply the brakes at the same instant. The skid marks of one of the cars are twice as long as the skid marks of the other vehicle. Assuming that the brakes of both cars apply the same force, what conclusions can you draw about the motion of the cars?

6. When a punter kicks a football, is he doing work on the ball while his toe is in contact with it? Is he doing work on the ball after the ball loses contact with his toe? Are any forces doing work on the ball while the ball is in flight?

Practice problems

7. A person lifts a 4.5 kg cement block a vertical distance 1.2 m and then carries the block horizontally a distance 7.3 m. Determine the work done by the person and by the force of gravity in this process. (See Sample Problem 5A.)

8. A flight attendant pulls her 70.0 N flight bag a distance of 253 m along a level airport floor at a constant speed. The force she exerts is 40.0 N at an angle of 52.0° above the horizontal. Find the following:
   a. the work she does on the flight bag
   b. the work done by the force of friction on the flight bag
   c. the coefficient of kinetic friction between the flight bag and the floor

   (See Sample Problem 5A.)

9. A plane designed for vertical takeoff has a mass of 8.0×10^3 kg. Find the net work done by all forces on the plane as it accelerates upward at 1.0 m/s^2 through a distance of 30.0 m after starting from rest. (See Sample Problem 5A.)

10. A catcher "gives" with a baseball when catching it. If the baseball exerts a force of 475 N on the glove, so that the glove is displaced 10.0 cm, how much work is done by the ball? (See Sample Problem 5A.)

ENERGY

Review questions

11. A person drops a ball from the top of a building while another person on the ground observes the ball's motion. Will these two people always agree on the following?
   a. the ball's potential energy
   b. the ball's change in potential energy
   c. the ball's kinetic energy

12. Can the kinetic energy of an object be negative? Explain.

13. Can the gravitational potential energy of an object be negative? Explain.

14. Two identical objects move with speeds of 5.0 m/s and 25.0 m/s. What is the ratio of their kinetic energies?

15. Each of the following objects possesses energy. Which forms of energy are mechanical and which are nonmechanical?
    a. glowing embers in a campfire
    b. a strong wind
    c. a swinging pendulum
    d. a person sitting on a mattress
    e. a rocket being launched into space

Practice problems

16. What is the kinetic energy of an automobile with a mass of 1250 kg traveling with a speed of 11 m/s? (See Sample Problem 5B.)

17. What speed would a fly with a mass of 0.55 g need in order to have the same kinetic energy as the automobile in item 16? (See Sample Problem 5B.)

18. A 60.0 kg skier is at the top of a slope, as in **Figure 5-19.** At the initial point **A,** the skier is 10.0 m vertically above the final point **B.**
    a. Set the zero level for gravitational potential energy at **B,** and find the gravitational potential energy of the skier at **A** and at **B.** Then find the difference in potential energy between these two points.
    b. Repeat this problem with the zero level at point **A.**
    c. Repeat this problem with the zero level midway down the slope, at a height of 5.0 m.
(See Sample Problem 5C.)

Figure 5-19

19. A 2.00 kg ball is attached to a ceiling by a 1.00 m long string. The height of the room is 3.00 m. What is the gravitational potential energy of the ball relative to each of the following?
    a. the ceiling
    b. the floor
    c. a point at the same elevation as the ball
(See Sample Problem 5C.)

20. A spring has a force constant of 500.0 N/m. Show that the energy stored in the spring is as follows:
    a. 0.400 J when the spring is stretched 4.00 cm from equilibrium
    b. 0.225 J when the spring is compressed 3.00 cm from equilibrium
    c. zero when the spring is unstretched
(See Sample Problem 5C.)

CONSERVATION OF MECHANICAL ENERGY

Review questions

21. Discuss the energy transformations that occur during the pole-vault event shown in **Figure 5-20.** Disregard rotational motion and air resistance.

Figure 5-20

22. A bowling ball is suspended from the center of the ceiling of a lecture hall by a strong cord. The ball is drawn up to the tip of a lecturer's nose at the front of the room and then released. If the lecturer remains stationary, explain why the lecturer is not struck by the ball on its return swing. Would this person be safe if the ball were given a slight push from its starting position at the person's nose?

Conceptual questions

23. A ball is thrown straight up. At what position is its kinetic energy at its maximum? At what position is gravitational potential energy at its maximum?

24. Advertisements for a toy ball once stated that it would rebound to a height greater than the height from which it was dropped. Is this possible?

25. A weight is connected to a spring that is suspended vertically from the ceiling. If the weight is displaced downward from its equilibrium position and released, it will oscillate up and down. How many forms of potential energy are involved? If air resistance and friction are disregarded, will the total mechanical energy be conserved? Explain.

Practice problems

26. A 215 g particle is released from rest at point **A** inside a smooth hemispherical bowl of radius 30.0 cm, as shown in **Figure 5-21.** Calculate the following:

Figure 5-21

   a. the gravitational potential energy at **A** relative to **B**
   b. the particle's kinetic energy at **B**
   c. the particle's speed at **B**
   d. the kinetic energy and potential energy at **C**
(See Sample Problem 5D.)

27. A child and sled with a combined mass of 50.0 kg slide down a frictionless hill. If the sled starts from rest and has a speed of 12.0 m/s at the bottom, what is the height of the hill?
(See Sample Problem 5D.)

28. Tarzan swings on a 30.0 m long vine initially inclined at an angle of 37.0° with the vertical. What is his speed at the bottom of the swing if he does the following?

   a. starts from rest
   b. pushes off with a speed of 4.00 m/s
(See Sample Problem 5D.)

29. A 50.0 kg pole vaulter running at 10.0 m/s vaults over the bar. Assuming that the vaulter's horizontal component of velocity over the bar is 1.0 m/s and disregarding air resistance, how high was the jump? (See Sample Problem 5D.)

30. Tarzan and Jane, whose total mass is 130.0 kg, start their swing on a 5.0 m long vine when the vine is at an angle of 30.0° with the horizontal. At the bottom of the arc, Jane, whose mass is 50.0 kg, releases the vine. What is the maximum height at which Tarzan can land on a branch after his swing continues? (Hint: Treat Tarzan's and Jane's energies as separate quantities.)
(See Sample Problem 5D.)

31. A 0.250 kg block on a vertical spring with a spring constant of 5.00×10^3 N/m is pushed downward, compressing the spring 0.100 m. When released, the block leaves the spring and travels upward vertically. How high does it rise above the point of release? (See Sample Problem 5D.)

WORK–KINETIC ENERGY THEOREM AND POWER

Conceptual questions

32. Discuss the production and dissipation of mechanical energy as an athlete does the following:

   a. lifts a weight
   b. holds the weight up in a fixed position
   c. lowers the weight slowly

33. A satellite is in a circular orbit above Earth's surface. Why is the work done on the satellite by the gravitational force zero? What does the work–kinetic energy theorem predict about the satellite's speed?

34. A car traveling at 50.0 km/h skids a distance of 35 m after its brakes lock. Estimate how far it will skid if its brakes lock when its initial speed is 100.0 km/h. What happens to the car's kinetic energy as it comes to rest?

35. Explain why more energy is needed to walk down stairs than to walk horizontally at the same speed.

36. How can the work–kinetic energy theorem explain why the force of sliding friction usually reduces the kinetic energy of a particle?

Practice problems

37. A 50.0 kg diver steps off a 10.0 m high diving board and drops straight down into the water. If the diver comes to rest 5.0 m below the surface of the water, determine the average resistance force exerted on the diver by the water.
(See Sample Problem 5E.)

38. A person doing a chin-up weighs 700.0 N, disregarding the weight of the arms. During the first 25.0 cm of the lift, each arm exerts an upward force of 355 N on the torso. If the upward movement starts from rest, what is the person's speed at this point?
(See Sample Problem 5E.)

39. In a circus performance, a monkey on a sled is given an initial speed of 4.0 m/s up a 25° incline. The combined mass of the monkey and the sled is 20.0 kg, and the coefficient of kinetic friction between the sled and the incline is 0.20. How far up the incline does the sled move?
(See Sample Problem 5E.)

40. An 80.0 N box of clothes is pulled 20.0 m up a 30.0° ramp by a force of 115 N that points along the ramp. If the coefficient of kinetic friction between the box and ramp is 0.22, calculate the change in the box's kinetic energy.
(See Sample Problem 5E.)

41. A 98.0 N grocery cart is pushed 12.0 m along an aisle by a shopper who exerts a constant horizontal force of 40.0 N. If all frictional forces are neglected and the cart starts from rest, what is the grocery cart's final speed?
(See Sample Problem 5E.)

42. When an automobile moves with constant velocity, the power developed is used to overcome the frictional forces exerted by air and road. If the power developed in an engine is 50.0 hp, what total frictional force acts on the car at 24.6 m/s? (Hint: Note that one horsepower, 1 hp, is equal to 746 W.)
(See Sample Problem 5F.)

43. Water flows over a section of Niagara Falls at the rate of 1.2×10^6 kg/s and falls 50.0 m. How much power is generated by the falling water?
(See Sample Problem 5F.)

MIXED REVIEW PROBLEMS

44. Three identical balls, all with the same initial speed, are thrown by a juggling clown on a tightrope. The first ball is thrown horizontally, the second is thrown at some angle above the horizontal, and the third is thrown at some angle below the horizontal. Disregarding air resistance, describe the motions of the three balls, and compare the speed of the balls as they reach the ground.

45. A 0.60 kg rubber ball has a speed of 2.0 m/s at point A and kinetic energy of 7.5 J at point B. Determine the following:
  a. the ball's kinetic energy at A
  b. the ball's speed at B
  c. the total work done on the ball as it moves from A to B

46. Starting from rest, a 5.0 kg block slides 2.5 m down a rough 30.0° incline in 2.0 s. Determine the following:
  a. the work done by the force of gravity
  b. the mechanical energy lost to friction
  c. the work done by the normal force between the block and the incline

47. A 70.0 kg base runner begins his slide into second base while moving at a speed of 4.0 m/s. The coefficient of friction between his clothes and Earth is 0.70. He slides so that his speed is zero just as he reaches the base.
  a. How much mechanical energy is lost due to friction acting on the runner?
  b. How far does he slide?

48. A horizontal force of 150 N is used to push a 40.0 kg packing crate a distance of 6.00 m on a rough horizontal surface. If the crate moves at constant speed, calculate the following:
  a. the work done by the force
  b. the coefficient of kinetic friction

49. A 5.00 g bullet moving at 600.0 m/s penetrates a tree trunk to a depth of 4.00 cm.
  a. Use work and energy considerations to find the average frictional force that stops the bullet.
  b. Assuming that the frictional force is constant, determine how much time elapses between the moment the bullet enters the tree and the moment the bullet stops moving.

50. A skier of mass 70.0 kg is pulled up a slope by a motor-driven cable. How much work is required to pull the skier 60.0 m up a 35° slope (assumed to be frictionless) at a constant speed of 2.0 m/s?

51. A 2.50×10^3 kg car requires 5.0 kJ of work to move from rest to some final speed. During this time, the car moves 25.0 m. Neglecting friction between the car and the road, find the following:

  a. the final speed
  b. the horizontal force exerted on the car

52. A ski jumper starts from rest 50.0 m above the ground on a frictionless track, and flies off the track at a 45.0° angle above the horizontal and at a height of 10.0 m from the ground. Disregard air resistance.

  a. What is the skier's speed when leaving the track?
  b. What is the maximum height attained?

53. Figure 5-22 is a graph of the gravitational potential energy and kinetic energy of a 75 g yo-yo as it moves up and down on its string. Use the graph to answer the following questions:

  a. By what amount does the mechanical energy of the yo-yo decrease after 6.0 s?
  b. What is the speed of the yo-yo after 4.5 s?
  c. What is the maximum height of the yo-yo?

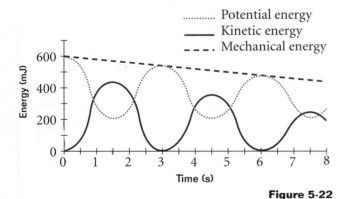

Figure 5-22

54. A skier starts from rest at the top of a hill that is inclined at 10.5° with the horizontal. The hillside is 200.0 m long, and the coefficient of friction between the snow and the skis is 0.0750. At the bottom of the hill, the snow is level and the coefficient of friction is unchanged. How far does the skier move along the horizontal portion of the snow before coming to rest?

55. Starting from rest, a 10.0 kg suitcase slides 3.00 m down a frictionless ramp inclined at 30.0° from the floor. The suitcase then slides an additional 5.00 m along the floor before coming to a stop. Determine the following:

  a. the speed of the suitcase at the bottom of the ramp
  b. the coefficient of kinetic friction between the suitcase and the floor
  c. the mechanical energy lost due to friction

56. A surprising demonstration involves dropping an egg from a third-floor window so that the egg lands on a foam-rubber pad without breaking. If a 56.0 g egg falls 12.0 m from rest and the 5.00 cm thick foam pad stops it in 6.25 ms, by how much is the pad compressed? Assume constant upward acceleration as the egg compresses the foam-rubber pad. (Hint: Assume that the gravitational potential energy that the egg gains while the pad is being compressed is negligible.)

57. A 75 kg man jumps from a window 1.0 m above a sidewalk.

  a. What is his speed just before his feet strike the pavement?
  b. If the man jumps with his knees and ankles locked, the only cushion for his fall is approximately 0.50 cm in the pads of his feet. Calculate the average force exerted on him by the ground in this situation.

58. A projectile of mass 5.0 kg is shot horizontally with an initial speed of 17 m/s from a height of 25.0 m above a flat desert surface. For the instant before the projectile hits the surface, calculate each of the following quantities:

  a. the work done on the projectile by gravity
  b. the change in kinetic energy since the projectile was fired
  c. the final kinetic energy of the projectile

59. A light horizontal spring has a spring constant of 105 N/m. A 2.00 kg block is pressed against one end of the spring, compressing the spring 0.100 m. After the block is released, the block moves 0.250 m to the right before coming to rest. What is the coefficient of kinetic friction between the horizontal surface and the block?

60. A 5.0 kg block is pushed 3.0 m at a constant speed up a vertical wall by a constant force applied at an angle of 30.0° with the horizontal, as shown in **Figure 5-23.** If the coefficient of kinetic friction between the block and the wall is 0.30, determine:

Figure 5-23

   a. the work done by the force on the block
   b. the work done by gravity on the block
   c. the normal force between the block and the wall

61. A 25 kg child on a 2.0 m long swing is released from rest when the swing supports make an angle of 30.0° with the vertical.

   a. What is the maximum potential energy that the child has?
   b. Disregarding friction, find the child's speed at the lowest position.
   c. What is the child's total mechanical energy?
   d. If the speed of the child at the lowest position is 2.00 m/s, what is the mechanical energy lost due to friction?

Technology & Learning

Graphing calculators

Program your graphing calculator to create a table for work done, given an applied force and an angle. Use the program to determine how much work is done on a sled by a person pulling on the sled on level ground in the following situations:

   a. a constant force of 225 N at an angle of 35° for a distance of 15 m
   b. the same force at the same angle for a distance of 22 m
   c. a constant force of 215 N at an angle of 25° for a distance of 15 m
   d. the same force at the same angle for a distance of 22 m

First, be certain the calculator is in degree mode by pressing [MODE] [▼] [▼] [►] [ENTER]. Press [Y] [=] [CLEAR] to clear any functions.

Open a new program by pressing [PRGM] [►] [►] [ENTER]. Name the program "WORK" and press [ENTER]. Then enter the program in the table below.

To exit the program editor, press [2nd] [QUIT]. To run the program, press [PRGM], select "WORK," and press [ENTER] [ENTER]. Enter the values for force and the angle, pressing [ENTER] after each. The calculator will provide a table of the work done (Y1) for the given displacement X. Press [ENTER] to exit the table.

Keystrokes	**Display**
	PROGRAM: WORK
1. [PRGM] [►] [2] [ALPHA] [F] [ENTER]	:PROMPT F
2. [PRGM] [►] [2] [ALPHA] [θ] [ENTER]	:PROMPT θ
3. [ALPHA] ["] [ALPHA] [F] [X,T,θ] [COS] [ALPHA] [θ] [ALPHA] ["] [STO►] [2nd] [Y-VARS] [1] [1] [ENTER]	:"FXCOSθ" → Y1
4. [0] [STO►] [VARS] [6] [1] [ENTER]	:0→ TBLMIN
5. [1] [STO►] [VARS] [6] [2] [ENTER]	:1 → ΔTBL
6. [PRGM] [►] [5] [ENTER]	:DISPTABLE

62. A particle of mass 522 g starts at rest and slides down a frictionless track, as shown in **Figure 5-24**. It leaves the track horizontally, striking the ground.

    a. At what height above the ground does the ball start to move?

    b. What is the ball's velocity when it leaves the track?

    c. What is the ball's velocity when it hits the ground?

Figure 5-24

Alternative Assessment

Performance assessment

1. Design experiments for measuring your power output when doing pushups, running up a flight of stairs, pushing a car, loading boxes onto a truck, throwing a baseball, or performing other energy-transferring activities. What data do you need to measure or calculate? Form groups to present and discuss your plans. If your teacher approves your plans, perform the experiments.

2. Investigate the amount of kinetic energy involved when your car's speed is 60 km/h, 50 km/h, 40 km/h, 30 km/h, 20 km/h, and 10 km/h. (Hint: Find your car's mass in the owner's manual.) How much work does the brake system have to do to stop the car at each speed?

If the owner's manual includes a table of braking distances at different speeds, determine the force the braking system must exert. Organize your findings in charts and graphs to study the questions and to present your conclusions.

3. Investigate the energy transformations of your body as you swing on a swingset. Working with a partner, measure the height of the swing at the high and low points of your motion. What points involve a maximum gravitational potential energy? What points involve a maximum kinetic energy? For three other points in the path of the swing, calculate the gravitational potential energy, the kinetic energy, and the velocity. Organize your findings in bar graphs.

Portfolio projects

4. In order to save fuel, an airline executive recommended the following changes in the airlines' largest jet flights:

    a. restrict the weight of personal luggage

    b. remove pillows, blankets, and magazines from the cabin

    c. lower flight altitudes by 5 percent

    d. reduce flying speeds by 5 percent

Research the information necessary to calculate the approximate kinetic and potential energy of a large passenger aircraft. Which of the measures described above would result in significant savings? What might be their other consequences? Summarize your conclusions in a presentation or report.

5. Make a chart of the kinetic energies your body can have. Measure your mass and speed when walking, running, sprinting, riding a bicycle, and driving a car. Make a poster graphically comparing these findings.

6. You are trying to find a way to bring electricity to a remote village in order to run a water-purifying device. A donor is willing to provide battery chargers that connect to bicycles. Assuming the water-purification device requires 18.6 kW•h daily, how many bicycles would a village need if a person can average 100 W while riding a bicycle? Is this a useful way to help the village? How would you schedule the use of these chargers? Summarize your comments and suggestions in a letter to the donor.

CHAPTER 5
Laboratory Exercise

OBJECTIVES

- Determine the spring constant of a spring.
- Calculate elastic potential energy.
- Calculate gravitational potential energy.
- Determine whether mechanical energy is conserved in an oscillating spring.

MATERIALS LIST

✔ meterstick
✔ set of masses
✔ support stand and clamp

PROCEDURE

CBL AND SENSORS

✔ C-clamp
✔ CBL
✔ CBL motion detector
✔ force sensor with CBL-DIN adapter
✔ graphing calculator with link cable
✔ lattice rod and right angle clamp
✔ spring
✔ tape
✔ wire letter basket

HOOKE'S LAW APPARATUS

✔ Hooke's law apparatus
✔ rubber bands

CONSERVATION OF MECHANICAL ENERGY

A mass on a spring will oscillate vertically when it is lifted to the length of the relaxed spring and released. The gravitational potential energy increases from a minimum at the lowest point to a maximum at the highest point. The elastic potential energy in the spring increases from a minimum at the highest point, where the spring is relaxed, to a maximum at the lowest point, where the spring is stretched. Because the mass is temporarily at rest, the kinetic energy of the mass is zero at the highest and lowest points. Thus, the total mechanical energy at those points is the sum of the elastic potential energy and the gravitational potential energy.

SAFETY

- **Tie back long hair, secure loose clothing, and remove loose jewelry to prevent their getting caught in moving or rotating parts.**
- **Attach masses securely. Perform this experiment in a clear area. Swinging or dropped masses can cause serious injury.**

PREPARATION

1. Determine whether you will be using the CBL and sensors or the Hooke's law apparatus to perform this experiment. Read the entire lab procedure for the appropriate method. Plan the steps you will take.

2. Prepare a data table in your lab notebook with four columns and seven rows. In the first row, label the first through fourth columns *Trial, Mass (kg), Stretched spring (m),* and *Force (N).* In the first column, label the second through seventh rows *1, 2, 3, 4, 5,* and *6.* Above or below the data table, make a space to enter the value for *Initial spring (m).*

3. Prepare a second data table in your lab notebook with three columns and seven rows. In the first row, label the first through third columns *Trial, Highest point (m),* and *Lowest point (m).* In the first column, label the second through seventh rows *1, 2, 3, 4, 5,* and *6.* Above or below the data table, make a space to enter the value for *Initial distance (m).*

Hooke's law apparatus procedure begins on page 203.

PROCEDURE

CBL AND SENSORS

Spring constant

4. Set up the CBL, graphing calculator, force sensor, and motion detector as shown in **Figure 5-25**.

5. Connect the CBL unit to the calculator with the unit-to-unit link cable using the ports located on each unit. Connect the force sensor to the CH1 port on the CBL unit, and connect the motion detector to the SONIC port.

6. Place the ring stand near the edge of the lab table. Use the C-clamp to clamp the base of the ring stand securely to the table. Position the clamp so that it protrudes as little as possible from the edge of the table. Attach the force sensor to the ring stand with the lattice rod and clamp.

7. Hook one end of the spring securely onto the force sensor. Attach the mass hanger securely to the spring. Tape the motion detector onto a lab stool directly below the force sensor so that the motion detector faces up. The motion detector should be more than 0.5 m away from the mass hanger on the bottom of the spring. Place the wire letter basket upside down over the motion detector to protect the sensor in case the masses fall.

8. Measure the distance from the floor to the top of the motion detector. Record this as *Initial distance (m)* in your data table. This distance must remain constant throughout the lab.

9. Turn on the CBL and the graphing calculator. Start the program PHYSICS on the graphing calculator.

   a. Select option *SET UP PROBES* from the MAIN MENU. Enter 2 for the number of probes. Select the motion detector, and then select the force sensor from the list. Your teacher will tell you what kind of force sensor you are using. Enter 1 for the channel number. Select *USE STORED* from the CALIBRATION menu.

   b. Select the *COLLECT DATA* option from the MAIN MENU. Select the *TIME GRAPH* option from the DATA COLLECTION menu. Enter 0.02 for the time between samples. Enter 99 for the number of samples. Check the values you entered, and press ENTER. Press ENTER to continue. If you made a mistake entering the time values, select MODIFY SETUP, reenter the values, and continue.

Figure 5-25

Step 6: Attach the force sensor securely to the ring stand. Tape the force sensor lead to the stand to keep it out of the way while you work.

Step 7: Make sure the motion detector is directly below the hanging mass. Make sure the force sensor is far enough over the edge of the table so that the motion detector will read the position of the mass without interference from the tabletop.

Step 9: In this part of the lab, you will collect data to find the spring constant of the spring.

Step 14: In this part of the lab, you will oscillate a mass on the spring to find out whether mechanical energy is conserved.

10. Press ENTER on the graphing calculator to begin collecting data. The motion detector will begin to click as it collects data. When the motion detector stops clicking and the CBL shows DONE, press ENTER on the graphing calculator.

11. Select the *SONIC* option from the SELECT CHANNELS menu. Select *DISTANCE* to plot a graph of the distance in meters against the time in seconds. Press TRACE on the graphing calculator, and use the arrow keys to trace the graph. The distance (y) values should be fairly constant. Record this value as *Initial spring (m)* in your data table. Press ENTER on the graphing calculator. Select *RETURN* from the SELECT CHANNEL menu. Select *RETURN* again. Select *YES* from the REPEAT? menu.

12. Add enough mass to stretch the spring to about 1.25 times its original length. Record the mass in the first data table. Press ENTER on the graphing calculator. The motion detector will begin to click as it collects data. When the motion detector stops clicking and the CBL shows DONE, press ENTER on the graphing calculator.

   a. Select the *ANALOG* option from the SELECT CHANNELS menu. This graphs the force in newtons for each second. Use the arrow keys to trace the graph. The force (y) values should be fairly constant. Record this value in the first data table. Sketch the graph in your lab notebook. Press ENTER on the graphing calculator.

   b. Select the *SONIC* option from the SELECT CHANNELS menu. Select *DISTANCE* to plot a graph of the distance in meters against the time in seconds. Use the arrow keys to trace the graph. The distance (y) values should be fairly constant. Record this value as *Stretched spring (m)* in your data table. Press ENTER on the graphing calculator. Select *RETURN* from the SELECT CHANNEL menu. Select *RETURN* again. Select *YES* from the REPEAT? menu.

13. Perform several trials with increasing masses. Record the mass, force, and distance measurements in the first data table for each trial.

Conservation of mechanical energy

14. Starting with a small mass and gradually increasing the mass in small increments, place masses on the mass hanger until you find a mass that will stretch the spring to about twice its original length. Record the mass in the second data table. Leave the mass in place on the hanger so that the spring remains stretched.

15. Raise the mass hanger until the mass hanger is at the zero position, the position where you measured the *Initial spring* measurement.

16. Press ENTER on the graphing calculator and simultaneously release the hanger gently to let the hanger drop. The motion detector will begin to click as it collects data. It is best to release the hanger from above and pull your hand out quickly to the side. If your hand passes between the hanger and the motion detector it will seriously affect your measurements.

17. When the motion detector stops clicking and the CBL shows DONE, press ENTER on the graphing calculator so that the calculator will receive the lists of data collected by the CBL.

18. Select *SONIC* from the SELECT CHANNELS menu. Select DISTANCE to plot a graph of the distance in meters against the time in seconds. Press TRACE on the graphing calculator, and use the arrow keys to trace the graph. The graph should move between high points and low points to reflect the oscillation of the mass on the spring. Record the distance (y) values of the *Highest point* and *Lowest point* in your data table. Sketch the graph in your lab notebook. Press ENTER on the graphing calculator.

19. Select *RETURN* from the SELECT CHANNEL menu. Select *RETURN* again. Select *YES* from the REPEAT? menu to continue to perform more trials.

20. Perform several more trials, using a different mass for each trial. Record all data in your data table.

Analysis and Interpretation begins on page 204.

PROCEDURE

HOOKE'S LAW APPARATUS

Spring constant

4. Set up the Hooke's law apparatus as shown in **Figure 5-26.**

5. Place a rubber band around the scale at the initial resting position of the pointer, or adjust the scale or pan to read 0.0 cm. Record this position of the pointer as *Initial spring (m)*. If you have set the scale at 0.0 cm, record 0.00 m as the initial spring position.

6. Measure the distance from the floor to the rubber band on the scale. Record this in the second data table under *Initial distance (m)*. This distance must remain constant throughout the lab.

7. Find a mass that will stretch the spring so that the pointer moves approximately one-quarter of the way down the scale.

8. Record the value of the mass. Also record the position of the pointer under *Stretched spring* in the data table.

9. Perform several trials with increasing masses until the spring stretches to the bottom of the scale. Record the mass and the position of the pointer for each trial.

Conservation of mechanical energy

10. Find a mass that will stretch the spring to about twice its original length. Record the mass in the second data table. Leave the mass in place on the pan.

11. Raise the pan until the pointer is at the zero position, the position where you measured the *Initial spring* measurement.

12. Gently release the pan to let the pan drop. Watch closely to identify the high and low points of the oscillation.

13. Use a rubber band to mark the lowest position to which the pan falls, as indicated by the pointer. This is the lowest point of the oscillation. Record the values as *Highest point* and *Lowest point* in your data table.

14. Perform several more trials, using a different mass for each trial. Record all data in your data table.

Figure 5-26

Step 5: If the scale is adjusted to read 0.0 cm, record 0.0 as the initial spring length in your data table.

Step 7: In this part of the lab, you will collect data to find the spring constant of the spring.

Step 10: In this part of the lab, you will oscillate a mass on the spring to find out whether mechanical energy is conserved.

ANALYSIS AND INTERPRETATION

Calculations and data analysis

CBL and sensors

Figure 5-27

1. **Organizing data**   Use your data from the first data table to calculate the elongation of the spring.

   a. **CBL and sensors**   Use the equation *elongation = initial spring – stretched spring.*

   b. **Hooke's law apparatus**   Use the equation *elongation = stretched spring – initial spring.*

   c. **Hooke's law apparatus**   Convert the masses used to measure the spring constant to their force equivalents.

2. **Evaluating data**   For each trial, calculate the spring constant using the equation $k = \dfrac{force}{elongation}$. Take the average of all trials, and use this value as the spring constant.

3. **Analyzing results**   How would using a stiffer spring affect the value for the spring constant? How would this affect the values for the elastic and gravitational potential energies?

4. **Organizing data**   Using your data from the second data table, calculate the elongation of the spring at the highest point of each trial.

   a. **CBL and sensors**   Use the equation *elongation = initial spring – highest point.*

   b. **Hooke's law apparatus**   Use the equation *elongation = highest point – initial spring.*

5. **Organizing data**   Calculate the elongation of the spring at the lowest point of each trial.

   a. **CBL and sensors**   Use the equation *elongation = initial spring – lowest point.*

   b. **Hooke's law apparatus**   Use the equation *elongation = lowest point – initial spring*

6. **Analyzing information**   For each trial, calculate the elastic potential energy, $PE_{elastic} = \frac{1}{2}kx^2$, at the highest point of the oscillation.

7. **Analyzing information**   For each trial, calculate the elastic potential energy at the lowest point of the oscillation.

8. **Analyzing results**   Based on your calculations in items 6 and 7, where is the elastic potential energy greatest? Where is it the least? Explain this in terms of the energy stored in the spring.

9. Organizing data   Calculate the height of the mass at the highest point of each trial.

   a. CBL and sensors   Use the equation *highest = initial distance + highest point*.

   b. Hooke's law apparatus   Use the equation *highest = initial distance − elongation*.

10. Organizing data   Calculate the height of the mass at the lowest point of each trial.

   a. CBL and sensors   Use the equation *lowest = initial distance + lowest point*.

   b. Hooke's law apparatus   Use the equation *lowest = initial distance − elongation*.

11. Applying ideas   For each trial, calculate the gravitational potential energy, $PE_g = mgh$, at the highest point of the oscillation.

12. Applying ideas   For each trial, calculate the gravitational potential energy at the lowest point of the oscillation.

13. Analyzing results   According to your calculations in items 11 and 12, where is the gravitational potential energy the greatest? Where is it the least? Explain this in terms of gravity and the height of the mass and the spring.

14. Evaluating data   Find the total potential energy at the top of the oscillation and at the bottom of the oscillation.

Conclusions

15. Drawing conclusions   Based on your data, is mechanical energy conserved in the oscillating mass on the spring? Explain how your data support your answers.

Extensions

16. Extending ideas   Use your data to find the midpoint of the oscillation for each trial. Calculate the gravitational potential energy and the elastic potential energy at the midpoint. Use the principle of the conservation of mechanical energy to find the kinetic energy and the speed of the mass at the midpoint.

Figure 5-28

CHAPTER 6

Momentum and Collisions

PHYSICS IN ACTION

Soccer players must consider an enormous amount of information every time they set the ball—or themselves—into motion. Once a player knows where the ball should go, the player has to decide how to get it there. The player also has to consider the ball's speed and direction in order to stop it or change its direction. The player in the photograph must determine how much force to exert on the ball and how much follow-through is needed. To do this, he must understand his own motion as well as the motion of the ball.

- *International regulations specify the mass of official soccer balls. How does the mass of a ball affect the way it behaves when kicked?*

- *How does the velocity of the player's foot affect the final velocity of the ball?*

CONCEPT REVIEW

Newton's laws of motion
(Sections 4-2 and 4-3)

Kinetic energy (Section 5-2)

Conservation of energy
(Section 5-3)

6-1
Momentum and impulse

- **Compare the momentum of different moving objects.**

- **Compare the momentum of the same object moving with different velocities.**

- **Identify examples of change in the momentum of an object.**

- **Describe changes in momentum in terms of force and time.**

momentum

a vector quantity defined as the product of an object's mass and velocity

LINEAR MOMENTUM

When a soccer player heads a moving ball during a game, the ball's velocity changes rapidly. The speed of the ball and the direction of the ball's motion change once it is struck so that the ball moves across the soccer field with a different speed than it had and in a different direction than it was traveling before the collision.

The quantities and kinematic equations from Chapter 2 can be used to describe the motion of the ball before and after the ball is struck. The concept of force and Newton's laws from Chapter 4 can be used to explain *why* the motion of the ball changes when it is struck. In this chapter, we will examine how the force and the duration of the collision between the ball and the soccer player affect the motion of the ball.

Momentum describes an object's motion

To address such questions, we need a new concept, **momentum.** *Momentum* is a word we use every day in a variety of situations. In physics, of course, this word has a specific meaning. The linear momentum of an object of mass m moving with a velocity $\mathbf{v}$ is defined as the product of the mass and the velocity. Momentum is represented by the symbol $\mathbf{p}$.

> **MOMENTUM**
>
> $$\mathbf{p} = m\mathbf{v}$$
>
> momentum = mass × velocity

As its definition shows, momentum is a vector quantity, with its direction matching that of the velocity. Momentum has dimensions mass × length/time, and its SI units are kilogram-meters per second (kg•m/s).

If you think about some examples of the way the word *momentum* is used in everyday speech, you will see that the physics definition conveys a similar meaning. Imagine coasting down a hill of uniform slope on your bike without pedaling or using the brakes. Because of the force of gravity, you will accelerate at a constant rate so that your velocity will increase with time. This is often expressed by saying that you are "picking up speed" or "gathering momentum." The faster you move, the more momentum you have and the more difficult it is to come to a stop.

Figure 6-1
When the bowling ball strikes the pin, the acceleration of the pin depends on the ball's momentum, which is the product of its mass and its velocity.

Imagine rolling a bowling ball down one lane at a bowling alley and rolling a playground ball down another lane at the same speed. The more-massive bowling ball, shown in **Figure 6-1,** will give the pins a greater acceleration because the bowling ball has more momentum than the playground ball. When we think of a massive object moving at a high velocity, we often say that the object has a large momentum. A less massive object with the same velocity has a smaller momentum.

On the other hand, a small object moving with a very high velocity has a large momentum. One example of this is hailstones falling from very high clouds. By the time they reach Earth, they can have enough momentum to hurt you or cause serious damage to cars and buildings

---

SAMPLE PROBLEM 6A

Momentum

PROBLEM

A 2250 kg pickup truck has a velocity of 25 m/s to the east. What is the momentum of the truck?

SOLUTION

Given: $m = 2250$ kg $\mathbf{v} = 25$ m/s to the east

Unknown: $\mathbf{p} = ?$

Use the momentum equation from page 208.
$$\mathbf{p} = m\mathbf{v} = (2250 \text{ kg})(25 \text{ m/s})$$

$$\boxed{\mathbf{p} = 5.6 \times 10^4 \text{ kg} \cdot \text{m/s to the east}}$$

CALCULATOR SOLUTION

Your calculator will give you the answer 56250 for the momentum. The value for the velocity has only two significant figures, so the answer must be reported as 5.6×10^4.

PRACTICE 6A

Momentum

1. What velocity must a car with a mass of 1210 kg have in order to have the same momentum as the pickup truck in Sample Problem 6A?

2. An ostrich with a mass of 146 kg is running to the right with a velocity of 17 m/s. Find the momentum of the ostrich.

3. A 21 kg child is riding a 5.9 kg bike with a velocity of 4.5 m/s to the northwest.
   a. What is the total momentum of the child and the bike together?
   b. What is the momentum of the child?
   c. What is the momentum of the bike?

Figure 6-2
When the ball is moving very fast, the player must exert a large force to change the ball's momentum and bring the ball to a stop.

impulse

for a constant external force, the product of the force and the time over which it acts on an object

A change in momentum takes force and time

Figure 6-2 shows a player stopping a moving soccer ball. In a given time interval, he must exert more force to stop a fast ball than to stop a ball that is moving more slowly. You have probably noticed that a ball moving very fast stings your hands when you catch it, while a slow-moving ball causes no discomfort when you catch it.

Imagine a toy truck and a real dump truck starting from rest and rolling down the same hill at the same time. They would accelerate at the same rate, so their velocity at any instant would be the same, but it would take much more force to stop the massive dump truck than to stop the toy truck in the same time interval.

From examples like these, we see that momentum is closely related to force. In fact, when Newton first expressed his second law mathematically, he wrote it not as $\mathbf{F} = m\mathbf{a}$, but in the following form.

$$\mathbf{F} = \frac{\Delta \mathbf{p}}{\Delta t} \qquad \text{force} = \frac{\text{change in momentum}}{\text{time interval}}$$

We can rearrange this equation to find the change in momentum in terms of the net external force and the time interval required to make this change.

IMPULSE-MOMENTUM THEOREM

$$\mathbf{F}\Delta t = \Delta \mathbf{p} \qquad \text{or} \qquad \mathbf{F}\Delta t = \Delta \mathbf{p} = m\mathbf{v_f} - m\mathbf{v_i}$$

$$\text{force} \times \text{time interval} = \text{change in momentum}$$

This equation states that a net external force, $\mathbf{F}$, applied to an object for a certain time interval, Δt, will cause a change in the object's momentum equal to the product of the force and the time interval. In simple terms, this equation means that a large constant force will cause a change in an object's momentum in a short time but that a small constant force will take a much longer time to cause the same change. In this book, all forces exerted on an object are assumed to be constant unless otherwise stated.

The expression $\mathbf{F}\Delta t = \Delta \mathbf{p}$ is called the impulse-momentum theorem. The term on the left side of the equation, $\mathbf{F}\Delta t$, is called the **impulse** of the force $\mathbf{F}$ for the time interval Δt.

The equation $\mathbf{F}\Delta t = \Delta \mathbf{p}$ explains why follow-through is important in so many sports, from karate and billiards to softball and croquet. For example, when a batter hits a ball, the ball will experience a greater change in momentum if the batter follows through and keeps the bat in contact with the ball for a longer time. Follow through is also important in many everyday activities, such as pushing a shopping cart or moving furniture. Extending the time interval over which a constant force is applied allows a smaller force to cause a greater change in momentum than would result if the force were applied for a very short time.

Force and momentum

PROBLEM

A 1400 kg car moving westward with a velocity of 15 m/s collides with a utility pole and is brought to rest in 0.30 s. Find the magnitude of the force exerted on the car during the collision.

SOLUTION

Given: $m = 1400$ kg $v_i = 15$ m/s to the west $v_f = 0$ m/s
$\Delta t = 0.30$ s

Unknown: $F = $?

Use the impulse-momentum theorem.

$$F\Delta t = \Delta p = mv_f - mv_i$$

$$F = \frac{mv_f - mv_i}{\Delta t}$$

$$F = \frac{(1400 \text{ kg} \times 0 \text{ m/s}) - (1400 \text{ kg} \times 15 \text{ m/s})}{0.30 \text{ s}} = \frac{-21\,000 \text{ kg} \cdot \text{m/s}}{0.30 \text{ s}}$$

$$F = -7.0 \times 10^4 \text{ kg} \cdot \text{m/s}^2 \text{ to the west} = 7.0 \times 10^4 \text{ N to the east}$$

Force and momentum

1. A 0.50 kg football is thrown with a velocity of 15 m/s to the right. A stationary receiver catches the ball and brings it to rest in 0.020 s. What is the force exerted on the receiver?

2. A 0.40 kg soccer ball approaches a player horizontally with a velocity of 18 m/s to the north. The player strikes the ball and causes it to move in the opposite direction with a velocity of 22 m/s. What impulse was delivered to the ball by the player?

3. A 0.50 kg object is at rest. A 3.00 N force to the right acts on the object during a time interval of 1.50 s.
   a. What is the velocity of the object at the end of this interval?
   b. At the end of this interval, a constant force of 4.00 N to the left is applied for 3.00 s. What is the velocity at the end of the 3.00 s?

4. An 82 kg man drops from rest on a diving board 3.0 m above the surface of the water and comes to rest 0.55 s after reaching the water. What force does the water exert on him?

Stopping times and distances depend on the impulse-momentum theorem

The impulse-momentum theorem is the formula that highway-safety engineers use to determine stopping times and safe following distances for cars and trucks. For example, the truck in **Figure 6-3** has two times as much mass as the small car. Therefore, if the car and the truck are both traveling at 48 km/h, the truck has two times as much momentum as the car. If we assume that the brakes on the truck exert about the same force as the brakes on the car, we find that the stopping time for the truck is two times longer than the stopping time for the car. Furthermore, the stopping distance for the truck is four times greater than the stopping distance for the car.

It takes longer to stop a car on a wet or icy road because the total force opposing the car's motion is less when the force of friction between the road and the tires is reduced. This lower force must be applied for a longer time in order to cause the same change in momentum.

Stopping distances

48 km/h (30 mi/h)

48 km/h (30 mi/h)

Figure 6-3
The truck must undergo a greater change in momentum than the car in order to stop.

SAMPLE PROBLEM 6C

Stopping distance

PROBLEM

A 2250 kg car traveling to the west is slowed down uniformly from 20.0 m/s to 5.00 m/s in 4.00 s. What constant force acted on the car during this time? How far did the car travel during the deceleration?

SOLUTION

Given:

$m = 2250$ kg $\mathbf{v_i} = 20.0$ m/s to the west
$\mathbf{v_f} = 5.00$ m/s to the west
$\Delta t = 4.00$ s

Unknown: $\mathbf{F} = ?$ $\Delta \mathbf{x} = ?$

Use the impulse-momentum theorem from page 210.

$$\mathbf{F}\Delta t = \Delta \mathbf{p}$$

$$\mathbf{F} = \frac{\Delta \mathbf{p}}{\Delta t} = \frac{m\mathbf{v_f} - m\mathbf{v_i}}{\Delta t}$$

$$\mathbf{F} = \frac{2250 \text{ kg}(5.00 \text{ m/s}) - 2250 \text{ kg}(20.0 \text{ m/s})}{4.00 \text{ s}}$$

$$\boxed{\mathbf{F} = -8.45 \times 10^3 \text{ N to the west} = 8.45 \times 10^3 \text{ N to the east}}$$

$$\Delta \mathbf{x} = \tfrac{1}{2}(\mathbf{v_i} + \mathbf{v_f})\Delta t$$

$$\Delta \mathbf{x} = \tfrac{1}{2}(20.0 \text{ m/s} + 5.00 \text{ m/s})(4.00 \text{ s})$$

$$\boxed{\Delta \mathbf{x} = 50.0 \text{ m to the west}}$$

Stopping distance

1. Assume a constant acceleration.
   a. How long would it take the car in Sample Problem 6C to come to a stop from 20.0 m/s to the west?
   b. How far would the car move before stopping?

2. Assume that the car in Sample Problem 6C has a mass of 3250 kg.
   a. How much force would be required to cause the same acceleration as in item 1? Use the impulse-momentum theorem.
   b. How far would the car move before stopping?

3. A 2500 kg car traveling to the north is slowed down uniformly from an initial velocity of 20.0 m/s by a 6250 N braking force acting opposite the car's motion. Use the impulse-momentum theorem to answer the following questions:
   a. What is the car's velocity after 2.50 s?
   b. How far does the car move during 2.50 s?
   c. How long does it take the car to come to a complete stop?

A change in momentum over a longer time requires less force

The impulse-momentum theorem is used to design safety equipment that reduces the force exerted on the human body during collisions. Examples of this are the nets and giant air mattresses firefighters use to catch people who must jump out of tall burning buildings. The relationship is also used to design sports equipment and games.

Figure 6-4 shows an Inupiat family playing a traditional game. Common sense tells us that it is much better for the girl to fall onto the outstretched blanket than onto the hard ground. In both cases, however, the change in momentum of the falling girl is exactly the same. The difference is that the blanket "gives way" and extends the time of collision so that the change in the girl's momentum occurs over a longer time interval. A longer time interval requires a smaller force to achieve the same change in the girl's momentum. Therefore, the force exerted on the girl when she lands on the outstretched blanket is less than the force would be if she were to land on the ground.

Figure 6-4
In this game, the girl is protected from injury because the blanket reduces the force of the collision by allowing it to take place over a longer time interval.

(a)

(b)

Now consider a falling egg. When the egg hits a hard surface, like the plate in **Figure 6-5(a),** the egg comes to rest in a very short time interval. The force the hard plate exerts on the egg due to the collision is large. When the egg hits a floor covered with a pillow, as in **Figure 6-5(b),** the egg undergoes the same change in momentum, but over a much longer time interval. In this case, the force required to accelerate the egg to rest is much smaller. By applying a small force to the egg over a longer time interval, the pillow causes the same change in the egg's momentum as the hard plate, which applies a large force over a short time interval. Because the force in the second situation is smaller, the egg can withstand it without breaking.

Figure 6-5

A large force exerted over a short time **(a)** causes the same change in the egg's momentum as a small force exerted over a longer time **(b).**

Section Review

1. The speed of a particle is doubled.
   a. By what factor is its momentum changed?
   b. What happens to its kinetic energy?

2. A pitcher claims he can throw a 0.145 kg baseball with as much momentum as a speeding bullet. Assume that a 3.00 g bullet moves at a speed of 1.50×10^3 m/s.
   a. What must the baseball's speed be if the pitcher's claim is valid?
   b. Which has greater kinetic energy, the ball or the bullet?

3. When a force is exerted on an object, does a large force always produce a larger change in the object's momentum than a smaller force does? Explain.

4. What is the relationship between impulse and momentum?

5. **Physics in Action**   A 0.42 kg soccer ball is moving downfield with a velocity of 12 m/s. A player kicks the ball so that it has a final velocity of 18 m/s downfield.
   a. What is the change in the ball's momentum?
   b. Find the constant force exerted by the player's foot on the ball if the two are in contact for 0.020 s.

6-2
Conservation of momentum

MOMENTUM IS CONSERVED

Figure 6-6 shows a stationary soccer ball set into motion when it collides with a moving soccer ball. Looking at this in terms of momentum, we see that the momentum of ball B was equal to zero before the collision with ball A. Because of the collision with the moving ball, ball B gains momentum during the collision. Furthermore, ball A loses the same amount of momentum during the collision. This happens whenever one isolated object collides with another isolated object. So far in this chapter, we have considered the momentum of only one object at a time. Now, in order to discover exactly how ball B gains momentum and how much momentum it gains as a result of this collision, we must also examine the momentum of ball A before and after the collision.

6-2 SECTION OBJECTIVES

- Describe the interaction between two objects in terms of the change in momentum of each object.

- Compare the total momentum of two objects before and after they interact.

- State the law of conservation of momentum.

- Predict the final velocities of objects after collisions, given the initial velocities.

(a)

A   B

(b)

A   B

Figure 6-6
Before the collision **(a)**, ball A has momentum $\mathbf{p_A}$ and ball B has no momentum. After the collision **(b)**, ball B gains momentum $\mathbf{p_B}$.

Table 6-1 shows the velocity and momentum of each soccer ball both before and after the collision. The momentum of each ball changes due to the collision, but the *total* momentum of the two balls together remains constant.

Table 6-1	Momentum in a collision					
	Ball A			**Ball B**		
	Mass	Velocity	Momentum	Mass	Velocity	Momentum
Before collision	0.47 kg	0.84 m/s	0.40 kg•m/s	0.47 kg	0 m/s	0 kg•m/s
After collision	0.47 kg	0.04 m/s	0.02 kg•m/s	0.47 kg	0.80 m/s	0.38 kg•m/s

In other words, the momentum of ball A plus the momentum of ball B before the collision is equal to the momentum of ball A plus the momentum of ball B after the collision.

$$\mathbf{p_{A,i}} + \mathbf{p_{B,i}} = \mathbf{p_{A,f}} + \mathbf{p_{B,f}}$$

This relationship is true for all interactions between isolated objects and is known as the *law of conservation of momentum.*

CONSERVATION OF MOMENTUM

$$m_1\mathbf{v_{1,i}} + m_2\mathbf{v_{2,i}} = m_1\mathbf{v_{1,f}} + m_2\mathbf{v_{2,f}}$$

total initial momentum = total final momentum

In its most general form, the law of conservation of momentum can be stated as follows:

The total momentum of all objects interacting with one another remains constant regardless of the nature of the forces between the objects.

Momentum is conserved in collisions

In the soccer-ball example, the momentum of ball A does not remain constant and the momentum of ball B does not remain constant, but the total momentum of ball A and ball B does remain constant. In general, the total momentum remains constant for a system of objects that interact with one another. In this case, the soccer balls are the only two objects interacting. If a third object were to exert a force on either ball A or ball B during the collision, the total momentum of ball A, ball B, and the third object would remain constant.

In this book, most conservation-of-momentum problems deal with only two isolated objects. However, when you use conservation of momentum to solve a problem or investigate a situation, it is important to include all objects that are involved in the interaction. Frictional forces—such as the frictional force between the soccer balls and the grass—will be disregarded in most conservation-of-momentum problems in this book.

Momentum is conserved for objects pushing away from each other

Another example of conservation of momentum is when two or more interacting objects that initially have no momentum begin moving away from each other. Imagine that you initially stand at rest and then jump up, leaving the ground with a velocity **v.** Obviously, *your* momentum is not conserved; before the jump, it was zero, and it became $m\mathbf{v}$ as you began to rise. However, the total momentum remains constant if you include Earth in your analysis. The total momentum for you and Earth remains constant.

You exert a downward force on Earth when you jump, and Earth exerts an equal but upward force on you. Thus, as you move upward with some momentum, $\mathbf{p_1} = m_1\mathbf{v_1}$, Earth moves in the opposite direction with momen-

Conceptual Challenge

1. Ice skating

If a reckless ice skater collides with another skater who is standing on the ice, is it possible for both skaters to be at rest after the collision?

2. Space travel

A spacecraft undergoes a change of velocity when its rockets are fired. How does the spacecraft change velocity in empty space, where there is nothing for the gases emitted by the rockets to push against?

tum of the same magnitude, $\mathbf{p}_2 = -m_2\mathbf{v}_2$. Therefore, the total momentum of you and Earth after the interaction is zero, which is equal to the total momentum of you and Earth before the interaction.

Imagine two skaters pushing away from each other, as shown in **Figure 6-7.** The skaters are both initially at rest with a momentum of $\mathbf{p}_{1,i} = \mathbf{p}_{2,i} = 0$. When they push away from each other, they move in opposite directions with equal but opposite momentum so that the total final momentum is also zero ($\mathbf{p}_{1,f} + \mathbf{p}_{2,f} = 0$).

(a)　　　　　　　　　　**(b)**

Figure 6-7

When the skaters stand facing each other **(a),** both skaters have zero momentum, so the total momentum of both skaters is zero.

When the skaters push away from each other **(b),** their momentum is equal but opposite, so the total momentum is still zero.

Consumer Focus　　*Surviving a Collision*

*P*ucks and carts collide in physics labs all the time with little damage. But when cars collide on a freeway, the resulting rapid change in speed can cause injury or death to the drivers and any passengers.

Many types of collisions are dangerous, but head-on collisions involve the greatest accelerations and thus the greatest forces. When two cars going 100 km/h (62 mi/h) collide head-on, each car dissipates the same amount of kinetic energy that it would dissipate if it hit the ground after being dropped from the roof of a 12-story building.

The key to many automobile-safety features is the concept of impulse. One way today's cars make use of the concept of impulse is by crumpling during impact. Pliable sheet metal and frame structures absorb energy until the force reaches the passenger compartment, which is built of rigid metal for protection. Because the crumpling slows the car gradually, it is an important factor in keeping the driver alive.

Even taking into account this built-in safety feature, the National Safety Council estimates that high-speed collisions involve accelerations of 20 times the free-fall acceleration. In other words, an 89 N (20 lb) infant could experience a force of 1780 N (400 lb) in a collision. If you are holding a baby in your lap during a collision, it is very likely that these large forces will break your hold on the baby. Because of inertia, the baby will continue at the car's original velocity and collide with the front windshield.

Seat belts are necessary to protect a body from forces of such large magnitudes. They stretch and extend the time it takes a passenger's body to stop, thereby reducing the force on the person. Seat belts also prevent passengers from hitting the inside frame of the car. During a collision, a person not wearing a seat belt is likely to hit the windshield, the steering wheel, or the dashboard—often with traumatic results.

Conservation of momentum

PROBLEM

A 76 kg boater, initially at rest in a stationary 45 kg boat, steps out of the boat and onto the dock. If the boater moves out of the boat with a velocity of 2.5 m/s to the right, what is the final velocity of the boat?

SOLUTION

1. DEFINE   **Given:** $m_1 = 76$ kg $m_2 = 45$ kg $\mathbf{v_{1,i}} = 0$
$\mathbf{v_{2,i}} = 0$ $\mathbf{v_{1,f}} = 2.5$ m/s to the right

Unknown: $\mathbf{v_{2,f}} = ?$

Diagram: $m_1 = 76$ kg $\mathbf{v_{1,f}} = 2.5$ m/s

$m_2 = 45$ kg

2. PLAN   **Choose an equation or situation:** Because the total momentum of an isolated system remains constant, the total initial momentum of the boater and the boat will be equal to the total final momentum of the boater and the boat.

$$m_1\mathbf{v_{1,i}} + m_2\mathbf{v_{2,i}} = m_1\mathbf{v_{1,f}} + m_2\mathbf{v_{2,f}}$$

Because the boater and the boat are initially at rest, the total initial momentum of the system is equal to zero.

$$m_1\mathbf{v_{1,i}} + m_2\mathbf{v_{2,i}} = 0$$

Therefore, the final momentum of the system must also be equal to zero.

$$m_1\mathbf{v_{1,f}} + m_2\mathbf{v_{2,f}} = 0$$

3. CALCULATE   **Substitute the values into the equation(s) and solve:**

$$m_1\mathbf{v_{1,f}} + m_2\mathbf{v_{2,f}} = (76 \text{ kg} \times 2.5 \text{ m/s}) + (45 \text{ kg} \times \mathbf{v_{2,f}})$$

$$190 \text{ kg} \cdot \text{m/s} + 45 \text{ kg}(\mathbf{v_{2,f}}) = 0$$

$$45 \text{ kg}(\mathbf{v_{2,f}}) = -190 \text{ kg} \cdot \text{m/s}$$

$$\mathbf{v_{2,f}} = \frac{-190 \text{ kg} \cdot \text{m/s}}{45 \text{ kg}}$$

$$\boxed{\mathbf{v_{2,f}} = -4.2 \text{ m/s}}$$

4. EVALUATE   The negative sign for $\mathbf{v_{2,f}}$ indicates that the boat is moving to the left, in the direction *opposite* the motion of the boater.

$$\boxed{\mathbf{v_{2,f}} = 4.2 \text{ m/s to the left}}$$

Conservation of momentum

1. A 63.0 kg astronaut is on a spacewalk when the tether line to the shuttle breaks. The astronaut is able to throw a 10.0 kg oxygen tank in a direction away from the shuttle with a speed of 12.0 m/s, propelling the astronaut back to the shuttle.

   a. Assuming that the astronaut starts from rest, find the final speed of the astronaut after throwing the tank.

   b. Determine the maximum distance the astronaut can be from the craft when the line breaks in order to return to the craft within 60.0 s.

2. An 85.0 kg fisherman jumps from a dock into a 135.0 kg rowboat at rest on the west side of the dock. If the velocity of the fisherman is 4.30 m/s to the west as he leaves the dock, what is the final velocity of the fisherman and the boat?

3. Each croquet ball in a set has a mass of 0.50 kg. The green ball, traveling at 12.0 m/s, strikes the blue ball, which is at rest. Assuming that all collisions are head-on, find the final speed of the blue ball in each of the following situations:

   a. The green ball stops moving after it strikes the blue ball.

   b. The green ball continues moving after the collision at 2.4 m/s in the same direction.

   c. The green ball continues moving after the collision at 0.3 m/s in the same direction.

   d. The blue ball and the green ball move in the same direction after the collision; the green ball has a speed of 1.6 m/s.

Newton's third law leads to conservation of momentum

Consider two isolated bumper cars, m_1 and m_2, before and after they collide. Before the collision, the velocities of the two bumper cars are $\mathbf{v_{1,i}}$ and $\mathbf{v_{2,i}}$, respectively. After the collision, their velocities are $\mathbf{v_{1,f}}$ and $\mathbf{v_{2,f}}$, respectively. The impulse-momentum theorem, $\mathbf{F}\Delta t = \Delta \mathbf{p}$, describes the change in momentum of one of the bumper cars. Applied to m_1, the impulse-momentum theorem gives the following:

$$\mathbf{F_1}\Delta t = m_1\mathbf{v_{1,f}} - m_1\mathbf{v_{1,i}}$$

Likewise, for m_2 it gives the following:

$$\mathbf{F_2}\Delta t = m_2\mathbf{v_{2,f}} - m_2\mathbf{v_{2,i}}$$

$\mathbf{F_1}$ is the force that m_2 exerts on m_1 during the collision, and $\mathbf{F_2}$ is the force that m_1 exerts on m_2 during the collision, as shown in **Figure 6-8.** Because the only forces acting in the collision are the forces the two bumper cars exert on each other, Newton's third law tells us that the force on m_1 is equal to and opposite the force on m_2 ($\mathbf{F_1} = -\mathbf{F_2}$). Additionally, the two forces act over the same time interval. Therefore, the force m_2 exerts on m_1 multiplied by the time interval is equal to the force m_1 exerts on m_2 multiplied by the time interval, or $\mathbf{F_1}\Delta t = -\mathbf{F_2}\Delta t$. That is, the impulse on m_1 is equal to and opposite the impulse on m_2. This relationship is true in every collision or interaction between two isolated objects.

Because impulse is equal to the change in momentum, and the impulse on m_1 is equal to and opposite the impulse on m_2, the change in momentum of m_1 is equal to and opposite the change in momentum of m_2. This means that in every interaction between two isolated objects, the change in momentum of the first object is equal to and opposite the change in momentum of the second object. In equation form, this is expressed by the following equation.

$$m_1\mathbf{v_{1,f}} - m_1\mathbf{v_{1,i}} = -(m_2\mathbf{v_{2,f}} - m_2\mathbf{v_{2,i}})$$

This equation means that if the momentum of one object increases after a collision, then the momentum of the other object in the situation must decrease by an equal amount.

Rearranging this equation gives the following equation for the conservation of momentum.

$$m_1\mathbf{v_{1,i}} + m_2\mathbf{v_{2,i}} = m_1\mathbf{v_{1,f}} + m_2\mathbf{v_{2,f}}$$

As mentioned in Section 6-1, the forces involved in a collision are treated as though they are constant. In a real collision, however, the forces may vary in time in a complicated way. **Figure 6-9** shows the forces acting during the collision of the two bumper cars. At all times during the collision, the forces on the two cars are equal and opposite in direction. However, the magnitudes of the forces change throughout the collision—increasing, reaching a maximum, and then decreasing.

The value used for the force in problem-solving is equal to the average force during the collision. In Chapter 2, you learned that the average velocity of an object undergoing a constant acceleration is equal to the constant velocity required for the object to travel the same displacement in the same time interval. Similarly, the average force during a collision is equal to the constant force required to cause the same change in momentum as the real, changing force.

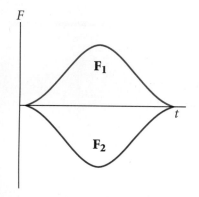

1. A 44 kg student on in-line skates is playing with a 22 kg exercise ball. Disregarding friction, explain what happens during the following situations.

   a. The student is holding the ball, and both are at rest. The student then throws the ball horizontally, causing the student to glide back at 3.5 m/s.

   b. Explain what happens to the ball in part (a) in terms of the momentum of the student and the momentum of the ball.

   c. The student is initially at rest. The student then catches the ball, which is initially moving to the right at 4.6 m/s.

   d. Explain what happens in part (c) in terms of the momentum of the student and the momentum of the ball.

2. A boy stands at one end of a floating raft that is stationary relative to the shore. He then walks in a straight line to the opposite end of the raft, away from the shore.

   a. Does the raft move? Explain.

   b. What is the total momentum of the boy and the raft before the boy walks across the raft?

   c. What is the total momentum of the boy and the raft after the boy walks across the raft?

3. High-speed stroboscopic photographs show the head of a 215 g golf club traveling at 55.0 m/s just before it strikes a 46 g golf ball at rest on a tee. After the collision, the club travels (in the same direction) at 42.0 m/s. Use the law of conservation of momentum to find the speed of the golf ball just after impact.

4. Two isolated objects have a head-on collision. For each of the following questions, explain your answer.

   a. If you know the change in momentum of one object, can you find the change in momentum of the other object?

   b. If you know the initial and final velocity of one object and the mass of the other object, do you have enough information to find the final velocity of the second object?

   c. If you know the masses of both objects and the final velocities of both objects, do you have enough information to find the initial velocities of both objects?

   d. If you know the masses and initial velocities of both objects and the final velocity of one object, do you have enough information to find the final velocity of the other object?

   e. If you know the change in momentum of one object and the initial and final velocities of the other object, do you have enough information to find the mass of either object?

6-3
Elastic and inelastic collisions

6-3 SECTION OBJECTIVES

- **Identify different types of collisions.**

- **Determine the decrease in kinetic energy during perfectly inelastic collisions.**

- **Compare conservation of momentum and conservation of kinetic energy in perfectly inelastic and elastic collisions.**

- **Find the final velocity of an object in perfectly inelastic and elastic collisions.**

perfectly inelastic collision

a collision in which two objects stick together and move with a common velocity after colliding

COLLISIONS

As you go about your day-to-day activities, you probably witness many collisions without really thinking about them. In some collisions, two objects collide and stick together so that they travel together after the impact. An example of this is a collision between an arrow and a target, as shown in **Figure 6-10.** The arrow, sailing forward, collides with the target at rest. In an isolated system, the target and the arrow would both move together after the collision with a momentum equal to their combined momentum before the collision. In other collisions, like a collision between a tennis racquet and a tennis ball, two objects collide and bounce so that they move away with two different velocities.

The total momentum remains constant in any type of collision. However, the total kinetic energy is generally not conserved in a collision because some of the kinetic energy is converted to thermal energy and internal elastic potential energy when the objects deform. In this section, we will examine the different types of collisions and determine whether kinetic energy is conserved in each type.

In the remainder of this section, we will learn about collisions by exploring the two extreme types, perfectly inelastic and elastic.

Perfectly inelastic collisions

When two objects collide and move together as one mass, like the arrow and the target described above, the collision is called **perfectly inelastic.** Likewise, if a meteorite collides head on with Earth, it becomes buried in Earth and the collision is considered perfectly inelastic.

Figure 6-10
When an arrow pierces a target and remains stuck in the target, the arrow and target have undergone a perfectly inelastic collision.

Perfectly inelastic collisions are easy to analyze in terms of momentum because the objects become essentially one object after the collision. The final mass is equal to the combined mass of the two objects, and they move with the same velocity after colliding.

Consider two cars of masses m_1 and m_2 moving with initial velocities of $\mathbf{v_{1,i}}$ and $\mathbf{v_{2,i}}$ along a straight line, as shown in **Figure 6-11.** The two cars stick together and move with some common velocity, $\mathbf{v_f}$, along the same line of motion after the collision. The total momentum of the two cars before the collision is equal to the total momentum of the two cars after the collision.

(a)

(b)

PERFECTLY INELASTIC COLLISION

$$m_1\mathbf{v_{1,i}} + m_2\mathbf{v_{2,i}} = (m_1 + m_2)\,\mathbf{v_f}$$

Figure 6-11
The total momentum of the two cars before the collision **(a)** is the same as the total momentum of the two cars after the inelastic collision **(b)**.

This simplified version of the equation for conservation of momentum is useful in analyzing perfectly inelastic collisions. When using this equation, it is important to pay attention to signs that indicate direction. In **Figure 6-11**, $\mathbf{v_{1,i}}$ has a positive value (m_1 moving to the right), while $\mathbf{v_{2,i}}$ has a negative value (m_2 moving to the left).

Perfectly inelastic collision

PROBLEM

A 1850 kg luxury sedan stopped at a traffic light is struck from the rear by a compact car with a mass of 975 kg. The two cars become entangled as a result of the collision. If the compact car was moving at a velocity of 22.0 m/s to the north before the collision, what is the velocity of the entangled mass after the collision?

SOLUTION

Given: $m_1 = 1850\ \text{kg}$ $\qquad m_2 = 975\ \text{kg}$ $\qquad \mathbf{v_{1,i}} = 0\ \text{m/s}$
$\mathbf{v_{2,i}} = 22.0$ m/s to the north

Unknown: $\mathbf{v_f} = ?$

Use the equation for a perfectly inelastic collision.

$$m_1\mathbf{v_{1,i}} + m_2\mathbf{v_{2,i}} = (m_1 + m_2)\,\mathbf{v_f}$$

$$(1850\ \text{kg} \times 0\ \text{m/s}) + (975\ \text{kg} \times 22.0\ \text{m/s}) = (1850\ \text{kg} + 975\ \text{kg})\,\mathbf{v_f}$$

$$(2.14 \times 10^4\ \text{kg} \cdot \text{m/s}) = (2820\ \text{kg})\,\mathbf{v_f}$$

$$\mathbf{v_f} = \frac{2.14 \times 10^4\ \text{kg} \cdot \text{m/s}}{2820\ \text{kg}}$$

$$\boxed{\mathbf{v_f} = 7.59\ \text{m/s to the north}}$$

Perfectly inelastic collision

1. A 1500 kg car traveling at 15.0 m/s to the south collides with a 4500 kg truck that is initially at rest at a stoplight. The car and truck stick together and move together after the collision. What is the final velocity of the two-vehicle mass?

2. A grocery shopper tosses a 9.0 kg bag of rice into a stationary 18.0 kg grocery cart. The bag hits the cart with a horizontal speed of 5.5 m/s toward the front of the cart. What is the final speed of the cart and bag?

3. A 1.5×10^4 kg railroad car moving at 7.00 m/s to the north collides with and sticks to another railroad car of the same mass that is moving in the same direction at 1.50 m/s. What is the velocity of the joined cars after the collision?

4. A dry cleaner throws a 22 kg bag of laundry onto a stationary 9.0 kg cart. The cart and laundry bag begin moving at 3.0 m/s to the right. Find the velocity of the laundry bag before the collision.

5. A 47.4 kg student runs down the sidewalk and jumps with a horizontal speed of 4.20 m/s onto a stationary skateboard. The student and skateboard move down the sidewalk with a speed of 3.95 m/s. Find the following:
    a. the mass of the skateboard
    b. how fast the student would have to jump to have a final speed of 5.00 m/s

CONCEPT PREVIEW

Chapter 10 will present a more thorough discussion of internal energy.

Kinetic energy does not remain constant in inelastic collisions

In a perfectly inelastic collision, the total kinetic energy does not remain constant when the objects collide and stick together. Some of the kinetic energy is converted to sound energy, internal energy, and internal elastic potential energy as the objects deform and lose their original shapes when they stick together as a result of the collision.

This phenomenon helps make sense of the special physics use of the words *elastic* and *inelastic*. In physics, just as in everyday language, *elastic* refers to things that retain their original shape. We normally think of *elastic* as referring to something that always returns to, or keeps, its original shape. In physics, the most important characteristic of an elastic collision is that the objects maintain their original shapes and are not deformed by the action of forces. Objects in an *inelastic* collision, on the other hand, are deformed during the collision and lose some kinetic energy. Objects in a *perfectly inelastic* collision are joined together as one mass after the collision.

The decrease in the total kinetic energy during an inelastic collision can be calculated using the formula for kinetic energy from Chapter 5. It is important to remember that not all of the initial kinetic energy is necessarily lost in a perfectly inelastic collision.

Changes in kinetic energy for perfectly inelastic collisions

PROBLEM

Two clay balls collide head-on in a perfectly inelastic collision. The first ball has a mass of 0.500 kg and an initial velocity of 4.00 m/s to the right. The mass of the second ball is 0.250 kg, and it has an initial velocity of 3.00 m/s to the left. What is the final velocity of the composite ball of clay after the collision? What is the decrease in kinetic energy during the collision?

SOLUTION

Given: $m_1 = 0.500$ kg $\qquad m_2 = 0.250$ kg $\qquad \mathbf{v_{1,i}} = 4.00$ m/s to the right

$\mathbf{v_{2,i}} = 3.00$ m/s to the left

Unknown: $\mathbf{v_f} = ?$

Use the equation for perfectly inelastic collisions from page 223.

$$m_1\mathbf{v_{1,i}} + m_2\mathbf{v_{2,i}} = (m_1 + m_2)\,\mathbf{v_f}$$

$$(0.500 \text{ kg} \times 4.00 \text{ m/s}) + (0.250 \text{ kg} \times -3.00 \text{ m/s}) = (0.500 \text{ kg} + 0.250 \text{ kg})\,\mathbf{v_f}$$

$$1.25 \text{ kg} \cdot \text{m/s} = (0.750 \text{ kg})\,\mathbf{v_f}$$

$$\boxed{\mathbf{v_f} = 1.67 \text{ m/s to the right}}$$

Use the equation for kinetic energy from Chapter 5.

Initial: $\qquad KE_i = KE_{1,i} + KE_{2,i}$

$$KE_i = \tfrac{1}{2}m_1 v_{1,i}^2 + \tfrac{1}{2}m_2 v_{2,i}^2$$

$$KE_i = \tfrac{1}{2}(0.500 \text{ kg})(4.00 \text{ m/s})^2 + \tfrac{1}{2}(0.250 \text{ kg})(-3.00 \text{ m/s})^2$$

$$KE_i = 5.12 \text{ J}$$

Final: $\qquad KE_f = KE_{1,f} + KE_{2,f}$

$$KE_f = \tfrac{1}{2}(m_1 + m_2)v_f^2$$

$$KE_f = \tfrac{1}{2}(0.750 \text{ kg})(1.67 \text{ m/s})^2$$

$$KE_f = 1.05 \text{ J}$$

$$\boxed{KE_i - KE_f = 4.07 \text{ J}}$$

Changes in kinetic energy for perfectly inelastic collisions

1. A 0.25 kg arrow with a velocity of 12 m/s to the west strikes and pierces the center of a 6.8 kg target.
   a. What is the final velocity of the combined mass?
   b. What is the decrease in kinetic energy during the collision?

2. During practice, a student kicks a 0.40 kg soccer ball with a velocity of 8.5 m/s to the south into a 0.15 kg bucket lying on its side. The bucket travels with the ball after the collision.
   a. What is the final velocity of the combined mass?
   b. What is the decrease in kinetic energy during the collision?

3. A 56 kg ice skater traveling at 4.0 m/s to the north suddenly grabs the hand of a 65 kg skater traveling at 12.0 m/s in the opposite direction as they pass. The two skaters continue skating together with joined hands.
   a. What is the final velocity of the two skaters?
   b. What is the decrease in kinetic energy during the collision?

ELASTIC COLLISIONS

When a player kicks a soccer ball, the collision between the ball and the player's foot is much closer to elastic than the collisions we have studied so far. In this case, *elastic* means that the ball and the player's foot remain separate after the collision.

elastic collision

a collision in which the total momentum and the total kinetic energy remain constant

In an **elastic collision,** two objects collide and return to their original shapes with no change in total kinetic energy. After the collision, the two objects move separately. In an elastic collision, both the total momentum and the total kinetic energy remain constant.

Most collisions are neither elastic nor perfectly inelastic

In the everyday world, most collisions are not perfectly inelastic. That is, colliding objects do not usually stick together and continue to move as one object. However, most collisions are not elastic, either. Even nearly elastic collisions, such as those between billiard balls or between a football player's foot and the ball, result in some decrease in kinetic energy. For example, a football deforms when it is kicked. During this deformation, some of the kinetic energy is converted to internal elastic potential energy. In most collisions, some of the kinetic energy is also converted into sound, such as the click of billiard balls colliding. In fact, any collision that produces sound is not elastic; the sound represents a decrease in kinetic energy.

Elastic and perfectly inelastic collisions are limiting cases; most collisions actually fall into a category between these two extremes. In this third category of collisions, called *inelastic collisions,* the colliding objects bounce and move separately after the collision, but the total kinetic energy decreases in the collision. *For the problems in this book, we will consider all collisions in which the objects do not stick together to be elastic collisions.* This means that we will assume that the total momentum and the total kinetic energy remain constant in all collisions that are not perfectly inelastic.

Kinetic energy is conserved in elastic collisions

Figure 6-12 shows a head-on collision between two soccer balls. The two balls are assumed to undergo an elastic head-on collision. Both balls have the same mass. The first ball is moving to the right when it collides with the second ball, which is moving to the left. When considered together, the entire system has momentum to the left.

After the elastic collision, the first ball moves to the left and the second ball moves to the right. The magnitude of the momentum of the first ball, which is now moving to the left, is greater than the magnitude of the momentum of the second ball, which is now moving to the right. When considered together, the entire system has momentum to the left, just as before the collision.

Another example of a nearly elastic collision is the collision between a golf ball and a club. After a golf club strikes a stationary golf ball, the golf ball moves at a very high speed in the same direction as the golf club. The golf club continues to move in the same direction, but its velocity decreases so that the momentum lost by the golf club is equal to and opposite the momentum gained by the golf ball. In both situations, we assume that *the total momentum and the total kinetic energy remain constant throughout the collision.*

MOMENTUM AND KINETIC ENERGY REMAIN CONSTANT IN AN ELASTIC COLLISION

$$m_1 \mathbf{v_{1,i}} + m_2 \mathbf{v_{2,i}} = m_1 \mathbf{v_{1,f}} + m_2 \mathbf{v_{2,f}}$$

$$\tfrac{1}{2} m_1 v_{1,i}^2 + \tfrac{1}{2} m_2 v_{2,i}^2 = \tfrac{1}{2} m_1 v_{1,f}^2 + \tfrac{1}{2} m_2 v_{2,f}^2$$

Remember that v is positive if an object moves to the right and negative if it moves to the left.

(a) Initial   **(b)** Impulse   **(c)** Final

p_A p_B $\Delta p_A = F \Delta t$ $\Delta p_B = -F \Delta t$ p_A p_B

A   B   A   B   A   B

Figure 6-12
In an elastic collision like this one **(b),** both objects return to their original shapes and move separately after the collision **(c).**

Elastic collisions

PROBLEM

A 0.015 kg marble moving to the right at 0.225 m/s makes an elastic head-on collision with a 0.030 kg shooter marble moving to the left at 0.180 m/s. After the collision, the smaller marble moves to the left at 0.315 m/s. What is the velocity of the 0.030 kg marble after the collision?

SOLUTION

1. DEFINE

Given: $m_1 = 0.015$ kg $m_2 = 0.030$ kg

$\mathbf{v_{1,i}} = 0.225$ m/s to the right

$\mathbf{v_{2,i}} = 0.180$ m/s to the left

$\mathbf{v_{1,f}} = 0.315$ m/s to the left

Unknown: $\mathbf{v_{2,f}} = ?$

Diagram:

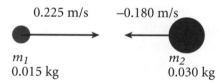

0.225 m/s   −0.180 m/s

m_1
0.015 kg

m_2
0.030 kg

2. PLAN

Choose equation(s) or situation: Use the equation for the conservation of momentum to find the final velocity of m_2, the 0.030 kg marble.

$$m_1\mathbf{v_{1,i}} + m_2\mathbf{v_{2,i}} = m_1\mathbf{v_{1,f}} + m_2\mathbf{v_{2,f}}$$

Rearrange the equation(s) to solve for the unknown: Rearrange the equation to isolate the final velocity of m_2.

$$m_2\mathbf{v_{2,f}} = m_1\mathbf{v_{1,i}} + m_2\mathbf{v_{2,i}} - m_1\mathbf{v_{1,f}}$$

$$\mathbf{v_{2,f}} = \frac{m_1\mathbf{v_{1,i}} + m_2\mathbf{v_{2,i}} - m_1\mathbf{v_{1,f}}}{m_2}$$

3. CALCULATE

Substitute the values into the equation(s) and solve: The rearranged conservation-of-momentum equation will allow you to isolate and solve for the final velocity.

$$\mathbf{v_{2,f}} = \frac{(0.015 \text{ kg})(0.225 \text{ m/s}) + (0.030 \text{ kg})(-0.180 \text{ m/s}) - (0.015 \text{ kg})(-0.315 \text{ m/s})}{0.030 \text{ kg}}$$

$$\mathbf{v_{2,f}} = \frac{(3.4 \times 10^{-3} \text{ kg} \cdot \text{m/s}) + (-5.4 \times 10^{-3} \text{ kg} \cdot \text{m/s}) - (-4.7 \times 10^{-3} \text{ kg} \cdot \text{m/s})}{0.030 \text{ kg}}$$

$$\mathbf{v_{2,f}} = \frac{2.7 \times 10^{-3} \text{ kg} \cdot \text{m/s}}{3.0 \times 10^{-2} \text{ kg}}$$

$$\boxed{\mathbf{v_{2,f}} = 9.0 \times 10^{-2} \text{ m/s to the right}}$$

4. EVALUATE   Confirm your answer by making sure kinetic energy is also conserved using these values.

Conservation of kinetic energy

$$\tfrac{1}{2}m_1v_{1,i}^2 + \tfrac{1}{2}m_2v_{2,i}^2 = \tfrac{1}{2}m_1v_{1,f}^2 + \tfrac{1}{2}m_2v_{2,f}^2$$

$$KE_i = \tfrac{1}{2}(0.015\ \text{kg})(0.225\ \text{m/s})^2 + \tfrac{1}{2}(0.030\ \text{kg})(-0.180\ \text{m/s})^2 =$$
$$8.7 \times 10^{-4}\ \text{kg}\bullet\text{m}^2/\text{s}^2 = 8.7 \times 10^{-4}\ \text{J}$$

$$KE_f = \tfrac{1}{2}(0.015\ \text{kg})(0.315\ \text{m/s})^2 + \tfrac{1}{2}(0.030\ \text{kg})(0.090\ \text{m/s})^2 =$$
$$8.7 \times 10^{-4}\ \text{kg}\bullet\text{m}^2/\text{s}^2 = 8.7 \times 10^{-4}\ \text{J}$$

Kinetic energy is conserved.

Elastic collisions

1. A 0.015 kg marble moving to the right at 22.5 cm/s makes an elastic head-on collision with a 0.015 kg marble moving to the left at 18.0 cm/s. After the collision, the first marble moves to the left at 18.0 cm/s.

   a. Find the velocity of the second marble after the collision.

   b. Verify your answer by calculating the total kinetic energy before and after the collision.

2. A 16.0 kg canoe moving to the left at 12 m/s makes an elastic head-on collision with a 4.0 kg raft moving to the right at 6.0 m/s. After the collision, the raft moves to the left at 22.7 m/s.

   a. Find the velocity of the canoe after the collision.

   b. Verify your answer by calculating the total kinetic energy before and after the collision.

3. A 4.0 kg bowling ball moving to the right at 8.0 m/s has an elastic head-on collision with another 4.0 kg bowling ball initially at rest. The first ball stops after the collision.

   a. Find the velocity of the second ball after the collision.

   b. Verify your answer by calculating the total kinetic energy before and after the collision.

4. A 25 kg bumper car moving to the right at 5.5 m/s overtakes and collides elastically with a 35 kg bumper car moving to the right at 2.0 m/s. After the collision, the 25 kg bumper car slows to 1.4 m/s to the right.

   a. Find the velocity of the 35 kg bumper car after the collision.

   b. Verify your answer by calculating the total kinetic energy before and after the collision.

Table 6-2   Types of collisions

Type of collision	Diagram	What happens	Conserved quantity
perfectly inelastic		The two objects stick together after the collision so that their final velocities are the same.	momentum
elastic		The two objects bounce after the collision so that they move separately.	momentum kinetic energy
inelastic		The two objects deform during the collision so that the total kinetic energy decreases, but the objects move separately after the collision.	momentum

Section Review

1. Give two examples of elastic collisions and two examples of perfectly inelastic collisions.

2. If two automobiles collide, they usually do not stick together. Does this mean the collision is elastic?

3. A 90.0 kg fullback moving south with a speed of 5.0 m/s has a perfectly inelastic collision with a 95.0 kg opponent running north at 3.0 m/s.
   a. Calculate the velocity of the players just after the tackle.
   b. Calculate the decrease in total kinetic energy as a result of the collision.

4. A rubber ball collides elastically with the sidewalk.
   a. Does each object have the same kinetic energy after the collision as it had before the collision? Explain.
   b. Does each object have the same momentum after the collision as it had before the collision? Explain.

5. **Physics in Action**   Two 0.40 kg soccer balls collide elastically in a head-on collision. The first ball starts at rest, and the second ball has a speed of 3.5 m/s. After the collision, the second ball is at rest.
   a. What is the final speed of the first ball?
   b. What is the kinetic energy of the first ball before the collision?
   c. What is the kinetic energy of the second ball after the collision?

CHAPTER 6
Summary

KEY IDEAS

Section 6-1 Momentum and impulse
- Momentum is a vector quantity defined as the product of an object's mass and velocity, $\mathbf{p} = m\mathbf{v}$.
- A net external force applied constantly to an object for a certain time interval will cause a change in the object's momentum equal to the product of the force and the time interval, $\mathbf{F}\Delta t = \Delta \mathbf{p}$.
- The product of the constant applied force and the time interval during which the force is applied is called the impulse of the force for the time interval.

Section 6-2 Conservation of momentum
- In all interactions between isolated objects, momentum is conserved.
- In every interaction between two isolated objects, the change in momentum of the first object is equal to and opposite the change in momentum of the second object.

Section 6-3 Elastic and inelastic collisions
- In a perfectly inelastic collision, two objects stick together and move as one mass after the collision.
- Momentum is conserved but kinetic energy is not conserved in a perfectly inelastic collision.
- In an inelastic collision, kinetic energy is converted to internal elastic potential energy when the objects deform. Some kinetic energy is also converted to sound energy and thermal energy.
- In an elastic collision, two objects return to their original shapes and move away from the collision separately.
- Both momentum and kinetic energy are conserved in an elastic collision.
- Few collisions are elastic or perfectly inelastic.

KEY TERMS

elastic collision (p. 226)

impulse (p. 210)

momentum (p. 208)

perfectly inelastic collision (p. 222)

Variable symbols

Quantities		Units
$\mathbf{p}$	momentum	kg•m/s kilogram-meters per second
$\mathbf{F}\Delta t$	impulse	N•s Newton-seconds = kilogram-meters per second

CHAPTER 6
Review and Assess

MOMENTUM AND IMPULSE

Review questions

1. If an object is not moving, what is its momentum?

2. If a particle's kinetic energy is zero, what is its momentum?

3. If two particles have equal kinetic energies, do they have the same momentum? Explain.

4. Show that $\mathbf{F} = m\mathbf{a}$ and $\mathbf{F} = \dfrac{\Delta \mathbf{p}}{\Delta t}$ are equivalent.

Conceptual questions

5. A truck loaded with sand is moving down the highway in a straight path.
   a. What happens to the momentum of the truck if the truck's velocity is increasing?
   b. What happens to the momentum of the truck if sand leaks at a constant rate through a hole in the truck bed while the truck maintains a constant velocity?

6. Gymnasts always perform on padded mats. Use the impulse-momentum theorem to discuss how these mats protect the athletes.

7. When a car collision occurs, an air bag is inflated, protecting the passenger from serious injury. How does the air bag soften the blow? Discuss the physics involved in terms of momentum and impulse.

8. A karate expert can break a stack of boards in half by hitting the boards with the side of one bare hand. Will the boards break more easily if they are struck swiftly or slowly? Explain.

9. Consider a field of insects, all of which have essentially the same mass.
   a. If the total momentum of the insects is zero, what does this imply about their motion?
   b. If the total kinetic energy of the insects is zero, what does this imply about their motion?

10. Two students hold an open bed sheet loosely by its corners to form a "catching net." The instructor asks a third student to throw an egg into the middle of the sheet as hard as possible. Why doesn't the egg's shell break?

11. How do car bumpers that collapse on impact help protect a driver?

Practice problems

12. Calculate the linear momentum for each of the following cases:
    a. a proton with mass 1.67×10^{-27} kg moving with a velocity of 5.00×10^{6} m/s straight up
    b. a 15.0 g bullet moving with a velocity of 325 m/s to the right
    c. a 75.0 kg sprinter running with a velocity of 10.0 m/s southwest
    d. Earth ($m = 5.98 \times 10^{24}$ kg) moving in its orbit with a velocity equal to 2.98×10^{4} m/s west
    (See Sample Problem 6A.)

13. If a 0.150 kg baseball has a momentum of $\mathbf{p} = 6.90$ kg•m/s as it is thrown from home to second base, what is its velocity?
    (See Sample Problem 6A.)

14. A 0.10 kg ball of dough is thrown straight up into the air with an initial velocity of 15 m/s.
    a. Find the momentum of the ball of dough at its maximum height.
    b. Find the momentum of the ball of dough halfway to its maximum height on the way up.
    (See Sample Problem 6A.)

15. What is the momentum of a 0.150 kg baseball thrown with a velocity of 35 m/s toward home plate?
    (See Sample Problem 6A.)

16. A 2.5 kg ball strikes a wall with a velocity of 8.5 m/s to the left. The ball bounces off with a velocity of 7.5 m/s to the right. If the ball is in contact with the

wall for 0.25 s, what is the constant force exerted on the ball by the wall?
(See Sample Problem 6B.)

17. A football punter accelerates a 0.55 kg football from rest to a speed of 8.0 m/s in 0.25 s. What constant force does the punter exert on the ball?
(See Sample Problem 6B.)

18. A constant force of 2.5 N to the right acts on a 1.5 kg mass for 0.50 s.
    a. Find the final velocity of the mass if it is initially at rest.
    b. Find the final velocity of the mass if it is initially moving along the x-axis with a velocity of 2.0 m/s to the left.
(See Sample Problem 6B.)

19. A 55 kg pole-vaulter falls from rest from a height of 5.0 m onto a foam-rubber pad. The pole-vaulter comes to rest 0.3 s after landing on the pad.
    a. Calculate the athlete's velocity just before reaching the pad.
    b. Calculate the constant force exerted on the pole-vaulter due to the collision.
(See Sample Problem 6B.)

20. A 0.150 kg baseball moving at +26 m/s is slowed to a stop by a catcher in 0.010 s. What constant force did the catcher exert on the ball during this time? How far did the ball travel before stopping?
(See Sample Problem 6C.)

21. A 0.025 kg golf ball moving at 18 m/s crashes through the window of a house in 5.0×10^{-4} s. After the crash, the ball continues in the same direction with a speed of 10 m/s. Assuming the force exerted on the ball by the window was constant, what was the magnitude of this force?
(See Sample Problem 6C.)

CONSERVATION OF MOMENTUM

Review questions

22. Two skaters initially at rest push against each other so that they move in opposite directions. What is the total momentum of the two skaters when they begin moving? Explain.

23. In a collision between two soccer balls, momentum is conserved. Is momentum conserved for each soccer ball? Explain.

24. Explain how momentum is conserved when a ball bounces against a floor.

Conceptual questions

25. As a ball falls toward Earth, the momentum of the ball increases. How would you reconcile this observation with the law of conservation of momentum?

26. In the early 1900s, Robert Goddard proposed sending a rocket to the moon. Critics took the position that in a vacuum such as exists between Earth and the moon, the gases emitted by the rocket would have nothing to push against to propel the rocket. To settle the debate, Goddard placed a gun in a vacuum and fired a blank cartridge from it. (A blank cartridge fires only the hot gases of the burning gunpowder.) What happened when the gun was fired? Explain your answer.

27. A magician places some dishes and silverware on a table covered by a tablecloth. He then rapidly removes the tablecloth from the table without disturbing the dishes and utensils on the table. On the basis of what you learned in this chapter, explain how this trick is possible.

28. When a bullet is fired from a gun, what happens to the gun? Explain, using the principles of momentum discussed in this chapter.

Practice problems

29. A 65.0 kg ice skater moving forward with a velocity of 2.50 m/s throws a 0.150 kg snowball forward with a velocity of 32.0 m/s.
    a. What is the velocity of the ice skater after throwing the snowball? Disregard the friction between the skates and the ice.
    b. A second skater initially at rest with a mass of 60.0 kg catches the snowball. What is the velocity of the second skater after catching the snowball in a perfectly inelastic collision?
(See Sample Problem 6D.)

30. A tennis player places a 55 kg ball machine on a frictionless surface, as in **Figure 6-13.** The machine fires a 0.057 kg tennis ball horizontally with a velocity of 36 m/s toward the north. What is the final velocity of the machine?
(See Sample Problem 6D.)

Figure 6-13

31. A 7.50 kg laundry bag is dropped from rest at an initial height of 3.00 m.

    a. What is the speed of Earth toward the bag just before the bag hits the ground? Use the value 5.98×10^{24} kg as the mass of Earth.
(See Sample Problem 6D.)

    b. Use your answer to part **(a)** to justify disregarding the motion of Earth when dealing with the motion of objects on Earth.

32. After being struck by a bowling ball, a 1.5 kg bowling pin moving to the right at 3.0 m/s collides head-on with another 1.5 kg bowling pin initially at rest. Find the final velocity of the second pin in the following situations:

    a. the first pin moves to the right after the collision at 0.5 m/s

    b. the first pin stops moving when it hits the second pin
(See Sample Problem 6D.)

ELASTIC AND INELASTIC COLLISIONS

Review questions

33. Consider a perfectly inelastic head-on collision between a small car and a large truck traveling at the same speed. Which vehicle has a greater change in kinetic energy as a result of the collision?

34. Given the masses of two objects and their velocities before and after a head-on collision, how could you determine whether the collision was elastic, inelastic, or perfectly inelastic? Explain.

35. In an elastic collision between two objects, do both objects have the same kinetic energy after the collision as before? Explain.

36. If two objects collide and one is initially at rest, is it possible for both to be at rest after the collision? Is it possible for one to be at rest after the collision? Explain.

Practice problems

37. A 1550 kg car moving south at 10.0 m/s collides with a 2550 kg car moving north. The cars stick together and move as a unit after the collision at a velocity of 5.22 m/s to the north. Find the velocity of the 2550 kg car before the collision.
(See Sample Problem 6E.)

38. Two carts with masses of 4.0 kg and 3.0 kg, respectively, move on a frictionless track with velocities of 5.0 m/s and 4.0 m/s. The carts stick together after colliding head-on. Find the final speed.
(See Sample Problem 6E.)

39. Two carts with masses of 10.0 kg and 2.5 kg, respectively, move in opposite directions on a frictionless horizontal track with speeds of 6.0 m/s and 3.0 m/s, repectively. The carts stick together after colliding head on. Find the final speed of the two carts.
(See Sample Problem 6E.)

40. A 1.20 kg skateboard is coasting along the pavement at a speed of 5.00 m/s when a 0.800 kg cat drops from a tree vertically downward onto the skateboard. What is the speed of the skateboard-cat combination?
(See Sample Problem 6E.)

41. A railroad car with a mass of 2.00×10^{4} kg moving at 3.00 m/s collides and joins with two railroad cars already joined together, each with the same mass as the single car and initially moving in the same direction at 1.20 m/s.

    a. What is the speed of the three joined cars after the collision?

    b. What is the decrease in kinetic energy during the collision?
(See Sample Problem 6F.)

42. A 2150 kg car moving east at 10.0 m/s collides with a 3250 kg car moving east. The cars stick together and move east as a unit after the collision at a velocity of 5.22 m/s.
   a. Find the velocity of the 3250 kg car before the collision.
   b. What is the decrease in kinetic energy during the collision?
(See Sample Problem 6F.)

43. A 91 kg fullback moving east with a speed of 5.0 m/s is tackled by a 95 kg opponent running west at 3.0 m/s, and the collision is perfectly inelastic. Calculate the following:
   a. the velocity of the players just after the tackle
   b. the decrease in kinetic energy during the collision
(See Sample Problem 6F.)

44. A 5.0 g coin moving to the right at 25.0 cm/s makes an elastic head-on collision with a 15.0 g coin that is initially at rest. After the collision, the 5.0 g coin moves to the left at 12.5 cm/s.
   a. Find the final velocity of the other coin.
   b. Find the amount of kinetic energy transferred to the 15.0 g coin.
(See Sample Problem 6G.)

45. A billiard ball traveling at 4.0 m/s has an elastic head-on collision with a billiard ball of equal mass that is initially at rest. The first ball is at rest after the collision. What is the speed of the second ball after the collision?
(See Sample Problem 6G.)

46. A 0.400 kg bead slides on a straight frictionless wire with a velocity of 3.50 cm/s to the right, as shown in **Figure 6-14.** The bead collides elastically with a larger 0.600 kg bead initially at rest. After the collision, the smaller bead moves to the left with a velocity of 0.70 cm/s. Find the distance the larger bead moves along the wire in the first 5.0 s following the collision.
(See Sample Problem 6G.)

Figure 6-14

47. A 25.0 g marble moving to the right at 20.0 cm/s overtakes and collides elastically with a 10.0 g marble moving in the same direction at 15.0 cm/s. After the collision, the 10.0 g marble moves to the right at 22.1 cm/s. Find the velocity of the 25.0 g marble after the collision.
(See Sample Problem 6G.)

48. A 15.0 g toy car moving to the right at 20.0 cm/s has an elastic head-on collision with a 20.0 g toy car moving in the opposite direction at 30.0 cm/s. After colliding, the 15.0 g car moves with a velocity of 37.1 cm/s to the left. Find the velocity of the 20.0 g car after the collision.
(See Sample Problem 6G.)

49. Two shuffleboard disks of equal mass, one orange and the other yellow, are involved in an elastic collision. The yellow disk is initially at rest and is struck by the orange disk moving initially to the right at 5.00 m/s. After the collision, the orange disk is at rest. What is the velocity of the yellow disk after the collision?
(See Sample Problem 6G.)

MIXED REVIEW PROBLEMS

50. A moving object has a kinetic energy of 150 J and a momentum with a magnitude of 30.0 kg•m/s. Determine the mass and speed of the object.

51. The bird perched on the swing in **Figure 6-15** has a mass of 52.0 g, and the base of the swing has a mass of 153 g. The swing and bird are originally at rest, and then the bird takes off horizontally at 2.00 m/s. How high will the base of the swing rise above its original level? Disregard friction.

8.00 cm

Figure 6-15

52. Two billiard balls with identical masses and moving in opposite directions have an elastic head-on collision. Before the collision, each ball has a speed of 22 cm/s. Find the speed of each billiard ball immediately after the collision. (See Appendix A for hints on solving simultaneous equations.)

53. A 3.00 kg mud ball has a perfectly inelastic collision with a second mud ball that is initially at rest. The composite system moves with a speed equal to one-third the original speed of the 3.00 kg mud ball. What is the mass of the second mud ball?

54. A 5.5 g bullet is fired into a block of wood with a mass of 22.6 g. The wood block is initially at rest on a 1.5 m tall post. After the collision, the wood block and bullet land 2.5 m from the base of the post. Find the initial speed of the bullet.

Technology & Learning

Graphing calculators

Program your graphing calculator to create a graph of force versus time for a 0.43 kg soccer ball in the situations below. Then use the graph to determine the force that must be exerted in the given time interval to cause the given changes in momentum.

a. the ball slows from 15 m/s to 0 m/s in 0.025 s

b. the ball slows from 15 m/s to 0 m/s in 0.75 s

c. the ball speeds up from 5.0 m/s in one direction to 22 m/s in the opposite direction in 0.045 s

d. the ball speeds up from 5.0 m/s in one direction to 22 m/s in the opposite direction in 0.55 s

Press Y= and CLEAR to clear any functions.
Open a new program by pressing PRGM ▶ ▶ ENTER.

Name the program "MOMENTUM" and press ENTER. Then enter the program shown in the table below.

To exit the program editor, press 2nd QUIT. To run the program, press PRGM, select "MOMENTUM," and press ENTER ENTER. Enter the value for the mass, initial velocity, and final velocity, pressing ENTER after each one.

The calculator will provide a graph of the force applied versus the time interval. (If the graph is not visible, press WINDOW and change the settings for the graph window, then press GRAPH.)

Press TRACE, and use the arrow keys to trace along the curve. The x value corresponds to the time in seconds and the y value corresponds to the force in newtons. (Note that the force will be negative in cases where it opposes the ball's initial velocity.)

Keystrokes	Display
	PROGRAM: MOMENTUM
1. PRGM ▶ 2 ALPHA M ENTER	:PROMPT M
2. PRGM ▶ 2 ALPHA I ENTER	:PROMPT I
3. PRGM ▶ 2 ALPHA F ENTER	:PROMPT F
4. ALPHA " ALPHA M (ALPHA F − ALPHA I) ÷ X,T,θ ALPHA " STO▶ 2nd Y-VARS 1 1 ENTER	:"M(F−I)/X" → Y₁
5. PRGM ▶ 4 ENTER	:DISPGRAPH

55. A 730 N student stands in the middle of a frozen pond having a radius of 5.0 m. He is unable to get to the other side because of a lack of friction between his shoes and the ice. To overcome this difficulty, he throws his 2.6 kg physics textbook horizontally toward the north shore at a speed of 5.0 m/s. How long does it take him to reach the south shore?

56. A 2250 kg car traveling at 10.0 m/s collides with a 2750 kg car that is initially at rest at a stoplight. The cars stick together and move 2.50 m before friction causes them to stop. Determine the coefficient of kinetic friction between the cars and the road, assuming that the negative acceleration is constant and that all wheels on both cars lock at the time of impact.

57. An 8.0 g bullet is fired into a 2.5 kg pendulum bob initially at rest and becomes embedded in it. If the pendulum rises a vertical distance of 6.0 cm, calculate the initial speed of the bullet.

58. An 85.0 kg astronaut is working on the engines of a spaceship that is drifting through space with a constant velocity. The astronaut turns away to look at Earth and seconds later is 30.0 m behind the ship, at rest relative to the spaceship. The only way to return to the ship without a thruster is to throw a 0.500 kg wrench directly away from the ship. If the astronaut throws the wrench with a speed of 20.0 m/s, how long does it take the astronaut to reach the ship?

59. An unstable nucleus with a mass of 17.0×10^{-27} kg initially at rest disintegrates into three particles. One of the particles, of mass 5.0×10^{-27} kg, moves along the positive y-axis with a speed of 6.0×10^6 m/s. Another particle, of mass 8.4×10^{-27} kg, moves along the positive x-axis with a speed of 4.0×10^6 m/s. Determine the third particle's speed and direction of motion. (Assume that mass is conserved.)

Alternative Assessment

Performance assessment

1. Design an experiment that uses a dynamics cart with other easily found equipment to test whether it is safer to crash into a steel railing or into a container filled with sand. How can you measure the force applied to the cart as it crashes into the barrier? If your teacher approves your plan, perform the experiment.

2. Obtain a videotape of one of your school's sports teams in action. Create a play-by-play description of a short segment of the videotape, explaining how momentum and kinetic energy change during impacts that take place in the segment.

3. An inventor has asked an Olympic biathlon team to test his new rifles during the target-shooting segment of the event. The new 0.75 kg guns shoot 25.0 g bullets at 615 m/s. The team's coach has hired you to advise him about how these guns could affect the biathletes' accuracy. Prepare figures to justify your answer. Be ready to defend your position.

Portfolio projects

4. Investigate the elastic collisions between atomic particles. What happens after an elastic collision between a hydrogen atom at rest and a helium atom moving at 150 m/s? Which direction will each particle move after the collision? Which particle will have a higher speed after the collision? What happens when a neutron moving at 150 m/s hits a hydrogen atom at rest? Research the masses of the particles involved. Draw diagrams of each collision.

5. An engineer working on a space mission claims that if momentum concerns are taken into account, a spaceship will need far less fuel for its return trip than it did for the first half of the mission. Prepare a detailed report on the validity of this hypothesis. Research the principles of rocket operations. Select specific examples of space missions, and study the nature of each mission and the amounts of fuel used. Your report should include diagrams and calculations.

CHAPTER 6
Laboratory Exercise

OBJECTIVES

- Measure the mass and velocity of two carts.
- Calculate the momentum of each cart.
- Verify the law of conservation of momentum.

MATERIALS LIST

✔ **two carts, one with a spring mechanism**

✔ **balance**

✔ **metric ruler**

PROCEDURE

CBL AND SENSORS

✔ **CBL**

✔ **CBL motion detector**

✔ **graphing calculator with link cable**

✔ **support stand with clamp**

✔ **set of masses**

✔ **tape**

✔ **two 25 × 25 cm squares of poster board**

RECORDING TIMER

✔ **recording timer**

✔ **paper tape**

✔ **stopwatch**

CONSERVATION OF MOMENTUM

The product of the mass of a moving object and its velocity is called its *momentum.* Studying momentum helps physicists understand the relationship between the motion of two interacting objects.

According to the impulse-momentum theorem, the change in an object's momentum is equal to the product of the force acting on the object and the time interval during which the force acts. Newton's third law states that every action is accompanied by an equal and opposite reaction. Thus, when a spring-loaded cart pushes off against another cart, the force on the first cart is accompanied by an equal and opposite force on the second cart. Both of these forces act for exactly the same time interval, so the change in momentum of the first cart is equal and opposite to the change in momentum of the second cart, in the absence of other forces.

In this experiment you will study the momentum of two carts with unequal masses. The carts will be placed together and will move apart when a compressed spring between them is released. You will find the mass and velocity of each cart in order to compare the momentum before and after the carts move apart.

SAFETY

- **Tie back long hair, secure loose clothing, and remove loose jewelry to prevent their getting caught in moving or rotating parts.**

PREPARATION

1. Determine whether you will be using the CBL and sensors or the recording timer to perform this experiment. Read the entire lab procedure for the appropriate method. Plan the steps you will take.

2. Prepare a data table in your lab notebook with seven columns and four rows. In the first row, label the first through seventh columns *Trial, m_1 (kg), m_2 (kg), Cart 1 Distance (m), Cart 2 Distance (m), Cart 1 Time interval (s),* and *Cart 2 Time interval (s).* In the first column, label the second through fourth rows *1, 2,* and *3.*

3. Choose a location where both carts will be able to move at least 1.0 m without any obstacles.

Recording timer procedure begins on page 240.

PROCEDURE

CBL AND SENSORS

Conservation of momentum

4. Connect the CBL to the calculator with the unit-to-unit link cable using the link ports located on each unit. Connect the motion detector to the SONIC port. Turn on the CBL and the graphing calculator.

5. Start the program PHYSICS on your graphing calculator.

   a. Select option *SET UP PROBES* from the MAIN MENU. Enter 1 for the number of probes. Select the motion detector from the list.

   b. Select the *COLLECT DATA* option from the MAIN MENU. Select the *TIME GRAPH* option from the DATA COLLECTION menu. Enter 0.02 for the time between samples. Enter 99 for the number of samples.

   c. Check the values you entered and press ENTER. If the values are correct, select *USE TIME SETUP* to continue. If you made a mistake entering the time values, select *MODIFY SETUP,* reenter the values, and continue.

   d. On the TIME GRAPH menu, select *NON-LIVE DISPLAY.*

6. Set up the apparatus, as shown in **Figure 6-16.** Position the motion detector so that it will be in a straight line with the motion of the carts. To keep the motion detector from moving during the experiment, clamp it to the support stand. Place a piece of tape 1.5 m in front of the motion detector to serve as a starting line for the cart.

7. Tape a square of poster board to the back of each cart to make a vertical surface. Label the carts *Cart 1* and *Cart 2.* Find the mass of cart 1, and record it in your data table. Securely tape a 1.0 kg mass to cart 2. Find the mass of cart 2 and the 1.0 kg mass, and record it in your data table.

8. Compress the spring mechanism and position the carts together, as shown in **Figure 6-16.** The poster board on cart 1 should be in a straight line with the motion detector, and it should be at least 1.5 m away from the motion detector. Use a piece of tape to mark the starting line on the table top. Cart 2 should be positioned to move away from the motion detector.

9. Press ENTER on the calculator. When the motion detector begins to click, quickly press the spring mechanism release on the carts. The carts will move away from each other. Let cart 1 move about 1.0 m, but catch the carts before they reach the edges of the table. *Do not let the carts hit the motion detector or fall off the table.*

Figure 6-16
This photo shows all the equipment necessary to complete this lab, but the equipment is not placed at the appropriate distances for the experiment. Follow the written directions for correct placement.

Step 8: If the spring mechanism has more than one notch, choose the first notch. Make sure there is at least 1.5 m between the motion detector and the cart. Make sure the other cart is at least 1.0 m from the edge of the table.

Step 9: Let the carts move at least 1.0 m before you catch them, but do not let the carts hit the motion detector or fall off the table.

Step 13: Switch the positions of the carts to record data for the second cart.

10. When the motion detector stops clicking and the CBL displays *DONE,* press ENTER on the graphing calculator. Select the *SONIC* option from the SELECT CHANNELS menu. Select *DISTANCE* to plot a graph of the distance between the cart and the motion detector in meters against time in seconds. Use the arrow keys to trace along the curve. On the far left and the far right, the curve represents the position of the cart before and after its motion. The middle section of the curve should be a straight line, and it represents the motion of the cart. Use the arrow keys to choose a point on the curve near the beginning of this middle section and another point near the end.

11. Find the difference between the *y* values of these two points, and record it as the cart 1 distance for trial 1 in your data table. Find the difference between the *x* values for these two readings to find the time elapsed between measurements. Record this as the cart 1 time interval for trial 1 in your data table. Press ENTER on the calculator.

12. Select the *SONIC* option again and select the *VELOCITY* option to plot a graph of the velocity against time. Examine how the velocity of the cart changed during the experiment. Make a sketch of the graph in your lab notebook. Press ENTER.

13. Select the *SONIC* option again and select the *ACCELERATION* option to plot a graph of the acceleration against time. Examine how the acceleration of the cart changed during the experiment. Make a sketch of the graph. Press ENTER.

14. To find the values for cart 2 distance and time interval, repeat the experiment by compressing the spring mechanism and repositioning the carts. Reverse the carts so that cart 2 is in a straight line with the motion detector while cart 1 moves away from the motion detector. Repeat step 8 through step 13. Record these values as the cart 2 distance and time interval in the data table for trial 1.

15. Using different masses, repeat the experiment two more times, for trials 2 and 3. For each trial, measure and record the values for cart 1 and for cart 2.

Analysis and interpretation begins on page 241.

PROCEDURE

RECORDING TIMER

Conservation of momentum

4. Set up the apparatus as shown in **Figure 6-17.** *Do not plug in the timer until your teacher approves your setup. Do not close the switch.*

5. If you have not used the recording timer before, refer to the Chapter 2 lab for instructions. Calibrate the recording timer with the stopwatch, or use the previously determined value for the timer's period.

6. Record the value for the timer's period on a line near the data table.

7. Measure the mass of one cart, and record it in the data table. Add a 1.0 kg mass to the second cart, and record the mass of the cart plus the 1.0 kg mass.

8. Fasten a timing tape to one end of each cart. Because both tapes pass through the same timer, place two carbon paper disks back to back between the paper tapes.

9. Compress the spring and position the carts. When your teacher approves your setup, plug the recording timer into the wall outlet. Start the timer and release the spring simultaneously.

10. Catch the carts before they reach the edge of the table and then stop the timer. *Do not let the carts fall off the table.* Remove the tapes. Label each tape so that it corresponds to the cart to which it was attached.

11. On each tape, find a portion where the distance between dots is fairly constant. Use the metric ruler to measure three distances between successive dots.

12. Find the average of these three values and record the average as the distance for that cart in your data table. Record the period of the timer as the time interval in your data table.

13. Using different masses, repeat the experiment two more times for trial 2 and trial 3.

Figure 6-17

Step 7: The recording timer will mark the tapes for both carts at the same time. Place two carbon disks back to back with one tape above and one tape below.

Step 9: If the spring mechanism has more than one notch, choose the first notch. Press straight down to release the spring mechanism so that you do not affect the motion of the carts. Let the carts move at least 1.0 m before you catch them, but do not let the carts fall off the table.

ANALYSIS AND INTERPRETATION

Calculations and data analysis

1. Organizing data   For each trial, find the velocities v_1 and v_2. Because the carts are moving in opposite directions, assign one of the carts a negative velocity to indicate direction.

2. Organizing data   For each trial, calculate the momentum of each cart by multiplying its mass by its velocity.

3. Organizing data   For each trial, find the total momentum of the two carts.

4. Applying ideas   For each trial, what is the total momentum of the two carts before they start moving?

Conclusions

5. Evaluating information   Conservation of velocity would mean that the total velocity for both carts is the same after the spring mechanism is released as it was before the release. Is velocity conserved in this experiment? Support your answer with data from the experiment.

6. Evaluating information   On the basis of your data, is momentum conserved in this experiment? Support your answer with data from the experiment.

7. Evaluating methods   How would using two carts with identical masses affect your answers to items 5 and 6?

Rotational Motion and the Law of Gravity

PHYSICS IN ACTION

When riding this spinning amusement-park ride, people feel as if a force is pressing them against the padding on the inside walls of the ride. However, it is actually inertia that causes their bodies to press against the padding. The inertia of their bodies tends to maintain motion in a straight-line path, while the walls of the ride exert a force on their bodies that makes them follow a circular path. This chapter will discuss the force that maintains circular motion and other rotational-motion quantities.

- *How can you determine the riders' average linear speed or acceleration during the ride?*
- *In what direction are the forces pushing or pulling the riders?*

CONCEPT REVIEW

Displacement   (Section 2-1)

Velocity   (Section 2-1)

Acceleration   (Section 2-2)

Force   (Section 4-1)

7-1
Measuring rotational motion

- **Relate radians to degrees.**

- **Calculate angular displacement using the arc length and the distance from the axis of rotation.**

- **Calculate angular speed or angular acceleration.**

- **Solve problems using the kinematic equations for rotational motion.**

rotational motion

motion of a body that spins about an axis

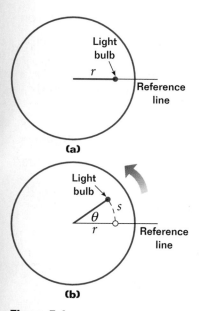

(a)

(b)

Figure 7-1

A light bulb on a rotating Ferris wheel **(a)** begins at a point along a reference line and **(b)** moves through an arc length *s*, and therefore through the angle *θ*.

ROTATIONAL QUANTITIES

When an object spins, it is said to undergo **rotational motion.** Consider a spinning Ferris wheel. The *axis of rotation* is the line about which the rotation occurs. In this case, it is a line perpendicular to the side of the Ferris wheel and passing through the wheel's center. How can we measure the distance traveled by an object on the edge of the Ferris wheel?

A point on an object that rotates about a single axis undergoes *circular motion* around that axis. In other words, regardless of the shape of the object, any single point on the object travels in a circle around the axis of rotation. It is difficult to describe the motion of a point moving in a circle using only the linear quantities introduced in Chapter 2 because the direction of motion in a circular path is constantly changing. For this reason, circular motion is described in terms of the angle through which the point on an object moves. When rotational motion is described using angles, all points on a rigid rotating object, except the points on the axis, move through the same angle during any time interval.

In **Figure 7-1,** a light bulb at a distance *r* from the center of a Ferris wheel, like the one shown in **Figure 7-2,** moves about the axis in a circle of radius *r*. In fact, every point on the wheel undergoes circular motion about the center. To analyze such motion, it is convenient to set up a *fixed* reference line. Let us assume that at time *t* = 0, the bulb is on the reference line, as in **Figure 7-1(a),** and that a line is drawn from the center of the wheel to the bulb. After a time interval Δ*t*, the bulb advances to a new position, as shown in **Figure 7-1(b).** In this time interval, the line from the center to the bulb (depicted with a red line in both diagrams) moved through the angle *θ* with respect to the reference line. Likewise, the bulb moved a distance *s*, measured along the circumference of the circle; *s* is the *arc length.*

Figure 7-2

Any point on a Ferris wheel that spins about a fixed axis undergoes circular motion.

Angles can be measured in radians

In the situations we have encountered so far, angles have been measured in degrees. However, in science, angles are often measured in **radians** (rad) rather than in degrees. Almost all of the equations used in this chapter and the next require that angles be measured in radians. In **Figure 7-1(b),** when the arc length, s, is equal to the length of the radius, r, the angle θ swept by r is equal to 1 rad. In general, any angle θ measured in radians is defined by the following:

$$\theta = \frac{s}{r}$$

The radian is a pure number, with no dimensions. Because θ is the ratio of an arc length (a distance) to the length of the radius (also a distance), the units cancel and the abbreviation *rad* is substituted in their place.

When the bulb on the Ferris wheel moves through an angle of 360° (one revolution of the wheel), the arc length s is equal to the circumference of the circle, or $2\pi r$. Substituting this value for s in the above equation gives the corresponding angle in radians.

$$\theta = \frac{s}{r} = \frac{2\pi r}{r} = 2\pi \text{ rad}$$

Thus, 360° equals 2π rad, or one complete revolution. In other words, one revolution corresponds to an angle of approximately $2(3.14) = 6.28$ rad. **Figure 7-3** depicts a circle marked with both radians and degrees.

It follows that any angle in degrees can be converted to an angle in radians by multiplying the angle measured in degrees by $2\pi/360°$. In this way, the degrees cancel out and the measurement is left in radians. The conversion relationship can be simplified as follows:

$$\theta(\text{rad}) = \frac{\pi}{180°}\theta(\text{deg})$$

radian

an angle whose arc length is equal to its radius, which is approximately equal to 57.3°

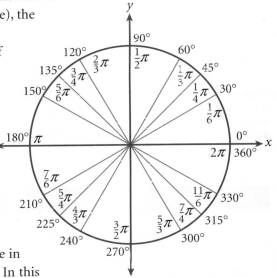

Figure 7-3
Angular motion is measured in units of radians. Because there are 2π radians in a full circle, radians are often expressed as a multiple of π.

Quick Lab

Radians and Arc Length

MATERIALS

✔ drawing compass
✔ paper
✔ thin wire
✔ wire cutters or scissors

Use the compass to draw a circle on a sheet of paper, and mark the center point of the circle. Measure the distance from the center point to the outside of the circle. This is the radius of the circle. Using the wire cutters, cut several pieces of wire equal to the length of this radius. Bend the pieces of wire, and lay them along the circle you drew with your compass. Approximately how many pieces of wire do you use to go all the way around the circle? Draw lines from the center of the circle to each end of one of the wires. Note that the angle between these two lines equals 1 rad. How many of these angles are there in this circle? Draw a larger circle using your compass. How many pieces of wire (cut to the length of the radius) do you use to go all the way around this circle?

Angular displacement describes how much an object has rotated

Just as an angle in radians is defined by the ratio of the arc length to the radius, the **angular displacement** traveled by the bulb on the Ferris wheel equals the change in the arc length, Δs, divided by the distance of the bulb from the axis of rotation. This relationship is depicted in **Figure 7-4**.

ANGULAR DISPLACEMENT

$$\Delta \theta = \frac{\Delta s}{r}$$

$$\text{angular displacement (in radians)} = \frac{\text{change in arc length}}{\text{distance from axis}}$$

For the purposes of this textbook, when a rotating object is viewed from above, the arc length, s, is considered positive when the point rotates counterclockwise and negative when it rotates clockwise. In other words, $\Delta \theta$ is positive when the object rotates counterclockwise and negative when the object rotates clockwise.

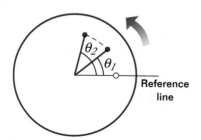

Figure 7-4
A light bulb on a rotating Ferris wheel rotates through an angular displacement of $\Delta \theta = \theta_2 - \theta_1$.

SAMPLE PROBLEM 7A

Angular displacement

PROBLEM

While riding on a carousel that is rotating clockwise, a child travels through an arc length of 11.5 m. If the carousel has a diameter of 8.00 m, through what angular displacement does the child travel? Convert this angular displacement to degrees.

SOLUTION

Given: $r = \dfrac{8.00 \text{ m}}{2} = 4.00 \text{ m}$ $\Delta s = -11.5 \text{ m}$

Unknown: $\Delta \theta = ? \text{ rad}$ $\Delta \theta = ?°$

Use the angular displacement equation on this page.

$$\Delta \theta = \frac{\Delta s}{r} = \frac{-11.5 \text{ m}}{4.00 \text{ m}}$$

$$\boxed{\Delta \theta = -2.88 \text{ rad}}$$

CALCULATOR SOLUTION

Most calculators have a key labeled DRG▶ that converts from degrees to radians.

$$\theta (\text{deg}) = \frac{180°}{\pi} \theta (\text{rad}) = \frac{180°}{\pi} (-2.88 \text{ rad})$$

$$\boxed{\theta (\text{deg}) = -165°}$$

Angular displacement

1. A girl sits on a merry-go-round at a distance of 1.5 m from the center. If the girl moves through an arc length of 2.5 m, through what angular displacement does she move?

2. A beetle sits at the top of a bicycle wheel with a diameter of 0.75 m. Assuming the wheel turns counterclockwise, what is the angular displacement of the beetle before it is squashed under the wheel? What arc length does the beetle travel through before it is squashed?

3. A passenger cart on a Ferris wheel moves through a distance of 12 m before it stops to drop off passengers. If the passenger carts are all 35 m from the axis of rotation of the Ferris wheel, what angular displacement does each cart move through during this part of the ride?

4. Fill in the unknown quantities in the following table:

	$\Delta\theta$	s	r
a.	? rad	+0.25 m	0.10 m
b.	+0.75 rad	?	8.5 m
c.	? degrees	−4.2 m	0.75 m
d.	+135°	+2.6 m	?

Angular speed describes rate of rotation

Recall that linear speed describes the distance traveled in a specified interval of time. **Angular speed** is similarly defined. The average angular speed, ω_{avg} (ω is the Greek letter *omega*), of a rotating rigid object is the ratio of the angular displacement, $\Delta\theta$, to the time interval, Δt, it takes the object to undergo that displacement. It describes how quickly the rotation occurs.

angular speed

the rate at which a body rotates about an axis, usually expressed in radians per second

ANGULAR SPEED

$$\omega_{avg} = \frac{\Delta\theta}{\Delta t}$$

$$\text{average angular speed} = \frac{\text{angular displacement}}{\text{time interval}}$$

Angular speed is given in units of radians per second (rad/s). Sometimes angular speeds are given in revolutions per unit time. Recall that 1 rev = 2π rad.

Angular speed

PROBLEM

A child at an ice cream parlor spins on a stool. If the child turns counter-clockwise through 10.0π rad during a 10.0 s interval, what is the average angular speed of the child's feet?

SOLUTION

Given: $\Delta\theta = 10.0\pi$ rad $\qquad \Delta t = 10.0$ s

Unknown: $\omega_{avg} = ?$

Use the angular speed equation from page 247.

$$\omega_{avg} = \frac{\Delta\theta}{\Delta t}$$

$$\omega_{avg} = \frac{10.0\pi \text{ rad}}{10.0 \text{ s}} = \pi \text{ rad/s}$$

$$\boxed{\omega_{avg} = 3.14 \text{ rad/s}}$$

PRACTICE 7B

Angular speed

1. A car tire rotates counterclockwise 3.5 times during a time interval of 0.75 s. What is the angular speed of the tire?

2. A girl ties a toy airplane to the end of a string and swings it around her head. What is the plane's angular speed if the plane moves through an angular displacement of 3.3 rad during 1.5 s?

3. Assuming Earth is perfectly spherical, what is the angular speed of some-one standing on the equator? Consider Earth's rotation to be counter-clockwise. State your answer in terms of rad/s. (Hint: Earth rotates about its axis once per day.)

4. Fill in the unknown quantities in the following table:

	ω_{avg}	$\Delta\theta$	Δt
a.	?	+2.3 rad	10.0 s
b.	+0.75 rev/s	?	0.05 s
c.	?	−1.2 turns	1.2 s
d.	+2π rad/s	+1.5π rad	?

Angular acceleration occurs when angular speed changes

Figure 7-5 shows a bicycle turned upside down so that a repair person can work on the rear wheel. The bicycle pedals are turned so that at time t_1 the wheel has angular speed ω_1, as shown in **Figure 7-5(a)**, and at a later time, t_2, it has angular speed ω_2, as shown in **Figure 7-5(b).**

The average **angular acceleration,** α_{avg} (α is the Greek letter *alpha*), of an object is given by the relationship shown below. Angular acceleration has the units radians per second per second (rad/s^2).

angular acceleration

the time rate of change of angular speed, expressed in radians per second per second

ANGULAR ACCELERATION

$$\alpha_{avg} = \frac{\omega_2 - \omega_1}{t_2 - t_1} = \frac{\Delta\omega}{\Delta t}$$

$$\text{average angular acceleration} = \frac{\text{change in angular speed}}{\text{time interval}}$$

SAMPLE PROBLEM 7C

Angular acceleration

PROBLEM

A car's tire rotates at an initial angular speed of 21.5 rad/s. The driver accelerates, and after 3.5 s the tire's angular speed is 28.0 rad/s. What is the tire's average angular acceleration during the 3.5 s time interval?

SOLUTION

Given: $\omega_1 = 21.5$ rad/s $\omega_2 = 28.0$ rad/s $\Delta t = 3.5$ s

Unknown: $\alpha_{avg} = ?$

Use the angular acceleration equation on this page.

$$\alpha_{avg} = \frac{\omega_2 - \omega_1}{\Delta t} = \frac{28.0 \text{ rad/s} - 21.5 \text{ rad/s}}{3.5 \text{ s}} = \frac{6.5 \text{ rad/s}}{3.5 \text{ s}}$$

$$\boxed{\alpha_{avg} = 1.9 \text{ rad/s}^2}$$

Angular acceleration

1. A figure skater begins spinning counterclockwise at an angular speed of 4.0π rad/s. During a 3.0 s interval, she slowly pulls her arms inward and finally spins at 8.0π rad/s. What is her average angular acceleration during this time interval?

2. What angular acceleration is necessary to increase the angular speed of a fan blade from 8.5 rad/s to 15.4 rad/s in 5.2 s?

3. Fill in the unknown quantities in the following table:

	α_{avg}	$\Delta\omega$	Δt
a.	?	+121.5 rad/s	7.0 s
b.	+0.75 rad/s^2	?	0.050 s
c.	?	−1.2 turns/s	1.2 s

All points on a rotating rigid object have the same angular acceleration and angular speed

If a point on the rim of a bicycle wheel had an angular speed greater than a point nearer the center, the shape of the wheel would be changing. Thus, for a rotating object to remain rigid, as does a bicycle wheel or a Ferris wheel, every portion of the object must have the same angular speed and the same angular acceleration. This fact is precisely what makes angular speed and angular acceleration so useful for describing rotational motion.

COMPARING ANGULAR AND LINEAR QUANTITIES

Table 7-1

Angular substitutes for linear quantities

Linear	Angular
x	θ
v	ω
a	α

Compare the equations we have found thus far for rotational motion with those we found for linear motion in Chapter 2. For example, compare the following defining equation for average angular speed with the defining equation for average linear speed:

$$\omega_{avg} = \frac{\theta_f - \theta_i}{t_f - t_i} = \frac{\Delta\theta}{\Delta t} \qquad v_{avg} = \frac{x_f - x_i}{t_f - t_i} = \frac{\Delta x}{\Delta t}$$

The equations are similar, with θ replacing x and ω replacing v. Take careful note of such similarities as you study rotational motion because nearly every linear quantity we have encountered thus far has a corresponding twin in rotational motion, as shown in **Table 7-1.**

Use kinematic equations for constant angular acceleration

In light of the similarities between variables in linear motion and those in rotational motion, it should be no surprise that the kinematic equations of rotational motion are similar to the linear kinematic equations in Chapter 2. The equations of rotational kinematics under constant angular acceleration, along with the corresponding equations for linear motion under constant acceleration, are summarized in **Table 7-2.** Note that the following rotational motion equations apply only for objects rotating about a fixed axis.

Table 7-2	Rotational and linear kinematic equations
Rotational motion with constant angular acceleration	**Linear motion with constant acceleration**
$\omega_f = \omega_i + \alpha \Delta t$	$v_f = v_i + a \Delta t$
$\Delta \theta = \omega_i \Delta t + \frac{1}{2}\alpha(\Delta t)^2$	$\Delta x = v_i \Delta t + \frac{1}{2}a(\Delta t)^2$
$\omega_f^2 = \omega_i^2 + 2\alpha(\Delta \theta)$	$v_f^2 = v_i^2 + 2a(\Delta x)$

Again, note the correlation between the rotational equations involving the angular variables θ, ω, and α and the equations of linear motion involving the variables x, v, and a.

The quantity ω in these equations represents the *instantaneous angular speed* of the rotating object rather than the average angular speed.

SAMPLE PROBLEM 7D

Angular kinematics

PROBLEM

The wheel on an upside-down bicycle rotates with a constant angular acceleration of 3.5 rad/s². If the initial angular speed of the wheel is 2.0 rad/s, through what angular displacement does the wheel rotate in 2.0 s?

SOLUTION

Given: $\omega_i = 2.0$ rad/s $\alpha = 3.5$ rad/s² $\Delta t = 2.0$ s

Unknown: $\theta = ?$

Use the second angular kinematic equation from **Table 7-2.**

$$\Delta\theta = \omega_i \Delta t + \frac{1}{2}\alpha(\Delta t)^2$$

$$\Delta\theta = (2.0 \text{ rad/s})(2.0 \text{ s}) + \frac{1}{2}(3.5 \text{ rad/s}^2)(2.0 \text{ s})^2$$

$$\boxed{\Delta\theta = 11 \text{ rad}}$$

Angular kinematics

1. What is the angular speed of the upside-down bicycle wheel in Sample Problem 7D at $t = 2.0$ s?

2. A diver performing a double somersault spins at an angular speed of 4.0π rad/s precisely 0.50 s after leaving the platform. Assuming the diver begins with zero initial angular speed and accelerates at a constant rate, what is the diver's angular acceleration during the double somersault?

3. A fish swimming behind an oil tanker gets caught in a whirlpool created by the ship's propellers. The fish has an angular speed of 1.0 rad/s. If the water in the whirlpool accelerates at a constant rate of 3.0 rad/s², what will the fish's instantaneous angular speed be 4.5 s later?

4. A remote-controlled car's wheel accelerates at 22.4 rad/s². If the wheel begins with an angular speed of 10.8 rad/s, what is the wheel's angular speed after exactly 3 full turns?

5. How long does the wheel in item 4 take to make the three turns?

Section Review

1. Convert the following angles in degrees to radians:
   a. 25°
   b. 35°
   c. 128°
   d. 270°

2. A mosquito lands on a phonograph record 5.0 cm from the record's center. If the record turns clockwise so that the mosquito travels along an arc length of 5.0 cm, what is the mosquito's angular displacement?

3. A bicyclist rides along a circular track. If the bicyclist travels around exactly half the track in 10.0 s, what is his average angular speed?

4. **Physics in Action**   Find the angular acceleration of a spinning amusement-park ride that initially travels at 0.50 rad/s then accelerates to 0.60 rad/s during a 0.50 s time interval.

5. **Physics in Action**   What is the instantaneous angular speed of a spinning amusement-park ride that accelerates from 0.50 rad/s at a constant angular acceleration of 0.20 rad/s² for 1.0 s?

7-2
Tangential and centripetal acceleration

RELATIONSHIPS BETWEEN ANGULAR AND LINEAR QUANTITIES

As described at the beginning of Section 7-1, the motion of a point on a rotating object is most easily described in terms of an angle from a fixed reference line. In some cases, however, it is useful to understand how the angular speed and angular acceleration of a rotating object relate to the linear speed and linear acceleration of a point on the object.

Imagine a golfer swinging a golf club. It turns out that the most effective method for hitting a golf ball a long distance involves swinging the club in an approximate circle around the body. If the club head undergoes a large angular acceleration, then the linear acceleration of the club head as it is swung will be large. This large linear acceleration causes the club head to strike the ball at a high speed and produce a significant force on the ball. This section will explore the relationships between angular and linear quantities.

Objects in circular motion have a tangential speed

Imagine a carousel at an amusement park rotating about its center. Because a carousel is a rigid object, any two horses attached to the carousel have the same angular speed and angular acceleration regardless of their respective distances from the axis of rotation. However, if the two horses are different distances from the axis of rotation, they have different **tangential speeds.** The tangential speed of any point rotating about an axis is also called the instantaneous linear speed of that point. The tangential speed of a horse on the carousel is its speed along a line drawn tangent to its circular path. (Recall that the tangent to a circle is the line that touches the circle at one and only one point.) The tangential speeds of two horses at different distances from the center of a carousel are represented in **Figure 7-6.**

Note that the speed of the horse at point *A* is represented by a longer arrow than the one that represents the speed of the horse at point *B*; this reflects the difference between the tangential speeds of the two horses. The horse on the outside must travel the same angular displacement during the same amount of time as the horse on the inside. To achieve this, the horse on the outside must travel a greater distance, Δs, than the horse on the inside. Thus, an object that is farther from the axis of a rigid rotating body, such as a carousel or a Ferris wheel, must travel at a higher tangential speed around the circular path, Δs, to travel the same angular displacement as would an object closer to the axis.

7-2 SECTION OBJECTIVES

- **Find the tangential speed of a point on a rigid rotating object using the angular speed and the radius.**
- **Solve problems involving tangential acceleration.**
- **Solve problems involving centripetal acceleration.**

tangential speed

the instantaneous linear speed of an object directed along the tangent to the object's circular path

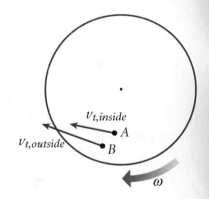

Figure 7-6
Horses on a carousel move at the same angular speed but different tangential speeds.

How can you find the tangential speed? Again consider the rotating carousel. If the carousel rotates through an angle $\Delta\theta$, a horse rotates through an arc length Δs in the interval Δt. The angular displacement of the horse is given by the equation for angular displacement.

$$\Delta\theta = \frac{\Delta s}{r}$$

To find the tangential speed of the horse, divide both sides of the equation by the time the horse takes to travel the distance Δs.

$$\frac{\Delta\theta}{\Delta t} = \frac{1}{r}\frac{\Delta s}{\Delta t}$$

From Section 7-1, you know that the left side of the equation equals ω_{avg}. Similarly, Δs is a linear distance, so Δs divided by Δt is a linear speed along an arc length. If Δt is very short, then Δs is so small it is nearly tangent to the circle, so the speed is the tangential speed.

TANGENTIAL SPEED

$$v_t = r\omega$$

Tangential speed = distance from axis × angular speed

Note that ω is the instantaneous angular speed, rather than the average angular speed, because the time interval is so short. This equation is valid only when ω is measured in radians per unit of time. Other measures of angular speed, such as degrees per second and revolutions per second, must not be used in this equation.

SAMPLE PROBLEM 7E

Tangential speed

PROBLEM

If the radius of a CD in a computer is 0.0600 m and the disc turns at a constant angular speed of 31.4 rad/s, what is the tangential speed of a microbe riding on the disc's rim?

SOLUTION

Given: $r = 0.0600$ m $\omega = 31.4$ rad/s

Unknown: $v_t = ?$

Use the tangential speed equation on this page.

$$v_t = r\omega = (0.0600 \text{ m})(31.4 \text{ rad/s})$$

$$\boxed{v_t = 1.88 \text{ m/s}}$$

Tangential speed

1. A revolving door turns at an angular speed of 1.75 rad/s. If a woman passes through the door at a distance of 1.0 m from the center of the door, what is the woman's linear speed?

2. While pitching, a softball pitcher swings the ball with an angular speed of 10.5 rad/s. If the pitcher's arm is 0.66 m long, what is the tangential speed of the ball just before the pitcher releases it?

3. An athlete spins in a circle before letting go of a discus. If the athlete spins at an angular speed of 12.3 rad/s and holds the discus at a distance of 0.75 m from the center of the torso, what is the discus's linear speed when the athlete releases it?

4. Fill in the unknown quantities in the following table:

	v_t	ω	r
a.	?	121.5 rad/s	0.030 m
b.	0.75 m/s	?	0.050 m
c.	?	1.2 turns/s	3.8 m
d.	2.0π m/s	1.5π rad/s	?

Tangential acceleration is tangent to the circular path

If a carousel speeds up, the horses on it experience an angular acceleration. The linear acceleration related to this angular acceleration is tangent to the circular path and is called the **tangential acceleration.**

Imagine that an object rotating about a fixed axis changes its angular speed by $\Delta\omega$ in the interval Δt. At the end of this time, the speed of a point on the object has changed by the amount Δv_t. Using the equation for tangential velocity on page 254 gives the following:

tangential acceleration

the instantaneous linear acceleration of an object directed along the tangent to the object's circular path

$$\Delta v_t = r\Delta\omega$$

Dividing by Δt gives $\quad \dfrac{\Delta v_t}{\Delta t} = r\dfrac{\Delta\omega}{\Delta t}$

If the time interval Δt is very small, then the left side of this relationship is the tangential acceleration of that point, and the angular speed divided by the time interval on the right side is the angular acceleration. Thus, the tangential acceleration of a point on a rotating object is given by the relationship on the following page.

TANGENTIAL ACCELERATION

$$a_t = r\alpha$$

Tangential acceleration = distance from axis × angular acceleration

Again, the angular acceleration in this equation refers to the instantaneous angular acceleration. This equation is valid only when the angular acceleration is expressed in units of radians per second per second.

SAMPLE PROBLEM 7F

Tangential acceleration

PROBLEM

A spinning ride at a carnival has an angular acceleration of 0.50 rad/s². Find the tangential acceleration of a rider who sits 6.5 m from the center.

SOLUTION

Given: $\alpha = 0.50$ rad/s² $r = 6.5$ m

Unknown: $a_t = ?$

Use the tangential acceleration equation on this page.

$$a_t = r\alpha = (6.5 \text{ m})(0.50 \text{ rad/s}^2)$$

$$\boxed{a_t = 3.3 \text{ m/s}^2}$$

PRACTICE 7F

Tangential acceleration

1. The computer disc ($r = 0.0600$ m) in Sample Problem 7E accelerates at a rate of 35.2 rad/s². Find the tangential acceleration of the microbe riding on the edge of the disc. 2.1

2. A young boy swings a yo-yo horizontally above his head at an angular acceleration of 0.35 rad/s². If the yo-yo string is 0.50 m long, what is the tangential acceleration of the yo-yo at the end of the string?

3. A dog sits 1.5 m from the center of a merry-go-round. If the dog undergoes a 1.5 m/s² linear acceleration, what is the angular acceleration of the merry-go-round? a.2

CENTRIPETAL ACCELERATION

Figure 7-7 shows a car moving in a circular path with a constant tangential speed of 30 km/h. Even though the car moves at a constant speed, it still has an acceleration. To see why this is, consider the defining equation for acceleration.

$$\mathbf{a} = \frac{\mathbf{v_f} - \mathbf{v_i}}{t_f - t_i}$$

Note that acceleration depends on a change in the velocity. Because velocity is a vector, there are two ways an acceleration can be produced: by a change in the *magnitude* of the velocity and by a change in the *direction* of the velocity. For a car moving in a circular path with constant speed, the acceleration is due to a change in direction. An acceleration of this nature is called a **centripetal** (center-seeking) **acceleration.** Its magnitude is given by the following equation:

$$a_c = \frac{v_t^2}{r}$$

Figure 7-7

Although the car moves at a constant speed of 30 km/h, the car still has an acceleration because the direction of the velocity changes.

Consider **Figure 7-8(a).** An object is seen first at point *A*, with tangential velocity $\mathbf{v_i}$ at time t_i, and then at point *B*, with tangential velocity $\mathbf{v_f}$ at a later time, t_f. Assume that $\mathbf{v_i}$ and $\mathbf{v_f}$ differ in direction only and their magnitudes are the same.

The change in velocity, $\Delta\mathbf{v} = \mathbf{v_f} - \mathbf{v_i}$, can be determined graphically, as shown by the vector triangle in **Figure 7-8(b).** Note that when Δt is very small, $\mathbf{v_f}$ will be almost parallel to $\mathbf{v_i}$ and the vector $\Delta\mathbf{v}$ will be approximately perpendicular to them, pointing toward the center of the circle. This means that the acceleration will also be directed toward the center of the circle because it is in the direction of $\Delta\mathbf{v}$.

Because the tangential speed is related to the angular speed through the relationship $v_t = r\omega$, the centripetal acceleration can be found using the angular speed as well.

centripetal acceleration

acceleration directed toward the center of a circular path

(a)

(b)

$$\Delta\mathbf{v} = \mathbf{v_f} - \mathbf{v_i} = \mathbf{v_f} + (-\mathbf{v_i})$$

Figure 7-8

(a) As the particle moves from *A* to *B*, the direction of the particle's velocity vector changes. **(b)** Vector addition is used to determine the direction of the change in velocity, $\Delta\mathbf{v}$, which for short time intervals is toward the center of the circle.

CENTRIPETAL ACCELERATION

$$a_c = \frac{v_t^2}{r}$$

$$a_c = r\omega^2$$

$$\text{centripetal acceleration} = \frac{(\text{tangential speed})^2}{\text{distance from axis}}$$

$$\text{centripetal acceleration} = \text{distance from axis} \times (\text{angular speed})^2$$

Centripetal acceleration

PROBLEM

A test car moves at a constant speed of 19.7 m/s around a circular track. If the distance from the car to the center of the track is 48.2 m, what is the centripetal acceleration of the car?

SOLUTION

Given: $v_t = 19.7$ m/s $r = 48.2$ m

Unknown: $a_c = ?$

Use the first centripetal acceleration equation from page 257.

$$a_c = \frac{v_t^2}{r} = \frac{(19.7 \text{ m/s})^2}{48.2 \text{ m}}$$

$$\boxed{a_c = 8.05 \text{ m/s}^2}$$

Centripetal acceleration

1. A girl sits on a tire that is attached to an overhanging tree limb by a rope. The girl's father pushes her with a tangential speed of 2.5 m/s, and the girl travels in a horizontal circle with a diameter of 4.2 m. What is the centripetal acceleration acting on the girl?

2. A young boy swings a yo-yo horizontally above his head at an angular speed of 22.5 rad/s. If the string is 0.50 m long, what is the centripetal acceleration of the yo-yo at the end of the string?

3. A dog sits 1.5 m from the center of a merry-go-round. If the dog undergoes a 1.5 m/s^2 centripetal acceleration, what is the dog's linear speed? What is the angular speed of the merry-go-round?

4. The test car from Sample Problem 7G moves at an angular speed of 0.512 rad/s while moving on the circular track. Find the centripetal acceleration of the car.

5. A piece of clay sits 0.20 m from the center of a potter's wheel. If the potter spins the wheel at an angular speed of 20.5 rad/s, what is the magnitude of the centripetal acceleration of the piece of clay on the wheel?

Tangential and centripetal accelerations are perpendicular

Centripetal and tangential acceleration are not the same. To understand why, consider a car moving around a circular track. Because the car is moving in a circular path, it always has a centripetal component of acceleration because its direction of travel, and hence the direction of its velocity, is continually changing. If the car's speed is increasing or decreasing, it also has a tangential component of acceleration. To summarize, the tangential component of acceleration is due to changing speed; the centripetal component of acceleration is due to changing direction.

Find the total acceleration using the Pythagorean theorem

When both components of acceleration exist simultaneously, the tangential acceleration is tangent to the circular path and the centripetal acceleration points toward the center of the circular path. Because these components of acceleration are perpendicular to each other, the magnitude of the *total acceleration* can be found using the Pythagorean theorem, as follows:

$$a_{total} = \sqrt{a_t^2 + a_c^2}$$

The direction of the total acceleration, as shown in **Figure 7-9,** depends on the magnitude of each component of acceleration and can be found using the inverse of the tangent function.

$$\theta = \tan^{-1} \frac{a_c}{a_t}$$

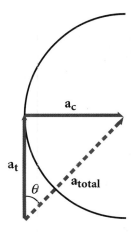

Figure 7-9
The direction of the total acceleration of a rotating object can be found using the tangent function.

Section Review

1. Find the tangential speed of a ball swung at a constant angular speed of 5.0 rad/s on a rope that is 5.0 m long.

2. If an object has a tangential acceleration of 10.0 m/s², the angular speed will do which of the following?
    a. decrease
    b. stay the same
    c. increase

3. **Physics in Action**   Find the tangential acceleration of a person standing 9.5 m from the center of a spinning amusement-park ride that has an angular acceleration of 0.15 rad/s².

4. **Physics in Action**   If a spinning amusement-park ride has an angular speed of 1.2 rad/s, what is the centripetal acceleration of a person standing 12 m from the center of the ride?

7-3

Causes of circular motion

- **Calculate the force that maintains circular motion.**

- **Explain how the apparent existence of an outward force in circular motion can be explained as inertia resisting the force that maintains circular motion.**

- **Apply Newton's universal law of gravitation to find the gravitational force between two masses.**

Figure 7-10

When a ball is whirled in a circle, a force acts on it directed toward the center of the ball's circular path.

FORCE THAT MAINTAINS CIRCULAR MOTION

Consider a ball of mass m tied to a string of length r that is being whirled in a horizontal circular path, as shown in **Figure 7-10.** Assume that the ball moves with constant speed. Because the velocity vector, **v,** changes direction continuously during the motion, the ball experiences a centripetal acceleration directed toward the center of motion, as described in Section 7-2, with magnitude given by the following equation:

$$a_c = \frac{v_t^2}{r}$$

The inertia of the ball tends to maintain the ball's motion in a straight-line path; however, the string counteracts this by exerting a force on the ball that makes the ball follow a circular path. This force is directed along the length of the string toward the center of the circle, as shown in **Figure 7-10.** The magnitude of this force can be found by applying Newton's second law along the radial direction.

$$F_c = ma_c$$

The net force on an object directed toward the center of the object's circular path is the force that maintains the object's circular motion.

FORCE THAT MAINTAINS CIRCULAR MOTION

$$F_c = \frac{mv_t^2}{r}$$

$$F_c = mr\omega^2$$

$$\text{force that maintains circular motion} = \text{mass} \times \frac{(\text{tangential speed})^2}{\text{distance to axis}}$$

$$\begin{array}{l}\text{force that maintains} \\ \text{circular motion}\end{array} = \text{mass} \times \text{distance to axis} \times (\text{angular speed})^2$$

The force that maintains circular motion is measured in the SI unit of newtons. This force is no different from any of the other forces we have studied. For example, friction between a race car's tires and a circular racetrack provides the force that enables the car to travel in a circular path. As another example, the gravitational force exerted on the moon by Earth provides the force necessary to keep the moon in its orbit.

Force that maintains circular motion

PROBLEM

A 70.5 kg pilot is flying a small plane at 30.0 m/s in a circular path with a radius of 100.0 m. Find the magnitude of the force that maintains the circular motion of the pilot.

SOLUTION

Given: $v_t = 30.0$ m/s $r = 100.0$ m $m = 70.5$ kg

Unknown: $F_c = ?$

Use the equation for force that maintains circular motion from page 260.

$$F_c = m\frac{v_t^2}{r} = (70.5 \text{ kg})\frac{(30.0 \text{ m/s})^2}{100.0 \text{ m}}$$

$$\boxed{F_c = 635 \text{ N}}$$

Force that maintains circular motion

1. A 29.4 kg girl sits in a tire that is attached to an overhanging tree limb by a rope. The girl's father pushes her with a linear speed of 2.5 m/s so that she travels in a horizontal circle with a diameter of 4.2 m. What is the magnitude of the force that maintains the girl's circular motion?

2. An 86.5 kg bicyclist is riding at a linear speed of 13.2 m/s around a circular track with a radius of 40.0 m. Find the magnitude of the force that maintains the bike's circular motion.

3. An 18.5 kg dog sits 1.5 m from the center of a merry-go-round. If the merry-go-round rotates at an angular speed of 6.5 rad/s, what is the force that acts on the dog to maintain its circular motion?

4. A test car moves around a 3.25 km circular track at a linear speed of 35.0 m/s. Find the magnitude of the force that maintains the car's circular motion if the test car has a mass of 905 kg.

5. A 40.0 kg child takes a ride on a Ferris wheel that rotates with an angular speed of 0.50 rad/s. Find the magnitude of the force that maintains the circular motion of the child if the distance from the center of the Ferris wheel to the child is 18.0 m.

Figure 7-11
A ball is whirled in a vertical circular path on the end of a string. When the string breaks at the position shown in **(a)**, the ball moves vertically upward in free fall. **(b)** When the string breaks at the top of the ball's path, the ball moves along a parabolic path.

Conceptual Challenge

1. Pizza

Pizza makers traditionally form the crust by throwing the dough up in the air and spinning it. Why does this make the pizza crust bigger?

2. Swings

The amusement-park ride pictured below spins riders around on swings attached by cables from above. What causes the swings to move away from the center of the ride when the center column begins to turn?

A force directed toward the center is necessary for circular motion

Because the force that maintains circular motion acts at right angles to the motion, it causes a change in the direction of the velocity. If this force vanishes, the object does not continue to move in its circular path. Instead, it moves along a straight-line path tangent to the circle. To illustrate this point, consider a ball that is attached to a string and is being whirled in a vertical circle, as shown in **Figure 7-11.** If the string breaks when the ball is at the position shown in **Figure 7-11(a),** the force that maintains circular motion will vanish and the ball will move vertically upward. Its motion will be that of a free-falling body. If the string breaks when the ball is at the top of its circular path, as shown in **Figure 7-11(b),** the ball will fly off horizontally in a direction tangent to the path and then move in the parabolic path of a projectile.

DESCRIBING THE MOTION OF A ROTATING SYSTEM

To better understand the motion of a rotating system, consider a car approaching a curved exit ramp to the left at high speed. As the driver makes the sharp left turn, the passenger slides to the right and hits the door. At that point, the force of the door keeps the passenger from being ejected from the car. What causes the passenger to move toward the door? A popular but *erroneous* explanation is that some mysterious force pushes the passenger outward. This is sometimes called the centrifugal force, but that term often creates confusion, so it is not used in this textbook.

Inertia is often misinterpreted as a force

The phenomenon is correctly explained as follows: Before the car enters the ramp, the passenger is moving in a straight-line path. As the car enters the ramp and travels along a curved path, the passenger, because of inertia, tends to move along the original straight-line path. This is in accordance with Newton's first law, which states that the natural tendency of a body is to continue moving in a straight line. However, if a sufficiently large force that maintains circular motion (toward the center of curvature) acts on the passenger, the person moves in a curved path, along with the car. The origin of the force that maintains the circular motion of the passenger is the force of friction between the passenger and the car seat. If this frictional force is not sufficient, the passenger slides across the seat as the car turns underneath. Because of inertia, the passenger continues to move in a straight-line path. Eventually, the passenger encounters the door, which provides a large enough force that enables the passenger to follow the same curved path as the car. The passenger slides toward the door not because of some mysterious outward force but because the force that maintains circular motion is not great enough to enable the passenger to travel along the circular path followed by the car.

NEWTON'S UNIVERSAL LAW OF GRAVITATION

Note that planets move in nearly circular orbits around the sun. As mentioned earlier, the force that keeps these planets from coasting off in a straight line is a **gravitational force.** The gravitational force is a field force that always exists between two masses, regardless of the medium that separates them. It exists not just between large masses like the sun, Earth, and moon but between any two masses, regardless of size or composition. For instance, desks in a classroom have a mutual attraction due to gravitational force. The force between the desks, however, is small compared with the force between the moon and Earth because the gravitational force is proportional to the product of the objects' masses.

Gravitational force acts so that objects are always attracted to one another. Examine the illustration of Earth and the moon in **Figure 7-12.** Note that the gravitational force between Earth and the moon is attractive, and recall that Newton's third law states that the force exerted on Earth by the moon, $\mathbf{F_{mE}}$, is equal in magnitude to and in the opposite direction of the force exerted on the moon by Earth, $\mathbf{F_{Em}}$.

gravitational force

the mutual force of attraction between particles of matter

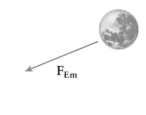

Figure 7-12
The gravitational force between Earth and the moon is attractive. According to Newton's third law, $F_{Em} = F_{mE}$.

Gravitational force is proportional to the distance between two masses

If particles have masses m_1 and m_2 and are separated by distance r, the magnitude of the gravitational force is given by the following equation:

NEWTON'S UNIVERSAL LAW OF GRAVITATION

$$F_g = G\frac{m_1m_2}{r^2}$$

$$\text{gravitational force} = \text{constant} \times \frac{\text{mass 1} \times \text{mass 2}}{(\text{distance between center of masses})^2}$$

G is a universal constant called the *constant of universal gravitation;* it can be used to calculate gravitational forces between any two particles and it has been measured experimentally.

$$G = 6.673 \times 10^{-11} \frac{\text{N} \cdot \text{m}^2}{\text{kg}^2}$$

The universal law of gravitation is an example of an *inverse-square law* in that the force varies as the inverse square of the separation. That is, the force between two masses decreases as the masses move farther apart.

Gravitational force is localized to the center of a spherical mass

The gravitational force exerted by a spherical mass on a particle outside the sphere is the same as it would be if the entire mass of the sphere were concentrated at its center. For example, the force on an object of mass m at Earth's surface has the following magnitude:

$$F_g = G\frac{M_E m}{R_E^2}$$

M_E is Earth's mass and R_E is its radius. This force is directed toward the center of Earth. Note that this force is in fact the weight of the mass, mg.

$$mg = G\frac{M_E m}{R_E^2}$$

By substituting the actual values for the mass and radius of Earth, we can find the value for g and compare it with the value of free-fall acceleration used throughout this book.

Because m occurs on both sides of the equation above, these masses cancel.

$$g = G\frac{M_E}{R_E^2} = \left(6.673 \times 10^{-11}\,\frac{\text{N} \cdot \text{m}^2}{\text{kg}^2}\right)\frac{5.98 \times 10^{24}\,\text{kg}}{(6.37 \times 10^6\,\text{m})^2} = 9.83\,\text{m/s}^2$$

This value for g is approximately equal to the value used throughout this book. The difference is due to rounding of the values for Earth's mass and radius.

SAMPLE PROBLEM 7I

Gravitational force

PROBLEM

A 0.300 kg billiard ball is placed 0.300 m from a 0.400 kg billiard ball. Find the magnitude of the gravitational force between these two balls.

SOLUTION

Given: $m_1 = 0.300$ kg $m_2 = 0.400$ kg $r = 0.300$ m

$$G = 6.673 \times 10^{-11}\,\frac{\text{N} \cdot \text{m}^2}{\text{kg}^2}$$

Unknown: $F_g = ?$

Use Newton's universal law of gravitation from page 263.

$$F_g = G\frac{m_1 m_2}{r^2}$$

$$F_g = \left(6.673 \times 10^{-11}\,\frac{\text{N} \cdot \text{m}^2}{\text{kg}^2}\right)\frac{(0.300\,\text{kg})(0.400\,\text{kg})}{(0.300\,\text{m})^2}$$

$$\boxed{F_g = 8.90 \times 10^{-11}\,\text{N}}$$

Gravitational force

1. If the mass of each ball in Sample Problem 7I is 0.300 kg, then what is the gravitational force between the two balls? Assume the distance between the balls is the same

2. The gravitational force between two sumo wrestlers just before they collide ($r = 0.025$ m) is 2.77×10^{-3} N. If one wrestler has a mass of 157 kg, what is the mass of the other wrestler?

3. Find the force a 67.5 kg person would experience while standing on the surface of each of the following planets:

Planet	m	r
a. Earth	5.98×10^{24} kg	6.37×10^6 m
b. Mars	6.34×10^{23} kg	3.43×10^6 m
c. Pluto	5×10^{23} kg	4×10^5 m

Section Review

1. A roller coaster moves through a vertical loop at a constant speed, suspending its passengers upside down. In what direction is the force that causes the coaster and its passengers to move in a circle? What provides this force?

2. Identify the force that maintains the circular motion of the following:
   a. a *bicyclist* moving around a flat circular track
   b. a *bicycle* moving around a flat circular track
   c. a *rubber stopper* swung in a horizontal circle on its chain
   d. a *bobsled* turning a corner on its track

3. A 90.0 kg person stands 1.00 m from a 60.0 kg person sitting on a bench nearby. What is the magnitude of the gravitational force between them?

4. **Physics in Action**   A 90.0 kg person rides a spinning amusement-park ride that has an angular speed of 1.15 rad/s. If the radius of the ride is 11.5 m, what is the magnitude of the force that maintains the circular motion of the person?

5. **Physics in Action**   Calculate the mass that a planet with the same radius as Earth would need in order to exert the force on the person in item 4.

ORBITING SATELLITES AND BLACK HOLES

Projectiles and satellites

As explained in Chapter 3, when a ball is thrown parallel to the ground, the motion of the ball has two components of motion: a horizontal velocity, which remains unchanged, and a vertical acceleration, which equals free-fall acceleration. Given this analysis, it may seem confusing to think of the moon and other satellites in orbit around Earth as projectiles. But, in fact, satellites are projectiles. As shown in **Figure 7-13,** the larger the velocity parallel to Earth's surface, the farther the projectile moves before striking Earth. Note, however, that at some large velocity, the projectile returns to its point of origin without moving closer to Earth. In this case, the gravitational force between the projectile and Earth is just great enough to keep the projectile from moving along its inertial straight-line path. This is how satellites stay in orbit.

Figure 7-13
When the speed of a projectile is large enough, the projectile orbits Earth like a satellite.

Escape speed

When the speed of an object, such as a rocket, is greater than the speed required to keep it in orbit, the object can escape the gravitational pull of Earth and soar off into space. This happens when the object's initial speed moves it out of the range in which the gravitational force is significant. Mathematically, the value of this *escape speed (v_{esc})* is given by the following equation:

$$v_{esc} = \sqrt{\frac{2MG}{R}}$$

For Earth, its radius, R, is about 6.37×10^6 m and its mass is approximately 5.98×10^{24} kg. Thus, the escape speed of a projectile from Earth is 1.12×10^4 m/s. (Note that this value does not depend on the mass of the projectile in question.)

As the mass of a planet or other body increases and its radius decreases, the escape speed necessary for a projectile to escape the gravitational pull of that body increases, as shown in **Figure 7-14.** If the body has a very large mass and a small radius, the speed necessary for a projectile to escape the gravitational pull of that body reaches very high values. For example, an object with a mass three times that of the sun but with a diameter of about 10 km would require an escape speed equal to the speed of light. In other words, the force of gravity such an object exerts on a projectile is so great that even light does not move fast enough to escape it.

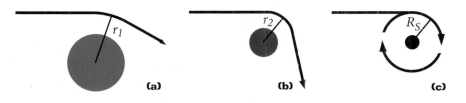

Figure 7-14

(a) A projectile that passes near any massive object will be bent from its trajectory by gravity. **(b)** The more compact the object, the nearer the projectile can approach and the greater the speed it needs to escape gravity. **(c)** If the object is so small and massive that a projectile's escape speed at distance R_S is greater than the speed of light, then the object is classified as a black hole. The radius from within which light cannot escape is called the Schwarzschild radius.

Black holes

The existence of such massive objects was first predicted in 1916 by Karl Schwarzschild, who used his solutions to Einstein's general-relativity equations to predict their properties. Thus, the distance from the center of the object to the circular orbit at which escape speed is equal to the speed of light is called the *Schwarzschild radius.* Because light cannot escape from any point within the sphere defined by the Schwarzschild radius, no information can be obtained about events that occur in this region. Hence, the edge of the sphere is called the *event horizon,* and the apparently lightless region within it is called a *black hole.*

Although the existence of black holes has been theoretically suggested, no black hole has been conclusively discovered. Nevertheless, numerous observations have provided evidence for their existence. Tremendous amounts of X rays and other radiation have been observed coming from regions that are near visible stars, although no stars appear to be the source of the radiation. If the visible star has a black hole as a companion, it could be losing some of its outer atmosphere to the black hole, and those atmospheric gases could be emitting radiation as they accelerate closer to the black hole. Candidates for black holes of these types include Scorpius X-1 and Cygnus X-1.

Figure 7-15

The gas jets and the central disk shown at right, created by combining an optical image with a radio telescope image of NGC 4261, show signs of a black hole in this galaxy's center.

The large amount of energy that galactic centers produce suggests to many astrophysicists that the energy sources are supermassive black holes. The galaxy NGC 4261, shown in **Figure 7-15,** is likely to have a black hole at its center. Some astronomers believe the Milky Way, our own galaxy, contains a black hole about the size of our solar system.

CHAPTER 7
Summary

KEY TERMS

angular acceleration (p. 249)

angular displacement
(p. 246)

angular speed (p. 247)

centripetal acceleration
(p. 257)

gravitational force (p. 263)

radian (p. 245)

rotational motion (p. 244)

tangential acceleration
(p. 255)

tangential speed (p. 253)

KEY IDEAS

Section 7-1 Measuring rotational motion
- The average angular speed, ω_{avg}, of a rigid, rotating object is defined as the ratio of the angular displacement, $\Delta\theta$, to the time interval, Δt.
- The average angular acceleration, α_{avg}, of a rigid, rotating object is defined as the ratio of the change in angular speed, $\Delta\omega$, to the time interval, Δt.

Section 7-2 Tangential and centripetal acceleration
- A point on an object rotating about a fixed axis has a tangential speed related to the object's angular speed. When the object's angular acceleration changes, the tangential acceleration of a point on the object changes.
- Uniform circular motion occurs when an acceleration of constant magnitude is perpendicular to the tangential velocity.

Section 7-3 Causes of circular motion
- Any object moving in a circular path must have a net force exerted on it that is directed toward the center of the circular path.
- Every particle in the universe attracts every other particle with a force that is directly proportional to the product of their masses and inversely proportional to the square of the distance between them.

Diagram symbols

Rotational motion	
Angle marking	

Variable symbols

Quantities		Units	
s	arc length	m	meters
$\Delta\theta$	angular displacement	rad	radians
ω	angular speed	rad/s	radians/second
α	angular acceleration	rad/s^2	radians/second^2
v_t	tangential speed	m/s	meters/second
a_t	tangential acceleration	m/s^2	meters/second^2
a_c	centripetal acceleration	m/s^2	meters/second^2
F_c	force that maintains circular motion	N	newtons
F_g	gravitational force	N	newtons
G	constant of universal gravitation	$\dfrac{\text{N} \cdot \text{m}^2}{\text{kg}^2}$	$\dfrac{\text{newtons} \cdot \text{meters}^2}{\text{kilograms}^2}$

RADIANS AND ANGULAR MOTION

Review questions

1. How many degrees equal π radians? How many revolutions?

2. What units must be used for θ, ω, and α in the kinematic equations for rotational motion listed in **Table 7-2**?

3. Distinguish between linear speed and angular speed.

4. When a wheel rotates about a fixed axis, do all points on the wheel have the same angular speed?

Practice problems

5. What is the angular displacement of the red line in each of the following cases? (Assume the red line starts from the horizontal black line.)

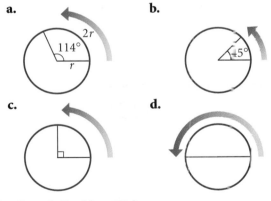

a.   b.

c.   d.

(See Sample Problem 7A.)

6. A wheel has a radius of 4.1 m. How far (in arc length) does a point on the circumference travel if the wheel is rotated through angles of 35°, 35 rad, and 35 rev, respectively?
(See Sample Problem 7A.)

7. What is the magnitude of the angular speed, ω, of the second hand of a clock? What is the angular acceleration, α, of the second hand?
(See Sample Problem 7B and 7C.)

8. Find the average angular speed of Earth about the sun in radians per second.
(See Sample Problem 7B. Hint: Remember that Earth orbits the sun once every 365.25 days.)

9. A phonograph record has an initial angular speed of 33 rev/min. The record slows to 11 rev/min in 2.0 s. What is the record's average angular acceleration during this time interval?
(See Sample Problem 7C.)

EQUATIONS FOR ANGULAR MOTION

Practice problems

10. A potter's wheel moves from rest to an angular speed of 0.20 rev/s in 30.0 s. Assuming constant angular acceleration, what is its angular acceleration in rad/s²?
(See Sample Problem 7D.)

11. A drill starts from rest. After 3.20 s of constant angular acceleration, the drill turns at a rate of 2628 rad/s.
    a. Find the drill's angular acceleration.
    b. Determine the angle through which the drill rotates during this period.
(See Sample Problem 7D.)

12. A tire placed on a balancing machine in a service station starts from rest and turns through 4.7 revs in 1.2 s before reaching its final angular speed. Assuming that the angular acceleration of the wheel is constant, calculate the wheel's angular acceleration.
(See Sample Problem 7D.)

13. The tub within a washer goes into its spin cycle, starting from rest and reaching an angular speed of 11π rad/s in 8.0 s. At this point, the lid is opened, and a safety switch turns off the washer. The tub slows to rest in 12.0 s. Through how many revolutions does the tub turn? Assume constant angular acceleration while the machine is starting and stopping.
(See Sample Problem 7D.)

TANGENTIAL AND CENTRIPETAL ACCELERATION

Review questions

14. When a wheel rotates about a fixed axis, do all the points on the wheel have the same tangential speed?

15. Correct the following statement: The racing car rounds the turn at a constant velocity of 90 mi/h.

16. Describe the path of a moving body whose acceleration is constant in magnitude at all times and is perpendicular to the velocity.

17. An object moves in a circular path with constant speed v.
    a. Is the object's velocity constant? Explain.
    b. Is its acceleration constant? Explain.

Conceptual questions

18. Give an example of a situation in which an automobile driver can have a centripetal acceleration but no tangential acceleration.

19. Can a car move around a circular racetrack so that it has a tangential acceleration but no centripetal acceleration?

20. The gas pedal and the brakes of a car accelerate and decelerate the car. Could a steering wheel fall into either of these categories? Explain.

21. It has been suggested that rotating cylinders about 10.0 mi long and 5.0 mi in diameter should be placed in space for future space colonies. The rotation would simulate gravity for the inhabitants of these colonies. Explain the concept behind this proposal.

Practice problems

22. The Emerald Suite, a revolving restaurant at the top of the Space Needle in Seattle, Washington, makes a complete turn once every hour. What is the tangential speed of a customer sitting 12.5 m from the restaurant's center?
    (See Sample Problem 7E.)

23. What is the magnitude of the centripetal acceleration of the customer in item 22?
    (See Sample Problem 7G.)

24. Find the centripetal accelerations of the following: (See Sample Problem 7G. See the table in the appendix for data on Earth.)
    a. a point on the equator of Earth
    b. a point at the North Pole of Earth

25. When the string is pulled in the correct direction on a window shade, a lever is released and the shaft that the window shade is wound around spins. If the angular acceleration of a 4.5 cm wide shaft is 3.8 rad/s^2, at what rate does the shade accelerate upward?
    (See Sample Problem 7F.)

FORCES THAT CAUSE CIRCULAR MOTION

Review questions

26. Imagine that you attach a heavy object to one end of a spring and then, while holding the spring's other end, whirl the spring and object in a horizontal circle. Does the spring stretch? Why? Discuss your answer in terms of the force that maintains circular motion.

27. Why does the water remain in a pail that is whirled in a vertical path, as shown in **Figure 7-16**?

Figure 7-16

28. Explain the difference between centripetal acceleration and angular acceleration.

29. Comment on the statement, "There is no gravity in outer space."

Conceptual questions

30. Explain why Earth is not spherical in shape and why it bulges at the equator.

31. Because of Earth's rotation, you would weigh slightly less at the equator than you would at the poles. Why?

32. Why does mud fly off a rapidly turning wheel?

33. Astronauts floating around inside the space shuttle are not actually in a zero-gravity environment. What is the real reason astronauts seem weightless?

34. A girl at a state fair swings a ball in a vertical circle at the end of a string. Is the force applied by the string greater than the weight of the ball at the bottom of the ball's path?

Practice problems

35. Tarzan ($m = 85$ kg) tries to cross a river by swinging from a 10.0 m long vine. His speed at the bottom of the swing, just as he clears the water, is 8.0 m/s. Tarzan doesn't know that the vine has a breaking strength of 1.0×10^3 N. Does he make it safely across the river? Justify your answer.
(See Sample Problem 7H.)

36. Approximate the gravitational force of attraction between a 50.0 kg girl and a 60.0 kg boy if they are sitting 2.50 m apart in physics class.
(See Sample Problem 7I.)

37. What is the gravitational force between the proton (1.67×10^{-27} kg) and the electron (9.11×10^{-31} kg) in a hydrogen atom if they are 1.00×10^{-10} m apart?
(See Sample Problem 7I.)

38. A 515 kg roller-coaster car rolls down past point A and then up past point B, as shown in **Figure 7-17.**

   a. If the vehicle has a speed of 20.0 m/s at point A, what is the force of the track on the vehicle at this point?

   b. What is the maximum speed the vehicle can have at B for gravity to hold it on the track?

(See Sample Problem 7H.)

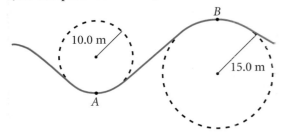

Figure 7-17

39. During a solar eclipse, the moon, Earth, and sun lie on the same line, with the moon between Earth and the sun. What force is exerted on

   a. the moon by the sun?
   b. the moon by Earth?
   c. Earth by the sun?

(See Sample Problem 7I. See the table in the appendix for data on the sun, moon, and Earth.)

MIXED REVIEW PROBLEMS

40. An airplane is flying in a horizontal circle at a speed of 105 m/s. The 80.0 kg pilot does not want his centripetal acceleration to exceed 7.00 times free-fall acceleration.

   a. What is the minimum radius of the circular path?

   b. At this radius, what is the *net* force that maintains circular motion exerted on the pilot by the seat belts, the friction between him and the seat, and so forth?

41. The driver of a car traveling at 30.0 m/s applies the brakes and undergoes a constant negative acceleration of magnitude 2.00 m/s^2. How many revolutions does each tire make before the car comes to a stop, assuming that the car does not skid and that the tires have radii of 0.300 m?

42. A coin with a diameter of 2.40 cm is dropped onto a horizontal surface. The coin starts out with an initial angular speed of 18.0 rad/s and rolls in a straight line without slipping. If the rotation slows with an angular acceleration of magnitude 1.90 rad/s^2, how far does the coin roll before coming to rest?

43. A 2.00×10^3 kg car rounds a circular turn of radius 20.0 m. If the road is flat and the coefficient of static friction between the tires and the road is 0.70, how fast can the car go without skidding?

44. A 13 500 N car traveling at 50.0 km/h rounds a curve of radius 2.00×10^2 m. Find the following:

   a. the centripetal acceleration of the car
   b. the force that maintains centripetal acceleration
   c. the minimum coefficient of static friction between the tires and the road that will allow the car to round the curve safely

45. A mass attached to a 50.0 cm string starts from rest and is rotated in a circular path exactly 40 times in 1.00 min before reaching a final angular speed. What is the angular speed of the mass after 1.00 min?

46. A copper block rests 30.0 cm from the center of a steel turntable. The coefficient of static friction between the block and the surface is 0.53. The turntable starts from rest and rotates with a constant angular acceleration of 0.50 rad/s². After what time interval will the block start to slip on the turntable? (Hint: The normal force in this case equals the weight of the block.)

47. You can determine the speed of a moving bullet by allowing the bullet to pass through two rotating paper disks mounted a distance, d, apart on the same axle, as shown in **Figure 7-18.** Find the bullet speed for the following data: $d = 80.0$ cm, $\omega = 905$ rev/min (angular speed of the disks), and $\Delta\theta = 0.54$ rad (angular displacement of the two bullet holes in the disks).

Figure 7-18

Technology & Learning

Graphing calculators

Program your graphing calculator to convert a given angular displacement in revolutions to radians, and create a graph of angular speed versus time so that you can identify the angular speed for the following situations:

   a. a bowl on a mixer stand that turns 2.0 rev in 3.0 s
   b. the same bowl on a mixer stand that has slowed down to 2.0 rev in 4.0 s
   c. a bicycle wheel turning 2.5 rev in 0.75 s
   d. the same bicycle wheel turning 2.5 rev in 0.35 s

First be certain the graphing calculator is in radian mode by pressing [MODE] [▼] [▼] [ENTER]. Press [Y=] and [CLEAR] to clear any functions.

Open a new program by pressing [PRGM] [►] [►] [ENTER]. Name the program "ANGSPEED" and press [ENTER]. Then enter the program shown in the table below.

To exit the program editor, press [2nd] [QUIT]. To run the program, press [PRGM], select "ANGSPEED," and press [ENTER] [ENTER]. Enter the value for the number of revolutions, and press [ENTER].

The calculator will provide a graph of the angular speed versus the time interval. (If the graph is not visible, press [WINDOW] and change the settings for the graph window; then press [GRAPH].)

Press [TRACE], and use the arrow keys to trace along the curve. The x value corresponds to the time interval in seconds, and the y value corresponds to the angular speed in rad/s.

Keystrokes	Display
	PROGRAM: ANGSPEED
1. [PRGM] [►] [2] [ALPHA] [θ] [ENTER]	:PROMPT θ
2. [ALPHA] ["] [(] [ALPHA] [θ] [2] [2nd] [π] [)] [÷] [X,T,θ] [ALPHA] ["] [STO►] [2nd] [Y-VARS] [1] [1] [ENTER]	:"(θ2π)/X" → Y₁
3. [PRGM] [►] [4] [ENTER]	: DISPGRAPH

48. An air puck of mass 0.025 kg is tied to a string and allowed to revolve in a circle of radius 1.0 m on a frictionless horizontal surface. The other end of the string passes through a hole in the center of the surface, and a mass of 1.0 kg is tied to it, as shown in **Figure 7-19.** The suspended mass remains in equilibrium while the puck revolves on the surface.

   a. What is the magnitude of the force that maintains circular motion acting on the puck?

   b. What is the linear speed of the puck?

49. In a popular amusement-park ride, a cylinder of radius 3.00 m is set in rotation at an angular speed of 5.00 rad/s, as shown in **Figure 7-20.** The floor then drops away, leaving the riders suspended against the wall in a vertical position. What minimum coefficient of friction between a rider's clothing and the wall of the cylinder is needed to keep the rider from slipping? (Hint: Recall that $F_s = \mu_s F_n$, where the normal force is the force that maintains circular motion.)

Figure 7-19

Figure 7-20

Alternative Assessment

Performance assessment

1. Turn a bicycle upside down. Make two marks on one spoke on the front wheel, one mark close to the rim, and another mark closer to the axle. Then spin the front wheel. Which point seems to be moving fastest? Have partners count the rotations of one mark for 10 or 20 s. Find the angular speed and the linear speed of each point. Reassign the observers to different points, and repeat the experiment. Make graphs to analyze the relationship between the linear and angular speeds.

2. When you ride a bicycle, the rotational motion you create on the pedals is transmitted to the back wheel through the primary sprocket wheel, the chain, and the secondary sprocket wheel. Study the connection between these components and measure how the angular and linear speeds change from one part of the bicycle to another. How does the velocity of the back wheel compare with that of the pedals on a bicycle? Demonstrate your findings in class.

Portfolio projects

3. Newton first applied his theory of gravitation to explain tides as follows: The moon exerts a force on Earth. Ocean water can flow freely, while the solid part of Earth cannot. As a result, the water bulges out on the side of Earth that faces the moon. Consider a sample body of water 1.0×10^3 km long, 1.0×10^3 km wide, and 1.0×10^2 m deep that is facing the moon, and an equal amount of water on the other side of Earth. Research data about the moon's mass and determine the distance from the moon to each side of Earth. Calculate the gravitational force of the moon on each body of water. Is the difference significant? Summarize your conclusions with diagrams and numerical calculations in a computer animation, poster, or report.

CHAPTER 7
Laboratory Exercise

CIRCULAR MOTION

In this experiment, you will construct a device for measuring the tangential speed of an object undergoing circular motion, and you will determine how the force and the radius affect the tangential speed of the object.

SAFETY

• Tie back long hair, secure loose clothing, and remove loose jewelry to prevent their getting caught in moving or rotating parts.

• Wear eye protection and perform this experiment in a clear area. Swinging or dropped masses can cause serious injury.

PREPARATION

1. Read the entire lab, and plan what measurements you will take.

2. Prepare a data table in your lab notebook with five columns and fifteen rows. In the first row, label the columns *Trial, Hanging mass (kg), Mass of stopper (kg), Total time (s), Radius (m)*. In the first column, label the second through fifteenth rows *1, 2, 3, 4, 5, 6, 7, 8, 9, 10, 11, 12, 13*, and *14*.

PROCEDURE

Constant radius with varying force

3. Measure the mass of the rubber stopper, and record it in your data table. Fasten one end of the nylon cord securely to the rubber stopper. Pass the other end of the cord through the PVC tube and securely fasten a 100 g mass to the other end, as shown in **Figure 7-21.** Leave approximately 0.75 m of cord between the top of the tube and the rubber stopper. Attach a piece of masking tape to the cord just below the bottom of the tube.

4. Make sure the area is clear of obstacles, and warn other students that you are beginning your experiment. Support the 100 g mass with one hand and hold the PVC tube in the other. Make the stopper at the end of the cord circle around the top of the tube by moving the tube in a circular motion.

5. Slowly release the 100 g mass, and adjust the speed of the stopper so that the masking tape stays just below the bottom of the tube. Make several practice runs before recording any data.

6. When you can keep the velocity of the stopper and the position of the masking tape relatively constant, measure the time required for 20 revolutions of the stopper. Record the time interval in your data table in the row labeled *Trial 1*. Repeat this trial and record the time interval in your data table as *Trial 2*.

7. Place the apparatus on the lab table. Extend the cord so that it is taut and the masking tape is in the same position it was in during the experiment. Measure the cord from the center of the top of the PVC tube to the center of the rubber stopper. Record this distance in the data table as *Radius* for *Trials 1* and *2*.

8. Repeat the procedure with three different masses for *Trials 3–8*. Keep the radius the same as in the first trial and use the same rubber stopper, but increase the mass at the end of the cord each time. Do not exceed 500 g. Attach all masses securely. Perform each trial two times, and record all data in your data table.

Constant force with varying radius

9. For *Trials 9–14*, use the same stopper and the 100 g mass and try three different values for the radius in the range 0.50 m to 1.00 m. Make sure that you have a clear area of at least 2.5 m in diameter to work in. Record all data in your data table.

Figure 7-21
Step 3: To attach masses, make a loop in the cord, place the mass inside the loop, and secure the mass with masking tape.
Step 4: You will need a clear area larger than two times the radius.
Step 5: Spin the stopper so that the cord makes a 90 degree angle with the PVC tube. Release the mass slowly without changing the speed.
Step7: Make sure the cord is held straight when you make your measurements.

ANALYSIS AND INTERPRETATION

Calculations and data analysis

1. Organizing data Calculate the weight of the hanging mass for each trial. This is the force that maintains circular motion, F_c.

2. Organizing data For each trial, find the time necessary for one revolution of the stopper by dividing the total time required for 20 revolutions by 20.

3. Organizing data Find the tangential speed for each trial.
a. Use the equation $v_t = \dfrac{2\pi r}{\Delta t}$.

b. Use the equation $v_t = \sqrt{\dfrac{F_c r}{m}}$, where r is the radius of revolution and m is the mass of the stopper.

4. Graphing data Plot the following graphs:
a. Use the data from *Trials 1–8* to plot a graph of force versus tangential speed.
b. Use the data from *Trials 9–14* to plot a graph of tangential speed versus radius.

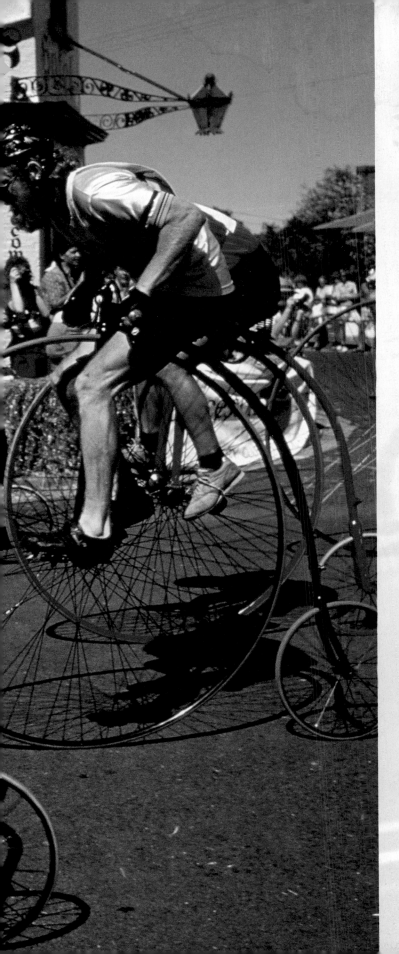

CHAPTER 8

Rotational Equilibrium and Dynamics

PHYSICS IN ACTION

One of the most popular early bicycles was the penny-farthing, first introduced in 1870. The bicycle was named for the relative sizes of its two wheels compared to the relative sizes of the penny and the farthing, two English coins. The penny-farthing had no gears, just pedals attached directly to the wheel axle. For every revolution of the pedals, the large wheel turned once. Unfortunately, as the bike moved faster, the pedals eventually rotated too fast for the rider to control. Gears and chains soon were introduced to solve this problem.

- *What makes a wheel difficult to rotate?*
- *How much does a wheel accelerate for a given applied force?*

CONCEPT REVIEW

Work (Section 5-1)

Energy (Section 5-2)

Momentum (Section 6-1)

Angular speed and acceleration (Section 7-1)

8-1
Torque

THE MAGNITUDE OF A TORQUE

You have been chosen to judge a race involving three objects: a solid sphere, a solid cylinder, and a hollow cylinder. The spectators for the race demand that the race be fair, so you make sure that all of the objects have the same mass and radius and that they all start from rest. Then you let the three objects roll down a long ramp. Is there a way to predict which one will win and which one will lose?

If you really performed such a race (see the Quick Lab on the next page), you would discover that the sphere would come in first and that the hollow cylinder would come in last. This is a little surprising because in the absence of friction the acceleration due to gravity is the same for all objects near the Earth's surface. Yet the acceleration of each of these objects is different.

In earlier chapters, the motion of an object was described by assuming the object was a point mass. This description, however, does not account for the differences in the motion of the objects in the race. This is because these objects are *extended objects*. An extended object is an object that has a definite, finite size and shape. It cannot be treated as a point mass. As we will see, a more sophisticated model that takes into account the properties of extended objects is needed to describe the motion of such objects.

Rotational and translational motion can be separated

Imagine that you roll a strike while bowling. What happens when the bowling ball strikes the pins, as shown in **Figure 8-1?** The pins fly backward, spinning in the air. The complicated motion of each pin can be separated into a translational motion and a rotational motion, each of which can be analyzed separately. For now, we will concentrate on an object's rotational motion. Then we will combine the rotational motion of an object with its translational motion.

Figure 8-1
In general, an extended object, such as one of these pins or this bowling ball, can exhibit rotational and translational motion.

Net torque produces rotation

Imagine a cat trying to leave a house by pushing perpendicularly on a cat-flap door. **Figure 8-2** shows a cat-flap door hinged at the top. In this configuration, the door is free to rotate around a line that passes through the hinge. This is the door's *axis of rotation.* When the cat pushes at the outer edge of the door with a force that is perpendicular to the door, the door opens. The ability of a force to rotate an object around some axis is measured by a quantity called **torque.**

Torque depends on a force and a lever arm

If a cat pushed on the door with the same force but at a point closer to the hinge, the door would be more difficult to rotate. How easily an object rotates depends not only on how much force is applied but also on where the force is applied. The farther the force is from the axis of rotation, the easier it is to rotate the object and the more torque is produced. The perpendicular distance from the axis of rotation to a line drawn along the direction of the force is called the **lever arm,** or moment arm.

Figure 8-3 shows a diagram of the force F applied by the pet perpendicular to the cat-flap door. If you examine the definition of *lever arm,* you will see that in this case the lever arm is the distance d shown in the figure, the distance from the pet's nose to the hinge. That is, d is the perpendicular distance from the axis of rotation to the line along which the applied force acts. If the pet pressed on the door at a higher point, the lever arm would be shorter. This shorter lever arm would correspond to a smaller torque than is shown in **Figure 8-3.**

torque

a quantity that measures the ability of a force to rotate an object around some axis

lever arm

the perpendicular distance from the axis of rotation to a line drawn along the direction of the force

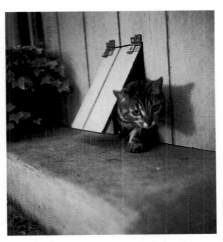

Figure 8-2

The cat-flap door rotates on a hinge, allowing pets to enter and leave a house at will.

Figure 8-3

A force applied to an extended object can produce a torque. This torque, in turn, causes the object to rotate.

Quick Lab

Two-Object Races

MATERIALS LIST

✔ various solid cylinders, such as unopened soup cans

✔ various hollow cylinders, such as empty soup cans with the tops and bottoms removed or PVC pipes of different diameters and lengths

✔ various spheres, such as a golf ball, tennis ball, and baseball

✔ an incline about 1 m long

Place any two objects from the above list at the top of the incline, and release them simultaneously. Note which object reaches the bottom first. Repeat the race with various combinations of objects. See if you can discover a general rule to predict which object will win. (Hint: You may wish to consider factors such as an object's mass, size, and shape.)

Most torque   **Less torque**   **Least torque**

Figure 8-4

In each example, the cat is pushing on the same door at the same distance from the axis and with the same amount of force, but it is producing different amounts of torque.

Torque also depends on the angle between a force and a lever arm

Forces do not have to be perpendicular to an object to cause the object to rotate. Imagine the cat-flap door again. What would happen if the cat pushed on the door at an angle to the door, rather than perpendicular to it as shown in **Figure 8-4?** The door would still rotate, but not as easily.

The symbol for torque is the Greek letter *tau* (τ), and the magnitude of the torque is given by the following equation:

TORQUE

$$\tau = Fd(\sin\theta)$$

torque = force × lever arm

The SI unit of torque is the N•m. Notice that the inclusion of the angle θ, the angle between the force and the distance from the axis, in this equation takes into account the changes in torque shown in **Figure 8-4.**

Figure 8-5 shows a wrench pivoted around a bolt. In this case, the applied force acts at an angle to the wrench. The quantity d is the distance from the axis of rotation to the point where force is applied. The quantity $d(\sin\theta)$, however, is the *perpendicular* distance from the axis of rotation to a line drawn along the direction of the force, so it is the lever arm.

Figure 8-5

The direction of the lever arm is always perpendicular to the direction of the applied force.

THE SIGN OF A TORQUE

A torque is positive or negative, depending on the direction the force tends to rotate an object. Recall the example of the cat-flap door. When the cat applies a force to the door, as in **Figure 8-4,** the force produces a torque that causes the door to rotate clockwise. Torques that produce clockwise rotation are defined to be negative. Torques that produce counterclockwise rotation are defined to be positive.

To determine the sign of a torque, imagine that it is the only torque acting on the object and that the object is free to rotate. Visualize the direction the object would rotate under these conditions. If more than one force is acting, then each force has a tendency to produce a rotation and should be treated separately. Be careful to associate the correct sign with each torque.

For example, imagine that you are pulling on a wishbone with a perpendicular force F_1 and that a friend is pulling in the opposite direction with a force F_2. If you pull the wishbone so that it would rotate counterclockwise, then you exert a positive torque of magnitude F_1d_1. Your friend, on the other hand, exerts a negative torque, $-F_2d_2$. To find the net torque acting on the wishbone, simply add up all of the individual torques.

$$\tau_{net} = \Sigma\tau = \tau_1 + \tau_2 = F_1d_1 + (-F_2d_2)$$

If you properly apply the sign convention, the sign of the net torque should tell you which way the object will rotate, if at all.

SAMPLE PROBLEM 8A

Torque

PROBLEM

A basketball is being pushed by two basketball players during tip-off. Assuming each force acts perpendicular to the axis of rotation through the center of the ball, find the net torque acting on the ball.

SOLUTION

1. DEFINE **Given:**

$F_1 = 15$ N $\qquad$ $F_2 = 11$ N

$d_1 = 0.14$ m $\qquad$ $d_2 = 0.070$ m

Unknown: $\tau_{net} = ?$

Diagram:

$F_2 = 11$ N

$d_1 = 0.14$ m

$d_2 = 0.070$ m

$F_1 = 15$ N

2. PLAN **Choose an equation(s) or situation:** Apply the definition of torque to each force and add up the individual torques.

$$\tau = Fd$$
$$\tau_{net} = \tau_1 + \tau_2 = F_1d_1 + F_2d_2$$

3. CALCULATE **Determine the torque produced by each force:** Because each force produces clockwise rotation, both torques are negative.

$$\tau_1 = F_1d_1 = -(15 \text{ N})(0.14 \text{ m}) = -2.1 \text{ N•m}$$

$$\tau_2 = F_2d_2 = -(11 \text{ N})(0.070 \text{ m}) = -0.77 \text{ N•m}$$

Add them to determine the net torque:

$$\tau_{net} = -2.1 \text{ N•m} - 0.77 \text{ N•m}$$

$$\boxed{\tau_{net} = -2.9 \text{ N•m}}$$

4. EVALUATE The net torque is negative, so the ball rotates in a clockwise direction.

CALCULATOR SOLUTION

Your calculator will give the answer as 2.87. Because of the significant figure rule for addition, the answer should be rounded to 2.9.

Torque

1. Find the torque produced by a 3.0 N force applied at an angle of 60.0° to a door 0.25 m from the hinge. What is the maximum torque this force could exert?

2. If the torque required to loosen a nut on the wheel of a car has a magnitude of 40.0 N•m, what *minimum* force must be exerted by a mechanic at the end of a 30.0 cm wrench to loosen the nut?

3. A simple pendulum consists of a 3.0 kg point mass hanging at the end of a 2.0 m long light string that is connected to a pivot point.

  a. Calculate the magnitude of the torque (due to the force of gravity) around this pivot point when the string makes a 5.0° angle with the vertical.

  b. Repeat this calculation for an angle of 15.0°.

Section Review

1. In which of the following situations should the object(s) be treated as a point mass? In which should the object(s) be treated as an extended object?

  a. a baseball hit high into center field
  b. a baseball rolling toward third base
  c. a pinwheel in the wind
  d. the Earth traveling around the sun

2. What is the rotational analog of a force? How does it differ from a force? On what quantities does it depend?

3. Calculate the torque for each force acting on the bar in **Figure 8-6.** Assume the axis is perpendicular to the page and passes through point *O*. In what direction will the object rotate?

4. How would the force needed to open a door change if you put the handle in the middle of the door?

5. **Physics in Action** How does the length of the pedal arm on a penny-farthing bicycle affect the amount of torque applied to the front wheel?

Figure 8-6

8-2
Rotation and inertia

CENTER OF MASS

Locating the axis of rotation for the cat-flap door is simple: it rotates on its hinges because the house applies a force that keeps the hinges in place. Now imagine you are playing fetch with your dog, and you throw a stick up into the air for the dog to retrieve. How can you determine the point around which the stick will rotate as it travels through the air? Unlike the cat-flap door, the stick is not attached to anything. There is a special point around which the stick rotates if gravity is the only force acting on the stick. This point is called the stick's **center of mass.**

Rotational and translational motion can be combined

The center of mass is also the point at which all the mass of the body can be considered to be concentrated. This means that the complete motion of the stick is a combination of both translational and rotational motion. The stick rotates in the air around its center of mass. The center of mass, in turn, moves as if the stick were a point mass, with all of its mass concentrated at that point for purposes of analyzing its translational motion.

Note that the hammer in **Figure 8-7** rotates about its center of mass as it moves through the air. As the rest of the hammer spins, the center of mass moves along the path of a projectile.

For regularly shaped objects, such as a sphere or a cube, the center of mass is at the geometric center of the object. For more complicated objects, finding the center of mass is more difficult and is beyond the scope of this book. While the center of mass is an average position of an object's mass, the *center of gravity* is the average position at which the gravitational force on the object acts. For most situations in this book, the center of mass and the center of gravity are equivalent.

8-2 SECTION OBJECTIVES

- **Identify the center of mass of an object.**
- **Distinguish between mass and moment of inertia.**
- **Define the second condition of equilibrium.**
- **Solve problems involving the first and second conditions of equilibrium.**

center of mass

the point at which all the mass of the body can be considered to be concentrated when analyzing translational motion

Figure 8-7
The point around which this object rotates is the center of mass. The center of mass traces out a parabola.

MOMENT OF INERTIA

Imagine you are rotating a baseball bat. There are many axes around which the bat can be rotated. But it is easier to rotate the bat around some axes than others, even though the bat's mass has not changed. The resistance of an object to changes in rotational motion is measured by a quantity called the **moment of inertia.** The term *moment* has a meaning in physics that is different from its everyday meaning. The moment of inertia of an object indicates how much an object's rotation will change.

moment of inertia

the measure of the resistance of an object to changes in rotational motion

Moment of inertia is the rotational analog of mass

The moment of inertia is similar to mass because they are both forms of inertia. However, there is an important difference between the inertia that resists changes in translational motion (mass) and the inertia that resists changes in rotational motion (moment of inertia). Although mass is an intrinsic property of an object, the moment of inertia is not. It depends on both the object's mass and the distribution of that mass around the axis of rotation. The farther the mass of an object is, on average, from the axis of rotation, the greater is the object's moment of inertia and the more difficult it is to rotate the object. This is why, in the race on page 278, the solid sphere came in first and the hollow cylinder came in last. The mass of the hollow cylinder is all concentrated around its rim (large moment of inertia), while the mass of the sphere is more evenly distributed throughout its volume (small moment of inertia).

Calculating the moment of inertia

According to Newton's second law, when a net force acts on an object, the resulting acceleration of the object depends on the object's mass. Similarly, when a net torque acts on an object, the resulting change in the rotational motion of the object depends on the object's moment of inertia.

Quick Lab

Finding the Center of Mass Experimentally

MATERIALS LIST

✔ cardboard
✔ scissors
✔ hole punch
✔ pushpin or nail
✔ corkboard or tackboard
✔ length of string, about 40 cm
✔ straightedge
✔ pencil or pen
✔ weight, such as a washer

Cut out an irregular shape from the cardboard, and punch 3–5 holes around the edge of the shape. Put the pushpin through one of the holes, and tack the shape to a corkboard so that the shape can rotate freely. (You may also hang the shape from a nail in the wall.)

Attach the weight to the end of the string and hang the string from the pushpin or nail. When the string stops moving, trace a line on the cardboard that follows the string.

Repeat this procedure for each of the holes in the cardboard. The point where the lines intersect is the center of mass.

The calculation of the moment of inertia is a straightforward but often tedious process. Fortunately, some simple formulas are available for common shapes. **Table 8-1** gives the moments of inertia for some common shapes. When the need arises, you can use this table to determine the moment of inertia of a body having one of the listed shapes.

The units for moment of inertia are $kg \cdot m^2$. To get an idea of the size of this unit, note that bowling balls typically have moments of inertia about an axis through their centers ranging from about $0.7 \ kg \cdot m^2$ to $1.8 \ kg \cdot m^2$, depending on the mass and size of the ball.

Notice that the moment of inertia for the solid sphere is indeed smaller than the moment of inertia for the thin hoop, as expected. In fact, the moment of inertia for the thin hoop about the symmetry axis through the center of mass is the largest moment of inertia that is possible for any shape.

Also notice that a point mass in a circular path, such as a ball on a string, has the same moment of inertia as the thin hoop if the distance of the point mass from its axis of rotation is equal to the radius of the thin hoop. This illustrates that only the distance of a mass from the axis of rotation is important in determining the moment of inertia for a shape. At a given radius from an axis, it does not matter how the mass is distributed around the axis.

Finally, recall the example of the spinning softball bat that began this section. A bat can be modeled as a rotating thin rod. **Table 8-1** shows that the

Table 8-1	The moment of inertia for a few shapes		
Shape	**Moment of inertia**	**Shape**	**Moment of inertia**
thin hoop about symmetry axis	MR^2	thin rod about perpendicular axis through center	$\frac{1}{12}M\ell^2$
thin hoop about diameter	$\frac{1}{2}MR^2$	thin rod about perpendicular axis through end	$\frac{1}{3}M\ell^2$
point mass about axis	MR^2	solid sphere about diameter	$\frac{2}{5}MR^2$
disk or cylinder about symmetry axis	$\frac{1}{2}MR^2$	thin spherical shell about diameter	$\frac{2}{3}MR^2$

moment of inertia for a thin rod is smaller if the rod is rotated around its center than if it is rotated around one of its ends. Thus, a bat is easier to swing if you hold it closer to the center of the bat than the end. Baseball players sometimes do this either because a bat is too heavy (large M) or is too long (large ℓ). In both cases, the player decreases the bat's moment of inertia.

ROTATIONAL EQUILIBRIUM

Figure 8-8
The two forces exerted on this table are equal and opposite, yet the table moves. How is this possible?

Imagine that you and a friend are trying to move a piece of heavy furniture and that you are both a little confused. Instead of pushing from the same side, you push on opposite sides, as shown in **Figure 8-8.** The two forces acting on the furniture are equal in magnitude and opposite in direction. Your friend thinks the condition for equilibrium is satisfied because the two forces balance each other. He says the piece of furniture shouldn't move. But it does; it rotates in place.

Equilibrium requires zero net force and zero net torque

The piece of furniture can move even though the net force acting on it is zero because the net torque acting on it is not zero. If the net force on an object is zero, the object is in *translational equilibrium.* If the net torque on an object is zero, the object is in *rotational equilibrium.* For an object to be completely in equilibrium, both rotational and translational, there must be both zero net force and zero net torque, as summarized in **Table 8-2.** The dependence of equilibrium on the absence of net torque is called the *second condition for equilibrium.*

To apply the first condition for equilibrium to an object, it is necessary to add up all of the forces acting on the object (see Chapter 4). To apply the second condition for equilibrium to an object, it is also necessary to choose an axis of rotation around which to calculate the torque. Which axis should be chosen? The answer is that it does not matter. The resultant torque acting on an object in rotational equilibrium is independent of where the axis is placed. This fact is useful in solving rotational equilibrium problems because an unknown force that acts along a line passing through this axis of rotation will not produce any torque. Beginning a diagram by arbitrarily setting an axis where a force acts can eliminate an unknown in the problem.

Table 8-2	**Conditions for equilibrium**	
Type of equilibrium	**Symbolic equation**	**Meaning**
translational	$\sum F = 0$	The net force on an object must be zero.
rotational	$\sum \tau = 0$	The net torque on an object must be zero.

Rotational equilibrium

PROBLEM

A 5.00 m long horizontal beam weighing 315 N is attached to a wall by a pin connection that allows the beam to rotate. Its far end is supported by a cable that makes an angle of 53.0° with the horizontal, and a 545 N person is standing 1.50 m from the wall. Find the force in the cable, F_T, and the force exerted on the beam by the wall, R, if the beam is in equilibrium.

SOLUTION

1. DEFINE   **Given:** $L = 5.00$ m $F_{g,b} = 315$ N $\theta = 53.0°$

$F_{g,p} = 545$ N $d = 1.50$ m

Unknown: $F_T = ?$ $R = ?$

Diagram: The weight of an extended object is assumed to be concentrated at the center of mass of the object.

2. PLAN   **Apply the first condition of equilibrium:** The unknowns are R_x, R_y, and F_T. The first condition of equilibrium for the x and y directions gives:

x component equation: $F_x = R_x - F_T(\cos \theta) = 0$

y component equation: $F_y = R_y + F_T(\sin \theta) - F_{g,p} - F_{g,b} = 0$

Because there are three unknowns and only two equations, we cannot find the solutions from only the first condition of equilibrium.

Choose a point for calculating the net torque: The pin connection is a convenient place to put the axis because the unknown force, R, will not contribute to the net torque about this point.

Apply the second condition of equilibrium: The necessary third equation can be found from the second condition of equilibrium.

$$\tau = F_T L(\sin \theta) - F_{g,b}\frac{L}{2} - F_{g,p}d = 0$$

3. CALCULATE   **Substitute the values into the equation(s) and solve:** The torque equation can be solved to give one of the unknowns immediately.

$$\tau = F_T(\sin 53.0°)(5.00 \text{ m}) - (315 \text{ N})(2.50 \text{ m}) -$$
$$(545 \text{ N})(1.50 \text{ m}) = 0$$

$$\tau = F_T (3.99 \text{ m}) - 738 \text{ N} \cdot \text{m} - 818 \text{ N} \cdot \text{m} = 0$$

$$F_T = \frac{1606 \text{ N} \cdot \text{m}}{3.99 \text{ m}}$$

$$\boxed{F_T = 403 \text{ N}}$$

continued on next page

This value for the force in the wire is then substituted into the x and y equations to find R.

$$F_x = R_x - F_T(\cos 53.0°) = 0$$

$$R_x = (403 \text{ N})(\cos 53.0°)$$

$$R_x = 243 \text{ N}$$

$$F_y = R_y + F_T(\sin 53.0°) - 860 \text{ N} = 0$$

$$R_y = -322 \text{ N} + 860 \text{ N}$$

$$R_y = 538 \text{ N}$$

$$R = \sqrt{R_x^2 + R_y^2}$$

$$R = \sqrt{(243 \text{ N})^2 + (538 \text{ N})^2}$$

$$\boxed{R = 5.90 \times 10^2 \text{ N}}$$

4. EVALUATE The sum of the y components of the force in the wire and the force exerted by the wall must equal the weight of the beam and the person. Thus, the force in the wire and the force exerted by the wall must be greater than the sum of the two weights.

$$403 + 590 > 545 + 315$$

PRACTICE 8B

Rotational equilibrium

1. Rework the example problem above with the axis of rotation passing through the center of mass of the beam. Verify that the answers do not change even though the axis is different.

2. A 400.0 N child and a 300.0 N child sit on either end of a 2.0 m long seesaw.
   a. Where along the seesaw should the pivot be placed to ensure rotational equilibrium?
   b. Suppose a 225 N child sits 0.200 m from the 400.0 N child. Where must a 325 N child sit to maintain rotational equilibrium?

3. A bridge 20.0 m long and weighing 4.00×10^5 N is supported by two pillars located 3.00 m from each end. If a 1.96×10^4 N car is parked 8.00 m from one end of the bridge, how much force does each pillar exert?

4. A 700.0 N window washer is standing on a scaffold supported by a vertical rope at each end. The scaffold weighs 200.0 N and is 3.00 m long. What is the force in each rope when the window washer stands 1.00 m from one end?

1. Where should the supporting pivot be located on the object in **Figure 8-9** to produce the following?

    a. a net positive torque
    b. a net negative torque
    c. no rotation

A B C D E F G

50 N

150 N

Figure 8-9

2. Describe the approximate location of the center of mass for the following objects:

    a. a meterstick
    b. a bowling ball
    c. an ice cube
    d. a doughnut
    e. a banana

3. A student says that moment of inertia and mass are the same thing. Explain what is wrong with this reasoning.

4. Identify which, if any, conditions of equilibrium hold for the following situations:

    a. a bicycle wheel rolling along a level highway at constant speed
    b. a bicycle parked against a curb
    c. the tires on a braking automobile that is still moving
    d. a football traveling through the air

5. A uniform 40.0 N board supports two children, one weighing 510 N and the other weighing 350 N. The support is under the center of mass of the board, and the 510 N child is 1.50 m from the center.

    a. Where should the 350 N child sit to balance the system?
    b. How much force does the support exert on the board?

6. **Physics in Action**   Why would it be beneficial for a bicycle to have a low center of mass when the rider rounds a turn?

7. **Physics in Action**   A bicycle designer recently modified a bicycle by adding cylindrical weights to the spokes of the wheels. He reasoned that this would make the mass of the wheel, on average, closer to the axle, in turn making the moment of inertia smaller and the wheel easier to rotate. Where did he go wrong?

8. **Physics in Action**   The front wheel of a penny-farthing bicycle is three times larger than the rear wheel. How much more massive must the rear wheel be to have the same moment of inertia as the front wheel?

8-3
Rotational dynamics

NEWTON'S SECOND LAW FOR ROTATION

You learned in Section 8-2 that there is a relationship between the net torque on an object and the angular acceleration given to the object. This is analogous to Newton's second law, which relates the net force on an object to the translational acceleration given to the object. Newton's second law for rotating objects can be written as follows:

NEWTON'S SECOND LAW FOR ROTATING OBJECTS

$$\tau_{net} = I\alpha$$

net torque = moment of inertia $\times$ angular acceleration

Figure 8-10
The continuous flow of water exerts a torque on the waterwheel.

Recall that a net positive torque causes an object to rotate counterclockwise. This means that the angular acceleration of the object is also counterclockwise. Similarly, a net negative torque will produce a clockwise angular acceleration. Thus, in calculating an object's angular acceleration, it is important to keep track of the signs of the torques acting on the object.

For example, consider **Figure 8-10,** which shows a continuous stream of water falling on a wheel. The force applied by the falling water exerts a force on the rim of the wheel, producing a net torque. This net torque, in turn, causes the wheel to rotate. The angular acceleration of the wheel is clockwise and has a magnitude that depends on the moment of inertia of the wheel as well as on the weight of the falling water.

The relationship between these translational and rotational quantities is summarized in **Table 8-3.**

Table 8-3	Newton's second law for translational and rotational motion	
Translation	$F = ma$	force = mass $\times$ acceleration
Rotation	$\tau = I\alpha$	torque = moment of inertia $\times$ angular acceleration

Newton's second law for rotating objects

PROBLEM

A catapult propels a 0.150 kg stone into the air. Assume that the length of the catapult arm is 0.350 m and that its moment of inertia is negligible. If the stone leaves the catapult with an acceleration of 1.00×10^2 m/s^2, what is the torque exerted on the stone?

SOLUTION

Given: $m = 0.150$ kg $a = 1.00 \times 10^2$ m/s^2
$d = 0.350$ m

Unknown: $\tau = ?$

Use the equation for Newton's second law for rotating objects, shown on page 290.

$$\tau = I\alpha, \text{ where } I = md^2 \text{ and } \alpha = \frac{a}{d}$$

$$\tau = md^2\left(\frac{a}{d}\right) = mda$$

$$\tau = (0.150 \text{ kg})(0.350 \text{ m})(1.00 \times 10^2 \text{ m/s}^2)$$

$$\boxed{\tau = 5.25 \text{ N} \cdot \text{m}}$$

Newton's second law for rotating objects

1. A potter's wheel of radius 0.50 m and mass 100.0 kg is freely rotating at 50.0 rev/min. The potter can stop the wheel in 6.0 s by pressing a wet rag against the rim and exerting a radially inward force of 70.0 N.
   a. What is the angular acceleration of the wheel?
   b. How much torque does the potter apply to the wheel?

2. A light string 4.00 m long is wrapped around a solid cylindrical spool with a radius of 0.075 m and a mass of 0.500 kg. A 5.00 kg mass is then attached to the free end of the string, causing the string to unwind from the spool.
   a. What is the angular acceleration of the spool?
   b. How fast will the spool be rotating after all of the string has unwound?

3. A bicycle tire of radius 0.33 m and mass 1.5 kg is rotating at 98.7 rad/s. What torque is necessary to stop the tire in 2.0 s?

MOMENTUM

Have you ever swung a sledgehammer or a similarly heavy object? You probably noticed that it took some effort to start the object rotating and that it also took an effort to stop it from rotating. This is because objects resist changes in their rotational motion as well as in their translational motion.

Rotating objects have angular momentum

Because a rotating object has inertia, it also possesses momentum associated with its rotation. This momentum is called **angular momentum.** Angular momentum is defined by the following equation:

ANGULAR MOMENTUM

$$L = I\omega$$

angular momentum = moment of inertia × angular speed

The unit of angular momentum is $kg \cdot m^2/s$. To get an idea of how large this unit is, note that when you swing a baseball bat, you give the bat an angular momentum of about $1\ kg \cdot m^2/s$. The relationship between these translational and rotational quantities is summarized in **Table 8-4.**

Table 8-4	Translational and angular momentum	
Translational	$p = mv$	momentum = mass × speed
Rotational	$L = I\omega$	rotational momentum = moment of inertia × angular speed

Figure 8-11
Angular momentum is conserved as the skater pulls his arms toward his body.

Angular momentum may be conserved

When the net external torque acting on an object or objects is zero, the angular momentum of the object(s) does not change. This is the law of *conservation of angular momentum.*

For example, assuming the friction between the skates and the ice is negligible, there is no torque acting on the skater in **Figure 8-11,** so his angular momentum is conserved. When he brings his hands and feet closer to his body, more of his mass, on average, is nearer his axis of rotation. As a result, the moment of inertia of his body decreases. Because his angular momentum is constant, his angular speed increases to compensate for his smaller moment of inertia.

Conservation of angular momentum

PROBLEM

A 65 kg student is spinning on a merry-go-round that has a mass of 115 kg and a radius of 2.0 m. She walks from the edge of the merry-go-round toward the center. If the angular speed of the merry-go-round is initially 2.0 rad/s, what is its angular speed when the student reaches a point 0.50 m from the center?

SOLUTION

1. DEFINE

Given: $M = 115$ kg $r_i = R = 2.0$ m $r_f = 0.50$ m
               $m = 65$ kg $\omega_i = 2.0$ rad/s

Unknown: $\omega_f = ?$

Diagram:

2. PLAN

Choose an equation(s) or situation: Because there are no external torques, the angular momentum of the system (merry-go-round plus student) is conserved.

$$L_i = L_f$$

$$L_{m,i} + L_{s,i} = L_{m,f} - L_{s,f}$$

Determine the moments of inertia. Treat the merry-go-round as a solid disk, and treat the student as a point mass.

$$I_m = \tfrac{1}{2}MR^2$$

$$I_{s,i} = mR^2$$

$$I_{s,f} = mr_f^2$$

3. CALCULATE

Substitute the values into the equation(s) and solve: Determine the initial moments of inertia and the initial angular momentum.

$$I_m = (0.5)(115 \text{ kg})(2.0 \text{ m})^2 = 230 \text{ kg} \cdot \text{m}^2$$

$$I_{s,i} = (65 \text{ kg})(2.0 \text{ m})^2 = 260 \text{ kg} \cdot \text{m}^2$$

$$L_i = L_{m,i} + L_{s,i} = I_m \omega_i - I_{s,i}\omega_i$$

$$L_i = (230 \text{ kg} \cdot \text{m}^2)(2.0 \text{ rad/s}) + (260 \text{ kg} \cdot \text{m}^2)(2.0 \text{ rad/s})$$

$$L_i = 980 \text{ kg} \cdot \text{m}^2/\text{s}$$

Determine the final moments of inertia and the final angular momentum.

$$I_{s,f} = (65 \text{ kg})(0.50 \text{ m})^2 = 16 \text{ kg} \cdot \text{m}^2$$

$$L_f = L_{m,f} + L_{s,f} = I_m \omega_f + I_{s,f}\omega_f$$

$$L_f = (230 \text{ kg} \cdot \text{m}^2 + 16 \text{ kg} \cdot \text{m}^2)\, \omega_f$$

$$L_f = (250 \text{ kg} \cdot \text{m}^2)\, \omega_f$$

continued on next page

Equate the initial and final angular momentum.

$$980 \text{ kg} \cdot \text{m}^2/\text{s} = (250 \text{ kg} \cdot \text{m}^2)\ \omega_f$$

$$\boxed{\omega_f = 3.9 \text{ rad/s}}$$

4. EVALUATE Because the total moment of inertia decreases as the student moves toward the axis, the final angular speed should be greater than the initial angular speed.

$$3.9 \text{ rad/s} > 2.0 \text{ rad/s}$$

PRACTICE 8D

Conservation of angular momentum

1. A merry-go-round rotates at the rate of 0.20 rev/s with an 80.0 kg man standing at a point 2.0 m from the axis of rotation. What is the new angular speed when the man walks to a point 1.0 m from the center? Assume that the merry-go-round is a solid 25 kg cylinder with a radius of 2.0 m.

2. A 2.0 kg bicycle wheel with a radius of 0.30 m turns at a constant angular speed of 25 rad/s when a 0.30 kg reflector is at a distance of 0.15 m from the axle. What is the angular speed of the wheel when the reflector slides to a distance of 0.25 m from the axle?

3. As Halley's comet orbits the sun, its distance from the sun changes dramatically, from 8.8×10^{10} m to 5.2×10^{12} m. If the comet's speed at closest approach is 5.4×10^4 m/s, what is its speed when it is farthest from the sun if angular momentum is conserved?

4. A solid, horizontal cylinder with a mass of 10.0 kg and a radius of 1.00 m rotates with an angular speed of 7.00 rad/s about a fixed vertical axis through its center. A 0.250 kg piece of putty is dropped vertically at a point 0.900 m from the cylinder's center of rotation and sticks to the cylinder. Determine the final angular speed of the system.

5. The entrance of a science museum features a funnel into which marbles are rolled one at a time. The marbles circle around the wall of the funnel, eventually spiraling down into the neck of the funnel. The internal radius of the funnel at the top is 1.50 m. At the bottom, the funnel's neck narrows to an internal radius of 0.025 m. A 5.0×10^{-3} kg marble begins rolling a large circular orbit around the funnel's rim at 0.65 rev/s. If it continues moving in a roughly circular path, what will the marble's angular speed be as it passes throught the neck of the funnel? (Consider only the effects of the conservation of angular momentum.)

KINETIC ENERGY

In Chapter 5 you learned that the mechanical energy of an object includes translational kinetic energy and potential energy, but that was for objects that can be modeled as point masses. In other words, this approach did not consider the possibility that objects could have rotational motion along with translational motion.

Rotating objects have rotational kinetic energy

Rotating objects possess kinetic energy associated with their angular speed. This form of energy is called **rotational kinetic energy** and is expressed by the following equation:

rotational kinetic energy

energy of an object due to its rotational motion

CALCULATING ROTATIONAL KINETIC ENERGY

$$KE_{rot} = \tfrac{1}{2}I\omega^2$$

rotational kinetic energy $= \tfrac{1}{2} \times$ **moment of inertia** $\times$ **(angular speed)**^{2}

This is analogous to the translational kinetic energy of a particle, given by the expression $\tfrac{1}{2}mv^2$, where the moment of inertia replaces the mass and the angular speed replaces the translational speed. The unit of rotational kinetic energy is the joule, the SI unit for energy (see Chapter 5). The relationship between these translational and rotational quantities is summarized in **Table 8-5.**

Table 8-5	Translational and rotational kinetic energy	
Translational	$KE_{trans} = \tfrac{1}{2}mv^2$	translational kinetic energy $= \tfrac{1}{2}$mass $\times$ (speed)^2
Rotational	$KE_{rot} = \tfrac{1}{2}I\omega^2$	rotational kinetic energy $= \tfrac{1}{2}$moment of inertia $\times$ (angular speed)^2

Mechanical energy may be conserved

Recall the race between two objects on page 278. Because it is assumed that gravity is the only external force acting on the cylinders and spheres, the mechanical energy associated with each object is conserved. Unlike the examples of energy conservation in Chapter 5, however, the objects in this example are rotating. Recalling that mechanical energy is the sum of all types of kinetic and potential energy, we must include a rotational kinetic energy term in our formula for mechanical energy, as follows:

$$ME = KE_{trans} + KE_{rot} + PE_g$$
$$ME = \tfrac{1}{2}mv^2 + \tfrac{1}{2}I\omega^2 + mgh$$

Conservation of mechanical energy

PROBLEM

A solid ball with a mass of 3.25 kg and a radius of 0.75 m starts from rest at a height of 2.00 m and rolls down a 30.0° slope, as shown in Figure 8-15. What is the translational speed of the ball when it leaves the incline?

SOLUTION

1. DEFINE **Given:**

$h = 2.00 \text{ m}$ $\quad \theta = 30.0°$ $\quad m = 3.25 \text{ kg}$

$r = 0.75 \text{ m}$ $\quad v_i = 0.0 \text{ m/s}$

Unknown: $\quad v_f = ?$

Diagram:

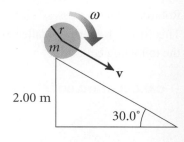

2.00 m

30.0°

2. PLAN **Choose an equation(s) or situation:** Apply the conservation of mechanical energy.

$$ME_i = ME_f$$

Initially, the system possesses only gravitational potential energy. When the ball reaches the bottom of the ramp, this potential energy has been converted to translational and rotational kinetic energy.

$$mgh = \tfrac{1}{2}mv_f^2 + \tfrac{1}{2}I\omega_f^2 \quad \text{where } \omega_f = \frac{v_f}{r}$$

The moment of inertia for a solid ball can be found in **Table 8-1,** on page 285.

$$I = \tfrac{2}{5}mr^2$$

Equate the initial and final mechanical energy.

$$mgh = \tfrac{1}{2}mv_f^2 + \tfrac{1}{2}\left(\tfrac{2}{5}mr^2\right)\left(\frac{v_f}{r}\right)^2 = \tfrac{1}{2}mv_f^2 + \tfrac{1}{5}mv_f^2 = \tfrac{7}{10}mv_f^2$$

Rearrange the equation(s) to isolate the unknown(s):

$$v_f^2 = \tfrac{10}{7}gh$$

3. CALCULATE **Substitute the values into the equation(s) and solve:**

$$v_f^2 = \tfrac{10}{7}(9.81 \text{ m/s}^2)(2.00 \text{ m})$$

$$\boxed{v_f = 5.29 \text{ m/s}}$$

4. EVALUATE This speed should be less than the speed of an object undergoing free fall from the same height because part of the energy goes into rotation.

$$v_f(\text{free fall}) = \sqrt{2gh} = 6.26 \text{ m/s}$$

$$5.29 \text{ m/s} < 6.26 \text{ m/s}$$

Conservation of mechanical energy

1. Repeat Sample Problem 8E using a solid cylinder of the same mass and radius as the ball and releasing it from the same height. In a race between these two objects on an incline, which would win?

2. A regulation basketball has a 25 cm diameter and may be approximated as a thin spherical shell. How long will it take a basketball starting from rest to roll without slipping 4.0 m down an incline that makes an angle of 30.0° with the horizontal?

3. A horizontal 800.0 N merry-go-round with a radius of 1.5 m is started from rest by a constant horizontal force of 50.0 N applied tangentially to the merry-go-round. Find the kinetic energy of the merry-go-round after 3.0 s. (Hint: Assume the merry-go-round is a solid disk.)

Section Review

1. A student holds a 3.0 kg mass in each hand while sitting on a rotating stool. When his arms are extended horizontally, the masses are 1.0 m from the axis of rotation and he rotates with an angular speed of 0.75 rad/s. If the student pulls the masses horizontally to 0.30 m from the axis of rotation, what is his new angular speed? Assume the combined moment of inertia of the student and the stool together is $3.0 \text{ kg} \cdot \text{m}^2$ and is constant.

2. A 4.0 kg mass is connected by a massless string over a massless and frictionless pulley to the center of an 8.0 kg wheel. Assume that the wheel has a radius of 0.50 m and a moment of inertia of $2.0 \text{ kg} \cdot \text{m}^2$, as shown in **Figure 8-12.** The mass is released from rest at a height of 2.0 m above the ground. What will its speed be just before it strikes the ground? (Hint: Apply conservation of mechanical energy.)

Figure 8-12

3. **Physics in Action** A bicyclist exerts a constant force of 40.0 N on a pedal 0.15 m from the axis of rotation of a penny-farthing bicycle wheel with a radius of 50.0 cm. If his speed is 2.25 m/s after 3.0 s, what is the moment of inertia of the wheel? (Disregard friction and the inertia of the small wheel.)

8-4
Simple machines

8-4 SECTION OBJECTIVES

- Identify the six types of simple machines.

- Explain how the operation of a simple machine alters the applied force and the distance moved.

- Calculate the mechanical advantage of a simple machine.

- Calculate the efficiency of a simple machine.

TYPES OF SIMPLE MACHINES

What do you do when you need to drive a nail into a board? You probably hit the nail with a hammer. Similarly, you would probably use scissors to cut paper or a bottle opener to pry a cap off a bottle. All of these devices make your task easier. These devices are *machines.*

The term *machine* may bring to mind intricate systems with multicolored wires and complex gear-and-pulley systems. Compared with internal-combustion engines or airplanes, simple devices such as hammers, scissors, and bottle openers may not seem like machines, but they are.

A machine is any device that transmits or modifies force, usually by changing the force applied to an object. All machines are combinations or modifications of six fundamental types of machines, called *simple machines.* These six simple machines are the lever, pulley, inclined plane, wheel and axle, wedge, and screw, as shown in **Table 8-6.**

Table 8-6   Six simple machines

USING SIMPLE MACHINES

Because the purpose of a simple machine is to change the direction or magnitude of an input force, a useful way of characterizing a simple machine is to compare how large the output force is relative to the input force. This ratio, called the machine's *mechanical advantage,* is written as follows:

$$MA = \frac{\text{output force}}{\text{input force}} = \frac{F_{out}}{F_{in}}$$

A good example of mechanical advantage is the claw hammer, which is a type of lever, as shown in **Figure 8-13.**

A person applies an input force to one end of the handle. The handle, in turn, exerts an output force on the head of a nail stuck in a board. Rotational equilibrium is maintained, so the input torque must balance the output torque. This can be written as follows:

$$\tau_{in} = \tau_{out}$$
$$F_{in}d_{in} = F_{out}d_{out}$$

Substituting this expression into the definition of mechanical advantage gives the following result:

$$MA = \frac{F_{out}}{F_{in}} = \frac{d_{in}}{d_{out}}$$

The longer the input lever arm is compared with the output lever arm, the greater the mechanical advantage is. This in turn indicates the factor by which the input force is amplified. If the force of the board on the nail is 99 N and if the mechanical advantage is 10, then only a force of 10 N is needed to pull out the nail. Without a machine, the nail could not be removed unless the force was greater than 100 N.

Machines can alter the force and the distance moved

You have learned that mechanical energy is conserved in the absence of friction. This law holds for machines as well. A machine can increase (or decrease) the force acting on an object at the expense (or gain) of the distance moved, but the product of the two—the work done on the object—is constant.

For example, imagine an incline. **Figure 8-14** shows two examples of a refrigerator being loaded onto a flatbed truck. In one example, the refrigerator is lifted directly onto the truck. In the other example, an incline is used.

In the first example, a force (F_1) of 1200 N is required to lift the refrigerator, which moves through a distance (d_1) of 1.5 m. This requires 1800 N•m of work. In the second example, a lesser force (F_2) of only 360 N is needed, but the refrigerator must be pushed a greater distance (d_2) of 5.0 m. This also requires 1800 N•m of work. As a result, the two methods require the same amount of energy.

Figure 8-13
A hammer makes it easier to pry a nail from a board by multiplying the input force. The hammer swivels around the point marked with a black dot.

Figure 8-14
Simple machines can alter both the force needed to perform a task and the distance through which the force acts.

Human Extenders

A cyborg, as any science-fiction aficionado knows, is part human and part machine and is able to perform extraordinary tasks. Although cyborgs are still more fiction than science, Dr. Homayoon Kazerooni, of the University of California at Berkeley, has been inventing machines called *human extenders* that can give mere mortals superhuman strength.

"Human extenders are robotic systems worn by a human to move heavy objects," Dr. Kazerooni says. One of the first machines Dr. Kazerooni designed is a 1.5 m (5 ft) long steel arm that weighs thousands of newtons (several hundred pounds) and is attached to a pedestal on the floor. The operator inserts one arm into the device, and an attached computer senses the arm's movement and uses hydraulic pressure to move the extender in conjunction with the operator's arm. The extender gives the operator a mechanical advantage. For example, when operating the extender, a person can lift objects weighing as much as 890 N (200 lb) while exerting a force of only 89 N (20 lb). In this case, the mechanical advantage is 10 (890 N/89 N = 10).

Dr. Kazerooni is developing a complete suit of human extenders that will be powered by electricity. Controlled completely by the movement of the user, the suit has two arms that sense and respond to both the force applied by the human and the weight of the object being lifted, taking most of the effort away from the operator. The machine's legs are able to balance the weight of the equipment, and they attach at the operator's feet to allow movement around the room.

Dr. Kazerooni envisions human extenders being used primarily as labor aids for factory workers. Approximately 30 percent of all workplace accidents in the United States are related to back injuries, and they are usually the result of a repeated lifting and moving of heavy objects. Human extenders could solve that problem. "The person who is wearing the machine," Dr. Kazerooni says, "will feel less force and less fatigue, and therefore the potential for back injuries or any kind of injury would be less."

Figure 8-15

Efficiency is a measure of how well a machine works

The simple machines we have considered so far are ideal, frictionless machines. Real machines, however, are not frictionless. They dissipate energy. The *efficiency* of a machine is a measure of how much input energy is lost compared with how much energy is used to perform work on an object. It is defined by the following equation:

$$eff = \frac{W_{out}}{W_{in}}$$

If a machine is frictionless, then mechanical energy is conserved. This means that the work done on the machine (input work) equals the work done by the machine (output work) because work is a measure of energy transfer. Thus, the mechanical efficiency of an ideal machine is 1, or 100%. This is the best efficiency a machine can have. Because all real machines have at least a little bit of friction, the efficiency of machines is always less than 1. The efficiencies for a number of activities are given in **Table 8-7.**

Table 8-7
Efficiencies for a few activities

Activity	% Efficiency
swimming	2.9–7.4
ice skating	11.0
walking	19.6–35.2
cycling	24.4–34.4

Section Review

1. **Figure 8-16** shows an example of a Rube Goldberg machine. Identify two types of simple machines in this compound machine.

2. The efficiency of a squeaky pulley system is 73 percent. The pulleys are used to raise a mass. What force is exerted on the machine if a rope is pulled 18.0 m in order to raise a 58 kg mass a height of 3.0 m?

Figure 8-16

3. A person pushes a 950 N box up an incline. If the person exerts a force of 350 N along the incline, what is the mechanical advantage of the incline?

4. A person must move a large stone in her backyard. She gets a 20.0 kg plank that is 3.50 m long to use as a lever, and she wedges one end of the plank under the large stone. A smaller stone, 0.750 m from the large one, serves as a pivot. The plank makes an angle of 20.0° with the ground. When she pushes down on the end of the plank with a force of 210 N, the large stone begins to move.

   a. What upward force is being exerted against the large stone?
   b. What is the mechanical advantage of the lever?

5. **Physics in Action** A bicycle is a combination of simple machines. Identify three types of simple machines used to propel a typical bicycle.

Quantum Angular Momentum

Earlier in this chapter, we discussed angular momentum and its effects in the macroscopic world of your everyday experience. In the early twentieth century, scientists realized that they must modify their ideas about angular momentum when working with the microscopic world of atoms and subatomic particles.

Electron orbital angular momentum

In 1911, Ernest Rutherford proposed a model of the atom in which negatively charged particles called *electrons* orbit a positively charged nucleus containing particles called *protons,* much as the Earth orbits the sun, as shown in **Figure 8-17(a).** Because the electron orbits the nucleus, it has an orbital angular momentum.

Further investigations into the microscopic realm revealed that the electron cannot be precisely located in space and therefore cannot be visualized as orbiting the proton. Instead, in modern theory the electron's location is depicted by an electron cloud, as shown in **Figure 8-17(b),** whose density varies throughout the cloud in proportion to the probability of finding the electron at a particular location in the cloud. Even though the electron does not orbit the nucleus in this model, the electron still has an orbital angular momentum that is very different from the angular momentum discussed earlier in this chapter.

For most of the history of science, it was assumed that angular momentum could have any possible value. But investigations at the atomic level have shown that this is not the case. The orbital angular momentum of the electron can have only certain possible values. Such a quantity is said to be discrete, and the angular momentum is said to be *quantized.* The branch of modern theory that deals with quanta is called *quantum mechanics.*

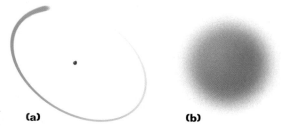

(a)   (b)

Figure 8-17

(a) In Rutherford's model of the atom, electrons orbit the nucleus. **(b)** In quantum mechanics, an electron cloud is used to show the probability that the electron will be at different points. The densest regions of the cloud represent the most probable locations for the electron.

Electron spin

In addition to the orbital angular momentum of the electron, certain experimental evidence led scientists to postulate another type of angular momentum of the electron. This type of angular momentum is known as *spin* because the effects it explains are those that would result if the electron were to spin on its axis, much like the Earth spins on its axis as it orbits the sun. Scientists first imagined that the electron actually spins in this way, but it soon became clear that electron spin is not a literal description. Instead, electron spin is a property that is independent of the electron's location in space. In this respect, electron spin is very different from the spin of the Earth.

Just as a wheel can turn either clockwise or counterclockwise, there are two possible types of electron spin, *spin up* and *spin down*, as shown in **Figure 8-18.** Thus, like orbital angular momentum, spin is quantized. Because the electron isn't really spinning in space, it should not be assumed that **Figure 8-18** is a physical description of the electron's motion.

Conservation of angular momentum

Although the quantum-mechanical concept of angular momentum is radically different from the classical concept of angular momentum, there is one fundamental similarity between the two models. Earlier in this chapter, you learned that angular momentum is always conserved. This principle still holds in quantum mechanics, where the total angular momentum, that is, the sum of the orbital angular momentum and spin, is always conserved.

As you have seen, the quantum-mechanical model of the atom cannot be visualized in the same way that previous atomic models could be. Although this may initially seem like a flaw of the modern theory, the accuracy of predictions based on quantum mechanics has convinced many scientists that physical models based on our experiences in the macroscopic realm cannot provide a complete picture of nature. Consequently, mathematical models must be used to describe the microscopic realm of atoms and subatomic particles.

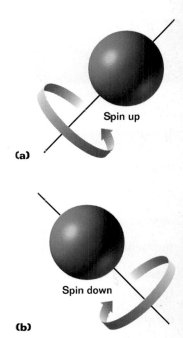

(a)

Spin up

Spin down

(b)

Figure 8-18
In the quantum-mechanical model of the atom, the electron has both an orbital angular momentum and an intrinsic angular momentum, known as spin. **(a)** Spin up and **(b)** spin down are the only possible values for electron spin.

Table 8-8	Angular momentum
Classical angular momentum	**Quantum angular momentum**
corresponds to a literal rotation	does not correspond to a literal rotation
can have any possible value	can have only certain discrete values
total angular momentum (orbital + rotational) conserved	total angular momentum (orbital angular momentum + spin) conserved

CHAPTER 8
Summary

KEY TERMS

angular momentum (p. 292)

center of mass (p. 283)

lever arm (p. 279)

moment of inertia (p. 284)

rotational kinetic energy (p. 295)

torque (p. 279)

KEY IDEAS

Section 8-1 Torque

- Torque is a measure of a force's ability to rotate an object.
- The torque on an object depends on the magnitude of the applied force and on the length of the lever arm, according to the following equation:

$$\tau = Fd(\sin\theta)$$

Section 8-2 Rotation and inertia

- The moment of inertia of an object is a measure of the resistance of the object to changes in rotational motion.
- For an extended object to be in complete equilibrium, it must be in both translational and rotational equilibrium.

Section 8-3 Rotational dynamics

- The rotational equation analogous to Newton's second law can be described as follows:

$$\tau = I\alpha$$

- A rotating object possesses angular momentum, which is conserved in the absence of any external forces on the object.
- A rotating object possesses rotational kinetic energy, which is conserved in the absence of any external forces on the object.

Section 8-4 Simple machines

- A simple machine can alter the force applied to an object or the distance an applied force moves an object.
- Simple machines can provide a mechanical advantage.

Key Symbols

Quantities		Units		Conversions
τ	torque	N•m	newton meter	$= kg•m^2/s^2$
$d(\sin\theta)$	lever arm	m	meter	
I	moment of inertia	$kg•m^2$	kilogram meter squared	
L	angular momentum	$kg•m^2/s$	kilogram meter squared per second	
KE_{rot}	rotational kinetic energy	J	joule	$= N•m$ $= kg•m^2/s^2$

TORQUE AND MOMENT OF INERTIA

Conceptual questions

1. How does an orthodontist use torque to realign teeth?

2. Which of the forces acting on the rod in **Figure 8-19** will produce a torque about the axis at the left end of the rod?

axis of rotation

F_1

F_2

Figure 8-19

3. Two children are rolling automobile tires down a hill. One child claims that the tire will roll faster if one of them curls up in the tire's center. The other child claims that will cause the tire to roll more slowly. Which child is correct?

4. The moment of inertia of Earth was recently measured to be $0.331MR^2$. What does this tell you about the distribution of mass inside the Earth? (Hint: Compare this value with the moments of inertia in **Table 8-1**.)

5. The moment of inertia for a regular object can never be larger than MR^2, where M is the mass and R is the size of the object. Why is this so? (Hint: Which object has a moment of inertia of MR^2?)

6. Two forces of equal magnitude act on a wheel, as shown in **Figure 8-20**. Which force will produce the greater torque on the wheel?

F_1

F_2

Figure 8-20

7. Two forces equal in magnitude but opposite in direction act at the same point on an object. Is it possible for there to be a net torque on the object? Explain.

8. It is more difficult to do a sit-up with your hands behind your head than with your arms stretched out in front of you. Why?

Practice problems

9. A mechanic jacks up a car to an angle of 8.0° to change the front tires. The car is 3.05 m long and has a mass of 1130 kg. Its center of mass is located 1.12 m from the front end. The rear wheels are 0.40 m from the back end. Calculate the torque exerted by the car around the back wheels. (See Sample Problem 8A.)

10. A bucket filled with water has a mass of 54 kg and is attached to a rope that is wound around a 0.050 m radius cylinder. What torque does the bucket produce around the center of the cylinder? (See Sample Problem 8A.)

11. A bucket filled with water has a mass of 75 kg and is attached to a rope that is wound around a 0.075 m radius cylinder. A crank with a turning radius of 0.25 m is attached to the end of the cylinder. What minimum force directed perpendicularly to the crank handle is required to raise the bucket? (See Sample Problem 8A.)

12. The arm of a crane is 15.0 m long and makes an angle of 20.0° with the horizontal. Assume that the maximum load for the crane is limited by the amount of torque the load produces around the base of the arm.

    a. What is the maximum torque the crane can withstand if the maximum load is 450 N?

    b. What is the maximum load for this crane at an angle of 40.0°?

(See Sample Problem 8A.)

CENTER OF MASS AND ROTATIONAL EQUILIBRIUM

Review questions

13. A juggler is throwing two spinning clubs, one heavier than the other. Which of the following statements is true?
    a. The smaller club is likely to have a larger moment of inertia.
    b. The ends of each club will trace out parabolas as the club is thrown.
    c. The center of mass of each club will trace out a parabola as the club is thrown.

14. When the juggler in the previous problem stands up straight and holds each club at arm's length, his center of mass will probably be
    a. exactly in the middle of his body
    b. slightly to the side where he is holding the light club
    c. slightly to the side where he is holding the heavy club

15. What are the conditions for equilibrium? Explain how they apply to children attempting to balance a seesaw.

16. What must be true about the velocity of a moving object in equilibrium?

17. A twirler throws a baton in the air.
    a. Describe the motion of the ends of the baton.
    b. Decribe the motion of the center of mass of the baton.

Conceptual questions

18. A projectile is fired into the air and suddenly explodes into several fragments. What can be said about the motion of the center of mass of the fragments after the explosion?

19. Is it possible to balance two masses of different weights on a simple balance beam? Explain.

20. A particle moves in a straight line, and you are told that the torque acting on it is zero about some unspecified origin. Does this necessarily imply that the total force on the particle is zero? Can you conclude that its angular velocity is constant? Explain.

Practice problems

21. A 0.100 kg meterstick is supported at its 40.0 cm mark by a string attached to the ceiling. A 0.700 kg mass hangs vertically from the 5.00 cm mark. A mass is attached somewhere on the meterstick to keep it horizontal and in *both* rotational and translational equilibrium. If the force applied by the string attaching the meterstick to the ceiling is 19.6 N, determine the following:
    a. the value of the unknown mass
    b. the point where the mass attaches to the stick
    (See Sample Problem 8B.)

22. A uniform ladder 8.00 m long and weighing 200.0 N rests against a smooth wall. The coefficient of static friction between the ladder and the ground is 0.60, and the ladder makes a 50.0° angle with the ground. How far up the ladder can an 800.0 N person climb before the ladder begins to slip?
    (See Sample Problem 8B.)

23. A floodlight with a mass of 20.0 kg is used to illuminate the parking lot in front of a library. The floodlight is supported at the end of a horizontal beam that is hinged to a vertical pole, as shown in **Figure 8-21**. A cable that makes an angle of 30.0° with the beam is attached to the pole to help support the floodlight. Find the following, assuming the mass of the beam is negligible when compared with the mass of the floodlight:

    Figure 8-21

    a. the force provided by the cable
    b. the horizontal and vertical forces exerted on the beam by the pole
    (See Sample Problem 8B.)

24. A window washer is standing on a scaffold supported by a vertical rope at each end. The scaffold weighs 205 N and is 3.00 m long. What is the force each rope exerts on the scaffold when the 675 N worker stands 1.00 m from one end of the scaffold?
    (See Sample Problem 8B.)

25. A 1200.0 N uniform boom is supported by a cable, as shown in **Figure 8-22**. The boom is pivoted at the bottom, and a 2000.0 N weight hangs from its top. Find the force applied by the supporting cable and the components of the reaction force on the bottom of the boom.
(See Sample Problem 8B.)

25°

$\frac{3}{4}L$ L

2000.0 N

65°

Figure 8-22

26. A uniform 10.0 N picture frame is supported as shown in **Figure 8-23**. Find the force in the cords and the magnitude of the horizontal force at P that are required to hold the frame in this position.
(See Sample Problem 8B.)

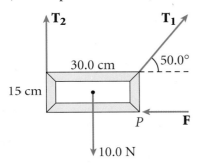

T_2 T_1

30.0 cm   50.0°

15 cm

P F

10.0 N   **Figure 8-23**

NEWTON'S SECOND LAW FOR ROTATION

Conceptual questions

27. An object rotates with a constant angular velocity. Can there be a net torque acting on the object? Explain your answer.

28. If an object is at rest, can you be certain that no external torques are acting on it?

29. Two uniformly solid disks of equal radius roll down an incline without slipping. The first disk has twice the mass of the second disk. How much torque was exerted on the first disk compared with the amount exerted on the second disk?

Practice problems

30. A cylindrical fishing reel has a mass of 0.85 kg and a radius of 4.0 cm. A friction clutch in the reel exerts a restraining torque of 1.3 N•m if a fish pulls on the line. The fisherman gets a bite, and the reel begins to spin with an angular acceleration of 66 rad/s^2. Find the following:
  a. the force of the fish on the line
  b. the amount of line that unwinds in 0.50 s
(See Sample Problem 8C.)

31. A 150 kg merry-go-round in the shape of a horizontal disk with a radius of 1.50 m is set in motion by wrapping a rope about the rim of the disk and pulling on the rope. What constant force would have to be exerted on the rope to bring the merry-go-round from rest to an angular speed of 0.500 rev/s in 2.00 s?
(See Sample Problem 8C.)

32. The combination of an applied force and a frictional force produces a constant torque of 36 N•m on a wheel rotating about a fixed axis. The applied force acts for 6.0 s, during which time the angular speed of the wheel increases from 0 to 12 rad/s. The applied force is then removed, and the wheel comes to rest in 65 s. Answer the following questions:
  a. What is the moment of inertia of the wheel?
  b. What is the magnitude of the frictional torque?
  c. How many revolutions does the wheel make?
(See Sample Problem 8C.)

33. A cable passes over a pulley. Because of friction, the force in the cable is not the same on opposite sides of the pulley. The force on one side is 120.0 N, and the force on the other side is 100.0 N. Assuming that the pulley is a uniform disk with a mass of 2.1 kg and a radius of 0.81 m, determine its angular acceleration.
(See Sample Problem 8C.)

34. An airliner lands with a constant speed of 50.0 m/s. Each wheel of the plane has a radius of 1.25 m and a moment of inertia of 110 kg•m^2. At touchdown the wheels begin to spin under the action of friction. Each wheel supports a weight of 1.40×10^4 N, and the wheels attain the angular speed of rolling without slipping in 0.480 s. What is the coefficient of kinetic friction between the wheels and the runway?
(See Sample Problem 8C.)

35. A pulley has a moment of inertia of 5.0 kg•m^2 and a radius of 0.50 m. A cord is wrapped over the pulley and attached to a hanging object on either end. Assume the cord does not slip, the axle is frictionless, and the two hanging objects have masses of 2.0 kg and 5.0 kg.

   a. Find the acceleration of each mass.

   b. Find the force in the cord supporting each mass. (Note that they are different.)

(See Sample Problem 8C.)

36. A 4.0 kg mass is connected by a light cord to a 3.0 kg mass on a smooth surface as shown in **Figure 8-24.** The pulley rotates about a frictionless axle and has a moment of inertia of 0.50 kg•m^2 and a radius of 0.30 m. Assuming that the cord does not slip on the pulley, answer the following questions:

   a. What is the acceleration of the two masses?

   b. What are the forces in the string F_1 and F_2?

(See Sample Problem 8C.)

Figure 8-24

ANGULAR MOMENTUM AND ROTATIONAL KINETIC ENERGY

Review questions

37. Is angular momentum always conserved? Explain.

38. Is it possible for two objects with the same mass and the same rotational speeds to have different values of angular momentum? Explain.

39. A child on a merry-go-round moves from near the axis to the outer edge of the merry-go-round. What happens to the rotational speed of the merry-go-round? Explain.

40. Is it possible for an ice skater to change her rotational speed without any external torque? Explain.

Conceptual questions

41. Ice skaters use the conservation of angular momentum to produce high-speed spins when they bring their arms close to the rotation axis. Imagine a skater moves her arms inward, cutting the moment of inertia in half and therefore doubling the angular speed. If we consider the rotational kinetic energy, we see that the energy is *doubled* in this situation. Thus, angular momentum is conserved, but kinetic energy is not. Where does this extra energy come from?

42. A solid 2.0 kg ball with a radius of 0.50 m starts at a height of 3.0 m and rolls down a 20° slope. A solid disk and a ring start at the same time and the same height. Both the ring and the disk have the same mass and radius as the ball. Which of the three wins the race to the bottom if all roll without slipping?

Practice problems

43. Calculate the following:

   a. the angular momentum of Earth that arises from its spinning motion on its axis

   b. the angular momentum of Earth that arises from its orbital motion about the sun

(See Sample Problem 8D. Hint: See item 4 on page 305 and Appendix D.)

44. A 65 kg woman stands at the rim of a horizontal turntable with a moment of inertia of 530 kg•m^2 and a radius of 2.0 m. The system is initially at rest, and the turntable is free to rotate about a frictionless vertical axle through its center. The woman then starts walking clockwise (when viewed from above) around the rim at a constant speed of 1.5 m/s relative to the Earth.

   a. In what direction and with what angular speed does the turntable rotate?

   b. How much work does the woman do to set the system in motion?

(See Sample Problem 8D.)

45. A solid, frictionless cylindrical pulley with a mass of 3.00 kg and a 0.400 m radius is used to draw water from a well. A 2.00 kg bucket is attached to a cord that is wrapped around the pulley. If the bucket starts from rest at the top of the well and falls for 3.00 s before hitting the water, how far does it fall? (See Sample Problem 8E.)

46. A coin with a diameter of 3.00 cm rolls up a 30.0° inclined plane. The coin starts with an initial angular speed of 60.0 rad/s and rolls in a straight line without slipping. How far does it roll up the inclined plane?
(See Sample Problem 8E.)

47. A solid sphere rolls along a horizontal, smooth surface at a constant linear speed without slipping. Show that the rotational kinetic energy about the center of the sphere is two-sevenths of its total kinetic energy.
(See Sample Problem 8E.)

48. A horizontal 800.0 N merry-go-round with a radius of 1.5 m is started from rest by a constant horizontal force of 50.0 N applied tangentially to the merry-go-round. Find the kinetic energy of the merry-go-round after 3.0 s. Assume it is a solid cylinder.
(See Sample Problem 8E.)

49. A top has a moment of inertia of 4.00×10^{-4} kg•m^2 and is initially at rest. It is free to rotate about a vertical stationary axis. A string around a peg along the axis of the top is pulled, maintaining a constant tension of 5.57 N in the string. If the string does not slip while it is wound around the peg, what is the angular speed of the top after 80.0 cm of string has been pulled off the peg?
(See Sample Problem 8E. Hint: Consider the work done.)

50. A skater spins with an angular speed of 12.0 rad/s with his arms outstretched. He lowers his arms, decreasing his moment of inertia from 41 kg•m^2 to 36 kg•m^2.
   a. Calculate his initial and final rotational kinetic energy.
   b. Is the rotational kinetic energy increased or decreased?
   c. How do you account for this change in kinetic energy?
(See Sample Problem 8E.)

51. A solid 240 N ball with a radius of 0.20 m rolls 6.0 m down a ramp that is inclined at 37° with the horizontal. What is the angular speed of the ball at the bottom of the ramp if it starts from rest?
(See Sample Problem 8E.)

SIMPLE MACHINES

Review questions

52. Why is it easier to loosen the lid from the top of a paint can with a long-handled screwdriver than with a short-handled screwdriver?

53. If a machine cannot multiply the amount of work, what is the advantage of using such a machine?

Conceptual questions

54. You are attempting to move a large rock using a long lever. Is it more effective to place the lever's axis of rotation nearer to your hands or nearer to the rock? Explain.

55. You are attempting to move a large rock using a long lever. Will the work you do on the lever be greater than, the same as, or less than the work done by the lever on the rock? Explain.

56. A perpetual motion machine is a machine that, when set in motion, will never come to a halt. Why is such a machine not possible?

57. If you were to use a machine to increase the output force, what factor would have to be sacrificed? Give an example.

MIXED REVIEW PROBLEMS

58. Two spheres look identical and have the same mass. One is hollow, and the other is solid. Which method would determine which is which?
   a. roll them down an incline
   b. drop them from the same height
   c. weigh them on a scale

59. A ladder with a length of 15.0 m and a weight of 520.0 N rests against a frictionless wall, making an angle of 60.0° with the horizontal.
   a. Find the horizontal and vertical forces exerted on the base of the ladder by the Earth when an 800.0 N firefighter is 4.00 m from the bottom.
   b. If the ladder is just on the verge of slipping when the firefighter is 9.00 m up, what is the coefficient of static friction between the ladder and the ground?

60. The efficiency of a pulley system is 73 percent. The pulleys are used to raise a mass of 58 kg to a height of 3.0 m. What force is exerted on the string of the pulley system if the string is pulled for 18.0 m in order to raise the mass to the required height?

61. If the torque required to loosen a nut that holds a wheel on a car has a magnitude of 40.0 N•m, what *minimum* force must be exerted at the end of a 0.30 m lug wrench to loosen the nut?

62. A 0.0200 m diameter coin rolls up a 15.0° inclined plane. The coin starts with an initial angular speed of 45.0 rad/s and rolls in a straight line without slipping. How much vertical distance does it gain before it stops rolling?

63. A simple pendulum consists of a 3.0 kg point mass hanging at the end of a 2.0 m long light string that is connected to a pivot point. Calculate the magnitude of the torque (due to the force of gravity) about this pivot point when the string makes a 5.0° angle with the vertical.

64. A 23.0 cm screwdriver is used to pry open a can of paint. If the axis of rotation is 2.00 cm from the end of the driver blade and a force of 84.3 N is exerted at the end of the handle, what force is applied to the lid?

65. A person is standing on tiptoe, and the person's total weight is supported by the force on the toe. A mechanical model for the situation is shown in **Figure 8-25,** where *T* is the force in the Achilles tendon and *R* is the force on the foot due to the tibia. Assume the total weight is 700.0 N, and find the values of *T* and *R*, if the angle labeled θ is 21.2°.

Figure 8-25

66. The net work done in accelerating a propeller from rest to an angular speed of 220 rad/s is 3000.0 J. What is the moment of inertia of the propeller?

67. In a circus performance, a large 4.0 kg hoop with a radius of 2.0 m rolls without slipping. If the hoop is given an angular speed of 6.0 rad/s while rolling on the horizontal and is allowed to roll up a ramp inclined at 15° with the horizontal, how far (measured along the incline) does the hoop roll?

68. A car is designed to get its energy from a rotating flywheel with a radius of 2.00 m and a mass of 500.0 kg. Before a trip, the disk-shaped flywheel is attached to an electric motor, which brings the flywheel's rotational speed up to 1000.0 rev/min.
  a. Find the kinetic energy stored in the flywheel.
  b. If the flywheel is to supply as much energy to the car as a 7457 W motor would, find the length of time the car can run before the flywheel has to be brought back up to speed again.

69. A 12 kg mass is attached to a cord that is wrapped around a wheel with a radius of 10.0 cm, as shown in **Figure 8-26.** The acceleration of the mass down the frictionless incline is measured to be 2.0 m/s². Assuming the axle of the wheel to be frictionless, determine
  a. the force in the rope.
  b. the moment of inertia of the wheel.
  c. the angular speed of the wheel 2.0 s after it begins rotating, starting from rest.

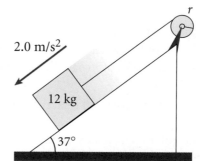

Figure 8-26

70. A cylindrical 5.00 kg pulley with a radius of 0.600 m is used to lower a 3.00 kg bucket into a well. The bucket starts from rest and falls for 4.00 s.
  a. What is the linear acceleration of the falling bucket?
  b. How far does it drop?
  c. What is the angular acceleration of the cylindrical pulley?

71. During a circus performance, a 5.0 kg hoop with a radius of 3.0 m rolls without slipping. If the hoop is given an angular speed of 3.0 rad/s while rolling on the horizontal and is allowed to roll up a ramp inclined at 20.0° with the horizontal, how far (measured along the incline) does the hoop roll?

72. A uniform 6.0 m ladder is leaning against a frictionless vertical wall. The ladder has a weight of 250 N. The ladder slips when it makes a 60.0° angle with the horizontal floor. Determine the coefficient of friction between the ladder and the floor.

Technology & Learning

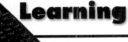

Graphing calculators

Program your graphing calculator to create a graph of torque versus angle of applied force to determine the torque involved in each of the following situations:

a. a force of 15.0 N that is applied 0.45 m from a door's hinges makes an angle of 75° with the door

b. the same force makes an angle of 45° with the door

c. a force of 15.0 N that is applied 0.25 m from a door's hinges makes an angle of 45° with the door

d. the same force makes an angle of 25° with the door

Press Y= and CLEAR to clear any functions. Press MODE ▼ ▼ ► ENTER to be certain the calculator is in degree mode.

Open a new program by pressing PRGM ► ► ENTER. Name the program "TORQUE" and press ENTER. Then enter the program shown in the table below.

To exit the program editor, press 2nd QUIT. To run the program, press PRGM, select "TORQUE," and press ENTER ENTER. Enter the value for the force and the distance, pressing ENTER after each one.

The calculator will provide a graph of the torque versus the angle of the applied force. (If the graph is not visible, press WINDOW and change the settings for the graph window, then press GRAPH.)

Press TRACE, and use the arrow keys to trace along the curve. The x value corresponds to the angle in degrees, and the y value corresponds to the torque in newton•meters.

Press 2nd QUIT to run the program for other forces and distances.

Keystrokes	Display
	PROGRAM: TORQUE
1. PRGM ► 2 ALPHA F ENTER	:PROMPT F
2. PRGM ► 2 ALPHA D ENTER	:PROMPT D
3. ALPHA " ALPHA F × ALPHA D × SIN X,T,θ ALPHA " STO► 2nd Y-VARS 1 1 ENTER	:"F*D*SIN X" → Y1
4. 0 STO► VARS 1 1 ENTER	0 → XMIN
5. 1 8 0 STO► VARS 1 2 ENTER	180 → XMAX
6. PRGM ► 4 ENTER	:DISPGRAPH

73. A crate is pulled 2.0 m at constant velocity along a 15° incline. The coefficient of kinetic friction between the crate and the plane is 0.160. Calculate the efficiency of this procedure.

74. The hands of the clock in the famous Parliament Clock Tower in London are 2.7 m and 4.5 m long and have masses of 60.0 kg and 100.0 kg, respectively. Calculate the torque around the center of the clock due to the weight of these hands at 5:20. (Model the hands as thin rods.)

75. A pulley system has an efficiency of 87.5 percent. How much of the rope must be pulled in if a force of 648 N is needed to lift a 150 kg desk 2.46 m?

76. A pulley system is used to lift a piano 3.0 m. If a force of 2200 N is applied to the rope as the rope is pulled in 14 m, what is the efficiency of the machine? Assume the mass of the piano is 750 kg.

77. Figure 8-27 shows a system of point masses that rotates at an angular speed of 2.0 rev/s. The masses are connected by light, flexible spokes that can be lengthened or shortened. What is the new angular speed if the spokes are shortened to 0.50 m? (An effect similar to this occurred in the early stages of the formation of our galaxy. As the massive cloud of gas and dust contracted, an initially small rotation increased with time.)

Figure 8-27

Alternative Assessment

Performance assessment

1. Imagine a balance with unequal arms. An earring placed in the left basket was balanced by 5.00 g of standard masses on the right. When placed in the right basket, the same earring required 15.00 g on the left to balance. Which was the longer arm? Do you need to know the exact length of each arm to determine the mass of the earring?

2. You have 32 identical beads, 30 of which are assembled in clusters of 16, 8, 4, and 2. Design and build a mobile that will balance, using all the beads and clusters. Explain your design in terms of torque and rotational equilibrium.

3. A well-known problem in architecture is to stack bricks on top of one another in a way that provides a maximum offset. Design an experiment to determine how much offset you can have by stacking two, three, and four physics textbooks. How many books would be needed to prevent the center of mass of the top book from being directly over the bottom book? (Alternatively, try this with a deck of playing cards.)

Portfolio projects

4. Describe exactly which measurements you would need to make in order to identify the torques at work during a ride on a specific bicycle. (Your plans should include measurements you can make with equipment available to you.) If others in the class analyzed different bicycle models, compare the models for efficiency and mechanical advantage.

5. Prepare a poster or a series of models of simple machines, explaining their use and how they work. Include a schematic diagram next to each sample or picture to identify the fulcrum, lever arm, and resistance. Add your own examples to the following list: nail clipper, wheelbarrow, can opener, nutcracker, electric drill, screwdriver, tweezers, key in lock.

6. Research what architects do, and create a presentation on how they use physics in their work. What studies and training are necessary? What are some areas of specialization in architecture? What associations and professional groups keep architects informed about new developments?

CHAPTER 8
Laboratory Exercise

MACHINES AND EFFICIENCY

In this experiment, you will raise objects using two different types of machines. You will find the work input and the work output for each machine. The ratio of the useful work output to the work input is called the *efficiency* of the machine. By calculating efficiency, you will be able to compare different machines for different jobs.

SAFETY

- Tie back long hair, secure loose clothing, and remove loose jewelry to prevent their getting caught in moving parts and pulleys.
- Attach string to masses and objects securely. Falling or dropped masses can cause serious injury.

PREPARATION

1. Read the entire lab, and plan what measurements you will take.

2. Prepare a data table with six columns and seven rows in your lab notebook. In the first row, label the first through sixth columns *Trial*, *Machine*, *mass$_1$ (kg)*, *Δh (m)*, *mass$_2$ (kg)*, and *Δd (m)*. In the first column, label the second through seventh rows *1, 2, 3, 4, 5*, and *6*.

OBJECTIVES

- Measure the work input and work output of several machines.
- Calculate the efficiency of each machine.
- Compare machines based on their efficiencies, and determine what factors affect efficiency.

MATERIALS LIST

- ✔ balance
- ✔ C-clamp
- ✔ cord
- ✔ dynamics cart
- ✔ inclined plane
- ✔ mass hanger
- ✔ pulleys, single and tandem
- ✔ meterstick
- ✔ set of hooked masses
- ✔ right-angle clamp
- ✔ support stand
- ✔ suspension clamp

Figure 8-28

Step 3: Choose any angle, but make sure the top of the plane is at least 20 cm above the table.

Step 4: Make sure the string is long enough to help prevent the cart from falling off the top of the plane. Attach the mass hanger securely to the end of the string.

Step 7: Keep the angle the same for all trials.

PROCEDURE

Inclined plane

3. Set up the inclined plane as shown in **Figure 8-28** on page 313. Set the incline securely to any angle. Keep the angle constant during this part of the experiment. Place the inclined plane away from the edge of the table, or clamp its base to the edge of the table.

4. Measure the mass of the cart. Attach a piece of cord through the hole on the body of the cart. The cord should be long enough so that the other end of the cord reaches the table top before the cart reaches the top of the incline. Place the cart on the plane and run the cord over the pulley at the top of the plane. Attach a mass hanger to the free end of the cord.

5. Place a 200 g mass in the cart. Record the total mass of the cart and its contents as $mass_1$. Attach masses to the mass hanger until you find the lowest mass that will allow the cart to move up the plane with a constant velocity. Stop the cart before it reaches the top of the incline. Record the mass of the mass hanger plus the added mass as $mass_2$ in your data table.

6. Measure the distances, and record them. Δh is the *vertical* distance the cart moves, while the mass hanger on the cord moves the distance Δd.

7. Repeat steps 5 and 6 several times, increasing the mass in the cart by 100 g and finding the mass that will allow the cart to move with a constant velocity each time. Record all data for each trial in your data table.

Pulley

8. Set up a pulley system like the one shown in **Figure 8-29.** For the first trial, use five pulleys. Keep the area beneath the pulley system clear throughout the experiment. Measure the mass of the bottom set of pulleys before including them in the setup. Attach a 500 g mass to the bottom, as shown. Record the total mass of the 500 g mass plus the bottom set of pulleys as $mass_1$ in your data table.

9. Starting with 50 g, add enough mass to the mass hanger to prevent the pulleys from moving when released. Place the mass hanger just below the 500 g mass, and measure the initial positions of both masses by measuring the height of each mass above the base.

10. Add masses to the mass hanger until you find the mass that will make the 500 g mass move up with constant velocity once it has been started. Record the mass of the mass hanger plus the added mass as $mass_2$ in your data table.

11. Measure the final positions of both masses, and record the distances (final position – initial position) in your data table. Δh is the *vertical* dis-

tance through which the mass on the pulley is raised, while the mass on the mass hanger moves down through the distance Δd.

12. Using the same 500 g $mass_1$, perform two more trials using different pulley systems (four pulleys, six pulleys, and so on). Record all data. Be sure to include the mass of the bottom set of pulleys in the total mass that is raised in each trial.

ANALYSIS AND INTERPRETATION

Calculations and data analysis

1. **Organizing data** For each trial, make the following calculations:

    a. the weight of the mass being raised

    b. the weight of the mass on the string

    c. the work input and the work output

2. **Analyzing results** In which trial did a machine perform the most work? In which trial did a machine perform the least work?

3. **Analyzing data** Calculate the efficiency for each trial.

4. **Evaluating data** Is the machine that performed the most work also the most efficient? Is the machine that performed the least work also the least efficient? What is the relationship between work and efficiency?

5. **Analyzing results** Based on your calculations in item 4, which is more efficient, a pulley system or an inclined plane?

Conclusions

6. **Evaluating methods** Why is it important to calculate the work input and the work output from measurements made when the object is moving with constant velocity?

Extensions

7. **Designing experiments** The lever is another type of simple machine. Design an experiment to measure the efficiency of different lever setups. If there is time and your teacher approves, test your lever setups in the lab. How does the efficiency of a lever compare with the efficiency of the other types of machines you have studied?

8. **Building models** Compare the trial with the highest efficiency to the trial with the lowest efficiency. Based on the differences between them, design a machine that will be more efficient than the most efficient one you built in the lab. If there is time and your teacher approves, test the machine to find out if it is more efficient.

Figure 8-29

Step 8: Clamp a meterstick parallel to the stand to take measurements throughout the lab.

Step 9: Use another ruler as a straight edge to help you measure the positions.

Step 10: The pulleys should not begin moving when the mass is added, but they should move with a constant velocity after a gentle push.

Step 11: Measure and record the distance moved by the mass on the pulley as Δh and the mass hanger distance as Δd.

CHAPTER 9

Fluid Mechanics

PHYSICS IN ACTION

The vampire squid is thought to live as deep as 5000 m beneath the water's surface. Although vampire squids have been caught in commercial fishing nets, only one has been seen in its natural habitat. Exploration of the deep-sea environment is difficult because of the enormous pressure that exists at such depths. Vampire squids were once thought to be evil because they have such an odd appearance and because they turn black when brought to the surface.

The body of the squid is well adapted to its deep-sea environment. For instance, a squid moves by jet propulsion, using a small tube near its head to eject a stream of water. The squid uses its fins to help steer it through the water.

- *Why is pressure so great at large depths?*
- *How can a squid float underwater?*

CONCEPT REVIEW

Force (Section 4-1)

Energy (Section 5-2)

Conservation laws (Section 5-3)

9-1
Fluids and buoyant force

9-1 SECTION OBJECTIVES

- **Define a fluid.**
- **Distinguish a liquid from a gas.**
- **Determine the magnitude of the buoyant force exerted on a floating object or a submerged object.**
- **Explain why some objects float and some objects sink.**

fluid

a nonsolid state of matter in which the atoms or molecules are free to move past each other, as in gas or liquid

DEFINING A FLUID

Matter is normally classified as being in one of three states—solid, liquid, or gaseous. This book's discussion of motion and its causes has dealt primarily with the behavior of solid objects. This chapter concerns the mechanics of liquids and gases.

Figure 9-1(a) is a photo of a liquid; **Figure 9-1(b)** shows an example of a gas. Pause a moment and see if you can identify a common trait between them. One property they have in common is the ability to flow and to alter their shape in the process. Materials that exhibit these properties are called **fluids.** Solid objects are not considered to be fluids because they have a definite shape and therefore cannot flow.

Liquids have a definite volume; gases do not

Even though both gases and liquids are fluids, there is a difference between them: one has a definite volume, and the other does not. Liquids, like solids, have a definite volume, but unlike solids, they do not have a definite shape. Imagine filling the tank of a lawn mower. The gasoline, a liquid, changes its shape from that of its original container to that of the tank. If there is a gallon of gasoline in the container before you pour, there will be a gallon in the tank after you pour. Gases, on the other hand, have neither definite volume nor definite shape. When a gas is poured from one container into another, the gas not only changes its shape to fit the new container but also spreads out to fill the container.

Figure 9-1

Both **(a)** liquids and **(b)** gases are fluids because they can flow and change shape.

(a)

(b)

DENSITY AND BUOYANT FORCE

Have you ever felt confined in a crowded elevator? You probably felt that way because there were too many people in the elevator for the amount of space available. In other words, the *density* of people was too high. In general, density is a measure of how much there is of a quantity in a given amount of space. The quantity can be anything from people or trees to mass or energy.

Mass density is mass per unit volume of a substance

When the word *density* is used to describe a fluid, what is really being measured is the fluid's **mass density.** Mass density is the mass per unit volume of a substance. It is often represented by the Greek letter *rho* (ρ).

MASS DENSITY

$$\rho = \frac{m}{V}$$

$$\text{mass density} = \frac{\text{mass}}{\text{volume}}$$

The SI unit of mass density is kilograms per cubic meter (kg/m^3). In this book we will follow the convention of using the word *density* to refer to *mass density*. **Table 9-1** lists the densities of some fluids and a few important solids.

Solids and liquids tend to be almost incompressible, meaning that their density changes very little with changes in pressure. Thus, the densities listed in **Table 9-1** for solids and liquids are approximately independent of pressure. Gases, on the other hand, are not incompressible and can have densities over a wide range of values. Thus, there is not a standard density for a gas, as there is for solids and liquids. The densities listed for gases in **Table 9-1** are the values of the density at a stated temperature and pressure. For deviations of temperature and pressure from these values, the density will vary significantly.

Buoyant forces can keep objects afloat

Have you ever wondered why a brick feels heavier in air than it does in water? The reason is that a fluid exerts an upward force on objects that are partially or completely submerged in it. This upward force is called a **buoyant force.** If you have ever rested on an air mattress in a swimming pool, you have experienced a buoyant force. The buoyant force kept you and the mattress afloat.

Because the buoyant force acts in a direction opposite the force of gravity, objects submerged in a fluid such as water have a net force on them that is smaller than their weight. This means that they appear to weigh less in water than they do in air. The weight of an object immersed in a fluid is the object's *apparent weight*. In the case of the brick, its apparent weight is less in water than in air, but it still sinks in water because the buoyant force is not enough to keep it afloat.

mass density

mass per unit volume of a substance

**Table 9-1
Density of some
common substances***

Substance	ρ (kg/m^3)
Hydrogen	0.0899
Helium	0.179
Steam (100°C)	0.598
Air	1.29
Oxygen	1.43
Carbon dioxide	1.98
Ethanol	0.806×10^3
Ice	0.917×10^3
Fresh water (4°C)	1.00×10^3
Sea water (15°C)	1.025×10^3
Iron	7.86×10^3
Mercury	13.6×10^3
Gold	19.3×10^3

*All densities are measured at 0°C and 1 atm unless otherwise noted.

buoyant force

a force that acts upward on an object submerged in a liquid or floating on the liquid's surface

Figure 9-2

(a) (b) (c) (d)

Archimedes' principle determines the amount of buoyancy

Imagine that you submerge a brick in a container of water, as shown in **Figure 9-2.** A spout on the side of the container at the water's surface allows water to flow out of the container. As the brick sinks, the water level rises and water flows through the spout into a smaller container. The total volume of water that collects in the smaller container is the *displaced volume* of water. The displaced volume of water is equal to the volume of the portion of the brick that is underwater. Knowledge of the concept of displaced volume is essential to understanding buoyant forces.

The magnitude of the buoyant force acting on the brick at any given time can be calculated by using a rule known as *Archimedes' principle.* This principle can be stated as follows: *Any object completely or partially submerged in a fluid experiences an upward buoyant force equal in magnitude to the weight of the fluid displaced by the object.* Everyone has experienced Archimedes' principle. For example, recall that it is relatively easy to lift someone if you are both standing in a swimming pool even if lifting that same individual on dry land would be a difficult task. Using m_f to represent the mass of the displaced fluid, Archimedes' principle can be written symbolically as follows:

BUOYANT FORCE

$$F_B = F_g \,(displaced\ fluid) = m_f g$$

magnitude of buoyant force = weight of fluid displaced

Whether an object will float or sink depends on the net force acting on it. This net force is the object's apparent weight and can be calculated as follows:

$$F_{net} = F_B - F_g \,(object)$$

Now we can apply Archimedes' principle, using m_o to represent the mass of the submerged object.

$$F_{net} = m_f g - m_o g$$

Remembering that $m = \rho V$, the expression can be rewritten as follows:

$$F_{net} = (\rho_f V_f - \rho_o V_o)g$$

Remember that in this expression, the fluid quantities refer to the *displaced* fluid.

A floating object cannot be denser than the fluid in which it floats

Archimedes' principle provides additional information about floating objects. The expression for the net force on an object floating on the surface, which makes use of Archimedes' principle, gives the following result:

$$F_{net} = 0 = (\rho_f V_f - \rho_o V_o)g$$

$$\frac{\rho_f}{\rho_o} = \frac{V_o}{V_f}$$

We know that the displaced volume of fluid can never be greater than the volume of the object. This means that for an object to float, the object's density can never be greater than the density of the fluid in which it floats. If the densities are equal, the entire object is submerged.

Devices that alter the buoyancy of an object do so by changing the object's average density. Such devices include life jackets, the ballast tanks of submarines, and the hollow hulls of ships. A fish can adjust its average density by inflating or deflating an organ called a *swim bladder*. A swim bladder functions in much the same way that ballast tanks function in a submarine—each controls buoyancy. In submarines, compressed air is pumped into the ballast tanks (and water is pumped out) to make the submarine rise to the surface. A fish fills its swim bladder with gas by either gulping air at the surface or by secreting gas from its gas gland into the swim bladder.

The human brain is immersed in a fluid of density 1007 kg/m³, which is slightly less than the average density of the brain, 1040 kg/m³. Consequently, most of the weight of the brain is supported by the buoyant force of the surrounding fluid. During clinical procedures in which a portion of this fluid is removed, the nerves and blood vessels in the brain experience great strain and care must be exercised until the volume of brain fluid is restored by the body.

For floating objects, the buoyant force equals the object's weight

Imagine a raft with cargo floating on a lake. There are two forces acting on the raft and its cargo: the downward force of gravity and the upward buoyant force of the water. Because the raft is floating on the water, the raft is in equilibrium and the two forces are balanced, as shown in **Figure 9-3.** This means that *for floating objects, the buoyant force is equal to the weight of the object.* This can be expressed as follows:

BUOYANT FORCE ON FLOATING OBJECTS

$$F_B = F_g(object) = m_o g$$

buoyant force = weight of floating object

Notice that for a floating object the buoyant force can be found by using only the first condition for equilibrium. Archimedes' principle is not needed.

Figure 9-3
The raft and cargo are floating because their weight and the buoyant force are balanced.

Figure 9-4
The raft and cargo sink because their density is greater than the density of water.

The apparent weight of a submerged object depends on density

Imagine that a hole is accidentally punched in the raft shown in **Figure 9-3** and that the raft begins to sink. The cargo and raft eventually sink below the water's surface, as shown in **Figure 9-4.** The net force on the raft and cargo is the difference between the buoyant force and the weight of the raft and cargo. As the volume of the raft decreases, the volume of water displaced by the raft and cargo also decreases, as does the magnitude of the buoyant force. This can be written by using the expression for the net force:

$$F_{net} = (\rho_f V_f - \rho_o V_o)g$$

Because the raft and cargo are completely submerged, the two volumes are equal:

$$F_{net} = (\rho_f - \rho_o)Vg$$

Notice that both the direction and the magnitude of the net force depend on the difference between the density of the object and the density of the fluid in which it is immersed. If the object's density is greater than the fluid density, the net force is negative (downward) and the object sinks. If the object's density is less than the fluid density, the net force is positive (upward) and the object rises to the surface and floats. If the densities are the same, the object floats underwater.

A simple relationship between the weight of a submerged object and the buoyant force on the object can be found by considering their ratio as follows:

$$\frac{F_g(object)}{F_B} = \frac{\rho_o \cancel{Vg}}{\rho_f \cancel{Vg}}$$

$$\frac{F_g(object)}{F_B} = \frac{\rho_o}{\rho_f}$$

This expression is often useful in solving buoyancy problems.

Conceptual Challenge

1. Neutral buoyancy Astronauts sometimes train underwater to simulate conditions in space. Explain why this is so.

2. More gravity A student claims that if the strength of Earth's gravity doubled, people would be unable to float on water. Do you agree or disagree with this statement? Why?

3. Ballooning Explain why balloonists use helium instead of pure oxygen in balloons.

Buoyant force

PROBLEM

A bargain hunter purchases a "gold" crown, like the one shown in Figure 9-5, at a flea market. After she gets home, she hangs the crown from a scale and finds its weight to be 7.84 N. She then weighs the crown while it is immersed in water, and the scale reads 6.86 N. Is the crown made of pure gold? Explain.

Figure 9-5

SOLUTION

1. DEFINE **Given:** $F_g = 7.84$ N   apparent $F_g = 6.86$ N $\rho_{water} = 1.00 \times 10^3$ kg/m^3

Unknown: $\rho_o = ?$

Diagram:

In air   In water

2. PLAN **Choose an equation(s) or situation:** Because the object is completely submerged, consider the ratio of the weight to the buoyant force.

$$F_g - F_B = \text{apparent } F_g$$

$$\frac{F_g}{F_B} = \frac{\rho_o}{\rho_f}$$

Rearrange the equation(s) to isolate the unknown(s):

$$F_B = F_g - (\text{apparent } F_g)$$

$$\rho_o = \frac{F_g}{F_B}\rho_f$$

3. CALCULATE **Substitute the values into the equation(s) and solve:**

$$F_B = 7.84 \text{ N} - 6.86 \text{ N} = 0.98 \text{ N}$$

$$\rho_o = \frac{F_g}{F_B}\rho_f = \frac{7.84 \text{ N}}{0.98 \text{ N}}(1.00 \times 10^3 \text{ kg/m}^3)$$

$$\boxed{\rho_o = 8.0 \times 10^3 \text{ kg/m}^3}$$

4. EVALUATE From **Table 9-1**, we know the density of gold is 19.3×10^3 kg/m^3. Because 8.0×10^3 kg/m$^3 < 19.3 \times 10^3$ kg/m^3, the crown is either hollow or not pure gold.

Buoyant force

1. A piece of metal weighs 50.0 N in air, 36.0 N in water, and 41.0 N in oil. Find the densities of the following:
   a. the metal
   b. the oil

2. An empty rubber balloon has a mass of 0.0120 kg. The balloon is filled with helium at 0°C, 1 atm pressure, and a density of 0.181 kg/m³. The filled balloon has a radius of 0.500 m.
   a. What is the buoyant force acting on the balloon? (Hint: See **Table 9-1** for the density of air.)
   b. What is the net force acting on the balloon?

3. A 2.3 kg rectangular air mattress is 2.0 m long, 0.50 m wide, and 0.10 m thick. What mass can it support in water before sinking?

4. A ferry boat is 4.0 m wide and 6.0 m long. When a truck pulls onto it, the boat sinks 4.00 cm in the water. What is the weight of the truck?

Section Review

1. What is the difference between a solid and a fluid? What is the difference between a gas and a liquid?

2. Which of the following objects will float in a tub of mercury?
   a. a solid gold bead
   b. an ice cube
   c. an iron bolt
   d. 5 mL of water

3. A 650 kg weather balloon is designed to lift a 4600 kg package. What volume should the balloon have after being inflated with helium at 0°C and 1 atm pressure to lift the total load? (Hint: Use the density values in **Table 9-1.**)

4. **Physics in Action**   A squid alters its buoyancy so that it begins to slowly sink toward the bottom. Is the density of the squid greater than or less than the density of the sea water that it swims in?

5. **Physics in Action**   A submerged squid alters its buoyancy so that it initially accelerates upward at 0.050 m/s². What is the squid's average density at this time compared with the density of the sea water?

Fluid pressure and temperature

PRESSURE

Deep-sea explorers wear atmospheric diving suits like the one shown in **Figure 9-6** to resist the forces exerted by ocean fluids. You experience these forces on your ears when you dive to the bottom of a swimming pool, drive up a mountain, or ride in an airplane. These effects are due to fluids pressing against your eardrums.

Pressure is force per unit area

The fluids are exerting **pressure** on your eardrums. Pressure is a measure of how much force is applied over a given area. It can be written as follows:

PRESSURE

$$P = \frac{F}{A}$$

$$\text{pressure} = \frac{\text{force}}{\text{area}}$$

The SI unit of pressure is N/m², which is called a *pascal* (Pa). The pascal is a small unit of pressure. The pressure of the atmosphere at sea level is about 10^5 Pa. This amount of air pressure under normal conditions is the basis for another unit, the *atmosphere* (atm). When calculating pressure, 10^5 Pa is about the same as 1 atm. The total air pressure in a typical automobile tire is about 3×10^5 Pa, or 3 atm. **Table 9-2** lists some additional pressures.

Table 9-2   Some pressures

Location	P (Pa)
Center of the sun	2×10^{16}
Center of Earth	4×10^{11}
Bottom of the Pacific Ocean	6×10^{7}
Atmosphere at sea level	1.01×10^{5}
Atmosphere at 10 km above sea level	2.8×10^{4}
Best vacuum in a laboratory	1×10^{-12}

pressure

force per unit area

Figure 9-6
Atmospheric diving suits allow divers to withstand the pressure exerted by the fluid in the ocean at depths of up to 610 m.

A fluid exerts pressure

When you pump a bicycle tire, you apply a force on the piston that in turn exerts a force on the gas inside the tire. The gas responds by pushing against not only the piston but also the walls of the tire. In fact, the pressure exerted by the gas is the same throughout the volume of the gas.

Blood pressure is the pressure that blood exerts against the walls of the arteries. To measure a person's blood pressure, a cuff is wrapped around the patient's upper arm and a stethoscope is placed over the arteries of the forearm. Air is pumped into the cuff until the pressure exerted by the cuff stops the flow of blood. The doctor or nurse then listens to the person's pulse as air is let out slowly until the pressure of the cuff is less than the blood pressure when the heart contracts; this pressure is called the *systolic* pressure. More air is released until the pulsing of the heart is no longer audible; this pressure, called the diastolic pressure, is the blood pressure when the heart relaxes.

An important use of pressure is in the hydraulic press, shown in **Figure 9-7.** Compressed air exerts a force on a small piston, increasing the pressure in the fluid. The pressure is transmitted through the fluid to a larger piston on which an automobile rests. Because the pressure is the same on both pistons, $P = F_1/A_1 = F_2/A_2$. The magnitude of the force, F_1, needed to keep the car suspended is smaller than the weight of the car by a factor of A_1/A_2. Hydraulic brakes, hydraulic jacks, forklifts, and other machines also make use of this principle.

Figure 9-7

Because the pressure is the same on both sides of the enclosed fluid in a hydraulic press, a small force on the left piston produces a much larger force on the right piston.

Foot Pressure

MATERIALS LIST

✔ single sheet of graph paper
✔ pencil or pen

Stand on a sheet of graph paper and draw an outline of your foot. Then count the number of squares on the paper that were under your foot and multiply this number by the area of a single square in square meters. This gives you the area of your foot. Divide your weight in newtons by this number to calculate the pressure exerted by your foot on the floor when you stand on one leg. How does the pressure exerted by your foot compare with atmospheric pressure? Would the pressure that your foot exerts on the floor be larger or smaller if your foot were smaller? How would the pressure change if you weighed less?

Pressure

PROBLEM

A car weighing 1.20×10^4 N sits on a hydraulic press piston with an area of 0.90 m^2. Compressed air exerts a force on the second piston, which has an area of 0.20 m^2. How large must this force be to support the car?

SOLUTION

Given: $A_1 = 0.20$ m^2 $A_2 = 0.90$ m^2
$F_2 = 1.20 \times 10^4$ N

Unknown: $F_1 = ?$

Use the equation for pressure from page 325.

$$\frac{F_1}{A_1} = \frac{F_2}{A_2}$$

$$F_1 = \left(\frac{A_1}{A_2}\right)F_2 = \left(\frac{0.20 \text{ m}^2}{0.90 \text{ m}^2}\right)(1.20 \times 10^4 \text{ N})$$

$$\boxed{F_1 = 2.7 \times 10^3 \text{ N}}$$

Pressure

1. In a car lift, compressed air exerts a force on a piston with a radius of 5.00 cm. This pressure is transmitted to a second piston with a radius of 15.0 cm.
   a. What force must the compressed air exert to lift a 1.33×10^4 N car?
   b. What air pressure produces this force? Neglect the weight of the pistons.

2. A 1.5 m wide by 2.5 m long water bed weighs 1025 N. Find the pressure that the water bed exerts on the floor. Assume that the entire lower surface of the bed makes contact with the floor.

3. A person rides up a lift to a mountaintop, but the person's ears fail to "pop"—that is, the pressure of the inner ear does not equalize with the outside atmosphere. The radius of each eardrum is 0.40 cm. The pressure of the atmosphere drops from 1.010×10^5 Pa at the bottom of the lift to 0.998×10^5 Pa at the top.
   a. What is the pressure on the inner ear at the top of the mountain?
   b. What is the net force on each eardrum?

Pressure varies with depth in a fluid

As a submarine dives deeper in the water, the pressure of the water against the hull of the submarine increases, and the resistance of the hull must be strong enough to withstand large pressures. Water pressure increases with depth because the water at a given depth must support the weight of the water above it.

Imagine a small area on the hull of a submarine. The weight of the entire column of water above that area exerts a force on the area. The column of water has a volume equal to Ah, where A is the cross-sectional area of the column and h is its height. Hence the mass of this column of water is $m = \rho V = \rho Ah$. Using the definitions of density and pressure, the pressure at this depth due to the weight of the column of water can be calculated as follows:

$$P = \frac{F}{A} = \frac{mg}{A} = \frac{\rho V g}{A} = \frac{\rho Ahg}{A} = \rho hg$$

This pressure is referred to as *gauge pressure*. It is not the total pressure at this depth because the atmosphere itself also exerts a pressure at the surface. Thus, the gauge pressure is actually the total pressure minus the atmospheric pressure. By using the symbol P_o for the atmospheric pressure at the surface, we can express the total pressure, or *absolute pressure*, at a given depth in a fluid of density ρ as follows:

Figure 9-8
The fluid pressure at the bottom of the box is greater than the fluid pressure at the top of the box.

FLUID PRESSURE AS A FUNCTION OF DEPTH

$$P = P_o + \rho gh$$

absolute pressure =
atmospheric pressure + (density × free-fall acceleration × depth)

This expression for pressure in a fluid can be used to help understand why buoyant forces are present in a fluid. Consider the situation in **Figure 9-8.** A rectangular box is submerged in a container of water. We know that the water pressure pushing down on the top of the box is $-(P_o + \rho gh_1)$ and that the

Conceptual Challenge

1. Atmospheric pressure Why doesn't the roof of a building collapse under the tremendous pressure exerted by our atmosphere?

2. Force and work In a hydraulic press, which of the two pistons (large or small) moves through a longer distance while the hydraulic press is lifting an object? (Hint: Remember that for an ideal machine, the input work equals the output work.)

3. Snowshoes A woman wearing snowshoes stands safely in the snow. If she removes her snowshoes, she quickly begins to sink. Explain this in terms of force and pressure.

water pressure pushing up on the bottom of the box is $P_0 + \rho g h_2$. The net pressure on the box is the sum of these two pressures.

$$P_{net} = P_{bottom} + P_{top} = (P_0 + \rho g h_2) - (P_0 + \rho g h_1) = \rho g (h_2 - h_1) = \rho g L$$

From this result, we can find the net force due to the pressure on the box as follows:

$$F_{net} = P_{net} A = \rho g L A = \rho g V = m_f g$$

This is an expression of Archimedes' principle. Thus, buoyancy forces arise from the differences in fluid pressure between the top and the bottom of an immersed object.

Atmospheric pressure is pressure from above

The weight of the air in the upper portion of Earth's atmosphere exerts pressure on the layers of air below. This pressure is called *atmospheric pressure;* the force it exerts on our bodies (assuming a body area of 2 m^2) is extremely large, on the order of 200 000 N (40 000 lb). How can we exist under such tremendous forces attempting to collapse our bodies? The answer is that our body cavities and tissues are permeated with fluids and gases that are pushing outward with a pressure equal to that of the atmosphere. Consequently, our bodies are in equilibrium—the force of the atmosphere pushing in equals the internal force pushing out.

An instrument that is commonly used to measure atmospheric pressure is the *mercury barometer,* shown in **Figure 9-9.** A long tube that is open at one end and closed at the other is filled with mercury and then inverted into a dish of mercury. Once inverted, the mercury does not empty into the bowl; rather, the atmosphere exerts a pressure on the mercury in the bowl and pushes the mercury in the tube to some height above the bowl. In this way, the force exerted on the bowl of mercury by the atmosphere is equal to the weight of the column of mercury in the tube. Any change in the height of the column of mercury means that the atmosphere's pressure has changed.

Kinetic theory of gases can describe the origin of gas pressure

Many models of a gas have been developed over the years. Almost all of these models attempt to explain the macroscopic properties of a gas, such as pressure, in terms of events occurring in the gas on a microscopic scale. One of these models is called the *kinetic theory of gases.*

In kinetic theory, gas particles are likened to a collection of billiard balls that constantly collide with one another. This simple model is successful in explaining many of the macroscopic properties of a gas. For instance, as these particles strike a wall of a container, they transfer some of their momentum during the collision. The rate of transfer of momentum to the container wall is equal to the force exerted by the gas on the container wall (see Chapter 6). This force per unit area is the gas pressure.

Mercury

Figure 9-9
The height of the mercury in the tube of a barometer indicates the atmospheric pressure.

Pressure as a function of depth

PROBLEM

Calculate the absolute pressure at an ocean depth of 1.00×10^3 m. Assume that the density of the water is 1.025×10^3 kg/m³ and that $P_0 = 1.01 \times 10^5$ Pa.

SOLUTION

Given: $\quad h = 1.00 \times 10^3$ m $\quad P_0 = 1.01 \times 10^5$ Pa $\quad \rho = 1.025 \times 10^3$ kg/m³
$\quad g = 9.81$ m/s²

Unknown: $\quad P = ?$

Use the equation for fluid pressure as a function of depth from page 328.

$$P = P_o + \rho g h$$

$$P = 1.01 \times 10^5 \text{ Pa} + (1.025 \times 10^3 \text{ kg/m}^3)(9.81 \text{ m/s}^2)$$
$$(1.00 \times 10^3 \text{ m})$$

$$P = 1.01 \times 10^5 \text{ Pa} + 1.01 \times 10^7 \text{ Pa}$$

$$\boxed{P = 1.02 \times 10^7 \text{ Pa}}$$

Pressure as a function of depth

1. The Mariana Trench, in the Pacific Ocean, is about 11.0 km deep. If atmospheric pressure at sea level is 1.01×10^5 Pa, how much pressure would a submarine need to be able to withstand to reach this depth? (Hint: Use the value for the density of sea water given in **Table 9-1.**)

2. Two fish swim in a freshwater lake, one at a depth of 14.0 m and the other at a depth of 98.0 m. Assuming that the atmospheric pressure at the lake's surface is 1.01×10^5 Pa, what is the difference in pressure on the two fish? (Hint: Use the value for the density of water from **Table 9-1.**)

3. A beaker filled with mercury to a height of 0.20 m is placed inside a vacuum chamber in a laboratory. What is the pressure at the bottom of the beaker? (Hint: See **Table 9-1** for the density of mercury. Think carefully about what value to use for atmospheric pressure.)

4. A container is filled with water to a depth of 20.0 cm. On top of the water floats a 30.0 cm thick layer of oil with a density of 0.70×10^3 kg/m³.
   a. What is the pressure at the surface of the water?
   b. What is the absolute pressure at the bottom of the container?

TEMPERATURE

Density and pressure are not the only two quantities useful in describing a fluid. The **temperature** of a fluid is also important. We often associate the concept of temperature with how hot or cold an object feels when we touch it. Thus, our senses provide us with qualitative indications of temperature. But to understand what the temperature of a fluid really measures, we must turn again to the kinetic theory of gases.

Like pressure, temperature in a gas can be understood on the basis of what is happening on the atomic scale. Kinetic theory predicts that temperature is related to the average kinetic energy of the particles in the gas. The higher the temperature of the gas, the faster the particles move. As the speed of the particles increases, there are more collisions of the particles against the walls of their container. More momentum is transferred to the container walls in a given time interval, resulting in an increase in pressure. Thus, kinetic theory predicts that the pressure and temperature of a gas are related. As we will see later in this chapter, this is indeed the case.

The SI units for temperature are kelvins and degrees Celsius (written K and °C). To quickly convert from the Celsius scale to the Kelvin scale, add 273. Room temperature is about 293 K (20°C).

temperature

a measure of the average kinetic energy of the particles in a substance

CONCEPT PREVIEW

Temperature and temperature scales will be discussed further in Chapter 10.

Section Review

1. Which of the following exerts the most pressure while resting on a floor?
   a. a 25 N box with 1.5 m sides
   b. a 15 N cylinder with a base radius of 1.0 m
   c. a 25 N box with 2.0 m sides
   d. a 25 N cylinder with a base radius of 1.0 m

2. Water is to be pumped to the top of the Empire State Building, which is 366 m high. What gauge pressure is needed in the water line at the base of the building to raise the water to this height? (Hint: See **Table 9-1** for the density of water.)

3. A room on the first floor of a hospital has a temperature of 20°C. A room on the top floor has a temperature of 22°C. In which of these two rooms is the average kinetic energy of the air particles greater?

4. The temperature of the air outside on a cool morning is 11°C. What is this temperature on the Kelvin scale?

5. **Physics in Action** When a vampire squid dives to a depth of 5.0×10^3 m, how much pressure, in Pa, must its body be able to withstand? How many times larger is this pressure compared with the pressure at the surface? (Hint: See **Table 9-1** for the density of sea water.)

9-3
Fluids in motion

9-3 SECTION OBJECTIVES

- Examine the motion of a fluid using the continuity equation.

- Apply Bernoulli's equation to solve fluid-flow problems.

- Recognize the effects of Bernoulli's principle on fluid motion.

FLUID FLOW

Have you ever gone canoeing or rafting down a river? If so, you may have noticed that part of the river flowed smoothly, allowing you to float calmly or to simply paddle along. At other places in the river, there may have been rocks or dramatic bends that created foamy whitewater rapids.

When a fluid, such as river water, is in motion, the flow can be characterized in one of two ways. The flow is said to be *laminar* if every particle that passes a particular point moves along the same smooth path traveled by the particles that passed that point earlier. This path is called a *streamline.* Different streamlines cannot cross each other, and the streamline at any point coincides with the direction of fluid velocity at that point. The smooth stretches of a river are regions of laminar flow. Another example is the continuous, small stream of water from a barely open faucet.

In contrast, the flow of a fluid becomes irregular, or *turbulent,* above a certain velocity or under conditions that can cause abrupt changes in velocity, such as where there are obstacles or sharp turns in a river. Irregular motions of the fluid, called *eddy currents,* are characteristic of turbulent flow. Examples of turbulent flow are found in water in the wake of a ship or in the air currents of a severe thunderstorm.

The difference between laminar flow and turbulent flow can be seen in **Figure 9-10.** This is a photograph of water flowing past a cylinder. Hydrogen bubbles were added to the water to make the streamlines and the eddy currents visible. Notice the dramatic difference in flow patterns between the laminar flow and the turbulent flow. Laminar flow is much easier to model because it is predictable. Turbulent flow is extremely chaotic and unpredictable.

Figure 9-10
The water flowing around this cylinder exhibits laminar flow and turbulent flow.

Ideal fluid model simplifies fluid-flow analysis

Many features of fluid motion can be understood by considering the behavior of an **ideal fluid.** Although the ideal fluid model does not perfectly match any real fluids, it does explain many properties of real fluids.

While discussing density and buoyancy, we assumed all of the fluids used in problems were almost incompressible. Incompressibility is one of the defining characteristics of an ideal fluid. Saying that a fluid is incompressible is equivalent to saying that the density of the fluid remains constant.

ideal fluid

a fluid that has no internal friction or viscosity and is incompressible

Ideal fluids are also nonviscous. The term *viscosity* refers to the amount of internal friction within a fluid. Internal friction can occur when one layer of fluid slides against another layer. This sliding motion is hindered by kinetic friction between the two fluid layers. As a fluid flows, part of the kinetic energy of the fluid is converted into thermal energy because of internal friction. A fluid with a high viscosity will flow more slowly through a pipe than a fluid with a low viscosity.

We will also consider ideal *flow* of an ideal fluid. Ideal fluids are also characterized by a steady flow. In other words, the velocity, density, and pressure at each point in the fluid do not change in time.

The final characteristic of an ideal fluid is nonturbulent flow. This implies that each element of the fluid has zero angular speed about its center; that is, there can be no eddy currents present in the moving fluid.

The rest of our discussion of fluid flow will assume that we are dealing with ideal fluids.

CONSERVATION LAWS IN FLUIDS

Imagine that a liquid flows into one end of a pipe and flows out the other end, as shown in **Figure 9-11.** The mass that flows into the bottom of the pipe must equal the mass that flows out of the top of the pipe in the same time interval. This is a statement of conservation of mass and can be written as follows:

$$m_1 = m_2$$

This expression can be used to predict changes in the speed of flow. First, it can be rewritten by recalling that $m = \rho V$ and by using the formula for the volume of a cylinder ($V = A\Delta x$).

$$\rho_1 V_1 = \rho_2 V_2$$
$$\rho_1 A_1 \Delta x_1 = \rho_2 A_2 \Delta x_2$$

In steady flow, the distance is the speed multiplied by the time interval.

$$\rho_1 A_1 v_1 \Delta t = \rho_2 A_2 v_2 \Delta t$$

Both the time interval and the density are the same on each side of the equation in an incompressible fluid, so they can be canceled from the equation.

$$A_1 v_1 = A_2 v_2$$

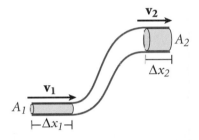

Figure 9-11
The mass flowing into the pipe must equal the mass flowing out of the pipe in the same time interval.

The continuity equation results from mass conservation

In fluid mechanics, this equation is referred to as the *continuity equation*. A_1 and A_2 represent the two different cross-sectional areas of the pipe, and v_1 and v_2 are the fluid speeds at those areas. Note that the equation is based on the principle of conservation of mass. It implies that the fluid speed is large where the tube is narrow and small where the tube is wide. The product Av, which has the dimension of volume per unit time, is called the *flow rate.*

Continuous-flow heart pump

Ordinarily, a patient with no pulse is in deep trouble. But that may not always be the case in the future. Dr. Leonard Golding, at the Cleveland Clinic Foundation in Cleveland, Ohio, has designed a new heart-replacement pump that sends blood through the body at a constant flow, keeping the patient alive while eliminating the person's pulse.

When a person's heart fails, it is commonly repaired with an artificial pump. Until now, pumps have been designed to imitate the rhythmic thumping of the heart, on the assumption that a pulse is necessary to maintain life. To imitate a pulse, heart pumps include many complex, moving parts: two constantly opening and closing valves, a moving diaphragm, and complicated electronics. All of these components make the pump very expensive and too large to be implanted into children or other people with a small chest cavity.

Dr. Golding's continuous-flow pump, on the other hand, is extremely simple and has only one moving part: a rotor that spins at 3000 rev/min. The pump attaches to the heart and the circulatory system, and the rotor forces blood through the arteries. The speed at which the rotor pumps blood can be adjusted electronically for each patient.

Dr. Golding's pump is also much smaller, 4.3 cm (1.75 in.) long and 3.8 cm (1.5 in.) in diameter. Because it has no complex electronics, the continuous-flow pump is also significantly less expensive than current technology.

Originally, the pump was designed to be a temporary fix for a patient awaiting a transplant, but now Dr. Golding is actively pursuing ways to make the device permanently

implantable. Golding must now show that the pump is able to function for long periods of time, providing enough blood flow at the correct pressure without causing damage to the blood itself. If tests determine that the pump can accomplish these things successfully, then some people may soon be living out their lives without a heartbeat.

Bernoulli's equation results from energy conservation

You have already learned that there is no internal friction in nonviscous fluid flow. Thus, it is not surprising that if a fluid is nonviscous, the energy in a small volume of the fluid does not change as the volume moves along a given streamline. In fluid mechanics, this law is referred to as *Bernoulli's equation*. It is important to realize, however, that this equation is really just an expression of the conservation of energy.

The expression for the conservation of energy in fluids differs slightly from the familiar form given in Chapter 5. In fluids, the expression includes an additional term: pressure. This is because a small volume of fluid can change shape. If the gas changes shape, either the gas has done work on the environment or work has been done on the gas. Changes in the pressure of a small volume of fluid can be related to the transfer of energy into or out of the volume. This energy must be accounted for in the conservation of energy.

As a fluid moves through a pipe of varying cross section and elevation, the pressure and speed of the fluid along a given streamline in the pipe can change, but the total energy does not. Bernoulli's equation can be written as follows:

BERNOULLI'S EQUATION

$$P + \frac{1}{2}\rho v^2 + \rho gh = \text{constant}$$

pressure + kinetic energy per unit volume + gravitational potential energy per unit volume = constant along a given streamline

If you wish to compare the energy in a fluid between two points, Bernoulli's equation takes the following equivalent form:

$$P_1 + \frac{1}{2}\rho v_1^2 + \rho gh_1 = P_2 + \frac{1}{2}\rho v_2^2 + \rho gh_2$$

A few special cases of Bernoulli's equation are worth mentioning. First, if the fluid is not moving, then both speeds are zero. If the initial height is also zero, then Bernoulli's equation reduces to the equation for pressure as a function of depth, shown in Section 9-2.

$$P_1 = P_2 + \rho gh_2$$

Second, imagine a fluid flowing through a horizontal pipe with a constriction. According to the continuity equation, the product Av is constant along the pipe: $A_1v_1 = A_2v_2$. Thus, if A_1 is larger than A_2 at some point in the pipe, then v_1 is less than v_2. This means that *the flow speed in a constriction must be greater than the flow speed before or after it.* This effect can be seen in rivers and streams. When the stream narrows or gets more shallow, the water's speed increases.

Because the height of the fluid is constant, the gravitational potential energy does not change. Bernoulli's equation then reduces to the following:

$$P_1 + \frac{1}{2}\rho v_1^2 = P_2 + \frac{1}{2}\rho v_2^2$$

This expression implies that if v_1 is greater than v_2 at some point in the flow, then P_1 must be less than P_2. Thus, *swiftly moving fluids exert less pressure than do slowly moving fluids,* as shown in **Figure 9-12.** This concept is sometimes referred to as **Bernoulli's principle;** its effects can be disastrous in the case of hurricanes and tornadoes, when high-speed winds create areas of low pressure, sometimes tearing homes apart.

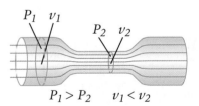

$$P_1 > P_2 \qquad v_1 < v_2$$

Figure 9-12
In the constriction, the pressure decreases and the fluid speed increases.

Bernoulli's principle

the pressure in a fluid decreases as its velocity increases

Bernoulli's equation

PROBLEM

A water tank has a spigot near its bottom. If the top of the tank is open to the atmosphere, determine the speed at which the water leaves the spigot when the water level is 0.500 m above the spigot.

SOLUTION

1. DEFINE **Given:** $h_2 - h_1 = 0.500$ m

Unknown: $v_1 = ?$

Diagram:

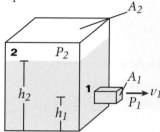

2. PLAN **Choose an equation(s) or situation:** Because this problem involves fluid flow and differences in height, it requires the application of Bernoulli's equation.

$$P_1 + \tfrac{1}{2}\rho v_1^2 + \rho g h_1 = P_2 + \tfrac{1}{2}\rho v_2^2 + \rho g h_2$$

Point 1 is at the hole, and point 2 is at the top of the tank. If we assume that the hole is small, then the water level drops very slowly and we can assume that v_2 is approximately zero. Also, note that $P_1 = P_0$ and $P_2 = P_0$ because both the top of the tank and the spigot are open to the atmosphere.

$$P_0 + \tfrac{1}{2}\rho v_1^2 + \rho g h_1 = P_0 + \rho g h_2$$

Rearrange the equation(s) to isolate the unknown(s):

$$\tfrac{1}{2}\rho v_1^2 = \rho g h_2 - \rho g h_1$$

$$v_1^2 = 2g(h_2 - h_1)$$

$$v_1 = \sqrt{2g(h_2 - h_1)}$$

3. CALCULATE **Substitute the values into the equation(s) and solve:**

$$v_1 = \sqrt{2(9.81 \text{ m/s}^2)(0.500 \text{ m})}$$

$$\boxed{v_1 = 3.13 \text{ m/s}}$$

4. EVALUATE A quick estimate gives the following:

$$v_1 \approx \sqrt{2(10)(0.5)} \approx 3$$

Bernoulli's equation

1. A large storage tank, open to the atmosphere at the top and filled with water, develops a small hole in its side at a point 16 m below the water level. If the rate of flow of water from the leak is 2.5×10^{-3} m³/min, determine the following:

   a. the speed at which the water leaves the hole
   b. the diameter of the hole

2. A liquid with a density of 1.65×10^3 kg/m³ flows through two horizontal sections of tubing joined end to end. In the first section, the cross-sectional area is 10.0 cm², the flow speed is 275 cm/s, and the pressure is 1.20×10^5 Pa. In the second section, the cross-sectional area is 2.50 cm². Calculate the following:

   a. the flow speed in the smaller section
   b. the pressure in the smaller section

3. When a person inhales, air moves down the windpipe at 15 cm/s. The average flow speed of the air doubles when passing through a constriction in the bronchus. Assuming incompressible flow, determine the pressure drop in the constriction.

Section Review

1. The time required to fill a bucket with water from a certain garden hose is 30.0 s. If you cover part of the hose's nozzle with your thumb so that the speed of the water leaving the nozzle doubles, how long does it take to fill the bucket?

2. Water at a pressure of 3.00×10^5 Pa flows through a horizontal pipe at a speed of 1.00 m/s. The pipe narrows to one-fourth its original diameter. Find the following:

   a. the flow speed in the narrow section
   b. the pressure in the narrow section

3. The water supply of a building is fed through a main entrance pipe that is 6.0 cm in diameter. A 2.0 cm diameter faucet tap positioned 2.0 m above the main pipe fills a 25 L container in 30.0 s.

   a. What is the speed at which the water leaves the faucet?
   b. What is the gauge pressure in the main pipe?

9-4
Properties of gases

- Define the general properties of an ideal gas.

- Use the ideal gas law to predict the properties of an ideal gas under different conditions.

GAS LAWS

When the density of a gas is sufficiently low, the pressure, volume, and temperature of the gas tend to be related to one another in a fairly simple way. In addition, the relationship is a good approximation for the behavior of many real gases over a wide range of temperatures and pressures. These observations have led scientists to develop the concept of an *ideal gas*.

Volume, pressure, and temperature are the three variables that completely describe the macroscopic state of an ideal gas. One of the most important equations in all of fluid mechanics is the relationship between these three quantities.

The ideal gas law relates gas volume, pressure, and temperature

The relationship that relates the volume, pressure, and temperature of a gas is the *ideal gas law*. This relationship can be written as follows:

IDEAL GAS LAW

$$PV = Nk_BT$$

**pressure × volume =
number of gas particles × Boltzmann's constant × temperature**

The symbol k_B represents a constant called *Boltzmann's constant*. Its value has been experimentally determined to be 1.38×10^{-23} J/K. Note that when applying the ideal gas law, you must express the temperature in the Kelvin scale (see Section 9-2). Also, the ideal gas law makes no mention of the composition of the gas. The gas particles could be oxygen, carbon dioxide, or any other gas. In this sense, the ideal gas law is universally applicable to all gases.

If a gas undergoes a change in volume, pressure, or temperature (or any combination of these), the ideal gas law can be expressed in a particularly useful form. If the number of particles in the gas is constant, the initial and final states of the gas are related as follows:

$$N_1 = N_2$$
$$\frac{P_1V_1}{T_1} = \frac{P_2V_2}{T_2}$$

This relation is illustrated in the experiment shown in **Figure 9-13.** In this experiment, a flask filled with air (V_1 equals the volume of the flask) at room temperature (T_1) and atmospheric pressure ($P_1 = P_0$) is placed over a heat

Figure 9-13
The balloon is inflated because the volume and pressure of the air inside are both increasing.

source, and a balloon is placed over the opening. As the flask sits over the burner, the temperature of the air inside it increases from T_1 to T_2. According to the ideal gas law, when the temperature increases, the pressure and volume must also increase. Thus, the air inside the flask exerts a pressure (P_2) on the balloon that serves to inflate the balloon. Because the flask is not completely closed, the air expands to a larger volume (V_2) to fill the balloon. When the flask is taken off the burner, the pressure, volume, and temperature of the air inside will slowly return to their initial states.

Another alternative form of the ideal gas law indicates the law's dependence on mass density. Assuming each particle in the gas has a mass m, the total mass of the gas is $N \times m = M$. The ideal gas law can then be written as follows:

$$PV = Nk_BT = \frac{Mk_BT}{m}$$

$$P = \frac{Mk_BT}{mV} = \left(\frac{M}{V}\right)\frac{k_BT}{m} = \frac{\rho k_BT}{m}$$

A real gas can often be modeled as an ideal gas

An ideal gas is defined as a gas whose behavior is accurately described by the ideal gas law. Although no real gas obeys the ideal gas law exactly for all temperatures and pressures, the ideal gas law holds for a broad range of physical conditions for all gases. The behavior of real gases departs from the behavior of an ideal gas at high pressures or low temperatures, conditions under which the gas nearly liquefies. However, when a real gas has a relatively high temperature and a relatively low pressure, such as at room temperature and atmospheric pressure, the behavior of most gases is very nearly that of an ideal gas.

For problems involving the motion of fluids, we have assumed that all gases and liquids are ideal fluids. Recall that an ideal fluid is a liquid or gas that is assumed to be incompressible. This is usually a good assumption because it is difficult to compress a fluid—even a gas—when it is not confined to a container. A fluid will tend to flow under the action of a force, changing its shape while maintaining a constant volume, rather than compress.

Ideal Gas Law

MATERIALS

✔ 1 plastic 1 L bottle
✔ 1 quarter

Make sure the bottle is empty, and remove the cap. Place the bottle in the freezer for at least 10 min. Wet the quarter with water, and place the quarter over the bottle's opening as you take the bottle out of the freezer. Set the bottle on a nearby tabletop; then observe the bottle and quarter while the air in the bottle warms up. As the air inside the bottle begins to return to room temperature, the quarter begins to jiggle around on top of the bottle. What does this movement tell you about the pressure and volume inside the bottle? What causes this increase in pressure and volume? Hypothesize as to why you need to wet the quarter before placing it on top of the bottle.

In this section, however, we are concerned with a gas that is confined to a container. This means that when a force is applied to the gas, the gas is unable to flow in response to the force and so it compresses. Thus, even though an ideal gas behaves like an ideal fluid in many situations, it can no longer be treated as incompressible in situations when it is confined to a container.

SAMPLE PROBLEM 9E

Gas laws

PROBLEM

Pure helium gas is contained in a leakproof cylinder containing a movable piston, as shown in Figure 9-14. The initial volume, pressure, and temperature of the gas are 15 L, 2.0 atm, and 310 K, respectively. If the volume is decreased to 12 L and the pressure is increased to 3.5 atm, find the final temperature of the gas.

Figure 9-14

SOLUTION

1. DEFINE   **Given:**

$V_1 = 15$ L	$P_1 = 2.0$ atm	$T_1 = 310$ K
$V_2 = 12$ L	$P_2 = 3.5$ atm	

Unknown: $T_2 = ?$

2. PLAN   **Choose an equation(s) or situation:** Because the gas undergoes a change and no gas particles are lost, the form of the ideal gas law relating the initial and final states should be used.

$$\frac{P_1V_1}{T_1} = \frac{P_2V_2}{T_2}$$

Rearrange the equation(s) to isolate the unknown(s):

$$T_2P_1V_1 = T_1P_2V_2$$

$$T_2 = T_1\left(\frac{P_2V_2}{P_1V_1}\right)$$

3. CALCULATE   **Substitute the values into the equation(s) and solve:**

$$T_2 = (310 \text{ K})\left[\frac{(3.5 \text{ atm})(12 \text{ L})}{(2.0 \text{ atm})(15 \text{ L})}\right]$$

$$\boxed{T_2 = 4.3 \times 10^2 \text{ K}}$$

> **CALCULATOR SOLUTION**
>
> Your calculator should give the answer as 434. However, because the values in the problem are known to only two significant figures, the answer should be rounded to 430.

4. EVALUATE   Because the gas was compressed and the pressure increased, the gas temperature should have increased.

$$430 \text{ K} > 310 \text{ K}$$

Gas laws

1. Gas is confined in a tank at a pressure of 1.0×10^8 Pa and a temperature of 15.0°C. If half the gas is withdrawn and the temperature is raised to 65.0°C, what is the new pressure in the tank in Pa?

2. A gas bubble with a volume of 0.10 cm^3 is formed at the bottom of a 10.0 cm deep container of mercury. If the temperature is 27°C at the bottom of the container and 37°C at the top, what is the volume of the bubble just beneath the surface of the mercury? Assume that the surface is at atmospheric pressure. (Hint: Use the density of mercury from **Table 9-1.**)

3. A cylinder with a movable piston contains gas at a temperature of 27°C, with a volume of 1.5 m^3 and a pressure of 0.20×10^5 Pa. What will be the final temperature of the gas if it is compressed to 0.70 m^3 and its pressure is increased to 0.80×10^5 Pa?

Section Review

1. Name some conditions under which a real gas is likely to behave like an ideal gas.

2. Two identical cylinders at the same temperature contain the same kind of gas. If cylinder A contains three times as many gas particles as cylinder B, what can you say about the relative pressures in the cylinders?

3. The pressure on an ideal gas is cut in half, resulting in a decrease in temperature to three-fourths the original value. Calculate the ratio of the final volume to the original volume of the gas.

4. A container of oxygen gas in a chemistry lab room is at a pressure of 6.0 atm and a temperature of 27°C.
    a. If the gas is heated at constant volume until the pressure triples, what is the final temperature?
    b. If the gas is heated so that both the pressure and volume are doubled, what is the final temperature?

5. **Physics in Action**   Some relatives of the squid use internal air chambers to maintain their buoyancy in water. Explain why these creatures cannot live at the great depths that a squid can.

CHAPTER 9
Summary

KEY IDEAS

Section 9-1 Fluids and buoyant force

- A fluid is a material that can flow, and thus it has no definite shape. Both gases and liquids are fluids.
- Buoyant force is an upward force exerted by a fluid on an object floating on or submerged in the fluid.
- The magnitude of a buoyant force for a submerged object is determined by Archimedes' principle and is equal to the weight of the displaced fluid.

Section 9-2 Fluid pressure and temperature

- Pressure is a measure of how much force is exerted over a given area.
- The pressure in a fluid increases with depth.

Section 9-3 Fluids in motion

- An ideal fluid is nonviscous, incompressible, steady, and nonturbulent.
- Moving fluids can exhibit laminar (smooth) flow or turbulent flow.
- According to the continuity equation, the amount of fluid leaving a pipe during some time interval equals the amount entering the pipe during that same time interval.
- According to Bernoulli's equation, swift-moving fluids exert less pressure than slower-moving fluids.

Section 9-4 Properties of gases

- An ideal gas obeys the ideal gas law. The ideal gas law is a relationship between the volume, pressure, and temperature of a gas.

Variable symbols

Quantities		Units		Conversions
ρ	density	kg/m^3	kilogram per meter^3	$= 10^{-3}\ g/cm^3$
P	pressure	Pa	pascal	$= N/m^2$
				$= 10^{-5}\ atm$
T	temperature	K	kelvin	
		°C	degrees Celsius	$= K - 273$
k_B	Boltzmann's constant	J/K	joules per kelvin	

CHAPTER 9
Review and Assess

DENSITY AND BUOYANCY

Conceptual questions

1. If an inflated beach ball is placed beneath the surface of a pool of water and released, it shoots upward, out of the water. Use Archimedes' principle to explain why.

2. Will an ice cube float higher in water or in mercury? (Hint: See **Table 9-1,** on page 319.)

3. An ice cube is submerged in a glass of water. What happens to the level of the water as the ice melts?

4. Will a ship ride higher in an inland freshwater lake or in the ocean? Why?

5. Steel is much denser than water. How, then, do steel boats float?

6. A small piece of steel is tied to a block of wood. When the wood is placed in a tub of water with the steel on top, half the block is submerged. If the block is inverted so that the steel is underwater, will the amount of the wooden block that is submerged increase, decrease, or remain the same?

7. A fish rests on the bottom of a bucket of water while the bucket is being weighed. When the fish begins to swim around, does the reading on the scale change?

Practice problems

8. A frog in a hemi-spherical bowl, as shown in **Figure 9-15,** just floats in a fluid with a density of 1.35 $\times\ 10^3$ kg/m^3. If the bowl has a radius of 6.00 cm and negligible mass, what is the mass of the frog?
(See Sample Problem 9A.)

Figure 9-15

9. An engineer weighs a sample of mercury ($\rho = 13.6 \times 10^3$ kg/m^3) and finds that the weight of the sample is 4.5 N. What is the sample's volume.

10. When a load of 1.0×10^6 N is placed on a battleship, the ship sinks only 2.5 cm in the water. Estimate the cross-sectional area of the ship at water level.
(See Sample Problem 9A. Hint: See **Table 9-1** for the density of sea water.)

11. A 1.0 kg beaker containing 2.0 kg of oil with a density of 916 kg/m^3 rests on a scale. A 2.0 kg block of iron is suspended from a spring scale and completely submerged in the oil, as shown in **Figure 9-16.** Find the equilibrium readings of both scales.
(See Sample Problem 9A. Hint: See **Table 9-1** for the density of iron.)

Figure 9-16

12. An object weighs 315 N in air. When tied to a string, connected to a balance, and immersed in water, it weighs 265 N. When it is immersed in oil, it weighs 275 N. Find the following:
   a. the density of the object
   b. the density of the oil
(See Sample Problem 9A.)

13. A sample of an unknown material weighs 300.0 N in air and 200.0 N when submerged in an alcohol solution with a density of 0.70×10^3 kg/m^3. What is the density of the material?
(See Sample Problem 9A.)

14. A raft is constructed of wood having a density of 600.0 kg/m^3. Its surface area is 5.7 m^2, and its volume is 0.60 m^3. When the raft is placed in fresh water having a density of 1.0×10^3 kg/m^3, how much of it is below water level?
(See Sample Problem 9A.)

PRESSURE

Conceptual questions

15. After a long class, a physics teacher stretches out for a nap on a bed of nails. How is this possible?

16. If you lay a steel needle horizontally on water, it will float. If you place the needle vertically into the water, it will sink. Explain why.

17. A typical silo on a farm has many bands wrapped around its perimeter, as shown in **Figure 9-17**. Why is the spacing between successive bands smaller toward the bottom?

Figure 9-17

18. Which dam must be stronger, one that holds back 1.0×10^5 m^3 of water 10 m deep or one that holds back 1000 m^3 of water 20 m deep?

19. In terms of the kinetic theory of gases, explain why gases do the following:
    a. expand when heated
    b. exert pressure

20. When drinking through a straw, you reduce the pressure in your mouth and the atmosphere moves the liquid. Could you use a straw to drink on the moon?

Practice problems

21. How much force does the atmosphere exert on 1.00 km^2 of land at sea level?
    (See Sample Problem 9C.)

22. The four tires of an automobile are inflated to an absolute pressure of 2.0×10^5 Pa. Each tire has an area of 0.024 m^2 in contact with the ground. Determine the weight of the automobile.
    (See Sample Problem 9B.)

23. A 70.0 kg man sits in a 5.0 kg chair so that his weight is evenly distributed on the legs of the chair. Assume that each leg makes contact with the floor over a circular area with a radius of 1.0 cm. What is the pressure exerted on the floor by each leg?
    (See Sample Problem 9B.)

24. A pipe contains water at 5.00×10^5 Pa above atmospheric pressure. If you patch a 4.00 mm diameter hole in the pipe with a piece of bubble gum, how much force must the gum be able to withstand?
    (See Sample Problem 9B.)

25. A submarine is at an ocean depth of 2.50 km.
    a. Calculate the absolute pressure at this depth. Assume that the density of water is 1.025×10^3 kg/m^3 and that atmospheric pressure is 1.01×10^5 Pa.
    (See Sample Problem 9C.)
    b. Calculate the total force exerted at this depth on a circular submarine window with a diameter of 30.0 cm.
    (See Sample Problem 9B.)

26. A piston, A, has a diameter of 0.64 cm, as in **Figure 9-18**. A second piston, B, has a diameter of 3.8 cm. In the absence of friction, determine the force, **F**, necessary to support the 500.0 N weight.
    (See Sample Problem 9B.)

Figure 9-18

27. A circular swimming pool at sea level has a flat bottom and a 6.00 m diameter. It is filled with water to a depth of 1.50 m.
    a. What is the absolute pressure at the bottom?
    (See Sample Problem 9C.)
    b. Two people with a combined mass of 150 kg float in the pool. What is the resulting increase in the absolute pressure at the bottom?
    (See Sample Problem 9B.)

CONTINUITY EQUATION AND BERNOULLI'S EQUATION

Conceptual questions

28. Municipal water supplies are often provided by reservoirs built on high ground. Why does water from such a reservoir flow more rapidly out of a faucet on the ground floor of a building than out of an identical faucet on a higher floor?

29. If air from a hair dryer is blown over the top of a table-tennis ball, the ball can be suspended in air. Explain how this is possible.

30. Prairie dogs live in underground burrows with at least two entrances. They ventilate their burrows by building a mound around one entrance, which is open to a stream of air. A second entrance at ground level is open to almost stagnant air. Use Bernoulli's principle to explain how this construction creates air flow through the burrow.

Practice problems

31. A dairy farmer notices that a circular water trough near the barn has become rusty and now has a hole near the base. The hole is 0.30 m below the level of the water that is in the tank. If the top of the trough is open to the atmosphere, what is the speed of the water as it leaves the hole?
(See Sample Problem 9D.)

32. The hypodermic syringe shown in **Figure 9-19** contains a medicine with the same density as water. The barrel of the syringe has a cross-sectional area of 2.50×10^{-5} m^2. The cross-sectional area of the needle is 1.00×10^{-8} m^2. In the absence of a force on the plunger, the pressure everywhere is 1.00 atm. A 2.00 N force is exerted on the plunger, making medicine squirt from the needle. Determine the speed of the emerging fluid. Assume that the pressure in the needle remains at 1.00 atm, that the syringe is horizontal, and that the speed of the emerging fluid is the same as the speed of the fluid in the needle.
(See Sample Problem 9D.)

Figure 9-19

33. The wind blows with a speed of 30.0 m/s over the roof of your house.

    a. Assuming the air inside the house is relatively stagnant, what is the pressure difference at the roof between the inside air and the outside air?

    b. What net force does this pressure difference produce on a roof having an area of 175 m^2?
(See Sample Problem 9D.)

34. A bag of blood with a density of 1050 kg/m^3 is raised about 1.00 m higher than the level of a patient's arm. How much greater is the blood pressure at this height than it would be if the bag were at the same level as the patient's arm?
(See Sample Problem 9D.)

GAS LAWS

Review questions

35. Why do underwater bubbles grow as they rise?

36. What happens to a helium-filled balloon released into the air? Does it expand or contract? Does it stop rising at some height?

Conceptual questions

37. What increase of pressure is required to change the temperature of a sample of nitrogen by 1.00 percent? Assume the volume of the sample remains constant.

38. A balloon filled with air is compressed to half its initial volume. If the temperature inside the balloon remains constant, what happens to the pressure of the air inside the balloon?

Practice problems

39. An ideal gas is contained in a vessel of fixed volume at a temperature of 300.0 K. The temperature is increased to 900.0 K. By what factor is the pressure in the vessel multiplied?
(See Sample Problem 9E.)

40. The pressure in a constant-volume gas thermometer is 0.700 atm at 100.0°C and 0.512 atm at 0.0°C.

    a. What is the temperature when the pressure is 0.0400 atm?

    b. What is the pressure at 450°C?
(See Sample Problem 9E.)

41. The density of helium gas at 0.0°C is 0.179 kg/m^3. The temperature is then raised to 100.0°C, but the pressure is kept constant. Assuming that helium is an ideal gas, calculate the new density of the gas.
(See Sample Problem 9E.)

42. A swimmer has 0.820 L of dry air in his lungs when he dives into a lake. Assuming the pressure of the dry air is 95 percent of the external pressure at all times, what is the volume of the dry air at a depth of 10.0 m? Assume that the atmospheric pressure at the surface is 1.013×10^5 Pa and that the density of the lake water is 1.00×10^3 kg/m³.
(See Sample Problem 9E.)

43. An air bubble has a volume of 1.50 cm³ when it is released by a submarine 100.0 m below the surface of the sea. What is the volume of the bubble when it reaches the surface? Assume that the temperature of the air in the bubble remains constant during ascent.
(See Sample Problem 9E.)

44. A weather balloon is designed to expand to a maximum radius of 20.0 m when the air pressure is 0.030 atm and the temperature of the air surrounding it is 200.0 K. If the balloon is filled at a pressure of 1.00 atm and 300.0 K, what is the radius of the balloon at the time of liftoff?
(See Sample Problem 9E.)

45. Before beginning a long trip on a hot day, a driver inflates an automobile tire to a gauge pressure of 1.8 atm at 293 K. At the end of the trip, the pressure in the tire has increased to 2.1 atm.

    a. Assuming the volume of the air inside the tire has remained constant, what is its temperature at the end of the trip?

    b. What volume of air (measured at atmospheric pressure) should be released from the tire so that the pressure returns to its initial value? Assume that the air is released during a short time interval during which the temperature remains at the value found in part **(a)**. Write your answer in terms of the initial volume, V_i.

(See Sample Problem 9E.)

46. A cylindrical diving bell 3.0 m in diameter and 4.0 m tall with an open bottom is submerged to a depth of 220 m in the ocean. The surface temperature of the water is 25°C, and the temperature 220 m down is 5.0°C. The density of sea water is 1025 kg/m³. How high does the sea water rise in the bell when the bell is submerged?
(See Sample Problem 9E.)

MIXED REVIEW PROBLEMS

47. A physics book has a height of 26 cm, a width of 21 cm, and a thickness of 3.5 cm.

    a. What is the density of the physics book if it weighs 19 N?

    b. Find the pressure that the physics book exerts on a desktop when the book lies face up.

    c. Find the pressure that the physics book exerts on the surface of a desktop when the book is resting on its spine.

48. A jet of water squirts horizontally from a hole near the bottom of the tank in **Figure 9-20**. If the hole has a diameter of 3.50 mm and the top of the tank is open, what is the height of the water in the tank?

Figure 9-20

49. A water tank open to the atmosphere at the top has two holes punched in its side, one above the other. The holes are 5.00 cm and 12.0 cm above the ground. What is the height of the water in the tank if the two streams of water hit the ground at the same place?

50. A hydraulic brake system is shown in **Figure 9-21**. The area of the piston in the master cylinder is 6.40 cm², and the area of the piston in the brake cylinder is 1.75 cm². The coefficient of friction between the brake shoe and the wheel drum is 0.50. Determine the frictional force between the brake shoe and the wheel drum when a force of 44 N is exerted on the pedal.

Figure 9-21

51. A natural-gas pipeline with a diameter of 0.250 m delivers 1.55 m³ of gas per second. What is the flow speed of the gas?

52. A 2.0 cm thick bar of soap is floating in water, with 1.5 cm of the bar underwater. Bath oil with a density of 600.0 kg/m^3 is added and floats on top of the water. What is the depth of the oil layer when the top of the soap is just level with the upper surface of the oil?

53. Oil having a density of 930 kg/m^3 floats on water. A rectangular block of wood 4.00 cm high and with a density of 960 kg/m^3 floats partly in the oil and partly in the water. The oil completely covers the block. How far below the interface between the two liquids is the bottom of the block?

54. A block of wood weighs 50.0 N in air. A sinker is attached to the block, and the weight of the wood-sinker combination is 200.0 N when the sinker alone is immersed in water. Finally, the wood-sinker combination is completely immersed and the weight is 140.0 N. Find the density of the block.

55. Water flows through a 0.30 m radius pipe at the rate of 0.20 m^3/s. The pressure in the pipe is atmospheric. The pipe slants downhill and feeds into a second pipe with a radius of 0.15 m, positioned 0.60 m lower. What is the gauge pressure in the lower pipe?

56. In a time interval of 1.0 s, 5.0×10^{23} nitrogen molecules strike a wall area of 8.0 cm^2. The mass of one nitrogen molecule is 4.68×10^{-26} kg. If the molecules move at 300.0 m/s and strike the wall head-on in an elastic collision, what is the pressure exerted on the wall?

57. **Figure 9-22** shows a water tank with a valve at the bottom. If this valve is opened, what is the maximum height attained by the water stream coming out of the right side of the tank? Assume that $h = 10.0$ m, $L = 2.0$ m, and $\theta = 30.0°$ and that the cross-sectional area at A is very large compared with that at B.

Figure 9-22

58. An air bubble originating from a deep-sea diver has a radius of 2.0 mm at the depth of the diver. When the bubble reaches the surface of the water, it has a

radius of 3.0 mm. Assuming that the temperature of the air in the bubble remains constant, determine the following:
   a. the depth of the diver
   b. the absolute pressure at this depth

59. A light spring with a spring constant of 90.0 N/m rests vertically on a table, as shown in **Figure 9-23(a)**. A 2.00 g balloon is filled with helium (0°C and 1 atm pressure) to a volume of 5.00 m^3 and connected to the spring, causing the spring to stretch and expand, as in **Figure 9-23(b)**. How much does the spring stretch when the balloon-and-spring system is in equilibrium?
(Hint: See **Table 9-1** for the density of helium. The force exerted by the spring equals $-k\Delta x$.)

(a)   (b)   **Figure 9-23**

60. An aorta has a cross-sectional area of 2.0 cm^2.
   a. Calculate the flow rate (in grams per second) of blood ($\rho = 1.0$ g/cm^3) in the aorta if the flow speed is 42 cm/s.
   b. Assume that the aorta branches to form a large number of capillaries with a combined cross-sectional area of 3.0×10^3 cm^2. What is the flow speed in the capillaries?

61. The approximate inside diameter of the aorta is 0.50 cm, and that of a capillary is 1.0×10^{-6} m. The average flow speed is about 1.0 m/s in the aorta and 1.0 cm/s in the capillaries. If all the blood in the aorta eventually flows through the capillaries, estimate the number of capillaries in the circulatory system.

62. A cowboy at a ranch fills a water trough that is 1.5 m long, 65 cm wide, and 45 cm deep. He uses a hose having a diameter of 2.0 cm, and the water emerges from the hose at 1.5 m/s. How long does it take the cowboy to fill the trough?

63. A light balloon is filled with helium at 0.0°C and 1.0 atm and then released from the ground. Determine its initial acceleration.
(Hint: See **Table 9-1** for information on the densities of helium and air.)

64. A 1.0 kg hollow ball with a radius of 0.10 m is filled with air and is released from rest at the bottom of a 2.0 m deep pool of water. How high above the water does the ball rise? Disregard friction and the ball's motion when it is only partially submerged.

65. A small sphere 0.60 times as dense as water is dropped from a height of 10.0 m above the surface of a smooth lake. Determine the maximum depth to which the sphere will sink. Disregard any energy transferred to the water during impact and sinking.

66. A sealed glass bottle at 27°C contains air at a pressure of 1.0 atm and has a volume of 30.0 cm^3. The bottle is tossed into an open fire. When the temperature of the air in the bottle reaches 225°C, what is the pressure inside the bottle? Assume the volume of the bottle is constant.

Technology & Learning

Press [Y=] and [CLEAR] to clear any functions. Open a new program by pressing [PRGM] [▶] [▶] [ENTER]. Name the program "FLOWRATE" and press [ENTER]. Then enter the program in the table shown below.

To exit the program editor, press [2nd] [QUIT]. To run the program, press [PRGM], select "FLOWRATE," and press [ENTER] [ENTER]. Enter the value for the speed of the water, and press [ENTER].

The calculator will provide a table of flow rates in cm^3/s (Y$_1$) versus hose diameters in cm (X). Cursor down the table to find the values you need. Press [ENTER] only when you are ready to end the program and exit the table. Run the program again to check flow rates for different speeds.

Graphing calculators

Program your graphing calculator to build a table of the flow rates in centimeters cubed per second for the following hose diameters and flow speeds:

a. a 4.5 cm diameter firehose with water traveling through it at 275 cm/s

b. a 2.5 cm diameter firehose with water traveling through it at 275 cm/s

c. a 3.5 cm diameter firehose with water traveling through it at 425 cm/s

d. a 5.5 cm diameter firehose with water traveling through it at 425 cm/s

Keystrokes

1. [PRGM] [▶] [2] [ALPHA] [V] [ENTER]

2. [ALPHA] ["] [2nd] [π] [×] [ALPHA] [V] [(] [X,T,θ] [÷] [2] [)] [x²] [ALPHA] ["] [STO▶] [2nd] [Y-VARS] [1] [1] [ENTER]

3. [0] [STO▶] [VARS] [6] [1] [ENTER]

4. [0] [.] [5] [STO▶] [VARS] [6] [2] [ENTER]

5. [PRGM] [▶] [5] [ENTER]

Display

PROGRAM: FLOWRATE

:PROMPT V

:"π*V(X/2)²" → Y1

:0 → TBLMIN

:0.5 → ΔTBL

:DISPTABLE

67. Superman leaps in front of Lois Lane to save her from a volley of bullets. In a 1.00 min interval, an automatic weapon fires 150 bullets, each with a mass of 8.0 g, at 400.0 m/s. The bullets strike Superman's chest, which has an area of 0.75 m². Find the pressure exerted on Superman's chest if the bullets bounce back after an elastic head-on collision.

68. A thin spherical shell with a mass of 4.00 kg and diameter of 0.200 m is filled with helium at 0°C and 1 atm pressure. It is then released from rest on the bottom of a pool of water that is 4.00 m deep.
   a. Determine the upward acceleration of the shell.
   b. How long will it take for the top of the shell to reach the surface? Disregard frictional effects.
   (Hint: See **Table 9-1** on page 319.)

69. A light spring with a spring constant of 16.0 N/m rests vertically on the bottom of a large beaker of water, as shown in **Figure 9-24(a)**. A 5.00×10^{-3} kg block of wood with a density of 650 kg/m³ is connected to the spring, and the mass-spring system is allowed to come to static equilibrium, as shown in **Figure 9-24(b)**. How much does the spring stretch?

(a) (b) **Figure 9-24**

Alternative Assessment

Performance assessment

1. Build a hydrometer from a long test tube with some sand at the bottom and a stopper. Adjust the amount of sand as needed so that the tube floats in most liquids. Calibrate it, and place a label with markings on the tube. Measure the densities of the following liquid foods: skim milk, whole milk, vegetable oil, pancake syrup, and molasses. Summarize your findings in a chart or table.

2. Explain how you can use differences in pressure to measure changes in altitude, assuming air density is constant. How accurate would your barometer need to be to provide an answer accurate to one meter for a 55 m tall building, a 255 m tall building, and a 2200 m tall mountain?

3. The owner of a fleet of tractor-trailers has contacted you after a series of accidents involving tractor-trailers passing each other on the highway. The owner wants to know how drivers can minimize the pull exerted as one tractor-trailer passes another going in the same direction. Should the passing tractor-trailer try to pass as quickly as possible or as slowly as possible? Design experiments to deter-

mine the answer by using model motor boats in a swimming pool. Indicate exactly what you will measure and how. If your teacher approves your plan and you are able to locate the necessary equipment, perform the experiment.

Portfolio projects

4. Record any examples of pumps in the tools, machines, and appliances you encounter in one week, and briefly describe the appearance and function of each pump. Research how one of these pumps works, contrasting it with a water pump in a car and an air pump used by bicyclists. Share your findings in a group meeting and create a presentation, model, or diagram that summarizes the group's findings.

5. You have been hired as a consultant to help the instructors of a diving school. They want you to develop materials that explain the physics involved in the following diving-safety rules: diving tanks must be kept immersed in cold water while they are being filled, and divers must exhale while ascending to the surface. Use the gas laws to explain what dangers (if any) these rules are designed to prevent.

CHAPTER 9
Laboratory Exercise

OBJECTIVES

• **Measure the volume and pressure of a gas at constant temperature.**

• **Explore the relationships between the volume and pressure of a gas.**

MATERIALS LIST

✔ **Check list for appropriate procedure.**

PROCEDURE

CBL AND SENSORS

✔ **CBL**

✔ **graphing calculator with link cable**

✔ **CBL pressure sensor with CBL-DIN adapter and syringe**

✔ **airline tubing (10 cm)**

BOYLE'S LAW APPARATUS

✔ **Boyle's law apparatus**

✔ **set of five 1 kg masses**

BOYLE'S LAW

The ideal gas law states the relationship between the temperature, pressure, and volume of an ideal gas. At room temperature and atmospheric pressure, air behaves like an ideal gas. In this lab, you will hold the temperature constant and explore the relationship between the volume and pressure of a gas at a constant temperature. Because the air will be contained in an airtight syringe, the quantity of gas will be constant throughout the experiment.

You will perform this experiment using either a CBL with pressure sensor or the Boyle's law apparatus.

• **CBL and sensors** You will use the pressure sensor to measure the pressure of the gas at different volumes, starting with an initial volume of 10 cm^3 and decreasing by 1 cm^3 increments. You will graph your data and analyze the graphs to find the relationship between pressure and volume for a gas.

• **Boyle's law apparatus** You will increase the pressure on a fixed quantity of gas in a syringe by adding weight to the end of the plunger. As the pressure is increased, you will measure the change in volume using the markings on the syringe. You will graph your data and analyze the graphs to find the relationship between pressure and volume for a gas.

SAFETY

• **Tie back long hair, secure loose clothing, and remove loose jewelry to prevent their getting caught in moving or rotating parts.**

• **Wear eye protection. Contents under pressure may become projectiles and cause serious injury.**

PREPARATION

1. Determine whether you will be using the CBL and sensors procedure or the Boyle's law apparatus. Read the entire lab for the appropriate procedure, and plan what steps you will take.

Boyle's law apparatus procedure begins on page 352.

PROCEDURE

CBL AND SENSORS

Pressure and volume of a gas

2. Prepare a data table in your lab notebook with four columns and nine rows. In the first row, label the first through fourth columns *Volume (cm³), Trial 1 Pressure (atm), Trial 2 Pressure (atm),* and *Trial 3 Pressure (atm).*

3. Set up the pressure sensor, CBL, and graphing calculator as shown in **Figure 9-25.** Connect the pressure sensor to the CH1 port on the CBL. Turn on the CBL and the graphing calculator.

4. Start the program PHYSICS on the calculator. Select option *SET UP PROBES* from the MAIN MENU. Enter 1 for the number of probes. Select the pressure sensor from the list. Enter 1 for the channel number. Select *USE STORED* from the CALIBRATION menu. Select *ATM* from the PRESSURE UNITS menu.

5. Select the *COLLECT DATA* option from the MAIN MENU. Select the *TRIGGER* option from the DATA COLLECTION menu.

6. Turn the stopcock so that the valve handle points downward. This will allow the syringe to fill with air. Pull the plunger on the syringe to the 10 cm³ mark. Turn the stopcock so that the valve handle points upward to set the volume of air in the syringe to 10 cm³. Attach one end of the tubing to the end of the syringe and attach the other end to the pressure sensor.

7. Push in the plunger until the volume of air in the syringe is near 8 cm³. Press TRIGGER on the CBL to collect the pressure reading at this volume. Record the reading from the CBL under *Trial 1 Pressure* in your data table. Read the volume, and record it in your data table. Select *CONTINUE* from the TRIGGER menu on the graphing calculator.

8. Push in the plunger until the volume of air in the syringe is near 7 cm³. Press TRIGGER on the CBL to collect the pressure reading. Record the reading under *Trial 1 Pressure* in your data table. Read the volume, and record it in your data table. Select *CONTINUE* on the graphing calculator.

9. Repeat several times, decreasing the volume each time by 1 cm³ until the volume is 2 cm³.

10. Repeat steps 4–9 two times, and record the volume and pressure values in the data table for *Trial 2* and *Trial 3.*

Analysis and interpretation begins on page 353.

Figure 9-25

Step 6: Set the volume of air in the syringe and attach the tubing securely to the syringe and pressure sensor.

Step 7: Record each volume in your data table, and use the same volumes for each trial.

Step 9: Decrease the volume by 1 cm³ until you reach 2 cm³ or until the plunger will no longer move.

PROCEDURE

BOYLE'S LAW APPARATUS

Pressure and volume of a gas

2. Prepare a data table in your lab notebook with four columns and six rows. In the first row, label the first through fourth columns *Number of weights, Trial 1 Volume (cm^3), Trial 2 Volume (cm^3)*, and *Trial 3 Volume (cm^3)*. In the first column, label the second through sixth rows *0, 1, 2, 3,* and *4*.

3. Remove the plastic cap, and adjust the piston head so that it reads between 30 cm^3 and 35 cm^3. See **Figure 9-26**.

4. While holding the piston in place, carefully replace the cap. Twist the piston several times to allow the head to overcome any frictional forces.

5. When the piston comes to rest, read the volume to the nearest 0.25 cm^3. Record this value as the volume for zero weight in your data table.

6. Carefully place one 1 kg mass on the piston. Twist the piston several times.

7. When the piston comes to rest, read the volume and record it in your data table.

8. Carefully add another 1 kg mass to the piston so that the total mass on the piston is 2 kg. Twist the piston several times.

9. When the piston comes to rest, read the volume and record it in your data table.

10. Carefully add another 1 kg mass to the piston so that the total mass on the piston is 3 kg. Twist the piston several times.

11. When the piston comes to rest, read the volume and record it in your data table.

12. Add another 1 kg mass to the piston. Twist the piston several times. When the piston comes to rest, read the volume and record it in your data table.

13. Repeat steps 3–12 two times, and record the values in the data table under *Trial 2* and *Trial 3*.

Figure 9-26

Step 3: Adjust the piston head to set the volume of air in the syringe between 30 cm^3 and 35 cm^3.

Step 5: Wait for the piston to come to rest before reading the volume.

ANALYSIS AND INTERPRETATION

Calculations and data analysis

1. Organizing data Using data from all three trials, make the following calculations:

    a. CBL and sensors Calculate the average pressure at each volume of air in the syringe.

    b. Boyle's law apparatus Calculate the average volume for each level of weight on the piston.

2. Organizing data Calculate the inverse of each of the pressures or volumes from item 1.

3. Graphing data Plot a graph using the calculated averages from item 1. Use a graphing calculator, computer, or graph paper.

    a. CBL and sensors Graph *Average Pressure* versus *Volume.*

    b. Boyle's law apparatus Graph *Average Volume* versus *Number of Weights.*

4. Graphing data Using a graphing calculator, computer, or graph paper, make a second graph using the inverse averages from item 2.

    a. CBL and sensors Plot a graph of the *Inverse Average Pressure* versus *Volume.*

    b. Boyle's law apparatus Plot a graph of the *Inverse Average Volume* versus *Number of Weights.*

Conclusions

5. Analyzing graphs Based on your graphs, what is the relationship between the volume and the pressure of a gas? Explain how your graphs support your answer.

6. Evaluating methods

    a. CBL and sensors Because the pressure sensor was not calibrated to your altitude, the pressure readings do not accurately reflect the pressure of the gas in the syringe. Explain why calibrating the probe is unnecessary for finding the relationship between the pressure readings and the volume of the gas.

    b. Boyle's law apparatus In plotting the graphs, the number of weights was used instead of the amount of pressure. Explain how the weight on the piston serves as a measure of the pressure of the air inside the syringe.

Physics and Its World *Timeline 1690–1785*

1690
1700
1710
1720
1730
1740

1695 – The Ashanti, the last of the major African kingdoms, emerges in what is now Ghana. The Ashanti's strong centralized government and effective bureaucracy enable them to control the region for nearly two centuries.

1712

$$eff = \frac{W_{net}}{Q_h}$$

Thomas Newcomen invents the first practical steam engine. Over 60 years later, **James Watt** makes significant improvements to the Newcomen engine.

1715 – Chinese writer **Ts'ao Chen** is born. His book *The Dream of the Red Chamber* is widely regarded today as the greatest Chinese novel.

1721 – **Johann Sebastian Bach** composes the six *Brandenburg Concertos*.

1735 – **John Harrison** constructs the first of four chronometers that will allow navigators to accurately determine a ship's longitude.

1738 – Under the leadership of **Nadir Shah,** the Persian Empire expands into India as the Moghul Empire enters a stage of decline.

1738

$$P + \frac{1}{2}\rho v^2 + \rho g h = \text{constant}$$

Daniel Bernoulli's *Hydrodynamics,* which includes his research on the mechanical behavior of fluids, is published.

1752

Benjamin Franklin builds on the first studies of electricity performed earlier in the century by describing electricity as having positive and negative charge. He also performs the dangerous "kite experiment," in which he demonstrates that lightning consists of electrical charge.

1744 – Contrary to the favored idea that heat is a fluid, Russian chemist **Mikhail V. Lomonosov** suggests that heat is the result of motion. Four years later, Lomonosov formulates conservation laws for mass and energy.

1756 – The Seven Years War begins.

1757 – German musician **William Herschel** emigrates to England to avoid fighting in the Seven Years War. Over the next 60 years he pursues astronomy, constructing the largest reflecting telescopes of the era and discovering new objects such as binary stars and the planet Uranus.

1770 – **Antoine Laurent Lavoisier** begins his research on chemical reactions, notably oxidation and combustion.

1782 – **Caroline Herschel,** sister of astronomer **William Herschel,** joins her brother in England. She compiles the most comprehensive star catalog of the era, and discovers several nebulous objects that are eventually recognized as galaxies.

1775 – The American Revolution begins.

1785

$$F_{electric} = k_c \left(\frac{q_1 q_2}{r^2} \right)$$

Charles Augustin Coulomb begins a series of experiments that will systematically and conclusively prove the inverse-square law for electric force. The law has been suggested for over 30 years by scientists such as **Daniel Bernoulli, Joseph Priestly,** and **Henry Cavendish.**

1740

1750

1760

1770

1780

1790

CHAPTER 10

Heat

PHYSICS IN ACTION

Whether you pop corn by putting the kernels in a pan of hot oil or in a microwave oven, the hard kernels will absorb energy until, at a high temperature, they rupture. At this point, superheated water suddenly turns to steam and rushes outward, and the kernels burst open to form the fluffy, edible puffs, or flakes, of starch. But what actually happens when water turns into steam, and what do we mean when we talk about heat and temperature?

In this chapter you will study what distinguishes temperature and heat and how different substances behave when energy is added or removed from them, causing a change in their temperature or phase.

- *Why does popcorn require steam, not just superheated water, to produce flakes?*
- *What role does oil play in the preparation of popcorn?*

CONCEPT REVIEW

Work (Section 5-1)

Energy (Section 5-2)

Conservation of energy (Section 5-3)

DEFINING TEMPERATURE

When you hold a glass of lemonade with ice, like that shown in **Figure 10-1,** you feel a sharp sensation in your hand that we describe as "cold." Likewise, you experience a "hot" feeling when you touch a cup of hot chocolate. We often associate temperature with how hot or cold an object feels when we touch it. Our sense of touch serves as a qualitative indicator of temperature. However, this sensation of hot or cold also depends on the temperature of the skin and therefore is misleading. The same object may feel warm or cool, depending on the properties of the object and on the conditions of your body.

Determining an object's temperature with precision requires a standard definition of temperature and a procedure for making measurements that establish how "hot" or "cold" objects are.

Figure 10-1

Objects at low temperatures feel cold to the touch, while objects at high temperatures feel hot.

Adding or removing energy changes temperature

Consider what happens when you use an electric range to cook food. By turning the dial that controls the electric current delivered to the heating element, you can adjust the element's temperature. As the current is increased, the temperature of the element increases. Similarly, as the current is reduced, the temperature of the element decreases. In general, energy must be either added to or removed from a substance to change its temperature.

Quick Lab

Sensing Temperature

MATERIALS LIST

✔ 3 identical basins

✔ hot and cold tap water

✔ ice

SAFETY CAUTION

Use only hot tap water. The temperature of the hot water must not exceed 50°C (122°F).

Fill one basin with hot tap water. Fill another with cold tap water, and add ice until about one-third of the mixture is ice.

Fill the third basin with an equal mixture of hot and cold tap water.

Place your left hand in the hot water and your right hand in the cold water for 15 s. Then place both hands in the basin of lukewarm water for 15 s. Describe whether the water feels hot or cold to either of your hands.

Temperature is proportional to the kinetic energy of atoms and molecules

In Section 9-2 you learned that temperature is a measure of the average kinetic energy of particles in a substance. A substance's temperature increases as a direct result of added energy being distributed among the particles of the substance, as shown in **Figure 10-2.**

For a monatomic gas, temperature can be understood in terms of the translational kinetic energy of the atoms in the gas. For other kinds of substances, molecules can rotate or vibrate, so rotational kinetic energy or vibrational kinetic and potential energies also exist (see **Table 10-1**).

The energies associated with atomic motion are referred to as **internal energy,** which is proportional to the substance's temperature. For an ideal gas, the internal energy depends only on the temperature of the gas. For gases with two or more atoms per molecule, as well as for liquids and solids, other properties besides temperature contribute to the internal energy. The symbol U stands for internal energy, and the symbol ΔU stands for a change in internal energy.

Energy added

(a)　　　(b)

Figure 10-2
The low average kinetic energy of the particles **(a),** and thus the temperature of the gas, increases when energy is added to the gas **(b).**

internal energy

the energy of a substance due to the random motions of its component particles and equal to the total energy of those particles

Temperature is meaningful only when it is stable

Imagine a can of warm fruit juice immersed in a large beaker of cold water. After about 15 minutes, the can of fruit juice will be cooler and the water surrounding it will be slightly warmer. Eventually, both the can of fruit juice and

Table 10-1	Examples of different forms of energy		
Form of energy	**Macroscopic examples**	**Microscopic examples**	**Energy type**
Translational	airplane in flight, roller coaster at bottom of rise	CO_2 molecule in linear motion	kinetic energy
Rotational	spinning top	CO_2 molecule spinning about its center of mass	kinetic energy
Vibrational	plucked guitar string	bending and stretching of bonds between atoms in a CO_2 molecule	kinetic and potential energy

thermal equilibrium

the state in which two bodies in physical contact with each other have identical temperatures

the water will be at the same temperature. That temperature will not change as long as conditions remain unchanged in the beaker. Another way of expressing this is to say that the water and can of juice are in **thermal equilibrium** with each other.

Thermal equilibrium is the basis for measuring temperature with thermometers. By placing a thermometer in contact with an object and waiting until the column of liquid in the thermometer stops rising or falling, you can find the temperature of the object. This is because the thermometer is at the same temperature as, or is in thermal equilibrium with, the object. Just as in the case of the can of fruit juice in the cold water, the temperature of any two objects at thermal equilibrium always lies between their initial temperatures.

Matter expands as its temperature increases

You have learned that increasing the temperature of a gas may cause the volume of the gas to increase. This occurs not only for gases, but also for liquids and solids. In general, if the temperature of a substance increases, so does its volume. This phenomenon is known as *thermal expansion*.

You may have noticed that the concrete roadway segments of a bridge are separated by gaps several centimeters wide. This is necessary because concrete expands with increasing temperature. Without these gaps, the force from the thermal expansion would cause the segments to push against each other, and they would eventually buckle and break apart.

Different substances undergo different amounts of expansion for a given temperature change. The thermal expansion characteristics of a material are indicated by a quantity called the *coefficient of volume expansion*. Gases have the largest values for this coefficient. Liquids have much smaller values.

In general, the volume of a liquid tends to increase with increasing temperature. However, the volume of water increases with decreasing temperature in the range between 0°C and 4°C. This explains why ice floats in liquid water. It also explains why a pond freezes from the top down instead of from the bottom up. If this did not happen, fish would likely not survive in freezing temperatures.

Solids typically have the smallest coefficient of volume expansion values. For this reason, liquids in solid containers expand more than the container. This property allows some liquids to be used to measure changes in temperature.

MEASURING TEMPERATURE

In order for a device to be used as a thermometer, it must make use of a change in some physical property that corresponds to changing temperature, such as the volume of a gas or liquid, or the pressure of a gas at constant volume. The most common thermometers use a thin glass tube containing mercury, colored alcohol, or colored mineral spirits. When the thermometer is heated, the volume of the liquid expands. Because the cross-sectional area of the tube remains nearly constant during temperature changes, the change in length of the liquid column is proportional to the temperature change (see **Figure 10-3**).

(a)

Volume of mercury at
0°C = 0.100 mL = V_i

0°C

(b)

50°C

Volume of mercury at
50°C = 0.101 mL =
V_i + 0.001 mL

0°C

Figure 10-3
The change in the mercury's volume from a temperature of 0°C **(a)** to a temperature of 50°C **(b)** is small, but because the mercury is limited to expansion in only one direction, the linear change is large.

Calibrating thermometers requires fixed temperatures

A thermometer must be more than an unmarked, thin glass tube of liquid. For a thermometer to measure temperature in a variety of situations, the length of the liquid column at different temperatures must be known. One reference point is etched on the tube and refers to when the thermometer is in thermal equilibrium with a mixture of water and ice at one atmosphere of pressure. This temperature is called the *ice point* of water and is defined as zero degrees Celsius, or 0°C. A second reference mark is made at the point when the thermometer is in thermal equilibrium with a mixture of steam and water at one atmosphere of pressure. This temperature is called the *steam point* of water and is defined as 100°C.

A temperature scale can be made by dividing the distance between the reference marks into equally spaced units, called *degrees*.

Temperature units depend on the scale used

The temperature scales most widely used today are the Fahrenheit, Celsius, and Kelvin (or absolute) scales. The Fahrenheit scale is commonly used in the United States. The Celsius scale is used in countries that have adopted the metric system and by the scientific community worldwide.

Celsius and Fahrenheit temperature measurements can be converted to each other using this equation.

CELSIUS-FAHRENHEIT TEMPERATURE CONVERSION

$$T_F = \frac{9}{5}T_C + 32.0$$

Fahrenheit temperature $= \left(\frac{9}{5} \times \text{Celsius temperature}\right) + 32.0$

The number 32.0 in the equation indicates the difference between the ice point value in each scale. The point at which water freezes is indicated by 0.0 degrees in the Celsius scale and 32.0 degrees in the Fahrenheit scale.

Temperature values in the Celsius and Fahrenheit scales can have positive, negative, or zero values. Because the kinetic energy of the atoms and molecules in a substance has a positive value, the temperature that is a measure of that energy should have positive magnitudes also. A temperature scale with

Volume-Temperature Graph for an Ideal Gas

$-273.15°C = 0 K$

Figure 10-4

If an ideal gas could be compressed to zero volume, its temperature would be $-273.15°C$, or 0 K.

only positive values is suggested in the graph of volume versus temperature for an ideal gas, shown in **Figure 10-4.** As the temperature of the gas decreases, so does its volume. If it were possible to compress the gas to zero volume, the gas temperature would equal $-273.15°C$. This temperature is designated in the Kelvin scale as 0.00 K, where K is the symbol for the temperature unit called the kelvin. Temperatures in this scale are indicated by the symbol T.

A temperature difference of one degree is the same on the Celsius and Kelvin scales. The two scales differ only in the choice of zero point. Thus, the ice point (0.00°C) equals 273.15 K, and the steam point (100.00°C) equals 373.15 K (see **Table 10-2**). The Celsius temperature can therefore be converted to the Kelvin temperature by adding 273.15.

CELSIUS-KELVIN TEMPERATURE CONVERSION

$$T = T_C + 273.15$$

Kelvin temperature = Celsius temperature + 273.15

Kelvin temperatures for various physical processes can range from around 1 000 000 000 K (10^9 K), which is the temperature of the interiors of the most massive stars, to less than 1 K, which is slightly cooler than the boiling point of liquid helium. The temperature 0 K is often referred to as *absolute zero*. Absolute zero has never been reached, although laboratory experiments have reached temperatures of 0.000 001 K.

Table 10-2	**Temperature scales and their uses**		
Scale	**Ice point**	**Steam point**	**Applications**
Fahrenheit	32°F	212°F	meteorology, medicine, and non-scientific uses (U.S.)
Celsius	0°C	100°C	meteorology, medicine, and non-scientific uses (outside U.S.); other sciences (international)
Kelvin (absolute)	273.15 K	373.15 K	physical chemistry, gas laws, astrophysics, thermodynamics, low-temperature physics

Temperature conversion

PROBLEM

What are the equivalent Celsius and Kelvin temperatures of 50.0°F?

SOLUTION

Given: $T_F = 50.0°F$

Unknown: $T_C = ?$ $T = ?$

Use the Celsius-Fahrenheit equation from page 361.

$$T_F = \frac{9}{5}T_C + 32.0$$

$$T_C = \frac{5}{9}(T_F - 32.0)$$

$$T_C = \frac{5}{9}(50.0 - 32.0)°C = 10.0°C$$

Use the Celsius-Kelvin equation from page 362.

$$T = T_C + 273.15$$

$$T = (10.0 + 273.2)K = 283.2\ K$$

$$\boxed{\begin{array}{l} T_C = 10.0°C \\ T = 283.2\ K \end{array}}$$

Temperature conversion

1. A pan of water is heated from 23°C to 78°C. What is the change in its temperature on the Kelvin and Fahrenheit scales?

2. The lowest outdoor temperature ever recorded on Earth is −128.6°F, recorded at Vostok Station, Antarctica, in 1983. What is this temperature on the Celsius and Kelvin scales?

3. Liquid nitrogen is used to cool substances to very low temperatures. Express the boiling point of liquid nitrogen (−195.81°C at 1 atm of pressure) in degrees Fahrenheit and in kelvins.

4. The temperatures of one northeastern state range from 105°F in the summer to −25°F in winter. Express this temperature range in degrees Celsius.

5. The normal human body temperature is 98.6°F. A person with a fever may record 102°F. Express these temperatures in degrees Celsius.

1. Two gases that are in physical contact with each other consist of particles of identical mass. In what order should the images shown in **Figure 10-5** be placed to correctly describe the changing distribution of kinetic energy among the gas particles? Which group of particles has the highest temperature at any time? Explain.

(a)   (b)   (c)

Figure 10-5

2. A hot copper pan is dropped into a tub of water. If the water's temperature rises, what happens to the temperature of the pan? How will you know when the water and copper pan reach thermal equilibrium?

3. Oxygen condenses into a liquid at approximately 90.2 K. To what temperature does this correspond on both the Celsius and Fahrenheit temperature scales?

4. The boiling point of sulfur is 444.6°C. Sulfur's melting point is 586.1°F lower than its boiling point.

   a. Determine the melting point of sulfur in degrees Celsius.
   b. Find the melting and boiling points in degrees Fahrenheit.
   c. Find the melting and boiling points in kelvins.

5. **Physics in Action**   Which of the following is true for the water molecules inside popcorn kernels during popping?

   a. Their temperature increases.
   b. They are destroyed.
   c. Their kinetic energy increases.
   d. Their mass changes.

6. **Physics in Action**   Referring to **Figure 10-6,** determine which of the following pairs represent objects that are in thermal equilibrium with each other.

   a. the hot plate and the glass pot
   b. the hot oil and the popcorn kernels
   c. the outside air and the hot plate

Figure 10-6

HEAT AND ENERGY

Thermal physics often appears mysterious at the macroscopic level. Hot objects become cool without any obvious cause. To understand thermal processes, it is helpful to shift attention to the behavior of atoms and molecules. Mechanics can be used to explain much of what is happening at the molecular, or microscopic, level. This in turn accounts for what you observe at the macroscopic level. Throughout this chapter, the focus will shift between these two viewpoints.

Recall the can of warm fruit juice immersed in the beaker of cold water (shown in **Figure 10-7**). The temperature of the can and the juice in it is lowered, and the water's temperature is slightly increased, until at thermal equilibrium both final temperatures are the same. Energy is transferred from the can of juice to the water because the two objects are at different temperatures. This transfer of energy is called **heat.**

Energy is transferred between substances by heat

From a macroscopic viewpoint, energy transferred by heat always moves from an object at high temperature to an object at low temperature. This is similar to the mechanical behavior of objects moving from a higher gravitational potential energy to a lower gravitational potential energy. Just as a pencil will drop from your desk to the floor but will not jump from the floor to your desk, so energy will travel spontaneously from an object at high temperature to one at lower temperature and not the other way around.

heat

the process by which energy is exchanged between objects because of a difference in their temperatures

Figure 10-7
Energy is transferred by the process of heat from objects with higher temperatures (the fruit juice and can) to those with lower temperatures (the cold water).

Figure 10-8

Energy is transferred by heat from the higher-energy particles to lower-energy particles **(a).** The net energy transferred is zero when thermal equilibrium is reached **(b).**

Metal atoms in can

Molecules in fruit juice   Water molecules

(a)

Direction of energy transfer

$T_{water} = 5°C$
$T_{juice} = 45°C$

(b)

Direction of energy transfer

$T_{water} = 11°C$
$T_{juice} = 11°C$

Heat's preferred direction can be explained at the atomic level. At first, the molecules in the fruit juice have higher average kinetic energies than do the water molecules that surround the can, as shown in **Figure 10-8.** This energy is transferred from the juice to the can by the molecules in the juice colliding with the metal atoms of the can. The atoms vibrate more because of their increased energy, and this energy is transferred to the surrounding water molecules.

As the energy of the water molecules gradually increases, the energy of the molecules in the fruit juice and the atoms of the can decreases until all of the particles have, on the average, equal kinetic energies. However, it is also possible for some of the energy to be transferred through collisions from the lower-energy water molecules to the higher-energy metal atoms and fruit-juice particles. Therefore, energy can move in both directions. Because the average kinetic energy of particles is higher in the body at higher temperature, more energy is transferred out of it by heat than is transferred into it. The net result is that energy is transferred by heat in only one direction.

Energy transfer by heat alters an object's temperature

Thermal equilibrium may be understood in terms of energy exchange between two objects at equal temperature. When the can of fruit juice and the surrounding water are at the same temperature, as depicted in **Figure 10-9,** the quantity of energy transferred by heat from the can of fruit juice to the water is the same as the energy transferred by heat from the water to the can of juice. The net energy transferred between the two objects is zero.

This reveals the difference between temperature and heat. The atoms of all objects are in continuous motion, so all objects have some internal energy. Because temperature is a measure of that energy, all objects have some temperature. Heat, on the other hand, is a process by which energy is transferred from one object to another because of the temperature difference between them. When there is no temperature difference between a substance and its surroundings, no net energy is transferred by heat.

Heat depends on the difference of the temperatures, much like the potential energy associated with the pencil on your desk depends on the magnitude of the distance between the level of your desktop and the level of the floor. The greater the temperature difference between two objects, the greater the amount of energy that is transferred between them by heat.

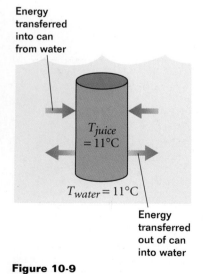

Energy transferred into can from water

$T_{juice} = 11°C$

$T_{water} = 11°C$

Energy transferred out of can into water

Figure 10-9

At thermal equilibrium, the net energy exchanged by heat between two objects equals zero.

For example, in winter, energy is transferred by heat from a car's surface at 30°C to a cold raindrop at 5°C. In the summer, energy is transferred by heat from a car's surface at 45°C to a warm raindrop at 20°C. In each case, the energy transferred by heat is the same, because the substances and the temperature difference (25°C) are the same (see **Figure 10-10**).

The concepts of heat and temperature help to explain why hands held in separate bowls containing hot and cold water subsequently sense the temperature of lukewarm water differently. The nerves in the outer skin of your hand detect energy passing through the skin from objects with temperatures different than your body temperature. If one hand is at thermal equilibrium with cold water, more energy is transferred from the outer layers of your hand than can be replaced by the blood, which has a temperature of about 37.0°C (98.6°F). When the hand is immediately placed in water that is at a higher temperature, energy is transferred from the water to the cooler hand. The energy transferred into the skin causes the water to feel warm. Likewise, the hand that has been in hot water temporarily gains energy from the water. The loss of this energy to the lukewarm water makes that water feel cool.

Figure 10-10
The energy transferred by heat from the car's surface to the raindrop is the same for low temperatures **(a)** as for high temperatures **(b)**, provided the temperature differences are the same.

Heat has units of joules

Before scientists arrived at the current model for heat, the units used for measuring heat had already been developed. These units are still widely used in many applications and therefore are listed in **Table 10-3**. Because heat, like work, is a transfer of energy, all heat units can be converted to joules, the SI unit for energy.

Just as other forms of energy and energy transfer have a symbol that identifies them (*PE* for potential energy, *KE* for kinetic energy, *U* for internal energy, *W* for work), heat is indicated by the symbol *Q*.

Table 10-3   Thermal units and their values in joules

Heat unit	Equivalent value	Uses
joule (J)	equal to $1 \text{ kg} \cdot \left(\dfrac{\text{m}^2}{\text{s}^2}\right)$	SI unit of energy
calorie (cal)	4.186 J	non-SI unit of heat; found especially in older works of physics and chemistry
kilocalorie (kcal)	4.186×10^3 J	non-SI unit of heat
Calorie, or dietary Calorie	4.186×10^3 J = 1 kcal	food and nutritional science
British thermal unit (Btu)	1.055×10^3 J	English unit of heat; used in engineering, air-conditioning, and refrigeration
therm	1.055×10^8 J	equal to 100 000 Btu; used to measure natural-gas usage

TRANSFERRING ENERGY BY HEAT AND WORK

Hammer a nail into a block of wood. After several minutes, pry the nail loose from the block and touch the side of the nail. It feels warm to the touch, indicating that energy is being transferred from the nail to your hand. Work is done in pulling the nail out of the wood. The nail encounters friction with the wood, and most of the energy required to overcome this friction is transformed into internal energy. The increase in the internal energy of the nail raises the nail's temperature, and the temperature difference between the nail and your hand results in the transfer of energy to your hand by heat.

Friction is only one mechanism for increasing a substance's internal energy. In the case of solids, internal energy can be increased by deforming their structure. Common examples of this are when a rubber band is stretched or a piece of metal is bent.

Total energy is conserved

When the concept of mechanical energy was introduced in Chapter 5, you discovered that whenever friction between two objects exists, not all of the work done in overcoming friction appears as mechanical energy. Similarly, not all of the kinetic energy in inelastic collisions remains as kinetic energy. Some of this energy is absorbed by the objects as internal energy. This is why, in the case of the nail pulled from the wood, the nail (and if you could touch it, the wood inside the hole) feels warm. If changes in internal energy are taken into account along with changes in mechanical energy, the total energy is a universally conserved property.

CONSERVATION OF ENERGY

$$\Delta PE + \Delta KE + \Delta U = 0$$

the change in potential energy + the change in kinetic energy + the change in internal energy = 0

Quick Lab

Transferring Energy by Work and Heat

MATERIALS LIST

✔ 1 large rubber band about 7–10 mm wide

SAFETY CAUTION

To avoid breaking the rubber band, do not stretch it more than a few inches. Do not point a stretched rubber band at another person.

Hold the rubber band between your thumbs. Touch the middle section of the rubber band to your lip and note how it feels. Rapidly stretch the rubber band and keep it stretched. Touch the middle section of the rubber band to your lip again. Notice whether the rubber band's temperature has increased. (You may have to repeat this procedure several times before you can clearly distinguish the temperature difference.)

Conservation of energy

PROBLEM

An arrangement similar to the one used to demonstrate energy conservation is shown at right. A vessel contains water. Paddles that are propelled by falling masses turn in the water. This agitation increases the internal energy of the water. The temperature of the water is then measured, giving an indication of the water's internal-energy increase. If a total mass of 11.5 kg falls 1.3 m and all of the mechanical energy is converted to internal energy, by how much will the internal energy of the water increase? (Assume no energy is transferred by heat out of the vessel to the surroundings or from the surroundings to the vessel's interior.)

SOLUTION

1. DEFINE

Given: $m = 11.5$ kg $\quad h = 1.3$ m $\quad g = 9.81$ m/s^2

Unknown: $\Delta PE = ?$ $\quad \Delta KE = ?$ $\quad \Delta U = ?$

2. PLAN

Choose an equation(s) or situation: The equation for conservation of energy can be expressed as the initial total energy equal to the final total energy. Because there is no kinetic energy in the apparatus when the mass is released or when it comes to rest, both KE_i and KE_f equal zero. Because all of the potential energy is assumed to be converted to internal energy, PE_t can be set equal to mgh if PE_f is set equal to zero.

$$\Delta PE + \Delta KE + \Delta U = 0$$
$$PE_i + KE_i + U_i = PE_f - KE_f + U_f$$
$$PE_i = mgh$$
$$PE_f = 0$$
$$KE_i = 0$$
$$KE_f = 0$$
$$mgh + 0 + U_i = 0 + 0 + U_f$$
$$\Delta U = U_f - U_i = mgh$$

3. CALCULATE

Substitute values into the equation(s) and solve:

$$\Delta U = (11.5 \text{ kg})(9.81 \text{ m/s}^2)(1.3 \text{ m})$$
$$= 1.5 \times 10^2 \text{ J}$$

$$\boxed{\Delta U = 1.5 \times 10^2 \text{ J}}$$

CALCULATOR SOLUTION

Because the minimum number of significant figures in the data is two, the calculator answer, 146.6595 J, should be rounded to two digits.

4. EVALUATE

The answer can be estimated using rounded values for m and g. If $m \approx 10$ kg and $g \approx 10$ m/s^2, then $\Delta U \approx 130$ J, which is close to the actual value calculated.

Conservation of energy

1. In the arrangement described in Sample Problem 10B, how far would the mass have to fall to increase the water's internal energy by 755 J?

2. A 2.5 kg block of ice at a temperature of 0.0°C and an initial speed of 5.7 m/s slides across a level floor. If 3.3×10^5 J are required to melt 1.0 kg of ice, how much ice melts, assuming that the initial kinetic energy of the ice block is entirely converted to the ice's internal energy?

3. The amount of internal energy needed to raise the temperature of 0.25 kg of water by 0.2°C is 209.3 J. How fast must a 0.25 kg baseball travel in order for its kinetic energy to equal this internal energy?

4. A worker drives a 0.500 kg spike into a rail tie with a 2.50 kg sledgehammer. The hammer hits the spike with a speed of 65.0 m/s. If one-third of the hammer's kinetic energy is converted to the internal energy of the hammer and spike, how much does the total internal energy increase?

5. A 3.0×10^{-3} kg copper penny drops a distance of 50.0 m to the ground. If 65 percent of the initial potential energy goes into increasing the internal energy of the penny, determine the magnitude of that increase.

Section Review

1. A bottle of water at room temperature is placed in a freezer for a short time. An identical bottle of water that has been lying in the sunlight is placed in a refrigerator for the same amount of time. What must you know to determine which situation involves more energy transfer?

2. Use the microscopic interpretations of temperature and heat to explain how you can blow on your hands to warm them and also blow on a bowl of hot soup to cool it.

3. If a bottle of water is shaken vigorously, will the internal energy of the water change? Why or why not?

4. Water at the top of Niagara Falls has a temperature of 10.0°C. Assume that all of the potential energy goes into increasing the internal energy of the water and that it takes 4186 J/kg to increase the water's temperature by 1°C. If 505 kg of water falls a distance of 50.0 m, what will the temperature of the water be at the bottom of the falls?

SPECIFIC HEAT CAPACITY

You have probably noticed on a hot day that the air around a swimming pool (like the one shown in **Figure 10-11**) is hot but the pool water is cool. This may seem odd, because both the air and water receive energy from sunlight. As it turns out, there is a property, not only of air and water but of all substances, that causes their temperatures to vary by different amounts when equal amounts of energy are added to or removed from them.

This property can be explained in terms of the ease with which atoms and molecules move within a substance, which in turn affects how much the substance's temperature changes for a given amount of energy that is added or removed. Each substance has a unique value for the energy required to change the temperature of 1 kg of that substance by 1°C. This value, known as the **specific heat capacity** (or sometimes just specific heat) of the substance, relates mass, temperature change, and energy transferred by heat.

The specific heat capacity is mathematically related to energy transferred by heat, mass, and temperature change by the following equation:

SPECIFIC HEAT CAPACITY

$$c_p = \frac{Q}{m\Delta T}$$

$$\text{specific heat capacity} = \frac{\text{energy transferred}}{\text{mass} \times \text{change in temperature}}$$

The subscript p indicates that the specific heat capacity is measured at constant pressure. Maintaining constant pressure is an important detail when determining certain thermal properties of gases, which are much more affected by changes in pressure than are solids or liquids.

Note that while energy is usually transferred by heat, Q, it can be transferred by other means. Also recall that a temperature change of 1°C is equal in magnitude to a temperature change of 1 K, so that ΔT gives the temperature change in either scale.

The equation for specific heat capacity applies to both substances that absorb energy from their surroundings and those that transfer energy to their surroundings. When the temperature increases, ΔT and Q are taken to be positive, which corresponds to energy transferred into the substance. Likewise, when the temperature decreases, ΔT and Q are negative and energy is

10-3 SECTION OBJECTIVES

- **Perform calculations with specific heat capacity.**

- **Perform calculations involving latent heat.**

- **Interpret the various sections of a heating curve.**

Figure 10-11
The air around the pool and the water in the pool receive energy from sunlight. However, the increase in temperature is greater for the air than for the water.

specific heat capacity

the quantity of energy needed to raise the temperature of 1 kg of a substance by 1°C at constant pressure

Table 10-4
Specific heat capacities

Substance	c_p (J/kg•°C)
aluminum	8.99×10^2
copper	3.87×10^2
glass	8.37×10^2
gold	1.29×10^2
ice	2.09×10^3
iron	4.48×10^2
lead	1.28×10^2
mercury	1.38×10^2
silver	2.34×10^2
steam	2.01×10^3
water	4.186×10^3

calorimetry

an experimental procedure used to measure the energy transferred by heat from one substance to another

transferred from the substance. **Table 10-4** lists specific heat capacities that have been determined for several substances.

Determining specific heat capacity

To measure the specific heat capacity of a substance, it is necessary to measure mass, temperature change, and energy transferred by heat. Mass and temperature change are directly measurable, but the direct measurement of heat is difficult. However, the specific heat capacity of water (4.186 kJ/kg•°C) is well known, so the energy transferred by heat between an object of unknown specific heat capacity and a known quantity of water can be measured.

If a hot substance is placed in an insulated container of cool water, energy conservation requires that the energy the substance gives up must equal the energy absorbed by the water. Although some energy is transferred to the surrounding container, this effect is small and, for simplicity, will be ignored in this discussion. Energy conservation can be used to calculate the specific heat capacity, $c_{p,x}$, of the substance (indicated by the subscript x). For simplicity, a subscript w will always stand for "water" in problems involving specific heat capacities.

energy absorbed by water = energy released by the substance

$$Q_w = Q_x$$

$$c_{p,w} m_w \Delta T_w = c_{p,x} m_x \Delta T_x$$

The energy gained by a substance is usually expressed as a positive quantity, and energy released usually has a negative value. The minus sign of the latter quantity can be eliminated if ΔT_x and ΔT_{water} are written as the larger temperature value minus the smaller one. Therefore, ΔT should always be written as a positive quantity for this equation.

This approach to determining a substance's specific heat capacity is called **calorimetry,** and devices that are used for making this measurement are called *calorimeters.* A calorimeter also contains a thermometer for measuring the final temperature when the substances are at thermal equilibrium and a stirrer to ensure the uniform mixture of energy throughout the water (see **Figure 10-12**).

Stirrer · Thermometer · Insulated outer container · Lid · Inner container · Water · Test substance

Figure 10-12
A simple calorimeter allows the specific heat capacity of a substance to be determined.

Calorimetry

PROBLEM

A 0.0500 kg metal bolt is heated to 100.0°C. It is then dropped into a beaker containing 0.400 kg of water with an initial temperature of 20.0°C. If the final temperature of the bolt and water is 22.1°C, find the specific heat capacity of the metal. Identify the metal using Table 10-4.

SOLUTION

1. DEFINE

Given:

$$m_{metal} = m_m = 0.0500 \text{ kg} \qquad T_{metal} = T_m = 100.0°C$$
$$m_{water} = m_w = 0.400 \text{ kg} \qquad T_{water} = T_w = 20.0°C$$
$$c_{p,w} = 4186 \text{ J/kg} \cdot °C \qquad T_{final} = T_f = 22.1°C$$

Unknown: $c_{p,m} = ?$

Diagram:

Before placing hot sample in calorimeter

After thermal equilibrium has been reached

$$m_m = 0.0500 \text{ kg} \qquad m_w = 0.400 \text{ kg} \qquad T_f = 22.1°C$$
$$T_m = 100.0°C \qquad T_w = 20.0°C$$

2. PLAN

Choose an equation(s) or situation: Equate the energy removed from the bolt to the energy absorbed by the water.

energy removed from metal = energy absorbed by water

$$c_{p,m} m_m \Delta T_m = c_{p,w} m_w \Delta T_w$$

Rearrange the equation(s) to isolate the unknown(s):

$$c_{p,m} = \frac{m_w c_{p,w} \Delta T_w}{m_m \Delta T_m}$$

3. CALCULATE

Substitute values into the equation(s) and solve:

Note that ΔT_m and ΔT_w have both been made positive.

$$\Delta T_m = T_m - T_f = 100.0°C - 22.1°C = 77.9°C$$

$$\Delta T_w = T_f - T_w = 22.1°C - 20.0°C = 2.1°C$$

$$c_{p,m} = \frac{(0.400 \text{ kg})\left(\dfrac{4186 \text{ J}}{\text{kg} \cdot °C}\right)(2.1°C)}{(0.0500 \text{ kg})(77.9°C)}$$

$$= \frac{3.5 \times 10^3 \dfrac{\text{J}}{\text{kg} \cdot °C} \cdot \text{kg} \cdot °C}{3.90 \text{ kg} \cdot °C}$$

continued on next page

$$c_{p,m} = 9.0 \times 10^2 \frac{\text{J}}{\text{kg} \cdot {}^\circ\text{C}}$$

$$\boxed{c_{p,m} = 9.0 \times 10^2 \frac{\text{J}}{\text{kg} \cdot {}^\circ\text{C}}}$$

4. EVALUATE   The bolt is most likely aluminum ($c_p = 899$ J/kg•°C), which has a value closer to 900 J/kg•°C than any other metal in **Table 10-4.**

PRACTICE 10C

Calorimetry

1. A cup is made of an experimental material that can hold hot liquids without significantly increasing its own temperature. The 0.75 kg cup has an initial temperature of 36.5°C when it is submerged in 1.25 kg of water with an initial temperature of 20.0°C. What is the cup's specific heat capacity if the final temperature is 24.4°C?

2. How many kilograms of water at 25°C must come to thermal equilibrium with a 3.0 kg gold bar at 99°C in order to lower the bar's temperature to 47°C?

3. A 0.225 kg sample of tin is heated to 97.5°C. It is then dropped into 0.115 kg of water with a temperature of 10.0°C. If the equilibrium temperature for the tin-and-water mixture is 18.5°C, what is the specific heat capacity of tin?

4. Brass is an alloy made from copper and zinc. A 0.59 kg brass sample at 98.0°C is dropped into 2.80 kg of water at 5.0°C. If the equilibrium temperature is 6.8°C, what is the specific heat capacity of brass?

5. What is the final temperature when 0.032 kg of milk at 11°C is added to 0.16 kg of coffee at 91°C? Assume the specific heat capacities of the two liquids are the same as water, and disregard any energy transfer to the liquids' surroundings.

6. The air temperature above coastal areas is profoundly influenced by the large specific heat capacity of water. How large of a volume of air can be cooled by 1.0°C if energy is transferred by heat from the air to the water, thus increasing the temperature of 1.0 kg of water by 1.0°C? The specific heat capacity of air is approximately 1000.0 J/kg•°C, and the density of air is approximately 1.29 kg/m^3.

Heating and Cooling from the Ground Up

As the earliest cave dwellers knew, a good way to stay warm in the winter and cool in the summer is to go underground. Now scientists and engineers are using the same premise to heat and cool aboveground homes for a fraction of the cost of conventional air-conditioning and heating systems.

"At any given occasion, the earth temperature is the seasonal average temperature," said Gunnar Walmet, of the New York State Energy Research and Development Authority (NYSERDA). "In New York state, that's typically about 50°F all year long."

Although the average specific heat capacity of earth has a smaller value than the specific heat capacity of air, the earth has a greater density. That means there are more kilograms of earth than there are of air near a house and that a 1°C change in temperature involves transferring more energy to or from the ground than to or from the air. Thus, in the wintertime, the ground will probably have a higher temperature than the air above it, while in the summer, the ground will likely have a lower temperature than the air.

An earth-coupled heat pump enables homeowners to tap the earth's belowground temperature to heat their homes in the winter or cool them during the summer. The system includes a network of plastic pipes placed in trenches or inserted in holes drilled 2 to 3 m (6 to 10 ft) beneath the ground's surface. To heat a home, a fluid circulates through the pipe, absorbs energy from the surrounding earth, and transfers this energy to a heat pump inside the house.

The heat pump uses a compressor, tubing, and refrigerant to transfer the energy from the liquid to the air inside the house. A blower-and-duct system distributes the warm air through the home. According to NYSERDA, the system can deliver up to four times as much energy by heat into the house as the electrical energy needed to drive it.

Like other heat pumps, the system is reversible. In the summer, it can transfer energy by heat from the air in the house to the system of pipes belowground.

There are currently tens of thousands of earth-coupled heat pumps installed throughout the United States. Although the system can function anywhere on Earth's surface, it is most appropriate in severe climates, where dramatic temperature swings may not be ideal for air-based systems.

LATENT HEAT

If you place an ice cube that has a temperature of −25°C in a pan and place the pan on a hot range element or burner, the temperature of the ice increases. By knowing the mass and specific heat capacity of ice, you can calculate to a fair approximation how much energy is being added to the ice from the element. However, this procedure only works as long as the ice remains ice and its temperature continues to rise as energy is transferred to it by heat.

The graph in **Figure 10-13** and data in **Table 10-5** show how the temperature of 10.0 g of ice changes as energy is added. You can see that as the ice is heated there is a steady increase in temperature from −25°C to 0°C (segment **A** of the graph).

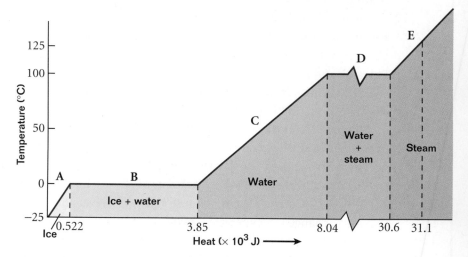

Figure 10-13
This heating curve shows the temperature change of 10.0 g of ice with added energy.

The situation at 0°C is very different. Despite the fact that energy is continuously being added, there is no change in temperature. Instead, the nature of the ice changes. The ice begins to melt and change into water at 0°C (segment **B**). The ice-and-water mixture remains at this temperature until all of the ice melts. From 0°C to 100°C, the water's temperature steadily increases (segment **C**). At 100°C, however, the temperature stops rising and the water turns into

Table 10-5	Changes occurring during the heating of 10.0 g of ice		
Segment of graph	Type of change	Amount of energy transferred by heat	Temperature range of segment
A	temperature of ice increases	522 J	−25°C to 0°C
B	ice melts; becomes water	3.33×10^3 J	0°C
C	temperature of water increases	4.19×10^3 J	0°C to 100°C
D	water boils; becomes steam	2.26×10^4 J	100°C
E	temperature of steam increases	502 J	100°C to 125°C

steam (segment **D**). Once the water has completely vaporized, the temperature of the steam increases (segment **E**). Steam whose temperature is greater than the boiling point of water is referred to as *superheated.*

When substances melt, freeze, boil, condense, or sublime (change from a solid to vapor or from vapor to a solid), the energy added or removed changes the internal energy of the substance without changing its temperature. These changes in matter are called **phase changes.**

The existence of phase changes requires that the definition of heat be expanded. *Heat is the process by which energy is exchanged, either between two bodies at different temperatures or between two bodies at the same temperature when one of them is undergoing a phase change.*

phase change

the physical change of a substance from one state (solid, liquid, or gas) to another at constant temperature and pressure

Phase changes involve potential energy between particles

To understand the behavior of a substance undergoing a phase change, you will need to recall how energy is transferred in collisions. Potential energy is the energy an object has because of its position relative to another object. Examples of potential energy are a pencil about to fall from your desk or a rubber band held in a tightly stretched position. Potential energy is present among a collection of particles in a solid or a liquid in the form of attractive bonds. These bonds result from the charges within atoms and molecules. Potential energy is associated with the electric forces between these charges.

The equilibrium separation between atoms or molecules corresponds to a position at which there is a minimum potential energy. The potential energy increases with increasing atomic separation from the equilibrium position. This resembles the elastic potential energy of a spring, as discussed in Chapter 5. For this reason, a collection of individual atoms or molecules and the bonds between them are often modeled as masses at the ends of springs.

If the particles are far enough apart, the bonds between them can break. The work needed to increase potential energy and ultimately break a bond is provided by collisions with energetic atoms or molecules, as shown in **Figure 10-14.** Just as bonds can be broken, new bonds can be formed if atoms or molecules are brought close together. This involves the collection of particles going from a high potential energy (large average separation) to a lower potential energy (small average separation). This decrease in potential energy involves a release of energy in the form of increasing kinetic energy of nearby particles.

(a)   (b)

Figure 10-14

Energy added to a substance **(a)** can increase the vibrational kinetic energy of its particles or break the bonds between those particles **(b).**

Energy required to melt a substance goes into rearranging the molecules

Phase changes result from a change in the potential energy between particles of a substance. When energy is added to or removed from a substance undergoing a phase change, the particles of the substance rearrange themselves to make up for their change of energy. This occurs without a change in the average kinetic energy of the particles.

For instance, if ice is melting, the absorbed energy is sufficient to break the weak bonds that hold the water molecules together as a well-ordered crystal. New but different bonds form between the liquid water molecules that have separated from the crystal, so some of the absorbed energy is released again. The difference between the potential energies of the broken bonds and the newly formed bonds is equal to the net energy added to the ice, as shown in **Figure 10-15.** As a result, the energy used to rearrange the molecules is not available to increase the molecules' kinetic energy, and therefore no increase in the temperature of the ice-and-water mixture occurs.

Figure 10-15
The heat of fusion is the difference between the energy needed to break bonds in a solid and the energy released when bonds form in a liquid.

For any substance, the energy added to the substance during melting equals the difference between the total potential energies for particles in the solid and the liquid phases. This energy per unit mass is called the **heat of fusion.**

heat of fusion

the energy per unit mass transferred in order to change a substance from solid to liquid or from liquid to solid at constant temperature and pressure

Energy required to vaporize a substance mostly goes into separating the molecules

The molecules are close together even in liquid water, although not as close together as they are in a solid. As a result, the forces between liquid molecules are stronger than those that exist between the more widely separated water molecules in steam. Therefore, at 100°C, all the energy absorbed goes into overcoming the attractive forces between the liquid water molecules. None is available to increase the kinetic energy of the molecules.

The energy added to a substance during vaporization equals the difference in the potential energy of attraction between the particles of a liquid and the potential energy of attraction between the gas particles (see **Figure 10-16**). This energy per unit mass is called the **heat of vaporization.**

heat of vaporization

the energy per unit mass transferred in order to change a substance from liquid to vapor or from vapor to liquid at constant temperature and pressure

Because they have few close neighbors, the particles in the gas phase gain very little energy from weak bonding. Therefore, more energy is required to vaporize a given mass of substance than to melt it. As a result, the heat of vaporization is much greater than the heat of fusion. Both the heat of fusion and the heat of vaporization are classified as **latent heat.**

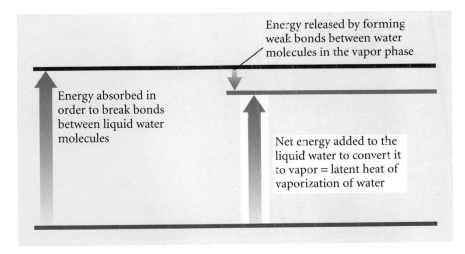

latent heat

the energy per unit mass that is transferred during a phase change of a substance

Figure 10-16
The heat of vaporization is mostly the energy required to separate molecules from the liquid phase.

LATENT HEAT

$$Q = mL$$

Energy transferred by heat during a phase change = mass × latent heat

For calculations involving melting or freezing, the latent heat of fusion is noted by the symbol L_f. Similarly, for calculations involving vaporizing or condensing, the symbol L_v is used for latent heat of vaporization. **Table 10-6** lists latent heats for a few substances.

Table 10-6	Latent heats of fusion and vaporization at standard pressure			
Substance	**Melting point (°C)**	**L_f (J/kg)**	**Boiling point (°C)**	**L_v (J/kg)**
nitrogen	−209.97	2.55×10^4	−195.81	2.01×10^5
oxygen	−218.79	1.38×10^4	−182.97	2.13×10^5
ethyl alcohol	−114	1.04×10^5	78	8.54×10^5
water	0.00	3.33×10^5	100.00	2.26×10^6
lead	327.3	2.45×10^4	1745	8.70×10^5
aluminum	660.4	3.97×10^5	2467	1.14×10^7

Heat of phase change

PROBLEM

How much energy is removed when 10.0 g of water is cooled from steam at 133.0°C to liquid at 53.0°C?

SOLUTION

1. DEFINE   **Given:** $T_{steam} = T_s = 133.0 \ ^\circ C$ $T_{water} = T_w = 53.0 ^\circ C$

$c_{p,steam} = c_{p,s} = 2.01 \times 10^3 \text{ J/kg} \cdot ^\circ C$

$c_{p,water} = c_{p,w} = 4.186 \times 10^3 \text{ J/kg} \cdot ^\circ C$

$L_v = 2.26 \times 10^6 \text{ J/kg}$

$m = 10.0 \text{ g} = 10.0 \times 10^{-3} \text{ kg}$

Unknown: $Q_{total} = ?$

Diagram:

2. PLAN   **Choose an equation(s) or situation:** Heat is calculated by using $Q = mc_p \Delta T$ when no phase changes occur. When steam changes to liquid water, a phase change occurs and the equation for the heat of vaporization, $Q = mL_v$, must be used. Be sure that ΔT is positive for each step.

To cool the steam to 100.0°C: $Q_1 = mc_{p,s} \Delta T$

To change steam to water at 100.0°C: $Q_2 = mL_v$

To cool the water to 53.0°C: $Q_3 = mc_{p,w} \Delta T$

3. CALCULATE   **Substitute values into the equation(s) and solve:** Find ΔT for steam cooling and water cooling. Calculate Q for both cooling steps and the phase change.

For the cooling steam:

$$\Delta T_s = 133.0^\circ C - 100.0^\circ C = 33.0^\circ C$$

$$Q_1 = mc_{p,s} \Delta T = (10.0 \times 10^{-3} \text{ kg}) \left(2.01 \times 10^3 \frac{J}{kg \cdot ^\circ C} \right) (33.0^\circ C)$$

$$= 663 \text{ J}$$

For the steam condensing to water:

$$Q_2 = mL_v = (10.0 \times 10^{-3} \text{ kg}) \left(2.26 \times 10^6 \frac{J}{kg} \right)$$

$$= 2.26 \times 10^4 \text{ J}$$

For the cooling water:

$$\Delta T_w = 100.0°C - 53.0°C = 47.0°C$$

$$Q_3 = mc_{p,w}\Delta T = (10.0 \times 10^{-3} \text{ kg})\left(4.186 \times 10^3 \frac{\text{J}}{\text{kg} \cdot °C}\right)(47.0°C)$$

$$= 1.97 \times 10^3 \text{ J}$$

$$Q_{total} = Q_1 + Q_2 + Q_3 =$$
$$663 \text{ J} + (2.26 \times 10^4 \text{ J})$$
$$+ (1.97 \times 10^3 \text{ J}) = 2.52 \times 10^4 \text{ J}$$

$$\boxed{Q_{total} = 2.52 \times 10^4 \text{ J removed}}$$

CALCULATOR SOLUTION

Because of the significant figure rule for addition, the calculator answer, 25233, should be rounded to 2.52×10^4.

4. EVALUATE   Most of the energy is added to or removed from a substance during phase changes. In this example, about 90 percent of the energy removed from the steam is due to heat of vaporization.

Heat of phase change

1. How much energy is required to change a 42 g ice cube from ice at −11°C to steam at 111°C? (Hint: Refer to **Tables 10-4** and **10-6**.)

2. Liquid nitrogen, which has a boiling point of 77 K, is commonly used to cool substances to low temperatures. How much energy must be removed from 1.0 kg of gaseous nitrogen at 77 K for it to completely liquefy?

3. How much energy is needed to melt 0.225 kg of lead so that it can be used to make a lead sinker for fishing? The sample has an initial temperature of 27.3°C and is poured in the mold immediately after it has melted.

4. How much heat is needed to melt exactly 1000 aluminum cans, each with a mass of 14.0 g, for recycling? Assume an initial temperature of 26.4°C.

5. A 0.011 kg cube of ice at 0.0°C is added to 0.450 kg of soup at 80.0°C. Assuming that the soup has the same specific heat capacity as water, find the final temperature of the soup after the ice has melted. (Hint: There is a temperature change after the ice melts.)

6. At a foundry, 25 kg of molten aluminum with a temperature of 660.4°C is poured into a mold. If this is carried out in a room containing 130 kg of air at 25°C, what is the temperature of the air after the aluminum is completely solidified? Assume that the specific heat capacity of air is 1.0×10^3 J/kg·°C.

1. A jeweler working with a heated 47 g gold ring must lower the ring's temperature to make it safe to handle. If the ring is initially at 99°C, what mass of water at 25°C is needed to lower the ring's temperature to 38°C?

2. Using the concepts of latent heat and internal energy, explain why it is difficult to build a fire with damp wood.

3. Why does steam at 100°C cause more severe burns than does liquid water at 100°C?

4. From the heating curve for a 15 g sample, as shown in **Figure 10-17,** estimate the following properties of the substance.

   a. the specific heat capacity of the liquid
   b. the latent heat of fusion
   c. the specific heat capacity of the solid
   d. the specific heat capacity of the vapor
   e. the latent heat of vaporization

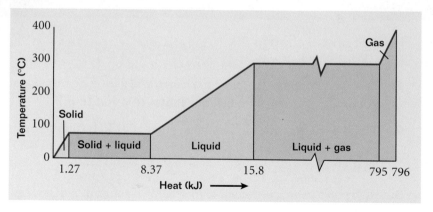

Figure 10-17

5. **Physics in Action**   How much energy must be added to a bowl of 125 popcorn kernels in order for them to reach a popping temperature of 175°C? Assume that their initial temperature is 21°C, that the specific heat capacity of popcorn is 1650 J/kg•°C, and that each kernel has a mass of 0.105 g.

6. **Physics in Action**   Because of the pressure inside a popcorn kernel, water does not vaporize at 100°C. Instead, it stays liquid until its temperature is about 175°C, at which point the kernel ruptures and the superheated water turns into steam. How much energy is needed to pop 95.0 g of corn if 14 percent of a kernel's mass consists of water? Assume that the latent heat of vaporization for water at 175°C is 0.90 times its value at 100°C and that the kernels have an initial temperature of 175°C.

THERMAL CONDUCTION

When you first place an iron skillet on a range burner or element, the metal handle feels comfortable to the touch. But after a few minutes the handle becomes too hot to touch without a cooking mitt. During that time, energy is transferred by heat from the high-temperature burner to the skillet. This type of energy transfer is called **thermal conduction.**

Thermal conduction can be understood by the behavior of atoms in a metal. Before the skillet is placed on the heating element, the skillet's iron atoms have an energy proportional to the temperature of the room. As the skillet is heated, the atoms nearest the heating element vibrate with greater energy. These vibrating atoms jostle their less-energetic neighbors and transfer some of their energy in the process. Gradually, iron atoms farther away from the element gain more energy.

The rate of thermal conduction depends on the properties of the substance being heated. A metal ice tray and a package of frozen food removed from the freezer are at the same temperature. However, the metal tray feels colder because metal conducts energy more easily and more rapidly than cardboard at the place where it comes into contact with your hand. In contrast, a piece of ceramic conducts energy very slowly, as may be seen in **Figure 10-18.** The end of the ceramic piece that is embedded in ice is barely affected by the energy of the flame surrounding the other end. Substances that rapidly transfer energy by heat are called *thermal conductors,* while those that slowly transfer energy by heat are called *thermal insulators.*

In general, metals are good thermal conductors. Materials such as asbestos, cork, ceramic, cardboard, and fiberglass are poor thermal conductors (and therefore good thermal insulators). Gases also are poor thermal conductors. The gas particles are so far apart with respect to their size that collisions between them are rare, and their kinetic energy is transferred slowly.

Although cooking oil is not any better as a thermal conductor than most nonmetals, it is useful for transferring energy uniformly around the surface of the food being cooked. When popping popcorn, for instance, coating the kernels with oil improves the energy transfer to each kernel, so that a higher percentage of them pop.

thermal conduction

the process by which energy is transferred by heat through a material between two points at different temperatures

Figure 10-18
Ceramics are poor thermal conductors, as indicated in this photograph.

Convection and radiation also transfer energy

There are two other mechanisms for transferring energy between places or objects at different temperatures. *Convection* involves the displacement of cold matter by hot matter, such as when hot air over a flame rises upward. This mechanism does not involve heat alone. Instead, it uses the combined effects of conduction and buoyancy. In the case of air over a flame, the air is heated through particle collisions (conduction), causing it to expand and its density to decrease. The warm air is then displaced by denser, colder air from above.

The other principal energy transfer mechanism is *electromagnetic radiation*, which includes visible light. Unlike convection, energy in this form does not involve the transfer of matter. Instead, objects reduce their internal energy by radiating electromagnetic radiation with particular wavelengths. This energy transfer often takes place from high temperature to low temperature, so that radiation is frequently associated with heat. The human body emits energy in the infrared portion of the electromagnetic spectrum.

CONCEPT PREVIEW

Electromagnetic radiation will be discussed in more detail in Chapter 14.

CLOTHING AND CLIMATE

To remain healthy, the human body must maintain a temperature close to 37.0°C (98.6°F). This becomes increasingly difficult as the surrounding air becomes hotter or colder than body temperature.

Without proper insulation, the body's temperature will drop in its attempt to reach thermal equilibrium with very cold surroundings. If this situation is not corrected in time, the body will enter a state of hypothermia, which lowers pulse, blood pressure, and respiration. Once the body temperature reaches 32.2°C (90.0°F), the person can lose consciousness. When the body temperature reaches 25.6°C (78.0°F), hypothermia is almost always fatal.

Insulating materials retain energy for cold climates

To prevent hypothermia, the transfer of energy from the human body to the surrounding air must be hindered. This is done by surrounding the body with heat-insulating material. An extremely effective and common thermal insulator is air. Like most gases, air is an extremely poor thermal conductor, so even a thin layer of air near the skin provides a barrier to energy transfer.

The Inupiat Eskimo people of northern Alaska have designed clothing to protect them from the severe Arctic climate, where average air temperatures range from 10°C (50°F) to −37°C (−35°F). The Inupiat clothing is made from animal skins that make use of air's insulating properties. Until recently, the traditional parka *(atigi)* was made from caribou skins. Two separate parkas are worn in layers, with the fur lining the inside of the inner parka and the outside of the outer parka. Insulation is provided mostly by air trapped between the short inner hairs and within the long, hollow hairs of the fur. Today, inner parkas are made from sheepskin (see **Figure 10-19**).

Figure 10-19
The Inupiat parka, called an *atigi*, consists today of a canvas shell over sheepskin. The wool provides layers of insulating air between the wearer and the cold.

Evaporation aids energy transfer in hot climates

At the other extreme, the Bedouins of the Arabian Desert have developed clothing that permits them to survive another of the harshest environments on Earth. Bedouin garments cover most of the body, thus protecting the wearer from direct sunlight and preventing excessive loss of body water from evaporation. These clothes are also designed to cool the wearer. The Bedouins must keep their body temperatures from becoming too high in desert temperatures, which often are in excess of 38°C (100°F). Heat exhaustion or heatstroke will result if the body's temperature becomes too high.

Although there are a number of differences among the types of clothing worn by different tribes and by men and women within tribes, a few basic garments are common to all Bedouins. One of these is the loose-fitting, elongated linen shirt called a *dish-dash* or *dish-dasha*, depending on whether it is worn by men or women, respectively. This shirt is worn close to the body, usually over an undergarment.

The loose fit and flared cut of the *dish-dash* permits air to flow over the wearer's skin. This causes any perspiration that has collected on the skin's surface to evaporate. During evaporation, water molecules enter the vapor phase. Because of the high specific heat capacity and latent heat of vaporization for water, evaporation removes a good deal of energy from the skin and air, thus causing the skin to cool.

Another common article of clothing is the *kefiyah*, a headcloth worn by Bedouin men, as shown in **Figure 10-20.** A similar garment made of two separate cloths, which are called a *mandil* and a *hatta*, is worn by Bedouin women. Firmly wrapped around the head of the wearer, the cloth absorbs perspiration and cools the wearer during evaporation. This same garment is also useful during cold periods in the desert. Wound snugly around the head, the garment traps air within its folds, thus providing an insulating layer to keep the head warm.

Figure 10-20
The Bedouin headcloth, called a *kefiyah,* employs evaporation to remove energy from the air close to the head, thus cooling the wearer.

Section Review

1. Why do fluffy down comforters provide more warmth than thin cloth blankets?

2. Explain how conduction causes the surface of a bridge to freeze sooner than the road surface on either side of the bridge.

3. If you place a heavy piece of canvas on top of a down sleeping bag, you will later feel colder than if you were to place the sleeping bag on top of the canvas. Explain why this happens. (Hint: A large amount of air is present in an uncrushed sleeping bag.)

CHAPTER 10
Summary

KEY IDEAS

Section 10-1 Temperature and thermal equilibrium
- Temperature can be changed by transferring energy to or from a substance.
- Thermal equilibrium is the condition in which the temperature of two objects in physical contact with each other is the same.

Section 10-2 Defining heat
- Energy transferred by heat always moves from objects at higher temperatures to objects at lower temperatures.
- Energy is conserved when mechanical energy and internal energy are taken into account.

Section 10-3 Changes in temperature and phase
- Specific heat capacity, which is a measure of the energy needed to change a substance's temperature, is described by the following formula:

$$c_p = \frac{Q}{m\Delta T}$$

- Latent heat, the energy required to change the phase of a substance, is described by the following formula:

$$L = \frac{Q}{m}$$

Section 10-4 Controlling heat
- Energy is transferred by thermal conduction through particle collisions.

Variable symbols

Quantities		Units	
T	temperature (Kelvin)	K	kelvins
T_C	temperature (Celsius)	°C	degrees Celsius
T_F	temperature (Fahrenheit)	°F	degrees Fahrenheit
ΔU	change in internal energy	J	joules
Q	heat	J	joules
c_p	specific heat capacity at constant pressure	$\dfrac{J}{kg \cdot °C}$	
L	latent heat	$\dfrac{J}{kg}$	

TEMPERATURE AND THERMAL EQUILIBRIUM

Review questions

1. What is the relationship between temperature and internal energy?

2. What property of two objects determines if the two are in a state of thermal equilibrium?

3. What are some physical properties that could be used in developing a temperature scale?

4. What property must a substance have in order to be used for calibrating a thermometer?

Conceptual questions

5. Which object in each of the following pairs has greater total internal energy, assuming that both objects in each pair are in thermal equilibrium? Explain your reasoning in each case.
   a. a metal knife in thermal equilibrium with a hot griddle
   b. a 1 kg block of ice at $-25°C$ or seven 12 g ice cubes at $-25°C$

6. Assume that each pair of objects in item 5 has the same internal energy instead of the same temperature. Which item in each pair will have the higher temperature?

7. Why are the steam and ice points of water better fixed points for a thermometer than the temperature of a human body?

8. How does the temperature of a tub of hot water as measured by a thermometer differ from the water's temperature before the measurement is made? What property of a thermometer is necessary for the difference between these two temperatures to be minimized?

Practice problems

9. The highest recorded temperature on Earth was $136°F$, at Azizia, Libya, in 1922. Express this temperature in degrees Celsius.
   (See Sample Problem 10A.)

10. Convert the following temperatures to degrees Fahrenheit and kelvins.
    a. the boiling point of liquid hydrogen ($-252.87°C$)
    b. the temperature of a room at $20.5°C$
    (See Sample Problem 10A.)

11. The melting point of gold is $1064°C$. Express this temperature in degrees Fahrenheit and kelvins.
    (See Sample Problem 10A.)

12. Show that the temperature $-40°$ is unique in that it has the same numerical value on the Celsius and Fahrenheit scales.
    (See Sample Problem 10A.)

13. At what Fahrenheit temperature are the Kelvin and Fahrenheit temperatures numerically equal?
    (See Sample Problem 10A.)

DEFINING HEAT

Review questions

14. Which drawing in **Figure 10-21** correctly shows the direction in which the net energy is transferred by heat between an ice cube and the freezer walls when the temperature of both is $-10°C$? Explain your answer.

(a)   (b)   (c)

Figure 10-21

15. A glass of water has a temperature of 8°C. In which situation will more energy be transferred by heat, when the air's temperature is 25°C or 35°C?

16. How much energy is transferred by heat between a piece of toast and an oven when both are at a temperature of 55°C? Explain.

Conceptual questions

17. If water in a sealed, insulated container is stirred, is its temperature likely to increase slightly, decrease slightly, or stay the same? Explain your answer.

18. Given your answer to item 17, why does stirring a hot cup of coffee cool it down?

19. Given any two bodies, the one with the higher temperature contains more heat. What is wrong with this statement?

20. Use the kinetic theory of atoms and molecules to explain why energy that is transferred by heat always goes from objects at higher temperatures to those at lower temperatures.

21. In which of the two situations described is more energy transferred by heat? Explain your answer.
   a. a cup of hot chocolate with a temperature of 40°C inside a freezer at −20°C
   b. the same cup of hot chocolate at 90°C in a room at 25°C

Practice problems

22. A 3.0 kg rock is initially at rest at the top of a cliff. Assuming the rock falls into the sea at the foot of the cliff and that its kinetic energy is transferred entirely to the water, how high is the cliff if the temperature of 1.0 kg of water is raised 0.10°C? (See Sample Problem 10B.)

23. A 0.75 kg spike is hammered into a railroad tie. The initial speed of the spike is equal to 3.0 m/s.
   a. If the tie and spike together absorb 85 percent of the spike's initial kinetic energy as internal energy, calculate the increase in internal energy of the tie and spike.
   b. What happens to the remaining energy?
   (See Sample Problem 10B.)

24. A force of 315 N is applied horizontally to a wooden crate in order to displace it 35.0 m across a level floor at a constant velocity. As a result of this work the crate's internal energy is increased by an amount equal to 14 percent of the crate's initial internal energy. Calculate the initial internal energy of the crate. (See Sample Problem 10B.)

CHANGES IN TEMPERATURE AND PHASE

Review questions

25. What data are required in order to determine the specific heat capacity of an unknown substance by means of calorimetry?

26. What principle permits calorimetry to be used to determine the specific heat capacity of a substance? Explain.

27. Why does the temperature of melting ice not change even though energy is being transferred by heat to the ice?

Conceptual questions

28. Why does the evaporation of water cool the air near the water's surface?

29. Ethyl alcohol has about one-half the specific heat capacity of water. If equal masses of alcohol and water in separate beakers at the same temperature are supplied by heat with the same amount of energy, which will have the higher final temperature?

30. Until refrigerators were invented, many people stored fruits and vegetables in underground cellars. Why was this more effective than keeping them in the open air?

31. During the winter, the people mentioned in item 30 would often place an open barrel of water in the cellar alongside their produce. Explain why this was done and why it would be effective.

32. During a cold spell, Florida orange growers often spray a mist of water over their trees during the night. What does this accomplish?

33. From the heating curve for a 23 g sample (see **Figure 10-22**), estimate the following properties of the substance.

    a. the specific heat capacity of the liquid
    b. the latent heat of fusion
    c. the specific heat capacity of the solid
    d. the specific heat capacity of the vapor
    e. the latent heat of vaporization

Figure 10-22

Practice problems

34. A 25.5 g ring that appears to be silver is heated to a temperature of 84.0°C, and then placed in a calorimeter containing 5.00×10^{-2} kg of water at 24.0°C. The calorimeter is not perfectly insulated, however, so that 0.14 kJ of energy is transferred by heat to the surroundings by the time a temperature of 25.0°C is reached. From the information provided, can you determine the specific heat capacity of the ring? Is the ring truly made of silver? (Refer to **Table 10-4.**)
(See Sample Problem 10C.)

35. When a driver brakes an automobile, friction between the brake disks and the brake pads converts part of the car's translational kinetic energy to internal energy. If a 1500 kg automobile traveling at 32 m/s comes to a halt after its brakes are applied, how much can the temperature rise in each of the four 3.5 kg steel brake disks? Assume the disks are made of iron ($c_p = 448$ J/kg•°C) and that all of the kinetic energy is distributed in equal parts to the internal energy of the brakes.
(See Sample Problem 10C.)

36. A 75 kg cross-country skier moves across snow. The coefficient of kinetic friction between the skis and the snow is 0.20. Assume that all the snow beneath the skis is at 0°C. If all of the energy is absorbed by the snow, how far would the skier have to travel in order to melt 1.0 kg of snow?
(See Sample Problem 10D.)

37. A plastic-foam container used as a picnic cooler contains a block of ice at 0.0°C. If 225 g of ice melts in 1.0 h, how much energy passes per second through the wall of the container?
(See Sample Problem 10D.)

THERMAL CONDUCTION AND INSULATION

Review questions

38. How does a metal rod conduct energy from one end, which has been placed in a fire, to the other end, which is at room temperature?

39. How does air within winter clothing keep you warm on cold winter days?

Conceptual questions

40. A metal spoon is placed in one of two identical cups of hot coffee. Which cup will be cooler after a few minutes?

41. A tile floor may feel uncomfortably cold to your bare feet, but a carpeted floor in an adjoining room at the same temperature feels warm. Why?

42. Why is it recommended that several items of clothing be worn in layers on cold days?

43. Why does a fan make you feel cooler on a hot day?

44. A paper cup is filled with water and then placed over an open flame, as shown in **Figure 10-23.** Explain why the cup does not catch fire and burn.

Figure 10-23

MIXED REVIEW PROBLEMS

45. Absolute zero on the Rankine temperature scale is $T_R = 0°R$, and the scale's unit is the same size as the Fahrenheit degree.

    a. Write a formula that relates the Rankine scale to the Fahrenheit scale.

    b. Write a formula that relates the Rankine scale to the Kelvin scale.

46. The freezing and boiling points of water on the imaginary "Too Hot" temperature scale are selected to be exactly 50 and 200 degrees TH.

    a. Derive an equation relating the Too Hot scale to the Celsius scale. (Hint: Make a graph of one temperature scale versus the other, and solve for the equation of the line.)

    b. Calculate absolute zero in degrees TH.

Technology & Learning

Graphing calculators

Program your graphing calculator to create a heating curve to determine the temperature of a 0.050 kg piece of aluminum foil (specific heat capacity equals 899 J/kg•°C) originally at 25°C that absorbs the following amounts of energy by heat:

    a. 75 J

    b. 225 J

    c. 475 J

    d. 825 J

Press Y= and CLEAR to clear any functions.

Open a new program by pressing PRGM ▶ ▶ ENTER. Name the program "HEAT" and press ENTER. Then enter the following program:

To exit the program editor, press 2nd QUIT. To run the program, press PRGM, select "HEAT," and press ENTER ENTER. Enter the value for the initial temperature, the mass, and the specific heat capacity, pressing ENTER after each one.

The calculator will provide a graph of the temperature versus the energy absorbed. (If the graph is not visible, press WINDOW and change the settings for the graph window so that Xmin is the lowest energy value required and Xmax is the highest value required, then press GRAPH.)

Press TRACE, and use the arrow keys to trace along the curve. The x value corresponds to the absorbed energy, and the y value corresponds to the temperature.

Keystrokes	Display
	PROGRAM: HEAT
1. PRGM ▶ 2 ALPHA T ENTER	:PROMPT T
2. PRGM ▶ 2 ALPHA M ENTER	:PROMPT M
3. PRGM ▶ 2 ALPHA C ENTER	:PROMPT C
4. ALPHA " ALPHA T + (X,T,θ ÷ (ALPHA M × ALPHA C)) ALPHA " STO▶ 2nd Y-VARS 1 1 ENTER	:"T+(X/(M∗C))" → Y₁
5. PRGM ▶ 4 ENTER	:DISPGRAPH

47. A hot-water heater is operated by solar power. If the solar collector has an area of 6.0 m² and the power delivered by sunlight is 550 W/m², how long will it take to increase the temperature of 1.0 m³ of water from 21°C to 61°C?

48. A student drops two metallic objects into a 120 g steel container holding 150 g of water at 25°C. One object is a 253 g cube of copper that is initially at 85°C, and the other is a chunk of aluminum that is initially at 5°C. To the surprise of the student, the water reaches a final temperature of 25°C, its initial temperature. What is the mass of the aluminum chunk?

49. A 250 g aluminum cup holds and is in thermal equilibrium with 850 g of water at 83°C. The combination of cup and water is cooled uniformly so that the temperature decreases by 1.5°C per minute. At what rate is energy being removed by heat?

50. A jar of tea is placed in sunlight until it reaches an equilibrium temperature of 32°C. In an attempt to cool the liquid, which has a mass of 180 g, 112 g of ice at 0.0°C is added. At the time at which the temperature of the tea is 15°C, determine the mass of the remaining ice in the jar. Assume the specific heat capacity of the tea to be that of pure liquid water.

Alternative Assessment

Performance assessment

1. According to legend, Archimedes determined whether the king's crown was pure gold by comparing its water displacement with the displacement of a piece of pure gold of equal mass. But this procedure is difficult to apply to very small objects. Design a method for determining whether a ring is pure gold using the concept of specific heat capacity. Present your plan to the class, and ask others to suggest improvements to your design. Discuss each suggestion's advantages and disadvantages.

2. The host of a cooking show on television claims that you can greatly reduce the baking time for potatoes by inserting a nail through each potato. Explain whether this advice has a scientific basis. Would this approach be more efficient than wrapping the potatoes in aluminum foil? Discuss and list all arguments.

3. The graph of decreasing temperature versus time of a hot object is called its cooling curve. Design and perform an experiment to determine the cooling curve of water in containers of various materials and shapes. Draw cooling curves for each one. Which trends represent good insulation? Use your findings and graphs to design a lunch box that keeps food warm or cold.

Portfolio projects

4. Research the life and work of James Prescott Joule, who is best known for his apparatus demonstrating the equivalence of work and heat and the conservation of energy. Many scientists of the day initially did not accept Joule's conclusions. Research the reasoning behind their objections. Prepare a presentation for a class discussion either supporting the objections of Joule's critics or defending Joule's conclusion before England's Royal Academy of Sciences.

5. Get information on solar water heaters available where you live. How does each type work? Compare prices and operating expenses for solar water heaters versus gas water heaters. What are some of the other advantages and limitations of solar water heaters? Prepare an informative brochure for homeowners interested in this technology.

6. Research how scientists measure the temperature of the following: the sun, a flame, a volcano, outer space, liquid hydrogen, mice, and insects. Find out what instruments are used in each case and how they are calibrated to known temperatures. Using what you learn, prepare a chart or other presentation on the tools used to measure temperature and the limitations on their ranges.

CHAPTER 10
Laboratory Exercise

MATERIALS LIST

✔ 2 beakers
✔ samples of various metals
✔ hot plate
✔ metal calorimeter and stirring rod
✔ ice
✔ balance
✔ metal heating vessel with metal heating dipper
✔ small plastic dish

PROCEDURE

CBL AND SENSORS
✔ CBL
✔ graphing calculator with link cable
✔ 2 temperature probes

THERMOMETER
✔ hand-held magnifying lens
✔ 2 thermometers

SPECIFIC HEAT CAPACITY

In this experiment, you will use calorimetry to identify various metals. In each trial, you will heat a sample of metal by placing it above a bath of water and bringing the water to a boil. When the sample is heated, you will place it in a calorimeter containing cold water. The water in the calorimeter will be warmed by the metal as the metal cools. According to the principle of energy conservation, the total amount of energy transferred by heat out of the metal sample as it cools equals the energy transferred by heat into the water and calorimeter as they are warmed. In this lab, you will use your measurements to determine the specific heat capacity and identity of each metal.

SAFETY

- When using a burner or hot plate, always wear goggles and an apron to protect your eyes and clothing. Tie back long hair, secure loose clothing, and remove loose jewelry. If your clothing catches on fire, walk to the emergency lab shower and use the shower to put out the fire.
- Never leave a hot plate unattended while it is turned on.
- If a thermometer breaks, notify the teacher immediately.
- Do not heat glassware that is broken, chipped, or cracked. Use tongs or a mitt to handle heated glassware and other equipment because it does not always look hot when it is hot. Allow all equipment to cool before storing it.
- Never put broken glass or ceramics in a regular waste container. Use a dustpan, brush, and heavy gloves to carefully pick up broken pieces and dispose of them in a container specifically provided for this purpose.

PREPARATION

1. Determine whether you will be using the CBL and sensors procedure or the thermometers. Read the entire lab for the appropriate procedure, and plan what steps you will take. Plan efficiently. Make sure you know which steps can be performed while you are waiting for the water to heat.

2. Prepare a data table with four columns and eight rows in your lab notebook. In the first row, label the second through fourth columns *Trial 1, Trial 2,* and *Trial 3.* In the first column, label the second through eighth rows *Sample number, Mass of metal, Mass of calorimeter cup and stirrer, Mass of water, Initial temperature of metal, Initial temperature of water and calorimeter,* and *Final temperature of metal, water, and calorimeter.*

3. In Appendix D look up the specific heat capacity of the material the calorimeter is made of and record the information in the top left corner of your data table.

Thermometer procedure begins on page 395.

PROCEDURE

CBL AND SENSORS

Finding the specific heat capacity of a metal

4. Choose a location where you can set up the experiment away from the edge of the table and away from other groups. Make sure the hot plate is in the "off" position before you plug it in.

5. Fill a metal heating vessel with 200 mL of water and place it on the hot plate. Turn on the hot plate and adjust the heating controls to heat the water.

6. Set up the temperature probe, CBL, and graphing calculator as shown in **Figure 10-24.** Connect the CBL to the graphing calculator with the unit-to-unit link cable using the I/O ports located on each unit. Connect the first temperature probe to the CH1 port. Connect the second temperature probe to the CH2 port. Turn on the CBL and the graphing calculator. Start the program PHYSICS on the graphing calculator.

a. Select option *SET UP PROBES* from the MAIN MENU. Enter 2 for the number of probes. Select the temperature probe from the list. Enter 1 for the channel number. Select the temperature probe from the list again, and enter 2 for the channel number.

b. Select the *COLLECT DATA* option from the MAIN MENU. Select the *TRIGGER* option from the DATA COLLECTION menu.

7. Obtain about 100 g of the metal sample. First find the mass of the small plastic dish. Place the metal shot in the dish and determine the mass of the shot. Record the number and the mass of the sample in your data table. Place one temperature probe in the metal heating dipper, and carefully pour the sample into the metal heating dipper. Make sure the temperature probe is surrounded by the metal sample.

Figure 10-24

Step 5: Start heating the water before you set up the CBL and temperature probes. Never leave a hot plate unattended when it is turned on.

Step 7: Be very careful when pouring the metal sample in the dipper around the temperature probe.

Step 17: Begin taking temperature readings a few seconds before adding the sample to the calorimeter.

Step 19: Record the *highest* temperature reached by the water, sample, and calorimeter combination, not the final temperature.

8. Place the dipper with metal contents into the top of the heating vessel, as shown in **Figure 10-24.** Make sure the temperature probe leads do not touch the hot plate or any heated surface.

9. While the sample is heating, find the mass of the empty inner cup of the calorimeter and the stirring rod. Record the mass in your data table. Do not leave the hot plate unattended.

10. For the water in the calorimeter, you will need about 100 g of water that is a little colder than room temperature. Put the water in a beaker. Use the second CBL temperature probe to find room temperature. Look at the temperatures on the CBL and read the temperature reading for the second probe. Place the second sensor in the water to check the water's temperature. (Do not use water colder than 5°C below room temperature. You may need to use ice to get the initial temperature low enough, but make sure all the ice has melted before pouring the water into the calorimeter.)

11. Place the calorimeter and stirrer on the balance and carefully add 100 g of the water. Record the mass of the water in your data table. Replace the cup in its insulating shell, and cover.

12. When the CBL displays a constant temperature for several readings, press TRIGGER on the CBL to collect the temperature reading of the metal sample. Record the temperature reading in your data table as the metal's initial temperature. Select *CONTINUE* from the TRIGGER menu on the graphing calculator.

13. Carefully remove the first temperature probe from the dipper. Set the probe aside to cool.

14. Use the stirring rod to stir the water in the calorimeter. Place the second temperature probe in the calorimeter. When the CBL displays a constant temperature for several readings for the calorimeter water, press TRIGGER on the CBL to collect the temperature readings. Record the initial temperature of the water and calorimeter. Select *STOP* from the TRIGGER menu on the graphing calculator. Leave the probe in the calorimeter.

15. Select *COLLECT DATA* from the MAIN MENU on the graphing calculator. Select the *TIME GRAPH* option from the DATA COLLECTION menu. Enter 2.0 for the time between samples. Enter 99 for the number of samples. Check the values you entered, and then press ENTER. Press ENTER to continue. If you made a mistake entering the time values, select *MODIFY SETUP,* reenter the values, and continue.

16. From the TIME GRAPH menu, select *LIVE DISPLAY.* Enter 0 for *Ymin,* enter 100 for *Ymax,* and enter 5 for *Yscl.*

17. Press ENTER on the graphing calculator to begin collecting the temperature readings for the water in the calorimeter.

18. Quickly transfer the metal sample to the calorimeter of cold water and replace the cover. Use a mitt when handling the metal heating dipper. Use the stirring rod to gently agitate the sample and to stir the water in the calorimeter. If you are not doing any more trials, make sure the hot plate is turned off. Otherwise, make sure there is plenty of water in the heating vessel, and do not leave the hot plate unattended.

19. When the CBL displays DONE, use the arrow keys to trace the graph. Time in seconds is graphed on the *x*-axis, and the temperature readings are graphed on the *y*-axis. Record the highest temperature reading from the CBL in your data table.

20. Press ENTER on the graphing calculator. On the REPEAT? menu, select *NO.* If you are going to perform another trial, select the *COLLECT DATA* option from the MAIN MENU. Select *TRIGGER* from the DATA COLLECTION menu.

21. If time permits, make additional trials with other samples. Record data for all trials in your data table.

Analysis and Interpretation begins on page 396.

PROCEDURE

THERMOMETER

Finding the specific heat capacity of a metal

4. Choose a location where you can set up the experiment away from the edge of the table and from other groups. Make sure the hot plate is in the "off" position before you plug it in.

5. Fill a metal heating vessel with 200 mL of water and place it on the hot plate, as shown in **Figure 10-25.** Turn on the hot plate and adjust the heating control to heat the water.

6. Measure out about 100 g of the metal sample. Record the number of the metal sample in your data table. Hold the thermometer in the metal heating dipper, and very carefully pour the sample into the metal heating dipper. Make sure the bulb of the thermometer is surrounded by the metal. Place the dipper with metal contents into the heating vessel. Hold the thermometer while the sample is heating.

7. While the sample is heating, determine the mass of the stirring rod and empty inner cup of the calorimeter. Record the mass in your data table. Do not leave the hot plate unattended.

8. Use the second thermometer to measure room temperature. For the water in the calorimeter, you will need about 100 g of water that is a little colder than room temperature. Put the water in a beaker. Place the thermometer in the water to check the temperature of the water. (Do not use water colder than 5°C below room temperature. You may need to use ice to get the initial temperature low enough, but make sure all the ice has melted before pouring the water into the calorimeter.)

9. Place the calorimeter and stirrer on the balance, and carefully add 100 g of the water. Record the mass of the water in your data table. Replace the cup in its insulating shell, and cover.

10. Use the thermometer to measure the temperature of the sample when the water is boiling and the sample reaches a constant temperature. Record this temperature as the initial temperature of the metal sample. (Note: When making temperature readings, take care not to touch the hot plate and the water.) Use the hand-held magnifying lens to estimate to the nearest 0.5°C. Make sure that the

Figure 10-25

Step 5: Start heating the water before you begin the rest of the lab. Never leave a hot plate unattended when it is turned on.

Step 6: Be very careful when pouring the metal sample in the dipper around the thermometer. Make sure the thermometer bulb is surrounded by the metal sample.

Step 12: Begin taking temperature readings a few seconds before adding the sample to the calorimeter.

Step 15: Record the *highest* temperature reached by the water, sample, and calorimeter combination.

thermometer bulb is completely surrounded by the metal sample, and keep your line of sight at a right angle to the stem of the thermometer. Reading the thermometer at an angle will cause considerable errors in your measurements. Carefully remove the thermometer and set it aside in a secure place.

11. Use the stirring rod to gently stir the water in the calorimeter. **Do not use the thermometer to stir the water.**

12. Place the second thermometer in the covered calorimeter. Measure the temperature of the water in the calorimeter to the nearest 0.1°C. Record this temperature in your data table as the initial temperature of the water and calorimeter.

13. Quickly transfer the sample to the cold water in the calorimeter and replace the cover. Use a mitt when handling the metal heating dipper. If you are not doing any more trials, make sure the hot plate is turned off. Otherwise, make sure there is plenty of water in the heating vessel, and do not leave the hot plate unattended.

14. Use the stirring rod to gently agitate the sample and stir the water in the calorimeter. **Do not use the thermometer to stir the water.**

15. Take readings every 5.0 s until five consecutive readings are the same. Record the highest reading in your data table.

16. If time permits, make additional trials with other metals. Record the data for all trials in your data table.

ANALYSIS AND INTERPRETATION

Calculations and data analysis

1. **Organizing data**   For each trial, calculate the temperature change of the water and calorimeter.

2. **Analyzing data**   Use your data for each trial.

   a. Calculate the energy transferred to the calorimeter cup and stirring rod by heat, using the value for the specific heat capacity you found in step 3.

   b. Calculate the energy transferred to the water by heat.

3. **Applying ideas**   Calculate the total energy transferred by heat into the water and the calorimeter.

4. **Analyzing results**   For each trial, find the temperature change of the sample and calculate the specific heat capacity of the sample.

Conclusions

5. **Evaluating data**   Use the accepted values for the specific heat capacities of various metals in **Table 10-4** on page 372, to determine what metal each sample is made of.

6. Evaluating results Calculate the absolute and relative errors of the experimental values. Check with your teacher to see if you have correctly identified the metals.

    a. Use the following equation to compute the absolute error:

$$\text{absolute error} = |\text{experimental} - \text{accepted}|$$

    b. Use the following equation to compute the relative error:

$$\text{relative error} = \frac{(\text{experimental} - \text{accepted})}{\text{accepted}}$$

7. Evaluating methods Explain why the energy transferred by heat into the calorimeter and the water is equal to the energy transferred by heat from the metal sample.

8. Evaluating methods Explain why it is important to calculate the temperature change using the highest temperature as the final temperature, rather than the last temperature recorded.

9. Evaluating methods Why should the water be a few degrees colder than room temperature when the initial temperature is taken?

10. Applying conclusions How would your results be affected if the initial temperature of the water in the calorimeter were 50°C instead of slightly cooler than room temperature?

11. Relating ideas How is the temperature change of the calorimeter and the water within the calorimeter affected by the specific heat capacity of the metal? Did a metal with a high specific heat capacity raise the temperature of the water and the calorimeter more or less than a metal with a low specific heat capacity?

12. Building models An environmentally conscious engineering team wants to design tea kettles out of a metal that will allow the water to reach its boiling point using the least possible amount of energy from a range or other heating source. Using the values for specific heat capacity in **Table 10-4** on page 372, choose a material that would work well, considering only the implications of transfer of energy by heat. Explain how the specific heat capacity of water will affect the operation of the tea kettle.

Extensions

13. Evaluating methods What is the purpose of the outer shell of the calorimeter and the insulating ring in this experiment?

14. Designing experiments If there is time and your teacher approves, design an experiment to measure the specific heat capacity of the calorimeter. Compare this measured value with the accepted value from **Table 10-4** on page 372. Are they the same? If not, how would using the experimental value affect your results in this lab?

Climatic Warming

Scientists typically devise solutions to problems and then test the solution to determine if it indeed solves the problem. But sometimes the problem is only suggested by the evidence, and there are no chances to test the solutions. A current example of such a problem is climatic warming.

Data recorded from various locations around the world over the past century indicate that the average atmospheric temperature is 0.5°C higher now than it was 100 years ago. Although this sounds like a small amount, such an increase can have pronounced effects. Increased temperatures may eventually cause the ice in polar regions to melt, causing ocean levels to increase, which in turn may flood some coastal areas.

Small changes in temperature can also affect living organisms. Most trees can tolerate only about a 1°C increase in average temperature. If a tree does not reproduce often or easily enough to "migrate" through successive generations to a cooler location, it can become extinct in that region. Any organisms dependent on that type of tree also will suffer.

But such disasters depend on whether global temperatures continue to increase. Historical studies indicate that some short-term fluctuations in climate are natural, like the "little ice age" of the seventeenth century. If the current warming trend is part of a natural cycle, the dire predictions may be overstated or wrong.

Even if the warming is continuous, climatic systems are very complex, and involve many unexpected factors. For example, if polar ice melts, a sudden increase in humidity may result in snow in polar areas. This could counter the melting, thus causing ocean levels to remain stable.

Greenhouse Gases

Most of the current attention and concern about climatic warming has been focused on the increase in the amount of "greenhouse gases," primarily carbon dioxide and methane, in the atmosphere. Molecules of these gases absorb incoming solar infrared radiation and reradiate it in random directions, causing the radiation to be trapped and to warm the atmosphere, similar to the way the glass panes of a greenhouse trap heat and warm the air within.

While carbon dioxide and methane are natural components of the air, their levels have increased rapidly during the last hundred years. This has been determined by analyzing air trapped in the ice layers of Greenland. Deeper sections of the ice contain air from earlier times. During the last ice age, there were about 185 ppm of carbon dioxide, CO_2, in the air, but the concentration from 130 years ago was slightly below 300 ppm. Today, the levels are 350 ppm, an increase that can be accounted for by the increase in combustion reactions, primarily from coal and petroleum burning, and by the decrease in CO_2-consuming trees through deforestation.

But does the well-documented increase in greenhouse gas concentrations enable detailed predictions? Atmospheric physicists have greatly improved their models in recent years, and they are able to correctly predict past ice ages and account for the heat-absorbing qualities of oceans. But such models remain oversimplified, partly because of a lack of detailed long-term data. In addition, the impact of many variables, such as fluctuations in solar energy output and volcanic processes, are poorly understood and cannot be factored into predictions. To take all factors into account would require more-complex models and more-sophisticated supercomputers than are currently available. As a result, many question whether meaningful decisions and planning can occur.

Risk of Action and Inaction

The evidence for climatic warming is suggestive but not conclusive. What should be done? Basically, there are two choices: either do something or do nothing.

The risks of doing nothing are that the situation may worsen. But it is also possible that waiting for better evidence will allow for a greater consensus among the world's nations about how to solve the problem efficiently. Convincing the world's population that action taken now will have the desired benefit decades from now will not be easy.

Acting now also involves risks. Gas and coal could be rationed or taxed to limit consumption. The development of existing energy-efficient technologies, such as low-power electric lights and more efficient motors and engines, could cut use of coal and gasoline in half. However, the economic effects could be as severe as those resulting from climatic warming.

But none of these options can guarantee results. Even if the trend toward climatic warming stops, it will be hard to prove whether this was due to human reduction in greenhouse gases, to natural cyclic patterns, or to other causes.

This map shows the reflecting properties of the Earth's surface. Regions colored in blue or green absorb much of the energy striking them.

 Researching the Issue

1. Carbon dioxide levels in the atmosphere have varied during Earth's history. Research the roles of volcanoes, plants, and limestone formation, and determine whether these processes have any bearing on the current increase in CO_2 concentrations. Can you think of any practical means of using these processes to reduce CO_2 concentrations? What would be the advantages and disadvantages?

2. Find out what technological developments have been suggested for slowing climatic warming. Can they be easily implemented? What are the drawbacks of these methods?

3. Models have shown that clouds play a large role in determining how warm or cool the atmosphere is. Research how models predict temperature changes based on the types of clouds and rainfall in an area. Note where cloud cover is greatest and smallest on Earth. How do clouds contribute to both cooling and warming?

CHAPTER 11

Thermodynamics

PHYSICS IN ACTION

This balloon, which is used to lift scientific instruments into the upper atmosphere, is an example of a simple thermodynamic system. Whenever there is a temperature or pressure difference between the gas inside the balloon and the outside air, energy is transferred between the gas and air by either heat or work done on or by the gas. In either case, the internal energy of the balloon's gas changes.

In this chapter, you will study how work and heat serve to change a system's internal energy and how machine efficiency is thermodynamically limited.

- *Why must a heat engine operate between two temperatures?*

- *Why does a refrigerator expend more energy than is needed to freeze water?*

CONCEPT REVIEW

Work (Section 5-1)

Internal energy (Section 10-1)

Heat (Section 10–2)

Conservation of energy (Section 10-2)

11-1
Relationships between heat and work

11-1 SECTION OBJECTIVES

- **Recognize that a system can absorb or give up energy by heat in order for work to be done on or by the system, and that work done on or by a system can result in energy transfer by heat.**

- **Compute the amount of work done during a thermodynamic process.**

- **Distinguish between isovolumetric, isothermal, and adiabatic thermodynamic processes.**

HEAT, WORK, AND INTERNAL ENERGY

Recall from Chapter 10 how pulling a nail from a piece of wood (as shown in **Figure 11-1**) causes the temperature of the nail to increase. The work done to overcome friction between the nail and the wood fibers transfers energy to the iron atoms in the nail and the molecules in the wood. This increase in the kinetic energy of these particles accounts for the increase in the internal energies of the nail and wood along their surface of contact.

As long as a substance does not change phase, its internal energy is proportional to its temperature. The increase in internal energy of the nail's surface corresponds to an increase in the surface temperature, which is higher than the temperature of the nail's interior. As a result, energy is transferred from the surface to the interior of the nail by heat. When all portions of the nail reach thermal equilibrium, energy transfer by heat ceases.

The removal of the nail from the wood is an example of heating by changing internal energy through work. The amount of energy transferred by heat is proportional to the change in the internal energy, which is proportional to the work done pulling the nail out of the wood. The thermal-equilibrium temperature is greater than the initial temperatures of either the wood or the nail, indicating that the internal energy of both increased as a result of the work done on them.

Note that this description requires a more complete definition of energy than the one found in Chapter 5. The mechanical energy added to the nail and wood by work does not appear to be conserved. The conservation of mechanical energy discussed in Chapter 5 did not take into consideration changes in the internal energy or energy transferred by heat (as discussed in Chapter 10). In some cases, the principle of energy conservation can be more useful if its scope is broadened to include internal energy and heat.

Figure 11-1
Work increases the nail's internal energy at the nail's surface. This energy is transferred away from the nail's surface by heat.

Heat can be used to do work

Work can transfer energy to a substance, increasing the internal energy of the substance. This internal energy can then decrease through energy transfer by heat. The reverse is also possible. Energy can be transferred to a substance by heat and from the substance by work.

Consider a flask of water. A balloon is placed over the mouth of the flask, and the flask is heated until the water boils. Energy transferred by heat from the flame of the gas burner to the water increases the internal energy of the water. When the water's temperature reaches the boiling point, the water changes phase and becomes steam. At this constant temperature, the volume of the steam increases. The expansion of the steam provides a force that pushes the balloon outward against the force exerted by the atmosphere, as shown in **Figure 11-2.** Thus, the steam does work on the balloon, and the steam's internal energy decreases as a result of the principle of energy conservation.

Figure 11-2
Energy transferred by heat turns water into steam. Energy from the steam does work against the force exerted by air outside the balloon.

Heat and work are transfers of energy to or from a system

On a microscopic scale, heat and work are very similar. Neither are properties of a substance; rather, they are ways by which energy can be transferred to or from a substance, thus changing the substance's internal energy. This change in internal energy is apparent by the change in the substance's temperature or phase.

So far, the internal energy of a substance or combination of substances has been treated as a single quantity to which energy is added or taken away. Such a substance or combination of substances is called a **system.** All of a system's parts are in thermal equilibrium with each other before and after a process adds or removes energy.

An example of a system would be the flask, balloon, water, and steam that was heated over the burner. As the burner transferred energy by heat to the system, that system's internal energy increased. When the expanding steam, a part of the system, did work on the balloon, the system's internal energy decreased. Some of the energy transferred to the system by heat was transferred out of the system by work done on the balloon.

Although a system is often treated as being isolated, in most cases it interacts with its surroundings. In the example above, a heat interaction occurs between the burner and the system, and work is done by the system on the surroundings (the balloon pushes on the outside air). Energy is also transferred by heat to the air surrounding the flask because of the temperature difference between the flask and the surrounding air. The surroundings with which the system interacts are referred to as its **environment.**

system

a collection of matter within a clearly defined boundary across which no matter passes

environment

everything outside a system that can affect or be affected by the system's behavior

Work done on or by a system is the pressure multiplied by the change in the volume of a gas

As defined in Chapter 5, work is the product of a force applied to an object and the distance moved by that object in the direction of the force. In thermodynamic systems, the simplest description of work is that work is the product of the change in the volume of a gas and the pressure applied on or by the gas. This chapter will use only this description of work. The expression in Chapter 5 can be derived from the equation for work using the definition for pressure (force divided by area) and the definition for the change of volume (area multiplied by the displacement).

Figure 11-3
Work done on or by the gas is the product of the volume change (area A multiplied by the displacement d) and the pressure of the gas.

DEFINING WORK IN TERMS OF CHANGING VOLUME

$$W = Fd$$

work = force × distance moved

$$W = Fd\left(\frac{A}{A}\right) = \left(\frac{F}{A}\right)(Ad) = P\Delta V$$

work = pressure × volume change

Because P is constant, work can be written as $P\Delta V$ rather than as $\Delta(PV)$. If the gas expands, as shown in **Figure 11-3,** d and ΔV are positive quantities. Thus, the work done *by* the gas on the piston is positive. If the gas is compressed, d and ΔV are negative quantities. Thus, the work done *on* the gas by the piston is negative. When the gas volume remains constant, there is no displacement and no work is done on or by the system.

Although the pressure can change during a process, work is done only if the volume changes. A situation in which pressure increases and volume remains constant is comparable to one in which a force does not displace a mass even as the force is increased. Work is not done in either situation.

SAMPLE PROBLEM 11A

Work done on or by a gas

PROBLEM

An engine cylinder has a cross-sectional area of 0.010 m². How much work can be done by a gas in the cylinder if the gas exerts a constant pressure of 7.5×10^5 Pa on the piston, moving it a distance of 0.040 m?

SOLUTION

Given: $A = 0.010 \text{ m}^2$ $d = 0.040 \text{ m}$

$P = 7.5 \times 10^5 \text{ Pa} = 7.5 \times 10^5 \text{ N/m}^2$

Unknown: $\Delta V = ?$ $W = ?$

Use the area-times-distance formula for volume change. Use the definition of work in terms of changing volume on this page.

$$\Delta V = Ad$$

$$W = P\Delta V$$

$$\Delta V = (0.010 \text{ m}^2)(0.040 \text{ m}) = 4.0 \times 10^{-4} \text{ m}^3$$

$$W = (7.5 \times 10^5 \text{ N/m}^2)(4.0 \times 10^{-4} \text{ m}^3) = 3.0 \times 10^2 \text{ J}$$

$$\boxed{W \text{ done by the gas} = 3.0 \times 10^2 \text{ J}}$$

Work done on or by a gas

1. Gas in a container is at a pressure of 1.6×10^5 Pa and a volume of 4.0 m^3. What is the work done on or by the gas if
   a. it expands at constant pressure to twice its initial volume?
   b. it is compressed at constant pressure to one-quarter of its initial volume?

2. A gas is enclosed in a container fitted with a piston. The applied pressure is maintained at 599.5 kPa as the piston moves inward, changing the volume of the gas from 5.317×10^{-4} m^3 to 2.523×10^{-4} m^3. How much work is done? Is the work done *on* or *by* the gas? Explain your answer.

3. A toy balloon is inflated with helium at a constant pressure that is 4.3×10^5 Pa in excess of atmospheric pressure. If the balloon inflates from a volume of 1.8×10^{-4} m^3 to 9.5×10^{-4} m^3, how much work is done by the balloon on the surrounding air?

4. Steam moves into the cylinder of a steam engine at a constant pressure of 2.0×10^5 Pa. The diameter of the piston is 1.6 cm, and the piston travels 2.1 cm in one stroke. How much work is done on the piston?

THERMODYNAMIC PROCESSES

In this section three distinct quantities have been related to each other: internal energy (U), heat (Q), and work (W). However, they are not necessarily linked to each other. Work can be performed in some processes with a change in internal energy and with no energy transferred by heat. In other cases, internal energy can change as energy is transferred by heat without work being done. In reality, processes that involve only work or only heat are rare. In most processes, energy is transferred to or from the system by both heat and work. However, a real process can often be approximated and described by one of the ideal processes.

No work is done in a constant-volume process

Suppose a car with closed windows and doors is parked inside a hot garage. The internal energy of the system (inside the car) increases as energy is transferred by heat into the car from the hot air in the garage. The car's heavy steel walls and sealed windows keep the system's volume nearly constant. As a result, no work is done by the system. All changes in the system's internal energy are due to energy transfer by heat.

Insulated calorimeter with water

Thermometer

Bomb

Bomb lid with valve for introducing oxygen

Electrodes

Combustion crucible with reactants

Figure 11-4
The volume inside the bomb calorimeter is nearly constant, so most of the energy transfer to or from the calorimeter is by heat.

In general, when a gas undergoes a change in temperature but no change in volume, no work is done on or by the system. Such a process is called a constant-volume, or **isovolumetric,** process.

Another example of an isovolumetric process takes place inside a *bomb calorimeter,* shown in **Figure 11-4.** This device is a thick container in which a small quantity of a substance undergoes a combustion reaction. The energy released by the reaction increases the pressure and temperature of the gaseous reaction products. Because the container's walls are thick, there is no change in the volume of the gas. The energy can be transferred from the container only by heat. As in the case of the simple calorimeter discussed in Chapter 10, the increase in the temperature of water surrounding the bomb calorimeter provides information for calculating the total amount of energy produced by the reaction.

Internal energy is constant in a constant-temperature process

Although you may think of a toy balloon that has been inflated and sealed as a static system, it is subject to continuous thermodynamic effects. Consider what happens to such a balloon during an approaching storm. During the few hours before the storm arrives, the barometric pressure of the atmosphere steadily decreases by about 2000 Pa. If you are indoors and the temperature of the building is controlled, any change in outside temperature will not take place indoors. But because no building is perfectly sealed, changes in the pressure of the air outside also take place inside.

As the atmospheric pressure inside the building slowly decreases, the balloon expands, slowly doing work on the air outside the balloon. As this happens, energy is slowly transferred into the balloon by heat. The net result of these two processes is that the air inside the balloon is at the same temperature as the air outside the balloon. So the internal energy of the balloon's air does not change, and the energy transferred out of the balloon by work is matched by the energy transferred into the balloon by heat (see **Figure 11-5**).

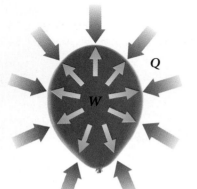

Q

W

Figure 11-5
An isothermal process can be approximated if energy is slowly removed from a system by work while an equivalent amount of energy is added by heat.

(a)

(b)

(c)

This procedure is a close approximation of an **isothermal process.** In an isothermal process, the system's temperature remains constant and internal energy does not change when energy is transferred to or from the system by heat or work.

You may wonder how energy can be transferred by heat from the air outside the balloon to the air inside when both gases are at the same constant temperature. After all, if no temperature difference exists, then energy cannot be transferred by heat. However, energy transfer by heat can occur in an isothermal process if it is assumed that the process takes place as a large number of very gradual, very small changes, as shown in **Figure 11-6.**

When the air inside the balloon expands, its internal energy and temperature decrease slightly. But as soon as that happens, energy is transferred by heat from the higher-temperature outside air to the air inside the balloon. This raises the temperature and internal energy of the air inside the balloon to their original values. Because the decrease and increase in the internal energy occur more rapidly than do the overall processes of transferring energy by work or heat, the internal energy of the balloon's air effectively remains constant.

Energy is not transferred by heat in an adiabatic process

When a tank of compressed gas is opened to fill a toy balloon, the process of inflation occurs rapidly, unlike the gradual inflation in the isothermal process previously described. The internal energy of the gas does not remain constant. Instead, as the pressure of the gas in the tank decreases, so does the gas's internal energy and temperature.

If the balloon and the tank are thermally insulated, no energy can be transferred from the expanding gas by heat because there is not enough time for this to occur. When energy is not transferred to or from a system by heat, the process is called **adiabatic.** The decrease in internal energy must therefore be

isothermal process

a thermodynamic process that takes place at constant temperature and in which the internal energy of a system remains unchanged

Did you know?

The absence of a change in the internal energy of an isothermal process is true only for systems in which there is no phase change. During a phase change, such as when water becomes steam, the temperature remains constant but internal energy increases.

adiabatic process

a thermodynamic process during which work is done on or by the system but no energy is transferred to or from the system by heat

Figure 11-7

As the gas inside the tank and balloon rapidly expands, its internal energy decreases. This energy leaves the system by means of work done against the outside air.

equal to the energy transferred from the gas by work. This work is done by the gas pushing against the inner wall of the balloon and overcoming the pressure exerted by the air outside the balloon. This causes the balloon to inflate, as shown in **Figure 11-7.**

Notice that this rapid inflation of the balloon in the present example is a process that is only approximately adiabatic. Some transfer of energy by heat actually does take place because neither the balloon nor the tank is perfectly insulated. The decrease in the internal energy and the temperature of the rapidly expanding gas accounts for the sudden drop in temperature of the outside surface of the tank when a compressed gas is being released. Once the adiabatic expansion is complete, the temperature of the gas gradually increases as energy from the outside air is transferred by heat into the tank.

The adiabatic expansion and compression of gases is found in many applications. As you will learn in the next section, both refrigerators and internal combustion engines require that gases be compressed or expanded rapidly. By assuming these processes to be adiabatic, predictions about how a machine will operate can be made.

Section Review

1. In which of the situations listed below is energy being transferred by heat to the system in order for the system to do work? In which is work being done on the system in order for energy to be transferred from the system by heat?

   a. Two sticks are rubbed together to start a fire.
   b. A firecracker explodes.
   c. A red-hot iron bar is set aside to cool.

2. Identify the following processes as isothermal, isovolumetric, or adiabatic:

   a. a tire being rapidly inflated
   b. a tire expanding gradually with heating
   c. a tire being heated while in a rigid metal container

3. A mixture of gasoline vapor and air is placed in an engine cylinder. The piston has an area of 7.4×10^{-3} m^2 and is displaced inward by 7.2×10^{-2} m. Assuming that 9.5×10^5 Pa of pressure is placed on the piston, how much work is done during this process? Is work being done on or by the gas mixture?

4. **Physics in Action**   A weather balloon slowly expands as energy is transferred by heat from the outside air. If the average net pressure is 1.5×10^3 Pa and the balloon's volume increases by 5.4×10^{-5} m^3, how much work is done by the expanding gas? What thermodynamic process does this resemble?

THE FIRST LAW OF THERMODYNAMICS

Imagine a roller coaster that operates without friction The car is raised against the force of gravity by work. Once the car is freely moving, it will have a certain kinetic energy (*KE*) and a certain potential energy (*PE*). The coaster will move slower (have a small *KE*) at the top of the rise (have a large *PE*) and faster (have a larger *KE*) at low points in the track (have a smaller *PE*). However, the mechanical energy, *KE* + *PE*, remains constant throughout the ride's duration.

If friction is taken into account, mechanical energy is not conserved, as shown in **Figure 11-8.** A steady decrease in the car's total mechanical energy occurs because of work being done against the friction between the car's axles and its bearings and between the car's wheels and the coaster track. Mechanical energy is transferred to the atoms and molecules throughout the entire roller coaster (both the car and the track). Thus, the roller coaster's internal energy increases by an amount equal to the decrease in the mechanical energy. Most of this energy is then gradually dissipated to the air surrounding the roller coaster by energy-transfer mechanisms, such as heat and sound. If the internal energy for the roller coaster (the system) and the energy dissipated to the surrounding air (the environment) are taken into account, then the total energy will be constant

11-2 SECTION OBJECTIVES

- **Illustrate how the first law of thermodynamics is a statement of energy conservation.**

- **Calculate heat, work, and the change in internal energy by applying the first law of thermodynamics.**

- **Apply the first law of thermodynamics to describe cyclic processes.**

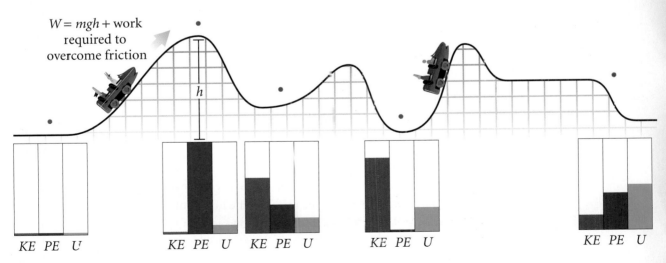

Figure 11-8
In the presence of friction, the internal energy (*U*) of the roller coaster increases as *KE* + *PE* decreases.

The principle of energy conservation that takes into account a system's internal energy as well as the transfer of energy to or from the system by work and heat is called the *first law of thermodynamics.*

Imagine that the isothermally expanding toy balloon in the previous section is squeezed rapidly. The process is no longer isothermal. Instead, it is a combination of two processes. On the one hand, work (W) is done on the system. The balloon and the air inside it (the system) are compressed, so that the air's internal energy and temperature increase. Work is being done on the system by the environment, so W is a negative quantity. This step, which is adiabatic, can be expressed mathematically as $\Delta U = -W$.

After the compression step, energy is transferred from the system by heat (Q). Some of the internal energy of the air inside the balloon is transferred to the air outside the balloon. During this step, the internal energy of the gas decreases, so ΔU has a negative value. Similarly, because energy is conveyed from the system, Q has a negative value. The change in internal energy for this step, which is isovolumetric, can be expressed as $-\Delta U = -Q$, or $\Delta U = Q$.

The signs for heat and work for a system are summarized in **Table 11-1.**

Did you know?

Not all ways of transferring energy can be classified simply by work or by heat. Other processes that can change the internal energy of a substance include changes in the chemical and magnetic properties of the substance.

Table 11-1	Signs of Q and W for a system	
$Q > 0$	energy added to system by heat	internal energy increases if $W = 0$
$Q < 0$	energy removed from system by heat	internal energy decreases if $W = 0$
$Q = 0$	no transfer of energy by heat	no internal energy change if $W = 0$
$W > 0$	work done by system (expansion of gas)	internal energy decreases if $Q = 0$
$W < 0$	work done on system (compression of gas)	internal energy increases if $Q = 0$
$W = 0$	no work done	no internal energy change if $Q = 0$

The first law of thermodynamics can be expressed mathematically

Throughout the entire process in which the balloon expands, energy is conserved. To describe the overall change in the system's internal energy, one must account for the transfer of energy to or from the system by heat and work. The total change in the internal energy is the difference between the final internal energy value (U_f) and the initial internal energy value (U_i). That is, $\Delta U = U_f - U_i$. Energy conservation requires that the total change in internal energy from its initial to its final equilibrium conditions be equal to the transfer of energy by both heat and work. This statement of total energy conservation is the first law of thermodynamics.

THE FIRST LAW OF THERMODYNAMICS

$$\Delta U = Q - W$$

Change in system's internal energy = energy transferred to or from system by heat − energy transferred to or from system by work

When using this equation, all quantities must have the same energy units. Throughout this chapter, the SI unit for energy, the joule, will be used.

According to the first law of thermodynamics, a system's internal energy can be changed by transferring energy by either work, heat, or a combination of the two. The thermodynamic processes discussed on pages 405–408 can therefore be expressed using the equation for the first law of thermodynamics, as shown in **Table 11-2.**

Table 11-2	First law of thermodynamics for special processes		
Process	**Conditions**	**First law of thermodynamics**	**Interpretation**
Isovolumetric	no work done	$\Delta V = 0$, so $P\Delta V = 0$ and $W = 0$; therefore $\Delta U = Q$	Energy added to the system by heat ($Q > 0$) increases the system's internal energy.
			Energy removed from the system by heat ($Q < 0$) decreases the system's internal energy.
Isothermal	no change in temperature and internal energy	$\Delta T = 0$, so $\Delta U = 0$; therefore, $\Delta U = Q - W = 0$, or $Q = W$	Energy added to the system by heat is removed from the system as work done by the system.
			Energy added to the system by work done on it is removed from the system by heat.
Adiabatic	no energy transferred by heat	$Q = 0$, so $\Delta U = -W$	Work done on the system ($W < 0$) increases the system's internal energy.
			Work done by the system ($W > 0$) decreases the system's internal energy.
Isolated system	no heat or work interaction with surroundings	$Q = W = 0$, so $\Delta U = 0$ and $U_i = U_f$	There is no change in the system's internal energy.

The first law of thermodynamics

PROBLEM

A total of 135 J of work is done on a gaseous refrigerant as it undergoes compression. If the internal energy of the gas increases by 114 J during the process, what is the total amount of energy transferred by heat? Has energy been added to or removed from the refrigerant by heat?

SOLUTION

1. DEFINE   **Given:** $W = -135 \text{ J}$ $\Delta U = 114 \text{ J}$

Work is done on the gas, so work (W) has a negative value. The internal energy increases during the process, so the change in internal energy (ΔU) has a positive value.

Unknown: $Q = ?$

Diagram:

$W = -135 \text{ J}$

$\Delta U = 114 \text{ J}$ $Q = ?$

2. PLAN   **Choose an equation(s) or situation:** Apply the first law of thermodynamics using the values for the change in internal energy (ΔU) and the work (W) done on the system in order to find the value for heat (Q).

$$\Delta U = Q - W$$

Rearrange the equation(s) to isolate the unknown(s):

$$Q = \Delta U + W$$

3. CALCULATE   **Substitute the values into the equation(s) and solve:**

$$Q = 114 \text{ J} + (-135 \text{ J}) = -21 \text{ J}$$

$$\boxed{Q = -21 \text{ J}}$$

The sign for the value of Q is negative. From **Table 11-1,** $Q < 0$ indicates that energy is transferred by heat *from* the refrigerant.

4. EVALUATE   Although the internal energy of the refrigerant increases under compression, more energy is added by work than can be accounted for by the increase in the internal energy. This energy is removed from the gas by heat, as indicated by the minus sign preceding the value for Q.

The first law of thermodynamics

1. The internal energy of a system is initially 27 J. A total of 33 J of energy is added to the system by heat while the system does 26 J of work. What is the system's final internal energy?

2. The internal energy of a gas decreases by 344 J. If the process is adiabatic, how much energy is transferred by heat? How much work is done on or by the gas?

3. The internal energy of the gas in a gasoline engine's cylinder decreases by 195 J. If 52.0 J of work is done by the gas, how much energy is transferred by heat? Does heat add energy to or remove energy from the gas?

4. A steam engine's boiler completely converts 155 kg of water to steam. This process involves the transfer of 3.50×10^8 J by heat. If steam escaping through a safety valve does 1.76×10^8 J of work expanding against the outside atmosphere, what is the net change in the internal energy of the water-steam system?

5. Water with a mass of 2.0 kg is held at constant volume in a pressure cooker while 1.00×10^4 J of energy is steadily added by heat from a range element. The container is not well insulated, and 2.0×10^3 J is transferred by heat to the surrounding air. How large is the change in the system's internal energy?

CYCLIC PROCESSES

A refrigerator performs work to create a temperature difference between its closed interior and its environment (the air in the room). A refrigerator can be represented schematically as a system that transfers energy from a body at low temperature, T_{cold} or T_c, to one at a high temperature, T_{hot} or T_h (see **Figure 11-9**).

The process by which a refrigerator accomplishes this task consists of four basic steps. The system to and from which energy is transferred is defined here as the refrigerant contained within the inner surface of the tubing.

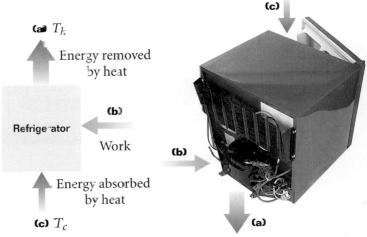

(a) T_h
Energy removed by heat

(b)
Refrigerator
Work

(c) T_c
Energy absorbed by heat

Figure 11-9
A refrigerator does work **(b)** in order to transfer energy by heat from a low-temperature region (the inside of the refrigerator) at T_c **(c)** to a high-temperature region (the air outside the refrigerator) at T_h **(a)**.

The entire process is shown in **Figure 11-10.** Initially, liquid refrigerant is at a low temperature and pressure so that it is colder than the air inside the refrigerator. The refrigerant absorbs energy from inside the refrigerator and lowers the refrigerator's interior temperature. This transfer of energy by heat increases the temperature of the liquid refrigerant until it begins to boil, as shown in **(a).** The refrigerant continues to absorb energy at the constant boiling temperature until it has completely vaporized.

Once it is in the vapor phase, the refrigerant is passed through a *compressor.* The compressor does work on the gas by decreasing its volume without transferring energy by heat, as shown in **(b).** This adiabatic process increases the pressure and internal energy (temperature) of the gaseous refrigerant.

In the next step, the refrigerant is moved to the outer parts of the refrigerator, where thermal contact is made with the air in the room. The refrigerant gives up energy to the environment, which is at a lower temperature, by means of heat, as shown in **(c).** The gaseous refrigerant at high pressure then condenses at a constant temperature to a liquid.

The liquefied refrigerant is brought back into the refrigerator. Just outside the low-temperature interior, the refrigerant is expanded adiabatically through what is called an *expansion valve.* Work is then done by the liquid as it expands from a region of high pressure to one of low pressure and its volume increases, as shown in **(d).** By doing work against the spring in the valve, the refrigerant reduces its internal energy.

Figure 11-10

In each of the four steps of a refrigeration cycle, energy is transferred to or from the refrigerant either by heat or by work.

Table 11-3 Thermodynamics of a refrigerant

Step	Q	W	ΔU
A	+	0	+
B	0	−	+
C	−	0	−
D	0	+	−

The refrigerant now has the same internal energy and phase as that at the start of the process. If its temperature is still lower than that of the air inside the refrigerator, the cycle will repeat.

The first law of thermodynamics can be used to describe the signs of each thermodynamic quantity in the four steps listed, as indicated in **Table 11-3.**

The change in internal energy of a system is zero in a cyclic process

The fact that the refrigerant's final internal energy is the same as its initial internal energy is extremely important, not only with refrigerators but with all machines that use heat to do work or that do work to create temperature differences. If a system's properties at the end of a process are identical to the system's properties before the process took place, the final and initial values of internal energy are the same and the change in internal energy is zero.

$$\Delta U_{net} = 0 \text{ and } Q_{net} = W_{net}$$

This resembles an isothermal process in that all energy is transferred by work and heat. But now the process is repeated with no net change in the system's internal energy. Such a process is called a **cyclic process.**

In a refrigerator, the net amount of work done during each complete cycle must equal the net amount of energy transferred by heat to and from the refrigerant. Energy is transferred by heat between the cold interior of the refrigerator and the colder evaporating refrigerant (Q_{cold}, or Q_c). Energy is also transferred by heat between the hot condensing refrigerant and the relatively cooler air outside the refrigerator (Q_{hot}, or Q_h). Therefore the difference between Q_h and Q_c equals the net energy transferred by heat, and thus the net work done, during one cycle of the refrigeration process.

$$W_{net} = Q_h - Q_c \text{ where } Q_h > Q_c$$

The colder you want the inside of a refrigerator to be, the greater the net energy transferred by heat ($Q_h - Q_c$) must be. The net energy transferred by heat can be increased only if the refrigerator does more work.

Did you know?

The process of changing phase can involve work. The volume of a liquid increases as the liquid vaporizes, thus doing work on the gases above the liquid. Similarly, work is done on a gas that condenses to a smaller-volume liquid. Because the system for a refrigerator is defined as the refrigerant within the tubing, energy is not transferred by work between the refrigerant and its surroundings outside the tubing during vaporization or condensation.

cyclic process

a thermodynamic process in which a system returns to the same conditions under which it started

Deep-Sea Air Conditioning

Deep beneath the ocean, about half a mile down, sunlight barely penetrates the still waters. Scientists at Makai Ocean Engineering in Hawaii are now tapping into that pitch-dark region as a resource for air conditioning.

In tropical locations where buildings are cooled year-round, air-conditioning systems operate with cold water. Compressors cool the water, and pumps circulate it throughout the walls of a building, where the water absorbs heat from the rooms. Unfortunately, powering these compressors is neither cheap nor efficient.

Instead of using compressors to cool the water in their operating system, the systems designed by Makai use frigid water from the ocean's depths. First, engineers install a pipeline that reaches deep into the ocean, where the water is nearly freezing. Then, powerful pumps on the shoreline move the water directly into a building's air-conditioning system. There, a system of heat exchangers uses the sea water to cool the fresh water in the air-conditioning system.

One complicating factor is that the water must also be returned to the ocean in a manner that will not disrupt the local ecosystem. It must be either piped to a depth of a few hundred feet, where its temperature is close to that of the ocean at that level, or poured into onshore pits, where it eventually seeps through the land and comes to an acceptable temperature by the time it reaches the ocean.

"This deep-sea air conditioning benefits the environment by operating with a renewable resource instead of freon," said Dr. Van Ryzin, the president of Makai. "Because the system eliminates the need for compressors, it uses only about 10 percent of the electricity of current methods, saving fossil fuels and a lot of money." However, deep-sea air conditioning technology only works for buildings within a few kilometers of the shore and carries a hefty installation cost of several million dollars. For this reason, Dr. Van Ryzin thinks this type of system is most appropriate for large central air-conditioning systems, such as those necessary to cool resorts or large manufacturing plants, where the electricity savings can eventually make up for the installation costs. Under the right circumstances, air conditioning with sea water can be provided at one-third to one-half the cost of conventional air conditioning.

Figure 11-11
A heat engine is able to do work **(b)** by transferring energy from a high-temperature substance (the boiler) at T_h **(a)** to a substance at a lower temperature (the air surrounding the engine) at T_c **(c)**.

Heat engines use heat to do work

A refrigerator uses mechanical work to create a difference in temperature and thus transfers energy by heat. A heat engine is a device that does the opposite. It uses heat to do mechanical work.

One analogy for a heat engine is a water wheel. A water wheel uses the energy of water falling from one level above Earth's surface to another. The change in potential energy increases the water's kinetic energy so that the water can do work on one side of the wheel and thus turn it. The greater the difference is between the initial and final values of the potential energy, the greater the amount of work that can be done.

Instead of using the difference in potential energy to do work, heat engines do work by making use of a difference in the energy transferred by heat between two substances at different temperatures, as indicated in **Figure 11-11.** For each complete cycle of the heat engine, the net work done will equal the difference between the energy transferred by heat from a high-temperature substance to the engine (Q_h) and the energy transferred by heat from the engine to a low-temperature substance (Q_c).

$$W_{net} = Q_h - Q_c$$

The larger the difference is between the amount of energy transferred by heat into the engine and out of the engine, the more work the engine can do.

The internal-combustion engine found in most vehicles is an example of a heat engine. Internal-combustion engines burn fuel within a closed chamber (the cylinder). The potential energy of the chemical bonds in the reactant gases is converted to kinetic energy of the particle products of the reaction. These gaseous products push against a piston, thus doing work on the environment (in this case, a crankshaft that transforms the linear motion of the piston to the rotational motion of the axle and wheels).

Although the basic operation of any internal-combustion engine resembles that of an ideal heat engine, certain steps do not fit the model. When gas is taken in or removed from the cylinder, matter enters or leaves the system so that the matter in the system is not isolated. No heat engine operates perfectly. Only part of the available internal energy leaves the engine as work done on the environment; most of the energy is removed by heat.

In **Figure 11-12,** the steps in one cycle of operation for a gasoline engine (one type of internal combustion engine) are shown. During compression, shown in **(a),** work is done by the piston as it adiabatically compresses the fuel-and-air mixture in the cylinder. Once maximum compression of the gas is reached, combustion takes place. The chemical potential energy released during combustion increases the internal energy of the gas, as shown in **(b).** The hot high-pressure gases from the combustion reaction expand in volume, causing the piston to do work on the crankshaft, as shown in **(c).** Once all of the work is done by the piston, energy is transferred by heat through the walls of the cylinder and by the physical transfer of the hot exhaust gases from the cylinder, as shown in **(d).** A new fuel-air mixture is then drawn through the intake valve into the cylinder by the downward-moving piston, as shown in **(e).**

Figure 11-12
The steps below show one complete cycle of a gasoline engine.

Spark plug fires

(b) Ignition

Expanding combustion-product gases

(c) Expansion

Intake valve closed
Spark plug
Exhaust valve closed
Fuel-air mixture
Cylinder
Piston
Connecting rod
Crankshaft

(a) Compression

Intake valve open
Exhaust valve closed
Fuel-air mixture

(e) Fuel intake

Intake valve closed
Exhaust valve open
Combustion-product gases

(d) Exhaust

Section Review

1. Use the first law of thermodynamics to show that the internal energy of an isolated system is always conserved.

2. In the systems listed below, identify where energy is transferred by heat and work and where changes in internal energy occur. Is energy conserved in each case?
   a. the steam in a steam engine consisting of a boiler, a firebox, a cylinder, a piston, and a flywheel
   b. the drill bit of a power drill and a metal block into which a hole is being drilled

3. Does the system's overall internal energy increase, decrease, or remain unchanged in either of the situations in item 2? Explain your answer in terms of the first law of thermodynamics.

4. A compressor for a jackhammer expands the air in the hammer's cylinder at a constant pressure of 8.6×10^5 Pa. The increase in the hammer's volume is 4.05×10^{-4} m^3. During the process, 9.5 J of energy is transferred out of the cylinder by means of heat.
   a. What is the work done by the air?
   b. What is the change in the air's internal energy?
   c. What type of ideal thermodynamic process does this approximate?

5. A mixture of fuel and air is enclosed in an engine cylinder fitted with a piston. The gas pressure is maintained at 7.07×10^5 Pa as the piston moves slowly inward. If the gas volume decreases by 1.1×10^{-4} m^3 and the internal energy of the gas increases by 62 J, how much energy is added to or removed from the system by heat?

6. Using what you learned in this section, explain why opening the refrigerator door on a hot day does not cause your kitchen to become cooler.

7. Over several cycles, a refrigerator does 1.51×10^4 J of work on the refrigerant. The refrigerant in turn removes 7.55×10^4 J by heat from the air inside the refrigerator.
   a. How much energy is transferred by heat from the refrigerator's inner compartment to the outside air?
   b. What is the net change in the internal energy of the refrigerant?
   c. What is the amount of work done on the air inside the refrigerator?
   d. What is the net change in the internal energy of the air inside the refrigerator?

8. **Physics in Action** If a weather balloon in flight gives up 15 J of energy by heat and the gas within it does 13 J of work on the outside air, by how much does its internal energy change?

11-3
Efficiency of heat engines

11-3 SECTION OBJECTIVES

- **Recognize why the second law of thermodynamics requires two bodies at different temperatures for work to be done.**

- **Calculate the efficiency of a heat engine.**

THE SECOND LAW OF THERMODYNAMICS

In the previous section, you learned how a heat engine absorbs a quantity of energy from a high-temperature body by means of heat, does work on the environment, and then gives up energy to a low-temperature body by means of heat. The net work done by the engine was defined as being equal to the net energy transferred by heat for the system during a cyclic process ($W_{net} = Q_{net} = Q_h - Q_c$).

This equation, obtained from the first law of thermodynamics, indicates that all energy entering and leaving the system is accounted for and is thus conserved. The equation also suggests that more work is gained by taking more energy at a higher temperature and giving up less energy at a lower temperature. If no energy is given up at the lower temperature ($Q_c = 0$), then it seems that work could be obtained from energy transferred by heat from any body, such as the air around the engine. Such an engine would be able to do more work on hot days than on cold days, but it would always do work as long as the engine's temperature were less than the temperature of the surrounding air.

A heat engine cannot transfer all energy from heat to do work

Unfortunately, it is impossible to make such an engine. While the transfer of energy by heat from the high-temperature source to the engine would cause the engine to do work, it would not be a cyclic process. In order for the cycle to be completed, the engine would have to transfer energy away by heat. Because the only body to which this energy can be transferred is the high-temperature source, the engine must do work to transfer this energy. This is the same amount of work that was made available through the energy transferred by heat from the high-temperature body in the first place. Thus, no net work is obtained from this engine in a cyclic process.

The requirement that a heat engine must give up some energy at a lower temperature in order to do work does not follow from the first law of thermodynamics. This requirement is the basis of what is called the *second law of thermodynamics*. The second law of thermodynamics can be stated as follows: *No machine can be made that only absorbs energy by heat and then entirely transfers the energy out of the engine by an equal amount of work.*

According to the second law of thermodynamics, W can never be equal to Q_h in a cyclic process. Put another way, some energy must always be transferred by heat to the system's surroundings ($Q_c > 0$).

Solar Thermal Power Systems

With the fossil fuels used to run our generators being rapidly depleted, we must find new methods of producing electricity. While water and wind power are already in use, it seems that the most promising source of electricity may be something Earth has more than enough of—sunlight.

At Sandia National Laboratories, in Albuquerque, New Mexico, engineers are working to harness the sun's energy to generate electricity. One of their projects involves the Stirling engine, a machine that was invented by Robert Stirling in 1816. A large dish-shaped mirror is used to reflect sunlight onto an absorber, which collects the energy and uses it to increase the internal energy of helium inside the engine. At that point, the engine works much like an automobile engine, with the heated helium gas being used to move a piston. But instead of spinning a set of wheels, this piston turns an electric generator.

The Stirling engine operates very efficiently; it holds a world record for converting solar energy into electricity. It is ideal for remote locations, where normal power lines cannot be run, or to power-specific devices, such as water pumps for agricultural purposes.

Sandia is also developing a solar power plant that uses the sun's energy to melt large quantities of salt. The energy transferred by heat from the salt is then used to generate steam, which can turn a turbine to make electricity. Also, the hot salt can be kept in insulated tanks, enabling its high internal energy to be stored. Previous solar power systems simply heated water to the boiling point, but the water boiled only while the sun was shining.

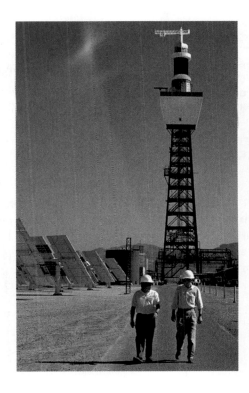

Sandia's salt-heated device stores energy more efficiently than water and maintains the higher temperature long enough to produce electricity even at night.

Greg Kolb, an engineer at Sandia, envisions such a power source replacing the central power stations we have today. "Imagine a tower about the size of the Washington Monument surrounded by a field of mirrors on the ground approximately one square mile in area," Kolb says. "The mirrors are reflecting the sunlight to the top of the tower, where all the light is focused and the energy is absorbed in a large heat exchanger." The engineer estimates that about 10 000 such setups spread throughout the nation could provide as much energy as the United States consumes annually.

Table 11-4
Typical efficiencies for engines

Engine type	eff (calculated maximum values)
steam engine	0.29
steam turbine	0.40
gasoline engine	0.60
diesel engine	0.56

Engine type	eff (measured values)
steam engine	0.17
steam turbine	0.30
gasoline engine	0.25
diesel engine	0.35

THERMODYNAMIC EFFICIENCY

A cyclic process cannot completely convert energy transferred by heat into work, nor can it transfer energy by heat from a low-temperature body to a high-temperature body without performing work. However, a cyclic process can be made to approach these ideal situations. A measure of how well an engine operates is given by the engine's *efficiency* (*eff*). In general, efficiency is a measure of the useful energy taken out of a process with respect to the total energy that is put into the process. Efficiencies for different types of engines are listed in **Table 11-4.**

Recall from the first law of thermodynamics that the work done on the environment by the engine is equal to the difference between the energy transferred to and from the system by heat. For a heat engine, the efficiency is the ratio of work done by the engine to the energy added to the system by heat during one cycle.

EQUATION FOR THE EFFICIENCY OF A HEAT ENGINE

$$eff = \frac{W_{net}}{Q_h} = \frac{Q_h - Q_c}{Q_h} = 1 - \frac{Q_c}{Q_h}$$

$$\text{efficiency} = \frac{\text{net work done by engine}}{\text{energy added to engine by heat}}$$

$$= \frac{\text{energy added by heat} - \text{energy removed by heat}}{\text{energy added by heat}}$$

$$= 1 - \frac{\text{energy removed by heat}}{\text{energy added by heat}}$$

Notice that efficiency is a unitless quantity that can be calculated using only the *magnitudes* for the energies added to and taken away from the engine.

This equation confirms that a heat engine has 100 percent efficiency (*eff* = 1) only if there is no energy transferred away from the engine by heat ($Q_c = 0$).

Conceptual Challenge

1. Cooling engines Use the second law of thermodynamics to explain why an automobile engine requires a cooling system to operate.

2. Power plants Why are many coal-burning and nuclear power plants located near rivers?

Unfortunately, there is no such machine, so the efficiencies of all engines are less than 1.0. The smaller the fraction of usable energy that an engine can provide, the lower its efficiency is.

The equation also provides some important information for increasing engine efficiency. By increasing the amount of energy added to the system by heat or by reducing the amount of energy given up by the system, the ratio of Q_c/Q_h becomes much smaller and the engine's efficiency comes closer to 1.0.

The efficiency equation gives only a maximum value for an engine's efficiency. Friction and thermal conduction in the engine hinder the engine's performance, and experimentally measured efficiencies are usually lower than the calculated efficiencies (see **Table 11-4**).

Heat-engine efficiency

PROBLEM

Find the efficiency of a gasoline engine that, during one cycle, receives 204.5 J of energy from combustion and loses 153.3 J by heat to the exhaust.

SOLUTION

1. DEFINE   **Given:** $Q_h = 204.5 \text{ J}$ $Q_c = 153.3 \text{ J}$

Unknown: $eff = ?$

Diagram:

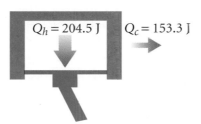

$Q_h = 204.5 \text{ J}$ $Q_c = 153.3 \text{ J}$

2. PLAN   **Choose an equation(s) or situation:** The efficiency of a heat engine is the ratio of the work done by the engine to the energy transferred to it by heat.

$$eff = \frac{W_{net}}{Q_h} = 1 - \frac{Q_c}{Q_h}$$

3. CALCULATE   **Substitute the values into the equation(s) and solve:**

$$eff = 1 - \frac{153.3 \text{ J}}{204.5 \text{ J}} = 0.2504$$

$$\boxed{eff = 0.2504}$$

CALCULATOR SOLUTION

Because the minimum number of significant figures for the data is four, the calculator answer, 0.250366748, should be rounded to four significant figures.

4. EVALUATE   Only about 25 percent of the energy added by heat is used by the engine to do work. As expected, the efficiency is less than 1.0.

Heat-engine efficiency

1. If a steam engine takes in 2.254×10^4 kJ from the boiler and gives up 1.915×10^4 kJ in exhaust during one cycle, what is the engine's efficiency?

2. If a gasoline engine has an efficiency of 21 percent and loses 780 J to the cooling system and exhaust during each cycle, how much work is done by the engine?

3. A steam engine absorbs 1.98×10^5 J and expels 1.49×10^5 J in each cycle. Assume that all of the remaining energy is used to do work.
   a. What is the engine's efficiency?
   b. How much work is done in each cycle?

4. A certain diesel engine performs 372 J of work in each cycle with an efficiency of 33.0 percent. How much energy is transferred from the engine to the exhaust and cooling system by heat?

5. If the energy transferred by heat from an engine during one cycle is 6.0×10^2 J, how much energy must be added to the engine in order for it to operate at 31 percent efficiency?

6. A test model for an experimental gasoline engine does 45 J of work in one cycle and gives up 31 J by means of heat. What is the engine's efficiency?

Section Review

1. Is it possible to construct a heat engine that doesn't transfer energy to its surroundings? Explain.

2. A steam-driven turbine is one major component of an electric power plant. Why is it advantageous to increase the steam's temperature as much as possible?

3. An engineer claims to have built an engine that takes in 75 000 J and expels 35 000 J.
   a. How much energy can the engine provide by doing work?
   b. What is the efficiency of the engine?
   c. Is this efficiency possible? Explain your answer.
   d. Compare the calculated efficiency for the proposed engine with the measured efficiencies for engines in **Table 11-4.** Is the value for the proposed engine's efficiency probable? Explain your answer.

HEAT AND ENTROPY

A forest like the one shown in the background of **Figure 11-13** appears to have random spacing between the trees. However, if you were to encounter a forest where all the trees appear to be equally spaced, like the one shown in the foreground of **Figure 11-13,** you would conclude that someone had planted the trees.

In general, if the laws of nature are allowed to act without interference, it is believed that a disorderly arrangement is much more likely to result than an orderly one. For instance, when you shuffle a deck of cards, the cards are most likely to be all mixed up. It is highly improbable that shuffled cards would end up separated by suit and in numerical sequence. Such a highly ordered arrangement can be formed in only a few ways, but there are more than 8×10^{67} ways to arrange 52 cards.

Entropy is a measure of a system's disorder

The assertion that a disordered arrangement has a vastly greater probability of forming than does a highly ordered arrangement can be demonstrated with a smaller number of components. If two light blue marbles and two purple marbles are placed in two groups of two, four possible combinations can be formed. Two combinations have all of the marbles separated by color. Two combinations have two marbles of each color in each group. There is only one way to form each of the first two combinations, but there are two ways to form

11-4 SECTION OBJECTIVES

- **Relate the disorder of a system to its ability to do work or transfer energy by heat.**

- **Identify systems with high and low entropy.**

- **Distinguish between entropy changes within systems and the entropy change for the universe as a whole.**

Figure 11-13

An orchard represents a well-ordered system, whereas the randomly spaced trees in the forest make for a fairly disordered system.

Table 11-5
**Ordered and
disordered
arrangements**

First arrangement –
one possible combination

Second arrangement –
one possible combination

Third arrangement –
two possible combinations

Fourth arrangement –
two possible combinations

entropy

*a measure of the disorder of a
system*

each of the last two combinations. These different arrangements are illustrated in **Table 11-5.**

This set of marbles may be thought of as a simplified thermodynamic system. Think of the purple marbles as high-energy particles and the light blue marbles as low-energy particles. There are two states with ordered, unmixed energies. These are described by the first two combinations (two purple and two light blue, or two light blue and two purple). There are, by contrast, four relatively disordered, mixed-energy states. These are indicated by the last two combinations. Thus, there is a 2-to-1 probability that the particles will be in the mixed energy, low-order states.

In thermodynamics, a system left to itself tends to go from a state with a very ordered set of energies (one that has only a small probability of being randomly formed) to one in which there is less order (or that has a high probability of being randomly formed). The measure of a system's disorder is called the **entropy** of the system. The greater the entropy of a system is, the greater its disorder.

Systems with maximum disorder are favored

To understand how entropy applies to a natural process, imagine a box that contains four pits into which the marbles can fit. Two pits are on one side of the box and two are on the other. The purple marbles are placed on one side of the box and the light blue marbles are placed on the other. If the box is closed and then shaken, the marbles are twice as likely to be mixed than unmixed. If the box is shaken again, the marbles are still likely to be mixed.

The greater probability of a disordered arrangement indicates that an ordered system (whether the system is composed of separated marbles or particles of separate energies) is likely to become disordered. Put another way, the entropy of a system increases. This greater probability also reduces the chance that a disordered system will become ordered at random. Thus, once a system has reached a state of greatest disorder, it will tend to remain in that state and have *maximum entropy.*

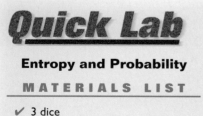

Entropy and Probability

MATERIALS LIST

✔ 3 dice
✔ a sheet of paper
✔ a pencil

Take two dice from a board game. Record all the possible ways to obtain the numbers 2 through 12 on the sheet of paper. How many possible dice combinations can be rolled? How many combinations of both dice will produce the number 5? the number 8? the number 11? What number(s) from 2 through 12 is most probable? How many ways out of the total number of ways can this be rolled? What number(s) from 2 through 12 is least probable? How many ways out of the total number of ways can this be rolled?

Repeat the experiment with three dice. Write down all of the possible combinations that will produce the numbers 3 through 18. What number is most probable?

Increasing disorder reduces the energy available for work

Entropy's role with respect to the second law of thermodynamics still requires explanation. You now know that a system will move toward a state of disorder on its own. But how does this tendency toward disorder affect the ability of a system to do work?

Consider a ball thrown toward a wall, as shown in **Figure 11-14.** The kinetic energy of the particles in the ball consists of their individual random motions and the kinetic energy of the ball as a whole. The wide range of kinetic energies that the particles have because of their random motions make up the ball's internal energy. These energies are in a disordered state. The translational kinetic energy of the particles due to the motion of the entire ball in one direction and with one velocity is, by contrast, well ordered.

When the ball hits the wall, the wall itself does not appear to move and the ball does not fall apart. But the particles within each object undergo collisions with some particles in the other object. These collisions increase the random individual motions of the particles. Thus, some particles within the wall increase their kinetic energy. Some particles in the ball will also increase their kinetic energy, but the ball as a whole still moves in one direction.

According to the first law of thermodynamics, this increase in internal energy must be balanced by a decrease of energy elsewhere. The kinetic energy of the entire ball is thus reduced. Before the collision, the ball could do a certain amount of work. With the proper amount of energy, it could knock over a bucket, for example. With the transformation of part of this ordered energy into disordered internal energy, this capability of doing work is reduced. The ball rebounds with less total kinetic energy than it originally had.

Greater disorder means there is less energy to do work

In a similar way, heat engines are limited in that only some of the energy added by heat can be used to do work. Not all of the gas particles move in an orderly fashion toward the piston and give up all of their energy in collision with the piston, as shown on the left in **Figure 11-15.** Instead, they move in all available directions, as shown on the right in **Figure 11-15,** transferring energy through collisions with the walls of the engine cylinder as well as with themselves. Although energy is conserved, not all of it is available to do useful work. The motion of the particles of a system (in this case, the gas in the cylinder) is not well ordered and therefore is less useful for doing work.

KE_ball $\quad$ **U_wall** $\quad$ **U_ball**
Before collision

KE_ball $\quad$ **U_wall** $\quad$ **U_ball**
After collision

Figure 11-14
The kinetic energies of the particles in the ball and the wall increase at the expense of the kinetic energy of the ball as a whole.

Well-ordered; high efficiency and highly improbable distribution of velocities

Highly disordered; average efficiency and highly probable distribution of velocities

Figure 11-15
If all gas particles moved toward the piston, all of the internal energy could be used to do work. This extremely well-ordered situation is highly improbable.

1. Flipping a coin

Explain why the repeated flipping of a coin does not produce a perfectly ordered, alternating pattern of heads and tails, even though the overall odds are 50:50.

2. Boiling water

A pan of boiling water is mixed with a pan of ice-cold water. The resulting lukewarm contents are then separated back into the two pans. Is there a change in the total energy of the system? Is there a change in entropy? Explain. (Hint: Compare this situation to the mixing of different-colored marbles.)

The second law of thermodynamics can be expressed in terms of entropy change

When an ice cube is surrounded by warm air, it melts at a constant temperature. The water molecules go from an ordered crystalline arrangement with a narrow range of molecular energies to a fairly disordered liquid with a wider range of energies. The entropy of the system increases because energy is transferred by heat to the system. Heat and entropy are therefore related.

When energy is added to or removed from a substance by heat, the temperature of the substance will usually change as well. The exception to this is when the substance changes phase. In this case, the temperature remains constant while the entropy of the system changes. This is why liquids solidify and become more ordered when energy is removed from them and why liquids evaporate and become less ordered when energy is transferred to them.

Because of the connection between a system's entropy, its ability to do work, and the direction of heat, the second law of thermodynamics can also be expressed in terms of entropy change. This applies to the entire universe and not only to a system that interacts with its environment. So the second law can be stated as follows: *The entropy of the universe increases in all natural processes.*

Entropy can increase or decrease within a system

Entropy can decrease for parts of systems, such as the water in the freezer shown in **Figure 11-16,** provided this decrease is offset by a greater increase in entropy elsewhere in the universe.

By doing work on a system, the system's entropy can be decreased. Just as it takes work to put a messy room in order or to put the hundreds of pieces of a

Small decrease in entropy

Water before freezing

Ice after freezing

Freezer compartment

Ice tray

Heat exhaust

Large increase in entropy

Air before water freezes

Air after ice is frozen

Figure 11-16
Because of the refrigerator's less-than-perfect efficiency, the entropy of the outside air molecules increases more than the entropy of the freezing water decreases.

jigsaw puzzle together to make one cohesive picture, work is done by the freezer to reduce the entropy of the water in the ice tray. In each of these examples, the environment's entropy increases to offset the decrease in the system's entropy. The surrounding air's entropy increases because of energy transferred to it by heat, either from the person cleaning the room or the freezer freezing the water.

As a system's entropy decreases by some amount, the entropy of the system's environment increases by a greater amount. The water's entropy decreases as it becomes ice, but the entropy of the air in the room is increased by a greater amount as energy is transferred by heat from the refrigerator. The result is that the total entropy of the refrigerator and the room together has increased.

Ultimately, the entropy of the universe should reach a maximum value. At that time, the universe will be in a state of thermal equilibrium and its temperature will be uniform throughout. All of the energy that is present now will still be in the universe. However, because there will be no difference in temperature anywhere in the universe, the transfer of energy by heat—and thus work—will be impossible. All physical, chemical, and biological processes will cease because a state of perfect disorder implies an absence of energy that can be used to do work. This gloomy state of affairs is sometimes referred to as an ultimate "heat death" of the universe. Estimates based on present models of stellar formation and evolution place this time of universal thermal equilibrium about 100 trillion years in the future.

Did you know?

Entropy decreases in many systems on Earth. These appear to be spontaneous because we think of the Earth itself as a closed system. So much energy comes from the sun that the disorder in chemical and biological systems is reduced, while the total entropy of the Earth, sun, and intervening space increases.

Section Review

1. Use the discussion on pp. 425–426 as a model to show that three purple marbles and three light blue marbles in two groups of three marbles each can be arranged in four combinations: two with only one possible arrangement each and two with nine possible arrangements each.

2. Which of the following systems have high entropy? Which systems have low entropy?
   a. papers scattered randomly across a desk
   b. a freshly opened pack of cards
   c. a cultivated field of cabbages
   d. a room after a party

3. Some molecules have been observed to form spontaneously, even though they are more ordered than their components. Interpret the second law of thermodynamics at the particle level to explain why this can occur.

4. Discuss three common examples of natural processes that involve decreases in entropy. Identify the corresponding entropy increases in the environments of these processes.

CHAPTER 11
Summary

KEY TERMS

adiabatic process (p. 407)

cyclic process (p. 415)

entropy (p. 426)

environment (p. 403)

isothermal process (p. 407)

isovolumetric process
(p. 406)

system (p. 403)

Diagram symbols

Energy transfer
by heat

Energy transfer
by work

Thermodynamic
cycle

KEY IDEAS

Section 11-1 Relationships between heat and work
- An object or grouping of objects that are in thermal equilibrium and contain an unchanging amount of matter make up a system, while their surroundings make up the system's environment.
- Heat and work can transfer energy to or from a system, changing its internal energy in the process.
- For thermodynamic systems, work is defined as the product of gas pressure and the change in the volume of the gas. $\boxed{W = P\Delta V}$

Section 11-2 Thermodynamic processes
- Energy is conserved for any system and its environment and is described by the first law of thermodynamics. $\boxed{\Delta U = Q - W}$
- A cyclic process returns a system to conditions identical to those it had before the process began, so that its internal energy is unchanged.

Section 11-3 Efficiency of heat engines
- The second law of thermodynamics states that no machine can transfer all of its absorbed energy by means of work.
- The efficiency of a heat engine depends on the amount of energy transferred by heat to and from the engine. $\boxed{eff = 1 - \dfrac{Q_c}{Q_h}}$

Section 11-4 Entropy
- Entropy is a measure of the disorder of a system. The more disordered a system is, the less energy that is available to do work.
- The entropy of a system can increase or decrease, but the total entropy of the universe is always increasing.

Variable symbols

Quantities		Units	
ΔU	change in internal energy	J	joules
Q	heat	J	joules
W	work	J	joules
eff	efficiency		(unitless)

CHAPTER 11
Review and Assess

HEAT, WORK, AND INTERNAL ENERGY

Review questions

1. Define a thermodynamic system and its environment.

2. In what two ways can the internal energy of a system be increased according to the first law of thermodynamics?

3. Which of the following expressions have units that are equivalent to the units of work?
   - **a.** mg
   - **b.** $\frac{1}{2}mv^2$
   - **c.** mgh
   - **d.** Fd
   - **e.** $P\Delta V$
   - **f.** $V\Delta T$

4. For each of the following, which thermodynamic quantities have values equal to zero?
   - **a.** an isothermal process
   - **b.** an adiabatic process
   - **c.** an isovolumetric process

Conceptual questions

5. Can energy be added to or removed from a substance without causing the substance's temperature to rise or its phase to change? Explain your answer.

6. When an ideal gas expands adiabatically, it does work on its surroundings. Describe the various transfers of energy that take place.

7. In each of the following cases, trace the chain of energy transfers (by heat or by work) as well as changes in internal energy.
   - **a.** You rub your hands together to warm them on a cold day.
   - **b.** A hole is drilled into a block of metal. When the drill bit and block are placed in a tub of water, steam rises from the tub.

8. Paint from an aerosol can is sprayed continuously for 30 s. The can was initially at room temperature, but now it feels cold to the touch. What type of thermodynamic process occurs for a small sample of gas as it leaves the high-pressure interior of the can and moves to the outside atmosphere?

9. The can of spray paint in item 8 is set aside for an hour. During this time the contents of the can return to room temperature. What type of thermodynamic process takes place in the can during the time the can is not in use?

Practice problems

10. How much work is done when a tire's volume increases from 35.25×10^{-3} m³ to 39.47×10^{-3} m³ at a pressure of 2.55×10^{5} Pa in excess of atmospheric pressure? Is work done on or by the gas? (See Sample Problem 11A.)

11. Helium in a toy balloon does 3.50×10^{2} J of work on its surroundings as it expands with a constant pressure of 2.52×10^{5} Pa in excess of atmospheric pressure. The balloon's final volume is 1.50×10^{-3} m³. From this information, determine the initial volume of the gas in the balloon. (See Sample Problem 11A.)

ENERGY CONSERVATION AND CYCLIC PROCESSES

Review questions

12. Write the equation for the first law of thermodynamics and explain why it is an expression of energy conservation.

13. Rewrite the equation for the first law of thermodynamics for each of the following special thermodynamic processes:
   - **a.** an isothermal process
   - **b.** an adiabatic process
   - **c.** an isovolumetric process

14. List the four thermodynamic processes that take place in one cycle of operation for a refrigerator. What is the difference between the system's internal energy before and after one cycle?

15. How is energy conserved if more energy is transferred by heat from a refrigerator to the outside air than is removed from the inside air of the refrigerator?

Conceptual questions

16. A bomb calorimeter is placed in a water bath and remains at constant volume while a mixture of fuel and oxygen is burned inside it. The temperature of the water is observed to rise during the combustion reaction. The calorimeter and the water remain at constant volume.

  a. If the reaction products are the system, which thermodynamic quantities—ΔU, Q, or W— are positive and which are negative?

  b. If the water bath is the system, which thermodynamic quantities—ΔU, Q, or W—are positive and which are negative?

17. Which of the thermodynamic values (ΔU, Q, or W) would be negative for the following systems?

  a. a steel rail (system) undergoing slow thermal expansion on a hot day displaces the spikes and ties that hold the rail in place

  b. a closed refrigerator (system) in a kitchen

  c. the helium in a thermally insulated weather balloon (system) expands during inflation

18. A system consists of steam within the confines of a steam engine (boiler, steam pipes, cylinder and piston). Construct a table similar to **Table 11-3,** and determine the signs of the quantities ΔU, Q, and W in the following steps of the engine's cycle:

  a. Water in a rigid boiler is heated until it vaporizes.

  b. Steam is conveyed through steam pipes from the boiler to the cylinder of the engine, where it rapidly pushes the piston outward from the cylinder.

  c. The steam condenses to liquid water at constant volume within the cylinder.

  d. The piston moves into the cylinder, pushing the liquid water out and back into the boiler.

Practice problems

19. A gas expands when 606 J of energy is added to it by heat. The expanding gas does 418 J of work on its surroundings.

  a. What is the overall change in the internal energy of the gas?

  b. If the work done by the gas equals 1212 J, how much energy must have been added by heat in order for the internal energy at the end of the process to equal the initial internal energy?

(See Sample Problem 11B.)

20. The lid of a pressure cooker forms a nearly airtight seal. Steam builds up pressure and increases temperature within the pressure cooker so that food cooks faster than it does in an ordinary pot. The system is defined as the pressure cooker and the water and steam within it.

  a. If 2.0 g of water is sealed in a pressure cooker and then vaporized by heating, what happens to the water's internal energy?

  b. Is energy transferred by heat to or from the system?

  c. Is energy transferred by work to or from the system?

  d. If 5175 J must be added by heat to completely vaporize the water, what is the change in the water's internal energy?

(See Sample Problem 11B.)

21. Water at 100.0°C is placed in an open pan and vaporized at 101 kPa when 647 kJ is added. The initial volume of the water is 255 cm^3, and the final volume of the steam is 4.26×10^5 cm^3. Find the following:

  a. the work done by the steam

  b. the change in the internal energy of the system

(See Sample Problem 11B.)

EFFICIENCY OF HEAT ENGINES

Review questions

22. The first law of thermodynamics states that you cannot obtain more energy from a process than you originally put in. The second law states that you cannot obtain as much usable energy from a system as you put into it. Explain why these two statements do not contradict each other.

23. What conditions are necessary for a heat engine to have an efficiency of 1.0?

24. How do the temperature of combustion and the temperatures of coolant and exhaust affect the efficiency of automobile engines?

Conceptual questions

25. If a cup of very hot water is used as an energy source and a cup of cold water is used as an energy "sink," they can, in principle, be used to do work, as shown in **Figure 11-17.** If they are mixed together and the resulting lukewarm contents are separated into two cups, no work can be done. Use the second law of thermodynamics to explain this. Has the first law of thermodynamics been violated by mixing and separating the contents of the two cups?

Figure 11-17

26. What happens to the temperature of a room if an air conditioner is left running on a table in the middle of the room? Take into account the energy transferred by heat from the motor that drives the air conditioner's compressor.

27. Suppose the waste heat at a power plant is exhausted to a pond of water. Could the efficiency of the plant be increased by refrigerating the water in the pond?

Practice problems

28. In one cycle, an engine burning a mixture of air and methanol (methyl alcohol) absorbs 525 J and expels

415 J. How much work is done by this engine? What is the engine's efficiency?
(See Sample Problem 11C.)

29. The energy provided each hour by heat to the turbine in an electric power plant is 9.5×10^{12} J. If the efficiency of this heat engine is 32 percent, how much energy is exhausted each hour from the engine? How much work can the engine do in 1 h?
(See Sample Problem 11C.)

30. The efficiency of a heat engine is 41 percent. The engine absorbs 850 J of energy per cycle from a high-temperature source. Determine the energy expelled and the work done during each cycle.
(See Sample Problem 11C.)

ENTROPY

Review questions

31. Explain how increasing entropy reduces the ability of energy to do work when you hammer a nail into a piece of wood.

32. In which of the following systems is entropy increasing?
  a. An egg is broken and scrambled.
  b. A cluttered room is cleaned and organized.
  c. A thin stick is placed in a glass of sugar-saturated water, and sugar crystals form on the stick.

33. A thermodynamic process occurs in which the entropy of a system decreases. From the second law of thermodynamics, what can you conclude about the entropy change of the environment?

34. Why is it not possible for all of the energy transferred by heat from a high-temperature source to be expelled from an engine by work?

Conceptual questions

35. A salt solution is placed in a bowl and set in sunlight. The salt crystals that remain after the water has evaporated are more highly ordered than the randomly dispersed sodium and chloride ions in the solution. Has the requirement that total entropy increase been violated? Explain your answer.

36. Use a discussion of internal energy and entropy to explain why the statement, "Energy is not conserved in an inelastic collision," is not true.

37. An ideal heat engine uses energy transferred by heat from a high-temperature body to do work. It then transfers energy by heat to a low-temperature body in order to complete the cycle. Find the sign of the entropy changes for the following:

    a. the high-temperature body
    b. the low-temperature body
    c. the engine
    d. the universe

38. One way to look at the transfer of energy between substances is to think of energy transferred by heat as a "disorganized" form of energy and energy transferred by work as an "organized" form. Use this interpretation to show the following:

    a. A heat engine can never have an efficiency of 1.0.
    b. The increased order obtained by freezing water is less than the total disorder that results from the freezer used to form the ice.
    c. The increased order obtained from cleaning a room is less than the total disorder that results from the heat engine (you) used to do the work.

Technology & Learning

Graphing calculators

In 1824, Sadi Carnot, a French engineer, discovered that even a perfectly functioning heat engine cannot achieve 100 percent efficiency. Efficiency depends on the temperatures of the bodies from which and to which energy is transferred. Carnot discovered that the maximum efficiency can be determined by the following equation:

$$highest\ theoretical\ efficiency = 1 - \frac{T_c}{T_h}$$

Use your graphing calculator to predict the highest theoretical efficiency for a Carnot engine operating between the following sets of temperatures:

    a. 435 K and 295 K
    b. 495 K and 295 K
    c. 295 K and 245 K

Open a new program by pressing [PRGM] [▶] [▶] [ENTER]. Name the program "CARNOT" and press [ENTER]. Then enter the program shown in the table below.

To exit the program editor, press [2nd] [QUIT]. To run the program, press [PRGM], select "CARNOT," and press [ENTER] [ENTER]. Enter the value for the hotter temperature, then the value for the cooler temperature, pressing [ENTER] after each value has been entered. The calculator will provide the highest theoretical efficiency. Due to friction and other problems, the actual efficiency of a heat engine in these situations will be lower than the calculated efficiency.

Keystrokes	Display
	PROGRAM: CARNOT
1. [PRGM] [▶] [2] [ALPHA] [H] [ENTER]	:PROMPT H
2. [PRGM] [▶] [2] [ALPHA] [C] [ENTER]	:PROMPT C
3. [1] [–] [(] [ALPHA] [C] [÷] [ALPHA] [H] [)] [STO▶] [ALPHA] [E] [ENTER]	:1–(C/H) → E
4. [PRGM] [▶] [3] [ALPHA] [E] [ENTER]	:DISP E

MIXED REVIEW

39. A 150 kg steel rod in a building under construction supports a load of 6050 kg. During the day the rod's temperature increases from 22°C to 47°C, causing the rod to thermally expand and raise the load 5.5 mm.

a. Find the work done in this process. Is work done on or by the rod?

b. Find the energy transferred by heat to or from the rod. (Hint: Assume the specific heat capacity of steel is the same as for iron.)

c. How great is the change in the rod's internal energy? Does the rod's internal energy increase or decrease?

40. A power plant has a power output of 1055 MW and operates with an efficiency of 33.0 percent. Excess energy is carried away by heat from the plant to a nearby river that has a flow rate of 1.1×10^6 kg/s. How much energy is transferred by heat to the river each second? What is the rise in temperature of the flowing water?

Alternative Assessment

Performance assessment

1. Work in groups to create a classroom presentation on the life, times, and work of James Watt, inventor of the first commercially successful steam engine in the early nineteenth century. Include material about how this machine affected transportation and industry in the United States.

2. Talk to someone who works on air conditioners or refrigerators to find out what fluids are used in these systems. What properties should refrigerant fluids have? Research the use of freon and freon substitutes. Why is using freon forbidden by international treaty? What fluids are now used in refrigerators and car air conditioners? For what temperature ranges are these fluids appropriate? What are the advantages and disadvantages of each fluid? Summarize your research in the form of a presentation or report.

3. The law of entropy can also be called the law of increasing disorder, but this law seems to contradict the existence of living organisms that are able to organize chemicals into organic molecules. Prepare for a class debate on the validity of the following arguments:

a. Living things are not subject to the laws of thermodynamics.

b. The increase in the universe's entropy due to life processes is greater than the decrease in entropy within a living organism.

Portfolio projects

4. During one day, record examples of any processes involving energy transfers that you observe. Identify whether entropy increases in each case. Display your examples, including an explanation for each, on a poster for a collective class exhibit on entropy.

5. Research how an internal-combustion engine operates. Describe the four steps of a combustion cycle. What materials go in and out of the engine during each step? How many cylinders are involved in one cycle? What energy processes take place during each stroke? In which steps is work done? Summarize your findings with diagrams or in a report. Contact an expert auto mechanic, and ask the mechanic to review your report for accuracy.

6. Imagine that an inventor is asking you to invest your savings in the development of a new turbine that will produce cheap electricity. It will take in 1000 J of energy from fuel to supply 650 J of work, which can then be used to power a generator. The energy removed by heat to a cooling system will raise the temperature of 0.10 kg of water by 1.2°C. Are these figures consistent with the first and second laws of thermodynamics? Would you consider investing in this project? Write a business letter to the inventor explaining how your analysis affected your decision.

CHAPTER 12

Vibrations and Waves

PHYSICS IN ACTION

A mechanical metronome consists of a pendulum that vibrates around a pivot. Below the pivot is a counterweight. A sliding weight above the pivot can be positioned to change the rate of vibration. As the pendulum vibrates, the metronome produces a ticking sound, which musicians use to keep a steady tempo.

The vibrations of a metronome are an example of a periodic motion known as *simple harmonic motion*. In this chapter you will study simple harmonic motion and learn about the relationship between simple harmonic vibrations and wave motions.

- *What is the relationship between the period and the frequency of a metronome?*
- *Are all pendulums examples of simple harmonic motion?*

CONCEPT REVIEW

Elastic potential energy
(Section 5-2)

Gravitational potential energy
(Section 5-2)

12-1
Simple harmonic motion

12-1 SECTION OBJECTIVES

- **Identify the conditions of simple harmonic motion.**

- **Explain how force, velocity, and acceleration change as an object vibrates with simple harmonic motion.**

- **Calculate the spring force using Hooke's law.**

HOOKE'S LAW

A repeated motion, such as that of an acrobat swinging on a trapeze, is called a periodic motion. Other periodic motions include those made by a child on a playground swing, a wrecking ball swaying to and fro, and the pendulum of a grandfather clock or a metronome. In each of these cases, the periodic motion is back and forth over the same path.

One of the simplest types of back-and-forth periodic motion is a mass attached to a spring, as shown in **Figure 12-1.** Let us assume that the mass moves on a frictionless horizontal surface. When the spring is stretched or compressed and then released, it vibrates back and forth around its unstretched position. We will begin by considering this example, and then we will apply our conclusions to the swinging motion of a trapeze acrobat.

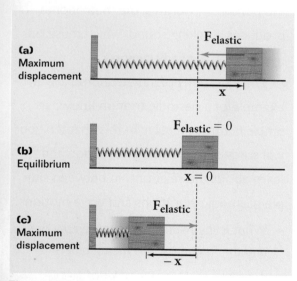

Figure 12-1
The direction of the force acting on the mass (**F**$_{elastic}$) is always opposite the direction of the mass's displacement from equilibrium (**x** = 0).
(a) When the spring is stretched to the right, the spring force pulls the mass to the left. **(b)** When the spring is unstretched, the spring force is zero.
(c) When the spring is compressed to the left, the spring force is directed to the right.

At the equilibrium position, velocity reaches a maximum

In **Figure 12-1(a),** the spring is stretched away from its unstretched, or equilibrium, position ($x = 0$). When released, the spring exerts a force on the mass toward the equilibrium position. This spring force decreases as the spring moves toward the equilibrium position, and it reaches zero at equilibrium, as illustrated in **Figure 12-1(b).** The mass's acceleration also becomes zero at equilibrium.

Though the spring force and acceleration decrease as the mass moves toward the equilibrium position, the velocity of the mass increases. At the equilibrium position, when acceleration reaches zero, the velocity reaches a maximum. At that point, although no net force is acting on the mass, the mass's momentum causes it to overshoot the equilibrium position and compress the spring.

At maximum displacement, spring force and acceleration reach a maximum

As the mass moves beyond equilibrium, the spring force and the acceleration increase. But the direction of the spring force and the acceleration (toward equilibrium) is opposite the mass's direction of motion (away from equilibrium), and the mass begins to slow down.

When the spring's compression is equal to the distance the spring was originally stretched away from the equilibrium position (x), as shown in **Figure 12-1(c),** the mass is at maximum displacement, and the spring force and acceleration of the mass reach a maximum. At this point, the velocity of the mass becomes zero. The spring force acting to the right causes the mass to change its direction, and the mass begins moving back toward the equilibrium position. Then the entire process begins again, and the mass continues to oscillate back and forth over the same path.

In an ideal system, the mass-spring system would oscillate indefinitely. But in the physical world, friction retards the motion of the vibrating mass, and the mass-spring system eventually comes to rest. This effect is called *damping.* In most cases, the effect of damping is minimal over a short period of time, so the ideal mass-spring system provides an approximation for the motion of a physical mass-spring system.

In simple harmonic motion, restoring force is proportional to displacement

As you have seen, the spring force always pushes or pulls the mass back toward its original equilibrium position. For this reason, it is sometimes called a *restoring force.* Measurements show that the restoring force is directly proportional to the displacement of the mass. Any periodic motion that is the result of a restoring force that is proportional to displacement is described by the term **simple harmonic motion.** Because simple harmonic motion involves a restoring force, every simple harmonic motion is a back-and-forth motion over the same path.

In the case of a mass-spring system, the relationship between force and displacement, discovered by Robert Hooke in 1678, is known as Hooke's law. The following equation describes this relationship mathematically:

HOOKE'S LAW

$$F_{elastic} = -kx$$

spring force = −(spring constant)(displacement)

The negative sign in the equation signifies that the direction of the spring force is always opposite the direction of the mass's displacement. In other words, the negative sign shows that the spring force is a restoring force that will tend to move the object back to its equilibrium position.

As mentioned in Chapter 5, the term k is a positive constant called the spring constant. The value of the spring constant is a measure of the stiffness of the spring. A greater value of k means a stiffer spring because a greater force is needed to stretch or compress that spring. The SI units of k are N/m since this will yield N as the unit of the spring force when the spring constant (N/m) is multiplied by the displacement (m).

Conceptual Challenge

1. Earth's orbit
The motion of Earth orbiting the sun is periodic. Is this motion simple harmonic? Why or why not?

2. Pinball
In pinball games, the force exerted by a compressed spring is used to release a ball. If the distance the spring is compressed is doubled, how will the force acting on the ball change? If the spring is replaced with one that is half as stiff, how will the force acting on the ball change?

Hooke's law

PROBLEM

If a mass of 0.55 kg attached to a vertical spring stretches the spring 2.0 cm from its equilibrium position, as shown in Figure 12-2, what is the spring constant?

SOLUTION

1. DEFINE **Given:**
$m = 0.55$ kg $x = -2.0$ cm $= -0.020$ m
$g = 9.81$ m/s^2

Unknown: $k = ?$

$x = 2.0$ cm

Figure 12-2

Diagram:

2. PLAN **Choose an equation(s) or situation:** When the mass is attached to the spring, the equilibrium position changes. At the new equilibrium position, the net force acting on the mass is zero. So the spring force (given by Hooke's law) must be equal and opposite to the weight of the mass.

$$\mathbf{F_{net}} = 0 = \mathbf{F_{elastic}} + \mathbf{F_g}$$

$$F_{elastic} = -kx$$

$$F_g = -mg$$

$$-kx - mg = 0$$

Rearrange the equation(s) to isolate the unknown(s):

$$kx = -mg$$

$$k = \frac{-mg}{x}$$

3. CALCULATE **Substitute the values into the equation(s) and solve:**

$$k = \frac{-(0.55 \text{ kg})(9.81 \text{ m/s}^2)}{-0.020 \text{ m}}$$

$$\boxed{k = 270 \text{ N/m}}$$

CALCULATOR SOLUTION

The calculator answer for k is 269.775. This answer is rounded to two significant figures, 270 N/m.

4. EVALUATE The value of k implies that about 300 N of force is required to displace the spring 1 m.

Hooke's law

1. Suppose the spring in Sample Problem 12A is replaced with a spring that stretches 36 cm from its equilibrium position.
   a. What is the spring constant in this case?
   b. Is this spring stiffer or less stiff than the one in Sample Problem 12A?

2. A slingshot consists of a light leather cup attached between two rubber bands.
   a. If it takes a force of 32 N to stretch the bands 1.2 cm, what is the equivalent spring constant of the rubber bands?
   b. How much force is required to pull the cup of this slingshot 3.0 cm from its equilibrium position?

3. A load of 45 N attached to a spring that is hanging vertically stretches the spring 0.14 m. What is the spring constant?

A stretched or compressed spring has elastic potential energy

As you saw in Chapter 5, a stretched or compressed spring stores elastic potential energy. To see how mechanical energy is conserved in an ideal mass-spring system, consider an archer shooting an arrow from a bow, as shown in **Figure 12-3.** Bending the bow by pulling back the bowstring is analogous to stretching a spring. To simplify this situation, we will disregard friction and internal energy.

Once the bowstring has been pulled back, the bow stores elastic potential energy. Because the bow, arrow, and bowstring (the system) are now at rest, the kinetic energy of the system is zero, and the mechanical energy of the system is solely elastic potential energy.

When the bowstring is released, the bow's elastic potential energy is converted to the kinetic energy of the arrow. At the moment the arrow leaves the bowstring, it gains most of the elastic potential energy originally stored in the bow. (The rest of the elastic potential energy is converted to the kinetic energy of the bow and the bowstring.) Thus, once the arrow has been released, the mechanical energy of the bow-and-arrow system is solely kinetic. Because mechanical energy must be conserved, the kinetic energy of the bow, arrow, and bowstring is equal to the elastic potential energy originally stored in the bow.

Figure 12-3
The elastic potential energy stored in this stretched bow is converted into the kinetic energy of the arrow.

*B*umps in the road are certainly a nuisance, but without strategic use of damping devices, they could also prove deadly. To control a car going 110 km/h (70 mi/h), a driver needs all the wheels on the ground. Bumps in the road lift the wheels off the ground and rob the driver of control. A good solution is to fit the car with springs at each wheel. The springs absorb energy as the wheels rise over the bumps and push the wheels back to the pavement to keep the wheels on the road. However, once set in motion, springs tend to continue to go up and down in simple harmonic motion. This affects the driver's control of the car and also can be very uncomfortable.

One way to cut down on unwanted vibrations is to use stiff springs that compress only a few centimeters under thousands of newtons of force. Such springs have very high spring constants and thus do not vibrate as freely as softer springs with lower constants. However, this solution reduces the driver's ability to keep the car's wheels on the road.

To completely solve the problem, energy-absorbing devices known as shock absorbers are placed parallel to the springs in some automobiles, as shown in **Figure 12-4(a).** Shock absorbers are fluid-filled tubes that turn the simple harmonic motion of the springs into damped harmonic motion. In damped harmonic motion, each cycle of stretch and compression of the spring is much smaller than the previous cycle. Modern auto suspensions are set up so that all of a spring's energy is absorbed by the shock absorbers, eliminating vibrations in just one up-and-down cycle. This keeps the car from continually bouncing without sacrificing the spring's ability to keep the wheels on the road.

Different spring constants and shock absorber damping are combined to give a wide variety of road responses. For example, larger vehicles have heavy-duty leaf springs made of stacks of steel strips, which have a larger spring constant than coil springs do. In this type of suspension system, the shock absorber is perpendicular to the spring, as shown in **Figure 12-4(b).** The stiffness of the spring can affect steering response time, traction, and the general feel of the car.

As a result of the variety of combinations that are possible, your driving experiences can range from the luxurious floating of a limousine to the bone-rattling road feel of a sports car.

(a) Shock absorber — Coil spring

(b) Shock absorber — Leaf spring

Figure 12-4

THE SIMPLE PENDULUM

As you have seen, the periodic motion of a mass-spring system is one example of simple harmonic motion. Now consider the trapeze acrobats shown in **Figure 12-5(a).** Like the vibrating mass-spring system, the swinging motion of a trapeze acrobat is a periodic vibration. Is a trapeze acrobat's motion an example of simple harmonic motion?

To answer this question, we will use a simple pendulum as a model of the acrobat's motion, which is a physical pendulum. A simple pendulum consists of a mass called a *bob,* which is attached to a fixed string, as shown in **Figure 12-5(b).** When working with a simple pendulum, we assume that the mass of the bob is concentrated at a point and that the mass of the string is negligible. Furthermore, we disregard the effects of friction and air resistance. For a physical pendulum, on the other hand, the distribution of the mass must be considered and friction and air resistance also must be taken into account. To simplify our analysis, we will disregard these complications and use a simple pendulum to approximate a physical pendulum in all of our examples.

(a)

(b)

Figure 12-5
(a) The motion of these trapeze acrobats is modeled by **(b)** a simple pendulum.

The restoring force of a pendulum is a component of the bob's weight

To see whether the pendulum's motion is simple harmonic, we must first examine the forces exerted on the pendulum's bob to determine which force acts as the restoring force. If the restoring force is proportional to the displacement, then the pendulum's motion is simple harmonic. Let us select a coordinate system in which the x-axis is tangent to the direction of motion and the y-axis is perpendicular to the direction of motion. Because the bob is always changing its position, these axes will change at each point of the bob's motion.

The forces acting on the bob at any point include the force exerted by the string and the bob's weight. The force exerted by the string always acts along the y-axis, which is along the string. At any point other than the equilibrium position, the bob's weight can be resolved into two components along the chosen axes, as shown in **Figure 12-6.** Because both the force exerted by the string and the y component of the bob's weight are perpendicular to the bob's motion, the x component of the bob's weight is the net force acting on the bob in the direction of its motion. In this case, the x component of the bob's weight always pushes or pulls the bob toward its equilibrium position and hence is the restoring force.

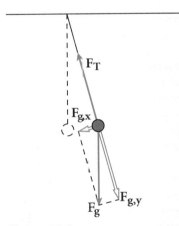

Figure 12-6
At any displacement from equilibrium, the weight of the bob (F_g) can be resolved into two components. The x component $(F_{g,x})$, which is perpendicular to the string, is the only force acting on the bob in the direction of its motion.

For small angles, the pendulum's motion is simple harmonic

As with a mass-spring system, the restoring force of a simple pendulum is not constant. Instead, the magnitude of the restoring force varies with the bob's distance from the equilibrium position. The magnitude of the restoring force decreases as the bob moves toward the equilibrium position and becomes zero at the equilibrium position ($\theta = 0°$). When the angle of displacement is relatively small (<15°), the restoring force is proportional to the displacement. For such small angles of displacement, the pendulum's motion is simple harmonic. We will assume a small angle of displacement for the remainder of this chapter unless otherwise noted.

Because a simple pendulum vibrates with simple harmonic motion, many of our earlier conclusions for a mass-spring system apply here. At maximum displacement, the restoring force and acceleration reach a maximum while the velocity becomes zero. Conversely, at equilibrium the restoring force and acceleration become zero and velocity reaches a maximum. **Table 12-1** on the following page illustrates the analogy between a simple pendulum and a mass-spring system.

At any displacement, a simple pendulum has gravitational potential energy

As with the mass-spring system, the mechanical energy of a simple pendulum is conserved in an ideal (frictionless) system. However, the spring's potential energy is elastic, while the pendulum's potential energy is gravitational.

Figure 12-7 illustrates how a pendulum's mechanical energy changes as the pendulum oscillates. At maximum displacement from equilibrium, a pendulum's energy is entirely gravitational potential energy. As the pendulum swings toward equilibrium, it gains kinetic energy and loses potential energy. At the equilibrium position, its energy becomes solely kinetic.

As the pendulum swings past its equilibrium position, the kinetic energy decreases while the gravitational potential energy increases. At maximum displacement from equilibrium, the pendulum's energy is once again entirely gravitational potential energy.

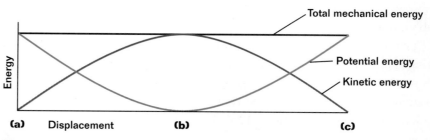

Figure 12-7
Whether at maximum displacement **(a)**, equilibrium **(b)**, or maximum displacement in the other direction **(c)**, the pendulum's total mechanical energy remains the same. However, as the graph shows, the pendulum's kinetic energy and potential energy are constantly changing.

Table 12-1   Simple harmonic motion

Maximum displacement		$F_x = F_{max}$ $a = a_{max}$ $v = 0$
Equilibrium		$F_x = 0$ $a = 0$ $v = v_{max}$
Maximum displacement		$F_x = F_{max}$ $a = a_{max}$ $v = 0$
Equilibrium		$F_x = 0$ $a = 0$ $v = v_{max}$
Maximum displacement		$F_x = F_{max}$ $a = a_{max}$ $v = 0$

$-A \quad 0 \quad A$ x

Section Review

1. Which of these periodic motions are simple harmonic?
   a. a child swinging on a playground swing (at a small angle)
   b. a record rotating on a turntable
   c. an oscillating clock pendulum

2. A pinball machine uses a spring that is compressed 4.0 cm to launch a ball. If the spring constant is 13 N/m, what is the force on the ball at the moment the spring is released?

3. How does the restoring force acting on a pendulum bob change as the bob swings toward the equilibrium position? How do the bob's acceleration (along the direction of motion) and velocity change?

4. When an acrobat reaches the equilibrium position, the net force acting along the direction of motion is zero. Why does the acrobat swing past the equilibrium position?

12-2
Measuring simple harmonic motion

12-2 SECTION OBJECTIVES

- **Identify the amplitude of vibration.**

- **Recognize the relationship between period and frequency.**

- **Calculate the period and frequency of an object vibrating with simple harmonic motion.**

amplitude

maximum displacement from equilibrium

period

time it takes to execute a complete cycle of motion

frequency

number of cycles or vibrations per unit of time

AMPLITUDE, PERIOD, AND FREQUENCY

In the absence of friction, a moving trapeze always returns to the same maximum displacement after each swing. This maximum displacement from the equilibrium position is the **amplitude.** A pendulum's amplitude can be measured by the angle between the pendulum's equilibrium position and its maximum displacement. For a mass-spring system, the amplitude is the maximum amount the spring is stretched or compressed from its equilibrium position.

Period and frequency measure time

Imagine the ride shown in **Figure 12-8** swinging from maximum displacement on one side of equilibrium to maximum displacement on the other side, and then back again. This is considered a complete cycle of motion. The **period,** T, is the time it takes for this complete cycle of motion. For example, if one complete cycle takes 20 s, then the period of this motion is 20 s. Note that during the time T, the displacement is zero.

The number of complete cycles the ride swings through in a unit of time is the ride's **frequency,** f. If one complete cycle takes 20 s, then the ride's frequency is $\frac{1}{20}$ cycles/s, or 0.05 cycles/s. The SI unit of frequency is s^{-1}, known as hertz (Hz). In this case, the ride's frequency is 0.05 Hz.

Period and frequency can be confusing because both are concepts involving time in simple harmonic motion. Notice that the period is the time per cycle and that the frequency is the number of cycles per unit time, so they are inversely related.

$$f = \frac{1}{T} \text{ or } T = \frac{1}{f}$$

This relationship was used to determine the frequency of the ride.

$$f = \frac{1}{T} = \frac{1}{20 \text{ s}} = 0.05 \text{ Hz}$$

In any problem where you have a value for period or frequency, you can use this relationship to calculate the other value.

Figure 12-8

For any periodic motion—such as the motion of this amusement park ride in Helsinki, Finland—period and frequency are inversely related.

Table 12-2   Measures of simple harmonic motion

Term	Example	Definition	SI unit
Amplitude		maximum displacement from equilibrium	radian, rad meter, m
Period, T		time it takes to execute a complete cycle of motion	second, s
Frequency, f		number of cycles or vibrations per unit of time	hertz, Hz ($Hz = s^{-1}$)

The period of a simple pendulum depends on string length and free-fall acceleration

Although both a simple pendulum and a mass-spring system vibrate with simple harmonic motion, calculating the period and frequency of each requires a separate equation. This is because in each, the period and frequency depend on different physical factors.

Consider an experimental setup of two pendulums of the same length but with bobs of different masses. If you were to pull each bob aside the same distance and then release them at the same time, each pendulum would complete one vibration in the same amount of time. In other words, they would have the same period. If you then changed the amplitude of one of the pendulums, you would find that they would still have the same period. Thus, neither mass nor amplitude affect the period of a pendulum (for small angles).

However, changing the string length of a pendulum *does* affect its period. A change in the free-fall acceleration also affects the period of a pendulum. The exact relationship between these variables can be derived mathematically or found experimentally.

PERIOD OF A SIMPLE PENDULUM IN SIMPLE HARMONIC MOTION

$$T = 2\pi \sqrt{\frac{L}{g}}$$

period = 2π × square root of (length divided by free-fall acceleration)

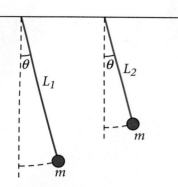

Figure 12-9
When the string length of one pendulum is decreased, the distance that the pendulum travels to equilibrium is also decreased. Because the accelerations of the two pendulums are equal, the shorter pendulum will have a smaller period.

Why does the period of a pendulum depend on string length and free-fall acceleration? When two pendulums have different lengths but the same amplitude, the shorter pendulum will have a smaller arc to travel through, as shown in **Figure 12-9.** Because the distance the mass travels from maximum displacement to equilibrium is less while the acceleration of both pendulums remains the same, the shorter pendulum will have a shorter period.

As discussed earlier, the restoring force is a component of the bob's weight. As g increases, the net acceleration increases, and so the period decreases.

Why don't mass and amplitude affect the period of a pendulum? When the bobs of two pendulums differ in mass, the heavier mass provides a larger restoring force, but it also needs a larger force to achieve the same acceleration. This is similar to the situation for objects in free fall, which all have the same acceleration regardless of their mass. Because the acceleration of both pendulums is the same, the period for both is also the same.

When the amplitude of a pendulum is increased, the restoring force also increases. Because force is proportional to acceleration, the initial acceleration will be greater. However, the distance this pendulum must cover is also greater, and its period remains the same.

SAMPLE PROBLEM 12B

Period of a simple pendulum

PROBLEM

You need to know the height of a tower, but darkness obscures the ceiling. You note that a pendulum extending from the ceiling almost touches the floor and that its period is 12 s. How tall is the tower?

SOLUTION

Given: $T = 12$ s $g = 9.81$ m/s^2

Unknown: $L = ?$

Use the equation given on page 447 to solve for L.

$$T = 2\pi\sqrt{\frac{L}{g}}$$

$$\frac{T\sqrt{g}}{2\pi} = \sqrt{L}$$

$$\frac{T^2 g}{4\pi^2} = L$$

$$L = \frac{(12 \text{ s})^2(9.81 \text{ m/s}^2)}{4\pi^2}$$

$$\boxed{L = 36 \text{ m}}$$

Period of a simple pendulum

1. If the length of the pendulum in Sample Problem 12B were halved, what would its period of vibration be?

2. The cables of a trapeze are approximately 3.5 m long. What is the period of an acrobat swinging on this trapeze?

3. What is the frequency of an acrobat swinging on the trapeze described in item 2?

4. Calculate the period and frequency of a 3.500 m long pendulum at the following locations:
   a. the North Pole, where $g = 9.832$ m/s^2
   b. Chicago, where $g = 9.803$ m/s^2
   c. Jakarta, Indonesia, where $g = 9.782$ m/s^2

Period of a mass-spring system depends on mass and spring constant

Now consider the period of a mass-spring system. In this case, according to Hooke's law, the restoring force acting on the mass is determined by the displacement of the mass and by the spring constant ($F_{elastic} = -kx$). The magnitude of the mass does not affect the restoring force. So unlike the case of the pendulum, where a heavier mass increased both the force on the bob and the bob's inertia, a heavier mass attached to a spring increases inertia without providing a compensating increase in force. Due to this increase in inertia, a heavy mass has a smaller acceleration than a light mass has. Thus, a heavy mass will take more time to complete one cycle of motion. In other words, the heavy mass has a greater period. Thus, as mass increases, the period of vibration likewise increases.

Conceptual Challenge

1. Pendulum on the moon

The free-fall acceleration on the surface of the moon is approximately one-sixth of the free-fall acceleration on the surface of Earth. Compare the period of a pendulum on Earth with that of an identical pendulum set in motion on the moon.

2. Pendulum clocks

Why is a pendulum a reliable time-keeping device, even if its oscillations gradually decrease in amplitude over time?

The greater the spring constant (k), the stiffer the spring; hence a greater force is required to stretch or compress the spring. When force is greater, acceleration is greater and the amount of time required for a single cycle should decrease (assuming that the amplitude remains constant). Thus, for a given amplitude, a stiffer spring will take less time to complete one cycle of motion than one that is less stiff.

As with the pendulum, the equation for the period of a mass-spring system can be derived mathematically or found experimentally.

PERIOD OF A MASS-SPRING SYSTEM IN SIMPLE HARMONIC MOTION

$$T = 2\pi \sqrt{\frac{m}{k}}$$

period = 2π × square root of (mass divided by spring constant)

Note that, as with the pendulum, changing the amplitude of the vibration does not affect the period.

SAMPLE PROBLEM 12C

Period of a mass-spring system

PROBLEM

The body of a 1275 kg car is supported on a frame by four springs, each of which has a spring constant of 2.0×10^4 N/m. Two people riding in the car have a combined mass of 153 kg. Find the period of vibration of the car when it is driven over a pothole in the road.

SOLUTION

Given: $\qquad m = \dfrac{(1275 \text{ kg} + 153 \text{ kg})}{4} = 357.0 \text{ kg} \qquad k = 2.0 \times 10^4 \text{ N/m}$

Unknown: $\qquad T = ?$

Use the equation for the period of a mass-spring system given on this page.

$$T = 2\pi \sqrt{\frac{m}{k}}$$

$$T = 2\pi \sqrt{\frac{357.0 \text{ kg}}{2.0 \times 10^4 \text{ N/m}}}$$

$$T = 2\pi \sqrt{0.01785 \text{ s}^2}$$

$$\boxed{T = 0.84 \text{ s}}$$

Period of a mass-spring system

1. What is the frequency of vibration in Sample Problem 12C?

2. When two more people get into the car described in Sample Problem 12C, the total mass of all four occupants of the car becomes 255 kg. Now what is the period of vibration of the car when it is driven over a pothole in the road?

3. How long will it take the car in item 2 to complete three vibrations?

4. A spring of spring constant 30.0 N/m is attached to different masses and the system is set in motion. Find the period and frequency of vibration for masses of the following magnitudes:
   a. 2.3 kg
   b. 15 g
   c. 1.9 kg

Section Review

1. Two mass-spring systems vibrate with simple harmonic motion. If the spring constants of each system are equal and the mass of one is twice that of the other, which system has a greater period?

2. A child swings on a playground swing with a 2.5 m long chain.
   a. What is the period of the child's motion?
   b. What is the frequency of vibration?

3. A 0.75 kg mass attached to a vertical spring stretches the spring 0.30 m.
   a. What is the spring constant?
   b. The mass-spring system is now placed on a horizontal surface and set vibrating. What is the period of the vibration?

4. A pendulum swings from maximum displacement on one side of equilibrium to maximum displacement on the opposite side of equilibrium. If the pendulum swings through a total of 24°, what is the amplitude of this vibration?

5. **Physics in Action** The reading on a metronome indicates the number of oscillations per minute. What are the period and frequency of the metronome's vibration when the metronome is set at 180?

12-3
Properties of waves

Figure 12-10
A pebble dropped into a pond creates ripple waves similar to those shown here.

medium

material through which a disturbance travels

mechanical wave

a wave whose propagation requires the existence of a medium

WAVE MOTION

What happens when you drop a pebble into a pond? The disturbance created by the pebble generates water waves that travel away from the disturbance, as seen in **Figure 12-10.** If you were to carefully examine the motion of a leaf floating near the disturbance, you would see that the leaf moves up and down and back and forth about its original position. However, the leaf does not undergo any net displacement from the motion of the waves.

The leaf's motion indicates the motion of the water's particles. The water molecules move locally, like the leaf does, but they do not travel across the pond. That is, the water wave moves from one place to another, but the water itself is not carried with it.

A wave is the motion of a disturbance

Ripple waves are formed by the vibrations of water molecules. As the vibrations spread to more molecules, the waves travel outward. Therefore, we can consider a *wave* to be the motion of a disturbance. Particles within a wave vibrate around an equilibrium position, and changes in their vibration allow the net disturbance to travel from one location to another.

In our example, the molecules of water are the **medium** through which the disturbance travels. The medium provides the particles that vibrate. Note that the medium does not travel with the wave. After the wave has passed, the particles of the medium return to their original positions.

In most familiar cases, air is the medium for sound waves. A bell vibrating in a chamber filled with air will produce a sound, but when all of the air is removed from the chamber, no sound is heard. Since these sound waves consist of the vibrations of air particles, they cannot exist in a vacuum. Waves that cannot exist without a medium, such as sound waves, are called **mechanical waves.**

Not all wave propagation requires a medium. Electromagnetic waves, such as visible light, radio waves, microwaves, and X rays, can travel through a vacuum. You will study electromagnetic waves in Chapters 14–16.

WAVE TYPES

One of the simplest ways to demonstrate wave motion is to flip one end of a taut rope whose opposite end is fixed, as shown in **Figure 12-11.** The flip of your wrist creates a pulse that travels to the fixed end with a definite speed. A wave that consists of a single traveling pulse is called a **pulse wave.**

Now imagine that you continue to generate pulses at one end of the rope. Together, these pulses form what is called a **periodic wave.** Whenever the source of a wave's motion is a periodic motion, such as the motion of your hand moving up and down repeatedly, a periodic wave is produced.

Figure 12-11
A single flip of a wrist on a taut rope creates a pulse wave.

Sine waves describe particles vibrating with simple harmonic motion

Figure 12-12 depicts a periodic wave on a string whose source is a blade vibrating with simple harmonic motion. As the wave travels to the right, any single point on the string vibrates up and down. Because the blade is vibrating with simple harmonic motion, the vibration of each point of the string is also simple harmonic. A wave whose source vibrates with simple harmonic motion is called a *sine wave.* Thus, a sine wave is a special case of a periodic wave in which the periodic motion is simple harmonic. The wave in **Figure 12-12** is called a sine wave because a graph of the trigonometric function $y = \sin x$ produces this curve when plotted.

Imagine that each particle of the sine wave shown in **Figure 12-12** is a mass attached to a vibrating spring. As the wave travels to the right, each spring would vibrate around its equilibrium position with simple harmonic motion. This relationship between simple harmonic motion and wave motion enables us to use some of the terms and concepts from simple harmonic motion in our study of wave motion.

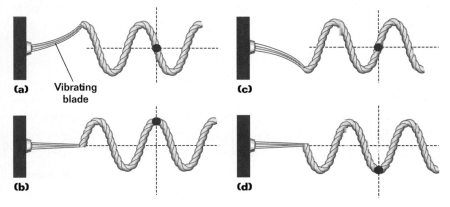

(a) Vibrating blade

(b)

(c)

(d)

Figure 12-12
As the sine wave created by this vibrating blade travels to the right, a single point on the string vibrates up and down with simple harmonic motion.

Vibrations of a transverse wave are perpendicular to the wave motion

Figure 12-13(a) is a representation of the wave shown in **Figure 12-12** (on page 453) at a specific instant of time, *t*. This wave travels to the right as the particles of the rope vibrate up and down. Thus, the vibrations are perpendicular to the direction of the wave's motion. A wave such as this, in which the particles of the disturbed medium move perpendicularly to the wave motion, is called a **transverse wave.**

The wave shown in **Figure 12-13(a)** can be placed on a coordinate system, as shown in **Figure 12-13(b).** A picture of a wave like the one in **Figure 12-13(b)** is sometimes called a *waveform*. A waveform can represent either the displacements of each point of the wave at a single moment in time or the displacements of a single particle as time passes.

In this case, the waveform depicts the displacements at a single instant. The *x*-axis represents the equilibrium position of the string, and the *y* coordinates of the curve represent the displacement of each point of the string at time *t*. For example, points where the curve crosses the *x*-axis (where $y = 0$) have zero displacement. Conversely, at the highest and lowest points of the curve, where displacement is greatest, the absolute values of *y* are greatest.

A wave is measured in terms of both its displacement from equilibrium and the distance between neighboring displacements. The highest point above the equilibrium position is called the wave **crest.** The lowest point below the equilibrium position is the **trough** of the wave. As in simple harmonic motion, amplitude is a measure of maximum displacement from equilibrium. Since the *x*-axis represents the equilibrium position of the string, the amplitude of a wave is the distance from the equilibrium position to a crest or to a trough, as shown in **Figure 12-13(b).**

Notice that there is a series of crests and troughs in the waveform shown in **Figure 12-13(b)** and that the distance between adjacent crests or troughs is always the same. Thus, a wave can be thought of as a cyclical motion. A particle in the wave is displaced first in one direction, then in the other direction, finally returning to its original equilibrium position ready to repeat the cycle. The distance the wave travels during one cycle is called the **wavelength,** λ (the Greek letter *lambda*). This is also the distance between neighboring displacements. The most practical way to find the wavelength is to measure the distance between two adjacent similar points of the wave, such as from crest to crest or from trough to trough.

---

transverse wave

a wave whose particles vibrate perpendicularly to the direction of wave motion

crest

the highest point above the equilibrium position

trough

the lowest point below the equilibrium position

wavelength

the distance between two adjacent similar points of the wave, such as from crest to crest or from trough to trough

---

Figure 12-13

(a) A picture of a transverse wave at some instant *t* can be turned into **(b)** a graph. The *x*-axis represents the equilibrium position of the string. The curve shows the displacements of the string at time *t*.

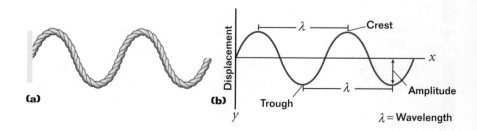

Vibrations of a longitudinal wave are parallel to the wave motion

You can create another type of wave with a spring Suppose that one end of the spring is fixed and that the free end is pumped back and forth along the length of the spring, as shown in **Figure 12-14.** This action produces compressed and stretched regions of the coil that travel along the spring. The displacement of the coils is in the direction of wave motion. In other words, the vibrations are parallel to the motion of the wave.

Compressed   Stretched   Compressed   Stretched

Figure 12-14

As this wave travels to the right, the coils of the spring are tighter in some regions and looser in others. The displacement of the coils is parallel to the direction of wave motion, so this wave is longitudinal.

When the particles of the medium vibrate parallel to the direction of wave motion, the wave is called a **longitudinal wave.** Sound waves in the air are longitudinal waves because air particles vibrate back and forth in a direction parallel to the direction of wave motion.

A longitudinal wave can also be described by a sine curve. Consider a longitudinal wave traveling on a spring. **Figure 12-15(a)** is a snapshot of the longitudinal wave at some instant *t,* and **Figure 12-15(b)** shows the sine curve representing the wave. The compressed regions correspond to the crests of the waveform, and the stretched regions correspond to troughs.

The type of wave represented by the curve in **Figure 12-15(b)** is often called a *density wave* or a *pressure wave* because the crests, where the spring coils are compressed, are regions of high density and pressure. Conversely, the troughs, where the coils are stretched, are regions of low density and pressure.

longitudinal wave

a wave whose particles vibrate parallel to the direction of wave motion

(a) x_1 x_2 x_3 x_4 (b)   y x_1 x_2 x_3 x_4

Figure 12-15

(a) A longitudinal wave at some instant *t* can also be represented by **(b)** a graph. The crests of this waveform correspond to compressed regions, and the troughs correspond to stretched regions.

PERIOD, FREQUENCY, AND WAVE SPEED

The up-and-down movement of your hand or a vibrating blade can generate waves on a string. Sound waves may begin, for example, with the vibrations of your vocal cords, a guitar string, or a taut drumhead. In each of these cases, the source of wave motion is a vibrating object.

The vibrating object that causes a sine wave always has a characteristic frequency. Because this motion is transferred to the particles in the wave, the frequency of vibration of the particles is equal to the frequency of the source. When the vibrating particles of the medium complete one full cycle, one complete wavelength passes any given point. Thus, wave frequency describes the number of crests or troughs that pass a given point in a unit of time.

The period of a wave is the amount of time required for one complete vibration of the particles of the medium. As the particles of the medium complete one full cycle of vibration at any point of the wave, one wavelength passes by that same point. Thus, the period of a wave describes the time it takes for a complete wavelength to pass a given point. The relationship between period and frequency seen earlier in this chapter holds true for waves as well; the period of a wave is inversely related to its frequency.

Wave speed equals frequency times wavelength

We can now derive an expression for the speed of a wave in terms of its period or frequency. We know that speed is equal to displacement divided by the time it takes to undergo that displacement.

$$v = \frac{\Delta x}{\Delta t}$$

For waves, a displacement of one wavelength (λ) occurs in a time interval equal to one period of the vibration (T).

$$v = \frac{\lambda}{T}$$

As you saw earlier in this chapter, frequency and period are inversely related.

$$f = \frac{1}{T}$$

Substituting this frequency relationship into the previous equation for speed gives a new equation for the speed of a wave.

$$v = \frac{\lambda}{T} = f\lambda$$

SPEED OF A WAVE

$$v = f\lambda$$

speed of a wave = frequency × wavelength

The speed of a mechanical wave is constant for any given medium. For example, at a concert, sound waves from different instruments reach your ears at the same moment, even when the frequencies of the sound waves are different. Thus, although the frequencies and wavelengths of the sounds produced by each instrument may be different, the product of the two, which is the speed of the sound waves, is always the same.

When a mechanical wave's frequency is increased, its wavelength must decrease in order for its speed to remain constant. The speed of a wave changes only when the wave moves from one medium to another or when certain properties of the medium are varied.

Wave speed

PROBLEM

The string of a piano that produces the note middle C vibrates with a frequency of 264 Hz. If the sound waves produced by this string have a wavelength in air of 1.30 m, what is the speed of sound in air?

SOLUTION

Given: $f = 264$ Hz $\qquad \lambda = 1.30$ m

Unknown: $v = ?$

Use the equation for the speed of a wave, given on page 456.

$$v = f\lambda$$
$$v = (264 \text{ Hz})(1.30 \text{ m})$$

$$\boxed{v = 343 \text{ m/s}}$$

Wave speed

1. A piano emits frequencies that range from a low of about 28 Hz to a high of about 4200 Hz. Find the range of wavelengths in air attained by this instrument when the speed of sound in air is 340 m/s.

2. An FM radio station broadcasts electromagnetic waves at a frequency of 125 MHz (M = mega = 10^6). These radio waves have a wavelength of 2.40 m. Find the speed of the radio waves.

3. The speed of the radio waves in item 2 is the speed of any electromagnetic waves traveling through empty space. Calculate the wavelength of electromagnetic waves emitted at the following frequencies:
   a. radio waves at 88.0 MHz
   b. visible light at 6.0×10^8 MHz
   c. X rays at 3.0×10^{12} MHz

4. What is the period of vibration for each of the frequencies in item 3?

5. A tuning fork produces a sound with a frequency of 256 Hz and a wavelength in air of 1.35 m.
   a. What value does this give for the speed of sound in air?
   b. What would be the wavelength of the wave produced by this tuning fork in water in which sound travels at 1500 m/s?

Waves transfer energy

When a pebble is dropped into a pond, the water wave that is produced carries a certain amount of energy. As the wave spreads to other parts of the pond, the energy likewise moves across the pond. Thus, the wave transfers energy from one place in the pond to another while the water remains in essentially the same place. In other words, waves transfer energy by transferring the *motion* of matter rather than by transferring matter itself. For this reason, waves are often able to transport energy efficiently.

The energy carried by a wave depends on the amplitude at which the particles of the medium are vibrating. The greater the amplitude, the more energy a wave carries in a given time interval. For a mechanical wave, the energy carried is proportional to the square of the wave's amplitude. When the amplitude of a mechanical wave is doubled, the energy it carries in a given time interval increases by a factor of four. Conversely, when the amplitude is halved, the energy decreases by a factor of four.

As with a mass-spring system or a simple pendulum, the amplitude of a wave gradually diminishes over time as its energy is dissipated. This effect, called *damping,* is usually minimal over relatively short distances. For this reason, we have disregarded damping in our analysis of wave motions.

Section Review

1. As waves pass by a duck floating on a lake, the duck bobs up and down but remains in essentially one place. Explain why the duck is not carried along by the wave motion.

2. Sketch each of the following waves on a spring that is attached to a wall at one end:
   a. a pulse wave that is longitudinal
   b. a periodic wave that is longitudinal
   c. a pulse wave that is transverse
   d. a periodic wave that is transverse

3. Draw a graph for each of the waves described in items (**b**) and (**d**) above, and label the *y*-axis of each graph with the appropriate variable. Label the following on each graph: crest, trough, wavelength, and amplitude.

4. If the amplitude of a sound wave is increased by a factor of four, how does the energy carried by the sound wave in a given time interval change?

5. The smallest insects that a bat can detect are approximately the size of one wavelength of the sound the bat makes. If a bat emits a chirp at a frequency of 60.0 kHz, what is the size of the smallest insect it can detect? Assume that the speed of sound in air is 340 m/s.

12-4
Wave interactions

WAVE INTERFERENCE

When two bumper boats collide, as shown in **Figure 12-16,** each bounces back in another direction. The two bumper boats cannot occupy the same space, and so they are forced to change the direction of their motion. This is true not just of bumper boats but of all matter. Two different material objects can never occupy the same space at the same time.

When two waves come together, they do not bounce back as bumper boats do. If you listen carefully at a concert, you can distinguish the sounds of different instruments. Trumpet sounds are different from flute sounds, even when the two instruments are played at the same time. This means the sound waves of each instrument are unaffected by the other waves that are passing through the same space at the same moment. Because mechanical waves are not matter but *displacements* of matter, two waves *can* occupy the same space at the same time. This is known as *superposition.*

Figure 12-17 shows the interference pattern of two waves in a ripple tank. As you can see, the two waves pass through one another without losing their own characteristics. Ripple tanks such as this one are often used to study wave interference patterns. Although the superposition of mechanical waves is fairly easy to observe, these are not the only kinds of waves that can pass through the same space at the same time. Visible light and other forms of electromagnetic radiation, such as microwaves and X rays, can also occupy the same space at the same time through superposition.

12-4 SECTION OBJECTIVES

- **Apply the superposition principle.**
- **Differentiate between constructive and destructive interference.**
- **Predict when a reflected wave will be inverted.**
- **Predict whether specific traveling waves will produce a standing wave.**
- **Identify nodes and antinodes of a standing wave.**

Figure 12-16
Two of these bumper boats cannot be in the same place at one time. Waves, on the other hand, can pass through one another without affecting each other.

Figure 12-17
This ripple tank demonstrates the interference of water waves.

Displacements in the same direction produce constructive interference

In **Figure 12-18(a),** two wave pulses are traveling toward each other on a stretched rope. The larger pulse is moving to the right, while the smaller pulse moves toward the left. At the moment the two wave pulses meet, a resultant wave is formed, as shown in **Figure 12-18(b).**

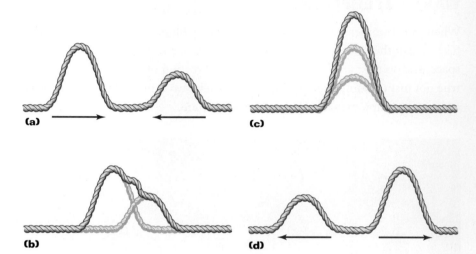

Figure 12-18
When these two wave pulses meet, the displacements at each point add up to form a resultant wave. This is an example of constructive interference.

At each point along the rope, the displacements due to the two pulses are added together, and the result is the displacement of the resultant wave. For example, when the two pulses exactly coincide, as they do in **Figure 12-18(c),** the amplitude of the resultant wave is equal to the sum of the amplitudes of each pulse. This method of summing the displacements of waves is known as the *superposition principle.* According to this principle, when two or more waves travel through a medium, the resultant wave is the sum of the displacements of the individual waves at each point. The superposition principle holds true for all types of waves, both mechanical and electromagnetic. However, experiments show that the superposition principle is valid only when the individual waves have small amplitudes of displacement—an assumption we make in all our examples.

Notice that after the two pulses pass through each other, each pulse has the same shape it had before the waves met and each is still traveling in the same direction, as shown in **Figure 12-18(d).** This is true for sound waves at a concert, water waves in a pond, light waves, and other types of waves. Each wave maintains its own characteristics after interference, just as the two pulses do in our example above.

You have seen that when more than one wave travels through the same space, the resultant wave is equal to the sum of the individual displacements. If the displacements are on the same side of equilibrium, as in **Figure 12-18,** they have the same sign. When added together, the resultant wave is larger than the individual displacements. This is called **constructive interference.**

constructive interference

interference in which individual displacements on the same side of the equilibrium position are added together to form the resultant wave

Displacements in opposite directions produce destructive interference

What happens if the pulses are on opposite sides of the equilibrium position, as they are in **Figure 12-19(a)**? In this case, the displacements have different signs, one positive and one negative. When the positive and negative displacements are added, as shown in **Figure 12-19(b)** and **(c)**, the resultant wave is the difference between the pulses. This is called **destructive interference.** After the pulses separate, their shapes are unchanged, as seen in **Figure 12-19(d).**

destructive interference

interference in which individual displacements on opposite sides of the equilibrium position are added together to form the resultant wave

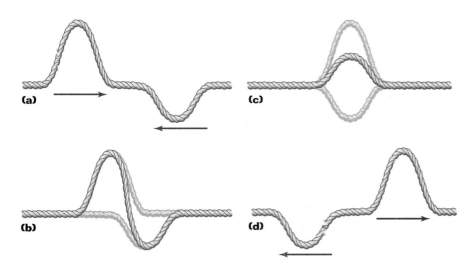

(a)

(c)

(b)

(d)

Figure 12-19
In this case, known as destructive interference, the displacement of one pulse is subtracted from the displacement of the other.

Figure 12-20 shows two pulses of equal amplitude but with displacements of opposite signs. When the two pulses coincide and the displacements are added, the resultant wave has a displacement of zero. In other words, the two pulses completely cancel each other; it is as if there were no disturbance at all at the instant the two pulses overlap. This situation is known as *complete destructive interference.*

If these waves were water waves coming together, one of the waves would be trying to pull an individual drop of water upward at the same instant and with the same force that another wave would be trying to pull it downward. The result would be no net force on the drop, and there would be no motion of the water at all at that moment.

Thus far, we have considered the interference produced by two transverse pulse waves. The superposition principle is valid for longitudinal waves as well. A *compression* involves a force on a particle in one direction, while a *rarefaction* involves a force on the same particle in the opposite direction. Hence, when a compression and a rarefaction interfere, there is destructive interference, and the net force on the particle is reduced.

In our examples, we have considered constructive and destructive interference separately, and we have dealt only with pulse waves. With periodic waves, complicated patterns arise that involve regions of constructive and destructive interference at different points, and the locations of these regions may vary with time as the individual waves travel.

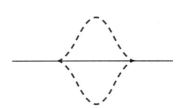

Figure 12-20
The resultant displacement at each point of the string is zero, so the two pulses cancel one another. This is complete destructive interference.

REFLECTION

In our discussion of waves so far, we have assumed that the waves being analyzed could travel indefinitely without striking anything that would stop them or otherwise change their motion. But what happens to the motion of a wave when it reaches a boundary?

At a free boundary, waves are reflected

Consider a pulse wave traveling on a stretched rope whose end forms a ring around a post, as shown in **Figure 12-21(a).** We will assume that the ring is free to slide along the post without friction.

As the pulse travels to the right, each point of the rope moves up once and then back down. When the pulse reaches the boundary, the rope is free to move up as usual, and it pulls the ring up with it. Then the ring falls back down to its previous level. The movement of the rope at the post is similar to the movement that would result if someone were to whip the rope upward to send a pulse to the left, which will cause a pulse to travel back along the rope to the left. This is called *reflection*. Note that the reflected pulse is identical to the incident pulse.

At a fixed boundary, waves are reflected and inverted

Now consider a pulse traveling on a stretched rope that is fixed at one end, as in **Figure 12-21(b).** When the pulse reaches the wall, the rope exerts an upward force on the wall, and the wall in turn exerts an equal and opposite reaction force on the rope. This downward force on the rope causes a displacement in the direction opposite the displacement of the original pulse. As a result, the pulse is inverted after reflection.

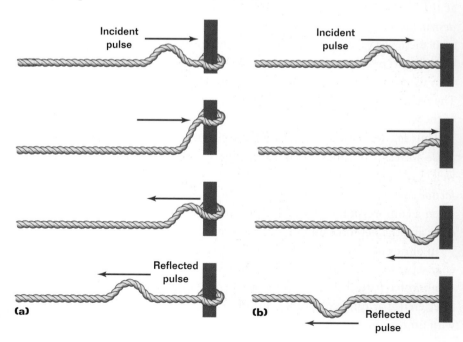

Figure 12-21

(a) When a pulse travels down a rope whose end is free to slide up the post, the pulse is reflected from the free end. **(b)** When a pulse travels down a rope that is fixed at one end, the reflected pulse is inverted.

STANDING WAVES

If a stretched string is clamped at both ends, traveling waves reflect from the fixed ends, creating waves traveling in both directions. The incident and reflected waves combine according to the superposition principle. When the string is vibrated at exactly the right frequency, a pattern will be established on the string that exhibits regions of zero displacement (at which the waves cancel) and regions of maximum displacement (at which the two waves add constructively). In the resulting pattern on the string, the wave appears to stand still—hence its name, **standing wave.**

Standing waves have nodes and antinodes

Figure 12-22(a) shows four possible standing waves for a given string length. The points at which the two waves cancel are called **nodes.** There is no motion in the string at the nodes, but midway between two adjacent nodes, the string vibrates with the largest amplitude. These points are called **antinodes.**

Figure 12-22(b) shows the oscillation of the second case shown in **Figure 12-22(a)** during half a cycle. All points on the string oscillate vertically with the same frequency, except for the nodes, which are stationary. In this case, there are three nodes (N) and two antinodes (A), as illustrated in the figure. Notice that different points of the string have different amplitudes.

standing wave

wave pattern that results when two waves of the same frequency, wavelength, and amplitude travel in opposite directions and interfere

node

point in a standing wave that always undergoes complete destructive interference and therefore is stationary

antinode

point in a standing wave, halfway between two nodes, at which the largest amplitude occurs

(b)

Figure 12-22
(a) This photograph shows four possible standing waves that can exist on a given string. **(b)** The diagram shows the progression of the second standing wave for one-half of a cycle.

Acoustic Levitation

In the movies, levitating objects are the products of a hefty special-effects budget. For Dr. Martin Barmatz, a physicist at Jet Propulsion Laboratory, in Pasadena, California, all it takes is sound.

Barmatz studies the properties of a chamber in which lightweight objects can be levitated, rotated, and oscillated by using sound waves.

"It's a rectangular chamber," he said. "It has two equal sides and a slightly larger third side. High-powered speakers introduce sound energy through a hole in the center of each of the chamber's sides. Three standing waves, each one perpendicular to the others, are produced within the chamber."

"The horizontal standing waves center the object along the vertical axis of the chamber. Then, the force of the vertical standing wave levitates the object from below," he said. These waves have a frequency of about 2000 Hz, well within the range of human hearing. Because the level of sound produced is around 160 decibels—loud enough to cause extreme pain to the ears— acoustic-levitation chambers must be very well insulated against sound leakage.

Barmatz said that this technology was originally designed for NASA as part of a space-

based furnace. In normal furnaces, substances being heated often become contaminated by their containers. By using these techniques in a space environment, however, the substances remain much purer because they are isolated from any container surfaces.

Acoustic levitation is used to study the properties of liquids and bubbles. A single drop of a liquid is isolated and levitated in the chamber. Then scientists study the path of bubbles in the liquid drop or the drop's behavior in a zero-gravity situation. The figure above shows an image of a rotating liquid drop in the Drop Physics Module, taken during the STS 50 Space Shuttle flight in June 1992 (shown below).

Only certain frequencies of vibration produce standing wave patterns. **Figure 12-23** shows different possible standing waves for a given string length. In each case, the curves represent the position of the string at different instants of time. If the string were vibrating rapidly, the several positions would blur together and give the appearance of loops, like those shown in the diagram. A single loop corresponds to either a crest or trough alone, while two loops correspond to a crest and a trough together, or one wavelength.

The ends of the string must be nodes because these points cannot vibrate. As you can see in **Figure 12-23,** standing waves can be produced for any wavelength that allows both ends of the string to be nodes. One possibility appears in **Figure 12-23(b).** In this case, each end is a node, and there are no nodes in between. Because a single loop corresponds to either a crest or trough alone, this standing wave corresponds to one-half of a wavelength. Thus, the wavelength in this case is equal to twice the string length ($2L$).

The next possible standing wave, shown in **Figure 12-23(c),** has three nodes: one at either end and one in the middle. In this case there are two loops, corresponding to a crest and a trough. Thus, this standing wave has a wavelength equal to the string length (L). The next case, shown in **Figure 12-23(d),** has a wavelength equal to two-thirds of the string length $\left(\frac{2}{3}L\right)$, and the pattern continues. Wavelengths between the values shown here do not produce standing waves because they do not allow both ends of the string to be nodes.

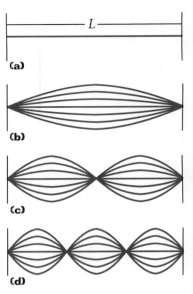

Figure 12-23
Only certain frequencies produce standing waves on this fixed string. The wavelength of these standing waves depends on the string length. Possible wavelengths include $2L$ **(b)**, L **(c),** and $\frac{2}{3}L$ **(d).**

Section Review

1. A wave of amplitude 0.30 m interferes with a second wave of amplitude 0.20 m. What is the largest resultant displacement that may occur?

2. A string is rigidly attached to a post at one end. A series of pulses of amplitude 0.15 m sent down the string are reflected at the post and travel back down the string without a loss of amplitude. What is the amplitude at a point on the string where two pulses cross? What type of interference is this?

3. How would your answer to item 2 change if the same pulses were sent down a string whose end is free? What type of interference is this?

4. Look at the standing wave shown in **Figure 12-24.** How many nodes does this wave have? How many antinodes?

Figure 12-24

5. A stretched string fixed at both ends is 2.0 m long. What are three wavelengths that will produce standing waves on this string? Name at least one wavelength that would not produce a standing wave pattern, and explain your answer.

De BROGLIE WAVES

Earlier in this chapter, we treated waves and particles as if there were a clear distinction between the two. For most of the history of science, this was believed to be the case. However, in the early twentieth century, scientists were confronted with experimental evidence suggesting that the distinction between waves and particles is not as clear-cut as everyone had assumed.

The dual nature of light

This scientific revolution began in 1900, when Max Planck proposed the possibility that energy comes in discrete units. In 1905, Einstein extended Planck's theory, suggesting that all electromagnetic waves (such as light) sometimes behave like particles. According to this theory, light is both a wave and a particle; some experiments reveal its wave nature, and other experiments display its particle nature. Although this idea was initially greeted with skepticism, it explained certain phenomena that the wave theory of light could not account for and was soon confirmed empirically in a variety of experiments.

Matter waves

The idea that light has a dual nature led Louis de Broglie to propose in his doctoral thesis that perhaps all matter has wavelike characteristics. De Broglie's thesis, submitted in 1924, was based on his belief that there should not be two separate branches of physics, one for electromagnetic waves and another for matter. At that time, there was no experimental evidence to support his theory.

De Broglie's calculations suggested that matter waves had a wavelength (λ), often called the de Broglie wavelength, given by the following equation:

$$\lambda = \frac{h}{p} = \frac{h}{mv}$$

The variable h in this equation is called Planck's constant, which is approximately equal to 6.63×10^{-34} J•s, and p is the object's momentum, which is equivalent to its mass, m, times its velocity, v. Note that the dual nature of matter suggested by de Broglie is seen by this equation, which includes both a wave concept (λ) and a particle concept (mv).

De Broglie's equation shows that the smaller the momentum of an object, the larger its de Broglie wavelength. But even when the momentum of an object is very small from our perspective, h is so small that the wavelength is still much too small for us to detect. In order to detect wavelengths this small, one must use an opening equal to or smaller than the wavelength because waves passing through such an opening will display patterns of constructive and destructive interference. When the opening is much larger than the wavelength, waves travel through it without being affected. The de Broglie wavelength of a 0.15 kg baseball moving at 30 m/s is about 1.5×10^{-34} m. This is almost a trillion trillion times smaller than the diameter of a typical air molecule—much smaller than any possible opening through which we could observe interference effects. This explains why the de Broglie wavelength of objects cannot be observed in our everyday experience.

However, in the microscopic world, the wave effects of matter can be observed. The distance between atoms in a crystal is about 10^{-10} m. Electrons ($m = 9.109 \times 10^{-31}$ kg) accelerated to a speed of 1.4×10^{7} m/s have a de Broglie wavelength of approximately this size. Thus, the atoms in a crystal can act as a three-dimensional grating that should diffract electron waves. Such an experiment was performed three years after de Broglie's thesis by Clinton J. Davisson and Lester H. Germer, and the electrons did create patterns of constructive and destructive interference. This experiment gave confirmation of de Broglie's theory of the dual nature of matter.

Figure 12-25

In this photograph, electron waves are diffracted by a crystal. Experiments such as this show the wave nature of electrons and thereby provide empirical evidence for de Broglie's theory of the dual nature of matter.

The electron microscope

A practical device that relies on the wave characteristics of matter is the electron microscope. In principle, the electron microscope is similar to an ordinary compound microscope. But while ordinary microscopes use lenses to bend rays of light that are reflected from a small object, electron microscopes use electric and magnetic fields to accelerate and focus a beam of electrons. Rather than examining the image through an eyepiece, as in an ordinary microscope, a magnetic lens forms an image on a fluorescent screen. Without the fluorescent screen, the image would not be visible.

Any microscope is capable of detecting details that are comparable in size to the wavelength of the radiation used to illuminate the object. Typically, the wavelengths of electrons are about 100 times shorter than those of the visible light used in optical microscopes. As a result, electron microscopes are able to distinguish details about 100 times smaller than optical microscopes. Because of their great resolving power, electron microscopes are widely used in many areas of scientific research.

Figure 12-26

This image of cat hairs, produced by an electron microscope, is magnified 500 times.

CHAPTER 12
Summary

KEY TERMS

amplitude (p. 446)

antinode (p. 463)

constructive interference (p. 460)

crest (p. 454)

destructive interference (p. 461)

frequency (p. 446)

longitudinal wave (p. 455)

mechanical wave (p. 452)

medium (p. 452)

node (p. 463)

period (p. 446)

periodic wave (p. 453)

pulse wave (p. 453)

simple harmonic motion (p. 439)

standing wave (p. 463)

transverse wave (p. 454)

trough (p. 454)

wavelength (p. 454)

KEY IDEAS

Section 12-1 Simple harmonic motion
- In simple harmonic motion, restoring force is proportional to displacement.
- A mass-spring system vibrates with simple harmonic motion, and the spring force is given by Hooke's law: $\boxed{F_{elastic} = -kx}$
- For small angles of displacement (<15°), a pendulum swings with simple harmonic motion.
- In simple harmonic motion, restoring force and acceleration are maximum at maximum displacement and velocity is maximum at equilibrium.

Section 12-2 Measuring simple harmonic motion
- The period of a mass-spring system depends only on the mass and the spring constant. The period of a simple pendulum depends only on the string length and the free-fall acceleration.
- Frequency is the inverse of period.

Section 12-3 Properties of waves
- Wave particles vibrate around an equilibrium position as the wave travels.
- In a transverse wave, vibrations are *perpendicular* to the direction of wave motion. In a longitudinal wave, vibrations are *parallel* to the direction of wave motion.
- Wave speed equals frequency times wavelength: $\boxed{v = f\lambda}$

Section 12-4 Wave interactions
- If two or more waves are moving through a medium, the resultant wave is found by adding the individual displacements together point by point.
- Standing waves are formed when two waves having the same frequency, amplitude, and wavelength travel in opposite directions through a medium and interfere.

Variable symbols

Quantities		Units	
$F_{elastic}$	spring force	N	newtons
k	spring constant	N/m	newtons/meter
T	period	s	seconds
f	frequency	Hz	hertz = s^{-1}
λ	wavelength	m	meters

CHAPTER 12
Review and Assess

SIMPLE HARMONIC MOTION

Review questions

1. What characterizes an object's motion as simple harmonic?

2. List four examples of simple harmonic motion.

3. Does the acceleration of a simple harmonic oscillator remain constant during its motion? Is the acceleration ever zero? Explain.

4. A pendulum is pulled aside 40° from its equilibrium position and released. Is its motion simple harmonic?

5. April is about to release the bob of a pendulum. Before she lets go, what sort of potential energy does the bob have? How does the energy of the bob change as it swings through one full cycle of motion?

Conceptual questions

6. An ideal mass-spring system vibrating with simple harmonic motion would oscillate indefinitely. Explain why.

7. In a simple pendulum, the weight of the bob can be divided into two components, one tangent to the bob's direction of motion and the other perpendicular to the bob's direction of motion. Which of these is the restoring force, and why?

Practice problems

8. In an arcade game, a 0.12 kg disk is shot across a frictionless horizontal surface by being compressed against a spring and then released. If the spring has a spring constant of 230 N/m and is compressed from its equilibrium position by 6.0 cm, what is the magnitude of the spring force on the disk at the moment it is released?
(See Sample Problem 12A.)

9. Janet wants to find the spring constant of a given spring, so she hangs the spring vertically and attaches a 0.40 kg mass to the spring's other end. If the spring stretches 3.0 cm from its equilibrium position, what is the spring constant?
(See Sample Problem 12A.)

10. In preparing to shoot an arrow, an archer pulls a bow string back 0.40 m by exerting a force that increases uniformly from 0 to 230 N. What is the equivalent spring constant of the bow?
(See Sample Problem 12A.)

11. A child's toy consists of a piece of plastic attached to a spring, as shown in **Figure 12-27.** The spring is compressed against the floor a distance of 2.0 cm and released. If the spring constant is 85 N/m, what is the magnitude of the spring force acting on the toy at the moment it is released?
(See Sample Problem 12A.)

Figure 12-27

PERIOD AND FREQUENCY

Review questions

12. A child swings on a playground swing. How many times does the child swing through the swing's equilibrium position during the course of a single period of motion?

13. What is the total distance traveled by an object moving back and forth in simple harmonic motion in a time interval equal to its period when its amplitude is equal to A?

14. How is the period of a simple harmonic vibration related to its frequency?

15. What happens to the period of a simple pendulum when the pendulum's length is doubled? What happens when the suspended mass is doubled?

16. A pendulum bob is made with a ball filled with water. What would happen to the frequency of vibration of this pendulum if there were a hole in the ball that allowed water to slowly leak out?

17. If a pendulum clock keeps perfect time at the base of a mountain, will it also keep perfect time when moved to the top of the mountain? Explain.

18. If a grandfather clock were running slow, how could you adjust the length of the pendulum to correct the time?

19. A simple pendulum can be used as an altimeter on a plane. How will the period of the pendulum vary as the plane moves from the runway to its cruising altitude of 1.00×10^4 m?

20. Will the period of a vibrating mass-spring system on Earth be different from the period of an identical mass-spring system on the moon? Why or why not?

Practice problems ◼▬▬▬

21. Find the period and frequency of a 9.8 m long pendulum.
   (See Sample Problem 12B.)

22. A spring with a spring constant of 1.8×10^2 N/m is attached to a 1.5 kg mass and then set in motion.
   a. What is the period of the mass-spring system?
   b. What is the frequency of the vibration?
   (See Sample Problem 12C.)

23. A pendulum that moves through its equilibrium position once every 1.000 s is sometimes called a "seconds pendulum."
   a. What is the period of any seconds pendulum?
   b. In Cambridge, England, a seconds pendulum is 0.9942 m long. What is the free-fall acceleration in Cambridge?
   c. In Tokyo, Japan, a seconds pendulum is 0.9927 m long. What is the free-fall acceleration in Tokyo?
   (See Sample Problem 12B.)

24. A visitor to a lighthouse wishes to determine the height of the tower. The visitor ties a spool of thread to a small rock to make a simple pendulum, then hangs the pendulum down a spiral staircase in the center of the tower. The period of oscillation is 9.49 s. What is the height of the tower?
   (See Sample Problem 12B.)

PROPERTIES OF WAVES

Review questions ◼▬▬▬

25. What is common to all waves?

26. How do transverse and longitudinal waves differ?

27. **Figure 12-28** depicts a pulse wave traveling on a spring.
   a. In which direction are the particles of the medium vibrating?
   b. Is this wave transverse or longitudinal?

Figure 12-28

28. In a stretched spring, several coils are pinched together and others are spread farther apart than usual. What sort of wave is this?

29. How far does a wave travel in one period?

30. If you were to shake the end of a rope up and down three times each second, what would be the period of the waves set up in the rope? What would be the frequency?

31. Give three examples of mechanical waves. How are these different from electromagnetic waves, such as light waves?

Conceptual questions ◼▬▬▬

32. How does a single point on a string move as a transverse wave passes by that point?

33. What happens to the wavelength of a wave on a string when the frequency is doubled? What happens to the speed of the wave?

34. Why do sound waves need a medium through which to travel?

35. Two tuning forks with frequencies of 256 Hz and 512 Hz are struck. Which of the sounds will move faster through the air?

36. What is one advantage of transferring energy by electromagnetic waves?

Practice problems

37. A wave traveling in the positive x direction with a frequency of 25.0 Hz is shown in **Figure 12-29**. Find the following values for this wave:
  - **a.** amplitude
  - **b.** wavelength
  - **c.** period
  - **d.** speed

(See Sample Problem 12D.)

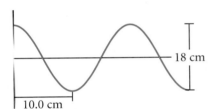

Figure 12-29

38. Green light has a wavelength of 5.20×10^{-7} m and travels through the air at a speed of 3.00×10^{8} m/s. Calculate the period and the frequency of green light waves with this wavelength.
(See Sample Problem 12D.)

39. Microwaves travel at the speed of light, 3.00×10^{8} m/s. When the frequency of microwaves is 9.00×10^{9} Hz, what is their wavelength?
(See Sample Problem 12D.)

WAVE INTERACTIONS

Review questions

40. Using the superposition principle, draw the resultant waves for each of the examples in **Figure 12-30**.

Figure 12-30

41. What is the difference between constructive interference and destructive interference?

42. Which waveform of those shown in **Figure 12-31** is the resultant waveform?

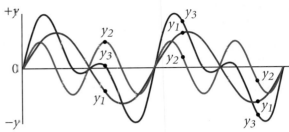

Figure 12-31

43. Anthony sends a series of pulses of amplitude 24 cm down a string that is attached to a post at one end. Assuming the pulses are reflected with no loss of amplitude, what is the amplitude at a point on the string where the two pulses are crossing if
  - **a.** the string is rigidly attached to the post?
  - **b.** the end at which reflection occurs is free to slide up and down?

44. A wave of 0.75 m interferes with a second wave of amplitude 0.53 m.
  - **a.** Find the amplitude of the resultant wave if the interference is constructive.
  - **b.** Find the amplitude of the resultant wave if the interference is destructive.

Conceptual questions

45. Can more than two waves interfere in a given medium?

46. What is the resultant displacement at a position where destructive interference is complete?

47. When two waves interfere, can the resultant wave be larger than either of the two original waves? If so, under what conditions?

48. Which of the following wavelengths will produce standing waves on a string that is 3.5 m long?
  - **a.** 1.75 m
  - **b.** 3.5 m
  - **c.** 5.0 m
  - **d.** 7.0 m

MIXED REVIEW PROBLEMS

49. You dip your finger into a pan of water twice each second, producing waves with crests that are separated by 0.15 m. Determine the frequency, period, and speed of these water waves.

50. What is the free-fall acceleration in a location where the period of a 0.850 m long pendulum is 1.86 s?

51. A sound wave traveling at 343 m/s is emitted by the foghorn of a tugboat. An echo is heard 2.60 s later. How far away is the reflecting object?

52. The notes produced by a violin range in frequency from approximately 196 Hz to 2637 Hz. Find the possible range of wavelengths in air produced by this instrument when the speed of sound in air is 340 m/s.

53. A mass-spring system oscillates with an amplitude of 3.5 cm. The spring constant is 250 N/m and the mass is 0.50 kg.

    a. Calculate the mechanical energy of the mass-spring system.

    b. Calculate the maximum acceleration of the mass-spring system.

Technology & Learning

Graphing calculators

Use your graphing calculator to predict the period of a clock pendulum with a period of 2.0 s on Earth if the pendulum were moved to the following locations, which have the free-fall accelerations indicated:

a. the surface of Mars, 3.71 m/s^2

b. the surface of Venus, 8.78 m/s^2

c. the surface of Neptune, 11.8 m/s^2

Press [Y=] and [CLEAR] to clear any functions.

Open a new program by pressing [PRGM] [▶] [▶] [ENTER]. Name the program "PEND" and press [ENTER]. Then enter the program shown in the table below.

To exit the program editor, press [2nd] [QUIT]. To run the program, press [PRGM], select "PEND," and press [ENTER] [ENTER]. Enter the value for the pendulum's period on Earth, and press [ENTER].

The calculator will provide a graph of the pendulum's period versus the free-fall acceleration. (If the graph is not visible, press [WINDOW] and change the settings for the graph window, then press [GRAPH].)

Press [TRACE] and use the arrow keys to trace along the curve. The x value corresponds to the free-fall acceleration in meters per second squared, and the y value corresponds to the period in seconds.

Keystrokes	Display
	PROGRAM: PEND
1. [PRGM] [▶] [2] [ALPHA] [T] [ENTER]	:PROMPT T
2. [(] [9] [.] [8] [1] [ALPHA] [T] [x²] [)] [÷] [(] [4] [2nd] [π] [2nd] [π] [)] [STO▶] [ALPHA] [L] [ENTER]	:(9.81T^2)/(4ππ) → L
3. [ALPHA] ["] [2] [2nd] [π] [2nd] [√] [(] [ALPHA] [L] [÷] [X,T,θ] [)] [ALPHA] ["] [STO▶] [2nd] [Y-VARS] [1] [1] [ENTER]	:"2π$\sqrt{(L/X)}$" → Y1
4. [PRGM] [▶] [4] [ENTER]	:DISPGRAPH

54. Yellow light travels through a certain glass block at a speed of 1.97×10^8 m/s. The wavelength of the light in this particular type of glass is 3.81×10^{-7} m (381 nm). What is the frequency of the yellow light in the glass block?

55. A 0.40 kg mass is attached to a spring with a spring constant of 160 N/m so that the mass is allowed to move on a horizontal frictionless surface. The mass is released from rest when the spring is compressed 0.15 m.

    a. Find the force on the mass at the instant the spring is released.

    b. Find the acceleration of the mass at the instant the spring is released.

    c. What are the maximum values of force and acceleration?

56. The distance between two successive crests of a certain transverse wave is 1.20 m. Eight crests pass a given point along the direction of travel every 12.0 s. Calculate the wave speed.

57. A simple 2.00 m long pendulum oscillates in a location where $g = 9.80$ m/s^2. How many complete oscillations does this pendulum make in 5.00 min?

58. A certain pendulum clock that works perfectly on Earth is taken to the moon, where $g = 1.63$ m/s^2. If the clock is started at 12:00:00 A.M., what will it read after 24 h?

59. A harmonic wave is traveling along a rope. The oscillator that generates the wave completes 40.0 vibrations in 30.0 s. A given maximum of the wave travels 425 cm along the rope in a time period of 10.0 s. What is the wavelength?

Alternative Assessment

Performance assessment

1. Design an experiment to compare the spring constant and period of oscillation of a system built with two (or more) springs connected in two ways: end to end and with all ends anchored to the same point. If your teacher approves your plan, obtain the necessary equipment and perform the experiment.

2. The rule that the period of a pendulum is determined by its length is a good approximation for amplitudes below 15°. Design an experiment to investigate how amplitudes of oscillation greater than 15° affect the motion of a pendulum.

    List what equipment you would need, what measurements you would perform, what data you would record, and what you would calculate. If your teacher approves your plan, obtain the necessary equipment and perform the experiment.

3. Imagine you are sitting on a small boat on a calm lake. A stone thrown in the water makes a splashing noise and some ripples. Predict whether the boat will oscillate before, after, or at the same time that you hear the splash. Write a justification supporting your prediction. Identify any additional information that would improve your prediction.

Portfolio projects

4. Investigate the relationship between uniform circular motion and simple harmonic motion by studying the motion of a crank handle and its shadow on the ground. Determine the displacement and period for both the handle and its shadow at different points of a cycle. You may create geometrical drawings, build a model, or videotape your experiment.

5. Research earthquakes and different kinds of seismic waves. Create a presentation about earthquakes that includes answers to the following questions as well as additional information: Do earthquakes travel through oceans? What is transferred from place to place as seismic waves propagate? What determines their speed?

6. Identify examples of periodic motion in nature. Create a chart describing the objects involved, their path of motion, their periods, and the forces involved. Which of the periodic motions are harmonic and which are not?

CHAPTER 12
Laboratory Exercise

THE PENDULUM AND SIMPLE HARMONIC MOTION

In this experiment, you will construct models of a simple pendulum using different masses and lengths of cord. For each model, you will measure how long it takes the pendulum to complete 20 cycles. You can then use the period—the time required for the pendulum to complete one cycle—and the length of the cord to calculate *g* at your geographical location.

PREPARATION

1. Read the entire lab, and plan what measurements you will take.

2. Prepare a data table with four columns and seven rows in your lab note-book. In the first row, label the second through fourth columns *Mass (kg)*, *Length (m)*, and *Time (s)*. In the first column, label the first row *Trial* and label the second through seventh rows *1, 2, 3, 4, 5,* and *6*.

PROCEDURE

Constant mass with varying length

3. Measure the mass of the bob. Record it in your data table.

4. Set up a ring stand with a clamp to serve as the support. Place the ring stand away from the table's edge. Use cord to tie the bob to the clamp on the ring stand, securing it at the desired length, about 75 cm. Choose a location away from other groups, where the pendulum can swing freely.

5. Measure the length of the pendulum to the center of the bob.

6. Use the protractor to find the position of the pendulum where the ampli-tude is equal to 10°. Lift the bob to this position. Make sure that the path is free of obstructions, and release the bob so that it swings freely.

7. Measure and record the time required for 20 cycles of the pendulum bob. Keep the amplitude in all trials between 5° and 15°. Do not exceed 15°.

8. Perform two more trials using the same mass but different cord lengths.

Constant length with varying mass

9. Replace the bob with a different mass, and repeat the entire procedure. Record the mass and length.

10. Perform two more trials using the same length with different masses.

ANALYSIS AND INTERPRETATION

Calculations and data analysis

1. Applying ideas For each trial, calculate the period of the pendulum.

2. Applying ideas Using the equation for the period of a pendulum, calculate the value for the free-fall acceleration, g, for each trial.

3. Analyzing results Use 9.81 m/s^2 as the accepted value for g.

    a. Compute the absolute error for each trial using the following equation:

$$\text{absolute error} = |\text{experimental} - \text{accepted}|$$

    b. Compute the relative error for each trial using the following equation:

$$\text{relative error} = \frac{(\text{experimental} - \text{accepted})}{\text{accepted}}$$

4. Graphing data Plot the following graphs:

    a. the period vs. the length for trials 1–3

    b. the period vs. the mass of the bob for trials 4–6

    c. the period vs. the square root of the length for trials 4–6

Conclusions

5. Evaluating results Based on your data and your graphs, how does the mass of the pendulum bob affect its period of vibration?

6. Evaluating results Based on your data and your graphs, how does the length of the pendulum affect its period of vibration?

Extensions

7. Building models On Earth, the value of g varies with the altitude. Develop a method to use a pendulum to find the altitude of your school. If there is time and your teacher approves your plan, test your method. Compare your result with the accepted value.

Figure 12-32
Step 6: Hold the bob so that the cord is perfectly straight while you measure the angle.

Step 7: Release the bob gently so that it swings smoothly. Practice counting and timing cycles to get good results.

1789 – The storming of the Bastille marks the beginning of the French Revolution.

1798 $$Q = mc_p \Delta T$$

Benjamin Thompson (Count Rumford) demonstrates that energy transferred by heat results from mechanical processes, rather than the release of caloric, the heat fluid that has been widely believed to exist in all substances.

1796 – Edward Jenner develops the smallpox vaccine.

1800 $$\Delta V = \frac{\Delta PE_{electric}}{q}$$

Alessandro Volta develops the first current-electricity cell using alternating plates of silver and zinc.

1802 $$m\lambda = d(\sin\theta)$$

Thomas Young demonstrates that light rays interfere, providing the first substantial support for a wave theory of light.

1804 – Saint-Domingue, under the control of the French-African majority led by **Toussaint-Louverture,** becomes the independent Republic of Haiti. Over the next two decades most of Europe's western colonies become independent.

1804 – Richard Trevithick builds and tests the first steam locomotive. It pulls 10 tons along a distance of 15 km at a speed of 8 km/h.

1811 – Mathematician **Sophie Germain** writes the first of three papers on the mathematics of vibrating surfaces. She later addresses one of the most famous problems in mathematics—Fermat's last theorem—proving it to be true for a wide range of conditions.

1810 – **Kamehameha I** unites the Hawaiian islands under a monarchy.

1814

$$\sin\theta = \frac{m\lambda}{a}$$

Augustin Fresnel begins his research in optics, the results of which will confirm and explain **Thomas Young's** discovery of interference and will firmly establish the wave model of light first suggested by **Christian Huygens** over a century earlier.

1818 – **Mary Shelley** writes *Frankenstein, or the Modern Prometheus*. Primarily thought of as a horror novel, the book's emphasis on science and its moral consequences also qualifies it as the first "science fiction" novel.

1820

$$F_{magnetic} = BI\ell$$

Hans Christian Oersted demonstrates that an electric current produces a magnetic field. (**Gian Dominico Romagnosi,** an amateur scientist, discovered the effect 18 years earlier, but at the time attracted no attention.) **André-Marie Ampere** repeats Oersted's experiment and formulates the law of electromagnetism that today bears his name.

1826 – **Katsushika Hokusai** begins his series of prints *Thirty-Six Views of Mount Fuji.*

1830 – **Hector Berlioz** composes his *Symphonie Fantastique,* one of the first Romantic works for large orchestra that tells a story with music.

1800

1810

1820

1830

Sound

PHYSICS IN ACTION

Some marine mammals, such as dolphins, use sound waves to locate distant objects. In this process, called *echolocation,* a dolphin produces a rapid train of short sound pulses that travel through the water, bounce off distant objects, and reflect back to the dolphin. From these echoes, dolphins can determine the size, shape, speed, and distance of their potential prey.

A dolphin's echolocation is extremely sophisticated. Experiments have shown that at a distance of 114 m, a blindfolded dolphin can locate a stainless-steel sphere with a diameter of 7.5 cm and can distinguish between a sheet of aluminum and a sheet of copper. In this chapter you will study sound waves and see how dolphins echolocate.

- *How does dolphin echolocation work?*
- *How does a dolphin determine the direction a fish is moving?*

CONCEPT REVIEW

Longitudinal waves (Section 12-3)

Wave speed (Section 12-3)

Standing waves (Section 12-4)

13-1
Sound waves

compression

the region of a longitudinal wave in which the density and pressure are greater than normal

rarefaction

the region of a longitudinal wave in which the density and pressure are less than normal

THE PRODUCTION OF SOUND WAVES

Whether a sound wave conveys the shrill whine of a jet engine or the melodic whistling of a bird, it begins with a vibrating object. We will explore how sound waves are produced by considering a vibrating tuning fork, as shown in **Figure 13-1(a).**

The vibrating prong of a tuning fork, shown in **Figure 13-1(b),** sets the air molecules near it in motion. As the prong swings to the right, as shown in **Figure 13-1(c),** the air molecules in front of the movement are forced closer together. (This situation is exaggerated in the figure for clarity.) Such a region of high molecular density and high air pressure is called a **compression.** As the prong moves to the left, as in **Figure 13-1(d),** the molecules to the right spread apart, and the density and air pressure in this region become lower than normal. This region of lower density and pressure is called a **rarefaction.**

As the tuning fork continues to vibrate, a series of compressions and rarefactions form and spread away from each prong. These compressions and rarefactions expand and spread out in all directions, like ripple waves on a pond. When the tuning fork vibrates with simple harmonic motion, the air molecules also vibrate back and forth with simple harmonic motion.

Figure 13-1

(a) The sound from a tuning fork is produced by **(b)** the vibrations of each of its prongs. **(c)** When a prong swings to the right, there is a region of high density and pressure. **(d)** When the prong swings back to the left, a region of lower density and pressure exists.

(a)

(c) Compression

(d) Rarefaction

(b)

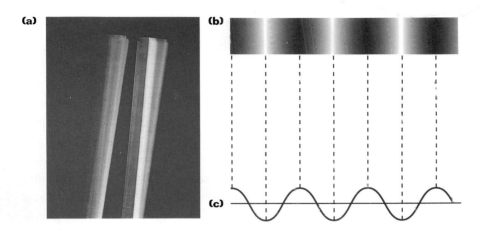

Figure 13-2
(a) As this tuning fork vibrates, **(b)** a series of compressions and rarefactions move away from each prong. **(c)** The crests of this sine wave correspond to compressions, and the troughs correspond to rarefactions.

Sound waves are longitudinal

In sound waves, the vibrations of air molecules are parallel to the direction of wave motion. Thus, sound waves are longitudinal. As you saw in Chapter 12, a longitudinal wave produced by a vibrating object can be represented by a sine curve. In **Figure 13-2** the crests of the sine curve correspond to compressions in the sound wave, and the troughs correspond to rarefactions. Because compressions are regions of higher pressure and rarefactions are regions of lower pressure, the sine curve represents the changes in air pressure due to the propagation of the sound waves.

CHARACTERISTICS OF SOUND WAVES

In Chapter 12, frequency was defined as the number of cycles per unit of time. Sound waves that the average human ear can hear, called *audible* sound waves, have frequencies between 20 and 20 000 Hz. (An individual's hearing depends on a variety of factors, including age and experiences with loud noises.) Sound waves with frequencies less than 20 Hz are called *infrasonic* waves, and those above 20 000 Hz are called *ultrasonic* waves.

It may seem confusing to use the term *sound waves* for infrasonic or ultrasonic waves since humans cannot hear these sounds, but ultrasonic and infrasonic waves consist of the same types of vibrations as the sounds that we can hear. The range of sound waves that are considered to be audible depends on the ability of the average human ear to detect their vibrations. Dogs can hear ultrasonic waves that humans cannot.

Frequency determines pitch

The frequency of an audible sound wave determines how high or low we perceive the sound to be, which is known as **pitch.** As the frequency of a sound wave increases, the pitch rises. The frequency of a wave is an objective quantity that can be measured, while pitch refers to how different frequencies are perceived by the human ear.

pitch

how high or low we perceive a sound to be, depending on the frequency of the sound wave

Figure 13-3
Ultrasound images, such as this one, are formed with reflected sound waves. This colorized image depicts a fetus after 21 weeks of development.

Table 13-1   Speed of sound in various media

Medium	v (m/s)
Gases	
air (0°C)	331
air (25°C)	346
air (100°C)	366
helium (0°C)	972
hydrogen (0°C)	1290
oxygen (0°C)	317
Liquids at 25°C	
methyl alcohol	1140
sea water	1530
water	1490
Solids	
aluminum	5100
copper	3560
iron	5130
lead	1320
vulcanized rubber	54

Ultrasonic waves can produce images of objects

As discussed in Chapter 12, wavelength decreases as frequency increases. Thus, infrasonic waves have longer wavelengths than audible sound waves, and ultrasonic waves have shorter wavelengths. Because of their short wavelengths, ultrasonic waves have widespread medical applications.

For example, ultrasonic waves can be used to produce images of objects inside the body. Such imaging is possible because sound waves are partially reflected when they reach a boundary between two materials of different densities. The images produced by ultrasonic waves are clearer and more detailed than those that could be produced by lower-frequency sound waves because the short wavelengths of ultrasonic waves are easily reflected off small objects. Audible and infrasonic sound waves are not as effective because their longer wavelengths pass around small objects.

Physicians commonly use ultrasonic waves to observe fetuses. In this process, a crystal emits ultrasonic pulses. The same crystal acts as a receiver and detects the reflected sound waves. These reflected sound waves are converted to an electric signal, which forms an image on a fluorescent screen. By repeating this process for different portions of the mother's abdomen, a physician can obtain a complete picture of the fetus. **Figure 13-3** shows the ultrasound image of a fetus in the womb after 21 weeks of development. In this profile view, the head is at the upper right of the image, and an outline of the spine and upper arm can also be seen. At this stage, the nose, lips, and chin are fully developed, and the fetus weighs about 500 g. Images such as this allow doctors to detect some types of fetal abnormalities.

Dolphin echolocation works in a similar manner. A dolphin sends out pulses of sound, which return in the form of reflected sound waves. These reflected waves allow the dolphin to form an image of the object that reflected the waves. Dolphins use high-frequency waves for echolocation because shorter wavelengths are most effective for detecting smaller objects.

Speed of sound depends on the medium

Sound waves can travel through solids, liquids, and gases. Because waves consist of particle vibrations, the speed of a wave depends on how quickly one particle can transfer its motion to another particle. For example, solid particles respond more rapidly to a disturbance than gas particles do because the molecules of a solid are closer together than those of a gas are. As a result, sound waves generally travel faster through solids than through gases.

The speed of sound also depends on the temperature of the medium. As temperature rises, the particles of a gas collide more frequently. Thus, in a gas, the disturbance can spread faster at higher temperatures than at lower temperatures. In liquids and solids, the particles are close enough together that the difference due to temperature changes is less noticeable. **Table 13-1** shows the speed of sound waves in various media.

Sound waves propagate in three dimensions

In Chapter 12, waves were shown as traveling in a single direction. But sound waves actually travel away from a vibrating source in all three dimensions. When a musician plays a saxophone in the middle of a room, the resulting sound can be heard throughout the room because the sound waves spread out in all directions. Such three-dimensional sound waves are approximately spherical. To simplify, we shall assume that sound waves are exactly spherical unless stated otherwise.

Spherical waves can be represented graphically in two dimensions with a series of circles surrounding the source, as shown in **Figure 13-4.** The circles represent the centers of compressions, called *wave fronts*. Because we are considering a three-dimensional phenomenon in two dimensions, each circle represents a spherical area.

Because each wave front corresponds to the center of a compression, the distance between adjacent wave fronts is equal to one wavelength, λ. The radial lines perpendicular to the wave fronts are called *rays*. Rays indicate the direction of the wave motion. The sine curve used in our previous representation of sound waves, also shown in **Figure 13-4,** corresponds to a single ray. Because crests of the sine curve represent compressions, each wave front crossed by this ray corresponds to a crest of the sine curve.

Now consider a small portion of a spherical wave front that is many wavelengths away from the source, as shown in **Figure 13-5.** In this case, the rays are nearly parallel lines, and the wave fronts are nearly parallel planes. Thus, at distances from the source that are great relative to the wavelength, we can approximate spherical wave fronts with parallel planes. Such waves are called *plane waves.* Any small portion of a spherical wave that is far from the source can be considered a plane wave. Plane waves can be treated as a series of identical one-dimensional waves, like those in Chapter 12, all traveling in the same direction.

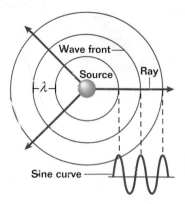

Figure 13-4
In this representation of a spherical wave, the wave fronts represent compressions and the rays show the direction of wave motion. Each wave front corresponds to a crest of the sine curve, which in turn corresponds to a single ray.

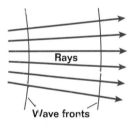

Figure 13-5
Spherical wave fronts that are a great distance from the source can be approximated with parallel planes known as plane waves.

Conceptual Challenge

1. A vibrating bell If a bell is ringing inside a glass container, we cease to hear the sound when the air is pumped out, even though we can still see the bell vibrating. What difference does this indicate between the properties of sound waves and light waves?

2. Hydrogen and air Hydrogen atoms have a smaller mass than the primary components of air, so they are accelerated much more easily. How does this account for the great difference in the speed of sound waves traveling through air and hydrogen, as shown in **Table 13-1** on page 482?

3. Lightning and thunder
Light waves travel nearly 1 million times faster than sound waves in air. With this in mind, explain how the distance to a lightning bolt can be determined by counting the seconds between the flash and the sound of the thunder.

Acoustic Bridge Inspection

When we drive over a bridge, we usually take its structural integrity for granted. Unfortunately, drivers should not always make that assumption. Many of the almost 600 000 bridges in the United States were built over 80 years ago, and most of the rest are 35 to 40 years old. As a bridge ages, cracks form in the steel that can weaken the bridge or even lead to eventual collapse. Inspectors search for those cracks visually, but that method is generally unreliable. David Prine, a senior research scientist at Northwestern University, thinks that the most reliable way to find damage in bridges is to listen to them.

"When a piece of steel cracks, high-frequency sound is emitted," explained Prine. These noises often sound like banging noises that echo throughout the bridge.

Prine has developed a way to inspect bridges using a system of acoustic-emissions sensors—sensitive microphones attached to the steel in a bridge—to capture audio signals from the structure. The signals are put into a computer, which filters out traffic and other noise and searches for sounds around 150 kHz, the frequency range of cracking steel. The computer locates where on the bridge each sound is com-

ing from and then determines whether the recorded sounds match the pattern of a spreading crack. Damage can then be tracked down and repaired.

The device works best as a preventive measure. "The name of the game is to determine what the problems are at the earliest possible stage so you can do a minimal level of repair and not wait until it gets too bad," Prine said.

Still, the acoustic-emissions sensor comes in handy even after a bridge has been fixed. The sensor can monitor different repair methods after they have been tried to determine which methods best correct the problem. This is a much more efficient means of checking repairs than the old way—waiting until the bridge falls apart.

THE DOPPLER EFFECT

If you stand on the street while someone drives by honking a car horn, you will notice the pitch of the horn change. The pitch will be higher as the car approaches you and will drop as the car moves away. As you read earlier in this section, the pitch of a sound depends on its frequency. But in this case, the car horn is not changing its frequency. How can we account for this change in pitch?

Figure 13-6
As this car moves to the left, an observer in front of the car, at point A, hears the car horn at a higher pitch than the driver, while an observer behind the car, at point B, hears a lower pitch.

Relative motion creates a change in frequency

In our earlier examples, we assumed that both the source of the sound waves and the listener were stationary. If a horn is honked in a parked car, an observer standing on the street hears the same pitch that the driver hears, as you would expect. For simplicity's sake, we will assume that the sound waves produced by the car horn are spherical.

When the car shown in **Figure 13-6** is moving, there is relative motion between the moving car and a stationary observer. This relative motion affects the way the wave fronts of the sound waves produced by the car's horn are perceived by an observer.

Although the frequency of the car horn (the source frequency) remains constant, the wave fronts reach an observer in front of the car, at point A, more often than they would if the car were stationary. This is because the source of the sound waves is moving toward the observer. Thus, the frequency heard by this observer is *greater* than the source frequency. (Note that the speed of the sound waves does not change.) For the same reason, the wave fronts reach an observer behind the car, at point B, less often than they would if the car were stationary. As a result, the frequency heard by this observer is *less* than the source frequency. This frequency shift is known as the **Doppler effect,** named for the Austrian physicist Christian Doppler (1803–1853), who discovered it.

Did you know?

The Doppler effect occurs with all types of waves. In the radar systems used by police to monitor car speeds, a computer compares the frequency of radar waves emitted with those reflected from a moving car and then uses this comparison to calculate the speed of the car.

Doppler effect

frequency shift that is the result of relative motion between the source of waves and an observer

Because frequency determines pitch, the Doppler effect affects the pitch heard by each listener on the street. The observer in front of the car hears a higher pitch, while the observer behind the car hears a lower pitch.

We have considered a moving source with respect to a stationary observer, but the Doppler effect also occurs when the observer is moving with respect to a stationary source or when both are moving at different speeds. In other words, the Doppler effect occurs whenever there is *relative motion* between the source of waves and an observer. Although the Doppler effect is most commonly experienced with sound waves, it is a phenomenon common to all waves, including electromagnetic waves, such as visible light.

Section Review

1. If you hear a higher pitch from a trumpet than from a saxophone, how do the frequencies of the sound waves from the trumpet compare with those from the saxophone?

2. Could a small portion of the innermost wave front shown in **Figure 13-7** be approximated by a plane wave? Why or why not?

Figure 13-7

3. **Figure 13-8** is a schematic diagram of the Doppler effect in a ripple tank. In which direction is the source of these ripple waves moving?

4. If the source of the waves in **Figure 13-8** is stationary, which way must the ripple tank be moving?

Figure 13-8

5. **Physics in Action**   Dolphins can produce sound waves with frequencies ranging from 0.25 kHz to 220 kHz, but only those at the upper end of this spectrum are used in echolocation. Explain why high-frequency waves work better than low-frequency waves.

6. **Physics in Action**   Sound pulses emitted by a dolphin travel through 20°C ocean water at a rate of 1450 m/s. In 20°C air, these pulses would travel 342.9 m/s. How can you account for this difference in speed?

7. **Physics in Action**   As a dolphin swims toward a fish, it sends out sound waves to determine the direction the fish is moving. If the frequency of the reflected waves is increased, is the dolphin catching up to the fish or falling behind?

13-2
Sound intensity and resonance

SOUND INTENSITY

13-2 SECTION OBJECTIVES

- **Calculate the intensity of sound waves.**

- **Relate intensity, decibel level, and perceived loudness.**

- **Explain why resonance occurs.**

When a piano player strikes a piano key, a hammer inside the piano strikes a wire and causes it to vibrate, as shown in **Figure 13-9.** The wire's vibrations are then transferred to the piano's soundboard. As the soundboard vibrates, it exerts a force on air molecules around it, causing air molecules to move. Because this force is exerted through displacement of the soundboard, the soundboard does work on the air. Thus, as the soundboard vibrates back and forth, its kinetic energy is converted into sound waves. This is one reason that the vibration of the soundboard gradually dies out.

Intensity is the rate of energy flow through a given area

As described in Section 13-1, sound waves traveling in air are longitudinal waves. As the sound waves travel outward from the source, energy is transferred from one air molecule to the next. The rate at which this energy is transferred through a unit area of the plane wave is called the **intensity** of the wave. Because power, P, is defined as the rate of energy transfer, intensity can also be described in terms of power.

intensity

rate at which energy flows through a unit area perpendicular to the direction of wave motion

$$\text{intensity} = \frac{\Delta E/\Delta t}{\text{area}} = \frac{P}{\text{area}}$$

As seen in Chapter 5, the SI unit for power is the watt. Thus, intensity has units of watts per square meter (W/m^2). In a spherical wave, energy propagates equally in all directions; no one direction is preferred over any other. In this case, the power emitted by the source (P) is distributed over a spherical surface (area $= 4\pi r^2$), assuming that there is no absorption in the medium.

INTENSITY OF A SPHERICAL WAVE

$$\text{intensity} = \frac{P}{4\pi r^2}$$

$$\text{intensity} = \frac{(\textbf{power})}{(4\pi)(\textbf{distance from the source})^2}$$

Figure 13-9
As this piano wire vibrates, it transfers energy to the piano's soundboard, which in turn transfers energy into the air in the form of sound.

This equation shows that the intensity of a sound wave decreases as the distance from the source (r) increases. This occurs because the same amount of energy is spread over a larger area.

Intensity of sound waves

PROBLEM

What is the intensity of the sound waves produced by a trumpet at a distance of 3.2 m when the power output of the trumpet is 0.20 W? Assume that the sound waves are spherical.

SOLUTION

Given: $P = 0.20 \text{ W}$ $r = 3.2 \text{ m}$

Unknown: Intensity = ?

Use the equation for the intensity of a spherical wave, given on page 487.

$$\text{Intensity} = \frac{P}{4\pi r^2}$$

$$\text{Intensity} = \frac{0.20 \text{ W}}{4\pi(3.2 \text{ m})^2}$$

$$\boxed{\text{Intensity} = 1.6 \times 10^{-3} \text{ W/m}^2}$$

CALCULATOR SOLUTION

The calculator answer for intensity is 0.0015543. This is rounded to 1.6×10^{-3} because each of the given quantities has two significant figures.

PRACTICE 13A

Intensity of sound waves

1. Calculate the intensity of the sound waves from an electric guitar's amplifier at a distance of 5.0 m when its power output is equal to each of the following values:
   a. 0.25 W
   b. 0.50 W
   c. 2.0 W

2. If the intensity of a person's voice is 4.6×10^{-7} W/m^2 at a distance of 2.0 m, how much sound power does that person generate?

3. How much power is radiated as sound from a band whose intensity is 1.6×10^{-3} W/m^2 at a distance of 15 m?

4. At a maximum level of loudness, the power output of a 75-piece orchestra radiated as sound is 70.0 W. What is the intensity of these sound waves to a listener who is sitting 25.0 m from the orchestra?

5. The power output of a tuba is 0.35 W. At what distance is the sound intensity of the tuba 1.2×10^{-3} W/m^2?

Intensity and frequency determine which sounds are audible

As you saw in Section 13-1, the frequency of sound waves heard by the average human ranges from 20 to 20 000 Hz. Intensity is also a factor in determining which sound waves are audible. **Figure 13-10** shows how the range of audibility of the average human ear depends on both frequency and intensity. As you can see in this graph, sounds at low frequencies (those below 50 Hz) or high frequencies (those above 12 000 Hz) must be relatively intense to be heard, whereas sounds in the middle of the spectrum are audible at lower intensities.

The softest sounds that can be heard by the average human ear occur at a frequency of about 1000 Hz and an intensity of 1.0×10^{-12} W/m^2. Such a sound is said to be at the *threshold of hearing*. (Note that some humans can hear slightly softer sounds, at a frequency of about 3300 Hz.) The threshold of hearing at each frequency is represented by the lowest curve in **Figure 13-10**. At the threshold of hearing, the changes in pressure due to compressions and rarefactions are about three ten-billionths of atmospheric pressure.

The maximum displacement of an air molecule at the threshold of hearing is approximately 1×10^{-11} m. Comparing this number to the diameter of a typical air molecule (about 1×10^{-10} m) reveals that the ear is an extremely sensitive detector of sound waves.

The loudest sounds that the human ear can tolerate have an intensity of about 1.0 W/m^2. This is known as the *threshold of pain* because sounds with greater intensities produce pain in addition to hearing. The highest curve in **Figure 13-10** represents the threshold of pain at each frequency. Exposure to sounds above the threshold of pain can cause immediate damage to the ear, even if no pain is felt. Prolonged exposure to sounds of lower intensities can also damage the ear. For this reason, many rock musicians wear earplugs during their performances, and some rock stars must wear hearing aids. Note that the threshold of hearing and the threshold of pain merge at both high and low ends of the spectrum.

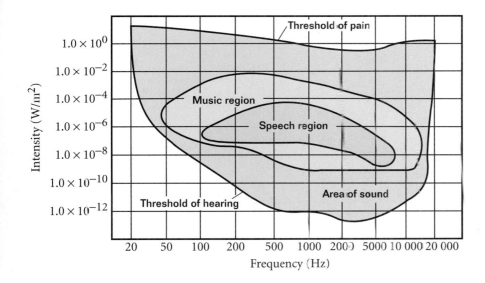

Figure 13-10
Human hearing depends on both the frequency and the intensity of sound waves. Sounds in the middle of the spectrum of frequencies can be heard more easily (at lower intensities) than those at lower and higher frequencies.

Relative intensity, or decibel level, is measured in decibels

Just as the frequency of a sound wave determines its pitch, the intensity of a wave determines its loudness, or volume. However, volume is not directly proportional to intensity. For example, a sound twice the intensity of the faintest audible sound is not perceived as being twice as loud. This is because the sensation of loudness is approximately logarithmic in the human ear.

Relative intensity, which is found by relating the intensity of a given sound wave to the intensity at the threshold of hearing, corresponds more closely to human perceptions of loudness. Relative intensity is also referred to as **decibel level** because relative intensity is measured in units called *decibels* (dB). The decibel is a dimensionless unit because it relates one intensity to another.

The conversion of intensity to decibel level is shown in **Table 13-2.** Notice in **Table 13-2** that when the intensity is multiplied by 10, 10 dB are added to the decibel level. A difference in 10 dB means the sound is approximately twice as loud. Although much more intensity (0.9 W/m^2) is added between 110 and 120 dB than between 10 and 20 dB ($9 \times 10^{-11} \text{ W/m}^2$), in each case the volume doubles. Because the volume doubles each time the decibel level increases by 10, sounds at the threshold of pain are 4096 times as loud as sounds at the threshold of hearing.

decibel level

relative intensity, determined by relating the intensity of a sound wave to the intensity at the threshold of hearing

Table 13-2	Conversion of intensity to decibel level	
Intensity (W/m^2)	**Decibel level (dB)**	**Examples**
1.0×10^{-12}	0	threshold of hearing
1.0×10^{-11}	10	rustling leaves
1.0×10^{-10}	20	quiet whisper
1.0×10^{-9}	30	whisper
1.0×10^{-8}	40	mosquito buzzing
1.0×10^{-7}	50	normal conversation
1.0×10^{-6}	60	air conditioning at 6 m
1.0×10^{-5}	70	vacuum cleaner
1.0×10^{-4}	80	busy traffic, alarm clock
1.0×10^{-3}	90	lawn mower
1.0×10^{-2}	100	subway, power motor
1.0×10^{-1}	110	auto horn at 1 m
1.0×10^{0}	120	threshold of pain
1.0×10^{1}	130	thunderclap, machine gun
1.0×10^{3}	150	nearby jet airplane

FORCED VIBRATIONS AND RESONANCE

When an isolated guitar string is held taut and plucked, hardly any sound is heard. When the same string is placed on a guitar and plucked, the intensity of the sound increases dramatically. What is responsible for this difference? To find the answer to this question, consider a set of pendulums suspended from a beam and bound by a loose rubber band, as shown in **Figure 13-11.** If one of the pendulums is set in motion, its vibrations are transferred by the rubber band to the other pendulums, which will also begin vibrating. This is called a *forced vibration.*

Figure 13-11

If one blue pendulum is set in motion, only the other blue pendulum, whose length is the same, will eventually oscillate with a large amplitude, or resonate.

The vibrating strings of a guitar force the bridge of the guitar to vibrate, and the bridge in turn transfers its vibrations to the guitar body. These forced vibrations are called *sympathetic vibrations.* The guitar body enables the strings' vibrations to be transferred to the air much more quickly because it has a larger area than the strings. As a result, the intensity of the sound is increased, and the strings' vibrations die out faster than they would if they were not attached to the body of the guitar. In other words, the guitar body allows the energy exchange between the strings and the air to happen more efficiently, thereby increasing the intensity of the sound produced.

In an electric guitar, string vibrations are translated into electrical impulses, which can be amplified as much as desired. An electric guitar can produce sounds that are much more intense than those of an unamplified acoustic guitar, which uses only the forced vibrations of the guitar's body to increase the intensity of the sound from the vibrating strings.

A forced vibration at the natural frequency produces resonance

As you saw in Chapter 12, the frequency of a pendulum depends on its string length. Thus, every pendulum will vibrate at a certain frequency, known as its *natural frequency.* In **Figure 13-11,** the two blue pendulums have the same natural frequency, while the red and green pendulums have different natural frequencies. When the first blue pendulum is set in motion, the red and green pendulums will vibrate only slightly, but the second blue pendulum will oscillate with a much larger amplitude because its natural frequency matches the

Resonance

MATERIALS LIST

✔ swing set

Go to a playground, and swing on one of the swings. Try pumping (or being pushed) at different rates—faster than, slower than, and equal to the natural frequency of the swing. Observe whether the rate at which you pump (or are pushed) affects how easily the amplitude of the vibration increases. Are some rates more effective at building your amplitude than others? You should find that the pushes are most effective when they match the swing's natural frequency. Explain how your results support the statement that resonance works best when the frequency of the applied force matches the system's natural frequency.

frequency of the pendulum that was initially set in motion. This system is said to be in **resonance.** Since energy is transferred from one pendulum to the other, the amplitude of vibration of the first blue pendulum will decrease as the second blue pendulum's amplitude increases.

A striking example of structural resonance occurred in 1940, when the Tacoma Narrows bridge, in Washington, shown in **Figure 13-12,** was set in motion by the wind. High winds set up standing waves in the bridge, causing the bridge to oscillate at one of its natural frequencies. The amplitude of the vibrations increased until the bridge collapsed. A more recent example of structural resonance occurred during the Loma Prieta earthquake near Oakland, California, in 1989, when part of the upper deck of a freeway collapsed. The collapse of this particular section of roadway has been traced to the fact that the earthquake waves had a frequency of 1.5 Hz, very close to the natural frequency of that section of the roadway.

Figure 13-12
On November 7, 1940, the Tacoma Narrows suspension bridge collapsed, just four months after it opened. Standing waves caused by strong winds set the bridge in motion and led to its collapse.

Conceptual Challenge

1. Concert If a 15-person musical ensemble gains 15 new members, so that its size doubles, will a listener perceive the music created by the ensemble to be twice as loud? Why or why not?

2. A noisy factory Federal regulations require that no office or factory worker be exposed to noise levels that average above 90 dB over an 8 h day. Thus, a factory that currently averages 100 dB must reduce its noise level by 10 dB. Assuming that each piece of machinery produces the same amount of noise, what percentage of equipment must be removed? Explain your answer.

3. Broken crystal Opera singers have been known to set crystal goblets in vibration with their powerful voices. In fact, an amplified human voice can shatter the glass, but only at certain fundamental frequencies. Speculate about why only certain fundamental frequencies will break the glass.

4. Electric guitars Electric guitars, which use electric amplifiers to magnify their sound, can have a variety of shapes, but acoustic guitars must have an hourglass shape. Explain why.

The human ear transmits vibrations that cause nerve impulses

The human ear is divided into three sections—outer, middle, and inner—as shown in **Figure 13-13.** Sound waves from the atmosphere travel down the ear canal of the outer ear. The ear canal terminates at a thin, flat piece of tissue called the eardrum.

The eardrum vibrates with the sound waves and transfers these vibrations to the three small bones of the middle ear, known as the hammer, the anvil, and the stirrup. These bones in turn transmit the vibrations to the inner ear, which contains a snail-shaped tube about 2 cm long called the cochlea.

The cochlea is divided along its length by the basilar membrane, which consists of small hairs and nerve fibers. This membrane has different natural frequencies at different positions. Sound waves of varying frequencies resonate at different spots along the basilar membrane, creating impulses in different nerve fibers. These impulses are then sent to the brain, which interprets them as sounds of varying frequencies.

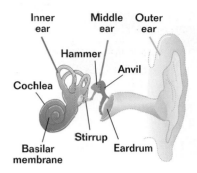

Figure 13-13
Sound waves travel through the three regions of the ear and are then transmitted to the brain as impulses through nerve endings on the basilar membrane.

Section Review

1. When the decibel level of traffic in the street goes from 40 to 60 dB, how much louder does the traffic noise seem? How much greater is the intensity?

2. If two flutists play their instruments together at the same intensity, is the sound twice as loud as that of either flutist playing alone at that intensity? Why or why not?

3. Which of the following factors change when a sound gets louder? Which change when a pitch gets higher?
   a. intensity
   b. speed of the sound waves
   c. frequency
   d. decibel level
   e. wavelength
   f. amplitude

4. A tuning fork consists of two metal prongs that vibrate at a single frequency when struck lightly. What will happen if a vibrating tuning fork is placed near another tuning fork of the same frequency? Explain.

5. **Physics in Action** A certain microphone placed in the ocean is sensitive to sounds emitted by dolphins. To produce a usable signal, sound waves striking the microphone must have a decibel level of 10 dB. If dolphins emit sound waves with a power of 0.050 W, how far can a dolphin be from the microphone and still be heard? (Disregard absorption of the sound waves.)

Figure 13-14
The vibrating strings of a violin produce standing waves whose frequencies depend on the string lengths.

fundamental frequency

the lowest frequency of vibration of a standing wave

STANDING WAVES ON A VIBRATING STRING

As discussed in Chapter 12, a variety of standing waves can occur when a string is fixed at both ends, and the wavelengths of these standing waves depend on the string length. When the string of a musical instrument vibrates, many of these standing waves exist at the same time. Because frequency is inversely proportional to wavelength, each of these standing waves has a different frequency. So the sounds you hear from a stringed instrument, even those of a single pitch, actually consist of multiple frequencies.

Consider a string on the violin shown in **Figure 13-14.** The ends of the string, which cannot vibrate, must always be nodes. The simplest vibration that can occur is shown in the first row of **Table 13-3,** on page 495. In this case, the center of the string experiences the most displacement, and so it is an antinode. Because the distance from one node to the next is always half a wavelength, the string length must equal $\lambda_1/2$. Thus, the wavelength is twice the string length ($\lambda_1 = 2L$).

As described in Chapter 12, the speed of a wave equals the frequency times the wavelength, which can be rearranged as shown.

$$v = f\lambda, \text{ so } f = \frac{v}{\lambda}$$

By substituting the value for wavelength found above into this equation for frequency, we see that the frequency of this vibration is equal to the speed of the wave divided by twice the string length.

$$\text{fundamental frequency} = f_1 = \frac{v}{\lambda_1} = \frac{v}{2L}$$

This frequency of vibration is called the **fundamental frequency** of the vibrating string. Because frequency is inversely proportional to wavelength and because we are considering the greatest possible wavelength, the fundamental frequency is the lowest possible frequency of a standing wave.

Harmonics are integral multiples of the fundamental frequency

The next possible standing wave for this violin string is shown in the second row of **Table 13-3.** In this case, there are three nodes instead of two, so the string length is equal to one wavelength. Because this wavelength is half the previous wavelength, the frequency of this wave is twice as much.

$$f_2 = 2f_1$$

This pattern continues, and the frequency of the standing wave shown in the third row of **Table 13-3** is three times the fundamental frequency. Hence, the frequencies of the standing wave patterns are all integral multiples of the fundamental frequency. These frequencies form what is called a **harmonic series.** The fundamental frequency (f_1) corresponds to the first harmonic, the next frequency (f_2) corresponds to the second harmonic, and so on.

harmonic series

series of frequencies that includes the fundamental frequency and integral multiples of the fundamental frequency

Table 13-3	The harmonic series			
	$\lambda_1 = 2L$	f_1		fundamental frequency, or first harmonic
	$\lambda_2 = L$	$f_2 = 2f_1$		second harmonic
	$\lambda_3 = \frac{2}{3}L$	$f_3 = 3f_1$		third harmonic
	$\lambda_4 = \frac{1}{2}L$	$f_4 = 4f_1$		fourth harmonic

Because each harmonic is an integral multiple of the fundamental frequency, the equation for the fundamental frequency can be generalized to include the entire harmonic series. Thus, $f_n = nf_1$, where f_1 is the fundamental frequency ($f_1 = \frac{v}{2L}$) and f_n is the frequency of the nth harmonic. Note that v is the speed of waves on the vibrating string and not the speed of the resultant sound waves in air.

HARMONIC SERIES OF STANDING WAVES ON A VIBRATING STRING

$$f_n = n\frac{v}{2L} \quad n = 1, 2, 3, \ldots$$

$$\text{frequency} = \text{harmonic number} \times \frac{(\text{speed of waves on the string})}{(2)(\text{length of vibrating string})}$$

When a guitar player presses down on a guitar string at any point, that point becomes a node and only a portion of the string vibrates. As a result, a single string can be used to create a variety of fundamental frequencies. In the previous equation, L refers to the portion of the string that is vibrating.

Figure 13-15
The harmonic series present in each of these organ pipes depends on whether the end of the pipe is open or closed.

Did you know?

A flute is similar to a pipe open at both ends. When all keys of a flute are closed, the length of the vibrating air column is approximately equal to the length of the flute. As the keys are opened one by one, the length of the vibrating air column decreases, and the fundamental frequency increases.

STANDING WAVES IN AN AIR COLUMN

Standing waves can also be set up in a tube of air, such as an organ pipe, the inside of a trumpet, or the column of a saxophone. While some waves travel down the tube, others are reflected back upward. These waves traveling in opposite directions combine to produce standing waves. Many brass instruments and woodwinds produce sound by means of these vibrating air columns.

If both ends of a pipe are open, all harmonics are present

The harmonic series present in a pipe depends on whether the reflecting end of the pipe is open or closed. To see why, we'll consider one of the organ pipes shown in **Figure 13-15.** When the reflecting end of the pipe is open, as is illustrated in **Figure 13-16,** the air molecules have complete freedom of motion, and an antinode exists at this end. So if a pipe is open at both ends, each end is an antinode. This is the exact opposite of a string fixed at both ends, where both ends are nodes.

Because the distance from one node to the next $(\frac{1}{2}\lambda)$ equals the distance from one antinode to the next, the pattern of standing waves that can occur in a pipe open at both ends is the same as that of a vibrating string. Thus, the entire harmonic series is present in this case, as shown in **Figure 13-16,** and our earlier equation for the harmonic series of a vibrating string can be used.

HARMONIC SERIES OF A PIPE OPEN AT BOTH ENDS

$$f_n = n\frac{v}{2L} \quad n = 1, 2, 3, \ldots$$

$$\text{frequency} = \text{harmonic number} \times \frac{\text{(speed of sound in the pipe)}}{\text{(2)(length of vibrating air column)}}$$

In this equation, L represents the length of the vibrating air column. Just as the fundamental frequency of a string instrument can be varied by changing the string length, the fundamental frequency of many woodwind and brass instruments can be varied by changing the length of the vibrating air column.

Harmonics in an open-ended pipe

Figure 13-16
In a pipe open at both ends, each end is an antinode, and all harmonics are present. Shown here are the first **(a)**, second **(b)**, and third **(c)** harmonics.

Harmonics in a pipe closed at one end

(a)

$\lambda_1 = 4L$

$f_1 = \dfrac{v}{4L}$

(b)

$\lambda_3 = \dfrac{4}{3}L$

$f_3 = \dfrac{3v}{4L} = 3f_1$

(c)

$\lambda_5 = \dfrac{4}{5}L$

$f_5 = \dfrac{5v}{4L} = 5f_1$

Figure 13-17
In a pipe closed at one end, the closed end is a node and the open end is an antinode. In this case, only the odd harmonics are present. The first **(a)**, third **(b)**, and fifth **(c)** harmonics are shown here.

If one end of a pipe is closed, only odd harmonics are present

When one end of an organ pipe is closed, as is illustrated in **Figure 13-17**, the movement of air molecules is restricted at this end, making this end a node. In this case, one end of the pipe is a node and the other is an antinode. As a result, a different set of standing waves can occur.

As shown in **Figure 13-17(a)**, the simplest possible standing wave that can exist in this pipe is equal to one-fourth of a wavelength. The wavelength of this standing wave equals four times the length of the pipe. Thus, in this case, the fundamental frequency equals the velocity divided by four times the pipe length.

$$f_1 = \frac{v}{\lambda_1} = \frac{v}{4L}$$

For the case shown in **Figure 13-17(b)**, there is three-fourths of a wavelength in the pipe, so the wavelength is four-thirds the length of the pipe ($\lambda_3 = \frac{4}{3}L$). Substituting this value into the equation for frequency gives the frequency of this harmonic.

$$f_3 = \frac{v}{\lambda_3} = \frac{v}{\frac{4}{3}L} = \frac{3v}{4L} = 3f_1$$

Notice that the frequency of this harmonic is *three* times the fundamental frequency. Repeating this calculation for the case shown in **Figure 13-17(c)** gives a frequency equal to *five* times the fundamental frequency. Thus, only the odd-numbered harmonics vibrate in a pipe closed at one end.

As with the vibrating string, we can generalize the equation for the harmonic series of a pipe closed at one end.

HARMONIC SERIES OF A PIPE CLOSED AT ONE END

$$f_n = n\frac{v}{4L} \quad n = 1, 3, 5, \ldots$$

$$\text{frequency} = \text{harmonic number} \times \frac{(\text{speed of sound in the pipe})}{(4)(\text{length of vibrating air column})}$$

Trumpets, saxophones, and clarinets are similar to a pipe closed at one end. Although a trumpet has two open ends, the player's mouth effectively closes one end of the instrument. In a saxophone or a clarinet, the reed closes one end.

Despite the similarity between these instruments and a pipe closed at one end, our equation for the harmonic series of pipes does not directly apply to such instruments because any deviation from the cylindrical shape of a pipe affects the harmonic series of an instrument. For example, a clarinet is primarily cylindrical, but because the open end of the instrument is bell-shaped, there are some even harmonics in a clarinet's tone at relatively small intensities. The shape of a saxophone is such that the harmonic series in a saxophone is similar to a cylindrical pipe open at both ends even though only one end of the saxophone is open. These deviations are in part responsible for the variety of sounds that can be produced by different instruments.

SAMPLE PROBLEM 13B

Harmonics

PROBLEM

What are the first three harmonics in a 2.45 m long pipe that is open at both ends? What are the first three harmonics of this pipe when one end of the pipe is closed? Assume that the speed of sound in air is 345 m/s for both of these situations.

SOLUTION

1. DEFINE   **Given:** $L = 2.45$ m $v = 345$ m/s

Unknown: Pipe open at both ends: f_1 f_2 f_3

Pipe closed at one end: f_1 f_3 f_5

2. PLAN   **Choose an equation(s) or situation:**

When the pipe is open, all harmonics are present. Thus, the fundamental frequency can be found by using the equation for the entire harmonic series, given on page 496:

$$f_n = n\frac{v}{2L}, \ n = 1, 2, 3, \ldots$$

When the pipe is closed at one end, only odd harmonics are present. In this case, the fundamental frequency is found by using the equation for the odd harmonic series, given on page 497:

$$f_n = n\frac{v}{4L}, \ n = 1, 3, 5, \ldots$$

In both cases, the second two harmonics can be found by multiplying the harmonic numbers by the fundamental frequency.

3. CALCULATE   For a pipe open at both ends:

$$f_1 = n\frac{v}{2L} = (1)\left(\frac{345 \text{ m/s}}{(2)(2.45 \text{ m})}\right) = \boxed{70.4 \text{ Hz}}$$

Because all harmonics are present in this case, the next two harmonics are the second and the third:

$$f_2 = 2f_1 = (2)(70.4 \text{ Hz}) = \boxed{141 \text{ Hz}}$$

$$f_3 = 3f_1 = (3)(70.4 \text{ Hz}) = \boxed{211 \text{ Hz}}$$

For a pipe closed at one end:

$$f_1 = n\frac{v}{4L} = (1)\left(\frac{345 \text{ m/s}}{(4)(2.45 \text{ m})}\right) = \boxed{35.2 \text{ Hz}}$$

Only the odd harmonics are present in this case, so the next possible harmonics are the third and the fifth:

$$f_3 = 3f_1 = (3)(35.2 \text{ Hz}) = \boxed{106 \text{ Hz}}$$

$$f_5 = 5f_1 = (5)(35.2 \text{ Hz}) = \boxed{176 \text{ Hz}}$$

4. EVALUATE   In a pipe open at both ends, the first possible wavelength is $2L$; in a pipe closed at one end, the first possible wavelength is $4L$. Because frequency and wavelength are inversely proportional, the fundamental frequency of the open pipe should be twice that of the closed pipe, that is, $70.4 = (2)(35.2)$.

PRACTICE 13B

Harmonics

1. What is the fundamental frequency of a 0.20 m long organ pipe that is closed at one end, when the speed of sound in the pipe is 352 m/s?

2. A flute is essentially a pipe open at both ends. The length of a flute is approximately 66.0 cm. What are the first three harmonics of a flute when all keys are closed, making the vibrating air column approximately equal to the length of the flute? The speed of sound in the flute is 340 m/s.

3. What is the fundamental frequency of a guitar string when the speed of waves on the string is 115 m/s and the effective string lengths are as follows:

   a. 70.0 cm   b. 50.0 cm   c. 40.0 cm

4. A violin string that is 50.0 cm long has a fundamental frequency of 440 Hz. What is the speed of the waves on this string?

Harmonics account for sound quality, or timbre

Table 13-4 shows the harmonics present in a tuning fork, a clarinet, and a viola when each sounds the musical note A-natural. Note that each instrument has its own characteristic mixture of harmonics at varying intensities.

The harmonics shown in the second column of **Table 13-4** add together according to the principle of superposition to give the resultant waveform shown in the third column. Since a tuning fork vibrates at only its fundamental frequency, its waveform is simply a sine wave. (Some tuning forks also vibrate at higher frequencies when they are struck hard enough.) The waveforms of the other instruments are more complex because they consist of many harmonics, each at different intensities. Each individual harmonic waveform is a sine wave, but the resultant wave is more complex than a sine wave because each individual waveform has a different frequency.

Even though the waveforms of a clarinet and a viola are more complex than those of a tuning fork, note that each consists of repeating patterns. Such waveforms are said to be *periodic*. These repeating patterns occur because each frequency is an integral multiple of the fundamental frequency.

The different waveforms shown in the third column of **Table 13-4** explain why a clarinet sounds different from a viola, even when both instruments are sounding the same fundamental frequency at the same decibel level. In music, the mixture of harmonics that produces the characteristic sound of an instru-

Consumer Focus   *Reverberation*

Auditoriums, churches, concert halls, libraries, and music rooms are designed with specific functions in mind. One auditorium may be made for rock concerts, while another is constructed for use as a lecture hall. Your school's auditorium, for instance, may allow you to hear a speaker well but make a band sound damped and muffled.

Rooms are often constructed so that sounds made by a speaker or a musical instrument bounce back and forth against the ceiling, walls, floor, and other surfaces. This repetitive echo is called *reverberation*. The reverberation time is the amount of time the sound audibly persists after the sound is produced.

For speech, the auditorium should be designed so that the reverberation time is relatively short. A repeated echo of each word could become confusing to listeners.

Music halls may also differ in construction depending on the type of music usually played there. For example, rock music is generally less pleasing with a large amount of reverberation, but more reverberation is sometimes desired for orchestral and choral music.

For these reasons, you may notice a difference in the way ceilings, walls, and furnishings are designed in different rooms. Ceilings designed for a lot of reverberation are flat and hard. Ceilings in libraries and other quiet places are often made of soft or textured material to muffle sounds. Padded furnishings and plants can also be strategically arranged to absorb sound. All of these different factors are considered and combined to accomodate the auditory function of a room.

Table 13-4	Harmonics of a tuning fork, a clarinet, and a viola at the same pitch

Tuning fork

Relative intensity — Harmonics (1 2 3 4 5 6 7 8 9 10) — Resultant waveform

Clarinet

Relative intensity — Harmonics (1 2 3 4 5 6 7 8 9 10) — Resultant waveform

Viola

Relative intensity — Harmonics (1 2 3 4 5 6 7 8 9 10) — Resultant waveform

ment is referred to as the spectrum of the sound, which results in a response in the listener called sound quality, or **timbre.** The rich harmonics of most instruments provide a much fuller sound than that of a tuning fork, which consists of a single frequency vibration.

The intensity of each harmonic varies within a particular instrument, depending on frequency, amplitude of vibration, and a variety of other factors. With a violin, for example, the intensity of each harmonic depends on where the string is bowed, the speed of the bow on the string, and the force the bow exerts on the string. Because there are so many factors involved, most instruments can produce a wide variety of tones.

timbre

the quality of a steady musical sound that is the result of a mixture of harmonics present at different intensities

Fundamental frequency determines pitch

As you saw in Section 13-1, the frequency of a sound determines its pitch. In musical instruments, the fundamental frequency of a vibration typically determines pitch. Other harmonics are sometimes referred to as overtones. In the chromatic (half-step) musical scale, there are 12 notes, each of which has a characteristic frequency. The frequency of the thirteenth note is exactly twice that of the first note, and together the 13 notes constitute an *octave*. Hence, the frequency of the second harmonic of a note corresponds to the frequency of the octave above that note.

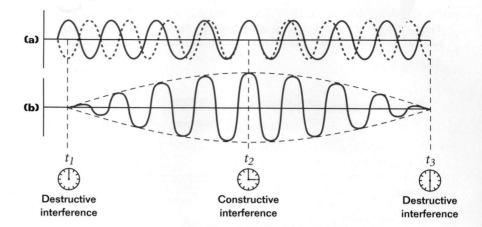

Figure 13-18

Beats are formed by the interference of two waves of slightly different frequencies traveling in the same direction. In this case, one beat occurs at t_2, where constructive interference is greatest.

(a)

(b)

t_1 — Destructive interference

t_2 — Constructive interference

t_3 — Destructive interference

BEATS

So far, we have considered the superposition of waves in a harmonic series, where each frequency is an integral multiple of the fundamental frequency. When two waves of *slightly* different frequencies interfere, the interference pattern varies in such a way that a listener hears an alternation between loudness and softness. The variation from soft to loud and back to soft is called a **beat.**

beat

interference of waves of slightly different frequencies traveling in the same direction, perceived as a variation in loudness

Sound waves at slightly different frequencies produce beats

Figure 13-18 shows how beats occur. In **Figure 13-18(a),** the waves produced by two tuning forks of different frequencies start exactly opposite one another. These waves combine according to the superposition principle, as shown in **Figure 13-18(b).** When the two waves are exactly opposite one another, they are said to be *out of phase,* and complete destructive interference occurs. For this reason, no sound is heard at t_1.

Because these waves have different frequencies, after a few more cycles, the crest of the blue wave matches up with the crest of the red wave, as at t_2. At this

Conceptual Challenge

1. Piano tuning How does a piano tuner use a tuning fork to adjust a piano wire to a certain fundamental frequency?

2. Concert violins Before a performance, musicians tune their instruments to match their fundamental frequencies. If a conductor hears the number of beats decreasing as two violin players are tuning, are the fundamental frequencies of these violins becoming closer together or farther apart? Explain.

3. Sounds from a guitar Will the speed of waves on a vibrating guitar string be the same as the speed of the sound waves in the air that are generated by this vibration? How will the frequency and wavelength of the waves on the string compare with the frequency and wavelength of the sound waves in the air?

point, the waves are said to be *in phase*. Now constructive interference occurs, and the sound is louder. Because the blue wave has a higher frequency than the red wave, the waves are out of phase again at t_3, and no sound is heard.

As time passes, the waves continue to be in and out of phase, the interference constantly shifts between constructive interference and destructive interference, and the listener hears the sound getting softer and louder and then softer again. You may have noticed a similar phenomenon on a playground swing set. If two people are swinging next to one another at different frequencies, the two swings may alternate between being in phase and being out of phase.

The number of beats per second corresponds to the difference between frequencies

In our previous example, there is one beat, which occurs at t_2. One beat corresponds to the blue wave gaining one entire cycle on the red wave. This is because to go from one destructive interference to the next, the red wave must lag one entire cycle behind the blue wave. If the time that lapses from t_1 to t_3 is one second, then the blue wave completes one more cycle per second than the red wave. In other words, its frequency is greater by 1 Hz. By generalizing this, you can see that the frequency difference between two sounds can be found by the number of beats heard per second.

Section Review

1. On a piano, the note middle C has a fundamental frequency of 264 Hz. What is the second harmonic of this note?

2. If the piano wire in item 1 is 66.0 cm long, what is the speed of waves on this wire?

3. A piano tuner using a 392 Hz tuning fork to tune the wire for G-natural hears four beats per second. What are the two possible frequencies of vibration of this piano wire?

4. In a clarinet, the reed end of the instrument acts as a node and the first open hole acts as an antinode. Because the shape of the clarinet is nearly cylindrical, its harmonic series approximately follows that of a pipe closed at one end. What harmonic series is predominant in a clarinet?

5. Which of the following must be different for a trumpet and a banjo when notes are being played by both at the same fundamental frequency?
   a. wavelength in air of the first harmonic
   b. number of harmonics present
   c. intensity of each harmonic
   d. speed of sound in air

The Doppler Effect and the BIG BANG

Earlier in this chapter, you learned that relative motion between the source of sound waves and an observer creates a frequency shift known as the Doppler effect. For visible light, the Doppler effect is observed as a change in color because the frequency of a light wave determines its color.

Frequency shifts

Of the colors of the visible spectrum, red light has the lowest frequency and violet light has the highest. When the source of electromagnetic waves is moving toward an observer, the frequency detected is higher than the source frequency. This corresponds to a shift toward the blue end of the spectrum. When the source of electromagnetic waves is moving away from an observer, the observer detects a lower frequency, which corresponds to a shift toward the red end of the spectrum. These two types of frequency shifts are known as *blue shift* and *red shift*, respectively, even though this shift occurs for any type of radiation, not just visible light.

In astronomy, such frequency shifts can be analyzed by a process called *spectroscopy*, in which electromagnetic waves emitted by distant objects and partially absorbed by another object are first passed through a telescope, then through a narrow slit, and finally through a prism or other device that separates the radiation into separate bands. Each band corresponds to one of the various frequencies contained in the radiation.

Table 13-5   The Doppler effect for light

Stationary source	$v = 0$	no shift
Approaching source	v	blue shift
Receding source	v	red shift

The expansion of the universe

As scientists began to study other galaxies with spectroscopy, the results were astonishing: nearly all of the galaxies that were observed exhibited a red shift, which suggested that they were moving away from Earth. If all galaxies are moving away from Earth, the universe must be expanding. This does not suggest that Earth is at the center of the expansion; from any other point in the universe, the same phenomenon would be observed.

The expansion of the universe suggests that at some point in the past the universe must have been confined to a point of infinite density. The eruption of the universe is often referred to as the *big bang*, which is generally considered to have occurred between 10 billion and 20 billion years ago. Current models indicate that the big bang involved such great amounts of energy in such a small space that matter could not form clumps or even individual atoms. It took about 700 000 years for the universe to cool from around 10^{32} K to around 3000 K, a temperature cool enough for atoms to begin forming.

Figure 13-19
Penzias and Wilson detected microwave background radiation, presumably left over from the big bang, with the horn antenna (in background) at Bell Telephone Laboratories, in New Jersey.

Experimental verification

In the 1960s, a group of scientists at Princeton predicted that the explosion of the big bang was so momentous that a small amount of radiation—the leftover glow from the big bang—should still be found in the universe. Around this time, Arno Penzias and Robert Wilson, of Bell Labs, noticed a faint background hiss interfering with satellite communications experiments they were conducting. This signal, which was detected in equal amounts in all directions, remained despite all attempts to remove it. Penzias and Wilson learned of the Princeton group's work and realized that the interference they were experiencing matched the characteristics of the radiation expected from the big bang. Subsequent experiments have confirmed the existence of this radiation, known as *cosmic microwave background radiation*. This background radiation is considered to be the most conclusive evidence for the big bang theory.

The big bang theory is generally accepted by scientists today. Research now focuses on more-detailed issues. However, there are certain phenomena that the standard big bang model cannot account for, such as the uniform distribution of matter on a large scale and the large-scale clustering of galaxies. As a result, some scientists are currently working on modifications and refinements to the standard big bang theory.

In December 1995, the Hubble Space Telescope obtained an image that reveals galaxies so far away from Earth that their light must have left them 10 billion to 20 billion years ago. This image shows the galaxies as they existed 10 billion to 20 billion years in the past, when the universe was less than a billion years old. As technology improves, scientists may see galaxies even farther away, and hence even farther back in time. Such observations may resolve many of the current questions regarding the origin of the universe.

Figure 13-20
This image, called the Hubble Deep Field, is a composite of 342 separate exposures taken by NASA's Hubble Space Telescope during 10 consecutive days. Most of the objects are galaxies, each containing billions of stars. The full image contains over 1500 galaxies, the youngest perhaps dating back to when galaxies first began forming.

CHAPTER 13
Summary

KEY TERMS

beat (p. 502)

compression (p. 480)

decibel level (p. 490)

Doppler effect (p. 485)

fundamental frequency
(p. 494)

harmonic series (p. 495)

intensity (p. 487)

pitch (p. 481)

rarefaction (p. 480)

resonance (p. 492)

timbre (p. 501)

KEY IDEAS

Section 13-1 Sound waves
- The frequency of a sound wave determines its pitch.
- The speed of sound depends on the medium.
- The relative motion between the source of waves and an observer creates an apparent frequency shift known as the Doppler effect.

Section 13-2 Sound intensity and resonance
- The sound intensity of a spherical wave is the power per area, as follows:

$$\text{Intensity} = \frac{P}{4\pi r^2}$$

- Decibel level is relative intensity.
- A forced vibration at the natural frequency produces resonance.

Section 13-3 Harmonics
- Harmonics of a vibrating string or a pipe open at both ends can be found with the following equation:

$$f_n = n\frac{v}{2L}, n = 1, 2, 3, \ldots$$

- Harmonics of a pipe closed at one end can be found with the following equation:

$$f_n = n\frac{v}{4L}, n = 1, 3, 5, \ldots$$

- The number and intensity of harmonics account for the sound quality of an instrument, also known as timbre.

Variable symbols

	Quantities	Units	
	sound intensity	W/m^2	watts/meters squared
	decibel level	dB	decibels
f_n	frequency of the nth harmonic	Hz	Hertz = s^{-1}
L	length of a vibrating string or an air column	m	meters

SOUND WAVES

Review questions

1. Why are sound waves in air characterized as longitudinal?

2. Draw the sine curve that corresponds to the sound wave depicted in **Figure 13-21**.

Figure 13-21

3. What is the difference between frequency and pitch?

4. Why can a dog hear a sound produced by a dog whistle, while his owner cannot?

5. What are the differences between infrasonic, audible, and ultrasonic sound waves?

6. Explain why the speed of sound depends on the temperature of the medium. Why is this temperature dependence more noticeable in a gas than in a solid or a liquid?

7. The Doppler effect occurs when
   a. a source of sound moves toward a listener.
   b. a listener moves toward a source of sound.
   c. a listener and a source of sound move away from each other.
   d. a listener and a source of sound move toward each other.
   e. All of the above

8. You are at a street corner and hear an ambulance siren. Without looking, how can you tell when the ambulance passes by?

9. Ultrasound waves are often used to produce images of objects inside the body. Why are ultrasound waves effective for this purpose?

Conceptual questions

10. If the wavelength of a sound source is reduced by a factor of 2, what happens to the wave's frequency? What happens to its speed?

11. As a result of a distant explosion, an observer first senses a ground tremor, then hears the explosion. What accounts for this time lag?

12. By listening to a band or an orchestra, how can you determine that the speed of sound is the same for all frequencies?

13. A sound wave travels in air at a frequency of 500 Hz. If part of the wave travels from air into water, does its frequency change? Does its wavelength change? Note that the speed of sound in air is about 340 m/s, whereas the speed of sound in water is about 1500 m/s.

14. A fire engine is moving at 40 m/s and sounding its horn. A car in front of the fire engine is moving at 30 m/s, and a van in front of the car is stationary. Which observer hears the fire engine's horn at a higher pitch, the driver of the car or the driver of the van?

15. A bat flying toward a wall emits a chirp at 40 kHz. Is the frequency of the echo received by the bat greater than, less than, or equal to 40 kHz?

SOUND INTENSITY AND RESONANCE

Review questions

16. If a sound seems to be getting louder, which of the following is probably increasing?
   a. intensity
   b. frequency
   c. speed of sound
   d. wavelength

17. What is the difference between intensity, decibel level, and volume?

18. Using **Table 13-2** (page 490) as a guide, estimate the decibel levels of the following sounds: a cheering crowd at a football game, background noise in a church, the pages of this textbook being turned, light traffic.

19. Why is the threshold of hearing represented as a curve in **Figure 13-10** (page 489) rather than as a single point?

20. Under what conditions does resonance occur?

Conceptual questions

21. If the distance from a point source of sound is tripled, by what factor does the sound intensity decrease? Assume there are no reflections from nearby objects to affect your results.

22. Why is the intensity of an echo less than that of the original sound?

23. The decibel level of an orchestra is 90 dB, and a single violin achieves a level of 70 dB. How do the intensity and volume of the sound of the full orchestra compare with those of the violin's sound?

24. A noisy machine in a factory produces a decibel rating of 80 dB. How many identical machines could you add to the factory without exceeding the 90 dB limit set by federal regulations?

25. Why are pushes given to a playground swing more effective if they are given at certain, regular intervals than if they are given at random positions in the swing's cycle?

26. Although soldiers are usually required to march together in step, they must break their march when crossing a bridge. Explain the possible danger of crossing a rickety bridge without taking this precaution.

Practice problems

27. A man shouting loudly produces a 70 dB sound at a distance of 5.0 m. How many watts of sound power does the man emit? (See Sample Problem 13A, and use **Table 13-2** on page 490 to convert decibel level to intensity.)

28. A stereo speaker represented by P in **Figure 13-22** emits sound waves with a power output of 100.0 W. What is the intensity of the sound waves at point x when $r = 10.0$ m? (See Sample Problem 13A.)

Figure 13-22

29. The area of a typical eardrum is approximately 5.0×10^{-5} m^2. Calculate the sound power (the energy per second) incident on the eardrum at

    a. the threshold of hearing.

    b. the threshold of pain.

(See Sample Problem 13A.)

HARMONICS

Review questions

30. What is fundamental frequency? How are harmonics related to the fundamental frequency?

31. **Figure 13-23** shows a stretched string vibrating in several of its modes. If the length of the string is 2.0 m, what is the wavelength of the wave on the string in **(a)**, **(b)**, **(c)**, and **(d)**?

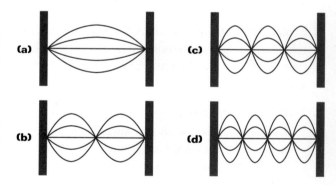

Figure 13-23

32. Why does a pipe closed at one end have a different harmonic series than an open pipe?

33. Explain why a saxophone sounds different from a clarinet, even when they sound the same fundamental frequency at the same decibel level.

34. Two violin players tuning their instruments together hear six beats in 2 s. What is the frequency difference between the two violins?

Conceptual questions

35. A student records the first 10 harmonics for a pipe. Is it possible to determine whether the pipe is open or closed by comparing the difference in frequencies between the adjacent harmonics with the fundamental frequency? Explain.

36. What is the purpose of the slide on a trombone and the valves on a trumpet?

37. A flute is similar to a pipe open at both ends, while a clarinet is similar to a pipe closed at one end. Explain why the fundamental frequency of a flute is about twice that of the clarinet, even though the length of these two instruments is approximately the same.

38. Why does a vibrating guitar string sound louder when it is on the instrument than it does when it is stretched on a work bench?

39. The fundamental frequency of any note produced by a flute will vary slightly with temperature changes in the air. For any given note, will an increase in temperature produce a slightly higher fundamental frequency or a slightly lower one?

Practice problems

40. What are the first three harmonics of a note produced on a 31.0 cm long violin string if waves on this string have a speed of 274.4 m/s? (See Sample Problem 13B.)

41. A pipe that is open at both ends has a fundamental frequency of 320 Hz when the speed of sound in air is 331 m/s.
    a. What is the length of this pipe?
    b. What are the next two harmonics?
    c. What is the fundamental frequency of this pipe when the speed of sound in air is increased to 367 m/s due to a rise in the temperature of the air?
    (See Sample Problem 13B.)

42. The human ear canal is about 2.8 cm long and can be regarded as a tube open at one end and closed at the eardrum. What is the fundamental frequency around which we would expect hearing to be best when the speed of sound in air is 340 m/s? (See Sample Problem 13B.)

MIXED REVIEW

43. The frequency of a tuning fork can be found by the method shown in **Figure 13-24**. A long tube open at both ends is submerged in a beaker of water, and the vibrating tuning fork is placed near the top of the tube. The length of the air column, L, is adjusted by moving the tube vertically. The sound waves generated by the fork are reinforced when the length of the air column corresponds to one of the resonant frequencies of the tube. The smallest value for L for which a peak occurs in sound intensity is 9.00 cm. (Use 345 m/s as the speed of sound in air.)

Figure 13-24

   a. What is the frequency of the tuning fork?
   b. What is the value of L for the next two harmonics?

44. When two tuning forks of 132 Hz and 137 Hz, respectively, are sounded simultaneously, how many beats per second are heard?

45. The range of human hearing extends from approximately 20 Hz to 20 000 Hz. Find the wavelengths of these extremes when the speed of sound in air is equal to 343 m/s.

46. A dolphin in 25°C sea water emits a sound directed toward the bottom of the ocean 150 m below. How much time passes before it hears an echo? (See **Table 13-1** for the speed of the sound waves.)

47. An open organ pipe is 2.46 m long, and the speed of the air in the pipe is 345 m/s.
   a. What is the fundamental frequency of this pipe?
   b. How many harmonics are possible in the normal hearing range, 20 Hz to 20 000 Hz?

48. The greatest value ever achieved for the speed of sound in air is about 1.0×10^4 m/s, and the highest frequency ever produced is about 2.0×10^{10} Hz. Find the wavelength of this wave.

49. If you blow across the open end of a soda bottle and produce a tone of 250 Hz, what will be the frequency of the next harmonic heard if you blow much harder?

50. A rock group is playing in a club. Sound emerging outdoors from an open door spreads uniformly in all directions. If the decibel level is 70 dB at a distance of 1.0 m from the door, at what distance is the music just barely audible to a person with a normal threshold of hearing? Disregard absorption.

51. The fundamental frequency of an open organ pipe corresponds to the note middle C ($f = 261.6$ Hz on the chromatic musical scale). The third harmonic (f_3) of another organ pipe that is closed at one end has the same frequency. Compare the lengths of these two pipes.

52. Some studies indicate that the upper frequency limit of hearing is determined by the diameter of the eardrum. The wavelength of the sound wave and the diameter of the eardrum are approximately equal at this upper limit. If this is so, what is the diameter of the eardrum of a person capable of hearing 2.0×10^4 Hz? Assume 378 m/s is the speed of sound in the ear.

53. The decibel level of the noise from a jet aircraft is 130 dB when measured 20.0 m from the aircraft.
  a. How much sound power does the jet aircraft emit?
  b. How much sound power would strike the eardrum of an airport worker 20.0 m from the aircraft? (Use the diameter found in item 52 to calculate the area of the eardrum.)

54. A typical decibel level for a buzzing mosquito is 40 dB, and normal conversation is approximately 50 dB. How many buzzing mosquitoes will produce a sound intensity equal to that of normal conversation?

Alternative Assessment

Performance assessment

1. A new airport is being built 750 m from your school. The noise level 50 m from planes that will land at the airport is 130 dB. In open spaces, such as the fields between the school and the airport, the level decreases by 20 dB each time the distance increases tenfold. Work in a cooperative group to research the options for keeping the noise level tolerable at the school. How far away would the school have to be moved to make the sound manageable? Research the cost of land near your school. What options are available for soundproofing the school's buildings? How expensive are these options? Have each member in the group present the advantages and disadvantages of such options.

2. Use soft-drink bottles and water to make a musical instrument. Adjust the amount of water in different bottles to create musical notes. Play them as percussion instruments (by tapping the bottles) or as wind instruments (by blowing over the mouths of individual bottles). What media are vibrating in each case? What affects the fundamental frequency? Use a microphone and an oscilloscope to analyze your performance and to demonstrate the effects of tuning your instrument.

Portfolio projects

3. Interview members of the medical profession to learn about human hearing. What are some types of hearing disabilities? How are hearing disabilities related to disease, age, and occupational or environmental hazards? What procedures and instruments are used to test hearing? How do hearing aids help? What are the limitations of hearing aids? Present your findings to the class.

4. Do research on the types of architectural acoustics that would affect a restaurant. What are some of the acoustics problems in places where many people gather? How do odd-shaped ceilings, decorative panels, draperies, and glass windows affect echo and noise? Find the shortest wavelengths of sounds that should be absorbed, considering that conversation sounds range from 500 to 5000 Hz. Prepare a plan or a model of your school cafeteria showing what approaches you would use to keep the level of noise to a minimum.

Technology & Learning

Graphing calculators

Program your graphing calculator to graph the frequency of a sound versus its apparent frequency to a stationary observer. Determine the apparent frequencies in each of the following cases if v_{sound} is 346 m/s:

a. a car horn tuned to middle C (264 Hz) passing the listener at a speed of 25 m/s

b. a car horn tuned to G (392 Hz) passing the listener at a speed of 25 m/s

c. a trumpet player playing middle C (264 Hz) on a parade float that passes the listener at a speed of 5.0 m/s

d. a trumpet player playing G (392 Hz) on a parade float that passes the listener at a speed of 5.0 m/s

Press $\boxed{Y=}$ and $\boxed{CLEAR}$ to clear any functions. Open a new program by pressing $\boxed{PRGM}$ $\boxed{\blacktriangleright}$ $\boxed{\blacktriangleright}$ $\boxed{ENTER}$. Name the program "DOPPLER" and press $\boxed{ENTER}$. Then enter the program in the table below.

To exit the program editor, press $\boxed{2nd}$ $\boxed{QUIT}$. To run the program, press $\boxed{PRGM}$, select "DOPPLER," and press $\boxed{ENTER}$ $\boxed{ENTER}$. Enter the value for the speed of sound and the speed of the source, pressing $\boxed{ENTER}$ after each one.

The calculator will provide a graph of the actual frequency versus the apparent frequencies. (If the graph is not visible, press $\boxed{WINDOW}$, change the settings for the graph window, and then press $\boxed{GRAPH}$.)

Press $\boxed{TRACE}$, and use the arrow keys to trace along the curve. The x value corresponds to the source frequency in hertz, the upper y value corresponds to the frequency heard by the observer as the source approaches him, and the lower y value corresponds to the frequency heard by the observer as the source moves away from him. Use the up and down arrows to toggle between the two graphs.

After you have finished using the graph for one source velocity, press $\boxed{2nd}$ $\boxed{QUIT}$ and run the program for the next one.

Keystrokes	Display
	PROGRAM:DOPPLER
1. $\boxed{PRGM}$ $\boxed{\blacktriangleright}$ $\boxed{3}$ $\boxed{2nd}$ $\boxed{A\text{-}LOCK}$ $\boxed{"}$ $\boxed{V}$ $\boxed{S}$ $\boxed{O}$ $\boxed{U}$ $\boxed{N}$ $\boxed{D}$ $\boxed{ALPHA}$ $\boxed{2nd}$ $\boxed{TEST}$ $\boxed{1}$ $\boxed{ALPHA}$ $\boxed{"}$ $\boxed{ENTER}$	:DISP "VSOUND="
2. $\boxed{PRGM}$ $\boxed{\blacktriangleright}$ $\boxed{1}$ $\boxed{ALPHA}$ $\boxed{S}$ $\boxed{ENTER}$	:INPUT S
3. $\boxed{PRGM}$ $\boxed{\blacktriangleright}$ $\boxed{3}$ $\boxed{ALPHA}$ $\boxed{"}$ $\boxed{ALPHA}$ $\boxed{V}$ $\boxed{2nd}$ $\boxed{TEST}$ $\boxed{1}$ $\boxed{ALPHA}$ $\boxed{"}$ $\boxed{ENTER}$	:DISP "V="
4. $\boxed{PRGM}$ $\boxed{\blacktriangleright}$ $\boxed{1}$ $\boxed{ALPHA}$ $\boxed{V}$ $\boxed{ENTER}$	:INPUT V
5. $\boxed{ALPHA}$ $\boxed{"}$ $\boxed{ALPHA}$ $\boxed{S}$ $\boxed{X,T,\theta}$ $\boxed{\div}$ $\boxed{(}$ $\boxed{ALPHA}$ $\boxed{S}$ $\boxed{-}$ $\boxed{ALPHA}$ $\boxed{V}$ $\boxed{)}$ $\boxed{ALPHA}$ $\boxed{"}$ $\boxed{STO\blacktriangleright}$ $\boxed{2nd}$ $\boxed{Y\text{-}VARS}$ $\boxed{1}$ $\boxed{1}$ $\boxed{ENTER}$	:"SX/(S–V)" → Y1
6. $\boxed{ALPHA}$ $\boxed{"}$ $\boxed{ALPHA}$ $\boxed{S}$ $\boxed{X,T,\theta}$ $\boxed{\div}$ $\boxed{(}$ $\boxed{ALPHA}$ $\boxed{S}$ $\boxed{+}$ $\boxed{ALPHA}$ $\boxed{V}$ $\boxed{)}$ $\boxed{ALPHA}$ $\boxed{"}$ $\boxed{STO\blacktriangleright}$ $\boxed{2nd}$ $\boxed{Y\text{-}VARS}$ $\boxed{1}$ $\boxed{2}$ $\boxed{ENTER}$	:"SX/(S+V)" → Y2
7. $\boxed{PRGM}$ $\boxed{\blacktriangleright}$ $\boxed{4}$ $\boxed{ENTER}$	:DISPGRAPH

CHAPTER 13
Laboratory Exercise

OBJECTIVES

- Find the speed of sound in air.

MATERIALS LIST

✔ Check list for appropriate procedure.

PROCEDURE

CBL AND SENSORS

✔ cardboard tube
✔ CBL
✔ CBL microphone
✔ graphing calculator with link cable
✔ masking tape
✔ meterstick
✔ support stand with clamp
✔ CBL temperature sensor

RESONANCE APPARATUS

✔ 4 tuning forks of different frequencies
✔ Erlenmeyer flask, 1000 mL
✔ resonance apparatus with clamp
✔ thermometer
✔ tuning-fork hammer
✔ water

SPEED OF SOUND

Sound waves can travel through solids, liquids, and gases. The speed of sound in a medium depends on the density of the particles that make up the medium. The speed also depends on the temperature, especially in a gas like air. In air, sound travels faster at higher temperatures and slower at lower temperatures. In this experiment, you will measure the speed of sound in air using one of the methods described below.

- **CBL and sensors**   The speed of sound will be determined using a CBL microphone placed directly above the opening of a large tube. A short, sharp noise will be recorded by the microphone at the top of the tube and again after the sound travels down the tube and reflects back to the microphone. You can use the time between recordings and distance traveled by the sound to determine the speed of sound in air.

- **Resonance apparatus**   The speed of sound will be determined using a tuning fork to produce resonance in a closed tube. The wavelength of the sound may be calculated from the resonant length of the tube, and the speed of the sound can be calculated from the equation $v = f\lambda$, where v is the speed of sound, f is the frequency of the sound produced by the tuning fork, and λ is the wavelength of the sound.

SAFETY

- **Never put broken glass or ceramics in a regular waste container. Use a dustpan, brush, and heavy gloves to carefully pick up broken pieces and dispose of them in a container specifically provided for this purpose.**

- **If a thermometer breaks, notify the teacher immediately.**

PREPARATION

1. Determine whether you will be using the CBL and sensors procedure or the resonance apparatus procedure. Read the entire lab for the appropriate procedure, and plan what steps you will take.

Resonance apparatus procedure begins on page 514.

PROCEDURE

CBL AND SENSORS

Finding the speed of sound

2. Prepare a data table in your lab notebook with four columns and five rows. In the first row, label the first through fourth columns *Trial, Distance from microphone to bottom of tube (m), Temperature (°C),* and *Time interval (s)*. In the first column, label the second through fifth rows *1, 2, 3,* and *4.*

3. Set up the temperature probe, CBL microphone, ring stand, tube, CBL, and calculator, as shown in **Figure 13-25.** Tape or clamp the tube securely in place. Clamp the CBL microphone to the edge of the table or to a ring stand so that the microphone points down and is directly above the open end of the tube. Connect the CBL to the graphing calculator. Connect the CBL microphone to the CH1 port and the temperature probe to the CH2 port on the CBL unit. Hang the temperature probe inside the tube to measure the air temperature.

4. Turn on the CBL unit and the calculator. Start the program PHYSICS on the calculator.

   a. Select the *SET UP PROBES* option from the MAIN MENU. Enter 1 for the number of probes. Select the *TEMPERATURE* probe. Enter 2 for the channel number.

   b. Select the *MONITOR INPUT* option from the MAIN MENU. Record the temperature reading in your data table. Press "+" to return to the MAIN MENU.

5. From the MAIN MENU, select the *SET UP PROBES* option. Enter 1 for the number of probes. Select the *MICROPHONE.* Your teacher will tell you what type of microphone you are using. Select the appropriate description from the list on the calculator. From the COLLECTION MODE menu, select *WAVEFORM/TRIGR.* Press ENTER on the graphing calculator.

6. Make a loud, short noise—such as a snap of the fingers—directly above the tube. This will trigger the CBL to collect the sound data.

7. When the CBL unit displays DONE, press ENTER on the calculator.

8. Use the metric ruler to measure the length from the bottom of the CBL microphone to the bottom of the tube. Record this length to the nearest millimeter in the data table.

9. Look at the graph on the graphing calculator, which shows the sound plotted against time in seconds. There should be two peaks on the graph, one near the beginning and one a little later. The first peak is the sound and the second peak is the echo of the sound. Use the arrow keys to trace the graph.

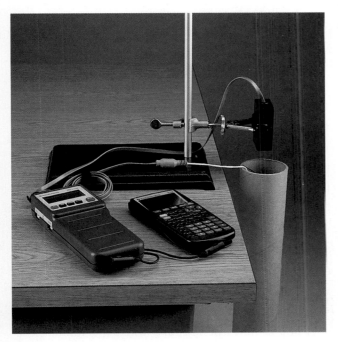

Figure 13-25

Step 6: The CBL will begin collecting sound data as soon as you make a sound, so work quietly until you are ready to begin the experiment. Remain quiet until the CBL displays DONE. Background noise may affect your results.

Step 9: On the graph, the first and second peaks may not be the same height, but they should both be noticeably higher than the other points on the graph. If the sound was too loud, the graph will show many high and low points. Repeat with a softer sound for better results.

Find the difference between the *x* values of the two peaks to find the time interval between them. Record the time interval in your data table. Sketch the graph in your lab notebook. Press ENTER on the calculator.

10. Repeat the procedure for several trials. Try different sounds, such as a soft noise, a loud noise, a high-pitched sound, or a low-pitched sound. Record all data in your data table.

Analysis and Interpretation begins on page 515.

PROCEDURE

RESONANCE APPARATUS

Finding the speed of sound

2. Prepare a data table in your lab notebook with four columns and five rows. In the first row, label the first through fourth columns *Trial, Length of tube (m), Frequency (Hz),* and *Temperature (°C)*. In the first column, label the second through fifth rows *1, 2, 3,* and *4.*

3. Set up the resonance apparatus as shown in **Figure 13-26.**

4. Raise the reservoir so that the top is level with the top of the tube. Fill the reservoir with water until the level in the tube is at the 5 cm mark.

Figure 13-26
Step 7: From the position of greatest resonance, move the reservoir up 2 cm and down again until you find the exact position.

5. Measure and record the temperature of the air inside the tube. Select a tuning fork, and record the frequency of the fork in the data table.

6. Securely clamp the tuning fork in place as shown in the figure, with the lower tine about 1 cm above the end of the tube. Strike the tuning fork sharply, but not too hard, with the tuning-fork hammer to create a vibration. A few practice strikes may be helpful to distinguish the tonal sound of the tuning fork from the unwanted metallic "ringing" sound that may result from striking the fork too hard. *Do not strike the fork with anything other than a hard rubber mallet.*

7. While the tuning fork is vibrating directly above the tube, slowly lower the reservoir about 20 cm or until you locate the position of the reservoir where the resonance is loudest. (Note: To locate the exact position of the resonance, you may need to strike the tuning fork again while the water level is falling.) Raise the reservoir to about 2 cm above the approximate level where you think the resonance is loudest. Strike the tuning fork with the tuning fork hammer and carefully lower the reservoir about 5 cm until you find the exact position of resonance.

8. Using the scale marked on the tube, record the level of the water in the tube when the resonance is loudest. Record this level to the nearest millimeter in your data table.

9. Repeat the procedure for several trials, using tuning forks of different frequencies.

ANALYSIS AND INTERPRETATION

Calculations and data analysis

1. **Organizing data**
   a. **CBL and sensors** For each trial, calculate the total distance the sound traveled by multiplying the distance measured by 2.
   b. **Resonance apparatus** For each trial, calculate the wavelength of the sound by using the equation for the fundamental wavelength: $\lambda = 4L$, where L is the length of the tube.

2. **Analyzing data** For each trial, find the speed of sound.
   a. **CBL and sensors** Use the values for distance traveled and the time interval from your data table to find the speed for each trial.
   b. **Resonance apparatus** Use the equation $v = f\lambda$, where f is the frequency of the tuning fork.

3. **Evaluating data** Find the *accepted* value for the speed of sound in air at room temperature (see page 482, **Table 13-1**). Find the average of your results for the speed of sound, and use the average as the experimental value.
   a. Compute the absolute error using the following equation:

   $$\text{absolute error} = |\text{experimental} - \text{accepted}|$$

   b. Compute the relative error using the following equation:

   $$\text{relative error} = \frac{(\text{experimental} - \text{accepted})}{\text{accepted}}$$

Conclusions

4. **Applying conclusions** Based on your results, is the speed of sound in air at a given temperature the same for all sounds, or do some sounds move more quickly or more slowly than other sounds? Explain.

5. **Applying ideas** How could you find the speed of sound in air at different temperatures?

Extensions

6. **Evaluating methods** How could you modify the experiment to find the length of an open pipe? If there is time and your teacher approves your plan, carry out the experiment.

7. **Research and communications** Many musical instruments operate by resonating air in open or closed tubes. In a pipe organ, for example, both open and closed tubes are used to create music. Research a pipe instrument, and find out how different notes are produced.

$\mathcal{S}$uppose you are spending some quiet time alone–reading, studying, or just daydreaming. Suddenly your peaceful mood is shattered by the sound of a lawn mower, loud music, or an airplane taking off. If this has happened to you, then you have experienced noise pollution.

Noise is defined as any loud, discordant, or disagreeable sound, so classifying sounds as noise is often a matter of personal opinion. When you are at a party, you might enjoy listening to loud music, but when you are at home trying to sleep, you may find the same music very disturbing.

There are two kinds of noise pollution, both of which can result in long-term hearing problems and even physical damage to the ear. Chapter 13 explains how we receive and interpret sound.

How can noise damage hearing?

The small bones and hairlike cells of the inner ear are delicate and very sensitive to the compression waves we interpret as sounds. The first type of noise pollution involves noises that are so loud they endanger the sensitive parts of the ear. Prolonged exposure to sounds of about 85 dB can begin to damage hearing irreversibly. Certain sounds above 120 dB can cause immediate damage. The sound level produced by a food blender or by diesel truck traffic is about 85 dB. A jet engine heard from a few meters away is about 140 dB.

Have you ever noticed the "headphones" worn by ground crew at an airport or by workers using chain saws or jackhammers? In most cases, these are ear protectors worn to prevent the hearing loss brought on by damage to the inner ear.

Whose noise annoys?

The second kind of noise pollution is more controversial because it involves noises that are considered annoyances. No one knows for sure how to measure levels of annoyance, but sometimes annoying noise becomes intolerable. Lack of sleep due to noise causes people to have slow reaction times and poor judgment, which can result in mistakes at work or school and accidents on the job or on the road. Scientists have found that continuous, irritating noise often produces high blood pressure, which leads to other health problems.

A major debate involves noise made by aircraft. Airport traffic in the United States nearly doubled from 1980 to 1990 and continues to grow at a rapid pace. People who live near airports once found aircraft noise an occasional annoyance, but because of increased traffic and runways added to accommodate growth, they now suffer sleep disruptions and other health effects.

Many people have organized groups to oppose airport expansion. Their primary concerns are the increase in noise and the decrease in property values associated with airport expansion.

But, city governments argue that an airport benefits the entire community both socially and economically and that airports must expand to meet the needs of increased populations. Officials have also argued that people knew they were taking chances by building or buying near an airport and that the community cannot compensate for their losses. Airlines contend that attempts to reduce noise by using less power during takeoffs or by veering away from populated areas can pose a serious threat to passenger safety.

Other annoyances

Besides airports, people currently complain most about noise pollution from nearby construction sites, jet skis, loud stereos in homes and cars, all-terrain vehicles, snowmobiles, and power lawn equipment, such as mowers and leaf blowers. Many people want to control such noise by passing laws to limit the use of this equipment to certain times of the day or by requiring that sound-muffling devices be used.

Opponents to these measures argue that much of this activity takes place on private property and that, in the case of building sites and industries, noise limitation would increase costs. Some public officials would like to control annoying noise but point out that laws to do so fall under the category of nuisance laws, which are notoriously difficult to enforce.

Noise pollution is also a problem in areas where few or no people live. Unwanted noise in wilderness areas can affect animal behavior and reproduction. Sometimes animals are simply scared away from their habitats. For this reason, the government has taken action in some national parks to reduce sightseeing flights, get rid of noisy campers, and limit or eliminate certain noisy vehicles. Some parks have drastically limited the number of people who can be in a park at any one time.

Researching the Issue

1. Obtain a sound-level meter, and measure the noise level at places where you and your friends might be during an average week. Also make some measurements at locations where sound is annoyingly loud. Be sure to hold the meter at head level and read the meter for 30 seconds to obtain an average. Present your findings to the class in a graphic display.

2. Measure the sound levels at increasing distances from two sources of steady, loud noise. Record all of your locations and measurements. Graph your data, and write an interpretation describing how sound level varies with distance from the source.

3. Is there a source of noise in your community that most people recognize to be a problem? If so, find out what causes the noise and what people want to do to relieve the problem. Hold a panel discussion to analyze the opinions of each side, and propose your own solution.

Light and Reflection

PHYSICS IN ACTION

Although much larger and different in appearance, the radio telescope at Arecibo, Puerto Rico, operates on the same principles as an optical telescope. Just as rays of visible light form images by reflecting from an optical telescope's curved mirror, radio waves reflect from the metal sides of the radio telescope's "mirror" to form radio images.

The two types of instruments function similarly because both visible light and radio waves are forms of electromagnetic radiation and, as such, reflect from certain materials. In this chapter, the nature of electromagnetic waves and their behavior during reflection will be examined.

- *Why are telescope mirrors always concave rather than flat or convex?*
- *How can the location and size of mirror images be predicted?*

CONCEPT REVIEW

Properties of waves   (Section 12-3)

Reflection of waves   (Section 12-4)

14-1
Characteristics of light

14-1 SECTION OBJECTIVES

- **Identify the components of the electromagnetic spectrum.**

- **Calculate the frequency or wavelength of electromagnetic radiation.**

- **Recognize that light has a finite speed.**

- **Describe how the brightness of a light source is affected by distance.**

electromagnetic wave

a transverse wave consisting of oscillating electric and magnetic fields at right angles to each other

ELECTROMAGNETIC WAVES

Nearly everyone has experienced light. When most people think of light, they think of light they can see. Some examples include the bright, white light that is produced by a light bulb or the sun. However, there is more to light than this.

When you hold a piece of green glass or plastic in front of a source of white light, you see green light pass through. This is also true for other colors. What your eyes recognize as "white" light is actually light that can be separated into six elementary colors of the visible *spectrum:* red, orange, yellow, green, blue, and violet.

If you examine a glass prism, like the one shown in **Figure 14-1,** or any thick, triangular-shaped piece of glass, you will find that sunlight passes through the glass and emerges as a rainbowlike band of colors.

The spectrum includes more than visible light

Not all light is visible to the human eye. If you were to examine the light dispersed through a prism using certain types of photographic film, you would find that the film records a much wider spectrum than the one you see. A variety of forms of radiation—including X rays, microwaves, and radio waves—have many of the same properties as visible light. This is because they are all examples of **electromagnetic waves.**

Light has been described as a particle, as a wave, and even as a combination of the two. While the current model has incorporated aspects of both particle and wave theories, the wave model is best suited for an introductory discussion of light, and it is the one that will be used in Chapters 14–16.

Figure 14-1
A prism separates light into its component colors.

Electromagnetic waves vary depending on frequency and wavelength

In classical electromagnetic wave theory, light is a wave composed of oscillating electric and magnetic fields. These fields are perpendicular to the direction in which the wave moves, as shown in **Figure 14-2.** Therefore, electromagnetic waves are transverse waves. The electric and magnetic fields are also at right angles to each other.

Electromagnetic waves are distinguished by their different frequencies and wavelengths. In visible light, these differences in frequency and wavelength account for different colors. The difference in frequencies and wavelengths also distinguishes visible light from invisible electromagnetic radiation, such as X rays.

Types of electromagnetic waves are listed in **Table 14-1.** Note the wide range of wavelengths and frequencies. Although specific ranges are indicated in the table, the electromagnetic spectrum is, in reality, continuous. There is no sharp division between one kind of wave and the next. Some types of waves even have overlapping ranges.

Figure 14-2
An electromagnetic wave consists of electric and magnetic field waves at right angles to each other.

Table 14-1   The electromagnetic spectrum

Classification	Range	Applications
Radio waves	$\lambda > 30$ cm $f < 1.0 \times 10^9$ Hz	AM and FM radio; television
Microwaves	30 cm $> \lambda > 1$ mm 1.0×10^9 Hz $< f < 3.0 \times 10^{11}$ Hz	radar; atomic and molecular research; aircraft navigation; microwave ovens
Infrared (IR) waves	1 mm $> \lambda > 700$ nm 3.0×10^{11} Hz $< f < 4.3 \times 10^{14}$ Hz	molecular vibrational spectra; infrared photography; physical therapy
Visible light	700 nm (red) $> \lambda > 400$ nm (violet) 4.3×10^{14} Hz $< f < 7.5 \times 10^{14}$ Hz	visible-light photography; optical microscopy; optical astronomy
Ultraviolet (UV) light	400 nm $> \lambda > 60$ nm 7.5×10^{14} Hz $< f < 5.0 \times 10^{15}$ Hz	sterilization of medical instruments; identification of fluorescent minerals
X rays	60 nm $> \lambda > 10^{-4}$ nm 5.0×10^{15} Hz $< f < 3.0 \times 10^{2}$ Hz	medical examination of bones, teeth, and vital organs; treatment for types of cancer
Gamma rays	0.1 nm $> \lambda > 10^{-5}$ nm 3.0×10^{18} Hz $< f < 3.0 \times 10^{22}$ Hz	examination of thick materials for structural flaws; treatment of types of cancer; food irradiation

CONCEPT PREVIEW

Electric fields will be discussed in greater detail in Chapter 17. Magnetic fields will be discussed in Chapter 21.

All electromagnetic waves move at the speed of light

All forms of electromagnetic radiation travel at a single high speed in a vacuum. Early experimental attempts to determine the speed of light failed because this speed is so great. As experimental techniques improved, especially during the nineteenth and early-twentieth centuries, the speed of light was determined with increasing accuracy and precision. By the mid-twentieth century, the experimental error was less than 0.001 percent. The currently accepted value for light traveling in a vacuum is $2.997\ 924\ 58 \times 10^8$ m/s. Light travels slightly slower in air, with a speed of $2.997\ 09 \times 10^8$ m/s. For calculations in this book, the value used for both situations will be 3.00×10^8 m/s.

The relationship between frequency, wavelength, and speed described in Chapter 12 also holds true for light waves.

WAVE SPEED EQUATION

$$c = f\lambda$$

speed of light = frequency × wavelength

SAMPLE PROBLEM 14A

Electromagnetic waves

PROBLEM

The AM radio band extends from 5.4×10^5 Hz to 1.7×10^6 Hz. What are the longest and shortest wavelengths in this frequency range?

SOLUTION

Given: $f_1 = 5.4 \times 10^5$ Hz $f_2 = 1.7 \times 10^6$ Hz $c = 3.00 \times 10^8$ m/s

Unknown: $\lambda_1 = ?$ $\lambda_2 = ?$

Use the wave speed equation on this page:

$$c = f\lambda \quad \lambda = \frac{c}{f}$$

$$\lambda_1 = \frac{3.00 \times 10^8 \text{ m/s}}{5.4 \times 10^5 \text{ Hz}}$$

$$\boxed{\lambda_1 = 5.6 \times 10^2 \text{ m}}$$

$$\lambda_2 = \frac{3.00 \times 10^8 \text{ m/s}}{1.7 \times 10^6 \text{ Hz}}$$

$$\boxed{\lambda_2 = 1.8 \times 10^2 \text{ m}}$$

CALCULATOR SOLUTION

Although the calculator solutions are 555.5555556 m and 176.470588 m, both answers must be rounded to two digits because the frequencies have only two significant figures.

Electromagnetic waves

1. What is the wavelength range for the FM radio band (88 MHz–108 MHz)?

2. What is the frequency of an electromagnetic wave if it has a wavelength of 1.0 km?

3. Shortwave radio is broadcast between 3.50 and 29.7 MHz. To what range of wavelengths does this correspond? Why do you suppose this part of the spectrum is called shortwave radio?

4. Gamma-ray bursters are objects in the universe that emit pulses of gamma rays with high energies. The frequency of the most energetic bursts has been measured at around 3.0×10^{21} Hz. What is the wavelength of these gamma rays?

5. The portion of the visible spectrum that appears brightest to the human eye is around 560 nm in wavelength, which corresponds to yellow-green. What is the frequency of 560 nm light?

6. What is the frequency of highly energetic ultraviolet radiation that has a wavelength of 125 nm?

Waves can be approximated as rays

Consider an ocean wave coming toward the shore. The broad crest of the wave that is perpendicular to the wave's motion consists of a line of water particles. Similarly, another line of water particles forms a low-lying trough in the wave, and still another line of particles forms another crest. In any type of wave, these lines of particles are called *wave fronts.*

All the points on the wave front of a plane wave can be treated as point sources. A few of these points are shown on the initial wave front in **Figure 14-3.** Each of these point sources produces a circular or spherical secondary wave, or *wavelet.* The radii of these wavelets are indicated by the blue arrows in **Figure 14-3.** The line that is tangent to each of these wavelets at some later time determines the new position of the initial wave front (the new wave front in **Figure 14-3**). This approach to analyzing waves is called Huygens' principle, named for the physicist Christian Huygens, who developed it.

Huygens' principle can be used to derive the properties of any wave (including light) that interacts with matter, but the same results can be obtained by treating the propagating wave as a straight line perpendicular to the wave front. This line is called a *ray,* and this simplification is called the *ray approximation.*

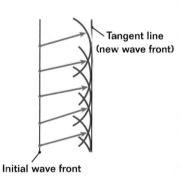

Figure 14-3

According to Huygens' principle, a wave front can be divided into point sources. The line tangent to the wavelets from these sources marks the wave front's new position.

Sulfur Light Bulbs

A new kind of lamp uses sulfur and microwaves to create light that is bright and energy-efficient and looks a lot like sunlight.

The sulfur bulb shown at the right of a metal-halide bulb in the photograph below is flooded with microwave energy. In a microwave oven, an electric field creates microwave radiation that causes water molecules to rotate and the food's temperature to increase. In the lamp, the electric field accelerates electrons that strike sulfur molecules, causing them to become excited and emit light.

In the photo at right, light from two 3000 W microwave sulfur lamps is routed through light pipes to illuminate a region 85 m wide. Because of its tremendous intensity, the lamp is not practical for home use, says Michael Ury, vice-president of research and development at Fusion Lighting, in Rockville, Maryland. "It certainly will not be in your kitchen until we can make a lower-power version. So for the next few years, you'll find this being used in factories, and

perhaps in sports arenas, aircraft hangars, and shopping malls, where the ceilings are high," says Ury. The lamp cannot be used where the high temperature of overhead lighting is considered to be a negative factor, such as in hockey rinks. But, adds Ury, "this is one of the few light sources with which you can light plants to solar levels without cooking them."

Compared with other forms of outdoor lighting, the sulfur lamp makes it easier to discern a full spectrum of color. For instance, if you are looking for your blue-green car in a parking lot at night, you may not recognize your car because the high-pressure sodium lamps used in most parking lots are deficient in the blue and green frequency ranges, making your car look black. By contrast, says Ury, "The sulfur lamp spectrum contains all the colors. If we were to light up a parking lot with this light, you'd find your car; you'd recognize its color."

Other advantages of the sulfur lamp are its high efficiency and reliability. It operates at about 1350 W and produces nearly six times as much light per watt as a 100 W incandescent bulb. A sulfur light bulb is designed to last 60 000 hours, outlasting its microwave source, which usually has to be replaced between 15 000 and 20 000 hours.

Brightness decreases by the square of the distance from the source

You have probably noticed that it is easier to read a book when a lamp that is 1 m away from you has a 100 W bulb installed in it instead of a 25 W bulb. This experience suggests that the brightness of light depends on how much light is actually emitted from a source. However, the amount of light that you detect also depends on your distance from the source.

The farther you are from a light source, the less bright the light appears to be. This is because the light emitted by the source spreads outward in all directions. The farther the light is from the source, the more spread out the light becomes. Therefore, less light is available per unit area at a greater distance from the source than at a smaller one. The brightness you perceive from a light source is related to the amount of light that falls on a unit surface area at some distance from the source. As you may note from **Figure 14-4,** the apparent brightness is proportional to the actual brightness of the source divided by the square of the distance between the source and the observer. For example, if you move twice as far away from the light source, one-fourth as much light falls on the book.

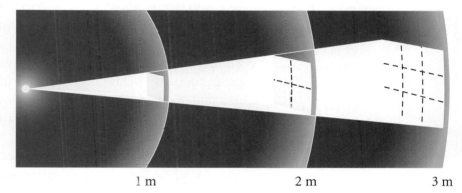

1 m   2 m   3 m

Figure 14-4

Less light falls on each unit square as the distance from the source increases.

Section Review

1. Identify which portions of the electromagnetic spectrum are used in each of the devices listed.

   a. a microwave oven
   b. a television set
   c. a single-lens reflex camera

2. If an electromagnetic wave has a frequency of 7.57×10^{14} Hz, what is its wavelength? To what part of the spectrum does this wave belong?

3. Galileo performed an experiment to measure the speed of light by timing how long it took light to travel from a lamp he was holding to an assistant about 1.5 km away and back again. Why was Galileo unable to conclude that light had a finite speed?

4. How bright would the sun appear to an observer on Earth if the sun were four times farther from Earth than it actually is? Express your answer as a fraction of the sun's brightness on Earth's surface.

14-2
Flat mirrors

14-2 SECTION OBJECTIVES

- **Distinguish between specular and diffuse reflection of light.**

- **Apply the law of reflection for flat mirrors.**

- **Describe the nature of images formed by flat mirrors.**

reflection

the turning back of an electro-magnetic wave at the surface of a substance

Figure 14-5
Mirrors reflect nearly all incoming light, so multiple images of an object between two mirrors are easily formed.

REFLECTION OF LIGHT

Suppose you have just had your hair cut and you want to know what the back of your head looks like. You can do this seemingly impossible task by using two mirrors to direct light from behind your head to your eyes. Redirecting light with mirrors reveals a basic property of light's interaction with matter.

Light traveling through a uniform substance, whether it is air, water, or a vacuum, always travels in a straight line. However, when the light encounters a different substance, its path will change. If a material is opaque to the light, such as the dark, highly polished surface of a wooden table, the light will not pass into the table more than a few wavelengths. Part of the light is absorbed, and the rest of it is deflected at the surface. This change in the direction of the light is called **reflection.**

Most substances absorb at least some of the incoming light and reflect the rest. A mirror reflects almost all incoming light, as shown in **Figure 14-5.**

The texture of a surface affects how it reflects light

The manner in which light is reflected from a surface depends on the surface's smoothness. Light that is reflected from a rough, textured surface, such as paper, cloth, or unpolished wood, is reflected in many different directions, as shown in **Figure 14-6(a).** This type of reflection is called *diffuse reflection.* Diffuse reflection will be discussed further in Section 14-4.

Light reflected from smooth, shiny surfaces, such as a mirror or water in a pond, is reflected in one direction only, as shown in **Figure 14-6(b).** This type of reflection is called *specular reflection.*

A surface is considered smooth if its surface variations are small compared with the wavelength of the incoming light. For our discussion, reflection will be used to mean only specular reflection.

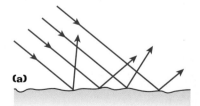

Figure 14-6
Diffusely reflected light is reflected in many directions **(a),** whereas specularly reflected light is reflected in the same forward direction only **(b).**

(b)

Figure 14-7
The symmetry of reflected light **(a)** is described by the law of reflection, which states that the angles of the incoming and reflected rays are equal **(b).**

(a)

Incoming and reflected angles are equal

You probably have noticed that when incoming rays of light strike a smooth reflecting surface, such as a polished table or mirror, at an angle close to the surface, the reflected rays are also close to the surface. When the incoming rays are high above the reflecting surface, the reflected rays are also high above the surface. An example of this similarity between incoming and reflected rays is shown in **Figure 14-7(a).**

If a straight line is drawn perpendicular to the reflecting surface at the point where the incoming ray strikes the surface, the **angle of incidence** and the **angle of reflection** can be defined with respect to the line. Careful measurements of the incident and reflected angles θ and θ', respectively, reveal that the angles are equal, as illustrated in **Figure 14-7(b).**

$$\theta = \theta'$$

angle of incoming light ray = angle of reflected light ray

Note that the line perpendicular to the reflecting surface is referred to as the *normal* to the surface. It therefore follows that the angle between the incoming ray and the surface equals $90° - \theta$, and the angle between the reflected ray and the surface equals $90° - \theta'$.

angle of incidence

the angle between a ray that strikes a surface and the normal to that surface at the point of contact

angle of reflection

the angle formed by the line normal to a surface and the direction in which a reflected ray moves

FLAT MIRRORS

The simplest mirror is the *flat mirror.* If an object, such as a pencil, is placed at a distance in front of a flat mirror and light is bounced off the pencil, light rays will spread out from the pencil and reflect from the mirror's surface. To an observer looking at the mirror, these rays appear to come from a location on the other side of the mirror. As a convention, an object's image is said to be at this location behind the mirror. The relationship between the *object distance* from the mirror, which is represented as p, and the *image distance* (that is, the distance the image appears to be behind the mirror's surface), which is represented as q, is such that the object and image distances are equal. Similarly, the image of the object is the same size as the object.

The image formed by rays that appear to come together at the image point behind the mirror—but never really do—is called a **virtual image.** As shown in **Figure 14-8(a),** a flat mirror always forms a virtual image, which can only be seen "behind" the surface of the mirror. For this reason, a virtual image can never be displayed on a physical surface.

Image location can be predicted with ray diagrams

Ray diagrams, such as the one shown in **Figure 14-8(b),** are drawings that use simple geometry to locate an image formed by a mirror. Suppose you want to make a ray diagram for a pencil placed in front of a flat mirror. First, sketch the situation. Draw the location and arrangement of the mirror and the position of the pencil with respect to the mirror. Construct the drawing so that the object and the image distances (p and q, respectively) are proportional to their actual sizes. To simplify matters, we will consider only the tip of the pencil.

To pinpoint the location of the pencil tip's image, draw two rays on your diagram. Draw the first ray from the pencil tip perpendicular to the mirror's surface. Because this ray makes an angle of 0° with the normal to the mirror, the angle of reflection also equals 0°, causing the ray to reflect back on itself. In **Figure 14-8(b),** this ray is denoted as **1** and is shown with arrows pointing in both directions because the incident ray reflects back on itself.

Draw the second ray from the tip of the pencil to the mirror, but this time place the ray at an angle that is not perpendicular to the surface of the mirror. Then draw the reflected ray, keeping in mind that it will reflect away from the surface of the mirror at an angle, θ', equal to the angle of incidence, θ. This ray is denoted in **Figure 14-8(b)** by the number **2.**

Next, trace both reflected rays back to the point from which they appear to have originated, that is, behind the mirror. Use dotted lines when drawing these apparent rays behind the mirror to distinguish them from the actual rays of light (the solid lines) in front of the mirror. The point at which these dotted lines meet is the image point, which in this case is where the image of the pencil's tip forms.

By continuing this process for all of the other parts of the pencil, you can locate the complete virtual image of the pencil. Note that the pencil's image appears as far behind the mirror as the pencil is in front of the mirror ($p = q$). Likewise, the object height, h, equals the image height, h'.

(a)

(b)   Mirror

Figure 14-8

The position and size of the virtual image that forms in a flat mirror **(a)** can be predicted by constructing a ray diagram **(b).**

This ray-tracing procedure will work for any object placed in front of a flat mirror. By selecting a single point on the object (usually its uppermost tip or edge), you can use ray tracing to locate the same point on the image. The rest of the image can be added once the image point and image distance have been determined.

The image formed by a flat mirror appears to have right-to-left reversal; that is, the right side of an object is the image's left side. You can see this by placing a watch in front of a mirror, as shown in **Figure 14-9.** In the mirror, the numbers on the watch are turned around and the hands point in the opposite direction.

Figure 14-9
The right side of an object becomes the left side of its image.

Section Review

1. Which of the following are examples of specular reflection and which are examples of diffuse reflection?
   a. reflection of light from the surface of a lake on a calm day
   b. reflection of light from a plastic trash bag
   c. reflection of light from the lens of eyeglasses
   d. reflection of light from a carpet

2. The photograph in **Figure 14-5** on page 526 shows multiple images that were created by multiple reflections between two flat mirrors. What conclusion can you make about the relative orientation of the mirrors? Explain your answer.

3. Suppose you are holding a flat mirror and standing at the center of a giant clock face built into the floor. Someone standing at 12 o'clock shines a beam of light toward you, and you want to use the mirror to reflect the beam toward an observer standing at 5 o'clock. What should the angle of incidence be to achieve this? What should the angle of reflection be?

4. Some department-store windows are slanted inward at the bottom. This is to decrease the glare from brightly illuminated buildings across the street, which would make it difficult for shoppers to see the display inside and near the bottom of the window. Sketch a light ray reflecting from such a window to show how this technique works.

5. If one wall of a room consists of a large flat mirror, how much larger will the room appear to be? Explain your answer.

6. Why does a flat mirror appear to reverse images left to right, but not up and down?

14-3
Curved mirrors

14-3 SECTION OBJECTIVES

- **Calculate distances and focal lengths using the mirror equation for concave and convex spherical mirrors.**

- **Draw ray diagrams to find the image distance and magnification for concave and convex spherical mirrors.**

- **Distinguish between real and virtual images.**

- **Describe how parabolic mirrors differ from spherical mirrors.**

concave spherical mirror

an inwardly curved, mirrored surface that is a portion of a sphere and that converges incoming light rays

CONCAVE SPHERICAL MIRRORS

You may have noticed small circular mirrors on dressing tables. Although such mirrors may appear at first glance to be the same as flat mirrors, the images they form differ from those formed by flat mirrors. For example, the images for objects close to the mirror are larger than the object, as shown in **Figure 14-10(a),** while the images of objects far from the mirror are smaller and upside down, as shown in **Figure 14-10(b).** Images such as these are characteristic of curved mirrors.

Concave mirrors focus light to form real images

One basic type of curved mirror is the spherical mirror. A spherical mirror, as its name implies, has the shape of part of a sphere's surface. A spherical mirror with light reflecting from its silvered, concave surface (that is, the inner surface of a sphere) is called a **concave spherical mirror.** Concave spherical mirrors are used whenever a magnified image of an object is needed, as in the case of the dressing-table mirror.

One factor that determines where the image will appear in a concave spherical mirror and how large that image will be is the amount by which the mirror is curved. This in turn depends on the radius of curvature, R, of the mirror. The radius of curvature is the same as the radius of a sphere whose curvature would be identical to that of the mirror; R therefore is the distance from the mirror's surface to the center of curvature, C.

(a)   (b)

Figure 14-10
Curved mirrors can be used to form images that are larger **(a)** or smaller **(b)** than the object.

(a)

(b)

Imagine that the pencil in **Figure 14-8,** on page 528, is placed upright at a distance p from a concave spherical mirror, as shown in **Figure 14-11(a).** The eraser end of the pencil is placed along the mirror's principal axis, which is the line that extends infinitely from the center of the mirror's surface through the center of curvature, C. Light rays will diverge from the pencil, reflect from the mirror's surface, and converge at some distance, q, in front of the mirror. Because the light rays reflected by the mirror actually pass through the image point, which in this case is below the principal axis, the image forms in front of the mirror.

If you place a piece of white paper at the image point, you will see on the paper a sharp and clear image of the pencil. As you move the paper in either direction away from the image point, the rays diverge and the image becomes unfocused. An image of this type is called a **real image.** An example of a real image is shown in the lower left corner of **Figure 14-11(b).** Unlike the virtual images that are always formed by flat mirrors, real images can be displayed on a surface, like the images on a movie screen.

real image

an image formed when rays of light actually intersect at a single point

Image location can be predicted with the mirror equation

By looking at **Figure 14-11(a),** you can see that object distance, image distance, and radius of curvature are interdependent. If the object distance and radius of curvature of the mirror are known, you can predict where the image will appear. Alternatively, the radius of curvature of a mirror can be determined if you know where the image appears for a given object distance. The equation relating object distance, image distance, and the radius of curvature is called the mirror equation.

$$\frac{1}{p} + \frac{1}{q} = \frac{2}{R}$$

$$\frac{1}{\text{object distance}} + \frac{1}{\text{image distance}} = \frac{2}{\text{radius of curvature}}$$

If the pencil is placed very far from the mirror, the object distance, p, is great enough compared with R that $1/p$ is almost 0. In this case, q is almost $R/2$, so the image forms halfway between the center of curvature and the center of the mirror's surface. The image point, as shown in **Figure 14-12(a)** and **(b)**, is in this special case called the *focal point* of the mirror and is denoted by the capital letter F. Because the light rays are reversible, the reflected rays from a light source at the focal point will emerge parallel to each other.

When the image point is at the focal point, F, the image distance is called the *focal length,* and it is denoted by the lowercase letter f. For a spherical mirror, the focal length is equal to half the radius of curvature of the mirror. The mirror equation can therefore be expressed in terms of the focal length.

MIRROR EQUATION

$$\frac{1}{p} + \frac{1}{q} = \frac{1}{f}$$

$$\frac{1}{\text{object distance}} + \frac{1}{\text{image distance}} = \frac{1}{\text{focal length}}$$

CONCEPT PREVIEW

When expressed in terms of focal length, the mirror equation becomes identical to the equation for a simple thin lens. The properties of lenses will be discussed in Chapter 15.

To use the mirror equation, a set of sign conventions for the three variables must be established. The region in which light rays reflect and form real images is called the front side of the mirror. The other side, where light rays do not exist—and where virtual images are formed—is called the back side of the mirror. The mirror is usually drawn so that the front side is to the left of the mirror's surface and the back side is to the right.

Object and image distances have a positive sign when measured from the center of the mirror to any point on the mirror's front side. Distances for images that form on the back side of the mirror always have a negative sign. Because the mirrored surface is on the front side of a concave mirror, its focal length always has a positive sign. The object and image heights are positive when both are above the principal axis and negative when either is below. **Table 14-4,** on page 538, lists these and other sign conventions for mirrors.

(a)

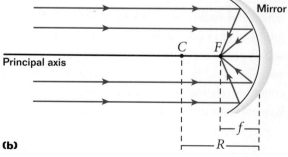

(b)

Figure 14-12
Light rays that are parallel converge at a single point **(a),** which can be represented in a diagram **(b),** when the rays are assumed to be from a distant object ($p \approx \infty$).

Magnification relates image and object sizes

Unlike flat mirrors, curved mirrors form images that are not the same size as the object. The measure of how much larger or smaller the image is with respect to the original object's size is called the *magnification* of the image.

If you know where the pencil's image will form for a given object distance, you can determine the magnification of the image. Magnification, M, is defined as the ratio of the height of the pencil's image to the pencil's actual height. M also equals the negative of the ratio of the image distance to the object distance. If an image is smaller than the object, the magnitude of its magnification is less than 1. If the image is larger than the object, the magnitude of its magnification is greater than 1. Magnification is a unitless quantity.

EQUATION FOR MAGNIFICATION

$$M = \frac{h'}{h} = -\frac{q}{p}$$

$$\text{magnification} = \frac{\text{image height}}{\text{object height}} = -\frac{\text{image distance}}{\text{object distance}}$$

For an image in front of the mirror, M is negative and the image is upside down, or *inverted*, with respect to the object. When the image is behind the mirror, M is positive and the image is *upright* with respect to the object. The conventions for magnification are listed in **Table 14-2.**

Table 14-2	Sign conventions for magnification	
Orientation of image with respect to object	**Sign of M**	**Type of image this applies to**
upright	+	virtual
inverted	−	real

Ray diagrams can be used for concave spherical mirrors

Ray diagrams are useful for checking values calculated from the mirror and magnification equations. The techniques for ray diagrams that were used to locate the image for an object in front of a flat mirror can also be used for concave spherical mirrors. When drawing ray diagrams for concave mirrors, follow the basic procedure for a flat mirror, but also measure all distances along the principal axis and mark the center of curvature, C, and the focal point, F. As with a flat mirror, draw the diagram to scale. For instance, if the object distance is 50 cm, you can draw the object distance as 5 cm.

For spherical mirrors, three reference rays are used to find the image point. The intersection of any *two* rays locates the image. The third ray should intersect

Quick Lab

Curved Mirrors

MATERIALS LIST

✔ stainless-steel or silver spoon
✔ short pencil

Observe the pencil's reflection in the inner portion of the spoon. Slowly move the spoon closer to the pencil. Note any changes in the appearance of the pencil's reflection. Repeat these steps using the other side of the spoon as the mirror.

at the same point and can be used to check the diagram. These reference rays are described in **Table 14-3.**

Table 14-3	Rules for drawing reference rays	
Ray	Line drawn from object to mirror	Line drawn from mirror to image after reflection
1	parallel to principal axis	through focal point F
2	through focal point F	parallel to principal axis
3	through center of curvature C	back along itself through C

The image distance in the diagram should agree with the value for q calculated from the mirror equation. However, the image distance may differ because of inaccuracies that arise from drawing the ray diagrams at a reduced scale. Ray diagrams should therefore be used to obtain approximate values only; they should not be relied on for the best quantitative results.

When an object is moved toward a concave spherical mirror, its image undergoes changes, as shown in **Figure 14-13.** For object distances greater than the focal length, the image is real and inverted, as shown in **(a).** When the object is at the focal point, the image is infinitely far to the left and therefore is not seen, as is indicated in **(b).** When the object lies between the focal point and the mirror surface, the image forms again, only now it becomes virtual and upright, as shown in **(c).**

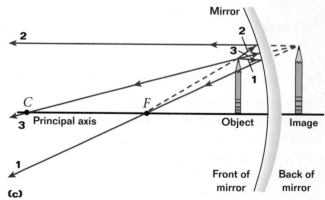

Figure 14-13
The image produced by a concave spherical mirror depends on whether the object distance is **(a)** greater than, **(b)** equal to, or **(c)** less than the focal length of the mirror. In each drawing, the rays are numbered according to their description in **Table 14-3.**

Concave mirrors

PROBLEM

A concave spherical mirror has a focal length of 10.0 cm. Locate the image of a pencil that is placed upright 30.0 cm from the mirror. Find the magnification of the image. Draw a ray diagram to confirm your answer.

SOLUTION

1. DEFINE

Given: $f = +10.0$ cm $p = +30.0$ cm

The mirror is concave, so f is positive. The object is in front of the mirror, so p is positive.

Unknown: $q = ?$ $M = ?$

Diagram:

Use the rules on page 534 to construct a ray diagram.

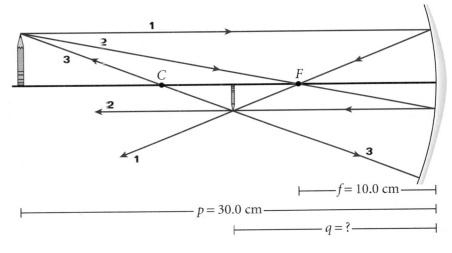

$f = 10.0$ cm

$p = 30.0$ cm

$q = ?$

2. PLAN

Choose an equation(s) or situation: Use the mirror equation that relates the object and image distances to focal length.

$$\frac{1}{p} + \frac{1}{q} = \frac{1}{f}$$

Use the magnification equation in terms of object and image distances.

$$M = -\frac{q}{p}$$

Rearrange the equation(s) to isolate the unknown(s): Subtract the reciprocal of the object distance from the reciprocal of the focal length to obtain an expression for the unknown image distance.

$$\frac{1}{q} = \frac{1}{f} - \frac{1}{p}$$

continued on next page

3. CALCULATE **Substitute the values into the equation(s) and solve:** Substitute the values for f and p into the mirror equation and the magnification equation to find the image distance and magnification.

$$\frac{1}{q} = \frac{1}{10.0 \text{ cm}} - \frac{1}{30.0 \text{ cm}} = \frac{0.100}{1 \text{ cm}} - \frac{0.033}{1 \text{ cm}} = \frac{0.067}{1 \text{ cm}}$$

$$\boxed{q = 15 \text{ cm}}$$

$$\boxed{M = -\frac{q}{p} = \frac{15 \text{ cm}}{30.0 \text{ cm}} = -0.50}$$

4. EVALUATE The image appears between the focal point (10.0 cm) and the center of curvature (20.0 cm), as confirmed by the ray diagram. The image is smaller than the object and inverted ($M < 0$), as is also confirmed by the ray diagram. The image is therefore real.

PRACTICE 14B

Concave mirrors

1. Find the image distance and magnification of the mirror in the sample problem when the object distances are 10.0 cm and 5.00 cm. Are the images real or virtual? Are the images inverted or upright? Draw a ray diagram for each case to confirm your results.

2. A concave makeup mirror is designed so that a person 25.0 cm in front of it sees an upright image at a distance of 50.0 cm behind the mirror. What is the radius of curvature of the mirror? What is the magnification of the image? Is the image real or virtual?

3. A concave shaving mirror has a focal length of 33 cm. Calculate the image position of a cologne bottle placed in front of the mirror at a distance of 93 cm. Calculate the magnification of the image. Is the image real or virtual? Is the image inverted or upright? Draw a ray diagram to show where the image forms and how large it is with respect to the object.

4. A pen placed 11.0 cm from a concave spherical mirror produces a real image 13.2 cm from the mirror. What is the focal length of the mirror? What is the magnification of the image? If the pen is placed 27.0 cm from the mirror, what is the new position of the image? What is the magnification of the new image? Is the new image real or virtual? Draw ray diagrams to confirm your results.

CONVEX SPHERICAL MIRRORS

On recent models of automobiles, there is a side-view mirror on the passenger's side of the car. Unlike the flat mirror on the driver's side, which produces unmagnified images, the passenger's mirror bulges outward at the center. Images in this mirror are distorted near the mirror's edges, and the image is smaller than the object. This type of mirror is called a **convex spherical mirror.**

A convex spherical mirror is a segment of a sphere that is silvered so that light is reflected from the sphere's outer, convex surface. This type of mirror is also called a diverging mirror because the incoming rays diverge after reflection as though they were coming from some point behind the mirror. The resulting image is therefore always virtual, and the image distance is always negative. Because the mirrored surface is on the side opposite the radius of curvature, a convex spherical mirror also has a negative focal length. The sign conventions for all mirrors are summarized in **Table 14-4** on page 538.

The technique for drawing ray diagrams for a convex mirror differs slightly from that for concave mirrors. The focal point and center of curvature are situated behind the mirror's surface. Dotted lines are extended along the reflected reference rays to points behind the mirror, as shown in **Figure 14-14(a).** A virtual, upright image forms where the three apparent rays intersect. Magnification for convex mirrors is always less than 1, as shown in **Figure 14-14(b).**

Convex spherical mirrors take the objects in a large field of view and produce a small image, so they are well suited for providing a fixed observer with a complete view of a large area. Convex mirrors are often placed in stores to help employees monitor customers and at the intersections of busy hallways so that people in both hallways can tell when others are approaching.

The side-view mirror on the passenger's side of a car is another application of the convex mirror. This mirror usually carries the warning, "objects are closer than they appear." Without this warning, a driver might think that he or she is looking into a flat mirror, which does not alter the size of the image. The driver could therefore be fooled into believing that a vehicle is farther away than it is.

convex spherical mirror

an outwardly curved, mirrored surface that is a portion of a sphere and that diverges incoming light rays

(a)

(b)

Figure 14-14
Light rays diverge upon reflection with a convex mirror **(a)**, forming a virtual image that is always smaller than the object **(b)**.

Table 14-4   Sign conventions for mirrors

Symbol	Situation	Sign	
p	the object is in front of the mirror (real object)	+	$p > 0$
q	the image is in front of the mirror (real image)	+	$q > 0$
q	the image is behind the mirror (virtual image)	−	$q < 0$
R, f	the center of curvature is in front of the mirror (concave spherical mirror)	+	$R > 0$ $f > 0$
R, f	the center of curvature is behind the mirror (convex spherical mirror)	−	$R < 0$ $f < 0$
R, f	the mirror has no curvature (flat mirror)	∞	$R, f \to \infty$
h'	the image is above the principal axis	+	$h, h' > 0$
h'	the image is below the principal axis	−	$h > 0, h' < 0$

Convex mirrors

PROBLEM

An upright pencil is placed 10.0 cm from a convex spherical mirror with a focal length of 8.00 cm. Find the position and the magnification of the image.

SOLUTION

1. DEFINE

Given: $f = -8.00 \text{ cm}$ $p = +10.0 \text{ cm}$

Because the mirror is convex, the focal length is negative.
The object is in front of the mirror, so p is positive.

Unknown: $q = ?$ $M = ?$

Diagram: Use the rules on page 534 to construct a ray diagram.

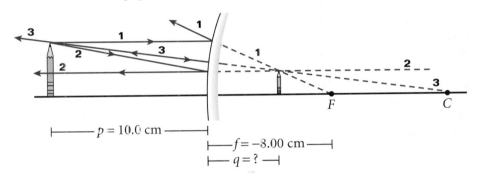

2. PLAN

Choose an equation(s) or situation: Use the mirror equation for focal length.

$$\frac{1}{p} + \frac{1}{q} = \frac{1}{f}$$

Use the magnification formula

$$M = -\frac{q}{p}$$

Rearrange the equation(s) to isolate the unknown(s):

$$\frac{1}{q} = \frac{1}{f} - \frac{1}{p}$$

3. CALCULATE

Substitute the values into the equation(s) and solve:

$$\frac{1}{q} = \frac{1}{(-8.00 \text{ cm})} - \frac{1}{10.0 \text{ cm}} =$$

$$\frac{-0.125}{1 \text{ cm}} - \frac{0.100}{1 \text{ cm}} = \frac{-0.225}{1 \text{ cm}}$$

$$\boxed{q = -4.44 \text{ cm}}$$

continued on
next page

> **CALCULATOR SOLUTION**
>
> Because the number of significant figures after subtraction is three, the calculator answer −4.444444444 should be rounded to three significant figures.

Substitute the values for p and q to find the magnification of the image.

$$M = -\left(\frac{-4.44 \text{ cm}}{10.0 \text{ cm}}\right)$$

$$\boxed{M = 0.444}$$

4. EVALUATE The image appears at a distance from the mirror that is shorter than the focal length (-8.00 cm), as confirmed by the ray diagram. The image is smaller than the object ($M < 1$) and is upright ($M > 0$), as is also confirmed by the ray diagram. The image is therefore virtual.

PRACTICE 14C

Convex mirrors

1. A convex mirror with a radius of curvature of 0.550 m is placed above the aisles in a store. Determine the image distance and magnification of a customer lying on the floor 3.1 m below the mirror. Is the image virtual or real? Is the image inverted or upright?

2. A spherical glass ornament is 6.00 cm in diameter. If an object is placed 10.5 cm away from the ornament, where will its image form? What is the magnification? Is the image virtual or real? Is the image inverted or upright? Draw a ray diagram to confirm your results.

3. What is the image distance for an automobile 5.5 m in front of a convex mirror with a 0.25 m focal length? What is the magnification? Is the image virtual or real? Is the image inverted or upright?

4. A soda bottle is placed 44 cm from a convex mirror. If the mirror's focal length is 33 cm, how far from the mirror's surface does the bottle's image form? What is its magnification? Is the image virtual or real? Is the image inverted or upright? Draw a ray diagram to confirm your results.

5. A candle is 49 cm in front of a convex spherical mirror that has a focal length of 35 cm. What are the image distance and magnification? Is the image virtual or real? Is the image inverted or upright? Draw a ray diagram to confirm your results.

6. The image of a crayon appears to be 23.0 cm behind the surface of a convex mirror. If the mirror's focal length is 46.0 cm, how far in front of the mirror is the crayon positioned? What is the magnification? Is the image virtual or real? Is the image inverted or upright?

PARABOLIC MIRRORS

You have probably noticed that certain rays in ray diagrams do not intersect exactly at the image point. This occurs especially with rays that reflect at the mirror's surface far from the principal axis. The situation also occurs with real light rays and real spherical mirrors.

If light rays from an object are near the principal axis, all of the reflected rays pass through the image point. Rays that reflect at points on the mirror far from the principal axis converge at slightly different points on the principal axis, as shown in **Figure 14-15.** This produces a blurred image. This effect, called *spherical aberration,* is present to some extent in any spherical mirror.

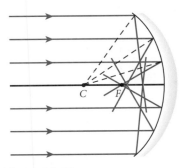

Figure 14-15
Spherical aberration occurs when parallel rays far from the principal axis converge away from the mirror's focal point.

Parabolic mirrors eliminate spherical aberration

A simple way to reduce the effect of spherical aberration is to use a mirror with a small diameter; that way, the rays are never far from the principal axis. If the mirror is large to begin with, shielding its outer portion will limit how much of the mirror is used and thus will accomplish the same effect. However, many concave mirrors, such as those used in astronomical telescopes, are made large so that they will collect a large amount of light. Therefore, it is not desirable to limit how much of the mirror is used in order to reduce spherical aberration. An alternative approach is to use a mirror that is not a segment of a sphere but still focuses light rays in a manner similar to a small spherical concave mirror. This is accomplished with a parabolic mirror.

Parabolic mirrors are segments of a paraboloid (a three-dimensional parabola) whose inner surface is reflecting. All rays parallel to the principal axis converge at the focal point regardless of where on the mirror's surface the rays reflect. Thus, a real image forms without spherical aberration, as illustrated in **Figure 14-16.** Similarly, light rays from an object at the focal point of a parabolic mirror will be reflected from the mirror in parallel rays. Parabolic reflectors are ideal for flashlights and automobile headlights.

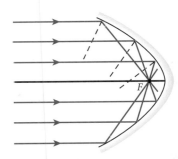

Figure 14-16
All parallel rays converge at a parabolic mirror's focal point. The curvature in this figure is much greater than it is in real parabolic mirrors.

Reflecting telescopes use parabolic mirrors

A telescope permits you to view distant objects, whether they are buildings a few kilometers away or galaxies that are millions of light-years from Earth. Not all telescopes are intended for visible light. Because all electromagnetic radiation obeys the law of reflection, parabolic surfaces can be constructed to reflect and focus electromagnetic radiation of different wavelengths. For instance, a radio telescope consists of a large metal parabolic surface that reflects radio waves in order to receive radio signals from objects in space.

There are two types of telescopes that use visible light. One type, called a *refracting telescope,* uses a combination of lenses to form an image. It will be discussed in Chapter 15. The other kind uses a curved mirror and small lenses to form an image. This type of telescope is called a *reflecting telescope.*

F

Small mirror

Parabolic objective mirror

Eyepiece   *a*

Figure 14-17
The parabolic objective mirror in a Cassegrain reflector focuses incoming light.

Reflecting telescopes employ a parabolic mirror (called an *objective mirror*) to focus light. One common type of reflecting telescope, called a *Cassegrain reflector,* is shown in **Figure 14-17.** Parallel light rays pass down the barrel of the telescope and are reflected by the parabolic objective mirror at the telescope's base. These rays converge toward the objective mirror's focal point, *F,* where a real image would normally form. However, a small curved mirror that lies in the path of the light rays reflects the light back toward the center of the objective mirror. The light then passes through a small hole in the center of the objective mirror and comes to a focus at point *a.* An eyepiece near point *a* magnifies the image.

You may wonder how a hole can be placed in the objective mirror without affecting the final image formed by the telescope. Each portion of the mirror's surface reflects light from distant objects so that a complete image is always formed. The presence of the hole merely reduces the amount of light that is reflected. Even that is not severely affected by the hole because the light-gathering capacity of an objective mirror is dependent on the mirror's area. For instance, a 1 m diameter hole in a mirror that is 4 m in diameter reduces the mirror's reflecting surface by only $\frac{1}{16}$, or 6.25 percent.

Section Review

1. A steel ball bearing with a radius of 1.5 cm forms an image of an object that has been placed 1.1 cm away from the bearing's surface. Determine the image distance and magnification. Is the image virtual or real? Is the image inverted or upright? Draw a ray diagram to confirm your results.

2. Why is an image formed by a parabolic mirror brighter than the image of the same object formed by a concave spherical mirror?

3. A spherical mirror is to be used in a motion-picture projector to form an inverted, real image 95 times as tall as the picture in a single frame of film. The image is projected onto a screen 13 m from the mirror. What type of mirror is required and how far should it be from the film?

4. Which of the following images are real and which are virtual?
   a. the image of a distant illuminated building projected onto a piece of heavy, white cardboard by a small reflecting telescope
   b. the image of an automobile in a flat rearview mirror
   c. the image of shop aisles in a convex observation mirror

5. **Physics in Action** The reflector of the radio telescope at Arecibo has a radius of curvature of 265.0 m. How far above the reflector must the radio-detecting equipment be placed in order to obtain clear radio images?

COLOR

You have probably noticed that the color of an object can appear different under different lighting conditions. A plant that appears green in sunlight will appear black under a red light. These differences are due to differences in the reflecting and light-absorbing properties of the object being illuminated.

So far, we have assumed that objects are either like mirrors, which reflect almost all light uniformly, or like rough objects, which reflect light diffusely in several directions. But as mentioned in Section 14-1, objects absorb certain wavelengths from the light falling on them and reflect the rest. The color of an object depends on which wavelengths of light shine on the object and which wavelengths are reflected (see **Figure 14-18**).

If all wavelengths of incoming light are completely reflected by an object, that object appears the same color as the light illuminating it. This gives the object the same appearance as a white object illuminated by the light. An object of a particular color, such as the green leaf in **Figure 14-18,** absorbs light of all colors except the light whose color is the same as the object's color. By contrast, an object that reflects no light appears black. Green leaves appear black under red light because there is no green light present for them to reflect and the red light is absorbed.

Additive primary colors produce white light when combined

Because white light can be dispersed into its elementary colors, it is reasonable to suppose that elementary colors can be combined to form white light. One way of doing this is to use a prism to recombine light that has been dispersed by another prism. Another way is to combine light that has been passed through red, green, and blue filters. These colors are called the *additive primary colors* because when they are added in varying proportions they can form all of the colors of the spectrum.

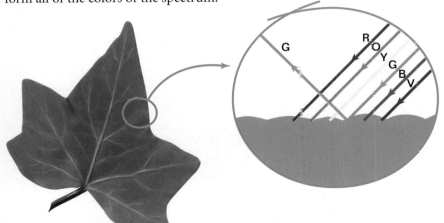

Figure 14-18
A leaf would appear green under white light because only green light would be reflected by the pigment in the leaf.

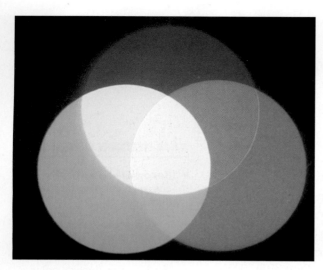

Figure 14-19
The combination of the additive primary colors in any two circles produces the complementary color of the third additive primary color.

Figure 14-20
The brightness of the red, green, and blue pixels of a color television screen are adjusted to produce all of the colors in a single picture.

When light passed through a red filter is combined with green light produced with a green filter, a patch of yellow light appears. If this yellow light is combined with blue light, the resulting light will be colorless, or "white," as shown in **Figure 14-19.** Because yellow is the color added to the primary additive color blue to produce white light, yellow is called the *complementary* color of blue. Two primary colors combine to produce the complement of the third primary color, as indicated in **Table 14-5.**

An example of the application of additive primary colors is the use of certain chemical compounds to give color to glass. Iron compounds give glass a green color. Manganese compounds give glass a magenta, or reddish blue, color. Green and magenta are complementary colors, so the right proportions of these compounds will produce an equal combination of green and magenta light, and the resulting glass will appear colorless.

Another example of additive colors is the image produced on a color television screen. A television screen consists of small, luminous dots, or *pixels*, that glow either red, green, or blue when they are struck by electrons (see **Figure 14-20**). By varying the brightness of different pixels in different parts of the picture, a picture with many colors present at one time is produced.

Humans can see in color because there are three kinds of color receptors in the eye. Each receptor, called a *cone cell*, is sensitive to either red, green, or blue light. Light of different wavelengths stimulates a combination of these receptors so that a wide range of colors can be perceived.

Table 14-5	Additive and subtractive primary colors	
Colors	**Additive (mixing light)**	**Subtractive (mixing pigments)**
Red	primary	complementary to cyan
Green	primary	complementary to magenta
Blue	primary	complementary to yellow
Cyan (blue green)	complementary to red	primary
Magenta (red blue)	complementary to green	primary
Yellow	complementary to blue	primary

Subtractive primary colors filter out all light when combined

When blue light and yellow light are mixed, white light results. However, if you mix a blue pigment (such as paint or the colored wax of a crayon) with a yellow pigment, the resulting color is green, not white. This difference is due to the fact that pigments rely on colors of light that are absorbed, or subtracted, from the incoming light.

For example, yellow pigment subtracts blue and violet colors from white light and reflects red, orange, yellow, and green light. Blue pigment subtracts red, orange, and yellow from the light and reflects green, blue, and violet. When yellow and blue pigments are combined, only green light is reflected.

When pigments are mixed, each one subtracts certain colors from white light, and the resulting color depends on the frequencies that are not absorbed. The primary pigments (or *primary subtractive colors,* as they are sometimes called) are cyan, magenta, and yellow. These are the same colors that are complementary to the additive primary colors (see **Table 14-5**). When any two primary subtractive colors are combined, they produce either red, green, or blue pigments. When the three primary pigments are mixed together in the proper proportions, all of the colors are subtracted from white light and the mixture is black, as shown in **Figure 14-21.**

Combining yellow pigment and its complementary color, blue, should produce a black pigment. Yet earlier, blue and yellow were combined to produce green. The difference between these two situations is explained by the broad use of color names. The "blue" pigment that is added to a "yellow" pigment to produce green is not a pure blue. If it were, only blue light would be reflected from it. Similarly, a pure yellow pigment will reflect only yellow light. Because most pigments found in paints and dyes are combinations of different substances, they reflect light from nearby parts of the visible spectrum. Without knowledge of the light-absorption characteristics of these pigments, it is hard to predict exactly what colors will result from different combinations.

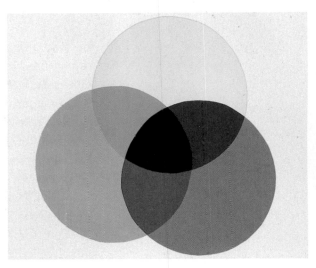

Figure 14-21
The combination of the subtractive primary colors by any two filters produces the complementary color of the third subtractive primary color.

Conceptual Challenge

1. Colors in a blanket   Brown is a mixture of yellow with small amounts of red and green. If you shine red light on a brown woolen blanket, what color will the blanket appear? Will it appear lighter or darker than it would under white light? Explain your answers.

2. Blueprints   If a blueprint (a blue drawing on a white background) is viewed under blue light, will you still be able to perceive the drawing? What will the blueprint look like under yellow light?

POLARIZATION OF LIGHT WAVES

You have probably seen sunglasses with Polaroid™ lenses that reduce glare without blocking the light entirely. There is a property of light that allows some of the light to be filtered by certain materials in the lenses.

In an electromagnetic wave, the electric field is at right angles to both the magnetic field and the direction of propagation. Light from a typical source consists of waves that have electric fields oscillating in random directions, as shown in **Figure 14-22.** Light of this sort is said to be *unpolarized.*

Electric-field oscillations of unpolarized light waves can be treated as combinations of vertical and horizontal electric-field oscillations. There are certain processes that separate waves with electric-field oscillations in the vertical direction from those in the horizontal direction, producing a beam of light with electric-field waves oriented in the same direction, as shown in **Figure 14-23.** These waves are said to have **linear polarization.**

Light can be linearly polarized through transmission

Certain transparent crystals cause unpolarized light that passes through them to become linearly polarized. The direction in which the electric fields are polarized is determined by the arrangement of the atoms or molecules in the

linear polarization

the alignment of electromagnetic waves in such a way that the vibrations of the electric fields in each of the waves are parallel to each other

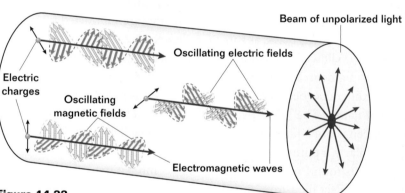

Figure 14-22
Randomly oscillating charges produce unpolarized light.

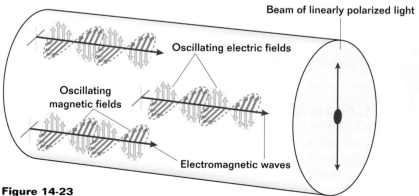

Figure 14-23
Light waves with aligned electric fields are linearly polarized.

crystal. The effect is similar to sending a transverse wave along a rope or spring through the slats of a picket fence, as shown in **Figure 14-24.** Only transverse waves in the up-and-down direction can pass through the fence.

For substances that polarize light by transmission, the line along which light is polarized is called the *transmission axis* of the substance. Only light waves that are linearly polarized with respect to the transmission axis of the polarizing substance can pass freely through the substance. All light that is polarized at an angle of 90° to the transmission axis does not pass through.

A polarizing substance can be used not only to linearly polarize light but also to determine if and how light is linearly polarized. By rotating a polarizing substance as a beam of polarized light passes through it, a change in the intensity of the light can be seen (see **Figure 14-25**). The light is brightest when its plane of polarization is parallel to the transmission axis. The larger the angle is between the electric-field waves and the transmission axis, the smaller the component of light that passes through the polarizer will be and the less bright the light will be. When the transmission axis is perpendicular to the plane of polarization for the light, no light passes through.

Figure 14-24
Only transverse waves that are aligned in the direction of the slats pass through the fence.

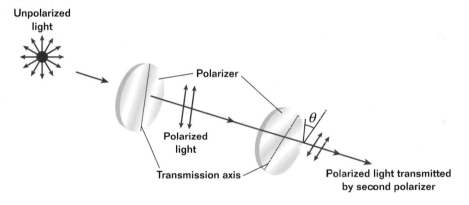

Unpolarized light

Polarizer

Polarized light

Transmission axis

θ

Polarized light transmitted by second polarizer

Figure 14-25
The brightness of the polarized light decreases as the angle, θ, increases between the transmission axis of the second polarizer and the plane of polarization of the light.

Light can be linearly polarized by reflection and scattering

When light is reflected at a certain angle from a surface, the reflected light is completely polarized parallel to the reflecting surface. If the surface is parallel to the ground, the light is polarized horizontally. This is the case with glaring light that reflects at a low angle from roads, bodies of water, and car hoods.

Quick Lab

Polarization of Sunlight

MATERIALS LIST

✔ a sheet of Polaroid filter or sunglasses with polarizing lenses

 SAFETY CAUTION

Never look directly at the sun.

During mid-morning or mid-afternoon, when the sun is well above the horizon but not directly overhead, look directly up at the sky through the polarizing filter. Note how the light's intensity is reduced.

Rotate the polarizer. Take note of which orientations of the polarizer make the sky darker and thus best reduce the amount of transmitted light.

Repeat the test with light from other parts of the sky. Test light reflected off a table near a window. Compare the results of these various experiments.

Because the light that causes glare is in most cases horizontally polarized, it can be filtered out by a polarizing substance whose transmission axis is oriented vertically. This is the case with polarizing sunglasses. As shown in **Figure 14-26,** the angle between the polarized reflected light and the transmission axis of the polarizer is 90°. Thus, none of the polarized light passes through.

In addition to reflection and absorption, scattering can also polarize light. Scattering, or the absorption and reradiation of light by particles in the atmosphere, causes sunlight to be polarized, as shown in **Figure 14-27.** When an unpolarized beam of sunlight strikes air molecules, the electrons in the molecules begin vibrating in the same plane as the electric field of the incoming wave. The reradiated light is polarized in the direction of the electron oscillations, and so the component of the polarized light that is parallel to Earth's surface is also polarized. Thus, an observer with his or her back to the sun will see polarized light when looking up toward the sky.

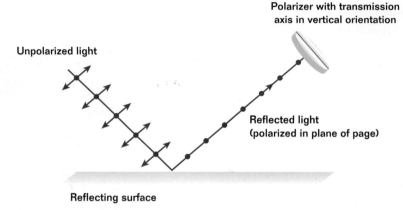

Figure 14-26
Reflected light is polarized horizontally. This light can be blocked by aligning the transmission axes of the sunglasses vertically.

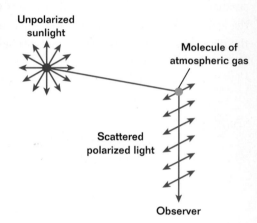

Figure 14-27
The sunlight scattered by air molecules is polarized for an observer on Earth's surface.

Section Review

1. A lens for a spotlight is coated so that it does not transmit yellow light. If the light source is white, what color is the spotlight?

2. A house is painted with pigments that reflect red and blue light but absorb all other colors. What color does the house appear to be when it is illuminated by white light? What color does it appear to be under red light?

3. What primary pigments would an artist need to mix to obtain a pale yellow green color? What primary additive colors would a theater-lighting designer need to mix in order to produce the same color with light?

4. The light reflected from the surface of a pool of water is observed through a polarizer. How can you tell if the reflected light is polarized?

CHAPTER 14
Summary

KEY IDEAS

Section 14-1 Characteristics of light
- Light is electromagnetic radiation that consists of oscillating electric and magnetic fields with different wavelengths.
- The relationship between the frequency, wavelength, and speed of electromagnetic radiation is given by the equation at right. $$c = f\lambda$$
- The brightness of light is inversely proportional to the square of the distance from the light source.

Section 14-2 Flat mirrors
- Light obeys the law of reflection, which states that the incident and reflected angles of light are equal.
- Flat mirrors form virtual images that are the same distance from the mirror's surface as the object is.

Section 14-3 Curved mirrors
- The mirror equation, at right, relates object distance, image distance, and focal length of a spherical mirror.
- The magnification equation, at right, relates image height or distance to object height or distance, respectively.

$$\frac{1}{p} + \frac{1}{q} = \frac{1}{f}$$

$$M = \frac{h'}{h} = -\frac{q}{p}$$

Section 14-4 Color and polarization
- Light of different colors can be produced by adding light consisting of the primary additive colors (red, green, and blue).
- Pigments can be produced by combining subtractive colors (magenta, yellow, and cyan).
- Light can be linearly polarized by transmission, reflection, or scattering.

KEY TERMS

angle of incidence (p. 527)

angle of reflection (p. 527)

concave spherical mirror (p. 530)

convex spherical mirror (p. 537)

electromagnetic wave (p. 520)

linear polarization (p. 546)

real image (p. 531)

reflection (p. 526)

virtual image (p. 528)

Diagram symbols

Light rays (real)	
Light rays (apparent)	‒ ‒ ‒ ‒ ‒► ‒ ‒ ‒
Normal lines	
Flat mirror	

Concave mirror   Convex mirror

Variable symbols

Quantities		Units	
p	object distance	m	meters
q	image distance	m	meters
R	radius of curvature	m	meters
f	focal length	m	meters
M	magnification		(unitless)

CHARACTERISTICS OF LIGHT

Review questions

1. Which band of the electromagnetic spectrum has
   a. the lowest frequency?
   b. the shortest wavelength?

2. Which of the following electromagnetic waves has the highest frequency?
   a. radio
   b. ultraviolet radiation
   c. blue light
   d. infrared radiation

3. Why can light be used to measure distances accurately? What must be known in order to make distance measurements?

4. For the diagram in **Figure 14-28,** use Huygens' principle to show what the wave front at point **a** will look like at point **b.** How would you represent this wave front in the ray approximation?

Source   New wavefront
             position
          a   b

Figure 14-28

5. What is the relationship between the actual brightness of a light source and its apparent brightness from where you see it?

Conceptual questions

6. Suppose an intelligent society capable of receiving and transmitting radio signals lives on a planet orbiting Procyon, a star 95 light-years away from Earth. If a signal were sent toward Procyon in 1999, what is the earliest year that Earth could expect to receive a return message? (Hint: A light-year is the distance a ray of light travels in one year.)

7. How fast do X rays travel in a vacuum?

8. Why do astronomers observing distant galaxies talk about looking backward in time?

9. Do the brightest stars that you see in the night sky necessarily give off more light than dimmer stars? Explain your answer.

Practice problems

10. The compound eyes of bees and other insects are highly sensitive to light in the ultraviolet portion of the spectrum, specifically light with wavelengths between 300.0 nm and 400.0 nm. To what frequencies do these wavelengths correspond? (See Sample Problem 14A.)

11. The brightest light detected from the star Antares has a wavelength of about 10^3 nm. What is the frequency of this light? (See Sample Problem 14A.)

12. What is the wavelength for an FM radio signal if the number on the dial reads 99.5 MHz? (See Sample Problem 14A.)

13. What is the wavelength of a radar signal that has a frequency of 33 GHz? (See Sample Problem 14A.)

FLAT MIRRORS

Review questions

14. For each of the objects listed below, identify whether light is reflected diffusely or specularly.
    a. a concrete driveway
    b. an undisturbed pond
    c. a polished silver tray
    d. a sheet of paper
    e. a mercury column in a thermometer

15. If you are stranded on an island, where would you align a mirror to use sunlight to signal a searching aircraft?

16. If you are standing 2 m in front of a flat mirror, how far behind the mirror is your image? What is the magnification of the image? Where is the image's right side with respect to your right side?

Conceptual questions

17. When you shine a flashlight across a room, you see the beam of light on the wall. Why do you not see the light in the air?

18. How can an object be a specular reflector for some electromagnetic waves yet be diffuse for others?

19. A flat mirror that is 0.85 m tall is nailed to a wall so that its upper edge is 1.7 m above the floor. Use the law of reflection and a ray diagram to determine if this mirror will show a person who is 1.7 m tall his or her complete reflection.

20. Two flat mirrors make an angle of 90.0° with each other, as diagrammed in **Figure 14-29.** An incoming ray makes an angle of 35° with the normal of mirror *A.* Use the law of reflection to determine the angle of reflection from mirror *B.* What is unusual about the incoming and reflected rays of light for this arrangement of mirrors?

$\theta = 35°$

Mirror B

Mirror A

Figure 14-29

21. If you walk 1.2 m/s toward a flat mirror, how fast does your image move? In what direction does your image move with respect to you?

22. Why do the images produced by two opposing flat mirrors appear to be progressively smaller?

CURVED MIRRORS

Review questions

23. What type of mirror should be used to project movie images on a large screen?

24. If an object is placed outside the focal length of a concave mirror, what type of image will be formed? Will it appear in front of or behind the mirror?

25. Can you use a convex mirror to burn a hole in paper by focusing light rays at the mirror's focal point?

26. Can the image produced by a convex mirror ever be larger than the object?

27. Why are parabolic mirrors preferred over spherical concave mirrors for use in reflecting telescopes?

Conceptual questions

28. Where does a ray of light that is parallel to the principal axis of a concave mirror go after it is reflected at the mirror's surface?

29. What happens to the real image produced by a concave mirror if you move the original object to the location of the image?

30. Consider a concave spherical mirror and a real object. Is the image always inverted? Is the image always real? Give conditions for your answers.

31. Explain why magnified images seem dimmer than the original objects.

32. What test could you perform to determine if an image is real or virtual?

33. You've been given a concave mirror that may or may not be parabolic. What simple test could you perform to determine whether it is parabolic?

Practice problems

34. A concave shaving mirror has a radius of curvature of 25.0 cm. For each of the following cases, find the magnification and determine whether the image formed is real or virtual and upright or inverted.
   a. an upright pencil placed 45.0 cm from the mirror
   b. an upright pencil placed 25.0 cm from the mirror
   c. an upright pencil placed 5.00 cm from the mirror

(See Sample Problem 14B.)

35. A concave spherical mirror can be used to project an image onto a sheet of paper, allowing the magnified image of an illuminated real object to be accurately traced. If you have a concave mirror with a focal length of 8.5 cm, where would you place a sheet of paper so that the image projected onto it is twice as far from the mirror as the object is? Is the image upright or inverted, real or virtual? What would the magnification of the image be?
(See Sample Problem 14B.)

36. The real image of a tree is magnified −0.085 times by a telescope's primary mirror. If the tree's image forms 35 cm in front of the mirror, what is the distance between the mirror and the tree? What is the focal length of the mirror? What is the value for the mirror's radius of curvature? Is the image virtual or real? Is the image inverted or upright?
(See Sample Problem 14B.)

37. A candlestick holder has a concave reflector behind the candle, as shown in **Figure 14-30.** The reflector magnifies a candle −0.75 times and forms an image 4.6 cm away from the reflector's surface. Is the image inverted or upright? What are the object distance and the reflector's focal length? Is the image virtual or real?
(See Sample Problem 14B.)

Figure 14-30

38. A glowing electric light bulb placed 15 cm from a concave spherical mirror produces a real image 8.5 cm from the mirror. If the light bulb is moved to a position 25 cm from the mirror, what is the position of the image? Is the final image real or virtual? What are the magnifications of the first and final images? Are the two images inverted or upright?
(See Sample Problem 14B.)

39. A 5.75 cm pencil is placed upright at a distance 53.5 cm away from the center of a convex mirror. The mirror's radius of curvature is 45.0 cm. Calculate the image distance. Is the image real or virtual? What is the magnification? Is the image inverted or upright?
(See Sample Problem 14C.)

40. A convex mirror is placed on the ceiling at the intersection of two hallways. If a young man stands directly underneath the mirror, his shoe, which is a distance of 195 cm from the mirror, forms an image that appears 12.8 cm behind the mirror's surface. What is the mirror's focal length? What is the magnification of the image? Is the image real or virtual? Is the image upright or inverted?
(See Sample Problem 14C.)

41. A child holds a candy bar 15.5 cm in front of the convex side-view mirror of an automobile. The image height is reduced by one-half. What is the radius of curvature of the mirror?
(See Sample Problem 14C.)

COLOR AND POLARIZATION

Review questions

42. What are the three primary additive colors? What happens when you mix them?

43. What are the three primary subtractive colors (or primary pigments)? What happens when you mix them?

44. Explain why a polarizing disk used to analyze light can block light from a beam that has been passed through another polarizer. What is the relative orientation of the two polarizing disks?

Conceptual questions

45. Explain what could happen when you mix the following:
   a. cyan and yellow pigment
   b. blue and yellow light
   c. pure blue and pure yellow pigment
   d. green and red light
   e. pure green and pure blue pigment

46. What color would an opaque magenta shirt appear to be under the following colors of light?

    a. white   **d.** green

    b. red   **e.** yellow

    c. cyan

47. A substance is known to reflect green and blue light. What color would it appear to be when it is illuminated by white light? by blue light?

48. How can you tell if a pair of sunglasses has polarizing lenses?

49. Why would sunglasses with polarizing lenses remove the glare from your view of the hood of your car or a distant body of water but not from a tall metal tank used for storing liquids?

50. Is light from the sky polarized? Why do clouds seen through Polaroid™ glasses stand out in bold contrast to the sky?

MIXED REVIEW PROBLEMS

51. The side-view mirror of an automobile has a radius of curvature of 11.3 cm. The mirror produces a virtual image one-third the size of the object. How far is the object from the mirror?

52. An object is placed 10.0 cm in front of a mirror. What type must the mirror be to form an image of the object on a wall 2.00 m away from the mirror? What is the magnification of the image? Is the image real or virtual? Is the image inverted or upright?

53. The reflecting surfaces of two intersecting flat mirrors are at an angle of θ ($0° < \theta < 90°$), as shown in **Figure 14-31**. A light ray strikes the horizontal mirror. Use the law of reflection to show that the emerging ray will intersect the incident ray at an angle of $\phi = 180° - 2\theta$.

Figure 14-31

54. Show that if a flat mirror is assumed to have an "infinite" radius of curvature, the mirror equation reduces to $q = -p$.

55. A real object is placed at the zero end of a meterstick. A large concave mirror at the 100.0 cm end of the meterstick forms an image of the object at the 70.0 cm position. A small convex mirror placed at the 20.0 cm position forms a final image at the 10.0 cm point. What is the radius of curvature of the convex mirror?

56. A dedicated sports-car enthusiast polishes the inside and outside surfaces of a hubcap that is a section of a sphere. When he looks into one side of the hubcap, he sees an image of his face 30.0 cm behind the hubcap. He then turns the hubcap over and sees another image of his face 10.0 cm behind the hubcap.

    a. How far is his face from the hubcap?

    b. What is the radius of curvature of the hubcap?

    c. What is the magnification for each image?

    d. Are the images real or virtual?

    e. Are the images upright or inverted?

57. An object 2.70 cm tall is placed 12.0 cm in front of a mirror. What type of mirror and what radius of curvature are needed to create an upright image that is 5.40 cm in height? What is the magnification of the image? Is the image real or virtual?

58. A "floating coin" illusion consists of two parabolic mirrors, each with a focal length of 7.5 cm, facing each other so that their centers are 7.5 cm apart (see **Figure 14-32**). If a few coins are placed on the lower mirror, an image of the coins forms in the small opening at the center of the top mirror. Use the mirror equation and draw a ray diagram to show that the final image forms at that location. Show that the magnification is 1 and that the image is real and upright. (Note: A flashlight beam shone on these images has a very startling effect. Even at a glancing angle, the incoming light beam is seemingly reflected off the images of the coins. Do you understand why?)

Figure 14-32

59. Use the mirror equation and the equation for magnification to prove that the image of a real object formed by a convex mirror is always upright, virtual, and smaller than the object. Use the same equations to prove that the image of a real object placed in front of any spherical mirror is always virtual and upright when $p < |f|$.

60. Use trigonometry to derive the mirror and magnification equations from the ray diagram in **Figure 14-11** on page 531. (Hint: Note that the incoming ray between the pencil's tip and the mirror forms the hypotenuse of a right triangle. The reflected ray between the image point and the mirror is also the hypotenuse of a right triangle.)

Alternative Assessment

Performance assessment

1. Suntan lotions include compounds that absorb the ultraviolet radiation in sunlight and therefore prevent the ultraviolet radiation from damaging skin cells. Design experiments to test the properties of varying grades (SPFs) of suntan lotions. Plan to use blueprint paper, film, plants, or other light-sensitive items. Write down the questions that will guide your inquiry, the materials you will need, the procedures you plan to follow, and the measurements you will take. If your teacher approves your plan, perform the experiments and report or demonstrate your findings in class.

2. The Egyptian scholar Alhazen studied lenses, mirrors, rainbows, and other light phenomena early in the Middle Ages. Research his scholarly work, his life, and his relationship with the Caliph al-Hakim. How advanced were Alhazen's inventions and theories? Summarize your findings and report them to the class.

3. Work in cooperative groups to explore the use of corner and ceiling mirrors as low-tech surveillance devices. Make a floor plan of an existing store, or devise a floor plan for an imaginary one. Determine how much of the store could be monitored by a clerk if flat mirrors were placed in the corners. If you could use curved mirrors in such a system, would you use concave or convex mirrors? Where would you place them? Identify which parts of the store could be observed with the curved mirrors in place. Note any disadvantages that your choice of mirrors may have.

Portfolio projects

4. Research the characteristics, effects, and applications of a specific type of electromagnetic wave in the spectrum. Find information about the range of wavelengths, frequencies, and energies; natural and artificial sources of the waves; and the methods used to detect them. Find out how they were discovered and how they affect matter. Learn about any dangers associated with them and about their uses in technology. Work together with others in the class who are researching other parts of the spectrum to build a group presentation, brochure, chart, or Web page that covers the entire spectrum.

5. The Chinese astronomer Chang Heng (A.D. 78–139) recognized that moonlight was a reflection of sunlight. He applied this theory to explain lunar eclipses. Make diagrams showing how Heng might have represented the moon's illumination and the path of light when the Earth, moon, and sun were in various positions on ordinary nights and on nights when there were lunar eclipses. Find out more about Heng's other scientific work, and report your findings to the class.

6. Explore how many images are produced when you stand between two flat mirrors whose reflecting surfaces face each other. What are the locations of the images? Are they identical? Investigate these questions with diagrams and calculations. Then test your calculated results with parallel mirrors, perpendicular mirrors, and mirrors at angles in between. Which angles produce one, two, three, five, and seven images? Summarize your results with a chart, diagram, or computer presentation.

Technology & Learning

Graphing calculators

The mirror equation (given on page 532) allows you to calculate the image distance for a given object distance and a particular focal length. From this information, the image's magnification may be determined as well. Program your graphing calculator to create a table of object distances versus image distances in order to predict the image distance, magnification, and characteristics of images in each of the following situations:

    a. concave mirror of focal length +0.32 m, object distance of 0.20 m

    b. concave mirror of focal length +0.32 m, object distance of 0.70 m

    c. convex mirror of focal length −0.50 m, object distance of 0.40 m

    d. convex mirror of focal length −0.50 m, object distance of 0.85 m

Press [Y=] and [CLEAR] to clear any functions. Open a new program by pressing [PRGM] [▶] [▶] [ENTER].

Name the program "MIRROR" and press [ENTER]. Then enter the program shown in the table below.

To exit the program editor, press [2nd] [QUIT]. To run the program, press [PRGM], select "MIRROR," and press [ENTER] [ENTER]. Enter the value for the focal length, and press [ENTER].

The calculator will provide a table of image distances in meters (Y_1) versus object distances in meters (X). Scroll down the table with the arrow keys to find the values you need. The column labeled Y_2 gives the value of the magnification. Recall that negative magnification values indicate that an image is real and inverted, while positive magnification values indicate that an image is virtual and upright. Magnification values greater than 1 or less than −1 indicate that the image is larger than the object.

Press [ENTER] only when you're ready to end the program and exit the table.

Run the program again to calculate the image distances for an object placed in front of a mirror with a different focal length.

Keystrokes	Display
	PROGRAM: MIRROR
1. [PRGM] [▶] [2] [ALPHA] [F] [ENTER]	:PROMPT F
2. [ALPHA] ["] [(] [X,T,θ] [×] [ALPHA] [F] [)] [÷] [(] [X,T,θ] [−] [ALPHA] [F] [)] [ALPHA] ["] [STO▶] [2nd] [Y-VARS] [1] [1] [ENTER]	:"(X*F)/(X−F)" → Y_1
3. [ALPHA] ["] [(-)] [2nd] [Y-VARS] [1] [1] [−] [X,T,θ] [ALPHA] ["] [STO▶] [2nd] [Y-VARS] [1] [2] [ENTER]	:"−Y_1/X" → Y_2
4. [0] [.] [0] [5] [STO▶] [VARS] [6] [─] [ENTER]	:0.05 → TBLMIN
5. [0] [.] [0] [5] [STO▶] [VARS] [6] [─] [ENTER]	:0.05 → ΔTBL
6. [PRGM] [▶] [5] [ENTER]	:DISPTABLE

CHAPTER 14
Laboratory Exercise

BRIGHTNESS OF LIGHT

The brightness, or intensity, of a light source may be measured with a light meter. In this lab, you will use a light meter to measure the intensity of light at different distances from the light source. The measured brightness of a light depends on the distance between the light meter and the light source. This relationship is an example of an inverse-square law. According to the inverse-square law, the brightness of light at a certain point is proportional to the square of the distance from the light source to the light meter. You will use your results from this experiment to investigate the relationship between the distance and the brightness of a light source and to examine the inverse-square law as it relates to the brightness of light. You will use your data to calculate the square of the distance, and you will analyze the relationship using graphs of your data.

PREPARATION

1. Determine whether you will be using the CBL and sensors procedure or the light meter. Read the entire lab for the appropriate procedure, and plan what steps you will take.

2. Prepare a data table in your lab notebook with two columns and nine rows. In the first row, label the columns *Distance (m)* and *Intensity*.

Light meter procedure begins on page 558.

PROCEDURE

CBL AND SENSORS

Brightness of light

3. In the first column of your data table, label the second through ninth rows *0.10, 0.15, 0.20, 0.25, 0.30, 0.50, 0.75,* and *1.00.* These values represent the distances at which you will take readings.

4. Set up the meterstick, meterstick supports, light source (bulb and socket), and power supply, as shown in **Figure 14-33.** Carefully screw the bulb into the lamp socket and tighten carefully. Tape the meterstick and its supports to the lab table.

5. Set up the CBL light probe with aperture, CBL, and graphing calculator as shown in **Figure 14-33.** Set the CBL light probe directly above the 0.00 m mark on the meterstick, as shown. Connect the CBL to the graphing calculator with the unit-to-unit link cable using the ports located on each unit. Connect the light probe to the CH1 port. Turn on the CBL and the graphing calculator. Start the program PHYSICS on the graphing calculator.

    a. Select option *SET UP PROBES* from the MAIN MENU. Enter 1 for the number of probes. Select MORE PROBES, then select the light probe from the list. Enter 1 for the channel number.

    b. Select the *COLLECT DATA* option from the MAIN MENU. Select the *TRIGGER* option from the DATA COLLECTION menu.

    c. Draw a line above or below your data table, and label it *Background.* Press TRIGGER on the CBL to record the value for the background intensity. Record this value as *Background.* On the calculator, select *STOP.* From the MAIN MENU, select *TRIGGER/PROMPT.*

6. Set the bulb and socket 0.10 m from the end of the CBL sensor. Carefully align the sensor clamp and the aperture of the sensor so that the aperture is level, pointing parallel to the meterstick, and at the same height as the hole in the tube that covers the bulb. Readjust the bulb socket to the 0.10 m mark if necessary.

7. Set the power supply at 4.5 V, and connect it carefully with the wires from the light socket. ***Do not plug in the power supply until your teacher has approved your setup.*** When your teacher has approved your setup, carefully plug the power supply into the wall outlet to light the lamp.

8. Press TRIGGER on the CBL to collect data for the light intensity. The calculator will prompt you for

Figure 14-33

Step 4: Make sure the apparatus is set up securely. The meterstick should be taped to the table so that it cannot move during the experiment. Use a support stand and clamp to hold the light probe in place.

Step 6: Use the meterstick to place the light source at the correct position. Make sure the light probe and the light source are lined up.

another value. Enter 0.10 as the value of the distance for this trial.

9. Select MORE DATA on the graphing calculator.

10. Carefully move the bulb to 0.15 m. Press TRIGGER on the CBL to collect data for the light intensity. When prompted, enter 0.15 for distance in this trial.

11. Repeat this procedure for all the distances in your data table. After each trial, select MORE DATA on the graphing calculator.

12. After the last trial, select QUIT on the graphing calculator. Carefully unplug the power supply from the wall outlet.

13. Record the data from all the trials in your data table. On the calculator, press STAT. Select EDIT. The column under L1 contains the distance values you entered for each trial. The column under L2 contains the light intensity values recorded by the CBL. Record the intensity values in the appropriate rows in your data table.

Analysis and interpretation begins on page 559.

PROCEDURE

LIGHT METER

Brightness of light

3. In the first column of your data table, label the second through ninth rows *0.20, 0.25, 0.30, 0.35, 0.40, 0.50, 0.75,* and *1.00*. These values represent the distances at which you will take readings.

4. Set up the meterstick, meterstick supports, light source (bulb and socket), power supply, and light meter with aperture as shown in **Figure 14-34.** Carefully screw the bulb into the socket. Tape the meterstick and supports to the lab table. Set the 0.00 m mark on the meterstick directly below the face of the light meter as shown.

5. Set the bulb socket at a distance of 0.20 m from the light meter. Carefully align the clamp and the aperture of the detector so that the aperture is level, parallel to the meterstick, and at the same height as the hole in the tube covering the bulb. Adjust the bulb socket to the 0.20 m mark on the meterstick.

6. Set the power supply at 5.0 V, and connect it carefully with the wires from the light socket. ***Do not plug in the power supply until your teacher has approved your setup.*** When your teacher has approved your setup, carefully plug the power supply into the wall outlet to light the lamp.

Figure 14-34

Step 4: Make sure the apparatus is set up securely. The meterstick should be taped to the table so that it cannot move during the experiment. Use a support stand and clamp to hold the light meter in place.

Step 5: Use the meterstick to place the light source at the correct position. Make sure the light source and light meter are lined up.

7. Use the light meter to read the intensity. Select the "fast" mode, and use the "data hold" option if the intensity values continually fluctuate. Record the intensity value for that distance in your data table.

8. Carefully move the bulb and socket to the 0.25 m mark on the meterstick. Repeat the procedure and record the intensity value for that distance in your data table.

9. Repeat this procedure for all distances recorded in your data table.

10. After the last trial, carefully unplug the power supply from the wall outlet. Draw a line above or below your data table, and label it *Background*. Use this space to record the intensity reading of the light meter without the bulb illuminated.

ANALYSIS AND INTERPRETATION

Calculations and data analysis

1. **Organizing data**   For each trial, find the real value of the measured light intensity by subtracting the background from the measured value.

2. **Graphing data**   Using your answers from item 1, make a graph of the intensity plotted against the distance. Use a graphing calculator, computer, or graph paper.

3. **Organizing data**   For each trial, calculate $1/(Distance^2)$. This value represents the inverse of the distance squared.

4. **Graphing data**   Using your answers from item 1 and item 3, make a graph of the intensity plotted against the inverse of the distance squared. Use a graphing calculator, computer, or graph paper.

Conclusions

5. **Interpreting graphs**   Based on your graphs, what is the relationship between the intensity of the light and the distance from the light source? Explain how your graphs support your answer.

6. **Evaluating methods**   What is the purpose of the shields used on the light bulb and the detector? Why are they important?

Extensions

7. **Designing experiments**   Devise a way to use this experiment to compare the intensities of light sources of different colors. If there is time and if your teacher approves your plan, perform the experiment, and record your results. Use your data to answer questions 1–5 above for each color. Write a brief report detailing your procedure and evaluating your results. Explain how color affects the intensity of a light source.

CHAPTER 15

Refraction

PHYSICS IN ACTION

Most people associate rainbows with rain showers. Rainbows, however, are formed any time the air is filled with water droplets. Sunlight striking the droplets passes through their front surface and is partially reflected back toward the viewer from the back of the droplet. But why do we see the rainbow of colors? A rainbow occurs when sunlight is bent as it passes from air to water then from water to air. The degree to which the light bends depends on the frequency of the light. In this way, observers see only the frequency (the color) that is directed toward them from each droplet.

- *What causes the sunlight to bend as it passes through the droplets?*
- *Why do rainbows form in the shape of a semicircle?*

CONCEPT REVIEW

15-1
Refraction

15-1 SECTION OBJECTIVES

- **Recognize situations in which refraction will occur.**

- **Identify which direction light will bend when it passes from one medium to another.**

- **Solve problems using Snell's law.**

refraction

the bending of a wave disturbance as it passes at an angle from one medium into another

Figure 15-1
The flower looks small when viewed through the water droplet because the light from the flower is bent as it passes through the water.

REFRACTION OF LIGHT

Look at the tiny image of the flower that appears in the water droplet in **Figure 15-1.** The flower can be seen in the background of the photo. Why does the flower look different when viewed through the droplet? This phenomenon occurs because light is bent at the boundary between the water and the air around it. The bending of light as it travels from one medium to another is called **refraction.**

If light travels from one transparent medium to another at any angle other than straight on (parallel to the line normal to the surface), the light ray changes direction when it meets the boundary. As in the case of reflection, the angles of the incoming and refracted rays are measured with respect to the normal. For studying refraction, the normal line is extended into the refracting medium, as shown in **Figure 15-2.** The angle between the refracted ray and the normal is called the *angle of refraction,* θ_r. For refraction, the angle of incidence is designated as θ_i.

Refraction occurs when light's velocity changes

Glass, water, ice, diamonds, and quartz are all examples of transparent media through which light can pass. The speed of light in each of these materials is different. The speed of light in water, for instance, is less than the speed of light in air. And the speed of light in glass is less than the speed of light in water.

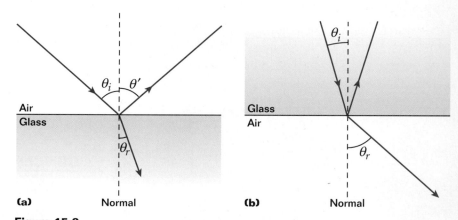

(a)   Normal   **(b)**   Normal

Figure 15-2
(a) When the light ray moves from air into glass, its path is bent toward the normal, **(b)** whereas the path of the light ray moving from glass into air is bent away from the normal.

When light moves from a material in which its speed is higher to a material in which its speed is lower, such as from air to glass, the ray is bent toward the normal, as shown in **Figure 15-2(a).** If the ray moves from a material in which its speed is lower to one in which its speed is higher, as in **Figure 15-2(b),** the ray is bent away from the normal. If the angle of incidence is parallel to the normal, then no refraction (bending) occurs in either case.

Note that the path of a light ray that crosses a boundary between two different media is reversible. If the ray in **Figure 15-2(a)** originated inside the glass block, it would follow the same path as shown in the figure, but the reflected ray would be inside the block.

Refraction can be explained in terms of the wave model of light

When a person rolls a barrel onto a lawn from a sidewalk, the barrel becomes harder to push on the lawn, just as it is harder to pedal a bicycle across a lawn. If the person does not push any harder when entering the lawn, the barrel will slow down. Now imagine that the person pushes the barrel at an angle to the lawn without pushing harder once the barrel reaches the lawn. One end of the barrel will go slower, while the other end will continue at the same speed because it is on the sidewalk. The slower end of the barrel will therefore act like a moving pivot, and the barrel will turn, as shown in **Figure 15-3.**

Light passing from one transparent medium into another can be thought of in a similar way. In **Figure 15-4,** wave fronts of a plane wave of light are traveling at an angle to the surface of a block of glass. As the light enters the glass, the wave fronts slow down, but the wave fronts that have not yet reached the surface of the glass continue traveling at the speed of light in air. During this time, the slower wave fronts travel a smaller distance than do the wave fronts in the air, so the entire plane wave changes directions.

Note the difference in wavelength (the space between the wave fronts) between the plane wave in air and the plane wave in the glass. Because the wave fronts inside the glass are traveling more slowly, in the same time interval they move through a shorter distance than the wave fronts that are still traveling in air. Thus, the wavelength of the light in the glass, λ_{glass}, is shorter than the wavelength of the incoming light, λ_{air}.

Figure 15-3
When this barrel is rolled at an angle from a sidewalk onto grass, the barrel turns because the gray end of the barrel, which is on the grass, travels slower than the maroon end, which is still on the sidewalk.

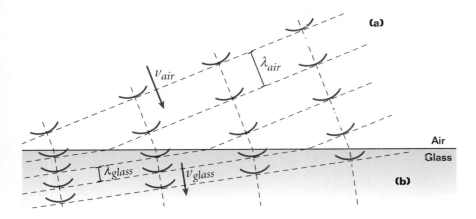

Figure 15-4
A plane wave traveling in air **(a)** has a wavelength of λ_{air} and velocity of v_{air}. Each wave front turns as it strikes the glass, just as the barrel turns when it is moving from the sidewalk onto the lawn. Because the speed of the wave fronts in the glass **(b)**, v_{glass}, is slower, the wavelength of the light becomes shorter and the wave fronts change direction.

index of refraction

the ratio of the speed of light in a vacuum to its speed in a given transparent medium

An important property of transparent substances is the **index of refraction.** The index of refraction for a substance is the ratio of the speed of light in a vacuum to the speed of light in that substance.

INDEX OF REFRACTION

$$n = \frac{c}{v}$$

$$\text{index of refraction} = \frac{\text{speed of light in vacuum}}{\text{speed of light in medium}}$$

Did you know?

The index of refraction of any medium can also be expressed as the ratio of the wavelength of light in a vacuum, λ_0, to the wavelength of light in that medium, λ_n, as shown in the following relation.

$$n = \frac{\lambda_0}{\lambda_n}$$

From this definition, we see that the index of refraction is a dimensionless number that is always greater than 1 because light always travels slower in a substance than in a vacuum. **Table 15-1** lists the indices of refraction for some representative substances. Note that the larger the index of refraction is, the slower light travels in that substance and the more a light ray will bend when it passes from a vacuum into that material.

Imagine, as an example, light passing between air and water. When light begins in the air (high speed of light and low index of refraction) and travels into the water (lower speed of light and higher index of refraction), the light rays are bent toward the normal. Conversely, when light passes from the water to the air, the light rays are bent away from the normal.

Note that the value for the index of refraction of air is nearly that of a vacuum. For simplicity, *use the value n = 1.00 for air when solving problems.*

Table 15-1	Indices of refraction for various substances*		
Solids at 20°C	**n**	**Liquids at 20°C**	**n**
Cubic zirconia	2.20	Benzene	1.501
Diamond	2.419	Carbon disulfide	1.628
Fluorite	1.434	Carbon tetrachloride	1.461
Fused quartz	1.458	Ethyl alcohol	1.361
Glass, crown	1.52	Glycerine	1.473
Glass, flint	1.66	Water	1.333
Ice (at 0°C)	1.309		
Polystyrene	1.49	**Gases at 0°C, 1 atm**	**n**
Sodium chloride	1.544	Air	1.000 293
Zircon	1.923	Carbon dioxide	1.000 450

*measured with light of vacuum wavelength = 589 nm

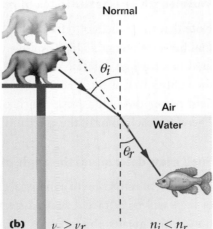

(a) $v_i < v_r$ $n_i > n_r$

(b) $v_i > v_r$ $n_i < n_r$

Figure 15-5
(a) To the cat on the pier, the fish looks closer to the surface than it really is. **(b)** To the fish, the cat seems to be farther from the surface than it actually is.

Objects appear to be in different positions due to refraction

When looking at a fish underwater, a cat sitting on a pier perceives the fish to be closer to the water's surface than it actually is, as shown in **Figure 15-5(a).** Conversely, the fish perceives the cat on the pier to be farther away from the water's surface than it actually is, as shown in **Figure 15-5(b).**

Because of the reversibility of refraction, both the fish and the cat see along the same path. However, the light ray that reaches the fish forms a smaller angle with respect to the normal than does the light ray from the cat to the water's surface. This is because light is bent toward the normal when it travels from a medium with a lower index of refraction (the air) to one with a higher index of refraction (the water). Extending this ray along a straight line shows the cat's image to be above the cat's actual position.

On the other hand, the light ray that reaches the cat from the water's surface forms a larger angle with respect to the normal. This is because the light from the fish travels from a medium with a higher index of refraction to one with a lower index of refraction. Note that the fish's image is closer to the water's surface than the fish actually is. An underwater object seen from the air above appears larger than its actual size because the image, which is the same size as the object, is closer to the observer.

Conceptual Challenge

1. The Invisible Man H. G. Wells wrote a famous novel about a man who made himself invisible by changing his index of refraction. What would his index of refraction have to be to accomplish this?

2. Visibility for the Invisible Man Would the invisible man be able to see anything?

3. Fishing When trying to catch a fish, should a pelican dive into the water horizontally in front of or behind the image of the fish it sees?

Wavelength affects the index of refraction

Note that the indices of refraction listed in **Table 15-1** are only valid for light that has a wavelength of 589 nm in a vacuum. This is because the amount that light bends when entering a different medium depends on the wavelength of the light as well as the speed. This is why a spectrum is produced when white light passes through a prism. Each color of light has a different wavelength. Therefore, each color of the spectrum is refracted by a different amount.

Snell's law determines the angle of refraction

The index of refraction of a material can be used to figure out how much a ray of light will be refracted as it passes from one medium to another. As mentioned, the greater the index of refraction, the more refraction occurs. But how can the angle of refraction be found?

In 1621, Willebrord Snell experimented with light passing through different media. By doing so, he developed a relationship called Snell's law, which can be used to find the angle of refraction for light traveling between any two media.

SNELL'S LAW

$$n_i(\sin \theta_i) = n_r(\sin \theta_r)$$

index of refraction of first medium × sine of the angle of incidence = index of refraction of second medium × sine of the angle of refraction

---

SAMPLE PROBLEM 15A

Snell's law

PROBLEM

A light ray of wavelength 589 nm (produced by a sodium lamp) traveling through air strikes a smooth, flat slab of crown glass at an angle of 30.0° to the normal. Find the angle of refraction, θ_r.

SOLUTION

Given: $\theta_i = 30.0°$ $n_i = 1.00$ $n_r = 1.52$

Unknown: $\theta_r = ?$

Use the equation for Snell's law.

$$n_i(\sin \theta_i) = n_r(\sin \theta_r)$$

$$\theta_r = \sin^{-1}\left[\frac{n_i}{n_r}(\sin \theta_i)\right] = \sin^{-1}\left[\frac{1.00}{1.52}(\sin 30.0°)\right]$$

$$\boxed{\theta_r = 19.2°}$$

Snell's law

1. Find the angle of refraction for a ray of light that enters a bucket of water from air at an angle of 25.0° to the normal. (Hint: Use **Table 15-1.**)

2. A ray of light of vacuum wavelength 550 nm traveling in air enters a slab of transparent material. The incoming ray makes an angle of 40.0° with the normal, and the refracted ray makes an angle of 26.0° with the normal. Find the index of refraction of the transparent material. (Assume that the index of refraction of air for light of wavelength 550 nm is 1.00.)

3. For an incoming ray of light of vacuum wavelength 589 nm, fill in the unknown values in the following table. (Hint: Use **Table 15-1.**)

	from (medium)	to (medium)	θ_i	θ_r
a.	flint glass	crown glass	25.0°	?
b.	air	?	14.5°	9.80°
c.	air	diamond	?	12.5°

Section Review

1. In which of the following situations will light from a laser be refracted?
   a. traveling from air into a diamond at an angle of 30° to the normal
   b. traveling from water into ice along the normal
   c. upon striking a metal surface
   d. traveling from air into a glass of ice tea at an angle of 25° to the normal

2. For each of the following cases, will light rays be bent toward or away from the normal?
   a. $n_i > n_r$, where $\theta_i = 20°$
   b. $n_i < n_r$, where $\theta_i = 20°$
   c. from air to glass with an angle of incidence of 30°
   d. from glass to air with an angle of incidence of 30°

3. Find the angle of refraction of a ray of light that enters a diamond from air at an angle of 15.0° to the normal. (Hint: Use **Table 15-1.**)

4. **Physics in Action**   Sunlight passes into a raindrop at an angle of 22.5° from the normal at one point on the droplet. What is the angle of refraction?

- **Use ray diagrams to find the position of an image produced by a converging or diverging lens, and identify the image as real or virtual.**

- **Solve problems using the thin-lens equation.**

- **Calculate the magnification of lenses.**

- **Describe the positioning of lenses in compound microscopes and refracting telescopes.**

lens

a transparent object that refracts light rays, causing them to converge or diverge to create an image

Figure 15-6

When rays of light pass through **(a)** a converging lens (thicker at the middle), they are bent inward. When they pass through **(b)** a diverging lens (thicker at the edge), they are bent outward.

TYPES OF LENSES

When light traveling in air enters a pane of glass, it is bent toward the normal. As the light exits the pane of glass, it is bent again. When the light exits, however, its speed increases as it enters the air, so the light bends away from the normal. Because the amount of refraction is the same regardless of whether light is entering or exiting a medium, the light rays are bent as much on exiting the pane of glass as they were on entering. Thus, the exiting ray of light is parallel to the ray that entered the pane, but it is displaced sideways by an amount that depends on the thickness of the pane, the index of refraction of the glass, and the angle of incidence of the light ray.

Curved surfaces change the direction of light

When the surfaces of a medium are curved, the alignment of the normal line differs for each spot on the surface of the medium. Thus, when light passes through a medium that has one or more curved surfaces, the change in the direction of the light rays varies from point to point. This principle is applied in objects called **lenses.** Like mirrors, lenses form images, but lenses do so by refraction rather than by reflection. The images formed can be either real or virtual, depending on the type of lens and on the placement of the object. Lenses are commonly used to form images in optical instruments, such as cameras, telescopes, and microscopes. In fact, the front of the human eyeball acts as a type of lens, converging light toward the light-sensitive retina at the back of the eyeball.

A typical lens consists of a piece of glass or plastic ground so that each of its two refracting surfaces is a segment of either a sphere or a plane. **Figure 15-6** shows examples of lenses. Notice that the lenses are shaped differently. The lens that is thicker at the middle than it is at the rim, shown in **Figure 15-6(a),** is an example of a *converging* lens. The lens that is thinner at the mid-

(a)

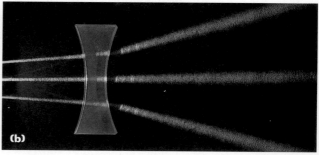

(b)

dle than it is at the rim, shown in **Figure 15-6(b)** is an example of a *diverging* lens. The light rays show why the names *converging* and *diverging* are applied to these lenses.

Focal length is the image distance for an infinite object distance

As with mirrors, it is convenient to define a point called the *focal point* for a lens. Note that light rays from an object far away are nearly parallel. The focal point of a converging lens is the location where the image of an object at an infinite distance from the lens is focused. For example, in **Figure 15-7(a)** a group of rays parallel to the principal axis passes through a focal point, *F*, after being bent inward by the lens. Unlike mirrors, every lens has a focal point on each side of the lens because light can pass through the lens from either side, as illustrated in **Figure 15-7**. The distance from the focal point to the center of the lens is called the *focal length, f.* The focal length is the image distance that corresponds to an infinite object distance.

Rays parallel to the principal axis diverge after passing through a diverging lens, as shown in **Figure 15-7(b).** In this case, the focal point is defined as the point from which the diverged rays appear to originate. Again, the focal length is defined as the distance from the center of the lens to the focal point.

Use ray diagrams to identify the image height and distance

Just as a set of standard rays and a ray diagram were used in Chapter 14 to predict the characteristics of images formed by spherical mirrors, a similar approach can be used for lenses. **Table 15-2** outlines the general rules for drawing these rays for lenses.

(a)

(b)

Figure 15-7
Both **(a)** converging lenses and **(b)** diverging lenses have two focal points but only one focal length.

Table 15-2	Rules for drawing reference rays	
Ray	**From object to lens**	**From *converging* lens to image**
Parallel ray	parallel to principal axis	passes through focal point, *F*
Central ray	to the center of the lens	from the center of the lens
Focal ray	passes through focal point, *F*	parallel to principal axis
Ray	**From object to lens**	**From *diverging* lens to image**
Parallel ray	parallel to principal axis	directed away from focal point, *F*
Central ray	to the center of the lens	from the center of the lens
Focal ray	proceeding toward back focal point, *F*	parallel to principal axis

The reasons why these rules work relate to concepts already covered in this textbook. From the definition of a focal point, we know that light traveling parallel to the principal axis (parallel ray) will be focused at the focal point. For a converging lens, this means that light will come together at the focal point in back of the lens. (In this book, the *front* of the lens is defined as the side of the lens that the light rays first encounter. The *back* of the lens refers to the side of the lens opposite where the light rays first encounter the lens.) But a similar ray passing through a diverging lens will exit the lens as if it originated from the focal point in front of the lens. Because refraction is reversible, a ray entering a converging lens from either focal point will be refracted so that it is parallel to the principal axis.

For both lenses, a ray passing through the center of the lens will continue in a straight line with no net refraction. This occurs because both sides of a lens are parallel to one another along any path through the center of the lens. As with a pane of glass, the exiting ray will be parallel to the ray that entered the lens. For ray diagrams, however, the usual assumption is that the lens is negligibly thin, so it is assumed that the ray is not displaced sideways but instead continues in a straight line.

CHARACTERISTICS OF LENSES

Table 15-3 summarizes the possible relationships between object and image positions for converging lenses. The rules for drawing reference rays were used to create each of these diagrams. Note that applications are listed along with each ray diagram to show the varied uses of the different configurations.

Converging lenses can produce real or virtual images

Notice that an object infinitely far away from a converging lens will create a point image at the focal point, as shown in the first diagram in **Table 15-3.** This image is real, which means that it can be projected on a screen, whereas a virtual image cannot be projected onto a screen.

As a distant object approaches the focal point, the image becomes larger and farther away, as shown in the second, third, and fourth diagrams in **Table 15-3.** When the object is at the focal point, as shown in the fifth diagram, the light rays from the object are refracted so that they exit the lens parallel to each other. (Note that because the object is at the focal point, it is impossible to draw a third ray that passes through that focal point, the lens, and the tip of the object.)

When the object is between a converging lens and its focal point, the light rays from the object diverge when they pass through the lens, as shown in the sixth diagram in **Table 15-3.** This image appears to an observer in back of the lens as being on the same side of the lens as the object. In other words, the brain interprets these diverging rays as coming from an object directly along the path of the rays that reach the eye. The ray diagram for this final case is less straightforward than those drawn for the other cases in the table. The first two

Focal Length

MATERIALS

✔ magnifying glass
✔ ruler

SAFETY CAUTION

Care should be taken not to focus the sunlight onto a flammable surface or any body parts, such as hands or arms. Also, do not look at the sun through the magnifying glass because serious eye injury can result.

On a sunny day, hold the magnifying glass, which is a converging lens, above a nonflammable surface, such as a sidewalk, so that a round spot of light is formed on the surface. Note where the spot formed by the lens is most distinct, or smallest. Use the ruler to measure the distance between the magnifying glass and the surface. This distance is the approximate focal length of the lens.

Table 15-3   Images created by converging lenses

Ray diagrams

1.

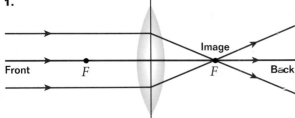

Configuration: object at infinity; point image at *F*

Applications: burning a hole with a magnifying glass

2.

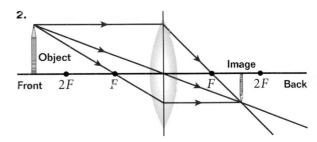

Configuration: object outside 2*F*; real, smaller image between *F* and 2*F*

Applications: lens of a camera, human eyeball lens, and objective lens of a refracting telescope

3.

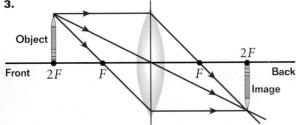

Configuration: object at 2*F*; real image at 2*F* same size as object

Applications: inverting lens of a field telescope

4.

Configuration: object between *F* and 2*F*; magnified real image outside 2*F*

Applications: motion-picture or slide projector and objective lens in a compound microscope

5.

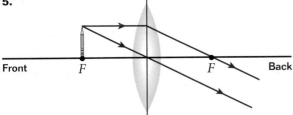

Configuration: object at *F*; image at infinity

Applications: lenses used in lighthouses and searchlights

6.

Configuration: object inside *F*; magnified virtual image on the same side of the lens as the object

Applications: magnifying with a magnifying glass; eyepiece lens of microscope, binoculars, and telescope rays (parallel to the axis and through the center of the lens) are drawn in the usual fashion. The third ray, however, is drawn so that if it were extended, it would connect the focal point in front of the lens, the tip of the object, and the lens in a straight line. To determine where the image is, draw lines extending from the rays exiting the lens back to the point where they would appear to have originated to an observer on the back side of the lens (these lines are dashed in the sixth diagram in **Table 15-3**).

A magnifying glass increases the angular size of an object

A magnifying glass is a converging lens and an example of a *simple magnifier*. As the name implies, this device is used to increase the apparent size of an object. When an object is placed just inside the focal point of a lens, a magnified virtual image appears. The last diagram in **Table 15-3** shows why the image appears upright, but why does the object's image appear larger?

The size of the image of an object formed at the retina of the eye depends on the *angular size* of the object. As the object moves closer, its angular size increases; as it moves farther away, its angular size decreases. For instance, consider **Figure 15-8.** When a person is standing 100 m from a house, the numbers on the house will not be visible. However, as the viewer moves closer to the house, the numbers become visible. If the viewer moves even closer, a

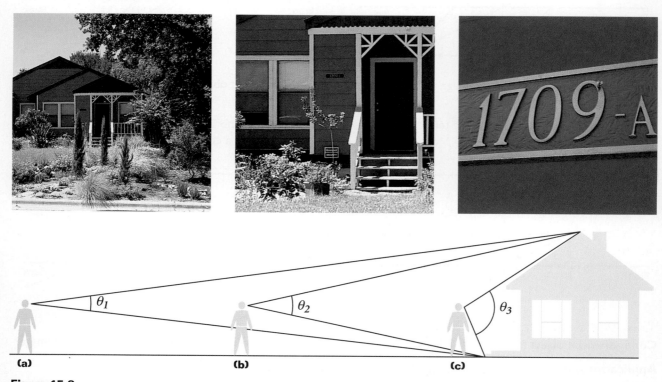

Figure 15-8
The angular size of the house is smaller at position **(a)** than it is when the viewer stands at position **(b).** At position **(c),** the angular size of the house is the largest and the most detail can be seen.

fly crawling across one of the numbers can be seen. Even more detail would be visible, such as the mouthparts of the fly, if the human eye could focus a very small distance from the object. What a simple magnifier does is enable the viewer to examine a small object by producing an enlarged image that fills a larger portion (angle) of the observer's field of vision.

Diverging lenses produce only a virtual image

As shown in **Figure 15-9,** diverging lenses can produce only one kind of image—virtual. Again, this image is upright, but diverging lenses *reduce* the size of the image. The image appears inside the focal point for any placement of the object.

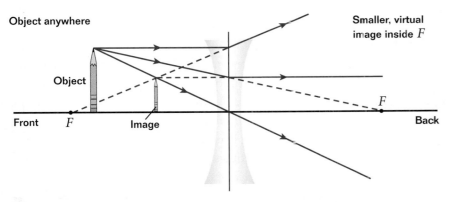

Figure 15-9
The image created by a diverging lens is always a virtual, smaller image.

The ray diagram shown in **Figure 15-9** for diverging lenses was created using the ray diagram rules for a diverging lens given in **Table 15-2.** The first ray, parallel to the axis, appears to come from the focal point on the same side of the lens as the object. This is indicated by the oblique dashed line. The second ray passes through the center of the lens and is not refracted. The third ray is drawn as if it were going to the focal point in back of the lens. As this ray passes through the lens, it is refracted parallel to the principal axis. Finally, this third ray must be extended backward, as shown by the dashed line. As with the sixth diagram in **Table 15-3,** the location of the tip of the image is the point at which the three rays appear to have originated.

THE THIN-LENS EQUATION AND MAGNIFICATION

Ray diagrams for lenses give an estimate of image size and distance, but it is possible to calculate these values. The equation that relates object and image distances for a lens is identical to the mirror equation in Chapter 14. This equation can be used to calculate any one of the three distances involved in the equation if the other two are known.

THIN-LENS EQUATION

$$\frac{1}{p} + \frac{1}{q} = \frac{1}{f}$$

$$\frac{1}{\text{distance from object to lens}} + \frac{1}{\text{distance from image to lens}} = \frac{1}{\text{focal length}}$$

This equation is called the *thin-lens equation* because it is derived using the assumption that the lens is very thin. In other words, this equation applies when the lens thickness is much smaller than its focal length. If this is true, it makes no difference whether we take the focal length to be the distance from the focal point to the surface of the lens or the distance from the focal point to the center of the lens.

The thin-lens equation can be applied to both converging and diverging lenses if we adhere to a set of sign conventions. **Table 15-4** gives the sign conventions for lenses. Under this convention, an image in back of the lens (that is, a real image) has a positive image distance, and an image in front of the lens, or a virtual image, has a negative image distance. A converging lens has a positive focal length and a diverging lens has a negative focal length. Because of this, converging lenses are sometimes called *positive lenses* and diverging lenses are sometimes called *negative lenses.*

Magnification of a lens depends on object and image distances

Recall that magnification (M) is defined as the ratio of image height to object height. The following equation can be used to calculate the magnification of both converging and diverging lenses.

MAGNIFICATION OF A LENS

$$M = \frac{h'}{h} = -\frac{q}{p}$$

$$\text{magnification} = \frac{\text{image height}}{\text{object height}} = -\frac{\text{distance from image to lens}}{\text{distance from object to lens}}$$

Note that the magnification equation for a lens is the same as the magnification equation for a mirror. If close attention is given to the sign conventions defined in **Table 15-4,** then the magnification will describe the image's size and orientation. When the magnitude of the magnification of an object is less than one, the image is smaller than the object. Conversely, when the magnitude of the magnification is greater than one, the image is larger than the object.

Additionally, a negative sign for the magnification indicates that the image is real and inverted. A positive magnification signifies that the image is upright and virtual.

Table 15-4
Sign conventions for lenses

	+	−
p	object in front of the lens	object in back of the lens
q	image in back of the lens	image in front of the lens
f	converging lens	diverging lens

Lenses

PROBLEM

An object is placed 30.0 cm in front of a converging lens and then 12.5 cm in front of a diverging lens. Both lenses have a focal length of 10.0 cm. For both cases, find the image distance and describe the image.

SOLUTION

1. DEFINE

Given:

$$f_{converging} = 10.0 \text{ cm} \qquad f_{diverging} = -10.0 \text{ cm}$$
$$p_{converging} = 30.0 \text{ cm} \qquad p_{diverging} = 12.5 \text{ cm}$$

Unknown:

$$q_{converging} = ? \qquad q_{diverging} = ?$$

Diagrams:

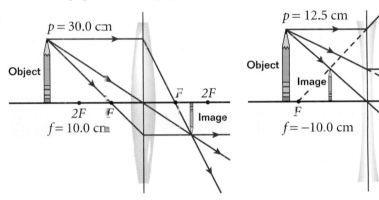

2. PLAN

Choose an equation(s) or situation:

The thin-lens equation can be used to find the image distance, while the equation for magnification will serve to describe the size and orientation of the image.

$$\frac{1}{p} + \frac{1}{q} = \frac{1}{f} \qquad M = -\frac{q}{p}$$

Rearrange the equation(s) to isolate the unknown(s):

$$\frac{1}{q} = \frac{1}{f} - \frac{1}{p}$$

3. CALCULATE

For the converging lens:

$$\frac{1}{q} = \frac{1}{f} - \frac{1}{p} = \frac{1}{10.0 \text{ cm}} - \frac{1}{30.0 \text{ cm}} = \frac{0.067}{1 \text{ cm}}$$

$$\boxed{q = 15 \text{ cm}}$$

$$M = -\frac{q}{p} = -\frac{15 \text{ cm}}{30.0 \text{ cm}}$$

$$\boxed{M = -0.50}$$

continued on next page

For the diverging lens:

$$\frac{1}{q} = \frac{1}{f} - \frac{1}{p} = \frac{1}{-10.0 \text{ cm}} - \frac{1}{12.5 \text{ cm}} = -\frac{0.180}{1 \text{ cm}}$$

$$\boxed{q = -5.56 \text{ cm}}$$

$$M = -\frac{q}{p} = -\frac{-5.56 \text{ cm}}{12.5 \text{ cm}}$$

$$\boxed{M = 0.445}$$

4. EVALUATE These values and signs for the converging lens indicate a real, inverted, smaller image. This is expected because the object distance is longer than twice the focal length of the converging lens. The values and signs for the diverging lens indicate a virtual, upright, smaller image formed inside the focal point. This is the only kind of image diverging lenses form.

PRACTICE 15B

Lenses

1. An object is placed 20.0 cm in front of a converging lens of focal length 10.0 cm. Find the image distance and describe the image.

2. Sherlock Holmes examines a clue by holding his magnifying glass (with a focal length of 15.0 cm) 10.0 cm away from an object. Find the image distance and describe the image that he observes.

3. An object is placed 20.0 cm in front of a diverging lens of focal length 10.0 cm. Find the image distance and describe the image.

4. Fill in the missing values in the following table.

f	p	q	M
Converging lens			
a. 6.0 cm	2.0 cm	?	?
b. ?	5.0 cm	7.0 cm	?
Diverging lens			
c. −6.0 cm	4.0 cm	?	?
d. ?	5.0 cm	?	0.50

EYEGLASSES AND CONTACT LENSES

The transparent front of the eyeball, called the *cornea,* acts like a lens, directing light rays toward the light-sensitive *retina* in the back of the eye. Although most of the refraction of light occurs at the cornea, the eye also contains a small lens, called the *crystalline lens,* that refracts light as well.

When the relaxed eye produces an image of a nearby object behind the retina, the abnormality is known as *hyperopia* and the person is said to be *farsighted.* With this defect, distant objects are seen clearly but near objects are blurred. Either the hyperopic eyeball is too short or the ciliary muscle that adjusts the shape of the lens cannot adjust enough to properly focus the image. **Table 15-5** shows how hyperopia can be corrected with a converging lens.

Another condition, known as *myopia,* or *nearsightedness,* occurs either when the eyeball is longer than normal or when the maximum focal length of the lens is insufficient to produce a clear image on the retina. In this case, light from a distant object is focused in front of the retina. The distinguishing feature of this imperfection is that distant objects are not seen clearly. Nearsightedness can be corrected with a diverging lens, as shown in **Table 15-5.**

A contact lens is simply a lens worn directly over the cornea of the eye. The lens floats on a thin layer of tears.

Table 15-5   Nearsighted and farsighted

Farsighted

Hyperopia

Corrected with a converging lens

Nearsighted

Myopia

Corrected with a diverging lens

COMBINATION OF THIN LENSES

If two lenses are used to form an image, the system can be treated in the following manner. First, the image of the first lens is calculated as though the second lens were not present. The light then approaches the second lens as if it had come from the image formed by the first lens. Hence, *the image formed by the first lens is treated as the object for the second lens.* The image formed by the second lens is the final image of the system. The overall magnification of a system of lenses is the product of the magnifications of the separate lenses. If the image formed by the first lens is in back of the second lens, then the image is treated as a virtual object for the second lens (that is, p is negative). The same procedure can be extended to a system of three or more lenses.

Compound microscopes use two converging lenses

A simple magnifier, such as a magnifying glass, provides only limited assistance when inspecting the minute details of an object. Greater magnification can be achieved by combining two lenses in a device called a compound microscope. It consists of two lenses: an objective lens (near the object) with a focal length of less than 1 cm and an eyepiece with a focal length of a few centimeters. As shown in **Figure 15-10,** the object placed just outside the focal point of the objective lens forms a real, inverted, and enlarged image that is at or just inside the focal point of the eyepiece. The eyepiece, which serves as a simple magnifier, uses this enlarged image as its object and produces an even more enlarged virtual image. The image viewed through a microscope is upside-down with respect to the actual orientation of the specimen, as shown in **Figure 15-10.**

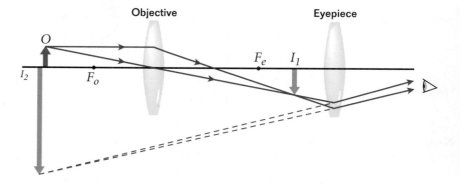

Figure 15-10

In a compound microscope, the real, inverted image produced by the objective lens is used as the object for the eyepiece lens.

The microscope has extended our vision into the previously unknown realm of incredibly small objects. A question that is often asked about microscopes is, "With extreme patience and care, would it be possible to construct a microscope that would enable us to see an atom?" As long as visible light is used to illuminate the object, the answer is no. In order to be seen, the object under a microscope must be at least as large as a wavelength of light. An atom is many times smaller than a wavelength of visible light, so its mysteries must be probed through other techniques.

Refracting telescopes also use two converging lenses

As mentioned in Chapter 14, there are two types of telescopes, reflecting and refracting. In a refracting telescope, an image is formed at the eye in much the same manner as is done with a microscope. A small, inverted image is formed at the focal point of the objective lens because the object is essentially at infinity. The eyepiece is positioned so that its focal point lies very close to the focal point of the objective lens, where the image is formed, as shown in **Figure 15-11.** Because the image is now just inside the focal point of the eyepiece, the eyepiece acts like a simple magnifier and allows the viewer to examine the object in detail.

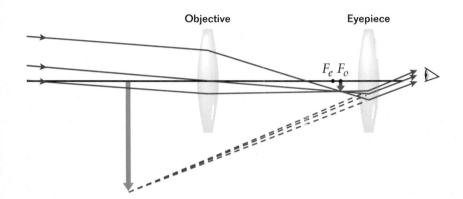

Figure 15-11
The image produced by the objective lens of a refracting telescope is a real, inverted image that is at its focal point. This inverted image, in turn, is the object from which the eyepiece creates a magnified, virtual image.

Section Review

1. Using a ray diagram, find the position and height of an image produced by a viewfinder in a camera, which is a diverging lens, with a focal length of 5.0 cm if the object is 1.0 cm tall and 10.0 cm in front of the lens.

2. What type of image, virtual or real, is produced in the following cases?
   a. an object at the focal point of a magnifying glass
   b. an object at the focal point of a camera's viewfinder
   c. an object inside the focal point of a camera lens
   d. an object outside the focal point of a refracting telescope's objective lens
   e. an object outside the focal point of a camera's viewfinder

3. Find the image position for an object placed 3.0 cm outside the focal point of a converging lens with a 4.0 cm focal length.

4. What is the magnification of the object from item 3?

5. Compare the length of a refracting telescope with the sum of the focal lengths of its two lenses.

6. What type of image is produced by the cornea and the lens on the retina?

15-3
Optical phenomena

total internal reflection

the complete reflection of light at the boundary of two transparent media; this effect occurs when the angle of incidence exceeds the critical angle

critical angle

the minimum angle of incidence for which total internal reflection occurs

TOTAL INTERNAL REFLECTION

An interesting effect called **total internal reflection** can occur when light moves along a path from a medium with a *higher* index of refraction to one with a *lower* index of refraction. Consider light rays traveling from water into air, as shown in **Figure 15-12(a).** Four possible directions of the rays are shown in the figure.

At some particular angle of incidence, called the **critical angle,** the refracted ray moves parallel to the boundary, making the angle of refraction equal to 90°, as shown in **Figure 15-12(b).** For angles of incidence greater than the critical angle, the ray is entirely reflected at the boundary, as shown in **Figure 15-12**. This ray is reflected at the boundary as though it had struck a perfectly reflecting surface. Its path and the path of all rays like it can be predicted by the law of reflection; that is, the angle of incidence equals the angle of reflection.

In optical equipment, prisms are arranged so that light entering the prism is totally internally reflected off the back surface of the prism. Prisms are used in place of silvered or aluminized mirrors because they reflect light more efficiently and are more scratch resistant.

Snell's law can be used to find the critical angle. As mentioned above, when the angle of incidence, θ_i, equals the critical angle, θ_c, then the angle of refraction, θ_r, equals 90°. Substituting these values into Snell's law gives the following relation.

$$n_i \sin \theta_c = n_r \sin(90°)$$

(a)   **(b)**

Figure 15-12
(a) This photo demonstrates several different paths of light radiated from the bottom of an aquarium. **(b)** At the critical angle, θ_c, a light ray will travel parallel to the boundary. Any rays with an angle of incidence greater than θ_c will be totally internally reflected at the boundary.

Because the sine of 90° equals 1, the following relationship results.

CRITICAL ANGLE

$$\sin \theta_c = \frac{n_r}{n_i} \text{ for } n_i > n_r$$

$$\text{sine (critical angle)} = \frac{\text{index of refraction of second medium}}{\text{index of refraction of first medium}}$$

but only if index of refraction of first medium >
index of refraction of second medium

Note that this equation can be used only when n_i is greater than n_r. In other words, *total internal reflection occurs only when light moves along a path from a medium of high index of refraction to a medium of lower index of refraction.* If n_i were less than n_r, this equation would give $\sin \theta_c > 1$, which is an impossible result because by definition the sine of an angle can never be greater than one.

When the second substance is air, the critical angle is small for substances with large indices of refraction. For instance, diamonds, which have an index of refraction of 2.419, have a critical angle of 24.4°. By comparison, the critical angle for crown glass, where $n = 1.52$, equals 41.0°. Because diamonds have such a small critical angle, most of the light that enters a cut diamond is totally internally reflected. The reflected light eventually exits the diamond from the most visible faces of the diamond. Jewelers intentionally cut diamonds so that the maximum light entering the upper surface is reflected back to these faces.

SAMPLE PROBLEM 15C

Critical angle

PROBLEM

Find the critical angle for a water-air boundary if the index of refraction of water is 1.333.

SOLUTION

Given: $n_i = 1.333$ $n_r = 1.00$

Unknown: $\theta_c = ?$

Use the equation for critical angle on this page.

$$\sin \theta_c = \frac{n_r}{n_i}$$

$$\theta_c = \sin^{-1}\left(\frac{n_r}{n_i}\right) = \sin^{-1}\left(\frac{1.00}{1.333}\right)$$

$$\boxed{\theta_c = 48.6°}$$

Critical angle

1. Find the critical angle for light traveling from glycerine ($n = 1.473$) into air.

2. Calculate the critical angle for light traveling from glycerine ($n = 1.473$) into water ($n = 1.333$).

3. Find the critical angle for light traveling from ice ($n = 1.309$) into air.

4. Which has a smaller critical angle in air, diamond ($n = 2.419$) or cubic zirconia ($n = 2.20$)? Show your work.

Fiber optics can guide light over a long distance

(a)

(b)

Another interesting application of total internal reflection is the use of glass or transparent plastic rods, like the ones shown in **Figure 15-13(a),** to transfer light from one place to another. As indicated in **Figure 15-13(b),** light is confined to traveling within the rods, even around gentle curves, as a result of successive internal reflections. Such a *light pipe* can be flexible if thin fibers rather than thick rods are used. If a bundle of parallel fibers is used to construct an optical transmission line, images can be transferred from one point to another.

This technique is used in a technology known as *fiber optics.* Very little light intensity is lost in these fibers as a result of reflections on the sides. Any loss of intensity is due essentially to reflections from the two ends and absorption by the fiber material. Fiber-optic devices are particularly useful for viewing images produced at inaccessible locations. For example, a fiber-optic cable can be threaded through the esophagus and into the stomach to look for ulcers.

The field of fiber optics is also being increasingly used in telecommunications because the fibers can carry much higher volumes of telephone calls and computer signals than can electrical wires.

Figure 15-13

(a) A fiber optic cable consists of several fibers. **(b)** Light is guided along a fiber by multiple internal reflections.

ATMOSPHERIC REFRACTION

We see an example of refraction every day: the sun can be seen even after it has passed below the horizon. Rays of light from the sun strike Earth's atmosphere and are bent because the atmosphere has an index of refraction different from that of the near-vacuum of space. The bending in this situation is gradual and continuous because the light moves through layers of air that have a continuously changing index of refraction. When the rays reach the observer, the eye follows them back along the direction from which they appear to have come.

Refracted light produces mirages

The *mirage* is another phenomenon of nature produced by refraction in the atmosphere. A mirage can be observed when the ground is so hot that the air directly above it is warmer than the air at higher elevations. The desert is, of course, a region in which such circumstances prevail, but mirages are also seen on heated roadways during the summer.

These layers of air at different heights above Earth have different densities and different refractive indices. The effect this can have is pictured in **Figure 15-14.** In this situation, the observer sees a tree in two different ways. One group of light rays reaches the observer by the straight-line path A, and the eye traces these rays back to see the tree in the normal fashion. In addition, a second group of rays travels along the curved path B. These rays are directed toward the ground and are then bent as a result of refraction. Consequently, the observer also sees an inverted image of the tree by tracing these rays back to the point at which they appear to have originated.

Because both an upright image and an inverted image are seen when the image of a tree is observed in a reflecting pool of water, the observer subconsciously calls upon this past experience and concludes that a pool of water must be in front of the tree.

Mirages also give the appearance of water even when no object is nearby. For instance, motorists driving along the road often see what appear to be wet spots on the road. In this case, light rays from the blue sky above are refracted by the warm air next to the dark, hot road.

Figure 15-14
A mirage is produced by the bending of light rays in the atmosphere when there are large temperature differences between the ground and the air.

DISPERSION

An important property of the index of refraction is that its value in anything but a vacuum depends on the wavelength of light. This phenomenon, described briefly in Chapter 14, is called **dispersion.** Since the index of refraction is a function of wavelength, Snell's law indicates that incoming light of different wavelengths is bent at different angles as it moves into a refracting material. As mentioned in Section 15-1, the index of refraction decreases with increasing wavelength. For instance, blue light ($\lambda \approx 470$ nm) bends more than red light ($\lambda \approx 650$ nm) when passing into a refracting material.

White light passed through a prism produces a visible spectrum

To understand how dispersion can affect light, consider what happens when light strikes a prism, as in **Figure 15-15.** Because of dispersion, the blue component of the incoming ray is bent more than the red component, and the rays that emerge from the second face of the prism fan out in a series of colors known as a *visible spectrum.* As mentioned in Chapter 14, these colors, in order of decreasing wavelength, are red, orange, yellow, green, blue, and violet.

dispersion

the process of separating polychromatic light into its component wavelengths

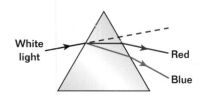

Figure 15-15
When white light enters a prism, the blue light is bent more than the red, and the prism disperses the white light into its various spectral components.

Rainbows are created by dispersion of light in water droplets

The dispersion of light into a spectrum is demonstrated most vividly in nature by a rainbow, often seen by an observer positioned between the sun and a rain shower. When a ray of sunlight strikes a drop of water in the atmosphere, it is first refracted at the front surface of the drop, with the violet light refracting the most and the red light the least. Then at the back surface of the drop, the light is

(a)

(b)

Figure 15-16

Rainbows **(a)** are produced because of dispersion of light in rain-drops. Sunlight is spread into a spectrum upon entering a spheri-cal raindrop **(b)**, then internally reflected on the back side of the raindrop. The perceived color of each water droplet then depends on the angle at which that drop is viewed.

reflected and returns to the front surface, where it again undergoes refraction as it moves from water into air. The rays leave the drop so that the angle between the incident white light and the returning violet ray is 40° and the angle between the white light and the returning red ray is 42°, as shown in **Figure 15-16(b).**

Now consider **Figure 15-16(a).** When an observer views a raindrop high in the sky, the red light reaches the observer, but the violet light, like the other spectral colors, passes over the observer because it deviates from the path of the white light more than the red light does. Hence, the observer sees this drop as being red. Similarly, a drop lower in the sky would direct violet light toward the observer and appear to be violet. (The red light from this drop would strike the ground and not be seen.) The remaining colors of the spectrum would reach the observer from raindrops lying between these two extreme positions.

Note that rainbows are most commonly seen above the horizon, where the ends of the rainbow disappear into the ground. However, if an observer is at an elevated vantage point, such as on an airplane or at the rim of a canyon, a complete circular rainbow can be seen.

LENS ABERRATIONS

One of the basic problems of lenses and lens systems is the imperfect quality of the images. The simple theory of mirrors and lenses assumes that rays make small angles with the principal axis and that all rays reaching the lens or mirror from a point source are focused at a single point, producing a sharp image. Clearly, this is not always true in the real world. Where the approximations used in this theory do not hold, imperfect images are formed.

As with spherical mirrors, *spherical aberration* occurs for lenses also. It results from the fact that the focal points of light rays far from the principal axis of a spherical lens are different from the focal points of rays with the same wavelength passing near the axis. Rays near the middle of the lens are focused farther from the lens than rays at the edges.

Another type of aberration, called **chromatic aberration,** arises from the wavelength dependence of refraction. Because the index of refraction of a material varies with wavelength, different wavelengths of light are focused at different focal points by a lens. For example, when white light passes through a lens, violet light is refracted more than red light, as shown in **Figure 15-17;** thus, the focal length for red light is greater than that for violet light. Other colors' wavelengths have intermediate focal points. Because a diverging lens has the opposite shape, the chromatic aberration for a diverging lens is opposite that for a converging lens. Chromatic aberration can be greatly reduced by the use of a combination of converging and diverging lenses made from two different types of glass.

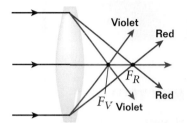

Figure 15-17
Because of dispersion, white light passing through a converging lens is focused at different focal points for each wavelength of light. (The angles in this figure are exaggerated for clarity.)

chromatic aberration

the focusing of different colors of light at different distances behind a lens

Section Review

1. Find the critical angle for light traveling from water ($n = 1.333$) into ice ($n = 1.309$).

2. Which of the following describe places where a mirage is likely to appear?
   a. above a warm lake on a warm day
   b. above an asphalt road on a hot day
   c. above a ski slope on a cold day
   d. above the sand on a beach on a hot day
   e. above a black car on a sunny day

3. When white light passes through a prism, which will be bent more, the red or green light?

4. **Physics in Action** After a storm, a man walks out onto his porch. Looking to the east, he sees a rainbow that has formed above his neighbor's house. What time of day is it, morning or evening?

CHAPTER 15
Summary

KEY TERMS

chromatic aberration (p. 585)

critical angle (p. 580)

dispersion (p. 583)

index of refraction (p. 564)

lens (p. 568)

refraction (p. 562)

total internal reflection (p. 580)

KEY IDEAS

Section 15-1 Refraction
- According to Snell's law, as a light ray travels from one medium into another medium where its speed is different, the light ray will change its direction unless it travels along the normal.
- When light passes from a medium with a smaller index of refraction to one with a larger index of refraction, the ray bends towards the normal. For the opposite situation, the ray bends away from the normal.

Section 15-2 Thin lenses
- The image produced by a converging lens is real and inverted when the object is outside the focal point and virtual and upright when the object is inside the focal point. Diverging lenses always produce upright, virtual images.
- The location of an image created by a lens can be found using either a ray diagram or the thin-lens equation.

Section 15-3 Optical phenomena
- Total internal reflection can occur when light attempts to move from a material with a higher index of refraction to one with a lower index of refraction. If the angle of incidence of a ray is greater than the critical angle, the ray is totally reflected at the boundary.
- Mirages and the visibility of the sun after it has physically set are natural phenomena that can be attributed to refraction of light in Earth's atmosphere.

Variable symbols

	Quantities		Units
θ_i	angle of incidence	°	degrees
θ_r	angle of refraction	°	degrees
n	index of refraction		
p	distance from object to lens	m	meters
q	distance from image to lens	m	meters
h'	image height	m	meters
h	object height	m	meters
θ_c	critical angle	°	degrees

REFRACTION AND SNELL'S LAW

Review questions

1. Does a light ray traveling from one medium into another always bend toward the normal?

2. As light travels from a vacuum ($n = 1$) to a medium such as glass ($n > 1$), does its wavelength change? Does its velocity change?

3. What is the relationship between the velocity of light and the index of refraction of a transparent substance?

4. Why does a clear stream always appear to be shallower than it actually is?

5. What are the three conditions that must be met for refraction to occur?

Conceptual questions

6. Two colors of light (X and Y) are sent through a glass prism, and X is bent more than Y. Which color travels more slowly in the prism?

7. Why does an oar appear to be bent when part of it is in the water?

8. A friend throws a coin into a pool. You close your eyes and dive toward the spot where you saw it from the edge of the pool. When you reach the bottom, will the coin be in front of you or behind you?

9. The level of water in a clear glass container is easily observed with the naked eye. The level of liquid helium in a clear glass container is extremely difficult to see with the naked eye. Explain why.

Practice problems

10. Light passes from air into water at an angle of incidence of 42.3°. Determine the angle of refraction in the water.
(See Sample Problem 15A.)

11. A ray of light enters the top of a glass of water at an angle of 36° with the vertical. What is the angle between the refracted ray and the vertical?
(See Sample Problem 15A.)

12. The angles of incidence and refraction for light going from air into a material with a higher index of refraction are 63.5° and 42.9°, respectively. What is the index of refraction of this material?
(See Sample Problem 15A.)

13. A person shines a light at a friend who is underwater. If the ray in the water makes an angle of 36.2° with the normal, what is the angle of incidence?
(See Sample Problem 15A.)

14. A narrow ray of yellow light from glowing sodium ($\lambda_0 = 589$ nm) traveling in air strikes a smooth surface of water at an angle of $\theta_i = 35.0°$. Determine the angle of refraction, θ_r.
(See Sample Problem 15A.)

15. A ray of light traveling in air strikes a flat 2.00 cm thick block of glass ($n = 1.50$) at an angle of 30.0° with the normal. Trace the light ray through the glass, and find the angles of incidence and refraction at each surface.
(See Sample Problem 15A.)

16. The light ray shown in **Figure 15-18** makes an angle of 20.0° with the normal line at the boundary of linseed oil and water. Determine the angles θ_1 and θ_2. Note that $n = 1.48$ for linseed oil.
(See Sample Problem 15A.)

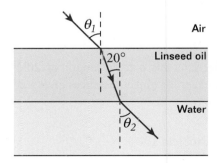

Figure 15-18

RAY DIAGRAMS AND THIN LENSES

Review questions

17. Which type of lens can focus the sun's rays?

18. Why is no image formed when an object is at the focal point of a converging lens?

19. Consider the image formed by a thin converging lens. Under what conditions will the image be
    a. inverted?
    b. upright?
    c. real?
    d. virtual?
    e. larger than the object?
    f. smaller than the object?

20. Repeat a–f of item 19 for a thin diverging lens.

21. Explain this statement: The focal point of a converging lens is the location of an image of a point object at infinity. Based on this statement, can you think of a quick method for determining the focal length of a positive lens?

Conceptual questions

22. If a glass converging lens is submerged in water, will its focal length be longer or shorter than when it is in air?

23. In order to get an upright image, slides must be placed upside down in a slide projector. What type of lens must the slide projector have? Is the slide inside or outside the focal point of the lens?

24. If there are two converging lenses in a compound microscope, why is the image still inverted?

25. In a Jules Verne novel, a piece of ice is shaped into the form of a magnifying lens to focus sunlight and thereby start a fire. Is this possible?

Practice problems

26. A converging lens has a focal length of 20.0 cm. Locate the images for object distances of
    a. 40.0 cm
    b. 10.0 cm
    (See Sample Problem 15B.)

27. For each case in item 26, state whether the image is real or virtual and upright or inverted, and find the magnification.
    (See Sample Problem 15B.)

28. A diverging lens has a focal length of 20.0 cm. Locate the images for object distances of
    a. 40.0 cm
    b. 20.0 cm
    c. 10.0 cm
    (See Sample Problem 15B.)

29. For each case in item 28, state whether the image is real or virtual and upright or inverted, and find the magnification.
    (See Sample Problem 15B.)

30. A magnifying glass has a converging lens of focal length 15.0 cm. At what distance from a nickel should you hold this lens to get an image with a magnification of +2.00?
    (See Sample Problem 15B.)

31. Where must an object be placed to have a magnification of 2.00 in each of the following cases? Show your work.
    a. a converging lens of focal length 12.0 cm
    b. a diverging lens of focal length 12.0 cm
    (See Sample Problem 15B.)

32. A diverging lens is used to form a virtual image of an object. The object is 80.0 cm in front of the lens, and the image is 40.0 cm in front of the lens. Determine the focal length of the lens.
    (See Sample Problem 15B.)

33. A microscope slide is placed in front of a converging lens with a focal length of 2.44 cm. The lens forms an image of the slide 12.9 cm from the slide.
    a. How far is the lens from the slide if the image is real?
    b. How far is the lens from the slide if the image is virtual?
    (See Sample Problem 15B.)

34. Where must an object be placed to form an image 30.0 cm from a diverging lens with a focal length of 40.0 cm? Determine the magnification of the image.
    (See Sample Problem 15B.)

35. An object's distance from a converging lens is 10 times the focal length. How far is the image from the lens? Express the answer as a fraction of the focal length.
(See Sample Problem 15B.)

36. A person looks at a gem using a converging lens with a focal length of 12.5 cm. The lens forms a virtual image 30.0 cm from the lens. Determine the magnification. Is the image upright or inverted?
(See Sample Problem 15B.)

TOTAL INTERNAL REFLECTION, ATMOSPHERIC REFRACTION, AND ABERRATIONS

Review questions

37. Is it possible to have total internal reflection for light incident from air on water? Explain.

38. What are the conditions necessary for the occurrence of a mirage?

39. On a hot day, what is it that we are seeing when we observe a "water on the road" mirage?

40. Why does the arc of a rainbow appear with red colors on top and violet colors on the bottom?

41. What type of aberration is involved in each of the following situations?
   a. The edges of the image appear reddish.
   b. The central portion of the image cannot be clearly focused.
   c. The outer portion of the image cannot be clearly focused.
   d. The central portion of the image is enlarged relative to the outer portions.

Conceptual questions

42. A laser beam passing through a nonhomogeneous sugar solution follows a curved path. Explain.

43. On a warm day, the image of a boat floating on cold water appears above the boat. Explain.

44. Explain why a mirror cannot give rise to chromatic aberration.

45. Why does a diamond show flashes of color when observed under ordinary white light?

Practice problems

46. Calculate the critical angle for light going from glycerine into air.
(See Sample Problem 15C.)

47. Assuming that $\lambda = 589$ nm, calculate the critical angles for the following materials when surrounded by air:
   a. zircon
   b. fluorite
   c. ice
(See Sample Problem 15C.)

48. Light traveling in air enters the flat side of a prism made of crown glass ($n = 1.52$), as shown in **Figure 15-19**. Will the light pass through the other side of the prism or will it be totally internally reflected? Show your work.

Figure 15-19

49. A fiber-optic cable has an index of refraction of 1.53. For total internal reflection, what is the minimum angle of incidence to the inside wall of the cable if the cable is in the following:
   a. air
   b. water
(See Sample Problem 15C.)

50. Light strikes the surface of a prism, $n = 1.8$, as shown in **Figure 15-20**. If the prism is surrounded by a fluid, what is the maximum index of refraction of the fluid that will still cause total internal reflection within the prism?
(See Sample Problem 15C.)

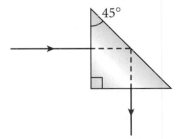

Figure 15-20

51. A fiber-optic rod consists of a central strand of material surrounded by an outer coating. The interior portion of the rod has an index of refraction of 1.60. If all rays striking the interior walls of the rod with incident angles greater than 59.5° are subject to total internal reflection, what is the index of refraction of the coating?
(See Sample Problem 15C.)

MIXED REVIEW

52. What is the index of refraction of a material in which the speed of light is 1.85×10^8 m/s? Look at the indices of refraction in **Table 15-1** to identify this material.

53. Light moves from flint glass into water at an angle of incidence of 28.7°.

   a. What is the angle of refraction?
   b. At what angle would the light have to be incident to give an angle of refraction of 90.0°?

54. The image of the United States postage stamps in **Figure 15-21** is 1.50 times the size of the actual stamps in front of the lens. Determine the focal length of the lens if the distance from the lens to the stamps is 2.84 cm.

Figure 15-21

55. The index of refraction for red light in water is 1.331, and that for blue light is 1.340. If a ray of white light traveling in air enters the water at an angle of incidence of 83.0°, what are the angles of refraction for the red and blue components of the light?

56. A ray of light traveling in air strikes the surface of mineral oil at an angle of 23.1° with the normal to the surface. If the light travels at 2.17×10^8 m/s through the oil, what is the angle of refraction? (Hint: Remember the definition of the index of refraction.)

57. A ray of light traveling in air strikes the surface of a liquid. If the angle of incidence is 30.0° and angle of refraction is 22.0°, find the critical angle for light traveling from the liquid back into the air.

58. The laws of refraction and reflection are the same for sound and for light. The speed of sound is 340 m/s in air and 1510 m/s in water. If a sound wave traveling in air approaches a flat water surface at an angle of incidence of 12.0°, what is the angle of refraction?

59. A jewel thief hides a diamond by placing it at the bottom of a fountain. He places a circular piece of wood on the surface of the water and anchors it directly above the diamond, as shown in **Figure 15-22**. If the fountain is 2.00 m deep, find the minimum diameter of the piece of wood that would prevent the diamond from being seen.

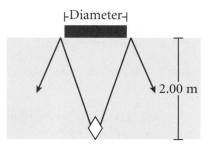

Figure 15-22

60. A ray of light traveling in air strikes the surface of a block of clear ice at an angle of 40.0° with the normal. Part of the light is reflected and part is refracted. Find the angle between the reflected and refracted light.

61. A ray of light traveling in air strikes the midpoint of one face of an equiangular glass prism ($n = 1.50$) at an angle of exactly 30°, as shown in **Figure 15-23**.

   a. Trace the path of the light ray through the glass and find the angle of incidence of the ray at the bottom of the prism.

   b. Will the ray pass through the bottom surface of the prism or will it be totally internally reflected?

Figure 15-23

62. A flashlight on the bottom of a 4.00 m deep swimming pool sends a ray upward and at an angle so that the ray strikes the surface of the water 2.00 m from the point directly above the flashlight. What angle (in air) does the emerging ray make with the water's surface? (Hint: To determine the angle of incidence, consider the right triangle formed by the light ray, the pool bottom, and the imaginary line straight down from where the ray strikes the surface of the water.)

63. A submarine is 325 m horizontally out from the shore and 115 m beneath the surface of the water. A laser beam is sent from the sub so that it strikes the surface of the water at a point 205 m from the shore. If the beam strikes the top of a building standing directly at the water's edge, find the height of the building. (Hint: To determine the angle of incidence, consider the right triangle formed by the light beam, the horizontal line drawn at the depth of the submarine, and the imaginary line straight down from where the beam strikes the surface of the water.)

64. A laser beam traveling in air strikes the midpoint of one end of a slab of material as shown in **Figure 15-24**. The index of refraction of the slab is 1.48. Determine the number of internal reflections of the beam before it emerges from the opposite end of the slab.

Figure 15-24

Alternative Assessment

Performance assessment

1. Interview an optometrist, optician, or ophthalmologist. Find out what equipment and tools they use. What kinds of eye problems are they able to correct? What training is necessary for each career?

2. Obtain permission to use a microscope and slides from your school's biology teacher. Identify the optical components (lenses, mirror, object, and light source) and knobs. Find out how they function at different magnifications and what adjustments must be made to obtain a clear image. Sketch a ray diagram for the microscope's image formation. Estimate the size of the images you see, and calculate the approximate size of the actual cells or microorganisms you observe. How closely do your estimates match the magnification indicated on the microscope?

3. Construct your own telescope with mailing tubes (one small enough to slide inside the other), two lenses, cardboard disks for mounting the lenses, glue, and masking tape. Test your instrument at night. Try to combine different lenses and explore ways to improve your telescope's performance. Keep records of your results to make a brochure documenting the development of your telescope.

Portfolio projects

4. Research how phone, television, and radio signals are transmitted over long distances through fiber-optic devices. Obtain information from telephone or cable television companies. What materials are fiber-optic cables made of? What are their most important properties? Are there limits on the kind of light that travels in these cables? What are the advantages of fiber-optic technology over broadcast transmission? Produce a brochure or informational video to explain this technology to consumers.

5. When the Indian physicist Venkata Raman first saw the Mediterranean Sea, he proposed that its blue color was due to the structure of water molecules rather than to the scattering of light from suspended particles. Later, he won the Nobel Prize for work relating to the implications of this hypothesis. Research Raman's life and work. Find out about his background and the challenges and opportunities he met on his way to becoming a physicist. Create a presentation about him in the form of a report, poster, short video, or computer presentation.

Technology & Learning

Graphing calculators

Program your graphing calculator to create a graph of the angle of incidence versus the angle of refraction to determine the index of refraction. Use this program to find the index of refraction for the following situations:

a. a light ray moving from air into a substance with an angle of incidence of 40° and an angle of refraction of 30°

b. a light ray moving from air into a substance with an angle of incidence of 40° and an angle of refraction of 25°

c. a light ray moving from air into a substance with an angle of incidence of 60° and an angle of refraction of 45°

d. a light ray moving from air into a substance with an angle of incidence of 60° and an angle of refraction of 30°

Press [Y=] and [CLEAR] to clear any functions. Press [MODE] [▼] [▼] [▶] [ENTER] to set the calculator in "Degree" mode.

Open a new program by pressing [PRGM] [▶] [▶] [ENTER]. Name the program "REFRACT" and press [ENTER]. Then enter the program in the table below.

To exit the program editor, press [2nd] [QUIT]. To run the program, press [PRGM], select "REFRACT," and press [ENTER] [ENTER]. Enter the value for the angle of incidence and press [ENTER].

The calculator will provide a graph of the index of refraction versus the angle of refraction. (If the graph is not visible, press [WINDOW], change the settings for the graph window, then press [GRAPH].)

Press [TRACE] and use the arrow keys to trace along the curve. The *x* value corresponds to the angle of refraction in degrees, and the *y* value corresponds to the index of refraction.

After you have finished using the graph for one angle of incidence, press [2nd] [QUIT] to run the program for the next angle of incidence.

Keystrokes	Display
	PROGRAM: REFRACT
1. [PRGM] [▶] [3] [2nd] [A-LOCK] ["] [θ] [I] [N] [C] [ALPHA] [2nd] [TEST] [1] [ALPHA] ["] [ENTER]	:"θINC="
2. [PRGM] [▶] [1] [ALPHA] [I] [ENTER]	:INPUT I
3. [ALPHA] ["] [SIN] [ALPHA] [I] [÷] [SIN] [X,T,θ] [ALPHA] ["] [STO▶] [2nd] [Y-VARS] [1] [1] [ENTER]	:"SIN I/SIN X" → Y1
4. [0] [STO▶] [VARS] [1] [1] [ENTER]	:0 → XMIN
5. [9] [0] [STO▶] [VARS] [1] [2] [ENTER]	:90 → XMAX
6. [0] [STO▶] [VARS] [1] [4] [ENTER]	:0 → YMIN
7. [2] [STO▶] [VARS] [1] [5] [ENTER]	:2 → YMAX
8. [PRGM] [▶] [4] [ENTER]	:DISPGRAPH

CONVERGING LENSES

Converging lenses can produce both real and virtual images, and they can produce images that are smaller, the same size, or larger than the object. In this experiment you will study image formation using a converging lens.

SAFETY

- **Use a hot mitt to handle resistors, light sources, and other equipment that may be hot. Allow all equipment to cool before storing it.**

- **Never put broken glass or ceramics in a regular waste container. Use a dustpan, brush, and heavy gloves to carefully pick up broken pieces, and dispose of them in a container specifically provided for this purpose.**

PREPARATION

1. Read the entire lab, and plan what measurements you will take.

2. Prepare a data table in your lab notebook with eight columns and six rows. Label this table *Focal Length*. In the first row, label the columns *Trial, Position of lens (cm), Position of object (cm), Position of image (cm), q (cm), p (cm), h_o (cm)*, and *h_i (cm)*. In the first column, label the second through sixth rows *1, 2, 3, 4*, and *5*. Above or below the data table, prepare a space to record the focal length, *f*, of the lens in centimeters.

PROCEDURE

Finding the focal length

3. Set up the meterstick, meterstick supports, image screen, and lens as shown in **Figure 15-25.** Make sure the image screen is securely held in the screen support rider to prevent its moving during the experiment. Locate and mark the point on the mounted screen where it intercepts the principal axis of the mounted lens.

4. Place the lens at the 50 cm mark and the image screen near the 70 cm mark on the meterstick. Through a laboratory window, choose an object, such as a building or tree, several hundred meters away, and point the mounted lens toward it. Stand with your back to the object, and carefully align the meterstick until the object's image is observed on the image screen.

OBJECTIVES

- Determine the focal length of a converging lens.

- Investigate the relationships between the positions of the lens and object, and the position and size of the image.

MATERIALS LIST

- ✔ 2 screen support riders
- ✔ cardboard image screen with metric scale
- ✔ converging lens
- ✔ dc power supply
- ✔ insulated copper wire, 2 lengths
- ✔ lens support rider
- ✔ meterstick and meterstick supports
- ✔ metric ruler
- ✔ miniature lamp and base on rider
- ✔ object screen

5. While viewing the image on the screen, move the screen along the meterstick until the image is as distinct as possible. Jot down the distance between the lens and the screen. Move the lens to the 60 cm position, and repeat the procedure using a different distant object. Average the two results for the distance between the lens and the screen. Record this average image distance as the *focal length* of the lens in your data table.

Figure 15-25

Step 4: Move the end of the meterstick until you find the position where the object, the lens, and the image screen are all in alignment.

Step 5: Find the position of the image screen where the image is most distinct, then move the lens and repeat. The average distance between the lens and the screen is the focal length.

Step 6: Use the illuminated object screen as the object for this part of the lab.

Formation of images

6. Place the illuminated object screen at one end of the meterstick. Make adjustments so that the center of the object screen coincides with the principal axis of the lens.

7. Place the lens far enough from the object screen to give an object distance greater than twice the focal length of the lens. Move the image screen along the meterstick until the image is as well defined as possible. Read and record in the data table the positions of the object, lens, and image on the meterstick. Also record the object distance, p, the image distance, q, the height of the object, h_o, and the height of the image, h_i.

8. For the second trial, place the lens at a position for an object distance exactly twice the focal length of the lens. Adjust the image screen for maximum image definition. Read and record in the data table the positions of the object, lens, and image on the meterstick. Also record the object distance, p, the image distance, q, and the height of the image, h_i. Record the height of the object, h_o, from step 7.

9. For the third trial, place the lens between one and two focal lengths from the object screen. Adjust the image screen for maximum image definition, and make all your measurements. Record all measurements in your data table.

10. For the fourth trial, place the lens exactly one focal length away from the object. Adjust the image screen for maximum image definition, and record all measurements or place X's in your data table.

11. For the fifth trial, place the lens less than one focal length away from the object. Adjust the image screen for maximum image definition, and record all measurements or place X's in your data table. Remove the image screen, and place your eye close to the lens. Look through the lens at the object. Record your observations in your lab notebook.

ANALYSIS AND INTERPRETATION

Calculations and data analysis

1. Organizing data   For each trial recorded in the data table, perform the following calculations:

   a. Find the reciprocal of the object distance, p.

   b. Find the reciprocal of the image distance, q.

   c. Add the reciprocals found in **(a)** and **(b)**.

2. Analyzing data   Compare the sum of the reciprocals for each trial with the focal length of the lens. What is the relationship? Is this true for all trials? Explain.

3. Organizing data   For each trial, perform the following calculations:

   a. Find the ratio between q and p.

   b. Find the ratio between h_i and h_o.

Conclusions

4. Analyzing data   For each trial, compare the ratios found in item 3.

   a. Based on your results, what physical quantity is expressed by each of the ratios found in item 3?

   b. What is the relationship between the two ratios for each trial? Is this true for all trials? Explain.

5. Graphing data   Use a graphing calculator, computer, or graph paper. Plot a graph of the ratio between h_i and h_o (the magnification) versus p (the object distance).

6. Evaluating results   What does the shape of the graph reveal about the relationship between the magnification of the image and the distance of the object from the lens?

CHAPTER 16

Interference and Diffraction

PHYSICS IN ACTION

The streaks of colored light you see reflected from a compact disc resemble the colors that appear when white light passes through a prism. However, the compact disc does not separate light by means of refraction. Instead, the light waves undergo interference.

In interference, light waves combine to produce resultant waves that are either brighter or less bright than the component waves. For light reflected from the compact disc, certain wavelengths are visible only at particular angles. Devices called diffraction gratings use the principle of interference to separate light into its component colors.

- *Why are light waves not easily observed bending around obstacles?*

- *What limits the separation of the colored light reflected from a compact disc?*

CONCEPT REVIEW

Superposition principle
   (Section 12-4)
Interference of waves   (Section 12-4)

16-1
Interference

16-1 SECTION OBJECTIVES

- **Describe how light waves interfere with each other to produce bright and dark fringes.**

- **Identify the conditions required for interference to occur.**

- **Predict the location of interference fringes using the equation for double-slit interference.**

LIGHT WAVES COMBINE WITH EACH OTHER

You have probably noticed the bands of color that form on the surface of a soap bubble, as shown in **Figure 16-1.** Unlike the colors that appear when light passes through a refracting substance, these colors are the result of light waves combining with each other.

To understand how light waves combine with each other, it helps to review how other kinds of waves combine. If a sound source is positioned near a wall so that you can hear both the original sound and its reflection from the wall, you will notice that at certain regularly spaced positions between the source and the wall, the sound becomes louder. Between these positions, the sound becomes softer. This effect involves not only reflection but also the wave phenomenon known as *interference,* which was discussed in Chapter 12.

Interference takes place when waves combine by superposition

Consider mechanical waves, such as sound waves in air or ripples in water. If two mechanical waves with identical wavelengths cross each other's paths, they combine to form a resultant wave. This resultant wave has the same wavelength as the component waves, but according to the superposition principle, its displacement at any instant equals the sum of the displacements of each component wave. Put another way, the resultant wave is the consequence of the two component waves interfering with each other.

Note that in **Figure 16-2** the superposition of waves does not disturb the waves themselves, so the waves pass through each other without being destroyed or altered. In the case of *constructive interference,* the component waves combine to form a resultant wave with an amplitude that is greater than the amplitude of either of the individual component waves. In the case of

Figure 16-1
Light waves interfere to form bands of color on a soap bubble's surface.

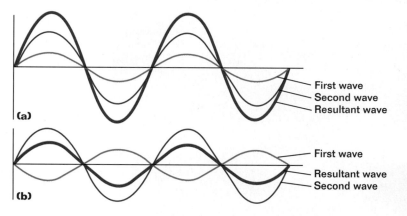

First wave
Second wave
Resultant wave

(a)

First wave
Resultant wave
Second wave

(b)

Figure 16-2
Two waves can interfere **(a)** constructively or **(b)** destructively. In interference, energy is not lost but is instead redistributed.

destructive interference, the resultant amplitude is less than the amplitude of the larger component wave. Because of energy conservation, energy is not destroyed at points where destructive interference occurs. Instead, it is redistributed to points where constructive interference takes place.

All interference associated with electromagnetic waves arises from the combining of the electric and magnetic fields that constitute each wave. The distance between points where constructive and destructive interference occur is proportional to the wavelength of the component waves. Interference is therefore more easily detected in electromagnetic waves with long wavelengths. FM radio waves have wavelengths of a few meters, so the distance between the points where constructive and destructive interference occurs between FM radio waves is also more than a meter long. The effects of interference in visible light waves are not easy to observe because of their short wavelengths (from about 4×10^{-7} m to about 7×10^{-7} m). The distance between neighboring points where constructive and destructive interference takes place in visible light is very small (about 0.000 0002 m).

Waves must have a constant phase difference for interference to be observed

Two sources, each producing a traveling periodic wave, are needed to create interference. To produce a stable interference pattern, the phases of the individual waves must remain unchanged with respect to one another. If the crest of one wave overlaps the crest of another wave, as in **Figure 16-3(a),** the two have a phase difference of 0° and are said to be *in phase.* If the crest of one wave overlaps the trough of the other wave, as in **Figure 16-3(b),** the two waves have a phase difference of 180° and are said to be *out of phase.*

When the phase difference between two waves is constant and the waves do not shift relative to each other as time passes, the waves are said to have **coherence.** Sources of such waves are said to be *coherent.*

A single source can be used to produce coherent waves. For example, the sound waves emitted by two side-by-side loudspeakers that are powered by a single amplifier are in phase. Because each speaker responds to the amplifier in the same way at the same time, the waves from each speaker can exhibit interference.

CONCEPT PREVIEW

Coherence and noncoherence in light is discussed in greater detail in Section 16-3.

coherence

the property by which two waves with identical wavelengths maintain a constant phase relationship

(a)

(b)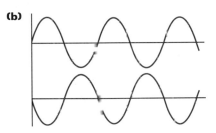

Figure 16-3
The features of two waves in phase completely match **(a),** whereas they are opposite each other in waves that are 180° out of phase **(b).**

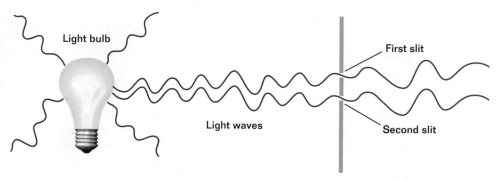

Light bulb

Light waves

First slit

Second slit

Figure 16-4

Passing a single wave front (shown here as two individual waves that are part of one wave front) through two slits yields two coherent sources of light. Changes that occur in the wave front also occur in the light from both slits.

Figure 16-5

When waves of white light from two coherent sources interfere, the pattern is indistinct because different colors interfere constructively at different positions.

When two light bulbs are placed side by side, no interference is observed. This is because the light waves from one light bulb are emitted independently of the waves from the other bulb. Changes occurring in the light from one bulb do not necessarily occur in the light from the other bulb. Thus, the phase difference between the light waves from the two bulbs is not constant. The light waves still interfere, but the conditions for that interference change with each phase change and, therefore, no single interference pattern is observed. Light sources of this type are said to be *noncoherent*.

A common method of producing two sources of visible light that will undergo interference is shown in **Figure 16-4.** If light from a single source is used to illuminate a screen containing two small slits, the light emerging from the two slits will be coherent. The slits serve only to separate the original beam into two parts in a manner similar to the separation of a sound signal into two identical signals from each of two speakers. Any random change in the light emitted by the source will occur in the two separate beams at the same time, and interference effects can be observed.

A stable interference pattern requires component waves with the same wavelength

While coherence is essential for interference to occur, the waves must also have the same wavelength if interference is to be observed. Light that has this property is said to be *monochromatic,* which means single-colored. When two coherent light waves of different wavelength combine, their amplitudes add to form an interference pattern that varies with time. This is similar to the phenomenon of beats in sound waves, which you studied in Chapter 13. Beats occur when two sound waves of similar but not identical frequency or wavelength interfere with each other.

In the case of light, if a white light source is used to observe interference, the situation becomes more complicated because the light source emits waves of many wavelengths. An example of a white light interference pattern is shown in **Figure 16-5.** Although these waves interfere with each other, the interference pattern is not stable or well-defined, except at those positions where light of a given wavelength constructively interferes with light of the same wavelength. This explains the bands of color on either side of the middle band of white light as well as the bands of color seen on a soap bubble's surface.

DEMONSTRATING INTERFERENCE

Interference in light waves from two sources can be demonstrated in the following way. Light that is passed through a narrow slit is then passed through two narrow parallel slits. These slits serve as a pair of coherent light sources because the waves emerging from them come from the same source.

If monochromatic light is used, the light from the two slits produces a series of bright and dark parallel bands, or *fringes,* on a distant viewing screen, as shown in **Figure 16-6.** When the light from the two slits arrives at a point on the viewing screen where constructive interference occurs, a bright fringe appears at that location. When the light from the two slits combines destructively at a point on the viewing screen, a dark fringe appears at that location.

Figure 16-7 illustrates some of the ways that two waves leaving the slits can combine at the viewing screen. When the two waves arrive at the central point of the screen, as in **Figure 16-7(a),** they have traveled equal distances. Thus, they arrive in phase at the center of the viewing screen, constructive interference occurs, and a bright fringe forms at that location.

When the two light waves combine at a certain point off the center of the screen, as in **Figure 16-7(b),** the wave from the more distant slit must travel one wavelength farther than the wave from the nearer slit. Because the first wave is out of phase with the second wave by exactly one wavelength, the two waves still are in phase when they combine at the screen. Constructive interference therefore occurs, and a second bright fringe appears on the screen.

If the waves meet midway between the locations of the two bright fringes, as in **Figure 16-7(c),** the first wave travels half a wavelength farther than the second wave. In this case, the trough of the first wave overlaps the crest of the second wave, giving rise to destructive interference. Consequently, a dark fringe appears on the viewing screen between the bright fringes.

Figure 16-6
An interference pattern consists of alternating light and dark fringes.

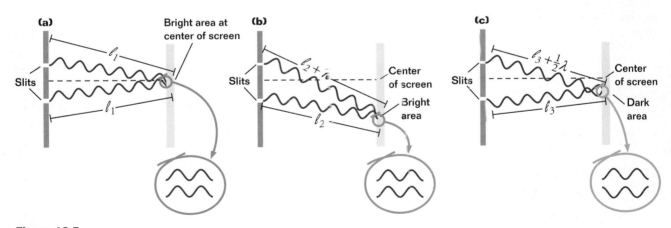

Figure 16-7
(a) When both waves of light travel the same distance (ℓ_1), they arrive at the screen in phase and interfere constructively. **(b)** If the difference between the distances traveled by the light from each source equals a whole wavelength, the waves still interfere constructively. **(c)** If the distances traveled by the light differ by a half wavelength, the waves interfere destructively.

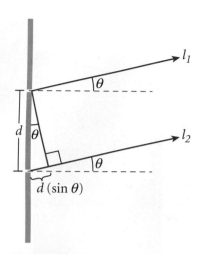

Figure 16-8

The path difference for two light waves equals $d \, (\sin \theta)$. In order to emphasize the path difference, the figure is not drawn to scale.

path difference

the difference in the distance traveled by two interfering light waves

order number

the number assigned to interference fringes with respect to the central bright fringe

Predicting the location of interference fringes

Consider two narrow slits that are separated by a distance d, as shown in **Figure 16-8,** and through which two coherent, monochromatic light waves, l_1 and l_2, pass. If the distance from the slits to the viewing screen is very large compared with the distance between the slits, then l_1 and l_2 are nearly parallel. As a result of this approximation, l_1 and l_2 make the same angle, θ, with the horizontal dotted lines that are perpendicular to the slit separation, d. The angle θ also indicates the position at which the waves combine with respect to the central point of the viewing screen.

The difference in the distance traveled by the two waves is called their **path difference.** Study the right triangle shown in **Figure 16-8,** and note that the path difference is equal to $d \, (\sin \theta)$. The value for the path difference varies with angle θ because the waves travel different distances for each fringe position on the distant viewing screen.

The value of the path difference determines whether the two waves are in or out of phase when they arrive at the viewing screen. If the path difference is either zero or some whole-number multiple of the wavelength, the two waves are in phase, and constructive interference results. The condition for bright fringes (constructive interference) is given by the following equation:

EQUATION FOR CONSTRUCTIVE INTERFERENCE

$$d \, (\sin \theta) = m\lambda \quad m = 0, \pm 1, \pm 2, \ldots$$

the path difference between two waves =
a whole-number multiple of the two waves' wavelength

In this equation, m is the **order number** of the fringe. The central bright fringe at $\theta = 0$ ($m = 0$) is called the *zeroth-order maximum*, or the *central maximum;* the first maximum on either side of the central maximum, which occurs when $m = \pm 1$, is called the *first-order maximum,* and so forth.

Similarly, when the path difference is an odd multiple of $\frac{1}{2}\lambda$, the two waves arriving at the screen are 180° out of phase, giving rise to destructive interference. The condition for dark fringes, or destructive interference, is given by the following equation:

EQUATION FOR DESTRUCTIVE INTERFERENCE

$$d \, (\sin \theta) = (m + \tfrac{1}{2})\lambda \quad m = 0, \pm 1, \pm 2, \ldots$$

the path difference between two waves =
an odd number of half wavelengths

If $m = 0$ in this equation, the path difference is $\frac{1}{2}\lambda$, which is the condition under which the first dark fringe forms on either side of the bright central maximum.

Likewise, if $m = \pm 1$, the path difference is $\frac{3}{2}\lambda$, which is the condition for the second dark fringe on each side of the central maximum, and so forth.

A representation of the interference pattern formed by double-slit interference is shown in **Figure 16-9.** The numbers indicate the two *maxima* (the plural of maximum) that form on either side of the central (zeroth-order) maximum. The darkest areas indicate the positions of the dark fringes, or *minima* (the plural of minimum), that also appear in the pattern.

Because the separation between interference fringes varies for light of different wavelengths, double-slit interference provides a method of measuring the wavelength of light. In fact, this technique was used to make the first measurement of the wavelength of light.

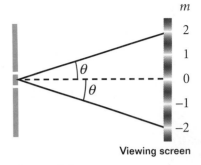

Figure 16-9
The higher-order ($m = \pm 1, \pm 2$) maxima appear on either side of the central maximum ($m = 0$).

Interference

PROBLEM

The distance between the two slits is 0.030 mm. The second-order bright fringe ($m = 2$) is measured on a viewing screen at an angle of 2.15° from the central maximum. Determine the wavelength of the light.

SOLUTION

1. DEFINE   **Given:** $d = 3.0 \times 10^{-5}$ m $m = 2$ $\theta = 2.15°$

   Unknown: $\lambda = ?$

   Diagram:

$d = 0.030$ mm $\theta = 2.15°$

Second-order
bright fringe
($m = 2$)

Zeroth-order
bright fringe
($m = 0$)

Diagram not to scale

2. PLAN   **Choose an equation(s) or situation:** Use the equation for constructive interference.

$$d(\sin \theta) = m\lambda$$

   Rearrange the equation(s) to isolate the unknown(s):

$$\lambda = \frac{d(\sin \theta)}{m}$$

3. CALCULATE   **Substitute the values into the equation(s) and solve:**

$$\lambda = \frac{(3.0 \times 10^{-5} \text{ m})(\sin 2.15°)}{2}$$

$$\lambda = 5.6 \times 10^{-7} \text{ m} = 5.6 \times 10^{2} \text{ nm}$$

$$\boxed{\lambda = 5.6 \times 10^{2} \text{ nm}}$$

CALCULATOR SOLUTION

Because the minimum number of significant figures for the data is two, the calculator answer $5 627366 \times 10^{-7}$ should be rounded to two significant figures.

4. EVALUATE   As indicated by **Table 14-1** on page 521, this light is in the visible spectrum. The wavelength corresponds to light of a yellow-green color.

Interference and Diffraction   **603**

Interference

1. A double-slit interference experiment is performed with blue-green light from an argon-gas laser (lasers will be discussed further in Section 16-3). The separation between the slits is 0.50 mm, and the first-order maximum of the interference pattern is at an angle of 0.059° from the center of the pattern. What is the wavelength of argon laser light?

2. A pair of narrow parallel slits separated by a distance of 0.250 mm are illuminated by the green component from a mercury vapor lamp ($\lambda = 546.1$ nm). Calculate the angle from the central maximum to the first bright fringe on either side of the central maximum.

3. Using the data from item 2, determine the angle between the central maximum and the second dark fringe in the interference pattern.

4. Light with a wavelength of 575 nm falls on a double slit, and the first bright fringe is seen at an angle of 16.5° with respect to the central maximum. Find the distance between the slits.

Section Review

1. What is the necessary condition for a path length difference between two waves that interfere constructively? destructively?

2. If white light is used instead of monochromatic light to demonstrate interference, how does the interference pattern change?

3. If the distance between two slits is 0.0550 mm, find the angle between the first-order and second-order bright fringes for yellow light with a wavelength of 605 nm.

4. Two radio antennas simultaneously transmit identical signals with a wavelength of 3.35 m, as shown in **Figure 16-10.** A radio in a car traveling parallel to and

Figure 16-10

several miles from the antennas receives the signals. If the second maximum is located at an angle of 1.28° north of the central maximum for the interfering signals, what is the distance, d, between the two antennas?

16-2
Diffraction

LIGHT WAVES BEND

If you stand near the corner of a building, you can hear someone who is talking around the corner but you cannot see the person. This is because sound waves are able to bend around the corner. In a similar fashion, water waves bend around obstacles, such as the barrier shown in **Figure 16-11.** Light waves can also bend around obstacles, but because of their short wavelengths, the amount they bend is too small to be easily observed.

If light traveled only in straight lines, you would not be able to observe an interference pattern in the double-slit demonstration. Instead, you would see two thin strips of light where each slit and the source were lined up perfectly. The rest of the screen would be completely dark. The edges of the slits would appear on the screen as sharply defined shadows. But this does not happen. Light bends to reach other parts of the screen.

The bending of light as it passes through each of the two slits can be understood using Huygens' principle, which states that any point on a wave front can be treated as a point source of waves. Because each slit serves as a point source of light, the waves spread out from the slits. The result is that light deviates from a straight-line path and enters the region that would otherwise be shadowed. This divergence of light from its initial line of travel is called **diffraction.**

In general, diffraction occurs when waves pass through small openings, around obstacles, or by sharp edges. For example, when a wide slit (1 mm or more) is placed between a distant light source and a screen, the light produces a bright rectangle with clearly marked edges. But if the slit is narrowed, the

16-2 SECTION OBJECTIVES

- **Describe how light waves diffract around obstacles and produce bright and dark fringes.**

- **Calculate the positions of fringes for a diffraction grating.**

- **Describe how diffraction determines an optical instrument's ability to resolve images.**

diffraction

the spreading of light into a region behind an obstruction

Figure 16-11
A property of all waves is that they bend, or *diffract,* around objects.

Interference and Diffraction   605

d   0.8 d   0.2 d

Figure 16-12
Diffraction becomes more evident
as the width of the slit is narrowed.
(Note: The wavelength of this light
is 510 nm.)

Did you know?

Diffraction patterns disappear in
light passing through a wider slit
because the slit no longer resembles
a point source. The light from broad
sources is responsible for the sharp
shadows produced by obstacles.

light begins to spread out and produce a *diffraction pattern,* like that shown in
Figure 16-12. Like the interference fringes in the double-slit demonstration,
this pattern of light and dark bands arises from the combination of light waves.

Wavelets in a wave front interfere with each other

Diffraction patterns resemble interference patterns because they also result
from constructive and destructive interference. In the case of interference, it is
assumed that the slits behave as point sources of light. For diffraction, the
actual width of a single slit is considered.

According to Huygens' principle, each portion of a slit acts as a source of
waves. Hence, light from one portion of the slit can interfere with light from
another portion. The resultant intensity of the diffracted light on the screen
depends on the angle, θ, that the light is diffracted.

To help you understand the single-slit diffraction pattern, consider **Figure
16-13(a),** which shows an incoming plane wave passing through a slit of
width a. Each point within the slit is a source of Huygens wavelets. To simplify the figure, only five of these sources are shown. As with double-slit interference, the viewing screen is assumed to be so far from the slit that the rays
emerging from the slit are nearly parallel. At the viewing screen's midpoint, all
rays from the slit travel the same distance, so a bright fringe appears.

The wavelets from the five sources can also interfere destructively when
they arrive at the screen, as shown in **Figure 16-13(b).** The wave from source
1 travels the shortest distance to the screen, and the wave from source 5 travels
the farthest. The first dark fringe occurs when the extra distance traveled by
the wave from source 3 is one-half a wavelength. In this case, the wavelets
from sources 1 and 3 are entirely out of phase and interfere destructively upon
reaching the screen. In fact, at this angle, each wavelet from the upper half of
the slit cancels a wavelet that travels one-half wavelength farther from the
lower half, and a dark fringe results.

For angles other than those at which destructive interference completely
occurs, some of the light waves remain uncanceled. At these angles light
appears on the screen as part of a bright band. The brightest band appears in
the pattern's center, while the bands to either side are much dimmer.

Figure 16-13
(a) By treating the light coming
through the slit as a line of point
sources along the slit's width, **(b)**
the conditions at which destructive
interference occurs between the
waves in the upper half of the slit
and the waves in the lower half can
be determined.

Figure 16-14

In a diffraction pattern, the central maximum is twice as wide as the secondary maxima.

Light diffracted by an obstacle also produces a pattern

The diffraction pattern that results from monochromatic light passing through a single slit consists of a broad, intense central band—the *central maximum*—flanked by a series of narrower, less intense secondary bands (called *secondary maxima*) and a series of dark bands, or *minima*. An example of such a pattern is shown in **Figure 16-14.** The points at which maximum constructive interference occurs lie approximately halfway between the dark fringes. Note that the central bright fringe is twice as wide as the next brightest maxima and is about 22 times as bright.

Diffraction occurs around the edges of all objects. **Figure 16-15** shows the diffraction pattern that appears in the shadow of a penny. The pattern consists of the shadow, with a bright spot at its center, and a series of bright and dark bands of light that continue to the shadow's edge. The penny is large compared with the wavelength of the light, and a magnifying glass is required to observe the pattern.

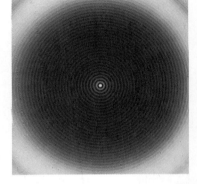

Figure 16-15

A diffraction pattern forms in the penny's shadow when light is diffracted at the penny's edge. Note the bright spot that is formed at the center of the shadow.

DIFFRACTION GRATINGS

You have probably noticed that a compact disc disperses light in streaks of color. This is because the digital information (alternating pits and smooth reflecting surfaces) on the disc forms closely spaced rows. These rows of data do not reflect nearly as much light as the thin portions of the disc that separate them. These areas consist entirely of reflecting material, so light reflected from them undergoes constructive interference in certain directions. This constructive interference depends on the direction of the incoming light, the orientation of the disc, and the light's wavelength. When white light is reflected from the disc, as shown in **Figure 16-16,** each wavelength of light can be seen at a particular angle with respect to the disc's surface, causing you to see a "rainbow" of color.

Figure 16-16

Compact discs disperse light into its component colors in a manner similar to that of a diffraction grating.

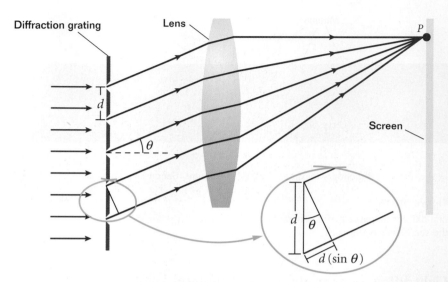

Figure 16-17
Light of a single wavelength passes through each of the slits of a diffraction grating to constructively interfere at a particular angle θ.

This phenomenon has been put to practical use in a device called a *diffraction grating*. A diffraction grating, which can be constructed to either transmit or reflect light, uses diffraction and interference to disperse light into its component colors with an effect similar to that of a glass prism. A transmission type of diffraction grating consists of many equally spaced parallel slits. These can be made by scratching parallel lines on a glass plate with a precision-machining technique. The spaces between the scratches are transparent to the light and hence act as separate slits. A typical grating contains several thousand lines per centimeter.

Figure 16-17 shows a schematic diagram of a section of a diffraction grating. A monochromatic plane wave is incoming from the left, normal to the plane of the grating. The waves that emerge nearly parallel from the grating are brought together at a point P on the screen by the lens. The intensity of the pattern on the screen is the result of the combined effects of interference and diffraction. Each slit produces diffraction, and the diffracted beams in turn interfere with one another to produce the pattern.

For some arbitrary angle, θ, measured from the horizontal, the waves must travel *different* path lengths before reaching point P on the screen. Note that the path difference between waves from any two adjacent slits is $d (\sin \theta)$. If this path difference equals one wavelength or some integral multiple of a wavelength, waves from all slits will be in phase at P, and a bright line will be observed. The condition for bright line formation at angle θ is therefore given by the equation for constructive interference:

$$d (\sin \theta) = m\lambda \qquad m = 0, \pm 1, \pm 2, \ldots$$

This equation can be used to calculate the wavelength of light if you know the grating spacing and the angle of deviation. The integer m is the order number for the bright lines of a given wavelength. If the incident radiation contains several wavelengths, each wavelength deviates by a specific angle, which can be determined from the equation.

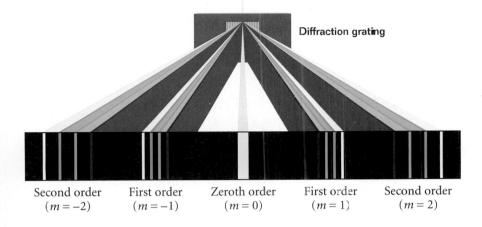

Diffraction grating

| Second order $(m = -2)$ | First order $(m = -1)$ | Zeroth order $(m = 0)$ | First order $(m = 1)$ | Second order $(m = 2)$ |

Figure 16-18
Light is dispersed by a diffraction grating. The angle of deviation for the first-order maximum is smaller for blue light than for yellow light.

Note in **Figure 16-18** that all wavelengths combine at $\theta = 0$, which corresponds to $m = 0$. This is called the *zeroth-order maximum*. The *first-order maximum*, corresponding to $m = \pm 1$, is observed at an angle that satisfies the relationship $\sin \theta = \lambda/d$. The *second-order maximum*, corresponding to $m = \pm 2$, is observed at an angle that satisfies the relationship $\sin \theta = 2\lambda/d$.

The sharpness of the principal maxima and the broad range of the dark areas depend on the number of lines in a grating. The number of lines per unit length in a grating is the inverse of the line separation d. For example, a grating ruled with 5000 lines/cm has a slit spacing, d, equal to the inverse of this number; hence, $d = (1/5000)$ cm $= 2 \times 10^{-4}$ cm. The greater the number of lines per unit length in a grating, the less separation between the lines and the farther spread apart the individual wavelengths of light are.

Diffraction gratings are frequently used in devices called spectrometers, which separate the light from a source into its monochromatic components. A diagram of the basic components of a spectrometer is shown in **Figure 16-19.** The light to be analyzed passes through a slit and is formed into a parallel beam by a lens. The light then passes through the grating. The diffracted light leaves the grating at angles that satisfy the diffraction grating equation. A telescope with a calibrated scale is used to observe the first-order maxima and to measure the angles at which they appear. From these measurements, the wavelengths of the light can be determined and the chemical composition of the light source can be identified. An example of a spectrum produced by a spectrometer is shown in **Figure 16-20.** Spectrometers are used extensively in astronomy to study the chemical compositions and temperatures of stars, interstellar gas clouds, and galaxies.

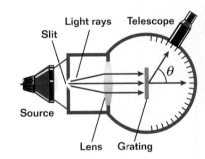

Figure 16-19
The spectrometer uses a grating to disperse the light from a source.

Figure 16-20
The light from mercury vapor is passed through a diffraction grating, producing the spectrum shown.

Diffraction gratings

PROBLEM

Monochromatic light from a helium-neon laser ($\lambda = 632.8$ nm) shines at a right angle to the surface of a diffraction grating that contains 150 500 lines/m. Find the angles at which one would observe the first-order and second-order maxima.

SOLUTION

1. DEFINE

Given:

$$\lambda = 632.8 \text{ nm} = 6.328 \times 10^{-7} \text{ m} \qquad m = 1 \text{ and } 2$$

$$d = \frac{1}{150\ 500\dfrac{\text{lines}}{\text{m}}} = \frac{1}{150\ 500} \text{ m}$$

Unknown: $\theta_1 = ? \qquad \theta_2 = ?$

Diagram:

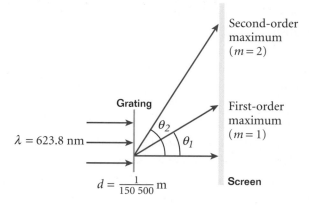

2. PLAN

Choose an equation(s) or situation: Use the equation for a diffraction grating.

$$d\,(\sin\theta) = m\lambda$$

Rearrange the equation(s) to isolate the unknown(s):

$$\theta = \sin^{-1}\left(\frac{m\lambda}{d}\right)$$

3. CALCULATE

Substitute the values into the equation(s) and solve:

For the first-order maximum, $m = 1$:

$$\theta_1 = \sin^{-1}\left(\frac{\lambda}{d}\right) = \sin^{-1}\left(\frac{6.328 \times 10^{-7}\ \cancel{\text{m}}}{\dfrac{1}{150\ 500}\cancel{\text{m}}}\right)$$

$$\boxed{\theta_1 = 5.465°}$$

For $m = 2$:

$$\theta_2 = \sin^{-1}\left(\frac{2\lambda}{d}\right)$$

$$\theta_2 = \sin^{-1}\left|\frac{2(6.328 \times 10^{-7}\ \text{m})}{\dfrac{1}{150\ 500}\ \text{m}}\right|$$

$$\boxed{\theta_2 = 10.98°}$$

4. EVALUATE   The second-order maximum is spread slightly more than twice as far from the center as the first-order maximum. This grating does not have high dispersion, and it can produce spectra up to the tenth order ($\sin \theta = 0.9524$).

PRACTICE 16B

Diffraction gratings

1. A diffraction grating is calibrated by using the 546.1 nm line of mercury vapor. The first-order maximum is found at an angle of 21.2°. Calculate the number of lines per centimeter on this grating.

2. A grating with 1555 lines/cm is illuminated with light of wavelength 565 nm. What is the highest-order number that can be observed with this grating? (Hint: Remember that $\sin \theta$ can never be greater than 1 for a diffraction grating.)

3. Repeat item 2, but for a diffraction grating with 15 550 lines/cm.

4. A diffraction grating with 2.500×10^3 lines/cm is used to examine the sodium spectrum. Calculate the angular separation of the two closely spaced yellow lines of sodium (588.995 nm and 589.592 nm) in each of the first three orders.

5. A diffraction grating with 4525 lines/cm is illuminated by sunlight. The first-order solar spectrum is spread out on a white wall opposite the grating. At what angle does the first-order maximum for blue light with a wavelength of 422 nm appear? At what angle does the first-order maximum for red light with a wavelength of 655 nm appear?

6. A diffraction grating has 1950 lines/cm. The angle between the first-order maximum and the zeroth-order maximum for monochromatic light is 27°. What is the wavelength of the light?

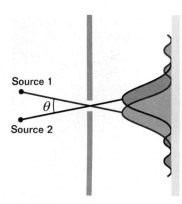

Figure 16-21
Each of two distant point sources produces a diffraction pattern.

resolving power

the ability of an optical instrument to separate two images that are close together

DIFFRACTION AND INSTRUMENT RESOLUTION

The ability of an optical system, such as a microscope or a telescope, to distinguish between closely spaced objects is limited by the wave nature of light. To understand this limitation, consider **Figure 16-21,** which shows two light sources far from a narrow slit. The sources can be taken as two point sources that are not coherent. For example, they could be two distant stars that appear close to each other in the night sky.

If no diffraction occurred, you would observe two distinct bright spots (or images) on the screen at the far right. However, because of diffraction, each source is shown to have a bright central region flanked by weaker bright and dark rings. What is observed on the screen is the resultant from the superposition of two diffraction patterns, one from each source.

Resolution depends on wavelength and aperture width

If the two sources are separated so that their central maxima do not overlap, as in **Figure 16-22,** their images can just be distinguished, and are said to be barely *resolved.* The angle between the resolved objects should be as small as possible for high resolution, or **resolving power.** The shorter the wavelength of the incoming light or the wider the opening, or *aperture,* through which the light passes, the smaller the angle of resolution, θ, will be and the greater the resolving power will be. For visible-light telescopes, the aperture width, D, is approximately equal to the diameter of the mirror or lens. The equation to determine the limiting angle of resolution in radians for an optical instrument with a circular aperture is as follows:

$$\theta = 1.22\frac{\lambda}{D}$$

The constant 1.22 comes from the derivation of the equation for circular apertures and is absent for square apertures. The equation indicates that for light with a short wavelength, such as an X ray, a small aperture is sufficient for high resolution. On the other hand, if the wavelength of the light is long, as in the case of a radio wave, the aperture must be large in order to resolve distant objects. This explains why radio telescopes have large dishlike antennas.

Yet even with their large sizes, radio telescopes cannot resolve sources as easily as visible-light telescopes. At the shortest radio wavelength (1 mm),

Figure 16-22
Two point sources are barely resolved if the central maxima of their diffraction patterns do not overlap.

the largest single antenna for a radio telescope—the 305 m dish at Arecibo, Puerto Rico—has a resolution angle of 4×10^{-6} rad. The same resolution angle can be obtained for the longest visible light waves (700 nm) by an optical telescope with a 21 cm mirror. A Cassegrain reflector telescope with a mirror of this size can easily fit in the trunk of a car. By contrast, the radio dish at Arecibo is built into the top of a mountain.

To compensate for the poor resolution due to radio waves being 10 000 times longer than visible light, several radio telescopes can be combined to function like a much larger telescope. An example of this is shown in **Figure 16-23.** By arranging the radio antennas in a line and using computers to process the signals that each receives, the resolution of the radio "images" obtained is the same as would be achieved if the radio telescope had a diameter of several kilometers.

It should be noted that the resolving power for optical telescopes on Earth is limited by the constantly moving layers of air in the atmosphere, which blur the light from objects in space. The images from the Hubble Space Telescope are of superior quality largely because the telescope operates in the vacuum of space. Under these conditions, the actual resolving power of the telescope is close to the telescope's theoretical resolving power.

Figure 16-23

The 27 antennas at the Very Large Array in New Mexico are used together to provide improved resolution for observing distant radio sources. The antennas can be arranged to have the resolving power of a 36 km wide radio telescope.

Section Review

1. A point source of light is inside a container that is opaque except for a single hole. Discuss what happens to the image of the point source projected onto a screen as the hole's diameter is reduced.

2. Describe the change in width of the central maximum of the single-slit diffraction pattern as the width of the slit is made smaller.

3. Which object would produce the most visible diffraction pattern, an apple, a pencil lead, or a human hair? Explain your answer.

4. Would orange light or blue light produce a wider diffraction pattern? Why is this the case?

5. Light passes through a diffraction grating with 3550 lines/cm and forms a first-order maximum at an angle of 12.07°.
   a. What is the wavelength of the light?
   b. At what angle will the second maximum appear?

6. Would it be easier to resolve nearby objects if you detected them using ultraviolet radiation rather than visible light? Why?

16-3
Coherence

laser

a device that produces an intense, nearly parallel beam of coherent light

LASERS AND COHERENCE

In the previous two chapters, light has been treated as electromagnetic radiation that is produced by a glowing, or *incandescent,* source, such as a light bulb, a candle flame, or the sun. These are familiar sources of light, but there is another form of light that has become common and yet has very different characteristics from the light produced by any of the sources mentioned. This other kind of light is produced by a device called a **laser.**

To understand what makes laser light different from conventional light, consider the properties of light from an incandescent light bulb, as shown in **Figure 16-24.** Variations in the structure of the filament and in the flow of electric charges through the filament cause individual electromagnetic waves to be emitted at different intensities from different parts of the filament at different times and in different directions. Typically, this light is noncoherent, so its component waves are not in phase at all points in space and time. The light also covers a large range of the electromagnetic spectrum. The wave fronts of noncoherent light are like the wave fronts that result when rain falls on the surface of a pond. No two wave fronts are caused by the same event, and they are therefore not in phase.

Lasers, on the other hand, typically produce a narrow beam of coherent light. The waves emitted by a laser do not shift relative to each other as time progresses. The individual waves effectively behave like a single wave. The fact that these light waves are coherent also means that they must have the same wavelength. As a result of these properties, laser light's intensity can be made much greater than that of noncoherent light.

Coherent light

Noncoherent light

Figure 16-24

Waves in noncoherent light have different directions, phases, and wavelengths, unlike waves in coherent light.

Lasers transform energy into coherent light

A laser is a device that converts light, electrical energy, or chemical energy into coherent light. There are a variety of different types of lasers, but they all have some common features. They all use a substance, called the *active medium*, to which energy can be added.

The basic operation of a laser is shown in **Figure 16-25.** When high-energy light or electrical or chemical energy is added to the active medium, as in **Figure 16-25(a),** the atoms in the active medium absorb some of the energy. The atoms later release the energy in the form of light waves that have the same wavelength and phase.

After one atom spontaneously releases its energy in the form of a light wave, this initial wave can cause other energized atoms to release their excess energy in the form of a light wave with the same wavelength, phase, and direction as the initial light wave, as shown in **Figure 16-25(b).** This process of using a light wave to produce more waves with properties identical to those of the first wave is called *stimulated emission.*

While some of the light produced by stimulated emission passes through the sides of the active medium, other light waves move along the length of the active medium. Mirrors on the ends of the material return these coherent light waves into the active medium, where they stimulate the emission of more coherent light waves, as shown in **Figure 16-25(c).** One of these mirrors is slightly transparent, so some of the coherent light is emitted by the laser.

CONCEPT PREVIEW

The absorption and emission of light by atoms will be discussed in greater detail in Chapter 23.

(a)

Atoms or molecules with added energy

Mirror   Active medium   Energy input   Mirror (partially transparent)

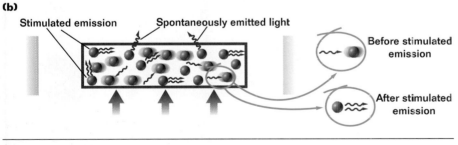

(b)

Stimulated emission   Spontaneously emitted light

Before stimulated emission

After stimulated emission

(c)

Coherent light output of laser

Figure 16-25
(a) Atoms or molecules in the active medium of a laser store energy from an external source.
(b) When a spontaneously emitted light wave interacts with an atom, it may cause the atom to emit an identical light wave. **(c)** Stimulated emission increases the amount of coherent light in the active medium, and the coherent waves behave as a single wave.

Consumer Focus *Holograms*

*O*nce considered a modern miracle, holograms are now so commonplace that these three-dimensional images can be found practically everywhere, from credit cards to magazine covers to postage stamps. But how can such three-dimensional images be made from just a laser, some mirrors, and film?

Holography, the technique for making holograms, makes use of the fact that all the light leaving a laser is in phase. One way to make a hologram is to begin by splitting the laser beam with a mirror or prism. Half of the laser beam, called the reference beam, is directed by mirrors toward a light-sensitive film. The other half of the laser beam is reflected off the object toward the film.

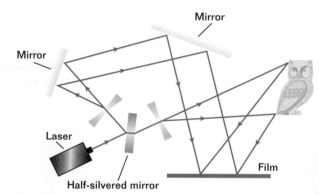

Because these two halves of the laser beam have not traveled the same distance, they are no longer in phase when they meet at the film. The degree to which they are out of phase at any spot on the film depends on the shape of the object. As a result of the phase difference, the two beams interfere with each other, producing what appears to be a pattern of dots and spirals on the film.

Once developed, the film acts like a diffraction grating. When a laser is shined onto the hologram from the same direction as the reference beam, the laser light interacts with the patterns on the film, changing the direction of the light waves in this beam. When viewed from the side of the film opposite the laser, the waves appear to come from the original illuminated object. The resulting three-dimensional image is a virtual image that appears to hang in the air on the same side of the film as the laser. A real image is also produced. This image appears on the same side as the observer and appears inverted, like a reflection from a concave mirror.

Several varieties of holograms exist. The type just described, *transmission* holograms, are illuminated from behind. They can also be illuminated with white light, such as sunlight, but this often creates rainbow-like bands of color across the image. This occurs because each wavelength of light is diffracted a different amount by the film. *Reflection* holograms are lighted from the front and can be viewed with white light. *Embossed* holograms are similar to reflection holograms in that they are lighted from the front with white light; however, they are simply transmission holograms that are backed by a mirror. Embossed holograms are a low-cost alternative to reflection holograms. Finally, *pulsed* holograms use short bursts of light from high-powered lasers to make holograms of moving objects. With this technique, holograms can be made of people, scenes, and very large objects, and the short exposure time allows holographers to create a series of three-dimensional holograms of objects in motion.

APPLICATIONS OF LASERS

Of the properties of laser light, the one that is most evident is that it emerges from the laser as a narrow beam. Unlike the light from a light bulb or even the light that is focused by a parabolic reflector, the light from a laser undergoes very little spreading with distance. This allows it to be pointed at distant reflectors and detected again. Because laser light is still narrow and bright after traveling long distances, it is used by surveyors to measure distances and to guarantee that segments of bridges and tunnels are in line.

As shown in **Figure 16-26,** astronomers direct laser light at particular points of the moon's surface to determine the Earth-to-moon distance. A pulse of light is directed toward one of several 0.25 m^2 reflectors that were placed on the moon's surface by astronauts during the *Apollo* missions. By measuring the time the light takes to travel to the moon and back, the Earth-to-moon distance (3.84×10^5 km) can be measured. Repeated measurements are used to record changes of just a few centimeters in the height of the Earth's crust that are due to geological processes.

Lasers improve information storage and retrieval

A recent application of the laser is the compact-disc (CD) player. A CD player contains the mechanism depicted in **Figure 16-27.** Light from a laser passes through a glass plate and is then redirected by a mirror through a lens toward the compact disc, on which the music has been *digitally recorded.*

In digital recording, a sound signal is sampled at regular intervals of time. Each sampling is converted to an electrical signal, which in turn is converted into a series of binary numbers (numbers consisting only of zeros and ones). The binary numbers contain information about the signal in a sample, including the frequencies and harmonics that are present, the volume for the left and right channels, and the speed of the motor that rotates the disc. Altogether, 44 000 samples of 16-digit (or 16-*bit*) binary numbers are taken each second.

Figure 16-26
A laser beam is fired at reflectors on the moon, which is more than 380 000 km away.

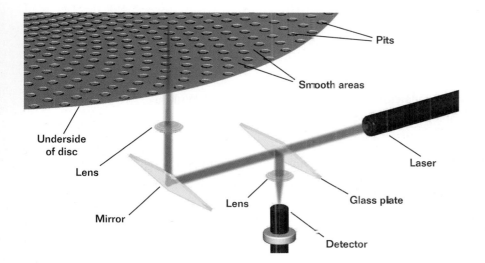

Pits

Smooth areas

Underside of disc

Lens

Mirror

Lens

Glass plate

Laser

Detector

Figure 16-27
Light from a laser is directed toward the surface of the compact disc. Smooth parts of the disc reflect the light back to the detector.

This sequence of binary numbers is recorded by a laser, which encodes the binary sequence by either burning a tiny pit into the disc or passing over a spot, leaving the disc's surface at that point smooth and reflecting.

When a compact disc is played, the laser light in the CD player is reflected sequentially from the string of binary bits etched on the disc. When the light is reflected from one of the smooth places on the disc, it reaches the detector. When the light strikes a pit on the rotating disc, it reflects in some random direction away from the detector. For each bit of data sampled, a change between returned and deflected light is interpreted as a binary 1. No change in the light signal is interpreted as a binary 0. Electronic circuits connected to the detector translate the binary data to an electrical signal, which is then amplified so that it drives the stereo unit's loudspeakers. The resulting sound is a reconstruction of the original recorded sound.

Lasers are widely used in medical procedures

Many of the medical applications of laser light make use of the tendency of certain substances to absorb light of different wavelengths. For instance, *glaucoma* is a condition in which the fluid pressure within the eye is too great. Left untreated, glaucoma can lead to damage of the optic nerve and eventual blindness. By focusing a laser at the clogged membrane, a tiny hole can be burned in it, relieving the pressure.

Water can be vaporized by high-intensity infrared light of a wavelength equal to 10 μm. Such light is produced by carbon dioxide lasers. By heating and vaporizing the water within muscle tissue cells, a laser that uses only 100 W of power can cut through the tissue like a knife. Unlike a knife, however, the energy from the laser also coagulates blood in the newly opened blood vessels, thus sealing them. The "laser knife" therefore can be used as accurately as a steel scalpel but without the resulting blood loss or risk of infection.

Section Review

1. How does light from a laser differ from light whose waves all have the same wavelength but are not in phase?

2. The process of stimulated emission involves producing a second wave that is identical to the first. Does this gaining of a second wave violate the principle of energy conservation? Explain your answer.

3. Fiber-optics systems transmit light by means of internal reflection within thin strands of extremely pure glass. In these fiber-optics systems, laser light is used instead of white light to transmit the signal. Apply your knowledge of refraction to explain why this is.

CHAPTER 16
Summary

KEY IDEAS

Section 16-1 Interference

- Light waves with the same wavelength and constant phase differences interfere with each other to produce light and dark interference patterns.
- In double-slit interference, the position of a bright fringe requires the path difference between two interfering point sources to equal a whole number of wavelengths.

$$d \, (\sin \theta) = m\lambda \quad m = 0, \pm1, \pm2, \ldots$$

- In double-slit interference, the position of a dark fringe requires the path difference between two interfering point sources to equal an odd number of half-wavelengths.

$$d \, (\sin \theta) = \left(m + \tfrac{1}{2}\right)\lambda \quad m = 0, \pm1, \pm2, \ldots$$

Section 16-2 Diffraction

- Light waves form a diffraction pattern by passing around an obstacle or bending through a slit and interfering with each other.
- The position of a maximum in a pattern created by a diffraction grating depends on the separation of the slits in the grating, the order of the maximum, and the wavelength of the light.

$$d \, (\sin \theta) = m\lambda \quad m = 0, \pm1, \pm2, \ldots$$

Section 16-3 Coherence

- A laser is a device that transforms energy into a beam of coherent monochromatic light.

KEY TERMS

coherence (p. 599)

diffraction (p. 605)

laser (p. 614)

order number (p. 602)

path difference (p. 602)

resolving power (p. 612)

Variable symbols

Quantities		Units	
λ	wavelength	m	meters
θ	angle from the center of an interference pattern	°	degrees
d	slit separation	m	meters
m	order number		(unitless)

CHAPTER 16
Review and Assess

INTERFERENCE

Review questions

1. What happens if two light waves with the same amplitude interfere constructively? What happens if they interfere destructively?

2. If one slit of a double-slit experiment is covered, how will the intensity of the maxima and minima change? Why? (Assume no diffraction occurs.)

3. A double-slit interference experiment is performed with red light and then again with blue light. In what ways do the two interference patterns differ? (Hint: Consider the difference in wavelength for the two colors of light.)

4. What data would you need to collect to correctly calculate the wavelength of light in a double-slit interference experiment?

Conceptual questions

5. If a double-slit experiment were performed underwater, how would the observed interference pattern be affected? (Hint: Consider how light changes in a medium with a higher index of refraction.)

6. Because of their great distance from us, stars are essentially point sources of light. If two stars were near each other in the sky, would the light from them produce an interference pattern? Explain your answer.

7. Assume that white light is provided by a single source in a double-slit experiment. Describe the pattern on the screen if one slit is covered with a red filter and the other slit is covered with a blue filter.

8. An interference pattern is formed by using green light and an apparatus in which the two slits can move. If the slits are moved farther apart, will the separation of the bright fringes in the pattern decrease, increase, or remain unchanged? Why?

Practice problems

9. A sodium-vapor street lamp produces light that is nearly monochromatic. If the light shines on a wooden door in which there are two straight, parallel cracks, an interference pattern will form on a distant wall behind the door. The slits have a separation of 0.3096 mm, and the second-order maximum occurs at an angle of 0.218° from the central maximum. Determine the following quantities:
    a. the wavelength of the light
    b. the angle of the third-order maximum
    c. the angle of the fourth-order minimum
(See Sample Problem 16A.)

10. Light of wavelength 460 nm falls on two slits spaced 0.33 mm apart. What is the angle between the first and second dark fringes?
(See Sample Problem 16A.)

11. A double-slit interference experiment is performed using blue light from a hydrogen discharge tube ($\lambda = 486$ nm). The fifth-order bright fringe in the interference pattern is 0.578° from the central maximum. How far apart are the two slits separated?
(See Sample Problem 16A.)

12. All but two gaps within a set of venetian blinds have been blocked off to create a double-slit system. These gaps are separated by a distance of 3.2 cm. Infrared radiation with a wavelength of 155 μm is then passed through the two gaps in the blinds. What is the angle between the central and the second-order maxima in the interference pattern?
(See Sample Problem 16A.)

DIFFRACTION

Review questions

13. Why does light produce a pattern similar to an interference pattern when it passes through a single slit?

14. How does the width of the central region of a single-slit diffraction pattern change as the wavelength of the light increases?

15. Why is white light separated into a whole spectrum of colors when it is passed through a diffraction grating?

16. Why are orbiting telescopes designed for use in all of the electromagnetic spectrum except for radio?

Conceptual questions

17. Monochromatic light shines through two different diffraction gratings. The second grating produces a pattern in which the first-order and second-order maxima are more widely spread apart. Use this information to tell if there are more or fewer lines per centimeter in the second grating than in the first.

18. Why is the resolving power of your eye better at night than during the day?

19. Globular clusters, such as the one shown in **Figure 16-28,** are spherical groupings of stars that orbit the Milky Way galaxy. Because there are several thousand stars in a single cluster and because they are distant, resolving individual stars within the cluster is a challenge. Of the following conditions, which would make it easier to resolve the component stars? Which would make it more difficult?

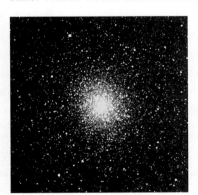

Figure 16-28

a. The number of stars per unit volume is half as great.
b. The cluster is twice as far away.
c. The cluster is observed in the ultraviolet portion instead of in the visible region of the electromagnetic spectrum.
d. The telescope's mirror or lens is twice as wide.

Practice problems

20. By attaching a diffraction-grating spectroscope to an astronomical telescope, the spectral lines from a star can be measured and the star's chemical composition can be determined. Assume the grating has 3661 slits/cm.
    a. If three first-order spectral lines occur at angles of 10.09°, 13.71°, and 14.77°, what are the wavelengths of the star's light?
    b. At what angles are these lines found in the second-order spectrum?
(See Sample Problem 16B.)

21. Visible light from an incandescent light bulb ranges from 400.0 nm to 700.0 nm. When this light is focused on a diffraction grating, the entire first-order spectrum is seen, but none of the second-order spectrum is seen. What is the maximum spacing between lines on this grating?
(See Sample Problem 16B.)

22. Light containing two different wavelengths passes through a diffraction grating with 795 slits/cm. The second-order maximum of the shorter wavelength and the first-order maximum of the longer wavelength are at the same angle, 3.22°, from the central maximum. What are the values for the two wavelengths?
(See Sample Problem 16B.)

COHERENCE

Review questions

23. What properties does laser light have that are not found in the light used to light your home?

24. Laser light is commonly used to demonstrate double-slit interference. Explain why laser light is preferable to light from other sources for observing interference.

25. Give two examples in which the uniform direction of laser light is advantageous. Give two examples in which the high intensity of laser light is advantageous.

26. Laser light is often linearly polarized. How would you show this to be true?

MIXED REVIEW PROBLEMS

27. A beam containing light of wavelengths λ_1 and λ_2 passes through a set of parallel slits. In the interference pattern, the fourth bright line of the λ_1 light occurs at the same position as the fifth bright line of the λ_2 light. If λ_1 is known to be 540.0 nm, what is the value of λ_2?

28. The 546.1 nm line in mercury is measured at an angle of 81.0° in the third-order spectrum of a diffraction grating. Calculate the number of lines per millimeter for the grating.

29. In an arrangement to demonstrate double-slit interference, $\lambda = 643$ nm, $\theta = 0.737°$, and $d = 0.150$ mm. For light from the two slits interfering at this angle, what is the path difference both in millimeters and in terms of the number of wavelengths? Will the interference correspond to a maximum, a minimum, or an intermediate condition?

30. Recall from Section 11-4 (pages 425–429) that the entropy of a system is a measure of that system's disorder. Why is it appropriate to describe a laser as an entropy-reducing device?

Alternative Assessment

Performance assessment

1. Design simulations of interference patterns. Use a computer to draw many concentric circles at regular distances to represent waves traveling from a point source. Photocopy the page onto two transparencies, and lay them on an overhead projector. Vary the distances between "source points," and observe how these variations affect interference patterns. Design transparencies with thicker lines with larger separations to explore the effect of wavelength on interference.

2. Investigate the effect of slit separation on interference patterns. Wrap a flashlight or a pen light tightly with tin foil and make pinholes in the foil. First record the pattern you see on a screen a few inches away with one hole, then do the same with two holes. How does the distance between the holes affect the distance between the bright parts of the pattern? Draw schematic diagrams of your observations, and compare them with the results of double-slit interference. How would you improve your equipment?

3. Soap bubbles exhibit different colors because light that is reflected from the outer layer of the soap film interferes with light that is refracted and then reflected from the inner layer of the soap film. Given a refractive index of $n = 1.35$ and thicknesses ranging from 600 nm to 1000 nm for a soap film, can you predict the colors of a bubble? Test your answer by making soap bubbles and observing the order in which the different colors appear. Can you tell the thickness of a soap bubble from its colors? Organize your findings into a chart, or create a computer program to predict the thickness of a bubble based on the wavelength of light it appears to reflect.

Portfolio projects

4. Thomas Young's 1803 experiment provided crucial evidence for the wave nature of light, but it was met with strong opposition in England until Augustin Fresnel presented his wave theory of light to the French Academy of Sciences in 1819. Research the lives and careers of these two scientists. Create a presentation about one of them. The presentation can be in the form of a report, poster, short video, or computer presentation.

5. Research waves that surround you, and learn their characteristics. What kind of waves travel between the base and the receiver of your cordless phone? between a radio station and your radio? between the radio and you? What is their wavelength? Draw a diagram showing how each type of wave might travel through a doorway. Are the waves diffracted? How can you tell? What properties make the diffraction of sound more evident in daily experience than the diffraction of light? Write a report citing your sources of information and reasoning.

Technology & Learning

Graphing calculators

Program your graphing calculator to build a table for identifying the separations on a screen due to double-slit interference between the first three bright fringes, given the following situations:

a. a yellow light of 589 nm that passes through two slits 2.00 mm apart and strikes a screen

b. a green light of 546 nm that passes through two slits 2.00 mm apart and strikes a screen

c. a violet light of 437 nm that passes through two slits 3.50 mm apart and strikes a screen

d. a red light of 660 nm that passes through two slits 3.50 mm apart and strikes a screen

Press Y= and CLEAR to clear any functions. Press MODE ▼ ▼ ► ENTER to be certain the calculator is in degree mode.

Open a new program by pressing PRGM ► ► ENTER. Name the program "INTERFER" and press ENTER. Then enter the program shown in the table below.

To exit the program editor, press 2nd QUIT. To run the program, press PRGM, select "INTERFER," and press ENTER ENTER. Enter the values for the wavelength and the slit separation, pressing ENTER after each one. (Remember to use 2nd EE to enter exponents and the (-) key to indicate negative exponents.)

The calculator will provide a table of fringe angles in degrees (Y1) versus order numbers (X). Move the cursor down the table to find the values you need. Remember that only the first few fringes will be bright enough to be visible. Press ENTER only when you are ready to end the program. Press ENTER again to run the program for a different set of data.

Keystrokes	Display
	PROGRAM: INTERFER
1. PRGM ► 3 2nd A-LOCK " L A M B D A 2nd TEST 1 ALPHA " ENTER	:DISP "LAMBDA="
2. PRGM ► 1 ALPHA W ENTER	:INPUT W
3. PRGM ► 3 2nd A-LOCK " S L I T 2nd TEST 1 ALPHA " ENTER	:DISP "SLIT="
4. PRGM ► 1 ALPHA D ENTER	:INPUT D
5. ALPHA " 2nd SIN⁻¹ (X,T,θ ALPHA W ÷ ALPHA D) ALPHA " STO► 2nd Y-VARS 1 1 ENTER	:"$\sin^{-1}(XW/D)$" $\rightarrow$ Y1
6. 1 STO► VARS 6 1 ENTER	:1 $\rightarrow$ TBLMIN
7. 1 STO► VARS 6 2 ENTER	:1 $\rightarrow$ ΔTBL
8. PRGM ► 5 ENTER	:DISPTABLE

CHAPTER 16
Laboratory Exercise

OBJECTIVES

• Find wavelengths of diffracted light.

MATERIALS LIST

✔ bent paper-clip riders for meterstick
✔ black cardboard
✔ cellophane tape
✔ diffraction grating
✔ grating holder and support
✔ incandescent light source and power supply
✔ meterstick and 2 supports
✔ metric scale and slit

DIFFRACTION

In this experiment, you will pass white light through a diffraction grating and use your measurement to determine wavelengths of the light's components.

SAFETY

• Use a hot mitt to handle resistors, light sources, and other equipment that may be hot. Allow all equipment to cool before storing it.

• If a bulb breaks, notify your teacher immediately. Do not remove broken bulbs from sockets.

• Never put broken glass or ceramics in a regular waste container. Use a dustpan, brush, and heavy gloves to carefully pick up broken pieces and dispose of them in a container specifically provided for this purpose.

• Avoid looking directly at a light source. Looking directly at a light source can cause permanent eye damage.

PREPARATION

1. Read the entire lab, and plan the steps you will take.

2. Prepare a data table in your lab notebook with six columns and four rows. In the first row, label the columns *Light source, Image color, Order, Image 1 (m), Image 2 (m),* and *Slit (m).* In the first column, label the second through fourth rows *White.* Above or below the data table, prepare a space to record the slit spacing, *d,* of the grating.

PROCEDURE

Wavelengths of white light

3. Set up the optical bench as shown in **Figure 16-29.** Mount the scale and slit on one end of the optical bench, and place a piece of tape over the slit. Place a cardboard shield around the light source to direct all the light through the slit. Illuminate the slit with white light. Mount the grating near the opposite end of the optical bench.

4. Adjust the apparatus so that the white-light source is centered on the slit and the slit scale is perpendicular to the optical bench. Tape the optical bench and the white-light source securely in place.

5. With your eye close to the grating, observe the first-order spectra. Move the grating forward or backward as required so that the entire spectrum appears on each side of the scale. Place a bent paper-clip rider on the scale at the point in each first-order spectrum where the yellow light is the purest. Adjust the grating and slit scale by rotating the grating around its vertical axis so that the two yellow points end up equidistant from the slit. Reposition the riders if necessary.

Figure 16-29

Step 3: Use the cardboard to make a shield around the light source. Make sure the light is directed through the slit.

6. Use the scale to measure the distance from the slit to each rider. Record these distances in your data table as *Image 1* and *Image 2*. Also measure the distance from the slit to the grating. Record this distance in your data table as the *Slit (m)*. Record the order number and the image color.

Step 4: From above, the slit scale should form right angles with the meterstick. Measurements can be strongly affected if the equipment is moved even slightly during the procedure.

7. Adjust the grating and slit to find the clearest first-order continuous spectrum. Measure and record the distance from the slit to the grating. Place a rider on the scale at the point in each first-order spectrum where you see the extreme end of the violet spectrum. Measure and record the distance from the slit to each rider.

Step 5: Place a bent-paperclip rider to mark the position of the images on the scale.

8. Repeat step 7 for the extreme red end of the spectrum. Record all data in your data table.

ANALYSIS AND INTERPRETATION

Calculations and data analysis

1. **Organizing data**   Use your data for each trial.

   a. For each trial, find the average image position.

   b. Use the average image position and the distance from the slit to the grating to find the distance from the grating to the image for each trial. (*Hint:* use the Pythagorean theorem.)

   c. To find $\sin\theta$ for each trial, divide the average image position by the distance found in (b).

Conclusions

2. **Organizing information**   For each trial, find the wavelength of the light using the equation $\lambda = \dfrac{d\,(\sin\theta)}{m}$, where λ is the wavelength of light (m), d is the diffraction-grating spacing (1/[number of lines/m]), and m is the order number of the spectrum containing the image.

CHAPTER 1

Electric Forces and Fields

PHYSICS IN ACTION

In this factory in Bowling Green, Kentucky, a fresh coat of paint is being applied to an automobile by spray guns. With ordinary spray guns, any paint that does not happen to hit the body of the car is wasted. A special type of spray painting, known as *electrostatic spray painting*, utilizes electric force to minimize the amount of paint that is wasted. Electrostatic spray painting is used in a variety of industries. According to one estimate, electrostatic spray painting saves industries in the United States up to $50 million each year.

In this chapter, you will study electric force and its effects and see how this force is used in electrostatic spray painting.

- *How does an electrostatic spray gun work?*
- *Why are electrostatic spray guns more efficient than typical spray guns?*

CONCEPT REVIEW

Vector addition (Section 3-2)

Field forces (Section 4-1)

17-1
Electric charge

17-1 SECTION OBJECTIVES

- **Understand the basic properties of electric charge.**

- **Differentiate between conductors and insulators.**

- **Distinguish between charging by contact, charging by induction, and charging by polarization.**

CONCEPT PREVIEW

This chapter and Chapter 18 are concerned with stationary charges, known as static electricity or *electrostatics*. Chapters 19 and 20 discuss charges in motion, or *electrodynamics*.

PROPERTIES OF ELECTRIC CHARGE

You have probably noticed that after running a plastic comb through your hair on a dry day, the comb attracts strands of your hair or small pieces of paper. Another simple experiment is to rub an inflated balloon back and forth across your hair. You may find that the balloon is attracted to your hair, as shown in **Figure 17-1(a).** On a dry day, a rubbed balloon will stick to the wall of a room, often for hours. When materials behave this way, they are said to have become *electrically charged.* Experiments such as these work best on a dry day because excessive moisture can provide a pathway for charge to leak off a charged object.

You can give your body an electric charge by vigorously rubbing your shoes on a wool rug or by sliding across a car seat. You can then remove the charge on your body by lightly touching another person. Under the right conditions, you will see a spark when you touch, and both of you will feel a slight tingle.

Another way to observe static electricity is to rub two balloons across your hair and then hold them near one another, as shown in **Figure 17-1(b).** In this case, you will see the two balloons pushing each other apart. Why is a rubbed balloon attracted to your hair but repelled by another rubbed balloon?

There are two kinds of electric charge

The two balloons must have the same kind of charge because each became charged in the same way. Because the two charged balloons repel one another, we see that *like charges repel.* Conversely, a rubbed balloon and your hair, which do not have the same kind of charge, are attracted to one another. Thus, *unlike charges attract.*

(a)

(b)

Figure 17-1

(a) If you rub a balloon across your hair on a dry day, the balloon and your hair become charged and are attracted to one another. **(b)** Two charged balloons, on the other hand, repel one another.

Benjamin Franklin (1706–1790) named the two different kinds of charge *positive* and *negative*. By convention, when you rub a balloon across your hair, the charge on your hair is *positive* and that on the balloon is *negative,* as shown in **Figure 17-2.** Positive and negative charges are said to be *opposite* because an object with an equal amount of positive and negative charge has no net charge.

Electrostatic spray painting utilizes the principle of attraction between unlike charges. Paint droplets are given a negative charge, and the object to be painted is given a positive charge. In ordinary spray painting, many paint droplets drift past the object being painted. But in electrostatic spray painting, the negatively charged paint droplets are attracted to the positively charged target object, so more of the paint droplets hit the object being painted and less paint is wasted.

Electric charge is conserved

When you rub a balloon across your hair, how do the balloon and your hair become electrically charged? To answer this question, you'll need to know a little about the atoms that make up the matter you see around you. Every atom contains even smaller particles. Positively charged particles, called *protons,* and neutral particles, called *neutrons,* are located in the center of the atom, called the *nucleus.* Negatively charged particles, known as *electrons,* are located outside the nucleus and move around it. (You will study the structure of the atom and the particles within the atom in greater detail in Chapters 23 and 25, respectively.)

Protons and neutrons are relatively fixed in the nucleus of the atom, but electrons are easily transferred from one atom to another. When the electrons in an atom are balanced by an equal number of protons, the atom has no net charge. If an electron is transferred from one neutral atom to another, one of the atoms gains a negative charge and the other loses a negative charge, thereby becoming positive. Atoms that are positively or negatively charged are called *ions.*

Both a balloon and your hair contain a very large number of neutral atoms. Charge has a natural tendency to be transferred between unlike materials. Rubbing the two materials together serves to increase the area of contact and thus enhance the charge-transfer process. When a balloon is rubbed against your hair, some of your hair's electrons are transferred to the balloon. Thus, the balloon gains a certain amount of negative charge while your hair loses an equal amount of negative charge and hence is left with a positive charge. In this and similar experiments, only a small portion of the total available charge is transferred from one object to another.

The positive charge on your hair can be shown to be equal in magnitude to the negative charge on the balloon. This means that electric charge is conserved in this process; no charge is created or destroyed. This principle of conservation of charge is one of the fundamental laws of nature.

(a)

(b)

Figure 17-2

(a) This negatively charged balloon is attracted to positively charged hair because the two have opposite charges. **(b)** Two negatively charged balloons repel one another because they have the same charge.

Electric charge is quantized

In 1909, Robert Millikan (1886–1953) performed an experiment at the University of Chicago in which he observed the motion of tiny oil droplets between two parallel metal plates, as shown in **Figure 17-3.** The oil droplets were charged by friction in an atomizer and allowed to pass through a hole in the top plate. Initially the droplets fell due to their weight. The top plate was given a positive charge as the droplets fell, and the droplets with a negative charge were attracted back upward toward the positively charged plate. By turning the charge on this plate on and off, Millikan was able to watch a single oil droplet for many hours as it alternately rose and fell.

Figure 17-3

This is a schematic view of the apparatus used by Millikan in his oil-drop experiment. In this experiment, Millikan found that there is a fundamental unit of charge.

After repeating this process for thousands of drops, Millikan found that when an object is charged, its charge is always a multiple of a fundamental unit of charge, symbolized by the letter e. In modern terms, charge is said to be *quantized*. This means that charge occurs as discrete amounts in nature. Thus, an object may have a charge of $\pm e$, or $\pm 2e$, or $\pm 3e$, and so on.

Other experiments in Millikan's time demonstrated that the electron has a charge of $-e$ and the proton has an equal and opposite charge, $+e$. The value of e has since been determined to be $1.602\ 19 \times 10^{-19}$ C, where the coulomb (C) is the SI unit of electric charge. For calculations, this book will use the approximate value given in **Table 17-1.** A total charge of -1.0 C contains 6.2×10^{18} electrons ($1/e$). Comparing this with the number of free electrons in 1 cm^3 of copper, which is on the order of 10^{23}, shows that 1.0 C is a substantial amount of charge.

CONCEPT PREVIEW

Certain experiments have suggested the existence of fundamental particles, called *quarks,* that have charges of $\pm\frac{1}{3}e$ or $\pm\frac{2}{3}e$. You will learn about these particles and their properties in Chapter 25.

Table 17-1	Charge and mass of atomic particles	
Particle	**Charge (C)**	**Mass (kg)**
electron	-1.60×10^{-19}	9.109×10^{-31}
proton	$+1.60 \times 10^{-19}$	1.673×10^{-27}
neutron	0	1.675×10^{-27}

TRANSFER OF ELECTRIC CHARGE

When a balloon and your hair are charged by rubbing, only the rubbed areas become charged, and there is no tendency for the charge to move into other regions of the material. In contrast, when materials such as copper, aluminum, and silver are charged in some small region, the charge readily distributes itself over the entire surface of the material. For this reason, it is convenient to classify substances in terms of their ability to transfer electric charge.

Materials in which electric charges move freely, such as copper and aluminum, are called **conductors.** Most metals are conductors. Materials in which electric charges do not move freely, such as glass, rubber, silk, and plastic, are called **insulators.**

Semiconductors are a third class of materials characterized by electrical properties that are somewhere between those of insulators and conductors. In their pure state, semiconductors are insulators. But the carefully controlled addition of specific atoms as impurities can dramatically increase a semiconductor's ability to conduct electric charge. Silicon and germanium are two well-known semiconductors that are used in a variety of electronic devices.

Certain metals belong to a fourth class of materials, called *superconductors.* Superconductors become perfect conductors when they are at or below a certain temperature. You will study semiconductors in greater detail in Chapter 24, and you will learn more about superconductors in Chapters 19 and 24.

Insulators and conductors can be charged by contact

In the experiments discussed above, a balloon and hair become charged because they are rubbed together. This process is known as *charging by contact.* Another example of charging by contact is a common experiment in which a glass rod is rubbed with silk and a rubber rod is rubbed with wool or fur. The two rods become oppositely charged and attract one another, like a balloon and your hair do. If two glass rods are charged, the rods have the same charge and repel each other, just as two charged balloons do. Likewise, two charged rubber rods repel one another. All of the materials used in these experiments—glass, rubber, silk, wool, and fur—are insulators. Can conductors also be charged by contact?

If you try a similar experiment with a copper rod, the rod does not attract or repel another charged rod. This might suggest that a metal cannot be charged by contact. However, if you hold the copper rod with an insulator and then rub it with wool or fur, the rod attracts a charged glass rod and repels a charged rubber rod.

In the first case, the electric charges produced by rubbing readily move from the copper through your body and finally to Earth because copper is a conductor. So the copper rod does become charged but it soon becomes neutral again. In the second case, the insulating handle prevents the flow of charge to Earth, and the copper rod remains charged. Thus, both insulators and conductors can become charged by contact.

conductor

material that transfers charge easily

insulator

material that does not transfer charge easily

Conceptual Challenge

1. Plastic wrap
Plastic wrap becomes electrically charged as it is pulled from its container, and, as a result, it is attracted to objects such as food containers. Explain why plastic is a good material for this purpose.

2. Charge transfer
If a glass rod is rubbed with silk, the glass becomes positive and the silk becomes negative. Compare the mass of the glass rod before and after it is charged.

3. Electrons
Many objects in the large-scale world have no net charge, even though they contain an extremely large amount of electrons. How is this possible?

Polarization

MATERIALS LIST

✔ balloon
✔ water faucet

Turn on a water faucet and adjust the flow of water so that you have a small but steady stream. The stream should be as slow as possible without producing individual droplets. Inflate the balloon, tie it, and rub it across your hair. Hold the charged end of the balloon near the stream without letting the balloon get wet. What happens to the stream of water? What might be causing this to happen?

induction

the process of charging a conductor by bringing it near another charged object and grounding the conductor

Conductors can be charged by induction

When a conductor is connected to Earth by means of a conducting wire or copper pipe, the conductor is said to be *grounded*. The Earth can be considered an infinite reservoir for electrons because it can accept or supply an unlimited number of electrons. This is the key to understanding another method of charging a conductor.

Consider a negatively charged rubber rod brought near a neutral (uncharged) conducting sphere that is insulated so that there is no conducting path to ground. The repulsive force between the electrons in the rod and those in the sphere causes a redistribution of negative charge on the sphere, as shown in **Figure 17-4(a).** As a result, the region of the sphere nearest the negatively charged rod has an excess of positive charge.

If a grounded conducting wire is then connected to the sphere, as shown in **Figure 17-4(b),** some of the electrons leave the sphere and travel to Earth. If the wire to ground is then removed while the negatively charged rod is held in place, as shown in **Figure 17-4(c),** the conducting sphere is left with an excess of induced positive charge. Finally, when the rubber rod is removed from the vicinity of the sphere, as in **Figure 17-4(d),** the induced positive charge remains on the ungrounded sphere. The motion of negative charges on the sphere causes the positive charge to become uniformly distributed over the outside surface of the ungrounded sphere. This process is known as **induction,** and the charge is said to be *induced* on the sphere.

Notice that charging an object by induction requires no contact with the object inducing the charge but does require contact with a third object, which serves as either a source or a sink of electrons. In the process of inducing a charge on the sphere, the charged rubber rod did not come in contact with the sphere and thus did not lose any of its negative charge. This is in contrast to charging an object by contact, in which charges are transferred directly from one object to another.

Figure 17-4
(a) When a charged rubber rod is brought near a metal sphere, the charges on the sphere become redistributed. **(b)** If the sphere is grounded, some of the electrons travel through the wire to the ground. **(c)** When this wire is removed, the sphere has an excess of positive charge, which **(d)** becomes evenly distributed on the surface of the sphere when the rod is removed.

A surface charge can be induced on insulators by polarization

A process very similar to charging by induction in conductors takes place in insulators. In most neutral atoms or molecules, the center of positive charge coincides with the center of negative charge. However, in the presence of a charged object, these centers may shift slightly, resulting in more positive charge on one side of a molecule than on the other. This effect is known as *polarization*.

This realignment of charge within individual molecules produces an induced charge on the surface of the insulator, as shown in **Figure 17-5(a)**. When an object becomes polarized, it has no net charge but is still able to attract or repel objects due to this realignment of charge. This explains why a plastic comb can attract small pieces of paper that have no net charge, as shown in **Figure 17-5(b)**. As with induction, in polarization one object induces a charge on the surface of another object with no physical contact.

(a)

(b)

Figure 17-5
(a) The charged object on the left induces charges on the surface of an insulator, which is said to be *polarized*. **(b)** This charged comb induces a charge on the surface of small pieces of paper that have no net charge.

Section Review

1. When a rubber rod is rubbed with wool, the rod becomes negatively charged. What can you conclude about the magnitude of the wool's charge after the rubbing process? Why?

2. What did Millikan's oil-drop experiment reveal about the nature of electric charge?

3. A typical lightning bolt has about 10.0 C of charge. How many excess electrons are in a typical lightning bolt?

4. If you stick a piece of transparent tape on your desk and then quickly pull it off, you will find that the tape is attracted to other areas of your desk that are not charged. Why does this happen?

5. Metals, such as copper and silver, can become charged by induction, while plastic materials cannot. Explain why.

6. **Physics in Action** Why is an electrostatic spray gun more efficient than an ordinary spray gun?

17-2
Electric force

- **Calculate electric force using Coulomb's law.**

- **Compare electric force with gravitational force.**

- **Apply the superposition principle to find the resultant force on a charge and to find the position at which the net force on a charge is zero.**

COULOMB'S LAW

In Chapter 4, a force is defined as the cause of a change in motion. Because two charged objects near one another may experience motion either toward or away from each other, each object exerts a force on the other object. This force is called the *electric force*. The two balloon experiments described in Section 17-1 demonstrate that the electric force is attractive between opposite charges and repulsive between like charges. What determines how small or large the electric force will be?

The closer two charges are, the greater the force between them

If you rub a balloon against your hair, you will find that the closer the balloon is to your hair, the stronger the attraction. Likewise, the repulsion between two charged balloons becomes stronger as the distance between the balloons decreases. Thus, the distance between two objects affects the magnitude of the electric force between them. Further, it seems reasonable that the amount of charge on the objects will also affect the magnitude of the electric force. What is the precise relationship between distance, charge, and the electric force?

In the 1780s, Charles Coulomb conducted a variety of experiments in an attempt to determine the magnitude of the electric force between two charged objects. Coulomb found that the electric force between two charges is proportional to the product of the two charges. Hence, if one charge is doubled, the electric force likewise doubles, and if both charges are doubled, the electric force increases by a factor of four. Coulomb also found that the electric force is inversely proportional to the square of the distance between the charges. Thus, when the distance between two charges is halved, the force between them increases by a factor of four. The following equation, known as Coulomb's law, expresses these conclusions mathematically for two charges separated by a distance, r.

COULOMB'S LAW

$$F_{electric} = k_C \left(\frac{q_1 q_2}{r^2} \right)$$

$$\text{electric force} = \text{Coulomb constant} \times \frac{(\text{charge 1})(\text{charge 2})}{(\text{distance})^2}$$

The symbol k_C, called the Coulomb constant, has SI units of $N \cdot m^2/C^2$ because this gives N as the unit of electric force. The value of k_C depends on the choice of units. Experiments have determined that in SI units, k_C has the value $8.9875 \times 10^9 \ N \cdot m^2/C^2$. This book will simplify calculations by using the approximate value $8.99 \times 10^9 \ N \cdot m^2/C^2$.

When dealing with Coulomb's law, remember that force is a vector quantity and must be treated accordingly. The electric force between two objects always acts along the line between the objects. Also note that Coulomb's law applies exactly only to point charges or particles and to spherical distributions of charge. When applying Coulomb's law to spherical distributions of charge, use the distance between the centers of the spheres as r.

Coulomb's law

PROBLEM

The electron and proton of a hydrogen atom are separated, on average, by a distance of about 5.3×10^{-11} m. Find the magnitudes of the electric force and the gravitational force that each particle exerts on the other.

SOLUTION

1. DEFINE   **Given:**

$$r = 5.3 \times 10^{-1} \ m$$
$$k_C = 8.99 \times 10^9 \ N \cdot m^2/C^2$$
$$m_e = 9.109 \times 10^{-31} \ kg$$
$$m_p = 1.673 \times 10^{-27} \ kg$$
$$q_e = -1.60 \times 10^{-19} \ C$$
$$q_p = +1.60 \times 10^{-19} \ C$$
$$G = 6.67 \times 10^{-11} \ N \cdot m^2/kg^2$$

Unknown: $F_{electric} = ?$ $F_g = ?$

2. PLAN   **Choose an equation(s) or situation:**
Find the magnitude of the electric force using Coulomb's law and the magnitude of the gravitational force using Newton's law of gravitation (introduced in Chapter 7).

$$F_{electric} = k_C \frac{q_1 q_2}{r^2} \qquad F_g = G \frac{m_e m_p}{r^2}$$

3. CALCULATE   **Substitute the values into the equations(s) and solve:**
Because we are finding the magnitude of the electric force, which is a scalar, we can disregard the sign of each charge in our calculation.

continued on next page

$$F_{electric} = k_C \frac{q_e q_p}{r^2} = \left(8.99 \times 10^9 \frac{N \cdot m^2}{C^2}\right)\left(\frac{(1.60 \times 10^{-19} \text{ C})^2}{(5.3 \times 10^{-11} \text{ m})^2}\right)$$

$$\boxed{F_{electric} = 8.2 \times 10^{-8} \text{ N}}$$

$$F_g = G \frac{m_e m_p}{r^2} =$$

$$\left(6.67 \times 10^{-11} \frac{N \cdot m^2}{kg^2}\right)\left(\frac{(9.109 \times 10^{-31} \text{ kg})(1.673 \times 10^{-27} \text{ kg})}{(5.3 \times 10^{-11} \text{ m})^2}\right)$$

$$\boxed{F_g = 3.6 \times 10^{-47} \text{ N}}$$

4. EVALUATE The electron and the proton have opposite signs, so the electric force between the two particles is attractive. The ratio $F_{electric}/F_g \approx 2 \times 10^{39}$; hence, the gravitational force between the particles is negligible compared with the electric force between them. Because each force is inversely proportional to distance squared, this result is independent of the distance between the two particles.

PRACTICE 17A

Coulomb's law

1. A small cork with an excess charge of $+6.0$ μC (1 μC $= 10^{-6}$ C) is placed 0.12 m from another cork, which carries a charge of -4.3 μC.
   a. What is the magnitude of the electric force between the corks?
   b. Is this force attractive or repulsive?
   c. How many excess electrons are on the negative cork?
   d. How many electrons has the positive cork lost?

2. A balloon rubbed against denim gains a charge of -8.0 μC. What is the electric force between the balloon and the denim when the two are separated by a distance of 5.0 cm? (Assume that the charges are located at a point.)

3. Two electrostatic point charges of $+60.0$ μC and $+50.0$ μC exert a repulsive force on each other of 175 N. What is the distance between the two charges?

4. Two identical conducting spheres are placed with their centers 0.30 m apart. One is given a charge of $+12 \times 10^{-9}$ C and the other is given a charge of -18×10^{-9} C.
   a. Find the electric force exerted on one sphere by the other.
   b. The spheres are connected by a conducting wire. After equilibrium has occurred, find the electric force between the two spheres.

Electric force is a field force

The Coulomb force is the second example we have studied of a force that is exerted by one object on another even though there is no physical contact between the two objects. As you learned in Chapter 4, such a force is known as a *field force*. Recall that another example of a field force is gravitational attraction. Notice that the mathematical form of the Coulomb force is very similar to that of the gravitational force. That is, both forces are inversely proportional to the square of the distance of separation.

However, there are some important differences between electric and gravitational forces. First of all, as you have seen, electric forces can be either attractive or repulsive. Gravitational forces, on the other hand, are always attractive. This is because objects can have either a positive or a negative charge, while mass is always positive.

Another difference between the gravitational and the electric force is their relative strength. As shown in Sample Problem 17A, the electric force is significantly stronger than the gravitational force. As a result, the electric force between charged atomic particles is much stronger than their gravitational attraction to the Earth.

In the large-scale world, the relative strength of these two forces can be seen by noting that the amount of charge required to overcome the gravitational force is relatively small. For example, if you rub a balloon against your hair and hold the balloon directly above your hair, your hair will stand on end because it is attracted toward the balloon. Although only a small amount of charge is transferred from your hair to the balloon, the electric force between the two is nonetheless stronger than the gravitational force that usually pulls your hair toward the ground.

Resultant force on a charge is the vector sum of the individual forces on that charge

Frequently, more than two charges are present, and it is necessary to find the net electric force on one of them. As demonstrated in Sample Problem 17A, Coulomb's law gives the electric force between any pair of charges. Coulomb's law applies even when more than two charges are present. Thus, the resultant force on any single charge equals the vector sum of the individual forces exerted on that charge by all of the other individual charges that are present. This is an example of the *principle of superposition.*

This method was introduced in Chapter 3 and was used to add forces together vectorially in Chapter 4. The process is essentially the same here; the only difference is that in this chapter we are considering electric forces, whereas in Chapter 4 we worked primarily with other kinds of forces. Once the magnitudes of the individual electric forces are found by Coulomb's law, they are added together exactly as forces were added together in Chapter 4. This process is demonstrated in Sample Problem 17B.

The superposition principle

PROBLEM

Consider three point charges at the corners of a triangle, as shown in Figure 17-6, where $q_1 = 6.00 \times 10^{-9}$ C, $q_2 = -2.00 \times 10^{-9}$ C, and $q_3 = 5.00 \times 10^{-9}$ C. Find the magnitude and direction of the resultant force on q_3.

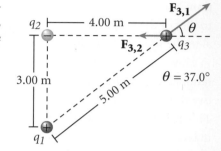

Figure 17-6

REASONING

According to the superposition principle, the resultant force on the charge q_3 is the vector sum of the forces exerted by q_1 and q_2 on q_3. First find the force exerted on q_3 by each, and then add these two forces together vectorially to get the resultant force on q_3.

SOLUTION

Given:
$$q_1 = +6.00 \times 10^{-9} \text{ C} \qquad r_{2,1} = 3.00 \text{ m}$$
$$q_2 = -2.00 \times 10^{-9} \text{ C} \qquad r_{3,2} = 4.00 \text{ m}$$
$$q_3 = +5.00 \times 10^{-9} \text{ C} \qquad r_{3,1} = 5.00 \text{ m}$$
$$k_C = 8.99 \times 10^9 \text{ N} \bullet \text{m}^2/\text{C}^2 \qquad \theta = 37.0°$$

Unknown: $\mathbf{F_{3,tot}} = ?$

Diagram:

Figure 17-7

1. **Calculate the magnitude of the forces with Coulomb's law:**

$$F_{3,1} = k_C \frac{q_3 q_1}{(r_{3,1})^2} = (8.99 \times 10^9 \text{ N} \bullet \text{m}^2/\text{C}^2) \left(\frac{(5.00 \times 10^{-9} \text{ C})(6.00 \times 10^{-9} \text{ C})}{(5.00 \text{ m})^2} \right)$$

$$F_{3,1} = 1.08 \times 10^{-8} \text{ N}$$

$$F_{3,2} = k_C \frac{q_3 q_2}{(r_{3,2})^2} = (8.99 \times 10^9 \text{ N} \bullet \text{m}^2/\text{C}^2) \left(\frac{(5.00 \times 10^{-9} \text{ C})(2.00 \times 10^{-9} \text{ C})}{(4.00 \text{ m})^2} \right)$$

$$F_{3,2} = 5.62 \times 10^{-9} \text{ N}$$

2. **Determine the direction of the forces by analyzing the charges:**

The force $\mathbf{F_{3,1}}$ is repulsive because q_1 and q_3 have the same sign.

The force $\mathbf{F_{3,2}}$ is attractive because q_2 and q_3 have opposite signs.

3. **Find the x and y components of each force:**

At this point, the direction of each component must be taken into account.

For $\mathbf{F_{3,1}}$: $F_x = (F_{3,1}) (\cos 37.0°) = (1.08 \times 10^{-8} \text{ N})(\cos 37.0°) = 8.63 \times 10^{-9} \text{ N}$

$F_y = (F_{3,1}) (\sin 37.0°) = (1.08 \times 10^{-8} \text{ N})(\sin 37.0°) = 6.50 \times 10^{-9} \text{ N}$

For $\mathbf{F_{3,2}}$: $\quad F_x = F_{3,2} = -5.62 \times 10^{-9}$ N

$\qquad\qquad F_y = 0$ N

4. **Calculate the magnitude of the total force acting in both directions:**

$F_{x,tot} = 8.63 \times 10^{-9}$ N $- 5.62 \times 10^{-9}$ N $= 3.01 \times 10^{-9}$ N

$F_{y,tot} = 6.50 \times 10^{-9}$ N $+ 0$ N $= 6.50 \times 10^{-9}$ N

5. **Use the Pythagorean theorem to find the magnitude of the resultant force:**

$$F_{3,tot} = \sqrt{(F_{x,tot})^2 + (F_{y,tot})^2} = \sqrt{(3.01 \times 10^{-9}\ N)^2 + (6.50 \times 10^{-9}\ N)^2}$$

$$\boxed{F_{3,tot} = 7.16 \times 10^{-9}\ N}$$

6. **Use a suitable trigonometric function to find the direction of the resultant force:**

In this case, you can use the inverse tangent function:

$$\tan \varphi = \frac{F_{y,tot}}{F_{x,tot}} = \frac{6.50 \times 10^{-9}\ N}{3.01 \times 10^{-9}\ N}$$

$$\boxed{\varphi = 65.2°}$$

Figure 17-8

7. **Evaluate your answer:**

Because $F_{3,1}$ is repulsive and $F_{3,2}$ is attractive, the magnitude of the resultant force ($F_{3,tot}$) should be between these two values:

1.08×10^{-8} N $(F_{3,1}) > 7.16 \times 10^{-9}$ N $(F_{3,tot}) > 5.62 \times 10^{-9}$ N $(F_{3,2})$.

PRACTICE 17B

The superposition principle

1. Three point charges, q_1, q_2, and q_3, lie along the x-axis at $x = 0$, $x = 3.0$ cm, and $x = 5.0$ cm, respectively. Calculate the magnitude and direction of the electric force on each of the three point charges when $q_1 = +6.0\ \mu C$, $q_2 = +1.5\ \mu C$, and $q_3 = -2.0\ \mu C$.

2. Four charged particles are placed so that each particle is at the corner of a square. The sides of the square are 15 cm. The charge at the upper left corner is $+3.0\ \mu C$, the charge at the upper right corner is $-6.0\ \mu C$, the charge at the lower left corner is $-2.4\ \mu C$, and the charge at the lower right corner is $-9.0\ \mu C$.

   a. What is the net electric force on the $+3.0\ \mu C$ charge?
   b. What is the net electric force on the $-6.0\ \mu C$ charge?
   c. What is the net electric force on the $-9.0\ \mu C$ charge?

As seen in Chapter 4, objects that are at rest are said to be in equilibrium. According to Newton's first law, the net external force acting on a body in equilibrium must equal zero. In electrostatic situations, the equilibrium position of a charge is the location at which the net electric force on the charge is zero. To find this location, you must find the position at which the electric force from one charge is equal and opposite the electric force from another charge. This can be done by setting the forces (found by Coulomb's law) equal and then solving for the distance between either charge and the equilibrium position. This process is demonstrated in Sample Problem 17C.

SAMPLE PROBLEM 17C

Equilibrium

PROBLEM

Three charges lie along the x-axis. One positive charge, $q_1 = 15\ \mu C$, is at $x = 2.0$ m, and another positive charge, $q_2 = 6.0\ \mu C$, is at the origin. At what point on the x-axis must a negative charge, q_3, be placed so that the resultant force on it is zero?

SOLUTION

1. DEFINE   **Given:**

$q_1 = 15\ \mu C\ (15 \times 10^{-6}\ C)$ $r_{3,1} = 2.0\ m - P$

$q_2 = 6.0\ \mu C\ (6.0 \times 10^{-6}\ C)$ $r_{3,2} = P$

Unknown: the distance (P) between the negative charge q_3 and the positive charge q_2 such that the resultant force on q_3 is zero

Diagram:

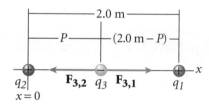

2. PLAN   **Choose an equation(s) or situation:**

The force exerted on q_3 by q_2 will be opposite the force exerted on q_3 by q_1 if q_3 lies on the x-axis between q_1 and q_2. Since we require that the resultant force on q_3 be zero, then $F_{3,1}$ and $F_{3,2}$, which can each be found by Coulomb's law, must equal one another.

$$F_{3,1} = k_C \left(\frac{q_3 q_1}{(r_{3,1})^2} \right) \text{ and } F_{3,2} = k_C \left(\frac{q_3 q_2}{(r_{3,2})^2} \right)$$

$$F_{3,1} = F_{3,2}$$

$$k_C \left(\frac{q_3 q_1}{(r_{3,1})^2} \right) = k_C \left(\frac{q_3 q_2}{(r_{3,2})^2} \right)$$

3. CALCULATE **Substitute the values into the equation(s) and solve:**

$$k_C\left(\frac{q_3(15 \times 10^{-6}\ C)}{(2.0\ m - P)^2}\right) = k_C\left(\frac{q_3(6.0 \times 10^{-6}\ C)}{P^2}\right)$$

Because k_C, 10^{-6}, and q_3 are common terms, these can be canceled from both sides of the equation. The unit C also cancels.

$$\frac{15}{(2.0\ m - P)^2} = \frac{6.0}{P^2}$$

Now solve for P to find the location of q_3.

$$(P^2)(15) = (2.0\ m - P)^2(6.0)$$

Take the square root of both sides, then isolate P.

$$P\sqrt{15} = (2.0\ m - P)\sqrt{6.0}$$

$$P = (2.0\ m - P)\sqrt{\frac{6.0}{15}}$$

$$P = 1.3\ m - (0.63)(P)$$

$$(1.63)(P) = 1.3\ m$$

$$\boxed{P = 0.80\ m\ \text{from}\ q_2}$$

4. EVALUATE Because q_1 is greater than q_2, we would expect the location of q_3 to be closer to q_2 in order for the forces to balance. Our answer seems reasonable because q_3 is 0.80 m from q_2 and 1.2 m (2.0 m − 0.80 m) from q_1.

PRACTICE 17C

Equilibrium

1. A charge of $+2.00 \times 10^{-9}$ C is placed at the origin, and another charge of $+4.00 \times 10^{-9}$ C is placed at $x = 1.5$ m. Find the point between these two charges where a charge of $+3.00 \times 10^{-9}$ C should be placed so that the net electric force on it is zero.

2. A charge q_1 of -5.00×10^{-9} C and a charge q_2 of -2.00×10^{-9} C are separated by a distance of 40.0 cm. Find the equilibrium position for a third charge of $+15.0 \times 10^{-9}$ C.

3. An electron is released above the Earth's surface. A second electron directly below it exerts just enough of an electric force on the first electron to cancel the gravitational force on it. Find the distance between the two electrons.

Coulomb quantified electric force with a torsion balance

Earlier in this chapter, you learned that Charles Coulomb was the first person to quantify the electric force and establish the inverse square law for electric charges. Coulomb measured electric forces between charged objects with a torsion balance, as shown in **Figure 17-9.** A torsion balance consists of two small spheres fixed to the ends of a light horizontal rod. The rod is made of an insulating material and is suspended by a silk thread.

In this experiment, one of the spheres is given a charge and another charged object is brought near the charged sphere. The attractive or repulsive force between the two causes the rod to rotate and to twist the suspension. The angle through which the rod rotates is measured by the deflection of a light beam reflected from a mirror attached to the suspension. The rod rotates through some angle against the restoring force of the twisted thread before reaching equilibrium. The value of the angle of rotation increases as the charge increases, thereby providing a quantitative measure of the electric force. With this experiment, Coulomb established the equation for electric force introduced at the beginning of this section. More-recent experiments have verified these results to within a very small uncertainty.

Charged object

Charged sphere

Figure 17-9
Coulomb's torsion balance was used to establish the inverse square law for the electric force between two charges.

Section Review

1. A small glass ball rubbed with silk gains a charge of +2.0 μC. The glass ball is placed 12 cm from a small charged rubber ball that carries a charge of −3.5 μC.
   a. What is the magnitude of the electric force between the two balls?
   b. Is this force attractive or repulsive?
   c. How many electrons has the glass ball lost in the rubbing process?

2. What are some similarities between the electric force and the gravitational force? What are some differences between the two?

3. A +2.2 × 10^{-9} C charge is on the x-axis at x = 1.5 m, a +5.4 × 10^{-9} C charge is on the x-axis at x = 2.0 m, and a +3.5 × 10^{-9} C charge is at the origin. Find the net force on the charge at the origin.

4. A charge q_1 of −6.00 × 10^{-9} C and a charge q_2 of −3.00 × 10^{-9} C are separated by a distance of 60.0 cm. Where could a third charge be placed so that the net electric force on it is zero?

5. **Physics in Action** The electric force between a negatively charged paint droplet and a positively charged automobile body is increased by a factor of two, but the charges on each remain constant. How has the distance between the two changed? (Assume that the charge on the automobile is located at a single point.)

ELECTRIC FIELD STRENGTH

As discussed earlier in this chapter, electric force, like gravitational force, is a field force. Unlike contact forces, which require physical contact between objects, field forces are capable of acting through space, producing an effect even when there is no physical contact between the objects involved. Field forces can be discussed in a variety of ways, but an approach developed by Michael Faraday (1791–1867) is of such practical value that we will devote much attention to it. In this approach, an **electric field** is said to exist in the region of space around a charged object. When another charged object enters this electric field, forces of an electrical nature arise.

To define an electric field more precisely, consider **Figure 17-10(a),** which shows an object with a small positive charge, q_0, placed near a second object with a larger positive charge, Q. The strength of the electric field, E, at the location of q_0 is defined as the magnitude of the electric force acting on q_0 divided by the charge of q_0:

$$E = \frac{F_{electric}}{q_0}$$

Note that this is the electric field at the location of q_0 produced by the charge Q, and *not* the field produced by q_0.

Because electric field strength is a ratio of force to charge, the SI units of E are newtons per coulomb (N/C). The electric field is a vector quantity. By convention, the direction of **E** at a point is defined as the direction of the electric force that would be exerted on a small *positive* charge (called a test charge) placed at that point. Thus, in **Figure 17-10(a),** the direction of the electric field is horizontal and to the right because a positive charge would be repelled by the positive sphere. In **Figure 17-10(b),** the direction of the electric field is to the left because a positive charge would be attracted toward the negatively charged sphere. In other words, the direction of **E** depends on the sign of the charge producing the field.

17-3 SECTION OBJECTIVES

- **Calculate electric field strength.**

- **Draw and interpret electric field lines.**

- **Identify the four properties associated with a conductor in electrostatic equilibrium.**

electric field

a field that permeates the space around a charged object and in which another charged object experiences an electric force

(a) **(b)**

Figure 17-10
(a) A small object with a positive charge placed near an object with a larger positive charge experiences an electric field, **E,** directed to the right. **(b)** A small object with a positive charge placed near a negatively charged object experiences an electric field, **E,** directed to the left.

Figure 17-11

We must assume a small test charge, as in **(a)**, because a larger test charge, as in **(b)**, can cause a redistribution of the charge on the sphere, which changes the electric field strength.

Now consider the positively charged conducting sphere in **Figure 17-11(a).** The field in the region surrounding the sphere could be explored by placing a positive test charge, q_0, in a variety of places near the sphere. To find the electric field at each point, you would first find the electric force on this charge, then divide this force by the magnitude of the test charge.

However, when the magnitude of the test charge is great enough to influence the charge on the conducting sphere, a difficulty with our definition arises. According to Coulomb's law, a strong test charge will cause a rearrangement of the charges on the sphere, as shown in **Figure 17-11(b).** As a result, the force exerted on the test charge is different from what it would be if the movement of charge on the sphere had not taken place. Furthermore, the strength of the measured electric field differs from what it would be in the absence of the test charge. To eliminate this problem, we assume that the test charge is small enough to have a negligible effect on the location of the charges on the sphere.

Electric field strength depends on charge and distance

To reformulate our equation for electric field strength from a point charge, consider a charge, q, located a distance, r, from a small test charge, q_0. According to Coulomb's law, the magnitude of the force on the test charge is given by the following equation:

$$F_{electric} = k_C \frac{qq_0}{r^2}$$

We can find the magnitude of the electric field due to the point charge q at the position of q_0 by substituting this value into our previous equation for electric field strength.

$$E = \frac{F_{electric}}{q_0} = k_C \frac{qq_0}{r^2 q_0}$$

Notice that q_0 cancels, and we have a new equation for electric field strength from a point charge.

CONCEPT PREVIEW

Just as gravitational potential energy depends on an object's position in a gravitational field, a type of potential energy known as electrical potential energy depends on a charge's position in an electric field. You will learn more about electrical potential energy in Chapter 18.

ELECTRIC FIELD STRENGTH FROM A POINT CHARGE

$$E = k_C \frac{q}{r^2}$$

$$\text{electric field strength} = \text{Coulomb constant} \times \frac{\text{charge producing the field}}{(\text{distance})^2}$$

As stated above, electric field, **E,** is a vector. If q is positive, the field due to this charge is directed outward radially from q. If q is negative, the field is directed toward q. As with electric force, the electric field due to more than one charge is calculated by applying the principle of superposition. This is demonstrated in Sample Problem 17D on page 646.

Our new equation for electric field strength points out an important property of electric fields. As the equation indicates, an electric field at a given point depends only on the charge, q, of the object setting up the field and on the distance, r, from that object to a specific point in space. As a result, we can say that an electric field exists at any point near a charged body even when there is no test charge at that point. **Table 17-2** shows the magnitudes of various electric fields.

Table 17-2	Electric fields
Examples	E, N/C
in a fluorescent lighting tube	10
in the atmosphere during fair weather	100
under a thundercloud or in a lightning bolt	10 000
at the electron in a hydrogen atom	5.1×10^{11}

Consumer Focus   *Microwave Ovens*

*I*t would be hard to find a town in America that does not have a microwave oven. Homes, convenience stores, and restaurants all have this marvelous invention that somehow heats only the soft parts of the food and leaves the inorganic and hard materials, like ceramic and bone, at approximately the same temperature. A neat trick, indeed, but how is it done?

Microwave ovens take advantage of a property of water molecules called *bipolarity*. Water molecules are considered bipolar because each molecule has a positive and a negative end. In other words, more of the electrons in these molecules are at one end of the molecule than the other.

Figure 17-12

Because microwaves are a high-frequency form of electromagnetic radiation, they supply an electric field that changes polarity billions of times a second. As this electric field passes a bipolar molecule, the positive side of the particle experiences a force in one direction, and the negative side of the particle is pushed or pulled in the other direction. When the field changes polarity, the directions of these forces are reversed. Instead of tearing apart, the particles simply spin about a central axis.

As the bipolar molecules spin, they rub against one another, producing friction. This friction in turn increases the internal energy of the food. Energy is transferred to the food by radiation (the microwaves) as opposed to conduction from hot air, as in a conventional oven.

Depending on the microwave oven's power and design, this rotational motion can generate up to about 3 J of internal energy each second in 1 g of water. At this rate, a top-power microwave oven can boil a cup (250 mL) of water in 2 min using about 0.033 kW•h of electricity.

Items such as bones, dry plates, and the air in the oven are unaffected by the fluctuating electric field because they are not polarized. Because energy is not wasted on heating these nonpolar items, the microwave oven cooks food faster and more efficiently than other ovens.

Electric field strength

PROBLEM

A charge $q_1 = +7.00 \ \mu C$ is at the origin, and a charge $q_2 = -5.00 \ \mu C$ is on the x-axis 0.300 m from the origin, as shown in Figure 17-13. Find the electric field strength at point P, which is on the y-axis 0.400 m from the origin.

Figure 17-13

REASONING

The principle of superposition must be applied in order to calculate the electric field due to a group of point charges. You must first calculate the electric field produced by each charge individually at point P, then add these fields together as vectors.

SOLUTION

Given:

$$q_1 = +7.00 \ \mu C \ (7.00 \times 10^{-6} \ C) \qquad r_1 = 0.400 \ m$$

$$q_2 = -5.00 \ \mu C \ (-5.00 \times 10^{-6} \ C) \qquad r_2 = 0.500 \ m$$

$$k_C = 8.99 \times 10^9 \ N \cdot m^2/C^2 \qquad \theta = 53.1°$$

Unknown: $\mathbf{E}$ at $P \ (y = 0.400 \ m)$

1. **Calculate the magnitude of the electric field strength produced by each charge:**

   Because we are finding the magnitude of the electric field, we can neglect the sign of each charge.

   $$E_1 = k_C \frac{q_1}{r_1^2} = (8.99 \times 10^9 \ N \cdot m^2/C^2)\left(\frac{7.00 \times 10^{-6} \ C}{(0.400 \ m)^2}\right) = 3.93 \times 10^5 \ N/C$$

   $$E_2 = k_C \frac{q_2}{r_2^2} = (8.99 \times 10^9 \ N \cdot m^2/C^2)\left(\frac{5.00 \times 10^{-6} \ C}{(0.500 \ m)^2}\right) = 1.80 \times 10^5 \ N/C$$

2. **Determine the direction of each electric field vector by analyzing the signs of the charges:**

   The field vector $\mathbf{E_1}$ at P due to q_1 is directed vertically upward, as shown in **Figure 17-13,** because q_1 is positive. Likewise, the field vector $\mathbf{E_2}$ at P due to q_2 is directed toward q_2 because q_2 is negative.

3. **Find the x and y components of each electric field vector:**

   At this point, the direction of each component must be taken into account.

   For $\mathbf{E_1}$: $E_{x,1} = 0 \ N/C$

   $\qquad E_{y,1} = 3.93 \times 10^5 \ N/C$

   For $\mathbf{E_2}$: $E_{x,2} = (E_2) \ (\cos 53.1°) = (1.80 \times 10^5 \ N/C)(\cos 53.1°) = 1.08 \times 10^5 \ N/C$

   $\qquad E_{y,2} = -(E_2) \ (\sin 53.1°) = (1.80 \times 10^5 \ N/C)(\sin 53.1°) = -1.44 \times 10^5 \ N/C$

4. Calculate the magnitude of the total electric field strength in both the x and y directions:

$$E_{x,tot} = E_{x,1} + E_{x,2} = 0 \text{ N/C} + 1.08 \times 10^5 \text{ N/C} = 1.08 \times 10^5 \text{ N/C}$$

$$E_{y,tot} = E_{y,1} + E_{y,2} = 3.93 \times 10^5 \text{ N/C} - 1.44 \times 10^5 \text{ N/C} = 2.49 \times 10^5 \text{ N/C}$$

5. Use the Pythagorean theorem to find the magnitude of the resultant electric field strength vector:

$$E_{tot} = \sqrt{(E_{x,tot})^2 + (E_{y,tot})^2} = \sqrt{(1.08 \times 10^5 \text{ N/C})^2 + (2.49 \times 10^5 \text{ N/C})^2}$$

$$\boxed{E_{tot} = 2.71 \times 10^5 \text{ N/C}}$$

6. Use a suitable trigonometric function to find the direction of the resultant electric field strength vector:

In this case, you can use the inverse tangent function:

$$\tan \varphi = \frac{E_{y,tot}}{E_{x,tot}} = \frac{2.49 \times 10^5 \text{ N/C}}{1.08 \times 10^5 \text{ N/C}}$$

$$\boxed{\varphi = 66.6°}$$

Figure 17-14

7. Evaluate your answer:

Because the electric field at point P is the result of a positive and a negative charge, E_{tot} should be between E_1 and E_2:

$$3.93 \times 10^5 (E_1) > 2.71 \times 10^5 (E_{tot}) > 1.80 \times 10^5 (E_2)$$

Electric field strength

1. A charge, $q_1 = 5.00 \ \mu C$, is at the origin, and a second charge, $q_2 = -3.00 \ \mu C$, is on the x-axis 0.800 m from the origin. Find the electric field at a point on the y-axis 0.500 m from the origin.

2. A proton and an electron in a hydrogen atom are separated on the average by about 5.3×10^{-11} m. What is the magnitude and direction of the electric field set up by the proton at the position of the electron?

3. An electric field of 2.0×10^4 N/C is directed along the positive x-axis.
   a. What is the electric force on an electron in this field?
   b. What is the electric force on a proton in this field?

ELECTRIC FIELD LINES

A convenient aid for visualizing electric field patterns is to draw lines pointing in the direction of the electric field, called **electric field lines.** Although electric field lines do not really exist, they offer a useful means of analyzing fields by representing both the strength and the direction of the field at different points in space. This is useful because the field at each point is often the result of more than one charge, as seen in Sample Problem 17D on page 646. Field lines make it easier to visualize the net field at each point.

The number of field lines is proportional to the electric field strength

By convention, electric field lines are drawn so that the electric field vector, **E,** is tangent to the lines at each point. Further, the number of lines per unit area through a surface perpendicular to the lines is proportional to the strength of the electric field in a given region. Thus, E is stronger where the field lines are close together and weaker where they are far apart.

Figure 17-15(a) shows some representative electric field lines for a positive point charge. Note that this two-dimensional drawing contains only the field lines that lie in the plane containing the point charge. The lines are actually directed outward radially from the charge in all directions, somewhat like quills radiate from the body of a porcupine. Because a positive test charge placed in this field would be repelled by the positive charge q, the lines are directed away from the positive charge, extending to infinity. Similarly, the electric field lines for a single negative point charge, which begin at infinity, are directed inward toward the charge, as shown in **Figure 17-15(b).** Note that the lines are closer together as they get near the charge, indicating that the strength of the field is increasing. This is consistent with our equation for electric field strength, which is inversely proportional to distance squared. **Figure 17-15(c)** depicts grass seeds in an insulating liquid. When a small charged conductor is placed in the center, these seeds align with the electric field produced by the charged body.

The rules for drawing electric field lines are summarized in **Table 17-3.** Note that no two field lines can cross one another. This is because at every point in space, the electric field vector points in a single direction and any field line at that point must also point in that direction.

(a)

(b)

(c)

Figure 17-15
The diagrams **(a)** and **(b)** show some representative electric field lines for a positive and a negative point charge. In **(c)**, grass seeds align with a similar field produced by a charged body.

Table 17-3	Rules for drawing electric field lines
The lines must begin on positive charges or at infinity and must terminate on negative charges or at infinity.	
The number of lines drawn leaving a positive charge or approaching a negative charge is proportional to the magnitude of the charge.	
No two field lines can cross each other.	

(a) **(b)**

Figure 17-16
(a) This diagram shows the electric field lines for two equal and opposite point charges. Note that the number of lines leaving the positive charge equals the number of lines terminating on the negative charge. **(b)** In this photograph, grass seeds in an insulating liquid align with a similar electric field produced by two oppositely charged conductors.

Figure 17-16 shows the electric field lines for two point charges of equal magnitudes but opposite signs. This charge configuration is called an *electric dipole*. In this case, the number of lines that begin at the positive charge must equal the number of lines that terminate on the negative charge. At points very near the charges, the lines are nearly radial. The high density of lines between the charges indicates a strong electric field in this region.

In electrostatic spray painting, field lines between a negatively charged spray gun and a positively charged target object are similar to those shown in **Figure 17-16.** As you can see, the field lines suggest that paint droplets that narrowly miss the target object still experience a force directed toward the object, sometimes causing them to wrap around from behind and hit it. This does in fact happen, and this increases the efficiency of an electrostatic spray gun.

(a) **(b)**

Figure 17-17
(a) This diagram shows the electric field lines for two positive point charges. **(b)** The photograph shows the analogous case for grass seeds in an insulating liquid around two conductors with the same charge.

Figure 17-17 shows the electric field lines in the vicinity of two equal positive point charges. Again, close to either charge, the lines are nearly radial. The same number of lines emerges from each charge because the charges are equal in magnitude. At great distances from the charges, the field approximately equals that of a single point charge of magnitude $2q$.

Finally, **Figure 17-18** is a sketch of the electric field lines associated with a positive charge $+2q$ and a negative charge $-q$. In this case, the number of lines leaving the charge $+2q$ is twice the number terminating on the charge $-q$. Hence, only half the lines that leave the positive charge end at the negative charge. The remaining half terminate at infinity. At distances that are great compared with the separation between the charges, the pattern of electric field lines is equivalent to that of a single charge, $+q$.

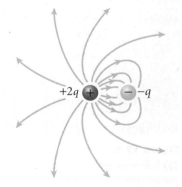

$+2q$ $-q$

Figure 17-18
In this case, only half the lines originating from the positive charge terminate on the negative charge because the positive charge is twice as great as the negative charge.

CONDUCTORS IN ELECTROSTATIC EQUILIBRIUM

A good electric conductor, such as copper, contains charges (electrons) that are not bound to any atoms and are free to move about within the material. When no net motion of charge is occurring within a conductor, the conductor is said to be in *electrostatic equilibrium.* As we shall see, such a conductor that is isolated has the four properties summarized in **Table 17-4.**

Table 17-4	Conductors in electrostatic equilibrium
The electric field is zero everywhere inside the conductor.	
Any excess charge on an isolated conductor resides entirely on the conductor's outer surface.	
The electric field just outside a charged conductor is perpendicular to the conductor's surface.	
On an irregularly shaped conductor, charge tends to accumulate where the radius of curvature of the surface is smallest, that is, at sharp points.	

The first property, which states that the electric field is zero inside a conductor in electrostatic equilibrium, can be understood by examining what would happen if this were not true. If there were an electric field inside a conductor, the free charges would move and a flow of charge, or current, would be created. However, if there were a net movement of charge, the conductor would no longer be in electrostatic equilibrium.

The fact that any excess charge resides on the outer surface of the conductor is a direct result of the repulsion between like charges described by Coulomb's law. If by some means an excess of charge is placed inside a conductor, the repulsive forces arising between the charges force them as far apart as possible, causing them to quickly migrate to the surface. Although we will not demonstrate it in this text, this property is a direct result of the fact that the electric force obeys an inverse square law. With any other power law, an excess of charge would still exist on the surface, but there would also be a distribution of charge, either of the same or opposite sign, inside the conductor.

We can understand why the electric field just outside a conductor must be perpendicular to the conductor's surface by considering what would happen if this were not true. If the electric field were not perpendicular to the surface, as in **Figure 17-19(a),** the electric field would have a component along the surface. This would cause the free negative charges within the conductor to move to the left. But if the charges moved, a current would be created and there would no longer be electrostatic equilibrium. Hence, **E** must be perpendicular to the surface, as in **Figure 17-19(b).**

To see why charge tends to accumulate at sharp points, consider a conductor that is fairly flat at one end and relatively pointed at the other. Any excess

(a) Charges in motion

(b) Charges in equilibrium

Figure 17-19

(a) If **E** were not perpendicular to the surface of the charged object, the component of the field that is along the surface would cause charges to move. **(b)** But charges are not moving, so **E** must instead be perpendicular to the surface.

charge placed on the object moves to its surface. **Figure 17-20** shows the forces between two charges at each end of such an object. At the flatter end, these forces are predominantly directed parallel to the surface. Thus, the charges move apart until repulsive forces from other nearby charges create a state of equilibrium.

At the sharp end, however, the forces of repulsion between two charges are directed predominantly perpendicular to the surface. As a result, there is less tendency for the charges to move apart along the surface and the amount of charge per unit area is greater than at the flat end. The cumulative effect of many such outward forces from nearby charges at the sharp end produces a large electric field directed away from the surface.

When the field becomes great enough, the air around the sharp end becomes ionized and a bluish glow called a *corona* is seen. Although air does not typically transfer electric charges easily, ionized air is a good conductor, and so charges leap from the surface into the surrounding air.

Electrostatic spray guns use this phenomenon to give paint droplets a negative charge. Electrostatic spray guns have a number of sharp points. When a spray gun is charged, the electric field around the sharp points can be strong enough to produce a corona around the gun. Air molecules in this area are ionized, and paint droplets pick up negative charges from these molecules as they move through the ionized air.

A Van de Graaff generator collects electric charge

In nuclear physics research, a Van de Graaff generator is often used to generate electric charge. If positively charged protons are introduced into a tube attached to the dome of a Van de Graaff generator, the large electric field of the dome exerts a repulsive force on the protons, causing them to accelerate to energies high enough to initiate nuclear reactions between the protons and various target nuclei.

A simple Van de Graaff generator is shown in **Figure 17-21.** To increase the amount of charge that can be generated, the Van de Graaff generator is designed to avoid ionizing the air, which would allow charge to "leak off" into the atmosphere.

Figure 17-20

When one end of a conductor is sharper than the other, excess charge tends to accumulate at the sharper end, resulting in a larger charge per unit area and therefore a larger repulsive electric force between charges at this end.

Figure 17-21

This person, insulated from the ground and touching the dome of a Van de Graaff generator, finds that her hair stands out on end because the strands become charged and repel one another.

Metal dome

(c)

Belt

(b)

Insulator

(a)

Ground

Figure 17-22
In a Van de Graaff generator, charge is transferred to the dome by a rotating belt that is kept in motion by a pulley **(a).** The charge is deposited on the belt at **(b)** and then transferred to the dome at **(c).**

Figure 17-22 shows the basic construction details of a Van de Graaff generator. A motor-driven pulley **(a)** moves a belt past positively charged comblike metallic needles **(b).** Negative charges are attracted to these needles from the belt, leaving the left side of the belt with a positive charge. The positive charges attract electrons onto the belt as it moves past a second comb of needles **(c),** increasing the excess positive charge on the dome. Because the electric field inside the dome is negligible, the positive charge on it can easily be increased, regardless of how much charge is already present. The result is that the metal dome is left with a large amount of positive charge.

This accumulation of charge on the dome cannot continue indefinitely because the magnitude of the electric field eventually becomes great enough to partially ionize the air near the surface. When this happens, charges on the dome have a pathway to leak off into the air, sometimes producing a spectacular lightning bolt. This occurs when the electric field strength in air exceeds 3.0×10^6 N/C. As discussed earlier, the electric field is greatest at points where the radius of curvature of the surface is smallest (the sharp points). Thus, a sphere is the most effective shape for building up large amounts of charge without producing a corona.

Section Review

1. Find the electric field at a point midway between two charges of $+40.0 \times 10^{-9}$ C and $+60.0 \times 10^{-9}$ C separated by a distance of 30.0 cm.

2. **Figure 17-23** shows the electric field lines for two point charges separated by a small distance.
   a. Determine the ratio q_1/q_2.
   b. What are the signs of q_1 and q_2?

q_2

q_1

Figure 17-23

3. Two point charges are a small distance apart.
   a. Sketch the electric field lines for the two if one has a charge four times that of the other and if both charges are positive.
   b. Repeat **(a),** but assume both charges are negative.

4. Why is it that the electric field inside a conductor in electrostatic equilibrium must be zero but the field outside the conductor must be perpendicular to its surface?

5. Explain why you're more likely to get a shock from static electricity by touching a metal object with your finger instead of with your entire hand.

6. **Physics in Action** In an electrostatic spray gun, paint droplets that miss the target object sometimes wrap around and hit the object from behind. Explain why.

CHAPTER 17
Summary

KEY IDEAS

Section 17-1 Electric charge

- There are two kinds of electric charge; likes repel, and unlikes attract.
- Electric charge is conserved.
- The fundamental unit of charge, e, is the charge of a single electron or proton.
- Conductors and insulators can be charged by contact. Conductors can also be charged by induction. A surface charge can be induced on an insulator by polarization.

Section 17-2 Electric force

- According to Coulomb's law, the electric force between two charges is proportional to the magnitude of the charges and inversely proportional to the square of the distance between them.

$$F_{electric} = k_C \frac{q_1 q_2}{r^2}$$

- The electric force is a field force.
- The resultant electric force on any charge is the vector sum of the individual electric forces on that charge.

Section 17-3 The electric field

- An electric field exists in the region around a charged object.
- Electric field strength depends on the magnitude of the charge producing the field and the distance between that charge and a point in the field.

$$E = \frac{F_{electric}}{q_0} = \frac{k_C\, q}{r^2}$$

- The direction of the electric field vector, **E,** is the direction in which an electric force would act on a positive test charge.
- Field lines are tangent to the electric field vector at any point, and the number of lines is proportional to the magnitude of the field strength.

KEY TERMS

conductor (p. 631)

electric field (p. 643)

electric field lines (p. 648)

induction (p. 632)

insulator (p. 631)

Diagram symbols

Positive charge	⊕ +q
Negative charge	⊖ −q
Electric field vector	**E**
Electric field lines	

Variable symbols

Quantities		Units		Conversions
$F_{electric}$	electric force	N	newtons	$= \text{kg} \cdot \text{m/s}^2$
q	charge	C	coulomb (SI unit of charge)	$= 6.3 \times 10^{18}\ e$
		e	fundamental unit of charge	$= 1.60 \times 10^{-19}\ \text{C}$
k_C	Coulomb constant	$\text{N} \cdot \dfrac{\text{m}^2}{\text{C}^2}$	newtons $\times \dfrac{\text{meters}^2}{\text{coulombs}^2}$	
E	electric field strength	N/C	newtons/coulomb	

CHAPTER 17
Review and Assess

ELECTRIC CHARGE

Review questions

1. How are conductors different from insulators?

2. When a conductor is charged by induction, is the induced surface charge on the conductor the same or opposite the charge of the object inducing the surface charge?

3. A negatively charged balloon has 3.5 μC of charge. How many excess electrons are on this balloon?

Conceptual questions

4. Which activity does not produce the same results as the other three?
   a. sliding over a plastic-covered automobile seat
   b. walking across a woolen carpet
   c. scraping food from a metal bowl with a metal spoon
   d. brushing dry hair with a plastic comb

5. Would life be different if the electron were positively charged and the proton were negatively charged? Explain your answer.

6. If a suspended object is attracted to another object that is charged, can you conclude that the suspended object is charged?

7. Explain from an atomic viewpoint why charge is usually transferred by electrons.

8. Because of a higher moisture content, air is a better conductor of charge in the summer than in the winter. Would you expect the shocks from static electricity to be more severe in summer or winter? Explain your answer.

9. A balloon is negatively charged by rubbing and then clings to a wall. Does this mean that the wall is positively charged?

10. Which effect proves more conclusively that an object is charged, attraction to or repulsion from another object? Explain.

ELECTRIC FORCE

Review questions

11. What determines the direction of the electric force between two charges?

12. In which direction will the electric force from the two equal positive charges pull the negative charge shown in **Figure 17-24**?

Figure 17-24

13. The gravitational force is always attractive, while the electric force is both attractive and repulsive. What accounts for this difference?

14. When more than one charged object is present in an area, how can the total electric force on one of the charged objects be found?

Conceptual questions

15. How does the electric force between two charges change when the distance between them is doubled? How does it change when the distance is halved?

16. According to Newton's third law, every action has an equal and opposite reaction. When a comb is charged and held near small pieces of paper, the comb exerts an electric force on the paper pieces and pulls them toward it. Why don't you observe the comb moving toward the paper pieces as well?

Practice problems

17. At the point of fission, a nucleus of ^{235}U with 92 protons is divided into two smaller spheres, each with 46 protons and a radius of 5.9×10^{-15} m. What is the repulsive force pushing these two spheres apart? (See Sample Problem 17A.)

18. What is the electric force between a glass ball with $+2.5\ \mu C$ of charge and a rubber ball with $-5.0\ \mu C$ of charge when they are separated by 5.0 cm? (See Sample Problem 17A.)

19. An alpha particle (charge $= +2.0e$) is sent at high speed toward a gold nucleus (charge $= +79e$). What is the electric force acting on the alpha particle when it is 2.0×10^{-14} m from the gold nucleus? (See Sample Problem 17A.)

20. Three positive point charges of 3.0 nC, 6.0 nC, and 2.0 nC, respectively, are arranged in a triangle, as shown in **Figure 17-25**. Find the magnitude and direction of the electric force on the 6.0 nC charge. (See Sample Problem 17B.)

Figure 17-25

21. Three point charges lie along the y-axis. A charge of $q_1 = -9.0\ \mu C$ is at $y = 6.0$ m, and a charge of $q_2 = -8.0\ \mu C$ is at $y = -4.0$ m. The net electric force on the third charge is zero. Where is this charge located? (See Sample Problem 17C.)

22. A charge of $+3.5$ nC and a charge of $+5.0$ nC are separated by 40.0 cm. Find the equilibrium position for a -6.0 nC charge. (See Sample Problem 17C.)

THE ELECTRIC FIELD

Review questions

23. What is an electric field?

24. Show that the definition of electric field strength ($E = F_{electric}/q_0$) is equivalent to the equation $E = k_C q / r^2$ for point charges.

25. In an irregularly shaped conductor, a corona forms around a sharp end sooner than around a smoother end. Explain why.

26. When electric field lines are being drawn, what determines the number of lines originating from a charge? What determines whether the lines originate from or terminate on a charge?

27. Draw some representative electric field lines for two charges of $+q$ and $-3q$ separated by a small distance.

28. Consider the electric field lines in **Figure 17-26**.
a. Where is charge density the highest? Where is it the lowest?
b. If an opposite charge were brought into the vicinity, where would charge on the pear-shaped object "leak off" most readily?

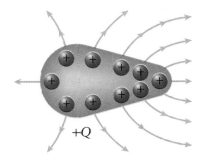

Figure 17-26

29. Do electric field lines actually exist?

30. Why does the dome of a Van de Graaff generator have a spherical surface?

Conceptual questions

31. When defining the electric field, why must the magnitude of the test charge be very small?

32. Why can't two field lines cross one another?

33. A student stands on a piece of insulating material, places her hand on a Van de Graaff generator, and then turns on the generator (see **Figure 17-21** on page 651). Is she shocked? Why or why not? The student finds that her hair stands on end. Why does this occur?

34. In **Figure 17-18** (page 649), where do the extra lines leaving the $+2q$ charge end?

35. A "free" electron and "free" proton are placed in an identical electric field. Compare the electric force on each particle. How do their accelerations compare?

Practice problems

36. Thunderstorms can have an electric field of up to 3.4×10^5 N/C. What is the magnitude of the electric force on an electron in such a field?
(See Sample Problem 17D.)

37. Find the electric field at a point midway between two charges of $+30.0 \times 10^{-9}$ C and $+60.0 \times 10^{-9}$ C separated by a distance of 30.0 cm.
(See Sample Problem 17D.)

38. A $+5.7$ μC point charge is on the x-axis at $x = -3.0$ m, and a $+2.0$ μC point charge is on the x-axis at $x = +1.0$ m. Determine the net electric field (magnitude and direction) on the y-axis at $y = +2.0$ m.
(See Sample Problem 17D.)

MIXED REVIEW

39. Calculate the net charge on a substance consisting of a combination of 7.0×10^{13} protons and 4.0×10^{13} electrons.

40. An electron moving through an electric field experiences an acceleration of 6.3×10^3 m/s^2.
  a. Find the electric force acting on the electron.
  b. What is the strength of the electric field?

41. One gram of copper has 9.48×10^{21} atoms, and each copper atom has 29 electrons.
  a. How many electrons are contained in 1.00 g of copper?
  b. What is the total charge of these electrons?

42. Consider three charges arranged as shown in **Figure 17-27.**
  a. What is the electric field strength at a point 1.0 cm to the left of the middle charge?
  b. What is the magnitude of the force on a -2.0 μC charge placed at this point?

6.0 μC   1.5 μC -2.0 μC

|— 3.0 cm —|— 2.0 cm —| **Figure 17-27**

43. Consider three charges arranged in a triangle as shown in **Figure 17-28.**
  a. What is the net electric force on the charge at the origin?
  b. What is the net electric field at the position of the charge at the origin?

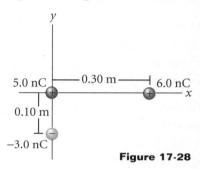

Figure 17-28

44. 1.00 g of hydrogen contains 6.02×10^{23} atoms, each with one electron and one proton. Suppose that 1.00 g of hydrogen is separated into protons and electrons, that the protons are placed at Earth's north pole, and that the electrons are placed at Earth's south pole. Find the magnitude of the resulting compressional force on Earth. (The radius of Earth is approximately 6.38×10^6 m.)

45. Sketch the electric field pattern set up by a positively charged hollow conducting sphere. Include regions both inside and outside the sphere.

46. The moon ($m = 7.36 \times 10^{22}$ kg) is bound to Earth ($m = 5.98 \times 10^{24}$ kg) by gravity. If, instead, the force of attraction were the result of each having a charge of the same magnitude but opposite in sign, find the quantity of charge that would have to be placed on each to produce the required force.

47. Two small metallic spheres, each with a mass of 0.20 g, are suspended as pendulums by light strings from a common point. They are given the same electric charge, and the two come to equilibrium when each string is at an angle of 5.0° with the vertical. If the string is 30.0 cm long, what is the magnitude of the charge on each sphere?

48. What are the magnitude and the direction of the electric field that will balance the weight of an electron? What are the magnitude and direction of the electric field that will balance the weight of a proton?

49. The nucleus of ^{208}Pb has 82 protons within a sphere of radius 6.34×10^{-15} m. Calculate the electric field at the surface of the nucleus. (Hint: Consider the properties of conductors in electrostatic equilibrium. Also, because the points on the surface are outside a spherically symmetrical charge distribution, the total charge may be considered as located at the center of the sphere.)

50. Three positive charges are arranged as shown in **Figure 17-29**. Find the electric field at the fourth corner of the rectangle.

Figure 17-29

51. An electron and a proton are each placed at rest in an external uniform electric field of 520 N/C. Calculate the speed of each particle after 48 ns.

52. The dome of a Van de Graaff generator receives a charge of 2.0×10^{-4} C. The radius of the dome is 1.0 m. Find the magnitude of the electric field strength at the following locations:

a. inside the dome
b. at the surface of the dome
c. 4.0 m from the center of the dome
(See the hint in item 49.)

53. Air becomes a conductor when the electric field strength exceeds 3.0×10^{6} N/C. Determine the maximum amount of charge that can be carried by a metal sphere 2.0 m in radius. (See the hint in item 49.)

54. A Van de Graaff generator is charged so that the electric field at its surface is 3.0×10^{4} N/C.

a. What is the electric force on a proton released at the surface of the generator?
b. Find the proton's acceleration at this instant.

55. Three identical charges $(q = +5.0\ \mu\text{C})$ are along a circle with a radius of 2.0 m at angles of 30°, 150°, and 270°, as shown in **Figure 17-30**. What is the resultant electric field at the center?

Figure 17-30

56. An object with a net charge of 24 μC is placed in a uniform electric field of 610 N/C, directed vertically. What is the mass of this object if it floats in this electric field?

57. A proton accelerates from rest in a uniform electric field of 640 N/C. At some time later, its speed is 1.20×10^{6} m/s.

a. What is the magnitude of the acceleration of the proton?
b. How long does it take the proton to reach this speed?
c. How far has it moved in this time interval?
d. What is its kinetic energy at the later time?

58. Three identical point charges, each of mass $m = 0.10$ kg, hang from three strings, as shown in **Figure 17-31**. If $L = 30.0$ cm and $\theta = 45°$, what is the value of q?

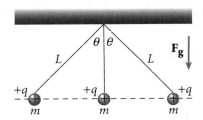

Figure 17-31

59. A small 2.0 g plastic ball is suspended by a 20.0 cm string in a uniform electric field of 1.0×10^{4} N/C, as shown in **Figure 17-32**.

a. Is the ball's charge positive or negative?
b. If the ball is in equilibrium when the string makes a 15° angle with the vertical as indicated, what is the net charge on the ball?

Figure 17-32

60. Five equal negative point charges are placed symmetrically around a circle of radius r. Calculate the electric field at the center of the circle.

61. Air breaks down (loses its insulating quality) and sparking results if the electric field strength is increased to about 3.0×10^6 N/C.

    a. What acceleration does an electron experience in such a field?

b. If the electron starts from rest, in what distance does it acquire a speed equal to 10.0 percent of the speed of light?

c. What acceleration does a proton experience in such a field?

Technology & Learning

Graphing calculators

Program your graphing calculator to create a graph of force versus distance for two positive charges in order to determine the forces involved in each of the following situations:

    a. 7.5×10^{-5} C and 3.2×10^{-6} C, 0.20 m apart
    b. 7.5×10^{-5} C and 3.2×10^{-6} C, 0.016 m apart
    c. 5.5×10^{-6} C and 3.2×10^{-5} C, 0.016 m apart
    d. 5.5×10^{-6} C and 3.2×10^{-5} C, 0.060 m apart

Press ⌷Y=⌷ and ⌷CLEAR⌷ to clear any functions. Open a new program by pressing ⌷PRGM⌷ ⌷▶⌷ ⌷▶⌷ ⌷ENTER⌷. Name the program "COULOMB" and press ⌷ENTER⌷. Then enter the program shown in the table below.

To exit the program editor, press ⌷2nd⌷ ⌷QUIT⌷. To run the program, press ⌷PRGM⌷, select "COULOMB," and press ⌷ENTER⌷ ⌷ENTER⌷. Enter the value for the charges, pressing ⌷ENTER⌷ after each one. (Remember to use ⌷2nd⌷ ⌷EE⌷ to enter exponents and the ⌷(-)⌷ key to indicate negative exponents.)

The calculator will provide a graph of the force applied versus the distance of separation. (If the graph is not visible, press ⌷WINDOW⌷, change the settings for the graph window, then press ⌷GRAPH⌷.)

Press ⌷TRACE⌷, and use the arrow keys to trace along the curve. The x value corresponds to the distance in meters, and the y value corresponds to the force in newtons.

After you have finished using the graph for one set of charges, press ⌷2nd⌷ ⌷QUIT⌷ to run the program for the next set.

Keystrokes	Display
	PROGRAM: COULOMB
1. ⌷PRGM⌷ ⌷▶⌷ ⌷3⌷ ⌷ALPHA⌷ ⌷"⌷ ⌷ALPHA⌷ ⌷Q⌷ ⌷1⌷ ⌷2nd⌷ ⌷TEST⌷ ⌷1⌷ ⌷ALPHA⌷ ⌷"⌷ ⌷ENTER⌷	:DISP "Q1="
2. ⌷PRGM⌷ ⌷▶⌷ ⌷1⌷ ⌷ALPHA⌷ ⌷A⌷ ⌷ENTER⌷	:INPUT A
3. ⌷PRGM⌷ ⌷▶⌷ ⌷3⌷ ⌷ALPHA⌷ ⌷"⌷ ⌷ALPHA⌷ ⌷Q⌷ ⌷2⌷ ⌷2nd⌷ ⌷TEST⌷ ⌷1⌷ ⌷ALPHA⌷ ⌷"⌷ ⌷ENTER⌷	:DISP "Q2="
4. ⌷PRGM⌷ ⌷▶⌷ ⌷1⌷ ⌷ALPHA⌷ ⌷B⌷ ⌷ENTER⌷	:INPUT B
5. ⌷ALPHA⌷ ⌷"⌷ ⌷8⌷ ⌷.⌷ ⌷9⌷ ⌷9⌷ ⌷2nd⌷ ⌷EE⌷ ⌷9⌷ ⌷(⌷ ⌷ALPHA⌷ ⌷A⌷ ⌷×⌷ ⌷ALPHA⌷ ⌷B⌷ ⌷÷⌷ ⌷X,T,θ⌷ ⌷x^2⌷ ⌷)⌷ ⌷ALPHA⌷ ⌷"⌷ ⌷STO▶⌷ ⌷2nd⌷ ⌷Y-VARS⌷ ⌷1⌷ ⌷1⌷ ⌷ENTER⌷	:"8.99E9(A∗B/X²)" → Y₁
6. ⌷PRGM⌷ ⌷▶⌷ ⌷4⌷ ⌷ENTER⌷	:DISPGRAPH

62. A DNA molecule (deoxyribonucleic acid) is 2.17 μm long. The ends of the molecule become singly ionized so that there is -1.60×10^{-19} C on one end and $+1.60 \times 10^{-19}$ C on the other. The helical molecule acts as a spring and compresses 1.00 percent upon becoming charged. Find the effective spring constant of the molecule.

63. An electron and a proton both start from rest and from the same point in a uniform electric field of 370.0 N/C. How far apart are they 1.00 μs after they are released? Ignore the attraction between the electron and the proton. (Hint: Imagine the experiment performed with the proton only, and then repeat with the electron only.)

64. An electron is accelerated by a constant electric field of 300.0 N/C.
   a. Find the acceleration of the electron.
   b. Find the electron's speed after 1.00×10^{-8} s, assuming it starts from rest.

65. A constant electric field directed along the positive x-axis has a strength of 2.0×10^3 N/C.
   a. Find the electric force exerted on a proton by the field.
   b. Find the acceleration of the proton.
   c. Find the time required for the proton to reach a speed of 1.00×10^6 m/s, assuming it starts from rest.

66. Consider an electron that is released from rest in a uniform electric field.
   a. If the electron is accelerated to 1.0 percent of the speed of light after traveling 2.0 mm, what is the strength of the electric field?
   b. What speed does the electron have after traveling 4.0 mm from rest?

67. Each of the protons in a particle beam has a kinetic energy of 3.25×10^{-15} J. What are the magnitude and direction of the electric field that will stop these protons in a distance of 1.25 m?

Alternative Assessment

Performance assessment

1. A metal can is placed on a wooden table. If a positively charged ball suspended by a thread is brought close to the can, the ball will swing toward the can, make contact, then move away. Explain why this happens and predict whether the ball is likely to make contact a second time. Sketch diagrams showing the charges on the ball and on the can at each phase. How can you test whether your explanation is correct? If your teacher approves of your plan, try testing your explanation.

2. The common copying machine was designed in the 1960s, after the American inventor Chester Carlson developed a practical device for attracting carbon-black to paper using localized electrostatic action. Research how this process works and determine why the last copy made when several hundred copies are made can be noticeably less sharp than the first copy. Create a report, poster, or brochure for office workers containing tips for using copiers.

Portfolio projects

3. Research how an electrostatic precipitator works to remove smoke and dust particles from the polluting emissions of fuel-burning industries. Find out what industries in your community use precipitators. What are their advantages and costs? What alternatives are available? Summarize your findings in a brochure, poster, or chart.

4. Imagine you are a member of a research team interested in lightning and you are preparing a grant proposal. Research information about the frequency, location, and effects of thunderstorms. Write a proposal that includes background information, research questions, a description of necessary equipment, and recommended locations for data collection.

5. Two 10^{-10} kg meteorites are traveling in deep space 1000 km apart. Each has 1.00 C of positive charge. Will their trajectories converge or diverge? How would your answer change if the meteorites had greater masses? What if they had greater charges?

CHAPTER 17
Laboratory Exercise

MATERIALS LIST

- ✔ 2 polystyrene rods
- ✔ 2 PVC rods
- ✔ insulated copper wire
- ✔ demonstration capacitor
- ✔ electroscope
- ✔ flint glass rod
- ✔ insulated wire with 2 alligator clips
- ✔ metric ruler
- ✔ nylon cord
- ✔ roll of cellophane tape
- ✔ silk cloth
- ✔ silk thread
- ✔ support stand with clamp
- ✔ suspension support for rod
- ✔ wool pad

ELECTROSTATICS

When objects made of two different materials are rubbed together, electric charges accumulate on both objects. This phenomenon is known as static electricity. When an object has an electric charge, it attracts some things and repels others. The charges can also be transferred to some objects and not to others. In this experiment, you will produce charges on different objects and distinguish between the types of charges produced. You will also use an electroscope to examine the transfer of charges and the conductivity of different materials.

SAFETY

- Never put broken glass or ceramics in a regular waste container. Use a dustpan, brush, and heavy gloves to carefully pick up broken pieces and dispose of them in a container specifically provided for this purpose.

PREPARATION

1. Read the entire lab, and plan what steps you will take.

2. In your lab notebook, prepare an observation table with two wide columns. Label the columns *Experiment* and *Observation*. For each part of the lab, you will write a brief description of what you do in each step under *Experiment*. In the *Observation* column, record your observations of what happens.

PROCEDURE

Electric charge

3. Take four strips of cellophane tape. Each strip should be 20 cm long. Fold over a tab at the end of each tape. Tape strips to the lab table, and label the strips *A, B, C,* and *D* with a pencil.

4. Vigorously rub tapes A and B with a wool pad. Grasp the tabbed ends of A and B and carefully remove the tapes from the table. Slowly bring the tapes close together, but do not allow them to touch. Observe how they affect one another. Record your observations in your lab notebook. Carefully place tapes A and B back on the lab table.

5. Carefully remove tape C from the lab table. Tape it firmly down on top of tape D. Carefully remove tapes C and D together from the lab table. Quickly separate them, being careful not to tangle the tapes. Bring the tapes close together—but not touching—and observe how they affect one another. Record your observations in your lab notebook. Place tape D back on the lab table, and place tape C down on top of tape D.

6. Vigorously rub tape A with a wool pad again. Grasp tape A by the tab and carefully remove it from the table. Remove C and D together from the table. Quickly pull C and D apart. Bring C close to tape A, but do not let them touch. Observe how they affect each other. Move C away, and bring D close to tape A. Record your observations in your lab notebook. Throw the four tapes away.

7. Tape a meterstick flat on the surface of the table so that the end of the meterstick extends over the edge of the table. Take another 20 cm long piece of tape, fold a tab on one end, and tape it down on the table. Vigorously rub the tape with a wool pad. Grasp the tab, and carefully remove the tape. Attach the tape to the end of the meterstick so that it freely hangs straight down.

8. Rub a polystyrene rod with wool. Bring the rod near the end of the tape that is hanging down, and observe the effect on the tape. Record your observations in your lab notebook. Throw away the tape, and remove the meterstick from the tabletop.

9. Tie the suspension support securely to a string, and suspend the string from the support stand and clamp. Attach a polystyrene rod to the support, and rub the rod with a wool pad. Rub a second polystyrene rod with wool, and bring this rod near one end of the suspended rod. Observe what happens, and record your observations in your lab notebook.

10. Rub the PVC rod with wool, and bring the rod near one end of the suspended polystyrene rod. Observe what happens, and record your observations.

11. Suspend a glass rod on the support, and rub the rod with silk. Rub the PVC rod with wool, and bring the rod near one end of the glass rod. Observe what happens, and record your observations.

12. Suspend a PVC rod on the support, and rub the rod with wool. Rub another PVC rod with wool, and bring the rod near one end of the suspended PVC rod. Observe what happens, and record your observations.

Figure 17-33

Step 9: Suspend the rod securely so that it hangs freely.

Step 10: Charge the rod by rubbing it vigorously with the wool pad. Bring the charged rod near one end of the suspended rod.

Charging an electroscope by conduction and induction

13. Charge a polystyrene rod, and touch it briefly against the knob of the electroscope. Record your observations.

14. Touch the knob of the electroscope with your hand. Observe what happens.

15. Bring a charged polystyrene rod near, but not touching, the electroscope knob. Observe what happens.

16. Continue holding the polystyrene rod near the electroscope knob. Briefly touch the knob of the electroscope with your finger. Observe what happens. Remove the rod, and observe what happens.

17. Discharge the electroscope by connecting a wire from it to a grounded object. Your teacher will tell you where to connect the wire.

18. Charge a glass rod, and repeat the procedure in steps 13–17 using the glass rod instead of the polystyrene rod.

Conductors, insulators, and capacitors

19. Set up the apparatus as shown in **Figure 17-34** but do not include the second capacitor plate until Step 22. The insulated wire has an alligator clip at each end. One alligator clip connects to the rod beneath the ball on the electroscope. Run the insulated copper wire from the other alligator clip to one of the plates of the demonstration capacitor.

20. Follow the procedure in steps 13–17, but this time bring the rod near the capacitor plate. Observe what happens to the leaves of the electroscope when the rod is brought near the capacitor plate. Record your observations.

21. Replace the copper wire with a piece of thread. Follow the procedure in steps 13–17, but this time bring the rod near the capacitor plate. Observe what happens to the leaves of the electroscope when the rod is brought near the capacitor plate. Record your observations.

Figure 17-34
Step 20: Charge a polystyrene rod, and bring it near plate B of the capacitor.

Step 21: Repeat the procedure using thread instead of the copper wire.

Step 22: Use copper wire to connect the electroscope to one plate of the capacitor. Touch the charged rod to the plate, and then move the second plate close to the first.

22. Connect the rod beneath the knob of the electroscope to one plate of the demonstration capacitor with a short piece of copper wire. Touch the charged polystyrene rod to the plate, and observe what happens to the leaves of the electroscope. Bring the second plate of the capacitor near, but not touching, the first. Observe what happens, and record your observations in your notebook.

23. Remove the second capacitor plate. Observe what happens. Record your observations in your notebook.

24. Bring the second plate near the first again. Using both capacitor plates, try to cause the same result as you obtained using only one plate.

ANALYSIS AND INTERPRETATION

Calculations and data analysis

1. **Organizing data**   Use examples from your observations to explain your answers to the following questions. Assume that the polystyrene rod takes a negative charge when it is rubbed with wool. To answer these questions, assume that like charges repel one another and unlike charges attract one another.

   a. What type of charge is on tape A?

   b. What type of charge is on tape B?

   c. Are the charges on C and D the same?

   d. Are the charges on C or D the same as the charges on A or B?

   e. What type of charge is on the charged suspended glass rod? Is the charge on the suspended glass rod the same or different from the charge on tape A?

   f. What type of charge is on the charged suspended polystyrene rod?

   g. What type of charge is on the second charged polystyrene rod?

   h. What type of charge is on the charged suspended PVC rod?

2. **Analyzing results**   Use your observations to answer the following:

   a. After you touch the knob of the electroscope with your hand, what type of charge is on the electroscope? Explain how your observations support this conclusion.

   b. When the charged polystyrene rod is used to charge an electroscope by induction, what type of charge is on the electroscope?

   c. What type of charge is on the electroscope when it is charged by induction using the charged glass rod?

3. **Analyzing information**   Is copper a conductor or an insulator? Is silk a conductor or an insulator? Use your observations to support your answers.

Conclusions

4. **Analyzing conclusions**   Based on your observations, how many types of charge are there? Explain how your observations support this conclusion.

5. **Organizing ideas**   Use your results to explain what a capacitor does.

CHAPTER 18

Electrical Energy and Capacitance

PHYSICS IN ACTION

During a thunderstorm, particles having different charges accumulate in different parts of a cloud. This separation of charges creates an electric field between a cloud and the ground. Normally, the charges remain separate because air is a nearly perfect insulator. But as charges continue to accumulate, the strength of the electric field increases, creating a potential difference of as much as 100 million volts. As the potential difference increases, a crucial *breakdown voltage* is sometimes reached; that is, the air is ionized by the potential difference and becomes a conductor. Electric charge then flows between the cloud and the ground, an event we perceive as lightning in the sky.

- *What is the relationship between electric potential and the electric field?*

- *How is a thunderstorm like a large natural capacitor?*

CONCEPT REVIEW

- **Potential energy** (Section 5-2)
- **Electric field** (Section 17-3)

18-1
Electrical potential energy

18-1 SECTION OBJECTIVES

- **Define electrical potential energy.**

- **Compute the electrical potential energy for various charge distributions.**

electrical potential energy

potential energy associated with an object due to its position relative to a source of electric force

ELECTRICAL ENERGY AND ELECTRIC FORCE

When two charges interact, there is an electric force between them, as described in Chapter 17. As with the gravitational force associated with an object's position relative to Earth, there is a potential energy associated with this force. This kind of potential energy is called **electrical potential energy.** Unlike gravitational potential energy, electrical potential energy results from the interaction of two objects' charges, not their masses.

Electrical potential energy is included in mechanical energy

Mechanical energy is conserved as long as friction and radiation are not present. As with gravitational and elastic potential energy, electrical potential energy can be included in the expression for mechanical energy (see Chapter 5). If gravitational force, elastic force, and electric force are all acting on an object, the mechanical energy can be written as follows:

$$ME = KE + PE_{grav} + PE_{elastic} + PE_{electric}$$

To account for the forces (except friction) that may also be present in a problem, the appropriate potential-energy terms associated with each force are added to the expression for mechanical energy.

Any time a charge moves because of an electric force, whether from a uniform electric field or from another charge or group of charges, work is done on that charge. At the same time, the electrical potential energy associated with the charge's position in the system decreases, as shown in **Figure 18-1.**

Figure 18-1

As the charges in these sparks move, the electrical potential energy decreases, just as gravitational potential energy decreases as an object falls.

Electrical potential energy can be associated with a charge in a uniform field

Consider a positive charge in a uniform electric field. (A uniform field is a field that has the same value and direction at all points.) Assume the charge is displaced at a constant velocity *in the same direction as the electric field,* as shown in **Figure 18-2.**

There is a change in the electrical potential energy associated with the charge's new position in the electric field. The change in the electrical potential energy depends on the charge, *q*, as well as the strength of the electric field, *E*, and the displacement, *d*. It can be written as follows:

$$\Delta PE_{electric} = -qE\Delta d$$

The negative sign indicates that the electrical potential energy will increase if the charge is negative and decrease if the charge is positive.

As with other forms of potential energy, it is the *difference* in electrical potential energy that is physically important. If the displacement in the expression above is chosen so that it is the distance in the direction of the field from the reference point, or zero level, then the initial electrical potential energy is zero and the expression can be rewritten as shown below. As with other forms of energy, the SI unit for electrical potential energy is the joule (J).

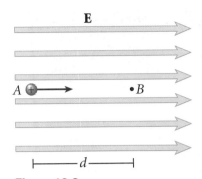

Figure 18-2
A positive charge moves from point A to point B in a uniform electric field, and the potential energy changes as a result.

ELECTRICAL POTENTIAL ENERGY IN A UNIFORM ELECTRIC FIELD

$$PE_{electric} = -qEd$$

**electrical potential energy =
−(charge × electric field strength × displacement from the reference point in the direction of the field)**

This equation is valid only for a uniform electric field. As described in Chapter 17, that the electric field lines for a point charge are closer together as they get nearer to the charge because the electric field is increasing. Thus, the electric field of a point charge is an example of a nonuniform field.

In calculating electrical potential energy, *d* is the magnitude of the displacement's component *in the direction of the electric field.* Any displacement of the charge in a direction perpendicular to the electric field does not change the electrical potential energy. This is similar to gravitational potential energy, in which only the vertical distance from the zero level is important.

Electrical potential energy can be associated with a pair of charges

Recall that a single point charge produces a nonuniform electric field. If a second charge is placed nearby, there will be an electrical potential energy associated with the two charges. Because the electric field is not uniform, the electrical potential energy of the system of two charges requires a different expression.

ELECTRICAL POTENTIAL ENERGY FOR A PAIR OF CHARGES

$$PE_{electric} = k_C \frac{q_1 q_2}{r}$$

$$\text{electrical potential energy} = \text{Coulomb constant} \times \frac{\text{charge 1} \times \text{charge 2}}{\text{distance}}$$

The quantity k_C is the *Coulomb constant,* which has an approximate value of $8.99 \times 10^9 \text{ N} \cdot \text{m}^2/\text{C}^2$.

There are several things to keep in mind regarding this expression. First, the reference point for the electrical potential energy is assumed to be at infinity. This can be verified by noting that the electrical potential energy goes to zero as the distance between the charges, r, goes to infinity. Second, because like charges repel, positive work must be done to bring them together, so the electrical potential energy is positive for like charges and negative for unlike charges.

This expression can be used to determine the electrical potential energy associated with more than two charges. In such cases, determine the electrical potential energy associated with *each pair* of charges, and then add the energies.

SAMPLE PROBLEM 18A

Electrical potential energy

PROBLEM

In one model of the hydrogen atom, an electron in its lowest energy state moves in a circular orbit about the nucleus (a single proton) at a distance of 5.29×10^{-11} m. Find the electrical potential energy of the hydrogen atom.

SOLUTION

Given: $q_1 = -1.60 \times 10^{-19}$ C $q_2 = +1.60 \times 10^{-19}$ C
$r = 5.29 \times 10^{-11}$ m

Unknown: $PE_{electric} = ?$

Use the equation for the electrical potential energy associated with a pair of charges.

$$PE_{electric} = k_C \frac{q_1 q_2}{r}$$

$$PE_{electric} = (8.99 \times 10^9 \text{ N} \cdot \text{m}^2/\text{C}^2) \left(\frac{(-1.60 \times 10^{-19} \text{ C})(+1.60 \times 10^{-19} \text{ C})}{(5.29 \times 10^{-11} \text{ m})} \right)$$

$$\boxed{PE_{electric} = -4.35 \times 10^{-18} \text{ J}}$$

Electrical potential energy

1. Two point charges are located on the y-axis—one, of 3.0×10^{-9} C, is at the origin, and the second, of 6.0×10^{-9} C, is at the point (0.0 cm, 30.0 cm).

   a. What is the electrical potential energy associated with the arrangement of charges if a third charge of 4.0×10^{-9} C is at the point (0.0 cm, 60.0 cm)?

   b. What if the third charge is at the point (0.0 cm, −60.0 cm)?

   c. What if a -6.0×10^{-9} C charge placed at (0.0 cm, −60.0 cm) is the third charge?

   (Hint: There are three pairs of interacting charges.)

2. What is the change in the electrical potential energy of a proton as it moves a distance of 2.0 cm in the direction of a uniform electric field with a strength of 215 N/C? (Hint: The electrical potential energy depends on the distance moved in the direction of the field.)

Section Review

1. What is the difference between $\Delta PE_{electric}$ and $PE_{electric}$?

2. In a uniform electric field, what factors does the electrical potential energy depend on?

3. Describe the conditions that are necessary for mechanical energy to be a conserved quantity.

4. Is there a single correct reference point from which all electrical potential energy measurements must be taken?

5. A uniform electric field with a magnitude of 250 N/C is directed in the positive x direction. A 12 μC charge moves from the origin to the point (20.0 cm, 50.0 cm). What is the change in the electrical potential energy of the system as a result of the change in position of this charge?

6. **Physics in Action** What is the change in the electrical potential energy in a lightning bolt if 1.0×10^5 C of charge travels to the ground from a cloud 2.5 km above the ground in the direction of the field? Assume the electric field is uniform and has a magnitude of 1.0×10^6 N/C.

18-2
Potential difference

- **Distinguish between electrical potential energy, electric potential, and potential difference.**

- **Compute the electric potential for various charge distributions.**

electric potential

the electrical potential energy associated with a charged particle divided by the charge of the particle

potential difference

the change in electrical potential energy associated with a charged particle divided by the charge of the particle

Figure 18-3

For a typical car battery, there is a potential difference of 12 V between the negative (black) and the positive (red) terminals.

CHANGING ELECTRIC POTENTIAL

Electrical potential energy is useful in solving problems, particularly those involving charged particles. But at any point in an electric field, as the value of the charge increases, the value of the electrical potential energy increases. A more practical concept in the study of electricity is **electric potential.**

The electric potential at some point is defined as the electrical potential energy associated with a charged particle in an electric field divided by the charge of the particle.

$$V = \frac{PE_{electric}}{q}$$

Although a greater charge will involve a greater amount of electrical potential energy, the ratio of that energy to the charge is the same as it would be if a smaller charge were at the same position in the field. In other words, the electric potential at a point *is independent of the charge at that point.*

Potential difference is a change in electric potential

Because the reference point for measuring electrical potential energy is arbitrary, the reference point for measuring electric potential is also arbitrary. Thus, only changes in electric potential are significant. The **potential difference** between two points can be expressed as follows:

POTENTIAL DIFFERENCE

$$\Delta V = \frac{\Delta PE_{electric}}{q}$$

$$\text{potential difference} = \frac{\text{change in electrical potential energy}}{\text{electric charge}}$$

Potential difference is a measure of the change in the electrical potential energy divided by the charge. The SI unit for potential difference (and electric potential) is the *volt,* V, and is equivalent to one joule per coulomb. As a 1 C charge moves through a potential difference of 1 V, the charge gains (or loses) 1 J of energy. The potential difference between the two terminals of a battery, for instance, can range from about 1.5 V for a small battery to about 12 V for a car battery like the one shown in **Figure 18-3.** The potential difference between the two slots in a household electrical outlet is about 120 V.

Remember that only electrical potential energy is a quantity of energy, with units in joules. Electric potential and potential difference are both measures of energy per unit charge (measured in units of volts), and potential difference describes a change in energy per unit charge.

The potential difference in a uniform field varies with the displacement from a reference point

The expression for potential difference can be combined with the expressions for electrical potential energy. The resulting equations are often simpler to apply in certain situations. For example, consider the electrical potential energy of a charge in a uniform electric field.

$$PE_{electric} = -qEd$$

This can be substituted into the equation for potential difference.

$$\Delta V = \frac{\Delta PE_{electric}}{q}$$

$$\Delta V = \frac{\Delta(-qEd)}{q}$$

As the charge moves in the electric field, the only quantity in the parentheses that changes is the displacement from the reference point. Thus, the potential difference in this case can be rewritten as follows:

POTENTIAL DIFFERENCE IN A UNIFORM ELECTRIC FIELD

$$\Delta V = -E\Delta d$$

potential difference =
−(magnitude of the electric field × displacement)

Again, keep in mind that the quantity Δd in this expression is the displacement moved in the direction of the field. Any displacement perpendicular to the field does not change the electrical potential energy.

The reference point for potential difference near a point charge is often at infinity

In Section 18-1, we were given the expression for the electrical potential energy associated with a pair of charges. To determine the potential difference between two points in the field of a point charge, we first calculate the electric potential associated with each point. Imagine a point charge q_2 in the electric field of a point charge q_1 at point B some distance away, as shown in **Figure 18-4.** The electric potential at point A due to q_1 can be expressed as follows:

$$V = \frac{PE_{electric}}{q_2} = k_C \frac{q_1 q_2}{r q_2} = k_C \frac{q_1}{r}$$

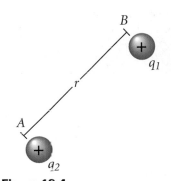

Figure 18-4
The electric potential at point A depends on the charge at point B and the distance r.

Do not confuse the two charges in this example. The charge q_1 is responsible for the electric potential at point A. Therefore, *an electric potential exists at some point in an electric field regardless of whether there is a charge at that point.* In this case, the electric potential at a point depends on only two quantities: the charge responsible for the electric potential (in this case q_1) and the distance r from this charge to the point in question.

To determine the potential difference between any two points near the point charge q_1, first note that the electric potential at each point depends only on the distance from each point to the charge q_1. If the two distances are r_1 and r_2, then the potential difference between these two points can be written as follows:

$$\Delta V = k_C \frac{q_1}{r_2} - k_C \frac{q_1}{r_1} = k_C q_1 \left(\frac{1}{r_2} - \frac{1}{r_1} \right)$$

If the distance r_1 is assumed to be infinitely far from the charge q_1, then the quantity $1/r_1$ is zero. The expression then simplifies to the following (dropping the subscripts):

POTENTIAL DIFFERENCE BETWEEN A POINT AT INFINITY AND SOME LOCATION NEAR A POINT CHARGE

$$\Delta V = k_C \frac{q}{r}$$

$$\text{potential difference} = \text{Coulomb constant} \times \frac{\text{value of the point charge}}{\text{distance to the point charge}}$$

This result for the potential difference associated with a point charge appears identical to the electric potential associated with a point charge. The two expressions look the same only because we have chosen a special reference point from which to measure the potential difference.

The superposition principle can be used to calculate the electric potential for a group of charges

The electric potential at a point near two or more charges is obtained by applying a rule called the *superposition principle.* This rule states that the total electric potential at some point near several point charges is the algebraic sum of the electric potentials resulting from each of the individual charges. While this is similar to the method used in Chapter 17 to find the resultant electric field at a point in space, here the summation is much easier to evaluate because the electric potentials are scalar quantities, not vector quantities. There are no components to worry about.

To evaluate the electric potential at a point near a group of point charges, you simply take the algebraic sum of the potentials resulting from all charges. Remember, you must keep track of signs. The electric potential at some point near a positive charge is positive, and the potential near a negative charge is negative.

Did you know?

Because it is measured in units of volts, potential difference is sometimes referred to as *voltage*.

Potential difference

PROBLEM

A 5.0 μC point charge is at the origin, and a point charge of -2.0 μC is on the x-axis at (3.0 m, 0.0 m), as shown in Figure 18-5. Find the total potential difference resulting from these charges between point P, with coordinates (0.0 m, 4.0 m), and a point infinitely far away.

Figure 18-5

SOLUTION

Given: $q_1 = 5.0 \times 10^{-6}$ C $q_2 = -2.0 \times 10^{-6}$ C
$r_1 = 4.0$ m

Unknown: $V = ?$

Use the equation for the potential difference near a point charge.

$$\Delta V_1 = k_C \frac{q_1}{r_1} = \left(8.99 \times 10^9 \frac{\text{N} \cdot \text{m}^2}{\text{C}^2}\right)\left(\frac{5.0 \times 10^{-6} \text{ C}}{4.0 \text{ m}}\right) = 1.1 \times 10^4 \text{ V}$$

$$r_2 = \sqrt{(3.0 \text{ m})^2 + (4.0 \text{ m})^2} = \sqrt{25 \text{ m}^2} = 5.0 \text{ m}$$

$$\Delta V_2 = k_C \frac{q_2}{r_2} = \left(8.99 \times 10^9 \frac{\text{N} \cdot \text{m}^2}{\text{C}^2}\right)\left(\frac{-2.0 \times 10^{-6} \text{ C}}{5.0 \text{ m}}\right) = -0.36 \times 10^4 \text{ V}$$

$$\Delta V = \Delta V_1 + \Delta V_2 = (1.1 \times 10^4 \text{ V}) - (0.36 \times 10^4 \text{ V})$$

$$\boxed{\Delta V = 7000 \text{ V}}$$

Potential difference

1. Find the potential difference between a point infinitely far away and a point 1.0 cm from a proton.

2. Two point charges of magnitude 5.0 nC and -3.0 nC are separated by 35.0 cm. What is the potential difference between a point infinitely far away and a point midway between the charges?

3. Four particles with charges of 5.0 μC, 3.0 μC, 3.0 μC, and -5.0 μC are placed at the corners of a 2.0 m $\times$ 2.0 m square. Determine the potential difference between the center of the square and infinity.

A potential difference within a battery causes charges to move

One of the best applications of the concepts of electric potential and potential difference is in the operation of a battery in some electrical apparatus. The battery is useful when it is connected by conducting wires to devices such as light bulbs, radios, power windows, motors, and so forth.

Recall that the reference point for determining the electric potential at some point is arbitrary. When a battery is connected by conductors to an electrical device, the reference point is often defined by *grounding* some point of the arrangement. (A point is said to be grounded when it is connected to an object having an electric potential of zero.) For example, imagine a typical 12 V automobile battery. Such a battery maintains a potential difference across its terminals, where the positive terminal is 12 V higher in potential than the negative terminal. If the negative plate of the battery is grounded, the positive plate would then have a potential of 12 V.

Consumer Focus — *Finding the Right Battery*

*H*eavy duty," "long-lasting alkaline," and "environmentally friendly rechargeable" are some of the labels that manufacturers put on batteries. But how do you know which one is the best?

The answer depends on how you will use it. Some batteries are used continuously, but others are turned off and on frequently, as in a stereo. Still others must be able to hold a charge without being used, especially if they will be used in smoke detectors and flashlights.

In terms of price, "heavy duty" batteries typically cost the least, but they last only about 30 percent as long as alkaline batteries. This makes them prohibitively expensive for most uses and makes them an unnecessary source of landfill clutter.

Alkaline batteries are more expensive but have longer lives, lasting up to 6 h in continuous use and up to 18 h in intermittent use. They hold a full charge for years, making them good for use in flashlights and similar devices. They are now less of an environmental problem because manufacturers stopped using mercury in such products several years ago. However, because they are single-use batteries, they also end up in landfills very quickly.

Rechargeable cells are the most expensive to purchase initially. They can cost up to $8, but if recycled, they are the most economical in the long term and are the most environmentally sound choice. These cells, often called NiCads because they contain nickel (Ni) and cadmium (Cd) metals, can be recharged hundreds of times. Although NiCads last only about half as long on one charge as alkaline batteries, the electricity to recharge them costs pennies. NiCads lose about 1 percent of their stored energy each day they are not used and should therefore never be put in smoke detectors or flashlights.

Now imagine a charge of 1 C moving around a battery connected to an electrical device. The charge moves inside the battery from the negative terminal (which is at an electrical potential of 0 V) to the positive terminal (which is at an electrical potential of 12 V). The battery does work on the charge to move it from the negative terminal to the positive terminal and to increase the electrical potential energy associated with the charge. The net result is an electrical potential increase of 12 V. This means that every coulomb of positive charge that leaves the positive terminal of the battery is associated with a total of 12 J of electrical potential energy.

As charge moves through the conductors and devices toward the negative battery terminal, it gives up its 12 J of electrical potential energy to the external devices. When the charge reaches the negative terminal, its electrical potential energy is zero. At this point, the battery provides another 12 J of energy to the charge as it is moved from the negative terminal to the positive terminal of the battery, allowing the charge to make another transit of the device and battery.

CONCEPT PREVIEW

The role of a battery in electric circuits will be discussed further in Chapters 19 and 20.

Section Review

1. The gap between electrodes in a spark plug is 0.060 cm. To produce an electric spark in a gasoline-air mixture, there must be an electric field of 3.0×10^6 V/m. What minimum potential difference must be supplied by the ignition circuit to start a car?

2. Given the electrical potential energy, how do you calculate electric potential?

3. Why is electric potential a more useful quantity for most calculations than electrical potential energy?

4. Explain how electric potential and potential difference are related. What units are used for each one?

5. A proton is released from rest in a uniform electric field with a magnitude of 8.0×10^4 V/m. The proton is displaced 0.50 m as a result.
   a. Find the potential difference between the proton's initial and final positions.
   b. Find the change in electrical potential energy of the proton as a result of this displacement.

6. **Physics in Action**   In a thunderstorm, the air must be ionized by a high voltage before a conducting path for a lightning bolt can be created. An electric field of about 1.0×10^6 V/m is required to ionize dry air. What would the breakdown voltage in air be if a thundercloud were 3.50 km above ground and the electric field between the cloud and the ground were uniform?

18-3
Capacitance

CAPACITORS AND CHARGE STORAGE

A capacitor is a device that is used in a variety of electric circuits to perform many functions. Uses include tuning the frequency of radio receivers, eliminating sparking in automobile ignition systems, and storing energy in electronic flash units.

A charged capacitor is useful because it acts as a storehouse of charge and energy that can be reclaimed when needed for a specific application. A typical design for a capacitor consists of two parallel metal plates separated by a small distance. This type of capacitor is called a *parallel-plate capacitor*.

When used in an electric circuit, the plates are connected to the two terminals of a battery or other potential difference, as shown in **Figure 18-6.** When this connection is made, charges are removed from one of the plates, leaving the plate with a net charge. An equal and opposite amount of charge accumulates on the other plate. Charge transfer between the plates stops when the potential difference between the plates is equal to the potential difference between the terminals of the battery. This charging process is illustrated in **Figure 18-6(b).**

Capacitance is the ratio of charge to potential difference

capacitance

the ability of a conductor to store energy in the form of electrically separated charges

The ability of a conductor to store energy in the form of electrically separated charges is measured by the **capacitance** of the conductor. The capacitance is defined as the ratio of the net charge on each plate to the potential difference created by the separated charges.

(a) No net charge on plates   **(b)** Small net charge on each plate   **(c)** Greater net charge on each plate

Before charging   During charging   After charging

Figure 18-6
When connected to a battery, the plates of a parallel-plate capacitor become oppositely charged.

CAPACITANCE

$$C = \frac{Q}{\Delta V}$$

$$\text{capacitance} = \frac{\text{magnitude of charge on each plate}}{\text{potential difference}}$$

The SI unit for capacitance is the *farad*, F, which is equivalent to a coulomb per volt (C/V). In practice, most typical capacitors have capacitances ranging from microfarads ($1\ \mu F = 1 \times 10^{-6}$ F) to picofarads ($1\ pF = 1 \times 10^{-12}$ F).

Capacitance depends on the size and shape of the capacitor

The capacitance of a parallel-plate capacitor with no material between its plates is given by the following expression:

CAPACITANCE FOR A PARALLEL-PLATE CAPACITOR IN A VACUUM

$$C = \varepsilon_0 \frac{A}{d}$$

$$\text{capacitance} = \text{permittivity of a vacuum} \times \frac{\text{area of one of the plates}}{\text{distance between the plates}}$$

In this expression, the Greek letter ε (epsilon) represents a constant called the *permittivity* of the medium. When it is followed by a subscripted zero, it refers to a vacuum. It has a magnitude of $8.85 \times 10^{-12}\ C^2/N \cdot m^2$.

Notice that the amount of charge a parallel-plate capacitor can store for a given potential difference increases as the plate area increases. A capacitor constructed from large plates has a larger capacitance than one having small plates if their plate separations are the same. For a given potential difference, the charge on the plates—and thus the capacitance—increases with decreasing plate separation (d).

Suppose an isolated conducting sphere has a radius R and a charge Q. The potential difference between the surface of the sphere and infinity is the same as it would be for an equal point charge at the center of the sphere.

$$\Delta V = k_C \frac{Q}{R}$$

Substituting this expression into the definition of capacitance results in the following expression:

$$C_{sphere} = \frac{Q}{\Delta V} = \frac{Q}{k_C \left(\dfrac{Q}{R}\right)} = \frac{R}{k_C}$$

This equation indicates that the capacitance of a sphere increases as the size of the sphere increases. Because Earth is so large, it has an extremely large capacitance. This means that Earth can provide or accept a large amount of charge without its electric potential changing too much. This is why Earth is often used as a ground in electric circuits. The ground is the reference point from which the potential differences in a circuit are measured, so it is important that this reference point not change.

The material between the plates of a capacitor can change its capacitance

So far, we have assumed that the space between the plates of a parallel-plate capacitor is a vacuum. However, in many parallel-plate capacitors, the space is filled with a material called a *dielectric*. A dielectric is an insulating material, such as air, rubber, glass, or waxed paper. When a dielectric is inserted between the plates of a capacitor, the capacitance increases. This is because the molecules in a dielectric can rotate so that there is an excess negative charge near the surface of the dielectric at the positive plate and an excess positive charge near the surface of the dielectric at the negative plate. The surface charge on the dielectric effectively reduces the charge on the capacitor plates, as shown in **Figure 18-7.** Thus, the plates can store more charge for a given potential difference. According to the expression $Q = C\Delta V$, if the charge increases and the potential difference is constant, the capacitance must increase. A capacitor with a dielectric can store more charge and energy for a given potential difference than can the same capacitor without a dielectric. In this book, problems will assume that capacitors are in a vacuum, with no dielectrics.

Discharging capacitors rapidly release their charge

Once a capacitor is charged, the battery or other source of potential difference that charged it can be removed from the circuit. The two plates of the capacitor will remain charged unless they are connected with a material that conducts. Once the plates are connected, the capacitor will *discharge.* This process

Figure 18-7
The effect of a dielectric is to reduce the strength of the electric field in a capacitor.

Conceptual Challenge

1. Charge on a capacitor plate A certain capacitor is designed so that one plate is large and the other is small. Do the plates have the same charge when connected to a battery?

2. Capacitor storage What does a capacitor store, given that the net charge in a parallel-plate capacitor is always zero?

3. Capacitors and batteries How is a capacitor similar to a battery? How is it different?

is the opposite of charging. The charges move back from one plate to another until both plates are uncharged again because this is the state of lowest potential energy.

One device that uses a capacitor is the flash attachment of a camera. A battery is used to charge the capacitor, and this stored charge is then released when the shutter-release button is pressed to take a picture. One advantage of using a discharging capacitor instead of a battery to power a flash is that with a capacitor, the stored charge can be delivered to a flash tube much faster, illuminating the subject at the instant more light is needed.

Computers make use of capacitors in many ways. For example, one type of computer keyboard has capacitors at the base of its keys, as shown in **Figure 18-8.** Each key is connected to a movable plate, which represents one side of the capacitor. The fixed plate on the bottom of the keyboard represents the other side of the capacitor. When a key is pressed, the capacitor spacing decreases, causing an increase in capacitance. External electronic circuits recognize that a key has been pressed when its capacitance changes.

Because the area of the plates and the distance between the plates can be controlled, the capacitance, and thus the electric field strength, can also be easily controlled.

Figure 18-8
A parallel-plate capacitor is often used in keyboards.

ENERGY AND CAPACITORS

A charged capacitor stores electrical potential energy because it requires work to move charges through a circuit to the opposite plates of a capacitor. The work done on these charges is a measure of the transfer of energy (see Chapter 5).

For example, if a capacitor is initially uncharged so that the plates are at the same electric potential, that is, if both plates are neutral, then almost no work is required to transfer a small amount of charge from one plate to the other. However, once a charge has been transferred, a small potential difference appears between the plates. As additional charge is transferred through this potential difference, the electrical potential energy of the system increases. This increase in energy is the result of work done on the charge. The electrical potential energy stored in a capacitor that is charged from zero to some charge, Q, is given by the following expression:

ELECTRICAL POTENTIAL ENERGY STORED IN A CHARGED CAPACITOR

$$PE_{electric} = \frac{1}{2}Q\Delta V$$

electrical potential energy =
$\frac{1}{2}$ **(charge on one plate)(final potential difference)**

By substituting the definition of capacitance ($C = Q/\Delta V$), these alternative forms can also be shown to be valid:

$$PE_{electric} = \tfrac{1}{2}C(\Delta V)^2$$

$$PE_{electric} = \frac{Q^2}{2C}$$

These results apply to any capacitor. In practice, there is a limit to the maximum energy (or charge) that can be stored because electrical breakdown ultimately occurs between the plates of the capacitor for a sufficiently large potential difference. For this reason, capacitors are usually labeled with a maximum operating potential difference. Electrical breakdown in a capacitor is similar to a lightning discharge in the atmosphere. **Figure 18-9** shows a pattern created in a block of Plexiglass that has undergone electrical breakdown. This book's problems assume that all potential differences are below the maximum.

Figure 18-9

The markings caused by electrical breakdown in this material look similar to the lightning bolts produced when air undergoes electrical breakdown.

SAMPLE PROBLEM 18C

Capacitance

PROBLEM

A 3.0 μF capacitor is connected to a 12 V battery. What is the magnitude of the charge on each plate of the capacitor, and how much energy is stored in the capacitor?

SOLUTION

Given: $C = 3.0\ \mu\text{F} = 3.0 \times 10^{-6}\ \text{F}$ $\Delta V = 12\ \text{V}$

Unknown: $Q = ?$ $PE_{electric} = ?$

To determine the charge, use the equation for capacitance on page 677.

$$Q = C\Delta V$$
$$Q = (3.0 \times 10^{-6}\ \text{F})(12\ \text{V}) = 36 \times 10^{-6}\ \text{C}$$

$$\boxed{Q = 36\ \mu\text{C}}$$

To determine the potential energy, use the alternative form of the equation for the potential energy of a charged capacitor shown on this page.

$$PE_{electric} = \tfrac{1}{2}C(\Delta V)^2$$
$$PE_{electric} = (0.5)(3.0 \times 10^{-6}\ \text{F})(12\ \text{V})^2$$

$$\boxed{PE_{electric} = 2.2 \times 10^{-4}\ \text{J}}$$

Capacitance

1. A parallel-plate capacitor has a charge of 6.0 μC when charged by a potential difference of 1.25 V.

    a. Find its capacitance.

    b. How much electrical potential energy is stored when this capacitor is connected to a 1.50 V battery?

2. You are asked to design a parallel-plate capacitor having a capacitance of 1.00 F and a plate separation of 1.00 mm. Calculate the required surface area of each plate. Is this a realistic size for a capacitor?

3. A 4.00 μF capacitor is connected to a 12.0 V battery.

    a. What is the charge on each plate of the capacitor?

    b. If this same capacitor is connected to a 1.50 V battery, how much electrical potential energy is stored?

4. A capacitor has a capacitance of 2.00 pF.

    a. What potential difference would be required to store 18.0 pC?

    b. How much charge is stored when the potential difference is 2.5 V?

Section Review

1. Explain why two metal plates near each other will not become charged unless they are connected to a source of potential difference.

2. A parallel-plate capacitor has an area of 2.0 cm^2, and the plates are separated by 2.0 mm.

    a. What is the capacitance?

    b. How much charge does this capacitor store when connected to a 6.0 V battery?

3. A parallel-plate capacitor has a capacitance of 1.35 pF. If a 12.0 V battery is connected to this capacitor, how much electrical potential energy would it store?

4. **Physics in Action** Assume Earth and a cloud layer 800.0 m above the Earth can be treated as plates of a parallel-plate capacitor.

    a. If the cloud layer has an area of 1.00×10^6 m^2, what is the capacitance?

    b. If an electric field strength of 2.0×10^6 N/C causes the air to conduct charge (lightning), what charge can the cloud hold?

Electrical Energy and Capacitance **681**

CHAPTER 18
Summary

KEY TERMS

capacitance (p. 676)

electric potential (p. 670)

electrical potential energy (p. 666)

potential difference (p. 670)

KEY IDEAS

Section 18-1 Electrical potential energy
- Electrical potential energy is energy associated with a charged object due to its position relative to a source of electric force.
- Electrical potential energy is a form of mechanical energy.

Section 18-2 Potential difference
- Electric potential is electrical potential energy divided by charge.
- The electric potential at a given point in an electric field is independent of the charge at that point.
- Only differences in electric potential (potential differences) from one position to another are useful in calculations.

Section 18-3 Capacitance
- The capacitance, C, of an object is the amount of charge, Q, the object can separate for a given potential difference, ΔV, as shown by the equation at right:

$$C = \frac{Q}{\Delta V}$$

- Capacitance depends only on the shape of an object, the distance between the plates, and the material it is made up of.
- A capacitor is a device that is used to store electrical potential energy.
- Capacitors will charge if a potential difference is applied. Once charged, a capacitor can discharge if its plates are connected by a conducting path.
- The potential energy stored in a charged capacitor depends on the charge and the final potential difference between the capacitor's two plates:

$$PE_{electric} = \tfrac{1}{2} Q \Delta V$$

Diagram symbols

Positive charge	+
Negative charge	−
Electric field vector	↑ E

Variable symbols

Quantities		Units		Conversions
$PE_{electric}$	electrical potential energy	J	joule	= N•m
				= kg•m²/s²
V	electric potential	V	volt	= J/C
ΔV	potential difference	V	volt	
C	capacitance	F	farad	= C/V

ELECTRICAL POTENTIAL ENERGY

Review questions

1. Explain the energy conversions that are involved when a positive charge moves because of a nearby uniform electric field. Be sure your discussion includes the following terms: *electrical potential energy, work,* and *kinetic energy.*

2. If a point charge is displaced perpendicular to a uniform electric field, which of the following expressions is likely to be equal to the change in electrical potential energy?

    a. $-qEd$
    b. 0
    c. $-k_c\left(\dfrac{q^2}{r^2}\right)$

3. Explain why the electrical potential energy is positive for a pair of like charges, but negative for a pair of unlike charges.

Practice problems

4. A point charge of 9.00×10^{-9} C is located at the origin. A positive charge of 3.00×10^{-9} C is brought in from infinity to a point that is exactly 30.0 cm away from the 9.00×10^{-9} C charge. What is the change in electrical potential energy?
    (See Sample Problem 18A.)

5. Three charges are situated at three corners of a rectangle, as shown in **Figure 18-10.** How much electrical potential energy would be expended in moving the 8.0 μC charge to infinity?
    (See Sample Problem 18A.)

2.0 μC   4.0 μC **Figure 18-10**

6. An electron is displaced from a point 55 cm away from a proton to a point 110 cm away from the proton. What is the change in the electrical potential energy as a result of this movement?
    (See Sample Problem 18A.)

ELECTRIC POTENTIAL AND POTENTIAL DIFFERENCE

Review questions

7. Differentiate between electrical potential energy and electric potential.

8. Differentiate between electric potential and potential difference.

9. At what location in relationship to a point charge is the electric potential considered by convention to be zero?

Conceptual questions

10. If the electric field in some region is zero, must the electric potential in that same region also be zero? Explain your answer.

11. If a proton is released from rest in a uniform electric field, does the corresponding electric potential at the proton's changing locations increase or decrease? What about the electrical potential energy?

12. If an electron is released from rest in a uniform electric field, does the corresponding electric potential at the electron's changing locations increase or decrease? What about the electrical potential energy?

Practice problems

13. The magnitude of a uniform electric field between the two plates is about 1.7×10^6 N/C. If the distance between these plates is 1.5 cm, find the potential difference between the plates.
    (See Sample Problem 18B.)

14. A pair of oppositely charged parallel plates are separated by 5.33 mm. A potential difference of 600.0 V exists between the plates.

   a. What is the magnitude of the electric field strength in the region that is located between the plates?

   b. What is the magnitude of the force on an electron that is in the region between the plates at a point that is exactly 2.90 mm from the positive plate?

   c. The electron is moved to the negative plate from an initial position 2.90 mm from the positive plate. What is the change in electrical potential energy due to the movement of this electron?

   (See Sample Problem 18B.)

15. An ion is displaced through a potential difference of 60.0 V and experiences an increase of electrical potential energy of 1.92×10^{-17} J. Calculate the charge on the ion.
   (See Sample Problem 18B.)

16. The three charges shown in **Figure 18-11** are located at the vertices of an isosceles triangle. Calculate the electric potential at the midpoint of the base if each one of the charges at the corners has a magnitude of 5.0×10^{-9} C.
   (See Sample Problem 18B.)

Figure 18-11

17. A force of 4.30×10^{-2} N is needed to move a charge of $56.0 \ \mu$C a distance of 20.0 cm in the direction of a uniform electric field. What is the potential difference that will provide this force?
   (See Sample Problem 18B.)

18. In **Figure 18-12,** find the electric potential at point P due to the grouping of charges at the other corners of the rectangle.
   (See Sample Problem 18B.)

$P_{\bullet}$ 8.0 μC

0.20 m

$-8.0 \ \mu$C ⊢— 0.35 m —⊣ $-12 \ \mu$C   **Figure 18-12**

CAPACITANCE

Review questions

19. What happens to the charge on a parallel-plate capacitor if the potential difference doubles?

20. You want to increase the maximum potential difference of a parallel-plate capacitor. Describe how you can do this for a fixed plate separation.

21. Why is the Earth considered a "ground" in electric terms? Can any other object act as a ground?

Conceptual questions

22. If the potential difference across a capacitor is doubled, by what factor is the electrical potential energy stored in the capacitor multiplied?

23. Two parallel plates are uncharged. Does the set of plates have a capacitance? Explain.

24. If you were asked to design a small capacitor with high capacitance, what factors would be important in your design?

25. If the area of the plates of a parallel-plate capacitor is doubled while the spacing between the plates is halved, how is the capacitance affected?

26. A parallel-plate capacitor is charged and then disconnected from a battery. How much does the stored energy change when the plate separation is doubled?

27. The potential difference between a pair of oppositely charged parallel plates is 400 V.

   a. If the spacing between the plates is doubled without altering the charge on the plates, what is the new potential difference between the plates?

   b. If the plate spacing is doubled while the potential difference between the plates is kept constant, what is the ratio of the final charge on one of the plates to the original charge?

28. Why is it dangerous to touch the terminals of a high-voltage capacitor even after the potential difference has been removed? What can be done to make the capacitor safe to handle?

29. Two capacitors have the same potential difference across them, but one has a large capacitance and the

other has a small capacitance. You would get a greater shock from touching the leads of the one with high capacitance than you would from touching the leads of the one with low capacitance. From this information, explain what causes the sensation of shock.

Practice problems

30. A 12.0 V battery is connected to a 6.0 pF parallel-plate capacitor. What is the charge on each plate? (See Sample Problem 18C.)

31. A potential difference of 100.0 V exists across the plates of a capacitor when the charge on each plate is 400.0 μC. What is the capacitance? (See Sample Problem 18C.)

32. A parallel-plate capacitor has a capacitance of 0.20 μF and is to be operated at 6500 V.
   a. Calculate the charge stored.
   b. What is the electrical potential energy stored in the capacitor at the operating potential difference?
(See Sample Problem 18C.)

33. Two devices with capacitances of 25 μF and 5.0 μF are each charged with separate 120 V power supplies. Calculate the total energy stored in the two capacitors. (See Sample Problem 18C.)

MIXED REVIEW

34. A charge of -3.00×10^{-9} C is at the origin of a coordinate system, and a charge of 8.00×10^{-9} C is on the x-axis at 2.00 m. At what two locations on the x-axis is the electric potential zero? (Hint: One location is between the charges, and the other is to the left of the y-axis.)

35. A circular parallel-plate capacitor with a spacing of 3.0 mm is charged to produce a uniform electric field with a strength of 3.0×10^6 N/C. What plate radius is required if the stored charge is $-1.0 \ \mu$C?

36. A 12 V battery is connected across two parallel metal plates separated by 0.30 cm. Find the magnitude of the electric field.

37. A parallel-plate capacitor has an area of 5.00 cm^2, and the plates are separated by 1.00 mm. The capacitor stores a charge of 400.0 pC.
   a. What is the potential difference across the plates of the capacitor?
   b. What is the magnitude of the uniform electric field in the region that is located between the plates?

38. A parallel-plate capacitor has a plate area of 175 cm^2 and a plate separation of 0.0400 mm. Determine the following:
   a. the capacitance
   b. the potential difference when the charge on the capacitor is 500.0 pC

39. A certain moving electron has a kinetic energy of 1.00×10^{-19} J.
   a. Calculate the speed necessary for the electron to have this energy.
   b. Repeat the calculation for a proton having a kinetic energy of 1.00×10^{-19} J.

40. A proton is accelerated from rest through a potential difference of 25 700 V.
   a. What is the kinetic energy of this proton in joules after this acceleration?
   b. What is the speed of the proton after this acceleration?

41. A proton is accelerated from rest through a potential difference of 120 V. Calculate the speed of this proton.

42. A pair of oppositely charged parallel plates are separated by a distance of 5.0 cm with a potential difference of 550 V between the plates. A proton is released from rest at the positive plate at the same time that an electron is released from rest at the negative plate. Disregard any interaction between the proton and the electron.
   a. How long does it take for the paths of the proton and the electron to cross?
   b. How fast will each particle be going when their paths cross?
   c. How much time will elapse before the proton reaches the opposite plate?
(See Appendix A for hints on solving simultaneous equations.)

43. A proton is accelerated through a potential difference of 4.5×10^6 V.

    a. How much kinetic energy has the proton acquired?

    b. If the proton started at rest, how fast is it moving?

44. A positron (a particle with a charge of $+e$ and a mass equal to that of an electron) that is accelerated from rest between two points at a fixed potential difference acquires a speed of 9.0×10^7 m/s. What speed is achieved by a *proton* accelerated from rest between the same two points? (Disregard relativistic effects.)

45. The speed of light is 3.00×10^8 m/s.

    a. Through what potential difference would an electron starting from rest need to accelerate to achieve a speed of 60.0% of the speed of light? (Disregard relativistic effects.)

    b. Repeat this calculation for a positron.

46. An electron moves from one plate to another, where there is a potential difference of 2200 V.

    a. Find the speed with which the electron strikes the positive plate.

    b. Repeat part (**a**) for a proton moving from the positive plate to the negative plate.

Technology & Learning

Graphing calculators

Program your graphing calculator to create a graph of potential difference versus electrical potential energy stored in a capacitor. Then use this graph to determine the potential difference required in the following situations:

    a. a 3.50 μF capacitor storing 1.20×10^{-4} J of energy

    b. the same 3.50 μF capacitor storing 3.80×10^{-4} J of energy

    c. a 24.0 μF capacitor storing 4.50×10^{-4} J of energy

    d. the same 24.0 μF capacitor storing 1.80×10^{-4} J of energy

Press [Y=] and [CLEAR] to clear any functions. Open a new program by pressing [PRGM] [▶] [▶] [ENTER]. Name

the program "CAPAC," and press [ENTER]. Then enter the program shown in the table below.

To exit the program editor, press [2nd] [QUIT]. To run the program, press [PRGM], select "CAPAC," and press [ENTER] [ENTER]. Enter the value for the capacitance, and press [ENTER].

The calculator will provide a graph of the electrical potential energy versus the potential difference. (If the graph is not visible, press [WINDOW], change the settings for the graph window, and then press [GRAPH].) Press [TRACE], and use the arrow keys to trace along the curve. The x value corresponds to the potential difference in volts, and the y value corresponds to the potential energy in joules.

After you have finished using the graph for one capacitance value, press [2nd] [QUIT] and run the program for the next one.

Keystrokes	Display
	PROGRAM: CAPAC
1. [PRGM] [▶] [2] [ALPHA] [C] [ENTER]	:PROMPT C
2. [ALPHA] ["] [ALPHA] [C] [X,T,θ] [x^2] [÷] [2] [ALPHA] ["] [STO▶] [2nd] [Y-VARS] [1] [1] [ENTER]	:"CX^2/2" → Y1
3. [PRGM] [▶] [4] [ENTER]	:DISPGRAPH

47. At some distance from a point charge, the electric potential is 600.0 V and the magnitude of the electric field is 200.0 N/C. Determine the charge and the distance from the charge.

48. Each plate on a 3750 pF capacitor carries a charge with a magnitude of 1.75×10^{-8} C.

   a. What is the potential difference across the plates when the capacitor has been fully charged?

   b. If the plates are 6.50×10^{-4} m apart, what is the magnitude of the electric field between the two plates?

49. A parallel-plate capacitor is made of two circular plates, each with a diameter of 2.50×10^{-3} m. The plates of this capacitor are separated by a space of 1.40×10^{-4} m.

   a. Assuming that the capacitor is operating in a vacuum and that the permittivity of a vacuum can be used, determine the capacitance for this arrangement.

   b. How much charge will be stored on each plate of this capacitor when it is connected across a potential difference of 0.12 V?

   c. What is the electrical potential energy stored in this capacitor when it is fully charged by the potential difference of 0.12 V?

   d. What is the potential difference between a point midway between the plates and a point that is 1.10×10^{-4} m from one of the plates?

   e. If the potential difference of 0.12 V is removed from the circuit and if the circuit is allowed to discharge until the charge on the plates has decreased to 70.7 percent of its fully charged value, what will the potential difference across the capacitor be?

Alternative Assessment

Performance assessment

1. If the electric potential in a certain region of space is zero, can you infer that there is no electric charge in that area? Come up with examples of sets of charges that support your inference, and be prepared to defend your conclusion in a class discussion.

2. Imagine that you are assisting nuclear scientists who need to accelerate electrons between electrically charged plates. Design and sketch a piece of equipment that could accelerate electrons to 10^7 m/s. What should the potential difference be between the plates? How would protons move inside this device? What would you change in order to accelerate the electrons to 100 m/s?

Portfolio projects

3. Tantalum is an element widely used in electrolytic capacitors. Research tantulum and its properties. Where on Earth is it found? In what form is it found? How expensive is it? Present your findings to the class in the form of a report, poster, or computer presentation.

4. Investigate how the shape of equally charged objects affects the potential around them. Examine the case of a point charge of 1 C, a hollow conducting sphere with a charge of 1 C, and a 1 m $\times$ 1 m square plate with a charge of 1 C. Find the electric potential at increasing distances from 0.1 m to 10 m along a line through the center of each charge. Draw graphs of the electric potential versus the distance from the charged object, and compare them.

5. Research what types of capacitors are used in different electrical and electronic devices. If possible, obtain old radios, telephones, or other electronic instruments that you can take apart. Find the capacitors, and describe them. Complete this research by visiting electronics stores or by examining catalogs of electrical and electronic equipment. Do the capacitors that are the largest in size have the largest capacitance values? Can you find out what substances are used to make these capacitors? Compile the class findings in a poster or an exhibit about these capacitors, and indicate their relative sizes, structures, capacitances, and uses.

CHAPTER 18
Laboratory Exercise

OBJECTIVES

- Explore the relationship between electrical energy and energy transferred by heat.
- Calculate the energy stored in a charged capacitor.

MATERIALS LIST

- ✔ 1-farad capacitor
- ✔ 10 Ω resistor
- ✔ insulated connecting wire
- ✔ low-calorie calorimeter with thermometer support
- ✔ momentary contact switch
- ✔ multimeter or dc voltmeter
- ✔ plastic electrical tape
- ✔ power supply
- ✔ stopwatch
- ✔ thermometer

CAPACITANCE AND ELECTRICAL ENERGY

When a capacitor is charged, it stores electrical potential energy, which can be measured by a change in temperature. In this experiment, you will charge a capacitor, then discharge it through a wire coil inside a special calorimeter. You will calculate the amount of energy transferred from the capacitor to the wire using the initial and final temperatures of the calorimeter.

SAFETY

- **Use a hot mitt to handle resistors, light sources, and other equipment that may be hot. Allow all equipment to cool before storing it.**

- **Never put broken glass or ceramics in a regular waste container. Use a dustpan, brush, and heavy gloves to carefully pick up broken pieces, and dispose of them in a container specifically provided for this purpose.**

PREPARATION

1. Read the entire lab, and plan the steps you will take.

2. Prepare a data table in your lab notebook with six columns and five rows. In the first row, label the columns *Trial, Mass of calorimeter (kg), T_i (°C), T_{max} (°C), ΔV_c (V)*, and *$C_{capacitor}$ (F)*. In the first column, label the second through fifth rows *1, 2, 3,* and *4*.

PROCEDURE

Charging the capacitor

3. Record the value of the capacitor in farads as $C_{capacitor}$.

4. Set up the apparatus as shown in **Figure 18-13.** Place the switch in front of you so that the switch moves from right to left. Using leads with alligator clips on both ends, connect the low-calorie calorimeter to the pins on the right side of the switch, and connect the capacitor to the center pins of the switch. Using leads with alligator clips on one end and banana terminals on the other, connect the resistor in series with the power supply and the pins on the left side of the switch. Connect the voltage meter to measure the potential difference across the capacitor. ***Do not close the switch until your teacher approves your circuit.***

5. Place the bulb end of the thermometer in the calorimeter. If necessary, carefully wrap one or two turns of electrical tape around the bulb to ensure a good fit. Place the other end of the thermometer in a support so that the thermometer is easy to read. Record the initial temperature of the calorimeter in your data table as T_i. **Do not close the switch until your teacher approves your circuit.**

6. When your teacher has approved your circuit, turn on the power supply and close the switch to the left in order to charge the capacitor. While the capacitor is charging, watch the voltage meter. When the potential difference across the capacitor remains constant for 30 s, record the value in your data table.

Figure 18-13

Step 4: Place the switch in front of you so that it moves from right to left. Check all connections carefully.

Step 5: Carefully place the bulb end of the thermometer in the calorimeter. Support the other end of the thermometer by placing it in a support, as shown.

Step 7: While the capacitor is discharging, read and record the temperature of the calorimeter at 5.0 s intervals.

Discharging the capacitor

7. Close the switch to the right to discharge the capacitor so that the current will be in the wire inside the calorimeter. Read the temperature of the calorimeter at 5.0 s intervals until five consecutive readings are the same. Record the maximum temperature reached in your data table.

8. Repeat the procedure for three more trials. **Do not close the switch until your teacher approves your circuit.** Record all data for all trials in your data table.

ANALYSIS AND INTERPRETATION

Calculations and data analysis

1. **Organizing data** For each trial recorded in your data table, perform the following calculations.

   a. Calculate the temperature change of the calorimeter.

   b. Your teacher will give you the value for the calibration constant of the calorimeter in J/°C. With that value, calculate the energy transferred to the calorimeter by heat.

2. **Organizing information** Use the equation $PE_{electric} = \frac{1}{2}C(\Delta V)^2$ to calculate the energy stored in the capacitor for each trial.

Conclusions

3. **Evaluating results** For each trial, compare the energy transferred to the calorimeter by heat to the energy stored in the capacitor. Based on your observations, is energy conserved in this experiment? Explain.

Are Electric Cars an Answer to Pollution?

In 1909, more than 50 percent of the automobiles in the United States were propelled by electric motors. These cars could go only a few miles before their batteries needed recharging, but they were more reliable than gasoline-powered cars, and starting them did not require hand cranking. Electric cars worked well for most in-city use, but as more roads were paved and as more people wanted to travel farther, electric cars were abandoned.

The return of electric cars

As industry spread and the number of cars on the road increased, the air in North America became more polluted and people searched for ways to reduce the pollution and its harmful effects on human health. In recent decades, federal and state laws have required industries and businesses–from steelmakers to dry cleaners–to limit polluting emissions. Although overall air quality has improved due to these regulations, pollution within many cities remains a serious problem, primarily because of emissions from motor-powered vehicles that use gasoline-burning internal combustion engines, or ICEs.

Gasoline-fueled cars emit nitrogen oxides, carbon monoxide, and unburned hydrocarbons—all of which, along with ozone, make up a major part of urban air pollution. In addition, ICEs give off large quantities of carbon dioxide, which contributes to Earth's greenhouse effect. So, because they emit no polluting exhaust fumes, people are interested once again in electric vehicles.

Modern electric vehicles

An electric vehicle, or EV, is powered by an electric motor with current supplied by an array of batteries. To recharge the batteries, the owner plugs the car into a recharging unit at home. The charging energy comes from the same electric-generating plants that produce household current. Besides producing no polluting exhaust, the main advantages of EVs are that they need no hydrocarbon fuel, they are quiet, and, because there are fewer moving parts to wear out, they are likely to last longer than cars with ICEs.

However, even EV proponents and manufacturers realize that EVs available now and in the near future have some major drawbacks. EVs can travel only about 65 km to 160 km before needing a recharge, which is not far enough for intercity travel or family trips. Also, EVs presently cost between $30,000 and $75,000, prices that are unacceptable to most consumers, especially when they consider the cars' limited range. Another problem is that the lead-acid batteries used in EVs, which cost about $3000, have to be replaced every two to three years.

The question of pollution

Many people wonder whether replacement of ICE vehicles by EVs will reduce air pollution and greenhouse gases or will increase the problem. After all, in charging a vehicle, the owner would be using electricity supplied by a power plant, which in its operation most likely causes air pollution. In some regions, such as southern California and the Pacific Northwest, abundant electric energy is available from relatively nonpolluting hydroelectric, nuclear, and natural-gas-burning power plants. The need to charge large numbers of EVs is unlikely to increase pollution at these sites.

On the other hand, 55 percent of generating plants in the United States are powered by heat from burning coal. Power plants will have to increase output by burning more coal, and it is even possible that new plants will have to be built. One scientist estimates that complete conversion to EVs would double the output of sulfur dioxide, a cause of acid rain, from coal-burning plants.

Supporters of EVs say that most people would recharge their vehicles overnight when power plants are operating far below their capacity. EV proponents also have estimated that 20 million EVs could be supported in the United States without building any new power plants.

In addition, they claim that the transfer of energy from burning coal to generate electric current, which ultimately powers an EV, is up to twice as efficient as burning gasoline to power a car.

To settle this question, the U.S. Department of Energy has assigned Argonne National Laboratories to perform a Total Energy Cycle Assessment comparing the energy efficiency of EVs with that of vehicles that run on gasoline. For gasoline-powered vehicles, technicians will consider every step, from producing crude oil to burning it for mechanical energy to move a car. For EVs, they will account for all steps, from mining coal to using the energy from a charged battery to move a car. In addition, they will keep track of all emissions, leftover material, and all activities involved in using and maintaining the vehicles. The results of this study should provide answers that will shape the destiny of electric vehicles.

Fuel production and transport • Electricity generation • Electricity transport and distribution • Battery charging • Electric vehicle operation

Crude oil production and transport • Oil refining • Gasoline transport • Vehicle fueling • ICE vehicle operation

Researching the Issue

1. If the Argonne study reveals that gasoline-powered cars are more energy-efficient than EVs, do you think that EVs should be discontinued? Account for your opinion.

2. The limited range of EVs is one of their biggest drawbacks. Do research to find out about hybrid electric vehicles, or HEVs. Describe how they operate and explain the differences between series and parallel HEVs. How might these vehicles overcome the range limitations of EVs?

3. The state of California has mandated that by the year 2003 at least 10 percent of the vehicles for sale in the state must be zero-emission vehicles, and EVs are the only vehicles that meet that requirement. Other states have passed similar laws. Because EVs are so expensive, the federal and state governments are offering subsidies and tax credits to people who will buy them. Hold a discussion or debate on the question, "Should the government spend taxpayers' money to subsidize the purchase of nonpolluting vehicles that people might not otherwise buy?"

CHAPTER 19

Current and Resistance

PHYSICS IN ACTION

Each device attached to a computer, such as a modem or a monitor, is typically controlled through a circuit board. These circuit boards are in turn connected to a main circuit board, called the *motherboard*. Each circuit board is studded with resistors, capacitors, and other tiny components that are involved with the movement and storage of electric charge. Copper "wires" printed onto the circuit boards during their manufacture conduct charges between components.

In this chapter, you will study the movement of electric charge and learn what factors affect the ease with which charges move through different materials.

- *What is the function of a resistor?*
- *What hinders the movement of charge?*

CONCEPT REVIEW

Power (Section 5-4)

Electrical potential energy (Section 18-1)

Potential difference (Section 18-2)

19-1
Electric current

CURRENT AND CHARGE MOVEMENT

Although many practical applications and devices are based on the principles of static electricity, electricity did not become an integral part of our daily lives until scientists learned to control the movement of electric charge, known as *current*. Electric currents power our lights, radios, television sets, air conditioners, and refrigerators. Currents also ignite the gasoline in automobile engines, travel through miniature components that make up the chips of computers, and perform countless other invaluable tasks.

Electric currents are even part of the human body. This connection between physics and biology was discovered by Luigi Galvani (1737–1798). While conducting electrical experiments near a frog he had recently dissected, Galvani noticed that electrical sparks caused the frog's legs to twitch and even convulse. After further research, Galvani concluded that electricity was present in the frog. Today, we know that electric currents are responsible for transmitting messages between body muscles and the brain. In fact, every action involving muscles is initiated by electrical activity.

Current is the rate of charge movement

A current exists whenever there is a net movement of electric charge through a medium. To define *current* more precisely, suppose positive charges are moving through a wire, as shown in **Figure 19-1.** The **current** is the rate at which these charges move through the cross section of the wire. If ΔQ is the amount of charge that passes through this area in a time interval, Δt, then the current, I, is the ratio of the amount of charge to the time interval.

Figure 19-1
The current in this wire is defined as the rate at which electric charges pass through a cross-sectional area of the wire.

current

the rate at which electric charges move through a given area

ELECTRIC CURRENT

$$I = \frac{\Delta Q}{\Delta t}$$

$$\text{electric current} = \frac{\text{charge passing through a given area}}{\text{time interval}}$$

The SI unit for current is the *ampere*, A. One ampere is equivalent to one coulomb of charge passing through a cross-sectional area in a time interval of one second (1 A = 1 C/s).

Relating current and charge

PROBLEM

The amount of charge that passes through the filament of a certain light bulb in 2.00 s is 1.67 C. Determine the current in the light bulb.

SOLUTION

Given: $\Delta Q = 1.67$ C $\Delta t = 2.00$ s

Unknown: $I = ?$

Solution:

Use the equation for electric current, given on page 694.

$$I = \frac{\Delta Q}{\Delta t}$$

$$I = \frac{1.67 \text{ C}}{2.00 \text{ s}}$$

$$\boxed{I = 0.835 \text{ A}}$$

Relating current and charge

1. How many electrons pass through the filament of the light bulb in Sample Problem 19A during the 2.00 s time interval?

2. A total charge of 9.0 mC passes through a cross-sectional area of a nichrome wire in 3.5 s.
   a. What is the current in the wire?
   b. How many electrons pass through the cross-sectional area in 10.0 s?
   c. If the number of charges that pass through the cross-sectional area during the given time interval doubles, what is the resulting current?

3. The compressor on an air conditioner draws 40.0 A when it starts up. If the start-up time is 0.50 s how much charge passes a cross-sectional area of the circuit in this time?

4. In a particular television tube, the measured beam current is 60.0 μA. How many electrons strike the screen every second?

5. If a current of 80.0 mA exists in a metal wire, how many electrons pass a given cross section of the wire in 10.0 min?

Conventional current is defined in terms of positive charge movement

The moving charges that make up a current can be positive, negative, or a combination of the two. In a common conductor, such as copper, current is due to the motion of negatively charged electrons. This is because the atomic structure of solid conductors allows the electrons to be transferred easily from one atom to the next, while the protons are relatively fixed inside the nucleus of the atom. In certain particle accelerators, a current exists when positively charged protons are set in motion. In some cases—in gases and dissolved salts, for example—current is the result of positive charges moving in one direction and negative charges moving in the opposite direction.

Positive and negative charges in motion are sometimes called *charge carriers. Conventional current* is defined as the current consisting of positive charge that would have the same effect as the actual motion of the charge carriers—regardless of whether the charge carriers are positive, negative, or a combination of the two. The three possible cases are shown in **Table 19-1.** We will use conventional current in this book unless stated otherwise.

Table 19-1   Conventional current

	First case	Second case	Third case
Motion of charge carriers	← ⊖	⊕ →	⊕ → ← ⊖
Equivalent conventional current	⊕ →	⊕ →	⊕ → ⊕ →

As was explained in Chapter 18, a potential difference sets charges in motion. For a material to be a good conductor, charge carriers in the material must move readily when a potential difference is applied across the material. Many metals are good conductors because metals usually contain a large number of free electrons. Body fluids and salt water are able to conduct electric charge because they contain charged atoms called *ions.* Because they can move through a solution easily, dissolved ions can be charge carriers. A solute that consists of charge carriers is called an *electrolyte.*

DRIFT VELOCITY

When you turn on a light switch, the light comes on almost immediately. For this reason, many people think that electrons flow very rapidly from the socket to the light bulb. However, this is not the case. When you turn on the switch, an electric field is established in the wire. This field, which sets electric charges in motion, travels through the wire at nearly 3.00×10^8 m/s. The charges themselves, however, do not travel nearly this quickly.

A Lemon Battery

MATERIALS LIST

- ✔ lemon
- ✔ copper wire
- ✔ paper clip

Straighten the paper clip, and insert it and the copper wire into the lemon to construct a chemical cell. Touch the ends of both wires with your tongue. Because a potential difference exists across the two metals and because your saliva provides an electrolytic solution that conducts electric current, you should feel a slight tingling sensation on your tongue.

Drift velocity is the net velocity of charge carriers

To see how the electrons move, consider a solid conductor in which the charge carriers are free electrons. When the conductor is in electrostatic equilibrium, the electrons move randomly, similar to the movement of molecules in a gas. When a potential difference is applied across the conductor, an electric field is set up inside the conductor. The force due to that field sets the electrons in motion, thereby creating a current.

These electrons do not move in straight lines along the conductor in a direction opposite the electric field. Instead, they undergo repeated collisions with the vibrating metal atoms of the conductor. If these collisions were charted, the result would be a complicated zigzag pattern like the one shown in **Figure 19-2.** The energy transferred from the electrons to the metal atoms during the collisions increases the vibrational energy of the atoms, and the conductor's temperature increases.

The energy gained by the electrons as they are accelerated by the electric field is greater than the average loss in energy due to the collisions. Thus, despite the internal collisions, the individual electrons move slowly along the conductor in a direction opposite the electric field, **E,** with a velocity known as the **drift velocity, v_{drift}.**

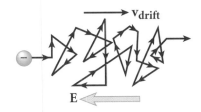

Figure 19-2
When an electron moves through a conductor, collisions with the vibrating metal atoms of the conductor force the electron to change its direction constantly.

drift velocity

the net velocity of a charge carrier moving in an electric field

Drift speeds are relatively small

The magnitudes of drift velocities, or drift speeds, are typically very small. In fact, the drift speed is much less than the average speed between collisions. For example, in a copper wire that has a current of 10.0 A, the drift speed of electrons is 2.46×10^{-4} m/s. These electrons would take about 68 min to travel 1 m! The electric field, on the other hand, reaches electrons throughout the wire at a speed approximately equal to the speed of light.

Conceptual Challenge

1. Electric field inside a conductor We concluded in our study of electrostatics that the field inside a conductor is zero, yet we have seen that an electric field exists inside a conductor that carries a current. How is this possible?

2. Turning on a light If charges travel very slowly through a metal (approximately 10^{-4} m/s), why doesn't it take several hours for a light to come on after you flip a switch?

3. Particle accelerator The positively charged dome of a Van de Graaff generator can be used to accelerate positively charged protons. A current exists due to the motion of these protons. In this case, how does the direction of conventional current compare with the direction in which the charge carriers move?

SOURCES AND TYPES OF CURRENT

When you drop a ball, it falls to the ground, moving from a place of higher gravitational potential energy to one of lower gravitational potential energy. As discussed in Chapter 18, charges have similar behavior. For example, free electrons in a conductor move randomly when all points in the conductor are at the same potential. But when a potential difference is applied across the conductor, they will move slowly from a higher electric potential to a lower electric potential. Thus, a difference in potential maintains current in a circuit.

Batteries and generators supply energy to charge carriers

Both batteries and generators maintain a potential difference across their terminals by converting other forms of energy into electrical energy. **Figure 19-3** shows an assortment of batteries, which convert *chemical* energy to electrical potential energy.

As charge carriers collide with the atoms of a device, such as a light bulb or a heater, their electrical potential energy is converted into kinetic energy. Note that electrical energy, not charge, is "used up" in this process. The battery continues to supply electrical energy to the charge carriers until its chemical energy is depleted. At this point, the battery must be replaced or recharged.

Because batteries must often be replaced or recharged, generators are sometimes preferable. Generators convert *mechanical* energy into electrical energy. One type of generator converts the kinetic energy of falling water into electrical energy, as shown in **Figure 19-4.** Generators are the source of the potential difference across the two holes of a socket in a wall outlet in your home. When you plug an appliance into an outlet, a potential difference of approximately 120 V is applied to the device, thereby generating a current.

Figure 19-3
Batteries maintain electric current by converting chemical energy into electrical energy.

Figure 19-4
In the electrical generators of this hydroelectric power plant, the mechanical energy of falling water is transformed into electrical energy.

Current can be direct or alternating

There are two different types of current: *direct current* (dc) and *alternating current* (ac). The difference between the two types of current is just what their names suggest. In direct current, charges move in only one direction. In alternating current, the motion of charges continuously changes in the forward and reverse directions.

Consider a light bulb connected to a battery. Because the positive terminal of the battery has a higher electric potential than the negative terminal has, charge carriers always move in one direction. Thus, the light bulb operates with a direct current. Because the potential difference between the terminals of a battery is fixed, batteries always generate a direct current.

In alternating current, the terminals of the source of potential difference are constantly changing sign. Hence, there is no net motion of the charge carriers in alternating current; they simply vibrate back and forth. If this vibration were slow enough, you would notice flickering in lights and similar effects in other appliances. To eliminate this problem, alternating current is made to change direction rapidly. In the United States, alternating current oscillates 60 times every second. Thus, its frequency is 60 Hz. The graphs in **Figure 19-5** compare direct and alternating current.

Unlike batteries, generators can produce either direct or alternating current, depending on their design. However, alternating current has advantages that make it more practical for use in transferring electrical energy. For this reason, the current supplied to your home by power companies is alternating current rather than direct current.

Figure 19-5
(a) The direction of direct current does not change, while **(b)** the direction of alternating current continually changes.

CONCEPT PREVIEW

Alternating current and generators will be discussed in greater detail in Chapter 22.

Section Review

1. Can the direction of conventional current ever be opposite the direction of charge movement? If so, when?

2. The charge that passes through the filament of a certain light bulb in 5.00 s is 3.0 C.
   a. What is the current in the light bulb?
   b. How many electrons pass through the filament of the light bulb in a time interval of 1.0 min?

3. In a conductor that carries a current, which is less, the drift speed of an electron or the average speed of the electron between collisions? Explain your answer.

4. What are the functions of batteries and generators?

5. In direct current, charge carriers have a drift velocity, but in alternating current, there is no net velocity of the charge carriers. Explain why.

19-2
Resistance

19-2 SECTION OBJECTIVES

- **Calculate resistance, current, and potential difference using the definition of resistance.**

- **Distinguish between ohmic and non-ohmic materials.**

- **Know what factors affect resistance.**

- **Describe what is unique about superconductors.**

resistance

ratio of the potential difference across a conductor to the current it carries

BEHAVIORS OF RESISTORS

When a light bulb is connected to a battery, the current in the bulb depends on the potential difference across the battery. For example, a 9.0 V battery connected to a light bulb generates a greater current than a 6.0 V battery connected to the same bulb. But potential difference is not the only factor that determines the current in the light bulb. The materials that make up the connecting wires and the bulb's filament also affect the current in the bulb. Even though most materials can be classified as conductors or insulators, some conductors allow charges to move through them more easily than others. The impedence of the motion of charge through a conductor is the conductor's *resistance*. More specifically, **resistance** is defined as the ratio of potential difference to current, as follows:

RESISTANCE

$$R = \frac{\Delta V}{I}$$

$$\text{resistance} = \frac{\text{potential difference}}{\text{current}}$$

The SI unit for resistance, the *ohm*, is equal to volts per ampere and is represented by the Greek letter Ω (*omega*). If a potential difference of 1 V across a conductor produces a current of 1 A, the resistance of the conductor is 1 Ω.

Resistance is constant over a range of potential differences

For many materials, including most metals, experiments show that *the resistance is constant over a wide range of applied potential differences.* This statement, known as Ohm's law, is named for Georg Simon Ohm (1789–1854), who was the first to conduct a systematic study of electrical resistance. Mathematically, Ohm's law is stated as follows:

$$\frac{\Delta V}{I} = \text{constant}$$

As can be seen by comparing the definition of resistance with Ohm's law, the constant of proportionality in the Ohm's law equation is resistance. It is common practice to express Ohm's law as $\Delta V = IR$, where R is understood to be independent of ΔV.

Ohm's law does not hold for all materials

Ohm's law is not a fundamental law of nature like the conservation of energy or the universal law of gravitation. Instead, it is a behavior that is valid only for certain materials. Materials that have a constant resistance over a wide range of potential differences are said to be *ohmic*. A graph of current versus potential difference for an ohmic material is linear, as shown in **Figure 19-6(a)**. This is because the slope of such a graph ($I/\Delta V$) is inversely proportional to resistance. When resistance is constant, the slope is constant and the resulting graph is a straight line.

Materials that do not function according to Ohm's law are said to be *non-ohmic*. **Figure 19-6(b)** shows a graph of current versus potential difference for a non-ohmic material. In this case, the slope is not constant because resistance varies. Hence, the resulting graph is nonlinear. One common semiconducting device that is non-ohmic is the *diode*. Its resistance is small for currents in one direction and large for currents in the reverse direction. Diodes are used in circuit boards to control the direction of current. This book assumes that all resistors function according to Ohm's law unless stated otherwise.

Resistance depends on length, cross-sectional area, material, and temperature

In Section 19-1 we pointed out that electrons do not move in straight-line paths through a conductor. Instead, they undergo repeated collisions with the metal atoms. These collisions affect the motion of charges somewhat as a force of internal friction would. This is the origin of a material's resistance. Thus, any factors that affect the number of collisions will also affect a material's resistance. Some of these factors are shown in **Table 19-2.**

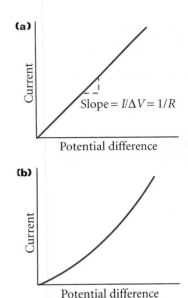

Figure 19-6
(a) The current–potential difference curve of an ohmic material is linear, and the slope is the inverse of the material's resistance. **(b)** The current–potential difference curve of a non-ohmic material is nonlinear.

Table 19-2   **Factors that affect resistance**

Factor	Less resistance	Greater resistance
Length	L_1	L_2
Cross-sectional area	A_1	A_2
Material	Copper	Aluminum
Temperature	T_1	T_2

Figure 19-7

Resistors, such as those shown here, are used to control current. The colors of the bands represent a code for the values of the resistances.

Resistors can be used to control the amount of current in a conductor

One way to change the current in a conductor is to change the potential difference across the ends of the conductor. But in many cases, such as in household circuits, the potential difference does not change. How can the current in a certain wire be changed if the potential difference remains constant?

According to the definition of resistance, if ΔV remains constant, current decreases when resistance increases. Thus, the current in a wire can be decreased by replacing the wire with one of higher resistance. The same effect can be accomplished by making the wire longer or by connecting a *resistor* to the wire. A resistor is a simple electrical element that provides a specified resistance. **Figure 19-7** shows a group of resistors in a circuit board. Resistors are sometimes used to control the current in an attached conductor because this is often more practical than changing the potential difference or the properties of the conductor.

CONCEPT PREVIEW

You will work with different combinations of resistors in Chapter 20.

SAMPLE PROBLEM 19B

Resistance

PROBLEM

All electrical devices are required to have identifying plates that specify their electrical characteristics. The plate on a certain steam iron states that the current in the iron is 6.4 A when the iron is connected across a potential difference of 120 V. What is the resistance of the steam iron?

SOLUTION

Given: $I = 6.4\ \text{A}$ $\Delta V = 120\ \text{V}$

Unknown: $R = ?$

Use the definition of resistance, given on page 700.

$$R = \frac{\Delta V}{I} = \frac{120\,\text{V}}{6.4\,\text{A}}$$

$$\boxed{R = 19\ \Omega}$$

Resistance

1. A typical color television draws 2.5 A of current when connected across a potential difference of 115 V. What is the effective resistance of the television set?

2. The current in a certain resistor is 0.50 A when it is connected to a potential difference of 110 V. What is the current in this same resistor if
   a. the operating potential difference is 90.0 V?
   b. the operating potential difference is 130 V?

3. Find the current in the following appliances when they are connected across a potential difference of 120 V.
   a. a stereo with a resistance of 65 Ω
   b. a hot plate with a resistance of 48 Ω
   c. a microwave oven with a resistance of 20.0 Ω

4. The current in a microwave oven is 6.25 A. If the resistance of the oven's circuitry is 17.6 Ω, what is the potential difference across the oven?

5. A 1.5 V battery is connected to a small light bulb with a resistance of 3.5 Ω. What is the current in the bulb?

Salt water and perspiration lower the body's resistance

The human body's resistance to current is on the order of 500 000 Ω when the skin is dry. However, the body's resistance decreases when the skin is wet. If the body is soaked with salt water, its resistance can be as low as 100 Ω. This is because ions in salt water readily conduct electric charge. Such low resistances can be dangerous if a large potential difference is applied between parts of the body because current increases as resistance decreases. Currents in the body that are less than 0.01 A either are imperceptible or generate a slight tingling feeling. Greater currents are painful and can disturb breathing, and currents above 0.15 A through the chest cavity can be fatal.

Perspiration also contains ions that conduct electric charge. In a *galvanic skin response* (GSR) test, commonly used as a stress test and as part of some lie detectors, a very small potential difference is set up across the body. Perspiration increases when a person is nervous or stressed, thereby decreasing the resistance of the body. In GSR tests, a state of low stress and high resistance, or "normal" state, is used as a control, and a state of higher stress is reflected as a decreased resistance compared with the normal state.

Did you know?

In reality, very large changes in potential difference will affect the resistance of a conductor. However, this variation is negligible at the level of potential differences supplied to homes and used in other common applications.

Electric
current

Diaphragm

Carbon
granules

Figure 19-8
In the carbon microphone, used in some telephones, changes in sound waves affect the resistance medium (the carbon granules). The resulting changes in current are transmitted through the phone line and then converted back to sound waves in the listener's earpiece.

CONCEPT PREVIEW ➤

Transformers will be described in greater detail in Chapter 22.

The carbon microphone uses varying resistance

Figure 19-8 illustrates the carbon microphone, commonly used in the mouthpiece of some telephones. The carbon microphone uses the inverse relationship between current and resistance to convert sound waves to electrical impulses. A flexible steel diaphragm is placed in contact with carbon granules inside a container. The carbon granules serve as the microphone's primary resistance medium. The microphone also contains a source of current and a transformer.

The magnitude of the current in the microphone changes when the compressions and rarefactions of a sound wave strike the diaphragm. When a compression arrives at the microphone, the diaphragm flexes inward, causing the carbon granules to press together into a smaller-than-normal volume. This corresponds to a decrease in the length of the resistance medium, which results in a lower resistance and hence a greater current. When a rarefaction arrives, the reverse process occurs, resulting in a decrease in current. These variations in current, following the changes of the sound wave, are sent through the transformer to the telephone company's transmission line. A speaker in the listener's earpiece then converts the electric signals back to sound waves.

Conceptual Challenge

1. Hair dryers While most wall sockets in England provide a potential difference of about 220 V, American outlets usually supply about 120 V. Why shouldn't you use a hair dryer designed for a 120 V American outlet in England without an adapter? Assume that the hair dryer is ohmic.

2. Light bulbs While working in the laboratory, you need to increase the glow of a light bulb, so you wish to increase the current in the bulb. List all of the different factors you could adjust to increase the current in the bulb.

3. Faulty outlet If you touch a faulty electrical outlet, there is a potential difference across your body that generates a current in your body. This situation is always dangerous, but the risk increases greatly if your body is wet. Explain why.

Tomorrow's Technology

Electroporation

Most people hate getting shots at the doctor's office. In the future, drugs may be delivered through a patient's skin without the use of needles—and without the pain they cause. Dr. Mark Prausnitz, of the Georgia Institute of Technology, has been working on a process that uses electricity to create tiny pores in the skin through which drug molecules can pass. This process is called electroporation.

Ordinarily, there are membranes in the outer part of the skin that prevent substances from entering the body. However, when high-voltage electrical pulses are applied to the skin, molecules are able to move through these membranes up to 10 000 times easier than under normal conditions.

"Charged molecules want to move in an electric field," explained Dr. Prausnitz. "But if there is a cell membrane in the way, suddenly they hit this membrane and they can't go anymore.

"As more and more of these charged molecules build up, you develop a voltage across this membrane. When the voltage gets high enough, the structure of the membrane itself changes to allow these molecules to cross the membrane, and this is the creation of an electropore."

This method could also be used to deliver drugs that would be destroyed by the stomach if taken in pill form. And it might add a level of convenience: Dr. Prausnitz envisions a device that could be worn like a watch that would deliver controlled doses of a drug over an entire day. Such a device would function like a nicotine patch except that it would also contain the electric equipment to carry out electroporation.

Although using electricity to deliver drugs through the skin is still in testing stages, electroporation is already being used to administer drugs to tumors in cancer patients. When the medication is injected into the patient's bloodstream, the cells of the tumor are electroporated, allowing more of the drug to enter the tumor and thus increasing the chance of successful treatment.

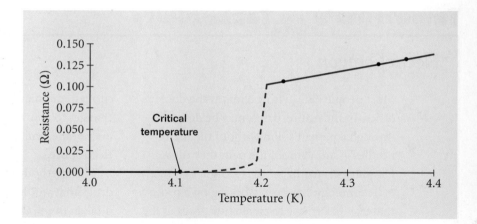

superconductor

a material whose resistance is zero at or below some critical temperature, which varies with each material

Superconductors have no resistance below a critical temperature

There is a class of materials that have zero resistance below a certain temperature, called the *critical temperature*. These materials are known as **superconductors.** The resistance-temperature graph for a superconductor resembles that of a normal metal at temperatures above the critical temperature. But when the temperature is at or below the critical temperature, the resistance suddenly drops to zero, as shown in **Figure 19-9.**

Today there are thousands of known superconductors, including common metals such as aluminum, tin, lead, and zinc. **Table 19-3** lists the critical temperatures of several superconductors. Interestingly, copper, silver, and gold, which are excellent conductors, do not exhibit superconductivity.

One of the truly remarkable features of superconductors is that once a current is established in them, the current continues even if the applied potential difference is removed. In fact, steady currents have been observed to persist for many years with no apparent decay in superconducting loops.

Figure 19-10 shows a small permanent magnet levitated above a disk of the superconductor $YBa_2Cu_3O_7$. As will be described in Chapter 21, electric currents produce magnetic effects. The interaction between a current in the superconductor and this magnet causes the magnet to float in the air over the

Table 19-3 Critical temperatures

Material	Degrees Kelvin
Zn	0.88
Al	1.19
Sn	3.72
Hg	4.15
Nb	9.46
Nb_3Ge	23.2
$YBa_2Cu_3O_7$	90
Tl-Ba-Ca-Cu-O	125

Figure 19-10

In this photograph, a small permanent magnet levitates above the superconductor $YBa_2Cu_3O_7$, which is at 77 K, 13 K below its critical temperature.

superconductor. This is known as the *Meissner effect*. One application of the Meissner effect is the high-speed express train shown in **Figure 19-11,** which levitates a few inches above the track.

An important recent development in physics is the discovery of high-temperature superconductors. The excitement began with a 1986 publication by scientists at the IBM Zurich Research Laboratory in Switzerland. In this publication, scientists reported evidence for superconductivity at a temperature near 30 K. More recently, scientists have found superconductivity at temperatures as high as 150 K. The search continues for a material that has superconducting qualities at room temperature. It is an important search that has both scientific and practical applications.

One useful application of superconductivity is superconducting magnets. Such magnets are being considered for storing energy. The idea of using superconducting power lines to transmit power more efficiently is also being researched. Modern superconducting electronic devices that consist of two thin-film superconductors separated by a thin insulator have been constructed. They include magnetometers (magnetic-field measuring devices) and various microwave devices.

Figure 19-11
This express train in Tokyo, Japan, which utilizes the Meissner effect, levitates above the track and is capable of speeds exceeding 225 km/h.

Section Review

1. How much current would a 10.2 Ω toaster oven draw when connected to a 120 V outlet?

2. An ammeter registers 2.5 A of current in a wire that is connected to a 9.0 V battery. What is the wire's resistance?

3. In a particular diode, the current triples when the applied potential difference is doubled. What can you conclude about the diode?

4. You have only one type of wire. If you are connecting a battery to a light bulb with this wire, how could you decrease the current in the wire?

5. How is the resistance of aluminum, which is a superconductor, different from that of gold, which does not exhibit superconductivity?

6. **Physics in Action** What is the function of resistors in a circuit board? What is the function of diodes in a circuit board?

7. **Physics in Action** Calculate the current in a 75 Ω resistor when a potential difference of 115 V is placed across it. What will the current be if the resistor is replaced with a 47 Ω resistor?

19-3
Electric power

19-3 SECTION OBJECTIVES

- **Relate electric power to the rate at which electrical energy is converted to other forms of energy.**

- **Calculate electric power.**

- **Calculate the cost of running electrical appliances.**

ENERGY TRANSFER

When a battery is used to maintain an electric current in a conductor, chemical energy stored in the battery is continuously converted to the electrical energy of the charge carriers. As the charge carriers move through the conductor, this electrical energy is converted to internal energy due to collisions between the charge carriers and other particles in the conductor.

For example, consider a light bulb connected to a battery, as shown in **Figure 19-12(a).** Imagine a charge Q moving from the battery's terminal to the light bulb and then back to the other terminal. The changes in electrical potential energy are shown in **Figure 19-12(b).** If we disregard the resistance of the connecting wire, no loss in energy occurs as the charge moves through the wire (A to B). But when the charge moves through the filament of the light bulb (B to C), which has a higher resistance than the wire has, it loses electrical potential energy due to collisions. This electrical energy is converted into internal energy, and the filament warms up.

When the charge first returns to the battery's terminal (D), its potential energy is zero, and the battery must do work on the charge. As the charge moves between the terminals of the battery (D to A), its electrical potential energy increases by $Q\Delta V$ (where ΔV is the potential difference across the two terminals). The battery's chemical energy decreases by the same amount. At this point, the process begins again. (Remember that this process happens very slowly compared with how quickly the bulb is illuminated.)

Electric power is the rate of conversion of electrical energy

In Chapter 5, power was described as the rate at which work is done. *Electric power,* then, is the rate at which charge carriers do work. Put another way, electric power is the rate at which charge carriers convert electrical potential energy to nonelectrical forms of energy.

$$P = \frac{W}{\Delta t} = \frac{\Delta PE}{\Delta t}$$

As discussed in Chapter 18, potential difference is defined as the change in potential energy per unit of charge.

$$\Delta V = \frac{\Delta PE}{q}$$

Figure 19-12
A charge leaves the battery at *A* with a certain amount of electrical potential energy. The charge loses this energy while moving from *B* to *C*, and then regains the energy as it moves from *D* to *A*.

This equation can be rewritten in terms of potential energy.

$$\Delta PE = q\Delta V$$

We can then substitute this expression for potential energy into the equation for power.

$$P = \frac{\Delta PE}{\Delta t} = \frac{q\Delta V}{\Delta t}$$

Because current, I, is defined as the rate of charge movement ($q/\Delta t$), we can express electric power as current multiplied by potential difference.

ELECTRIC POWER

$$P = I\Delta V$$

electric power = current × potential difference

This equation describes the rate at which charge carriers lose electrical potential energy. In other words, power is the rate of conversion of electrical energy. As described in Chapter 5, the SI unit of power is the *watt*, W. When considering the dissipation of electrical energy, 1 W is equivalent to 1 J of electrical energy being converted to other forms of energy per second.

Most light bulbs are labeled with their power ratings. The amount of heat and light given off by a bulb is related to the power rating, also known as wattage, of the bulb.

Because $\Delta V = IR$, we can express the power dissipated by a resistor in the following alternative forms:

$$P = I\Delta V = I(IR) = I^2R$$

$$P = I\Delta V = \left(\frac{\Delta V}{R}\right)\Delta V = \frac{(\Delta V)^2}{R}$$

The conversion of electrical energy to internal energy in a material of resistance R is called *joule heating*. It is also often referred to as an I^2R loss.

Conceptual Challenge

1. Power delivered to a light bulb Explain why the filament of a light bulb connected to a battery receives much more power than the wire connecting the bulb and the battery.

2. Power and resistance Compare the two alternative forms for the equation that expresses the power dissipated by a resistor. In the first equation ($P = I^2R$), power is proportional to resistance; in the second equation ($P = (\Delta V)^2/R$), power is *inversely* proportional to resistance. How can you reconcile this apparent discrepancy?

3. Different wattages Which has a greater resistance when connected to a 120 V outlet, a 40 W light bulb or a 100 W light bulb?

Electric power

PROBLEM

An electric space heater is connected across a 120 V outlet. The heater dissipates 3.5 kW of power in the form of electromagnetic radiation and heat. Calculate the resistance of the heater.

SOLUTION

Given: $\Delta V = 120 \text{ V}$ $P = 3.5 \text{ kW} = 3.5 \times 10^3 \text{ W}$

Unknown: $R = ?$

Because power and potential difference are given but resistance is unknown, use the third form of the power equation on page 709, which includes these three variables.

$$P = \frac{(\Delta V)^2}{R}$$

$$R = \frac{(\Delta V)^2}{P} = \frac{(120 \text{ V})^2}{3.5 \times 10^3 \text{ W}} = \frac{(120)^2 \text{ J}^2/\text{C}^2}{3.5 \times 10^3 \text{ J/s}}$$

$$R = \frac{(120)^2 \text{ J/C}}{3.5 \times 10^3 \text{ C/s}} = 4.1 \text{ V/A}$$

$$\boxed{R = 4.1 \ \Omega}$$

Electric power

1. An electric heater is operated by applying a potential difference of 50.0 V across a nichrome wire of total resistance 8.00 Ω. Find the current in the wire and the power rating of the heater.

2. For each of the following devices, calculate the unknown quantities.

	Device	P	R	I	ΔV
a.	Computer	?	92 Ω	1.2 A	?
b.	Portable stereo	12.0 W	?	?	3.0 V
c.	Coffee maker	600.0 W	?	5.0 A	?
d.	Graphing calculator	?	?	26.2 mA	6.0 V

Electric companies measure energy consumed in kilowatt-hours

Electric power, as discussed previously, is the rate of energy transfer. Power companies charge for energy, not power. However, the unit of energy used by electric companies to calculate consumption, the *kilowatt-hour,* is defined in terms of power. One kilowatt-hour (kW•h) is the energy delivered in 1 h at the constant rate of 1 kW. The following equation shows the relationship between the kilowatt-hour and the SI unit of energy, the joule:

$$1 \text{ kW} \cdot \text{h} \times \frac{10^3 \text{ W}}{1 \text{ kW}} \times \frac{60 \text{ min}}{1 \text{ h}} \times \frac{60 \text{ s}}{1 \text{ min}} = 3.6 \times 10^6 \text{ W} \cdot \text{s} = 3.6 \times 10^6 \text{ J}$$

On an electric bill, the electrical energy used in a given period is usually stated in multiples of kilowatt-hours, as shown in **Figure 19-13(a).** The cost of energy ranges from about 5 to 20 cents per kilowatt-hour, depending on where you live. An electric meter, like the one shown in **Figure 19-13(b),** is used by the electric company to determine how much energy is consumed over some period of time.

The electrical energy supplied by power companies is used to generate currents, which in turn are used to operate household appliances. As seen earlier in this section, as the charge carriers that make up a current encounter resistance, some of the electrical energy is converted to internal energy by collisions between moving electrons and atoms, and the conductor warms up. This effect is made useful in many common appliances, such as hair dryers, electric heaters, clothes dryers, toasters, and steam irons.

Hair dryers contain a long, thin heating coil that becomes very hot when the hair dryer is turned on. A fan behind the heating coil blows air through the area that contains the coils and out of the hair dryer. In this case, the warm air is used to dry hair; the same principle is used in clothes dryers and electric heaters.

Quick Lab

Energy Use in Home Appliances

MATERIALS LIST

- ✔ three small household appliances, such as a toaster, television, lamp, or stereo
- ✔ household electric-company bill (optional)

SAFETY CAUTION

Unplug appliances before examination. Use extreme caution when handling electrical equipment.

Look for a label on the back or bottom of each appliance. Record the power rating, which is given in units of watts (W). Use the billing statement to find the cost of energy per kilowatt-hour. (Prices usually range from $0.05 to $0.20. If you don't have a bill, choose a value from this range to use for your calculations.) Calculate the cost of running each appliance for 1 h. Estimate how many hours a day each appliance is used. Then calculate the monthly cost of using each appliance based on your daily estimate.

Figure 19-13

(a) Consumers are charged for the amount of energy they use in units of kilowatt-hours. **(b)** An electric meter, like the one shown here, records the amount of energy consumed.

In electric crock pots, a similar heating coil located at the base of the pot warms food inside the pot. In a steam iron, a heating coil warms the bottom of the iron and simultaneously turns water to steam, which is sprayed from jets in the bottom of the iron. Electric toasters have heating elements around the edges and in the center of the toaster. When the bread is loaded into the toaster, the heating coils turn on, and a timer determines the length of time the heating elements remain on before the bread pops up in the toaster.

SAMPLE PROBLEM 19D

Cost of electrical energy

PROBLEM

How much does it cost to operate a 100.0 W light bulb for 24 h if electrical energy costs $0.080 per kW•h?

SOLUTION

Given: Cost of energy = $0.080/kW•h
$P = 100.0$ W $= 0.1000$ kW $\Delta t = 24$ h

Unknown: Cost to operate the light bulb for 24 h

First calculate the energy used in units of kilowatt-hours by multiplying the power (in kW) by the time interval (in h). Then multiply the amount of energy by the cost per kilowatt-hour to find the total cost.

$$\text{Energy} = P\Delta t = (0.1000 \text{ kW})(24 \text{ h}) = 2.4 \text{ kW•h}$$
$$\text{Cost} = (2.4 \text{ kW•h})(\$0.080/\text{kW•h})$$

$$\boxed{\text{Cost} = \$0.19}$$

PRACTICE 19D

Cost of electrical energy

1. Assuming electrical energy costs $0.080 per kW•h, calculate the cost of running each of the following appliances for 24 h if 115 V is supplied to each:
   a. a 75.0 W stereo
   b. an electric oven that draws 20.0 A of current
   c. a television with a resistance of 60.0 Ω

2. Determine how many joules of energy are used by each appliance in item 1 in the 24 h period.

Electrical energy is transferred at high potential differences to minimize energy loss

When transporting electrical energy by power lines, such as those shown in **Figure 19-14,** power companies want to minimize the I^2R loss and maximize the energy delivered to a consumer. This can be done by decreasing either current or resistance. Although wires have little resistance, recall that resistance is proportional to length. Hence, resistance becomes a factor when power is transported over long distances. Even though power lines are designed to minimize resistance, some energy will be lost due to the length of the power lines.

As expressed by the equation $P = I^2R$, energy loss is proportional to the *square* of the current in the wire. For this reason, decreasing current is even more important than decreasing resistance. Because $P = I\Delta V$, the same amount of power can be transported either at high currents and low potential differences or at low currents and high potential differences. Thus, transferring electrical energy at low currents, thereby minimizing the I^2R loss, requires that electrical energy be transported at very high potential differences. Power plants transport electrical energy at potential differences of up to 765 000 V. In your city, this potential difference is reduced by a transformer to about 4000 V. At your home, this potential difference is reduced again to about 120 V by another transformer.

Figure 19-14
Power companies transfer electrical energy at high potential differences in order to minimize the I^2R loss.

Section Review

1. What does the power rating on a light bulb describe?

2. If the resistance of a light bulb is increased, how will the electrical energy used by the light bulb over the same time period change?

3. The potential difference across a resting neuron in the human body is about 70 mV, and the current in it is approximately 200 μA. How much power does the neuron release?

4. How much does it cost to watch an entire World Series (21 h) on a 90.0 W black-and-white television set? Assume that electrical energy costs $0.070/kW•h.

5. Explain why it is more efficient to transport electrical energy at high potential differences and low currents rather than at low potential differences and high currents.

Electron Tunneling

Earlier in this chapter we discussed current as the motion of charge carriers, which we treated as particles. But, as discussed in the "De Broglie Waves" feature in Chapter 12, the electron has both particle and wave characteristics. The wave nature of the electron leads to some strange consequences that cannot be explained in terms of classical physics. One example is *tunneling,* a phenomenon whereby electrons can pass into regions which, according to classical physics, they do not have the energy to reach.

Probability waves

To see how tunneling is possible, we must explore matter waves in greater detail. De Broglie's revolutionary idea that particles have a wave nature raised the question of how these matter waves behave. In 1926, Erwin Schrödinger proposed a wave equation that described the manner in which de Broglie matter waves change in space and time. Two years later, in an attempt to relate the wave and particle natures of matter, Max Born suggested that the square of the amplitude of a matter wave is proportional to the probability of finding the corresponding particle at that location.

Tunneling

Born's interpretation makes it possible for a particle to be found in a location that is not allowed by classical physics. Consider an electron with a potential energy of zero in the region between 0 and L (region II), which we call the *potential well,* and with a potential energy of some finite value U outside this

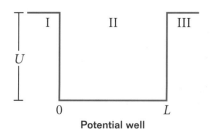
Potential well

Figure 19-15
An electron has a potential energy of zero inside the well and a potential energy of U outside the well. According to classical physics, if the electron's energy is less than U, it cannot escape the well without absorbing energy.

area (regions I and III), as shown in **Figure 19-15.** If the energy of the electron is less than U, then according to classical physics, the electron cannot escape the well without first acquiring additional energy.

The probability wave for this electron (in its lowest energy state) is shown in **Figure 19-16.** Between any two points of this curve, the area under the corresponding part of the curve is proportional to the probability of finding the electron in that region. The highest point of the curve corresponds to the most probable location of the electron, while the lower points correspond to less probable locations. Note that the curve never actually meets the x-axis. This means that the electron has some finite probability of being anywhere in space. Hence, there is a probability that the electron will actually be found outside the potential well. In other words, according to quantum mechanics, the electron is no longer confined to strict boundaries because of its energy. When the electron is found outside the boundaries established by classical physics, it is said to have *tunneled* to its new location.

The scanning tunneling microscope

In 1981, Gerd Binnig and Heinrich Rohrer, at IBM Zurich, discovered a practical application of tunneling current: a powerful microscope called the *scanning tunneling microscope,* or *STM.* The STM can produce highly detailed images with resolution comparable to the size of a single atom. The image of the surface of nickel shown in **Figure 19-17** demonstrates the power of the STM. Note that individual nickel atoms are recognizable. The smallest detail that can be discerned is about 0.2 nm, or approximately the size of an atom's radius. A typical optical microscope has a resolution no better than 200 nm, or about half the wavelength of visible light, and so it could never show the detail shown in **Figure 19-17.**

In the STM, a conducting probe with a very sharp tip (about the width of an atom) is brought near the surface to be studied. According to classical physics, electrons cannot move between the surface and the tip because they lack the energy to escape either material. But according to quantum theory, electrons can tunnel across the barrier, provided the distance is small enough (about 1 nm). By applying a potential difference between the surface and the tip, the electrons can be made to tunnel preferentially from surface to tip. In this way, the tip samples the distribution of electrons just above the surface.

The STM works because the probability of tunneling decreases exponentially with distance. By monitoring changes in the tunneling current as the tip is scanned over the surface, scientists obtain a sensitive measure of the topography of the electron distribution on the surface. The result is used to make images like the one in **Figure 19-17.** The STM can measure the height of surface features to within 0.001 nm, approximately 1/100 of an atomic diameter.

Although the STM was originally designed for imaging atoms, other practical applications are being developed. Engineers have greatly reduced the size of the STM and hope to someday develop a computer in which every piece of data is held by a single atom or by small groups of atoms and then read by an STM.

Probability wave

Figure 19-16
The probability curve for an electron in its lowest energy state shows that there is a certain probability of finding the electron outside the potential well.

Figure 19-17
A scanning tunneling microscope (STM) was used to produce this image of the surface of nickel. The contours represent the arrangement of individual nickel atoms on the surface. An STM enables scientists to see small details on surfaces with a lateral resolution of 0.2 nm and a vertical resolution of 0.001 nm.

CHAPTER 19
Summary

KEY TERMS

current (p. 694)

drift velocity (p. 697)

resistance (p. 700)

superconductor (p. 706)

KEY IDEAS

Section 19-1 Electric current

- Current is the rate of charge movement.
- Conventional current is defined in terms of *positive* charge movement.
- Drift velocity is the net velocity of charge carriers; its magnitude is much less than the average speed between collisions.
- Batteries and generators supply energy to charge carriers.
- In direct current, charges move in a single direction; in alternating current, the direction of charge movement continually alternates.

Section 19-2 Resistance

- According to the definition of resistance, potential difference equals current times resistance, as follows:

$$\Delta V = IR$$

- Resistance depends on length, cross-sectional area, temperature, and material.
- Superconductors are materials that have resistances of zero below a critical temperature, which varies with each metal.

Section 19-3 Electric power

- Electric power is the rate of conversion of electrical energy:

$$P = I\Delta V$$

- The power dissipated by a resistor can be calculated with the following equations:

$$P = I^2 R = \frac{(\Delta V)^2}{R}$$

- Electric companies measure energy consumed in kilowatt-hours.

Diagram symbols

Current	I
Positive charge	
Negative charge	

Variable symbols

Quantities		Units		Conversions	
ΔV	potential difference	V	volt	= J/C	= joules of energy/ coulomb of charge
I	current	A	ampere	= C/s	= coulombs of charge/second
R	resistance	Ω	ohm	= V/A	= volts of potential difference/ ampere of current
P	electric power	W	watt	= J/s	= joules of energy/second

ELECTRIC CURRENT

Review questions

1. What is electric current? What is the SI unit for electric current?

2. In a metal conductor, current is the result of moving electrons. Can charge carriers ever be positive?

3. What is meant by the term *conventional current*?

4. What is the difference between the drift speed of an electron in a metal wire and the average speed of the electron between collisions with the atoms of the metal wire?

5. There is a current in a metal wire due to the motion of electrons. Sketch a possible path for the motion of a single electron in this wire, the direction of the electric field vector, and the direction of conventional current.

6. What is an electrolyte?

7. What is the direction of conventional current in each case shown in **Figure 19-18**?

(a)   (b)

Figure 19-18

8. Why must energy be continuously pumped into a circuit by a battery or a generator to maintain an electric current?

9. Name at least two differences between batteries and generators.

10. What is the difference between direct current and alternating current? Which type of current is supplied to the appliances in your home?

Conceptual questions

11. In an analogy between traffic flow and electric current, what would correspond to the charge, Q? What would correspond to the current, I?

12. Is current ever "used up"? Explain your answer.

13. Why do wires usually warm up when an electric current is in them?

14. A student in your class claims that batteries supply the charges that move in a conductor to generate a current. What is wrong with this reasoning?

15. When a light bulb is connected to a battery, charges begin moving almost immediately, although each electron travels very slowly across the wire. Explain why the bulb lights up so quickly.

16. What is the drift velocity of an electron in a wire that has alternating current in it?

17. What is one advantage to using conventional current rather than considering current as the direction in which charge carriers are moving?

Practice problems

18. A net charge of 45 mC passes through the cross-sectional area of a wire in 15 s.
    a. What is the current in the wire?
    b. How many electrons pass the cross-sectional area in 1.0 min?
    (See Sample Problem 19A.)

19. A hair dryer draws a current of 9.1 A.
    a. How much charge passes through the hair dryer in 3.5 min?
    b. How many electrons does this represent?
    (See Sample Problem 19A.)

20. How much charge passes through a cross-sectional area of a copper wire in 1.0 s if $I = 5.0$ A?
    (See Sample Problem 19A.)

RESISTANCE

Review questions

21. What factors affect the resistance of a conductor?

22. Each of the wires shown in **Figure 19-19** is made of copper. Assuming each piece of wire is at the same temperature, which has the greatest resistance? Which has the least resistance?

Figure 19-19

23. Why are resistors used in circuit boards?

24. The critical temperature of aluminum is 1.19 K. What happens to the resistance of aluminum at temperatures lower than 1.19 K?

Conceptual questions

25. For a constant resistance, how are potential difference and current related?

26. If the potential difference across a conductor is constant, how is current dependent on resistance?

27. Using the atomic theory of matter, explain why the resistance of a material should increase as its temperature increases.

28. Recent discoveries have led some scientists to hope that a material will be found that is superconducting at room temperature. Why would such a material be useful?

Practice problems

29. A nichrome wire with a resistance of 15 Ω is connected across the terminals of a 3.0 V flashlight battery. How much current is in the wire?
(See Sample Problem 19B.)

30. How much current is drawn by a television with a resistance of 35 Ω that is connected across a potential difference of 120 V?
(See Sample Problem 19B.)

31. A potential difference of 12 V produces a current of 0.40 A in a piece of copper wire. What is the resistance of the wire?
(See Sample Problem 19B.)

32. Calculate the current that each resistor shown in **Figure 19-20** would draw when connected to a 9.0 V battery.
(See Sample Problem 19B.)

      Figure 19-20

ELECTRIC POWER

Review questions

33. Compare and contrast mechanical power with electric power.

34. What does an electric company charge consumers for?

35. What quantity is measured in kilowatt-hours?

36. If electrical energy is transmitted over long distances, the resistance of the wires becomes significant. Why?

37. How many joules of energy are dissipated by a 50.0 W light bulb in 1.00 s?

38. How many joules are in a kilowatt-hour?

Conceptual questions

39. A 40 W light bulb and a 75 W light bulb operate from 120 V. Which bulb has a greater current in it?

40. Two conductors of the same length and radius are connected across the same potential difference. One conductor has twice as much resistance as the other. Which conductor dissipates more power?

41. When a small lamp is connected to a battery, the filament becomes hot enough to emit electromagnetic radiation in the form of visible light, while the wires do not. What does this tell you about their relative resistances?

Practice problems

42. The operating potential difference of a light bulb is 120 V. The power rating of the bulb is 75 W. Find the current in the bulb and the bulb's resistance.
(See Sample Problem 19C.)

43. A color television has a power rating of 325 W. How much current does this set draw from a potential difference of 120 V?
(See Sample Problem 19C.)

44. How much would it cost to watch a football game on the television described in item 43 for 3.0 h if electrical energy costs $0.08/kW•h?
(See Sample Problem 19D.)

45. Calculate the cost of operating a 75 W light bulb continuously for a 30-day month when electrical energy costs $0.15/kW•h.
(See Sample Problem 19D.)

MIXED REVIEW

46. The current in a lightning bolt is 2.0×10^5 A. How many coulombs of charge pass through a cross-sectional area of the lightning bolt in 0.50 s?

47. A person notices a mild shock if the current along a path through the thumb and index finger exceeds 80.0 μA. Determine the maximum allowable potential difference without shock across the thumb and index finger for the following:
  a. a dry-skin resistance of 4.0×10^5 Ω
  b. a wet-skin resistance of 2.0×10^3 Ω

48. How much power is needed to operate a radio that draws 7.0 A of current when a potential difference of 115 V is applied across it?

49. It is estimated that in the United States (population 250 million) there is one electric clock per person, with each clock using energy at a rate of 2.5 W. Using this estimate, how much energy is consumed by all of the electric clocks in the United States in a year?

50. An X-ray tube used for cancer therapy operates at 4.0 MV with a beam current of 25 mA striking a metal target. Calculate the power of this beam.

51. A steam iron draws 6.0 A when connected to a potential difference of 120 V.
  a. What is the power rating of this iron?
  b. How many joules of energy are produced in 20.0 min?
  c. How much does it cost to run the iron for 20.0 min at $0.010/kW•h?

52. A high-voltage transmission line carries 1.0×10^3 A of current at 7.0×10^5 V for a distance of 160 km. The resistance in the wire is 0.30 Ω/km.
  a. What is the total power transmitted?
  b. What is the power dissipated due to resistive losses?
  c. What percent of the total power is lost due to resistance?

53. An 11.0 W energy-efficient fluorescent lamp is designed to produce the same illumination as a conventional 40.0 W lamp.
  a. How much energy does this lamp save during 100.0 h of use?
  b. If electrical energy costs $0.080/kW•h, how much money is saved in 100.0 h?

54. Use the electric bill shown in **Figure 19-21** to answer the following questions:
  a. How many joules of energy were consumed in this billing cycle?
  b. What is the average amount of energy consumed per day in joules and kilowatt-hours?
  c. If the cost of energy were increased to $0.15/kW•h, how much more would energy cost in this billing cycle? (Assume that the price of fuel remains constant.)

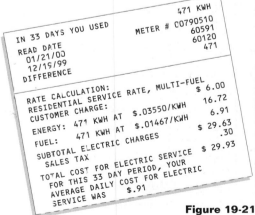

Figure 19-21

55. The mass of a gold atom is 3.27×10^{-25} kg. If 1.25 kg of gold is deposited on the negative electrode of an electrolytic cell in a period of 2.78 h, what is the current in the cell in this period? Assume that each gold ion carries one elementary unit of positive charge.

56. The power supplied to a typical black-and-white television is 90.0 W when the set is connected across a potential difference of 120 V. How much electrical energy does this set consume in 1.0 h?

57. A color television set draws about 2.5 A of current when connected to a potential difference of 120 V. How much time is required for it to consume the same energy that the black-and-white model described in item 56 consumes in 1.0 h?

58. The headlights on a car are rated at 80.0 W. If they are connected to a fully charged 90.0 A•h, 12.0 V battery, how long does it take the battery to completely discharge?

Technology & Learning

Graphing calculators

Program your graphing calculator to build a table of potential difference, resistance, and current, given the power dissipated in a resistor. Use your table to find the resistance of and current in the following:

 a. a 75.0 W bulb with a potential difference of 120.0 V across it

 b. a 75.0 W bulb with a potential difference of 20.0 V across it

 c. a 200.0 W bulb with a potential difference of 120.0 V across it

 d. a 200.0 W bulb with a potential difference of 20.0 V across it

Press [Y=] and [CLEAR] to clear any functions. Open a new program by pressing [PRGM] [▶] [▶] [ENTER]. Name the program "POWER" and press [ENTER]. Then enter the program in the table below.

To exit the program editor, press [2nd] [QUIT]. To run the program, press [PRGM], select "POWER," and press [ENTER] [ENTER]. Enter the value for the power dissipated, and press [ENTER].

The calculator will provide a table of resistances in ohms (Y1) and current in amperes (Y2) versus potential difference in volts (X). Cursor down the table to find the values you need. Press [ENTER] only when you're ready to end the program and exit the table.

Run the program again for different power values.

Keystrokes	Display
	PROGRAM: POWER
1. [PRGM] [▶] 2 [ALPHA] P [ENTER]	:PROMPT P
2. [ALPHA] ["] [X,T,θ] [x^2] [÷] [ALPHA] P [ALPHA] ["] [STO▶] [2nd] [Y-VARS] 1 1 [ENTER]	:"X^2/P" → Y1
3. [ALPHA] ["] [ALPHA] P [÷] [X,T,θ] [ALPHA] ["] [STO▶] [2nd] [Y-VARS] 1 2 [ENTER]	:"P/X" → Y2
4. 2 0 [STO▶] [VARS] 6 1 [ENTER]	:20→ TBLMIN
5. 2 0 [STO▶] [VARS] 6 2 [ENTER]	:20→ ΔTBL
6. [PRGM] [▶] 5 [ENTER]	:DISPTABLE

59. The current in a conductor varies over time as shown in **Figure 19-22.**

    a. How many coulombs of charge pass through a cross section of the conductor in the time interval $t = 0$ to $t = 5.0$ s?

    b. What constant current would transport the same total charge during the 5.0 s interval as does the actual current?

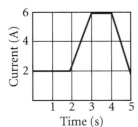

Time (s)   **Figure 19-22**

60. Birds resting on high-voltage power lines are a common sight. A certain copper power line carries a current of 50.0 A, and its resistance per unit length is 1.12×10^{-5} Ω/m. If a bird is standing on this line with its feet 4.0 cm apart, what is the potential difference across the bird's feet?

61. An electric car is designed to run on a bank of batteries with a total potential difference of 12 V and a total energy storage of 2.0×10^{7} J.

    a. If the electric motor draws 8.0 kW, what is the current delivered to the motor?

    b. If the electric motor draws 8.0 kW as the car moves at a steady speed of 20.0 m/s, how far will the car travel before it is "out of juice"?

Alternative Assessment

Performance assessment

1. Design an experiment to investigate how the characteristics of a conducting wire affect its resistance. In particular, plan to explore the effects of length, shape, mass, thickness, and the nature of the material. If your teacher approves your plan, obtain the necessary equipment and perform the experiment. Share the results of your experiment with your class.

2. Construct a voltaic pile like the first battery made by Alessandro Volta (1745–1827). Make a stack of alternating copper and zinc disks, inserting cardboard moistened in salt water between the disks. (Copper pennies and dimes can be used as well.) How many layers do you need to make an LED light up? How many layers are required to light a flashlight bulb? How could you measure the relationship between stack size and potential difference? If your teacher approves your plan, carry out an experiment testing the relationships between the stack size and potential difference. Compare your method and results with those of other students in your class.

Portfolio projects

3. When Edison invented the electric light bulb in 1879, his bulb lasted only a week. In 1881, Lewis Howard Latimer received patents for bulbs that could operate for months. Research the life and accomplishments of Latimer, and prepare a presentation in the form of a report, poster, short video, or computer presentation.

4. Visit an electric parts or electronic parts store or consult a print or on-line catalog to learn about different kinds of resistors. Find out what the different resistors look like, what they are made of, what their resistance is, how they are labeled, and what they are used for. Summarize your findings in a poster or a brochure entitled *A Consumer's Guide to Resistors*.

5. The units of measurement you learned about in this chapter were named after three famous scientists: Andre-Marie Ampere, Georg Simon Ohm, and Alessandro Volta. Research their lives, works, discoveries, and contributions. Create a presentation about one of these scientists. The presentation can be in the form of a report, poster, short video, or computer presentation.

CHAPTER 19
Laboratory Exercise

CURRENT AND RESISTANCE

Different substances offer different amounts of resistance to an electric current. Physicists have found that temperature, length, cross-sectional area, and the material the conductor is made of determine the resistance of a conductor. In this experiment, you will observe the effects of length, cross-sectional area, and material on the resistance of conductors.

You will use a set of mounted resistance coils, which will provide wire coils of different lengths, diameters, and metals. The resistance provided by each resistance coil will affect the current in the resistor. You will measure the potential difference across the resistance coil, and you will find the current in the conductor. Then you will use these values to calculate the resistance of each resistance coil using the definition of resistance.

SAFETY

• **Never close a circuit until it has been approved by your teacher. Never rewire or adjust any element of a closed circuit. Never work with electricity near water; be sure the floor and all work surfaces are dry.**

• **If the pointer on any kind of meter moves off scale, open the circuit immediately by opening the switch.**

• **Do not attempt this exercise with any batteries or electrical devices other than those provided by your teacher for this purpose.**

PREPARATION

1. Determine whether you will be using the CBL and sensors procedure or the meters procedure. Read the entire lab for the appropriate procedure, and plan what steps you will take.

2. Prepare a data table in your lab notebook with seven columns and six rows. For the CBL and sensors procedure, label the first through seventh columns *Trial, Metal, Gauge number, Length (cm), Cross-sectional area* (cm^2), ΔV_C *(V),* and ΔV_R *(V).* Prepare a space near the data table to record the resistance of the known resistor. For the meters procedure, label the first through seventh columns *Trial, Metal, Gauge number, Length (cm), Cross-sectional area* (cm^2), ΔV_x *(V),* and *I (A).* In the first column, label the second through sixth rows *1, 2, 3, 4,* and *5.*

Meters procedure begins on page 724.

PROCEDURE

CBL AND SENSORS

Potential difference and resistance

3. Set up the apparatus as shown in **Figure 19-23**. Construct a circuit that includes a power supply, a switch, a resistor of known resistance, and the mounted resistance coils. For each trial, you will measure the potential difference across one unknown resistance coil and then across the known resistor using the CBL voltage probe. *Do not turn on the power supply. Do not close the switch until your teacher has approved your circuit.*

4. With the switch open, connect the voltage probe to measure the potential difference across the first unknown resistance coil. Connect the black lead of the voltage probe to the side of the coil that is connected to the black pin on the power supply. Connect the red lead to the other side of the coil. *Do not close the switch.*

5. Connect the CBL and graphing calculator. Connect the voltage probe to CH1 on the CBL. Turn on the CBL and the graphing calculator, and start the program PHYSICS on the calculator.

6. Select option *SET UP PROBES* from the MAIN MENU. Enter 1 for the number of probes. Select *MORE PROBES* from the SELECT PROBE menu. Select the *VOLTAGE PROBE* from the list. Enter 1 for the channel number.

7. Select the *COLLECT DATA* option from the MAIN MENU. Select the *MONITOR INPUT* option from the DATA COLLECTION menu. The graphing calculator will begin to display values for the potential difference across the coil. *Do not close the switch.*

8. When your teacher has approved your circuit, make sure the power supply dial is turned completely counterclockwise. Turn on the power supply, and slowly turn the dial clockwise. Periodically close the switch briefly and read the value for the potential difference on the CBL. When the potential difference is approximately 0.5 V, read and record the value as ΔV_C in your data table. Open the switch.

9. Remove the leads of the voltage probe from the resistance coil, and connect the probe to the known resistor. Connect the black lead to the side of the resistor that is connected to the black pin on the power supply, and connect the red lead to the other side of the resistor. Have your teacher approve your circuit.

10. When your teacher has approved your circuit, close the switch and read the value for the potential difference across the known resistor. Record this value as ΔV_R in your data table.

Figure 19-23

Step 3: The set of mounted resistance coils shown includes five different resistance coils. In this lab, you will measure the potential difference across each coil in turn.

Step 4: Always make sure the black lead on the probe is connected to the side of the coil that connects to the black pin on the power supply. Use your finger to trace the circuit from the black pin on the power supply through the circuit to the red pin on the power supply to check for proper connections.

Step 8: Close the switch only long enough to take readings. Open the switch as soon as you have taken the reading.

11. When your teacher has approved your circuit, close the switch and read the value for the potential difference across the unknown resistance coil. Record this value as ΔV_C in your data table. Open the switch.

12. For Trial 2, remove the voltage probe from the known resistor and connect it to the next coil of unknown resistance. Connect the black lead of the probe to the side of the coil that is connected to the black pin on the power supply, and connect the red lead to the other side. Repeat the procedure in steps 8–11. Repeat the procedure until the potential difference across all five coils has been recorded. Record the potential difference across the known resistor for each trial. Your teacher will supply the length and cross-sectional area for each unknown resistance coil. Record these in your data table.

Analysis and Interpretation begins on page 725.

PROCEDURE

METERS

Current at varied resistances

3. Set up the apparatus as shown in **Figure 19-24.** Construct a circuit that includes a power supply, a switch, a current meter, a voltage meter, and the mounted resistance coils. For each trial, you will measure the current and the potential difference for one of the coils to determine the value of the resistance. ***Do not turn on the power supply. Do not close the switch until your teacher has approved your circuit.***

4. With the switch open, connect the current meter in a straight line with the mounted resistance coils. Make sure the black lead on the meter is connected to the black pin on the power supply. Connect the black lead on the voltage meter to the side of the first resistance coil that is connected to the black pin on the power supply, and connect the red lead to the other side of the coil. ***Do not close the switch until your teacher approves your circuit.***

5. When your teacher has approved your circuit, make sure the power supply dial is turned completely counterclockwise. Turn on the power supply, and slowly turn the dial clockwise. Periodically close the switch briefly and read the current value on the current meter. Adjust the dial until the current is approximately 0.15 A.

6. Close the switch. Quickly record the current in and the potential difference across the resistance coil in your data table. Open the switch immediately. Turn off the power supply by turning the dial completely counterclockwise. Your teacher will supply the length and cross-sectional area of the wire on the coil. Record these in your data table.

Figure 19-24

Step 3: The set of mounted resistance coils shown includes five different resistance coils. In this lab, you will measure the current and potential difference for each coil in turn.

Step 4: Use your finger to trace the circuit from the black pin on the power supply through the circuit to the red pin on the power supply to check for proper connections.

Step 6: Close the switch only long enough to take readings. Open the switch as soon as you have taken the reading.

7. Remove the leads of the voltmeter from the resistance coil, and connect them in parallel to the next adjacent coil. Repeat steps 5 and 6 until five coils have been studied. For each coil, adjust the current, and follow the same procedure as above. Record the current and potential difference readings for each coil. Your teacher will supply the length and cross-sectional area for each coil. Record these in your data table.

ANALYSIS AND INTERPRETATION

Calculations and data analysis

1. Organizing data Use the definition of resistance, $R = \dfrac{\Delta V}{i}$.

    a. CBL and sensors Use the value for the known resistance and the potential difference across the known resistor to calculate the current in the circuit for each trial. Use the value for the current to calculate the resistance, R_C, for each resistance coil you tested.

    b. Meters Use the measurements for current and potential difference to calculate the resistance, R_C, for each resistance coil you tested.

Conclusions

2. Analyzing data Rate the coils from lowest to highest resistance. Record your ratings.

    a. According to your results for this experiment, how does the length of the wire affect the resistance of the coil?

    b. According to your results for this experiment, how does the cross-sectional area affect the resistance of the coil?

3. Evaluating results Based on your results for the metals used in this experiment, which metal has the greatest resistance? Explain how you arrived at this conclusion.

4. Evaluating results Based on your results for the metals used in this experiment, which metal has the lowest resistance? Explain how you arrived at this conclusion.

Extension

5. Devise a method for identifying a resistance coil made of an unknown metal by placing the coil in a circuit and finding its resistance. Research and include in your plans a way to use the value for the resistance to identify the metal. If there is time and your teacher approves your plan, perform the experiment. Write a report detailing your procedure and results.

Physics and Its World *Timeline 1830–1890*

1831

$$\text{emf} = -N\Delta\frac{[AB(\cos\theta)]}{\Delta t}$$

Michael Faraday begins experiments demonstrating electromagnetic induction. Similar experiments are conducted around the same time by **Joseph Henry** in the United States, but at the time he doesn't publish the results of his work.

1831 – Charles Darwin sets sail on the H.M.S. *Beagle* to begin studies of life-forms in South America, New Zealand, and Australia. His discoveries form the foundation for the theory of natural selection.

1837 – Queen Victoria ascends the British throne at the age of 18. Her reign continues for 64 years, setting the tone for the Victorian era.

1839

Samuel Morse sends the first telegraph message from Washington, D. C. to Baltimore.

1843

$$\Delta U = Q - W$$

James Prescott Joule determines that mechanical energy is equivalent to energy transferred by heat, laying the foundation for the principle of energy conservation.

1843 – Richard Wagner's first major operatic success, *The Flying Dutchman*, premieres in Dresden, Germany.

1850 – Harriet Tubman, an ex-slave from Maryland, becomes a "conductor" on the Underground Railroad. Over the next decade, she helps more than 300 slaves escape to northern "free" states.

1850

$$W = Q_h - Q_c$$

Rudolph Clausius formulates the second law of thermodynamics, the first step in the transformation of thermodynamics into an exact science.

1820

1830

1840

1850

1860

1861 – **Benito Juárez** is elected president of Mexico. During his administration, the invasion by France and Austria is repelled and basic social reforms are implemented.

Scala/Art Resource, NY

1861 – The American Civil War begins at Fort Sumter in Charleston, South Carolina.

1873

$$c = \frac{1}{\sqrt{\mu_0 \varepsilon_0}}$$

James Clerk Maxwell completes his *Treatise on Electricity and Magnetism*. In this work, Maxwell gives **Michael Faraday's** discoveries a mathematical framework.

1874 – The first exhibition of impressionist paintings, including works by **Claude Monet, Camille Pissarro,** and **Pierre-Auguste Renoir**, takes place in Paris.

Giraudon/Art Resource, NY

1878 – The first commercial telephone exchange in the United States begins operation in New Haven, Connecticut.

1884 – *Huckleberry Finn*, by **Samuel L. Clemens** (better known as Mark Twain), is published.

1888

$$\lambda = \frac{c}{f}$$

Heinrich Hertz experimentally demonstrates the existence of electromagnetic waves, which were predicted by **James Clerk Maxwell.** **Oliver Lodge** makes the same discovery independently.

1860
1870
1880
1890
1900

Physics and Its World 1830–1890 **727**

Circuits and Circuit Elements

PHYSICS IN ACTION

For strings of decorative lights—like these that illuminate the Riverwalk in San Antonio, Texas—two types of electric circuits can be used. In the first type, called a series circuit, when a single bulb burns out, the entire string of lights goes dark. Most consumers prefer the second type of circuit, known as a parallel circuit. This type allows the other lights to remain lighted, even when one or more bulbs burn out. In this chapter, you will explore the basic properties of these two types of circuits.

- *How does the wiring of a circuit alter the current in and potential difference across each element?*

- *What happens when both types of circuits are combined in a single circuit?*

CONCEPT REVIEW

Potential difference (Section 18-2)

Current (Section 19-1)

Resistance and Ohm's law
  (Section 19-2)

20-1
Schematic diagrams and circuits

schematic diagram

a graphic representation of an electric circuit, with standardized symbols representing circuit components

SCHEMATIC DIAGRAMS

Take a few minutes to examine the battery and light bulb in **Figure 20-1(a),** then draw a diagram of each element in the photograph and its connection. How easily could your diagram be interpreted by someone else? Could the elements in your diagram be used to depict a string of decorative lights, such as those draped over the trees of the San Antonio Riverwalk?

A diagram that depicts the construction of an electrical apparatus is called a **schematic diagram.** The schematic diagram shown in **Figure 20-1(b)** uses symbols to represent the bulb, battery, and wire from **Figure 20-1(a).** Note that these same symbols can be used to describe these elements in any electrical apparatus. This way, schematic diagrams can be read by anyone familiar with the standard set of symbols.

Reading schematic diagrams is necessary to determine how the parts in an electrical device are arranged. In this chapter, you will see how the arrangement of resistors in an electrical device can affect the current in and potential difference across the other elements in the device. The ability to interpret schematic diagrams for complicated electrical equipment is an essential skill for solving problems involving electricity.

As shown in **Table 20-1,** each element used in a piece of electrical equipment is represented by a symbol in schematic diagrams that reflects the element's construction or function. For example, the schematic-diagram symbol that represents an open switch resembles the open knife switch that is shown in the corresponding photograph. Note that **Table 20-1** also includes other forms of schematic-diagram symbols; these alternative symbols will not be used in this book.

Figure 20-1

(a) When this battery is connected to a light bulb, the potential difference across the battery generates a current that illuminates the bulb.
(b) The connections between the light bulb and battery can be represented in a schematic diagram.

Table 20-1   Schematic diagram symbols

Component	Symbol used in this book	Other forms of this symbol	Explanation
Wire or conductor			• Wires that connect elements are conductors. • Because wires offer negligible resistance, they are represented by straight lines.
Resistor or circuit load			• Resistors are shown as wires with multiple bends, illustrating resistance to the movement of charges.
Bulb or lamp			• The multiple bends of the filament indicate that the light bulb is a resistor. • The symbol for the filament of the bulb is often enclosed in a circle to emphasize the enclosure of a resistor in a bulb.
Plug			• The plug symbol looks like a container for two prongs. • The potential difference between the two prongs of a plug is symbolized by lines of unequal height.
Battery		Multiple cells	• Differences in line height indicate a potential difference between positive and negative terminals of the battery. • The taller line represents the positive terminal of the battery.
Switch		Open / Closed	• The small circles indicate the two places where the switch makes contact with the wires. Most switches work by breaking only one of the contacts, not both.
Capacitor			• The two parallel plates of a capacitor are symbolized by two parallel lines of equal height. • One curved line indicates that the capacitor can be used with only direct current sources with the polarity as shown.

ELECTRIC CIRCUITS

Think about how you get the bulb in **Figure 20-2** to light up. Will the bulb stay lit if the switch is opened? Is there any way to light the bulb without connecting the wires to the battery?

Figure 20-2
When all electrical components are connected, charges can move freely in a circuit. The movement of charges in a circuit can be halted by opening the switch.

electric circuit

a set of electrical components connected so that they provide one or more complete paths for the movement of charges

The filament of the light bulb is a resistor. When a wire connects the terminals of the battery to the light bulb, as shown in **Figure 20-2,** charges built up on one terminal of the battery have a path to follow to reach the opposite charges on the other terminal. Because there are charges moving uniformly, a current exists. This current causes the filament to heat up and glow.

Together, the bulb, battery, switch, and wire form an **electric circuit.** An electric circuit is a path through which charges can be conducted. A schematic diagram for a circuit is sometimes called a circuit diagram.

Any element or group of elements in a circuit that dissipates energy is called a *load.* Therefore, a simple circuit consists of a source of potential difference and electrical energy, such as a battery, and a load, such as a bulb or group of bulbs. Because the connecting wire and switch have negligible resistance, we will not consider these elements as part of the load.

In **Figure 20-2,** the path from one battery terminal to the other is complete, a potential difference exists, and electrons move from one terminal to the other. In other words, there is a closed-loop path for electrons to follow. This is called a *closed circuit.* The switch in the circuit in **Figure 20-2** must be closed in order for a steady current to exist.

Without a complete path, there is no charge flow and therefore no current. This situation is an *open circuit.* If the switch in **Figure 20-2** were open, as shown in **Table 20-1,** the circuit would be open, the current would be zero, and the bulb would not light up.

Conceptual Challenge

1. Bird on a wire Why is it possible for a bird to be perched on a high-voltage wire without being electrocuted? (Hint: Consider the potential difference between the bird's two feet.)

2. Parachutist on a wire Suppose a parachutist lands on a high-voltage wire and grabs the wire in preparation to be rescued. Will the parachutist be electrocuted? If the wire breaks, why should the parachutist let go of the wire as it falls to the ground? (Hint: First consider the potential difference between the parachutist's two hands holding the wire. Then consider the potential difference between the wire and the ground.)

3. Avoiding electrocution When current stronger than 10 mA is in a person holding a live wire, the hand muscles contract and the person may be unable to let go of the live wire. What procedure would you use to try to save a person "frozen" to a live high-voltage wire without endangering your own life?

Light bulbs contain a complete conducting path

How does a light bulb contain a complete conducting path? When you look at a clear light bulb, you can see the twisted filament inside that provides a portion of the conducting path for the circuit. However, the bulb screws into a single socket; it seems to have only a single contact, the rounded part at the bulb's base.

Closer examination of the socket reveals that it has two contacts inside. One contact, in the bottom of the socket, is connected to the wire going to one side of the filament. The other contact is in the side of the socket, and it is connected to the wire going to the other side of the filament.

The placement of the contacts within the socket indicates how the bulb completes the circuit, as shown in **Figure 20-3.** Within the bulb, one side of the filament is connected with wires to the contact at the light bulb's base, **(a).** The other side of the filament is connected to the side of the metal base **(c).** Insulating material between the side of the base and the contact on the bottom prevents the wires from being connected to each other with a conducting material. In this way, charges have only one path to follow when passing through a light bulb—through the filament, **(b).**

When a light bulb is screwed in, the contact on one side of the socket touches the threads on the side of the bulb's base. The contact on the bottom of the socket touches the contact on the bottom of the bulb's base. Charges then enter through the bulb's base, move through the bulb to the filament, and exit the bulb through the threads. For most light bulbs, the bulb will glow regardless of which direction the charges move. Thus, the positive terminal of a battery can be connected to either the base of the bulb or the threads of the bulb, as long as the negative terminal is connected to the threads or base, respectively. All that matters is that there is a complete conducting path for the charges to move through the circuit.

Short circuits can be hazardous

Without a load, such as a bulb or other resistor, the circuit contains little resistance to the movement of charges. This situation is called a short circuit. For example, a short circuit occurs when a wire is connected from one terminal of a battery to the other by a wire with little resistance. This commonly occurs when uninsulated wires connected to different terminals come into contact with each other.

When short circuits occur in the wiring of your home, the increase in current can become unsafe. Most wires cannot withstand the increased current, and they begin to overheat. The wire's insulation may even melt or cause a fire.

(b)

(c)

(a)

Figure 20-3
Light bulbs contain a complete conducting path. When a light bulb is screwed in, charges can enter through the base **(a)**, move along the wire to the filament **(b)**, and exit the bulb through the threads **(c)**.

The source of potential difference and electrical energy is the circuit's emf

Is it possible to light a bulb using only wires and no battery? Without a potential difference, there is no charge flow and hence no current. In any circuit, a battery is necessary because the battery is the source of potential difference and electrical energy for the circuit. So the bulb must be connected to a battery to be lit.

Any device that increases the potential energy of charges circulating in a circuit is a source of **emf.** The emf is the energy per unit charge supplied by a source of electric current. Think of such a source as a "charge pump" that forces electrons to move in a certain direction. Batteries and generators are examples of emf sources.

emf

the energy per unit charge supplied by a source of electric current

For conventional current, the terminal voltage is less than the emf

Look at the battery attached to the light bulb in the circuit shown in **Figure 20-4.** As shown in the inset, instead of behaving only like a source of emf, the battery behaves as if it contains both an emf source and a resistor. The battery's internal resistance to current is the result of moving charges colliding with atoms inside the battery while the charges are traveling from one terminal to the other. Thus, when charges move conventionally in a battery, the potential difference across the battery's terminals, the *terminal voltage*, is actually slightly less than the emf.

Unless otherwise stated, any reference in this book to the potential difference across a battery should be thought of as the potential difference measured across the battery's terminals rather than as the emf of the battery. In other words, all examples and end-of-chapter problems will disregard internal resistance.

Figure 20-4
A battery **(a)** in a circuit behaves as if it contains both an emf source **(b)** and an internal resistance **(c).** For simplicity's sake, in problem solving it will be assumed that this internal resistance is insignificant.

Small internal resistance

Quick Lab

Simple Circuits

MATERIALS LIST

✔ 1 miniature light bulb
✔ 1 D-cell battery
✔ wires
✔ rubber band or tape

⚡ SAFETY CAUTION

Do not perform this lab with any batteries or electrical devices other than those listed here.

Never work with electricity near water. Be sure the floor and all work surfaces are dry.

Connect the bulb to the battery using two wires, using a rubber band or tape to

hold the wire to the battery. Once you have gotten the bulb to light, try different arrangements to see whether there is more than one way to get the bulb to light. Can you make the bulb light using just one wire? Diagram each arrangement that you try, and note whether it produces light.

Explain exactly which parts of the bulb, battery, and wire must be connected for the light bulb to produce light.

Potential difference across a load equals the terminal voltage

When a charge moves within a battery from one terminal to the other, the chemical energy of the battery is converted to the electrical potential energy of the charge. Then, as the charge leaves the battery terminal and moves through the circuit, its electrical potential energy is converted to other forms of energy. For instance, when the load is a resistor, the electrical potential energy of the charge is converted to the internal energy of the resistor and dissipated as thermal energy and light energy.

Because of conservation of energy, the charge must gain as much energy as it loses in one complete trip around the circuit (starting and ending at the same place). Thus, the electrical potential energy gained in the battery must equal the energy dissipated by the load. Because the potential difference is the measurement of potential energy per amount of charge, the potential increase across the battery must equal the potential decrease across the load.

Section Review

1. Identify the types of elements in the schematic diagram illustrated in **Figure 20-5** and the number of each type.

2. Using the symbols listed in **Table 20-1,** draw a schematic diagram that contains two resistors, an emf source, and a closed switch.

Figure 20-5

3. In which of the schematic diagrams shown below will there be no current?

Figure 20-6

Figure 20-7

Figure 20-8

Figure 20-9

4. If the potential difference across the bulb in a certain flashlight is 3.0 V, what is the potential difference across the combination of batteries used to power it?

5. **Physics in Action**   In what form is the electrical energy that is supplied to a string of decorative lights dissipated?

20-2
Resistors in series or in parallel

20-2 SECTION OBJECTIVES

- **Calculate the equivalent resistance for a circuit of resistors in series, and find the current in and potential difference across each resistor in the circuit.**

- **Calculate the equivalent resistance for a circuit of resistors in parallel, and find the current in and potential difference across each resistor in the circuit.**

series

describes a circuit or portion of a circuit that provides a single conducting path without junctions

RESISTORS IN SERIES

In a circuit that consists of a single bulb and a battery, the potential difference across the bulb equals the terminal voltage. The total current in the circuit can be found using the equation $\Delta V = IR$.

What happens when a second bulb is added to such a circuit, as shown in **Figure 20-10**? When moving through this circuit, charges that pass through one bulb must also move through the second bulb. Because all charges in the circuit must follow the same conducting path, these bulbs are said to be connected in **series.**

Resistors in series have the same current

Light-bulb filaments are resistors; thus, **Figure 20-10(b)** represents the two bulbs in **Figure 20-10(a)** as resistors. According to the conservation of charge, charges cannot build up or disappear at a point. For this reason, the amount of charge that enters one bulb in a given time interval equals the amount of charge that exits that bulb in the same amount of time. Because there is only one path for a charge to follow, the amount of charge entering and exiting the first bulb must equal the amount of charge that enters and exits the second bulb in the same time interval.

Because the current is the amount of charge moving past a point per unit of time, the current in the first bulb must equal the current in the second bulb. This is true for any number of resistors arranged in series. *When many resistors are connected in series, the current in each resistor is the same.*

The total current in a series circuit depends on how many resistors are present and on how much resistance each offers. Thus, to find the total current, first use the individual resistance values to find the total resistance of the circuit, called the *equivalent resistance.* Then the equivalent resistance can be used to find the current.

(a)

(b)

R_1 R_2

Figure 20-10
Because light-bulb filaments are resistors, the two bulbs in this series circuit **(a)** can be represented by two resistors in the schematic diagram **(b)** shown on the right.

The equivalent resistance in a series circuit is the sum of the circuit's resistances

As described in Section 20-1, the potential difference across the battery, ΔV, must equal the potential difference across the load, $\Delta V_1 + \Delta V_2$, where ΔV_1 is the potential difference across R_1 and ΔV_2 is the potential difference across R_2.

$$\Delta V = \Delta V_1 + \Delta V_2$$

According to $\Delta V = IR$, the potential difference across each resistor is equal to the current in that resistor multiplied by the resistance.

$$\Delta V = I_1 R_1 + I_2 R_2$$

Because the resistors are in series, the current in each is the same. For this reason, I_1 and I_2 can be replaced with a single variable for the current, I.

$$\Delta V = I(R_1 + R_2)$$

Finding a value for the equivalent resistance of the circuit is now possible. If you imagine the equivalent resistance replacing the original two resistors, as shown in **Figure 20-11,** you can treat the circuit as if it contains only one resistor and use $\Delta V = IR$ to relate the total potential difference, current, and equivalent resistance.

$$\Delta V = I(R_{eq})$$

Now set the last two equations for ΔV equal to each other, and divide by the current.

$$\Delta V = I(R_{eq}) = I(R_1 + R_2)$$

$$R_{eq} = R_1 + R_2$$

Thus, the equivalent resistance of the series combination is the sum of the individual resistances. An extension of this analysis shows that the equivalent resistance of two or more resistors connected in series can be calculated using the following equation.

Figure 20-11
The two resistors in the actual circuit **(a)** have the same effect on the current in the circuit as the equivalent resistor **(b).**

RESISTORS IN SERIES

$$R_{eq} = R_1 + R_2 + R_3 \ldots$$

Equivalent resistance equals the total of individual resistances in series.

Because R_{eq} represents the sum of the individual resistances that have been connected in series, *the equivalent resistance of a series combination of resistors is always greater than any individual resistance.*

To find the total current in a series circuit, first simplify the circuit to a single equivalent resistance using the boxed equation above, then use $\Delta V = IR$ to calculate the current.

$$I = \frac{\Delta V}{R_{eq}}$$

Because the current in each bulb is equal to the total current, you can also use $\Delta V = IR$ to calculate the potential difference across each resistor.

$$\Delta V_1 = IR_1 \text{ and } \Delta V_2 = IR_2$$

The method described above can be used to find the potential difference across resistors in a series circuit containing any number of resistors.

SAMPLE PROBLEM 20A

Resistors in series

PROBLEM

A 9.0 V battery is connected to four light bulbs, as shown in Figure 20-12. Find the equivalent resistance for the circuit and the current in the circuit.

Figure 20-12

SOLUTION

1. DEFINE **Given:**

$\Delta V = 9.0$ V	$R_1 = 2.0 \ \Omega$
$R_2 = 4.0 \ \Omega$	$R_3 = 5.0 \ \Omega$
$R_4 = 7.0 \ \Omega$	

Unknown: $R_{eq} = ?$ $I = ?$

Diagram:

4.0 Ω   5.0 Ω   7.0 Ω

2.0 Ω   9.0 V

2. PLAN **Choose an equation(s) or situation:** Because the resistors are connected end to end, they are in series. Thus, the equivalent resistance can be calculated with the equation from page 737.

$$R_{eq} = R_1 + R_2 + R_3 \ldots$$

The following equation can be used to calculate the current.

$$\Delta V = IR_{eq}$$

Rearrange the equation(s) to isolate the unknown(s): No rearrangement is necessary to calculate R_{eq}, but $\Delta V = IR_{eq}$ must be rearranged to calculate current.

$$I = \frac{\Delta V}{R_{eq}}$$

3. CALCULATE **Substitute the values into the equation(s) and solve:**

$$R_{eq} = 2.0 \ \Omega + 4.0 \ \Omega + 5.0 \ \Omega + 7.0 \ \Omega$$

$$\boxed{R_{eq} = 18.0 \ \Omega}$$

Substitute the equivalent resistance value into the equation for current.

$$I = \frac{\Delta V}{R_{eq}} = \frac{9.0 \text{ V}}{18.0 \text{ } \Omega}$$

$$\boxed{I = 0.50 \text{ A}}$$

4. EVALUATE For resistors connected in series, the equivalent resistance should be greater than the largest resistance in the circuit.

$$18.0 \text{ } \Omega > 7.0 \text{ } \Omega$$

Resistors in series

1. A 12.0 V storage battery is connected to three resistors, 6.75 Ω, 15.3 Ω, and 21.6 Ω, respectively. The resistors are joined in series.
   a. Calculate the equivalent resistance.
   b. What is the current in the circuit?

2. A 4.0 Ω resistor, an 8.0 Ω resistor, and a 12.0 Ω resistor are connected in series with a 24.0 V battery.
   a. Calculate the equivalent resistance.
   b. Calculate the current in the circuit.
   c. What is the current in each resistor?

3. Because the current in the equivalent resistor of Sample Problem 20A is 0.50 A, it must also be the current in each resistor of the original circuit. Find the potential difference across each resistor.

4. A series combination of two resistors, 7.25 Ω and 4.03 Ω, is connected to a 9.00 V battery.
   a. Calculate the equivalent resistance of the circuit and the current.
   b. What is the potential difference across each resistor?

5. A 7.0 Ω resistor is connected in series with another resistor and a 4.5 V battery. The current in the circuit is 0.60 A. Calculate the value of the unknown resistance.

6. Several light bulbs are connected in series across a 115 V source of emf.
   a. What is the equivalent resistance if the current in the circuit is 1.70 A?
   b. If each light bulb has a resistance of 1.50 Ω, how many light bulbs are in the circuit?

Series circuits require all elements to conduct

What happens to a series circuit when a single bulb burns out? Consider what a circuit diagram for a string of lights with one broken filament would look like. As the schematic diagram in **Figure 20-13** shows, the broken filament means that there is a gap in the conducting pathway used to make up the circuit. Because the circuit is no longer closed, there is no current in it and all of the bulbs go dark.

Why, then, would anyone arrange resistors in series? Resistors can be placed in series with a device in order to regulate the current in that device. In the case of decorative lights, adding an additional bulb will decrease the current in each bulb. Thus, the filament of each bulb need not withstand such a high current. Another advantage to knowing the effects of placing resistors in series is that several lesser resistances can be used to add up to a single greater resistance that is unavailable. Finally, in some cases, it is important to have a circuit that will have no current if any one of its component parts fails. This technique is used in a variety of contexts, including some burglar alarm systems.

RESISTORS IN PARALLEL

As discussed above, when a single bulb in a series light set burns out, the entire string of lights goes dark because the circuit is no longer closed. What would happen if there were alternative pathways for the movement of charge, as shown in **Figure 20-14**?

A wiring arrangement that provides alternative pathways for the movement of a charge is a **parallel** arrangement. The bulbs of the decorative light set shown in the schematic diagram in **Figure 20-14** are arranged in parallel with each other.

Resistors in parallel have the same potential differences across them

To explore the consequences of arranging resistors in parallel, consider the two bulbs connected to a battery in **Figure 20-15(a).** In this arrangement, the left

Figure 20-13

A burnt-out filament in a bulb has the same effect as an open switch. Because this series circuit is no longer complete, there is no current in the circuit.

parallel

describes two or more components in a circuit that are connected across common points or junctions, providing separate conducting paths for the current

Figure 20-14

These decorative lights are wired in parallel. Notice that in a parallel arrangement there is more than one path for current.

side of each bulb is connected to the positive terminal of the battery, and the right side of each bulb is connected to the negative terminal. Because the sides of each bulb are connected to common points, the potential difference across each bulb is the same. If the common points are the battery's terminals, as they are in the figure, the potential difference across each resistor is also equal to the terminal voltage of the battery. The current in each bulb, however, is not always the same.

Figure 20-15
(a) This simple parallel circuit with two bulbs connected to a battery can be represented by **(b)** the schematic diagram shown on the right.

The sum of currents in parallel resistors equals the total current

In **Figure 20-15**, when a certain amount of charge leaves the positive terminal and reaches the branch on the left side of the circuit, some of the charge moves through the top bulb and some moves through the bottom bulb. If one of the bulbs has less resistance, more charge moves through that bulb because the bulb offers less opposition to the flow of charges.

Because charge is conserved, the sum of the currents in each bulb equals the current delivered by the battery. This is true for all resistors in parallel.

$$I = I_1 + I_2 + I_3 \ldots$$

The parallel circuit shown in **Figure 20-15** can be simplified to an equivalent resistance with a method similar to the one used for series circuits. To do this, first show the relationship among the currents.

$$I = I_1 + I_2$$

Then substitute the equivalents for current according to $\Delta V = IR$.

$$\frac{\Delta V}{R_{eq}} = \frac{\Delta V_1}{R_1} + \frac{\Delta V_2}{R_2}$$

Quick Lab

Series and Parallel Circuits

MATERIALS LIST

✔ 4 regular drinking straws
✔ 4 stirring straws or coffee stirrers
✔ tape

Cut the regular drinking straws and thin stirring straws into equal lengths. Tape them end to end in long tubes to form series combinations. Form parallel combinations by taping the straws together side by side.

Try several combinations of like and unlike straws. Blow through each combination of tubes, holding your fingers in front of the opening(s) to compare the air flow (or current) that you achieve with each combination.

Straws in series

Straws in parallel

Rank the combinations according to how much resistance they offer. Classify them according to the amount of current created in each.

Conceptual Challenge

1. Car headlights

How can you tell that the headlights on a car are wired in parallel rather than in series? How would the brightness of the bulbs differ if they were wired in series across the same 12 V battery instead of in parallel?

2. Simple circuits

Sketch as many different circuits as you can using three light bulbs—each having the same resistance—and a battery.

Because the potential difference across each bulb in a parallel arrangement equals the terminal voltage ($\Delta V = \Delta V_1 = \Delta V_2$), you can divide each side of the equation by ΔV to get the following equation.

$$\frac{1}{R_{eq}} = \frac{1}{R_1} + \frac{1}{R_2}$$

An extension of this analysis shows that the equivalent resistance of two or more resistors connected in parallel can be calculated using the following equation.

RESISTORS IN PARALLEL

$$\frac{1}{R_{eq}} = \frac{1}{R_1} + \frac{1}{R_2} + \frac{1}{R_3} \ldots$$

The equivalent resistance of resistors in parallel can be calculated using a reciprocal relationship.

Notice that this equation does not give the value of the equivalent resistance directly. You must take the reciprocal of your answer to obtain the value of the equivalent resistance.

Because of the reciprocal relationship, *the equivalent resistance for a parallel arrangement of resistors must always be less than the smallest resistance in the group of resistors.*

The conclusions made about both series and parallel circuits are summarized in **Table 20-2.**

Table 20-2   Resistors in series or in parallel

Circuit type	Series	Parallel
Schematic diagram		
Current	$I = I_1 = I_2 = I_3 = \ldots$ = same for each resistor	$I = I_1 + I_2 + I_3 + \ldots$ = sum of currents
Potential difference	$\Delta V = \Delta V_1 + \Delta V_2 + \Delta V_3 \ldots$ = sum of potential differences	$\Delta V = \Delta V_1 = \Delta V_2 = \Delta V_3 \ldots$ = same for each resistor
Equivalent resistance	$R_{eq} = R_1 + R_2 + R_3 \ldots$ = sum of individual resistances	$\frac{1}{R_{eq}} = \frac{1}{R_1} + \frac{1}{R_2} + \frac{1}{R_3} \ldots$ = reciprocal sum of resistances

Resistors in parallel

PROBLEM

A 9.0 V battery is connected to four resistors, as shown in Figure 20-16. Find the equivalent resistance for the circuit and the total current in the circuit.

Figure 20-16

SOLUTION

1. DEFINE

Given:

$$\Delta V = 9.0 \text{ V} \qquad R_1 = 2.0 \ \Omega$$
$$R_2 = 4.0 \ \Omega \qquad R_3 = 5.0 \ \Omega$$
$$R_4 = 7.0 \ \Omega$$

Unknown: $R_{eq} = ?$ $I = ?$

Diagram:

2. PLAN

Choose an equation(s) or situation: Because both sides of each resistor are connected to common points, they are in parallel. Thus, the equivalent resistance can be calculated with the equation from p. 742.

$$\frac{1}{R_{eq}} = \frac{1}{R_1} + \frac{1}{R_2} + \frac{1}{R_3} \dots \text{ for parallel}$$

The following equation can be used to calculate the current.

$$\Delta V = I R_{eq}$$

Rearrange the equation(s) to isolate the unknown(s): No rearrangement is necessary to calculate R_{eq}; rearrange $\Delta V = I R_{eq}$ to calculate current.

$$I = \frac{\Delta V}{R_{eq}}$$

3. CALCULATE

Substitute the values into the equation(s) and solve: Remember to take the reciprocal in the final step.

$$\frac{1}{R_{eq}} = \frac{1}{2.0 \ \Omega} - \frac{1}{4.0 \ \Omega} + \frac{1}{5.0 \ \Omega} + \frac{1}{7.0 \ \Omega}$$

$$\frac{1}{R_{eq}} = \frac{0.50}{1 \ \Omega} + \frac{0.25}{1 \ \Omega} + \frac{0.20}{1 \ \Omega} + \frac{0.14}{1 \ \Omega} = \frac{1.09}{1 \ \Omega}$$

$$R_{eq} = \frac{1 \ \Omega}{1.09}$$

$$\boxed{R_{eq} = 0.917 \ \Omega}$$

continued on next page

Substitute that equivalent resistance value in the equation for current.

$$I = \frac{\Delta V_{tot}}{R_{eq}} = \frac{9.0 \text{ V}}{0.917 \text{ }\Omega}$$

$$\boxed{I = 9.8 \text{ A}}$$

4. EVALUATE For resistors connected in parallel, the equivalent resistance should be less than the smallest resistance.

$$0.917 \text{ }\Omega < 2.0 \text{ }\Omega$$

PRACTICE 20B

Resistors in parallel

1. The potential difference across the equivalent resistance in Sample Problem 20B equals the potential difference across each of the individual parallel resistors. Calculate the value for the current in each resistor.

2. A 4.0 Ω resistor, an 8.0 Ω resistor, and a 12.0 Ω resistor are connected in parallel across a 24.0 V battery.
    a. What is the equivalent resistance of the circuit?
    b. What is the current in each resistor?

3. An 18.0 Ω, 9.00 Ω, and 6.00 Ω resistor are connected in parallel to an emf source. A current of 4.00 A is in the 9.00 Ω resistor.
    a. Calculate the equivalent resistance of the circuit.
    b. What is the potential difference across the source?
    c. Calculate the current in the other resistors.

4. A length of wire is cut into five equal pieces. The five pieces are then connected in parallel, with the resulting resistance being 2.00 Ω. What was the resistance of the original length of wire before it was cut up?

$V = I R$

Parallel circuits do not require all elements to conduct

What happens when a bulb burns out in a string of decorative lights that is wired in parallel? There is no current in that branch of the circuit, but each of the parallel branches provides a separate alternative pathway for current. Thus, the potential difference supplied to the other branches and the current in these branches remain the same, and the bulbs in these branches remain lit.

When resistors are wired in parallel with an emf source, the potential difference across each resistor always equals the potential difference across the source. Because household circuits are arranged in parallel, appliance manufacturers are able to standardize their design, producing devices that all operate at the same potential difference. (Because the potential difference provided by a wall outlet in a home in North America is not the same as the potential difference that is standard on other continents, appliances made in North America are not always compatible with wall outlets in homes on other continents.)

Because household devices operate at the same potential difference, manufacturers can choose the resistance of the device to ensure that the current in the device will be neither too high nor too low for the internal wiring and other components that make up the device.

Additionally, the equivalent resistance of several parallel resistors is less than the resistance of any of the individual resistors. Thus, a low equivalent resistance can be created with a group of resistors of higher resistances.

Section Review

1. Two resistors are wired in series. In another circuit, the same two resistors are wired in parallel. In which circuit is the equivalent resistance greater?

2. A 5 Ω, a 10 Ω, and a 15 Ω resistor are connected in series.
   a. Which resistor has the most current in it?
   b. Which resistor has the largest potential difference across it?

3. A 5 Ω, a 10 Ω, and a 15 Ω resistor are connected in parallel.
   a. Which resistor has the most current in it?
   b. Which resistor has the largest potential difference across it?

4. Find the current in and potential difference across each of the resistors in the following circuits:
   a. a 2.0 Ω and a 4.0 Ω resistor wired in series with a 12 V source
   b. a 2.0 Ω and a 4.0 Ω resistor wired in parallel with a 12 V source
   c. a 4.0 Ω and a 12.0 Ω resistor wired in series with a 4.0 V source
   d. a 4.0 Ω and a 12.0 Ω resistor wired in parallel with a 4.0 V source

5. Find the current in and potential difference across each of the resistors in the following circuits:
   a. a 150 Ω and a 180 Ω resistor wired in series with a 12 V source
   b. a 150 Ω and a 180 Ω resistor wired in parallel with a 12 V source

6. **Physics in Action** A string of 35 miniature decorative lights is wired in series. If it draws 0.20 A of current when it is connected to a 120.0 V emf source, what is the resistance of each miniature bulb?

20-3
Complex resistor combinations

- **Calculate the equivalent resistance for a complex circuit involving both series and parallel portions.**

- **Calculate the current in and potential difference across individual elements within a complex circuit.**

RESISTORS COMBINED BOTH IN PARALLEL AND IN SERIES

Series and parallel circuits are not often encountered independent of one another. Most circuits today employ both series and parallel wiring to utilize the advantages of each type.

A common example of a complex circuit is the electrical wiring typical in a home. In a home, a fuse or circuit breaker is connected in series to numerous outlets, which are wired to one another in parallel. An example of a typical household circuit is shown in **Figure 20-17.**

As a result of the outlets being wired in parallel, all the appliances operate independently; if one is switched off, any others remain on. Wiring the outlets in parallel ensures that an identical potential difference exists across any appliance. This way, appliance manufacturers can produce appliances that all use the same standard potential difference.

To prevent excessive current, a fuse or circuit breaker must be placed in series with all of the outlets. Fuses and circuit breakers open the circuit when the current becomes too high. A fuse is a small metallic strip that melts if the current exceeds a certain value. After a fuse has melted, it must be replaced. A circuit breaker, a more modern device, triggers a switch when current reaches a certain value. The switch must be reset, rather than replaced, after the circuit overload has been removed. Both fuses and circuit breakers must be in series with the entire load to prevent excessive current from reaching any appliance. This is important because excessive currents could damage equipment, overheat wires, and perhaps cause a fire.

Fuses and circuit breakers are carefully selected to meet the demands of a circuit. If the circuit is to carry currents as large as 30 A, an appropriate fuse or circuit breaker must be used. Since the fuse or circuit breaker is placed in series with the rest of the circuit, the current in the fuse or circuit breaker is the same as the total current in the circuit. To find this current, the equivalent resistance must be determined.

When determining the equivalent resistance for a complex circuit, you must simplify the circuit into groups of series and parallel resistors and then find the equivalent resistance for each group by using the rules for finding the equivalent resistance of series and parallel resistors.

(a)

Toaster: 16.9 Ω

Microwave: 8.0 Ω

Popcorn popper: 10.0 Ω

$\Delta V = 120$ V   Circuit breaker: 0.01 Ω

(b)

Figure 20-17

(a) When all of these devices are plugged into the same household circuit, **(b)** the result is a parallel combination of resistors in series with a circuit breaker.

Equivalent resistance

PROBLEM

Determine the equivalent resistance of the complex circuit shown in Figure 20-18.

REASONING

The best approach is to divide the circuit into groups of series and parallel resistors. This way the methods presented in Sample Problems 20B and 20C can be used to calculate the equivalent resistance for each group.

Figure 20-18

SOLUTION

1. **Redraw the circuit as a group of resistors along one side of the circuit.**

   Because bends in a wire do not affect the circuit, they do not need to be represented in a schematic diagram. Redraw the circuit without the corners, keeping the arrangement of the circuit elements the same, as shown in **Figure 20-19.** For now, disregard the emf source and work only with the resistances.

Figure 20-19

2. **Identify components in series, and calculate their equivalent resistance.**

   Resistors in groups (**a**) and (**b**) in **Figure 20-20** are in series.
   For group (**a**): $R_{eq} = 3.0\ \Omega + 6.0\ \Omega = 9.0\ \Omega$
   For group (**b**): $R_{eq} = 6.0\ \Omega + 2.0\ \Omega = 8.0\ \Omega$

3. **Identify components in parallel, and calculate their equivalent resistance.**

   Resistors in group (**c**) in **Figure 20-20** are in parallel.

   For group (**c**):

   $$\frac{1}{R_{eq}} = \frac{1}{8.0\ \Omega} + \frac{1}{4.0\ \Omega} = \frac{0.12}{1\ \Omega} + \frac{0.25}{1\ \Omega} = \frac{0.37}{1\ \Omega}$$

   $$R_{eq} = 2.7\ \Omega$$

4. **Repeat steps 2 and 3 until the resistors in the circuit are reduced to a single equivalent resistance.**

   The remainder of the resistors, group (**d**) in **Figure 20-20**, are in series.

   For group (**d**): $R_{eq} = 9.0\ \Omega + 2.7\ \Omega + 1.0\ \Omega$

   $$\boxed{R_{eq} = 12.7\ \Omega}$$

Figure 20-20

5. **Redraw the circuit as in Figure 20-20, with the equivalent resistance connected to the original emf source.**

Equivalent resistance

1. **For each of the following sets of values, determine the equivalent resistance for the circuit shown in Figure 20-21.**

   a. $R_a = 25.0\ \Omega$ $R_b = 3.0\ \Omega$ $R_c = 40.0\ \Omega$

   b. $R_a = 12.0\ \Omega$ $R_b = 35.0\ \Omega$ $R_c = 25.0\ \Omega$

   c. $R_a = 15.0\ \Omega$ $R_b = 28.0\ \Omega$ $R_c = 12.0\ \Omega$

Figure 20-21

2. **For each of the following sets of values, determine the equivalent resistance for the circuit shown in Figure 20-22.**

   a. $R_a = 25.0\ \Omega$ $R_b = 3.0\ \Omega$ $R_c = 40.0\ \Omega$
   $R_d = 15.0\ \Omega$ $R_e = 18.0\ \Omega$

   b. $R_a = 12.0\ \Omega$ $R_b = 35.0\ \Omega$ $R_c = 25.0\ \Omega$
   $R_d = 50.0\ \Omega$ $R_e = 45.0\ \Omega$

Figure 20-22

Work backward to find the current in and potential difference across a part of a circuit

Now that the equivalent resistance for a complex circuit has been determined, you can work backward to find the current in and potential difference across any resistor in that circuit. In the household example, substitute potential difference and equivalent resistance in $\Delta V = IR$ to find the total current in the circuit. Because the fuse or circuit breaker is in series with the load, the current in it is equal to the total current. Once this total current is determined, $\Delta V = IR$ can again be used to find the potential difference across the fuse or circuit breaker.

There is no single formula for finding the current in and potential difference across a resistor buried inside a complex circuit. Instead, $\Delta V = IR$ and the rules reviewed in **Table 20-3** must be applied to smaller pieces of the circuit until the desired values are found.

Table 20-3	Series and parallel resistors	
	Series	**Parallel**
Current	same as total	add to find total
Potential difference	add to find total	same as total

Current in and potential difference across a resistor

PROBLEM

Determine the current in and potential difference across the 2.0 Ω resistor highlighted in Figure 20-23.

REASONING

First determine the total circuit current by reducing the resistors to a single equivalent resistance. Then rebuild the circuit in steps, calculating the current and potential difference for the equivalent resistance of each group until the current in and potential difference across the 2.0 Ω resistor are known.

Figure 20-23

SOLUTION

1. **Determine the equivalent resistance of the circuit.**

   The equivalent resistance of the circuit is 12.7 Ω; this value is calculated in Sample Problem 20C.

2. **Calculate the total current in the circuit.**

   Substitute the potential difference and equivalent resistance in $\Delta V = IR$, and rearrange the equation to find the current delivered by the battery.

   $$I = \frac{\Delta V}{R} = \frac{9.0\ \text{V}}{12.7\ \Omega} = 0.71\ \text{A}$$

3. **Determine a path from the equivalent resistance found in step 1 to the 2.0 Ω resistor.**

   Review the path taken to find the equivalent resistance in **Figure 20-24,** and work backward through this path. The equivalent resistance for the entire circuit is the same as the equivalent resistance for group **(d).** The center resistor in group **(d)** in turn is the equivalent resistance for group **(c).** The top resistor in group **(c)** is the equivalent resistance for group **(b),** and the right resistor in group **(b)** is the 2.0 Ω resistor.

4. **Follow the path determined in step 3, and calculate the current in and potential difference across each equivalent resistance. Repeat this process until the desired values are found.**

   Regroup, evaluate, and calculate.

   Replace the circuit's equivalent resistance with group

continued on next page

Figure 20-24

(d), as shown in **Figure 20-25.** The resistors in group **(d)** are in series; therefore, the current in each resistor is the same as the current in the equivalent resistance, which equals 0.71 A. The potential difference across the 2.7 Ω resistor in group **(d)** can be calculated using $\Delta V = IR$.

Figure 20-25

Given:	$I = 0.71$ A	$R = 2.7\ \Omega$
Unknown:	$\Delta V = ?$	

$$\Delta V = IR = (0.71\ \text{A})(2.7\ \Omega) = 1.9\ \text{V}$$

Regroup, evaluate, and calculate.

Replace the center resistor with group **(c),** as shown in **Figure 20-26.**

The resistors in group **(c)** are in parallel; therefore, the potential difference across each resistor is the same as the potential difference across the 2.7 Ω equivalent resistance, which equals 1.9 V. The current in the 8.0 Ω resistor in group **(c)** can be calculated using $\Delta V = IR$.

Figure 20-26

Given:	$\Delta V = 1.9$ V	$R = 8.0\ \Omega$
Unknown:	$I = ?$	

$$I = \frac{\Delta V}{R} = \frac{1.9\ \text{V}}{8.0\ \Omega} = 0.24\ \text{A}$$

Regroup, evaluate, and calculate.

Replace the 8.0 Ω resistor with group **(b),** as shown in **Figure 20-27.**

The resistors in group **(b)** are in series; therefore, the current in each resistor is the same as the current in the 8.0 Ω equivalent resistance, which equals 0.24 A.

$$\boxed{I = 0.24\ \text{A}}$$

Figure 20-27

The potential difference across the 2.0 Ω resistor can be calculated using $\Delta V = IR$.

Given:	$I = 0.24$ A	$R = 2.0\ \Omega$
Unknown:	$\Delta V = ?$	

$$\Delta V = IR = (0.24\ \text{A})(2.0\ \Omega) = 0.48\ \text{V}$$

$$\boxed{\Delta V = 0.48\ \text{V}}$$

Current in and potential difference across a resistor

1. Calculate the current in and potential difference across each of the resistors shown in the schematic diagram in **Figure 20-28**.

$R_a = 5.0\ \Omega$ $R_b = 7.0\ \Omega$

$R_c = 4.0\ \Omega$

$R_d = 4.0\ \Omega$ $R_e = 4.0\ \Omega$

14.0 V

$R_f = 2.0\ \Omega$

Figure 20-28

Consumer Focus *Decorative Lights and Bulbs*

*L*ight sets arranged in series cannot remain lit if a bulb burns out. Wiring in parallel can eliminate this problem, but each bulb must then be able to withstand 120 V. To eliminate the drawbacks of either approach, modern light sets typically contain two or three sections connected to each other in parallel, each of which contains bulbs in series.

When one bulb is removed from a modern light set, half or one-third of the lights in the set go dark because the bulbs in that section are wired in series. When a bulb *burns out,* however, all of the other bulbs in the set remain lit. How is this possible?

Modern decorative bulbs have a short loop of insulated wire called the *jumper,* that is wrapped around the wires connected to the filament, as shown in **Figure 20-29**. There is no current in the insulated wire when the bulb is functioning properly. When the filament breaks, however, the current in the section is zero and the potential difference across the two wires connected to the broken filament is then 120 V. This large potential difference creates a spark across the two wires that burns the insulation off the small loop of wire. Once that occurs, the small loop closes the circuit, and the other bulbs in the section remain lit.

Because the small loop in the burnt-out bulb has very little resistance, the equivalent resistance of that portion of the light set decreases and the current in it increases. This increased current results in a slight increase in the brightness of each bulb. As more bulbs burn out, the temperature in each bulb increases and can become a fire hazard; thus, bulbs should be replaced soon after burning out.

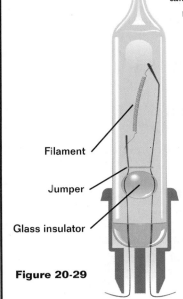

Filament

Jumper

Glass insulator

Figure 20-29

1. Find the equivalent resistance of the complex circuit shown in **Figure 20-30.**

2. What is the current in the 1.5 Ω resistor in the complex circuit shown in **Figure 20-30**?

Figure 20-30

3. What is the potential difference across the 1.5 Ω resistor in the circuit shown in **Figure 20-30**?

4. **Figure 20-31** depicts a household circuit containing several appliances and a circuit breaker attached to a 120 V source of potential difference.
   a. Is the current in the toaster equal to the current in the microwave?
   b. Is the potential difference across the microwave equal to the potential difference across the popcorn popper?
   c. Is the current in the circuit breaker equal to the current in all of the appliances combined?

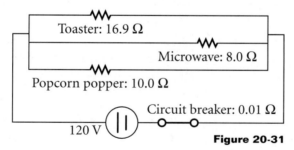

Figure 20-31

5. Determine the equivalent resistance for the household circuit shown in **Figure 20-31.**

6. Determine how much current is in the toaster in the household circuit shown in **Figure 20-31.**

7. **Physics in Action**   A certain strand of miniature lights contains 35 bulbs wired in series, with each bulb having a resistance of 15 Ω. What is the equivalent resistance when three such strands are connected in parallel across a potential difference of 120.0 V?

8. **Physics in Action**   What is the current in and potential difference across each of the bulbs in the strands of lights described in item 7?

9. **Physics in Action**   If one of the bulbs in one of the three strands of lights in item 7 goes out, what is the current in and potential difference across each of the lit bulbs?

CHAPTER 20
Summary

KEY IDEAS

Section 20-1 Schematic diagrams and circuits
- Schematic diagrams use standardized symbols to summarize the contents of electric circuits.
- A circuit is a set of electrical components connected so that they provide one or more complete paths for the movement of charges.
- Any device that transforms nonelectrical energy into electrical energy, such as a battery or a generator, is a source of emf.
- If the internal resistance of a battery is neglected, the emf can be considered equal to the terminal voltage, the potential difference across the source's two terminals.

Section 20-2 Resistors in series or in parallel
- The equivalent resistance of a set of resistors connected in series is the sum of the individual resistances.

$$R_{eq} = R_1 + R_2 + R_3 \ldots$$
For resistors in series

- The equivalent resistance of a set of resistors connected in parallel is calculated using an inverse relationship.

$$\frac{1}{R_{eq}} = \frac{1}{R_1} + \frac{1}{R_2} + \frac{1}{R_3} \ldots$$
For resistors in parallel

Section 20-3 Complex resistor combinations
- Complex circuits can be understood by isolating segments that are in series or in parallel and simplifying them to their equivalent resistances.

KEY TERMS

electric circuit (p. 732)

emf (p. 734)

parallel (p. 740)

schematic diagram (p. 730)

series (p. 736)

Diagram symbols

Wire or conductor	
Resistor or circuit load	
Bulb or lamp	
Plug	
Battery/ direct-current emf source	
Switch	
Capacitor	

Variable symbols

Quantities	Units	Conversions
I current	A amperes	= C/s = coulombs of charge per second
R resistance	Ω ohms	= V/A = volts per ampere of current
ΔV potential difference	V volts	= J/C = joules of energy per coulomb of charge

SCHEMATIC DIAGRAMS AND CIRCUITS

Review questions

1. Why are schematic diagrams useful?

2. Draw a circuit diagram containing three 5.0 Ω resistors, a 6.0 V battery, and a switch.

3. The switch in the circuit shown in **Figure 20-32** can be set to connect to points *A, B,* or *C.* Which of these connections will provide a complete circuit?

Figure 20-32

4. If the batteries in a cassette recorder provide a terminal voltage of 12.0 V, what is the potential difference across the entire recorder?

5. In a case in which the internal resistance of a battery is significant, which is greater?
   a. the terminal voltage
   b. the emf of the battery

Conceptual questions

6. Do charges move from a source of potential difference into a load or through both the source and the load?

7. Assuming that you want to create a circuit that has current in it, why should there be no openings in the circuit?

8. Suppose a 9 V battery is connected across a light bulb. In what form is the electrical energy supplied by the battery dissipated by the light bulb?

9. Why is it dangerous to turn on a light when you are in the bathtub?

10. Which of the switches in the circuit in **Figure 20-33** will complete the circuit when closed? Which will cause a short circuit?

Figure 20-33

RESISTORS IN SERIES OR IN PARALLEL

Review questions

11. If four resistors in a circuit are connected in series, which of the following is the same for the resistors in the circuit?
    a. potential difference across the resistors
    b. current in the resistors

12. If four resistors are in parallel, which of the following is the same for the resistors in the circuit?
    a. potential difference across the resistors
    b. current in the resistors

Conceptual questions

13. A short circuit is a circuit containing a path of very low resistance in parallel with some other part of the circuit. Discuss the effect of a short circuit on the current within that portion of the circuit.

14. Fuses protect electrical devices by opening a circuit if the current in the circuit is too high. Would a fuse work successfully if it were connected in parallel with the device that it is supposed to protect?

15. What might be an advantage of using two identical resistors in parallel that are connected in series with another identical parallel pair, as shown in **Figure 20-34**, instead of using a single resistor?

Figure 20-34

Practice problems

16. A length of wire is cut into five equal pieces. If each piece has a resistance of 0.15 Ω, what was the resistance of the original length of wire?
(See Sample Problem 20A.)

17. A 9.0 Ω resistor and a 6.0 Ω resistor are connected in series with an emf source. The potential difference across the 6.0 Ω resistor is measured with a voltmeter to be 12 V. Find the potential difference across the emf source.
(See Sample Problem 20A.)

18. A 4.0 Ω resistor, an 8.0 Ω resistor, and a 12 Ω resistor are connected in series with a 24 V battery. Determine the following:
  a. the equivalent resistance for the circuit
  b. the current in the circuit
  c. the current in each resistor
  d. the potential difference across each resistor
(See Sample Problem 20A.)

19. The resistors in item 18 are connected in parallel across a 24 V battery. Determine the following:
  a. the equivalent resistance for the circuit
  b. the current in the circuit
  c. the current in each resistor
  d. the potential difference across each resistor
(See Sample Problem 20B.)

20. An 18.0 Ω, 9.00 Ω, and 6.00 Ω resistor are connected in series with an emf source. The current in the 9.00 Ω resistor is measured to be 4.00 A.
  a. Calculate the equivalent resistance of the three resistors in the circuit.
  b. Find the potential difference across the emf source.
  c. Find the current in the other resistors.
(See Sample Problem 20B.)

21. An 18.0 Ω resistor, 9.00 Ω resistor, and 6.00 Ω resistor are connected in parallel across a 12 V battery. Determine the following:
  a. the equivalent resistance for the circuit
  b. the current in the circuit
  c. the current in each resistor
  d. the potential difference across each resistor
(See Sample Problem 20B.)

COMPLEX RESISTOR COMBINATIONS

Conceptual questions

22. A technician has two resistors, each with the same resistance, R.
  a. How many different resistances can the technician achieve?
  b. Express the effective resistance of each possibility in terms of R.

23. The technician in item 22 finds another resistor, so now there are three resistors with the same resistance.
  a. How many different resistances can the technician achieve?
  b. Express the effective resistance of each possibility in terms of R.

24. Three identical light bulbs are connected to a battery, as shown in **Figure 20-35**. Compare the level of brightness of each bulb when all are illuminated. What happens to the brightness of each bulb if the following changes are made?
  a. Bulb A is removed from its socket.
  b. Bulb C is removed from its socket.
  c. A wire is connected between points D and E.
  d. A wire is connected between points D and F.

Figure 20-35

Practice problems

25. Find the equivalent resistance of the circuit shown in **Figure 20-36.**
(See Sample Problem 20C.)

Figure 20-36

26. Find the equivalent resistance of the circuit shown in **Figure 20-37.**
(See Sample Problem 20C.)

Figure 20-37

27. Two identical parallel-wired strings of 25 bulbs are connected to each other in series. If the equivalent resistance of the combination is 150.0 Ω when it is connected across a potential difference of 120.0 V, what is the resistance of each individual bulb?
(See Sample Problem 20C.)

28. For the circuit shown in **Figure 20-38,** determine the following:

    a. the current in the 2.0 Ω resistor
    b. the potential difference across the 2.0 Ω resistor
    c. the potential difference across the 12.0 Ω resistor
    d. the current in the 12.0 Ω resistor

(See Sample Problem 20D.)

Figure 20-38

29. For the circuit shown in **Figure 20-39,** determine the following:

    a. the current in each resistor
    b. the potential difference across each resistor

(See Sample Problem 20D.)

Figure 20-39

MIXED REVIEW

30. An 8.0 Ω resistor and a 6.0 Ω resistor are connected in series with a battery. The potential difference across the 6.0 Ω resistor is measured as 12 V. Find the potential difference across the battery.

31. A 9.0 Ω resistor and a 6.0 Ω resistor are connected in parallel to a battery, and the current in the 9.0 Ω resistor is found to be 0.25 A. Find the potential difference across the battery.

32. A 9.0 Ω resistor and a 6.0 Ω resistor are connected in series to a battery, and the current through the 9.0 Ω resistor is 0.25 A. What is the potential difference across the battery?

33. The stockroom has only 20 Ω and 50 Ω resistors.

    a. You need a resistance of 45 Ω. How can this resistance be achieved under these circumstances?
    b. What can you do if you need a 35 Ω resistor?

34. The equivalent resistance of the circuit shown in **Figure 20-40** is 60.0 Ω. Determine the value of R.

Figure 20-40

35. **Figure 20-41** depicts five resistance diagrams Each individual resistance is 6.0 Ω .

    a. Which resistance combination has the largest equivalent resistance?

    b. Which resistance combination has the smallest equivalent resistance?

    c. Which resistance combination has an equivalent resistance of 4.0 Ω ?

    d. Which resistance combination has an equivalent resistance of 9.0 Ω ?

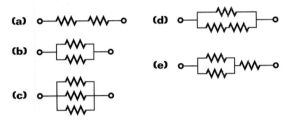

Figure 20-41

36. An 18.0 Ω resistor and a 6.0 Ω resistor are connected in series to an 18.0 V battery. Find the current in and the potential difference across each resistor.

37. The resistors described in item 36 are reconnected in parallel to the same 18.0 V battery. Find the current in each resistor and the potential difference across each resistor.

38. A 30.0 Ω resistor is connected in parallel to a 15.0 Ω resistor. These are joined in series to a 5.00 Ω resistor and a source with a potential difference of 30.0 V.

    a. Draw a schematic diagram for this circuit.

    b. Calculate the equivalent resistance for this circuit.

    c. Calculate the current in each resistor.

    d. Calculate the potential difference across each resistor.

39. A resistor with an unknown resistance is connected in parallel to a 12 Ω resistor. When both resistors are connected in parallel to an emf source of 12 V, the current across the unknown resistor is measured with an ammeter to be 3.0 A. What is the resistance of the unknown resistor?

40. Three small lamps are connected to a 9.0 V battery, as shown in **Figure 20-42.**

    a. What is the equivalent resistance of this circuit?

    b. What is the total current in this circuit?

    c. What is the current in each bulb?

    d. What is the potential difference across each bulb?

Figure 20-42

41. The equivalent resistance for the circuit shown in **Figure 20-43** drops to one-half its original value when the switch, S, is closed. Determine the value of R.

Figure 20-43

42. You can obtain only four 20.0 Ω resistors from the stockroom.

    a. How can you achieve a resistance of 50.0 Ω under these circumstances?

    b. What can you do if you need a 5.0 Ω resistor?

43. Four resistors are connected to a battery with a terminal voltage of 12.0 V, as shown in **Figure 20-44.** Determine the following:

    a. the equivalent resistance for the circuit

    b. the current in the battery

    c. the current in the 30.0 Ω resistor

    d. the power dissipated by the 50.0 Ω resistor

    e. the power dissipated by the 20.0 Ω resistor

(Hint: Remember that $P = \dfrac{(\Delta V)^2}{R} = I\Delta V$.)

Figure 20-44

44. Two resistors, A and B, are connected in series to a 6.0 V battery. A voltmeter connected across resistor A measures a potential difference of 4.0 V. When the two resistors are connected in parallel across the 6.0 V battery, the current in B is found to be 2.0 A. Find the resistances of A and B.

45. Draw a schematic diagram of nine 100 Ω resistors arranged in a series-parallel network so that the total resistance of the network is also 100 Ω. All nine resistors must be used.

46. For the circuit in **Figure 20-45,** find the following:
  a. the equivalent resistance of the circuit
  b. the current in the 5.0 Ω resistor

Figure 20-45

Technology Learning

Graphing calculators

Program your graphing calculator to calculate the equivalent resistance of any number of resistors in parallel. Use the program to determine the equivalent resistance for the following 15 resistors in parallel: 1.0 Ω, 2.0 Ω, 3.0 Ω, 4.0 Ω, 5.0 Ω, 6.0 Ω, 7.0 Ω, 8.0 Ω, 9.0 Ω, 10.0 Ω, 11.0 Ω, 12.0 Ω, 13.0 Ω, 14.0 Ω, and 15.0 Ω.

Open a new program by pressing [PRGM] [▶] [▶] [ENTER]. Name the program "PARALL" and press [ENTER]. Then enter the program shown in the table below.

To exit the program editor, press [2nd] [QUIT]. To run the program, press [PRGM], select "PARALL," and press [ENTER] [ENTER]. When prompted for N, enter the number of resistors that you want to have in your circuit and press [ENTER]. When prompted for R, enter the individual resistor values, pressing [ENTER] after each one.

When you have entered an appropriate number of values for the individual resistances, the calculator will perform the calculation and display the equivalent resistance for the parallel combination of those resistors.

Keystrokes	Display
	PROGRAM: PARALL
1. [0] [STO▶] [ALPHA] [Z] [ENTER]	:0 → Z
2. [PRGM] [▶] [2] [ALPHA] [N] [ENTER]	:PROMPT N
3. [PRGM] [4] [(] [ALPHA] [C] [,] [1] [,] [ALPHA] [N] [,] [1] [)] [ENTER]	:FOR (C,1,N,1)
4. [PRGM] [▶] [2] [ALPHA] [R] [ENTER]	:PROMPT R
5. [(] [1] [÷] [ALPHA] [R] [)] [+] [ALPHA] [Z] [STO▶] [ALPHA] [Z] [ENTER]	:(1/R) + Z → Z
6. [PRGM] [7] [ENTER]	:END
7. [PRGM] [▶] [3] [1] [÷] [ALPHA] [Z] [ENTER]	:DISP 1/Z

47. The power supplied to the circuit shown in **Figure 20-46** is 4.00 W. Determine the following:

   a. the equivalent resistance of the circuit
   b. the potential difference across the battery

(Hint: Remember that $P = \dfrac{(\Delta V)^2}{R}$.)

Figure 20-46

48. Your toaster oven and coffee maker each dissipate 1200 W of power. Can you operate them together if the 120 V line you use has a circuit breaker rated at 15 A? Explain.
(Hint: Recall that $P = I\Delta V$.)

49. An electric heater is rated at 1300 W, a toaster is rated at 1100 W, and an electric grill is rated at 1500 W. The three appliances are connected in parallel across a 120 V emf source.

   a. Find the current in each appliance.
   b. Is a 30.0 A circuit breaker sufficient in this situation? Explain.

Alternative Assessment

Performance assessment

1. How many ways can two or more batteries be connected in a circuit with a light bulb? How will the current change depending on the arrangement? First draw diagrams of the circuits you want to test. Then identify the measurements you need to make to answer the question. If your teacher approves your plan, obtain the necessary equipment and perform the experiment.

2. Propose an experimental procedure for measuring the resistance of a metal ring. Diagram the circuit you would use to test the ring and indicate how you would connect the measurement devices. What measurements would you make? If your teacher approves your plan, obtain the necessary equipment and perform the experiment.

3. Research the career of an electrical engineer or technician. Prepare materials for people interested in this career. Include information on where people in this career work, which tools and equipment they use, and the challenges of their field. Indicate what training is typically necessary to enter the field.

Portfolio projects

4. The manager of an automotive repair shop has been contacted by two competing firms that are selling ammeters to be used in testing automobile electrical systems. One firm claims that its ammeter is better because it has high internal resistance. The other claims that its ammeter is better because it has low resistance. Write a report with your recommendation to the manager of the automotive repair shop. Include diagrams and calculations that explain how you reached your conclusion.

5. You and your friend want to start a business exporting small electrical appliances. You have found people willing to be your partners to distribute these appliances in Germany. Write a letter to these potential partners that describes your product and asks for information about the electric power, sources, consumption, and distribution in Germany.

6. Contact an electrician, builder, or contractor, and ask to see a house electrical plan. Study the diagram to identify the circuit breakers, their connections to different appliances in the home, and the limitations they impose on the circuit's design. Find out how much current, on average, is in each appliance in the house. Draw a diagram of the house, showing which circuit breakers control which appliances and keeping the current in each of these appliances under the performance and safety limits.

CHAPTER 20
Laboratory Exercise

RESISTORS IN SERIES AND IN PARALLEL

In this lab, you will compare the circuits created by wiring two unknown resistors first in series and then in parallel. By taking measurements of the current in and the potential difference (voltage) across the resistors, and the voltage across the whole circuit, you will find the value of the resistance of each resistor and the equivalent resistance for both resistors to compare the total current in each circuit.

PREPARATION

1. Determine whether you will be using the CBL and sensors procedure or the meters procedure. Read the entire lab for the appropriate procedure, and plan what steps you will take.

2. Prepare a data table in your lab notebook with six columns and three rows. In the first column, label the second row *Series* and the third row *Parallel*. In the first row, label the second through sixth columns ΔV_T, ΔV_1, I_1, ΔV_2, and I_2.

Meters procedure begins on page 762.

PROCEDURE

CBL AND SENSORS

Resistors in series

3. Construct a circuit that includes a battery, a switch, and two unequal resistors in series. ***Do not close the switch until your teacher has approved your circuit.***

4. Connect the probes to measure the current in and the voltage across the first resistor. With the switch open, connect one current probe in series and one voltage probe in parallel with the first resistor, as shown in **Figure 20-47**.

5. Connect the CBL and graphing calculator. Connect the DIN1 lead on the amplifier box to one of the CBL-DIN adapters, and connect the adapter to the CH1 port on the CBL. Connect the DIN2 lead on the amplifier box to the other CBL-DIN adapter, and connect the adapter to the CH2 port. Connect the CURRENT1 probe to the PROBE1 port on the amplifier box, and connect the VOLTAGE1 probe to the PROBE2 port. Turn on the CBL and graphing calculator. Start the program PHYSICS on the calculator.

6. Select option *SET UP PROBES* from the MAIN MENU. Enter 2 for the number of probes. Select *MORE PROBES* from the SELECT PROBE menu. Select the *CV CURRENT* probe from the list. Enter 1 for the channel number. Select *USED STORED* from the CALIBRATION menu. Select *MORE PROBES* from the SELECT PROBE menu. Select the *CV VOLTAGE* probe from the list. Enter 2 for the channel number. Select *USED STORED* from the CALIBRATION menu.

7. Select the *COLLECT DATA* option from the MAIN MENU. Select the *MONITOR INPUT* option from the DATA COLLECTION menu. The calculator will begin to display values. ***Do not close the switch.***

8. When your teacher has approved your circuit, close the switch. Quickly take readings for the voltage and current. Open the switch, and record the readings in your data table as ΔV_1 and I_1.

9. Carefully remove the probes from the first resistor. Rewire the probes to measure the voltage across and the current in the second resistor. ***Do not close the switch.***

10. When your teacher has approved your circuit, close the switch. Measure the current in and voltage across the resistor, and open the switch. Record the information in your data table as ΔV_2 and I_2.

11. Leave the current probe in place, and carefully rewire the voltage probe to measure the potential difference across both resistors. Record this value in your data table as ΔV_T.

Resistors in parallel

12. Construct a circuit containing a power supply, a switch, and the two resistors wired in parallel. ***Do not close the switch until your teacher has approved your circuit.***

Figure 20-47

Step 6: Make sure all connections are correct and all plugs are pushed firmly in place.

Step 10: When you have recorded data for the first resistor, open the switch and connect the probes to take data for the second resistor.

Step 12: For this part of the lab, make sure the resistors are wired in parallel.

13. With the switch open, connect the current probe in series and the voltage probe in parallel with one of the resistors. ***Do not close the switch.***

14. When your teacher has approved your circuit, close the switch. Quickly record the readings for the voltage and current in your data table. Open the switch.

15. Rewire the probes to measure the voltage across and the current in the second resistor. ***Do not close the switch.***

16. When your teacher has approved your circuit, close the switch. Measure the current in and voltage across the resistor, and record the information in your data table. Open the switch.

17. Leave the current probe in place, and carefully rewire the voltage probe to measure the potential difference across the power supply. Record this value in your data table as ΔV_T.

Analysis and interpretation begins on page 763.

PROCEDURE

METERS

Resistors in series

3. Construct a circuit that includes a battery, a switch, and two unequal resistors in series. ***Do not close the switch until your teacher has approved your circuit.***

4. With the switch open, connect the current meter in series and the voltage meter in parallel with one of the resistors. ***Do not close the switch.***

5. When your teacher has approved your circuit, close the switch. Measure the current in and the potential difference across the resistor. Record the information in your data table. Open the switch.

6. Carefully remove the meters from the first resistor. Rewire the meters to measure the voltage across and the current in the second resistor. ***Do not close the switch.***

7. When your teacher has approved your circuit, close the switch. Measure the current in and potential difference across the resistor, and record the information in your data table. Open the switch.

8. Leave the current meter in place, and carefully rewire the voltage meter to measure the potential difference across both resistors. Record this value in your data table as ΔV_T.

Resistors in parallel

9. Construct a circuit containing a power supply, a switch, and the two resistors wired in parallel, as shown in **Figure 20-48**. ***Do not close the switch until your teacher has approved your circuit.***

10. With the switch open, connect the current meter in series and the voltage meter in parallel with one of the resistors. ***Do not close the switch.***

Figure 20-48

Step 4: Make sure all connections are correct. For this part of the lab, make sure the resistors are wired in series.

Step 7: When you have recorded data for the first resistor, open the switch and connect the probes to take data for the second resistor.

Step 9: For this part of the lab, make sure the resistors are wired in parallel, as shown in **Figure 20-48**.

11. When your teacher has approved your circuit, close the switch. Measure the current in and potential difference across the resistor, and record the information in your data table. Open the switch.

12. Rewire the meters to measure the potential difference across and current in the second resistor. **Do not close the switch until your teacher has approved your circuit.**

13. When your teacher has approved your circuit, close the switch. Measure the current in and potential difference across the resistor, and record the information in your data table. Open the switch.

14. Leave the current meter in place, and carefully rewire the voltage meter to measure the potential difference across the power supply. Record this value in your data table as ΔV_T.

ANALYSIS AND INTERPRETATION

Calculations and data analysis

1. **Analyzing data**   Using your measurements for voltage and current, compute the resistance values of R_1 and R_2 in each circuit.

2. **Comparing results**   Compare your results from item 1 for the different circuits.
   a. Do R_1 and R_2 have the same values in each circuit?
   b. Did you expect R_1 and R_2 to have the same values? Explain. If the results are different, explain what may have caused the difference.

3. **Analyzing data**   Compute the equivalent resistance R_{eq} using the values found in item 1 for each circuit.

Conclusions

4. **Comparing results**   Based on your calculations in item 3, did the two resistors provide the same equivalent resistance in both circuits? If not, which combination had the greater resistance? Explain how the combination of resistors affects the total resistance in the circuit.

5. **Analyzing data**   Compute the total current in each circuit using the calculated value for R_{eq} and the measured value for ΔV_T.

6. **Comparing results**   Based on your calculations in item 5, do both circuits have the same total current? If not, which circuit has the greater current? Explain how the combination of resistors affects the total current in the circuit.

7. **Analyzing information**   Compare the total current in each circuit with the current in each resistor. What is the relationship between the current in an individual resistor and the total current in the circuit?

8. **Organizing conclusions**   For each circuit, compare the voltage across each resistor with ΔV_T. What is the relationship?

Magnetism

PHYSICS IN ACTION

Some satellites contain loops of wire called *torque coils* that can be activated by a computer or a satellite operator on Earth.

When activated, a torque coil has a current in it. As you will learn in this chapter, the current-carrying coil behaves like a magnet. Because Earth also has magnetic properties, a magnetic force is exerted on the satellite, just as two magnets brought close together exert a force on one another. In this way, the satellite can be oriented so that its instruments point in the desired direction.

- *How does a current in the coil give the coil magnetic properties?*

- *How does the direction of the current in the wire affect the direction of the force on the satellite?*

CONCEPT REVIEW

Force (Section 4-1)

Force that maintains circular motion (Section 7-3)

Torque (Section 8-1)

Electric fields (Section 17-3)

Electric current (Section 19-1)

21-1
Magnets and magnetic fields

21-1 SECTION OBJECTIVES

- **For given situations, predict whether magnets will repel or attract each other.**

- **Describe the magnetic field around a permanent magnet.**

- **Describe the orientation of Earth's magnetic field.**

MAGNETS

Most people have had experience with different kinds of magnets, such as those shown in **Figure 21-1.** You are probably familiar with the horseshoe magnet, which can pick up iron-containing objects such as paper clips and nails, and flat magnets, such as those used to attach items to a refrigerator. In the following discussion, we will assume that the magnet has the shape of a bar. Iron objects are most strongly attracted to the ends of such a magnet. These ends are called *poles;* one is called the *north pole,* and the other is called the *south pole.* The names derive from the behavior of a magnet on Earth. If a bar magnet is suspended from its midpoint so that it can swing freely in a horizontal plane, it will rotate until its north pole points north and its south pole points south. In fact, a compass is just a magnetic needle that swings freely on a pivot.

The list of important technological applications of magnetism is very long. For instance, large electromagnets are used to pick up heavy loads. Magnets are also used in meters, motors, and loudspeakers. Magnetic tapes are routinely used in sound- and video-recording equipment, and magnetic recording material is used on computer discs. Superconducting magnets are currently being used to contain the plasmas used in controlled-nuclear-fusion research (heated to temperatures on the order of 10^8 K), and they are used to levitate modern trains. These so-called *maglev* trains are faster and provide a smoother ride than the ordinary track system because of the absence of friction between the train and the track.

Figure 21-1
Regardless of their shape, all magnets have both a north pole and a south pole.

Like poles repel each other, and unlike poles attract each other

The magnetic force between two magnets can be likened to the electric force between charged objects in that unlike poles of two magnets attract one another and like poles repel one another. Thus, the north pole of a magnet is attracted to the south pole of another magnet, and two north poles (or two south poles) brought close together repel each other. Electric charges differ from magnetic poles in that they can be isolated, while magnetic poles cannot. In fact, no matter how many times a permanent magnet is cut, each piece always has a north pole and a south pole. Thus, magnetic poles always occur in pairs.

Some materials can be made into permanent magnets

Just as two materials, such as rubber and wool, can become charged after they are rubbed together, an unmagnetized piece of iron can become a permanent magnet by being stroked with a permanent magnet. Magnetism can be induced by other means as well. For example, if a piece of unmagnetized iron is placed near a strong permanent magnet, the piece of iron will eventually become magnetized. The process can be reversed either by heating and cooling the iron or by hammering.

A magnetic piece of material is classified as magnetically *hard* or *soft,* depending on the extent to which it retains its magnetism. Soft magnetic materials, such as iron, are easily magnetized but also tend to lose their magnetism easily. In contrast, hard magnetic materials, such as cobalt and nickel, are difficult to magnetize, but once they are magnetized, they tend to retain their magnetism.

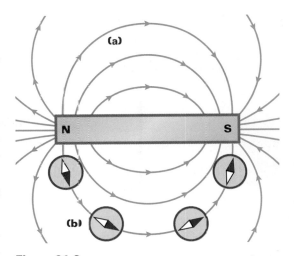

Figure 21-2
The magnetic field **(a)** of a bar magnet can be traced with a compass **(b).** Note that the north poles of the compasses point in the direction of the field lines from the magnet's north pole to its south pole.

MAGNETIC FIELDS

You know that the interaction between charged objects can be described using the concept of an electric field. A similar approach can be used to describe the **magnetic field** surrounding any magnetized material.

The direction of the magnetic field, **B,** at any location is defined as the direction in which the north pole of a compass needle points at that location. **Figure 21-2** shows how the magnetic field of a bar magnet can be traced with the aid of a compass. Note that the direction of the magnetic field is the same as the direction of the needles, and its magnitude is greatest close to the poles.

To indicate the direction of **B** when it points into or out of the page, use the conventions shown in **Table 21-1.** If **B** is directed into the page, we will use a series of blue *crosses,* representing the tails of arrows. If **B** is directed out of the page, we will use a series of blue *dots,* representing the tips of arrows.

When describing a small bar magnet as having north and south poles, it is more proper to say that it has a "north-seeking" pole and a "south-seeking" pole. This means that if such a magnet is used as a compass, the north pole of the magnet will seek, or point to, the geographic North Pole of Earth. Because unlike poles attract, we can deduce that the geographic North Pole of Earth corresponds to the magnetic south pole, and the geographic South Pole of Earth corresponds to the magnetic north pole.

The difference between true north, defined as the geographic North Pole, and north indicated by a compass varies from point to point on Earth, and the difference is referred to as *magnetic declination.* For example, along a line through South Carolina and the Great Lakes, a compass will point to true north (0° declination), whereas in Washington state it will point 25° east of true north (25° E declination).

magnetic field

a region in which a magnetic force can be detected

**Table 21-1
Conventions for representing the direction of a magnetic field**

In the plane of the page	↑
Into the page	✕
Out of the page	●

Magnetic south pole   Geographic north pole

Geographic south pole   Magnetic north pole

Figure 21-3
Earth's magnetic field has a configuration similar to a bar magnet's. Note that the magnetic south pole is near the geographic North Pole and that the magnetic north pole is near the geographic South Pole.

Note that the configuration of Earth's magnetic field, pictured in **Figure 21-3,** resembles the field that would be produced if a bar magnet were buried within Earth.

If a compass needle is allowed to rotate in the vertical plane as well as in the horizontal plane, the needle will be horizontal with respect to Earth's surface only near the equator. As the compass is moved northward, the needle will rotate so that it points more toward the surface of Earth. Finally, at a point just north of Hudson Bay, in Canada, the north pole of the needle will point directly downward. This site is considered to be the location of the magnetic south pole of Earth. It is approximately 1500 km from Earth's geographic North Pole. Similarly, the magnetic north pole of Earth is roughly the same distance from the geographic South Pole. Thus, it is only an approximation to say that a compass needle points toward the geographic North Pole.

Although Earth has large deposits of iron ore deep beneath its surface, the high temperatures in Earth's liquid core prevent the iron from retaining any permanent magnetization. It is considered more likely that the source of Earth's magnetic field is the movement of charges in convection currents in Earth's core. Charged ions or electrons circling in the liquid interior could produce a magnetic field. There is also evidence that the strength of a planet's magnetic field is related to the planet's rate of rotation. For example, Jupiter rotates at a faster rate than Earth, and recent space probes indicate that Jupiter's magnetic field is stronger than Earth's. Conversely, Venus rotates more slowly than Earth, and its magnetic field has been found to be weaker. Investigation into the cause of Earth's magnetism continues.

Naturally occurring magnetic materials, such as magnetite, achieve their magnetism because they have been subjected to Earth's magnetic field over very long periods of time. In fact, studies have shown that a type of anaerobic bacterium that lives in swamps has a magnetized chain of magnetite as part of its internal structure. (The term *anaerobic* means that these bacteria live and grow

Magnetic Field of a File Cabinet

MATERIALS LIST

✔ compass
✔ metal file cabinet

Stand in front of the file cabinet, and hold the compass face up and parallel to the ground. Now move the compass from the top of the file cabinet to the bottom. Making sure that the compass is parallel to the ground, check to see if the direction of the compass needle changes as it moves from the top of the cabinet to the bottom. If the compass needle changes direction, the file cabinet is magnetized. Can you

explain what might have caused the file cabinet to become magnetized? Remember that Earth's magnetic field has a vertical component as well as a horizontal component.

Try tracing the field around some large metal objects around your house. Can you find an object that has been magnetized by the horizontal component of Earth's magnetic field?

without oxygen; in fact, oxygen is toxic to some of them.) The magnetized chain acts as a compass needle, enabling the bacteria to align with Earth's magnetic field. When they find themselves out of the mud at the bottom of the swamp, they return to their oxygen-free environment by following the magnetic-field lines of Earth. Further evidence of their magnetic-sensing ability is the discovery that the bacteria in the Northern Hemisphere have internal magnetite chains that are opposite in polarity to that of similar bacteria in the Southern Hemisphere. This is consistent with the fact that in the Northern Hemisphere, Earth's magnetic field has a downward component, whereas in the Southern Hemisphere it has an upward component.

Section Review

1. For each of the cases in **Figure 21-4**, identify whether the magnets will attract or repel one another.

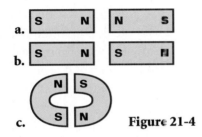

Figure 21-4

2. When you break a magnet in half, how many poles does each piece have?

3. Which of the compass-needle orientations in **Figure 21-5** might correctly describe the magnet's field at that point?

Figure 21-5

4. **Physics in Action** Satellite ground operators use the feedback from a device called a magnetometer, which senses the direction of Earth's magnetic field, to decide which torque coil to activate. What direction will the magnetometer read for Earth's magnetic field when the satellite passes over Earth's equator?

5. **Physics in Action** In order to protect other equipment, the body of a satellite must remain unmagnetized, even when the torque coils have been activated. Would hard or soft magnetic materials be best for building the rest of the satellite?

21-2
Electromagnetism and magnetic domains

- **Describe the magnetic field produced by the current in a straight conductor and in a solenoid.**

- **Explain magnetism in terms of the domain theory of magnetism.**

MAGNETIC FIELD OF A CURRENT-CARRYING WIRE

The experiment shown in **Figure 21-6(a)** uses iron filings to demonstrate that a current-carrying conductor produces a magnetic field. In a similar experiment, several compass needles are placed in a horizontal plane near a long vertical wire. When there is no current in the wire, all needles point in the same direction (that of Earth's magnetic field). However, when the wire carries a strong, steady current, all the needles deflect in directions tangent to concentric circles around the wire, pointing in the direction of **B**, the magnetic field, due to the current. When the current is reversed, the needles also reverse direction. These observations show that the direction of **B** is consistent with the following rule, known as the right-hand rule: If the wire is grasped in the right hand with the thumb in the direction of the current, as shown in **Figure 21-6(b)**, the fingers will curl in the direction of **B**.

As shown in **Figure 21-6(a)**, the lines of **B** form concentric circles about the wire. By symmetry, the magnitude of **B** is the same everywhere on a circular path centered on the wire and lying in a plane perpendicular to the wire. Experiments show that **B** is proportional to the current in the wire and inversely proportional to the distance from the wire.

(a)

(b)

Figure 21-6
(a) When the wire carries a strong current, the iron filings show that the magnetic field due to the current forms concentric circles around the wire. **(b)** Use the right-hand rule to find the direction of this magnetic field.

MAGNETIC FIELD OF A CURRENT LOOP

The right-hand rule can also be applied to find the direction of the magnetic field of a current-carrying loop, such as the loop represented in **Figure 21-7(a).** Regardless of where on the loop you apply the right-hand rule, the field within the loop points in the same direction—upward. Note that the field lines of the current-carrying loop resemble those of a bar magnet, as shown in **Figure 21-7(b).** If a long, straight wire is bent into a coil of several closely spaced loops, as shown in **Figure 21-8,** the resulting device is called a **solenoid.**

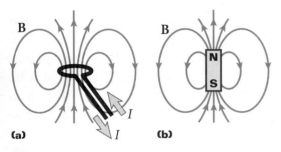

(a)

(b)

Figure 21-7
(a) The magnetic field of a current loop is similar to
(b) that of a bar magnet.

Solenoids produce a strong magnetic field by combining several loops

A solenoid is important in many applications because it acts as a magnet when it carries a current. The magnetic field inside a solenoid increases with the current and is proportional to the number of coils per unit length. The magnetic field of a solenoid can be increased by inserting an iron rod through the center of the coil; this device is often called an *electromagnet*. The magnetic field that is induced in the rod adds to the magnetic field of the solenoid, often creating a powerful magnet.

Figure 21-8 shows the magnetic field lines of a solenoid. Note that the field lines inside the solenoid are nearly parallel, are uniformly spaced, and are close together. This indicates that the field inside the solenoid is strong and nearly uniform. The field outside the solenoid is nonuniform and much weaker than the interior field.

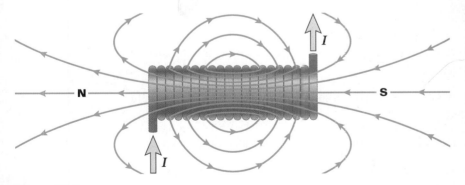

Figure 21-8
The magnetic field inside a solenoid is strong and nearly uniform.
Note that the field lines resemble those of a bar magnet, so a
solenoid effectively has north and south poles.

Quick Lab

Electromagnetism

MATERIALS LIST

✔ D-cell battery
✔ 1 m length of insulated wire
✔ large nail
✔ compass

Wind the wire around the nail as shown below. Remove the insulation from the ends of the wire, and hold these ends against the metal

terminals of the battery. Use the compass to determine whether the nail is magnetized. Next, flip the battery so that the direction of the current is reversed. Again bring the compass toward the same part of the nail. Can you explain why the compass needle now points in a different direction?

Figure 21-9
When a substance is unmagnetized, its domains are randomly oriented.

domain

a microscopic magnetic region composed of a group of atoms whose magnetic fields are aligned in a common direction

MAGNETIC DOMAINS

The magnetic properties of many materials are explained in terms of a model in which an electron is said to spin on its axis much like a top does. (This classical description should not be taken literally. The property of electron spin can be understood only with the methods of quantum mechanics.) The spinning electron represents a charge in motion that produces a magnetic field. In atoms containing many electrons, the electrons usually pair up with their spins opposite each other, and their fields cancel each other. That is why most substances, such as wood and plastic, are not magnets. However, in materials such as iron, cobalt, and nickel, the magnetic fields produced by the electron spins do not cancel completely. Such materials are said to be *ferromagnetic*. In ferromagnetic materials, strong coupling occurs between neighboring atoms to form large groups of atoms whose net spins are aligned; these groups are called **domains.** Domains typically range in size from about 10^{-4} cm to 0.1 cm. In an unmagnetized substance, the domains are randomly oriented, as shown in **Figure 21-9.** When an external field is applied, the orientation of the magnetic fields of each domain may change slightly to more closely align with the external magnetic field, or the domains that are already aligned with the external field may grow at the expense of the other domains.

In hard magnetic materials, domain alignment persists after the external magnetic field is removed; the result is a permanent magnet. In soft magnetic materials, such as iron, once the external field is removed, the random motion of the particles in the material changes the orientation of the domains and the material returns to an unmagnetized state.

As mentioned earlier, the strength of a solenoid can be increased dramatically by the insertion of an iron rod into the coil's center. The magnetic field produced by the current in the loops causes alignment of the domains in the iron, producing a large net external field.

Section Review

1. What is the shape of the magnetic field produced by a straight current-carrying wire?

2. Why is the magnetic field inside a solenoid stronger than the magnetic field outside?

3. If electrons behave like magnets, then why aren't all atoms magnets?

4. **Physics in Action**   In some satellites, torque coils are replaced by devices called torque rods. In torque rods, a ferromagnetic material is inserted inside the coil. Why does a torque rod have a stronger magnetic field than a torque coil?

21-3
Magnetic force

CHARGED PARTICLES IN A MAGNETIC FIELD

Although experiments show that a stationary charged particle does not inter-act with a constant magnetic field, charges moving through a magnetic field do experience a magnetic force. This force has its maximum value when the charge moves perpendicular to the magnetic field, decreases in value at other angles, and becomes zero when the particle moves along the field lines. For the purposes of this book, we will limit our discussion to situations in which charges move parallel or perpendicular to the magnetic-field lines.

A charge moving through a magnetic field experiences a force

In our discussion of electric forces, the electric field at a point in space was defined as the electric force per unit charge acting on some test charge placed at that point. In a similar manner, we can describe the properties of the mag-netic field, **B,** in terms of the magnetic force exerted on a test charge at that point. Our test object is assumed to be a positive charge, q, moving with veloc-ity **v.** It has been found experimentally that the strength of the magnetic force on the particle moving perpendicular to the field is equal to the product of the magnitude of the charge, q, the magnitude of the velocity, v, and the strength of the external magnetic field, B, as shown by the following relationship.

$$F_{magnetic} = qvB$$

This expression can be rearranged to define the magnitude of the magnetic field as follows:

MAGNITUDE OF A MAGNETIC FIELD

$$B = \frac{F_{magnetic}}{qv}$$

$$\text{magnetic field} = \frac{\text{magnetic force on a charged particle}}{\text{(magnitude of charge)(speed of charge)}}$$

If the force is in newtons, the charge is in coulombs, and the speed is in meters per second, the SI unit of magnetic field strength is the tesla (T). Thus, if a 1 C charge moving at 1 m/s perpendicular to a magnetic field experiences a magnetic force of 1 N, the magnitude of the magnetic field equals 1 T. We can express the units of the magnetic field as follows:

$$T = N/(C \bullet m/s) = N/(A \bullet m) = (V \bullet s)/m^2$$

B

$F_{magnetic}$ **v**

Figure 21-10

Use the right-hand rule to find the
direction of the magnetic force on a
positive charge.

Conventional laboratory magnets can produce magnetic fields as large as
about 2.5 T. Superconducting magnets that can generate magnetic fields as great
as 30 T have been constructed. These values can be compared with the value of
Earth's magnetic field near its surface, which is about 50 μT (5×10^{-5} T).

Use the right-hand rule to find the direction of the magnetic force

Experiments show that the direction of the magnetic force is always perpendicular to both **v** and **B.** To determine the direction of the force, use the right-
hand rule. As before, place your fingers in the direction of **B** with your thumb
pointing in the direction of **v,** as illustrated in **Figure 21-10.** The magnetic
force, $\mathbf{F_{magnetic}}$, on a positive charge is directed *out* of the palm of your hand.

If the charge is negative rather than positive, the force is directed *opposite*
that shown in **Figure 21-10.** That is, if q is negative, simply use the right-hand
rule to find the direction of $\mathbf{F_{magnetic}}$ for positive q, and then reverse this
direction for the negative charge.

The force on a moving charge due to a magnetic field is used to create pictures on a television screen. The main component of a television is the *cathode
ray tube,* which is essentially a vacuum tube in which electric fields are used to
form a beam of electrons. This beam causes phosphor on the television screen
to glow when struck by the electrons in the beam. Without magnetism, however, only the center of the screen would be illuminated by the beam. The
direction of the beam is changed by two electromagnets, one deflecting the
beam horizontally, the other deflecting the beam vertically. The direction of
the force on the beam can be changed by changing the direction of the current
in each electromagnet. In this way, the beam illuminates the entire screen.

In a color television, three different colors of phosphor—red, green, and
blue—make up the screen. Three electron beams, one for each color, scan over
the screen to produce a color picture.

SAMPLE PROBLEM 21A

Magnitude of a magnetic field

PROBLEM

**A proton moving east at 1.0×10^5 m/s experiences a force of 8.8×10^{-19} N
upward (away from Earth) due to Earth's magnetic field. What is the magnitude and direction of Earth's magnetic field at this location?**

SOLUTION

Given: $q = 1.60 \times 10^{-19}$ C $v = 1.0 \times 10^5$ m/s

               $F_{magnetic} = 8.8 \times 10^{-19}$ N

Unknown: $B = ?$

Use the equation for the magnitude of a magnetic field from page 773.

$$B = \frac{F_{magnetic}}{qv}$$

$$B = \frac{8.8 \times 10^{-19} \text{ N}}{(1.60 \times 10^{-19} \text{ C})(1.0 \times 10^5 \text{ m/s})}$$

$$\boxed{B = 5.5 \times 10^{-5} \text{ T}}$$

The direction of the field can be found using the right-hand rule. Imagine standing at this location and facing north. Turn the palm of your right hand upward (the direction of the force) with your thumb pointing east (the direction of the velocity). If your palm and thumb point in these directions, your fingers point directly north. Therefore, Earth's magnetic field points north at this location.

Magnitude of a magnetic field

1. A proton traveling at a speed of 3.5×10^6 m/s passes perpendicular to a uniform magnetic field of 4.2×10^{-2} T. What is the magnitude of the force on the proton while the proton is in the magnetic field?

2. A uniform 1.5 T magnetic field points north. If an electron moves vertically downward (toward the ground) with a speed of 2.5×10^7 m/s through this field, what force (magnitude and direction) will act on it?

3. A proton moves straight upward (away from the ground) through a uniform magnetic field that points from east to west and has a magnitude of 2.5 T. If the proton moves with a speed of 1.5×10^7 m/s through this field, what force (magnitude and direction) will act on it?

4. A proton traveling to the right along the x-axis enters a region where there is a magnetic field of magnitude 2.5 T directed upward along the y-axis. If the proton experiences a force of 3.2×10^{-12} N, find the speed of the proton.

5. If an electron in an electron beam experiences a force of 2.0×10^{-14} N down while traveling north at a speed of 1.5×10^6 m/s, then what is the magnitude and direction of the magnetic field that deflects the electron?

6. An alpha particle (the nucleus of a helium atom, carrying a charge of 3.2×10^{-19} C) moves at 5.5×10^7 m/s at a right angle to a magnetic field. If the particle experiences a force of 1.5×10^{-14} N due to the magnetic field, then what is the magnitude of the magnetic field?

Figure 21-11

When the velocity, **v**, of a charged particle is perpendicular to a uniform magnetic field, the particle moves in a circle whose plane is perpendicular to **B**.

A charge moving through a magnetic field follows a circular path

Consider a positively charged particle moving in a uniform magnetic field so that the direction of the particle's velocity is perpendicular to the field, as in **Figure 21-11.** Application of the right-hand rule for the charge q shows that the direction of the magnetic force, **F**$_{magnetic}$, at the charge's location is to the left. This causes the particle to alter its direction and to follow a curved path. Application of the right-hand rule at any point shows that the magnetic force is always directed toward the center of the circular path. Therefore, the magnetic force is, in effect, a force that maintains circular motion and changes only the direction of **v,** not its magnitude.

Now consider a charged particle traveling through a uniform magnetic field with a velocity that is neither parallel nor perpendicular to the direction of the magnetic field. In this case, the particle will follow a helical path along the direction of the magnetic field.

MAGNETIC FORCE ON A CURRENT-CARRYING CONDUCTOR

Recall that current is a collection of many charged particles in motion. If a force is exerted on a single charged particle when the particle moves through a magnetic field, it should be no surprise that a current-carrying wire also experiences a force when it is placed in a magnetic field. The resultant force on the wire is due to the sum of the individual forces on the charged particles. The force on the particles is transmitted to the bulk of the wire through collisions with the atoms making up the wire.

Consider a straight segment of wire of length ℓ carrying current, I, in a uniform external magnetic field, **B,** as in **Figure 21-12.** The magnitude of the total magnetic force on the wire is given by the following relationship.

FORCE ON A CURRENT-CARRYING CONDUCTOR PERPENDICULAR TO A MAGNETIC FIELD

$$F_{magnetic} = BI\ell$$

magnitude of magnetic force = (magnitude of magnetic field) (current)(length of conductor within B)

This equation can be used only when the current and the magnetic field are at right angles to each other.

The direction of the magnetic force on a wire can be obtained by using the right-hand rule. However, in this case, you must place your thumb in the direction of the current rather than in the direction of the velocity, **v.** In **Figure 21-12,** the direction of the magnetic force on the wire is to the left. When the current is either in the direction of the field or opposite the direction of the field, the magnetic force on the wire is zero.

Figure 21-12

A current-carrying conductor in a magnetic field experiences a force that is perpendicular to the direction of the current.

Two parallel conducting wires exert a force on one another

Since a current in a conductor creates its own magnetic field, it is easy to understand that two current-carrying wires placed close together exert magnetic forces on each other. When the two conductors are parallel to each other, the direction of the magnetic field created by one is perpendicular to the direction of the current of the other, and vice versa. In this way, a force of $F_{magnetic} = BI\ell$ acts on each wire, where B is the magnitude of the magnetic field created by the other wire.

Consider the two long, straight, parallel wires shown in **Figure 21-13.** When the current in each is in the same direction, as shown in **Figure 21-13(a)**, the two wires attract one another. You can confirm this by using the right-hand rule. Point your thumb in the direction of current in one wire, and point your fingers in the direction of the field produced by the other wire. By doing this, you find that the direction of the force (pointing out from the palm of your hand) is toward the other wire. When the currents in each wire are in opposite directions, as shown in **Figure 21-13(b),** the wires repel one another.

Loudspeakers use magnetic force to produce sound

The loudspeakers in most sound systems use a magnetic force acting on a current-carrying wire in a magnetic field to produce sound waves. One speaker design, shown in **Figure 21-14,** consists of a coil of wire, a flexible paper cone that acts as the speaker, and a permanent magnet. When an electric signal is sent to the coil, producing a current in the wire, a magnetic force acts on the coil. When the current reverses direction, the magnetic force on the coil reverses direction, and the cone accelerates in the opposite direction. This alternating force on the speaker results in vibrations of the cone, which produce variations in the density of the air in front of it. In this way, an electric signal is converted to a sound wave that closely resembles the sound wave produced by the source.

Figure 21-13

Two parallel wires, each carrying a steady current, exert forces on each other. The force is **(a)** attractive if the currents have the same direction and **(b)** repulsive if the two currents have opposite directions.

Figure 21-14

In a loudspeaker, when the direction and magnitude of the current in the coil of wire change, the paper cone attached to the coil moves, producing sound waves.

Force on a current-carrying conductor

PROBLEM

A wire 36 m long carries a current of 22 A from east to west. Find the magnetic force on the wire if the magnetic field of Earth at this location is directed from south to north and has a magnitude of 5.0×10^{-5} T.

SOLUTION

Given: $B = 5.0 \times 10^{-5}$ T $I = 22$ A $\ell = 36$ m

Unknown: $F_{magnetic} = ?$

Use the equation for force on a current-carrying conductor perpendicular to a magnetic field, shown on page 776.

$$F_{magnetic} = BI\ell = (5.0 \times 10^{-5} \text{ T})(22 \text{ A})(36 \text{ m})$$

$$\boxed{F_{magnetic} = 4.0 \times 10^{-2} \text{ N}}$$

Using the right-hand rule, face north with your thumb pointing to the west (in the direction of the current) and your fingers pointing north (in the direction of Earth's magnetic field). The palm of your hand points down. Thus, the force on the wire is directed toward Earth.

Force on a current-carrying conductor

1. What is the force in Sample Problem 21B if the direction of the current points west to east?

2. A wire 1.0 m long experiences a magnetic force of 0.50 N due to a perpendicular uniform magnetic field. If the wire carries a current of 10.0 A, what is the magnitude of the magnetic field?

3. The magnetic force acting on a wire that is perpendicular to a 1.5 T uniform magnetic field is 4.4 N. If the current in the wire is 5.0 A, what is the length of the wire that is inside the magnetic field?

4. A 2.5 N magnetic force acts on a 475 m wire that is perpendicular to a 0.50 T magnetic field. What is the current in the wire?

5. The magnetic force on a straight 0.15 m segment of wire carrying a current of 4.5 A is 1.0 N. What is the magnitude of the component of the magnetic field that is perpendicular to the wire?

GALVANOMETERS

A *galvanometer* is a device used in the construction of both ammeters and voltmeters. Its operation is based on the idea that a torque acts on a current loop in the presence of a magnetic field. **Figure 21-15** shows a simplified arrangement of the main components of a galvanometer. It consists of a coil of wire wrapped around a soft iron core mounted so that it is free to pivot in the magnetic field provided by the permanent magnet. The torque experienced by the coil is proportional to the current in the coil. This means that the larger the current, the greater the torque and the more the coil will rotate before the spring tightens enough to stop the movement. Hence, the amount of deflection of the needle is proportional to the current in the coil. When there is no current in the coil, the spring returns the needle to zero. Once the instrument is properly calibrated, it can be used in conjunction with other circuit elements as an ammeter (to measure currents) or as a voltmeter (to measure potential differences).

Figure 21-15

In a galvanometer, when current enters the coil, which is in a magnetic field, the magnetic force causes the coil to twist.

Section Review

1. A particle with a charge of 0.030 C experiences a magnetic force of 1.5 N while moving at right angles to a uniform magnetic field. If the speed of the charge is 620 m/s, what is the magnitude of the magnetic field the particle passes through?

2. An electron moving north encounters a uniform magnetic field. If the magnetic field points east, what is the direction of the magnetic force on the electron?

3. A straight segment of wire has a length of 25 cm and carries a current of 5.0 A. If the wire is perpendicular to a magnetic field of 0.6 T, then what is the magnitude of the magnetic force on this segment of the wire?

4. Two parallel wires have charges moving in the same direction. Is the force between them attractive or repulsive?

5. Find the direction of the magnetic force on the current-carrying wire in **Figure 21-16.**

Figure 21-16

CHAPTER 21
Summary

KEY TERMS

domain (p. 772)

magnetic field (p. 767)

solenoid (p. 771)

KEY IDEAS

Section 21-1 Magnets and magnetic fields
- Like magnetic poles repel, and unlike poles attract.
- The direction of any magnetic field is defined as the direction the north pole of a magnet would point if placed in the field. The magnetic field of a magnet points from the north pole of the magnet to the south pole.
- The magnetic north pole of Earth corresponds to the geographic South Pole, and the magnetic south pole corresponds to the geographic North Pole.

Section 21-2 Electromagnetism and magnetic domains
- A magnetic field exists around any current-carrying wire; the direction of the magnetic field follows a circular path around the wire.
- The magnetic field created by a solenoid or coil is similar to the magnetic field of a permanent magnet.
- A domain is a group of atoms whose magnetic fields are aligned.

Section 21-3 Magnetic force
- The direction of the force on a positive charge moving through a magnetic field can be found using the right-hand rule. The magnitude of a magnetic field is given by the relation $B = \dfrac{F_{magnetic}}{qv}$.
- A length of wire, ℓ, in an external magnetic field undergoes a magnetic force with a magnitude of $F_{magnetic} = BI\ell$. The direction of the magnetic force on the wire can be found using the right-hand rule.
- Two parallel current-carrying wires exert a force on one another. If the currents are in the same direction, the two wires attract one another. If the currents are in opposite directions, the wires repel one another.

Diagram symbols

Magnetic field vector	
Magnetic field pointing into the page	
Magnetic field pointing out of the page	

Variable symbols

Quantities		Units		Conversions
B	magnetic field	T	tesla	$= \dfrac{N}{C \cdot m/s} = \dfrac{N}{A \cdot m}$
$F_{magnetic}$	magnetic force	N	newtons	$= \dfrac{kg \cdot m}{s^2}$
ℓ	length of conductor in field	m	meters	

MAGNETS AND MAGNETIC FIELDS

Review questions

1. What is the minimum number of poles for a magnet?

2. When you break a magnet in half, how many poles does each piece have?

3. The north pole of a magnet is attracted to the geographic North Pole of Earth, yet like poles repel. Can you explain this?

4. Which way would a compass needle point if you were at the magnetic north pole?

Conceptual questions

5. You are an astronaut stranded on a planet with no test equipment or minerals around. The planet does not even have a magnetic field. You have two iron bars in your possession; one is magnetized, one is not. How can you determine which one is magnetized?

6. In **Figure 21-17,** two permanent magnets with holes bored through their centers are placed one over the other. Because the poles of the upper magnet are the reverse of those of the lower, the upper magnet levitates above the lower magnet. If the upper magnet were displaced slightly, either up or down, would the resulting motion be periodic? Explain. What would happen if the upper magnet were inverted?

Figure 21-17

ELECTROMAGNETISM AND MAGNETIC DOMAINS

Review questions

7. What is a magnetic domain?

8. Why are iron atoms so strongly affected by magnetic fields?

9. When a magnetized steel needle is strongly heated in a Bunsen burner flame, it becomes demagnetized. Explain why.

10. What indicates that a piece of iron is magnetic, its attraction to or repulsion from another piece of iron?

11. Why does a very strong magnet attract both poles of a weak magnet?

12. A magnet attracts a piece of iron. The iron can then attract another piece of iron. Explain, on the basis of alignment of domains, what happens in each piece of iron.

13. When a small magnet is repeatedly dropped, it becomes demagnetized. Explain what happens to the magnet subatomically.

14. A conductor carrying a current is arranged so that electrons flow in one segment from east to west. If a compass is held over this segment of the wire, in what direction is the needle deflected?

15. What factors does the strength of the magnetic field of a solenoid depend on?

Conceptual questions

16. A solenoid with ends marked A and B is suspended by a thread so that the core can rotate in the horizontal plane. A current is maintained in the coil so that the electrons move clockwise when viewed from end A toward end B. How will the coil align itself in Earth's magnetic field?

17. Is it possible to orient a current-carrying loop of wire in a uniform magnetic field so that the loop will not tend to rotate?

18. If a solenoid were suspended by a string so that it could rotate freely, could it be used as a compass when it carried a direct current? Could it also be used if the current were alternating in direction?

MAGNETIC FORCE

Review questions

19. Two charged particles are projected into a region where there is a magnetic field perpendicular to their velocities. If the particles are deflected in opposite directions, what can you say about them?

20. Suppose an electron is chasing a proton up this page when suddenly a magnetic field pointing into the page is applied. What would happen to the particles?

21. Why does the picture on a television screen become distorted when a magnet is brought near the screen?

22. A proton moving horizontally enters a region where there is a uniform magnetic field perpendicular to the proton's velocity, as shown in **Figure 21-18**. Describe the proton's subsequent motion. How would an electron behave under the same circumstances?

Figure 21-18

23. Explain why two parallel wires carrying currents in opposite directions repel each other.

24. Can a stationary magnetic field set a resting electron in motion? Explain.

25. At a given instant, a proton moves in the positive x direction in a region where there is a magnetic field in the negative z direction. What is the direction of the magnetic force? Does the proton continue to move in the positive x direction? Explain.

Conceptual questions

26. A stream of electrons is projected horizontally to the right. A straight conductor carrying a current is supported parallel to and above the electron stream.
  a. What is the effect on the electron stream if the direction of the current in the conductor is from left to right?
  b. What is the effect if the current is reversed?

27. If the conductor in item 26 is replaced by a magnet with a downward magnetic field, what is the effect on the electron stream?

28. Two wires carrying equal but opposite currents are twisted together in the construction of a circuit. Why does this technique reduce stray magnetic fields?

Practice problems

29. A duck flying due east at 15 m/s passes over Atlanta, where the magnetic field of the Earth is 5.0×10^{-5} T directed north. The duck has a positive charge of 4.0×10^{-8} C. What is the magnetic force acting on the duck?
(See Sample Problem 21A.)

30. A proton moves at 2.50×10^6 m/s horizontally at a right angle to a magnetic field.
  a. What is the strength of the magnetic field required to exactly balance the weight of the proton and keep it moving horizontally?
  b. Should the direction of the magnetic field be in a horizontal or a vertical plane?
(See Sample Problem 21A.)

31. Find the direction of the force on a proton moving through each magnetic field in **Figure 21-19**.
(See Sample Problem 21A.)

Figure 21-19

32. Find the direction of the force on an electron moving through each magnetic field in **Figure 21-19.** (See Sample Problem 21A.)

33. In **Figure 21-19,** assume that in each case the velocity vector shown is replaced with a wire carrying a current in the direction of the velocity vector. Find the direction of the magnetic force acting on each wire. (See Sample Problem 21B.)

34. Find the direction of the magnetic field for a positively charged particle moving in each situation in **Figure 21-20** if the direction of the magnetic force acting on it is as indicated. (See Sample Problem 21A.)

Figure 21-20

35. A wire carries a 10.0 A current at an angle 90.0° from the direction of a magnetic field with a strength of 0.300 T. Find the magnitude of the magnetic force on a 5.00 m length of the wire. (See Sample Problem 21B.)

36. Sodium ions (Na$^+$) move at 0.851 m/s through the bloodstream in the arm of a person standing near a large magnet. The magnetic field has a strength of 0.254 T and makes an angle of 90.0° with the motion of the sodium ions. The arm contains 100.0 cm^3 of blood with 3.00×10^{20} Na$^+$ ions per cubic centimeter. What is the magnetic force on the arm? (See Sample Problem 21A. Hint: The charge of a sodium ion equals the charge of a single proton.)

37. A thin 1.00 m long copper rod has a mass of 50.0 g. What is the minimum current needed in the rod to cause it to float in a magnetic field of 2.00 T? (See Sample Problem 21B.)

38. A proton moves eastward in the plane of Earth's magnetic equator so that its distance from the ground remains constant. What is the speed of the proton if Earth's magnetic field points north and has a magnitude of 5.0×10^{-5} T? (See Sample Problem 21A.)

MIXED REVIEW

39. A proton moves at a speed of 2.0×10^7 m/s at right angles to a magnetic field with a magnitude of 0.10 T. Find the magnitude of the acceleration of the proton.

40. A proton travels with a speed of 3.0×10^6 m/s at an angle of 37° west of north. A magnetic field of 0.30 T points to the north. Determine the following:
  a. the magnitude of the magnetic force on the proton
  b. the direction of the magnetic force on the proton
  c. the proton's acceleration
(Hint: the magnetic force is proportional to the component of the proton's velocity that is perpendicular to the magnetic field.)

41. A proton moves perpendicular to a uniform magnetic field, **B,** at 1.0×10^7 m/s and experiences an acceleration of 2.0×10^{13} m/s^2 in the positive x direction when its velocity is in the positive z direction. Determine the magnitude and direction of the field.

42. In **Figure 21-21,** a 15 cm length of conductor that is free to move is held in place between two thin conductors. When a 5.0 A current is in the wire, the wire segment moves upward at a constant velocity. Assuming the wire slides without friction on the two vertical conductors and has a mass of 0.15 kg, find the magnitude and direction of the minimum magnetic field required to move the wire.

Figure 21-21

43. A current, $I = 15$ A, is directed along the positive x-axis and perpendicular to a magnetic field. The conductor experiences a magnetic force per unit length of 0.12 N/m in the negative y direction. Calculate the magnitude and direction of the magnetic field in the region through which the current passes.

44. A proton moves in a circular path perpendicular to a constant magnetic field so that it takes 1.00×10^{-6} s to complete one revolution. Determine the strength of the magnetic field.

(Hint: The magnetic force exerted on the proton is the force that maintains circular motion, and the number of radians per time interval is the angular speed.)

Technology & Learning

Graphing calculators

Program your graphing calculator to use line-fitting techniques on given data to predict the magnetic field for the following:

a. a current of 2.37 A in a solenoid that has a magnetic field of 2.54×10^{-2} T when the current is 3.35 A and 5.20×10^{-2} T when the current is 6.90 A

b. a current of 3.54 A in a solenoid that has a magnetic field of 5.50×10^{-3} T when the current is 1.25 A and 1.74×10^{-2} T when the current is 3.80 A

Press [Y=] and [CLEAR] to clear any functions. Clear the lists by pressing [STAT] [4] [2nd] [L₁] [ENTER] and [STAT] [4] [2nd] [L₂] [ENTER]. Press [STAT] [1], and enter the current data into list [L₁] and the mag-

netic field data into list [L₂]. (Remember to use [2nd] [EE] and the [(-)] key to enter exponents.)

Open a new program by pressing [PRGM] [►] [►] [ENTER]. Name the program "SOLENOID" and press [ENTER]. Then enter the program shown in the table below.

To exit the program editor, press [2nd] [QUIT]. To run the program, press [PRGM], select "SOLENOID," and press [ENTER] [ENTER]. Enter the value for the current and press [ENTER].

The calculator will provide the magnetic field strength in units of teslas. After you have finished using the graph for one situation, press [2nd] [QUIT], run the program again and enter the data for the next situation.

Keystrokes	Display
	PROGRAM: SOLENOID
1. [STAT] [►] [5] [2nd] [L₁] [,] [2nd] [L₂] [ENTER]	:LINREG (AX+B) L₁, L₂
2. [ALPHA] ["] [VARS] [5] [►] [►] [1] [X,T,θ] [+] [VARS] [5] [►] [►] [2] [ALPHA] ["] [STO►] [2nd] [Y-VARS] [1] [1] [ENTER]	:"AX + B" → Y₁
3. [PRGM] [►] [2] [ALPHA] [I]	:PROMPT I
4. [ALPHA] [I] [STO►] [X,T,θ] [ENTER]	:I → X
5. [PRGM] [►] [8] [ENTER]	:CLRHOME
6. [PRGM] [►] [3] [ALPHA] ["] [ALPHA] [B] [2nd] [TEST] [1] [ALPHA] ["] [ENTER]	:DISP "B="
7. [PRGM] [►] [3] [2nd] [Y-VARS] [1] [1] [ENTER]	:DISP Y₁

45. A singly charged positive ion with a mass of 6.68×10^{-27} kg moves clockwise with a speed of 1.00×10^4 m/s in a circular path with a radius of 3.00 cm. Find the direction and strength of the magnetic field. (Hint: The magnetic force exerted on the ion is the force that maintains circular motion, and the speed of the ion given is its tangential speed.)

46. What speed would a proton need to achieve in order to circle Earth 1000.0 km above the magnetic equator, where Earth's magnetic field is directed over a line between magnetic north and south and has an intensity of 4.00×10^{-8} T? (Hint: The mag-

netic force exerted on the proton is equal to the force that maintains circular motion, and the speed needed by the proton is its tangential speed. Remember that the radius of the circular orbit should also include the radius of Earth.)

47. An electron moves in a circular path perpendicular to a magnetic field of magnitude 1.00×10^{-3} T. If the angular momentum of the electron about the center of the circle is 4.00×10^{-25} J•s, determine the following:

   a. the radius of the circular path
   b. the speed of the electron

Alternative Assessment

Performance assessment

1. During a field trip you find a roundish chunk of metal that attracts iron objects. Design a procedure to determine whether the object is magnetic and, if so, to locate its poles. Describe the limitations of your method. What materials would you need? How would you draw your conclusions? List all the possible results you can anticipate and the conclusions you could draw from each result.

2. Imagine you have been hired by a manufacturer interested in making kitchen magnets. The manufacturer wants you to determine how to combine several magnets to get a very strong magnet. He also wants to know what protective material to use to cover the magnets. Develop a method for measuring the strength of different magnets by recording the maximum number of paper clips they can hold under various conditions. First open a paper clip to use as a hook. Test the strength of different magnets and combinations of magnets by holding up the magnet, placing the open clip on the magnet, and hooking the rest of the paper clips so that they hang below the magnet. Examine the effect of layering different materials between the magnet and the clips. Organize your data in tables and graphs to present your conclusions.

Portfolio projects

3. Research phenomena related to one of the following topics, and prepare a report or presentation with pictures and data.

   a. How does Earth's magnetic field vary with latitude, with longitude, with its distance from Earth, and in time?
   b. How do people who rely on compasses account for these differences?
   c. What is the Van Allen Belt?
   d. How do solar flares occur?
   e. How do solar flares affect Earth?

4. Obtain old buzzers, bells, telephone receivers, speakers, motors from power or kitchen tools, and so on, to take apart. Identify the mechanical and electromagnetic components. Examine their connections. How do they produce magnetic fields? Work in a cooperative group to describe and organize your findings about several devices for a display entitled "Anatomy of Electromagnetic Devices."

5. William Gilbert (1544–1603) believed Earth's magnetic field was due to a large lodestone, a magnetic mineral, inside Earth's core. Research the properties of Earth's core and the properties of lodestone. Is this theory still plausible? Write a letter to Gilbert explaining the new information that supports or invalidates his theory.

CHAPTER 21
Laboratory Exercise

MATERIALS LIST

✔ 1 Ω resistor
✔ galvanometer
✔ insulated connecting wires and bare copper wire
✔ masking tape
✔ power supply
✔ switch

PROCEDURE

CBL AND SENSORS

✔ alligator clips
✔ CBL
✔ CBL magnetic field sensor
✔ CBL voltage probe
✔ graphing calculator with link cable
✔ support stand and clamp

COMPASS

✔ compass
✔ multimeter or dc ammeter

MAGNETIC FIELD OF A CONDUCTING WIRE

In this lab, you will study the magnetic field that occurs around a current-carrying wire. You will construct a circuit with a current-carrying wire and use a magnetic compass needle or a CBL and magnetic field sensor to investigate the relationship between the magnetic field and the current in the wire. You will be able to determine the magnitude and direction of the magnetic field surrounding the wire.

SAFETY

- **Never close a circuit until it has been approved by your teacher. Never rewire or adjust any element of a closed circuit. Never work with electricity near water; be sure the floor and all work surfaces are dry.**

- **If the pointer on any kind of meter moves off scale, open the circuit immediately by opening the switch.**

- **Do not attempt this exercise with any batteries, electrical devices, or magnets other than those provided by your teacher for this purpose.**

- **Wire coils may heat up rapidly during this experiment. If heating occurs, open the switch immediately and handle the equipment with a hot mitt. Allow all equipment to cool before storing it.**

PREPARATION

1. Determine whether you will be using the CBL and sensors procedure or the compass procedure. Read the entire lab for the appropriate procedure, and plan what steps you will take.

2. Prepare a data table in your lab notebook.

   - **CBL and sensors** Prepare a table with four columns and thirteen rows. In the first row, label the columns *Trial, Current Direction, ΔV_R (V)*, and $B_{Measured}$ (*T*). Label the 2nd through 13th rows *1* through *12*.

   - **Compass** Prepare a table with four columns and nine rows. In the first row, label the columns *Turns, Current (A), Current direction*, and *Compass reading*. In the first column, label the second through ninth rows *One, One, Two, Two, Three, Three, Four,* and *Four*.

Compass procedure begins on page 788.

PROCEDURE

CBL AND SENSORS

Magnetic field strength

3. Set up the apparatus as shown in **Figure 21-22**. Use 1 m of copper wire to make a square loop around the coil support pins on the galvanometer apparatus. Attach alligator clips to the ends of the wire. Label one clip A and label the other B. Place the galvanometer apparatus so that you are facing the plane of the coil.

4. Use masking tape to mark a line on the stand of the galvanometer directly under the top of the coil. Make another tape line perpendicular to the first, as shown in **Figure 21-22**. The two tapes should cross in the middle of the apparatus. On the second tape, on the side away from you, mark the point 2 cm from the center. Using this point as the center point, draw a circle with a 1 cm radius.

5. Construct a circuit that contains the power supply and a 1 Ω resistor wired in series through the middle set of posts on the switch. Place the switch so that it moves from left to right. Connect the front right post of the switch to the end of the coil

Figure 21-22

Step 3: Loop the copper wire around the support pins and attach alligator clips to the ends. Place the galvanometer with one support pin on the left and one on the right.

Step 4: Use two pieces of tape to mark perpendicular lines, and mark a circle to use as a reference for placing the sensor.

Step 5: Place the switch in front of you so that it moves from left to right. Check all connections carefully.

marked A and connect the rear right post of the switch to the end of the coil marked B. Now connect the front left post of the switch to the end of the coil marked B and the rear left post of the switch to the end of the coil marked A. **Do not close the switch or turn on the power supply until your teacher has approved your circuit.**

6. Connect the CBL to the calculator with the unit-to-unit link cable. Connect the CBL voltage probe to the CH1 port on the CBL and the magnetic field probe to the CH2 port. Connect the CBL voltage probe to measure the voltage across the resistor.

   • Turn on the CBL and the graphing calculator. Start the program PHYSICS on the calculator. Select option *SET UP PROBES* from the MAIN MENU. Enter 2 for the number of probes. Select *MORE PROBES* from the SELECT PROBE menu. Select the *VOLTAGE* probe from the list. Enter 1 for the channel number.

   • Select *MORE PROBES* from the SELECT PROBE menu. Select the *MAGNETIC FIELD* probe from the list. Enter 2 for the channel number. From the CALIBRATION menu, select *USE STORED*. For the MAGNETIC FIELD SETTING, select *HIGH (MTESLA)*.

7. Select *OPTIONS* from the MAIN MENU. Select option *ZERO SENSOR* from the PHYSICS OPTIONS menu. Select *CHANNEL 2* to zero the magnetic field sensor.

8. Hold the magnetic field sensor vertically with the white dot facing north. The CBL will display the sensor readings in volts. When the CBL displays a constant value for the field strength, press TRIGGER on the CBL to zero the sensor.

9. Select the *COLLECT DATA* option from the MAIN MENU. Select the *MONITOR INPUT* option from the DATA COLLECTION menu. The graphing calculator will begin to display values.

10. Set up a support stand with a buret clamp to hold the magnetic field sensor vertically. Position the magnetic sensor securely so that the white dot is facing you and the sensor is directly above the 1 cm circle marked on the tape.

11. Make sure the dial on the power supply is turned completely counterclockwise. When your teacher has approved your circuit, turn the dial on the power supply about halfway to its full value. Close the switch briefly.

12. Read the potential difference across the resistor and the strength of the magnetic field. Open the switch as soon as you have made your observations. Record ΔV_R (V) and $B_{Measured}$ (T) for *Trial 1* in your data table. Determine and record the *Current Direction* (A to B or B to A).

13. Reverse the direction of the current by closing the switch in the opposite direction. Read and record the potential difference and the strength of the magnetic field for *Trial 2*. Open the switch as soon

as you have made your observations. Determine and record the *Current Direction* (A to B or B to A).

14. Disconnect the alligator clips from A and B on the wire loop, and turn the wire loop 180°. Reconnect the alligator clips, making sure that clip A is on the same end of the wire it was for previous trials. Repeat steps 12 and 13 as *Trials 3 and 4*. Record all data in your data table. Always open the switch as soon as you have made your readings.

15. Return the apparatus to the same position as it was in *Trial 1*. Increase the setting on the power supply to about two-thirds of the maximum setting on the dial. Repeat the procedure in steps 10 through 14. Record all data in your data table for *Trials 5 through 8*.

16. Repeat step 15 with the power supply set to one-third of the maximum setting. Record all data in your data table as *Trials 9 through 12*.

Analysis and interpretation begins on page 789.

PROCEDURE

COMPASS

Magnetic field of a current-carrying wire

3. Wrap the wire once around the galvanometer. Place the large compass on the stand of the galvanometer so that the compass needle is parallel to and directly below the wire, as shown in **Figure 21-23.** Turn the galvanometer until the turn of wire is in the north-to-south plane, as indicated by the compass needle.

4. Construct a circuit that contains the power supply, a current meter, a 1 Ω resistor, and a switch, all wired in series with the galvanometer. Connect the galvanometer so that the direction of the current will be from south to north through the segment of the loop above the compass needle. ***Do not close the switch until your teacher has approved your circuit.***

5. Set the power supply to its lowest output. When your teacher has approved your circuit, close the switch

briefly. Using the power supply, adjust the current in the circuit to 1.5 A. Use the power supply to maintain this current throughout the lab. Record the current, the current direction, and the compass reading in your data table.

6. Reverse the direction of the current in the segments of the loop above the needle by reversing the wires connecting to the galvanometer.

7. Close the switch. Adjust the power supply to 1.5 A. Record your observations in your data table. Open the switch as soon as you have made your observations.

8. Remove the galvanometer from the circuit. Add a second turn of wire, and reconnect the galvanometer to the circuit so that the current direction will be south to north.

Figure 21-23
Step 3: Use the support pins on the galvanometer to wrap the wire into a loop. Adjust the apparatus so that the needle and wire are in the north-to-south plane.

9. Close the switch. Adjust the power supply to 1.5 A. Record your observations in your data table. Open the switch immediately.

10. Reverse the direction of the current through the segments of the loop above the needle by reversing the wires connecting to the galvanometer.

11. Close the switch. Adjust the power supply to 1.5 A.

12. Repeat the experiment for three turns and then four turns. For each, connect the circuit so that the direction of the current is from south to north and then north to south. Record all information in your data table.

ANALYSIS AND INTERPRETATION

Calculations and data analysis

1. **Analyzing data**   Use the data for each trial.
   a. **CBL and sensors**   Find the current using the equation $\Delta V = IR$.
   b. **Compass**   Find the tangent of the angle of deflection for the compass needle.

2. **Graphing data**   Use a computer, graphing calculator, or graph paper.
   a. **CBL and sensors**   Use the data from *Trials 1, 5,* and *9* to plot a graph of B_{wire} in teslas against the current in the circuit. Also plot graphs for *Trials 2, 6,* and *10; Trials 3, 7,* and *11;* and *Trials 4, 8,* and *12.*
   b. **Compass**   Plot a graph of the tangents found in item 1 against the number of turns in the wire.

Conclusions

3. **Analyzing graphs**   Use your graphs to answer the following questions.
   a. **CBL and sensors**   For each position, what is the relationship between the current in the wire loop and the magnetic field strength?
   b. **Compass**   What is the relationship between the tangent of the angle and the number of turns? Explain.

4. **Applying conclusions**   What is the relationship between the direction of current in the wire and the direction of the magnetic field? Explain.

ELECTROMAGNETIC FIELDS: CAN THEY AFFECT YOUR HEALTH?

In the 1970s, many people became concerned about the electromagnetic radiation being produced by electric devices they used at work and at home. People already knew that microwaves could cook food and that exposure to ultraviolet light contributed to skin cancer. So if all these effects were possible, people reasoned, couldn't electromagnetic radiation given off by standard 60 Hz alternating current also cause harm?

Electromagnetic waves are produced when a charged particle undergoes acceleration. Accordingly, a 60 Hz alternating current in a wire produces 60 Hz electromagnetic radiation. This is fairly low on the electromagnetic spectrum, considering that AM radio waves have frequencies around 10^6 Hz, which is itself fairly low on the electromagnetic spectrum. The region of space through which electromagnetic radiation passes is an electromagnetic field. Electromagnetic waves produced by 60 Hz alternating current produce what is called an extremely low frequency electromagnetic field, or ELF.

Problems with power lines

In 1979, scientists reported that children who lived near high-voltage power-transmission lines were twice as likely to suffer from childhood leukemia as children who did not live near power lines. In 1986, another study seemed to confirm that occurrences of leukemia and other childhood cancers were linked to the presence of power lines. Scientists generally thought that the 60 Hz electromagnetic fields from the power lines were responsible.

Many scientists criticized these studies because the researchers did not measure the strengths of the fields the people were exposed to. Instead, they had estimated the amount of exposure from the way the power lines were arranged, the current running through the lines, and the distance of the lines from each house. Critics also pointed out that the research consisted only of epidemiological studies, which mathematically correlate the frequency of an illness to factors in the surroundings.

Partly as a result of this criticism, researchers were challenged to discover a mechanism (a specific biological change that would lead to the development of cancer) by which ELFs could affect biological systems. Soon, researchers began to report that ELFs could damage cell membranes, cause unusual expression of genes, increase the production of the hormone estrogen, and reduce the pineal gland's production of melatonin, a hormone that can limit the growth of cancerous cells.

From 1991 to 1995, scientists conducted another epidemiological study to relate the health problems of 130 000 electric utility workers to their on-the-job exposure to ELFs. The researchers made a few measurements of field strength in order to estimate the amount of exposure for each type of job. To their surprise, they did not find an increased risk of leukemia, as they had expected. Instead, they found that brain cancer occurred more than twice as often among these workers as it did among other kinds of workers. However, two other studies conducted at nearly the same time found the opposite results or no correlation at all. In these last two studies, scientists measured the ELF exposure of every worker.

A need for conclusions

By 1995, several billion dollars had been spent on research that essentially provided no conclusive results, so government and other institutions were becoming wary of pouring more money into further study. The public was also becoming increasingly uneasy over the conflicting claims about ELFs. In addition, a whole industry had built up around people's fears of ELFs. Companies were selling everything from useful devices, such as gaussmeters, which measure magnetic field strength, to questionable gadgets that promised to absorb ELFs and reradiate them in a "coherent" form that was supposedly beneficial to health.

In 1995, the American Physical Society (APS) reviewed all of the research and declared that the studies had failed to show any connection between electromagnetic fields and cancer. They added that researchers had not found any mechanism by which ELFs might cause cancer. The National Academy of Sciences (NAS) came to a similar conclusion in 1996, although it conceded that a correlation did exist between childhood leukemia and the presence of power lines. The NAS suggested that scientists should continue

to search for a reason for this correlation. In 1997, the U.S. Department of Energy announced that it would no longer fund ELF programs.

Some scientists believe funding should be continued, saying that more-refined research would reveal a firm

correlation. Others have criticized the APS, saying that the organization dismissed epidemiological studies too easily and was too focused on the lack of a confirmed mechanism. Still others were pleased that NAS supported continued research into the connection between power lines and leukemia. Scientists who defend the actions of the APS and NAS point out that research money is no longer easy to get and that it should be used in more-promising kinds of cancer research.

 Researching the Issue

1. Evidence indicates that the incidence of cancer is more frequent among children who live near power-transmission lines but that the cancers are not caused by electromagnetic fields. What other factors would you suggest that scientists examine? The factors do not have to involve electricity.

2. Interpret the following statement in light of the public's perception of the disagreements over ELFs: "You can prove something to be unsafe, but you can never prove something to be completely safe."

3. Find Internet sites that offer products that claim to help people avoid exposure to electromagnetic fields. List and describe products that you think would be useful and those that you think would be a waste of money. Defend your classification of each item.

4. Electromagnetic fields from household devices, especially those with electric motors, are usually stronger than fields from nearby power lines when the fields are measured in the home. How can you account for this phenomenon?

Induction and Alternating Current

PHYSICS IN ACTION

In an electric guitar, the vibrations of the strings are converted to an electric signal, which is then amplified outside the guitar and heard as sound from a loudspeaker.

Yet the electric guitar is not plugged directly into an electric source. Instead, it generates electric current by a process called induction. By changing the magnetic field near a coil of wire, an electric current can be induced in the coil by the vibrations of the guitar strings.

This chapter explores how induction produces and changes alternating currents.

- *Why does the generated current last only as long as the string vibrates?*

- *Why must the strings be ferromagnetic in order for an electric guitar to work?*

CONCEPT REVIEW

Resistance (Section 19–2)

emf (Section 20–1)

Magnetic force (Section 21–3)

22-1
Induced current

22-1 SECTION OBJECTIVES

- **Describe how the change in the number of magnetic field lines through a circuit loop affects the magnitude and direction of the induced current.**

- **Apply Lenz's law to determine the direction of an induced current.**

- **Calculate the induced emf and current using Faraday's law of induction.**

electromagnetic induction

production of an emf in a conducting circuit by a change in the strength, position, or orientation of an external magnetic field

MAGNETIC FIELDS AND INDUCED EMFS

Recall that in Chapter 20 you were asked if it was possible to produce an electric current using only wires and no battery. So far, all electric circuits that you have studied have used a battery or direct-current power supply to create a potential difference within a circuit. In both of these cases, an emf increases the electrical potential energy of charges in the circuit, causing them to move through the circuit and create a current.

It is also possible to *induce* a current in a circuit without the use of a battery or an electrical power supply. Just as a magnetic field can be formed by a current in a circuit (as shown in the previous chapter), a current can be formed by moving a portion of a closed electric circuit through an external magnetic field, as indicated in **Figure 22-1.** The process of inducing a current in a circuit with a changing magnetic field is called **electromagnetic induction.**

Consider a circuit consisting of only a resistor in the vicinity of a magnet. There is no battery to supply a current. If neither the magnet nor the circuit is moving with respect to the other, no current will be present in the circuit. But if the circuit moves toward or away from the magnet or the magnet moves toward or away from the circuit, a current is induced. As long as there is relative motion between the two, a current can form in the circuit.

The separation of charges by the magnetic force induces an emf

It may seem strange that there can be an induced emf and a corresponding induced current without a battery or similar source of electrical energy. Recall that in the previous chapter a moving charge can be deflected by a magnetic field. This deflection can be used to explain how an emf occurs in a wire that moves through a magnetic field.

Figure 22-1

When the circuit loop crosses the lines of the magnetic field, a current is induced in the circuit, as indicated by the movement of the galvanometer needle.

Consider a conducting wire pulled through a magnetic field, as shown on the left in **Figure 22-2.** You learned in Chapter 21 that positive charges moving with a velocity at an angle to the magnetic field will experience a magnetic force. According to the right-hand rule, this force will be directed perpendicular to both the magnetic field and the motion of the charges. For positive charges in the wire, the force is directed downward along the wire. For negative charges, the force is upward. This effect is equivalent to replacing the segment of wire and the magnetic field with a battery that has a potential difference, or emf, between its terminals, as shown on the right in **Figure 22-2.** As long as the conducting wire moves through the magnetic field, the emf will be maintained.

The polarity of the induced emf—and thus the direction of the induced current in the circuit—depends on the direction in which the wire is moved through the magnetic field. For instance, if the wire in **Figure 22-2** is moved to the right, the right-hand rule predicts that the positive charges will be pushed downward. If the wire is moved to the left, the positive charges will be pushed upward. The magnitude of the induced emf depends on the velocity with which the wire is moved through the magnetic field, the length of the wire, and the strength of the magnetic field.

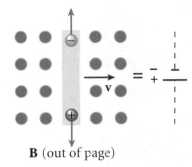

B (out of page)

Figure 22-2
The separation of positive and negative moving charges by the magnetic force creates a potential difference (emf) between the ends of the conductor.

The angle between a magnetic field and a circuit affects induction

To induce an emf in a wire loop, part of the loop must move through a magnetic field or the entire loop must pass into or out of the magnetic field. No emf is induced if the loop is static or the magnetic field is constant.

The magnitude of the induced emf and current depends on how the loop is oriented to the magnetic field, as shown in **Figure 22-3.** The induced current is largest when the plane of the loop is perpendicular to the magnetic field, as in **(a)**; it is less when the plane is tilted into the field, as in **(b)**; and it is zero when the plane is parallel to the field, as in **(c).**

The role of orientation on induced current can be understood in terms of the force exerted by a magnetic field on charges in the moving loop. The smaller the component of the magnetic field perpendicular to both the plane and the motion of the loop, the smaller the magnetic force on the charges in the loop. When the area of the loop is moved parallel to the magnetic field, there is no magnetic field component perpendicular to the plane of the loop and therefore no force that moves the charges through the circuit.

(a)　　　　　　**(b)**　　　　　　**(c)**

Figure 22-3
The induced emf and current are largest when the plane of the loop is perpendicular to the magnetic field **(a)**, smaller when the plane of the loop is tilted into the field **(b)**, and zero when the plane of the loop and the magnetic field are parallel **(c).**

Change in the number of magnetic field lines induces a current

So far, you have learned that moving a circuit loop into or out of a magnetic field can induce an emf and a current in the circuit. Changing the size of the loop or the strength of the magnetic field also will induce an emf in the circuit.

One way to predict whether a current will be induced in a given situation involves the concept of changes in magnetic field lines. For example, moving the circuit into the magnetic field causes some lines to move into the loop. Changing the size of the circuit loop or rotating the loop changes the number of field lines passing through the loop, as does changing the magnetic field's strength. **Table 22-1** summarizes these three ways of inducing a current.

CHARACTERISTICS OF INDUCED CURRENT

Suppose a bar magnet is pushed into a coil of wire. As the magnet moves into the coil, the strength of the magnetic field within the coil increases, and a current is induced in the circuit. This induced current in turn produces its own magnetic field, whose direction can be found by using the right-hand rule. If you were to apply this rule for several cases, you would notice that the induced magnetic field direction depends on the change in the applied field.

As the magnet approaches, the magnetic field lines passing through the coil increase in strength. The induced current in the coil must be in a direction that produces a magnetic field that opposes the increasing strength of the approaching field. The induced magnetic field is therefore in the direction opposite that of the approaching magnetic field.

Table 22-1   Ways of inducing a current in a circuit

Description	Before	After
Circuit is moved into or out of magnetic field (either circuit or magnet moving).		
Circuit is rotated in the magnetic field (angle between area of circuit and magnetic field changes).		
Intensity of magnetic field is varied.		

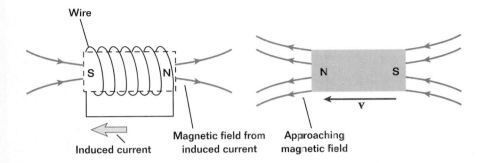

Magnetic field from
induced current

Approaching
magnetic field

Induced current

Figure 22-4
The approaching magnetic field is
opposed by the induced magnetic
field, which behaves like a bar magnet with the orientation shown.

The induced magnetic field is like the field of a bar magnet oriented as
shown in **Figure 22-4.** Note that the coil and magnet repel each other.

If the magnet is moved away from the coil, the magnetic field lines passing
through the coil decrease in strength. Again, the direction of current induced
in the coil must be such that it produces a magnetic field that opposes the
decreasing strength of the receding field. This means that the magnetic field
set up by the coil must be in the same direction as the receding magnetic field.

The induced magnetic field is like the field of a bar magnet oriented as
shown in **Figure 22-5.** Note that the coil and magnet attract each other.

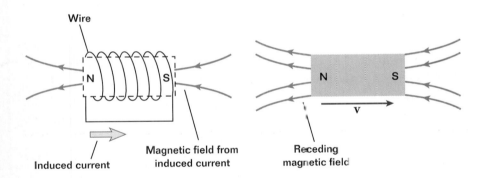

Magnetic field from
induced current

Receding
magnetic field

Induced current

Figure 22-5
The receding magnetic field is
attracted by the induced magnetic
field, which behaves like a bar magnet with the orientation shown.

Conceptual Challenge

1. Falling magnet A bar magnet is dropped
toward the floor, on which lies a large ring of conducting metal. The magnet's length—and thus the
poles of the magnet—is parallel to the direction of
motion. Disregarding air resistance, does the magnet
during its fall toward the ring move with the same
constant acceleration as a freely falling body? Explain
your answer.

2. Induction in a bracelet Suppose you are
wearing a bracelet that is an unbroken ring of copper. If
you walk briskly into a strong magnetic field
while wearing the bracelet, how would
you hold your wrist with respect
to the magnetic field in
order to avoid inducing a
current in the bracelet?

The rule for finding the direction of the induced current is called *Lenz's law* and is expressed as follows:

The magnetic field of the induced current opposes the change in the applied magnetic field.

Note that the field of the induced current does not oppose the applied field but rather the change in the applied field. If the applied field changes, the induced field attempts to keep the total field strength constant, according to the principle of energy conservation.

Faraday's law of induction

Because of the principle of energy conservation, Lenz's law allows you to determine the direction of an induced current in a circuit. Lenz's law does not provide information on the magnitude of the induced current or the induced emf. To calculate the magnitude of the induced emf, you must use *Faraday's law of magnetic induction.* For a single loop of a circuit, this may be expressed as follows:

$$\text{emf} = -\frac{\Delta[AB(\cos\theta)]}{\Delta t}$$

Certain features of this equation should be noted. First, a change with time of any of the three variables—applied magnetic field strength, B, circuit area, A, or angle of orientation, θ—can give rise to an induced emf. The term $B(\cos\theta)$ represents the component of the magnetic field perpendicular to the plane of the loop. The angle θ is measured between the applied magnetic field and the normal to the plane of the loop, as indicated in **Figure 22-6.**

The minus sign in front of the equation is included to indicate the polarity of the induced emf. It indicates that the induced magnetic field opposes the changing applied magnetic field according to Lenz's law.

If a circuit contains a number, N, of tightly wound loops, the average induced emf is simply N times the induced emf for a single loop. The equation thus takes the general form of Faraday's law of magnetic induction.

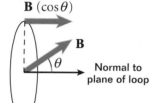

Figure 22-6
The angle θ is defined as the angle between the magnetic field and the normal to the plane of the loop. $B(\cos\theta)$ equals the strength of the magnetic field perpendicular to the plane of the loop.

FARADAY'S LAW OF MAGNETIC INDUCTION

$$\text{emf} = -N\frac{\Delta[AB(\cos\theta)]}{\Delta t}$$

**average induced emf = −the number of loops in the circuit ×
the rate of change of (circuit loop area × magnetic field component
normal to the plane of loop)**

In this chapter, N is always assumed to be a whole number.

Recall that the SI unit for magnetic field strength is the tesla (T), which equals one newton per ampere-meter, or $N/(A \cdot m)$. When calculating induced emf, express the tesla in units of one volt-second per meter squared, or $(V \cdot s)/m^2$.

Induced emf and current

PROBLEM

A coil with 25 turns of wire is wrapped around a hollow tube with an area of 1.8 m². Each turn has the same area as the tube. A uniform magnetic field is applied at a right angle to the plane of the coil. If the field increases uniformly from 0.00 T to 0.55 T in 0.85 s, find the magnitude of the induced emf in the coil. If the resistance in the coil is 2.5 Ω, find the magnitude of the induced current in the coil.

SOLUTION

1. DEFINE   **Given:**

$$\Delta t = 0.85 \text{ s} \qquad A = 1.8 \text{ m}^2 \qquad \theta = 0.0° \qquad N = 25$$

$$B_i = 0.00 \text{ T} = 0.00 \text{ V} \cdot \text{s/m}^2 \qquad B_f = 0.55 \text{ T} = 0.55 \text{ V} \cdot \text{s/m}^2$$

$$R = 2.5 \text{ Ω}$$

Unknown: $\text{emf} = ? \qquad I = ?$

Diagram: Show the coil before and after the change in the magnetic field.

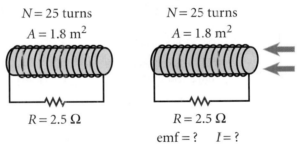

$N = 25$ turns $N = 25$ turns

$A = 1.8 \text{ m}^2$ $A = 1.8 \text{ m}^2$

$R = 2.5 \text{ Ω}$ $R = 2.5 \text{ Ω}$

$\text{emf} = ? \qquad I = ?$

$B = 0.00 \text{ T at } t = 0.00 \text{ s}$ $B = 0.55 \text{ T at } t = 0.85 \text{ s}$

2. PLAN   **Choose an equation(s) or situation:** Use Faraday's law of magnetic induction to find the induced emf in the coil.

$$\text{emf} = -N \frac{\Delta[AB(\cos \theta)]}{\Delta t}$$

Substitute the induced emf into the definition of resistance to determine the induced current in the coil.

$$I = \frac{\text{emf}}{R}$$

Rearrange the equation(s) to isolate the unknown(s): In this example, only the magnetic field strength changes with time. The other components (the coil area and the angle between the magnetic field and the coil) remain constant.

$$\text{emf} = -NA(\cos \theta) \frac{\Delta B}{\Delta t}$$

continued on next page

3. CALCULATE   Substitute the values into the equation(s) and solve:

$$\text{emf} = -(25)(1.8 \text{ m}^2)(\cos 0.0°) \frac{\left((0.55 - 0.00)\frac{\text{V} \cdot \text{s}}{\text{m}^2}\right)}{(0.85 \text{ s})} = -29 \text{ V}$$

$$I = \frac{-29 \text{ V}}{2.5 \text{ }\Omega} = -12 \text{ A}$$

> emf = −29 V
> $I = -12$ A

4. EVALUATE   The induced emf, and therefore the induced current, are directed through the coil so that the magnetic field produced by the induced current opposes the change in the applied magnetic field. For the diagram shown on page 799, the induced magnetic field is directed to the right and the current that produces it is directed from left to right through the resistor.

PRACTICE 22A

Induced emf and current

1. A single circular loop with a radius of 22 cm is placed in a uniform external magnetic field with a strength of 0.50 T so that the plane of the coil is perpendicular to the field. The coil is pulled steadily out of the field in 0.25 s. Find the average induced emf during this interval.

2. A coil with 205 turns of wire, a total resistance of 23 Ω, and a cross-sectional area of 0.25 m^2 is positioned with its plane perpendicular to the field of a powerful electromagnet. What average current is induced in the coil during the 0.25 s that the magnetic field drops from 1.6 T to 0.0 T?

3. A circular wire loop with a radius of 0.33 m is located in an external magnetic field of strength +0.35 T that is perpendicular to the plane of the loop. The field strength changes to −0.25 T in 1.5 s. (The plus and minus signs for a magnetic field refer to opposite directions through the coil.) Find the magnitude of the average induced emf during this interval.

4. A 505-turn circular-loop coil with a diameter of 15.5 cm is initially aligned so that its plane is perpendicular to the Earth's magnetic field. In 2.77 ms the coil is rotated 90.0° so that its plane is parallel to the Earth's magnetic field. If an average emf of 0.166 V is induced in the coil, what is the value of the Earth's magnetic field?

APPLICATIONS OF INDUCTION

In electric circuits, the need often arises for a temporary or continuously changing current to be produced. This kind of current can be generated through electromagnetic induction.

Door bells

Certain types of door bells chime when the button is briefly pushed. A hint to how these door bells work is the small electric light bulb often found behind the doorbell button. When you press the button, the light briefly goes out. This indicates that the door bell's circuit has been opened and that the current has been temporarily discontinued.

You can see the effect of opening the circuit in **Figure 22-7.** While the current is constant in the first circuit, the magnetic field in the coil of this circuit is steady. As long as this field does not change, no current is induced in the coil of the second circuit. When the current in the first circuit is interrupted by pressing the doorbell button, the magnetic field in the first coil drops rapidly, inducing a current in the second circuit and causing a magnetic field to quickly rise along the axis of the second coil. This induced magnetic field is strong enough to push the iron plunger against the chime.

Figure 22-7
The sudden drop in current in the first circuit induces a current in the second circuit. The resulting magnetic field pushes the plunger against the door-bell chime.

Tape recorders

One common use of induced currents and emfs is found in the tape recorder. Many different types of tape recorders are made, but the same basic principles apply for all. A magnetic tape moves past a recording head and a playback head. The tape is a plastic ribbon coated with either iron oxide or chromium dioxide.

A microphone transforms a sound wave into a fluctuating electric current. This current is amplified and allowed to pass through a wire coiled around an iron ring, as shown in **Figure 22-8,** which functions as the recording head. The iron ring and wire constitute an electromagnet; the lines of the magnetic field are contained completely inside the iron except at the point where a gap is cut in the ring. The magnetic tape is passed over this gap.

Because the magnetic field does not pass as easily through the air of the gap as it does through the nearby small pieces of metal oxide in the tape, the magnetic field passes around the gap and magnetizes the metal oxide particles. As the tape moves past the slot, it becomes magnetized in a pattern that corresponds to both the frequency and the intensity of the sound signal entering the microphone.

Figure 22-8
The signal fluctuations in the current induce a fluctuating magnetic field, which is recorded along the length of the tape. During playback, the changing magnetic field of the tape will induce in the coil a fluctuating current that can be converted to reproduce the original recorded sound.

In the recording process, the magnetic field is produced by an applied current. During the playback process, induction is used to create a current from a changing magnetic field. The sound signal is reconstructed by passing the tape over the playback head, which is an iron ring with wire wound around it. In some recorders, one head is used for both playback and recording.

When the tape moves past the playback head, the varying magnetic fields on the tape produce changing magnetic-field lines through the wire coil, inducing a current in the coil. The current corresponds to the current in the recording head that originally produced the recording on the tape. This changing electric current can be amplified and used to drive a speaker. Playback is thus an example of induction of a current by a moving magnet.

Section Review

1. A circular current loop made of flexible wire is located in a magnetic field. Describe three ways an emf can be induced in the loop.

2. A spacecraft orbiting Earth has a coil of wire in it. An astronaut measures a small current in the coil, even though there is no battery connected to it and there are no magnets on the spacecraft. What is causing the current?

3. A bar magnet is positioned near a coil of wire, as shown in **Figure 22-9.** What is the direction of the current through the resistor when the magnet is moved to the left, as in (**a**)? To the right, as in (**b**)?

Figure 22-9

4. A 256-turn coil with a cross-sectional area of 0.0025 m^2 is placed in a uniform external magnetic field of strength 0.25 T so that the plane of the coil is perpendicular to the field. The coil is pulled steadily out of the field in 0.75 s. Find the average induced emf during this interval.

5. **Physics in Action**   Electric guitar strings are made of ferromagnetic materials that can be magnetized. The strings lie closely over and perpendicular to a coil of wire. Inside the coil are permanent magnets that magnetize the segments of the strings overhead. Using this arrangement, explain how the vibrations of a plucked string produce an electric signal at the same frequency as the vibration of the string.

6. **Physics in Action**   The magnetic field strength of a magnetized electric guitar string is 9.0×10^{-4} T. The pickup coil consists of 5200 turns of wire and has an effective area for each string of 5.4×10^{-5} m^2. If the string vibrates with a frequency of 440 Hz, what is the average induced emf? (Hint: Assume the magnetic field strength varies from a minimum value of 0.0 T to its maximum value during one fourth of the string's vibration cycle.)

22-2

*Alternating current, generators,
and motors*

GENERATORS AND ALTERNATING CURRENT

In the previous section you learned that a current can be induced in a circuit either by changing the magnetic field strength or by moving the circuit loop in or out of the magnetic field. Another way to induce a current is to change the orientation of the loop with respect to the magnetic field.

This second approach to inducing a current represents a means of generating electrical energy. In effect, the mechanical energy used to turn the loop is converted to electrical energy. A device that does this is called an electric **generator.**

In most commercial power plants, mechanical energy is provided in the form of rotational motion. For example, in a hydroelectric plant, falling water directed against the blades of a turbine causes the turbine to turn; in a coal or natural-gas-burning plant, energy produced by burning fuel is used to convert water to steam, and this steam is directed against the turbine blades to turn the turbine.

Basically, a generator uses the turbine's rotary motion to turn a wire loop in a magnetic field. A simple generator is shown in **Figure 22-10.** As the loop rotates, the effective area of the loop changes with time, inducing an emf and a current in an external circuit connected to the ends of the loop.

A generator produces a continuously changing emf

Consider a single loop of wire that is rotated with a constant angular frequency in a uniform magnetic field. The loop can be thought of as four conducting wires similar to the conducting wire discussed on page 795 of Section 22-1. In this example, the loop is rotating counterclockwise within a magnetic field directed to the left.

22-2 SECTION OBJECTIVES

- **Calculate the maximum emf for an electric generator.**

- **Calculate rms current and potential difference for ac circuits.**

- **Describe how an electric motor relates to an electric generator.**

generator

a device that uses induction to convert mechanical energy to electrical energy

Figure 22-10

In a simple generator, the rotation of conducting loops (located on the left end of the axis) through a constant magnetic field induces an alternating current in the loops.

When the area of the loop is perpendicular to the magnetic field lines, as shown in **Figure 22-11(a),** segments *a* and *c* move parallel to the magnetic field lines. At this instant, they do not cross the lines and the magnetic field therefore does not exert a force on the charges in the segments. The induced emf in each segment is therefore zero. The magnetic forces on charges in segments *b* and *d* are always perpendicular to these wire segments, so these segments carry no induced currents and never contribute to the induced emf.

As the loop rotates, segments *a* and *c* begin to cross magnetic field lines so that the magnetic force on the charges in these segments, and thus the induced emf, increases. The greatest magnetic force on the charges and the greatest induced emf occur at the instant when segments *a* and *c* move perpendicular to the magnetic field lines, as shown in **Figure 22-11(b).** This occurs when the plane of the loop is parallel to the magnetic field lines.

Because segment *a* moves downward through the field while segment *c* moves upward, their emfs are in opposite directions, but both produce a counter-clockwise current. As the loop continues to rotate, segments *a* and *c* cross fewer lines, and the emf decreases. When the plane of the loop is perpendicular to the magnetic field, the motion of segments *a* and *c* is again parallel to the magnetic lines and the induced emf is again zero, as shown in **Figure 22-11(c).** Segments *a* and *c* now move in directions opposite those in which they moved from their positions in **(a)** to those in **(b).** As a result, the polarity of the induced emf and the direction of the current are reversed, as shown in **Figure 22-11(d).**

Figure 22-11

For a rotating loop in a magnetic field, the induced emf is zero when the loop is perpendicular to the magnetic field, as in **(a)** and **(c),** and is at a maximum when the loop is parallel to the field, as in **(b)** and **(d).**

A graph of the change in emf versus time as the loop rotates is shown in **Figure 22-12.** Note the similarities between this graph and a sine curve.

The induced emf is the result of the steady change in the angle between the magnetic field lines and the normal to the loop. The following equation for the emf produced by a generator can be derived from Faraday's law of induction. The derivation is not shown here because it requires the use of calculus. In this equation, the angle of orientation, θ, has been replaced with the equivalent expression ωt, where ω is the angular frequency of rotation $(2\pi f)$.

$$emf = NAB\omega\,(\sin\,\omega t)$$

The equation describes the sinusoidal variation of emf with time, as graphed in **Figure 22-12.**

The emf has a maximum value when the plane of the loop is parallel to the magnetic field, that is, when $\sin\,(\omega t) = 1$, which occurs when $\omega t = \theta = 90°$. In this case, the expression above reduces to the following:

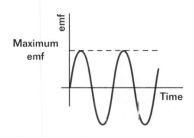

Figure 22-12
The change with time of the induced emf is depicted by a sine wave.

MAXIMUM EMF FOR A GENERATOR

$$\text{maximum emf} = NAB\omega$$

maximum induced emf = number of loops × cross-sectional area of loops × magnetic field strength × angular frequency of rotation of loops

---

Induction in generators

PROBLEM

A generator consists of exactly eight turns of wire, each with an area $A = 0.095$ m^2 and a total resistance of 12 Ω. The loop rotates in a magnetic field of 0.55 T at a constant frequency of 60.0 Hz. Find the maximum induced emf and maximum induced current in the loop.

SOLUTION

1. DEFINE

Given: $f = 60.0$ Hz $A = 0.095$ m^2 $R = 12\,\Omega$
$B = 0.55$ T $= 0.55$ V·s/m^2 $N = 8$

Unknown: $\omega = ?$ maximum emf $= ?$ $I_{mcx} = ?$

Diagram:

$f = 60.0$ Hz

$B = 0.55$ T

$R = 12\,\Omega$

$A = 0.095$ m^2

$N = 8$ turns

continued on next page

2. PLAN **Choose an equation(s) or situation:** Use the maximum emf equation for a generator. Use the definition of angular frequency to convert f to ω. The maximum current can be obtained from the definition for resistance.

$$\text{maximum emf} = NAB\omega \qquad \omega = 2\pi f$$

$$I_{max} = \frac{\text{maximum emf}}{R}$$

Rearrange the equation(s) to isolate the unknown(s): Substitute the angular frequency expression into the maximum emf equation.

$$\text{maximum emf} = NAB(2\pi f)$$

3. CALCULATE **Substitute the values into the equation(s) and solve:**

$$\text{maximum emf} = 8(0.095 \text{ m}^2)(0.55 \text{ T})(2\pi)(60.0 \text{ Hz})$$

$$\boxed{\text{maximum emf} = 1.6 \times 10^2 \text{ V}}$$

$$I_{max} = \frac{1.6 \times 10^2 \text{ V}}{12 \ \Omega} = 13 \text{ A}$$

$$\boxed{I_{max} = 13 \text{ A}}$$

CALCULATOR SOLUTION

Because the minimum number of significant figures for the data is two, the calculator answer, 157.5822875, should be rounded to two digits.

4. EVALUATE By expressing the units used in the calculation in terms of equivalent units ($1 \text{ T} = 1 \ (\text{V} \cdot \text{s/m}^2)$ and $1 \text{ Hz} = 1/\text{s}$), you can see which terms cancel. In this case, m^2 and s cancel to leave the answer for emf in units of volts.

PRACTICE 22B

Induction in generators

1. In a model generator, a 510-turn rectangular coil 0.082 m by 0.25 m rotates with an angular frequency of 12.8 rad/s in a uniform magnetic field of 0.65 T. What is the maximum emf induced in the coil?

2. A circular coil with a radius of $R = 0.22$ m and 17 turns is rotated in a uniform magnetic field of 1.7 T. The coil rotates at a constant frequency of 2.0 Hz. Determine the maximum value of the emf induced in the coil.

3. A square coil with an area of 0.045 m^2 consists of 120 turns of wire. The coil rotates about a vertical axis at 157 rad/s. The horizontal component of Earth's magnetic field at the location of the loop is 2.0×10^{-5} T. Calculate the maximum emf induced in the coil.

4. A maximum emf of 90.4 V is induced in a generator coil rotating with a frequency of 65 Hz. If the coil has an area of 230 cm^2 and rotates in a magnetic field of 1.2 T, how many turns are in the coil?

Alternating current changes direction at a constant frequency

The output emf of a typical generator has a sinusoidal pattern, as you can see in the graph in **Figure 22-12** on page 805. Note that the emf alternates from positive to negative. As a result, the output current from the generator changes its direction at regular intervals. This variety of current is called **alternating current,** or, more commonly, *ac.*

The rate at which the coil in an ac generator rotates determines the maximum generated emf. The frequency of the alternating current can differ from country to country. In the United States, Canada, and Central America, the frequency of rotation for commercial generators is 60 Hz. This means that the emf undergoes one full cycle of changing direction 60 times each second. In the United Kingdom, Europe, and most of Asia and Africa, 50 Hz is used. (Recall that $\omega = 2\pi f$, where f is the frequency in Hz.)

Resistors can be used in either alternating- or direct-current applications. A resistor resists the motion of charges regardless of whether they move in one continuous direction or shift direction periodically. Thus, if the definition for resistance holds for circuit elements in a dc circuit, it will also hold for the same circuit elements with alternating currents and emfs.

Effective current and potential difference are measured in ac circuits

An ac circuit consists of combinations of circuit elements and an ac generator or an ac power supply, which provides the alternating current. As shown earlier, the emf produced by a typical ac generator is sinusoidal and varies with time. The induced emf equals the instantaneous ac potential difference, which is written as Δv. The quantity for the maximum emf can be written as the maximum potential difference ΔV_{max}, and the emf produced by a generator can be expressed as follows:

$$\Delta v = \Delta V_{max} \sin \omega t$$

Because all circuits have some resistance, a simple ac circuit can be treated as an equivalent resistance and an ac source. In a circuit diagram, the ac source is represented by the symbol $\ominus$, as shown in **Figure 22-13.**

The instantaneous current that changes with the potential difference can be determined using the definition for resistance. The instantaneous current, i, is related to maximum current by the following expression:

$$i = I_{max} \sin \omega t$$

The rate at which electrical energy is converted to internal energy in the resistor (the power, P) has the same form as in the case of direct current. The electrical energy converted to internal energy in a resistor is proportional to the *square* of the current and is independent of the direction—or the change of direction—of the current. However, the energy produced by an alternating current with a maximum value of I_{max} is not the same as that produced by a direct current of the same value. This is because the alternating current is at its maximum value for only a very brief instant of time during a cycle.

Did you know?

Although the light intensity from a 60 W incandescent light bulb appears to be constant, the current in the bulb fluctuates 60 times each second between −0.71 A and 0.71 A. The light appears to be steady because the fluctuations are too rapid for our eyes to perceive.

Figure 22-13
An ac circuit represented schematically consists of an ac source and an equivalent resistance.

rms current

the amount of direct current that dissipates as much energy in a resistor as an instantaneous alternating current does during a complete cycle

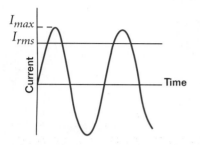

Figure 22-14
The rms current is a little more than two-thirds as large as the maximum current.

The important quantity for current in an ac circuit is the **rms current.** The rms (or *root-mean-square*) current is the same as the amount of direct current that would dissipate the same energy in a resistor as is dissipated by the instantaneous alternating current over a complete cycle.

Figure 22-14 shows a graph in which instantaneous and rms currents are compared. **Table 22-2** summarizes the notations used in this chapter for these and other ac quantities.

The equation for the power dissipated in an ac circuit has the same form as the equation for power dissipated in a dc circuit except that the dc current I is replaced by the rms current (I_{rms}).

$$P = (I_{rms})^2 R$$

This equation is identical in form to the one for direct current. However, the power dissipated in the ac circuit equals half the power dissipated in a dc circuit when the dc current equals I_{max}.

$$P = (I_{rms})^2 R = \frac{1}{2}(I_{max})^2 R$$

From this equation you may note that the rms current is related to the maximum value of the alternating current by the following equation:

$$(I_{rms})^2 = \frac{(I_{max})^2}{2}$$

$$I_{rms} = \frac{I_{max}}{\sqrt{2}} = 0.707 \, I_{max}$$

This equation says that an alternating current with a maximum value of 5 A produces the same heating effect in a resistor as a direct current of $(5/\sqrt{2})$ A, or about 3.5 A.

Alternating potential differences are also best discussed in terms of *rms potential differences,* with the relationship between rms and maximum values being identical to the one for currents. The rms potential difference, ΔV_{rms}, is related to the maximum value of the potential difference, ΔV_{max}, as follows:

$$\Delta V_{rms} = \frac{\Delta V_{max}}{\sqrt{2}} = 0.707 \, V_{max}$$

Table 22-2	Notation used for ac circuits	
	Potential difference	**Current**
instantaneous values	Δv	i
maximum values	ΔV_{max}	I_{max}
rms values	$\Delta V_{rms} = \dfrac{\Delta V_{max}}{\sqrt{2}}$	$I_{rms} = \dfrac{I_{max}}{\sqrt{2}}$

The ac potential difference of 120 V measured from an electric outlet is actually an rms potential difference of 120 V. A quick calculation shows that such an ac potential difference has a maximum value of about 170 V.

A resistor limits the current in an ac circuit just as it does in a dc circuit. If the definition of resistance is valid for an ac circuit, the rms potential difference across a resistor equals the rms current multiplied by the resistance. Thus, all maximum and rms values can be calculated if only one current or emf value and the circuit resistance are known.

Because ac ammeters and voltmeters measure rms values, all values of alternating current and alternating potential difference in this chapter will be given as rms values unless otherwise noted. The equations for ac circuits have the same form as those for dc circuits when rms values are used.

---

rms currents and potential differences

PROBLEM

A generator with a maximum output emf of 205 V is connected to a 115 Ω resistor. Calculate the rms potential difference. Find the rms current through the resistor. Find the maximum ac current in the circuit.

SOLUTION

1. DEFINE   **Given:** $\Delta V_{max} = 205$ V $R = 115$ Ω

Unknown: $\Delta V_{rms} = ?$ $I_{rms} = ?$ $I_{max} = ?$

Diagram:

$\Delta V_{max} = 205$ V
$\Delta V_{rms} = ?$

$I_{rms} = ?$ $I_{max} = ?$
$R = 115$ Ω

2. PLAN   **Choose an equation(s) or situation:** Use the equation for the rms potential difference to find ΔV_{rms}.

$$\Delta V_{rms} = 0.707\ \Delta V_{max}$$

Rearrange the definition for resistance to calculate I_{rms}.

$$I_{rms} = \frac{\Delta V_{rms}}{R}$$

Use the equation for rms current to find I_{max}.

$$I_{rms} = 0.707\ I_{max}$$

Rearrange the equation(s) to isolate the unknown(s):
Rearrange the equation relating rms current to maximum current so that maximum current is calculated.

$$I_{max} = \frac{I_{rms}}{0.707}$$

continued on next page

3. CALCULATE **Substitute the values into the equation(s) and solve:**

$$\Delta V_{rms} = (0.707)(205 \text{ V}) = 145 \text{ V}$$

$$I_{rms} = \frac{145 \text{ V}}{115 \text{ }\Omega} = 1.26 \text{ A}$$

$$I_{max} = \frac{1.26 \text{ A}}{0.707} = 1.78 \text{ A}$$

$$\boxed{\begin{array}{l} \Delta V_{rms} = 145 \text{ V} \\ I_{rms} = 1.26 \text{ A} \\ I_{max} = 1.78 \text{ A} \end{array}}$$

CALCULATOR SOLUTION

Because the minimum number of significant figures for the data is three, the calculator solution for the rms potential difference, 144.935, should be rounded to three digits.

4. EVALUATE The rms values for potential difference and current are a little more than two-thirds the maximum values, as expected.

PRACTICE 22C

rms currents and potential differences

1. What is the rms current in a light bulb that has a resistance of 25 Ω and an rms potential difference of 120 V? What are the maximum values for current and potential difference?

2. The current in an ac circuit is measured with an ammeter. The meter gives a reading of 5.5 A. Calculate the maximum ac current.

3. A toaster is plugged into a source of alternating potential difference with an rms value of 110 V. The heating element is designed to convey a current with a maximum value of 10.5 A. Find the following:
   a. the rms current in the heating element
   b. the resistance of the heating element

4. An audio amplifier provides an alternating rms potential difference of 15.0 V. A loudspeaker connected to the amplifier has a resistance of 10.4 Ω. What is the rms current in the speaker? What are the maximum values of the current and the potential difference?

5. An ac generator has a maximum potential difference output of 155 V.
   a. Find the rms potential difference output.
   b. Find the rms current in the circuit when the generator is connected to a 53 Ω resistor.

6. The largest potential difference that can be placed across a certain capacitor at any instant is 451 V. What is the largest rms potential difference that can be placed across the capacitor without damaging it?

AC Generator

Slip rings

N

S

Brush

Brush

Brush

DC Generator

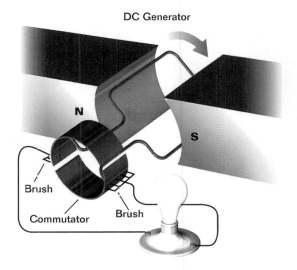

N

S

Brush

Commutator

Brush

Figure 22-15
A simple dc generator (shown on the right) employs the same design as an ac generator (shown on the left). A split slip ring converts alternating current to direct current.

Alternating current can be converted to direct current

The conducting loop in an ac generator must be free to rotate through the magnetic field. Yet it must also be part of an electric circuit at all times. To accomplish this, the ends of the loop are connected to conducting rings, called *slip rings,* that rotate with the loop. Connections to the external circuit are made by stationary graphite strips, called *brushes,* that make continuous contact with the slip rings. Because the current changes direction in the loop, the output current through the brushes alternates direction as well.

By varying this arrangement slightly, an ac generator can be converted to a dc generator. Note in **Figure 22-15** that the components of a dc generator are essentially the same as those of the ac generator except that the contacts to the rotating loop are made by a single split slip ring, called a *commutator.*

At the point in the loop's rotation when the current has dropped to zero and is about to change direction, each half of the commutator comes into contact with the brush that was previously in contact with the other half of the commutator. The reversed current in the loop changes directions again so that the output current has the same direction as it originally had, although it still changes from a maximum value to zero. A plot of this pulsating direct current is shown in **Figure 22-16.**

A steady direct current can be produced by using many loops and commutators distributed around the rotation axis of the dc generator. The sinusoidal currents from each loop overlap. The superposition of the currents produces a direct current output that is almost entirely free of fluctuations.

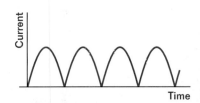

Figure 22-16
The output current for a dc generator is a sine wave with the negative parts of the curve made positive.

MOTORS

Motors are devices that convert electrical energy to mechanical energy. Instead of a current being generated by a rotating loop in a magnetic field, a current is supplied to the loop by an emf source and the magnetic force on the current loop causes it to rotate (see **Figure 22-17**).

A motor is almost identical in construction to a dc generator. The coil of wire is mounted on a rotating shaft and is positioned between the poles of a magnet. Brushes make contact with a commutator, which alternates the current in the coil. This alternation of the current causes the magnetic field produced by the current to regularly reverse and thus always be repelled by the fixed magnetic field. Thus, the coil and the shaft are kept in continuous rotational motion.

A motor can perform useful mechanical work when a shaft connected to its rotating coil is attached to some external device. As the coil in the motor rotates, however, the changing normal component of the magnetic field through it induces an emf that acts to reduce the current in the coil. If this were not the case, Lenz's law would be violated. This induced emf is called the **back emf.**

The back emf increases in magnitude as the magnetic field changes at a higher rate. In other words, the faster the coil rotates, the greater the back emf becomes. The potential difference available to supply current to the motor equals the difference between the applied potential difference and the back emf. Consequently, the current in the coil is also reduced because of the presence of back emf. The faster the motor turns, the smaller the net potential difference across the motor, and the smaller the net current in the coil, becomes.

back emf

the emf induced in a motor's coil that tends to reduce the current powering the motor

Figure 22-17

In a motor, the current in the coil interacts with the magnetic field, causing the coil and the shaft on which the coil is mounted to turn.

Consumer Focus   *Avoiding Electrocution*

A person can receive an electric shock by touching a conducting or "live" wire while in contact with a lower electric potential, or ground. The ground contact might be made by touching a water pipe (which is normally at zero potential) or by standing on the floor with wet feet (because impure water is a good conductor).

Electric shock can result in fatal burns or can cause the muscles of vital organs, such as the heart, to malfunction. The degree of damage to the body depends on the magnitude of the current, the length of time it acts, and the part of the body through which it passes. A current of 100 milliamps (mA) can be fatal. If the current is larger than about 10 mA, the hand muscles contract and the person may be unable to let go of the wire.

To prevent electrocution, any wires designed to have such currents in them are wrapped in insulation, usually plastic or rubber. However, with frequent use, electric cords can fray, exposing some of the conductors. To further prevent electrocution in these and other situations in which electrical contact can be made, devices called a Ground Fault Circuit Interrupter (GFCI) and a Ground Fault Interrupter (GFI) are mounted in electrical outlets and individual appliances.

GFCIs and GFIs provide protection by comparing the current in one side of the electrical outlet socket to the current in the other socket. If there is even a 5 mA difference, the interrupter opens the circuit in a few milliseconds (thousandths of a second). If you accidentally touch a bare wire and create an alternate conducting path through you to ground, the device detects this redirection of current and you get only a small shock or tingle.

Despite these safety devices, you can still be electrocuted. Never use electrical appliances near water or with wet hands. Use a battery-powered radio near water because batteries cannot supply enough current to harm you. It is also a good idea to replace old outlets with GFCI-equipped units or to install GFI-equipped circuit breakers.

Section Review

1. A loop with an area of 0.23 m^2 is rotating at 281 rad/s with its axis of rotation perpendicular to a uniform magnetic field. The magnetic field has a strength of 0.035 T. If the loop contains 37 turns of wire, what is the maximum potential difference induced in the loop?

2. A generator develops a maximum emf of 2.8 V. If the generator coil has 25 turns of wire, a cross-sectional area of 36 cm^2, and rotates with a constant frequency of 60.0 Hz, what is the strength of the magnetic field in which the coil rotates?

3. What is the purpose of a commutator in a motor? Explain what would happen if a commutator were not used in a motor.

4. **Physics in Action**   The rms current produced by a single coil of an electric guitar is 0.025 mA. How large is the maximum instantaneous current? If the coil's resistance is 4.3 kΩ, what are the rms and maximum potential differences produced by the coil?

22-3
Inductance

- **Describe how mutual induction occurs in circuits.**

- **Calculate the potential difference from a step-up or step-down transformer.**

- **Describe how self-induction occurs in an electric circuit.**

MUTUAL INDUCTANCE

The basic principle of electromagnetic induction was first demonstrated by Michael Faraday. His experimental apparatus, which resembled the arrangement shown in **Figure 22-18,** used a coil connected to a switch and a battery instead of a magnet to produce a magnetic field. This coil is called the *primary coil,* and its circuit is called the primary circuit. The magnetic field is strengthened by the magnetic properties of the iron ring around which the primary coil is wrapped.

A second coil is wrapped around another part of the iron ring and is connected to a galvanometer. An emf is induced in this coil, called the *secondary coil,* when the magnetic field of the primary coil is changed. When the switch in the primary circuit is closed, the galvanometer in the secondary circuit deflects in one direction and then returns to zero. When the switch is opened, the galvanometer deflects in the opposite direction and again returns to zero. When there is a steady current in the primary circuit, the galvanometer reads zero.

The magnitude of this emf is predicted by Faraday's law of induction. However, Faraday's law can be rewritten so that the induced emf is proportional to the changing current in the primary coil. This can be done because of the direct proportionality between the magnetic field produced by a current in a coil, or solenoid, and the current itself, as discussed in Chapter 21. The form of Faraday's law in terms of changing primary current is as follows:

$$\text{emf} = -N\frac{\Delta[AB\,(\cos\theta)]}{\Delta t} = -M\frac{\Delta I}{\Delta t}$$

mutual inductance

a measure of the ability of one circuit carrying a changing current to induce an emf in a nearby circuit

The constant, *M,* is called the **mutual inductance** of the two-coil system. The mutual inductance depends on the geometrical properties of the coils and

Figure 22-18

Faraday's electromagnetic-induction experiment used a changing current in one circuit to induce a current in another circuit.

Galvanometer

Primary coil   Iron ring   Secondary coil

their orientation to each other. Because these properties are kept constant, it follows that a changing current in the secondary coil can also induce an emf in the primary circuit. The equation holds as long as the coils remain unchanged with respect to each other, so that the mutual inductance is constant.

By changing the number of turns of wire in the secondary coil, the induced emf in the secondary circuit can be changed. This arrangement is the basis of an extremely useful electrical device: the transformer.

TRANSFORMERS

In many situations, it is desirable or necessary to change a small ac potential difference to a larger one or to change a large potential difference to a smaller one. The device that makes these conversions possible is the **transformer.**

In its simplest form, an ac transformer consists of two coils of wire wound around a core of soft iron, like the apparatus for the Faraday experiment. The coil on the left in **Figure 22-19** has N_1 turns and is connected to the input ac potential difference source. This coil is called the primary winding, or the *primary*. The coil on the right, which is connected to a resistor R and consists of N_2 turns, is the *secondary*. As in Faraday's experiment, the iron core provides a medium for nearly all magnetic field lines passing through the two coils.

Because the strength of the magnetic field in the iron core and the cross-sectional area of the core are the same for both the primary and secondary windings, the potential differences across the two windings differ only because of the different number of turns of wire for each. The ac potential difference that gives rise to the changing magnetic field in the primary is related to that changing field by Faraday's law of induction.

$$\Delta V_1 = -N_1 \frac{\Delta(AB \cos \theta)}{\Delta t}$$

Similarly, the induced potential difference (emf) across the secondary coil is

$$\Delta V_2 = -N_2 \frac{\Delta(AB \cos \theta)}{\Delta t}$$

Taking the ratio of ΔV_1 to ΔV_2 causes all terms on the right side of both equations except for N_1 and N_2 to cancel. This result is the transformer equation.

transformer

a device that changes one ac potential difference to a different ac potential difference

Figure 22-19
A transformer uses the alternating current in the primary circuit to induce an alternating current in the secondary circuit.

TRANSFORMER EQUATION

$$\Delta V_2 = \frac{N_2}{N_1} \Delta V_1$$

potential difference in secondary =
$$\left(\frac{\text{number of turns in secondary}}{\text{number of turns in primary}} \right) \text{potential difference in primary}$$

Another way to express this equation is to equate the ratio of the potential differences to the ratio of the number of turns.

$$\frac{\Delta V_2}{\Delta V_1} = \frac{N_2}{N_1}$$

When N_2 is greater than N_1, the secondary potential difference is greater than that of the primary, and the transformer is called a *step-up transformer*. When N_2 is less than N_1, the secondary potential difference is less than that of the primary, and the transformer is called a *step-down transformer*.

It may seem that a transformer provides something for nothing. For example, a step-up transformer can change an input potential difference from 10 V to 100 V. However, the power input at the primary must equal the power output at the secondary. An increase in potential difference at the secondary means that there must be a proportional decrease in current. If the potential difference at the secondary is 10 times that at the primary, then the current at the secondary is reduced by a factor of 10.

Real transformers are not perfectly efficient

The transformer equation assumes that there are no power losses between the transformer's primary and its secondary. Real transformers typically have efficiencies ranging from 90 percent to 99 percent. Power losses occur because of the small currents induced by changing magnetic fields in the iron core of the transformer and because of resistance in the wires of the windings.

When electric power is transmitted over large distances, it is economical to use a high potential difference and a low current. This is because the power lost to resistive heating in the transmission lines varies as I^2R. By reducing the current by a factor of 10, the power loss is reduced by a factor of 100. In practice, potential difference is stepped up to around 230 000 V at the generating station, then stepped down to 20 000 V at a regional distribution station, and finally stepped down to 120 V at the customer's utility pole. The high potential difference in long-distance transmission lines makes them especially dangerous when they are knocked down by high winds.

Coils in gasoline engines are transformers

An automobile ignition system uses a transformer, or *ignition coil*, to convert the car battery's 12 dc volts to a potential difference that is large enough to cause sparking between the gaps of the spark plugs. The diagram in **Figure 22-20** shows the type of ignition system that has been

Figure 22-20

The transformer in an automobile engine raises the potential difference across the gap in a spark plug so that sparking occurs.

Step-up transfomer (ignition coil)

Ignition switch

Computer

Crank angle sensor

12 V battery

Spark plug

used in automobiles since 1990. In this particular arrangement, each cylinder has its own transformer, and a photoelectric detector called a *crank angle sensor* determines from the crankshaft's position which cylinder's contents are at maximum compression. Upon receiving this signal, the computer closes the primary circuit to the cylinder's coil, causing the current in the primary to rapidly increase and the magnetic field in the transformer to change. This, in turn, induces a potential difference of about 20 000 V across the secondary.

Transformers

PROBLEM

A step-up transformer is used on a 120 V line to provide a potential difference of 2400 V. If the primary has 75 turns, how many turns must the secondary have?

SOLUTION

1. DEFINE **Given:** $\Delta V_1 = 120 \text{ V}$ $\Delta V_2 = 2400 \text{ V}$ $N_1 = 75 \text{ turns}$

Unknown: $N_2 = ?$

Diagram:

2. PLAN **Choose an equation(s) or situation:** Use the transformer equation.

$$\Delta V_2 = \frac{N_2}{N_i}\Delta V_1$$

Rearrange the equation(s) to isolate the unknown(s):

$$N_2 = \frac{\Delta V_2}{\Delta V_1}N_1$$

3. CALCULATE **Substitute the values into the equation(s) and solve:**

$$N_2 = \left(\frac{2400 \text{ V}}{120 \text{ V}}\right)75 \text{ turns} = 1500 \text{ turns}$$

$$\boxed{N_2 = 1500 \text{ turns}}$$

4. EVALUATE The greater number of turns in the secondary accounts for the increase in the potential difference in the secondary. The step-up factor for the transformer is 20:1.

Transformers

1. A step-down transformer providing electricity for a residential neighbor-hood has exactly 2680 turns in its primary and exactly 55 turns in its secondary. If the potential difference across the primary is 5850 V, what is the potential difference across the secondary?

2. A step-up transformer for long-range transmission of electric power is used to create a potential difference of 119 340 V across the secondary. If the potential difference across the primary is 117 V and the number of turns in the secondary is 25 500, what is the number of turns in the primary?

3. A potential difference of 0.750 V is needed to provide a large current for arc welding. If the potential difference across the primary of a step-down transformer is 117 V, what is the ratio of the number of turns of wire on the primary to the number of turns on the secondary?

4. A step-up transformer used in an automobile has a potential difference across the primary of 12 V and a potential difference across the secondary of 2.0×10^4 V. If the number of turns in the primary is 21, what is the number of turns in the secondary?

5. A television picture tube requires a high potential difference, which in older models is provided by a step-up transformer. The transformer has 12 turns in its primary and 2550 turns in its secondary. If 120 V is placed across the primary, what is the output potential difference?

6. A step-down transformer has 525 turns in its secondary and 12 500 turns in its primary. If the potential difference across the primary is 3510 V, what is the potential difference across the secondary?

Figure 22-21

The changing magnetic field that is produced by changing current induces an emf that opposes the applied emf.

SELF-INDUCTION

Consider a circuit consisting of a switch, a resistor, and a source of emf, as shown in **Figure 22-21.** When the switch is closed, the current does not immediately change from zero to its maximum value, I_{max}. Instead, the current increases with time, and the magnetic field through the loop due to this current also increases. The increasing field induces an emf in the circuit to oppose the change in magnetic field, according to Lenz's law, and so the polarity of the induced emf must oppose the direction of the original current. The induced emf is in the direction indicated by the dashed battery. The net potential difference across the resistor is the emf of the battery minus the induced emf.

As the current increases, the *rate* of increase lessens and the induced emf decreases, as shown in **Figure 22-22.** The decrease in the induced emf results in a gradual increase in the current. Similarly, when the switch is opened, the current gradually decreases to zero. This effect is called **self-induction** because the changing magnetic field through the circuit arises from the current in the circuit itself. The induced emf in this case is called *self-induced emf.*

An example of self-induction is seen in a coil wound on a cylindrical iron core. (A practical device would have several hundred turns.) When the current is in the direction shown in **Figure 22-23(a),** a magnetic field forms inside the coil. As the current changes with time, the field through the coil changes and induces an emf in the coil.

Lenz's law indicates that this induced emf opposes the change in the current. For increasing current, the induced emf is as pictured in **Figure 22-23(b),** and for decreasing current, the induced emf is as shown in **Figure 22-23(c).**

Faraday's law of induction takes the same form for self-induction as it does for mutual induction except that the symbol for mutual inductance, M, is replaced with the symbol for *self-inductance, L.*

$$emf = -N\frac{\Delta[AB(\cos\theta)]}{\Delta t} = -L\frac{\Delta I}{\Delta t}$$

The self-inductance of a coil depends on the number of turns of wire in the coil, the coil's cross-sectional area, and other geometric factors. The SI unit of inductance is the *henry* (H), which is equal to 1 volt-second per ampere.

self-induction

the process by which a changing current in a circuit induces an emf in that same circuit

Figure 22-22
The self-induced emf reduces the rate of increase of the current in the circuit immediately after the circuit is closed.

Lenz's law emf
for increasing I

Lenz's law emf
for decreasing I

(a)   **(b)**   **(c)**

Figure 22-23
The polarity of the self-induced emf is such that it can produce a current whose direction is opposite the change in the current in the coil.

Section Review

1. The centers of two circular loops are separated by a fixed distance. For what relative orientation of the loops will their mutual inductance be a maximum? For what orientation will it be a minimum?

2. A step-up transformer has exactly 50 turns in its primary and exactly 7000 turns in its secondary. If the potential difference across the primary is 120 V, what is the potential difference across the secondary?

3. Does the self-inductance L) of a coil depend on the current in the coil?

CHAPTER 22
Summary

KEY TERMS

alternating current (p. 807)

back emf (p. 812)

electromagnetic induction (p. 794)

generator (p. 803)

mutual inductance (p. 814)

rms current (p. 808)

self-induction (p. 819)

transformer (p. 815)

KEY IDEAS

Section 22-1 Induced current

- Changing the magnetic field strength near a conductor induces an emf.
- The direction of an induced current in a circuit is such that its magnetic field opposes the change in the applied magnetic field.
- Induced emf can be calculated using Faraday's law of magnetic induction.

$$emf = -N\frac{\Delta[AB(\cos\theta)]}{\Delta t}$$

Section 22-2 Alternating current, generators, and motors

- Generators use induction to convert mechanical energy into electrical energy.
- Alternating current is measured in terms of rms current.
- Motors use an arrangement similar to that of generators to convert electrical energy into mechanical energy.

Section 22-3 Inductance

- Mutual inductance involves the induction of a current in one circuit by means of a changing current in a nearby circuit.
- Transformers change the potential difference of an alternating current.
- Self-induction occurs when the changing current in a circuit induces an emf in the same circuit.

Diagram symbols

Induced emf	
ac generator/ alternating current emf source	

Variable symbols

Quantities		Units	
N	number of turns	(unitless)	
ΔV_{max}	maximum potential difference	V	volt
ΔV_{rms}	rms potential difference	V	volt
I_{max}	maximum current	A	ampere
I_{rms}	rms current	A	ampere
M	mutual inductance	H	henry $= \dfrac{\text{volt} \cdot \text{second}}{\text{ampere}}$
L	self-inductance	H	henry $= \dfrac{\text{volt} \cdot \text{second}}{\text{ampere}}$

INDUCED CURRENT

Review questions

1. Suppose you have two circuits. One consists of an electromagnet, a dc emf source, and a variable resistor that permits you to control the strength of the magnetic field. In the second circuit, you have a coil of wire and a galvanometer. List three ways that you can induce a current in the second circuit.

2. Explain how Lenz's law allows you to determine the direction of an induced current.

3. What four factors affect the induced emf?

4. If you have a fixed magnetic field and a length of wire, how can you increase the induced emf?

Conceptual questions

5. Rapidly inserting the north pole of a bar magnet into a coil of wire causes the needle of a galvanometer to deflect to the right. What will happen to the needle if you do the following?
   a. pull the magnet out of the coil
   b. let the magnet sit at rest in the coil
   c. thrust the south end of the magnet into the coil

6. An electromagnet is placed next to a coil of wire in the arrangement shown in **Figure 22-24**. According to Lenz's law, what will be the direction of the induced current in the resistor *R* in the following cases?
   a. the magnetic field suddenly decreases after the switch is opened
   b. the coil is moved closer to the electromagnet

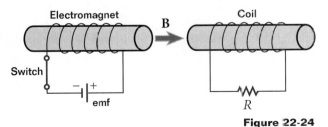

Figure 22-24

7. Explain how Lenz's law illustrates the principle of energy conservation.

8. Does dropping a bar magnet down a long copper tube induce a current in the tube? If so, how must the magnet be oriented with respect to the tube?

9. Two bar magnets are placed side by side so that the north pole of one magnet is next to the south pole of the other magnet. If these magnets are then pushed toward a coil of wire, would you expect an emf to be induced in the coil? Explain your answer.

Practice problems

10. A student attempts to make a simple generator by passing a single loop of wire between the poles of a horseshoe magnet with a 2.5×10^{-2} T field. The area of the loop is 7.54×10^{-3} m^2 and is moved perpendicular to the magnetic field lines. In what time interval will the student have to move the loop out of the magnetic field in order to induce an emf of 1.5 V? Is this a practical generator? (See Sample Problem 22A.)

11. The same student in item 10 modifies the simple generator by wrapping a much longer piece of wire around a cylinder with about one-fourth the area of the original loop (1.886×10^{-3} m^2). Again using a uniform magnetic field with a strength of 2.5×10^{-2} T, the student finds that by removing the coil perpendicular to the magnetic field lines during 0.25 s, an emf of 149 mV can be induced. How many turns of wire are wrapped around the coil? (See Sample Problem 22A.)

12. A rectangular coil 0.055 m by 0.085 m is positioned so that its cross-sectional area is perpendicular to the direction of a magnetic field, *B*. If the coil has 75 turns and a total resistance of 8.7 Ω, at what rate must the magnitude of *B* decrease to induce a current of 0.12 A in the coil? (See Sample Problem 22A.)

13. A coil of 325 turns and an area of 19.5×10^{-4} m^2 is removed from a uniform magnetic field at an angle of 45° in 1.25 s. If the induced emf is 15 mV, what is the magnetic field's strength?
(See Sample Problem 22A.)

14. A 52-turn coil with an area of 5.5×10^{-3} m^2 is dropped from a position where $B = 0.00$ T to a new position where $B = 0.55$ T. If the displacement occurs in 0.25 s and the area of the coil is perpendicular to the magnetic field lines, what is the resulting average emf induced in the coil?
(See Sample Problem 22A.)

15. A flexible loop of conducting wire has a radius of 0.12 m and is perpendicular to a uniform magnetic field with a strength of 0.15 T, as in **Figure 22-25(a)**. The loop is grasped at opposite ends and stretched until it closes to an area of 3×10^{-3} m^2, as in **Figure 22-25(b)**. If it takes 0.20 s to close the loop, find the magnitude of the average emf induced in the loop during this time.
(See Sample Problem 22A.)

 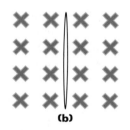

(a)　　　　(b)

Figure 22-25

ALTERNATING CURRENT, GENERATORS, AND MOTORS

Review questions

16. List the essential components of an electric generator, and explain the role of each component in generating an alternating emf.

17. A student turns the handle of a small generator attached to a lamp socket containing a 15 W bulb. The bulb barely glows. What should the student do to make the bulb glow more brightly?

18. What is meant by the term *frequency* in reference to an alternating current?

19. How can an ac generator be converted to a dc generator? Explain your answer.

20. In what way is the output of a dc generator different from the output of a battery?

21. What is meant by back emf? How is it induced in an electric motor?

Conceptual questions

22. When the plane of a rotating loop of wire is parallel to the magnetic field lines, the number of lines passing through the loop is zero. Why is the current at a maximum at this point in the loop's rotation?

23. The faster the coil of loops, or *armature,* of an ac generator rotates, the harder it is to turn the armature. Use Lenz's law to explain why this happens.

24. Voltmeters and ammeters that measure ac quantities measure the rms values of emf and current, respectively. Why would this be preferred to measuring the maximum emf or current? (Hint: Think about what a meter reading would look like if ac quantities other than rms values were measured.)

25. A bar magnet is attached perpendicular to a rotating shaft. It is then placed in the center of a coil of wire. In which of the arrangements shown in **Figure 22-26** could this device be used as an electric generator? Explain your choice.

Figure 22-26

Practice problems

26. A generator can be made using the component of Earth's magnetic field that is parallel to Earth's surface. A 112-turn square wire coil with an area of 4.41×10^{-2} m^2 is mounted on a shaft so that the cross-sectional area of the coil is perpendicular to the ground. The shaft then rotates with a frequency of 25.0 Hz. The horizontal component of Earth's magnetic field at the location of the loop is 5.00×10^{-5} T. Calculate the maximum emf induced in the coil by Earth's magnetic field.
(See Sample Problem 22B.)

27. An ac generator consists of 45 turns of wire with an area of 0.12 m^2. The loop rotates in a magnetic field of 0.118 T at a constant frequency of 60.0 Hz. The generator is connected across a circuit load with a total resistance of 35 Ω. Find the following:
    a. the maximum induced emf
    b. the maximum induced current
(See Sample Problem 22B.)

28. The rms potential difference across high-voltage transmission lines in Great Britain is 220 000 V. What is the maximum potential difference?
(See Sample Problem 22C.)

29. The maximum potential difference across certain heavy-duty appliances is 340 V. If the total resistance of an appliance is 120 Ω, calculate the following:
    a. the rms potential difference
    b. the rms current
(See Sample Problem 22C.)

30. The maximum current that can pass through a light bulb filament is 0.909 A when its resistance is 182 Ω.
    a. What is the rms current conducted by the filament of the bulb?
    b. What is the rms potential difference across the bulb's filament?
    c. How much power does the light bulb use?
(See Sample Problem 22C.)

31. A 996 W hair dryer is designed to carry a maximum current of 11.8 A.
    a. How large is the rms current in the hair dryer?
    b. What is the rms potential difference across the hair dryer?
(See Sample Problem 22C.)

INDUCTANCE

Review questions

32. Describe how mutual induction occurs.

33. What is the difference between a step-up transformer and a step-down transformer?

34. Does a step-up transformer increase power? Explain your answer.

35. Describe how self-induction occurs.

Conceptual questions

36. In many transformers, the wire around one winding is thicker, and therefore has lower resistance, than the wire around the other winding. If the thicker wire is wrapped around the secondary winding, is the device a step-up or a step-down transformer? Explain.

37. Would a transformer work with pulsating direct current? Explain your answer.

Practice problems

38. A transformer has 22 turns of wire in its primary and 88 turns in its secondary.
    a. Is this a step-up or step-down transformer?
    b. If 110 V ac is applied to the primary, what is the output potential difference?
(See Sample Problem 22D.)

39. A transformer is used to convert 120 V to 9.0 V for use in a portable CD player. If the primary, which is connected to the outlet, has 640 turns, how many turns does the secondary have?
(See Sample Problem 22D.)

40. The potential difference in the lines that carry electric power to homes is typically 20.0 kV. What is the ratio of the turns in the primary to the turns in the secondary of the transformer if the output potential difference is 117 V?
(See Sample Problem 22D.)

41. A transformer is used to convert 120 V to 6.3 V in order to power a toy electric train. If there are 210 turns in the primary, how many turns should there be in the secondary?
(See Sample Problem 22D.)

MIXED REVIEW PROBLEMS

42. A generator supplies 5.0×10^3 kW of power. The output potential difference is 4500 V before it is stepped up to 510 kV. The electricity travels 410 mi (6.44×10^5 m) through a transmission line that has a resistance per unit length of 4.5×10^{-4} Ω/m.

a. How much power is lost through transmission of the electrical energy along the line?

b. How much power would be lost through transmission if the generator's output potential difference were not stepped up? What does this answer tell you about the role of large potential differences in power transmission?

Technology 8 Learning

Graphing calculators

Program your graphing calculator to determine the instantaneous and root-mean-square values of the current in the following ac circuits:

a. an ac circuit with a maximum current of 0.250 A and a frequency of 60.0 Hz at $t = 3.27$ s

b. the same circuit at $t = 5.14$ s

c. an ac circuit with a maximum current of 0.110 A and a frequency of 110.0 Hz at $t = 2.50$ s

d. the same circuit at $t = 4.24$ s

Press [Y=] and [CLEAR] to clear any functions. Press [MODE] [▼] [▼] [ENTER] to be certain that the calculations are in radians. Open a new program by pressing [PRGM] [►] [►] [ENTER]. Name the program "AC" and press [ENTER]. Then enter the program shown in the table below.

To exit the program editor, press [2nd] [QUIT]. To run the program, press [PRGM], select "AC," and press [ENTER] [ENTER]. Enter the values for the frequency and the maximum current, pressing [ENTER] after each one.

The calculator will provide a sinusoidal graph of the current versus the time. (If the graph is not visible or not sinusoidal, press [WINDOW], change the settings for the graph window, and then press [GRAPH].)

Press [TRACE], and use the arrow keys to trace along the curve. The x value corresponds to the time in seconds, and the y value of the curve corresponds to the instantaneous current in amperes. The y value of the straight line gives the root-mean-square value for the current.

After you have finished using the graph for one circuit, press [2nd] [QUIT], and run the program for the next circuit.

Keystrokes	Display
	PROGRAM: AC
1. [PRGM] [►] [2] [ALPHA] [F] [ENTER]	:PROMPT F
2. [PRGM] [►] [2] [ALPHA] [I] [ENTER]	:PROMPT I
3. [ALPHA] ["] [ALPHA] [I] [SIN] [(] [2] [2nd] [π] [ALPHA] [F] [X,T,θ] [)] [ALPHA] ["] [STO►] [2nd] [Y-VARS] [1] [1] [ENTER]	:"ISIN (2πFX)" → Y1
4. [ALPHA] ["] [ALPHA] [I] [÷] [2nd] [√] [2] [ALPHA] ["] [STO►] [2nd] [Y-VARS] [1] [2] [ENTER]	:"I/$\sqrt{2}$" → Y2
5. [PRGM] [►] [4] [ENTER]	:DISPGRAPH

43. The alternating potential difference of a generator is represented by the equation emf = (245 V) sin 560t, where emf is in volts and t is in seconds. Find the frequency of the potential difference and the maximum potential difference output of the source.

44. A bolt of lightning, such as the one shown on the left in **Figure 22-27,** behaves like a vertical wire conducting electric current. As a result, it produces a magnetic field whose strength varies with the distance from the lightning. A 105-turn circular coil is oriented perpendicular to the magnetic field, as shown on the right in **Figure 22-27.** The coil has a radius of 0.833 m. If the magnetic field at the coil drops from 4.72×10^{-3} T to 0.00 T in 10.5 μs, what is the average emf induced in the coil?

Figure 22-27

Alternative Assessment

Performance assessment

1. Identify the chain of electromagnetic energy transformations involved in making the blades of a ceiling fan spin. Include the fan's motor, the transformers bringing electricity to the house, and the turbines generating the electricity.

2. Two identical magnets are dropped simultaneously from the same point. One of them passes through a coil of wire in a closed circuit. Predict whether the two magnets will hit the ground at the same time. Explain your reasoning, then plan an experiment to test which of the following variables measurably affect how long each magnet takes to fall: magnetic strength, coil cross-sectional area, and the number of loops the coil has. What measurements will you make? What are the limits of precision in your measurements? If your teacher approves your plan, obtain the necessary materials and perform the experiments. Report your results to the class, describing how you made your measurements, what you concluded, and what additional questions need to be investigated.

3. What do adapters do to potential difference, current, frequency, and power? Examine the input/output information on several adapters to find out. Do they contain step-up or step-down transformers? How does the output current compare to the input? What happens to the frequency? What percentage of the energy do they transfer? What are they used for?

Portfolio projects

4. Research the debate between the proponents of alternating current and those who favored direct current in the 1880–1890s. How were Thomas Edison and George Westinghouse involved in the controversy? What advantages and disadvantages did each side claim? What uses of electricity were anticipated? What kind of current was finally generated in the Niagara Falls hydroelectric plant? Had you been in a position to fund these projects at that time, which projects would you have funded? Prepare your arguments to re-enact a meeting of businesspeople in Buffalo in 1887.

5. Research the history of telecommunication. Who invented the telegraph? Who patented it in England? Who patented it in the United States? Research the contributions of Charles Wheatstone, Joseph Henry, and Samuel Morse. How did each of these men deal with issues of fame, wealth, and credit to other people's ideas? Write a summary of your findings, and prepare a class discussion about the effect patents and copyrights have had on modern technology.

CHAPTER 22
Laboratory Exercise

ELECTROMAGNETIC INDUCTION

In this laboratory, you will use a magnet, a conductor, and a galvanometer to explore electromagnets and the principle of self-induction.

SAFETY

- Never close a circuit until it has been approved by your teacher. Never rewire or adjust any element of a closed circuit. Never work with electricity near water; be sure the floor and all work surfaces are dry.
- If the pointer on any kind of meter moves off scale, open the circuit immediately by opening the switch.
- Do not attempt this exercise with any batteries, electrical devices, or magnets other than those provided by your teacher for this purpose.

PREPARATION

1. Read the entire lab, and plan what measurements you will take.

2. In your lab notebook, prepare an observation table with three wide columns. Label the columns *Sketch of setup, Experiment,* and *Observation.* For each part of the lab, you will sketch the apparatus and label the poles of the magnet, write a brief description, and record your observations.

PROCEDURE

Induction with a permanent magnet

3. Connect the ends of the smaller coil to the galvanometer. Hold the magnet still and move the coil quickly over the north pole of the magnet, as shown in **Figure 22-28.** Remove the coil quickly. Observe the galvanometer.

4. Repeat, moving the coil more slowly. Observe the galvanometer.

5. Turn the magnet over, and repeat steps 3 and 4, moving the coil over the south pole of the magnet with the magnet held still. Observe the galvanometer.

6. Hold the coil stationary and quickly move the north pole of the magnet in and out of the coil. Repeat, moving the magnet slowly. Turn the magnet, and repeat both quickly and slowly with the south pole. Observe the galvanometer.

Induction with an electromagnet

7. Connect the larger coil to the galvanometer. Connect the small coil in series with a switch, battery, and rheostat. Slip the smaller coil inside the larger coil, so that the arrangement resembles that shown in **Figure 22-29**. Close the switch. Adjust the rheostat so that the galvanometer reading registers on the scale. Observe the galvanometer.

8. Open the switch to interrupt the current in the small coil. Observe the galvanometer.

9. Close the switch again, and open it after a few seconds. Observe the galvanometer.

10. Adjust the rheostat to increase the current in the small coil. Close the switch, and observe the galvanometer.

11. Decrease the current in the circuit, and observe the galvanometer. Open the switch.

12. Reverse the direction of the current by reversing the battery connections. Close the switch, and observe the galvanometer.

13. Place an iron rod inside the small coil. Open and close the switch while observing the galvanometer. Record all observations in your notebook.

ANALYSIS AND INTERPRETATION

Calculations and data analysis

1. Organizing information   Based on your observations from the first part of the lab, did the speed of the motion have any effect on the galvanometer?

2. Organizing results   In the first part of the lab, did it make any difference whether the coil or the magnet moved? Explain why or why not.

Conclusions

3. Applying ideas   Explain what the galvanometer readings revealed to you about the magnet and the wire coil.

4. Evaluating results   Based on your observations, what conditions are required to induce a current in a wire?

5. Evaluating results   Based on your observations, what factors influence the direction and magnitude of the induced current?

Figure 22-28
Step 3: Connect the coil to the galvanometer. Holding the magnet still, move the coil over the magnet quickly.

Step 4: Holding the magnet still, move the coil over the magnet slowly.

Step 6: Repeat the procedure, but hold the coil still while moving the magnet.

Figure 22-29
Step 7: Connect the larger coil to the galvanometer, and connect the smaller coil in series with the battery, switch, and rheostat. Place the smaller coil inside the larger coil.

CHAPTER 23

Atomic Physics

PHYSICS IN ACTION

Colorful lights similar to these in Denali National Park, Alaska, are commonly seen in the sky in northern latitudes. This dazzling array of colors is known as the *aurora borealis,* or the *northern lights.* The northern lights, which can extend thousands of kilometers across the sky, appear as arcs, bands, or streaks of color, sometimes flickering or pulsating.

In this chapter, you will learn how classical physics has been superseded by a new theory known as *quantum mechanics.* As you will see, this scientific revolution has provided a new picture of the atom that accounts for the northern lights.

- *Why are only certain colors part of the northern lights?*

- *What do the colors of the northern lights reveal about our atmosphere?*

CONCEPT REVIEW

Standing waves (Section 12-4)

The wave model of light (Section 14-1)

Electromagnetic waves (Section 14-1)

23-1
Quantization of energy

- **Explain how Planck resolved the ultraviolet catastrophe in blackbody radiation.**

- **Calculate quanta of energy using Planck's equation.**

- **Solve problems involving maximum kinetic energy, work function, and threshold frequency in the photoelectric effect.**

BLACKBODY RADIATION

By the end of the nineteenth century, classical physics was thought to be nearly complete. One of the few remaining questions to be solved involved electromagnetic radiation and thermodynamics. Specifically, scientists were concerned with the glow of objects when they reach a high temperature.

All objects emit electromagnetic radiation. This radiation, which depends on the temperature and other properties of an object, typically consists of a continuous distribution of wavelengths from the infrared, visible, and ultraviolet portions of the spectrum. The distribution of the different wavelengths varies with temperature.

At low temperatures, radiation wavelengths are mainly in the infrared region and hence are not observable by the human eye. As the temperature of an object increases, the predominant wavelength emitted by the object shifts to the visible region of the electromagnetic spectrum. At sufficiently high temperatures, the object appears to have a red glow, like the charcoal shown in **Figure 23-1.** At even higher temperatures, the object appears to have a white glow, as in the hot tungsten filament of a light bulb.

Classical physics cannot account for blackbody radiation

One problem puzzling physicists at the end of the nineteenth century concerned the distribution of wavelengths emitted by a blackbody. Most objects absorb some incoming radiation and reflect the rest. An ideal system that absorbs all incoming radiation is called a blackbody. Physicists study **blackbody radiation** by observing a hollow object with a small opening, as shown in **Figure 23-2.** The system is a good approximation of a blackbody because it traps radiation. The light emitted by the small opening is in equilibrium with the walls of the object because it has been absorbed and re-emitted many times.

Figure 23-1
These charcoal briquets have a bright red glow because of their high temperature.

blackbody radiation

electromagnetic radiation emitted by a blackbody, which absorbs all incoming radiation and then emits radiation based only on its temperature

Figure 23-2
As light enters this hollow object through the small opening, part of it is reflected and part of it is absorbed on each reflection from the interior walls. After many reflections, essentially all of the incoming energy is absorbed.

(a)

(b)

Figure 23-3
(a) This graph shows the intensity of blackbody radiation at three different temperatures. **(b)** Classical theory's prediction for blackbody radiation (the blue curve) did not correspond to the experimental data (the red data points) at all wavelengths, while Planck's theory (the red curve) did.

Experimental data for the radiation emitted by an object at three different temperatures are shown in **Figure 23-3(a).** Note that as the temperature increases, the total energy emitted by the body (the area under the curve) also increases. In addition, as the temperature increases, the peak of the distribution shifts to shorter wavelengths.

Scientists could not account for these experimental results with classical physics. **Figure 23-3(b)** compares an experimental plot of the blackbody radiation spectrum (the red data points) with the theoretical picture of what this curve should look like based on classical theories (the blue curve). Classical theory predicts that as the wavelength approaches zero, the amount of energy being radiated should become infinite. This is contrary to the experimental data, which show that as the wavelength approaches zero, the amount of energy being radiated also approaches zero. This contradiction is often called the **ultraviolet catastrophe** because the disagreement occurs at the ultraviolet end of the spectrum.

Experimental data for blackbody radiation support the quantization of energy

In 1900, Max Planck (1858–1947) developed a formula for blackbody radiation that was in complete agreement with experimental data at all wavelengths. Planck's original theoretical approach is rather abstract in that it involves arguments based on entropy and thermodynamics. The arguments presented in this book are easier to visualize, and they convey the spirit and revolutionary impact of Planck's original work.

Planck proposed that blackbody radiation was produced by submicroscopic electric oscillators, which he called *resonators*. He assumed that the walls of a glowing cavity were composed of billions of these resonators, all vibrating at different frequencies. While most scientists naturally assumed that the energy of these resonators was continuous, Planck made the radical assumption that these resonators could only absorb and then re-emit certain discrete amounts of energy.

When he first discovered this idea, Planck was using a mathematical technique in which quantities that are known to be continuous are temporarily

ultraviolet catastrophe

contradiction between the predictions of classical physics and the experimental data for the electromagnetic radiation of a blackbody in the ultraviolet end of the spectrum considered to be discrete. After the calculations are made, the discrete units are taken to be infinitesimally small. Planck found that the calculations worked if he omitted this last step and considered energy to come in discrete units throughout his calculations. With this method, Planck found that the total energy of a resonator with frequency f is an integral multiple of hf, as follows:

$$E = nhf$$

In this equation, n is a positive integer called a *quantum number,* and the factor h is Planck's constant, which equals $6.626\ 075 \times 10^{-34}$ J•s. To simplify calculations, we will use the approximate value of $h = 6.63 \times 10^{-34}$ J•s in this textbook. Because the energy of each resonator comes in discrete units, it is said to be *quantized,* and the allowed energy states are called *quantum states* or *energy levels.* With the assumption that energy is quantized, Planck was able to derive the red curve shown in **Figure 23-3(b)** on page 831.

According to Planck's theory, the resonators absorb or emit energy in discrete units of light energy called *quanta* (now called *photons*) by "jumping" from one quantum state to another adjacent state. As seen by the equation above, if the quantum number (n) changes by one unit, the amount of energy radiated changes by hf. Hence, the energy of a light quantum, which corresponds to the energy difference between two adjacent levels, is given by the following equation:

ENERGY OF A LIGHT QUANTUM

$$E = hf$$

energy = Planck's constant × frequency

A resonator will radiate or absorb energy only when it changes quantum states. If a resonator remains in one quantum state, no energy is absorbed or emitted. The idea that energy comes in discrete units marked the birth of a new theory known as *quantum mechanics.*

If Planck's constant is expressed in units of J•s, the equation $E = hf$ gives the energy in joules. However, when dealing with the constituents of atoms, energy is often expressed in units of the electron volt, eV. An electron volt is defined as the energy that an electron or proton gains when it is accelerated through a potential difference of 1 V. Because 1 V = 1 J/C, the relation between the electron volt and the joule is as follows:

$$1\ \text{eV} = 1.60 \times 10^{-19}\ \text{C•V} = 1.60 \times 10^{-19}\ \text{C•J/C} = 1.60 \times 10^{-19}\ \text{J}$$

Planck's idea that energy is quantized was so radical that most scientists, including Planck himself, did not consider the quantization of energy to be realistic. Planck thought of his assumption as a mathematical contrivance to be used in calculations rather than a physical explanation. Therefore, he and other scientists continued to search for a more rational explanation of blackbody radiation that was consistent with classical physics.

Quantum energy

PROBLEM

The pendulum of a grandfather clock swings back and forth with a frequency of 2.0 Hz. If this were one of Planck's resonators, how much energy would be carried away from this vibration in a one-quantum change? Express your answer in both joules and electron volts.

SOLUTION

Given: $f = 2.0$ Hz $\qquad h = 6.63 \times 10^{-34}$ J•s

Unknown: $E = ?$ J $\qquad E = ?$ eV

Use the equation for the energy of a light quantum, given on page 832.

$$E = hf = (6.63 \times 10^{-34} \text{ J•s})(2.0 \text{ Hz})$$

$$\boxed{E = 1.3 \times 10^{-33} \text{ J}}$$

Now convert your answer to units of the electron volt.

$$E = \frac{1.3 \times 10^{-33} \text{ J}}{1.60 \times 10^{-19} \text{ J/eV}}$$

$$\boxed{E = 8.1 \times 10^{-15} \text{ eV}}$$

Quantum energy

1. Yellow light with a frequency of approximately 6.0×10^{14} Hz is the predominant frequency in sunlight. In units of the electron volt, what is the energy carried by one quantum (photon) of this light?

2. A vibrating mass-spring system has a frequency of 0.56 Hz. How much energy of this vibration is carried away in a one-quantum change?

3. A quantum of a certain color of visible light is found to have an energy of 5.0×10^{-19} J. What is the color of this light?

4. Radiation emitted from human skin reaches its peak at $\lambda = 940$ μm.
   a. What is the frequency of this radiation?
   b. What type of electromagnetic waves are these?
   c. How much energy (in electron volts) is carried by one quantum of these electromagnetic waves?

THE PHOTOELECTRIC EFFECT

Around this same time, scientists were attempting to explain a phenomenon first noticed by the German physicist Heinrich Hertz. While conducting an experiment that demonstrated the existence of the electromagnetic waves predicted by Maxwell, Hertz happened to notice that when light strikes certain metallic surfaces, electrons are emitted from the surface, as depicted schematically in **Figure 23-4.** This effect is called the **photoelectric effect.** The emitted electrons are called *photoelectrons,* and surfaces that exhibit this effect are said to be *photosensitive.*

Classical physics cannot explain the photoelectric effect

The fact that light waves can eject electrons from a metal surface does not contradict the principles of classical physics. Light waves have energy, and if that energy is great enough, an electron could be stripped from its atom and have enough energy to escape the metal. However, the details of the photoelectric effect cannot be explained by classical theories. In order to see where the conflict arises, we must consider what should happen according to classical theory and then compare these predictions with experimental observations.

As was stated in Chapter 12, the energy of a wave increases as its intensity increases. Thus, according to classical physics, light waves of any frequency should have sufficient energy to eject electrons from the metal if the intensity of the light is high enough. Even at lower intensities, electrons should be ejected if light shines on the metal for a sufficient time period because the electrons would take time to absorb the incoming energy before acquiring enough kinetic energy to escape from the metal. Furthermore, increasing the intensity of the light waves should increase the kinetic energy of the photoelectrons, and the maximum kinetic energy of any electron should be determined by the light's intensity. These classical predictions are summarized in the second column of **Table 23-1.**

Figure 23-4

A light beam shining on this metal may eject electrons from the metal. Because this interaction involves both light and electrons, it is called the photoelectric effect.

photoelectric effect

emission of electrons from a surface that occurs when light of certain frequencies shines on the surface

Table 23-1	The photoelectric effect	
	Classical predictions	**Experimental evidence**
Whether electrons are ejected depends on ...	the intensity of the light.	the frequency of the light.
The kinetic energy of ejected electrons depends on ...	the intensity of the light.	the frequency of the light.
At low intensities, electron ejection ...	takes time.	occurs almost instantaneously above a certain frequency.

Scientists found that *none* of these classical predictions are actually observed. No electrons are emitted if the frequency of the incoming light falls below a certain frequency, even if the intensity is very high. This frequency, known as the *threshold frequency* (f_t), varies with each metal.

If the light frequency exceeds the threshold frequency, the photoelectric effect is observed. The number of photoelectrons emitted is proportional to the light intensity, but the maximum kinetic energy of the photoelectrons is independent of the light intensity. Instead, the maximum kinetic energy of the photoelectrons increases with increasing frequency. Furthermore, electrons are emitted from the surface almost instantaneously, even at low intensities. These observations are summarized in the third column of **Table 23-1.**

Einstein proposed that all electromagnetic waves are quantized

Albert Einstein resolved this conflict in his paper on the photoelectric effect, for which he received the Nobel Prize in 1921, by extending Planck's concept of quantization to electromagnetic waves. Einstein assumed that electromagnetic waves of the same frequency can be viewed as a stream of particles called **photons.** Each photon has an energy, E, given by Planck's equation ($E = hf$). In this theory, each photon can be absorbed as a unit by an electron. When a photon's energy is transferred to an electron in a metal, the energy acquired by the electron is equal to hf.

photon

the discrete unit (or quantum) of light energy

Threshold frequency depends on the work function of the surface

In order to be ejected from a metal, an electron must escape from the metal by overcoming the force that binds it to the metal. The amount of energy the electron must have to escape the metal is known as the **work function** of the metal. The work function is equal to hf_t, where f_t is the threshold frequency for the metal. Photons with energy less than hf_t do not have enough energy to eject an electron from the metal. Because energy must be conserved, the maximum kinetic energy of the ejected photoelectrons is the difference between the photon energy and the work function of the metal. This relationship is expressed mathematically by the following equation:

work function

minimum amount of energy required for an electron to escape from a metal

---

MAXIMUM KINETIC ENERGY OF A PHOTOELECTRON

$$KE_{max} = hf - hf_t$$

maximum kinetic energy =
(Planck's constant × frequency of incoming photon) − work function

---

According to this equation, there should be a linear relationship between f and KE_{max} because h is a constant and the work function, hf_t, is constant for any given metal. Experiments have verified that this is indeed the case, as shown in **Figure 23-5,** and the slope of such a curve ($\Delta KE/\Delta f$) gives a value for h that corresponds to Planck's value.

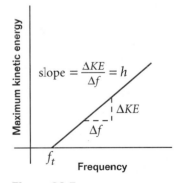

Figure 23-5

This graph shows a linear relationship between the maximum kinetic energy of emitted electrons and the frequency of incoming light. The intercept with the horizontal axis is the threshold frequency.

The photoelectric effect

PROBLEM

A sodium surface is illuminated with light with a frequency of 1.00×10^{15} Hz. The work function of sodium is 2.28 eV. Find the maximum kinetic energy of the photoelectrons in electron volts.

SOLUTION

Given: $f = 1.00 \times 10^{15}$ Hz $hf_t = 2.28$ eV

$h = 6.63 \times 10^{-34}$ J•s

Unknown: $KE_{max} = ?$ eV

Use the equation for maximum kinetic energy, given on page 835, and convert the first term to electron volts.

$$KE_{max} = hf - hf_t$$

$$KE_{max} = \left(\frac{6.63 \times 10^{-34} \text{ J•s}}{1.60 \times 10^{-19} \text{ J/eV}} \right)(1.00 \times 10^{15} \text{ Hz}) - (2.28 \text{ eV})$$

$$KE_{max} = 4.14 \text{ eV} - 2.28 \text{ eV}$$

$$\boxed{KE_{max} = 1.86 \text{ eV}}$$

PRACTICE 23B

The photoelectric effect

1. Calculate the threshold frequency of sodium using the information given in Sample Problem 23B.

2. Which of the following metals will exhibit the photoelectric effect when light of 7.0×10^{14} Hz frequency is shined on it?
   a. lithium, $hf_t = 2.3$ eV
   b. silver, $hf_t = 4.7$ eV
   c. cesium, $hf_t = 2.14$ eV

3. For the metals in item 2 that experience the photoelectric effect, what is the maximum kinetic energy of the photoelectrons?

4. Light of wavelength 350 nm falls on a potassium surface, and the photoelectrons have a maximum kinetic energy of 1.3 eV. What is the work function of potassium? What is the threshold frequency for potassium?

Photon theory accounts for observations of the photoelectric effect

The photon theory of light explains features of the photoelectric effect that cannot be understood using classical concepts. The photoelectric effect is not observed below a certain threshold frequency because the energy of the photon must be greater than or equal to the work function of the material. If the energy of each incoming photon is not equal to or greater than the work function, electrons will never be ejected from the surface, regardless of how many photons are present (how great the intensity is). Because the energy of each photon depends on the frequency of the incoming photon's waves ($E = hf$), the photoelectric effect is not observed when the waves of the incoming photon are below a certain frequency (f_t).

If the light intensity is doubled, the number of photons is doubled, and that in turn doubles the number of electrons ejected from the metal. However, the equation for the maximum kinetic energy of an electron shows that the kinetic energy depends only on the light frequency and the work function, not on the light intensity. Thus, even though there are more electrons ejected, the maximum kinetic energy of each electron does not change.

Finally, the fact that the electrons are emitted almost instantaneously is consistent with the particle theory of light, in which energy appears in small packets. Because each photon affects a single electron, there is no significant time delay between shining light on the metal and observing electrons being ejected.

Einstein's success in explaining the photoelectric effect by assuming that electromagnetic waves are quantized led scientists to realize that the quantization of energy must be considered a real description of the physical world rather than a mathematical contrivance, as most had initially supposed. The discreteness of energy had not been considered a viable possibility because the energy quantum is not detected in our everyday experiences. However, scientists began to believe that the true nature of energy is seen in the submicroscopic level of atoms and molecules, where quantum effects become important and measurable.

Conceptual Challenge

1. Photoelectric effect Even though bright red light delivers more total energy per second than dim violet light, the red light cannot eject electrons from a certain metallic surface, while the dimmer violet light can. How does Einstein's photon theory explain this observation?

2. Photographs Suppose a photograph were made of a person's face using only a few photons. According to Einstein's photon theory, would the result be simply a very faint image of the entire face? Why or why not?

3. Glowing objects As a hot object glows, the color of its glow depends on the object's temperature. As temperature increases, the color turns from red to orange to yellow and finally to white. Classical physics cannot explain this color change, while quantum mechanics can. What explanation is given by quantum mechanics?

Incoming photon   Stationary electron

(a)

(b)

Recoiling electron

Scattered photon

Figure 23-6

(a) When a photon collides with an electron, **(b)** the scattered photon has less energy and a longer wavelength than the incoming photon.

Compton shift

change in wavelength between incoming and scattered electromagnetic waves

Compton shift supports the photon theory of light

The American physicist Arthur Compton (1892–1962) realized that if light behaves like a particle, then a collision between an electron and a photon should be similar to a collision between two billiard balls. Hence, photons should have momentum as well as energy, and both quantities should be conserved in collisions. For example, when a photon collides with an electron initially at rest, as shown in **Figure 23-6,** the photon should transfer some of its energy and momentum to the electron. As a result, the energy and frequency of the scattered photon should be lowered and its wavelength should increase.

In 1923, to test this theory, Compton directed electromagnetic waves (X rays) toward a block of graphite. He found that the scattered waves had slightly less energy and slightly longer wavelengths than the incoming waves, just as he had predicted. This change in wavelength, known as the **Compton shift,** provides further support for Einstein's photon theory of light.

The amount that the wavelength shifts depends on the angle through which the photon is scattered and can range from about 10^{-6} nm to 10^{-3} nm. Note that even the largest change in wavelength is very small in relation to the wavelengths of visible light. For this reason, the Compton shift is difficult to detect using visible light, but it can be observed using electromagnetic waves with much shorter wavelengths, such as X rays.

The photoelectric effect has a variety of practical applications

Many practical devices in our everyday lives depend on the photoelectric effect. Such applications often use a *phototube,* which contains a cathode made of a photosensitive material and an anode. The cathode is connected to the negative terminal of a power source and the anode is connected to the positive terminal. Thus, a potential difference exists across the cathode and the anode. When a beam of light shines on the photosensitive cathode, electrons are ejected from it. Because of the potential difference, the photoelectrons move toward the anode and a current exists.

Figure 23-7 shows how the photoelectric effect is used to produce sound on movie film. The soundtrack of a movie is located along the side of the film in the form of an optical pattern of light and dark lines. A beam of light in the

Figure 23-7

The shading on the soundtrack varies the light intensity reaching the phototube, which varies the current sent to the speaker. This changing current reproduces the original sound waves in the speaker.

Soundtrack   Phototube

Light source   To speakers

projector is directed through the soundtrack toward a photo-tube. The variation in shading on the soundtrack varies the light intensity falling on the plate of the phototube. When the light intensity increases, the number of photoelectrons also increases because there are more photons striking the surface. Likewise, when the intensity decreases, the number of photoelectrons decreases. Hence, the current is constantly changing as the intensity changes. This changing current electrically simulates the original sound wave and reproduces it in the speaker.

Another common application of the photoelectric effect is a type of burglar alarm. In such alarms, a beam of ultraviolet light shines on a photosensitive surface in a phototube. (Ultraviolet rather than visible light is typically used to make the beam less obvious.) This beam causes the surface to emit electrons. The photoelectrons generate a current, which exists as long as the light continues to strike the surface. The current produced is amplified and used to energize an electromagnet that attracts a metal rod, as shown in **Figure 23-8(a).**

If an intruder breaks the light beam, light no longer shines on the photosensitive surface and electrons are no longer ejected. This stops the current, and the electromagnet switches off. When this occurs, the spring pulls the iron rod to the right, as shown in **Figure 23-8(b).** In this position, the circuit that contains the bur-glar alarm is complete, and a current activates the alarm.

Figure 23-8
(a) When light strikes the photoelectric tube, the current in the circuit on the left energizes the magnet, keeping the burglar-alarm circuit on the right open.
(b) When the light stops shining on the tube, the alarm circuit closes, and the alarm sounds.

Section Review

1. Describe the conflict known as the ultraviolet catastrophe. How did Planck resolve this conflict? How does Planck's assumption depart from classical physics?

2. What is the energy (in eV units) carried by one photon of violet light that has a wavelength of 4.5×10^{-7} m?

3. Why did scientists originally think that the intensity of light shining on a photosensitive surface should determine whether electrons are ejected from that surface?

4. How does Einstein's theory that electromagnetic waves are quantized explain the fact that the frequency of light (rather than the intensity) determines whether electrons are ejected from a photosensitive surface?

5. Light with a wavelength of 1.00×10^{-7} m shines on tungsten, which has a work function of 4.6 eV. Are electrons ejected from the tungsten? If so, what is their maximum kinetic energy?

23-2
Models of the atom

23-2 SECTION OBJECTIVES

- **Explain the strengths and weaknesses of Rutherford's model of the atom.**

- **Recognize that each element has a unique emission and absorption spectrum.**

- **Explain atomic spectra using Bohr's model of the atom.**

EARLY MODELS OF THE ATOM

The model of the atom in the days of Newton was that of a tiny, hard, indestructible sphere. This model was a good basis for the kinetic theory of gases. However, new models had to be devised when experiments revealed the electrical nature of atoms. The discovery of the electron in 1897 prompted J. J. Thomson (1856–1940) to suggest a new model of the atom. In Thomson's model, electrons are embedded in a spherical volume of positive charge like seeds in a watermelon, as shown in **Figure 23-9.**

Rutherford proposed a planetary model of the atom

In 1911, Hans Geiger and Ernest Marsden, under the supervision of Ernest Rutherford (1871–1937), performed a critical experiment showing that Thomson's model could not be correct. In this experiment, a beam of positively charged *alpha particles*—which consist of two protons and two neutrons—was projected against a thin metal foil, as shown in **Figure 23-10.** Most of the alpha particles passed through the foil as if it were empty space. Furthermore, some of the alpha particles were deflected from their original direction through very large angles. Some particles were even deflected backward. Such deflections were completely unexpected on the basis of the Thomson model. As Rutherford wrote, "It was quite the most incredible event that has ever happened to me in my life. It was almost as incredible as if you fired a 15-inch shell at a piece of tissue paper and it came back and hit you."

Such large deflections could not occur on the basis of Thomson's model, in which positive charge is evenly distributed throughout the atom, because the positively charged alpha particles would never come close to a positive charge concentrated enough to cause such large-angle deflections.

Electron   Sphere of positive charge

The Thomson model of the atom

Figure 23-9
In Thomson's model of the atom, electrons are embedded inside a larger region of positive charge like seeds in a watermelon.

Figure 23-10
In this experiment, positively charged alpha particles are directed at a thin metal foil. Because many particles pass through the foil and only a few are deflected, Rutherford concluded that the atom's positive charge is concentrated at the center of the atom.

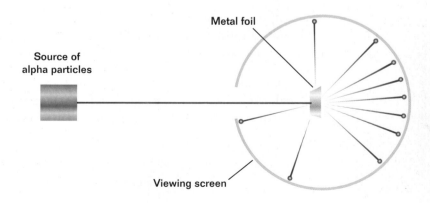

Metal foil

Source of alpha particles

Viewing screen

To explain his observations, Rutherford concluded that all of the positive charge in an atom and most of the atom's mass are concentrated in a region that is small relative to the size of the atom. He called this concentration of positive charge and mass the *nucleus* of the atom. Any electrons belonging to the atom were assumed to be in the relatively large volume outside the nucleus. Thus, according to Rutherford's theory, most alpha particles missed the nucleus entirely and passed through the foil, while only a few came close enough to the nucleus to be deflected.

Rutherford's model predicts that atoms are unstable

To explain why electrons in this outer region of the atom were not pulled into the nucleus, Rutherford viewed the electrons as moving in orbits about the nucleus, much like the planets orbit the sun, as shown in **Figure 23-11.**

However, this assumption posed a serious difficulty. If electrons orbited the nucleus, they would undergo a centripetal acceleration. According to Maxwell's theory of electromagnetism, accelerated charges should radiate electromagnetic waves, losing energy; hence, the radius of an atom's orbit would steadily decrease. This would lead to an ever-increasing frequency of emitted radiation and a rapid collapse of the atom as the electron plunged into the nucleus. In fact, calculations show that according to this model, the atom would collapse in about one-billionth of a second. This difficulty with Rutherford's model prompted scientists to continue searching for a new model of the atom.

ATOMIC SPECTRA

In addition to resolving the difficulty with Rutherford's planetary model, scientists hoped that a new model of the atom would explain another mysterious phenomenon involving gases. When an evacuated glass tube is filled with a pure atomic gas and a sufficiently high potential difference is applied between metal electrodes in the tube, a current is produced in the gas and the tube emits light, as shown in **Figure 23-12.** The light's color is characteristic of the gas in the tube. This is how a neon sign works. The variety of colors seen in neon signs is the result of the emission of light by different gases in the tubes.

CONCEPT PREVIEW

You will learn more about the nucleus of the atom in Chapter 25.

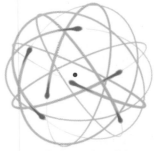

The Rutherford model

Figure 23-11
In Rutherford's model of the atom, electrons orbit the nucleus in a manner similar to planets orbiting the sun.

Figure 23-12
When a potential difference is applied across an atomic gas in a tube—here, hydrogen **(a)**, mercury **(b)**, and nitrogen **(c)**—the gas glows. The color of the glow depends on the type of gas.

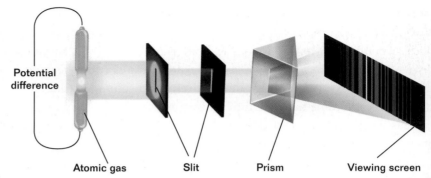

Figure 23-13
When the light from an atomic gas is passed through a prism, the dispersed light appears as a series of discrete, bright spectral lines.

emission spectrum

a unique series of spectral lines emitted by an atomic gas when a potential difference is applied across the gas

absorption spectrum

a continuous spectrum interrupted by dark lines characteristic of the medium through which the radiation has passed

Each gas has a unique emission and absorption spectrum

When the light emitted by an atomic gas is passed through a prism, as shown in **Figure 23-13,** a series of discrete bright lines is observed. Each line corresponds to a different wavelength, or color, of light. Such a series of spectral lines is commonly referred to as an **emission spectrum.**

As shown in **Figure 23-14,** the emission spectra for hydrogen, mercury, and helium are each unique. Further analysis of other substances reveals that every element has a distinct emission spectrum. In other words, the wavelengths contained in a given spectrum are characteristic of the element emitting the light. Because no two elements emit the same line spectrum, this phenomenon represents a reliable technique for identifying elements in a mixture.

In addition to emitting light at specific wavelengths, an element can also absorb light at specific wavelengths. The spectral lines corresponding to this process form what is known as an **absorption spectrum.** An absorption spectrum can be obtained by passing light containing all wavelengths through a

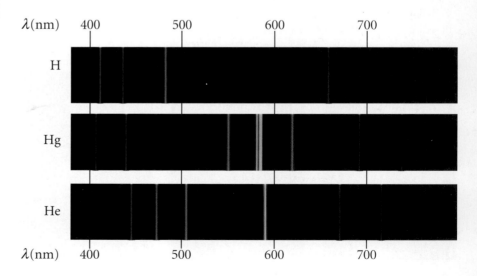

Figure 23-14
Each of these gases—hydrogen, mercury, and helium—has a unique emission spectrum.

Figure 23-15
Hydrogen's dark absorption lines occur at the same wavelengths as its bright emission lines.

vapor of the element being analyzed. The absorption spectrum consists of a series of dark lines superimposed on the otherwise continuous spectrum.

Each line in the absorption spectrum of a given element coincides with a line in the emission spectrum of that element, as shown in **Figure 23-15** for hydrogen. In practice, more emission lines are usually observed than absorption lines. The reason for this will be discussed shortly.

The absorption spectrum of an element has many practical applications. For example, the continuous spectrum of radiation emitted by the sun must pass through the cooler gases of the solar atmosphere and then through Earth's atmosphere. The various absorption lines observed in the solar spectrum have been used to identify elements in the solar atmosphere. Scientists are able to examine the light from stars other than our sun in this fashion, but elements other than those present on Earth have never been detected.

The phenomenon of atomic spectra was of great importance to scientists attempting to find a new model of the atom. Long after atomic spectra had been discovered, their cause remained unexplained. There was nothing in Rutherford's planetary model to account for the fact that each element has a unique series of spectral lines. Scientists hoped that a new model of the atom would explain why the atoms of a given element emit only certain lines and why the atoms absorb only those wavelengths that they emit.

THE BOHR MODEL OF THE HYDROGEN ATOM

In 1913, the Danish physicist Niels Bohr (1885–1962) proposed a new model of the simplest atom, hydrogen, that provided an explanation of atomic spectra. Bohr's model of hydrogen contains some classical features as well as some revolutionary postulates that could not be explained by classical physics.

Bohr's model is similar to Rutherford's in that the electron moves in circular orbits about the nucleus. The electric force between the positively charged proton inside the nucleus and the negatively charged electron is the force that holds the electron in orbit. However, in Bohr's model, only certain orbits are stable. The electron is never found between these orbits; instead, it is said to "jump" instantly from one orbit to another without ever being between orbits.

Bohr's model further departs from classical physics by assuming that the hydrogen atom does not emit energy in the form of radiation when the electron is in any of these stable orbits. Hence, the total energy of the atom remains constant and one difficulty with the Rutherford model (the instability of the atom) is resolved. Bohr claimed that rather than radiating energy continuously, the electron radiates energy when it jumps from an outer orbit to an inner one. The frequency of the radiation emitted in the jump is *independent of the frequency of the electron's orbital motion.* The frequency of the emitted radiation is instead related to the change in the atom's energy and is found by Planck's equation ($E = E_{initial} - E_{final} = hf$).

In Bohr's model, transitions between stable orbits with different energy levels account for the discrete spectral lines

The lowest energy state in the Bohr model, which corresponds to the shortest possible radius, is often called the *ground state* of the atom, and the radius of this orbit is called the *Bohr radius.* At ordinary temperatures, most electrons are in the ground state, with the electron relatively close to the nucleus. When light of a continuous spectrum shines on the atom, only the photons whose energy (hf) matches the energy separation between two levels can be absorbed by the atom. When this occurs, an electron jumps from a lower energy state to a higher energy state, which corresponds to an orbit farther from the nucleus, as shown in **Figure 23-16(a).** This is called an *excited state.* The absorbed photons account for the dark lines in the absorption spectrum.

Once an electron is in an excited state, there is a certain probability that it will jump back to a lower energy level by emitting a photon, as shown in **Figure 23-16(b).** This process is known as *spontaneous emission.* The emitted photons are responsible for the bright lines in the emission spectrum.

In both cases, there is a correlation between the "size" of an electron's jump and the energy of the photon. For example, an electron in the fourth energy level could jump to the third level, the second level, or the ground state. Because Planck's equation gives the energy from one level to the next level, a greater jump means that more energy is emitted. Thus, jumps between different levels correspond to the various spectral lines that are observed. The jumps that correspond to the four spectral lines in the visible spectrum of

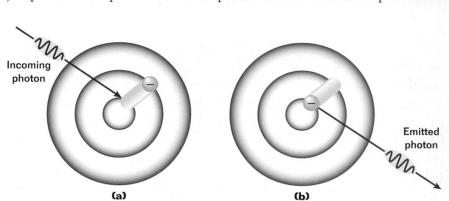

Figure 23-16
(a) When a photon is absorbed by an atom, an electron jumps to a higher energy level. **(b)** When the electron falls back to a lower energy level, the atom releases a photon.

Incoming photon

Emitted photon

(a)   **(b)**

hydrogen are shown in **Figure 23-17.** Bohr's calculations successfully predict the wavelengths of all the spectral lines of hydrogen.

As noted earlier, fewer absorption lines than emission lines are typically observed. This is because absorption spectra are usually observed when a gas is at room temperature. Thus, most electrons are in the ground state, so all transitions observed are from a single level (E_1) to higher levels. Emission spectra, on the other hand, are seen by raising a gas to a high temperature and viewing downward transitions between any two levels. In this case, all transitions are possible, so more spectral lines are observed.

Bohr's idea of the quantum jump between energy levels provides an explanation for the aurora borealis, or northern lights. Charged particles from the sun sometimes become trapped in Earth's magnetic field and are deposited around the northern and southern magnetic poles. (Light shows in southern latitudes are called *aurora australis,* or *southern lights.*) When deposited, these charged particles from the sun collide with the electrons of the atoms in our atmosphere and transfer energy to these electrons, causing them to jump to higher energy levels. When an electron returns to its original orbit, the extra energy is released as a photon. The northern lights are the result of billions of these quantum jumps happening at the same time.

The colors of the northern lights are determined by the type of gases in the atmosphere. The charged particles from the sun are most commonly released from Earth's magnetic field into a part of the atmosphere that contains oxygen. Oxygen releases green light; thus, green is the most common color of the northern lights. Red lights are the result of collisions with nitrogen atoms. Because each type of gas releases a unique color, the northern lights contain only a few distinct colors rather than a continuous spectrum.

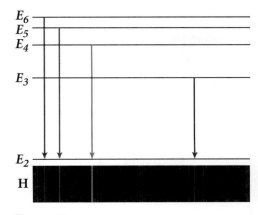

Figure 23-17
Every jump from one energy level to another corresponds to a specific spectral line. This example shows the transitions that result in the visible spectral lines of hydrogen. The lowest energy level, E_1, is not shown in this diagram.

Conceptual Challenge

1. Neon signs When a potential difference is placed across electrodes at the ends of a tube that contains neon, such as a neon sign, the neon glows. Is the light emitted by a neon sign composed of a continuous spectrum or only a few lines? Defend your answer.

2. Energy levels If a certain atom has four possible energy levels and an electron can jump between any two energy levels of the atom, how many different spectral lines could be emitted?

3. Identifying gases Neon is not the only type of gas used in neon signs. As you have seen, a variety of gases exhibit similar effects when there is a potential difference across them. While the colors observed are sometimes different, certain gases do glow with the same color. How could you distinguish two such gases?

Laser Surface Analyzer

Many homes contain a silent danger to children living in them. Paints manufactured 50 years ago contain lead—a toxic metal. If children swallow flakes of this paint, they are at risk of contracting lead poisoning and of developing learning disabilities.

In the past, testing paint flakes for lead required complicated procedures available only at chemical labs or the use of instruments containing radioactive sources.

David Cremers, a scientist at Los Alamos National Laboratory, has plans to change all that with a device called a laser surface analyzer. This device uses a laser to create a tiny spark. The spark is intensely hot, around 5811 K (10 000°F). The spark vaporizes a material to produce atoms that are then excited to emit light.

According to Cremers, "If we take this light from the spark and pass it through a prism to produce a spectrum, we'll see bright emissions in certain colors or regions of the spectrum. Because each element in the periodic table has a unique emission spectrum, by accurately determining the wavelengths of these emissions or the colors of these emissions, we can tell you what elements the material is composed of."

Although the laser surface analyzer was originally created to test walls for toxic paint, it can be used on any surface to test for any elements. Another possible use is screening materials for recycling. A backpack model of the device has already been created for environmental workers in the field, who can use it to monitor soil for contaminants. Because the technique depends on laser light, fiber optics can be used to test samples over long distances.

Cremers hopes to develop the device's software so that the computer can automatically analyze a material and print out the results. This way, the laser surface analyzer could be operated by nearly anyone interested in checking a home for the presence of lead.

Bohr's model is incomplete

The Bohr theory of hydrogen was a tremendous success in certain areas because it explained several features of the spectra of hydrogen that had previously defied explanation. Bohr's model gave an expression for the radius of the atom and predicted the energy levels of hydrogen. This model was also successful when applied to hydrogen-like atoms, that is, atoms that contain only one electron. But while many attempts were made to extend the Bohr theory to multi-electron atoms, the results were unsuccessful. Even today, only approximate methods are available for treating multi-electron atoms.

Bohr's model of the atom also raised new questions. For example, Bohr assumed that electrons do not radiate energy when they are in a stable orbit, but his model offered no explanation for this. Also, the model could not explain why electrons always have certain stable orbits, while other orbits are not allowed. Finally, the model seemed transitional because it followed classical physics in certain respects but radically departed from classical physics in other respects. For all of these reasons, Bohr's model was not considered to be a complete picture of the structure of the atom, and scientists continued to search for a new model that would resolve these difficulties.

Section Review

1. Based on the Thomson model of the atom, what did Rutherford expect to happen when he projected positively charged alpha particles against a metal foil?

2. Why did Rutherford conclude that an atom's positive charge and most of its mass are concentrated in the center of the atom?

3. What are two problems with Rutherford's model of the atom?

4. How could the atomic spectra of gases be used to identify the elements present in light from distant stars?

5. Bohr's model of the atom follows classical physics in some respects and quantum mechanics in others. Which assumptions of the Bohr model correspond to classical physics? Which correspond to quantum mechanics?

6. How does Bohr's model of the atom account for the emission and absorption spectra of an element?

7. **Physics in Action** A Norwegian scientist, Lars Vegard, determined the different wavelengths that are part of the northern lights. He found that only a few wavelengths of light, rather than a continuous spectrum, are present in the lights. How does Bohr's model of the atom account for this observation?

23-3
Quantum mechanics

23-3 SECTION OBJECTIVES

- **Recognize the dual nature of light.**

- **Calculate the de Broglie wavelength of matter waves.**

- **Distinguish between classical ideas of measurement and Heisenberg's uncertainty principle.**

- **Describe the quantum-mechanical picture of the atom, including the electron cloud and probability waves.**

THE DUAL NATURE OF LIGHT

As discussed in Section 23-1, there is considerable evidence for the photon theory of light. In this theory, all electromagnetic waves consist of photons, particle-like pulses that have energy and momentum. On the other hand, light and other electromagnetic waves exhibit interference and diffraction effects that are considered to be wave behaviors. The photon theory does not invalidate the evidence that light is a wave, and we do still discuss the frequency and wavelength of electromagnetic waves. So which model is correct? Is light a wave or a particle? The answer depends on the specific phenomenon being observed.

Light is both a wave and a particle

Some experiments can be better explained or only explained by the photon concept, whereas others are best described with a wave model. Most physicists accept both models and believe that the true nature of light is not describable in terms of a single classical picture.

For an example of how photons can be compatible with electromagnetic waves, consider radio waves at a frequency of 2.5 MHz. The energy of a photon having this frequency can be found using Planck's equation, as follows:

$$E = hf = (6.63 \times 10^{-34} \text{ J} \cdot \text{s})(2.5 \times 10^6 \text{ Hz}) = 1.7 \times 10^{-27} \text{ J}$$

From a practical viewpoint, this energy is too small to be detected as a single photon. A sensitive radio receiver might need as many as 10^{10} of these photons to produce a detectable signal. With such a large number of photons reaching the detector every second, we would not be able to detect the individual photons striking the antenna. Thus, the signal would appear as a continuous wave.

Now consider what happens as we go to higher frequencies and hence shorter wavelengths. In the visible region, it is possible to observe both the photon and the wave characteristics of light. As we mentioned earlier, a light beam can show interference phenomena and produce photoelectrons. The interference phenomena are best explained by the wave model of light, while the photoelectrons are best explained by the particle theory of light.

At even higher frequencies and correspondingly shorter wavelengths, the momentum and energy of the photons increase. Consequently, the photon nature of light becomes very evident. In addition, as the wavelength decreases, wave effects, such as interference and diffraction, become more difficult to observe. Very indirect methods are required to detect the wave nature of very high frequency radiation, such as gamma rays.

Thus, all forms of electromagnetic radiation can be described from two points of view. At one extreme, the electromagnetic wave description suits the overall interference pattern formed by a large number of photons. At the other extreme, the particle description is more suitable for dealing with highly energetic photons of very short wavelengths.

MATTER WAVES

In the world around us, we are accustomed to regarding things such as thrown baseballs solely as particles, and things such as sound waves solely as forms of wave motion. As already noted, this rigid distinction cannot be made with light, which has both wave and particle characteristics. In 1924, the French physicist Louis de Broglie (1892–1987) extended the wave-particle duality. In his doctoral dissertation, de Broglie proposed that all forms of matter may have both wave properties and particle properties. At that time, this was a highly revolutionary idea with no experimental support.

The wavelength of a photon is equal to Planck's constant (h) divided by the photon's momentum (p). De Broglie speculated that this relationship might also hold for matter waves, as follows:

WAVELENGTH OF MATTER WAVES

$$\lambda = \frac{h}{p} = \frac{h}{mv}$$

$$\text{de Broglie wavelength} = \frac{\text{Planck's constant}}{\text{momentum}}$$

As seen by this equation, the larger the momentum of an object, the smaller its wavelength. In an analogy with photons, de Broglie postulated that the frequency of a matter wave can be found with Planck's equation.

FREQUENCY OF MATTER WAVES

$$f = \frac{E}{h}$$

$$\text{de Broglie frequency} = \frac{\text{energy}}{\text{Planck's constant}}$$

The dual nature of matter suggested by de Broglie is quite apparent in these two equations, both of which contain particle concepts (E and mv) and wave concepts (λ and f).

Figure 23-18
(a) Electrons show interference patterns similar to **(b)** light waves. This demonstrates that electrons sometimes behave like waves.

De Broglie's proposal that all particles also exhibit wave properties was first regarded as pure speculation. If particles such as electrons had wave properties, then under the correct conditions they should exhibit interference phenomena. Three years after de Broglie's proposal, C. J. Davisson and L. Germer, of the United States, discovered that electrons can be diffracted by a single crystal of nickel. This important discovery provided the first experimental confirmation of the matter waves proposed by de Broglie. An example of electron diffraction compared with light diffraction is shown in **Figure 23-18.**

Electron diffraction by a crystal is possible because the de Broglie wavelength of a low-energy electron is approximately equal to the distance between atoms in a crystal. In principle, diffraction effects should be observable even for objects in our large-scale world. However, the wavelengths of material objects in our everyday world are much smaller than any possible aperture through which the object could pass, as shown below in Sample Problem 23C. This means that we could not observe diffraction effects, and as a result the wave properties of large-scale objects cannot be observed.

SAMPLE PROBLEM 23C

De Broglie waves

PROBLEM

What is the de Broglie wavelength of a 50.0 g rock with a speed of 40.0 m/s?

SOLUTION

Given:

$m = 50.0 \text{ g} = 50.0 \times 10^{-3} \text{ kg}$ $v = 40.0 \text{ m/s}$
$h = 6.63 \times 10^{-34} \text{ J} \cdot \text{s}$

Unknown: $\lambda = ?$

Use the equation for the de Broglie wavelength, given on page 849.

$$\lambda = \frac{h}{mv} = \frac{6.63 \times 10^{-34} \text{ J} \cdot \text{s}}{(50.0 \times 10^{-3} \text{ kg})(40.0 \text{ m/s})}$$

$$\boxed{\lambda = 3.32 \times 10^{-34} \text{ m}}$$

De Broglie waves

1. Calculate the de Broglie wavelength of an electron ($m = 9.109 \times 10^{-31}$ kg) moving at 1.00×10^7 m/s.

2. If the de Broglie wavelength of an electron is equal to 5.00×10^{-7} m, how fast is the electron moving?

3. What is the de Broglie wavelength of a 1375 kg car traveling at 43 km/h?

4. A bacterium moving across a petri dish at 3.5 μm/s has a de Broglie wavelength of 1.9×10^{-13} m. What is the bacterium's mass?

De Broglie waves account for the allowed orbits of Bohr's model

For more than a decade following the publication of Bohr's theory, no one was able to explain why only certain orbits were stable (allowed). Finally, de Broglie recognized a connection between his theory of the wave character of matter and the stable orbits in the Bohr model. De Broglie assumed that an electron orbit would be stable only if it contained an integral (whole) number of electron wavelengths, as shown in **Figure 23-19.** The first orbit contains one wavelength, the second orbit contains two wavelengths, and so on.

De Broglie's hypothesis is analogous to the example of standing waves that can exist on a vibrating string of a given length, as discussed in Chapter 12. (As with all analogies, this one is not perfect. For example, there are no points on the orbits that can be identified as nodes.) In this analogy, the circumference of the electron's orbit corresponds to the length of the string. Thus, the condition for an electron orbit is that the circumference must contain an integral multiple of electron wavelengths.

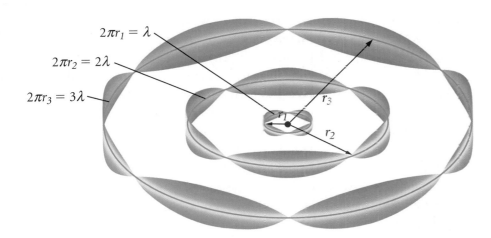

$2\pi r_1 = \lambda$

$2\pi r_2 = 2\lambda$

$2\pi r_3 = 3\lambda$

Figure 23-19
De Broglie's hypothesis that there is always an integral number of electron wavelengths around each circumference explains why only certain orbits are stable.

THE UNCERTAINTY PRINCIPLE

In classical mechanics, there is no limitation to the accuracy of our measurements in experiments. In principle, we could always make a more precise measurement using a more finely detailed meterstick or a stronger magnifier. This unlimited precision does not hold true in quantum mechanics. The absence of such precision is not due to the limitations of our instruments or to our perturbation of the system when we make measurements. It is a fundamental limitation inherent in nature due to the wave nature of particles.

Simultaneous measurements of position and momentum cannot be completely certain

In 1927, Werner Heisenberg argued that *it is fundamentally impossible to make simultaneous measurements of a particle's position and momentum with infinite accuracy.* In fact, the more we learn about a particle's momentum, the less we know of its position, and the reverse is also true. This principle is known as Heisenberg's **uncertainty principle.**

To understand this principle, consider a particle whose wavelength we know *exactly.* According to the de Broglie equation, $\lambda = \dfrac{h}{p}$, we then also know the momentum to infinite accuracy. **Figure 23-20(a)** shows a one-dimensional version of part of such a wave. In reality, this wave would exist throughout space. Notice that any region along this wave is the same as any other region. As a result, there is no particular location along the wave that we might identify with the particle. Thus, we have infinite uncertainty as to the position of the particle; that is, we know nothing about where it is. Perfect knowledge of the particle's momentum has cost us all information about its position.

With a range of wavelengths, a wave packet exists

In comparison, let us consider a particle whose momentum is uncertain. In this case, there is a range of possible values of momentum. According to the de Broglie equation, this situation will result in a range of wavelengths. Thus, the particle is represented not by a single wavelength but by a combination of all wavelengths within this range. Using the principle of superposition, we can imagine some point in space where all of the waves in this range add constructively. As we move away from this point, destructive interference will cause the resultant amplitude to fall. There will generally be destructive interference everywhere in space except in one region, as shown in **Figure 23-20(b).** This region is called a *wave packet.* The particle must be somewhere in the wave packet because there is a distinct difference between this region and the rest of space. Thus, by losing some information about the particle's momentum, we have gained information about its position.

If we were to lose all information about the momentum, then we would be adding together waves of all possible wavelengths. This would result in a wave packet of zero length. Thus, if we knew nothing about the momentum, we would know exactly where the particle is.

uncertainty principle

states that it is impossible to simultaneously measure both the position and momentum of an object with complete certainty

(a)

(b)

Figure 23-20

(a) When there is no uncertainty in the wavelength, the particle could be anywhere in space. **(b)** When there is a range of wavelengths, there is a wave packet in one region in space, and the particle is located somewhere in the packet.

The mathematical form of the uncertainty principle states that the product of the uncertainties in position and momentum will always be larger than some minimum value. Arguments similar to those given here show that this minimum value is Planck's constant (h) divided by 4π.

THE ELECTRON CLOUD

In 1926, Erwin Schrödinger proposed a wave equation that described the manner in which de Broglie's matter waves change in space and time. Although this equation and its derivation are beyond the scope of this book, we will consider Schrödinger's equation qualitatively. Solving Schrödinger's equation yields a quantity called the *wave function*, represented by ψ (Greek letter *psi*). A particle is represented by a wave function, ψ, that depends on the position of the object and time.

An electron's location is described by a probability wave

As discussed earlier, simultaneous measurements of position and momentum cannot be completely certain. Because the electron's location cannot be precisely determined, it is useful to discuss the *probability* of finding the electron at different locations. It turns out that the quantity $|\psi|^2$ is proportional to the probability of finding the electron at a given position. This interpretation of Schrödinger's wave function was first proposed by the German physicist Max Born in 1926.

Figure 23-21 shows the probability of finding the electron at various distances from the nucleus in the ground state of hydrogen. The height of the curve at each point is proportional to the probability of finding the electron, and the x coordinate represents the electron's distance from the nucleus. Note that there is zero probability of finding the electron in the nucleus at this energy level.

The peak of this curve represents the distance from the nucleus at which the electron is most likely to be found in the ground state. Schrödinger's wave equation predicts that this distance is 5.3×10^{-11} m, which is the value of the radius of the first electron orbit in Bohr's model of hydrogen. However, as the curve indicates, there is also a probability of finding the electron at various other distances from the nucleus. In other words, the electron is not confined to a particular orbital distance from the nucleus as is assumed in the Bohr model. The electron may be found at various distances from the nucleus, but the probability of finding it at a distance corresponding to the first Bohr orbit is greater than that of finding it at any other distance. This new model of the atom is consistent with Heisenberg's uncertainty principle, which states that we cannot know the electron's location with complete certainty. Thus, the quantum-mechanical model resolves another difficulty with the Bohr model of hydrogen, which violates the uncertainty principle.

Figure 23-21
The height of this curve is proportional to the probability of finding the electron at different distances from the nucleus in the ground state of hydrogen.

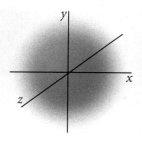

Figure 23-22

This spherical electron cloud for the ground state of hydrogen represents the probability of finding the electron at different locations. The darkest regions are the most probable, and the lightest are the least probable.

Quantum mechanics also predicts that the wave function for the hydrogen atom in the ground state is spherically symmetrical; hence, the electron can be found in a spherical region surrounding the nucleus. This is in contrast to the Bohr theory, which confines the position of the electron to points in a plane. This result is often interpreted by viewing the electron as a cloud surrounding the nucleus, called an *electron cloud,* as represented in **Figure 23-22.** The densest regions of the cloud in the figure represent the locations where the electron is most likely to be found. In this case, the densest region is a sphere, and the distance from any point on the sphere to the nucleus is equal to the first Bohr radius.

Analysis of each of the energy levels of hydrogen reveals that the most probable electron location in each case is in agreement with each of the radii predicted by the Bohr theory. The discrete energy levels that could not be explained by Bohr's theory can be derived from Schrödinger's wave equation, and the de Broglie wavelengths account for the allowed orbits that were unexplainable in Bohr's theory. Thus, the new quantum-mechanical model explains certain aspects of the structure of the atom that Bohr's model could not account for.

Although probability waves and electron clouds cannot be simply visualized as Bohr's planetary model could, they offer a mathematical picture of the atom that is more complete than Bohr's model. The material presented in this chapter is only an introduction to quantum theory. Quantum mechanics has been amazingly successful in calculating the behavior of atoms and is still progressing rapidly today. While most scientists believe that quantum mechanics may be nearly the final picture of the deepest levels of nature, a few continue to search for other explanations, and debates about the implications of quantum mechanics continue.

Section Review

1. Is light considered to be a wave or a particle? Explain your answer.

2. How did de Broglie account for the fact that the electrons in Bohr's model are always found at certain distinct distances from the nucleus?

3. Calculate the de Broglie wavelength of a proton moving at 1.00×10^4 m/s.

4. In classical physics, the accuracy of measurements has always been limited by the measuring instruments used, and no instrument is perfect. How is this limitation different from that formulated by Heisenberg in the uncertainty principle?

5. What is the physical significance of the square of the Schrödinger wave function, $|\psi|^2$?

6. What does the density of an electron cloud represent?

CHAPTER 23
Summary

KEY IDEAS

Section 23-1 Quantization of energy

- Blackbody radiation and the photoelectric effect contradict classical physics, but they can be explained with the assumption that energy comes in discrete units, or is quantized.
- The energy of a light quantum, or photon, depends on the frequency of the light, as follows:

$$E = hf$$

- The minimum energy required for an electron to escape from a metal depends on the threshold frequency of the metal, as follows:

$$\text{work function} = hf_t$$

- The maximum kinetic energy of photoelectrons depends on the work function and the frequency of the light shining on the metal, as follows:

$$KE_{max} = hf - hf_t$$

Section 23-2 Models of the atom

- Rutherford's scattering experiment revealed that all of an atom's positive charge and most of an atom's mass are concentrated at its center.
- Each gas has a unique emission and absorption spectrum.
- Atomic spectra are explained by Bohr's model of the atom, in which electrons move from one energy level to another when they absorb or emit photons.

Section 23-3 Quantum mechanics

- Light has both wave and particle characteristics.
- De Broglie proposed that matter has both wave and particle characteristics.
- The frequency and wavelength of de Broglie waves are found with the following expressions:

$$\lambda = \frac{h}{mv} \text{ and } f = \frac{E}{h}$$

- Simultaneous measurements of position and momentum cannot be completely certain.

KEY TERMS

absorption spectrum (p. 842)

blackbody radiation (p. 830)

Compton shift (p. 838)

emission spectrum (p. 842)

photoelectric effect (p. 834)

photon (p. 835)

ultraviolet catastrophe (p. 831)

uncertainty principle (p. 852)

work function (p. 835)

Variable symbols

Quantities		Units	
E	photon energy	J	joules
		eV	electron volts
f_t	threshold frequency	Hz	hertz
hf_t	work function	eV	electron volts
KE_{max}	maximum kinetic energy	eV	electron volts

CHAPTER 23
Review and Assess

QUANTIZATION OF ENERGY

Review questions

1. Why is the term *ultraviolet catastrophe* used to describe the discrepancy between the predictions of classical physics and the experimental data for blackbody radiation?

2. What is meant by the term *quantum*?

3. What did Planck assume in order to explain the experimental data for blackbody radiation? How did Planck's assumption contradict classical physics?

4. What is the relationship between a joule and an electron volt?

5. According to classical physics, when a light illuminates a photosensitive surface, what should determine whether electrons are ejected from the surface?

6. How do observations of the photoelectric effect conflict with the predictions of classical physics?

7. According to Einstein's photon theory of light, what does the frequency of light shining on a metal determine? What does the intensity of the light determine?

8. What does Compton scattering demonstrate?

Conceptual questions

9. Which has more energy, a photon of ultraviolet radiation or a photon of yellow light?

10. If the photoelectric effect is observed for one metal using light of a certain wavelength, can you conclude that the effect will also be observed for another metal under the same conditions?

11. What effect, if any, would you expect the temperature of a material to have on the ease with which electrons can be ejected from the metal in the photoelectric effect?

12. An X-ray photon is scattered by an electron. Does the frequency of this scattered photon increase, decrease, or stay the same relative to its frequency before being scattered?

13. A photon is deflected by a collision with an electron. Can the photon's wavelength ever become shorter due to the Compton shift? Explain your answer.

Practice problems

14. A quantum of electromagnetic radiation has an energy of 2.0 keV. What is its frequency?
(See Sample Problem 23A.)

15. Calculate the energy in electron volts of a photon having a wavelength in the following ranges:
    a. the microwave range, 5.00 cm
    b. the visible light range, 5.00×10^{-7} m
    c. the X-ray range, 5.00×10^{-8} m
(See Sample Problem 23A.)

16. Light of 1.5×10^{15} Hz illuminates a piece of tin, which has a work function of 4.97 eV.
    a. What is the maximum kinetic energy of the photoelectrons?
    b. What is the threshold frequency of tin?
(See Sample Problem 23B.)

17. Light of wavelength 3.0×10^{-7} m shines on the metals lithium, iron, and mercury, which have work functions of 2.3 eV, 3.9 eV, and 4.5 eV, respectively.
    a. Which of these metals will exhibit the photoelectric effect?
    b. For those metals that do exhibit the photoelectric effect, what is the maximum kinetic energy of the photoelectrons?
(See Sample Problem 23B.)

18. The threshold frequency of silver is 1.14×10^{15} Hz. What is the work function of silver?
(See Sample Problem 23B.)

MODELS OF THE ATOM

Review questions

19. What did Rutherford's foil experiment reveal?

20. If Rutherford's planetary model were correct, atoms would be extremely unstable. Explain why.

21. How is an emission spectrum observed? How is an absorption spectrum observed?

22. How can the absorption spectrum of a gas be used to identify the gas?

23. What restriction does the Bohr model place on the movement of an electron in an atom?

24. How is Bohr's model of the hydrogen atom similar to Rutherford's planetary model? How are the two models different?

25. How does Bohr's model account for atomic spectra?

Conceptual questions

26. Explain why all of the wavelengths in an element's absorption spectrum are also found in that element's emission spectrum.

27. More emission lines than absorption lines are usually observed in the atomic spectra of most elements. Explain why this occurs.

28. Suppose that the electron in the hydrogen atom obeyed classical mechanics rather than quantum mechanics. Why should such a hypothetical atom emit a continuous spectrum rather than the observed line spectrum?

QUANTUM MECHANICS

Review questions

29. Name two situations in which light behaves like a wave and two situations in which light behaves like a particle.

30. What does Heisenberg's uncertainty principle claim?

31. How do de Broglie's matter waves account for the "allowed" electron orbits?

32. Describe the quantum-mechanical model of the atom. How is this model similar to Bohr's model? How are the two different?

Conceptual questions

33. Explain why it is impossible to simultaneously measure the position and momentum of a particle with infinite accuracy.

34. How does Heisenberg's uncertainty principle conflict with the Bohr model of hydrogen?

35. Discuss whether the behavior of an electron is mainly wavelike or particle-like in each of the following situations:
    a. traversing a circular orbit in a magnetic field
    b. absorbing a photon and being photoelectrically ejected from the surface of a metal
    c. forming an interference pattern

36. Use de Broglie's equation to explain why the wave properties of an electron can be observed, while those of a speeding car cannot.

37. An electron and a proton are accelerated from rest through the same potential difference. Which particle has the longer wavelength?

38. Discuss why the term *electron cloud* is used to describe the arrangement of electrons in the quantum-mechanical view of the atom.

Practice problems

39. Calculate the de Broglie wavelength of an electron moving with a speed of 1.4×10^7 m/s. (See Sample Problem 23C.)

40. Calculate the de Broglie wavelength of a 0.15 kg baseball moving at 45 m/s. (See Sample Problem 23C.)

41. What is the speed of a proton with a de Broglie wavelength of 4.00×10^{-14} m? (See Sample Problem 23C.)

42. A mosquito moving at 12 m/s has a de Broglie wavelength of 5.5×10^{-30} m. What is the mass of this mosquito? (See Sample Problem 23C.)

MIXED REVIEW

43. Electrons are ejected from a surface with speeds ranging up to 4.6×10^5 m/s when light with a wavelength of $\lambda = 625$ nm is used.

    a. What is the work function of this surface?

    b. What is the threshold frequency for this surface?

44. What is the de Broglie wavelength of a proton traveling at 1.0×10^7 m/s?

45. A photon of a certain color of visible light has 2.8×10^{-19} J of energy. What color is the light?

46. A light source of wavelength λ illuminates a metal and ejects photoelectrons with a maximum kinetic energy of 1.00 eV. A second light source of wavelength $\frac{1}{2}\lambda$ ejects photoelectrons with a maximum kinetic energy of 4.00 eV. What is the work function of the metal?

Technology & Learning

Graphing calculators

Program your graphing calculator to create a graph of speed versus the de Broglie wavelength of a particle. Use your graph to determine the de Broglie wavelength for the following particles:

a. an electron ($m = 9.109 \times 10^{-31}$ kg) with a speed of 3.00×10^3 m/s

b. the same electron with a speed of 70.0 m/s

c. a neutron ($m = 1.675 \times 10^{-27}$ kg) with a speed of 3.00×10^3 m/s

d. the same neutron with a speed of 70.0 m/s

Press $\boxed{\text{Y=}}$ and $\boxed{\text{CLEAR}}$ to clear any functions. Open a new program by pressing $\boxed{\text{PRGM}}\ \boxed{\blacktriangleright}\ \boxed{\blacktriangleright}\ \boxed{\text{ENTER}}$. Name the program "DEBROGLI" and press $\boxed{\text{ENTER}}$. Then enter the program shown in the table below.

To exit the program editor, press $\boxed{\text{2nd}}\ \boxed{\text{QUIT}}$. To run the program, press $\boxed{\text{PRGM}}$, select "DEBROGLI," and press $\boxed{\text{ENTER}}\ \boxed{\text{ENTER}}$. Enter the value for the mass of the particle in kilograms and press $\boxed{\text{ENTER}}$. (Remember to press $\boxed{\text{2nd}}\ \boxed{\text{EE}}$ and use the $\boxed{\text{(-)}}$ key for entering negative exponents.)

The calculator will provide a graph of the particle's speed versus its wavelength. (If the graph is not visible, press $\boxed{\text{WINDOW}}$, change the settings for the graph window, and press $\boxed{\text{GRAPH}}$.)

Press $\boxed{\text{TRACE}}$, and use the arrow keys to trace along the curve. The x value corresponds to the speed in meters per second, and the y value corresponds to the wavelength in meters.

After you have finished using the graph for one particle, press $\boxed{\text{2nd}}\ \boxed{\text{QUIT}}$ to run the program for the next one.

Keystrokes	Display
	PROGRAM: DEBROGLI
1. $\boxed{\text{PRGM}}\ \boxed{\blacktriangleright}\ \boxed{2}\ \boxed{\text{ALPHA}}\ \boxed{\text{M}}\ \boxed{\text{ENTER}}$	:PROMPT M
2. $\boxed{\text{ALPHA}}\ \boxed{"}\ \boxed{6}\ \boxed{.}\ \boxed{6}\ \boxed{3}\ \boxed{\text{2nd}}\ \boxed{\text{EE}}$ $\boxed{\text{(-)}}\ \boxed{3}\ \boxed{4}\ \boxed{\div}\ \boxed{(}\ \boxed{\text{ALPHA}}\ \boxed{\text{M}}\ \boxed{\text{X,T,θ}}$ $\boxed{)}\ \boxed{\text{ALPHA}}\ \boxed{"}\ \boxed{\text{STO▶}}\ \boxed{\text{2nd}}\ \boxed{\text{Y-VARS}}\ \boxed{1}\ \boxed{1}$ $\boxed{\text{ENTER}}$	:"6.63E ‾34/(MX)" → Y₁
3. $\boxed{\text{PRGM}}\ \boxed{\blacktriangleright}\ \boxed{4}\ \boxed{\text{ENTER}}$	: DISPGRAPH

47. A 0.50 kg mass falls from a height of 3.0 m. If all of the energy of this mass could be converted to visible light of wavelength 5.0×10^{-7} m, how many photons would be produced?

48. Red light ($\lambda = 670.0$ nm) produces photoelectrons from a certain material. Green light ($\lambda = 520.0$ nm) produces photoelectrons from the same material with 1.50 times the previous maximum kinetic energy. What is the material's work function?

49. Find the de Broglie wavelength of a ball with a mass of 0.200 kg just before it strikes the Earth after it has been dropped from a building 50.0 m tall.

50. How many photons are emitted every 1.00 s by a 100.0 W sodium lamp if the wavelength of sodium light is 589.3 nm?

51. From the scattering of sunlight, Thomson found that the classical radius of the electron is 2.82×10^{-15} m. If sunlight with an intensity of 5.00×10^2 W/m^2 falls on a disk with this radius, estimate the time required to accumulate 1.0 eV of energy. Assume that light is a classical wave and that the light striking the disk is completely absorbed. How does your estimate compare with the observation that photoelectrons are emitted within 10^{-9} s?

52. Ultraviolet light is incident normally on the surface of a substance that has a work function of 3.44 eV. The incident light has an intensity of 0.055 W/m^2, and the electrons are photoelectrically emitted with a maximum speed of 5.2×10^5 m/s. How many electrons are emitted from a square centimeter of the surface every 1.0 s? Assume that 100.0 percent of the photons are absorbed.

53. The wave nature of electrons makes an electron microscope, which uses electrons rather than light, possible. The resolving power of any microscope is approximately equal to the wavelength used. A resolution of approximately 1.0×10^{-11} m would be required in order to "see" an atom.

    a. If electrons were used, what minimum kinetic energy of the electrons (in eV) would be required to obtain this degree of resolution?

    b. If photons were used, what minimum photon energy would be required?

Alternative Assessment

Performance assessment

1. Calculate the de Broglie wavelength for an electron, a neutron, a baseball, and your body, at speeds varying from 1.0 m/s to 3.0×10^7 m/s. Organize your findings in a table. The distance between atoms in a crystal is approximately 10^{-10} m. Which wavelengths could produce diffraction patterns using crystal as a diffraction grating? What can you infer about the wave characteristics of large objects? Explain your conclusions.

2. A student claims that any flame that has a blue color must always be hotter than any flame that is yellow. Is this always true? Can the same inference be made when comparing the temperatures of bluish stars and reddish stars? Research the topic to prepare for a classroom debate.

Portfolio projects

3. You have been hired by a children's science museum to prepare an exhibit on solar panels and the way they work. Research the structure, size, efficiency, costs, and limitations of solar panels. Then prepare either a model or a detailed plan for the exhibit.

4. Bohr, Einstein, Planck, and Heisenberg each received the Nobel Prize for their contributions to twentieth-century physics. Their lives were also affected by the extraordinary events of World War II. Research their stories and the ways the war affected their work. What were their opinions about science and politics during and after the war? Write a report about your findings and about the opinions in your groups regarding the involvement and responsibility of scientists in politics.

CHAPTER 23
Laboratory Exercise

OBJECTIVES

- Use a phototube and photoelectric-effect device to observe and measure the photoelectric effect.

- Use the measured value for the stopping voltage to calculate the maximum kinetic energy of the emitted electrons.

MATERIALS LIST

✔ adhesive tape

✔ black construction paper

✔ insulated connecting wire

✔ lens supports

✔ light sources and power supply

✔ meterstick and meterstick supports

✔ multimeter or dc voltmeter

✔ photoelectric effect device with amplifier and filters

✔ wood block

THE PHOTOELECTRIC EFFECT

In this laboratory, you will explore the photoelectric effect.

SAFETY

- **Avoid looking directly at a light source. Looking directly at a light may cause permanent eye damage.**

- **Never close a circuit until it has been approved by your teacher. Never rewire or adjust any element of a closed circuit. Never work with electricity near water; be sure the floor and all work surfaces are dry.**

- **If the pointer on any kind of meter moves off scale, open the circuit immediately by opening the switch.**

PREPARATION

1. Read the entire lab, and plan what measurements you will take.

2. Prepare a data table with thirteen columns and four rows. In the first row, label the columns *Filter*, I_1 *(mA)*, ΔV_1 *(V)*, I_2 *(mA)*, ΔV_2 *(V)*, I_3 *(mA)*, ΔV_3 *(V)*, I_4 *(mA)*, ΔV_4 *(V)*, I_5 *(mA)*, ΔV_5 *(V)*, I_6 *(mA)*, and ΔV_{stop} *(V)*. In the first column, label the second through fourth rows *Blue*, *Green*, and *Red*.

PROCEDURE

Stopping voltage

3. Set up the apparatus as shown in **Figure 23-23.** Connect the voltage meter to measure the potential difference across the photoelectric-effect device. ***Do not turn on the power supply or light source until your teacher approves your setup.***

4. When your teacher has approved your setup, read the current meter on the device. Turn on the power supply. Turn the knob on the power supply until the current meter on the photoelectric device reads 15 mA. Set the zero point by turning the voltage-adjustment knob on the photoelectric-effect device until the applied potential difference is enough to stop the photocurrent. (The current meter will go to the initial reading when the photocurrent is zero.) When you have found this point, adjust the "Zero adjust" until the current meter on the device reads zero.

5. Turn the voltage-adjustment knob counterclockwise until the voltage meter reads zero. Record 0 V as ΔV_1 in your data table. Adjust the power supply until the current meter on the photoelectric-effect device reads about 10 mA. Record this current in your data table as I_1 (mA).

6. Slowly increase the potential difference by turning the voltage-adjustment knob clockwise. When the current is 8.0 mA, record I_2 and ΔV_2 in your data table. Continue to increase the potential difference, and record I and ΔV when the current is 6.0 mA, 4.0 mA, and 2.0 mA.

7. When the current meter reads 0.0 mA, read ΔV. Make sure you find the lowest potential difference at which the current is equal to zero. This value is called the *stopping voltage*. Decrease the potential difference, and repeat to find ΔV when the current goes to zero four more times. Average all five values, and record the current as I_6 and the potential difference as ΔV_{stop} in your data table.

8. Turn the light source off, and replace the blue filter with the green filter. Turn on the light source, and repeat steps 5 through 7 for the green filter. Record all data in your data table.

9. Turn the light source off, and replace the green filter with the red filter. Replace the light source with the second light source. Place the light source close to the red filter. Turn on the light source, and repeat steps 5 through 7.

ANALYSIS AND INTERPRETATION

Calculations and data analysis

1. **Organizing data**   For each trial, calculate the maximum kinetic energy (in eV) of the emitted electrons using the equation $KE_{max} = \Delta V_{stop} \times e$, where ΔV_{stop} is the stopping voltage and $e = 1.60 \times 10^{-19}$ C.

2. **Graphing data**   For each trial, graph the kinetic energy of the electron versus the wavelength of the light source.

Conclusions

3. **Interpreting graphs**   Use your graph to answer the following questions.

   a. What is the relationship between the kinetic energy of the emitted electrons and the wavelength of the light?

   b. What is the wavelength of light at which the kinetic energy is zero?

4. **Evaluating data**   What is the relationship between the stopping voltage and the wavelength of light?

Figure 23-23

Step 4: When the photoelectric-effect device is operating, the current meter will probably not read zero even though there is no photocurrent. Set the meter to zero by starting a photocurrent and applying a potential difference to stop it. When the current meter returns to its original setting, set the meter to zero.

Step 5: Start a photocurrent in the device.

Step 6: Adjust the potential difference to set the photocurrent to different levels.

Physics and Its World *Timeline 1890–1950*

1895 – In Paris, the brothers **Auguste** and **Louis Lumière** show a motion picture to the public for the first time.

1898 Po, Ra

Marie and **Pierre Curie** are the first to isolate the radioactive elements polonium and radium.

1903 – **Wilbur** and **Orville Wright** fly the first successful heavier-than-air craft.

1905

$$E_0 = mc^2$$

Vol. 17 of *Annalen der Physik* contains three extraordinarily original and important papers by **Albert Einstein**. In one paper he introduces his special theory of relativity. In another he presents the quantum theory of light.

1913

$$E_n = \frac{13.6}{n^2}\ \text{eV}$$

Niels Bohr—building on the discoveries of **Ernest Rutherford** and **J. J. Thomson,** and the quantum theories of **Max Planck** and **Albert Einstein**—develops a model of atomic structure based on energy levels that accounts for emission spectra.

1912 – **Henrietta Leavitt** discovers the period-luminosity relation for variable stars, making them among the most accurate and useful objects for determining astronomical distances.

1914 – World War I begins.

1922 – James Joyce's *Ulysses* is published.

1926

$$p = \frac{h}{\lambda}$$

Erwin Schrödinger uses the wave-particle model for light and matter to develop the theory of wave mechanics, which describes atomic systems. About the same time, **Werner Heisenberg** develops a mathematically equivalent theory called quantum mechanics, by which the probability that matter has certain properties is determined.

1929 – The New York Stock Exchange collapses, ushering in a global economic crisis known in the United States as The Great Depression.

1937 – **Pablo Picasso** paints *Guernica* in outraged response to the Nazi bombing of that town during the Spanish Civil War.

1938

$$_{0}^{1}n + _{92}^{235}U \rightarrow _{56}^{141}Ba + _{36}^{92}Kr + 3\,_{0}^{1}n$$

Otto Hahn, Lise Meitner, and **Fritz Strassman** achieve nuclear fission. Early the next year, Meitner and her nephew **Otto Frisch** explain the process and introduce the term *fission* to describe the division of a nucleus into lighter nuclei.

1939 – World War II begins with the Nazi invasion of Poland.

1943

Shin'ichiro Tomonaga develops quantum electrodynamics, which describes the interactions between charged particles and light at the quantum level. The theory is later independently developed by **Richard Feynman** and **Julian Schwinger.**

1948 – **Martin Luther King Jr.** graduates from Morehouse College and enters Crozer Theological Seminary where he becomes acquainted with the principles of **Mohandas Gandhi**. During the next two decades he becomes one of the most forceful and articulate voices in the US civil rights movement.

1920

1930

1940

1950

Physics and Its World 1890–1950   **863**

CHAPTER 24

Modern Electronics

PHYSICS IN ACTION

The wafer shown here is made of purified polycrystalline silicon derived from sand. Although silicon is usually a semiconductor, the addition of a few atoms of an impurity can alter its conductivity dramatically. Careful addition of impurities, along with precise etching, can create tiny integrated circuits with specific electrical characteristics on the wafer's surface. If no flaws are found during the testing process, shown here, the wafer will be cut up into individual chips with a diamond saw and packaged for use in electronic devices.

- *What determines whether a material is a conductor, semiconductor, or insulator?*
- *How can components made of semiconductors be used to control current?*

CONCEPT REVIEW

Work (Section 5-1)

Electric current (Section 19-1)

Conductors, insulators, and semiconductors (Section 17-1)

24-1

Conduction in the solid state

24-1 SECTION OBJECTIVES

- **Distinguish between conductors, insulators, and semiconductors.**

- **Identify valence electrons.**

- **Describe the role of energy bands in electrical conductivity.**

CLASSIFICATION OF SOLIDS

As you learned in Chapter 17, materials can be classified according to their ability to conduct electricity. It is easy for the charge carriers in a good *conductor* to move because the conductor has low resistance, whereas it is difficult for the charge carriers in an *insulator* to move because an insulator has very high resistance. *Semiconductors* exhibit electronic properties between those of insulators and those of conductors.

One of the accomplishments of *solid-state physics* is the development of a theory that uses basic physical principles to explain some of the properties of these three categories of materials. For instance, in one simple model, a solid is represented as a collection of positively charged nuclei surrounded by their associated electrons. If some of the electrons are bound to their nuclei, then the material is an insulator. If the electrons are free to move within the solid and thus carry electrical current, then the material is a conductor.

A more sophisticated model of atoms and solids is needed

This simple model is not very accurate. For instance, it does not explain how a semiconductor differs from an insulator or a conductor. It also does not explain why electrons are sometimes bound and sometimes free or why the ability to conduct electricity differs not only between conductors and insulators but also among conductors and insulators themselves. A better model for the atom is needed as well as a better model for a solid.

Positively charged protons and neutral neutrons are contained in a small, dense nucleus at the center of an atom. The nucleus is surrounded by negatively charged electrons in a series of shells, such as those shown in **Figure 24-1.** As a whole, the atom is uncharged.

Figure 24-1

These are approximate shapes and sizes for the regions of space containing electrons of certain energy levels.

1s

2s

2p

3s

3p

Valence electrons determine an atom's chemical properties

The number of electrons in an atom can range from 1 to more than 100, depending on the type of atom. The complicated arrangement of electrons around the positively charged nucleus can be simplified using a model that groups the electrons into several sets, or shells, each within a space having a specific shape, such as that of a sphere or a dumbbell (see **Figure 24-1**).

In this model, the farther a shell is from the nucleus, the greater the energy of the electrons in the shell. An electron farther from the nucleus has greater energy because at greater distances the electrostatic forces between the electron and the positively charged nucleus decrease and the electron is more loosely bound to the atom.

Because the electrons in the outermost shell, called the **valence electrons,** are the most loosely bound, they are the ones that can interact more strongly with other atoms. As a result, the behavior of an atom's valence electrons determines the chemical properties of the atom. The inner electron shells and the nucleus can be thought of as a single point-charge surrounded by valence electrons.

Electrons occupy energy levels

The electrons in an atom can possess only certain amounts of energy. Because of this, the electrons are often said to occupy specific *energy levels*. Electrons in a shell sometimes form a set of closely spaced energy levels. Normally, electrons are in the lowest energy level available to them. The specific arrangement of electrons in which all are in the lowest possible energy levels of an atom is called the atom's **ground state.**

As described in Chapter 23, an atom can sometimes absorb energy from the environment. If the available energy is sufficient, one of the atom's electrons can move to a higher energy level. When this happens, the atom is said to be in an **excited state.** The electron may also absorb so much energy that it is no longer bound to the atom. The electron is then called a *free electron*.

BAND THEORY

One model that can be used to help understand why solids fall into the three categories of conductor, insulator, and semiconductor is called *band theory*. Band theory can explain the mechanisms of conduction in many solids and the large variation in the electrical conductivity of these materials.

When identical atoms are far apart, they have identical energy-level diagrams and identical wave functions. As the atoms are brought closer together, their wave functions overlap. Because no two electrons in the same system can occupy the same state, the energy level in an atom is altered by the influence of the electric field of another atom. In the case of two atoms, each given energy

CONCEPT PREVIEW

The structure within the nucleus will be studied in greater detail in Chapter 25.

valence electron

an electron in the outermost shell of an atom

ground state

the lowest energy state of a quantized system

excited state

the state of an atom that is no longer in its ground state

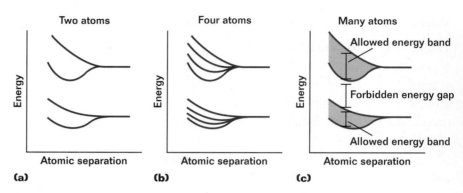

Figure 24-2

Energy levels split when two atoms are close together **(a).** Adding a few more nearby atoms causes further splitting **(b).** When many atoms interact, the energy levels are so closely spaced that they can be represented as energy bands **(c).**

level splits into two different energy levels. **Figure 24-2** shows the splitting of two energy levels as two atoms get closer. Notice that the energy difference between two new energy levels depends on the distance between the atoms.

When more atoms are brought close together, each energy level splits into more levels. The number of splittings depends on the number of interacting particles. If there are many atoms, the energy level splits so many times and the new energy levels are so closely spaced that they may be regarded as a continuous band of energies.

When atoms are close to each other, some energy levels become energy bands

When atoms are bound together in a solid, the clearly defined energy levels of a single atom widen and blur into *energy bands,* like those shown in **Figure 24-3.**

The most important energy band is the highest band containing occupied energy levels, known as the *valence band.* In solids that are semiconductors and insulators, electrons do not contribute to the solid's electrical conductivity while they are in the valence band. In solids that are conductors, the valence electrons are able to conduct electricity.

There can be many more bands of lower energy than the valence band, but these bands are completely filled and are of little consequence in determining the electrical properties of the solid.

There are additional unoccupied bands of higher energy besides the valence band. In semiconductors and insulators, the band immediately above the valence band is called the *conduction band.* If an atom is excited, valence electrons can sometimes move to this higher energy level. Then they can contribute to the conduction of electricity, as we will see.

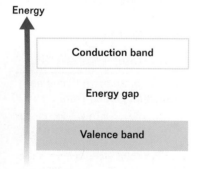

Figure 24-3

Energy levels of atoms become energy bands in solids. The valence band is the highest occupied band.

band gap

the minimum energy separation between the highest occupied state and the lowest empty state

There is often an energy gap between bands

The range of energies lying between the valence band and the conduction band is called the **band gap,** or *energy gap,* as shown in **Figure 24-3.** An electron in an insulator or semiconductor cannot have a value for its energy that would lie within the energy gap. Because these energies are not available for an electron in the insulator or semiconductor, they are often referred to collectively as "the forbidden energy gap."

The size of the energy gap differs with different materials, resulting in different properties. In an insulator, the gap is so large that it is unlikely an electron could ever gain enough energy to move from the valence band to the conduction band. In a semiconductor, the gap is somewhat smaller, making it more likely that an electron could move to the conduction band. In a conductor, the valence band is only partially filled, so there is essentially no gap between filled levels and available unoccupied levels.

A band can be full or partially full

Electrons in a solid normally occupy the lowest available energy levels within an atom. However, no two electrons can occupy the same energy level, so not all of them can occupy the lowest energy level. As electrons fill the energy levels of an atom, they occupy the lowest levels first. Normally there are no electrons in higher energy levels of an atom unless all of the lower energy levels are completely filled.

In a solid, if there are more electrons than there are energy levels in the lowest energy band, then the lowest energy band is full. Because no more electrons can move into an already full band, any additional electrons must occupy energy levels in the next higher band.

In some materials, there are more energy levels in a band than there are electrons to fill them. In such cases, the band remains partially full. Whether the highest energy band is completely full or only partially full is important in determining the electrical properties of a material.

Electrons can move between energy levels in a solid

Recall from Chapter 23 that when an electron in an atom absorbs energy, it can be excited to a higher energy level. However, the electron can absorb only certain amounts of energy that correspond to the differences in energy between the energy levels in the atom.

A similar process can occur in a solid. Electrons that absorb energy can be excited to higher energy levels. An electron must be given sufficient energy to occupy some higher available energy level.

Figure 24-4 is a schematic diagram showing the three highest bands in a solid with an energy gap between each band. Remember that these bands really consist of closely spaced energy levels. All of the energy levels in the bottom two bands are filled with electrons.

What transitions are possible for an electron in this solid? Because the only unfilled energy levels are in the conduction band, only the transitions represented by **(a)** and **(b)** are possible. However, transition **(a)** occurs much more easily than transition **(b)** does because transition **(a)** requires less energy. That is why the bands below the valence band do not appreciably affect the electrical properties of a material; the energy required for an electron in one of these low-lying bands to be excited into a higher unfilled energy level is usually too large.

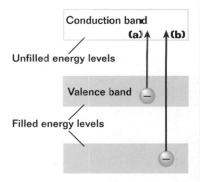

Figure 24-4
Only transitions into unfilled energy levels, such as those represented by **(a)** and **(b)**, are possible for electrons in a solid. However, transition **(b)** requires such a large amount of energy that it does not easily occur.

CONDUCTION AND ELECTRON TRANSITIONS

So far, we have considered the band structure of a solid and the way an electron can make transitions between the energy levels within or between these bands. These transitions do not represent a physical motion of the electrons. Rather, they represent changes in the energy of electrons.

The physical motion of electrons in a solid—the conduction of electricity—depends on the arrangement of the electrons in the bands of the solid because a moving electron requires an unfilled final energy level to move to.

Bound electrons need energy to escape the electrostatic forces that bind them to an individual atom. Electrons can be excited into higher energy levels by either of two important mechanisms: the application of an electric field or thermal excitation.

When an electric field is applied to a solid, the electric field does work on individual electrons, giving them enough energy to move to higher energy levels within the atom.

The absorption of thermal energy can also excite electrons in a solid. The atoms in a solid undergo random vibrations (thermal energy) that can occasionally transfer enough energy to an electron to excite it to a higher energy level. At room temperature, a few electrons near the unfilled energy levels are excited to unoccupied levels. The thermal energy available for this is very small, so only the uppermost electrons can move across the band gap.

A conductor has a partially filled valence band

If the valence band overlaps the conduction band, the solid is a *conductor*. For example, **Figure 24-5(a)** shows a valence band that is also the conduction band. The band is actually partly filled. The uppermost filled energy level lies in the middle of the band. If energy is added, electrons can be excited from filled energy levels to one of many higher unfilled energy levels.

A solid conductor has many electrons that require only a small amount of energy—either from the applied field or by thermal excitation—to be moved into nearby unfilled energy levels. These electrons are then able to move freely in the conductor with only a small applied field. An important feature of a conductor is the partially filled conduction band. The rest of a conductor's band structure, including the size of the energy gaps, is of little importance.

An insulator has a full valence band and a large energy gap

An *insulator* has an empty conduction band and a full valence band, as shown in **Figure 24-5(b).** It also has a very large energy gap (about 5–10 eV) between the conduction band and the valence band. In fact, the energy gap is so large that it is difficult for an electron to gain enough energy to be excited into the conduction band.

(a) Conductor

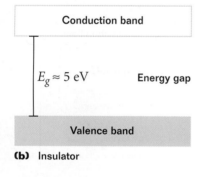

$E_g \approx 5$ eV   Energy gap

(b) Insulator

$E_g \approx 1$ eV   Energy gap

(c) Semiconductor

Figure 24-5

A conductor **(a)** has a partially filled valence band. Insulators **(b)** and semiconductors **(c)** have empty conduction bands and filled valence bands, but the energy gap in a semiconductor is smaller than it is in an insulator.

For example, at room temperature, thermal excitations typically give electrons about 0.025 eV, which is much smaller than the energy gap. At such a temperature, very few electrons are thermally excited into the conduction band. Thus, although an insulator has many vacant states in its conduction band, there are so few electrons occupying these states that the overall electrical conductivity is very small, resulting in the high resistance typical of substances that are insulators.

A semiconductor has a full valence band and a small energy gap

Intermediate between a conductor and an insulator is a *semiconductor*. The valence band of a semiconductor, like that of an insulator, is full, as shown in **Figure 24-5(c).** However, the energy gap in a semiconductor is much smaller than in an insulator (about 1 eV). In fact, the energy gap in many semiconductors is small enough for electrons to be thermally excited into the conduction band rather easily. Thus, the conductivity of many semiconductors is strongly dependent on temperature.

For example, at temperatures near 0 K, most electrons are in the valence band and there is little thermal energy available for excitation. This makes semiconductors poor conductors at very low temperatures. At higher temperatures, however, an appreciable number of electrons can be thermally excited from the valence band to the conduction band, which has many empty energy levels. Because thermal excitation across the narrow gap is more probable at higher temperatures, the conductivity of semiconductors improves rapidly with temperature. The application of an electric field to a semiconductor also does work on electrons, increasing their energy so that they can conduct and create a current.

Section Review

1. The resistance of conductors increases with increasing temperature, as described in Chapter 19. On the other hand, the resistance of a semiconductor decreases with increasing temperature. How can you explain this property of semiconductors?

2. Which of the following is likely to be a valence electron?
   a. the innermost electron of a uranium atom
   b. an electron in a calcium atom that is in the outermost energy level
   c. an electron in a bromine atom that is in the second-most outer energy level of the atom

3. Which band contains energy levels for electrons that are already free to move about within a semiconductor? Which band contains energy levels for electrons that cannot move within a semiconductor?

24-2
Semiconductor applications

hole

an energy level that is not occupied by an electron in a semiconductor

Figure 24-6

An electric field can excite valence electrons into the conduction band, where they are free to move through the material. Holes in the valence band can then move in the opposite direction.

SEMICONDUCTOR DOPING

Charge carriers in a semiconductor can be negative or positive. To see why this is so, consider the valence and conduction bands of a semiconductor, as shown in **Figure 24-6.** Imagine that a few electrons are excited from the valence band to the conduction band by an electric field. The electrons in the conduction band are free to move through the material. Normally, electrons in the valence band are unable to move because all nearby energy levels are occupied. But when an electron moves from the valence band into the conduction band, it leaves a vacancy, or **hole,** in an otherwise filled valence band. Because this hole creates an empty energy level in the valence band, another valence electron from this or a nearby atom is free to move into the hole. Whenever an electron does so, a new hole is created at its former location. Thus, the net effect can be viewed as a hole migrating through the material in a direction opposite the motion of the electrons in the conduction band.

In a material containing only one element or compound, there are an equal number of conduction electrons and holes. Such combinations of charges are called *electron-hole pairs,* and a semiconductor that contains such pairs is called an *intrinsic semiconductor.* **Figure 24-6** is a schematic of an intrinsic semiconductor. In the presence of an electric field, the holes move in the direction of the field and the conduction electrons move opposite the field. Keep in mind that the motion of holes is always in the direction opposite the motion of the electrons.

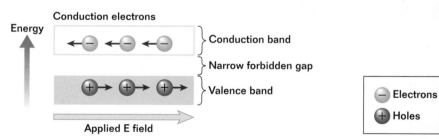

Doping adds impurities that enhance conduction

In the last section, it was explained that the concentration (the number per unit volume) of charge carriers in a semiconductor depends on temperature. Another way to change the concentration of charge carriers is to add *impurities,* atoms that are different from those of an intrinsic semiconductor.

The addition of just a few impurity atoms, a process called **doping,** can have a large effect on the resistance of a semiconductor. The conductivity of a semiconductor increases as the doping level increases. When conduction is dominated by impurities, the material is called an *extrinsic semiconductor.*

There are two methods for doping a semiconductor: either add impurities that have extra valence electrons or add impurities that have fewer valence electrons compared with the atoms in the intrinsic semiconductor.

Semiconductors used in commercial devices are usually doped silicon or germanium. These elements have four valence electrons. Semiconductors are doped by replacing an atom of silicon or germanium with one containing either three valence electrons or five valence electrons. Note that a doped semiconductor is electrically neutral because it is made of neutral atoms. The semiconductor atoms and the impurity atoms remain uncharged as before. The balance of positive and negative charges has not changed, but the number of charges that are free and able to move has, and these charges are therefore able to participate in electrical conduction.

doping

the addition of impurity atoms to a semiconductor

An n-type semiconductor has electrons as majority carriers

In **Figure 24-7(a),** an atom containing five valence electrons, such as arsenic, is added to a semiconductor. Four of the valence electrons participate in the bonding between neighboring atoms. One electron is left over. Such an impurity in effect donates an extra electron to the solid, so it is referred to as a *donor atom.* The impurity alters the band structure of the solid so that the extra electron occupies an energy level, or donor level, that lies just below the conduction band, as shown in **Figure 24-7(b).**

Because the energy spacings between donor levels and the bottom of the conduction band are very small (typically about 0.05 eV), only a small amount of thermal energy is needed to cause an electron in these donor levels to move into the conduction band. Semiconductors doped with donor atoms are called *n-type semiconductors* because most of the charge carriers are electrons with negative charges. Positive holes that form in the donor level do not move very easily.

Did you know?

The average thermal energy of an electron at room temperature (22°C) is about 0.025 eV.

(a)

(b)

$E_g = 1$ eV
$E_d \approx 0.05$ eV

Figure 24-7
An n-type semiconductor is doped with impurity atoms that have extra valence electrons.

Semiconductor atoms

Impurity atom with three valence electrons

Hole, or electron deficiency in a bond

Figure 24-8

A p-type semiconductor is doped with impurity atoms having fewer valence electrons.

(a)

(b)

Conduction band

E_g

Acceptor levels

E_a

Valence band

$E_g = 1 \text{ eV}$
$E_a \approx 0.05 \text{ eV}$

A p-type semiconductor has holes as majority carriers

If a semiconductor is doped with atoms containing three valence electrons, such as indium and aluminum, all three of these electrons form bonds with the neighboring atoms in the p-type semiconductor. This leaves an electron deficiency, or hole, in the fourth bond, as shown in **Figure 24-8(a).** The energy levels, or acceptor levels, of such impurities lie just above the valence band, as shown in **Figure 24-8(b).**

Electrons from the valence band have enough thermal energy at room temperature to fill these impurity levels, leaving a hole in the valence band. These holes can be filled by other nearby electrons, which leave new holes. Thus, positive charges (holes) can move throughout the material even if no electrons are in the conduction band.

Because such an impurity accepts an electron from the valence band, these impurities are referred to as *acceptors.* A semiconductor containing acceptors is known as a *p-type semiconductor* because the majority of the charge carriers are positively charged holes.

DIODES

diode

an electronic device that allows electric current to pass more easily in one direction than in the other

A **diode** is a device that has an almost infinite resistance in one direction and nearly zero resistance in the other direction. Thus, a diode is able to pass current in only one direction, similar to the way a one-way valve passes water into a pipeline. A diode used in this manner is called a *rectifier.* **Figure 24-9** shows the electrical circuit symbol for a diode. The arrow that is a part of the circuit symbol for the diode indicates the direction of the current in the diode under most situations.

The p-n junction is the contact between a p-type semiconductor and an n-type semiconductor

Consider what happens when a p-type semiconductor is joined to an n-type semiconductor to form a *p-n junction.* A device having one p-n junction can be used as a diode in electrical circuits. It will allow current to pass through the circuit in only one direction. This is because holes and electrons on either

Figure 24-9

The circuit diagram symbol for a diode indicates that it allows electric current in one direction only.

side of the p-n junction can migrate across the junction. In doing so, they create a potential barrier (an internal electric field) that allows charge to flow one way and not the other. Let us examine this effect in more detail.

Remember that an n-type semiconductor has free electrons and a p-type semiconductor has free holes. When an n-type semiconductor and a p-type semiconductor are brought together to form a p-n junction, these free positive and negative charges move because of thermal diffusion. Electrons from the n side nearest the junction, the blue area in **Figure 24-10(a),** diffuse toward the p side, leaving behind positive ions that are fixed in the solid. Similarly, on the p side nearest the junction, electrons diffuse so that holes move to the n side, leaving a region of fixed negative ions. When a free-moving electron and a free-moving hole meet, the charges cancel each other, leaving no charge carriers. As a result, the region where the p-type and the n-type semiconductors meet has no mobile charge carriers. For this reason, it is called a *depletion region*. The depletion region has a fixed size because the presence of the ions in it creates an internal electric field that opposes the further diffusion of electrons and holes that would cause the region to grow larger. This internal electric field is directed from right to left in **Figure 24-10(a).**

On either side of the depletion region are the p-type and n-type regions. Thus, the p-n junction in a diode consists of three distinct regions, as shown in **Figure 24-10(a).**

Figure 24-10

Diffusion of charge carriers across a p-n junction sets up an electric field within the depletion region.

Diodes allow movement of charge in only one direction

The different regions of the diode can be understood in terms of the electric potential diagram in **Figure 24-10(b).** Because of the electric field within the depletion region, one side of the junction is held at a higher electric potential than the other side is. Positive charge carriers cannot move from left to right because that would require extra energy, $q \cdot \Delta V_0$ (see Chapter 18), to overcome the internal electric field in the depletion region. For the same reason, negative charge carriers cannot move from right to left.

The extra energy needed to move negative charge carriers from right to left can be supplied by an external source of potential difference. If a large enough positive external voltage is applied to the p side of the junction, the electric potential on the left (positive) side is raised relative to the right (negative) side. Because the left side is now at a higher potential than the right side, charges will move, creating a current. When a diode is connected to an external source of potential difference in this manner, it is said to be *forward biased*. When a positive external voltage is applied to the n side of the junction, however, the potential barrier is increased even more, further limiting the current in the junction. Such a diode is said to be *reverse biased*.

Figure 24-11

The slope at any point on this curve is equal to the reciprocal of the resistance of the diode at that voltage and current.

Figure 24-11 shows a typical plot of the current across a diode versus the potential difference in the diode. Notice that a diode does not obey Ohm's law (see Chapter 19). Ohm's law predicts that a plot of current versus potential difference will be a straight line with a slope equal to the reciprocal of the resistance. The resistance of a diode, on the other hand, is not constant. When the diode is reverse biased, the curve is nearly horizontal, which implies that the resistance is effectively infinite. (The fact that the current is slightly negative means that, in reality, a small *leakage current* still flows in the "wrong" direction in a reverse-biased diode. Because the leakage current is typically very small, we will ignore its presence.) When the diode is forward biased, the resistance varies, approaching zero for larger currents. Note that the maximum potential difference across the diode under forward bias is small (about 0.5–0.8 V).

Diodes can be used to convert alternating current to direct current

Figure 24-12 shows the effect of a diode on an applied alternating potential difference. **Figure 24-12(a)** is the current produced by the generator without the diode, and **Figure 24-12(b)** is the current in the resistor with the diode in place. Only the positive part of the current remains because the diode is forward biased at these times and therefore has very little resistance. When the diode is reverse biased, it has a very large resistance. In this case, the negative part of the original signal is suppressed by the diode, so there is no current in the resistor from this part of the signal. This process of converting an alternating current into a direct current is called *rectification*. When a single diode is used as a rectifier, the direct current is not constant; instead, it occurs in pulses. This is referred to as a *pulsed direct current*.

A smoother direct current can be made from the alternating current if more than one diode and some capacitors are included in the rectifier circuit. An additional diode allows more pulses of direct current between the times of the pulses allowed by the first diode, as shown in **Figure 24-12(c).** The capacitor acts as a *filter* that smooths the output of the rectifier. Because capacitors store charge when a potential difference is applied and release it when there is no potential difference, they keep the current in the circuit steadier, as shown in **Figure 24-12(d).**

Figure 24-12

The diode rectifies an alternating current **(a)** into a pulsed direct current **(b).** With the addition of other diodes, more pulses can be added to the signal **(c).** Capacitors can act as filters that smooth out the variations in current **(d).**

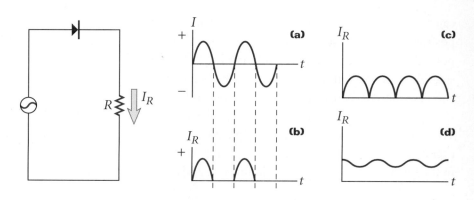

TRANSISTORS

A **transistor** is a more complicated electronic device that is used in many applications. Transistors have two p-n junctions instead of one. In this section, we will see how a transistor can be used to amplify a signal. This property of a transistor arises from the nature of the p-n junction.

There are many types of transistors, but the type we are concerned with is the *junction transistor*. The junction transistor shown in **Figure 24-13(a)** consists of a semiconducting material with a very narrow n region sandwiched between two p regions. This configuration is called a *pnp transistor*. Another configuration is the *npn transistor*, which consists of a p region sandwiched between two n regions. Because the operation of the two transistors is essentially the same, we will describe only the pnp transistor.

The structure of the pnp transistor, together with its circuit symbol, is shown in **Figure 24-13.** The arrow on the emitter lead in **Figure 24-13(b)** is necessary to distinguish a pnp transistor from an npn transistor. In an npn transistor, the arrow points in the opposite direction. The outer regions are called the *emitter* and *collector*, and the narrow central region is called the *base*. Notice that the junction transistor contains two p-n junctions: the emitter-base junction and the collector-base junction. Usually, the emitter is more heavily doped than the base, so there are more charge carriers in the emitter compared with what would be found in the base. The transistor, unlike most electrical components you have encountered, has three leads instead of two.

Setting the reference voltage is important for transistor operation

One potential difference (ΔV_{ec}) is applied between the emitter and the collector so that the emitter is at a higher electric potential than the collector, as shown at point A in **Figure 24-14.** The base is held at an electric potential between the emitter potential and the collector potential by the potential difference at point B (ΔV_{eb}). Remember from our discussion of diodes that if the

a device, typically containing three terminals, that can amplify a signal

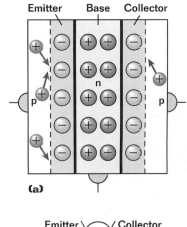

(a)

Emitter \\ / Collector

(b) | Base

Figure 24-13
(a) A pnp junction transistor consists of an n-type semiconductor sandwiched between two p-type semiconductors. **(b)** The circuit symbol for a transistor has three leads.

Figure 24-14
Two batteries are necessary to properly bias this transistor.

p region is at a higher electric potential than the n region across a p-n junction, the p-n junction is forward biased. If we think of the transistor as two diodes back to back, we see that the emitter-base junction is forward biased and that the base-collector junction is reverse biased. This particular biasing of the two junctions in a transistor is crucial for its proper operation.

The junction transistor can be used as an amplifier

Now we can see how a transistor can amplify a signal. First consider the emitter-base junction. It is forward biased so that current enters the transistor through the emitter terminal and charge readily flows across the emitter-base junction. Because the emitter is heavily doped relative to the base, nearly all of the current consists of holes moving from the p-type emitter to the base. Few electrons move from the base to the emitter. In addition, most of the holes do not recombine with electrons in the base because the base is very narrow.

Although only a small number of holes recombine in the base, those that do recombine limit the current that can go from the emitter to the collector through the base. This is because positive charge carriers accumulate in the base and prevent holes from flowing in.

Once the surviving holes diffuse through the base, they encounter the base-collector junction. This junction is reverse biased, so normally there is no current in this region. The base-collector barrier with its depletion region prevents electrons from migrating to the right and prevents holes from migrating to the left. In this case, however, the holes are on the n side of the junction, where the charge carriers are usually electrons. So the barrier has an opposite effect on holes migrating to the right; the holes are accelerated across the reverse-biased base-collector junction.

A small change in the properties of the base can have a great effect on the movement of charge from the emitter to the collector. One way to cause such a change is to connect the base to a second source of potential difference, labeled ΔV_{eb}, as shown at B in **Figure 24-14.** The current from this source, although small, draws some of the positive charge that would otherwise accumulate in the base, allowing more charge to pass through the base from the emitter to the collector. The small voltage to be amplified is placed in series with this battery. The input signal produces a small variation in the base current, resulting in a large change in collector current and hence a large change in potential difference across the output resistor.

If the transistor is properly biased, the collector (output) current is directly proportional to the base (input) current and the transistor acts as a current amplifier. This condition may be written as follows:

$$I_c = \beta I_b$$

The quantity β (beta) is called the *current gain*. Values of the current gain typically range from 10 to 100.

INTEGRATED CIRCUITS

The integrated circuit has been called the "most remarkable technology ever created by mankind." Integrated circuits form the foundation for computers, watches, cameras, automobiles, aircraft, robots, space vehicles, and all sorts of communication and switching networks.

In simplest terms, an integrated circuit is a collection of interconnected transistors, diodes, resistors, and capacitors fabricated onto a single piece of silicon, known as a *chip*. State-of-the-art chips easily contain several hundred thousand components in a very small area, as shown in **Figure 24-15.**

Integrated circuits were invented partly in an effort to achieve circuit miniaturization and partly to solve the interconnection problem spawned by the transistor. Before transistors, power and size considerations of individual components set modest limits on the number of components that could be interconnected in a given circuit. With the advent of the tiny, low-power, highly reliable transistor, design limits on the number of components disappeared and were replaced with the problem of wiring together hundreds of thousands of components. **Figure 24-16** shows a schematic diagram of one of the first types of integrated circuits, an operational amplifier.

Operational amplifiers, or *op amps,* are used extensively in electronics and computers. They are the basic element used to perform key mathematical operations, such as addition and multiplication. The numbers involved in the operation are the values of the input and output potential differences.

For example, in one configuration, a single input into an op-amp results in a single output. The magnitude of the potential difference of the output will be the magnitude of the potential difference of the input multiplied by the gain for the device.

In another configuration, several potential differences are connected as inputs to an op-amp, resulting in a single output that has a potential difference with a magnitude that is the sum of the magnitudes of the individual input potential differences.

Figure 24-15
Although it is smaller than a dime, this computer memory chip can store more than 1 million digital bits of information.

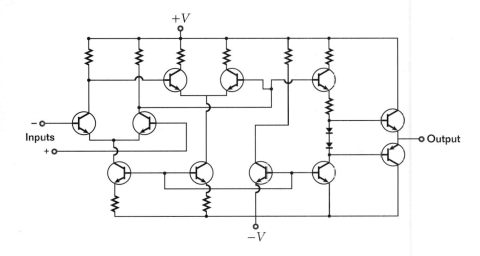

Figure 24-16
This is a simplified schematic diagram of an operational amplifier, one of the first types of integrated circuits. Notice the many resistors, diodes, transistors, and interconnections that make up the circuit.

In addition to solving the interconnection problem, integrated circuits have the advantages of miniaturization and fast response, two features that are critical for high-speed computer operation. The fast response results from the miniaturization and close packing of components. The response time of a circuit depends on the time it takes for electrical signals traveling at about 0.3 m/ns to pass from one component to another. This time is reduced by the closer packing of components. These advances, along with new parallel arrangements of processors that allow a computer to break difficult calculations into many pieces, have continued, and computers are getting smaller and faster every day. In 1997, a computer at Sandia National Laboratories became the first to perform more than 1 trillion calculations per second.

Section Review

1. Which of the following are equivalent to a conventional current from left to right?
   a. electrons traveling from left to right
   b. electrons traveling from right to left
   c. holes traveling from left to right
   d. holes traveling from right to left

2. Explain why it is not necessary for an n-type semiconductor to be negatively charged.

3. What type of fixed charge is predominant in the depletion region of a p-type semiconductor at a p-n junction?

4. A diode is connected to a source of alternating current. The current in the source fluctuates between −1.0 mA and 1.0 mA. What will be the range for the rectified current?

5. The current in the base terminal of a transistor is decreased. How will this affect the output current in the collector terminal?

6. Transistors are widely used as amplifiers in radio receivers as well as in microphones. This is because a typical radio signal from an antenna has only a few microamperes of current and a speaker often requires a current of about 0.1 A to work properly.
   a. If a transistor circuit is used to amplify a 2.5 μA signal to at least 0.1 A, what must be the minimum gain of the transistor circuit?
   b. Assume the amplifier consists of a number of transistors in series, each with a gain of 10. How many transistors are needed in this circuit? (Hint: Two such transistors in series would provide a total gain of $10 \times 10 = 100$.)

TEMPERATURE AND CONDUCTIVITY

Recall from Chapter 19 that the resistance of many solids (other than semiconductors) increases with increasing temperature. This is because at a nonzero temperature, the atoms in a solid are always vibrating, and the higher the temperature, the larger the amplitude of the vibrations. It is more difficult for electrons to move through the solid when the atoms are moving with large amplitudes. This is similar to walking through a crowded room. It is much harder to do so when the people are in motion than when they are standing still.

If the resistance depended only on atomic vibrations, we would expect the resistance of the material that is cooled to absolute zero to go gradually to zero as the superconductivity described in Chapter 19 began to occur. Experiments have shown, however, that this does not happen. In fact, the resistances of very cold solids behave in two very different ways—either the substance suddenly begins superconducting at temperatures above absolute zero or it never superconducts, no matter how cold it gets.

Lattice imperfections cause resistance in some materials

The graph in **Figure 24-17** shows the temperature dependence of the resistance of two similar objects, one made of silver and the other made of tin. The temperature dependence of the resistance of the silver object is similar to that of a typical metal. At higher temperatures, the resistance decreases as the metal is cooled. This suggests that the amplitude of the lattice vibrations is decreasing, as expected. But at a temperature of about 10 K, the curve levels off and the resistance is constant. Cooling the metal further does not appreciably lower the resistance, even though the vibrations of the metal's atoms have been lessened.

Part of the cause of this nonzero resistance, even at absolute zero, is *lattice imperfection*. The regular, geometric pattern of the crystal, or lattice, in a solid is often flawed. A lattice imperfection occurs when some of the atoms do not line up perfectly.

Imagine you are walking through a crowded room in which the people are standing in perfect rows. It would be easy to walk through the room between two rows. Now imagine that occasionally one person stands in the middle of the aisle instead of in the row, making it harder for you to pass. This is similar to the effect of a lattice imperfection. Even in the absence of thermal vibrations, many materials exhibit a *residual resistance* due to the imperfect geometric arrangement of their atoms.

Figure 24-17

The resistance of silver exhibits the behavior of a normal metal. The resistance of tin goes to zero at temperature T_c, the temperature at which tin becomes a superconductor.

Figure 24-17 shows that the resistance of tin goes to zero below a certain temperature that is well above absolute zero. A solid whose resistance is zero below a certain nonzero temperature is called a *superconductor,* and the temperature at which the resistance goes to zero is the critical temperature of the superconductor, as described in Chapter 19.

BCS THEORY

Before the discovery of superconductivity, it was thought that all materials should have some nonzero resistance due to lattice vibrations and lattice imperfections, much like the behavior of the silver in **Figure 24-17.**

The first complete microscopic theory of superconductivity was not developed until 1957, almost half a century after the discovery of superconductivity. This theory is called *BCS theory* after the three scientists who first developed it: John Bardeen, Leon Cooper, and Robert Schrieffer. The crucial breakthrough of BCS theory is a new understanding of the special way that electrons traveling in pairs move through the lattice of a superconductor. According to BCS theory, electrons do suffer collisions in a superconductor, just like they do in any other material, but the collisions do not alter the total momentum of the pair of electrons. The net effect is as if the electrons moved unimpeded through the lattice.

Imagine an electron moving through a lattice, such as Electron 1 in **Figure 24-18.** There is an attractive force between the electron and the nearby positively charged atoms in the lattice. As the electron passes by, the attractive force causes the lattice atoms to be pulled toward the electron, resulting in a concentration of positive charge near the electron. If a second electron is nearby, it can be attracted to this excess positive charge in the lattice before the lattice has had a chance to return to its equilibrium position.

Through the process of deforming the lattice, the first electron gives up some of its momentum. The deformed region of the lattice attracts the second electron, transferring excess momentum to the second electron. The net effect of this two-step process is a weak, delayed attractive force between the two electrons, resulting from the motion of the lattice as it is deformed by the first electron. The attractive force between these two electrons is an electron-lattice-electron interaction, where the lattice serves as the mediator of the attractive force. The two electrons travel through the lattice acting like a single particle. This particle is called a *Cooper pair.* In BCS theory, Cooper pairs are responsible for superconductivity.

The reason superconductivity has been found at only low temperatures so far is that Cooper pairs are weakly bound. Random thermal motions in the lattice tend to destroy the bonds between Cooper pairs. Even at very low temperatures, Cooper pairs are constantly being formed, destroyed, and reformed in a superconducting material, usually with different pairings of electrons.

Figure 24-18
The first electron deforms the lattice, and the deformation affects the second electron. The net result is as if the two electrons were loosely bound together. Such a two-electron bound state is called a *Cooper pair.*

Cooper pairs maintain their momentum as they move through the lattice

Calculations of the properties of a Cooper pair have shown that this peculiar bound state of two electrons has zero total momentum in the absence of an applied electric field. When an external electric field is applied, the Cooper pairs move through the lattice under the influence of the field. However, the center of mass for every Cooper pair has exactly the same momentum. This is the crucial feature of Cooper pairs that explains superconductivity. If one electron scatters, the other electron in a pair also scatters in a way that keeps the total momentum constant. The net result is that scattering due to lattice imperfections and lattice vibrations has no net effect on Cooper pairs.

APPLICATIONS OF SUPERCONDUCTIVITY

Notice in **Table 19-2,** on page 706, that in order to be superconducting, many materials have to be cooled to very close to absolute zero. This makes the use of these superconductors for everyday applications difficult because it is expensive to cool a material to such low temperatures. In fact, early superconductors required coolant baths of either liquefied helium, which is rare and expensive, or liquid hydrogen, which is very explosive.

As shown in **Table 19-2,** a new class of materials has been found that superconducts at much higher temperatures. In particular, such high-T_c superconductors can enter the superconducting state at temperatures above 77 K, which is the boiling point for liquid nitrogen. This is very important because liquid nitrogen is inexpensive, abundant, and inert. The search continues for materials that will superconduct at room temperatures. **Figure 24-19** illustrates the dramatic increase in the highest known critical temperature for a superconductor since the discovery of this phenomenon.

Superconductors can reduce energy loss and revolutionize electronics

The property of zero resistance to direct currents would be very advantageous in low-loss electrical power transmission. A significant fraction of electrical power is converted to internal energy in normal conductors. If power transmission lines could be made to be superconducting, these losses could be eliminated, and there would be substantial savings in energy costs.

Figure 24-19
The last 10 years have yielded a dramatic rise in the highest recorded T_c values for superconducting substances.

High-temperature superconductors could also have a major impact on the field of electronics. For instance, the junction of two superconductors, like that of two semiconductors, has special properties. Together, the two superconductors can act as an electronic switch. Superconducting film could be used to connect computer chips, enhancing the speed of computer operation.

In addition, superconducting rings could be used as storage devices for electrical current or energy. Because there is no resistance in a superconductor, a current introduced in a superconducting ring will continue indefinitely. The electrical energy in the current could be extracted at any later time.

Superconductors have special magnetic properties

Recall from Chapter 21 that when a conductor carries a current, a magnetic field is produced around the conductor. If a magnet is near the conductor, the magnet will be attracted to or repelled by the conductor. This is the basis of magnetic levitation, a phenomenon in which an object is suspended in the air because it is repelled by a magnet underneath. Such magnets are usually electromagnets. However, electromagnets dissipate a great deal of energy because of their electrical resistance to current. The solution to this problem is to use superconducting wires in the electromagnet.

Magnetic levitation has many potential applications in the field of transportation. In fact, a prototype for a train that runs on superconducting magnets has been constructed in Japan.

Superconducting magnets are already used in high-energy particle accelerators. Another important application of superconducting magnets is a diagnostic tool called *magnetic resonance imaging* (MRI). This technique has played a prominent role in diagnostic medicine because it uses relatively safe radio-frequency radiation rather than high-energy X rays to produce images of body sections. **Figure 24-20** shows a patient undergoing an MRI, along with the resulting images of the patient's brain.

Figure 24-20
Magnetic resonance imaging (MRI) is one medical application of superconducting magnets.

Section Review

1. A substance has a nonzero resistance even when cooled to absolute zero. What can you predict about the substance's structure?

2. Do electrons in a superconductor collide with atoms in the superconductor? Explain your answer.

3. How is a superconducting ring like a capacitor? How is it different?

4. MRI scans of the brain rely on radio-frequency waves instead of X rays. Calculate the energy of an X-ray photon with a wavelength of 1.0×10^{-10} m. Then calculate the energy carried by a radio-wave photon with a frequency of 100 MHz.

KEY IDEAS

Section 24-1 Conduction in the solid state

- Solids can be classified according to their electronic properties as conductors, insulators, or semiconductors.
- Electrons in a solid occupy sets of energy levels called bands.
- Electrons in a semiconductor can be excited from the valence band into a different band, called the conduction band. When this happens, the semiconductor conducts electric charge.

Section 24-2 Semiconductor applications

- Charge can move in a substance as electrons or as positively charged holes left by an electron-poor substance.
- The n-type semiconductor contains impurities of an atom that has five valence electrons instead of four. As a result, electrons are the majority charge carriers.
- The p-type semiconductor contains impurities of an atom that has three valence electrons instead of four. As a result, positively charged holes are the majority charge carriers.
- A diode allows current in only one direction.
- A transistor consisting of two diodes placed back to back and properly biased with batteries can be used to amplify a weak signal.

Section 24-3 Superconductors

- A superconductor is a solid whose resistance is zero below some temperature called the critical temperature.
- According to the BCS theory, electrons travel in groups and the momentum of the group doesn't change. If one electron undergoes a collision, the others adjust their course, so momentum is conserved.

KEY TERMS

band gap (p. 868)

diode (p. 874)

doping (p. 873)

excited state (p. 867)

ground state (p. 867)

hole (p. 872)

transistor (p. 877)

valence electrons (p. 867)

Diagram symbols

electron	−	electric current arrow	→
hole	+	diode	—▶|—
electric field vector	→	transistor	(symbol)

CHAPTER 24
Review and Assess

VALENCE ELECTRONS AND BAND THEORY

Review questions

1. Discuss the differences in the band structures of metals, insulators, and semiconductors. How does the band structure model enable you to better understand the electrical properties of these materials?

2. Which of the energy bands in **Figure 24-21** contain unexcited valence electrons?

Band A		Band D

Band B		Band E

Band C		Band F
Semiconductor		Conductor

Figure 24-21

3. Which of the following is likely to be able to move and conduct electricity?
   a. an electron in the innermost shell of an indium atom
   b. an electron in the innermost shell of a copper atom
   c. a valence electron in a copper atom in a wire
   d. a valence electron in the semiconductor selenium
   e. an excited electron in the semiconductor selenium
   f. an electron in the conduction band of the semiconductor germanium

4. Which is likely to have the larger band gap, iodine (an insulator) or silicon (a semiconductor)?

Conceptual questions

5. When a photon is absorbed by a semiconductor, an electron-hole pair is created. Using the energy-band model, explain how this enables the semiconductor to conduct electricity.

6. The energy of visible light ranges from 1.8 to 3.2 eV. Use this fact to explain why silicon, with an energy gap of 1.1 eV, appears opaque, whereas diamond, with an energy gap of 5.5 eV, appears transparent despite the many similarities in their structures and atoms.

SEMICONDUCTORS, DIODES, AND TRANSISTORS

Review questions

7. An electric field is oriented as shown in **Figure 24-22.** In which direction will electrons in this field move? In which direction will holes move?

Figure 24-22

8. Which is likely to contain the most holes, a semiconductor doped with atoms with three valence electrons, four valence electrons, or five valence electrons?

9. What are the majority charge carriers in an n-type semiconductor?

10. What are the majority charge carriers in a p-type semiconductor?

11. Explain how diodes differ from resistors.

12. When a single diode is used as a rectifier, does it provide a constant current?

13. In **Figure 24-23,** the p-n diode is conducting electricity.

    a. Which way do electrons move in the circuit?

    b. Which way do holes move in the circuit?

Circuit with a conducting diode   **Figure 24-23**

14. If the circuit in **Figure 24-23** had the battery's polarity in the opposite direction, would the diode still conduct electricity?

15. Explain how transistors differ from diodes.

16. In the pnp transistor described on page 877, between which two points is the input signal connected?

17. In the pnp transistor described on page 877, between which two points is the output signal connected?

Technology & Learning

Graphing calculators

Program your graphing calculator to calculate the number of free electrons per cubic centimeter of a substance. Use the program to determine the number of free electrons for the following materials:

a. copper, which has a density of 8.92 g/cm³, an average atomic mass of 63.546 u, and an average of one atom for each free electron

b. silicon, which has a density of 2.33 g/cm³, an average atomic mass of 28.086 u, and an average of 2×10^{12} atoms for each free electron

Open a new program by pressing [PRGM] [▶] [▶] [ENTER]. Name the program "FREE" and press [ENTER]. Then enter the program shown in the table below.

Press [2nd] [QUIT]. To run the program, press [PRGM], select "FREE," and press [ENTER] [ENTER]. A prompt for D means you should enter the mass density. M corresponds to the atomic mass, and N corresponds to the number of atoms per free electron. Press [ENTER] after entering each piece of data.

When you have entered the appropriate values, the calculator will perform the calculation and display the number of electrons per cubic centimeter for the substance. Press [2nd] [QUIT], and run the program again to calculate for a different substance.

Keystrokes	Display
	PROGRAM: FREE
1. [PRGM] [▶] [2] [ALPHA] [D] [ENTER]	:PROMPT D
2. [PRGM] [▶] [2] [ALPHA] [M] [ENTER]	:PROMPT M
3. [PRGM] [▶] [2] [ALPHA] [N] [ENTER]	:PROMPT N
4. [(] [ALPHA] [D] [×] [6] [.] [0] [2] [2nd] [EE] [2] [3] [)] [÷] [(] [ALPHA] [N] [×] [ALPHA] [M] [)] [STO▶] [ALPHA] [F] [ENTER]	:(D*6.02E23)/(N*M) → F
5. [PRGM] [▶] [3] [ALPHA] [F] [ENTER]	:DISP F
6. [PRGM] [7] [ENTER]	:END

18. Atoms with five valence electrons, such as arsenic, are donor atoms in a semiconductor, while those with three valence electrons, such as gallium, are acceptor atoms. Check the periodic table in Appendix E to determine what other elements might make good donors or acceptors.

19. Is the value for the current gain for an amplifying transistor likely to be one, more than one, or less than one?

SUPERCONDUCTORS

Review questions ▰▰▰▰

20. If a substance is superconducting, is it likely to contain lattice imperfections?

21. What is conserved as Cooper pairs travel through a superconductor?

22. Are electrons in Cooper pairs directly attracted to each other?

23. Would a superconductor make a good heating element in a toaster oven? Explain why or why not.

24. Would a superconductor make a good material for a high-voltage transmission line? Explain why or why not.

MIXED REVIEW

25. The energy gap for silicon at 300 K is 1.14 eV.
    a. Find the lowest frequency photon that will promote an electron in silicon from the valence band to the conduction band.
    b. What is the wavelength of this photon?

26. A light-emitting diode (LED) made of the semiconductor GaAsP emits red light with a wavelength of 650 nm. Determine the energy-band gap in the semiconductor.

27. Most solar radiation has a wavelength of 10^{-6} m or less. What energy gap should the material in a solar cell have in order to absorb this radiation?

Alternative Assessment

Performance assessment

1. Silicon, Si, atoms have four valence electrons. Arsenic, As, atoms used as impurities have five valence electrons. Will the resulting n-type semiconductor have a net negative charge? Draw diagrams to support or refute your claim, and present your arguments in a class discussion.

2. Design an experiment to investigate the effects of varying temperature over a range of 100°C on a metallic conductor's resistance. Review Ohm's law before planning your experiment. List the materials you will need and describe the procedure you will follow, including the measurements you will take. If your teacher approves your plan, obtain the necessary equipment and perform the experiment. What resistances do your results predict at absolute zero?

Portfolio projects

3. Research information about the physical properties, sources, and other uses of elements that can be used in superconductors. Obtain pictures of samples, if possible. Organize your findings in a brochure, poster, or computer presentation.

4. Interview someone in the electronics industry, or research careers in this industry. Find out about the types of jobs available and the education and training necessary for these jobs. Prepare a file documenting your search process, letters you wrote, notes from interviews, and other sources of information. Compile a summary report, brochure, or presentation based on your research that could be used by clients of a career guidance center.

RESISTORS AND DIODES

Ohm's law describes the relationship between the current and the potential difference for an ohmic resistor in a circuit. Ohmic resistors are used to regulate the current in a circuit. For a given potential difference, a higher resistance results in a smaller current, while a lower resistance results in a larger current.

Diodes are used in circuits because they have an almost infinite resistance in one direction (reverse biased) and nearly zero resistance in the other direction (forward biased). In this experiment, you will compare the performance of an ohmic resistor in a circuit with the performance of a diode in the same circuit.

SAFETY

- **Never close a circuit until it has been approved by your teacher. Never rewire or adjust any element of a closed circuit. Never work with electricity near water; be sure the floor and all work surfaces are dry.**

- **If the pointer on any kind of meter moves off scale, open the circuit immediately by opening the switch.**

- **Do not attempt this exercise with any batteries, electrical devices, or magnets other than those provided by your teacher for this purpose.**

PREPARATION

1. Read the entire lab, and plan the steps you will take.

2. Prepare a data table in your lab notebook with seven columns and eleven rows. In the first row, label the columns *Level*, I_R *(A)*, ΔV_R *(V)*, I_{D-F} *(A)*, ΔV_{D-F} *(V)*, I_{D-R} *(A)*, and ΔV_{D-R} *(V)*. In the first column, label the 2nd through 11th rows *1* through *10*.

PROCEDURE

Ohmic resistance

3. Construct a circuit that includes a power supply, a contact switch, a resistance box, a current meter, a resistor, and a voltage meter. ***Do not close the switch until your teacher approves your circuit.*** The current meter

OBJECTIVES

- Examine the relationships between current, potential difference, and resistance in an ohmic resistor circuit.

- Examine the relationships between current, potential difference, and resistance in a semiconductor diode circuit.

- Recognize the directional character of the resistance in the diode.

MATERIALS LIST

✔ 2 multimeters or dc ammeter and voltmeter
✔ diode
✔ momentary contact switch
✔ power supply
✔ resistance box
✔ resistor
✔ wire leads

should be connected in series with the power supply and the resistor. The voltage meter should be connected in parallel with the power supply. Make sure the voltage meter and the current meter are connected properly.

4. When your teacher has approved your circuit, make sure the power supply is turned to its lowest setting and the dials on the resistance box are turned all the way to the right. Turn on the power supply, and close the switch to read the voltage meter. Turn the dial on the power supply clockwise until the voltage meter reads 2.5 V. Open the switch, and turn off the power supply.

5. Remove the voltage meter from the power supply, and wire the voltage meter in parallel with the resistor. With the switch open, make sure that the meters are wired correctly. ***Do not close the switch or turn on the power supply until your teacher approves your circuit.***

6. When your teacher has approved your circuit, turn on the power supply, but do not close the switch. Slowly turn the dials on the resistance box to the left, starting with the 100 kΩ dial. Periodically close the switch just long enough to read the potential difference across the resistor. Turn the dial until the voltage meter reads 0.2 V. Record the potential difference across the resistor, ΔV_R, and the current in the resistor, I_R, in your data table under Level 1.

7. Repeat the procedure in step 6, turning the dials on the resistance box until the potential difference across the resistor is 0.4 V. Record ΔV_R and I_R in your data table under Level 2.

8. Repeat the procedure in step 6, increasing the potential difference across the resistor in 0.2 V steps to 2.0 V. Record the current and the potential difference for Levels 3 through 10. Open the switch.

Figure 24-24

Step 3: Make sure all connections are correct.

Step 4: Use the voltage meter to measure the potential difference across the power supply. Close the switch only long enough to take your measurements.

Step 5: Rewire the circuit to measure the potential difference across the resistor.

Step 9: Replace the resistor with the diode. Connect the end of the diode with the colored bands to the black terminal of the power supply.

Step 11: Reverse the diode and repeat.

Diode

9. Replace the resistor with the diode, as shown in **Figure 24-24.** The diode should be connected in the forward-biased position so that the end of the diode with the colored bands is connected to the wire leading to the black terminal of the power supply. Make sure that the meters are connected properly. ***Do not close the switch until your teacher approves your circuit.***

10. When your teacher has approved your circuit, repeat the procedure in steps 6 through 8 to find the current and the potential difference for the diode at each level. Adjust by steps of 0.2 V from 0.2 V to 2.0 V, and record the potential difference across the forward-biased diode, $\Delta V_{D\text{-}F}$, and the current in the forward-biased diode, $I_{D\text{-}F}$, for each level.

11. Remove the diode from the circuit, and reverse its connections in the circuit so that the end of the diode without the colored bands is connected to the black terminal of the power supply. **Do not close the switch until your teacher approves your circuit.**

12. When your teacher has approved your circuit, repeat the procedure in steps 6 through 8 above to find the current and the potential difference for the diode at each voltage level. Adjust the potential difference by steps of 0.2 V from 0.2 V to 2.0 V, and record the potential difference across the reverse-biased diode, $\Delta V_{D\text{-}R}$, and the current in the reverse-biased diode, $I_{D\text{-}R}$, for each level.

ANALYSIS AND INTERPRETATION

Calculations and data analysis

1. **Organizing data** For each level, calculate the ratio between the potential difference across the ohmic resistor and the current in the circuit.

2. **Graphing data** Using a graphing calculator, computer, or graph paper, plot the following graphs:
   a. I_R versus ΔV_R for the ohmic resistor
   b. $I_{D\text{-}F}$ versus $\Delta V_{D\text{-}F}$ for the forward-biased diode
   c. $I_{D\text{-}R}$ versus $\Delta V_{D\text{-}R}$ for the reverse-biased diode

Conclusions

3. **Analyzing results** Compare the ratios found in item 1. What is the relationship between the potential difference and the current? Is this true for all trials? Explain.

4. **Analyzing graphs** Use your graphs to answer the following questions.
   a. What is the relationship between current and voltage in the resistance circuit?
   b. What is the relationship between current and voltage in the diode circuit?

5. **Comparing results** Based on your results, explain the relationship between current, voltage, and resistance for the diode. Use examples from this experiment to explain both the forward-biased and reverse-biased diode.

WHAT CAN WE DO WITH NUCLEAR WASTE?

For about the past 40 years, people have been arguing about what to do with radioactive waste. Since the waste is harmful to humans—as well as to the environment—deciding where to put it is a serious problem.

Protection for 10 000 years

As radioactive isotopes decay, nuclear waste emits all common forms of radioactivity–α-particles, β-particles, γ-radiation, and X rays. When this radiation penetrates living cells, it knocks electrons away from atoms, causing them to become electrically charged ions. As a result, vital biological molecules break apart or form abnormal chemical bonds with other molecules. Often, a cell can repair this damage, but if too many molecules are disrupted, the cell will die. This ionizing radiation can also damage a cell's genetic material (DNA and RNA), which may cause the cell to divide again and again, out of control. This condition is called cancer.

Because of these hazards, nuclear waste must be sealed and stored until the radioactive isotopes in the waste decay to the point at which radiation reaches a safe level. Some kinds of radioactive waste will require safe storage for at least 10 000 years.

Questions of disposal

Low-level waste includes materials from the nuclear medicine departments at hospitals, where radioactive isotopes are used to diagnose and treat diseases. The greatest disposal problem involves high-

level waste, or HLW. Nearly all HLW consists of used fuel rods from reactors at nuclear power plants; about a third of these rods are replaced every year or two because their supply of fissionable uranium-235 becomes depleted, or spent.

When nuclear power plants in the United States began operating in 1957, engineers had planned to reprocess spent fuel to reclaim fissionable isotopes of uranium and plutonium to make new fuel rods. But people feared that the plutonium made available by reprocessing might be used to build bombs, so that plan was abandoned. Since that time, HLW has continued to accumulate at power plant sites in "temporary" storage facilities that are now nearly full. When there is no more storage space, plants will have to cease operation. Consequently, states and utility companies are demanding that the federal government honor the Nuclear Policy Act of 1982 in which the federal government agreed to provide permanent storage sites.

Disposal possibilities

Any site used for disposal of HLW must be far away from population centers and likely to remain geologically stable for thousands of years.

One possibility lies at certain deep spots of the oceans, where, some scientists claim, the seabed is geologically stable as well as devoid of life. Sealed stainless-steel canisters of waste could be packed into rocket-shaped carriers which would bury themselves deep into sediments when they hit the ocean bottom. Opponents say that the canisters have not been proven safe and that, if released, the radioactivity could kill off photosynthetic marine algae that replenish much of the world's oxygen. Proponents claim that the ocean bottom already contains many radioactive minerals and that the radioactivity from all HLWs in existence would not harm marine algae.

Scientists in the United States have considered other proposals as well, but since the Nuclear Policy Act of 1982, most of the attention has focused on the development of a disposal site beneath Yucca Mountain in Nevada. The design of this site includes sloping shafts that lead to a 570 hectare (1400 acre) storage area 300 m deep in the mountain's interior. (See cross-section on previous page.)

The U.S. Department of Energy is committed to developing Yucca Mountain. Engineers believe that it will be 2010 before the site is ready to receive waste. Until that time, there is a plan to begin moving HLW from power plants to a remote interim site in a western state. HLW would be transported to the storage site by truck or rail in sealed, steel canisters placed inside reinforced shipping casks.

Objections to Yucca Mountain

There are two main sources of opposition to the Yucca Mountain plan. One source maintains that Yucca Mountain has not been proven to be geologically secure, citing evidence that gases emitted at the lowest depth were able to reach the outside air. In addition, the group is concerned about the possibility of collisions or other accidents that might break the casks open while in transport.

The Department of Energy claims it has proven the casks safe. Several tests have been performed, including one in which a cask was loaded onto a flatbed trailer and crashed into a concrete wall at 135 km/h. In another test, a cask was struck by a locomotive at 130 km/h. No leakage occurred in these tests.

The other source of opposition to Yucca Mountain are people who maintain that the costs of overcoming legal challenges will ultimately make the plan financially infeasible. These people believe that the government should stop spending money on the Yucca Mountain project and resume the plan to reprocess waste to make new nuclear fuel.

 Researching the Issue

1. Learn about the policies of your city, county, or state concerning the transport and/or storage of nuclear waste. Write a report describing these policies and include your opinion of them. Give reasons for the stance you take.

2. Scientists have considered the possibility of packing waste into powerful rockets and blasting them into the sun or into solar orbit. Organize a classroom discussion of the benefits and hazards of this method.

3. Whenever public officials must decide on a location for a facility that people perceive as hazardous, they must find a way to overcome the NIMBY syndrome. What does *NIMBY* mean? How would you, as a public official, try to overcome this problem?

Subatomic Physics

PHYSICS IN ACTION

High-energy particles from space, called *cosmic rays,* continually create carbon-14 atoms from nitrogen in the atmosphere. Because carbon-14 atoms decay into other atoms at a specific rate, researchers can use carbon-14 to determine the age of organic materials in a process called *carbon dating.*

All living organisms have the same ratio of carbon-14 to carbon-12 atoms. When an organism dies, it no longer takes in carbon-14, and the ratio of carbon-14 to carbon-12 decreases with time as a result of the decay of carbon-14. It is therefore possible to determine the age of an organic material by measuring this ratio.

- *What makes up a carbon-14 nucleus?*
- *By what process does carbon-14 decay into other atoms?*

CONCEPT REVIEW

Electric force   (Section 17-2)

Atomic structure   (Section 23-2)

25-1
The nucleus

PROPERTIES OF THE NUCLEUS

In Chapter 17, you learned that atoms are composed of electrons, protons, and neutrons. Except for the ordinary hydrogen nucleus, which consists of a single proton, both protons and neutrons are found in the nucleus. Together, protons and neutrons are referred to as *nucleons*.

As seen in Chapter 23, Rutherford's scattering experiment led to the conclusion that all of an atom's positive charge and most of its mass are concentrated in the nucleus. Rutherford's calculations revealed that the nucleus has a radius of no greater than about 10^{-14} m. Because such small lengths are common in nuclear physics, a convenient unit of length is the *femtometer* (fm). Sometimes called the *fermi*, this unit is equal to 10^{-15} m.

A nucleus can be specified by an atomic number and a mass number

There are a few important quantities that are used to describe the charge and mass of the nucleus. **Table 25-1** lists these quantities and the symbols commonly used to represent them. The mass number (A) represents the number of protons and neutrons—or nucleons—in the nucleus. The atomic number (Z) represents the number of protons in the nucleus, and the neutron number (N) represents the number of neutrons in the nucleus.

Table 25-1	Symbols for nuclear quantities	
Symbol	**Name**	**Explanation**
A	mass number	the number of nucleons (protons and neutrons) in the nucleus
Z	atomic number	the number of protons in the nucleus
N	neutron number	the number of neutrons in the nucleus

As an example, consider a nucleus of aluminum. A typical atom of aluminum has a mass number of 27 and an atomic number of 13. Therefore, it has 13 protons and 14 neutrons ($27 - 13 = 14$). A periodic table of the elements usually includes the atomic number of each element above or near the element's chemical symbol.

Often, the mass number and the atomic number of the nucleus of an atom are combined with the atom's chemical symbol, as shown in **Figure 25-1.**

Mass number (A)

Chemical symbol

Atomic number (Z)

Figure 25-1
The chemical symbol of an element is often written with its mass number and atomic number, as shown here.

The chemical symbol for aluminum is Al. The superscript refers to the mass number A (27 in the case of aluminum), and the subscript refers to the atomic number Z (13 in the case of aluminum).

An element can be identified by its atomic number, Z. Because the number of protons determines the element, the atomic number of any given element does not change. Thus, the chemical symbol, such as Al, or the name of the element, such as aluminum, can always be used to determine the atomic number. For this reason, the atomic number is sometimes omitted.

Although atomic number does not change within an element, atoms of the same element can have different mass numbers. This is because the number of neutrons in a particular element can vary. Atoms that have the same atomic number but different neutron numbers (and thus different mass numbers) are called **isotopes.** The neutron number for an isotope is found from the following relationship:

$$A = Z + N$$

This expression says that the mass number of an atom (A) equals the number of protons (Z) plus the number of neutrons (N) in the nucleus of the atom. This expression was used to find the number of neutrons in aluminum.

The natural abundance of isotopes can vary greatly. For example, $^{11}_{6}C$, $^{12}_{6}C$, $^{13}_{6}C$, and $^{14}_{6}C$ are four isotopes of carbon. The natural abundance of the $^{12}_{6}C$ isotope is about 98.9 percent, while that of the $^{13}_{6}C$ isotope is only about 1.1 percent. Some isotopes do not occur naturally but can be produced in the laboratory. Even the simplest element, hydrogen, has isotopes: $^{1}_{1}H$, called hydrogen; $^{2}_{1}H$, called *deuterium;* and $^{3}_{1}H$, called *tritium.*

A nucleus is very dense

Experiments have shown that most nuclei are approximately spherical and that the volume of a nucleus is proportional to the total number of nucleons, and thus to the mass of the nucleus. This suggests that *all nuclei have nearly the same density,* which is about 2.3×10^{17} kg/m^3, 2.3×10^{14} times greater than the density of water (1.0×10^3 kg/m^3). Nucleons combine to form a nucleus as though they were tightly packed spheres, as shown in **Figure 25-2.**

The unified mass unit and rest energy are used to express the mass of a nucleus

Because the mass of a nucleus is extremely small, the *unified mass unit,* u, is often used for atomic masses. This unit is sometimes referred to as the *atomic mass unit.* 1 u is defined so that 12 u is equal to the mass of one atom of carbon-12. That is, the mass of a nucleus (or atom) is measured relative to the mass of an atom of the neutral carbon-12 isotope (the nucleus plus six electrons). Based on this definition, 1 u = $1.660\ 5402 \times 10^{-27}$ kg. The proton and neutron each have a mass of about 1 u, and the electron has a mass that is only a small fraction of 1 u, or about 5×10^{-4} u.

isotopes

atoms of an element having the same atomic number but different neutron and mass numbers

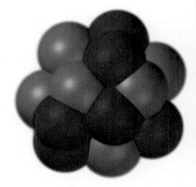

Figure 25-2
A nucleus can be visualized as a cluster of tightly packed spherical nucleons. The pink spheres represent protons, and the blue spheres represent neutrons.

Alternatively, the mass of the nucleus is often expressed in terms of rest energy. As seen in the Physics on the Edge feature in Chapter 5, a particle has a certain amount of energy, called *rest energy,* associated with its mass. (Some texts distinguish between a relativistic mass, m, and a rest mass, m_0. In this book, relativistic mass is not used, and m always refers to rest mass.) The following equation expresses the relationship between mass and rest energy mathematically:

RELATIONSHIP BETWEEN MASS AND REST ENERGY

$$m = \frac{E_o}{c^2}$$

$$\text{mass} = \frac{\text{rest energy}}{(\text{speed of light})^2}$$

This expression is often used because mass is not conserved in many nuclear processes, as we will see. When rest energy is measured in units of MeV, this equation gives mass in units of MeV/c^2. With these units, the energy that would be produced if mass were entirely converted to energy can be easily determined. For example, the mass of 1 u is 931.50 MeV/c^2. This is equivalent to a rest energy of $mc^2 = 931.50 \text{ MeV}/c^2 \times c^2$, or 931.50 MeV. Thus, the conversion of 1 u of mass into energy would produce 931.50 MeV.

The masses of the proton, neutron, and electron are summarized in **Table 25-2** using three different units. Notice that in order to distinguish between the mass of the proton and the mass of the neutron, you must know their masses to at least four significant figures in units of kg or u. The masses and some other properties of selected isotopes are provided in Appendix F.

Table 25-2	Mass of the proton, neutron, and electron		
Particle	**kg**	**u**	**MeV/c^2**
proton	1.673×10^{-27}	1.007 276	938.3
neutron	1.675×10^{-27}	1.008 665	939.6
electron	9.109×10^{-31}	0.000 549	0.5110

NUCLEAR STABILITY

Given that the nucleus consists of a closely packed collection of protons and neutrons, you might be surprised that it can exist. The very large repulsive electric forces between protons should cause the nucleus to fly apart. Nuclei are able to stay together despite the repulsive electric force between them because of a much stronger force called the *nuclear force,* or the **strong force.** The strong force is an attractive force that acts between all nucleons. At distances comparable to nuclear dimensions, the strong force is much greater

strong force

the interaction that binds nucleons together in a nucleus

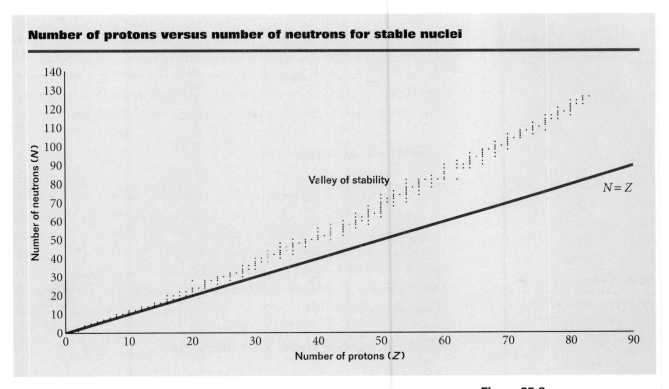

Figure 25-3

Each data point in this graph represents a stable nucleus. Note that as the number of protons increases, the ratio of neutrons to protons also increases. In other words, heavy nuclei have more neutrons per proton than lighter nuclei.

than the Coulomb repulsive force. Further, the strong force is independent of charge. In other words, the attractive strong forces associated with the proton-proton, proton-neutron, and neutron-neutron interactions are the same.

Neutrons help to stabilize a nucleus

A plot of neutron number versus atomic number (the number of protons) for stable nuclei is shown in **Figure 25-3.** The solid line in the plot shows the locations of nuclei that have an equal number of protons and neutrons ($N = Z$). Notice that only light nuclei are on this line, while all heavier nuclei fall above this line. Light nuclei are stable only if they contain about the same number of protons and neutrons. Heavy nuclei, on the other hand, are stable only when they have more neutrons than protons. Thus, heavy nuclei are neutron-rich compared with light nuclei.

This condition is necessary for the stability of a heavy nucleus. Remember that there are both attractive strong forces and repulsive Coulomb forces acting on the nucleons. Protons in a nucleus attract each other via the strong force and are also attracted to the neutrons. At the same time, the like charges on these protons repel other protons through the Coulomb force. Thus, the attractive forces of the neutrons on the protons help bind the nucleus together. The more protons there are in the nucleus, the greater the repulsive force; therefore, the more protons there are, the more neutrons that are needed to provide the attractive strong forces necessary to keep the nucleus stable.

For Z greater than 83, the repulsive forces between protons cannot be compensated by the addition of more neutrons. That is, *elements that contain more that 83 protons do not have stable nuclei.* The long, narrow region in **Figure 25-3** (on page 899), which contains the cluster of dots representing stable nuclei, is sometimes referred to as the *valley of stability.* Nuclei that are not stable decay into other nuclei until the decay product is in the valley of stability.

A nucleus has a binding energy

Nuclear stability can be understood not only in terms of a balancing of forces but also in terms of energy balance. A nucleus is stable if less energy is required for the nucleons to bind together than is required for the nucleons to be unbound. Thus, to separate a stable nucleus into protons and neutrons requires an input of energy. The energy that must be added, which is the difference in energy between the bound and unbound nucleons, is called the **binding energy** of the nucleus. Conversely, binding energy is the amount of energy unbound nucleons give up when they form a stable nucleus.

Binding energy is related to mass differences

Because of the equivalence between mass and energy, a group of unbound nucleons at rest has a certain amount of rest energy. If these nucleons spontaneously bind together into a single nucleus, there is also a binding energy associated with the nucleus. For energy to be conserved as the nucleons bind together, the binding energy must equal the rest energy of the unbound nucleons minus the rest energy of the bound nucleons.

$$E_{bind} = E_{0,unbound} - E_{0,bound}$$

Using the equation for rest energy on page 898, this can be written as follows:

$$E_{bind} = m_{unbound}c^2 - m_{bound}c^2 = (m_{unbound} - m_{bound})c^2$$

The mass of the unbound nucleons minus the mass of the bound nucleons is called the *mass defect* and is expressed as Δm. Thus, the previous equation for binding energy can be expressed as follows:

> **BINDING ENERGY OF A NUCLEUS**
>
> $$E_{bind} = \Delta mc^2$$
>
> **binding energy = mass defect $\times$ (speed of light)^2**

Note that the total mass of a stable nucleus (m_{bound}) is always less than the sum of the masses of its individual nucleons ($m_{unbound}$). It is often convenient to find the mass defect in terms of u so that it can be converted to energy with the equivalence given earlier in this chapter (1 u = 931.50 MeV).

The mass of the unbound nucleus is the sum of the individual nucleon masses, and the mass of the bound nucleus is about equal to the atomic mass minus

binding energy

the energy released when nucleons bind together to form a stable nucleus the mass of the electrons. Thus, $\Delta m = (Zm_p + Nm_n) -$ (atomic mass $- Zm_e$). One way to rearrange this equation is $\Delta m = (Zm_p + Zm_e) + Nm_n -$ (atomic mass). Because one proton and one electron are a hydrogen atom, the first term is equal to Z(atomic mass of H). Thus, the equation for mass defect can be rewritten as follows:

$$\Delta m = Z(\text{atomic mass of H}) + Nm_n - \text{atomic mass}$$

Use this equation and the atomic masses given in Appendix F to calculate mass defect when solving problems involving binding energy.

The binding energy per nucleon for light nuclei ($A < 20$) is much smaller than the binding energy per nucleon for heavier nuclei. In other words, particles in lighter nuclei are less tightly bound on average than particles in heavier nuclei. Except for the lighter nuclei, the average binding energy per nucleon is about 8 MeV. Of all nuclei, iron-58 has the greatest binding energy.

SAMPLE PROBLEM 25A

Binding energy

PROBLEM

The nucleus of the deuterium atom, called the *deuteron*, consists of a proton and a neutron. Given that the atomic mass of deuterium is 2.014 102 u, calculate the deuteron's binding energy in MeV.

SOLUTION

1. DEFINE **Given:**

$Z = 1$ atomic mass of deuterium = 2.014 102 u

$N = 1$ atomic mass of H = 1.007 825 u

$m_n = 1.008\ 665$ u

Unknown: $E_{bind} = ?$

2. PLAN **Choose an equation(s) or situation:**
First find the mass defect with the following relationship:

$$\Delta m = Z\ (\text{atomic mass of H}) + Nm_n - \text{atomic mass}$$

Then find the binding energy by converting the mass defect to rest energy.

3. CALCULATE **Substitute the values into the equation(s) and solve:**

$$\Delta m = 1(1.007\ 825\ \text{u}) + 1(1.008\ 665\ \text{u}) - 2.014\ 102\ \text{u}$$

$$\Delta m = 0.002\ 388\ \text{u}$$

$$E_{bind} = (0.002\ 388\ \text{u})\ (931.50\ \text{MeV/u})$$

$$\boxed{E_{bind} = 2.224\ \text{MeV}}$$

4. EVALUATE In order to separate a deuteron into its constituents—a proton and a neutron—it is necessary to add 2.224 MeV of energy.

Binding energy

1. Calculate the total binding energy of $^{20}_{10}\text{Ne}$ and $^{40}_{20}\text{Ca}$. (Refer to Appendix F for this and the following problems.)

2. Determine the difference in the binding energy of $^{3}_{1}\text{H}$ and $^{3}_{2}\text{He}$.

3. Find the binding energy per nucleon of $^{238}_{92}\text{U}$ in MeV.

4. Calculate the binding energy of the last neutron in the $^{43}_{20}\text{Ca}$ nucleus. (Hint: Compare the mass of $^{43}_{20}\text{Ca}$ with the mass of $^{42}_{20}\text{Ca}$ plus the mass of a neutron.)

5. Two isotopes having the same mass number are known as *isobars*. Calculate the difference in binding energy per nucleon for the isobars $^{23}_{11}\text{Na}$ and $^{23}_{12}\text{Mg}$. How do you account for this difference?

Section Review

1. Does the nuclear mass or the charge of the nucleus determine the element that an atom is?

2. Oxygen has several isotopes. What do these isotopes have in common? How do they differ?

3. Of atomic number, mass number, and neutron number, which are the same for each isotope of an element, and which are different?

4. The protons in a nucleus repel one another with the Coulomb force. What holds these protons together?

5. Describe the relationship between the number of protons, the number of neutrons, and the stability of a nucleus.

6. Calculate the total binding energy of the following:
   a. $^{93}_{41}\text{Nb}$
   b. $^{197}_{79}\text{Au}$
   c. $^{27}_{13}\text{Al}$
   (Refer to Appendix F.)

7. Physics in Action How many protons are there in the nucleus $^{14}_{6}\text{C}$? How many neutrons? How many electrons are there in the neutral atom?

25-2
Nuclear decay

NUCLEAR DECAY MODES

So far, we have considered what happens when nucleons are bound together to form stable nuclei. However, not all nuclei are stable. There are about 400 stable nuclei; hundreds of other nuclei are unstable and tend to break apart into other particles. This process is called *nuclear decay.*

The nuclear decay process can be a natural event or it can be induced artificially. In either case, when a nucleus decays, radiation is emitted in the form of particles, energy, or both. The spontaneous emission of such radiation is called *radioactivity.* The nucleus before decay is called the *parent nucleus,* and the nucleus remaining after decay is called the *daughter nucleus.* For example, the hands and numbers of the watch shown in **Figure 25-4** contain small amounts of radium salts. The nuclei within these salts decay, releasing light energy that causes the watch to glow in the dark. In this and all other nuclear reactions, the energy released is found by the equation $E = \Delta mc^2$.

A radioactive material can emit three types of radiation

Three types of radiation can be emitted by a nucleus as it undergoes radioactive decay: alpha (α) rays, in which the emitted particles are $^4_2$He nuclei; beta (β) rays, in which the emitted particles are either electrons or positrons (positively charged particles with a mass equal to that of the electron); and gamma (γ) rays, in which the emitted "rays" are high-energy photons. These three types of radiation are summarized in **Table 25-3.**

Figure 25-4
The radioactive decay of radium nuclei causes the hands and numbers of this watch to glow in the dark.

25-2 SECTION OBJECTIVES

- **Describe the three modes of nuclear decay.**

- **Predict the products of nuclear decay.**

- **Calculate the decay constant and the half-life of a radioactive substance.**

Table 25-3	Alpha, beta, and gamma radiation			
Particle	**Symbols**	**Composition**	**Charge**	**Effect on parent nucleus**
alpha	α ($^4_2$He)	2 protons, 2 neutrons	+2	mass loss; new element produced
beta	β^- ($^{\,0}_{-1}e$)	electron	−1	no significant change in mass; new element produced
	β^+ (^0_1e)	positron	−1	
gamma	γ	photon	0	energy loss

The ability of radiation to penetrate a material depends on the type of radiation. Alpha particles barely penetrate a piece of paper, beta particles can penetrate a few millimeters of aluminum, and gamma rays can penetrate several centimeters of pure lead.

Helium nuclei are emitted in alpha decay

When a nucleus undergoes alpha decay, it emits an alpha particle ($^4_2$He). Thus, the nucleus loses two protons and two neutrons. This makes the nucleus lighter and decreases its positive charge. (Because the electrons around the nuclei do not participate in nuclear reactions, they are ignored.)

For example, the nucleus of uranium-238 ($^{238}_{92}$U) can decay by alpha emission to a thorium-234 nucleus and an alpha particle. This process is written symbolically as follows:

$$^{238}_{92}\text{U} \rightarrow {}^{234}_{90}\text{Th} + {}^4_2\text{He}$$

This expression says that a parent nucleus, $^{238}_{92}$U, emits an alpha particle, $^4_2$He, and thereby changes to a daughter nucleus, $^{234}_{90}$Th (thorium-234). This reaction is governed by the rules summarized in **Table 25-4.** These two rules can be used to determine the unknown daughter atom when a parent atom undergoes alpha decay.

Table 25-4   **Rules for nuclear decay**
The total of the atomic numbers on the left is the same as the total on the right because charge must be conserved.
The total of the mass numbers on the left is the same as the total on the right because nucleon number must be conserved.

Electrons or positrons are emitted in beta decay

When a radioactive nucleus undergoes beta decay, the nucleus emits either an electron or a positron. Thus, the atomic number is increased or decreased by one, with an opposite change in the neutron number. Because the daughter nucleus contains the same number of nucleons as the parent nucleus, the mass number does not change. Thus, beta decay does not appreciably alter the mass of a nucleus. Instead, the ratio of neutrons to protons in a nucleus is changed. This ratio affects the stability of the nucleus, as seen in Section 25-1.

A typical beta decay event is the decay of carbon-14, as follows:

$$^{14}_6\text{C} \rightarrow {}^{14}_7\text{N} + {}^{\ 0}_{-1}e$$

This decay produces an electron, written as $^{\ 0}_{-1}e$. In this decay, the atomic number of the daughter nucleus is increased by 1.

CONCEPT PREVIEW

A positron is the antiparticle of the electron. An antiparticle is similar to a particle in most respects except that it has an opposite charge. Almost all particles have an antiparticle associated with them. Antiparticles are discussed in more detail in the feature at the end of this chapter.

Another beta decay event is the decay of nitrogen-12, as follows:

$$^{12}_{7}\text{N} \rightarrow {}^{12}_{6}\text{C} + {}^{0}_{1}e$$

This decay produces a positron, written as ${}^{0}_{1}e$. In this decay, the atomic number of the daughter nucleus is decreased by 1.

The superscripts and subscripts on the carbon and nitrogen nuclei follow our usual conventions, but those on the electron and the positron may need some explanation. The -1 indicates that the electron has a charge whose magnitude is equal to that of the proton but is negative. Similarly, the 1 indicates that the positron has a charge that is equal to that of the proton in magnitude and sign. Thus, the subscript can be thought of as the charge of the particle. The 0 used for the mass number of the electron and the positron indicates that their masses are almost zero relative to those of carbon and nitrogen nuclei. Notice that both numbers must balance in the equations for beta decay, just as in alpha decay.

Figure 25-5
The spiral in this bubble-chamber image is the track left by a positron after beta decay. This reaction took place in a magnetic field, which caused the positron to spiral.

Beta decay involves the conversion of neutrons and protons

A bubble-chamber image of beta decay is shown in **Figure 25-5.** The emission of electrons or positrons from a nucleus is surprising because the nucleus is made of only protons and neutrons. This apparent discrepancy can be explained by noting that in beta decay, either a neutron is transformed into a proton, creating an electron in the process, or a proton is transformed into a neutron, creating a positron in the process. These two beta decays can be written as follows:

$$^{1}_{0}n \rightarrow {}^{1}_{1}p + {}^{0}_{-1}e$$

$$^{1}_{1}p \rightarrow {}^{1}_{0}n + {}^{0}_{1}e$$

Decay events can be written in this way because other particles in the nucleus, much like the electrons around the nucleus, do not directly participate in the beta decay. The electrons and positrons involved in beta decay, on the other hand, are produced in the nuclear-decay process. Because they do not come from the shells around the nucleus, they cannot be ignored.

Neutrinos and antineutrinos are emitted in beta decay

Before we conclude our discussion of beta decay, there is one problem that must be resolved. In analyzing the experimental results of beta decay reactions, scientists noticed a disturbing fact. If carbon-14 beta decay actually occurred as described on page 904, energy, linear momentum, and angular momentum would not be conserved. In 1930, to solve this problem, Wolfgang Pauli proposed that a third particle must be missing from the equation. He reasoned that this new particle, called a *neutrino*, is necessary to conserve energy and momentum. Experimental evidence confirmed the existence of such a particle in 1956.

Table 25-5
Properties of the neutrino

The neutrino has zero electric charge.

The neutrino has a mass much smaller than that of the electron, and in fact, its mass may be zero.

The neutrino interacts very weakly with matter and is therefore very difficult to detect.

Did you know?

The word *neutrino* means "little neutral one." It was suggested by the physicist Enrico Fermi because the neutrino had to have zero electric charge and little or no mass.

The Greek letter nu (ν) is used to represent a neutrino. When a bar is drawn above the nu ($\overline{\nu}$), the particle is an antineutrino, or the antiparticle of a neutrino. The properties of the neutrino are summarized in **Table 25-5.** Note that the neutrino has no electric charge and that its mass is very small, perhaps even zero. As a result, the neutrino is difficult to detect experimentally.

With the neutrino, we can now describe the beta decay process of carbon-14 in a form that takes energy and momentum conservation into account, as follows:

$$^{14}_{6}\text{C} \rightarrow \,^{14}_{7}\text{N} + \,^{0}_{-1}e + \overline{\nu}$$

According to this expression, carbon-14 decays into a nitrogen nucleus, releasing an electron and an antineutrino in the process.

The decay of nitrogen-12 can also be rewritten, as follows:

$$^{12}_{7}\text{N} \rightarrow \,^{12}_{6}\text{C} + \,^{0}_{1}e + \nu$$

Here we see that when $^{12}_{7}\text{N}$ decays into $^{12}_{6}\text{C}$, a positron and a neutrino are produced. To avoid confusing these two types of beta decay, keep in mind this simple rule: *In beta decay, an electron is always accompanied by an antineutrino and a positron is always accompanied by a neutrino.*

High-energy photons are emitted in gamma decay

Very often, a nucleus that undergoes radioactive decay, either alpha or beta, is left in an excited energy state. The nucleus can then undergo a gamma decay in which one or more nucleons make transitions from a higher energy level to a lower energy level. In the process, one or more photons are emitted. Such photons, or *gamma rays,* have very high energy relative to the energy of visible light. The process of nuclear de-excitation, or gamma decay, is very similar to the emission of light by an atom, in which an electron makes a transition from a state of higher energy to a state of lower energy (as discussed in Chapter 23). Note that in gamma decay energy is emitted but the parts of the nucleus are left unchanged. Thus, both the atomic number and the mass number stay the same. Nonetheless, gamma decay is still considered to be a form of nuclear decay because it involves protons or neutrons in the nucleus.

Two common reasons for a nucleus being in an excited state are alpha and beta decay. The following sequence of events represents a typical situation in which gamma decay occurs:

$$^{12}_{5}\text{B} \rightarrow \,^{12}_{6}\text{C}^{\star} + \,^{0}_{-1}e + \overline{\nu}$$
$$^{12}_{6}\text{C}^{\star} \rightarrow \,^{12}_{6}\text{C} + \gamma$$

The first step is a beta decay in which $^{12}_{5}\text{B}$ decays to $^{12}_{6}\text{C}^{\star}$. The asterisk indicates that the carbon nucleus is left in an excited state following the decay. The excited carbon nucleus then decays in the second step to the ground state by emitting a gamma ray.

NUCLEAR DECAY SERIES

If the product of a nuclear decay is stable, the decay process ends. In other cases, the decay product—the daughter nucleus—is itself unstable. The daughter nucleus then becomes the parent nucleus for an additional decay process. Such a sequence is called a *decay series*.

Figure 25-6(a) depicts the number of protons versus neutrons for all stable nuclei. A small portion of this graph is enlarged in **Figure 25-6(b),** which shows a naturally occurring decay series beginning with thorium, Th, and ending with lead, Pb. Each square in **Figure 25-6(b)** corresponds to a possible nucleus. The black dots represent stable nuclei, and the red dots represent unstable nuclei. Thus, each black dot in **Figure 25-6(b)** corresponds to a data point in the circled portion of **Figure 25-6(a)**. The decay series continues until a stable nucleus is reached, in this case ^{208}Pb. Notice that there is a branch in the decay path; there are actually two ways that thorium can decay into lead.

The entire series in **Figure 25-6(b)** consists of 10 decays: 6 alpha decays and 4 beta decays. When α decay occurs, the nucleus moves down two squares and to the left two squares because it loses two protons and two neutrons. When β^- decay occurs, the nucleus moves down one square and to the right one square because it loses one neutron and gains one proton. Gamma decays are not represented because they do not alter the ratio of protons to neutrons.

The result of the decay series is to lighten the nucleus. The neutron-to-proton ratio in a parent nucleus is altered through alpha and beta decay. The proper ratio of neutrons to protons is important, as we have seen, in balancing the strong and Coulomb forces in the nucleus.

Figure 25-6
The heaviest nuclei in the graph of all stable nuclei **(a)** are represented by the black dots in the enlarged view **(b)**. Note that an unstable nucleus (represented by the red dots) will continue to decay until the daughter nucleus is stable.

Nuclear decay

PROBLEM

The element radium was discovered by Marie and Pierre Curie in 1898. One of the isotopes of radium, $^{226}_{88}Ra$, decays by alpha emission. What is the resulting daughter element?

SOLUTION

Given: The decay can be written symbolically as follows:

$$^{226}_{88}Ra \rightarrow X + {}^{4}_{2}He$$

Unknown: the daughter element (X)

The mass numbers and atomic numbers on the two sides of the expression must be the same so that both charge and nucleon number are conserved during the course of this particular decay.

$$\text{Mass number of } X = 226 - 4 = 222$$
$$\text{Atomic number of } X = 88 - 2 = 86$$
$$^{226}_{88}Ra \rightarrow {}^{222}_{86}X + {}^{4}_{2}He$$

The periodic table (Appendix E) shows that the nucleus with an atomic number of 86 is radon, Rn. Thus, the process is as follows:

$$\boxed{^{226}_{88}Ra \rightarrow {}^{222}_{86}Rn + {}^{4}_{2}He}$$

PRACTICE 25B

Nuclear decay

1. Complete the following radioactive-decay formulas:

  a. $^{12}_{5}B \rightarrow ? + {}^{0}_{-1}e + \overline{\nu}$

  b. $^{225}_{89}Ac \rightarrow {}^{221}_{87}Fr + ?$

  c. $? \rightarrow {}^{14}_{7}N + {}^{0}_{-1}e + \overline{\nu}$

  d. $^{212}_{83}Bi \rightarrow ? + {}^{4}_{2}He$

  (Refer to Appendix E for this and the following problems.)

2. Nickel-63 decays by β^- emission to copper-63. Write the complete decay formula for this process.

3. The isotope $^{56}_{26}Fe$ decays into the isotope $^{56}_{27}Co$.

  a. By what process will this decay occur?

  b. Write the decay formula for this process.

MEASURING NUCLEAR DECAY

Imagine that you are studying a sample of radioactive material. You know that the atoms in the material are decaying into other types of atoms. How many of the unstable parent atoms remain after a certain amount of time?

The decay constant indicates the rate of radioactive decay

If the sample contains N radioactive parent nuclei at some instant, the number of parent nuclei that decay into daughter nuclei (ΔN) in a small time interval (Δt) is proportional to N, as follows:

$$\Delta N = -\lambda N \Delta t$$

The negative sign signifies that N decreases with time; that is, ΔN is negative. The quantity λ is called the *decay constant*. The value of λ for any isotope indicates the rate at which that isotope decays. Isotopes with a large decay constant decay quickly, and those with a small decay constant decay slowly. The number of decays per unit time, $-\Delta N/\Delta t$, is called the *decay rate*, or *activity*, of the sample. Note that the activity of a sample equals the decay constant times the number of radioactive nuclei in the sample, as follows:

$$\text{activity} = -\Delta N/\Delta t = \lambda N$$

The SI unit of activity is the *becquerel* (Bq). One becquerel is equal to 1 decay/s. The *curie* (Ci), which was the original unit of activity, is the approximate activity of 1 g of radium. One curie is equal to 3.7×10^{10} Bq.

Half-life measures how long it takes half a sample to decay

Another quantity that is useful for characterizing radioactive decay is the **half-life,** written as $T_{1/2}$. The half-life of a radioactive substance is the time it takes for half a given number of radioactive nuclei to decay. The half-life of any substance is inversely proportional to the decay constant of the substance.

half-life

the time required for half the original nuclei of a radioactive material to undergo radioactive decay

Conceptual Challenge

1. Decay series
Suppose a radioactive parent substance with a very long half-life has a daughter with a very short half-life. Describe what happens to a freshly purified sample of the parent substance.

2. Probability of decay
"The more probable the decay, the shorter the half-life." Explain this statement.

3. Decay of radium
The radioactive nucleus $^{226}_{88}$Ra (radium-226) has a half-life of about 1.6×10^3 years. Although the solar system is approximately 5 billion years old, we still find this radium nucleus in nature. Explain how this is possible.

Thus, substances with large decay constants have short half-lives. The relationship between half-life and decay constant is expressed as follows:

HALF-LIFE

$$T_{1/2} = \frac{0.693}{\lambda}$$

$$\text{half-life} = \frac{0.693}{\textbf{decay constant}}$$

Consider a sample that begins with N radioactive parent nuclei. Such a sample will slowly decay into stable daughter nuclei. By definition, after an elapsed time of one half-life, $\frac{1}{2}N$ radioactive parent nuclei remain; the rest have decayed into daughter nuclei. After two half-lives, half the $\frac{1}{2}N$ parent nuclei will have decayed, so $\frac{1}{4}N$ radioactive parent nuclei remain. This means there will be $\frac{3}{4}N$ daughter nuclei. After three half-lives, there will be $\frac{1}{8}N$ parent nuclei and $\frac{7}{8}N$ daughter nuclei, and so on.

SAMPLE PROBLEM 25C

Measuring nuclear decay

PROBLEM

The half-life of the radioactive radium (^{226}Ra) nucleus is 5.0×10^{10} s. A sample contains 3.0×10^{16} nuclei. What is the decay constant for this decay? How many radium nuclei, in curies, will decay per second?

SOLUTION

1. DEFINE **Given:** $T_{1/2} = 5.0 \times 10^{10}$ s $N = 3.0 \times 10^{16}$

Unknown: $\lambda = ?$ activity $= ?$ Ci

2. PLAN **Choose an equation(s) or situation:**
To find the decay constant, use the equation for half-life, given on this page.

$$T_{1/2} = \frac{0.693}{\lambda}$$

The number of nuclei that decay per second is given by the equation for the activity of a sample, given on page 909:

$$\text{activity} = \lambda N$$

Rearrange the equation(s) to isolate the unknown(s):
The first equation must be rearranged to isolate the decay constant, λ.

$$\lambda = \frac{0.693}{T_{1/2}}$$

3. CALCULATE **Substitute the values into the equation(s) and solve:**

$$\lambda = \frac{0.693}{T_{1/2}} = \frac{0.693}{5.0 \times 10^{10} \text{ s}}$$

$$\boxed{\lambda = 1.4 \times 10^{-11} \text{s}^{-1}}$$

$$\text{activity} = \lambda N = (1.4 \times 10^{-11} \text{ s}^{-1})(3.0 \times 10^{16})$$

To convert the answer to Ci, divide by 3.7×10^{10} s^{-1}/Ci.

$$\text{activity} = \frac{(1.4 \times 10^{-11} \text{ s}^{-1})(3.0 \times 10^{16})}{3.7 \times 10^{10} \text{ s}^{-1}/\text{Ci}}$$

$$\boxed{\text{activity} = 1.1 \times 10^{-5} \text{ Ci}}$$

4. EVALUATE Because the half-life is on the order of 10^{10} s, the decay constant, which approximately equals 0.7 divided by the half-life, should equal a little less than 10^{-10} s^{-1}. Thus, 1.4×10^{-11} s^{-1} is a reasonable answer for the decay constant.

PRACTICE 25C

Measuring nuclear decay

1. Radon-222 ($^{222}_{86}$Rn) is a radioactive gas with a half-life of 3.82 days. A gas sample contains 4.0×10^3 radon atoms initially.

   a. Estimate how many radon atoms will remain after 12 days.
   b. Estimate how many radon nuclei will have decayed by this time.

2. Suppose that you start with 1.00×10^{-3} g of a pure radioactive substance and determine 2.0 h later that only 0.25×10^{-3} g of the substance is left undecayed. What is the half-life of this substance?

3. The half-life of iodine-131 is 8.07 days.

   a. Calculate the decay constant for this isotope.
   b. What is the activity of this isotope in Ci for a sample that contains 2.5×10^{10} iodine-131 nuclei?
   c. Find the number of iodine-131 nuclei necessary to produce a sample with an activity of 0.50 μCi.

4. Two samples of the same radioactive substance are prepared. Sample A has twice as much initial activity as sample B does.

   a. Compare the half-life of sample A with the half-life of sample B.
   b. After each sample has passed through five half-lives, what is the ratio of their activities?

A *decay curve* is a plot of the number of radioactive parent nuclei remaining in a sample as a function of time. A typical decay curve for a radioactive sample is shown in **Figure 25-7.** After each half-life, half the remaining parent nuclei have decayed. This is represented in the circles to the right of the decay curve. The blue spheres are the parent nuclei (carbon-14), and the red spheres are daughter nuclei (nitrogen-14). Notice that the total number of nuclei remains constant, while the number of carbon atoms continually decreases over time.

For example, the initial sample contains 8 carbon-14 atoms. After one half-life, there are 4 carbon-14 atoms and 4 nitrogen-14 atoms. By the next half-life, the number of carbon-14 atoms is reduced to 2, and the process continues. As the number of carbon-14 atoms decreases, the number of nitrogen-14 atoms increases.

Living organisms have a constant ratio of carbon-14 to carbon-12 because they continuously exchange carbon dioxide with their surroundings. When an organism dies, this ratio changes due to the decay of carbon-14. Measuring the ratio between carbon-14, which decays as shown in **Figure 25-7,** and carbon-12, which does not decay, provides an approximate date as to when the sample was alive.

Figure 25-7

The radioactive isotope carbon-14 has a half-life of 5730 years. In each successive 5730-year period, half the remaining mass of carbon-14 decays to nitrogen-14.

Section Review

1. Explain the main differences between alpha, beta, and gamma decays.

2. Complete the following radioactive decay formulas:
   a. $^{232}_{90}\text{Th} \rightarrow ? + ^{4}_{2}\text{He}$
   b. $^{12}_{5}\text{B} \rightarrow ? + ^{0}_{-1}e + \overline{\nu}$
   c. $? \rightarrow ^{4}_{2}\text{He} + ^{145}_{60}\text{Nd}$

3. A radioactive sample consists of 5.3×10^5 nuclei. There is one decay every 4.2 h.
   a. What is the decay constant for the sample?
   b. What is the half-life for the sample?

4. **Physics in Action**   The ^{14}C content decreases after the death of a living system with a half-life of 5730 years. If an archaeologist finds an ancient fire pit containing partially consumed firewood and if the ^{14}C content of the wood is only 12.5 percent that of an equal carbon sample from a present-day tree, what is the age of the ancient site?

25-3
Nuclear reactions

FISSION AND FUSION

Any process that involves a change in the nucleus of an atom is called a nuclear reaction. Nuclear reactions include *fission,* in which a nucleus splits into two or more nuclei, and *fusion,* in which one or more nuclei combine.

Stable nuclei can be made unstable

When a nucleus is bombarded with energetic particles, it may capture a particle, such as a neutron. As a result, the nucleus will no longer be stable and will disintegrate. For example, protons can be released when alpha particles collide with nitrogen atoms, as follows:

$$\,^{4}_{2}\text{He} + \,^{14}_{7}\text{N} \rightarrow \text{X} + \,^{1}_{1}\text{H}$$

According to this expression, an alpha particle ($^{4}_{2}\text{He}$) strikes a nitrogen nucleus ($^{14}_{7}\text{N}$) and produces an unknown product nucleus (X) and a proton ($^{1}_{1}\text{H}$). By balancing atomic numbers and mass numbers, we can conclude that the unknown product has a mass number of 17 and an atomic number of 8. Because the element with an atomic number of 8 is oxygen, the product can be written symbolically as $^{17}_{8}\text{O}$, and the reaction can be written as follows:

$$\,^{4}_{2}\text{He} + \,^{14}_{7}\text{N} \rightarrow \,^{17}_{8}\text{O} + \,^{1}_{1}\text{H}$$

This nuclear reaction starts with two stable isotopes—helium and nitrogen—that form an unstable intermediate nucleus ($^{18}_{9}\text{F}$). The intermediate nucleus then disintegrates into two different stable isotopes, hydrogen and oxygen. This reaction, which was the first nuclear reaction to be observed, was detected by Rutherford in 1919.

Heavy nuclei can undergo nuclear fission

Nuclear fission occurs when a heavy nucleus splits into two lighter nuclei. For fission to occur naturally, the nucleus must release energy. This means that the nucleons in the daughter nuclei must be more tightly bound and therefore have less mass than the nucleons in the parent nucleus. This decrease in mass per nucleon appears as released energy when fission occurs, often in forms such as photons or kinetic energy of the fission products. Because fission produces lighter nuclei, the binding energy per nucleon must *increase* with decreasing atomic number. **Figure 25-8** shows that this is possible only for atoms in which A > 58. Thus, *fission occurs naturally only for heavy atoms.*

25-3 SECTION OBJECTIVES

- **Distinguish between nuclear fission and nuclear fusion.**

- **Explain how a chain reaction is utilized by nuclear reactors.**

- **Compare fission and fusion reactors.**

Figure 25-8

Light nuclei are very loosely bound. The binding energy of heavy nuclei is roughly the same for all nuclei.

Subatomic Physics   913

One example of this process is the fission of uranium-235. First, the nucleus is bombarded with neutrons. When the nucleus absorbs a neutron, it becomes unstable and decays. The fission of ^{235}U can be represented as follows:

$$^{1}_{0}n + \,^{235}_{92}U \rightarrow \,^{236}_{92}U^{\star} \rightarrow X + Y + \text{neutrons}$$

The isotope $^{236}_{92}U^{\star}$ is an intermediate state that lasts only for about 10^{-12} s before splitting into X and Y. Many combinations of X and Y are possible. In the fission of uranium, about 90 different daughter nuclei can be formed. The process also results in the production of about two or three neutrons per fission event.

A typical reaction of this type is as follows:

$$^{1}_{0}n + \,^{235}_{92}U \rightarrow \,^{140}_{56}Ba + \,^{93}_{36}Kr + 3\,^{1}_{0}n$$

To estimate the energy released in a typical fission process, note that the binding energy per nucleon is about 7.6 MeV for heavy nuclei (those having a mass number of approximately 240) and about 8.5 MeV for nuclei of intermediate mass (see **Figure 25-8** on page 913). The amount of energy released in a fission event is the difference in these binding energies (8.5 MeV − 7.6 MeV, or about 0.9 MeV per nucleon). Assuming a total of 240 nucleons, this is about 220 MeV. This is a very large amount of energy relative to the energy released in typical chemical reactions. For example, the energy released in burning one molecule of the octane used in gasoline engines is about one hundred-millionth the energy released in a single fission event.

Neutrons released in fission can trigger a chain reaction

When ^{235}U undergoes fission, an average of about 2.5 neutrons are emitted per event. The released neutrons can be captured by other nuclei, making these nuclei unstable. This triggers additional fission events, which lead to the possibility of a *chain reaction,* as shown in **Figure 25-9.** Calculations show that if the chain reaction is not controlled—that is, if it does not proceed slowly—it could result in the release of an enormous amount of energy and a violent explosion. If the energy in 1 kg of ^{235}U were released, it would equal the energy released by the detonation of about 20 000 tons of TNT. This is the principle behind the first nuclear bomb, shown in **Figure 25-10,** which was essentially an uncontrolled fission reaction.

Figure 25-9

A nuclear chain reaction can be initiated by the capture of a neutron.

A *nuclear reactor* is a system designed to maintain a controlled, self-sustained chain reaction. Such a system was first achieved with uranium as the fuel in 1942 by Enrico Fermi, at the University of Chicago. Primarily, it is the uranium-235 isotope that releases energy through nuclear fission. Uranium from ore typically contains only about 0.7 percent of ^{235}U, with the remaining 99.3 percent being the ^{238}U isotope. Because uranium-238 tends to absorb neutrons instead of undergoing fission, reactor fuels must be processed to increase the proportion of ^{235}U so the reaction can sustain itself. This process is called *enrichment*.

At this time, all nuclear reactors operate through fission. One difficulty associated with fission reactors is the safe disposal of radioactive materials when the core is replaced. Transportation of reactor fuel and reactor wastes poses additional safety risks. As with all sources of energy, the risks must be weighed against the benefits and the availability of the energy source.

Light nuclei can undergo nuclear fusion

Nuclear fusion, the opposite of nuclear fission, occurs when two light nuclei combine to form a heavier nucleus. As with fission, the product of a fusion event must have a greater binding energy than the original nuclei for energy to be released in the reaction. Because fusion reactions produce heavier nuclei, the binding energy per nucleon must increase as atomic number increases. As shown in **Figure 25-8** (page 913), this is possible only for atoms with A less than 58. Hence, *fusion occurs naturally only for light atoms*.

One example of this process is the fusion reactions that occur in stars. All stars generate energy through fusion. About 90 percent of the stars, including our sun, fuse hydrogen and possibly helium. Some other stars fuse helium or other heavier elements. The *proton-proton cycle* is a series of three nuclear-fusion reactions that are believed to be stages in the liberation of energy in our sun and other stars rich in hydrogen. In the proton-proton cycle, four protons combine to form an alpha particle and two positrons, releasing 25 MeV of energy in the process. The first two steps in this cycle are as follows:

$$^1_1H + ^1_1H \rightarrow ^2_1H + ^0_1e + \nu$$

$$^1_1H + ^2_1H \rightarrow ^3_2He + \gamma$$

This is followed by either of the following processes:

$$^1_1H + ^3_2He \rightarrow ^4_2He + ^0_1e + \nu$$

$$^3_2He + ^3_2He \rightarrow ^4_2He + ^1_1H + ^1_1H$$

The released energy is carried primarily by gamma rays, positrons, and neutrinos. These energy-liberating fusion reactions are called *thermonuclear fusion reactions*. The hydrogen (fusion) bomb, first detonated in 1952, is an example of an uncontrolled thermonuclear fusion reaction.

Figure 25-10
The first nuclear fission bomb, often called the atomic bomb, was tested in New Mexico in 1945.

Did you know?

Stars do not normally fuse elements beyond iron-58 because it is the most stable element. Fusing elements beyond iron-58 would require an input of energy rather than producing energy.

Fusion reactors are being developed

The enormous amount of energy released in fusion reactions suggests the possibility of harnessing this energy for useful purposes on Earth. Efforts are under way to develop sustained and controllable thermonuclear reactions in the form of a *fusion reactor*. Because of the ready availability of its fuel source—water—controlled fusion is often called the ultimate energy source.

For example, if deuterium (^2_1H) were used as the fuel, 0.16 g of deuterium could be extracted from just 1 L of water at a cost of about one cent. Such rates would make the fuel costs of even an inefficient reactor almost insignificant. An additional advantage of fusion reactors is that comparatively few radioactive byproducts are formed. The proton-proton cycle shows that the end product of the fusion of hydrogen nuclei is safe, nonradioactive helium. Unfortunately, a thermonuclear reactor that can deliver a net power output over a reasonable time interval is not yet a reality, and many difficulties must be resolved before a successful device is constructed.

For example, the energy released in a gas undergoing nuclear fusion depends on the number of fusion reactions that can occur in a given amount of time. This varies with the density of the gas because collisions are more frequent in a denser gas. It also depends on the amount of time the gas is confined.

In addition, the Coulomb repulsion force between two charged nuclei must be overcome before they can fuse. The fundamental challenge is to give the two nuclei sufficient kinetic energy to overcome this repulsive force. This can be accomplished by heating the fuel to extremely high temperatures (about 10^8 K, or about 10 times greater than the interior temperature of the sun). Such high temperatures are not easy to obtain in a laboratory or a power plant.

Section Review

1. What are the similarities and differences between fission and fusion?

2. Explain how nuclear reactors utilize chain reactions.

3. Why would a fusion reactor produce less radioactive waste material than a fission reactor?

4. What is enrichment? Why is enrichment necessary when uranium is used as a reactor fuel?

5. A fission reaction leads to the formation of ^{141}Ba and ^{92}Kr when ^{235}U absorbs a neutron.
   a. How is this reaction expressed symbolically?
   b. How many neutrons are released in this reaction?

6. What are some advantages to fusion reactors (as opposed to fission reactors)? What are some difficulties in the development of a fusion reactor?

25-4
Particle physics

THE PARTICLE VIEW OF NATURE

Particle physics seeks to discover the ultimate structure of matter: *elementary particles*. Elementary particles, which are the fundamental units that compose matter, do not appear to be divisible and have neither size nor structure.

Many new particles have been produced in accelerators

Until 1932, scientists thought protons and electrons were elementary particles because they are stable. However, beginning in 1945, experiments at particle accelerators, such as the Stanford Linear Accelerator shown in **Figure 25-11,** have demonstrated that new particles are often formed in high-energy collisions between known particles. These new particles tend to be very unstable and have very short half-lives, ranging from 10^{-6}s to 10^{-23}s. So far, more than 300 new particles have been catalogued.

There are four fundamental interactions in nature

The key to understanding the properties of elementary particles is to be able to describe the interactions between them. All particles in nature are subject to four fundamental interactions: *strong, electromagnetic, weak,* and *gravitational.*

The strong interaction is responsible for the binding of neutrons and protons into nuclei, as we have seen. This interaction, which represents the "glue" that holds the nucleons together, is the strongest of all the fundamental interactions. It is very short-ranged and is negligible for separations greater than about 10^{-15} m (the approximate size of a nucleus).

The electromagnetic interaction, which is about 10^{-2} times the strength of the strong interaction at nuclear distances, is responsible for the attraction of unlike charges and the repulsion of like charges. This interaction is responsible for the binding of atoms and molecules. It is a long-range interaction that decreases in strength as the inverse square of the separation between interacting particles, as described in Chapter 17.

The weak interaction is a short-range nuclear interaction that is involved in beta decay. Its strength is only about 10^{-13} times that of the strong interaction. However, because the strength of an interaction depends on the distance through which it acts, the relative strengths of two interactions differ depending on what separation distance is used. The strength of the weak interaction, for example, is sometimes cited to be as large as 10^{-6} times that of the strong interaction. Keep in mind that these relative strengths are merely estimates and they depend on the assumed separation distance.

25-4 SECTION OBJECTIVES

- **Define the four fundamental interactions of nature.**
- **Identify the elementary particles that make up matter.**
- **Describe the standard model of the universe.**

Figure 25-11
The Stanford Linear Accelerator, in California, creates high-energy particle collisions that provide evidence of new particles.

Finally, the gravitational interaction is a long-range interaction with a strength of only about 10^{-38} times that of the strong interaction. Although this familiar interaction is what holds the planets, stars, and galaxies together, its effect on elementary particles is negligible. The gravitational interaction is the weakest of all four fundamental interactions.

A force can be thought of as mediated by an exchange of particles

Notice that in this section we have referred to a force as an *interaction*. This is because in particle physics the interaction of matter is usually described not in terms of forces but in terms of the exchange of special particles. In the case of the electromagnetic interaction, the particles are photons. Thus, it is said that the electromagnetic force is *mediated* by photons.

Figure 25-12 shows how two electrons might repel one another through the exchange of a photon. Because momentum is conserved, the electron emitting a photon changes direction slightly. As the photon is absorbed, the other electron's direction must also change. The net effect is that the two electrons change direction and move away from each other.

Likewise, the strong interaction is mediated by particles called *gluons*, the weak interaction is mediated by particles called the *W* and *Z bosons*, and the gravitational interaction is mediated by *gravitons*. All of these particles except the graviton have been detected. The four fundamental interactions of nature and their mediating field particles are summarized in **Table 25-6.**

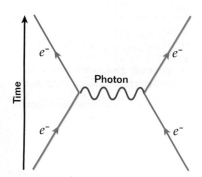

Figure 25-12

In particle physics, the electromagnetic interaction is modeled as an exchange of photons. The wavy red line represents a photon, and the blue lines represent electrons.

Table 25-6	The fundamental interactions of nature		
Interaction (force)	**Relative strength**	**Range of force**	**Mediating field particle**
strong	1	≈ 1 fm	gluon
electromagnetic	10^{-2}	proportional to $1/r^2$	photon
weak	10^{-13}	$< 10^{-3}$ fm	$W^{\pm}$ and Z bosons
gravitational	10^{-38}	proportional to $1/r^2$	graviton

CLASSIFICATION OF PARTICLES

All particles other than the mediating field particles can be classified into two broad categories: *leptons* and *hadrons*. The difference between the two is whether they interact through the strong interaction. Leptons are a group of particles that participate in the weak, gravitational, and electromagnetic interactions but not in the strong interaction. Hadrons are particles that interact through all four fundamental interactions, including the strong interaction.

Leptons are thought to be elementary particles

Electrons and neutrinos are both leptons. Like all leptons, they have no measurable size or internal structure and do not seem to break down into smaller units. Because of this, *leptons appear to be truly elementary.*

The number of known leptons is small. Currently, scientists believe there are only six leptons: the electron, the muon, the tau, and a neutrino associated with each. Each of these six leptons also has an antiparticle.

Hadrons include mesons and baryons

Hadrons, the strongly interacting particles, can be further divided into two classes: *mesons* and *baryons.* Originally, mesons and baryons were classified according to their masses. Baryons were heavier than mesons, and both were heavier than leptons. However, this distinction no longer holds. Today, mesons and baryons are distinguished by their internal structure.

All mesons are unstable. Because of this, they are not constituents of normal, everyday matter. Baryons have masses equal to or greater than the proton mass. The most common examples of baryons are protons and neutrons, which are constituents of normal, everyday matter. A summary of this classification of particles is given in **Figure 25-13.**

Hadrons are thought to be made of quarks

Particle-collision experiments involving hadrons seem to involve many short-lived particles, implying that hadrons are made up of more-fundamental particles. Furthermore, there are numerous hadrons, and many of them are known to decay into other hadrons. These facts strongly suggest that hadrons, unlike leptons, cannot be truly elementary.

In 1963, Murray Gell-Mann and George Zweig independently proposed that hadrons have a more elementary substructure. According to their model, all hadrons are composed of two or three fundamental particles, which came to be called *quarks.* In the original model, there were three types of quarks, designated by the symbols *u, d,* and *s.* These were given the arbitrary names *up, down,* and *sideways* (now more commonly referred to as *strange*). Associated with each quark is an antiquark of opposite charge.

The difference between mesons and baryons is due to the number of quarks that compose them. The compositions of all hadrons known when Gell-Mann and Zweig presented their models could be completely specified by three simple rules, which are summarized in **Table 25-7.**

Later evidence from collision experiments encouraged theorists to propose the existence of several more quarks, now known as *charm, top,* and *bottom.* These six quarks seem to fit together in pairs: up and down, charm and strange, and top and bottom.

All quarks have a charge associated with them. The charge of a hadron is equal to the sum of the charges of its constituent quarks and is either zero or a multiple of *e,* the fundamental unit of charge introduced in Chapter 17. This

Classification of particles

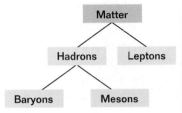

Figure 25-13
Leptons appear to be elementary, while hadrons consist of smaller particles, called quarks. As a result, hadrons can be further subdivided into baryons and mesons, based on their internal composition.

Table 25-7	Hadrons
Particle	**Composition**
meson	one quark and one antiquark
baryon	three quarks
antibaryon	three antiquarks

implies that quarks have a very unusual property—fractional electric charge. In other words, the charge of the electron is no longer thought to be the smallest possible nonzero charge that a particle can have. The charges for all six quarks that have been discovered and their corresponding antiquarks are summarized in **Table 25-8.**

Table 25-8   Quarks and their charges

Quark	Charge	Antiquark	Charge
up (u)	$+\frac{2}{3}e$	$\bar{u}$	$-\frac{2}{3}e$
down (d)	$-\frac{1}{3}e$	$\bar{d}$	$+\frac{1}{3}e$
charm (c)	$+\frac{2}{3}e$	$\bar{c}$	$-\frac{2}{3}e$
strange (s)	$-\frac{1}{3}e$	$\bar{s}$	$+\frac{1}{3}e$
top (t)	$+\frac{2}{3}e$	$\bar{t}$	$-\frac{2}{3}e$
bottom (b)	$-\frac{1}{3}e$	$\bar{b}$	$+\frac{1}{3}e$

Conceptual Challenge

1. Particle-antiparticle interactions

An antibaryon interacts with a meson. Can a baryon be produced in such an interaction? Explain.

2. Strong and weak interactions

Two protons in a nucleus interact via the strong interaction. Are they also subject to the weak interaction?

Figure 25-14 represents the quark compositions of several hadrons, both baryons and mesons. Just two of the quarks, u and d, are needed to construct the hadrons encountered in ordinary matter (protons and neutrons). The other quarks are needed only to construct rare forms of matter that are typically found only in high-energy situations, such as particle collisions.

The charges of the quarks that make up each hadron in **Figure 25-14** add up to zero or a multiple of e. For example, the proton contains three quarks (u, u, and d) having charges of $+\frac{2}{3}e$, $+\frac{2}{3}e$, and $-\frac{1}{3}e$. The total charge of the proton is $+e$, as you would expect. Likewise, the total charge of quarks in a neutron is zero ($+\frac{2}{3}e$, $-\frac{1}{3}e$, and $-\frac{1}{3}e$).

You may be wondering whether such discoveries will ever end. At present, physicists believe that six quarks and six leptons (and their antiparticles) are the fundamental particles.

Figure 25-14
Baryons contain three quarks, while mesons contain a quark and an antiquark. The baryons represented are a proton (p^+) and a neutron (n). The mesons shown are a pion (π^+) and a kaon (K^-), both rare particles.

Despite many extensive efforts, no isolated quark has ever been observed. Physicists now believe that quarks are permanently confined inside ordinary particles by the strong force. This force, often called the *color force* for quarks, is analogous to the electric force between charges; like colors repel, and opposite colors attract. Of course, quarks are not really colored. Color is merely a name given to the property of quarks that allows them to attract one another and form composite particles. The attractive force between nucleons is a byproduct of the strong force between quarks.

THE STANDARD MODEL

The current model used in particle physics to understand matter is called the *standard model*. This model was developed over many years by a variety of people. Although the details of the standard model are complex, the model's essential elements can be summarized using **Figure 25-15.** The strong force, mediated by gluons, holds quarks together to form composite particles, such as protons, neutrons, and mesons. Leptons participate only in the electromagnetic, gravitational, and weak interactions. The combination of composite particles, such as protons and neutrons, with leptons, such as electrons, makes the constituents of all matter, which are atoms.

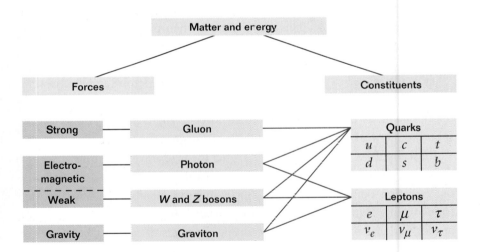

Figure 25-15
This schematic diagram summarizes the main elements of the standard model, including the fundamental forces, the mediating field particles, and the constituents of matter.

The standard model can help explain the early universe

Particle physics helps us understand not only the realm of the very small but also the origin and evolution of the universe. The current theory of the creation of the universe is called the *big bang*. According to the big bang theory, the universe erupted from a pointlike singularity about 15 billion to 20 billion years ago. In the brief instant after the big bang came such extremes in the density of matter and energy that all four fundamental interactions of physics operated in a single, unified way. The temperatures and energy present reduced everything into an undifferentiated "quark soup."

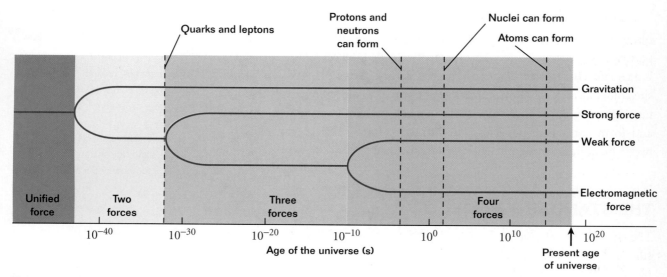

Quarks and leptons

Protons and neutrons can form

Nuclei can form

Atoms can form

Gravitation

Strong force

Weak force

Electromagnetic force

Unified force

Two forces

Three forces

Four forces

10^{-40} 10^{-30} 10^{-20} 10^{-10} 10^{0} 10^{10} 10^{20}

Age of the universe (s)

Present age of universe

Figure 25-16
The four fundamental interactions of nature were indistinguishable during the early moments of the big bang.

The evolution of the four fundamental interactions from the big bang to the present is shown in **Figure 25-16.** During the first 10^{-43} s, it is presumed that the strong, electroweak (electromagnetic and weak), and gravitational interactions were joined together. From 10^{-43} s to 10^{-32} s after the big bang, gravity broke free of this unification while the strong and electroweak interactions remained as one. This was a period when particle energies were so great (greater than 10^{16} GeV) that very massive particles that are now rare, as well as quarks, leptons, and their antiparticles, existed.

Then the universe rapidly expanded and cooled, the strong and electroweak interactions parted, and the grand unification was broken. About 10^{-10} s after the big bang, as the universe continued to cool, the electroweak interaction split into the weak interaction and the electromagnetic interaction.

Until about 7×10^5 years (2×10^{13} s) after the big bang, most of the energy in the universe was in the form of radiation rather than matter. This was the era of the radiation-dominated universe. Such intense radiation prevented matter from forming even single hydrogen atoms. Matter did exist, but only in the form of ions and electrons. Electrons are strong scatterers of photons, so matter at this time was opaque to radiation. Matter continuously absorbed and re-emitted photons, thereby ensuring thermal equilibrium of radiation and matter.

By the time the universe was about 7 million years (2×10^{14} s) old, it had expanded and cooled to about 3000 K. At this temperature, protons could bind to electrons to form hydrogen atoms. Without free electrons to scatter photons, the universe suddenly became transparent. Matter and radiation no longer interacted as strongly, and each evolved separately. By this time, most of the energy in the universe was in the form of matter. Clumps of neutral matter steadily grew: first atoms, followed by molecules, gas clouds, stars, and finally galaxies. This period, referred to as the matter-dominated universe, continues to this day.

The standard model is still incomplete

While particle physicists have been exploring the realm of the very small, cosmologists have been exploring cosmic history back to the first microsecond of the big bang. Observation of the events that occur when two particles collide in an accelerator is essential to reconstructing the early moments in cosmic history. Perhaps the key to understanding the early universe is to first understand the world of elementary particles. Cosmologists and particle physicists find that they have many common goals, and they are working together to attempt to study the physical world at its most fundamental level.

Our understanding of physics at short distances is far from complete. Particle physics still faces many questions. For example, why does the photon have no mass, while the W and Z bosons do? Because of this mass difference, the electromagnetic and weak forces are quite distinct at low energies, such as those in everyday life, but they behave in similar ways at very high energies.

To account for these changes, the standard model proposes the existence of a particle called the *Higgs boson,* which exists only at the high energies at which the electromagnetic and weak forces begin to merge. The Higgs boson has not yet been found. According to the standard model, its mass should be less than 1 TeV (10^{12} eV). International efforts are under way to build a device capable of reaching energies close to 1 TeV to search for the Higgs boson.

There are still other questions that the standard model has yet to answer. Is it possible to unify the strong and electroweak theories in a logical and consistent manner? Why do quarks and leptons form three similar but distinct families? Are muons the same as electrons (apart from their different masses), or do they have other subtle differences that have not been detected? Why are some particles charged and others neutral? Why do quarks carry a fractional charge? What determines the masses of the fundamental constituents? Can isolated quarks exist? The questions go on and on. Because of the rapid advances and new discoveries in the field of particle physics, by the time you read this book, some of these questions may have been resolved, while new questions may have emerged.

Section Review

1. Name the four fundamental interactions and the particles that mediate each interaction.

2. What are the differences between hadrons and leptons? What are the differences between baryons and mesons?

3. Describe the main stages of the evolution of the universe according to the big bang theory.

Antimatter

Startling discoveries made in the twentieth century have confirmed that electrons and other particles of matter have *antiparticles*. Antiparticles have the same mass as their corresponding particle but an opposite charge.

The discovery of antiparticles

The discovery of antiparticles began in the 1920s with work by the theoretical physicist Paul Adrien Maurice Dirac (1902–1984), who developed a version of quantum mechanics that incorporated Einstein's theory of special relativity. Dirac's theory was successful in many respects, but it had one major problem: its relativistic wave equation required solutions corresponding to negative energy states. This negative set of solutions suggested the existence of something like an electron but with an opposite charge, just as the negative energy states were opposite to an electron's typical energy states. At the time, there was no experimental evidence of such antiparticles.

In 1932, shortly after Dirac's theory was introduced, evidence of the anti-electron was discovered experimentally by the American physicist Carl Anderson. The anti-electron, also known as the *positron,* has the same mass as the electron but is positively charged. Anderson found the positron while examining tracks created by electronlike particles in a cloud chamber that was placed in a magnetic field. As described in Chapter 21, such a field will cause moving particles to follow curved paths. The direction in which a particle moves depends on whether its charge is positive or negative. Anderson noted that some of the tracks had deflections typical of an electron's mass, but in the opposite direction, corresponding to a positively charged particle.

Pair production and annihilation

Since Anderson's initial discovery, the positron has been observed in a number of experiments. In perhaps the most common process, a gamma ray with sufficiently high energy collides with a nucleus, creating an electron-positron pair. An example of this process, known as *pair production,* is shown in **Figure 25-17.**

During pair production, the energy of the photon is completely converted into the rest energy and kinetic energy of the electron and the positron. Thus, pair

Figure 25-17
The red and green spirals shown here are the paths of a positron and an electron moving through a magnetic field. Note that these paths have about the same shape but are opposite in direction.

production is a striking verification of the equivalence of mass (rest energy) and other forms of energy as predicted by Einstein's special theory of relativity. (The equivalence between mass and energy is discussed in the Physics on the Edge feature at the end of Chapter 5.)

Once formed, a positron will most likely soon collide with an oppositely charged electron in a process known as *pair annihilation*. This process is the inverse of pair production—an electron-positron pair produces two photons. In the simplest example of pair annihilation, an electron and a positron initially at rest combine with each other and disappear, leaving behind two photons. Because the initial momentum of the electron-positron pair is zero, it is impossible to produce a single photon. Momentum can be conserved only if two photons moving in opposite directions, both with the same energy and magnitude of momentum, are produced.

Antimatter produced in a particle accelerator

After the positron was discovered, physicists began to search for the anti-proton and anti-neutron. However, because the proton and neutron are much more massive than the electron, a much greater amount of energy is required to produce their antiparticles. By 1955, technological advances in particle accelerators made observations of evidence of the anti-proton possible, and evidence of the anti-neutron was found a year later.

The discovery of other antiparticles leads to the question of whether these antiparticles can be combined to form antimatter and, if so, how that antimatter would behave. In 1995, physicists at the CERN particle accelerator in Geneva, Switzerland, succeeded in producing anti-hydrogen atoms, that is, atoms with a single anti-electron orbiting an anti-proton. Researchers observed nine anti-hydrogen atoms during a three-week period. Unfortunately, the anti-hydrogen atoms had a short lifetime—less than 37 billionths of a second—because as soon as an anti-hydrogen atom encountered ordinary matter, the two annihilated one another. Attempts to produce antimatter for greater time periods are currently under way.

CHAPTER 25
Summary

KEY TERMS

binding energy (p. 900)

half-life (p. 909)

isotope (p. 897)

strong force (p. 898)

KEY IDEAS

Section 25-1 The nucleus

- The nucleus, which consists of protons and neutrons, is the small, dense core of an atom.
- A nucleus can be characterized by a mass number, A, an atomic number, Z, and a neutron number, N.
- The binding energy of a nucleus is the difference in energy between its nucleons when bound and its nucleons when unbound.

Section 25-2 Nuclear decay

- An unstable nucleus can decay in three ways: alpha (α) decay, beta (β) decay, or gamma (γ) decay.
- The decay constant, λ, indicates the rate of radioactive decay.
- The half-life, $T_{1/2}$, is the time required for half the original nuclei of a radioactive substance to undergo radioactive decay.

Section 25-3 Nuclear reactions

- Nuclear reactions involve a change in the nucleus of an atom.
- In fission, a heavy nucleus splits into two lighter nuclei. In fusion, two light nuclei combine to form a heavier nucleus.

Section 25-4 Particle physics

- There are four fundamental interactions in nature: strong, weak, gravitational, and electromagnetic.
- The constituents of matter can be classified as leptons or hadrons, and hadrons can be further divided into mesons and baryons. Electrons and neutrinos are leptons. Protons and neutrons are baryons.
- Mesons consist of a quark-antiquark pair; baryons consist of three quarks.

Particle symbols

Particle name	Symbol
alpha particle (helium nucleus)	α (^4_2He)
beta particle (electron)	β^- ($^0_{-1}e$)
beta particle (positron)	β^+ ($^0_{+1}e$)
gamma ray	γ
neutron	n ($^1_0 n$)
proton	p ($^1_1 p$)
neutrino	ν
antineutrino	$\bar{\nu}$

Variable symbols

Quantities		Units		Conversions
m	mass	u	unified mass unit or atomic mass unit	$= 1.660\ 559 \times 10^{-27}$ kg $= 931.50$ MeV/c^2
λN	activity or decay rate	Bq Ci	becquerel curie	$= 1$ decay/s $= 3.7 \times 10^{10}$ Bq
$T_{1/2}$	half-life	s	seconds	

CHAPTER 25
Review and Assess

THE NUCLEUS

Review questions

1. How many protons are there in the nucleus $^{197}_{79}$Au? How many neutrons? How many electrons are there in the neutral atom?

2. What are isotopes?

3. What holds the nucleons in a nucleus together?

Conceptual questions

4. Is it possible to accurately predict an atom's mass from its atomic number? Explain.

5. What would happen if the binding energy of a nucleus was zero?

6. Why do heavier elements require more neutrons to maintain stability?

Practice problems

7. Calculate the total binding energy of $^{12}_{6}$C. (See Sample Problem 25A and refer to Appendix F.)

8. Calculate the average binding energy per nucleon of $^{24}_{12}$Mg and $^{85}_{37}$Rb. (See Sample Problem 25A and refer to Appendix F.)

9. Calculate the total binding energy of tritium ($^{3}_{1}$H) and helium-3 ($^{3}_{2}$He). (See Sample Problem 25A and refer to Appendix F.)

NUCLEAR DECAY AND REACTIONS

Review questions

10. Explain the main differences between alpha, beta, and gamma rays.

11. What fraction of a radioactive sample has decayed after two half-lives have elapsed?

12. **Figure 25-18** shows the steps by which $^{235}_{92}$U decays to $^{207}_{82}$Pb. Draw this diagram, and enter the correct isotope symbol in each square.

Figure 25-18

13. What factors make a fusion reaction difficult to achieve?

Conceptual questions

14. If a film is kept in a box, alpha particles from a radioactive source outside the box cannot expose the film, but beta particles can. Explain.

15. An alpha particle has twice the charge of a beta particle. Why does the beta particle deflect more when both pass between electrically charged plates, assuming they both have the same speed?

16. If a nucleus has a half-life of one year, will it be completely decayed after two years? Explain.

17. Why is carbon dating unable to provide accurate estimates of very old materials?

18. Suppose it could be shown that cosmic ray intensity was much greater thousands of years ago. How would this affect the ages we assign to ancient samples of once-living matter?

19. A free neutron undergoes beta decay with a half-life of about 15 min. Can a free proton undergo a similar decay? (Hint: Compare the masses of the proton and the neutron.)

20. In a fission reactor, nuclear reactions produce energy to drive a generator. How is this energy produced?

21. Is it possible for a $^{12}_{6}C$ (12.000 000 u) nucleus to spontaneously decay into three alpha particles? Explain.

22. Why is the temperature required for deuterium-tritium fusion lower than that needed for deuterium-deuterium fusion? (Hint: Consider the Coulomb repulsion and nuclear attraction for each case.)

Practice problems

23. Determine the product of the following reaction:
$^{7}_{3}Li + ^{4}_{2}He \rightarrow ? + ^{1}_{0}n$
(See Sample Problem 25B.)

24. A nuclear reaction of significant historical note occurred in 1932, when a beryllium target was bombarded with alpha particles. Analysis of the experiment indicated that the following reaction occurred:
$^{4}_{2}He + ^{9}_{4}Be \rightarrow ^{12}_{6}C + X$
What is X in this reaction?
(See Sample Problem 25B.)

25. Complete the following nuclear reactions:
   a. $? + ^{14}_{7}N \rightarrow ^{1}_{1}H + ^{17}_{8}O$
   b. $^{7}_{3}Li + ^{1}_{1}H \rightarrow ^{4}_{2}He + ?$
(See Sample Problem 25B.)

26. How long will it take a sample of polonium-210 with a half-life of 140 days to decay to one-sixteenth its original strength?
(See Sample Problem 25C.)

27. A radioactive sample contains 1.67×10^{11} atoms of $^{108}_{47}Ag$ (half-life = 2.42 min) at some instant. What is the activity of this sample in mCi?
(See Sample Problem 25C.)

28. The amount of carbon-14 ($^{14}_{6}C$) in a wooden artifact is measured to be 6.25 percent the amount in a fresh sample of wood from the same region. The half-life of carbon-14 is 5730 years. Assuming the same amount of carbon-14 was initially present in the artifact, determine the age of the artifact.
(See Sample Problem 25C.)

29. A sample of organic material is found to contain 18 g of carbon. Based on samples of pottery found at the site, investigators believe the material is about 23 000 years old. Estimate what percentage of the material's carbon-14 has decayed.
(See Sample Problem 25C.)

PARTICLE PHYSICS

Review questions

30. Describe the properties of quarks.

31. What is the electrical charge of the particles with the following quark compositions?
   a. *udd*
   b. *uud*
   c. $u\bar{d}$

32. What is the electrical charge of the baryons with the following quark compositions?
   a. $\bar{u}\bar{u}\bar{d}$
   b. $\bar{u}\bar{d}\bar{d}$

33. What are each of the baryons in item 32 called?

34. How many quarks or antiquarks are there in the following particles?
   a. a baryon
   b. an antibaryon
   c. a meson
   d. an antimeson

Conceptual questions

35. Compare a neutrino with a photon.

36. Consider the statement, "All mesons are hadrons, but not all hadrons are mesons." Is this statement true? Discuss.

37. The *W* and *Z* bosons were first produced in 1983. Why was this an important discovery?

MIXED REVIEW

38. Find the diameter of a sphere of nuclear matter that would have a mass equal to that of Earth. Base your calculation on an Earth radius of 6.38×10^6 m, an average Earth density of 5.52×10^3 kg/m³, and a nuclear density of 2.3×10^{17} kg/m³.

39. A sample of a radioactive isotope is measured to have an activity of 240.0 mCi. If the sample has a half-life of 14 days, how many nuclei of the isotope are there at this time?

40. Find the energy released in the alpha decay of $^{238}_{92}\text{U}$. Use the masses in the following table:

Nucleus	Mass
$^{238}_{92}\text{U}$	238.050 784 u
$^{234}_{90}\text{Th}$	234.043 593 u
$^{4}_{2}\text{He}$	4.002 602 u

41. Certain stars are thought to collapse at the end of their lives, combining their protons and electrons to form a neutron star. Such a star could be thought of as a giant atomic nucleus. If a star with a mass equal to that of the sun (1.99×10^{30} kg) were to collapse into neutrons, what would be the radius of the star?

42. Two ways ^{235}U can undergo fission when bombarded with a neutron are described below. In each case, neutrons are also released. Find the number of neutrons released in each of the following:
  a. ^{140}Xe and ^{94}Sr released as fission fragments
  b. ^{132}Sn and ^{101}Mo released as fission fragments

43. When a proton traveling near the speed of light collides with a nucleus, it travels an average distance of 3.0×10^{-15} m before interacting. Estimate the time it takes for the strong interaction to occur.

44. Disregard binding energies and estimate the masses of the u and d quarks from the masses of the proton and neutron.

45. Natural gold has only one stable isotope, $^{197}_{79}\text{Au}$. If gold is bombarded with slow neutrons, β^- particles are emitted.
  a. Write the appropriate reaction equation.
  b. Calculate the maximum energy of the emitted beta particles.

46. Complete the following nuclear reactions:
  a. $^{27}_{13}\text{Al} + ^{4}_{2}\text{He} \rightarrow ? + ^{30}_{15}\text{P}$
  b. $^{1}_{0}n + ? \rightarrow ^{4}_{2}\text{He} + ^{7}_{3}\text{Li}$

47. When a $^{6}_{3}\text{Li}$ nucleus is struck by a proton, an alpha particle and a product nucleus are released. What is the product nucleus?

48. Suppose $^{10}_{5}\text{B}$ is struck by an alpha particle, releasing a proton and a product nucleus in the reaction. What is the product nucleus?

49. When ^{18}O is struck by a proton, ^{18}F and another particle are produced. What is the other particle?

50. Find the threshold kinetic energy that the incident neutron must have to produce the following reaction:
$^{1}_{0}n + ^{4}_{2}\text{He} \rightarrow ^{2}_{1}\text{H} + ^{3}_{1}\text{H}$

51. If the average energy released in a fission event is 208 MeV, find the total number of fission events required to provide enough energy to keep a 100.0 W light bulb burning for 1.0 h.

52. How many atoms of ^{235}U must undergo fission to operate a 1.0×10^3 MW power plant for one day if the conversion efficiency is 30.0 percent? Assume 208 MeV released per fission event.

53. An all-electric home uses about 2.0×10^3 kW•h of electrical energy per month. How many ^{235}U atoms would be required to provide this house with its energy needs for one year? Assume 100.0 percent conversion efficiency and 208 MeV released per fission.

54. Consider the hydrogen atom to be a sphere with a radius equal to the Bohr radius, 0.53×10^{-10} m, and calculate the approximate value of the ratio of atomic density to nuclear density.

55. A pair of nuclei for which $Z_1 = N_2$ and $Z_2 = N_1$ are called *mirror isobars* (the atomic and neutron numbers are interchangeable). Binding energy measurements on such pairs can be used to obtain evidence of the charge independence of nuclear forces. Charge independence means that the proton-proton, proton-neutron, and neutron-neutron forces are approximately equal. Calculate the difference in binding energy for the two mirror nuclei, $^{15}_{8}\text{O}$ (15.003 065 u) and $^{15}_{7}\text{N}$ (15.000 108 u).

56. What would be the gravitational force between two golf balls whose centers are 1.0 m apart if the golf balls were made of nuclear matter? Assume that the diameter of a golf ball is 3.5 cm.

57. It has been estimated that Earth has 9.1×10^{11} kg of natural uranium that can be economically mined. Of this total, 0.70 percent is ^{235}U. If all the world's energy needs (7.0×10^{12} J/s) were supplied by ^{235}U fission, how long would this supply last? Assume that 208 MeV of energy is released per fission event and that the mass of ^{235}U is about 3.9×10^{-25} kg.

58. A fission reaction that occurs when uranium-235 absorbs a neutron leads to the formation of barium-141 and krypton-92.

    a. Write the equation that describes this fission reaction.

    b. How many neutrons are released at the end of this reaction?

Technology & Learning

Graphing calculators

Program your graphing calculator to create a graph of time versus the amount of radioactive material remaining. Use your graph to determine the amount of radioactive material remaining for each of the following situations:

a. the amount of a 5.00 g sample of radium-226 with a half-life of 1600 years remaining after 250 years

b. the amount of the same sample of radium-226 remaining after 750 years

c. the amount of a 7.50 g sample of plutonium-236 with a half-life of 2.85 years remaining after 5 years

d. the amount of the same sample of plutonium-236 remaining after 25 years

Press [Y=] and [CLEAR] to clear any functions.
Open a new program by pressing [PRGM] [▶] [▶] [ENTER].

Name the program "NUCLEAR" and press [ENTER]. Then enter the program shown in the table below.

To exit the program editor, press [2nd] [QUIT]. To run the program, press [PRGM], select "NUCLEAR," and press [ENTER] [ENTER]. Enter the value for the half-life of the nuclide and the original mass of the sample, pressing [ENTER] after each one.

The calculator will provide a graph of the time versus the mass of the nuclide remaining. (If the graph is not visible, press [WINDOW], change the settings for the graph window, then press [GRAPH].)

Press [TRACE], and use the arrow keys to trace along the curve. The x value corresponds to the time in years, and the y value corresponds to the mass remaining in grams.

After you have finished using the graph for one sample, press [2nd] [QUIT] to run the program for the next one.

Keystrokes	Display
	PROGRAM: NUCLEAR
1. [PRGM] [▶] [2] [ALPHA] [H] [ENTER]	:PROMPT H
2. [PRGM] [▶] [2] [ALPHA] [M] [ENTER]	:PROMPT M
3. [ALPHA] ["] [ALPHA] [M] [×] [2nd] [e^x] [(] [(-)] [.] [6] [9] [3] [×] [X,T,θ] [÷] [ALPHA] [H] [)] [ALPHA] ["] [STO▶] [2nd] [Y-VARS] [1] [1] [ENTER]	:"M*e^(−.693*X/H)" → Y₁
4. [PRGM] [▶] [4] [ENTER]	:DISPGRAPH

59. A piece of charcoal known to be approximately 25 000 years old contains 7.96×10^{10} C-14 atoms.

    a. Determine the number of decays per minute expected from this sample.

    b. If the radioactive background in the counter without a sample is 20.0 counts/min and we assume 100.0 percent efficiency in counting, explain why 25 000 years is close to the limit of dating with this technique.

60. A photon with an energy of 2.09 GeV creates a proton-antiproton pair in which the proton has a kinetic energy of 95 MeV. What is the kinetic energy of the antiproton?

61. When a star has exhausted its hydrogen fuel, it may fuse other nuclear fuels, such as helium. At temperatures above 1.0×10^8 K, helium fusion can occur.

    a. Two alpha particles fuse to produce a nucleus, A, and a gamma ray. What is nucleus A?

    b. Nucleus A absorbs an alpha particle to produce a nucleus, B, and a gamma ray. What is nucleus B?

62. Two photons are produced when a proton and an antiproton annihilate each other. What is the minimum frequency of each photon? What is the minimum wavelength of each photon?

Alternative Assessment

Performance assessment

1. You are designing a nuclear power plant for a space station to be established on Mars. Material A is radioactive and has a half-life of two years. Material B is also radioactive and has a half-life of one year. Atoms of material B have one half the mass of atoms of material A. Discuss the benefits and drawbacks involved with each of these fuels.

2. Design a questionnaire to investigate what people in your community know about nuclear power and how they feel about it. Give the questionnaire to your classmates for their comments, and if your teacher approves, conduct a study with people in your community. Present your results in the form of a class presentation and discussion.

3. Investigate careers in nuclear medicine. Interview people who work with radiation or with isotopic tracers in a hospital. Find out what kind of patients they treat or test and the technology they use. What training is necessary for this type of career?

Portfolio projects

4. Research the lives and careers of female nuclear physicists such as Marie Curie, Lise Meitner, Ida Tacke Noddack, and Maria Goeppert-Mayer. Create a presentation about one of these scientists. The presentation can be in the form of a report, poster, short video, or computer presentation.

5. Research how radioactive decay is used to date archaeological remains and fossils. What nuclear reactions are involved in the carbon-14 dating technique? What assumptions are made when the carbon-14 dating technique is used? What time scale is the carbon-14 technique suitable for? Is the carbon-14 technique appropriate to determine the age of a painting suspected to be 375 years old? Summarize your findings in a brochure or poster for visitors to a science museum.

6. "In 50 years of producing electrical power and weapons from nuclear fuel, the United States has accumulated millions of cubic meters and tens of billions of curies of radioactive waste." This statement appeared in a June 1997 special issue of *Physics Today*. Research the problem of nuclear waste in the United States. How much is there? What kinds of radioactive waste are there? Where are they produced? What are the costs and hazards associated with different techniques for disposal of radioactive waste? How do other countries deal with the problem? Choose the disposal option you think is most appropriate, and write a position paper. Include information about all options and the reasons for your choice.

CHAPTER 25
Laboratory Exercise

HALF-LIFE

The half-life of a radioactive element is the time it takes for half a given number of atoms of the element to decay. In this experiment, the activity of a radioisotope with a short half-life will be measured using a nuclear-lab station over a period of 10 s. The resulting data will be plotted on a graph, and the half-life will be calculated from points on the graph.

SAFETY

- Do not eat or drink anything in the laboratory. Never taste chemicals or touch them with your bare hands.

- Tie back long hair, secure loose clothing, and remove loose jewelry to prevent their coming into contact with hazardous chemicals.

- Do not allow radioactive materials to come into contact with your skin, hair, clothing, or personal belongings. Although the materials used in this lab are not hazardous when used properly, radioactive materials can cause serious illness and may have permanent effects.

- Dispose of chemicals as instructed by your teacher. Never pour hazardous chemicals into a regular waste container. Never pour radioactive materials down the drain.

PREPARATION

1. Read the entire lab, and plan the steps you will take.

2. Prepare a data table in your lab notebook with 2 columns and 31 rows. Label this table *Data Table*. Label the columns *Time interval (s)* and *Total count*. In the first column, label the 2nd through 31st rows in increments of 10 from *10* to *300*. Above the table, make a space to record the *Background count (s^{-1})*.

PROCEDURE

3. Turn on the nuclear-lab station. Even when no radioactive substances are near the station, counts will register. This is caused by background radiation. Take the radiation count for 10 min, and divide the total by 600 s (10 min × 60 s/min). This will give you the background count per second. Record this value in the space provided.

4. Wearing goggles, gloves, and a protective apron, set up the isogenerator vertically on a stand and clamp it securely in place, as shown in **Figure 25-19.** Carefully loosen the cap on the isogenerator, and turn the stopcock. Release 3–4 mL of the barium solution into a small culture dish. The dish now contains the radioisotope Ba-137m, a metastable isomer.

5. Add a small drop of soap to the solution so that it spreads evenly over the bottom of the dish.

6. Immediately insert the dish into the nuclear lab station, and start the counter. Read the total count at the end of each 10 s interval, and record both the time interval and the count in your data table.

Figure 25-19

Step 3: The station will begin showing counts as soon as it is turned on. Find the background count per second so you can subtract this number from your counts to obtain an accurate result.

Step 4: Wear protective gear and work carefully when preparing the solution.

Step 6: As soon as the solution is prepared, insert the dish into the counter and begin. Record the count and time interval every 10 s until the count remains fairly constant for over a minute.

ANALYSIS AND INTERPRETATION

Calculations and data analysis

1. **Organizing data**   For each 10 s time interval, calculate the count per second by dividing the count by 10 s. This will give you the average count per second.

2. **Organizing data**   For each value found in item 1, calculate the actual count per second due to the source by subtracting the background count from the average count.

3. **Graphing data**   Plot a graph of the actual counts versus the total elapsed time. Use a graphing calculator, computer, or graph paper.

Conclusions

4. **Analyzing graphs**   Select a value for the actual count near the left end of the graph and read from the graph the amount of time it took for the activity to decrease to one-half that value. Record this value as the half-life.

5. **Analyzing graphs**   Repeat the procedure in step 4 three more times, each time starting at a different place on the graph. Find the average of the four values for the half-life.

6. **Analyzing graphs**   Why is using the graph a better way to find the half-life than simply using the data table?

Reference Section

Appendixes

Appendix A
Mathematical Review

Scientific Notation

Positive exponents Many quantities that scientists deal with often have very large or very small values. For example, the speed of light is about 300 000 000 m/s, and the ink required to make the dot over an i in this textbook has a mass of about 0.000 000 001 kg. Obviously, it is cumbersome to work with numbers such as these. We avoid this problem by using a method based on powers of the number 10.

$$10^0 = 1$$
$$10^1 = 10$$
$$10^2 = 10 \times 10 = 100$$
$$10^3 = 10 \times 10 \times 10 = 1000$$
$$10^4 = 10 \times 10 \times 10 \times 10 = 10\ 000$$
$$10^5 = 10 \times 10 \times 10 \times 10 \times 10 = 100\ 000$$

The number of zeros determines the power to which 10 is raised, or the *exponent* of 10. For example, the speed of light, 300 000 000 m/s, can be expressed as 3×10^8 m/s. In this case, the exponent of 10 is 8.

Negative exponents For numbers less than one, we note the following:

$$10^{-1} = \frac{1}{10} = 0.1$$

$$10^{-2} = \frac{1}{10 \times 10} = 0.01$$

$$10^{-3} = \frac{1}{10 \times 10 \times 10} = 0.001$$

$$10^{-4} = \frac{1}{10 \times 10 \times 10 \times 10} = 0.0001$$

$$10^{-5} = \frac{1}{10 \times 10 \times 10 \times 10 \times 10} = 0.000\ 01$$

The value of the negative exponent equals the number of places the decimal point must be moved to be to the right of the first nonzero digit (in these cases, the digit 1). Numbers that are expressed as a number between 1 and 10 multiplied by a power of 10 are said to be in *scientific notation*. For example, 5 943 000 000 is 5.943×10^9 when expressed in scientific notation, and 0.000 083 2 is 8.32×10^{-5} when expressed in scientific notation.

Multiplication and division in scientific notation When numbers expressed in scientific notation are being multiplied, the following general rule is very useful:

$$10^n \times 10^m = 10^{(n+m)}$$

Note that n and m can be any numbers; they are not necessarily integers. For example, $10^2 \times 10^5 = 10^7$, and $10^{1/4} \times 10^{1/2} = 10^{3/4}$. The rule also applies to negative exponents. For example, $10^3 \times 10^{-8} = 10^{-5}$. When dividing numbers expressed in scientific notation, note the following:

$$\frac{10^n}{10^m} = 10^n \times 10^{-m} = 10^{(n-m)}$$

For example, $\dfrac{10^3}{10^2} = 10^{(3-2)} = 10^1$.

Fractions

The rules for multiplying, dividing, adding, and subtracting fractions are summarized in **Table A-1,** where a, b, c, and d are four numbers.

Table A-1 Basic Operations for Fractions

Operation	Rule	Example
Multiplication	$\left(\dfrac{a}{b}\right)\left(\dfrac{c}{d}\right) = \dfrac{ac}{bd}$	$\left(\dfrac{2}{3}\right)\left(\dfrac{4}{5}\right) = \dfrac{(2)(4)}{(3)(5)} = \dfrac{8}{15}$
Division	$\dfrac{\left(\dfrac{a}{b}\right)}{\left(\dfrac{c}{d}\right)} = \dfrac{ad}{bc}$	$\dfrac{\left(\dfrac{2}{3}\right)}{\left(\dfrac{4}{5}\right)} = \dfrac{(2)(5)}{(3)(4)} = \dfrac{10}{12} = \dfrac{5}{6}$
Addition and subtraction	$\dfrac{a}{b} \pm \dfrac{c}{d} = \dfrac{ad \pm bc}{bd}$	$\dfrac{2}{3} - \dfrac{4}{5} = \dfrac{(2)(5) - (3)(4)}{(3)(5)} = -\dfrac{2}{15}$

Powers

Rules of exponents When powers of a given quantity, x, are multiplied, the rule used for scientific notation applies:

$$(x^n)(x^m) = x^{(n+m)}$$

For example, $(x^2)(x^4) = x^{(2+4)} = x^6$.

When dividing the powers of a given quantity, note the following:

$$\frac{x^n}{x^m} = x^{(n-m)}$$

For example, $\dfrac{x^8}{x^2} = x^{(8-2)} = x^6$.

A power that is a fraction, such as $\frac{1}{3}$, corresponds to a root as follows:

$$x^{1/n} = \sqrt[n]{x}$$

For example, $4^{1/3} = \sqrt[3]{4} = 1.5874$. (A scientific calculator is useful for such calculations.)

Finally, any quantity, x^n, that is raised to the mth power is as follows:

$$(x^n)^m = x^{nm}$$

For example, $(x^2)^3 = x^{(2)(3)} = x^6$.

The basic rules of exponents are summarized in **Table A-2.**

Table A-2 Rules of Exponents

$x^0 = 1$	$x^1 = x$	$(x^n)(x^m) = x^{(n+m)}$
$\dfrac{x^n}{x^m} = x^{(n-m)}$	$x^{(1/n)} = \sqrt[n]{x}$	$(x^n)^m = x^{(nm)}$

Algebra

Solving for unknowns When algebraic operations are performed, the laws of arithmetic apply. Symbols such as x, y, and z are usually used to represent quantities that are not specified. Such unspecified quantities are called *unknowns*.

First, consider the following equation:

$$8x = 32$$

If we wish to solve for x, we can divide each side of the equation by the same factor without disturbing the equality. In this case, if we divide both sides by 8, we have the following:

$$\frac{8x}{8} = \frac{32}{8}$$
$$x = 4$$

Next, consider the following equation:

$$x + 2 = 8$$

In this type of expression, we can add or subtract the same quantity from each side. If we subtract 2 from each side, we get the following:

$$x + 2 - 2 = 8 - 2$$
$$x = 6$$

In general, if $x + a = b$, then $x = b - a$.

Now, consider the following equation:

$$\frac{x}{5} = 9$$

If we multiply each side by 5, we are left with x isolated on the left and a value of 45 on the right.

$$(5)\left(\frac{x}{5}\right) = (9)(5)$$

$$x = 45$$

In all cases, *whatever operation is performed on the left side of the equation must also be performed on the right side.*

Factoring

Some useful formulas for factoring an equation are given in **Table A-3.** As an example of a common factor, consider the equation $5x + 5y + 5z = 0$. This equation can be expressed as $5(x + y + z) = 0$. The expression $a^2 + 2ab + b^2$, which is an example of a perfect square, is equivalent to the expression $(a + b)^2$. For example, if $a = 2$ and $b = 3$, then $2^2 + (2)(2)(3) + 3^2 = (2 + 3)^2$, or $(4 + 12 + 9) = 5^2 = 25$. Finally, for an example of the difference of two squares, let $a = 6$ and $b = 3$. In this case, $(6^2 - 3^2) = (6 + 3)(6 - 3)$, or $(36 - 9) = (9)(3) = 27$.

Table A-3 Factoring Equations

$ax + ay + az = a(x + y + z)$	common factor
$a^2 + 2ab + b^2 = (a + b)^2$	perfect square
$a^2 - b^2 = (a + b)(a - b)$	difference of two squares

Quadratic Equations

The general form of a quadratic equation is as follows:

$$ax^2 + bx + c = 0$$

In this equation, x is the unknown quantity and a, b, and c are numerical factors known as *coefficients*. This equation has two roots, given by the following:

$$x = \frac{-b \pm \sqrt{b^2 - 4ac}}{2a}$$

If $b^2 \geq 4ac$, the value inside the square-root symbol will be positive or zero and the roots will be real. If $b^2 < 4ac$, the value inside the square-root symbol will be negative and the roots will be imaginary. In problems in this physics book, imaginary roots should not occur.

Example

Find the solutions for the equation $x^2 + 5x + 4 = 0$.

Solution

The given equation can be expressed as $(1)x^2 + (5)x + (4) = 0$. In other words, $a = 1$, $b = 5$, and $c = 4$. The two roots of this equation can be found by substituting these values into the quadratic equation, as follows:

$$x = \frac{-b \pm \sqrt{b^2 - 4ac}}{2a} = \frac{-5 \pm \sqrt{5^2 - (4)(1)(4)}}{(2)(1)} = \frac{-5 \pm \sqrt{9}}{2} = \frac{-5 \pm 3}{2}$$

The two roots are $x = \dfrac{-5 + 3}{2} = -1$ and $x = \dfrac{-5 - 3}{2} = -4$.

$$\boxed{x = -1 \text{ and } x = -4}$$

We can evaluate these answers by substituting them into the given equation and verifying that the result is zero.

$$x^2 + 5x + 4 = 0$$

For $x = -1$, $(-1)^2 + 5(-1) + 4 = 1 - 5 + 4 = 0$.

For $x = -4$, $(-4)^2 + 5(-4) + 4 = 16 - 20 + 4 = 0$.

Example

Factor the equation $2x^2 - 3x - 4 = 0$.

Solution

In this case, the given equation can be expressed as $(2)x^2 + (-3)x + (-4) = 0$. Thus, $a = 2$, $b = -3$, and $c = -4$. Substitute these values into the quadratic equation to factor the given equation.

$$x = \frac{-b \pm \sqrt{b^2 - 4ac}}{2a} = \frac{3 \pm \sqrt{(-3)^2 - (4)(2)(-4)}}{(2)(2)} = \frac{3 \pm \sqrt{41}}{4} = \frac{3 \pm 6.403}{4}$$

The two roots are $x = \dfrac{3 + 6.403}{4} = 2.351$ and $x = \dfrac{3 - 6.403}{4} = -0.851$.

$$\boxed{x = 2.351 \text{ and } x = -0.851}$$

Again, evaluate these answers by substituting them into the given equation.

$$2x^2 - 3x - 4 = 0$$

For $x = 2.351$, $2(2.351)^2 - 3(2.351) - 4 = 11.054 - 7.053 - 4 \approx 0$.

For $x = -0.851$, $2(-0.851)^2 - 3(-0.851) - 4 = 1.448 + 2.553 - 4 \approx 0$.

Linear Equations

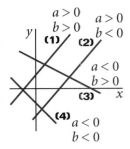

Figure A-1

Figure A-2

A linear equation has the following general form:

$$y = ax + b$$

In this equation, a and b are constants. This equation is called linear because the graph of y versus x is a straight line, as shown in **Figure A-1.** The constant b, called the *intercept*, represents the value of y where the straight line intersects the y-axis. The constant a is equal to the *slope* of the straight line and is also equal to the tangent of the angle that the line makes with the x-axis (θ). If any two points on the straight line are specified by the coordinates (x_1, y_1) and (x_2, y_2), as in **Figure A-1,** then the slope of the straight line can be expressed as follows:

$$\text{slope} = \frac{y_2 - y_1}{x_2 - x_1} = \frac{\Delta y}{\Delta x}$$

For example, if the two points shown in **Figure A-1** are $(2, 4)$ and $(6, 9)$, then the slope of the line is as follows:

$$\text{slope} = \frac{(9 - 4)}{(6 - 2)} = \frac{5}{4}$$

Note that a and b can have either positive or negative values. If $a > 0$, the straight line has a *positive* slope, as in **Figure A-1.** If $a < 0$, the straight line has a *negative* slope. Furthermore, if $b > 0$, the y intercept is positive (above the x-axis), while if $b < 0$, the y intercept is negative (below the x-axis). **Figure A-2** gives an example of each of these four possible cases, which are summarized in **Table A-4.**

Table A-4 Linear Equations

Constants	Slope	y intercept
$a > 0, b > 0$	positive slope	positive y intercept
$a > 0, b < 0$	positive slope	negative y intercept
$a < 0, b > 0$	negative slope	positive y intercept
$a < 0, b < 0$	negative slope	negative y intercept

Solving Simultaneous Linear Equations

Consider the following equation:

$$3x + 5y = 15$$

This equation has two unknowns, x and y. Such an equation does not have a unique solution. That is, $(x = 0, y = 3)$, $(x = 5, y = 0)$, and $\left(x = 2, y = \frac{9}{5}\right)$ are all solutions to this equation.

If a problem has two unknowns, a unique solution is possible only if there are two independent equations. In general, if a problem has n unknowns, its solution requires n independent equations. There are three basic methods that can be used to solve simultaneous equations. Each of these methods is discussed below, and an example is given for each.

First method: substitution One way to solve two simultaneous equations involving two unknowns, x and y, is to solve one of the equations for one of the unknown values in terms of the other unknown value. In other words, either solve one equation for x in terms of y or solve one equation for y in terms of x. Once you have an expression for either x or y, substitute this expression into the other original equation. At this point, the equation has only one unknown quantity. This unknown can be found through algebraic manipulations and then can be used to determine the other unknown.

Example
Solve the following two simultaneous equations:

1. $5x + y = -8$
2. $2x - 2y = 4$

Solution
First solve for either x or y in one of the equations. We'll begin by solving equation 2 for x.

2. $2x - 2y = 4$
$$2x = 4 + 2y$$
$$x = \frac{4 + 2y}{2} = 2 + y$$

Next, we substitute this equation for x into equation 1 and solve for y.

1. $5x + y = -8$
$$5(2 + y) + y = -8$$
$$10 + 5y + y = -8$$
$$6y = -18$$

$$\boxed{y = -3}$$

To find x, substitute this value for y into the equation for x derived from equation 2.

$$x = 2 + y = 2 + -3$$

$$\boxed{x = -1}$$

There is always more than one way to solve simultaneous equations by substitution. In this example, we first solved equation 2 for x. However, we could have begun by solving equation 2 for y or equation 1 for x or y. Any of these processes would result in the same answer.

Second method: canceling one term Simultaneous equations can also be solved by multiplying both sides of one of the equations by a value that will make either the x value or the y value in that equation equal to and opposite the corresponding value in the second equation. When the two equations are added together, that unknown value drops out and only one of the unknown values remains. This unknown can be found through algebraic manipulations and then can be used to determine the other unknown.

Example

Solve the following two simultaneous equations:

1. $3x + y = -6$
2. $-4x - 2y = 6$

Solution

First, multiply each term of one of the equations by a factor that will make either the x or the y values cancel when the two equations are added together. In this case, we can multiply each term in equation 1 by the factor 2. The positive $2y$ in equation 1 will then cancel the negative $2y$ in equation 2.

1. $3x + y = -6$
   $(2)(3x) + (2)(y) = -(2)(6)$
   $6x + 2y = -12$

Next, add the two equations together and solve for x.

2. $-4x - 2y = 6$
   $6x + 2y = -12$
   $2x = -6$

$$\boxed{x = -3}$$

Then substitute this value of x into either equation to find y.
1. $3x + y = -6$
   $y = -6 - 3x = -6 - (3)(-3) = -6 + 9$

$$\boxed{y = 3}$$

In this example, we multiplied both sides of equation 1 by 2 so that the y terms would cancel when the two equations were added together. As with substitution, this is only one of many possible ways to solve the equations. For example, we could have multiplied both sides of equation 2 by $\frac{3}{4}$ so that the x terms would cancel when the two equations were added together.

Third method: graphing the equations Two linear equations with two unknowns can also be solved by a graphical method. If the straight lines corresponding to the two equations are plotted in a conventional coordinate system, the intersection of the two lines represents the solution.

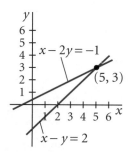

Figure A-3

Example

Solve the following two simultaneous equations:

1. $x - y = 2$
2. $x - 2y = -1$

Solution

These two equations are plotted in **Figure A-3.** To plot an equation, rewrite the equation in the form $y = ax + b$, where a is the slope and b is the y intercept. In this example, the equations can be rewritten as follows:

$$y = x - 2$$
$$y = \tfrac{1}{2}x + \tfrac{1}{2}$$

Once one point of a line is known, any other point on that line can be found with the slope of the line. For example, the slope of the first line is 1, and we know that $(0, -2)$ is a point on this line. If we choose the point $x = 2$, we have $(2, y_2)$. The coordinate y_2 can be found as follows:

$$\text{slope} = \frac{y_2 - y_1}{x_2 - x_1} = \frac{y_2 - (-2)}{2 - 0} = 1$$
$$y_2 = 0$$

Connecting the two known coordinates, $(0, -2)$ and $(2, 0)$, results in a graph of the line. The second line can be plotted with the same method.

As shown in **Figure A-3,** the intersection of the two lines has the coordinates $x = 5$, $y = 3$. This intersection represents the solution to the equations. You should check this solution using either of the analytical techniques discussed above.

Logarithms

Suppose that a quantity, x, is expressed as a power of another quantity, a.

$$x = a^y$$

The number a is called the *base number*. The *logarithm* of x with respect to the base, a, is equal to the exponent to which a must be raised in order to satisfy the expression $x = a^y$.

$$y = \log_a x$$

Conversely, the *antilogarithm* of y is the number x.

$$x = \text{antilog}_a y$$

Common and natural bases In practice, the two bases most often used are base 10, called the *common* logarithm base, and base $e = 2.718\ldots$, called the *natural* logarithm base. When common logarithms are used, y and x are related as follows:

$$y = \log_{10} x, \text{ or } x = 10^y$$

When natural logarithms are used, the symbol ln is used to signify that the logarithm has a base of e; in other words, $\log_e x = \ln x$.

$$y = \ln x, \text{ or } x = e^y$$

For example, $\log_{10} 52 = 1.716$, so antilog$_{10}$ $1.716 = 10^{1.716} = 52$. Likewise, $\ln 52 = 3.951$, so antiln $3.951 = e^{3.951} = 52$.

Note that you can convert between base 10 and base e with the equality

$$\ln x = (2.302\ 585)\log_{10} x.$$

Some useful properties of logarithms are summarized in **Table A-5.**

Table A-5 Properties of Logarithms

Rule	Example
$\log (ab) = \log a + \log b$	$\log (2)(5) = \log 2 + \log 5$
$\log \left(\dfrac{a}{b}\right) = \log a - \log b$	$\log \frac{3}{4} = \log 3 - \log 4$
$\log (a^n) = n \log a$	$\log 7^3 = 3 \log 7$
$\ln e = 1$	
$\ln e^a = a$	$\ln e^5 = 5$
$\ln \left(\dfrac{1}{a}\right) = -\ln a$	$\ln \frac{1}{8} = -\ln 8$

Conversions Between Fractions, Decimals, and Percentages

The rules for converting numbers from fractions to decimals and percentages and from percentages to decimals are summarized in **Table A-6.**

Table A-6 Conversions

Conversion	Rule	Example
Fraction to decimal	divide numerator by denominator	$\dfrac{31}{45} = 0.69$
Fraction to percentage	convert to decimal, then multiply by 100%	$\dfrac{31}{45} = (0.69)(100\%) = 69\%$
Percentage to decimal	move decimal point two places to the left, and remove the percent sign	$69\% = 0.69$

Geometry

Table A-7 provides equations for the area and volume of several geometric shapes used throughout this text.

Table A-7 Geometrical Areas and Volumes

Geometrical shape	Useful equations
rectangle	$\text{area} = lw$
circle	$\text{area} = \pi r^2$ $\text{circumference} = 2\pi r$
triangle	$\text{area} = \dfrac{1}{2}bh$
sphere	$\text{surface area} = 4\pi r^2$ $\text{volume} = \dfrac{4}{3}\pi r^3$
cylinder	$\text{volume} = \pi r^2 l$
rectangular box	$\text{surface area} = 2(lh + lw + hw)$ $\text{volume} = lwh$

Trigonometry and the Pythagorean Theorem

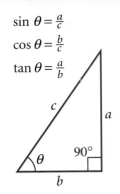

$\sin \theta = \frac{a}{c}$

$\cos \theta = \frac{b}{c}$

$\tan \theta = \frac{a}{b}$

Figure A-4

The portion of mathematics that is based on the special properties of a right triangle is called *trigonometry*. Many of the concepts of this branch of mathematics are of utmost importance in the study of physics. To review some of the basic concepts of trigonometry, consider the right triangle shown in **Figure A-4,** where side *a* is opposite the angle θ, side *b* is adjacent to the angle θ, and side *c* is the hypotenuse of the triangle (the side opposite the right angle). The most common trigonometry functions are summarized in **Table A-8,** using this figure as an example.

Table A-8 Trigonometry Functions

sine (sin)	$\sin \theta = \dfrac{\text{side opposite } \theta}{\text{hypotenuse}} = \dfrac{a}{c}$
cosine (cos)	$\cos \theta = \dfrac{\text{side adjacent to } \theta}{\text{hypotenuse}} = \dfrac{b}{c}$
tangent (tan)	$\tan \theta = \dfrac{\text{side opposite } \theta}{\text{side adjacent to } \theta} = \dfrac{a}{b}$
inverse sine ($\sin^{-1}$)	$\theta = \sin^{-1}\left(\dfrac{\text{side opposite } \theta}{\text{hypotenuse}}\right) = \sin^{-1}\left(\dfrac{a}{c}\right)$
inverse cosine ($\cos^{-1}$)	$\theta = \cos^{-1}\left(\dfrac{\text{side adjacent to } \theta}{\text{hypotenuse}}\right) = \cos^{-1}\left(\dfrac{b}{c}\right)$
inverse tangent ($\tan^{-1}$)	$\theta = \tan^{-1}\left(\dfrac{\text{side opposite } \theta}{\text{side adjacent to } \theta}\right) = \tan^{-1}\left(\dfrac{a}{b}\right)$

When $\theta = 30°$, for example, the ratio of *a* to *c* is always 0.50. In other words, $\sin 30° = 0.50$. Sine, cosine, and tangent are quantities without units because each represents the ratio of two lengths. Furthermore, note the following trigonometry identity:

$$\frac{\sin \theta}{\cos \theta} = \frac{\dfrac{\text{side opposite } \theta}{\text{hypotenuse}}}{\dfrac{\text{side adjacent to } \theta}{\text{hypotenuse}}} = \frac{\text{side opposite } \theta}{\text{side adjacent to } \theta} = \tan \theta$$

Some additional trigonometry identities are as follows:

$$\sin^2\theta + \cos^2\theta = 1$$
$$\sin \theta = \cos(90° - \theta)$$
$$\cos \theta = \sin(90° - \theta)$$

Determining an unknown side The first three functions given in **Table A-8** can be used to determine any unknown side of a right triangle when one side and one of the non-right angles are known. For example, if $\theta = 30°$ and $a = 1.0$ m, the other two sides of the triangle can be found as follows:

$$\sin \theta = \frac{a}{c}$$

$$c = \frac{a}{\sin \theta} = \frac{1.0 \text{ m}}{\sin 30°}$$

$$\boxed{c = 2.0 \text{ m}}$$

$$\tan \theta = \frac{a}{b}$$

$$b = \frac{a}{\tan \theta} = \frac{1.0 \text{ m}}{\tan 30°}$$

$$\boxed{b = 1.7 \text{ m}}$$

Determining an unknown angle In some cases, you might know the value of the sine, cosine, or tangent of an angle and need to know the value of the angle itself. The inverse sine, cosine, and tangent functions given in **Table A-8** can be used for this purpose. For example, in **Figure A-4** on page 947, suppose you know that side $a = 1.0$ m and side $c = 2.0$ m. To find the angle θ, you could use the inverse sine function, $\sin^{-1}$, as follows:

$$\theta = \sin^{-1}\left(\frac{a}{c}\right) = \sin^{-1}\left(\frac{1.0 \text{ m}}{2.0 \text{ m}}\right) = \sin^{-1}(0.50)$$

$$\boxed{\theta = 30°}$$

Pythagorean theorem Another useful equation when working with right triangles is the Pythagorean theorem. If a and b are the two legs of a right triangle and c is the hypotenuse, as in **Figure A-5**, the Pythagorean theorem can be expressed as follows:

$$c^2 = a^2 + b^2$$

In other words, the square of the hypotenuse of a right triangle equals the sum of the squares of the other two legs of the triangle. The Pythagorean theorem is useful when two sides of a right triangle are known but the third side is not. For example, if $c = 2.0$ m and $a = 1.0$ m, you could find b using the Pythagorean theorem as follows:

$$b = \sqrt{c^2 - a^2} = \sqrt{(2.0 \text{ m})^2 - (1.0 \text{ m})^2}$$
$$b = \sqrt{4.0 \text{ m}^2 - 1.0 \text{ m}^2} = \sqrt{3.0 \text{ m}^2}$$

$$\boxed{b = 1.7 \text{ m}}$$

Figure A-5

Accuracy in Laboratory Calculations

Absolute error Some of the laboratory experiments in this book involve finding a value that is already known, such as free-fall acceleration. In this type of experiment, the accuracy of your measurements can be determined by comparing your results with the accepted value. The absolute value of the difference between your experimental or calculated result and the accepted value is called the *absolute error*. Thus, absolute error can be found with the following equation:

$$\text{absolute error} = \left| \text{experimental} - \text{accepted} \right|$$

Be sure not to confuse accuracy with precision. The *accuracy* of a measurement refers to how close that measurement is to the accepted value for the quantity being measured. *Precision,* on the other hand, depends on the instruments used to measure a quantity. A meterstick that includes millimeters, for example, will give a more precise result than a meterstick whose smallest unit of measure is a centimeter. Thus, a measurement of 9.61 m/s^2 for free-fall acceleration is more precise than a measurement of 9.8 m/s^2, but 9.8 m/s^2 is more accurate than 9.61 m/s^2.

Relative error Note that a measurement that has a relatively large absolute error may be more accurate than a measurement that has a smaller absolute error if the first measurement involved much larger quantities. For this reason, the percentage error, or *relative error,* is often more meaningful than the absolute error. The relative error of a measured value can be found with the following equation:

$$\text{relative error} = \frac{(\text{experimental} - \text{accepted})}{\text{accepted}}$$

In other words, the relative error is the difference between the experimental value and the accepted value divided by the accepted value. Because relative error takes the size of the quantity being measured into account, the accuracy of two different measurements can be compared by comparing their relative errors.

For example, consider two laboratory experiments in which you are determining values that are fairly well known. In the first, you determine that free-fall acceleration at Earth's surface is 10.31 m/s^2. In the second, you find that the speed of sound in air at 25°C is 355 m/s. The accepted values for these quantities are 9.81 m/s^2 and 346 m/s. respectively. Now we'll find the absolute and relative errors for each experiment.

For the first experiment, the absolute and relative errors can be calculated as follows:

$$\text{absolute error} = \left| \text{experimental} - \text{accepted} \right| = \left| 10.31 \text{ m/s}^2 - 9.81 \text{ m/s}^2 \right|$$

$$\boxed{\text{absolute error} = 0.50 \text{ m/s}^2}$$

$$\text{relative error} = \frac{(\text{experimental} - \text{accepted})}{\text{accepted}} = \frac{(10.31 \text{ m/s}^2 - 9.81 \text{ m/s}^2)}{9.81 \text{ m/s}^2}$$

$$\boxed{\text{relative error} = 0.051 = 5.1\%}$$

For the second experiment, the absolute and relative errors can be calculated as follows:

$$\text{absolute error} = \left| \text{experimental} - \text{accepted} \right| = \left| 355 \text{ m/s} - 346 \text{ m/s} \right|$$

$$\boxed{\text{absolute error} = 9 \text{ m/s}}$$

$$\text{relative error} = \frac{(\text{experimental} - \text{accepted})}{\text{accepted}} = \frac{(355 \text{ m/s} - 346 \text{ m/s})}{346 \text{ m/s}}$$

$$\boxed{\text{relative error} = 0.026 = 2.6\%}$$

Note that the *absolute* error is less in the first experiment, while the *relative* error is less in the second experiment. The absolute error is less in the first experiment because typical values for free-fall acceleration are much smaller than typical values for the speed of sound in air. The relative errors take this difference into account. Thus, comparing the relative errors shows that the speed of sound is measured with greater accuracy than is the free-fall acceleration.

Appendix B Symbols

Diagram Symbols

The entries in this table are given roughly in order of appearance in the textbook, but consistency has been maintained in later chapters as well.

Mechanics

Symbol	Meaning
	displacement vector, component displacement
	velocity vector, component velocity
	acceleration vector
	force vector, component force
	momentum vector
	angle marking
	rotational motion

Thermodynamics

Symbol	Meaning
	energy transfer by heat
	energy transfer by work
	cycle or process

Waves and Electromagnetism

Symbol	Meaning
	ray (light or sound)
	positive charge
	negative charge
	electric field lines
	electric field vector
	electric current
	magnetic field lines
	magnetic field vector (into page, out of page)

Mathematical Symbols

Symbol	Meaning	Symbol	Meaning
Δ	(Greek *delta*) change in some quantity	$\leq$	less than or equal to
Σ	(Greek *sigma*) sum of quantities	$\propto$	is proportional to
θ	(Greek *theta*) any angle	$\approx$	is approximately equal to
$=$	equal to	$\lvert n \rvert$	absolute value or magnitude of
$>$	greater than	sin	sine
$\geq$	greater than or equal to	cos	cosine
$<$	less than	tan	tangent

Quantity Symbols Used Throughout

Symbols that are **boldfaced** refer to vector quantities that have both a magnitude and a direction. Symbols that are *italicized* refer to quantities with only a magnitude. Symbols that are neither are usually units (see Appendix C).

Symbol	Quantity
A	area
D	diameter
$\mathbf{F}, F$	force
m	mass
M	total mass
R	radius (of a spherical body, a curved mirror, or a curved lens)
r	radius (of sphere, shell, or disk)
t	time
V	volume

Translational Mechanics Symbols Used in This Book (Chapters 2–6)

Symbols that are **boldfaced** refer to vector quantities that have both a magnitude and a direction. Symbols that are *italicized* refer to quantities with only a magnitude. Symbols that are neither are usually units (see Appendix C).

Symbol	Quantity
$\mathbf{a}, a$	acceleration
$\mathbf{d}, d$	displacement
$\mathbf{F}\Delta t$	impulse
$\mathbf{F_g}, F_g$	gravitational force (weight)
$\mathbf{F_k}, F_k$	force of kinetic friction
$\mathbf{F_n}, F_n$	normal force
$\mathbf{F_{net}}, F_{net}$	net force
$\mathbf{F_R}, F_R$	force of air resistance
$\mathbf{F_s}, F_s$	force of static friction
$\mathbf{F_{s,max}}, F_{s,max}$	maximum force of static friction
h	height
k	spring constant
KE	kinetic energy
KE_{trans}	translational kinetic energy
MA	mechanical advantage
ME	mechanical energy (sum of all kinetic and potential energies)
μ_k	(Greek *mu*) coefficient of kinetic friction
μ_s	(Greek *mu*) coefficient of static friction
P	power
$\mathbf{p}, p$	momentum
PE	potential energy
$PE_{elastic}$	elastic potential energy
PE_g	gravitational potential energy
r	separation between point masses
$\mathbf{v}, v$	velocity or speed
W	work
$W_{friction}$	work done by a frictional force (or work required to overcome a frictional force)
W_{net}	net work done
$\Delta\mathbf{x}, \Delta x$	displacement in the x direction
$\Delta\mathbf{y}, \Delta y$	displacement in the y direction

Rotational Mechanics Symbols Used in This Book (Chapters 7–8)

Symbols that are **boldfaced** refer to vector quantities that have both a magnitude and a direction. Symbols that are *italicized* refer to quantities with only a magnitude. Symbols that are neither are usually units (see Appendix C).

Symbol	Quantity
a_t	tangential acceleration
a_c	centripetal acceleration
α	(Greek *alpha*) angular acceleration
$d\,(\sin\theta)$	length of lever arm (for torque calculations)
$\mathbf{F_c}$, F_c	force that maintains circular motion
I	moment of inertia
KE_{rot}	rotational kinetic energy
L	angular momentum
ℓ	length of a rotating rod
s	arc length
τ	(Greek *tau*) torque
τ_{net}	(Greek *tau*) net torque
θ	(Greek *theta*) angle of rotation
$\Delta\theta$	(Greek *delta* and *theta*) angular displacement (in radians)
v_t	tangential speed
ω	(Greek *omega*) angular speed

Fluid Dynamics and Thermodynamics Symbols Used in This Book (Chapters 9–11)

Symbols that are **boldfaced** refer to vector quantities that have both a magnitude and a direction. Symbols that are *italicized* refer to quantities with only a magnitude. Symbols that are neither are usually units (see Appendix C).

Symbol	Quantity
c_p	specific heat capacity
eff	efficiency of a simple machine, thermal efficiency of a heat engine
$\mathbf{F_B}$, F_B	buoyant force
L	latent heat
L_f	latent heat of fusion
L_v	latent heat of vaporization
N	number of gas particles or nuclei
P	pressure
P_0	initial pressure, gauge pressure
P_{net}	net pressure
ρ	(Greek *rho*) mass density
Q	heat
Q_c	energy transferred by heat to or from a low-temperature (cold) substance
Q_h	energy transferred by heat to or from a high-temperature (hot) substance
Q_{net}	net amount of energy transferred by heat to or from a system
T	temperature (absolute)
T_C	temperature in degrees Celsius
T_c	temperature of a low-temperature (cool) substance
T_F	temperature in degrees Fahrenheit
T_h	temperature of a high-temperature (hot) substance
U	internal energy

Vibrations, Waves, and Optics Symbols Used in This Book (Chapters 12–16)

Symbols that are **boldfaced** refer to vector quantities that have both a magnitude and a direction. Symbols that are *italicized* refer to quantities with only a magnitude. Symbols that are neither are usually units (see Appendix C).

Symbol	Quantity
C	center of curvature for spherical mirror
d	slit separation in double-slit interference of light
$d\,(\sin\theta)$	path difference for interfering light waves
$\mathbf{F}_{elastic}$, $F_{elastic}$	spring force
F	focal point
f	focal length
f	frequency
f_n	nth harmonic frequency
h	object height
h'	image height
k	spring constant
L	length of a pendulum, vibrating string, or vibrating column of air
ℓ	path length of light wave
λ	(Greek *lambda*) wavelength
m	order number for interference fringes
M	magnification of image
n	harmonic number (sound)
n	index of refraction
p	object distance
q	image distance
T	period of a pendulum (simple harmonic motion)
θ	(Greek *theta*) angle of incidence of a beam of light (reflection)
θ	(Greek *theta*) angle of fringe separation from center of interference pattern
θ'	(Greek *theta*) angle of reflection
θ_c	(Greek *theta*) critical angle of refraction
θ_i	(Greek *theta*) angle of incidence of a beam of light (refraction)
θ_r	(Greek *theta*) angle of refraction

Electromagnetism Symbols Used in This Book (Chapters 17–22)

Symbols that are **boldfaced** refer to vector quantities that have both a magnitude and a direction. Symbols that are *italicized* refer to quantities with only a magnitude. Symbols that are neither are usually units (see Appendix C).

Symbol	Quantity
$\mathbf{B}$, B	magnetic field
C	capacitance
d	separation of plates in a capacitor
$\mathbf{E}$, E	electric field
emf	emf (potential difference) produced by a battery or electromagnetic induction
$\mathbf{F}_{electric}$, $F_{electric}$	electric force
$\mathbf{F}_{magnetic}$, $F_{magnetic}$	magnetic force
I	electric current
i	instantaneous current (ac circuit)
I_{max}	maximum current (ac circuit)
I_{rms}	root-mean-square current (ac circuit)
L	self-inductance
ℓ	length of an electrical conductor in a magnetic field
M	mutual inductance
N	number of turns in a current-carrying loop or a transformer winding
$PE_{electric}$	electrical potential energy
Q	large charge or charge on a fully charged capacitor
q	charge
R	resistance
r	separation between charges
R_{eq}	equivalent resistance
V	electric potential
ΔV	potential difference
Δv	instantaneous potential difference (ac circuit)
ΔV_{max}	maximum potential difference (ac circuit)
ΔV_{rms}	root-mean-square potential difference (ac circuit)
ω	(Greek *omega*) angular frequency

Particle and Electronic Symbols Used in This Book (Chapters 23–25)

For this part of the book, two tables are given because some symbols refer to quantities and others refer to specific particles. The symbol's context should make clear which table should be consulted.

Symbol	Quantity
A	mass number
β	(Greek *beta*) current or potential difference gain of an amplifier
E	photon energy
E_0	rest energy
f_t	threshold frequency (photoelectric effect)
hf_t	work function (photoelectric effect)
KE_{max}	maximum energy of ejected photoelectron
λ	(Greek *lambda*) decay constant
λN	decay rate (activity)
N	neutron number, number of decayed particles
n	energy quantum number
$T_{1/2}$	half-life
Z	atomic number

Symbol	Particle
α	alpha particle
$b, \bar{b}$	bottom quark, antiquark
β^+	(Greek *beta*) positron (beta particle)
β^-	(Greek *beta*) electron (beta particle)
$c, \bar{c}$	charmed quark, antiquark
$d, \bar{d}$	down quark, antiquark
$e^+, {}^{0}_{+1}e$	positron
$e^-, {}^{0}_{-1}e$	electron
γ	(Greek *gamma*) photon (gamma rays)
${}^{4}_{2}\text{He}$	alpha particle (helium-4 nucleus)
μ	(Greek *mu*) muon
${}^{1}_{0}n$	neutron
${}^{1}_{1}p$	proton
$s, \bar{s}$	strange quark, antiquark
$t, \bar{t}$	top quark, antiquark
$u, \bar{u}$	up quark, antiquark
τ	(Greek *tau*) tauon
$\nu, \bar{\nu}$	(Greek *nu*) neutrino, antineutrino
W^+, W^-	boson (weak force)
Z	boson (weak force)

Appendix C SI Units

SI Base Units Used in This Book

Symbol	Name	Quantity
A	ampere	current
K	kelvin	absolute temperature
kg	kilogram	mass
m	meter	length
s	second	time

SI Prefixes

Symbol	Name	Numerical equivalent
a	atto	10^{-18}
f	femto	10^{-15}
p	pico	10^{-12}
n	nano	10^{-9}
μ	micro	10^{-6}
m	milli	10^{-3}
c	centi	10^{-2}
d	deci	10^{-1}
k	kilo	10^{3}
M	mega	10^{6}
G	giga	10^{9}
T	tera	10^{12}
P	peta	10^{15}
E	exa	10^{18}

Other Commonly Used Units

Symbol	Name	Quantity	Conversions
atm	standard atmosphere	pressure	$1.013\ 250 \times 10^5$ Pa
Btu	British thermal unit	energy	1.055×10^3 J
Ci	curie	decay rate or activity	3.7×10^{10} s^{-1}
Cal	food calorie	energy	$= 1$ kcal $= 4.186 \times 10^3$ J
cal	calorie	energy	4.186 J
°F	degree Fahrenheit	temperature	1.8°C
ft	foot	length	0.3048 m
ft•lb	foot-pound	work and energy	1.356 J
g	gram	mass	0.001 kg
gal	gallon	volume	3.785×10^{-3} m^3
hp	horsepower	power	746 W
in	inch	length	2.54×10^{-2} m
kcal	kilocalorie	energy	4.186×10^3 J
lb	pound	force	4.536×10^{-1} N
mi	mile	length	1.609×10^3 m
rev	revolution	angular displacement	2π rad
°	degrees	angular displacement	$= \left(\dfrac{2\pi}{360}\right)$ rad $= 1.745 \times 10^{-2}$ rad

Other Units Acceptable with SI

Symbol	Name	Quantity	Conversion
Bq	becquerel	decay rate or activity	$\dfrac{1}{s}$
C	coulomb	electric charge	$1\ A\cdot s$
°C	degree Celsius	temperature	$1\ K$
dB	decibel	relative intensity (sound)	(unitless)
eV	electron volt	energy	$1.60 \times 10^{-19}\ J$
F	farad	capacitance	$1\dfrac{A^2 \cdot s^4}{kg \cdot m^2} = 1\dfrac{C}{V}$
H	henry	inductance	$1\dfrac{kg \cdot m^2}{A^2 \cdot s^2} = 1\dfrac{J}{A^2}$
h	hour	time	$3.6 \times 10^3\ s$
Hz	hertz	frequency	$\dfrac{1}{s}$
J	joule	work and energy	$1\dfrac{kg \cdot m^2}{s^2} = 1\ N \cdot m$
kW•h	kilowatt-hour	energy	$3.60 \times 10^6\ J$
L	liter	volume	$10^{-3}\ m^3$
min	minute	time	$6.0 \times 10^1\ s$
N	newton	force	$1\dfrac{kg \cdot m}{s^2}$
Pa	pascal	pressure	$1\dfrac{kg}{m \cdot s^2} = 1\dfrac{N}{m^2}$
rad	radian	angular displacement	(unitless)
T	tesla	magnetic field strength	$1\dfrac{kg}{A \cdot s^2} = 1\dfrac{N}{A \cdot m} = 1\dfrac{V \cdot s}{m^2}$
u	unified unit	mass (atomic masses)	$1.660\,5402 \times 10^{-27}\ kg$
V	volt	electric potential difference	$1\dfrac{kg \cdot m^2}{A \cdot s^3} = 1\dfrac{J}{C}$
W	watt	power	$1\dfrac{kg \cdot m^2}{s^3} = 1\dfrac{J}{s}$
Ω	ohm	resistance	$1\dfrac{kg \cdot m^2}{A^2 \cdot s^3} = 1\dfrac{V}{A}$

Appendix D Useful Tables

Fundamental Constants

Symbol	Quantity	Established value	Value used for calculations in this book
c	speed of light in a vacuum	299 792 458 m/s	3.00×10^8 m/s
e^-	elementary charge	$1.602\ 177\ 33 \times 10^{-19}$ C	1.60×10^{-19} C
e^x	base of natural logarithms	2.718 2818 28	2.72
ε_0	(Greek *epsilon*) permittivity of a vacuum	$8.854\ 187\ 817 \times 10^{-12}$ C^2/(N•m^2)	8.85×10^{-12} C^2/(N•m^2)
G	constant of universal gravitation	$6.672\ 59 \times 10^{-11}$ N•m^2/kg^2	6.673×10^{-11} N•m^2/kg^2
g	free-fall acceleration at Earth's surface	9.806 65 m/s^2	9.81 m/s^2
h	Planck's constant	$6.626\ 0755 \times 10^{-34}$ J•s	6.63×10^{-34} J•s
k_B	Boltzmann's constant (R/N_A)	$1.380\ 658 \times 10^{-23}$ J/K	1.38×10^{-23} J/K
k_C	Coulomb constant	$8.987\ 551\ 788 \times 10^9$ N•m^2/C^2	8.99×10^9 N•m^2/C^2
R	molar (universal) gas constant	8.314 510 J/(mol•K)	8.31 J/(mol•K)
π	(Greek *pi*) ratio of the circumference to the diameter of a circle	3.141 592 654	calculator value

Coefficients of Friction (Approximate Values)

	μ_s	μ_k		μ_s	μ_k
Steel on steel	0.74	0.57	Waxed wood on wet snow	0.14	0.1
Aluminum on steel	0.61	0.47	Waxed wood on dry snow	—	0.04
Rubber on dry concrete	1.0	0.8	Metal on metal (lubricated)	0.15	0.06
Rubber on wet concrete	—	0.5	Ice on ice	0.1	0.03
Wood on wood	0.4	0.2	Teflon on Teflon	0.04	0.04
Glass on glass	0.9	0.4	Synovial joints in humans	0.01	0.003

Useful Astronomical Data

Symbol	Quantity	Value used for calculations in this book
I_E	moment of inertia of Earth	8.03×10^{31} kg•m^2
M_E	mass of Earth	5.98×10^{24} kg
R_E	radius of Earth	6.37×10^6 m
	Average Earth–moon distance	3.84×10^8 m
	Average Earth–sun distance	1.496×10^{11} m
	mass of the moon	7.36×10^{22} kg
	mass of the sun	1.99×10^{30} kg
yr	period of Earth's orbit	3.16×10^7 s

The Moment of Inertia For a Few Shapes

Shape		Moment of inertia
	thin hoop about symmetry axis	MR^2
	thin hoop about diameter	$\frac{1}{2}MR^2$
	point mass about axis	MR^2
	disk or cylinder about symmetry axis	$\frac{1}{2}MR^2$

Shape		Moment of inertia
	thin rod about perpendicular axis through center	$\frac{1}{12}M\ell^2$
	thin rod about perpendicular axis through end	$\frac{1}{3}M\ell^2$
	solid sphere about diameter	$\frac{2}{5}MR^2$
	thin spherical shell about diameter	$\frac{2}{3}MR^2$

Density of Some Common Substances*

Substance	ρ (kg/m^3)
Hydrogen	0.0899
Helium	0.179
Steam (100°C)	0.598
Air	1.29
Oxygen	1.43
Carbon dioxide	1.98
Ethanol	0.806×10^3
Ice	0.917×10^3
Fresh water (4°C)	1.00×10^3
Sea water (15°C)	1.025×10^3
Glycerine	1.26×10^3
Aluminum	2.70×10^3
Iron	7.86×10^3
Copper	8.92×10^3
Silver	10.5×10^3
Lead	11.3×10^3
Mercury	13.6×10^3
Gold	19.3×10^3

*All densities are measured at 0°C and 1 atm unless otherwise noted.

Specific Heat Capacities

Substance	c_p (J/kg·°C)
Aluminum	8.99×10^2
Copper	3.87×10^2
Glass	8.37×10^2
Gold	1.29×10^2
Ice	2.09×10^3
Iron	4.48×10^2
Lead	1.28×10^2
Mercury	1.38×10^2
Silver	2.34×10^2
Steam	2.01×10^3
Water	4.186×10^3

Latent Heats of Fusion and Vaporization at Standard Pressure

Substance	Melting point (°C)	L_f (J/kg)	Boiling point (°C)	L_v (J/kg)
nitrogen	−209.97	2.55×10^4	−195.81	2.01×10^5
oxygen	−218.79	1.38×10^4	−182.97	2.13×10^5
ethyl alcohol	−114	1.04×10^5	78	8.54×10^5
water	0.00	3.33×10^5	100.00	2.26×10^6
lead	327.3	2.45×10^4	1745	8.70×10^5
aluminum	660.4	3.97×10^5	2467	1.14×10^7

Speed of Sound in Various Media

Medium	v (m/s)	Medium	v (m/s)	Medium	v (m/s)
Gases		**Liquids at 25°C**		**Solids**	
air (0°C)	331	methyl alcohol	1140	aluminum	5100
air (25°C)	346	sea water	1530	copper	3560
air (100°C)	366	water	1490	iron	5130
helium (0°C)	972			lead	1320
hydrogen (0°C)	1290			vulcanized rubber	54
oxygen (0°C)	317				

Conversion of Intensity to Decibel Level

Intensity (W/m^2)	Decibel level (dB)	Examples
1.0×10^{-12}	0	threshold of hearing
1.0×10^{-11}	10	rustling leaves
1.0×10^{-10}	20	quiet whisper
1.0×10^{-9}	30	whisper
1.0×10^{-8}	40	mosquito buzzing
1.0×10^{-7}	50	normal conversation
1.0×10^{-6}	60	air conditioning at 6 m
1.0×10^{-5}	70	vacuum cleaner
1.0×10^{-4}	80	busy traffic, alarm clock
1.0×10^{-3}	90	lawn mower
1.0×10^{-2}	100	subway, power motor
1.0×10^{-1}	110	auto horn at 1 m
1.0×10^{0}	120	threshold of pain
1.0×10^{1}	130	thunderclap, machine gun
1.0×10^{3}	150	nearby jet airplane

Indices of Refraction for Various Substances*

Solids at 20°C	n	Liquids at 20°C	n	Gases at 0°C, 1 atm	n
Cubic zirconia	2.20	Benzene	1.501	Air	1.000 293
Diamond	2.419	Carbon disulfide	1.628	Carbon dioxide	1.000 450
Fluorite	1.434	Carbon tetrachloride	1.461		
Fused quartz	1.458	Ethyl alcohol	1.361		
Glass, crown	1.52	Glycerine	1.473		
Glass, flint	1.66	Water	1.333		
Ice (at 0°C)	1.309				
Polystyrene	1.49				
Sodium chloride	1.544				
Zircon	1.923				

*measured with light of vacuum wavelength = 589 nm

Useful Atomic Data

Symbol	Quantity	Established value	Value used for calculations in this book
m_e	mass of electron	$9.109\ 3897 \times 10^{-31}$ kg $5.485\ 799\ 03 \times 10^{-4}$ u $0.510\ 999\ 06$ MeV	9.109×10^{-31} kg 5.49×10^{-4} u 5.110×10^{-1} MeV
m_n	mass of neutron	$1.674\ 9286 \times 10^{-27}$ kg $1.008\ 664\ 904$ u $939.565\ 63$ MeV	1.675×10^{-27} kg $1.008\ 665$ u 9.396×10^{2} MeV
m_p	mass of proton	$1.672\ 6231 \times 10^{-27}$ kg $1.007\ 276\ 470$ u $938.272\ 31$ MeV	1.673×10^{-27} kg $1.007\ 276$ u 9.383×10^{2} MeV

Appendix E
Periodic Table of the Elements

Key:

6	— Atomic number
C	— Symbol
Carbon	— Name
12.011	— Average atomic mass
[He]$2s^2 2p^2$	— Electron configuration

Period

1
H
Hydrogen
1.00794
$1s^1$

Group 1

3
Li
Lithium
6.941
[He]$2s^1$

Group 2

4
Be
Beryllium
9.012 182
[He]$2s^2$

11
Na
Sodium
22.989 768
[Ne]$3s^1$

12
Mg
Magnesium
24.3050
[Ne]$3s^2$

Group 3	Group 4	Group 5	Group 6	Group 7	Group 8	Group 9
21 **Sc** Scandium 44.955 910 [Ar]$3d^1 4s^2$	22 **Ti** Titanium 47.88 [Ar]$3d^2 4s^2$	23 **V** Vanadium 50.9415 [Ar]$3d^3 4s^2$	24 **Cr** Chromium 51.9961 [Ar]$3d^5 4s^1$	25 **Mn** Manganese 54.938 05 [Ar]$3d^5 4s^2$	26 **Fe** Iron 55.847 [Ar]$3d^6 4s^2$	27 **Co** Cobalt 58.933 20 [Ar]$3d^7 4s^2$
39 **Y** Yttrium 88.905 85 [Kr]$4d^1 5s^2$	40 **Zr** Zirconium 91.224 [Kr]$4d^2 5s^2$	41 **Nb** Niobium 92.906 38 [Kr]$4d^4 5s^1$	42 **Mo** Molybdenum 95.94 [Kr]$4d^5 5s^1$	43 **Tc** Technetium (97.9072) [Kr]$4d^6 5s^1$	44 **Ru** Ruthenium 101.07 [Kr]$4d^7 5s^1$	45 **Rh** Rhodium 102.906 [Kr]$4d^8 5s^1$
57 **La** Lanthanum 138.9055 [Xe]$5d^1 6s^2$	72 **Hf** Hafnium 178.49 [Xe]$4f^{14}5d^2 6s^2$	73 **Ta** Tantalum 180.9479 [Xe]$4f^{14}5d^3 6s^2$	74 **W** Tungsten 183.84 [Xe]$4f^{14}5d^4 6s^2$	75 **Re** Rhenium 186.207 [Xe]$4f^{14}5d^5 6s^2$	76 **Os** Osmium 190.23 [Xe]$4f^{14}5d^6 6s^2$	77 **Ir** Iridium 192.22 [Xe]$4f^{14}5d^7 6s^2$
89 **Ac** Actinium (227.0278) [Rn]$6d^1 7s^2$	104 **Rf** Rutherfordium (261.11) [Rn]$5f^{14}6d^2 7s^2$	105 **Db** Dubnium (262.114) [Rn]$5f^{14}6d^3 7s^2$	106 **Sg** Seaborgium (263.118) [Rn]$5f^{14}6d^4 7s^2$	107 **Bh** Bohrium (262.12) [Rn]$5f^{14}6d^5 7s^2$	108 **Hs** Hassium (265)† [Rn]$5f^{14}6d^6 7s^2$	109 **Mt** Meitnerium (266)† [Rn]$5f^{14}6d^7 7s^2$

Period 4: 19 **K** Potassium 39.0983 [Ar]$4s^1$; 20 **Ca** Calcium 40.078 [Ar]$4s^2$

Period 5: 37 **Rb** Rubidium 85.4678 [Kr]$5s^1$; 38 **Sr** Strontium 87.62 [Kr]$5s^2$

Period 6: 55 **Cs** Cesium 132.905 43 [Xe]$6s^1$; 56 **Ba** Barium 137.327 [Xe]$6s^2$

Period 7: 87 **Fr** Francium (223.0197) [Rn]$7s^1$; 88 **Ra** Radium (226.0254) [Rn]$7s^2$

† Estimated from currently available IUPAC data.

58 **Ce** Cerium 140.115 [Xe]$4f^1 5d^1 6s^2$	59 **Pr** Praseodymium 140.908 [Xe]$4f^3 6s^2$	60 **Nd** Neodymium 144.24 [Xe]$4f^4 6s^2$	61 **Pm** Promethium (144.9127) [Xe]$4f^5 6s^2$	62 **Sm** Samarium 150.36 [Xe]$4f^6 6s^2$
90 **Th** Thorium 232.0381 [Rn]$6d^2 7s^2$	91 **Pa** Protactinium 231.035 88 [Rn]$5f^2 6d^1 7s^2$	92 **U** Uranium 238.0289 [Rn]$5f^3 6d^1 7s^2$	93 **Np** Neptunium (237.0482) [Rn]$5f^4 6d^1 7s^2$	94 **Pu** Plutonium 244.0642 [Rn]$5f^6 7s^2$

Group 18

2
He
Helium
4.002602
$1s^2$

Group 13	Group 14	Group 15	Group 16	Group 17
5	6	7	8	9
B	**C**	**N**	**O**	**F**
Boron	Carbon	Nitrogen	Oxygen	Fluorine
10.811	12.011	14.006 74	15.9994	18.998 4032
$[He]2s^22p^1$	$[He]2s^22p^2$	$[He]2s^22p^3$	$[He]2s^22p^4$	$[He]2s^22p^5$

10
Ne
Neon
20.1797
$[He]2s^22p^6$

13	14	15	16	17	18
Al	**Si**	**P**	**S**	**Cl**	**Ar**
Aluminum	Silicon	Phosphorus	Sulfur	Chlorine	Argon
26.985 39	28.0855	30.9738	32.066	35.4527	39.948
$[Ne]3s^23p^1$	$[Ne]3s^23p^2$	$[Ne]3s^23p^3$	$[Ne]3s^23p^4$	$[Ne]3s^23p^5$	$[Ne]3s^23p^6$

Group 10	Group 11	Group 12						
28	29	30	31	32	33	34	35	36
Ni	**Cu**	**Zn**	**Ga**	**Ge**	**As**	**Se**	**Br**	**Kr**
Nickel	Copper	Zinc	Gallium	Germanium	Arsenic	Selenium	Bromine	Krypton
58.6934	63.546	65.39	69.723	72.61	74.921 59	78.96	79.904	83.80
$[Ar]3d^84s^2$	$[Ar]3d^{10}4s^1$	$[Ar]3d^{10}4s^2$	$[Ar]3d^{10}4s^24p^1$	$[Ar]3d^{10}4s^24p^2$	$[Ar]3d^{10}4s^24p^3$	$[Ar]3d^{10}4s^24p^4$	$[Ar]3d^{10}4s^24p^5$	$[Ar]3d^{10}4s^24p^6$
46	47	48	49	50	51	52	53	54
Pd	**Ag**	**Cd**	**In**	**Sn**	**Sb**	**Te**	**I**	**Xe**
Palladium	Silver	Cadmium	Indium	Tin	Antimony	Tellurium	Iodine	Xenon
106.42	107.8682	112.411	114.818	118.710	121.757	127.60	126.904	131.29
$[Kr]4d^{10}5s^0$	$[Kr]4d^{10}5s^1$	$[Kr]4d^{10}5s^2$	$[Kr]4d^{10}5s^25p^1$	$[Kr]4d^{10}5s^25p^2$	$[Kr]4d^{10}5s^25p^3$	$[Kr]4d^{10}5s^25p^4$	$[Kr]4d^{10}5s^25p^5$	$[Kr]4d^{10}5s^25p^6$
78	79	80	81	82	83	84	85	86
Pt	**Au**	**Hg**	**Tl**	**Pb**	**Bi**	**Po**	**At**	**Rn**
Platinum	Gold	Mercury	Thallium	Lead	Bismuth	Polonium	Astatine	Radon
195.08	196.966 54	200.59	204.3833	207.2	208.980 37	(208.9824)	(209.9871)	(222.0176)
$[Xe]4f^{14}5d^96s^1$	$[Xe]4f^{14}5d^{10}6s^1$	$[Xe]4f^{14}5d^{10}6s^2$	$[Xe]4f^{14}5d^{10}6s^26p^1$	$[Xe]4f^{14}5d^{10}6s^26p^2$	$[Xe]4f^{14}5d^{10}6s^26p^3$	$[Xe]4f^{14}5d^{10}6s^26p^4$	$[Xe]4f^{14}5d^{10}6s^26p^5$	$[Xe]4f^{14}5d^{10}6s^26p^6$

63	64	65	66	67	68	69	70	71
Eu	**Gd**	**Tb**	**Dy**	**Ho**	**Er**	**Tm**	**Yb**	**Lu**
Europium	Gadolinium	Terbium	Dysprosium	Holmium	Erbium	Thulium	Ytterbium	Lutetium
151.966	157.25	158.925 34	162.50	164.930	167.26	168.934 21	173.04	174.967
$[Xe]4f^76s^2$	$[Xe]4f^75d^16s^2$	$[Xe]4f^96s^2$	$[Xe]4f^{10}6s^2$	$[Xe]4f^{11}6s^2$	$[Xe]4f^{12}6s^2$	$[Xe]4f^{13}6s^2$	$[Xe]4f^{14}6s^2$	$[Xe]4f^{14}5d^16s^2$
95	96	97	98	99	100	101	102	103
Am	**Cm**	**Bk**	**Cf**	**Es**	**Fm**	**Md**	**No**	**Lr**
Americium	Curium	Berkelium	Californium	Einsteinium	Fermium	Mendelevium	Nobelium	Lawrencium
(243.0614)	(247.0703)	(247.0703)	(251.0796)	(252.083)	(257.0951)	(258.10)	(259.1009)	(262.11)
$[Rn]5f^77s^2$	$[Rn]5f^76d^17s^2$	$[Rn]5f^97s^2$	$[Rn]5f^{10}7s^2$	$[Rn]5f^{11}7s^2$	$[Rn]5f^{12}7s^2$	$[Rn]5f^{13}7s^2$	$[Rn]5f^{14}7s^2$	$[Rn]5f^{14}6d^17s^2$

The atomic masses listed in this table reflect the precision of current measurements. (Values listed in parentheses are those of the element's most stable or most common isotope.) In calculations throughout the text, however, atomic masses have been rounded to two places to the right of the decimal.

Appendix F
Abbreviated Table of Isotopes and Atomic Masses

Z	Element	Symbol	Average atomic mass (u)	Mass number (* indicates radioactive) A	Atomic mass (u)	Percent abundance	Half-life (if radioactive) $T_{1/2}$
0	(Neutron)	n		1*	1.008 665		10.4 m
1	Hydrogen	H	1.0079	1	1.007 825	99.985	
	Deuterium	D		2	2.014 102	0.015	
	Tritium	T		3*	3.016 049		12.33 y
2	Helium	He	4.002 60	3	3.016 029	0.000 14	
				4	4.002 602	99.999 86	
				6*	6.018 886		0.81 s
3	Lithium	Li	6.941	6	6.015 121	7.5	
				7	7.016 003	92.5	
4	Beryllium	Be	9.0122	7*	7.016 928		53.3 d
				8	8.005 305		6.7×10^{-17} s
				9	9.012 174	100	
				10*	10.013 584		1.5×10^{6} y
5	Boron	B	10.81	10	10.012 936	19.9	
				11	11.009 305	80.1	
6	Carbon	C	12.011	10*	10.016 854		19.3 s
				11*	11.011 433		20.4 m
				12	12.000 000	98.9	
				13	13.003 355	1.10	
				14*	14. 003 242		5730 y
7	Nitrogen	N	14.0067	13*	13.005 738		996 m
				14	14.003 074	99.63	
				15	15.000 108	0.37	
				16*	16.006 100		7.13 s
8	Oxygen	O	15.9994	15*	15.003 065		122 s
				16	15.994 915	99.761	
				17	16.999 132	0.039	
				18	17.999 160	0.200	
				19*	19.003 577		26.9 s
9	Fluorine	F	18.998 40	18*	18.000 937		109.8 m
				19	18.998 404	100	
				20*	19.999 982		11.0 s
10	Neon	Ne	20.180	19*	19.001 880		17.2 s
				20	19.992 435	90.48	
				21	20.993 841	0.27	
				22	21.991 383	9.25	
11	Sodium	Na	22.989 87	22*	21.994 434		2.61 y
				23	22.989 767	100	
				24*	23.990 961		14.96 h
12	Magnesium	Mg	24.305	23*	22.994 124		11.3 s
				24	23.985 042	78.99	
				25	24.985 838	10.00	
				26	25.982 594	11.01	
13	Aluminum	Al	26.981 54	26*	25.986 892		7.4×10^{5} y
				27	26.981 534	100	

Z	Element	Symbol	Average atomic mass (u)	Mass number (* indicates radioactive) A	Atomic mass (u)	Percent abundance	Half-life (if radioactive) $T_{1/2}$
14	Silicon	Si	28.086	28	27.976 927	92.23	
				29	28.976 495	4.67	
				30	29.973 770	3.10	
15	Phosphorus	P	30.973 76	30*	29.978 307		2.50 m
				31	30.973 762	100	
16	Sulfur	S	32.066	32	31.972 071	95.02	
				33	32.971 459	0.75	
				34	33.967 867	4.21	
				35*	34.969 033		87.5 d
				36	35.967 081	0.02	
17	Chlorine	Cl	35.453	35	34.968 853	75.77	
				36*	35.968 307		3.0×10^5 y
				37	36.975 893	24.23	
18	Argon	Ar	39.948	36	35.967 547	0.337	
				37*	36.956 776		35.04 d
				38	37.962 732	0.063	
				39*	38.964 314		269 y
				40	39.962 384	99.600	
19	Potassium	K	39.0983	39	38.963 708	93.2581	
				40*	39.964 000	0.0117	1.28×10^9 y
				41	40.961 827	6.7302	
20	Calcium	Ca	40.08	40	39.962 591	96.941	
				41*	40.962 279		1.0×10^5 y
				42	41.958 618	0.647	
				43	42.958 767	0.135	
				44	43.955 481	2.086	
21	Scandium	Sc	44.9559	41*	40.969 250		0.596 s
				45	44.955 911	100	
22	Titanium	Ti	47.88	44*	43.959 691		49 y
				47	46.951 765	7.3	
				48	47.947 947	73.8	
23	Vanadium	V	50.9415	50*	49.947 161	0.25	1.5×10^{17} y
				51	50.943 962	99.75	
24	Chromium	Cr	51.996	48*	47.954 033		21.6 h
				52	51.940 511	83.79	
				53	52.940 652	9.50	
25	Manganese	Mn	54.938 05	54*	53.940 361		312.1 d
				55	54.938 048	100	
26	Iron	Fe	55.847	54	53.939 613	5.9	
				55*	54.938 297		2.7 y
				56	55.934 940	91.72	
27	Cobalt	Co	58.933 20	59	58.933 198	100	
				60*	59.933 820		5.27 y
28	Nickel	Ni	58.793	58	57.935 345	68.077	
				59*	58.934 350		7.5×10^4 y
				60	59.930 789	26.223	
29	Copper	Cu	63.54	63	62.929 599	69.17	
				65	64.927 791	30.83	
30	Zinc	Zn	65.39	64	63.929 144	48.6	
				66	65.926 035	27.9	
				67	66.927 129	4.1	
				68	67.924 845	18.8	

Z	Element	Symbol	Average atomic mass (u)	Mass number (* indicates radioactive) A	Atomic mass (u)	Percent abundance	Half-life (if radioactive) $T_{1/2}$
31	Gallium	Ga	69.723	69	68.925 580	60.108	
				71	70.924 703	39.892	
32	Germanium	Ge	72.61	70	69.924 250	21.23	
				72	71.922 079	27.66	
				73	72.923 462	7.73	
				74	73.921 177	35.94	
				76	75.921 402	7.44	
33	Arsenic	As	74.9216	75	74.921 594	100	
34	Selenium	Se	78.96	76	75.919 212	9.36	
				77	76.919 913	7.63	
				78	77.917 397	23.78	
				80	79.916 519	49.61	
				82*	81.916 697	8.73	1.4×10^{20} y
35	Bromine	Br	79.904	79	78.918 336	50.69	
				81	80.916 287	49.31	
36	Krypton	Kr	83.80	81*	80.916 589		2.1×10^{5} y
				82	81.913 481	11.6	
				83	82.914 136	11.4	
				84	83.911 508	57.0	
				85*	84.912 531		10.76 y
				86	85.910 615	17.3	
37	Rubidium	Rb	85.468	85	84.911 793	72.17	
				87*	86.909 186	27.83	4.75×10^{10} y
38	Strontium	Sr	87.62	86	85.909 266	9.86	
				87	86.908 883	7.00	
				88	87.905 618	82.58	
				90*	89.907 737		29.1 y
39	Yttrium	Y	88.9058	89	88.905 847	100	
40	Zirconium	Zr	91.224	90	89.904 702	51.45	
				91	90.905 643	11.22	
				92	91.905 038	17.15	
				93*	92.906 473		1.5×10^{6} y
				94	93.906 314	17.38	
41	Niobium	Nb	92.9064	93	92.906 376	100	
				94*	93.907 280		2×10^{4} y
42	Molybdenum	Mo	95.94	92	91.906 807	14.84	
				93*	92.906 811		3.5×10^{3} y
				94	93.905 085	9.25	
				95	94.905 841	15.92	
				96	95.904 678	16.68	
				97	96.906 020	9.55	
				98	97.905 407	24.13	
				100	99.907 476	9.63	
43	Technetium	Tc		97*	96.906 363		2.6×10^{6} y
				98*	97.907 215		4.2×10^{6} y
				99*	98.906 254		2.1×10^{5} y
44	Ruthenium	Ru	101.07	99	98.905 939	12.7	
				100	99.904 219	12.6	
				101	100.905 558	17.1	
				102	101.904 348	31.6	
				104	103.905 558	18.6	
45	Rhodium	Rh	102.9055	103	102.905 502	100	

Z	Element	Symbol	Average atomic mass (u)	Mass number (* indicates radioactive) A	Atomic mass (u)	Percent abundance	Half-life (if radioactive) $T_{1/2}$
46	Palladium	Pd	106.42	104	103.904 033	11.14	
				105	104.905 082	22.33	
				106	105.903 481	27.33	
				108	107.903 898	26.46	
				110	109.905 158	11.72	
47	Silver	Ag	107.868	107	106.905 091	51.84	
				109	108.904 754	48.16	
48	Cadmium	Cd	112.41	109*	108.904 984		462 d
				110	109.903 004	12.49	
				111	110.904 182	12.80	
				112	111.902 760	24.13	
				113*	112.904 401	12.22	9.3×10^{15} y
				114	113.903 359	28.73	
49	Indium	In	114.82	113	112.904 060	4.3	
				115	114.903 876	95.7	4.4×10^{14} y
50	Tin	Sn	118.71	116	115.901 743	14.53	
				117	116.902 953	7.58	
				118	117.901 605	24.22	
				119	118.903 308	8.58	
				120	119.902 197	32.59	
				121*	120.904 237		55 y
51	Antimony	Sb	121.76	121	120.903 820	57.36	
				123	122.904 215	42.64	
52	Tellurium	Te	127.60	125	124.904 429	7.12	
				126	125.903 309	18.93	
				128*	127.904 468	31.79	$> 8 \times 10^{24}$ y
				130*	129.906 228	33.87	$< 1.25 \times 10^{21}$ y
53	Iodine	I	126.9045	127	126.904 474	100	
				129*	128.904 984		1.6×10^{7} y
54	Xenon	Xe	131.29	129	128.904 779	26.4	
				131	130.905 069	21.2	
				132	131.904 141	26.9	
				134	133.905 394	10.4	
				136*	135.907 214	8.9	$> 2.36 \times 10^{21}$ y
55	Cesium	Cs	132.9054	133	132.905 436	100	
				135*	134.905 891		2×10^{6} y
				137*	136.907 078		30 y
56	Barium	Ba	137.33	133*	132.905 990		10.5 y
				137	136.905 816	11.23	
				138	137.905 236	71.70	
57	Lanthanum	La	138.905	138*	137.907 105	0.0902	1.05×10^{11} y
				139	138.906 346	99.9098	
58	Cerium	Ce	140.12	138	137.905 986	0.25	
				140	139.905 434	88.43	
				142*	141.909 241	11.13	$> 5 \times 10^{16}$ y
59	Praseodymium	Pr	140.9076	141	140.907 647	100	
60	Neodymium	Nd	144.24	142	141.907 718	27.13	
				143	142.909 809	12.18	
				144*	143.910 082	23.80	2.3×10^{15} y
				145	144.912 568	8.30	
				146	145.913 113	17.19	

Z	Element	Symbol	Average atomic mass (u)	Mass number (* indicates radioactive) A	Atomic mass (u)	Percent abundance	Half-life (if radioactive) $T_{1/2}$
61	Promethium	Pm		145*	144.912 745		17.7 y
				146*	145.914 968		5.5 y
62	Samarium	Sm	150.36	147*	146.914 894	15.0	1.06×10^{11} y
				148*	147.914 819	11.3	7×10^{15} y
				149*	148.917 180	13.8	$> 2 \times 10^{15}$ y
				150	149.917 273	7.4	
				152	151.919 728	26.7	
				154	153.922 206	22.7	
63	Europium	Eu	151.96	151	150.919 846	47.8	
				152*	151.921 740		13.5 y
				153	152.921 226	52.2	
64	Gadolinium	Gd	157.25	155	154.922 618	14.80	
				156	155.922 119	20.47	
				157	156.923 957	15.65	
				158	157.924 099	24.84	
				160	159.927 050	21.86	
65	Terbium	Tb	158.9253	159	158.925 345	100	
66	Dysprosium	Dy	162.5	161	160.926 930	18.9	
				162	161.926 796	25.5	
				163	162.928 729	24.9	
				164	163.929 172	28.2	
67	Holmium	Ho	164.9303	165	164.930 316	100	
68	Erbium	Er	167.26	166	165.930 292	33.6	
				167	166.932 047	22.95	
				168	167.932 369	27.8	
				170	169.935 462	14.9	
69	Thulium	Tm	168.9342	169	168.934 213	100	
				171*	170.936 428		1.92 y
70	Ytterbium	Yb	173.04	171	170.936 324	14.3	
				172	171.936 379	21.9	
				173	172.938 209	16.12	
				174	173.938 861	31.8	
				176	175.942 564	12.7	
71	Lutetium	Lu	174.967	175	174.940 772	97.41	
				176*	175.942 679	2.59	3.78×10^{10} y
72	Hafnium	Hf	178.49	177	176.943 218	18.606	
				178	177.943 697	27.297	
				179	178.945 813	13.029	
				180	179.946 547	35.100	
73	Tantalum	Ta	180.9479	181	180.947 993	99.988	
74	Tungsten	W	183.85	182	181.948 202	26.3	
				183	182.950 221	14.28	
				184	183.950 929	30.7	
				186	185.954 358	28.6	
75	Rhenium	Re	186.207	185	184.952 951	37.40	
				187*	186.955 746	62.60	4.4×10^{10} y
76	Osmium	Os	190.2	188	187.955 832	13.3	
				189	188.958 139	16.1	
				190	189.958 439	26.4	
				192	191.961 468	41.0	
77	Iridium	Ir	192.2	191	190.960 585	37.3	
				193	192.962 916	62.7	

Z	Element	Symbol	Average atomic mass (u)	Mass number (* indicates radioactive) A	Atomic mass (u)	Percent abundance	Half-life (if radioactive) $T_{1/2}$
78	Platinum	Pt	195.08	194	193.962 655	32.9	
				195	194.964 765	33.8	
				196	195.964 926	25.3	
79	Gold	Au	196.9665	197	196.966 543	100	
80	Mercury	Hg	200.59	198	197.966 743	9.97	
				199	198.968 253	16.87	
				200	199.968 299	23.10	
				201	200.970 276	13.10	
				202	201.970 617	29.86	
81	Thallium	Tl	204.383	203	202.972 320	29.524	
				204*	203.073 839		3.78 y
				205	204.974 400	70.476	
				208*	207.981 992		3.053 m
82	Lead	Pb	207.2	206	205.974 440	24.1	
				207	206.974 871	22.1	
				208	207.976 627	52.4	
				212*	211.991 872		10.64 h
83	Bismuth	Bi	208.9803	209	208.980 374	100	
				212*	211.991 259		60.6 m
84	Polonium	Po		209*	208.982 405		102 y
				212*	211.988 842		0.30 μs
				216*	216.001 889		0.145 s
85	Astatine	At		218*	218.008 685		1.6 s
				219*	219.011 294		0.9 m
86	Radon	Rn		220*	220.011 369		55.6 s
				222*	222.017 571		3.823 d
87	Francium	Fr		223*	223.019 733		22 m
88	Radium	Ra		224*	224.020 187		3.66 d
				226*	226.025 402		1.6×10^3 y
				228*	228.031 064		5.75 y
89	Actinium	Ac		227*	227.027 701		18.72 y
				228*	228.028 716		1.913 y
90	Thorium	Th		232*	232.038 051	100	1.40×10^{10} y
				234*	234.043 593		24.1 d
91	Protactinium	Pa		231*	231.035 880		32.760 y
				234*	234.043 300		6.7 h
92	Uranium	U		235*	235.043 924	0.720	7.04×10^8 y
				238*	238.050 784	99.2745	4.47×10^9 y
93	Neptunium	Np		236*	236.046 560		1.15×10^5 y
				237*	237.048 168		2.14×10^6 y
94	Plutonium	Pu		239*	239.052 157		2.412×10^5 y
				244*	244.064 200		8.1×10^7 y

Answers to Selected Problems

Practice 1A, p. 14
1. 5×10^{-5} m
3. 1.440×10^3 kg
5. 1×10^{-6} s

1 Review and Assess,
pp. 27–31
11. **a.** 2×10^2 mm
    b. 7.8×10^3 s
    c. 1.6×10^7 μs
    d. 7.5×10^4 cm
    e. 6.75×10^{-4} g
    f. 4.62×10^{-2} cm
    g. 9.7 m/s
13. 1.08×10^9 km
37. **a.** 22 cm; 38 cm^2
    b. 29.2 cm; 67.9 cm^2
39. 9.818×10^{-2} m
41. The ark (10^4 m^3) was about 10–100 times as large as a house (10^2–10^3 m^3).
43. 1.0×10^3 kg
45. **a.** 0.677 kg/m^3
    b. 4.30×10^{16} m^2

Practice 2A, p. 44
1. 0.98 m/s to the east
3. 7.2×10^{-2} km/min (1.2 m/s) to the north
5. 0.5 h

Practice 2B, p. 49
1. -6.00 m/s^2
3. -3.5×10^{-3} m/s^2
5. 27 s

Practice 2C, p. 53
1. 21 m
3. no; the plane needs 1 km to land.
5. 3.2 km

Practice 2D, p. 55
1. 36 km/h (9.9 m/s); $+0.030$ km
3. -7.5 m/s; 19 m

Practice 2E, p. 58
1. $+2.51$ m/s
3. -5 m/s
5. **a.** 16 m/s
   b. 7.0 s

Practice 2F, p. 64
1. 1.8 m; $+1.1$ m/s
3. **a.** 8.0 m/s
   b. 1.63 s
5. 110 s; -420 m/s

2 Review and Assess,
pp. 69–75
9. 19 km/h (5.3 m/s) to the east
11. 5.436 m/s
13. **a.** 53.5 km/h
    b. 91.0 km
15. 280 km/h
17. 0.2 km west of the flagpole
23. $+8.6$ m/s
25. **a.** $+1.6$ m/s^2
    b. $+24$ m/s
    c. 240 m
27. **a.** $+72$ m/s
    b. 45 s
29. **a.** -15 m/s
    b. -38 m
31. 110 m

33. 0.0 m/s^2; $+1.36$ m/s^2; $+0.680$ m/s^2
35. **a.** 2.0×10^1 s
    b. No; the plane needs at least 1.2 km to land.
41. **a.** $+17.5$ m/s
    b. 15.5 m
43. **a.** -2.0×10^1 m/s
    b. 2.0×10^1 m
45. 3.94 s
47. **a.** 31.9 m from its original position
    b. 2.55 s
    c. 2.63 s
    d. -25.0 m/s
49. **a.** 3.0 s
    b. -24.5 m/s for each
    c. 23.6 m
51. **a.** 2.00 min
    b. 1.00 min
    c. 2.00 min
53. -27 m/s; 31 m
55. 1.6 s
57. 5 s; 85 s; $+60$ m/s
59. -1500 m/s^2
61. **a.** 3.40 s
    b. -9.2 m/s
    c. -31.4 m/s; -33 m/s
63. **a.** 4.6 s after stock car starts
    b. 38 m
    c. $+17$ m/s (stock car), $+21$ m/s (sports car)
65. 4.17 m/s

CHAPTER 3

Practice 3A, p. 91
1. 45.6 m at 9.5° east of due north
3. 1.8 m at 49° below the horizontal

Practice 3B, p. 94

1. 95 km/h
3. 1.1×10^2 m, −53 m
5. 21 m/s, 5.7 m/s
7. 0 m, 5 m

Practice 3C, p. 97

1. 49 m at 7.3° to the right of down field
3. 13.0 m at 33° east of north

Practice 3D, p. 102

1. 5.0 m
3. 26.5 m/s at 31.9° below the horizontal

Practice 3E, p. 104

1. yes, $\Delta y = -2.3$ m
3. 6.2 m/s

Practice 3F, p. 109

1. 0 m/s
3. 3.9 m/s at $(4.0 \times 10^1)°$ north of east

3 Review and Assess, pp. 113–119

23. 108 m, −19.1 m
25. 8.07 m at 42.0° south of east
27. 31.5 m, 26.4 m
29. 2.40×10^2 m at 57.2° south of west
35. a. 2.77×10^5 m
    b. 284 s
37. 10.7 m
39. a. 41.7 m/s
    b. 3.81 s
    c. $v_{y,f} = -13.5$ m/s,
       $v_{x,f} = 34.2$ m/s,
       $v_f = 36.7$ m/s
41. 10.4 m/s
43. 11 m

51. a. 10.1 m/s at 8.53° east of north
    b. 48.8 m
53. 0.12 h
55. a. 12 m/s at 16° south of east
    b. 1.1×10^2 s
57. a. 22.2 s
    b. 2.00×10^2 s
59. 22.5 s
61. a. 32.5 m
    b. 1.78 s
63. a. 5.0×10^1 m/s
    b. 4.0×10^1 m
65. a. 57.7 km/h at 60.0° west of the vertical
    b. 28.8 km/h straight down
67. 18.0 m, 7.8 m
69. 6.19 m/s downfield

CHAPTER 4

Practice 4A, p. 133

1. a. 60.6 N
   b. 35.0 N
3. a. -3.0×10^1 N
   b. 329 N
   c. 3.30×10^2 N at 94.5° counterclockwise from the positive x-axis.

Practice 4B, p. 138

1. 23 m/s² forward
3. 6.8×10^3 N east
5. 2.1 kg

Practice 4C, p. 145

1. 0.23
3. a. 1.5
   b. 1.3

Practice 4D, p. 147

1. 0.609
3. 0.9 m/s²

4 Review and Assess, pp. 151–157

9. a. force of 185 N points forward, 155 N downward, 155 N upward
   b. force of 8.9 N downward, force of 2.1 N downward, force of 11.0 N upward
11. a. force of 114 N and force of 220 N, both directed to the right; force of 114 N directed to the right and force of 220 N directed to the left
    b. 114 N; 220 N
21. 3.52 m/s²
23. 480 s
25. a. 0.25 m/s²
    b. 12.5 m
    c. 2.5 m/s
27. a. 72.0 m
    b. 6.00 s
    c. 63.6 m/s
29. 13 N
31. 2.0×10^1 m/s
33. a. 2690 N
    b. 699 N
45. a. 0.883 N
    b. 14.0 N
47. a. zero
    b. 33.9 N
49. 51 N
51. a. 2 s
    b. the box will never move; the force exerted is not enough to overcome friction
53. 0.436
55. 1.4 m/s²
57. 0.816
59. 5.0×10^1 m
61. 32.1 N
63. 13 N, 13 N, 0 N, −26 N
65. a. Δx
    b. $1/4\Delta x$
67. a. 75 N
    b. 0.50

CHAPTER 5

Practice 5A, p. 170
1. 1.50×10^7 J
3. 1.6×10^3 J

Practice 5B, p. 173
1. 1.1×10^9 J
3. 2.4 J, 9.6 J; the bullet with the greater speed; 4 to 1

Practice 5C, p. 177
1. 98.7 N/m
3. 3.3 J

Practice 5D, p. 182
1. 20.7 m/s
3. 14.1 m/s
5. 1.9 m/s

Practice 5E, p. 186
1. 1.9 m/s
3. a. -1.9×10^2 J
   b. -2.8×10^2 J
   c. 7.5×10^2 J
   d. 2.8×10^2 J
   e. 7.6 m/s

Practice 5F, p. 188
1. 66 kW
3. 2.38×10^4 W (23.8 kW)

5 Review and Assess, pp. 193–199
7. 53 J; −53 J
9. 2.4×10^5 J
17. 1.7×10^4 m/s
19. a. −19.6 J
    b. 39.2 J
    c. 0 J
27. 7.34 m
29. 5.0 m
31. 10.2 m
37. -1.5×10^3 N
39. 1.3 m

41. 9.80 m/s
43. 5.9×10^8 W
45. a. 1.2 J
    b. 5.0 m/s
    c. 6.3 J
47. a. −560 J
    b. 1.2 m
49. a. −22 500 N
    b. 1.33×10^{-4} s
51. a. 2.0 m/s
    b. 2.0×10^2 N
53. a. 100 mJ
    b. 3.1 m/s
    c. 0.8 m
55. a. 5.42 m/s
    b. 0.300
    c. 147 J
57. a. 4.4 m/s
    b. 1.5×10^5 N
59. 0.107
61. a. 66 J
    b. 2.3 m/s
    c. 66 J
    d. 16 J

CHAPTER 6

Practice 6A, p. 209
1. 46 m/s to the east
3. a. 1.2×10^2 kg•m/s to the northwest
   b. 94 kg•m/s to the northwest
   c. 27 kg•m/s to the northwest

Practice 6B, p. 211
1. 3.8×10^2 N to the right
3. a. 9.0 m/s to the right
   b. 15 m/s to the left

Practice 6C, p. 213
1. a. 5.33 s
   b. 53.3 m
3. a. 14 m/s to the north
   b. 42 m
   c. 8.0 s

Practice 6D, p. 219
1. a. 1.90 m/s
   b. 114 m
3. a. 12.0 m/s
   b. 9.6 m/s
   c. 11.7 m/s
   d. 10.4 m/s

Practice 6E, p. 224
1. 3.8 m/s to the south
3. 4.0 m/s to the north
5. a. 3.0 kg
   b. 5.32 m/s

Practice 6F, p. 226
1. a. 0.43 m/s to the west
   b. 17 J
3. a. 4.6 m/s to the south
   b. 3.9×10^3 J

Practice 6G, p. 229
1. a. 22.5 cm/s to the right
   b. $KE_i = 6.2 \times 10^{-4}$ J $= KE_f$
3. a. 8.0 m/s to the right
   b. $KE_i = 1.3 \times 10^2$ J $= KE_f$

6 Review and Assess, pp. 232–237
13. 46.0 m/s toward second base
15. 5.2 kg•m/s toward home plate
17. 18 N
19. a. −9.9 m/s
    b. 2×10^3 N upward
21. 400 N
29. a. 2.43 m/s forward
    b. 7.97×10^{-2} m/s forward
31. a. 9.62×10^{-24} m/s, upward
37. 14.5 m/s to the north
39. 4.2 m/s
41. a. 1.80 m/s
    b. 2.16×10^4 J
43. a. 0.97 m/s to the east
    b. 1.4×10^3 J
45. 4.0 m/s

47. 17.2 cm/s to the right
49. 5.00 m/s to the right
51. 2.36×10^{-2} m
53. 6.00 kg
55. 29 s
57. 340 m/s
59. 1.3×10^7 m/s, 41° below the negative x-axis

CHAPTER 7

Practice 7A, p. 247
1. 1.7 rad
3. 0.34 rad

Practice 7B, p. 248
1. 29 rad/s
3. 7.3×10^{-5} rad/s

Practice 7C, p. 250
1. 4.2 rad/s²
3. **a.** 17 rad/s²
   b. 0.038 rad/s
   c. −6.3 rad/s²

Practice 7D, p. 252
1. 9.0 rad/s
3. 15 rad/s
5. 0.89 s

Practice 7E, p. 255
1. 1.8 m/s
3. 9.2 m/s

Practice 7F, p. 256
1. 2.11 m/s²
3. 1.0 rad/s²

Practice 7G, p. 258
1. 3.0 m/s²
3. 1.5 m/s, 1.0 rad/s
5. 84 m/s²

Practice 7H, p. 261
1. 88 N
3. 1.2×10^3 N
5. 1.8×10^2 N

Practice 7I, p. 265
1. 6.67×10^{-11} N
3. **a.** 664 N
   b. 243 N
   c. 1×10^4 N

7 Review and Assess, pp. 269–273
5. **a.** 1.99 rad
   b. 0.79 rad
   c. $\frac{\pi}{2}$ rad
   d. π rad
7. 0.105 rad/s, 0 rad/s²
9. −1.2 rad/s²
11. **a.** 821 rad/s²
   b. 4.20×10^3 rad
13. 55 rev
23. 3.81×10^{-5} m/s²
25. 0.086 m/s²
35. no, 1.37×10^3 N > 1.0×10^3 N
37. 1.02×10^{-47} N
39. **a.** 4.39×10^{20} N
   b. 1.99×10^{20} N
   c. 3.55×10^{22} N
41. 119 rev
43. 12 m/s
45. 8.38 rad/s
47. 140 m/s
49. 0.131

CHAPTER 8

Practice 8A, p. 282
1. 0.65 N•m
3. **a.** 5.1 N•m
   b. 15 N•m

Practice 8B, p. 288
1. 4.00×10^2 N; 592 N; slight differences due to rounding
3. 2.1×10^5 N; 2.1×10^5 N

Practice 8C, p. 291
1. **a.** 0.87 rad/s²
   b. 1.1×10^1 N•m
3. **a.** 7.8 N•m

Practice 8D, p. 294
1. 3.5 rad/s
3. 9.1×10^2 m/s
5. 1.5×10^4 rad/s

Practice 8E, p. 297
1. 5.11 m/s; the ball wins the race
3. 280 J

8 Review and Assess, pp. 305–312
9. 1.68×10^4 N•m
11. 2.2×10^2 N
21. **a.** 1.20 kg
   b. at the 0.593 m mark
23. **a.** 392 N
   b. $R_x = 339$ N, $R_y = 196$ N
25. 1.5×10^3 N; 1.4×10^3 N (x component) and 2.6×10^3 N (y component)
31. 1.8×10^2 N
33. 23 rad/s²
35. **a.** 1.1 m/s²; −1.1 m/s²
   b. 22 N; 44 N
43. **a.** 7.08×10^{33} kg•m²/s
   b. 2.67×10^{40} kg•m²/s
45. 25.2 m
49. 149 rad/s
51. 36 rad/s
59. **a.** 1.32×10^3 N; 273 N
   b. 0.324
61. 1.3×10^2 N
63. 5.1 N•m

65. $R = 2.4 \times 10^3$ N;
$T = 1.7 \times 10^3$ N

67. 57 m

69. a. 47 N
b. 0.24 kg•m^2
c. 4.0 × 10^1 rad/s

71. 24 m

73. 63%

75. 6.4 m

77. 8.0 rev/s

CHAPTER 9

Practice 9A, p. 324

1. a. 3.56 × 10^3 kg/m^3
b. 6.40 × 10^2 kg/m^3

3. 98 kg

Practice 9B, p. 327

1. a. 1.48 × 10^3 N
b. 1.88 × 10^5 Pa

3. a. 1.20 × 10^3 Pa
b. 6.0 × 10^{-2} N

Practice 9C, p. 330

1. 1.11 × 10^8 Pa

3. 2.7 × 10^4 Pa

Practice 9D, p. 337

1. a. 18 m/s
b. 1.7 × 10^{-3} m

3. −4.4 × 10^{-2} Pa

9 Review and Assess, pp. 343–349

9. 3.4 × 10^{-5} m^3

11. 17 N, 31 N

13. 2.1 × 10^3 kg/m^3

21. 1.01 × 10^{11} N

23. 5.9 × 10^5 Pa

25. a. 2.52 × 10^7 Pa
b. 1.78 × 10^6 N

27. a. 1.16 × 10^5 Pa
b. 52 Pa

31. 2.4 m/s

33. a. 5.80 × 10^2 Pa
b. 1.02 × 10^5 N upward

39. 3.000 times

41. 0.131 kg/m^3

43. 16.5 cm^3

45. a. 3.2 × 10^2 K
b. 0.1V_i

47. a. 1.0 × 10^3 kg/m^3
b. 3.5 × 10^2 Pa
c. 2.1 × 10^3 Pa

49. 17.0 cm

51. 31.6 m/s

53. 2 × 10^{-2} m

55. 2.2 × 10^3 Pa

57. 2.2 m above the spout opening

59. 0.605 m

61. 2.5 × 10^9 capillaries

63. 60.9 m/s^2

65. 15 m

67. 21 Pa

69. 1.7 × 10^{-3} m

CHAPTER 10

Practice 10A, p. 363

1. 55 K; 99°F

3. −320.5°F; 77.34 K

5. 37.0°C; 39°C

Practice 10B, p. 370

1. 6.69 m

3. 41 m/s

5. 0.96 J

Practice 10C, p. 374

1. 2500 J/kg•°C

3. 230 J/kg•°C

5. 79°C

Practice 10D, p. 381

1. 1.29 × 10^5 J

3. 1.415 × 10^4 J

5. 76.2°C

10 Review and Assess, pp. 387–391

9. 57.8°C

11. 1947°F; 1337 K

13. 574.6 K = 574.6°F

23. a. 2.9 J

33. a. 1.1 × 10^3 J/kg•°C
b. 4.4 × 10^5 J/kg
c. 5.0 × 10^2 J/kg•°C
d. 4 × 10^2 J/kg•°C
e. 3.6 × 10^7 J/kg

(Estimates on the specific heat capacities may vary.)

35. 120°C

37. 21 J/s

45. a. $T_R = T_F + 459.7$, or
$T_F = T_R − 459.7$
b. $T = \frac{5}{9} T_R$, or $T_R = \frac{9}{5} T$

47. 5.1 × 10^4 s, or 14 h

49. 5.6 × 10^3 J/min = 93 J/s

CHAPTER 11

Practice 11A, p. 405

1. a. 6.4 × 10^5 J
b. −4.8 × 10^5 J

3. 3.3 × 10^2 J

Practice 11B, p. 413

1. 34 J

3. −143 J removed by heat

5. 8.0 × 10^3 J

Practice 11C, p. 424

1. 0.1504

3. a. 0.247
b. 4.9 × 10^4 J

5. 8.7 × 10^2 J

11 Review and Assess, pp. 431–435

11. 1.1 × 10^{-4} m^3

19. a. $\Delta U = 188$ J
b. $Q = 1212$ J

21. a. 43.0 × 10^3 J (43.0 kJ)

b. 604×10^3 J (604 kJ)
29. 6.5×10^{12} J; 3.0×10^{12} J
39. a. 3.3×10^2 J; by the rod
  b. 1.7×10^6 J; to the rod
  c. 1.7×10^6 J; it increases

CHAPTER 12

Practice 12A, p. 441
1. a. 15 N/m
  b. less stiff
3. 3.2×10^2 N/m

Practice 12B, p. 449
1. 8.5 s
3. 0.26 Hz

Practice 12C, p. 451
1. 1.2 Hz
3. 2.6 s

Practice 12D, p. 457
1. 0.081 m $\leq \lambda \leq 12$ m
3. a. 3.41 m
  b. 5.0×10^{-7} m
  c. 1.0×10^{-10} m
5. a. 346 m/s
  b. 5.9 m

12 Review and Assess, pp. 469–473
9. 1.3×10^2 N/m
11. 1.7 N
21. 6.3 s; 0.16 Hz
23. a. 2.000 s
  b. 9.812 m/s^2
  c. 9.798 m/s^2
37. a. 9.0 cm
  b. 20.0 cm
  c. 0.0400 s
  d. 5.00 m/s
39. 0.0333 m
49. 2.0 Hz; 0.50 s; 0.30 m/s
51. 446 m
53. a. 0.15 J
  b. 18 m/s^2

55. a. 24 N
  b. 6.0×10^1 m/s^2
  c. 24 N; 6.0×10^1 m/s^2
57. 106 oscillations
59. 0.319 m

CHAPTER 13

Practice 13A, p. 488
1. a. 8.0×10^{-4} W/m^2
  b. 1.6×10^{-3} W/m^2
  c. 6.4×10^{-3} W/m^2
3. 4.5 W
5. 4.8 m

Practice 13B, p. 499
1. 440 Hz
3. a. 82.1 Hz
  b. 115 Hz
  c. 144 Hz

13 Review and Assess, pp. 507–511
27. 3.1×10^{-3} W
29. a. 5.0×10^{-17} W
  b. 5.0×10^{-5} W
41. a. 52 cm
  b. 640 Hz, 960 Hz
  c. 350 Hz
43. a. 958 Hz
  b. 27.0 cm, 45.0 cm
45. 20 m; 2×10^{-2} m
47. a. 70.1 Hz
  b. 285
49. 750 Hz
51. $L_{closed} = 1.5\,(L_{open})$
53. a. 5.0×10^4 W
  b. 2.8×10^{-3} W

CHAPTER 14

Practice 14A, p. 523
1. 3.4 m–2.78 m
3. 85.7 m–10.1 m; The wavelengths are shorter than

those of the AM radio band.
5. 5.4×10^{14} Hz

Practice 14B, p. 536
1. $p = 10.0$ cm: no image (infinite q); $p = 5.00$ cm: $q = -10.0$ cm, virtual, upright image, $M = 2.00$
3. $q = 53$ cm; $M = -0.57$, real, inverted image

Practice 14C, p. 540
1. $q = -0.25$ m; $M = 0.081$; virtual, upright image
3. $q = -0.24$ m; $M = 0.044$; virtual, upright image
5. $q = -2.0 \times 10^1$ cm; $M = 0.41$; virtual, upright image

14 Review and Assess, pp. 550–555
11. 3×10^{14} Hz
13. 9.1×10^{-3} m (9.1 mm)
35. $p = 13$ cm; real, inverted; $M = -2.0$
37. inverted; $p = 6.1$ cm; $f = 2.6$ cm; real
39. $q = -15.8$ cm; virtual; $M = 0.295$; upright
41. $R = -31.0$ cm
51. $p = 11.3$ cm
55. $R = -25.0$ cm
57. concave, $R = 48.1$ cm; $M = 2.00$; virtual

CHAPTER 15

Practice 15A, p. 567
1. 18.5°
3. a. 27.5°
  b. glycerine ($n = 1.47$)
  c. 31.6°

Practice 15B, p. 576

1. 2.0×10^1 cm; real, inverted image
3. -6.67 cm; virtual, upright image

Practice 15C, p. 582

1. $42.8°$
3. $49.8°$

15 Review and Assess,
pp. 587–592

11. $26°$
13. $51.9°$
15. $30.0°, 19.5°, 19.5°, 30.0°$
27. **a.** real, inverted, -1.00
    b. virtual, upright, 2.0
29. All are virtual and upright.
    a. 0.332
    b. 0.500
    c. 0.667
31. **a.** 6.00 cm
    b. A diverging lens cannot form an image larger than the object.
33. **a.** 3.01 cm
    b. 2.05 cm
35. $\dfrac{10}{9}f$
47. **a.** $31.3°$
    b. $44.2°$
    c. $49.8°$
49. **a.** $40.8°$
    b. $60.6°$
51. 1.38
53. **a.** $36.7°$
    b. $53.4°$
55. blue: $47.8°$, red: $48.2°$
57. $48.8°$
59. 4.54 m
61. **a.** $24.7°$
    b. It will pass through the bottom surface because $\theta_i < \theta_c$ ($\theta_c = 41.8°$).
63. 58.0 m

CHAPTER 16

Practice 16A, p. 604

1. 5.1×10^2 nm
3. $0.188°$

Practice 16B, p. 611

1. 6.62×10^3 lines/cm
3. 1
5. $11.0°; 17.2°$

16 Review and Assess,
pp. 620–623

9. **a.** 589 nm
   b. $0.327°$
   c. $0.491°$
11. 2.41×10^{-4} m
21. 8.000×10^{-7} m
27. 432.0 nm
29. 1.93×10^{-3} mm $= 3\,\lambda$; a maximum

CHAPTER 17

Practice 17A, p. 636

1. **a.** 16 N
   b. attractive
   c. 2.7×10^{13} electrons
   d. 3.8×10^{13} electrons
3. 39.3 cm

Practice 17B, p. 639

1. 47 N, along the negative x-axis; 157 N, along the positive x-axis; 11.0×10^1 N, along the negative x-axis

Practice 17C, p. 641

1. $x = 0.64$ m
3. 5.07 m

Practice 17D, p. 647

1. 1.66×10^5 N/C, $81.1°$ above the positive x-axis

3. **a.** 3.2×10^{-15} N, along the negative x-axis
   b. 3.2×10^{-15} N, along the positive x-axis

17 Review and Assess,
pp. 654–659

17. 3.5×10^3 N
19. 91 N (repulsive)
21. $y = 0.8$ m
37. 12.0×10^3 N/C, toward the 30.0×10^{-9} C charge
39. 4.8×10^{-6} C
41. **a.** 2.75×10^{23} electrons
    b. 4.40×10^4 C
43. **a.** 1.3×10^{-5} N, $77°$ below the negative x-axis
    b. 2.6×10^3 N/C, $77°$ below the negative x-axis
47. 7.2×10^{-9} C
49. 2.93×10^{21} N/C, directed away from the surface
51. $v_{electron} = 4.4 \times 10^6$ m/s; $v_{proton} = 2.4 \times 10^3$ m/s
53. 1.3×10^{-3} C
55. 0.0 N/C
57. **a.** 6.1×10^{10} m/s^2
    b. 2.0×10^{-5} s
    c. 12 m
    d. 1.20×10^{-15} J
59. **a.** positive
    b. 5.3×10^{-7} C
61. **a.** 5.3×10^{17} m/s^2
    b. 8.5×10^{-4} m
    c. 2.9×10^{14} m/s^2
63. 32.5 m
65. **a.** 3.2×10^{-16} N, along the positive x-axis
    b. 1.9×10^{11} m/s^2
    c. 5.3×10^{-6} s
67. 1.62×10^4 N/C, opposite the proton's velocity

CHAPTER 18

Practice 18A, p. 669

1. **a.** 14.4×10^{-7} J

b. 9.6×10^{-7} J
c. -0.9×10^{-7} J

Practice 18B, p. 673
1. 1.4×10^{-7} V
3. 3.8×10^{4} V

Practice 18C, p. 681
1. a. 4.8×10^{-6} F
b. 5.4×10^{-6} J
3. a. 4.80×10^{-5} C
b. 4.50×10^{-6} J

18 Review and Assess
pp. 683–687
5. 9.1 J
13. 2.6×10^{4} V
15. 3.20×10^{-19} C
17. −154 V
31. 4.000×10^{-6} F
33. 0.22 J
35. 0.11 m
37. a. 90.4 V
b. 9.04×10^{4} V/m
39. a. 4.69×10^{5} m/s
b. 1.09×10^{4} m/s
41. 1.5×10^{5} m/s
43. a. 7.2×10^{-13} J
b. 2.9×10^{7} m/s
45. a. -9.22×10^{4} V
b. 9.22×10^{4} V
47. 2.00×10^{-7} C; 3.000 m
49. a. 3.10×10^{-13} F
b. 3.7×10^{-14} C
c. 2.2×10^{-15} J
d. 3.4×10^{-2} V
e. 8.5×10^{-2} V

CHAPTER 19

Practice 19A, p. 695
1. 1.04×10^{19} electrons

3. 2.0×10^{1} C
5. 3.00×10^{20} electrons

Practice 19B, p. 703
1. 46 Ω
3. a. 1.8 A
b. 2.5 A
c. 6.0 A
5. 0.43 A

Practice 19C, p. 710
1. 6.25 A; 312 W

Practice 19D, p. 712
1. a. $0.14
b. $4.40
c. $0.42

19 Review and Assess,
pp. 717–721
19. a. 1.9×10^{3} C
b. 1.2×10^{22} electrons
29. 0.20 A
31. 3.0×10^{1} Ω
43. 2.7 A
45. $8.10
47. a. 32 V
b. 0.16 V
49. 2.0×10^{16} J
51. a. 720 W
b. 8.6×10^{5} J
c. $0.0024
53. a. 1.04×10^{7} J
b. $0.23
55. 61.1 A
57. 1.1×10^{3} s (18 min)
59. a. 18 C
b. 3.6 A
61. a. 670 A
b. 5.0×10^{4} m

CHAPTER 20

Practice 20A, p. 739
1. a. 43.6 Ω
b. 0.275 A
3. 1.0 V, 2.0 V, 2.5 V, 3.5 V
5. 0.5 Ω

Practice 20B, p. 744
1. 4.5 A, 2.2 A, 1.8 A, 1.3 A
3. a. 2.99 Ω
b. 36.0 V
c. 2.00 A, 6.00 A

Practice 20C, p. 748
1. a. 27.8 Ω
b. 26.6 Ω
c. 23.4 Ω

Practice 20D, p. 751
1. R_a: 0.50 A, 2.5 V
R_b: 0.50 A, 3.5 V
R_c: 1.5 A, 6.0 V
R_d: 1.0 A, 4.0 V
R_e: 1.0 A, 4.0 V
R_f: 2.0 A, 4.0 V

20 Review and Assess,
pp. 754–759
17. 3.0×10^{1} V
19. a. 2.2 Ω
b. 11 A
c. 6.0 A, 3.0 A, 2.0 A
d. 24 V, 24 V, 24 V
21. a. 2.99 Ω
b. 4.0 A
c. 0.67 A, 1.3 A, 2.0 A
d. 12 V, 12 V, 12 V
25. 15 Ω
27. 1875 Ω
29. a. 1.1 A, 0.72 A, 1.8 A
b. 6.5 V, 6.5 V, 5.4 V
31. 2.2 V
35. a. a
b. c
c. d
d. e

37. 18.0 Ω: 1.00 A, 18.0 V
6.0 Ω: 3.0 A, 18.0 V

39. 4.0 Ω

41. 13.96 Ω

43. a. 62.4 Ω
b. 0.192 A
c. 0.102 A
d. 0.520 W
e. 0.737 W

47. a. 5.1 Ω
b. 4.5 V

49. a. 11 A (heater), 9.2 A (toaster), 12 A (grill)
b. The total current is 32.2 A, so the 30.0 A circuit breaker will open the circuit if these appliances are all on.

CHAPTER 21

Practice 21A, p. 775

1. 2.4×10^{-14} N

3. 6.0×10^{-12} N south

5. 8.3×10^{-2} T west

Practice 21B, p. 778

1. 4.0×10^{-2} up, away from Earth

3. 0.59 m

5. 1.5 T

21 Review and Assess, pp. 781–785

29. 3.0×10^{-11} N upward

35. 15.0 N

37. 0.245 A

39. 1.9×10^{14} m/s^2

41. 2.1×10^{-2} T in the negative y direction

43. 8.0×10^{-3} T in the positive z direction

45. 1.39×10^{-2} T toward the observer

47. a. 5.00×10^{-2} m
b. 8.78×10^{6} m/s

CHAPTER 22

Practice 22A, p. 800

1. 0.30 V

3. 0.14 V

Practice 22B, p. 806

1. 87 V

3. 1.7×10^{-2} V

Practice 22C, p. 810

1. 4.8 A; 6.8 A, 170 V

3. a. 7.42 A
b. 15 Ω

5. a. 1.10×10^{2} V
b. 2.1 A

Practice 22D, p. 818

1. 1.20×10^{2} V

3. 156:1

5. 2.6×10^{4} V

22 Review and Assess, pp. 821–825

11. 790 turns

13. 4.2×10^{-2} T

15. 3.2×10^{-2} V

27. a. 2.4×10^{2} V
b. 6.9 A

29. a. 2.4×10^{2} V
b. 2.0 A

31. a. 8.34 A
b. 119 V

39. 48 turns

41. 11 turns

43. $f = 89$ Hz; 245 V

CHAPTER 23

Practice 23A, p. 833

1. 2.5 eV

3. violet

Practice 23B, p. 836

1. 5.50×10^{14} Hz

3. 0.6 eV; 1.0 eV

Practice 23C, p. 851

1. 7.28×10^{-11} m

3. 4.0×10^{-38} m

23 Review and Assess, pp. 856–859

15. a. 2.49×10^{-5} eV
b. 2.49 eV
c. 24.9 eV

17. a. lithium; iron
b. 1.8 eV; 0.2 eV

39. 5.2×10^{-11} m

41. 9.91×10^{6} m/s

43. a. 1.39 eV
b. 3.35×10^{14} Hz

45. red

47. 3.7×10^{19} photons

49. 1.06×10^{-34} m

51. 1.3×10^{7} s

53. a. 1.5×10^{4} eV (15 keV)
b. 1.2×10^{5} eV (120 keV)

CHAPTER 24

24 Review and Assess, pp. 886–888

25. a. 2.75×10^{14} Hz
b. 1.09×10^{-6} m

27. 1 eV

CHAPTER 25

Practice 25A, p. 902

1. 160.65 MeV; 342.06 MeV

3. 7.5702 MeV/nucleon

5. 0.2101 MeV

Practice 25B, p. 908

1. a. $^{12}_{6}$C
b. $^{4}_{2}$He

c. $^{14}_{6}C$

d. $^{208}_{81}Tl$

3. a. β^- decay

b. $^{56}_{26}Fe \rightarrow ^{56}_{27}Co + ^{0}_{-1}e + \overline{\nu}$

Practice 25C, p. 911

1. a. about 5.0×10^7 atoms

b. about 3.5×10^8 atoms

3. a. 9.94×10^{-7} s^{-1}

b. 6.7×10^{-7} Ci

c. 1.9×10^{10} nuclei

25 Review and Assess, pp. 927–931

7. 92.163 MeV

9. 8.482 MeV; 7.718 MeV

23. $^{10}_{5}B$

25. a. $^{4}_{2}He$

b. $^{4}_{2}He$

27. 22 mCi

29. 93.8%

39. 1.6×10^{16} nuclei

41. 1.3×10^4 m

43. 1.0×10^{-23} s

45. a. $^{1}_{0}n + ^{197}_{79}Au \rightarrow ^{198}_{80}Hg + ^{0}_{-1}e + \overline{\nu}$

b. 7.885 MeV

47. $^{3}_{2}He$

49. $^{1}_{0}n$

51. 1.1×10^{16} fission events

53. 2.6×10^{21} atoms

55. 3.53 MeV

57. 7.8×10^{10} s (2500 years)

59. a. 18.3 decays/min

61. a. $^{8}_{4}Be$

b. $^{12}_{6}C$

Credits

Illustrations

Photography

Front and Back Cover: The Image Bank **Background Tabs:** Interference pattern on oil on water/ Peter Aprahamian/Photo Researchers, Inc.; Concentric circle in colored pool/Mahau Kulyk/Science Library/Photo Researchers, Inc.: Computer circuit board/Charlotte Raymond/Science Source/Photo Researchers, Inc.; Colored bubble chamber showing subatomic particle tracks/Patrice Loiez/Science Photo Library/Photo Researchers, Inc. **Title Page:** The Image Bank **Table of Contents:** Page viii (tl), Richard Megna/Photo Researchers, Inc.; ix (cr),x (cl), Richard Megna/Fundamental Photographs; xi (tr), Robert Mathena/Fundamental Photographs; xii (c), xiii (tr),Richard Megna/Fundamental Photographs; xiv (tl), Michelle Bridwell/HRW Photo; xvii (br), Caltech Archives. **Chapter One:** Page 2-3 (c), Sharon Green/Pacific Stock; 4 (b), Ron Kimball ©1995; 6 (br), 7 (tl), Christine Galida/HRW Photo; 10 (bl), The National Institute of Standards and Technology; 11 (br), Stephen Dalton/Photo Researchers, Inc.; 12 (tl), Mike Fager/HRW Photo; 13 (tl), Sam Dudgeon/HRW Photo; 15 (all), 16 (all), Michelle Bridwell/HRW Photos; 17 (tr), Ron Thomas/FPG International, Inc.; 20 (bl), Richard Megna/Fundamental Photographs; 22 (bl), John P. Kelly/The Image Bank; 24 (b), Michelle Bridwell/HRW Photo; 28 (tr), Sam Dudgeon/HRW Photo. **Chapter Two:** Page 38-39, Tony Stone Images; 41 (c), FPG International, Inc.; 45 (tc), Photo Researchers, Inc.; 45 (bc), Michelle Bridwell/HRW Photo; 50 (tl), Eugene Gebhardt/FPG International, Inc.; 50 (br), Aaron Haupt/Photo Researchers, Inc.; 51 (b), Richard Megna/Fundamental Photographs; 57 (tc), Michelle Bridwell/HRW Photo; 60 (bl), James Sugar/Black Star; 61 (tr), (br), Richard Megna/Fundamental Photographs; 67 (br), Sam Dudgeon/HRW Photo; 70 (br), 72 (c), Educational Development Center;77 (bl), 79 (bl), Mike Fager/HRW Photo. **Chapter Three:** Page 82-83, Photo Researchers, Inc.; 84 (bl), 85 (br), Michelle Bridwell/HRW Photo; 98 (cl), Dennis O'Clair/Tony Stone Images; 99 (br), Richard Megna/Fundamental Photographs; 100; 107 (br), Corbis-Bettmann; 111 (bl), Caltech Archives; 121 (tr), Mike Fager/HRW Photo. **Chapter Four:** Page 122-123, Nicholas Pinturas/Tony Stone Images; 124 (all), 125 (br), Michelle Bridwell/HRW Photo; 127 (tr), William Means/Tony Stone Images; 129 (br), Photo Researchers, Inc.; 130 (cl), SuperStock; 131 (all), 132 (tr), Michelle Bridwell/HRW Photos; 135 (tr), Tony Freeman/Photo Edit; 136 (all),138 (bl),139 (cr), Michelle Bridwell/HRW Photo; 141 (cr), Photo Researchers, Inc.; 142 (all), Michelle Bridwell/HRW Photo; 144 (bl), Jess Stock/Tony Stone Images; 146 (tr), Michelle Bridwell/HRW Photo; 148 (bl), Ken Lax; 148 (br), Goodyear Tire and Rubber Company; 159(bl), 161 (bl), Mike Fager/HRW Photo. **Timeline (1540-1690):** 164 (tl), Giraudon/Art Resource; 164 (tc), Ann Ronan Picture Library/Image Select; 164 (tr), Corbis-Bettman; 164 (cl), Erich Lessing/Art Resource, NY; 164 (c), Archive Photos; 164 (bl), Image Select; 164 (bc), Photo AKG London/Ottario Leoni, t-83"T; 164 (br), Corbis-Bettmann; 165 (tl), Scala/Art Resource, NY; 165 (tc), Archive Photos/ Kean Archives; 165 (tr), Ann Ronan Picture Library/Image Select; 165 (cl), Burstein/Corbis-Bettmann; 165 (cl), J. Sowerby/ e.t. archive; 165 (bl), Sir Isaac Newton's Mathematical Principles of Natural Philosophy

Glossary

absorption spectrum a continuous spectrum interrupted by dark lines characteristic of the medium through which the radiation has passed (p. 842)

acceleration the rate of change of velocity (p. 48)

accuracy the extent to which a reported measurement approaches the true value of the quantity measured (p. 15)

action-reaction pair a pair of simultaneous equal but opposite forces resulting from the interaction of two objects (p. 139)

adiabatic process a thermodynamic process during which work is done on or by a system but no energy is transferred to or from the system by heat (p. 407)

alternating current an electric current that changes direction at regular intervals (p. 807)

amplitude maximum displacement from equilibrium (p. 446)

angle of incidence the angle between a ray that strikes a surface and the normal to that surface at the point of contact (p. 527)

angle of reflection the angle formed by the line normal to a surface and the direction in which a reflected ray moves (p. 527)

angular acceleration the time rate of change of angular speed, expressed in radians per second per second (p. 249)

angular displacement the angle through which a point, line, or body is rotated in a specified direction and about a specified axis (p. 246)

angular momentum the product of a rotating object's moment of inertia and the angular speed about the same axis (p. 292)

angular speed the rate at which a body rotates about an axis, usually expressed in radians per second (p. 247)

antinode the point in a standing wave, halfway between two nodes, at which the largest amplitude occurs (p. 463)

average velocity total displacement divided by the time interval during which the displacement occurred (p. 43)

B

back emf the emf induced in a motor's coil that tends to reduce the current powering the motor (p. 812)

band gap the minimum energy separation between the highest occupied state and the lowest empty state (p. 868)

beat the interference of waves of slightly different frequencies traveling in the same direction, perceived as a variation in loudness (p. 502)

Bernoulli's principle states that the pressure in a fluid decreases as its velocity increases (p. 335)

binding energy the energy released when nucleons bind together to form a stable nucleus (p. 900)

blackbody radiation electromagnetic radiation emitted by a blackbody, which absorbs all incoming radiation and then emits radiation based only on its temperature (p. 830)

buoyant force a force that acts upward on an object submerged in a liquid or floating on the liquid's surface (p. 319)

C

calorimetry an experimental procedure used to measure the energy transferred by heat from one substance to another (p. 372)

capacitance the ability of a conductor to store energy in the form of electrically separated charges (p. 676)

center of mass the point at which all the mass of the body can be considered to be concentrated when analyzing translational motion (p. 283)

centripetal acceleration acceleration directed toward the center of a circular path (p. 257)

chromatic aberration the focusing of different colors of light at different distances behind a lens (p. 585)

coefficient of friction the ratio of the force of friction to the normal force acting between two objects (p. 144)

coherence the property by which two waves with identical wavelengths maintain a constant phase relationship (p. 599)

components of a vector the projections of a vector along the axes of a coordinate system (p. 92)

compression the region of a longitudinal wave in which the density and pressure are greater than normal (p. 480)

Compton shift the change in wavelength between incoming and scattered electromagnetic waves (p. 838)

concave spherical mirror an inwardly curved, mirrored surface that is a portion of a sphere and that converges incoming light rays (p. 530)

conductor material that transfers charge easily (p. 631)

constructive interference interference in which individual displacements on the same side of the equilibrium position are added together to form the resultant wave (p. 460)

contact force force that arises from the physical contact of two objects (p. 125)

controlled experiment experiment involving manipulation of only a single variable or factor (p. 9)

convex spherical mirror an outwardly curved, mirrored surface that is a portion of a sphere and that diverges incoming light rays (p. 537)

crest the highest point above the equilibrium position (p. 454)

critical angle the minimum angle of incidence for which total internal reflection occurs (p. 580)

current the rate at which electric charges move through a given area (p. 694)

cyclic process a thermodynamic process in which a system returns to the same conditions under which it started (p. 415)

decibel level relative intensity determined by relating the intensity of a sound wave to the intensity at the threshold of hearing (p. 490)

destructive interference interference in which individual displacements on opposite sides of the equilibrium position are added together to form the resultant wave (p. 461)

diffraction the spreading of light into a region behind an obstruction (p. 605)

diode an electronic device that allows electric current to pass more easily in one direction than in the other (p. 874)

dispersion the process of separating polychromatic light into its component wavelengths (p. 583)

displacement the change in position of an object (p. 40)

domain a microscopic magnetic region composed of a group of atoms whose magnetic fields are aligned in a common direction (p. 772)

doping the addition of an impurity to a semiconductor (p. 873)

Doppler effect frequency shift that is the result of relative motion between the source of sound waves and an observer (p. 485)

drift velocity the net velocity of a charge carrier moving in an electric field (p. 697)

elastic collision a collision in which the total momentum and the total kinetic energy remain constant (p. 226)

elastic potential energy the potential energy in a stretched or compressed elastic object (p. 175)

electric circuit a set of electrical components connected so that they provide one or more complete paths for the movement of charges (p. 732)

electric field a field that permeates the space around a charged object and in which another charged object experiences an electric force (p. 643)

electric field lines lines that represent both the magnitude and the direction of the electric field (p. 648)

electric potential the electrical potential energy associated with a charged particle divided by the charge of the particle (p. 670)

electrical potential energy potential energy associated with an object due to its position relative to a source of electric force (p. 666)

electromagnetic induction production of an emf in a conducting circuit by a change in the strength, position, or orientation of an external magnetic field (p. 794)

electromagnetic wave a transverse wave consisting of oscillating electric and magnetic fields at right angles to each other (p. 520)

emf the energy per unit charge supplied by a source of electric current (p. 734)

emission spectrum a unique series of spectral lines emitted by an atomic gas when a potential difference is applied across the gas (p. 842)

entropy a measure of the disorder of a system (p. 426)

environment everything outside a system that can affect or be affected by the system's behavior (p. 403)

equilibrium the state of a body in which there is no change in its motion (p. 134)

excited state the state of an atom that is no longer in its ground state (p. 867)

field force force that can exist between objects, even in the absence of physical contact between the objects (p. 125)

fluid a nonsolid state of matter in which the atoms or molecules are free to move past each other, as in gas or liquid (p. 318)

force the cause of an acceleration or the change in an object's motion (p. 124)

force diagram a diagram of the objects involved in a situation and the forces exerted on the objects (p. 126)

frame of reference a coordinate system for specifying the precise location of objects in space (p. 106)

free fall the motion of an object falling with a constant acceleration (p. 60)

frequency the number of cycles or vibrations per unit of time (p. 446)

fundamental frequency the lowest frequency of vibration of a standing wave (p. 494)

G

generator a device that uses induction to convert mechanical energy to electrical energy (p. 803)

gravitational force the mutual force of attraction between particles of matter (p. 263)

gravitational potential energy potential energy associated with an object due to its position relative to Earth or some other gravitational source (p. 174)

ground state the lowest-energy state of a quantized system (p. 867)

H

half-life the time required for half the original nuclei of a radioactive material to undergo radioactive decay (p. 909)

harmonic series a series of frequencies that includes the fundamental frequency and integral multiples of the fundamental frequency (p. 495)

heat the process by which energy is exchanged between objects because of a difference in their temperatures or because one object is undergoing a phase change (p. 365)

heat of fusion the energy per unit mass transferred in order to change a substance from solid to liquid or from liquid to solid at constant temperature and pressure (p. 378)

heat of vaporization the energy per unit mass transferred in order to change a substance from liquid to vapor or from vapor to liquid at constant temperature and pressure (p. 378)

hole an energy level that is not occupied by an electron in a semiconductor (p. 872)

I

ideal fluid a fluid that has no internal friction or viscosity and that is incompressible (p. 332)

impulse for a constant external force, the product of the force and the time over which it acts on an object (p. 210)

index of refraction the ratio of the speed of light in a vacuum to its speed in a given transparent medium (p. 564)

induction the process of charging a conductor by bringing it near another charged object and grounding the conductor (p. 632)

inertia the tendency of an object to maintain its state of motion (p. 130)

insulator material that does not transfer charge easily (p. 631)

intensity the rate at which energy flows through a unit area perpendicular to the direction of wave motion (p. 487)

internal energy the energy of a substance due to the random motions of its component particles and equal to the total energy of those particles (p. 359)

isothermal process a thermodynamic process that takes place at constant temperature and in which the internal energy of a system remains unchanged (p. 407)

isotope an atom of an element having the same atomic number but different neutron and mass numbers (p. 897)

isovolumetric process a thermodynamic process that takes place at constant volume so that no work is done on or by the system (p. 406)

K

kinetic energy the energy of an object due to its motion (p. 172)

kinetic friction the force exerted on a moving object (p. 143)

L

laser a device that produces an intense, nearly parallel beam of coherent light (p. 614)

latent heat the energy per unit mass that is transferred during a phase change of a substance (p. 379)

lens a transparent object that refracts light rays, causing them to converge or diverge to create an image (p. 568)

lever arm the perpendicular distance from the axis of rotation to a line drawn along the direction of the force (p. 279)

linear polarization the alignment of electromagnetic waves in such a way that the vibrations of the electric fields in each of the waves are parallel to each other (p. 546)

longitudinal wave a wave whose particles vibrate parallel to the direction of wave motion (p. 455)

M

magnetic field a region in which a magnetic force can be detected (p. 767)

mass density mass per unit volume of a substance (p. 319)

mechanical energy the sum of kinetic energy and all forms of potential energy (p. 177)

mechanical wave a wave whose propagation requires the existence of a medium (p. 452)

medium material through which a disturbance travels (p. 452)

model a replica or description designed to show the structure or workings of an object, system, or concept (p. 6)

moment of inertia the measure of the resistance of an object to changes in rotational motion (p. 284)

momentum a vector quantity defined as the product of an object's mass and velocity (p. 208)

mutual inductance a measure of the ability of one circuit carrying a changing current to induce an emf in a nearby circuit (p. 814)

net external force the total force resulting from a combination of external forces on an object; sometimes called the resultant force (p. 131)

node the point in a standing wave that always undergoes complete destructive interference and therefore is stationary (p. 463)

normal force a contact force exerted by one object on another in a direction perpendicular to the surface of contact (p. 141)

O

order number the number assigned to interference fringes with respect to the central bright fringe (p. 602)

P

parallel describes two or more components in a circuit that are connected across common points or junctions, providing separate conducting paths for the current (p. 740)

path difference the difference in the distance traveled by two interfering light waves (p. 602)

perfectly inelastic collision a collision in which two objects stick together and move with a common velocity after colliding (p. 222)

period the time it takes to execute a complete cycle of motion (p. 446)

periodic wave a wave whose source is some form of periodic motion (p. 453)

phase change the physical change of a substance from one state (solid, liquid, or gas) to another at constant temperature and pressure (p. 377)

photoelectric effect the emission of electrons from a surface that occurs when light of certain frequencies shines on the surface (p. 834)

photon the discrete unit (or quantum) of light energy (p. 835)

pitch how high or low we perceive a sound to be, depending on the frequency of the sound wave (p. 481)

potential difference the change in electrical potential energy associated with a charged particle divided by the charge of the particle (p. 670)

potential energy energy associated with an object due to its position (p. 174)

power the rate at which energy is transferred (p. 186)

precision the degree of exactness or refinement of a measurement (p. 15)

pressure force per unit area (p. 325)

projectile motion the motion of objects moving in two dimensions under the influence of gravity (p. 99)

pulse wave a single nonperiodic disturbance (p. 453)

R

radian an angle whose arc length is equal to its radius, which is approximately equal to 57.3°(p. 245)

rarefaction the region of a longitudinal wave in which the density and pressure are less than normal (p. 480)

real image an image formed when rays of light actually intersect at a single point (p. 531)

reflection the turning back of an electromagnetic wave at the surface of a substance (p. 526)

refraction the bending of a wave disturbance as it passes at an angle from one medium to another (p. 562)

resistance the ratio of the potential difference across a conductor to the current it carries (p. 700)

resolving power the ability of an optical instrument to separate two images that are close together (p. 612)

resonance a condition that exists when the frequency of a force applied to a system matches the natural frequency of vibration of the system (p. 492)

resultant a vector representing the sum of two or more vectors (p. 85)

rms current the amount of direct current that dissipates as much energy in a resistor as an instantaneous alternating current does during a complete cycle (p. 808)

rotational kinetic energy the energy of an object due to its rotational motion (p. 295)

rotational motion the motion of a body that spins about an axis (p. 244)

scalar a physical quantity that has only a magnitude and no direction (p. 84)

schematic diagram a graphic representation of an electric circuit, with standardized symbols representing circuit components (p. 730)

self-induction the process by which a changing current in a circuit induces an emf in that circuit (p. 819)

series describes a circuit or portion of a circuit that provides a single conducting path without junctions (p. 736)

significant figures digits in a measurement that are known with certainty plus the first digit that is uncertain (p. 16)

simple harmonic motion vibration about an equilibrium position in which a restoring force is proportional to the displacement from equilibrium (p. 439)

solenoid a long, helically wound coil of insulated wire (p. 771)

specific heat capacity the quantity of energy needed to raise the temperature of 1 kg of a substance by 1°C at constant pressure (p. 371)

spring constant a parameter that expresses how resistant a spring is to being compressed or stretched (p. 175)

standing wave a wave pattern that results when two waves of the same frequency, wavelength, and amplitude travel in opposite directions and interfere (p. 463)

static friction the force exerted on a motionless body by its environment to resist an external force (p. 143)

strong force the interaction that binds nucleons together in a nucleus (p. 898)

superconductor a material whose resistance is zero at or below some critical temperature, which varies with each material (p. 706)

system a collection of matter within a clearly defined boundary across which no matter passes (p. 403)

system a set of items or interactions considered a distinct physical entity for the purpose of study (p. 7)

T

tangential acceleration the instantaneous linear acceleration of an object directed along the tangent to the object's circular path (p. 255)

tangential speed the instantaneous linear speed of an object directed along the tangent to the object's circular path (p. 253)

temperature a measure of the average kinetic energy of the particles in a substance (p. 331)

thermal conduction the process by which energy is transferred by heat through a material between two points at different temperatures (p. 383)

thermal equilibrium the state in which two bodies in physical contact with each other have identical temperatures (p. 360)

timbre the quality of a steady musical sound that is the result of a mixture of harmonics present at different intensities (p. 501)

torque a quantity that measures the ability of a force to rotate an object around some axis (p. 279)

total internal reflection the complete reflection of light at the boundary of two transparent media; this effect occurs when the angle of incidence exceeds the critical angle (p. 580)

transformer a device that changes one ac potential difference to a different ac potential difference (p. 815)

transistor a device, typically containing three terminals, that can amplify a signal (p. 877)

transverse wave a wave whose particles vibrate perpendicular to the direction of wave motion (p. 454)

trough the lowest point below the equilibrium position (p. 454)

U

ultraviolet catastrophe contradiction between the predictions of classical physics and the experimental data for the electromagnetic radiation of a blackbody in the ultraviolet end of the spectrum (p. 831)

uncertainty principle states that it is impossible to simultaneously measure both the position and the momentum of an object with complete certainty (p. 852)

V

valence electron an electron in the outermost shell of an atom (p. 867)

vector a physical quantity that has both a magnitude and a direction (p. 84)

virtual image an image formed by light rays that only appear to intersect (p. 528)

W

wavelength the distance between two adjacent similar points of the wave, such as from crest to crest or from trough to trough (p. 454)

weight the magnitude of the force of gravity acting on an object (p. 141)

work the product of the magnitudes of the component of a force along the direction of displacement and the displacement (p. 168)

work function the minimum amount of energy required for an electron to escape from a metal (p. 835)

work–kinetic energy theorem the net work done on an object is equal to the change in the kinetic energy of the object (p. 184)

Index

634; measurement of, 76, 617. *See also* displacement.

diverging lens(es), **568**, 569, 573, **573**, 576, **577**

diverging mirror(s), 537–540, *t* 538, 549

diving suit(s), **325**

DNA (deoxyribonucleic acid), 659, 892

dolphin(s), **478–479**, 479, 482, 486

door bell(s), 801, **801**

doping, of semiconductors, 872–874

Doppler, Christian, 485

Doppler effect, 485–486, 504–505, 506, 510

drift velocity, 696–697, 716

driving, friction and, 148

Dufay, Charles Francois de Cisternay, 354

E

ear(s), 493, **493**, 509

Earth: atmosphere of, 582–583, 586, 651; capacitance of, 678; magnetic field of, 765; magnetic poles of, 767–769, 780; mass of, 266; radius of, 248, 266; specific heat capacity of, 375

earthquake(s), resonance in, 492

echolocation, 479, 482, 486

eddy current(s), 332

efficiency: of electric vehicles, 690–691; of engines, *t* 422, 422–424, 427, 430, 434; friction and, 301; laboratory exercise on, 313–315; machines and, 301, 313–315; thermodynamics and, 413–419, 422–424, 430, 434; of transformers, 816

Einstein, Albert: electromagnetic waves and, 466; equation of, 191; photoelectric effect and, 837; probability waves and, 853; special theory of relativity and, 66–67, 110–111, 862, 898

elastic collision. *See* collision, elastic.

elastic potential energy, **175,** 175–176, 192, 200–205, 441

electric charge(s): of atomic particles, *t* 630, 653; conservation of, 629; Coulomb's law and, 634–642; current and, 694–696; electrical potential energy and, 667–669; as field force, 125, 637;

laboratory exercise on, 660–663; quantization of, 630; transfer of, 631–633, 679

electric current: circuitry and, 741, *t* 742, 748–751, 753; current gain, 878; electric power and, 708–709; induction of, 794–800, *t* 796, *t* 820; laboratory exercise on, 722–725; leakage of, 876; magnetic fields and, **770,** 770–771, **771,** 776–780, 786–789; overview of, 694–699, 716; resistance and, 700–701, 722–725; root mean square (rms) and, 807–810, 820, *t* 820; units of, *t* 716. *See also* resistance.

electric dipole, 649

electric energy. *See* electrical energy.

electric field(s): in the atmosphere, 651; current and, 696–697; electrical potential energy and, 667, **667,** 671; electromagnetic waves and, 521, **521, 546;** in electrostatic equilibrium, 650–652; lines of, **648,** *t* 648, 648–649, **649;** potential difference in, 671–672; strength of, **643,** 643–647, *t* 645, 653, *t* 653; television and, 683; units and symbols of, 643, *t* 653

electric force, 634–642, 653, *t* 653, 658

electric guitar, **792–793,** 793

electric meter(s), **711**

electric potential, 670–675, 682, *t* 682, 875

electric power, 688–689, 708–713, 716, *t* 716, 720, 883–884

electric vehicle(s), 690–691

electrical energy, 665–689; capacitance and, 662, 676–681; laboratory exercise on, 688–689; potential, 644, 666–669, 675, 679–682, *t* 682, 698

electrical storm(s), 633, **664–665,** 665

electricity, generation of, 421, 691

electrocution, 732, 813

electrolyte(s), 696, 702

electromagnet(s), 766, 827; laboratory exercise on, 771

electromagnetic induction, 794; laboratory exercise on, 826–827

electromagnetic interaction, 917, **918**

electromagnetic wave(s), 384, 520–525, 546, 549, 790–791. *See also* light.

electromagnetism, *t* 5, 780

electron(s): angular momentum of, **302,** 302–303, **303;** beta decay and, 904–905; conduction and, 870–871; de Broglie waves and, **850,** 850–851; drift velocity and, 696–697; electric charge and, 629–630, *t* 630; as elementary particles, 919; energy states of, 844, 867–869; forces on, 635–636; free, 867, 887; holes, **872,** 872–875, 878, 885, *t* 885; magnetic domains and, 772; mass of, 897, *t* 898; orbital angular momentum of, 302; orbits of, 845, 847, 851, 853; photoelectrons, 834–836, 844–845; potential energy of, **714,** 714–715, 860–861; thermal energy of, 873; uncertainty principle and, 852–854; valence, 867–868

electron cloud(s), 853–854, **854**

electron microscope(s), 467

electron spin, 303

electron tunneling, 714–715

electron volt(s), 671, 832–833, 898

electronics, 865–893

electroporation, 705

electroscope(s), 660–663

electrostatic equilibrium, 650–652, 660–663

electrostatic spray painting, **626–627,** 629, 649, 651

elementary particle(s), 917–918

elephant(s), 481

ELF (extremely low frequency electromagnetic field), 790–791

Elizabeth I, Queen of England, 164

embossed hologram(s), 616

emf: back, 812; generators and, 803–807; magnetic fields and, 794–796, 798–800; potential difference and, 734, 753; self-induced, 819

emission spectra, **609, 842,** 842–843, 855

emitter(s), 877–878

energy: binding, 900–902, **913,** 914, 926; chemical, 698; conservation of, 179–183, 191, 334–335, 368–370, 599; electric power and, 708–709, 883–884; heat and, 365–367; intensity of, 487–490; internal, 359, 368, *t* 386, 402–407, 409–415; mass and, 190; of photons, 832–833, 835–836, 838, 844,

ideal gas law, laboratory exercise on, 339
ignition coil(s), 816
image(s): distance, 527, 531–533, *t* 549, 575; in mirrors, 527–542, **528**, 555, 575; real, 531, **531**, *t* 538, 586. *See also* virtual image(s).
impulse, 210, 217, 219–220
impulse-momentum theorem, 210–214, 219–220, 231, 238
incandescence, 614. *See also* light bulb(s).
incidence, angle of, 527, 563, 580, 584, 586, *t* 586
inclined plane, 120–121, **298**, 298–299, **313**, 313–314
index of refraction, 563–566, *t* 564, 580–583, 585–586, *t* 586, 592
induction: alternating current and, 816; applications of, 801–802; charging of conductors by, 632–633, 653; of current, 793–802, *t* 796, *t* 820; Faraday's law and, 798–799, 805, 814, 820; generators and, 803–806; laboratory exercise on, 826–827; magnetic fields and, 794–802, *t* 796, **797**, 820, 826–827; mutual, 814–815, 820, *t* 820; self, **818**, 818–820, *t* 820
inelastic collision. *See* collision, inelastic.
inertia, 130–134, 150, 262, 304; laboratory exercise on, 134. *See also* moment of inertia.
infrared (IR) wave(s), *t* 521
infrasonic sound wave(s), 481
instrument resolution, diffraction and, 612–613
insulator(s): charging of, 631, 633, 653; classification of, 866–867; electron transitions and, **870**, 870–871; thermal, 383–384
integrated circuits, **864–865**, 865, 879–880
intensity. *See* sound, intensity of; light, intensity of.
interference: diffraction, 597–613, **605**, 619, 624–625; diffraction grating(s) and, 607–611, **608, 609**, 616, 619, 624–625; diffraction pattern(s) and, 606–607, **607, 612**; double-slit, 600–606, **603**, 619, 622; electrons and, 850, **850**; overview of, **598**, 598–600, **601**,

604. *See also* constructive interference; destructive interference.
interference fringe(s), **601**, 601–603, 607, 619
interference pattern(s), 600–603, **601**, *t* 619
internal energy, 359, 368, *t* 386, 402–407, 409–415
Inupiat Eskimo(s), 384
inverse-beta decay, 905
inverse-square law, 263
iodine, 911
ion(s), 629, 696, 702
IR. *See* infrared wave(s).
iron, *t* 319, *t* 372, 482, 544, 856
isobar(s), 902, 929
isothermal process(es), 406–407, **407**, *t* 411
isotope(s), 895, 897, 904–906, 912, **912**. *See also* radioactivity; nuclear decay.
isovolumetric process(es), 406, *t* 411

J

Jenner, Edward, 476
joule(s), 169, 172, 174, 192, 295, 367
Joule, James Prescott, 169, 391, 726
joule heating, 709
Juárez, Benito, 726
jumper(s), 751
junction transistor(s), 877–878
Jupiter, 149, 768

K

Kamehameha I, 476
kamikluuk, **384**
kaon(s), **920**
Kazerooni, Homayoon, 300
kefiyah, 385, **385**
kelvin(s), 331, 342, 361–363, *t* 362, *t* 386
Kepler, Johannes, 164
Kilby, Jack, 880
kilocalorie(s), *t* 367
kilogram(s), **10**, 11, *t* 11
kilowatt-hour(s), 711
kinematics, 43
kinetic energy: collisions and, 224–226, 227–229; conservation of, 179–180, 227–231, 295; entropy and, 427, **427**; of fluids, 335; overview of, 172–173; of

photoelectrons, 835–836; relativity and, 190–191; rotational, 295–297, 304, *t* 359; speed and, 172–173; temperature and, 359; units of, 192; work and, 184–186
kinetic friction, 143–145, 185–186
kinetic theory, 329, 331, 366, 383
King, Martin Luther, Jr., 862
Kolb, Greg, 421

L

laminar flow, 332, **332**
laser(s), 597, 614–618, **615**, 846
laser surface analyzer, 846, **846**
latent heat, 376–381, 386
Lavoisier, Antoine Laurent, 354
lead, *t* 372, *t* 379, *t* 482, 657, 846
Leavitt, Henrietta, 862
Leibniz, Gottfried Wilhelm, 209
lens(es): aberrations of, 585; characteristics of, 570–573; combinations of, 578–579; contact, 577; converging, **568**, 568–575, **577, 585**, 586, 593–595; diverging, **568**, 569, 573, **573**, 576, **577**; in eyeglasses, 577; in eyes, 561, **571**; focal length of, **569**, 569–570, **571**, 574, 585; laboratory exercises on, 546, 556–559; Polaroid, 546; ray diagrams for, **569**, 569–571, **571**, 573, **573**; refraction and, 568–579, 585–586; sign conventions for, *t* 574; telescopes and, **571**; thin-lens equation, 573–576; types of, 568–570; virtual images in, 570, 573, **573**, 586
Lenz's law, 798, 812, 819
lepton(s), 918–921, **919, 921**
leukemia, 790–791
lever(s), 279–280, **280**, 298, **298**, 304
levitation, 464, 884
libra, 125
lie detector(s), 702
light, 519–559; characteristics of, 520–525, 549; coherent, 599–600; Doppler effect and, 504–505; dual nature of, 466, 848–849, 855; emission spectra, **609, 842**, 842–843, 855; energy transfer and, 384; intensity of, 525, 547, 556–559, 614; monochromatic, 600–601, **608**, 610; phase differences in, 599; and photoelectric effect, 834–839,

458; of fluids, **332,** 332–337, 342; free-fall, 60–65, 68, 74, 99–106; laboratory exercises on, 33–34, 76–81; laws of, 123–150; measurement of, 34–37, 76–81; Newton's first law of, 130–135, 142, 150; Newton's second law of, 136–138, 150, 158–163, 210, 260, 290–292; Newton's third law of, 138–140, 150, 219–220; one-dimensional, 39–81; pendulum, 29, 443–444, *t* 447, 468, 474–475; periodic, 438–439; relative, 106–109, 112, 485–486; simple harmonic, 437–445, 446–451, 453, 468, 474–475; translational, 278, 283; two-dimensional, 83–121. *See also* projectile motion; rotational motion; wave(s).

motion detector(s), 34–37, 76–78, **77,** 239–240. *See also* CBL unit(s).

motor(s), 812–813, 820

motor oil(s), 333

MRI (Magnetic Resonance Imaging), 884, **884**

muon(s), 67, 919

music, physics of, 456–457, 487–488, 492, 494–501, 793, 802

myopia, 577, **577**

N

n-type semiconductor, **873,** 873–875, **877,** 877, 885

Nadir Shah, 354

negative (diverging) lens(es), **568,** 569, 573, **573,** 576, **577**

neon sign(s), 841, **841,** 845

net external force, 131–135, 136–139, 150

neutrino(s), 905–906, *t* 906, 919, 926

neutron(s): fission and, 914; mass of, *t* 630, *t* 898; nuclear stability and, 899, **899,** 907, 921

neutron number, *t* 896

neutron star(s), 902

Newcomen, Thomas, 354

newton(s), 11, 124–125, 260, *t* 780

Newton, Isaac: contributions of, 124; first law of, 130–135, 142, 150; Galileo and, 54; second law of, 136–138, 150, 158–163, 210, 260, 290–292; third law of,

138–140, 150, 219–220; unified model of mechanics and, 164; universal law of gravitation and, 263–264

NGC 4261, 267, **267**

NiCad batteries, 674

niobium, *t* 706

nitrogen, *t* 379, 845, 905

node(s), 463, 465, 497

noise pollution, 516–517

non-ohmic, 701

normal force, 141–144, **142,** 147, 150, 156, 527

northern lights, **828–829,** 829, 845

Noyce, Robert, 880

nuclear bomb(s), 914–915, **915**

nuclear chain reaction, 914, **914**

nuclear decay, 903–912, 913, 926, 930

nuclear fission, 191, 655, 862, 913–916

nuclear force, 898–902

nuclear fusion, 191, **191,** 913–916

Nuclear Policy Act of 1982, 892–893

nuclear power plant(s), 191, 892, 914, 916

nuclear waste, 892–893, 915

nucleon(s), 896–897, **897**

nucleus of an atom, 841, 896–902, 913–916, 926

O

object distance, 527

octave(s), 501

Oersted, Hans Christian, 476

ohm(s), 700

Ohm, Georg Simon, 476, 700

ohmic material(s), 701, 889–891

Ohm's law, 700–701

Onnes, H. Kamerlingh, 382

optics, *t* 5

orbit(s), 264, 266, 845, 847, 851, 853

order number(s), 602, *t* 619

order-of-magnitude estimation, 23–26

organ pipe(s), **496**

overtone(s) (harmonics), 494–495, 496–501, 506

oxygen, *t* 319, *t* 379, 482, 845

P

p-type semiconductor, **874,** 874–875, **877,** 877–878, 885

paint color (subtractive color), *t* 544, 544–545, **545,** 549

painting: colors and, *t* 544, 544–545, **545,** 549; electrostatic spray, **626–627,** 649, 651

pair annihilation, 925

pair production, 924

palladium, 129

parabola(s), **99,** 99–100, 112, 541–542

parallax, 15

parallel circuit. *See* circuit(s), parallel.

parallel-plate capacitor(s), 676–679, **679**

particle physics, 917–923, **921,** 926

pascal(s), 325, 342

Pasteur, Louis, 726

path difference(s), 602–603

Pauli, Wolfgang, 905

pendulum(s): bobs, 443–444, 447–448; energy of, 177, 444, 833; forces on, **443,** 443–445; laboratory exercises on, 444, 474–475; on metronomes, 437; motion of, 29, 443–444, *t* 447, 468, 474–475; periods of, 446–449, *t* 447, 472

penny–farthing bicycle(s), **276–277,** 277

Penzias, Arno, 505, **505**

period(s): in mass-spring systems, 449–451; pendulums and, 446–449, *t* 447, 468, 472; units of, *t* 468; of waves, 455–456, 500

periodic wave(s), 453, 461, 500

periscope(s), laboratory exercise on, 581

permittivity of a vacuum, 677

phase change(s), 377–381, 407

photoelectric effect, 834–839, 855; laboratory exercise on, 860–861

photon(s): electromagnetic interaction and, **918;** electron jumps and, 844, **844;** energy of, 832–833, 835–836, 838, 844, 855; gamma decay and, 906; particle physics and, **921;** photoelectric effect and, 837–838; quantum mechanics and, 848–849, 855 phototube(s), **838**, 838–839

physics: atomic, 829–861; mathematics and, 20–22; measurements in, 10–19; overview of, 4–5, 26, 56; particle, 917–923, **921**, 926; scientific method and, 6–9; solid-state, 866; subatomic, 895–933

pi, 245, **245**

piano(s), **487**

Picasso, Pablo, 862

pigment(s) (subtractive colors), t 544, 544–545, **545**, 549

pion(s), **920**

pitch, 481, 485–486, 501

pixel(s), 544

Place de la Concorde fountain, **82–83**, 83

Planck, Max, 466, 831–832, 862

Planck's constant, 466

Planck's equation, 835

plane wave(s), 483

plastic wrap, 631

plug(s), t 731

point charge(s), 649, 671–673

polarization: electrical, 632–633, **633**, 653; of light, **546**, 546–549

Polaroid lens(es), 546

poles of magnets, 766–767

polystyrene, t 564

popcorn, **356–357**, 357, 382, 383

positive (converging) lens(es), **568**, 568–575, **577, 585**, 586, 593–595

positron(s), 904–906, 924–925

potential difference: alternating current and, 699, 807–809; in batteries, 674–675; breakdown voltage and, 665; diodes and, 875–876; electrical energy transfer and, 713; emf and, 734, 753; international differences in, 745; magnetic fields and, 795, t 820; measurement of, 760–763; overview of, 670–672, 682; reference voltage, 877; resistance and, 700–702; root-mean-square (rms) currents and, 808–810, t 820; series and parallel circuits and, t 742, 748–751, 753; stopping voltage, 860–861; terminal voltage and, 735; units of, t 682, t 716

potential energy: chemical, 177; conservation of, 179–180; elastic, **175**, 175–176, 192, 200–205, 441; elec-

trical, 644, 666–669, 675, 679–682, t 682, 698; electric power and, 708–709; laboratory exercise on, 180; momentum and, 226, 231; overview of, 174–177; phase changes and, 377–378. *See also* gravitational potential energy.

potential well(s), 714, **714**

pound(s), 125

power: electric, 688–689, 708–713, 716, t 716, 720, 883–884; hydroelectric, 698, 803; nuclear, 191, 892, 914, 916; overview of, 186–189, 192; solar thermal, 421; units and symbols for, 187, t 192, 709; work and, 187

power rating(s), 188–189, 192

prairie dog(s), 345

Prausnitz, Mark, 705

precision, 15–19, 26

pressure, t 325, 325–330, 335, 342, 350–353; laboratory exercise on, 326

pressure wave(s), 455

primary color(s), 543–545, **544, 545**, 549

Prine, David, 484

prism(s), **520**, 543, 566, 580–581, 583. *See also* refraction.

probability wave(s), 714–715, 853–855

projectile motion: center of mass and, 283; laboratory exercise on, 120–121; relative motion and, 106, 112; satellites and, 266–267; two-dimensional, 98–105; velocity of, 120–121. *See also* free fall.

projection(s). *See* vector(s).

proton(s): charge and, 629–630, t 630; forces on, 635–636, 921; mass of, t 898; nuclear decay and, 903, 905, 907

proton-proton cycle, 915–916

Puerto Rico, 519

pulley, 298, **298**, 314–315, **315**

pulsar(s), 902

pulse wave(s), 453, 460–462

pulsed direct current, 876

pulsed hologram(s), 616

pump(s), 334, 375

pyramid(s), 89

Pythagorean theorem, 89–91, 93–96, 108, 112, 259

Q

quantum chromodynamics, 921

quantum electrodynamics (QED), 918

quantum mechanics, t 5, 302–303, 832, 834, 848–855, 862

quantum states, 832

quark(s), 630, **919**, t 919, 919–922, **920**, t 920

quartz, t 564

R

radian(s), 245–246, 249, 256, t 447; laboratory exercise on, 245

radiation: alpha, 840, t 903, 903–904, 908, 926; beta, t 903, 903–906, **905**, 917, 926; blackbody, 830–833, 855; cosmic microwave background, 505; electromagnetic waves, 384, 520–525, 546, 549, 790–791; gamma, t 903, 903–904, 906, 926; temperature and, 830–831, **831**, 845

radio telescope, **518–519**, 519, 612–613

radio wave(s), t 521, 599

radioactive waste, 892–893, 915

radioactivity, 892, 903–912; laboratory exercise on, 932–933

radium, 908–910

radius of a circle in a triangle, 29

radius of curvature, 274–275, 530–531, t 549, 650

radon, 908, 911

rainbow(s), **560–561**, 561, 584, **584**

Raman, Venkata, 591

Rankine temperature scale, 390

rarefaction of wave(s), 461, 480–481

ray(s): cosmic, 505, 895; of light, 523; reference, 533–534, 569, t 569; of sound, 483; X rays, t 521. *See also* radiation.

ray approximation, 523

ray diagram(s): for lenses, **569**, 569–571, **571**, 573, **573**; for mirrors, **528**, 528–529, **531**, 533–535, 537, 539–540

reaction time, 62

real image(s), 531, **531**, t 538

recording timer(s), 76, **79**, 79–80

rectifier(s), 874, 876

red shift, **504**, 504–505

processes in, 405–408; of a refrigerator, **413,** 413–415, **414,** *t* 415; second law of, 420–422

thermometer(s), 360–361, 395–396

thermonuclear fusion, 191, **191,** 913–916

thin-lens equation, 573–576

Thompson, Benjamin (Count Rumford), 476

Thomson, J. J., 840, **840**

thorium, 904

threshold of hearing, 489, *t* 490

threshold of pain, 489, *t* 490

timbre, 500–501, 506. *See also* sound.

time, 34–37, 56, 66; laboratory exercises on, 33–34, 76–81

time dilation, 66–67, **67,** 110

timeline(s), 164–165, 354–355, 476–477, 726–727, 862–863

timer(s), recording, 79, **79,** 161–162, 240–241, **241**

tin, *t* 706, **881,** 882

tire(s), 148, 210, 260, 325–326

Tomonaga, Shin'ichiro, 862

torque, 278–282, 286–288, 290–292, 304, 311

torque coils, 765

torsion balance(s), 642, **642**

Total Energy Cycle Assessment, 691

train(s), **38,** 39, 48, **50,** 707, **707,** 884

transformer(s), 713, 802, **815,** 815–818, 820

transistor(s), 877–878, 885, *t* 885

translational energy, *t* 359

translational equilibrium, 286, *t* 286

translational motion, 278, 283

transmission axis, 547

transmission hologram(s), 616

transverse wave(s), 453, 460–461

Trevithick, Richard, 476

triangle(s), Pythagorean theorem and, **89,** 89–91

triangle method of vector addition, 86–87, 112

trigonometric function(s), 90–93, 95–96

tritium, 896

trough of waves, 454

trumpet(s), 498

Ts'ao Chen, 354

Tubman, Harriet, 726

tug-of-war, 131, **131**

tuning fork(s), **480,** 480–481, **481,** 500, *t* 501, 514–515

turbulent flow, **332,** 332–333

U

ultrasonic sound wave(s), 481–482, **482**

ultraviolet catastrophe, 831

ultraviolet light, *t* 521, 831

uncertainty principle, 852–854, 855

Underwriters Laboratories (UL), 733

unified mass unit(s), 897, 926

unit(s). *See* Système International (SI) units.

universal gas constant, 339

universe, 429, 504–505, 921–922

uranium, 655, 904, 914–915, 927, 929

Ury, Michael, 524

V

vampire squid(s), **316–317,** 317

Van de Graaff generator(s), 651–652, **652**

van Wesel, Andries, 164

vaporization, heat of, 378–381, **379,** *t* 379

vector(s): addition of, 85–87, 94–97, 110–112; components of, 92–95, 98–105, 112; electric-field, 637–639, 646–647, 653; force, 126–128, 150; free fall and, 100–105; operations, 88–97; overview of, 84–87; resultant, 85, 89–91; symbols for, *t* 112; work, 169–170

velocity: acceleration and, 48–51, 54–56, 61–62; angular, 247–252, 254, 268, 272, 292; average, 43–46, 68, 80; drift, 696–697; escape, 266–267; free-fall, 61–65, 99–100, 120–121; instantaneous, 46; laboratory exercise on, 120–121; measurement of, 76–81; momentum and, 215–220, 227–228, 241; overview of, 43–46, 112; refraction and, 562–564; relative, 106–110; relativistic addition of, 110–111, 190; tangential, 255, 268, 274–275

velocity-time graph(s), 50, **50, 61**

Venus, 768

Vermeer, Jan, 164

Very Large Array, New Mexico, **613**

Vesalius, Andreas, 164

vibrational energy, *t* 359, 377, 487, 491–493, 494–495

Victoria, Queen of England, 726

viola(s), *t* 501

violin string(s), 494–495, 501

virtual image(s): holograms and, 616; in lenses, 570, 573, **573,** 586; for mirrors, 528, **528,** 534, 537, **537,** *t* 538

viscosity, 332

viscosity index, 333

vision, 544, 550, 561, 567, 571, 577

volt(s), 670

Volta, Alessandro, 476

voltage. *See* potential difference.

voltage meter(s), 762, 890–891

volume(s): of a cylinder, 333; displacement, 320–321; measurement of, 33, 350–353; expansion coefficient, 360; work and, 403–405, 430

W

Wagner, Richard, 726

walking, 301

water: density of, *t* 319; heating curve of, **376,** *t* 376; ice point of, 361, *t* 362; index of refraction of, *t* 564, 581, 590; latent heat of, *t* 379; specific heat capacity of, *t* 372; speed of sound in, *t* 482; steam point of, 361, *t* 362

Waterstrat, Richard, 129

watt(s), 187, 192, 487, 709

wave(s), 437–475; compression, 461, 480–481; de Broglie, 466–467, 714, 849–851, 858; electromagnetic, 384, 520–525, 546, 549, 790–791; frequency of, 455–456; infrared, *t* 521; interactions, 468; levitation by, 464; longitudinal, 455, **455,** 461, 481; of matter, 466–467, 849–851, 855; medium for, 452; motion of, 468; period of, 455–456, 500; photons and, 848–849; plane, 483; properties of, 452–458; pulse, 453, 460–462; reflection of, 462, 526–529, 547–549, 580; sound, 455–456, 460, 464, **464,** 480–483, 506; speed of, 456–457, 522, 562–563; spherical, 483, **483,** 487, 506, 523; standing, **463,** 463–465,

465, 468, 494–495, 496–501; transfer energy of, 458, 487; types of, 453–455. *See also* interference.

wave front(s), 523

waveform(s), 454

wave packet(s), 852

wave phenomena, *t* 5

wavelength(s): atomic emission and, 838, 845; coherence and, 600; color and, 543–544, 583–585; de Broglie, 466, 850, 858; diffraction and, 607–608, 624–625; frequency and, 494, 522; instrument resolution and, 612–613; interference and, 600–603, **601;** of matter waves, 849–850; overview of, 454, 456; refraction and, 563–564, 566, 583; in standing waves, 465, 497–501; units of, *t* 468, *t* 619

wavelet(s), 523

weak force, 917–918, *t* 918, 921, **921**

wedge, 298, **298**

weight, 124, 141, 150, 319–321

Wells, H. G., 565

wheel and axle, 298, **298**

Wilson, Robert, 505, **505**

wind instrument(s), 496–501

wire(s), *t* 731, 770, 777

wiring, 746, 760–763

wood, **144,** *t* 144

woodwind instrument(s), 496–501

work, 167–199; calculation of, 169–170, 198; definition of, 168, 192, 403–405; energy and, 167–205; entropy and, 427; force and, 168–170; gases and, 403–405; heat and, 368, 402–408, 410–413; kinetic energy and, 184–186; laboratory exercise on, 368; net, 169–171, 192; power and, 187; torque and, 281; units and sym-

bols for, 169, *t* 192, *t* 430; volume and, 403–405, 430

work-energy theorem, 184–186

work function of metal, 835, 855, *t* 855

Wright, Wilbur and Orville, 862

X

X ray(s), *t* 521

Y

Young, Thomas, 476, 601, 603, 623

Yucca Mountain disposal site, 893

Z

zinc, *t* 706

zircon, *t* 564

zirconium, 129, 582

Zweig, George, 919

Fundamental Constants

Symbol	Quantity	Established Value	Value used for calculations in this book
c	speed of light in a vacuum	299 792 458 m/s	3.00×10^8 m/s
e^-	elementary charge	$1.602\ 177\ 33 \times 10^{-19}$ C	1.60×10^{-19} C
ε_0	(Greek *epsilon*) permittivity of a vacuum	$8.854\ 187\ 817 \times 10^{-12}$ C^2/(N•m^2)	8.85×10^{-12} C^2/(N•m^2)
G	constant of universal gravitation	$6.672\ 59 \times 10^{-11}$ N•m^2/kg^2	6.673×10^{-11} N•m^2/kg^2
g	free-fall acceleration at Earth's surface	$9.806\ 65$ m/s^2	9.81 m/s^2
h	Planck's constant	$6.626\ 0755 \times 10^{-34}$ J•s	6.63×10^{-34} J•s
k_B	Boltzmann's constant (R/N$_A$)	$1.380\ 658 \times 10^{-23}$ J/K	1.38×10^{-23} J/K
k_C	Coulomb constant	$8.987\ 551\ 788 \times 10^9$ N•m^2/C^2	8.99×10^9 N•m^2/C^2
R	molar (universal) gas constant	$8.314\ 510$ J/(mol•K)	8.31 J/(mol•K)
π	(Greek *pi*) ratio of the circumference to the diameter of a circle	$3.141\ 592\ 654$	calculator value

Useful Astronomical Data

Symbol	Quantity	Value used for calculations in this book
I_E	moment of inertia of Earth	8.03×10^{31} kg•m^2
M_E	mass of Earth	5.98×10^{24} kg
R_E	radius of Earth	6.37×10^6 m

Useful Atomic Data

Symbol	Quantity	Established Value	Value used for calculations in this book
m_e	mass of electron	$9.109\ 3897 \times 10^{-31}$ kg $5.485\ 799\ 03 \times 10^{-4}$ u $0.510\ 999\ 06$ MeV	9.109×10^{-31} kg 5.49×10^{-4} u 5.110×10^{-1} MeV
m_n	mass of neutron	$1.674\ 9286 \times 10^{-27}$ kg $1.008\ 664\ 904$ u $939.565\ 63$ MeV	1.675×10^{-27} kg $1.008\ 665$ u 9.396×10^2 MeV
m_p	mass of proton	$1.672\ 6231 \times 10^{-27}$ kg $1.007\ 276\ 470$ u $938.272\ 31$ MeV	1.673×10^{-27} kg $1.007\ 276$ u 9.383×10^2 MeV